FOURTH EDITION

EXPERT DATA STRUCTURES WITH C

R. B. PATEL

(Professor)

Dept. of Computer Science & Engineering

Chandigarh College of Engineering & Technology, Chandigarh

KHANNA BOOK PUBLISHING CO. (P) LTD.

Publisher, of Science, Technology and Engineering Books

4C/4344, Ansari Road, Darya Ganj, New Delhi-110002

Phone: 011-23244447-48 **Mobile:** +91-99109 09320

E-mail: contact@khannabooks.com

Website: www.khannabooks.com

Dear Readers,

To prevent the piracy, this book is secured with HIGH SECURITY HOLOGRAM on the front title cover. In case you don't find the hologram on the front cover title, please write us to at contact@khannabooks.com or whatsapp us at +91-99109 09320 and avail special gift voucher for yourself.

Specimen of Hologram on front Cover title:

Moreover, there is a SPECIAL DISCOUNT COUPON for you with EVERY HOLOGRAM.

How to avail this SPECIAL DISCOUNT:

Step 1: Scratch the hologram
Step 2: Under the scratch area, your "coupon code" is available
Step 3: Logon to www.khannabooks.com
Step 4: Use your "coupon code" in the shopping cart and get your copy at a special discount
Step 5: Enjoy your reading!

Price: ₹ 550.00

ISBN: 978-93-86173-69-0

Expert Data Structures with C
by R.B. Patel

Fourth Edition: 2018
Reprint Edition : 2020, 2024, **2026**

To view complete list of books, Please scan the QR Code:

Published by:
Khanna Book Publishing Co. (P) Ltd.
CIN: U22110DL1998PTC095547

Visit us at: **www.khannabooks.com**
Write us at: **contact@khannabooks.com**

Printed in Bharat.

Preface To Fourth Edition

Heading in the direction "Easy ⇒ Easier ⇒ Easiest" some modifications and amendments edition. "A picture does work of thousand words and a memory of thousand pictures"'- I have done the first thousand, the second thousand is left for you. The primary objective of writing this book is to give an easy to understand"- pictorial treatment to such a subject of theoretical complexities as data structures. The book turns out to be voluminous owing to its pictorial nature. Don't get frightened by the number of pages, just take a glance at the figures and you would find the monster of data structures being tamed within no time. Just go through the book once and after that you'll just need to turn the pages over and back again.

To further strengthen the base of reade:s some new bricks are added to the foundation. Enhancement of literature is done in every chapter. Contains several changes, viz., all algorithm modified to give new look and clarity. In this edition tree chapter added new flavor to understand the application of binary tree. In Sorting and Searching chapter quick sort algorithm and other algorithms are also focused to view their very close watch in terms of performance and their implementation. Every chapter is added sets of simple multiple choice questions, provided entirely for reader's self-assessment, and are based on the most fundamental aspects of data structures and algorithms. The level of the questions is no more than that of what one would encounter in an introductory Programming and Data Structures.

Along with these new features this edition is backup by more examples, programs, and For Summative and Formative Assessment and of course sincere efforts to develop this book as an efficient learning tool in the field of Data Structures. At the end of each chapter a summary quiz is given in most of the chapters. A brief look on the contents is as follows.

This book starts with the fundamentals of data structures and finally leads to the much-detailed discussion on the subject. The very first chapter introduces the readers about the elementary concepts of C such as type conversions, structures, pointers, dynamic memory management, functions, flowchart. algorithm and fundamental of data structures.

The next chapter deals with recursion and involves factorials, various forms of exponential power, Fibonacci numbers, greatest common divisor of two integer numbers, much popular **Towers of Hanoi** problem, divide and conquer technique, function overhead and finally efficient recursion.

Chapter Three: covers the concepts of 'String Manipulation and Pattern Matching, incorporating structures of string storage, string functions and Markov algorithm.

Chapter Four: Arrays, an elementary subject of data structures is dealt next, covering the basic one-dimensional, two-dimensional and multidimensional arrays, algebra of matrix, triangular arrays, sparse arrays, etc.

Chapter Five: After getting firm hold on fundamentals we come to more specialized linked list, which introduces the readers with linear linked list and doubly linked lists. The operations such as traversal, insertions. deletions are performed on them for giving the in-depth knowledge on linked list. Further, the header-linked list, circular linked list, application of linked, searching and sorting have also been discussed.

Chapter Sixth deals with 'Stacks and Queues', another building block of data structures. This portion covers stack representations, stack operations- traversal, insertion, deletion, peep and update. Stack applications are also introduced in detail. The latter portion of the chapter conceptualizes queues- their implementation and types like circular queues, double ended queues and priority queues with adequate illustrations.

Chapter Seven: Exploring further we come across 'Trees', their representation as sequential and linked list. The binary tree and complete binary trees form the striking note to the chapter. Traversal of the binary tree preorder, inorder and postorder are covered. Another important concept of 'Huffman trees' is discussed next leading to applications of the binary trees. Search trees and deletion in binary search tree is discussed adequately. Balanced binary trees, AVL tree, Read-Black tree, m-way search tree, B-trees, paged tree, and threaded binary trees, relation between leaf nodes and non leaf nodes in binary tree, view of nodes in binary tree have been covered.

Chapter Eighth on "Graphs' gives its basic concepts, path, representation including sequential representation, shortest path algorithms such as "Warshall's algorithms, Dijkstra, Krushkal, Floyd", adjacency lists and graph traversal is discussed next. Depth and Breadth first searches and topological sorting, minimum spanning tree are also discussed.

Chapter Ninth Sorting and Searching' has been given special attention in which efficiency factor has been kept in mind. This chapter searches (linear, binary and hashing), and covers different types of sorting techniques such as Bubble sort, Insertion sort, Quick sort, Selection sort, Donald Shell sort, Merge sort. Heap sort. Radix sort, Radix exchange sort and external sorting

Chapter Ten: This chapter includes concepts of file systems-MS DOS FAT file system, UNIX file system, File Structure analysis concepts, secondary storage devices- Disk, Tape storage, File Organizations- Indexes, Sequential files, Index Sequential file, Inverted files, etc. External sorting is revisited in respect to file structures, Hashing- Linear hashing, Dynamic hashing, B-tree, B+-tree as secondary index.

Chapter Eleven: This chapter includes concepts of different variants of B-tree such as B-tree and B-tree, more detailed analysis of m-way search tree. B-tree performance is also added. Further index sequential file is revisited by giving more practical examples.

This textbook covers the syllabus of Semester College course on data structures. It provides both a strong theoretical base in data structures and an advanced approach to their representation in **C**. The text is useful to **C** professionals and programmers, as well as students of any branch of Engineering of graduate and postgraduate courses. The data structures are presented with in the context of complete working programs that have been tested both on a **UNIX** system and a personal computer using **Turbo-C++ 3.0** Compiler. The code is developed in a top-down fashion, typically with the low-level data structures implementation following the high-level application code. This approach foster good programming habits and makes subject matter more interesting.

The book has three goals- to develop a consistent programming methodology, to develop data structures access techniques and to introduce algorithms. The bulk of the text is developed to make a strong hold on data structures. Programming style and development methodology are introduced and its applications are presented. This has the advantage of allowing the reader to concentrate on the data structures, while illustrating how good practices make programming easier.

Final words of advice to readers is that, in case you find hard to grasp through words, go to figures and again come back to the text. This would reinforce the idea expressed and I am sure you will never find anything as easy as data structures.

Preface To First Edition

"A picture does work of thousand words and a memory of thousand pictures"- I have done the first thousand, the second thousand is left for you. The primary objective of writing this book is to give "an easy to understand"– pictorial treatment to such a subject of theoretical complexities as data structures. The book turns out to be voluminous owing to its pictorial nature. Don't get frightened by the number of pages, just take a glance at the figures and you would find the monster of data structures being tamed within no time. Just go through the book once and after that you'll just need to turn the pages over and back again.

This book starts with the fundamentals of data structures and finally lead to the much-detailed discussion on the subject. The very first chapter introduces the readers with elementary concepts of C as type conversions, structures, pointers, dynamic memory management, functions, flow-chart, algorithm and fundamental of data structures.

The next chapter deals with recursion and involves factorials, various forms of exponential power, Fibbonacci numbers, greatest common divisor of two integer numbers, much popular **Towers of Hanoi** problem, divide and conquer technique and finally function overhead.

Chapter Three covers the concepts of 'String Manipulation and Pattern Matching', incorporating structures of string storage, string functions and **Markov algorithm**.

Chapter Four: Arrays, an elementary subject of data structures is dealt next, covering the basic one-dimensional, two-dimensional and multidimensional arrays etc.

Chapter Five: After getting firm hold on fundamentals we come to more specialized linked list, which introduces the readers with linear linked list and doubly linked lists. The operations such as traversal, insertions, deletions are performed on them for giving the in-depth knowledge on linked list. Further, the header-linked list and the circular linked list have also been discussed.

Chapter Sixth deals with 'Stacks and Queues', another building block of data structures. This portion covers stack representations, stack operations- traversal, insertion, deletion, peep and update. Stack applications are also introduced. The latter portion of the chapter conceptualizes queues- their implementation and types like circular queues, double ended queues and priority queues with adequate illustrations.

Chapter Seven: Exploring further we come across 'Trees', their representation as sequential and linked list. The binary tree and complete binary trees form the striking note to the chapter. Traversal of the binary tree preorder, in-order and postorder are covered.

Another important concept of 'Huffman trees' is discussed next leading to applications of the binary trees. Search trees and deletion in binary search tree is discussed adequately. Balanced binary trees, AVL tree, B-trees and threaded binary trees have been covered.

Chapter eighth on 'Graphs' gives its basic concepts, path, representation including sequential representation, shortest path algorithms such as "Warshall's algorithms, Dijkstra, Floyd", adjacency lists and graph traversal is discussed next. Depth and Breadth first searches and topological sorting, mark the end of the chapter.

Chapterinth 'Sorting and Searching' has been given special attention in which efficiency factor has been kept in mind. This chapter searches (linear, binary and hashing), and covers different types of sorting techniques such as Bubble sort, Insertion sort, Quick sort, Selection sort, Donald Shell sort, Merge sort, Heap sort and Radix sort, Radix exchange sort.

This textbook covers the syllabus of Semester College course on data structures. It provides both a strong theoretical base in data structures and an advanced approach to their representation in **C**. The text is useful to **C** professionals and programmers, as well as students of any branch of Engineering of graduate and postgraduate courses. The data structures are presented with in the context of complete working programs that have been tested both on a **UNIX** system and a personal computer using **Turbo-C++,** Compiler. The code is developed in a top-down fashion, typically with the low-level data structures implementation following the high-level application code. This approach foster good programming habits and makes subject matter more interesting.

The book has three goals- to develop a consistent programming methodology, to develop data structures access techniques and to introduce algorithms. The bulk of the text is developed to make a strong hold on data structures. Programming style and development methodology are introduced and its applications are presented. This has the advantage of allowing the reader to concentrate on the data structures, while illustrating how good practices make programming easier.

Final words of advice to readers is that, in case you find hard to grasp through words, go to figures and again come back to the text. This would reinforce the idea expressed and I am sure you will never find anything as easy as data structures.

// Acknowledgement

Sitting on the seashore I had thought that it was an easy task to dive but it was only when I dived into one ocean of Computer and brought for you the pearl "Expert Data Structures With C". I realize how much helpful were so many people to us. Without these people this exploration could never have been materialized. I now realize that the acknowledgement is something that really comes from the bottom of the heart of every writer.

My primary obligation is to son of the soil Shri Tarsem Kumar Garg, Chancellor, M. M. University, Ambala. For those who knew him, no words are necessary and for those who do not know him, no words will suffice. Inspiration from these persons aided me immensely at all stages in the development and production of this book and without their guidance this book would not have seen the light of the day.

I am deeply indebted to the contributions made by my faculty members and friends especially Professor Manpreet Singh Gujral, Principal, Sunil Kumar Singh, and other faculty and staff of the Computer Science & Engineering, Chandigarh College of Engineering and Technology, Chandigarh whose moral boosting and support motivated me to work efficiently in the odd hours.

I am also deeply indebted to the contribution offered by Ms. Kanchan Lata and her friends. Last but not the least, the contribution of Ms. Rachita, Ms. Eishita and Shreshtham cannot be overlooked for thier pain staking efforts and finding even the minutest bugs that had creped into the manuscript and deserve sincere appreciation.

Suggestions and queries are most welcome through Publisher.

R. B. Patel

Contents

CHAPTER

1 Basics of Data Structures & Programming Language 'C'

Today we are living in the era of computers and computers are used in almost every field. Can one imagine railway reservation without the use of computers? No, doubt we can do that with computer also, but today this is look like impossible task. There are various other fields where computers are widely used. When we think of the computer working, we must remember that a computer purchased directly from the manufacturer is like a dead body, i.e., computer system should have programs to execute a job that is very much similar to giving life to it by feeding something to enable it to perform the desired function. As blood circulation is essential for existence of human beings, software is required to run the computers. The software provides the interface between computer and human beings. We have two main categories of software- System software, and Application software. For development of these softwares we need to some languages.

In this chapter we discuss about the evolution of computer languages. We have many languages; some languages are machine-level, middle-level, and some are high-level; even some languages are similar to natural language like English. But a computer can only understand the binary code, so we have translators to convert the high-level code into machine-readable code. We have also see, that when we move from machine-level languages to high-level languages, effort involved in programming decreases but time involved in execution increases.

Now let us see what a language is in general sense. We have so many languages; for example Hindi, English, French, etc. These are natural languages and people using a particular language are very much aware about those languages. For example, let us consider a sentence in English language: "**C is middle-level language.**"

We understand each character, each word of above sentence. We are also very much aware about the placing of the words in the sentence. The meaning is that we cannot put the words at random to form a sentence. We have well-defined rules and grammar for constructing a sentence. For example,

- Present Tense, Past tense, future tense,
- Each sentence should be terminated by a dot, etc.

We have categories of words, for example noun, pronoun, verb, adverb, etc. When we use some word in a sentence, we have meaning of that word. So, we can say, "**A language has a finite set of characters, characters form words, each word has some meaning, and a well-defined grammar that governs the construction of sentences.**"

The above facts are also applicable for computer languages; overall we are the designer of computer languages. We know that a computer cannot do any thing without instruction. So, there should be instructions and these instructions should be understand by computer system. If instructions are in machine language, a computer can understand directly and there is no need of any translator (or compiler). For example, consider some pseudo instructions of an assembly language:

Instruction	Meaning
ADD R1 R2	Add contents of registers R1 and R2 and store result into R1 register.

SUB R1 R3	Subtract content of register R3 from content of register R1 and store result into R1 register.

Now, suppose there is an assembler that converts the above instructions into binary code. We have defined the ADD, SUB, R1, R2, and R3 in binary as given below:

Mnemonics	Binary Code
ADD	001
SUB	010
R1	01
R2	10
R3	11

The previous two instructions are converted into binary code as given below:

001 01 10

010 01 11

The binary codes for the mnemonics are stored in system library files and definition of the words or functions are stored in system header files. For example, in C language we use header files like "stdio.h", "math.h", "conio.h", etc. and library function in library file "CS.LIB". In this chapter we will introduce about C language.

1.1 DEVELOPMENT OF C LANGUAGE

The concept of C language was put forward in the early 1970s at Bell Laboratories. It was developed in 1972 by ***Dennis Ritchie***. It is a successor of B language which is successor of BCPL. This is the reason why it is named as C. There is an interesting story behind the development of **C**. Actually it was not the motto to develop a language like **C** before a team lead by *Thompson* and *Ritchie* working at *AT&T Bell Labs*. It came into picture all of a sudden. The final shape of C language came into existence in 1973. At this time work on **UNIX** system development was going on and Thompson was writing the first UNIX version in assembly language. Thompson found difficulty in debugging a program written in assembly language. So, there was a need to develop higher-level language that may provide interface between a computer and human.

The concept of **C** was taken from Algol-60. With these concepts, a language B was developed and later on when some problems arose; language B was called by a new name **C**. Then **UNIX** operating system was written in **C** language. One of the most interesting things about the **C** language is that its compiler is written in C. Today it is one of the most used languages in system programming.

C is an imperative (procedural) systems implementation language. Its design goals were for it to be compiled using a relatively straightforward compiler, provide low-level access to memory, provide language constructs that map efficiently to machine instructions, and require minimal run-time support. **C** was therefore useful for many applications that had formerly been coded in assembly language. Despite its low-level capabilities, the language was designed to encourage machine-independent programming. A standards-compliant and portably written **C** program can be compiled for a very wide variety of computer platforms and operating systems with minimal change to its source code. The language has become available on a very wide range of platforms, from embedded microcontrollers to supercomputers.

1.2 FEATURES OF C LANGUAGE

C language possesses the features of both low-level and high-level languages and this is the reason why it is called middle-level language.

- C language provides facilities for programming at register level. It means we can access some hardware feature directly using C language. A program written in this language is much closer to the hardware and it takes less amount of time in execution as compared to the programs developed in high-level languages.
- C language is quite close to English language. So, it is very much convenient for programmers to use and this is the reason why program development is easier and less time consuming as compared to low-level languages.

We can program different types of tasks using C language. It is not limited to one field as some other languages are. It has great impact of system programming and general-purpose programming and this is why it does not loss its applicability even after 43 years of birth. Today many object-oriented and high-level languages can incorporate the program code written in C language. This shows the importance of this language. The place of C language in the spectrum of computer languages is shown in Table 1.1.

Table 1.1 Place of C language in Computer Languages

Level of Programming	Language
High-level	• COBOL • Pascal • Ada • FORTRAN • BASIC
Middle-level	• C • C++ • Other Fourth-generation Language
Low-level	• Assembly Language • Machine Language

C language is distinguished by the following characteristics:

- A simple, small core language, with extended functionality such as mathematical functions and file handling provided by library routines/functions/procedures.
- A procedural programming paradigm, with facilities to support structured programming as well.
- Low-level access to computer memory via the use of pointers.
- Prevents many operations that are not meaningful.
- A standardized C preprocessor for macro definition, source code files inclusion, conditional compilation, etc.
- A relatively small set of reserved keywords and easier to remember {**Table 1.2**}.
- Parameters that are passed by value; pass-by-reference semantics may be simulated by explicitly passing pointer values.
- Pointer to function and static variables, which allow for a rudimentary form of closures and runtime polymorphism.

- User-defined aggregate data types (struct, union, etc.) which allow related data to be combined and manipulated as a group.

There are 32 keywords in C language. Out of which 27 are given by ***Kernighan*** and ***Retchie de facto*** standard and remaining 5 added by **ANSI** standardization committee (ANSI-C). The keywords of **C** are shown in **Table 1.2.** The keywords with bold fonts represent the keywords given by the **ANSI-C** committee. Some features that C language lacks that are found in other languages:

·Automatic garbage collection

·Object-oriented programming features like inheritance that are provide by language like C++, Java, etc.

·Compile-time polymorphism in the form of function overloading and operator overloading.

·Native support for multithreading and networking, though these facilities are provided by standard libraries today.

Table 1.2 Keywords of C

auto	double	int	struct
break	else	long	switch
case	**enum**	register	typedef
char	extern	return	union
const	float	short	unsigned
continue	for	**signed**	**void**
default	goto	sizeof	**volatile**
do	if	static	while

1.3 HOW TO START PROGRAMMING?

A computer program consists of two parts: ***code*** and ***data***. The code is the set of instructions for performing a task, and the data is the set of "registers" or "memory locations" which contain the intermediate results which are used as the program performs its calculations.

Note that the code is relatively ***static*** while the data is ***dynamic***. Once we have gotten a program working, its code would not change. But every time we run it, it will typically be working with different data, so the memory locations will take on different values.

Once we have written a program, we have defined a new thing that a computer can do. The applications (text and graphic editors, spreadsheets, games, etc.) which a computer may already have are "just" programs, written by programmers using programming languages such as the one we are about to learn.

It is quite interesting to know *"HOW TO START PROGRAMMING IN C LANGUAGE"*. We have to understand some basic things before getting started. There are several elements which programming languages, and programs written in them, typically contain. These elements are found in all languages, not just in **C**. If we understand these elements and what they are for, not only will we understand **C** better. But we will also find learning other programming languages, and moving between different programming languages, much easier.

1. There are ***variables*** or ***objects***, in which we can store the pieces of data that a program is working on. Variables are the way we talk about memory locations (data), and are analogous to the "registers" in our pocket calculator. Variables may be ***global*** (i.e., accessible anywhere in a program) or ***local*** (i.e., private to certain parts of a program).

2. There are *expressions* which compute new values from old ones.
3. There are ***assignments*** which store values (of expressions, or other variables) into variables. In many languages, assignment is indicated by an equals (=) sign; thus, we might have

   b = 3 or c = d + e + 1

   The first sets the variable **b** to 3; the second sets the variable **c** to the sum of the variables **d** plus **e** plus 1.

   The use of an equals sign can be mildly confusing at first. In mathematics, an equal sign indicates equality, i.e., two things are stated to be inherently equal, for all time. In programming, there is a time element, and a notion of cause-and-effect: after the assignment, the thing on the left-hand side of the assignment statement is equal to what the stuff on the right-hand side was before. To remind meaning of this, we might want to read the equals sign in an assignment as "gets" or "receives"- a = 3 means "a gets 3" or "a receives 3."

   A few programming languages use a left arrow for assignment "a ← 3" to make the "receives" relation obvious. But this notation is not too popular, if for no other reason than that few character sets have left arrow in them, and the left arrow key on the keyboard usually moves the cursor rather than typing a left arrow. If assignment seems natural and non-confusing so far, consider the line

   i = i + 1

   What can this mean? In algebra, we had subtract i from both sides and end up with

   0 = 1

   which does not make much sense. In programming, however, lines like

   i = i + 1

   are extremely common, and as long as we remember how assignment works, they are not too hard to understand: the variable i receives (its new value is), as always, what we get when we evaluate the expression on the right-hand side. The expression says to fetch i's (old) value, and add 1 to it, and this new value is what will get stored into i. So i = i + 1 adds 1 to i; we say that it *increments* i. We will eventually see that, in C, assignments are just another kind of expression.
4. There are *conditionals* which can be used to determine whether some condition is true, such as whether one number is greater than another. In some languages, including **C**, conditionals are actually expressions which compare two values and compute a "true" or "false" value.
5. **Variables** and **expressions** may have ***types***, indicating the nature of the expected values. For instance, we might declare that one variable is expected to hold a number, and that another is expected to hold a piece of text. In many languages (including C), ***declarations*** of the names of the variables we plan to use and what types we expect them to hold must be explicit.

   There are all sorts of data types handled by various computer languages. There are single characters, integers, and "real" (floating point) numbers. There are text strings (i.e., strings of several characters), and there are *arrays* of integers, reals, or other types. There are types which reference (point at) values of other types. Finally, there may be user-defined data types, such as *structures* or *records*, which allow the programmer to build a more complicated data structure, describing a more complicated object, by accreting together several simpler types (or even other user-defined types).
6. There are *statements* which contain instructions describing what a program actually does. Statements may compute expressions, perform assignments, or call functions.

7. There are *control flow constructs* which determine what order statements are performed in. A certain statement might be performed only if a condition is true. A sequence of several statements might be repeated over and over, until some condition is met; this is called a *loop*.
8. An entire set of statements, declarations, and control flow constructs can be lumped together into a *function* also called *routine*, *subroutine*, or *procedure*.

   When we call a function, we transfer control to it and wait for it to do its job, after which it *returns* to us. It may also return a value as a result of what it has done. We may also pass values to the function on which it will operate or which otherwise direct its work.

   Placing code into functions not only avoids repetition if the same sequence of actions must be performed at several places within a program, but it also makes programs easy to understand, because we can see that some function is being called, and performing some (presumably) well-defined subtask, without always concerning programmer with the details of how that function does its job. If we have ever done any knitting, we know that knitting instructions are often written with little sub-instructions or patterns which describe a sequence of stitches and is to be performed multiple times during the course of the main piece. These sub-instructions are very much like function calls in programming.
9. A set of functions, global variables, and other elements makes up a *program*. An additional wrinkle is that the source code for a program may be distributed among one or more *source files*. In the other direction, it is also common for a suite of related programs to work closely together to perform some larger task, but we will not worry about that "large scale integration" for now.
10. In the process of specifying a program in a form suitable for a compiler, there are usually a few logical details to keep track of. These details may involve the specification of compiler parameters or interdependencies between different functions and other parts of the program. Specifying these details often involves miscellaneous syntax which does not fall into any of the other categories listed above, and which we might lump together as "boilerplate."

Many of these elements exist in a hierarchy. A program typically consists of functions and global variables. A function is made up of statements and statements usually contain expressions, expressions operate on objects. It is also possible to extend the hierarchy in the other direction; for instance, sometimes several interrelated but distinct programs are assembled into a suite, and used in concert to perform complex tasks. The various "office" packages-integrated word processor, spreadsheet, etc. are example.

As we mentioned, many of the concepts in programming are somewhat arbitrary. This is particularly, so for the terms *expression*, *statement*, and *function*. All of these could be defined as "an element of a program that actually does something." The differences are mainly in the level at which the "something" is done, and it is not necessary at this point to define those "levels." We will come to understand them as we begin to write programs.

1.4 PROGRAM ANALOGY

Just as a book is composed of chapters which are composed of sections which are composed of paragraphs which are composed of sentences which are composed of words which are composed of letters, so is a program composed of functions which are composed of statements which are composed of expressions which are in fact composed of smaller elements which we would not bother to define. Analogies are never perfect, though, and this one is weaker than most; it still does not tell us anything about what expressions, statements, and functions really *are*. If "expression" and "statement" and "function" seem like totally arbitrary words to us, use the analogy to understand that what they are, is arbitrary words describing arbitrary levels in the hierarchical composition of a program, just as "sentence," "paragraph," and "chapter" are different levels of structure within a book.

In the above section we have presented very general terms, describing features common to most conventional computer languages. If we understand these elements at a relatively abstract level, then learning a new computer language becomes a relatively simple matter of finding out how that language implements each of the elements. Of course, we cannot understand these abstract elements in isolation; it helps to have concrete examples to map them too. If we have never programmed before, most of this section has probably seemed like words without meaning.

Finally, there is no need to overdo the abstraction. For the simple programs we will be writing, in a language like C, the series of calculations and other operations that actually takes place as a program runs is a simpleminded translation (into terms the computer can understand) of the expressions, statements, functions, and other elements of the program. Expressions are evaluated and their results assigned to variables. Statements are executed one after the other, except when the control flow is modified by if/then conditionals and loops. Functions are called to perform subtasks, and return values to their callers which have been waiting for them.

There is one initial file <stdio.h> that is to be included in a program. The system library file "CS.lib" is automatically added to a program when compiler runs. So, we have not to include this into a program but we have to include the necessary header files. One thing noticeable about the header files that these all are ".h" files and included in a program starting with symbol '#' followed by the word "include" and the name of header file is enclosed in < > or " ". For example,

```
#include <stdion.h>
#include <math.h>
#include <conio.h>
```

We include the header files as per need in a program. For example, math.h header file is used when we need some mathematical calculations, but the header file stdio.h (stands for standard input/ output) is always there when we develop a program.

Now, the next part is the main function written as main(). This is the main body of a program. When a compiler compiles a program and that program runs, it is always started with the main function. So, we always have a main function while running a program. One cannot think about multiple main functions in a single program. We can have only one main function in a single program. A program written in C language is always saved as ".c" or ".C" file.

Function main() is a part of every C program. C permits different forms of main statement. The following forms are allowed:

- main()
- int main()
- void main()
- main(void)
- void main(void)
- int main(void)

Empty pair of parenthesis indicates that the function has no arguments. This may be explicitly indicated by using the keyword void inside the parenthesis. We may also specify the keyword int or void before the word main. The keyword void means that the function does not return any value to the operating system and int means that the function returns an integer value to the operating system. When int is specified, the last statement in the program must be "return 0". For the sake of simplicity, we use the first form in programs.

Now let us see the *structure of a C program* which is given in Figure 1.1. The document section consists of comment lines giving the name of the program, program author, etc. see Example 1.1. The link section provides instructions to the compiler to link functions from the system library. The definition section defines all symbolic constants. There are some variables which are used in the entire program are also defined here are called global parameters/variables. These parameters declared outside of every function used in the program segment.

Documentation section
Link section
Definition section
Global declaration section
int main ( ) Function Section
{
Declaration section
Executable code section
statement 1;
statement 2;
...
statement n;
}
	Main section

Subprogram section Function 1 Function 2 Function 3 ... Function n	User defined functions

Figure 1.1 An overview of a C Program

Every program has one main() function section. This section comprise of two parts- declaration section and executable code section. These two sections appear between '{' and '}' and there must be at least one executable statement. In the declaration section we define those parameters which have scope within the function main(). The program execution begins at opening brace '{' and ends at closing brace '}'. The closing brace of the function main is being logical end of the program. All the statements in the declaration and execution parts end with a semicolon. All the sections, except the main function section may be absent when they are not required. We can see that after the main function the opening curly bracket "{" is there and there are n number of statements ending in semicolon (;) and finally the closing curly bracket "}". Next we discuss about formatted input and output functions and specifier.

1.5 FORMATTED INPUT/OUTPUT

There are a number of related functions used for formatted input/output (I/O), each one determining the format of the I/O from a *format string*. For output, the format string consists of plain text, which is output unchanged, and embedded *format specifications* which call for some special processing of one of the remaining arguments to the function. On input, the plain text must match what is seen in the input stream; the format specifications again specify what the meaning of remaining arguments is. Each format specification is introduced by a % character, followed by the rest of the specification.

1.5.1 Output: the Printf Family

printf's name comes from **print** formatted. It generates output under the control of a *format string* (its first argument) which consists of literal characters to be printed and also special character sequences-*format specifiers* which request that other arguments be fetched, formatted, and inserted into the string. The very first program was nothing more than a call to printf, printing a constant string. For those functions performing output, the format specification takes the following form, with optional parts enclosed in brackets:

```
%<flags><field width><precision><length>conversion
```

The meaning of *flags, field width, precision, length*, and *conversion* are given in **Table 1.3**, although tersely. For example, see the following code:

```
printf("Hello, world!\n");
```

The second program also featured a call to printf:

```
printf("i is %d\n", i);
```

In this case, whenever printf printed the string "i is %d", it did not print it verbatim; it replaces the two characters %d with the value of the variable i. There are quite a number of format specifiers for printf which are given in **Table 1.4**.

It is also possible to specify the width and precision of numbers and strings as they are inserted (somewhat like FORTRAN format statements). A notation like %3d means to print an int in a field at least 3 spaces wide; a notation like %5.2f means to print a float or double in a field at least 5 spaces wide, with two places to the right of the decimal. To illustrate with a few more examples: the call

```
printf("%c %d %f %e %s %d%%\n", '1', 2, 3.14, 56000000., "eight", 9);
```

would print

```
1 2 3.140000 5.600000e+07 eight 9%
```

The call

```
printf("%d %o %x\n", 100, 100, 100);
```

would print

```
100 144 64
```

Successive calls to printf just build up the output a piece at a time, so the calls

```
printf("Hello, ");
printf("world!\n");
```

would also print Hello, world! (on one line of output).

Table 1.3 FORMAT flags

Flags	Meaning
-	Left justify the conversion within its field.
+	A signed conversion will always start with a plus or minus sign.
' ' space	If the first character of a signed conversion is not a sign, insert a space. Overridden by + if present.
#	Forces an alternative form of output. The first digit of an octal conversion will always be a 0; inserts 0X in front of a non-zero hexadecimal.
0	Pad d, i, o, u, x, X, e, E, f, F and G conversions on the left with zeros up to the field width. Overridden by the - flag. If a precision is specified for the d, i, o, u, x or X conversions, the flag is ignored. The behaviour is undefined for other conversions.
field width	A decimal integer specifying the minimum output field width. This will be exceeded if necessary. If an asterisk is used here, the next argument is converted to an integer and used for the value of the field width; if the value is negative it is treated as a - flag followed by a positive field width. Output that would be less than the field width is padded with spaces (zeros if the field width integer starts with a zero) to fit. The padding is on the left unless the left-adjustment flag is specified.
precision	This starts with a period '.'. It specifies the minimum number of digits for d, i, o, u, x, or X conversions; the number of digits after the decimal point for e, E, f conversions; the maximum number of digits for g and G conversions; the number of characters to be printed from a string for s conversion. The amount of padding overrides the field width. If an asterisk is used here, the next argument is converted to an integer and used for the value of the field width. If the value is negative, it is treated as if it were missing. If only the period is present, the precision is taken to be zero.
length	h preceding a specifier to print an integral type causes it to be treated as if it were a short. (Note that the various sorts of short are always promoted to one of the flavours of int when passed as an argument.) l works like h but applies to a long integral argument. L is used to indicate that a long double argument is to be printed, and only applies to the floating-point specifiers. These are cause undefined behaviour if they are used with the 'wrong' type of conversion see Table 1.4

Earlier we learned that C represents characters internally as small integers corresponding to the characters' values in the machine's character set (typically ASCII). This means that there is not really much difference between a character and an integer in C; most of the difference is in whether we choose to interpret an integer as an integer or a character. printf is one place where we get to make that choice: %d prints an integer value as a string of digits representing its decimal value, while %c prints the character corresponding to a character set value.

Table 1.4 DATA formatters

Specifier	Effect	Default precision
D	signed decimal	1
I	signed decimal	1
U	unsigned decimal	1
O	unsigned octal	1
x	unsigned hexadecimal (0–f)	1
X	unsigned hexadecimal (0–F)	1
Precision	Precision specifies minimum number of digits, expanded with leading zeros if necessary. Printing a value of zero with zero precision outputs no characters.	
f	Print a double with precision digits (rounded) after the decimal point. To suppress the decimal point use a precision of explicitly zero. Otherwise, at least one digit appears in front of the point.	6
e, E	Print a double in exponential format, rounded, with one digit before the decimal point, precision after it. A precision of zero suppresses the decimal point. There will be at least two digits in the exponent, which is printed as 1.23e15 in e format, or 1.23E15 in E format.	6
g,G	Use style f, or e (E with G) depending on the exponent. If the exponent is less than –4 or ≥ precision, f is not used. Trailing zeros are suppressed; a decimal point is only printed if there is a following digit.	unspecified
c	The int argument is converted to an unsigned char and the resultant character printed.	
s	Print·a string up to precision digits long. If precision is not specified, or is greater than the length of the string, the string must be NULL terminated.	infinite
P	Display the value of a (void *) pointer in a system-dependent way.	
n	The argument must be a pointer to an integer. The number of characters output so far by this call will be written into the integer.	
%	A %	
[^]	String char []* (character selection)	
%ud	Unsigned integer	
%uc	Unsigned character	
%uf	Unsigned floating point number	
%ld	Long integer	

So the lines

```
char c = 'A';
int i = 97;
printf("c = %c, i = %d\n", c, i);
```

would print c as the character A and i as the number 97. But if, on the other hand, we called

```
printf("c = %d, i = %c\n", c, i);
```

We had seen the decimal value (printed by %d) of the character 'A', followed by the character (whatever it is) which happens to have the decimal value 97.

We have to be careful when calling printf. It has no way of knowing how many arguments we have passed it or what their types are other than by looking for the format specifiers in the format string. If there are more format specifiers (that is, more % signs) than there are arguments, or if the arguments have the wrong types for the format specifiers, printf will misbehave badly, often printing nonsense numbers or (even worse) numbers which mislead us into thinking that some other part of a program is broken.

Because of some automatic conversion rules which we have not covered yet, we have a small amount of latitude in the types of the expressions we pass as arguments to printf. The argument for %c may be of type char or int, and the argument for %d may be of type char or int. The string argument for %s may be a string constant, an array of characters, or a pointer to some characters (though we have not really covered strings or pointers yet). Finally, the arguments corresponding to %e, %f, and %g may be of types float or double. But other combinations do *not* work reliably: %d will not print a long int or a float or a double; %ld will not print an int; %e, %f, and %g will also not print an int.

The functions that use these formats are described in **Table 1.5**. All need the inclusion of <stdio.h>. Their declarations are:

```
#include <stdio.h>
int fprintf(FILE *stream, const char *format, ...);
int printf(const char *format, ...);
int sprintf(char *s, const char *format, ...);

#include <stdarg.h> /* as well as stdio.h */
int vfprintf(FILE *stream, const char *format, va list arg);
int vprintf(const char *format, va list arg);
int vsprintf(char *s, const char *format, va list arg);
```

All of the above functions return the number of characters output, or a negative value on error. The trailing null is *not* counted by sprintf and vsprintf.

1.5.2 Input: the Scanf Family

A number of functions exist analogous to the printf family, but for the purposes of input instead. The most immediate difference between the two families is that the scanf group needs to be passed *pointers* to their arguments, so that the values read can be assigned to the proper destinations. Forgetting to pass a pointer is a very common error, and one which the compiler cannot detect-the variable argument list prevents it. The format string is used to control interpretation of a stream of input data, which generally contains values to be assigned to the objects pointed to by the remaining arguments to scanf. The contents of the format string may contain:

white space: This causes the input stream to be read up to the next non-white-space character.

ordinary character: Anything except white-space or % character. The next character in the input stream *must* match this character.

conversion specification: This is a % character, followed by an optional * character (which suppresses the conversion), followed by an optional nonzero decimal integer specifying the maximum field width, an optional h, l or L to control the length of the conversion and finally a non-optional conversion specifier. Note that use of h, l, or L will affect the type of pointer which may be used.

Table 1.5 Functions performing formatted output

Name	Purpose
fprintf	General formatted output as described. Output is written to the file indicated by stream.
printf	Identical to fprintf with a first argument equal to stdout.
sprintf	Identical to fprintf except that the output is not written to a file, but written into the character array pointed to by s.
vfprintf	Formatted output as for fprintf, but with the variable argument list replaced by arg which must have been initialized by va_start. va_end is not called by this function.
vprintf	Identical to vfprintf with a first argument equal to stdout.
vsprintf	Formatted output as for sprintf, but with the variable argument list replaced by arg which must have been initialized by va_start. va_end is not called by this function.

Except for the specifiers c, n and [, a field of input is a sequence of non-space characters starting at the first non-space character in the input. It terminates at the first conflicting character or when the input field width is reached.

The result is put into wherever the corresponding argument points, unless the assignment is suppressed using the * mentioned already. The conversion specifiers shown in **Table 1.6** may be used. The size specifiers have the effect shown in **Table 1.7**. The functions are described below, with the following declarations:

```
#include <stdio.h>
int fscanf(FILE *stream, const char *format, ...);
int sscanf(const char *s, const char *format, ...);
int scanf(const char *format, ...);
```

Table 1.6 Conversion specifiers

Specifier	Effect
d i o u x	Convert a signed integer, a signed integer in a form acceptable to strtol, an octal integer, an unsigned integer and a hexadecimal integer, respectively.
e f g	Convert a float (not a double).
s	Read a string, and add a null at the end. The string is terminated by whitespace on input (which is not read as part of the string).
[	Read a string. A list of characters, called the scan set follows the [. A] delimits the list. Characters are read until (but not including) the first character which is not in the scan set. If the first character in the list is a circumflex ^, then the scan set includes any character not in the list. If the initial sequence is [^] or [], the] is not a delimiter, but part of the list and another] will be needed to end the list. If there is a minus sign (-) in the list, it must be either the first or the last character; otherwise the meaning is implementation defined.
c	Read a single character; white space is significant here. To read the first non-white space character, use %1s. A field width indicates that an array of characters is to be read.
p	Read a (void *) pointer previously written out using the %p of one of the printfs.
%	A % is expected in the input, no assignment is made.
n	Return as an integer the number of characters read by this call so far.

Table 1.7 Size specifiers

Specifier	Modifies	Converts
l	d i o u x	long int
h	d i o u x	short int
l	e f	double
L	e f	long double

fscanf takes its input from the designated stream, scanf is identical to fscanf with a first argument of stdin, and sscanf takes its input from the designated character array. If an input failure occurs before any conversion, EOF is returned. Otherwise, the number of successful conversions is returned: this may be zero if no conversions are performed. An input failure is caused by reading EOF or reaching the end of the input string (as appropriate). A conversion failure is caused by a failure to match the proper pattern for a particular conversion.

1.6 COMPILING C PROGRAMS

Process of processing a program is shown in **Figure 1.2**. First we need to prepare source code (write a C program) then input to the system, at this stage if required edit the code before submitting it to the translator (compiler/assembler) otherwise forward directly to the compiler/assembler. Translator translates (compiles/assembles) the code as a whole and reports the errors if any with their appropriate type and statement and line number of the code. Translator at this stage reports only syntax errors. When all syntax errors are removed Translator generates object code. Then the linker is called which attaches the library files, required for the used library function (s). After linking the library file(s) it generates executable (binary) codes and forwards to the loader. Loader on receiving the code checks it. If any portion of the code is not properly compiled it compiles the same. Finally loader loads the executable codes into the system memory for the execution. Program during execution may ask for some input data. After getting input data during execution logical (semantic errors) and data errors are checked, if a data error is there new input data is provided and code is re-executed. If after feeding correct data to the code, result is not correct means there is semantic error in the code, sometimes an appropriate message (s) is displayed regarding semantic errors. Then control is transferred to edit the source code. The above process is repeated till all the existing errors are not removed.

- On a UNIX machine, type **cc program file -o object file** (if cc does not work, try gcc). This line invokes the C compiler called cc, asks it to compile **program file** and asks it to place the executable code into the object code file. For example if program file is **test1.c** and object file name is test1. Then the procedure to compile test1.c under UNIX/LINUX is

  $ cc test1.c

  or

  $ cc –o test1 test1.c

  or

  $ cc test1.c –o test1

  There are several options available with the compiler choose as per need of the program. The first option generates an executable file a.out that can be run by giving the command:

  $a.out

  or

$./a.out

Second and third option generates **test1** as an executable file which can be run as

$test1

or

$./test1

- On a DOS or Windows machine using TCC, at an MS-DOS prompt type **TCC test1.c -o test1.obj**. This line invokes the C compiler called TCC, asks it to compile **test1.c** and it places the object code in file it creates under the name **test1.obj**. To create executable codes for this object code use **tlink object code file** (here test1.obj) then it will generate an executable file with same name as object code was, i.e., test1.exe. To run the program, type **test1**. There are several options available with the compiler choose as per need of the program.
- If we are using Turbo-C compiler and using turbo editor simply press CRTL and F9 keys together to compile and run the code. It will create test1.exe if test1.c is compiled, if test2.c is compiled it will generate test2.exe executable code file. For viewing the result press ALT and F5 keys together to see the result(s).
- If we are working with some other compiler or development tool, we need to read and follow the directions for the compiler we are using to compile and executing the program.
- If a program is distributed across the several files, it can be compiled and run under UNIX environment as:

  $cc file1.c file2.c ... filen.c-o outputfile

  or

  $cc -o outputfile file1.c file2.c ... filen.c

  To run the code use the option as discussed earlier.

$./outputfile

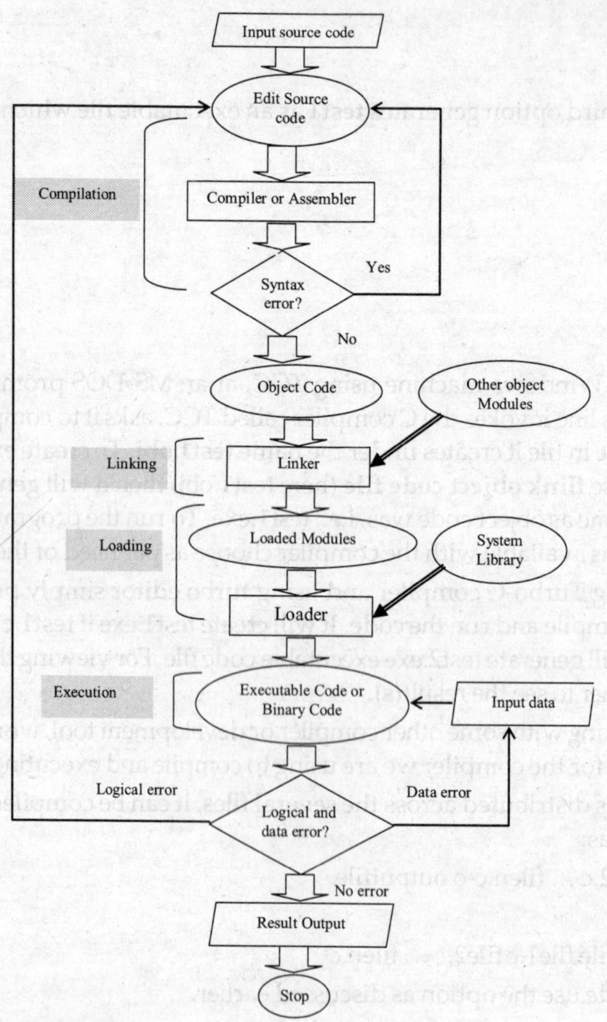

Figure 1.2 Processes of Compiling and Running a C Program

1.7 ADDRESS OPERATOR &

The & (address) operator yields a pointer to its operand. The operand must be an lvalue, a function designator, or a qualified name. It cannot be a bit field, nor can it have the storage class register. If the operand is an lvalue or function, the resulting type is a pointer to the expression type. For example, if the expression has type int, the result is a pointer to an object having type int. If the operand is a qualified name and the member is not static, the result is a pointer to a member of class and has the same type as the member. The result is not an lvalue. If p_to_y is defined as a pointer to an int and y as an int, the following expression assigns the address of the variable y to the pointer p_to_y :

```
p_to_y = &y;
```

1.8 INDIRECTION OPERATOR *

The * (indirection) operator determines the value referred to by the pointer-type operand. The operand cannot be a pointer to an incomplete type. If the operand points to an object, the operation yields an lvalue referring to that object. If the operand points to a function, the result is a function designator in C, an lvalue referring to the object to which the operand points. Arrays and functions are converted to pointers. The type of the operand determines the type of the result. For example, if the operand is a pointer to an int, the result has type int. Do not apply the indirection operator to any pointer that contains an address that is not valid, such as NULL. The result is not defined. If p_to_y is defined as a pointer to an int and y as an int, the expressions:

```
p_to_y = &y;
*p_to_y = 3;
```

These statements cause the variable y to receive the value 3.

1.9 ARITHMETIC OPERATOR WITH ASSIGNMENT

If we compare a C program with a program with a similar purpose written in another language, we may well find that C source file is shorter. One reason for this is that C has several operators that can compress often used programming statements. For example, consider the following code slice:

```
Total = Total + Number;
```

Here the value of **Number** is added to the value in **Total** and result is placed in **Total**. In **C,** this statement can be written as **Total += Number;** The effect is same; but the expression is more compact, as shown in **Figure 1.3**.

```
Total = Total + Number;
```

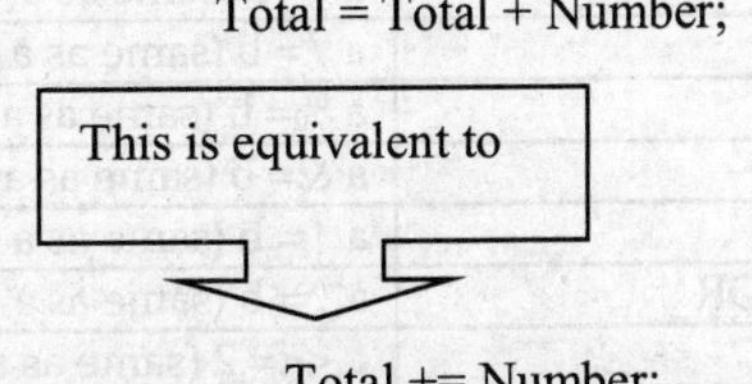

Figure 1.3 The arithmetic assignment operator

For example, consider the following program segment that implements the above discussion (ASSIGN.C):

```
/* ASSIGN.C */
#include <stdio.h>
void main(void)
{
 int total = 0;
 int count = 10;
 printf("\nTotal = %d\n", total);
 total += count;
 printf("Total = %d\n", total);
 total += count;
 printf("Total=%d\n", total);
}
```

The expressions such as **Total = Total + Number;** in which the variable on the left-hand side is repeated on the right, can be written as **Total += Number;** The operator += is called an assignment operator. Most binary operators have a corresponding assignment **op=**, where **op** is one of + - * / << & ^ |. For example, if **Total += Number;** then operator pair += tells the compiler to assign **Total**, the value of **Total** plus **Number**. If **exp_1** and **exp_2** are expressions, then **exp_1 op = exp_2;** is equivalent to **exp_1=(exp_1) op (exp_2);** except that **exp_1** is computed only once. For example: **a* = b +1;** means **a = a * (b + 1);** rather than **a = a * b + 1;** . See another example, which counts 1's in an integer number interpreting integer number as binary.

```
bc ( unsigned a) /* Counts number of 1's in a given number */
{
 int b = 0;
 for ( b; a!=0; a>>1)
 if (a &1)
 b += 1;
 return(b);
}
```

The parentheses '( )' and bracket '[ ]' are used to increase the precedence of expressions. The details of the assignment operators are given in **Table 1.8**.

Table 1.8 Assignment operators

Symbol	**Operator**	**Example**
=	Equal	a = b
+=	Addition	a += b (same as a = a + b)
-=	Subtraction	a -= b (same as a = a – b)
*=	Multiplication	a *= b (same as a = a * b)
/=	Division	a /= b (same as a = a / b)
%=	Remainder	a %= b (same as a = a %b)
&=	Bitwise AND	a &= b (same as a = a & b)
|=	Bitwise OR	a |= b (same as a = a | b)
^=	Bitwise exclusive OR	a ^= b (same as a = a ^ b)
<<=	Left shift	a <<= 2 (same as a = a << 2)
>>=	Right shift	a >>= 3 (same as a = a >> 3)

1.10 PRECEDENCE AND ASSOCIATIVITY OF THE OPERATORS

The data type and the value of an expression depend on the data types of the operands and the order of evaluation of operators which is determined by the precedence, and associativity of operators. *Precedence* is the order in which the compiler groups operands with operators. The C compiler evaluates certain operators and their operands before others. If operands are not grouped using parentheses, the compiler groups them according to its own rules. Most operators group from the left to the right but some group from the right to left. The grouping indicates how an expression containing several operators of the same precedence will be evaluated. For example,

Left to right grouping means the expression

a/b* c/d;

behaves as if it had been written:

(((a/b)*c)/d);

An operator that groups from the right to left causes the expression

a = b = c;

to behave as if it had been written:

a = (b = c);

means **a = (b = c),** In other words, first b=c is evaluated and then a=b, that is, right associativity.

a + b – c; means **(a + b) – c;**

Here + and – operators have same priority but associativity is left to right and hence first a+b is evaluated and then c is subtracted.

Let us first consider the order of evaluation. When expressions contain more than one operator, the order in which the operators are evaluated depends on their precedence levels. A higher precedence operator is evaluated before a lower precedence operator. When operators of the same precedence level appear in an expression, the order of evaluation is determined by the associativity (or grouping). Except for the assignment operator, associativity of most binary operators is left to right (LTR); associativity of the assignment operator and most unary operators is right to left (RTL).

The unary operators and assignment operators are right associative and the remaining operators are left associative. **Table 1.9** shows the precedence levels and associativity of all C operators. In the table, there are 15 precedence levels 0 through 14: higher level implies higher precedence. The precedence levels of operators are separated by solid lines with operators within solid lines having the same precedence level.

For example, binary arithmetic operators, *, / and % have the same precedence level which is higher than binary +, and -. Observe that the precedence of the assignment operator is lower than all but higher than comma operator. This is in accordance with the rule that the expression on the right side of an assignment is evaluated first, and then its value is assigned to the left hand side object. On the other hand, function call has the highest precedence, since a function *value* is treated like a variable reference in an expression. In any expression, parentheses may be used to over ride the precedence of the operators - innermost parentheses are always evaluated first.

The precedence of binary logical operators is lower than that of binary relational operators; that of binary relational operators is lower than that of binary arithmetic operators, and so forth. The unary NOT operator has a precedence higher than that of all binary operators.

1.11 EXPRESSION

Expressions acted on by operators, i.e., expressions are sequences of operators, operands, and punctuators that specify a computation. The evaluation of expressions is based on the operators that the expressions contain and the context in which they are used. A sequence of operators and operands may yield a single value. An expression is classified as per operands' data type and values used. An expression can result in a value and can produce *side effects*. A side effect is a change in the state of the execution environment. For example, the following is an expression containing two operands and one operator.

z = a + b;

Table 1.9 Precedence and Associativity of operators

Operator	Description	Associativity	Precedence
()	Parentheses (grouping)	LTR	14
[]	Brackets (array subscript)		
.	Member selection via object name		
->	Member selection via pointer		
++ --	Unary pre-increment/pre-decrement	RTL	13
+ -	Unary plus/minus		
! ~	Unary logical negation/bitwise complement		
(type)	Unary cast (change type)		
*	Dereference		
&	Address		
sizeof	Determine size in bytes		
* / %	Multiplication/division/modulus	LTR	12
+ -	Addition/subtraction	LTR	11
<< >>	Bitwise shift left, Bitwise shift right	LTR	10
< <=	Relational less than/less than or equal to	LTR	9
> >=	Relational greater than/greater than or equal to		
== !=	Relational is equal to/is not equal to	LTR	8
&	Bitwise AND	LTR	7
^	Bitwise exclusive OR	LTR	6
|	Bitwise inclusive OR	LTR	5
&&	Logical AND	LTR	4
||	Logical OR	LTR	3
?:	Ternary conditional	RTL	2
=	Assignment	RTL	1
+= -=	Addition/subtraction assignment		
*= /=	Multiplication/division assignment		
%= &=	Modulus/bitwise AND assignment		
^= |=	Bitwise exclusive/inclusive OR assignment		
<<= >>=	Bitwise shift left/right assignment		
,	Comma (separate expressions)	LTR	0

a and *b* are both operands of the + operator.

- There are several types of expressions such as Postfix expressions, Primary expressions, Lvalues and rvalues, Conditional expressions, Assignment expressions, Comma expressions, Unary expressions, Cast expressions and Binary expressions. But we are only interested in Lvalues and rvalues expression.

An ***lvalue*** (pronounced "el-value") is an expression that refers to a region of storage that can be manipulated, i.e., an *object* is a region of storage that can be examined and stored into. An *lvalue* is an expression that refers to such an object. An lvalue does not necessarily permit modification of the object it designates. For example, a const object is an lvalue that cannot be modified. The term *modifiable lvalue* is used to emphasize that the lvalue allows the designated object to be changed as well as examined. The following object types are lvalues, but not modifiable lvalues:

- An array type
- An incomplete type
- A const-qualified type
- A structure or union type with one of its members qualified as a const type

For example, all simple variables, like ints and floats are lvalues. An element of an array is also an lvalue; however an entire array is not. A member of a structure or union is an lvalue; an entire structure or union is not. Given the following declarations:

```
int *p, a, b;
int arr[4];
int func();
a /* lvalue */
a + b /* Not an lvalue */
p /* lvalue */
*p /* lvalue */
arr /* lvalue, but not modifiable */
*(arr + a) /* lvalue */
arr[a] /* lvalue, equivalent to *(arr+a) */
func /* Not an lvalue */
func() /* Not an lvalue */
```

Because these lvalues are not modifiable, they cannot appear on the left side of an assignment statement.

The term *rvalue* refers to a data value that is stored at some address in memory. An rvalue is an expression that cannot have a value assigned to it. Both a literal constant and a variable can serve as an rvalue. When an lvalue appears in a context that requires an rvalue, the lvalue is implicitly converted to an rvalue. The reverse, however, is not true: an rvalue cannot be converted to an lvalue. Rvalues always have complete types or the void type.

C defines a *function designator* as an expression that has function type. A function designator is distinct from an object type or an lvalue. It can be the name of a function or the result of dereferencing a function pointer. The C language also differentiates between its treatment of a function pointer and an object pointer. On the other hand, in C++, a function call that returns a reference is an lvalue. Otherwise, a function call is an rvalue expression. In C++, every expression produces an lvalue, an rvalue, or no value. In both C and C++, certain operators require lvalues for some of their operands. **Table 1.10** lists these operators and additional constraints on their usage.

Table 1.10 Operators participating in lvalue and rvalue expression

Operator	Requirement
& (unary)	Operand must be an lvalue.
++ --	Operand must be an lvalue. This applies to both prefix and postfix forms.
= += -= *= %= <<= >>= &= ^= |=	Left operand must be an lvalue.

For example, all assignment operators evaluate their right operand and assign that value to their left operand. The left operand must be a modifiable lvalue or a reference to a modifiable object. The address operator (&) requires an lvalue as an operand while the increment (++) and the decrement (—) operators require a modifiable lvalue as an operand. The following example shows expressions and their corresponding lvalues.

Expression	Lvalue
x = 42	x
*ptr = newvalue	*ptr
a++	a
int &f()	The function call to f() /* this valid in C++*/

1.12 HOW THE OVERFLOW ARISE?

C language uses 16 bit to represent variable type **int**. Most significant bit is used to represent the sign. If the most significant bit is zero then the value is treated as positive, if it is **1** then negative. For example consider the 16-bit integer number representation, which is illustrated in **Table 1.11**.

For example, consider the following program segment

```
/* OVERFLOW.C */
#include <stdio.h>
void main (void)
{
 int positive = 32767;
 int negative = -32768;
 printf("%d + 1 is %d\n", positive, positive+1);
 printf("%d - 1 is %d\n", negative, negative-1);
}
```

Table 1.11 Discuss of overflow condition

Binary Number				Decimal Equivalent
0000	0000	0000	0000	0
0000	0000	0000	0001	1
0000	0000	0000	0010	2
	...			...
0111	1111	1111	1101	32,765
0111	1111	1111	1110	32,766
0111	1111	1111	1111	32,767
If we add 1 to 32,767, we would expect the result to be 32,768. However, to C++, the value becomes -32,768, as follows:				
0111	1111	1111	1111	32,767
0000	0000	0000	0001	1
1000	0000	0000	0000	-32,768

1.13 STRUCTURES

A structure is a collection of fields in which the fields may be same or of different types. A structure declaration forms a template that can be used to create structures. The fields that make up the structure are called members of the structure. Generally all the member of a structure is logically related. For example, we consider the mailing list of all of the employees of GBPEC Company. The list contains the following information about the employees:

- Name
- Date of joining
- Grade
- Department
- Address

The list can be represented with the help of structure for the above details of the employees. The keyword **struct** is used to declare a structure. The syntax is

```
struct Tag name
{
    data type1 field1;
    data type2 field2;
    data type3 field3;
    ...
    ...
    ...
    data typen fieldn;
};
```

For example, the list of employees of GBPEC Company can be declared as:

```
struct Mailing_List
{
    char Name[20];
    char Join_Date [8];
    char Grade;
    char Department [30];
    char Address [120];
};

Maling_List List; /* List is a variable of type Mailing_List*/
```

Figure 1.4 illustrates the above structure of employees in memory. If one wants to access individual member of the structure then one requires to use a period (.) operator. The syntax is

Process (Structure_name →member_name) ; or Process (Structure_name.field_name);

Name	Joining Date	Grade	Department	Address
20 bytes	8 bytes	1 byte	30 bytes	120 bytes

Figure 1.4 List structure in the memory

For example, if one wants to input **Name** from an input device then it is possible with the help of input functions such as **gets(), scanf (), fread (), fscanf (),** etc. gets (List.Name);

Most common use of structures is found in the case of arrays of structures. To declare an array of structures, we must define a structure and then declare an array variable of that type. For example, if

GBPEC Company has 1000 employees and company manager wants to maintain a record of each employee in the computer, then one can maintain it with the help of an array. The following declaration defines array of 1000 records: Mailing_List List [1000];

When a structure variable is defined as a pointer type then individual fields can be processed with the help of arrow → operator. The pointer type declaration of structures can be implemented with the help of following syntax: Mailing_List *List [1000];

If one wants to process **Name** field then it is possible with the help of following syntax:

```
Process (List [i]->Name);
```

For example, if we want to maintain customer bank account for the following information:

- Name
- Account number
- Profession
- Address
  - Street
  - City
  - State
  - Pin code

Then the above information can be maintained with the help of following declarations:

```
/* Structure declaration for address */
struct Addr{
   char Street[30];
   char City [30];
   char State[20];
   long int Pin_Code;
};

/* Nested structure declaration */
struct Customer
{
   char Name[20];
   char Account_No [10];
   char Profession[30];
   Addr Address;
};

Customer *List [100];
```

To access information about individual field in the **List** one can do **List [index]->field name.** The program segment **STRUCT.C** illustrates the above discussion in detail.

```
/* Definition of structure */
/* STRUCT.C */
# include<stdio.h>
/* Structure declaration for address */
struct Addr
{
```

```
    char Street[30];
    char City [30];
    char State[20];
    long int Pin_Code;
};
/* Nested structure declaration */
struct Customer
{
    char Name[20];
    char Account_No [10];
    char Profession[30];
    struct Addr Address;
};
/* Function main */
void main()
{
    struct Customer *List[100];
    int i, n;
    printf("\n Input number of record you want to process: ");
    scanf("%d", &n);
    fflush(stdin);
    printf("\n Input the information of customer\n");
    for(i=0; i< n; i++)
    {
        printf("\n Name: ");
        gets(List[i]->Name);
        printf("\n Account Number:");
        gets(List[i]->Account_No);
        printf("\n Profession:");
        gets(List[i]->Profession);
        printf("\n*** Address***");
        printf("\n**************\n");
        printf("\n Street:");
        gets(List[i]->Address.Street);
        printf("\n City:");
        gets(List[i]->Address.City);
        printf("\n State:");
        gets(List[i]->Address.State);
        printf("\n Pin Code:");
        scanf("%ld", &List[i]->Address.Pin_Code);
        fflush(stdin);
    }
```

```
    printf("\n List of the customer");
    printf("\n *******************\n");
    for(i= 0; i< n; i++)
    {
        printf("\n Name: %s", List[i]->Name);
        printf("\n Account Number: %s", List[i]->Account_No);
        printf("\n Professiion: %s", List[i]->Profession);
        printf("\n *** Address ***\n");
        printf("\n **************\n");
        printf("\n Street: %s", List[i]->Address.Street);
        printf("\n City: %s", List[i]->Address.City);
        printf("\n State: %s", List[i]->Address.State);
        printf("\n Pin code: %ld", List[i]->Address.Pin_Code);
    }
}
```

1.14 UNION

A union is a memory location that is shared by two or more different type of variables; generally these variables can be used for different data types at different times. The syntax is:

union tag name{

```
 Datatype1 field1; Datatype2 field2; Datatype3 field3; ...
   ...
   ...
Datatypen fieldn;};
```

For example, consider the following declaration of union:

```
union Data_Types{
 char Ch; int Integer_Number; long int Int_Long_Number;
 float Float_Number;
 double Double_Number;
 };
```

The above declaration does not create any variables. We can declare a variable by either placing its name at the end of the declaration or by using a separate declaration statement. To declare a **union** variable data of type **Data_Types** we use the definition such that:

```
Data_Types Data;
```

In **Data**, character **Ch**, integer **Integer_Number**, long integer **Integer_Long_Number**, floating point number **Float_Number** and double **Double_Number** share the same memory locations. **Figure 1.5** illustrates the concepts of sharing memory. To access a member of **union**, same syntax is used as for structures. The dot (.), arrow, (→) pointer (*) and dot (.) operators will work in the case of union. If we want to operate direct on the union then we use dot operator, if the union is accessed through a pointer we use arrow operator or use pointer and dot operators. For example, assign **char 'c'** to the field variable **Ch** of **Data** we use:

```
Data.Ch = 'c';
```

If a pointer to **Data** is passed to a function them we use:

```
Data_Types Fun (Data_Types *Member)
{
      Member->Ch = 'c';
      Member->Integer_Number= 100;
      Member->Float_Number = 20.50;
      (*Member).Double_Number = 30.5;
      return (Member);
}
```

Using a union helps in the production of machine independent (portable) code. Because the compiler keeps track of the actual size of the union members, no machine dependencies are produced, which means that one should not be worry about the size of an **int, long; char, float, double** or whatever.

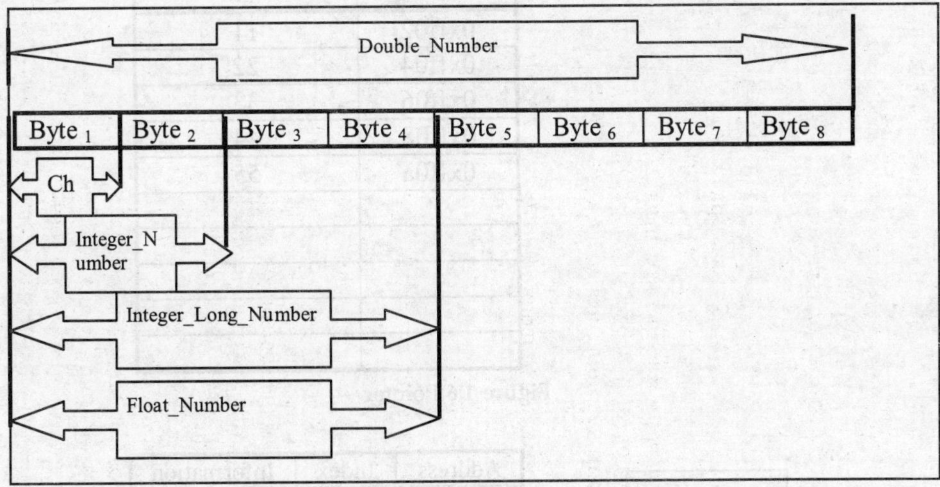

Figure 1.5 Data in memory

1.15 POINTERS

A pointer stores nothing but a memory address; this is its object value. It does not store a string, an integer, a double, etc. However, it may point to a storage location for such object value types. A pointer points to a memory location, and through the use of proper operators (& for address, * for value), the object value at the address to which it points can be retrieved or written. For example, **Figure 1.6** illustrates a pointer attached with some location in memory. If one is interested fetching the information, then one can easily obtain the information by using operator (*) with the pointer variable.

For example, consider the following code slice:

```
INFORMATION = *P;
```

where **P** contains the address 0xf f02 and the information stored at this location is 11, after this assignment we will get 11 in **INFORMATION**.

A pointer does not point to any single memory location. It can point to even through out **RAM** locations. For example, if **P** is a pointer (character) type variable then the following assignment is correct:

```
char *P;
P = "Expert Data Structures With C";
```

The initial value of **P** is called the base address. In the above example the base address holds **'E'**, base address plus 1 holds **'x'**, base address plus 2 holds **'p'** and base address +29 holds **'C'.** Above discussion can be illustrated with the help of **Figure 1.7**. Some times it is also required to declare a pointer variable to another pointer (pointer to pointer to variable). The syntax is:

Data type **variable name;

For example: int ** Pointer_To_Pointer_Integer;

The actual representation of this declaration is a two-dimensional array of infinite length and is illustrated in **Figure 1.8**

Pointer variable P

0xff02 →

ADDRESS	INFORMATIO N
0xff02	11
0xff04	22
0xff06	33
0xff08	44
0xff0a	55

Figure 1.6 Pointer

Base address →

Address	Index	Information
0xff04	0	E
0xff05	1	X
0xff06	2	P
0xff07	3	E
0xff08	4	R
0xff09	5	T
0xff0a	6	
…	7	D
…	8	A
…	9	T
	10	A
	11	
	12	S
	13	T
	14	R
	15	U

	16	C
	17	T
	18	U
	19	R
	20	E
	21	S
	22	
	23	W
	24	I
	25	T
	26	H
...	27	
...	28	C
...	29	
0xff22	30	
0xff23	31	
0xff24	32	
0xff25	33	

Figure 1.7 Pointer and base address

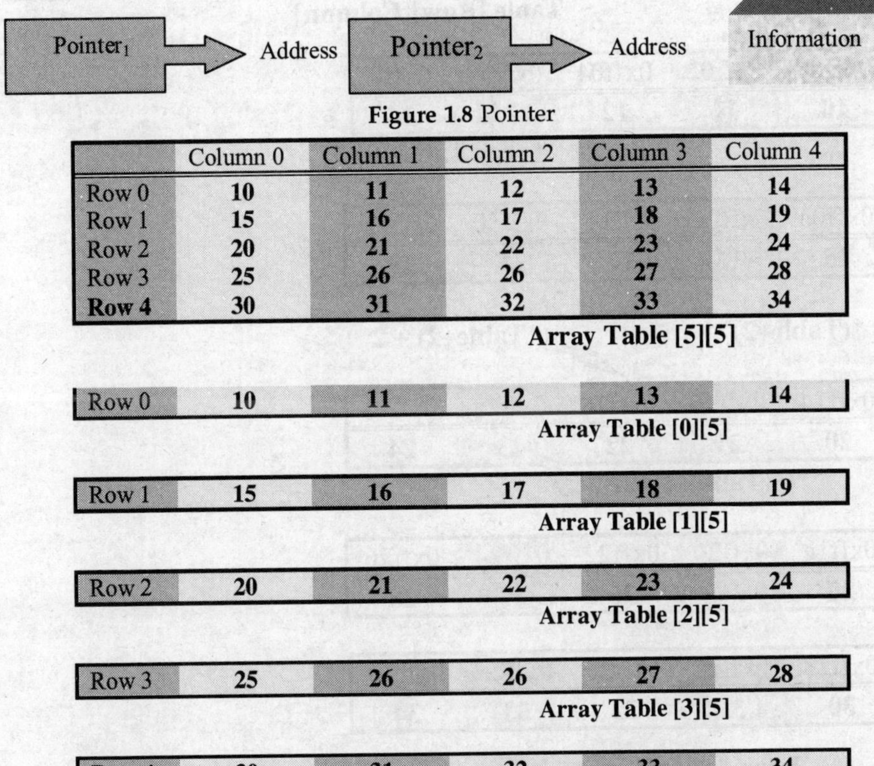

Figure 1.8 Pointer

	Column 0	Column 1	Column 2	Column 3	Column 4
Row 0	**10**	**11**	**12**	**13**	**14**
Row 1	**15**	**16**	**17**	**18**	**19**
Row 2	**20**	**21**	**22**	**23**	**24**
Row 3	**25**	**26**	**26**	**27**	**28**
Row 4	**30**	**31**	**32**	**33**	**34**

Array Table [5][5]

Row 0	10	11	12	13	14

Array Table [0][5]

Row 1	15	16	17	18	19

Array Table [1][5]

Row 2	20	21	22	23	24

Array Table [2][5]

Row 3	25	26	26	27	28

Array Table [3][5]

Row 4	30	31	32	33	34

Array Table [4][5]

Figure 1.9 Array and rows of array

For example, suppose we have an array as illustrated in **Figure 1.9**. Let's Figure out how to use pointers with reference to the third element in the third row of the array or **Table [2][2],** which is 22. First, the base address of the entire array is **Table**. Let's assume that the array starts at address **0xff00** in the memory, so **Table = 0xff00**. It is an integer array so each element will take two bytes. There are five elements in each row, so each row takes 10 bytes. Thus, each row starts 10 bytes further. Because row is a one-dimensional array, each of these one-dimensional arrays starts 10 bytes further along than the last one. **Figure 1.10** illustrates that the address of the third element is ***(Table+2)+2** and content of this location is ***(*(Table+2)+2),** whose value is **22**. Simply we can say that Table [i][j] = *(*Table +i)+ j);

Table + 1 = 0xff0a **Table = 0xff00**

	Index	Address	Column 0	Column 1	Column 2	Column 3	Column 4
Bytes			2	2	2	2	2
Index			0	1	2	3	4
Row 0	0	0xff00	10	11	12	13	14
Row 1	1	0xff0a	15	16	17	18	19
Row 2	2	0xff14	20	21	22	23	24
Row 3	3	0xff1e	25	26	26	27	28
Row 4	4	0xff28	30	31	32	33	34

Table [Row][Column]

Address	0xff00	0xff02	0xff04	0xff06	0xff8
Row 0	10	11	12	13	14

Array Table [0][5]

Address	0xff0a	0xff0c	0xff0e	0xff10	0xff12
Row 1	15	16	17	18	19

***(Table+2)** **(*Table+2) + 2**

Address	0xff14	0xff16	0xff18	0xff1a	0xff1c
Row 2	20	21	22	23	24

***(*(Table+2)+2)**

Address	0xff1e	0xff20	0xff22	0xff24	0xff26
Row 3	25	26	26	27	28

Address	0xff28	0xff2a	0xff2c	0xff2e	0xff30
Row 4	30	31	32	33	34

Figure 1.10 Pointing to element in two-dimensional Array

For example, if we will execute the program segment **POINTER.C** we will get the desired result.

```
/* Definition of Pointer and arrays */
/* pointer.c */
# include<stdio.h>
# define rows 5
# define cols 5
void main()
{
   int i, j;
   int Table[rows][cols] = {
                  {10,11,12,13,14},
                  {15,16,17,18,19},
                  {20,21,22,23,24},
                  {25,26,27,28,29},
                  {30,31,32,33,34}   };
   for (i = 0; i < 5; i++)
   {
      for (j = 0; j < 5; j++)
      {
         printf(" 0x%x", *(Table+i)+j);
         printf(" %d", *(*(Table+i)+j));
      }
      printf("\n");
   }
}
```

1.15.1 Arrays of Pointers and Pointer of Arrays

An array of pointers is similar to an array of any predefined data types. As a pointer variable contains an address, an array of pointers is a collection of addresses. These can be addresses of ordinary isolated variables or addresses of an array elements. The elements of an array of pointers are stored in the memory just like the elements of other kinds of array. The syntax for defining an array of pointer is the same as an array, except that pointer operator (*) precedes the array name. The syntax is: **Data type * array_ name [size of array];**

An array of pointer is useful for holding a pointer, pointing to a list of string. They can be utilized in implementing algorithms involving excessive information movements, we provide an example, where the use of pointer to pointer seems to be effective. The simplest way is to sort information by information movement. This method of sorting incurs many overheads in terms of both the time and space complexity, as it requires temporary space for exchanging the information between the records and has excessive information movement. This is especially large if the size of information is large. Pointers can be utilized to perform the same with much flexibility and less overhead. In this method, instead of information exchange, pointers are exchanged to accomplish the same task. The program segment **POINTSRT.C** illustrates the above discussion. In this program segment we have used **string [n] = new char(48);** statement that allocates 48 bytes to the **n**th element and stores its memory address in the array of pointers to strings indexed by **n**. This is C ++ language feature. The sorting procedure through the pointers is illustrated in **Figure 1.11(i)**.

```
sort (string, n);
```

The above statement invokes the sorting function by passing the array of pointers and information count as actual parameters.

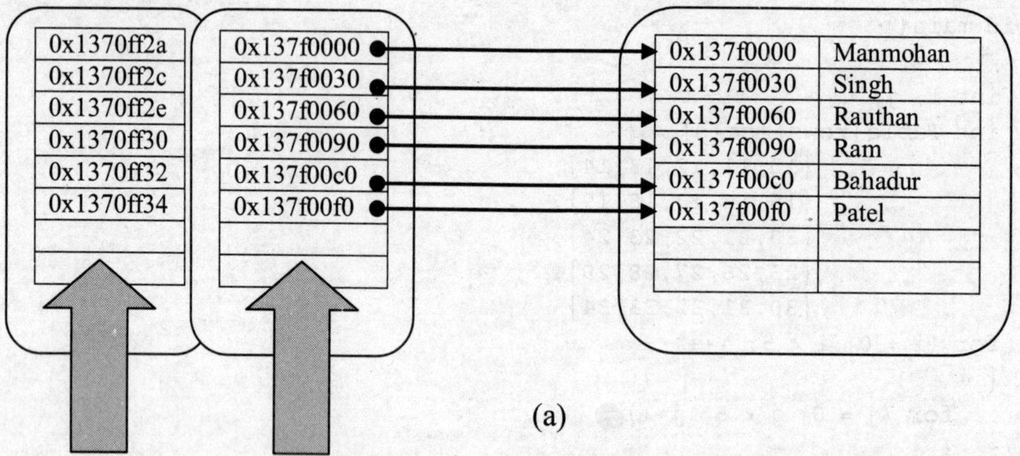

(a)

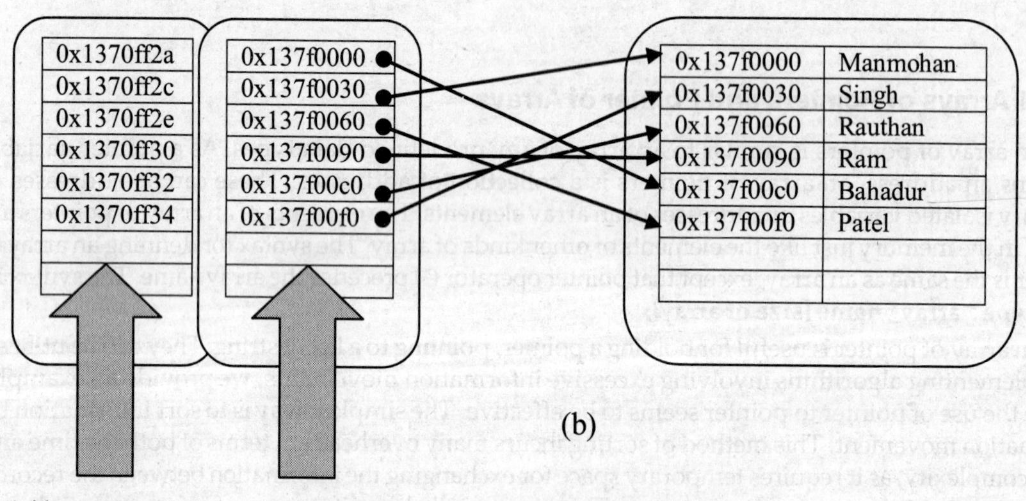

(b)

Figure 1.11(i) Sorting using pointers

```
/* Pointer and Array */
/* POINTSRT.C */
# include<stdio.h>
```

```
# include<string.h>
# include<ctype.h>

/* PROTOTYPE */
void sort(char **, int );
/* Definition of function */
void sort(char **str, int n)
{
    int i,j, flag;
    char *temp = (char *)malloc(50);
    for(i =0; i < n; i++)
    {
        flag = 1;
        for (j=0; j <(n-i-1); j++)
        {
            if (strcmp (str[j], str[j+1])>0)
            {
                flag = 0;
                temp = str[j];
                str[j] = str[j+1];
                str[j+1] = temp;
            }
        }
        if (flag)
            break;
    }
}
/* Function main */
void main()
{
    char choice;
    int i, n = 0;
    char *string[100];
    do
    {
        string[n] = (char *) malloc(50);
        printf("Input string: ");
        gets(string[n]);
        n++;
        fflush(stdin);
        printf("\n Input another Y/N? ");
```

```
        choice = getchar();
        fflush(stdin);
    }while(toupper(choice) == 'Y');
    printf("Unsorted list \n");
    printf("************\n");
    for (i = 0; i < n; i++)
    {
        printf(" 0x%x", &string[i]);
        printf(" ");
        printf("%s", string[i]);
        printf("\n");
    }
    sort(string, n);
    printf("\n Sorted list");
    printf("\n************\n");
    for (i = 0; i < n; i++)
    {
        printf(" 0x%x", &string[i]);
        printf(" %s", string[i]);
        printf("\n");
    }
}
```

Pointer of arrays refers to a pointer to a pointer is a form of multiple indirection, or a chain of pointers. Normally, a pointer contains the address of a variable. When we define a pointer to a pointer, the first pointer contains the address of the second pointer, which points to the location that contains the actual value as shown in **Figure 1.11(ii)**.

Figure 1.11(ii) Multiple indirection

A variable that is a pointer to a pointer must be declared as such. This is done by placing an additional asterisk in front of its name. For example, following is the declaration to declare a pointer to a pointer of type int:

```
int **pptr;
```

When a target value is indirectly pointed to by a pointer to a pointer, accessing that value requires that the asterisk operator be applied twice, as is shown in the following example.

```
int **pptr;

#include <stdio.h>

int main ()
```

```
{
 int var;
 int *ptr;
 int **pptr;

 var = 3000;

 /* take the address of var */
 ptr = &var;

 /* take the address of ptr using address of operator & */
 pptr = &ptr;

 /* take the value using pptr */
 printf("Value of var = %d\n", var );
 printf("Value available at *ptr = %d\n", *ptr );
 printf("Value available at **pptr = %d\n", **pptr);

 return 0;
}
```

When the above code is compiled and executed, it produces the following result:

```
Value of var = 3000
Value available at *ptr = 3000
Value available at **pptr = 3000
```

1.15.2 Pointer To Structure

A pointer can also hold the address of aggregate data types such as structures. Similar to pointers to basic data types, the pointers to aggregate data types can be initialized with address of statically or dynamically created information items. The syntax for defining a pointer to structures is given in **Figure 1.12**. The accessing procedure for members of a structure is discussed in previous section. For example, the program segment **STRUCT_S.C** illustrates the implementation of structures by sorting a list of structured information.

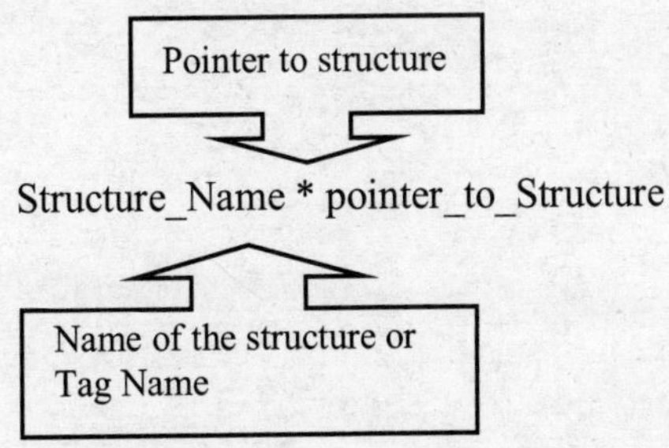

Figure 1.12 Pointer to structures

```
/* Pointer and structures */
/* STRUCT_S.C */
```

```
# include<string.h>
# include<stdio.h>
# include<malloc.h>
struct Record
{
    char *name;
    char *address;
    long Pin_code;
};
/* PROTOTYPE */
void sort(struct Record * , int );
void sort(struct Record *str, int n)
{
    int i,j, flag;
    struct Record temp;
    for(i =0; i <n-1; i++)
    {
        flag = 1;
        for (j=0; j <(n-i-1); j++)
        {
            if (strcmp (str[j].name, str[j+1].name)>0)
            {
                flag = 0;
                temp = str[j];
                str[j] = str[j+1];
                str[j+1] = temp;
            }
        }
        if (flag)
            break;
    }
}

/* Function main */
void main()
{
    char choice;
    int i, n = 0;
    struct Record string[10];
    printf("Input The List\n ");
    printf("\n*************\n");
```

```
    do
    {
        string[n].name = (char *) malloc(50);
        string[n].address= (char *) malloc(100);
        printf("Name: ");
        gets(string[n].name);
        printf("\n Address: ");
        gets(string[n].address);
        printf("Postal index number: ");
        scanf("%ld", &string[n].Pin_code);
        n++;
        fflush(stdin);
        printf("\n Input another y/n? ");
        choice = getchar();
        fflush(stdin);
    }while(choice == 'y');
    printf("Unsorted list \n");
    printf("\n*******************\n");
    for (i =0; i < n ; i++)
    {
        printf("\n %s", string[i].name);
        printf("\n %s", string[i].address);
        printf("\n %ld", string[i].Pin_code);
        printf("\n*******************\n");
    }
    getchar();
    sort(string, n);
    printf("\n Sorted list");
    printf("\n*******************\n");
    for (i =0; i < n ; i++)
    {
        printf("\n %s", string[i].name);
        printf("\n %s", string[i].address);
        printf("\n %ld", string[i].Pin_code);
        printf("\n*******************\n");
    }
    getchar();
}

/* Pointer and Array */
/* POINTSRT.C */
```

```
# include<stdio.h>
# include<string.h>
# include<ctype.h>

/* PROTOTYPE */
void sort(char **, int );
/* Definition of function */
void sort(char **str, int n)
{
    int i,j, flag;
    char *temp = (char *)malloc(50);
    for(i =0; i < n; i++)
    {
        flag = 1;
        for (j=0; j <(n-i-1); j++)
        {
            if (strcmp (str[j], str[j+1])>0)
            {
                flag = 0;
                temp = str[j];
                str[j] = str[j+1];
                str[j+1] = temp;
            }
        }if (flag)
            break;
    }
}

/* Function main */
void main()
{
    char choice;
    int i, n = 0;
    char *string[100];
    do{
        string[n] = (char *) malloc(50);
        printf("Input string: ");
        gets(string[n]);
        n++;
        fflush(stdin);
        printf("\n Input another Y/N? ");
```

```
        choice = getchar();
        fflush(stdin);
    }while(toupper(choice) == 'Y');
    printf("Unsorted list \n");
    printf("***********\n");
    for (i = 0; i < n; i++)
    {
        printf(" 0x%x", &string[i]);
        printf(" ");
        printf("%s", string[i]);
        printf("\n");
    }
    sort(string, n);
    printf("\n Sorted list");
    printf("\n***********\n");
    for (i = 0; i < n; i++)
    {
        printf(" 0x%x", &string[i]);
        printf(" %s", string[i]);
        printf("\n");
    }
}
```

1.16 DYNAMIC MEMORY ALLOCATION

When we declare an array in a program, the compiler allocates memory to hold the array prior to providing it. Some times it is required to change the size of the array and in that case it is required to edit and compile the program. To reduce the number of changes, it is required to allocate required memory during the run-time. For example, suppose we want to read a file into memory from the disk which contains information about students of a University? If we have prior information about the number of students and information associated with each student, then we can simply allocate required memory to an array and size of array is equal to the size of file. If the size of file is not known and we have to load it into memory and defining very large array, so that file can fit into the array. If the size of the array is larger than that of file then the space is wasted. If the size of file is larger then it is not possible to load the complete file into the array, leading to a need for dynamic memory allocation. In the dynamic memory allocation we use a pointer variable and it's size is allocated during the execution of the program. There are two principal functions in **C**, which are used to allocate required memory to pointer variable.

- malloc ()
- calloc ()

Both the **malloc ()** and **calloc ()** functions perform the operations and checks memory availability, based on the memory block size requested. When a suitable segment of memory is located, a pointer to the address of the allocated block is returned by the function.

The **malloc ()** function simply finds a free block in memory and then returns a pointer to it. The **calloc ()** function works in similar fashion, except that it is more convenient when allocating memory for storage units of more than one byte. Also, **calloc ()** clears all memory blocks as a part of its operation. This means that a block of pointer to block whose bytes have been set to **NULL**. For example, the program segment **CALLOC.C** illustrates the operation performed by **calloc ()** function. In this program segment **calloc ()** allocates 800*2 = 1600 bytes long block. The number of storage units is 800, but the size of each storage unit is 2 bytes. This program segment can safely address from 0 to 799 units in this block without overwriting memory. This means ***(p+799)** will access the 1599th and 1600th bytes in the allocated block. **Figure 1.13** illustrates the memory allocation by **calloc()** function and **Figure 1.14** shows the values written into allocated block.

```
/* calloc function */
/* CALLOC.C */
# include<malloc.h>
# include<stdlib.h>
# include<stdio.h>
/* Function main*/
void main()
{
    int *p, i;
    if((p =(int *) calloc(800, 2)) == NULL)
    {
        printf("\n Out of Memory \n");
        exit(0);
    }
    for (i = 0; i < 800; i++)
    {
        printf(" 0x%x", (p+i));
        printf(" %d", *(p+i));
    }
    getchar();
    for (i = 0; i < 800; i++)
    {
        *(p+i) = 77;
    }
    for (i = 0; i < 800; i++)
    {
        printf(" 0x%x", (p+i));
        printf(" %d", *(p+i));

    }
    getchar();
}
```

ADDRESS	INFORMATION
0x13580f0a	0
0x13580f0c	0
0x13580f0e	0
...	...
...	...
...	...
0x13581546	0
0x13581548	0

Figure 1.13 Before writing information calloc (800, 2)

ADDRESS	INFORMATION
0x13580f0a	77
0x13580f0c	77
0x13580f0e	77
...	...
...	...
...	...
0x13581546	77
0x13581548	77

Figure 1.14 After writing information calloc (800, 2)

The **malloc ()** function returns a pointer of type **void**, which means that we can assign it to any type of pointer. After a successful call **malloc ()** returns a pointer to the first byte of the block of memory which is allocated. If there is not enough available memory to satisfy the **malloc ()** request, an allocation failure occurs and **malloc ()** returns a **NULL**. For example:

```
int *p;
p = malloc (200*2);
```

After the assignment, **p** points to the 200*2 bytes of free memory. As we know that **malloc ()** returns a void pointer so a **cast operator** is required to change the returned pointer type according to need. The above statement can be written as:

```
int *p;
p = (int ) mallc(200*sizeof(int));
```

The allocated memory by **malloc ()** and **calloc ()** function are not free automatically and it is required to free the allocated space after the completion of the job. For this purpose **C++** has **free()** function that frees the allocated space. For example, the program segment **MALLOC.C** first of all allocates 400 bytes of memory space and frees these bytes. **Figure 1.15** illustrates operation performed by **malloc ()** function.

Address	Information
0x13450ef2	88
0x13450ef4	88
0x13450ef6	88
...	...
...	...
...	...
0x1345107e	88
0x13451080	88

Figure 1.15 malloc (200* sizeof (int))

```
/* malloc function*/
/* MALLOC.C */
# include<malloc.h>
# include<stdlib.h>
# include<stdio.h>
void main()
{
    int *p, i;
    p = (int *) malloc(200* sizeof(int));

    for (i = 0; i < 200; i++)
    {
        *(p+i) = 88;
    }

    for (i = 0; i < 200; i++)
    {
        printf(" 0x%x", (p+i));
        printf(" %d", *(p+i));
    }
    getchar();
}
```

1.17 ENUMERATION

These fall into the category of 'half baked'. They are not proper enumerated types, as in Pascal, and only really serve to help we reduce the number of #define statements in a program. Enumeration defines a set of constants of type int. The syntax for defining constants using enum is

`enum [tag] {name [=value], ...};`

The set can optionally be given a type tag name, it is the name of a constant that can optionally be assigned the (constant) value of *value*, etc. If *value* is missing, then a value is assumed to be the value of the previous constant in the list + 1. If this is the first constant in the list, the default value is 0. More precise, 'enum *tag*' becomes a new type which is equal in rights with any built-in type. If we give a type tag name, then we can declare variables of enumerated type using enum *tag variable-names*. For example,

```
enum e_tag
{
 a, b, c, d=20, e, f, g=20, h
}var;
```

Just as with structures and unions, the e_tag is the tag, and var is the definition of a variable. The names declared inside the enumeration are constants with int type. Their values are these,

```
a = 0
b = 1
c = 2
d = 20
e = 21
f = 22
g = 20
h = 21
```

So we can see that, in the absence of anything to the contrary, the values assigned start at zero and increase. A specific value can be given if we want, when the increase will continue one at a time afterwards; the specific value must be an *integral constant* that is representable in an int. It is possible for more than one of the names to have the same value. The only use for these things is to give a better-scoped version of this:

```
#define a 0
#define b 1
/* and so on */
```

It is better scoped because the declaration of enumerations follows the standard scope rules for C, whereas #define statements have file scope. Not that we are likely to care, but the C states that enumeration types are of a type that is compatible with an implementation-defined one of the integral types. So what? For interest's sake here is an illustration:

```
enum ee{a, b, c}e_var, *ep;
```

The names a, b, and c all behave as if they were int constants when we use them; e_var has type enum ee and ep is a pointer to enum ee. The compatibility requirement means that (amongst other implications) there will be an integral type whose address can be assigned to ep without violating the type-compatibility requirements for pointers.

1.18 BIT FIELD

A bit field is an element of a structure that is defined in terms of bits. Using a special type of struct definition, we can declare a structure element that can range from 1 to 16 bits in length. For example,

```
struct bit_field
 {
 int bit_1 : 1;
 int bits_2_to_5 : 4;
 int bit_6 : 1;
 int bits_7_to_16 : 10;
 } bit_var;
```

1.19 THE CONST AND VOLATILE

The idea of const has been borrowed from C++. The concepts of const and volatile are *completely independent*. A common misconception is to imagine that somehow const is the opposite of volatile and vice versa. They are unrelated and we should remember the fact. Since const declarations are the simpler, we will look at them first, but only after we see where both of these type qualifiers may be used. The complete list of relevant keywords is

char	long	float	volatile
short	signed	double	void
int	unsigned	const	

In the list, const and volatile are type qualifiers, the rest are *type specifiers*. Various combinations of type specifiers are permitted:

- char, signed char, unsigned char
- int, signed int, unsigned int
- short int, signed short int, unsigned short int
- long int, signed long int, unsigned long int
- float
- double
- long double

A few points should be noted. All declarations to do with an int will be signed anyway, so signed is redundant in that context. If *any* other type specifier or qualifier is present, then the int part may be dropped, as that is the default.

The keywords const and volatile can be applied to any declaration, including those of structures, unions, enumerated types or typedef names. Applying them to a declaration is called *qualifying* the declaration—that is why const and volatile are called type qualifiers, rather than type specifiers. Here are a few representative examples:

```
volatile i;
volatile int j;
const long q;
const volatile unsigned long int rt_clk;
struct
{
 const long int li;
 signed char sc;
}volatile vs;
```

Do not be put off; some of them are deliberately complicated: what they mean will be explained later. Remember that they could also be further complicated by introducing storage class specifications as well. In fact, the truly spectacular.

```
extern const volatile unsigned long int rt_clk;
```

is a strong possibility in some real time operating system kernels.

1.19.1 The const

Sometimes we want to keep some data types constant throughout the program. For this purpose we use *const* keyword in declaration of that identifier. Constant declarations are done with the help of keyword **const.** The values of these types of variables are not altered during program execution. The syntax for **const** is given below:

```
const data type variables;
```

For example,

- const ch='Y';
- const float float_constant = 3.17;
- const int num = 256;

See Example 1.1 which is implementing the above discussion.

Example 1.1: Write a C code to demonstrate the const.

Answer: The following program illustrates the idea and use of the **const** data types in C language.

```
#include<stdio.h>
void main()
   {
       const double a = 100000000.2234567;
       const float b = 1234.56 ;
       const int c = 34234 ;
       const char ch = 'Y' ;
       double d;
       d = a+b+c;
       printf("\n Value of a is: %lf",a);
       printf("\n Value of b is:%f",b);
       printf("\n Value ofc is:%d",c);
       printf("\n Value of ch is:%c",ch);
       }
```

If we write code like:

- a=a+1;
- c=256;
- ch='N';

Then we will get error message from the compiler because modification of *const data* type is not permitted in C. The **const** access modifier does not work with **long double** data type in C. For example, consider the following program:

```
#include<stdio.h>
void main()
{
    const long double num = 15.12345L;
printf("\n Value of num is: %lf ",num);
}
```

If we run the above program, the output comes -0.000000. In **const** declaration of **float**, character **L** or **l** is used after the last digit of the number. However this is optional.

If we are accessing a hardware port at a fixed memory address and promised only to read from it, then it would be declared to be const but not initialized. Taking the address of a data object of a type which is not const and putting it into a pointer to the const-qualified version of the same type is both safe and explicitly permitted; we will be able to use the pointer to inspect the object, but not modify it. Putting the address of a const type into a pointer to the unqualified type is much more dangerous and consequently prohibited (although we can get around this by using a cast). See Example 1.2 which is implementing the above discussion.

Example 1.2: Write a C code which implements const and pointer together and shows their alteration.

Answer: Following program segment implements the idea.

```
#include <stdio.h>
#include <stdlib.h>

main()
{
    int i;
    const int ci = 123;
     /* declare a pointer to a const.. */
     const int *cpi;
     /* ordinary pointer to a non-const */
     int *ncpi;
     cpi = &ci;
     ncpi = &i;
     /* this is allowed */
     cpi = ncpi;

     /* this needs a cast because it is usually a big mistake, see what it
permits below */
     ncpi = (int *)cpi;
     /** now to get undefined behaviour modify a const through a pointer */
     *ncpi = 0;
     exit(0);
}
```

As the example shows, it is possible to take the address of a constant object, generate a pointer to a non-constant, then use the new pointer. This is an *error* in the program and results in undefined behaviour.

The main intention of introducing const objects is to allow them to be put into read only store, and to permit compilers to do extra consistency checking in a program. Unless we defeat the intent by doing naughty things with pointers, a compiler is able to check that const objects are not modified explicitly by the user. An interesting extra feature pops up now. What does this mean?

```
char c;
char *const cp = &c;
```

It is simple really; cp is a pointer to a char, which is exactly what it would be if the const are not there. The const means that cp is not to be modified, although whatever it points to can be- the pointer is constant, not the thing that it points to. The other way round is

```
const char *cp;
```

which means that now cp is an ordinary, modifiable pointer, but the thing that it points to must not be modified. So, depending on what we choose to do, both the pointer and the thing it points to may be modifiable or not; just choose the appropriate declaration.

1.19.2 The volatile

C provides the luxury to change a constant data type during execution of program. The volatile modifier is used to tell the compiler that a variable value can be changed in the ways which are not explicitly specified by the program. It is also possible to use both (const, volatile) modifiers together. This type of declaration is used when we are writing software for communication purpose and during the software development; the communicating ports do not know it. For example,

```
const volatile unsigned char *port = 0x2d;
(Where 0x2d is the port address)
```

The reason for having this type qualifier is mainly to do with the problems that are encountered in real-time or embedded systems programming using C. Imagine that we are writing code that controls a hardware device by placing appropriate values in hardware registers at known absolute addresses.

Let us imagine that the device has two registers, each 16 bits long, at ascending memory addresses; the first one is the control and status register (csr) and the second is a data port. The traditional way of accessing such a device is like this:

```
/* Declare the device registers whether to use int or short is implementation
dependent*/
struct devregs
{
  unsigned short csr; /* control & status */
  unsigned short data; /* data port */
};

/* bit patterns in the csr */
#define ERROR 0x1
#define READY 0x2
#define RESET 0x4

/* absolute address of the device */
#define DEVADDR ((struct devregs *)0xffff0004)
/* number of such devices in system */
#define NDEVS 4
```

```
/* Busy-wait function to read a byte from device n, check range of device
number. Wait until READY or ERROR if no error, read byte, return it otherwise
reset error, return 0xffff */

unsigned int read_dev(unsigned devno)
{
 struct devregs *dvp = DEVADDR + devno;
 if(devno >= NDEVS)
 return(0xffff);
 while((dvp->csr & (READY | ERROR)) == 0)
 ; /* NULL - wait till done */

 if(dvp->csr & ERROR)
 {
 dvp->csr = RESET;
 return(0xffff);
 }
 return((dvp->data) & 0xff);
}
```

The technique of using a structure declaration to describe the device register layout and names is very common practice. Notice that there are not actually any objects of that type defined, so the declaration simply indicates the structure without using up any store.

To access the device registers, an appropriately cast constant is used as if it is pointing to such a structure, but of course it points to memory addresses instead.

However, a major problem with old C compilers would be in the while loop which tests the status register and waits for the ERROR or READY bit to come on. Any self-respecting optimizing compiler would notice that the loop tests the same memory address over and over again. It would almost certainly arrange to reference memory once only, and copy the value into a hardware register, thus speeding up the loop. This is, of course, exactly what we do not want; this is one of the few places where we must look at the place where the pointer points, every time around the loop.

Because of this problem, most C compilers have been unable to make that sort of optimization in the past. To remove the problem (and other similar ones to do with when to write to where a pointer points), the keyword volatile was introduced. It tells the compiler that the object is subject to sudden change for reasons which cannot be predicted from a study of the program itself, and forces every reference to such an object to be a genuine reference.

Here is how we would rewrite the example, making use of const and volatile to get what we want.

```
/* Declare the device registers whether to use int or short is implementation
dependent */

struct devregs
{
 unsigned short volatile csr;
 unsigned short const volatile data;
```

```
};

/* bit patterns in the csr */

#define ERROR 0x1
#define READY 0x2
#define RESET 0x4

/* absolute address of the device */

#define DEVADDR ((struct devregs *)0xffff0004)

/* number of such devices in system */

#define NDEVS 4
```

/* Busy-wait function to read a byte from device n, check range of device number. Wait until READY or ERROR if no error, read byte, return it otherwise reset error, return 0xffff */

```
unsigned int read_dev(unsigned devno)
{
    struct devregs * const dvp = DEVADDR + devno;

     if(devno >= NDEVS)
     return(0xffff);

     while((dvp->csr & (READY | ERROR)) == 0)
     ; /* NULL - wait till done */

     if(dvp->csr & ERROR){
     dvp->csr = RESET;
     return(0xffff);
  }

     return((dvp->data) & 0xff);
}
```

The rules about mixing volatile and regular types resemble those for const. A pointer to a volatile object can be assigned address of a regular object with safety, but it is dangerous (and needs a cast) to take the address of a volatile object and put it into a pointer to a regular object. It is found that using such a derived pointer results in undefined behaviour.

If an array, union or structure is declared with const or volatile attributes, then all of the members take on that attribute too. This makes sense when we think about it—how could a member of a const structure be modifiable?

That means that an alternative rewrite of the last example would be possible. Instead of declaring the device registers to be volatile in the structure, the pointer could have been declared to point to a volatile structure instead, like this:

```
struct devregs
{
 unsigned short csr; /* control & status */
 unsigned short data; /* data port */
};

volatile struct devregs *const dvp=DEVADDR+devno;
```

Since dvp points to a volatile object, it is not permitted to optimize references through the pointer. Although this would work, it is bad style. The volatile declaration belongs in the structure: it is the device registers which are volatile and that is where the information should be kept; it reinforces the fact for a reader.

So, for any object likely to be subject to modification either by hardware or asynchronous interrupt service routines, the volatile type qualifier is important. Now, just when we thought that we understood all that, here comes the final twist. A declaration like this:

```
volatile struct devregs
{
 /* stuff */
}v_decl;
```

The above statement declares the type struct devregs and also a volatile-qualified object of that type, called v_decl. A later declaration like this

```
struct devregs nv_decl;
```

The above statement declares nv_decl which is *not* qualified with volatile. The qualification is *not* part of the type of struct devregs but applies only to the declaration of v_decl. Look at the following declaration which is same as previous declaration.

```
struct devregs
{
 /* stuff */
}volatile v_decl;
```

If we do want to get a shorthand way of attaching a qualifier to another type, we can use typedef to do it:

```
struct x
{
 int a;
};
typedef const struct x csx;

csx const_sx;
```

```
struct x non_const_sx = {1};

const_sx = non_const_sx; /* error - attempt to modify a const */
```

Readers are advised reread this section after completion of pointer and arrays.

1.20 CONSTANTS

We have seen data types in C and we know that a variable can hold some data. The data can be assigned while writing a program or inputted through keyboard also. The data can be modified as per need of a programmer. But sometimes we need to make some data constant and it should not be altered during the program execution. A data may be modified knowingly or unknowingly. We have a special feature in C that makes a data constant throughout the execution of a program. For this, we use keyword const defined in C language. We can also make a data constant by using *define* directive in C. For example, the following directive creates a constant named Size and assigns value 25 to it.

```
#define Size 25
```

This directive (define) is instruction for the C preprocessor; the preprocessor will replace the constant name with its value.

There is a keyword **const** available in **C**, which is also used for the same purpose. With this keyword, one requires to use prefixes/suffixes, which are given in **Table 1.12**. The **const** ensures that the parameter defined and value associated will not alter during the lifetime of the program. The constants can be classified into five categories:

- Character Constants
- Integer constants
- Floating-point constants
- Literal constants (Strings, group of characters)
- Enumeration constants

Table 1.12 Constant suffixes/prefixes Example

Constant suffix/prefix	Example
L, l are used for long integer and double as suffix	6599L, 35471
F, f are used for float constant as suffix	46578F, 54328f
For hexadecimal constant 0x is used as prefix	0x35536
Single quote is used for character constant	'Y'
For integer constant simply const keyword is placed	const in num =7674

For example, the program *constant.c* discusses the constant declarations with the help of keyword **const**.

```
/* constant.c */
#include<stdio.h>
void main()
{
 const int num = 345;
```

```
    const long int LONG =999678647L;
    const float Float_num = 1234.30045f;
    const int Octal = 012345;
    const int Hex = 0x1abc;
    const int Unsigned_num = 1236u;
    printf ("\n Integer %d",num);
    printf ("\n Long integer %ld ",LONG);
    printf ("\n Float %f",Float_num);
    printf ("\n Octal %o",Octal);
    printf ("\n Hexadecimal %X",Hex);
    printf ("\nUnsigned integer: %u ",Unsigned_num);
    }
```

Output

```
Integer 234
Long integer 999678647
Float 1234.30045
Octal 12345
Hexadecimal 1ABC
Unsigned integer 1236
```

1.21 ALGORITHMS

So far we have considered the construct of C language a little bit. But we have not focus on this fact that what type of instructions should be given to a computer system for some specific work. We know that a computer cannot do anything itself. We have to program a computer. So, a program should be based on well-defined solution for a specific problem. If the solution is ill-defined, we cannot expect the right response from a computer system, because that computer is not properly instructed by the programmer. For details see Example 1.3, suppose we want to get the addition of two integers m and n. Let the variable *result* holds the addition of m and n, i.e.,

```
result = m+n;
```

Example 1.3: Write C code which adds two integer numbers.

Answer: Now, let us program the above work using C language. Computer does not know any thing about the operands m, n and result. So, we have to define these first to make the computer aware. If we use these terms without making the computer system aware, the compiler will raise error message. The following program *add.c* solves the purpose. We assume that m=20 and n=15.

```
/*** add.c ***/
#include<stdio.h>
main()
{
    int m, n, result;
```

```
m=20;
n=15;
result = m+n;
printf"("%d", result);
}
```

```
Output
```

```
35
```

Suppose the above program written as given below:

```
/** add1.c **/
#include<stdio.h>
main()
{
  m=20;
  n=15;
  result = m+n;
printf"("%d", result);
}
```

We will get error message by the compiler while compile the above program add1.c as:

"m, n, result are not defined"

Program *add.c* is based on the following steps:

1. Define the variables m, n, and result
2. Initialize the values of m and n, that is, m=20, n=15
3. Add m and n and assign the value into variable result, that is, result = m+n

If a program does not incorporate the above steps, it cannot produce the desired result as the program *add1.c* does. The above discussion indicates the notion of sequential or procedural processing. In other words, we can say that C language is sequential or procedural language. But it is structured also. Thus, fundamental knowledge necessary to solve problems using a computer is the notation of an algorithm. An algorithm is a precise specification of a sequence of instructions to be carried out in order to solve a given problem. Each instruction tells what task is to be performed. Specification of a sequence of instructions to do a job is used in many fields.

1.21.1 Concept of Algorithm

We have various problems in our life and we try to overcome of those. We have well- defined way to accomplish our work, assignments, etc. If we convert the well-defined way into steps then these steps give rise to the concept of algorithm. Whatever we do in this practical world is based on some well-defined thought. Starting from the civilization, people are used to find the simplest method to fulfill their daily needs and overcome of their problems. This is the origin of algorithm. When a man faces a problem or has some need, he tries to find the solution. It may be that first time he could not find simple solution, but he keeps on trying to get better solution. This is why we have so established society.

In every field, we have well defined means and methods to fulfill our needs. Let us think about computer system. A common man believes that a computer can do anything and everything that he imagines. It is very difficult to make people realize that it is not really the computer but the man behind computer who does everything.

In this Internet world, a man feels that just by entering what he wants to search into the computers, he can get information as desired by him and believes computer does that search. A common man seldom understands that a man made procedure called search has done the entire job and the only support provided by the computer is the executioner and organized storage of information.

In the above instance, a designer of the information system should know what one frequently searches for. He should make a structured organization of all those details to store in memory of the computer. Based on the requirement, the right information is brought out. This is accomplished through a set of instructions created by the designer of the information system to search the right information matching the requirement of the users. This set of instructions is termed as program. It should be evident by now that it is not the computer, which generates automatically the program but it is the designer of the information system who has created this. So, a computer can do those things what a designer can programmed. This indicates the limit of a computer system.

Therefore, the program is executed to perform all the activities as desired by a user. This indicates that programming a computer is more important than the computer itself while solving a problem. Even at this stage, one should not quickly jump to conclusion that coding is programming. Coding is perhaps the last stage in the process of programming a computer. Programming involves various activities form the stage of conceiving the problem up to the stage of creating a model to solve the problem. The formal representation of this model as a sequence of instructions is called an algorithm and coded algorithm in a specific computer language is called a program.

One can now experience that the focus is shifted from computer to computer programming and then to creating an algorithm. This is algorithm design which is heart of problem solving in the field of computer.

1.21.2 Definition

An algorithm is named after the ninth century scholar **Abu Jafar Muhammad Ibn Musu Al-Khowarizmi.** In mathematics and **computer** science, an algorithm is a step-by-step procedure for calculations. Algorithms are used for calculation, data processing, and automated reasoning. It is simply defined as follows.

1. An algorithm is a set of well-defined rules for carrying out calculation either by hand or on a machine.
2. An algorithm is a finite step-by-step procedure to achieve a required result.
3. An algorithm is a sequence of computational steps that transform the input into the output.
4. An algorithm is a sequence of operations performed on input (data) that have to be organized in data structures.
5. An algorithm is an abstraction of a program to be executed on a physical machine (model of Computation).

In more specific way "an algorithm can be classified as a finite sequence of instructions" which has the following basic properties:

- A number of quantities provided to an algorithm initially before the algorithm begins. These quantities are the inputs, which are processed by the algorithm.

- The processing rules specified in the algorithm must be precise and unambiguous and lead to a specific action.
- Each instruction must be sufficiently basic so that a person using paper and pencil can in principle carry it out in a finite time.
- The total time to carry out all the steps in the algorithm must be finite. As algorithms may contain instructions to repetitively carry out a group of instructions, this requirement implies that the total number of repetitions must be finite.
- An algorithm must have one or more outputs.
- Each step of an algorithm should be well-defined, it should not be ambiguous.

The most famous algorithm in history dates well before the time of the ancient Greeks and this is **Euclid's algorithm** for calculating the greatest common divisor of two integers.

1.21.3 Characteristics of an Algorithm

Let us try to present the scenario of a man brushing his own teeth (natural denture) step-by-step and say it is an algorithm.

Step 1. Take the tooth brush

Step 2. Apply the tooth paste

Step 3. Start brushing

Step 4. Rinse the brush

Step 5. Wash

Step 6. Stop

If one goes through all these steps without being aware of the statement of the problem, he/she could possibly feel that this is the algorithm for cleaning a toilet. This is because of several ambiguities while comprehending every step. The step 1 may imply toothbrush, paintbrush, toilet brush, etc. Such an ambiguity should not be an instruction (step) of an algorithmic. Thus, every step should be made unambiguous. An unambiguous step is called definite instruction. Even if the step 2 is rewritten as apply the toothpaste, to eliminate ambiguities yet the conflicts such as, where to apply the toothpaste and where the source of the toothpaste is, need to be resolved. Hence, the act of applying the toothpaste is not mentioned. Although unambiguous, such unrealizable steps cannot be included as an instruction (step) of an algorithmic as they are not effective.

The definiteness and effectiveness of an instruction implies the successful termination with desire output of that instruction. However the above two may not be sufficient to guarantee the termination of the algorithm. Therefore, while designing an algorithm care should be taken to provide a proper termination for algorithm.

Therefore, an algorithm can be defined as a sequence of definite and effective instructions, which terminates with the production of correct output from the given input.

In other words, viewed little more formally, an algorithm is a step-by-step formalization of a mapping function to map input set onto an output set.

Thus, every algorithm should have the following five characteristic features.

- Input
- Output
- Definiteness

- Effectiveness
- Termination

Algorithm Design and Analysis (ADA) is a branch of Computer Science that consists of designing and analyzing computer algorithms. The "**Design**" pertains to the description of algorithm at an abstract level by means of a pseudo language, and proof of correctness that is, the algorithm solves the given problem in all cases.

1.21.4 Algorithmic Notations

The pseudo code uses notations used in common languages like PASCAL and C language. For example, if-else structure, for loop structure, while loop structure, do-while loop structure. A conditional statement of an algorithm has the following form.

1. If-Else Structure:

```
If (condition) then
Block 1   // Instruction(s)
Else
Block 2   //Instruction(s)
          // End of Structure
```

Comments are given with the symbol // for better understanding of the instructions of an algorithm. It is good practice to give comments about the instructions of the algorithm. The above pseudo code executes Block 1 if the condition is true otherwise Block 2 is executed. A block is a set of instructions and it may contain one or more instructions. Sometimes, the If-Else structure is nested and appears as given below.

```
If (condition) then
Block 1   // Instruction(s)
Else If (condition) then
Block 2   //Instruction(s)
Else
Block 3   //Instruction(s)
          // End of Structure
```

2. For loop Structure: We use for loop structure to repeat to certain Block (instructions) up to fixed number of times. There is a counter, which keeps track of the number of repetitions. The structure of **for** loop is given below.

For Counter = i to j
{Instruction 1, Instruction 2… Instruction n}

There are three things hidden in the for loop structure.

(a) Counter initialization
(b) Condition checking
(c) Increment of Counter

3. While loop Structure: When we are not sure about the number of repetitions of a block then we use while loop structure as follows.

while (condition)
{Instruction 1, Instruction 2… Instruction n}

4. Do-while loop Structure: When we are not sure about the number of repetitions of a block (instructions) and want that the block could execute at least once then we use do-while loop structure as follows.

Do

{Instruction 1, Instruction 2... Instruction n} w**hile** (condition)

5. Conditions and Concatenation of Conditions: We use conditions to make the number of execution of a block finite or infinite, some times as there is need. We use some logical operators like AND, OR, NOT, etc. to concatenate the conditions. Conditions are expressions, which give the value TRUE (1) or FALSE (0). When we use the logical operators then we evaluate NOT, AND, and OR in sequence. If conditions are concatenated by AND operator then result is TRUE if and only all conditions are TRUE otherwise FALSE and in case of OR operator, result is TRUE if at least one of the conditions is TRUE and FALSE otherwise.

$C=C_1$ AND C_2 AND...AND C_n =TRUE if and only if $C_1=C_2=...=C_n$=TRUE, otherwise FALSE and $C=C_1$ OR C_2 OR...OR C_n =TRUE if at least one the $C_1, C_2,...,C_n$ is TRUE, otherwise FALSE. The NOT operator reverses the value of the condition. If C_1 is TRUE then NOT C_1 is FALSE.

For example, consider the following conditions and show their values after concatenation.

Condition	Value
C_1	1
C_2	1
C_3	0

(a) $C_4=C_1$ AND C_2

(b) $C_5=C_2$ AND C_3

(c) $C_6=C_1$ AND NOT C_3

Solution:

(a) C_4= 1 AND 1=1

(b) C_5=1 AND 0=0

(c) C_6=1 AND NOT 0= 1 AND 1=1

The fundamental knowledge to solve problems using a computer is the notation of an algorithm. For example, suppose we have an array **DATA** of numerical values with size **N** in memory. We want to find the location **K** and the value **MAX** of the largest element of **DATA**. An algorithm for this problem can be constructed as illustrated in **Figure 1.16**.

The execution of an algorithm begins at **Step1** and continues from there in sequential order unless the result of a condition tested or an unconditional transfer specifies otherwise. In the algorithm given in Figure 1.16, **Step 1** is executed first if the array **DATA** is empty, the algorithm terminates; otherwise **Step 2** is performed. In this step, **MAX** is initialized to the value of **DATA [I].** Firstly **I** is 1 and variable **I** is incremented by 1. **Step 3** leads to termination of this algorithm if we have already tested the last element of the array **DATA**; otherwise **Step 4** is performed. In this step, the value of **MAX** is compared with the value of next element of the array **DATA**. If **MAX** is less than the next element, **MAX** is assigned this new value (by calling Step 2). If the test fails, no reassignment takes place. The completion of **Step 4** is followed by **Step 5** where control returns to the **Step 2** when we assign new value to **MAX** and increment the subscript by 1.

It is very much advisable to the readers that before writing a program design an algorithm for a problem. Do not try hit and trial method. Sometimes it may be costly and may result into damaging the system. Keep in mid that C language is middle-level language. So, any bad instruction can damage the system. Designing an algorithm is simple for any problem when we have some solution for that. Derive the solution step by step considering the flow of processing. If some steps are missing or misplaced then result will be undesirable.

```
Step 1: [Initialization]
        I = 1
        K = 1
Step 2: [Increment counter]
        MAX = DATA [I]
        I = I + 1
Step 3: [Test counter]
        If (I > N) then
        Write K, MAX and Exit
Step 4: [Compare and update]
        If (MAX < DATA [I]) then
        K = I
Step 5: Go to Step 2
```

Figure. 1.16 search Algorith

1.21.5 Analysis of Algorithms

As soon as one can write an algorithm, it is necessary to learn how to analyze an algorithm. The first type of analysis that one encounters is of the correctness of an algorithm. Tracing the algorithm, reading the algorithm for logical correctness, implementing the algorithm and testing it on some data or using mathematical techniques to prove it correct can do this analysis. Another type of analysis is of the simplicity of the algorithm. Perhaps the algorithm can be expressed in a simpler way, so that it is easier to implement and perform other analysis on the algorithm. However, the simplest and most straightforward way of solving a problem is sometimes not the best one. Usually this occurs when the simplest approach involves the use of too much computer time or space. Thus, it is important to be able to analyze the time and space requirements of an algorithm to see if it is within acceptable limits. For example, if an algorithm to control the trajectory of a rocket required several seconds for each trajectory adjustment, it would be unacceptable.

Two important ways to characterize the effectiveness of an algorithm are its space complexity and time complexity. Time complexity of an algorithm concerns with determining an expression of the number of steps needed as a function of the problem size (input size). Since, the step count measure is somewhat coarse; one does not aim at obtaining an exact step count. Instead, one attempts only to get asymptotic bounds on the step count. Asymptotic analysis makes use of the **O**(*Big Oh*) notation. Two other notational constructs used by computer scientists in the analysis of algorithms are – (*Big Theta*) and Ω (*Big Omega*) notations. The performance evaluation of an algorithm is obtained by totaling the number of occurrences of each operation when running the algorithm. The performance of an algorithm is evaluated as a function of the input size **n** and is to be considered modulo a multiplicative constant.

1.21.6 Rate of Growth

Unfortunately it is generally not possible to perform a simple analysis of an algorithm to determine the exact amount of time required it. The first complication is that the exact amount of time will depend on the implementation of the algorithm on the actual machine. Another complication arises in doing time analysis in that the time requirements will normally depend on the amount of input data. For example, an algorithm that sums the values in an array can be expected to require more time for an array of size 10000 values that for one of size 100. As a result the estimate for the time required by an algorithm is usually expressed as a function of the size of the input data. Thus, if input has size **n**, as in the above example, where there are **n** values in the array, then the time is expressed as **T (n)** and space as **S (n),** where **T** and **S** are functions of the amount of data.

Before starting analysis of algorithms it is beneficial to recall the rates of growth for some functions that are often used to express **T** and **S**. In **Figure 1.17** we have plotted several functions. The functions that involve **n** as an exponent, 2^n, n^n and $n! \sim (n/2.56)^n$ are called exponential functions. Any algorithm whose execution time grows proportionally to an exponential function is too slow for some constant **c**, for example, n^3, n^2, $n \log_2 n$, **n** and $\log_2 n$ are said to be polynomial. Algorithms with polynomial time can solve rescannable sized problems if the constant in the exponent is small. For problems involving large amounts of data, it is necessary to find an algorithm whose execution time grows linearly, proportional to **n** or sub-linearly, for instance, proportional to $\log_2 n$.

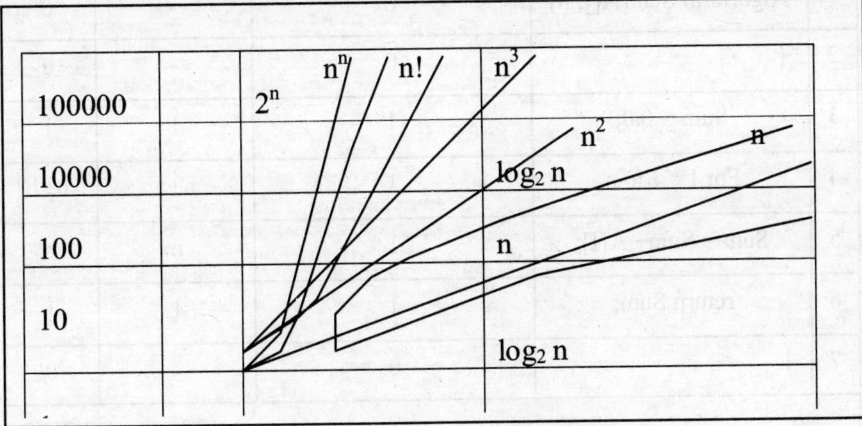

Figure. 1.17 Rate of Growth

1.21.7 Time Analysis

Time required T(P) to run a program P also consists of two components: (a) A fixed part: compile time which is independent of the problem instance → c (b) A variable part: run time which depends on the problem instance → t_p(instance). Thus, time complexity may be defined as.

$T(P) = c + t_p(\text{instance})$

As we have already discussed that calculation of exact amount of time required by an algorithm is very difficult, so we want an estimate of it. How to measure T(P)? If we measure experimentally, using a "stop watch" then T(P) is obtained in secs, msecs, etc. Another way to count program steps → T(P) obtained as a step count. We normally ignore the fixed part and only the variable part t_p() is measured. Usually this is most easily done by isolating a particular operation, sometimes called active operation, that is central to the algorithm and that is executed essentially as often as any other. Now it is important discuss. What is a program step? These are given in the following steps.

- If a+b+b*c+(a+b)/(a-b) is an expression then it is → one step;
- comments → zero steps;
- while (<expr>) do → step count equal to the number of times <expr> is executed.
- for i=<expr> to <expr1> do → step count equal to number of times <expr1> is checked.

For example, consider the algorithm **Summation** that finds summation of an array containing **n** values, given in **Figure 1.18.** In this algorithm, a good operation to isolate is the addition that occurs when another array value is added to the partial sum. The other operations in the algorithm, the assignments, the manipulations of index **I** and the accessing of a value in the array, occur no more often than the addition of the array values. These other operations are collectively called bookkeeping operations and are not generally counted. It is very important that none of the bookkeeping operations are executed significantly more often than the active operation. After the active operation is isolated, the number of times that it is executed is counted. If we follow this approach in the summation algorithm shown in **Figure 1.18**, the number of additions of values is **n.** As long as the active operation occurs at least as often as the others, then the execution time will increase in proportion to the number of times the active operation is executed. Thus, the above algorithm has execution time proportional to **n**. this discussion is summarized as follows.

	Statements	Statement/Expression	Frequency	Total
1	Algorithm Sum(A[], n)	0	-	0
2	{	0	-	0
3	Sum = 0.0;	1	1	1
4	For I = 1 to n	1	n+1	n+1
5	Sum = Sum+ A[I];	1	n	n
6	return Sum;	1	1	1
7	}	0	-	0
				2n+3

Consider another example, addition of two matrices of size **n x n** and are **M** and **N**, to form an **n x n** matrix **R.** The algorithm is given in **Figure 1.19.**

The actual size of the input for this algorithm is **2n²**, but it is convenient to use **n** as our measure of the size of the input in orders to simplify the calculations. For the active operations, we can select either the multiplication of **M [I][K]** and **N [I][K]** or addition of the above product to **Sum**. This follows since both are central operations and essentially occur as often as any other does. It is easy to see that either of these operations is executed $\mathbf{n^3}$ times, so that the time for the algorithm is proportional to $\mathbf{n^3}$.

Note that there are actually more assignments than multiplication or additions. There are **n** assignment to **I**, $\mathbf{n^2}$ assignments to **J** and **R**, $\mathbf{n^3}$ assignments to **K** and $\mathbf{n^2+n^3}$ assignments to **Sum**. This yields a total of $\mathbf{n + 3n^2 + 2n^3}$ assignments. Certainly assignment could have been selected as active operation, although it is questionable whether it is as central to the problem as either multiplication or addition. If it were used as the active operation, we would conclude that the time was proportional to $\mathbf{n + 3n^2 + 2n^3}$. Fortunately we are normally only interested in the order of magnitude of the time required. The order only considers the term that grows the fastest, $\mathbf{2n^3}$ and ignores the constant 2, associated with it. Thus, we obtain that the order of magnitude for the time required in $\mathbf{n^3}$, independent of which operation is chosen as active, but that just happens in this problem. In other cases, may be assignments would have to be active. **Question to reader formulate this analysis as done for algorithm given in Figure 1.18.**

```
Summation (A[], n)
{
Step 1: [Initialization]
   Sum = 0.0
Step 2: [Sum the values in array A]
   For I=1 to n
   Sum = Sum + A[I]
Step 3: [Finish]
   Return Sum
}
```

Figure 1.18 Summation of content of an array

```
Matrix_Addition(M, N, R)
Where M, N and R are nxn array
Step 1: [Perform multiplication operation]

Repeat through Step 3 for I = 1, 2, 3 … n
Repeat through Step 3 for J = 1, 2, 3 … n
Sum = 0.0
Repeat through Step 2 for K= 1, 2, 3 … n

Step 2:   Sum = Sum + M[I][K]*N[K][J]

Step 3:   R[I][J] = Sum

Step 4: [Finished]
Exit
```

Figure 1.19 Matrix Multiplication algorithm

1.21.8 Space Analysis

Memory space S(P) needed by a program P, consists of two components: (a) A fixed part: needed for instruction space (byte code), simple variable space, constants space, etc. → c (b) A variable part: dependent on a particular instance of input and output data. → S_p(instance). Thus, space complexity of program P may be written as.

$S(P) = c + S_p(\text{instance})$

See the following example in which only one statement is playing major role. If for every instance 3 computer words required to store variables: a, b, and c then $S_p() = 3$ {constant number of statements}, i.e., S(P) = 3.

```
Algorithm abc (a, b, c)
{
```

```
    return a+b+b*c+(a+b-c)/(a+b)+4.0;
}
```

See another example consider the algorithm given in **Figure 1.18** which finds summation of an array of n number. In this example every instance needs to store array A[] and n. Space needed to store n = 1 word, space needed to store A[ ] = n floating point words (or at least n words), and space needed to store I and s = 2 words. Thus, space complexity of the algorithm is

$S_p(n) = (n + 3)$. Hence $S(P) = (n + 3)$.

1.21.9 Asymptotic Notations

Now we might say, it is obvious how to measure the efficiency of an algorithm. Just code up the algorithm as a program and run the program on some test data. Measures the execution time, or the memory required, and there we are. If we want to know if one algorithm is more efficient than another, do this for both of them and compare the results. For this we need to discuss few notations which are as follows.

Big - Oh Notation: it is asymptotic Upper Bound

The Big O notation defines an upper bound of an algorithm; it bounds a function only from above. Big O of a function gives us 'rate of growth' of the step count function *f(n)*, in terms of a simple function *g(n)*, which is easy to compare. It is defined as "The function $f(n) = O(g(n))$ (big 'Oh' of g of n) if there exist positive constants c and n_0 such that $f(n) \le c^*g(n)$ for all n, $n \ge n_0$."

For example, consider the case of Insertion Sort. It takes linear time in best case and quadratic time in worst case. We can safely say that the time complexity of Insertion sort is $O(n^2)$. Note that $O(n^2)$ also covers linear time. If we use Θ notation to represent time complexity of Insertion sort, we have to use two statements for best and worst cases:

1. The worst case time complexity of Insertion Sort is $\Theta(n^2)$.
2. The best case time complexity of Insertion Sort is $\Theta(n)$.

See the following example for better understanding the Big Oh analysis.

(a) $f(n) = 3n+2$ is $O(n)$ because $3n+2 \le 4n$ for all $n \ge 2$, $c = 4$, $n_0 = 2$. Here $g(n) = n$.

(b) $f(n) = 10n^2+4n+2$ is $O(n^2)$ because $10n^2+4n+2 \le 11n^2$ for all $n \ge 5$.

(c) $f(n) = 6*2^n+n^2$ is $O(2^n)$ because $6*2^n+n^2 \le 7*2^n$ for all $n \ge 4$.

See the following example

Algorithm	*Cost*
sum = 0;	c_1
for(i=0; i<n; i++)	c_2
for(j=0; j<m; j++)	c_2
sum += arr[i][j];	c_3

In this algorithm it is observed that outer lop runs for (n) times whereas inner loop runs for n (m) times. When cost is summarized=> $c_1 + c_2 x n + c_2 x n x m + c_3 x n x m = O(n x m)$. If n and m are equal then $O(n^2)$

A characteristic of Big O is shown in **Figure 1.20**. Since "Big - Oh" is an upper bound, it is often used to state the complexity of a worst case analysis. If running cost of an algorithm is 30*n*+8. Then it is not less than *n anywhere for n*>0. It is not even less than 31*n* everywhere. But it is less than 31n everywhere to the right of n=8. This is shown in **Figure 1.21.**

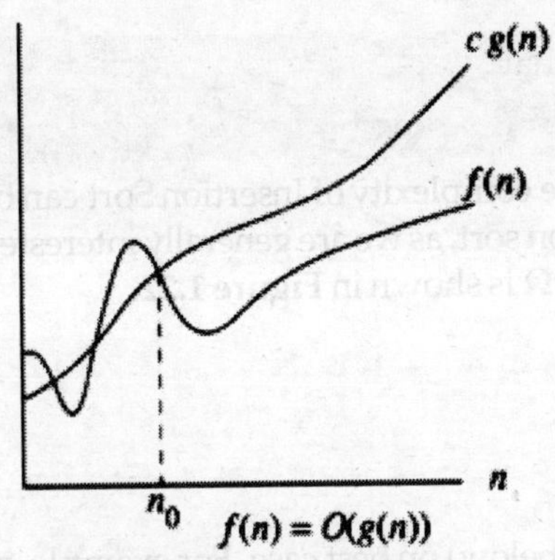

Figure 1.20 Big O Notation

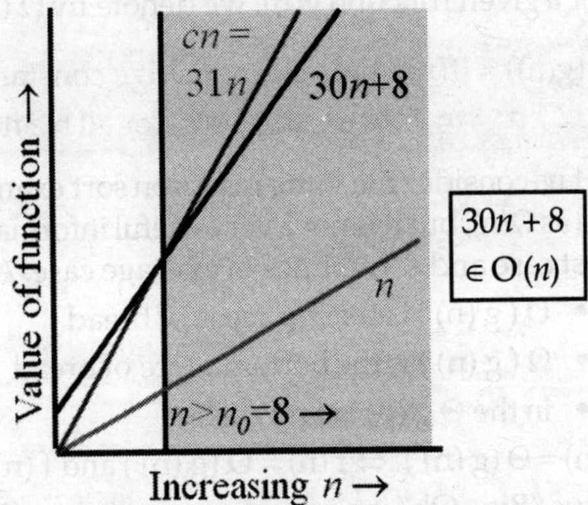

Figure 1.21 Big O the cost function 30n+8.

Θ- Notation:

The theta notation bounds functions from above and below, so it defines exact asymptotic behavior. A simple way to get Theta notation of an expression is to drop low order terms and ignore leading constants. For example, consider the following expression.

$3n^3 + 6n^2 + 6000 = \Theta(n^3)$

Dropping lower order terms is always fine because there will always be a n_0 after which $\Theta(n^3)$ beats $\Theta(n^2)$ irrespective of the constants involved.

For a given function g (n): Θ (g(n)) = { f (n) : there exist positive constants c_1, c_2, n_0 such that $0 \le c_1 g(n) \le f(n) \le c_2 g(n)$ for all $n \ge n_0$}. This definition means, iff(n) is theta of g(n), then the value f(n) is always between c1*g(n) and c2*g(n) for large values of n ($n \ge n_0$). The definition of theta also requires that f(n) must be positive for values of n greater than n0. In other words we can say that at some point f (n) is sandwiched between c_1 g (n) and c_2 g (n) as shown in **Figure 1.21**.

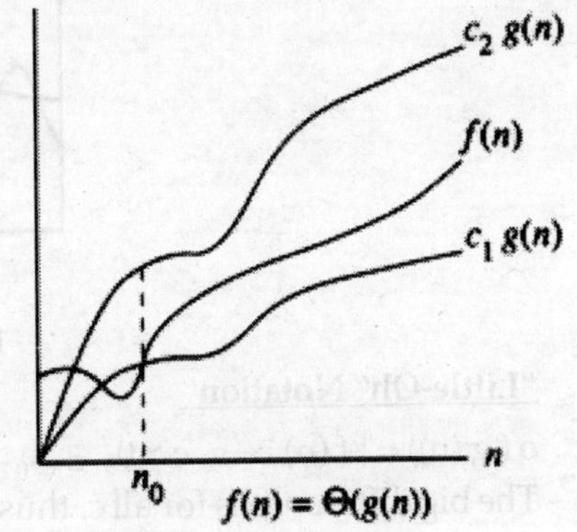

Figure 1.21 Θ notation

Θ(g (n)) is a set of functions, yet we write " f (n) = Θ(g (n))" to mean that f (n) ≥ Θ(g (n)). We use set notation because of sandwiching for n, f (n) is equal to g (n) to within a constant factor, therefore g(n) is an asymptotically tight bound for f (n). Note: The definition requires all f(n) ≥ Θ(g (n)) to be asymptotically positive. This means that g (n) must be as well.

For example: $n^2/2 - n/2 = \Theta(n^2)$ then compute value of c_1 and c_2

- **$\frac{1}{2} n^2 - \frac{1}{2} n \le \frac{1}{2} n^2 \ \forall\ n \ge 0 \Rightarrow c_2 = \frac{1}{2}$**
- **$\frac{1}{2} n^2 - \frac{1}{2} n \ge \frac{1}{2} n^2 - \frac{1}{2} n * \frac{1}{2} n \ (\forall\ n \ge 2) = \frac{1}{4} n^2 \quad \Rightarrow \quad c_1 = \frac{1}{4}$**

Ω (Omega) notation:

Just as Big O notation provides an asymptotic upper bound on a function, Ω notation provides an asymptotic lower bound. Ω Notation will be useful when we have lower bound on time complexity of an algorithm. The best case performance of an algorithm is generally not useful; the Ω notation is the least used notation among all three.

For a given function g(n), we denote by Ω (g(n)) the set of functions.

Ω (g(n)) = {f(n): there exist positive constants c and n0 such that
$0 \le cg(n) \le f(n)$ for all $n \ge n0$}.

Let us consider the same Insertion sort example here. The time complexity of Insertion Sort can be written as Ω(n), but it is not a very useful information about insertion sort, as we are generally interested in worst case and sometimes in average case. A characteristic of Ω is shown in **Figure 1.22.**

- **O** (g (n)) is the top piece of bread
- Ω (g (n)) is the bottom piece of bread
- in the Θ g (n)) sandwich

$f(n) = \Theta(g(n)) \Leftrightarrow f(n) = \mathbf{O}(g(n))$ and $f(n) = \Omega(g(n))$

Thus "Big - Oh" is a bound on worst case, Ω is a bound (from below) on best case. For example, in the case of insertion sort, for all inputs n:

$T(n) = \mathbf{O}(n^2) = \Omega(n)$

"Running time is Ω (g (n))" means that no matter what input the running time is at least c * g (n) for large n.

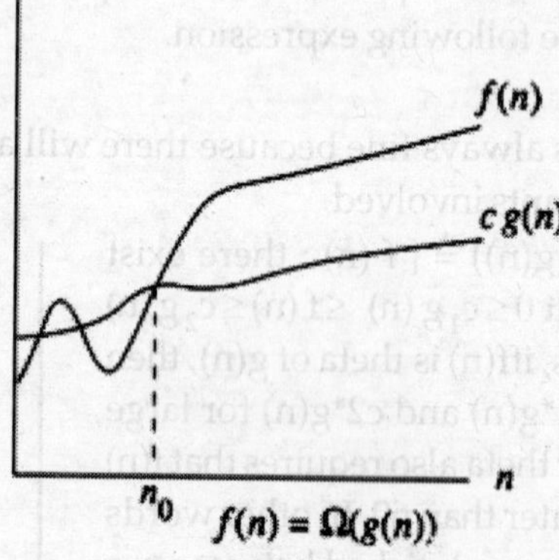

Figure 1.22 Big Ω Notation

"Little-Oh" Notation"

$\mathbf{o}(g(n)) = \{ f(n) :: \forall c > 0, \exists n_0 > 0 \ni 0 \le f(n) \le cg(n) \ \forall \ n \ge n_0 \}$

The big difference is for all c, thus this is an upper bound that is not tight. It also means that:

$$\lim_{n \to \infty} \frac{f(n)}{g(n)} = 0$$

ω Notation (ω is to **o** as Ω is to **O**)

$\omega(g(n)) = \{ f(n) :: \forall c > 0, \exists n_0 > 0 \ni 0 \le cg(n) \le f(n) \ \forall \ n \ge n_0 \}$

$$\lim_{n \to \infty} \frac{g(n)}{f(n)} = 0$$

Hence $f(n) = \omega(g(n)) \Leftrightarrow g(n) = \mathbf{o}(f(n))$

1.22 FLOWCHART

People always think about the better one and keep on trying. Similar thing is true for flowchart. In the previous section we have discussed about the algorithm. An algorithm provides solution for some specific problem in well-defined manner, i.e., step by step processing. Here we have better representation of steps of an algorithm in pictorial manner. Pictorial representation is very much readable and readers can understand the things quickly.

Flowchart is the pictorial representation of the steps involved in solving a problem. It depicts pictorial sequence in which instructions are carried out in an algorithm. Flowchart is used not only as an *aid* in developing algorithms but also to document algorithms. It is the next step towards problem solving. Usually the flowcharts are primarily used as an aid in formulating, writing and understanding the programs. For easy visual recognition, the standard convention is to use only pre-decided and accepted specific symbol for a particular operation only so that every computer professional interprets the flowcharts in the same manner. For example, suppose three numbers are given and we have to find out the largest one. Let **x, y** and **z** are three numbers. Algorithm can be constructed such as:

- Compare **x** with **y** if **x** is larger. Then compare it with **z**. If **x** is found larger than **z** then **x** is the largest; otherwise **z** is the largest.
- If in the first step **x** is smaller than or equal to **y** then **y** is compared with **z**. if **y** is larger than **z** then it is the largest number else **z** is the largest.

This algorithm can be represented by the flowchart shown in **Figure 1.23**. Different symbols used in flowchart are shown in **Figure 1.24**.

Now we define in detail the meaning and significance of each of these symbols. Oval is used for two purposes, to define the starting (START or BEGIN) point of flowchart and to define the ending point (END) of flowchart.

PARALLELOGRAM– Parallelogram is used for input-output. This is tne input symbol to indicate the input from standard input or output to standard output device.

RECTANGLE– anhold rectangle is used to indicate the processing. Inside, this processing box statements of processing are specified.

DIAMOND– The diamond shaped box is decision box. This has one entry point. There will be at least two exit points depending upon the decision taken inside the symbol. When a condition is tested, if the condition is true, the path for "yes" is followed. If the condition is false, the path for "no" is followed.

CIRCLE– If flowchart is discontinued at some point and continued again at another place, the connector symbol is used. It is a circle with a number written inside it. If a flowchart is discontinued at some point, a circle is drawn pointing away from the chart. Another circle with same number inside it is placed where the flowchart is to be continued.

SMALL PENTAGON– Some times due to spaces limitations or due to some other reasons, it becomes necessary to terminate a flowchart temporarily and continue from the next page. In such situations this off page connector is used. A number is written inside it. Same number is placed in another pentagon on next page where the flowchart is to be continued.

Comment symbol:– This symbol contains the comment. These comments are included for the documentation purpose to make the understanding of flowcharts easy.

PENTAGON (rectangle with five corners):– The symbol having five corners is used for indicating the input-output. This symbol indicates the input from or output to punched cards.

HEXAGON (flat)– This is the preparation box. This box contains the loop setting statement, *i.e.*,

ARROWS– These arrows are to indicate the direction of the flow of control. This means these statements indicate the next statement to be executed.

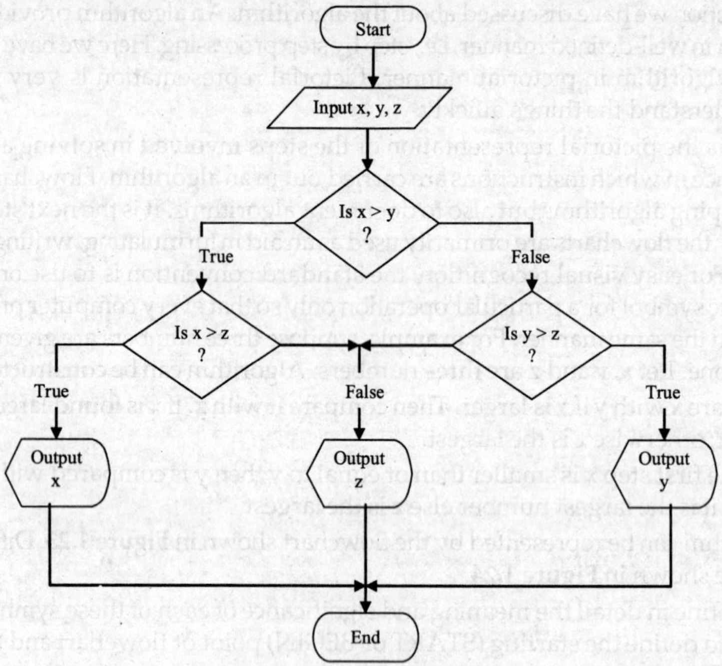

Figure 1.23 Largest of 3-numbers

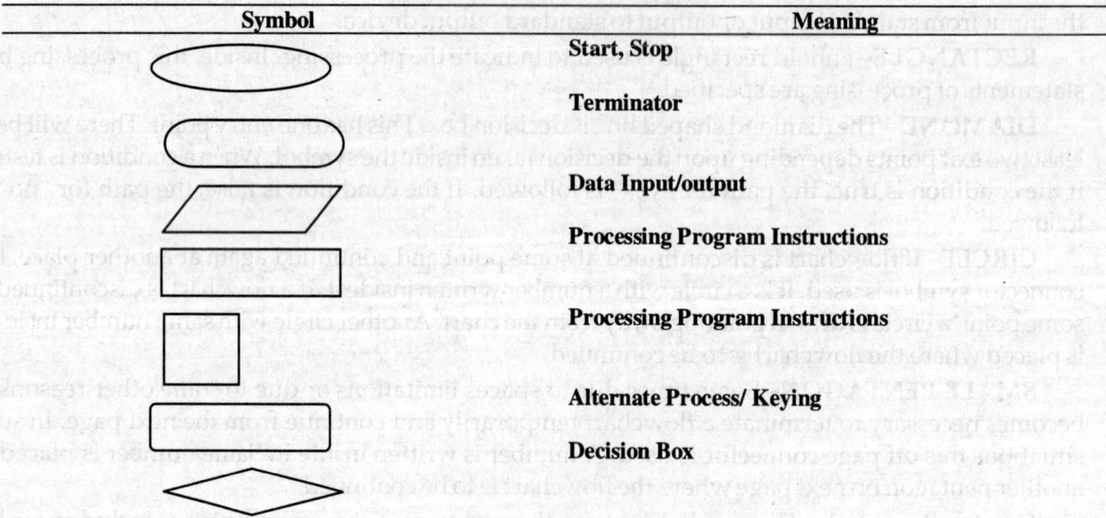

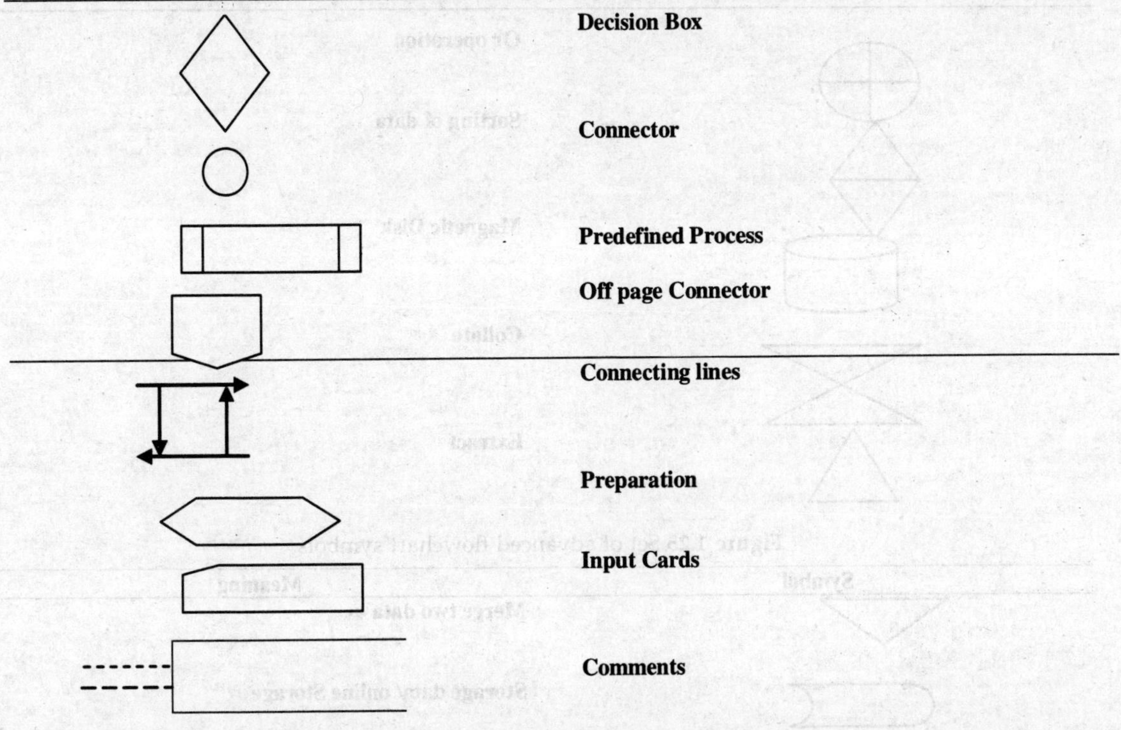

Figure 1.24 Set of flowchart symbols

Figures 1.25 and 1.26 show the flowcharting symbols for special processing and input-output purpose. These symbols are rarely used in flowcharting.

Symbol	Meaning
	Internal Storage
	Documents
	Multi-document
	Manual Input
	Manual Operation
	Punched tape

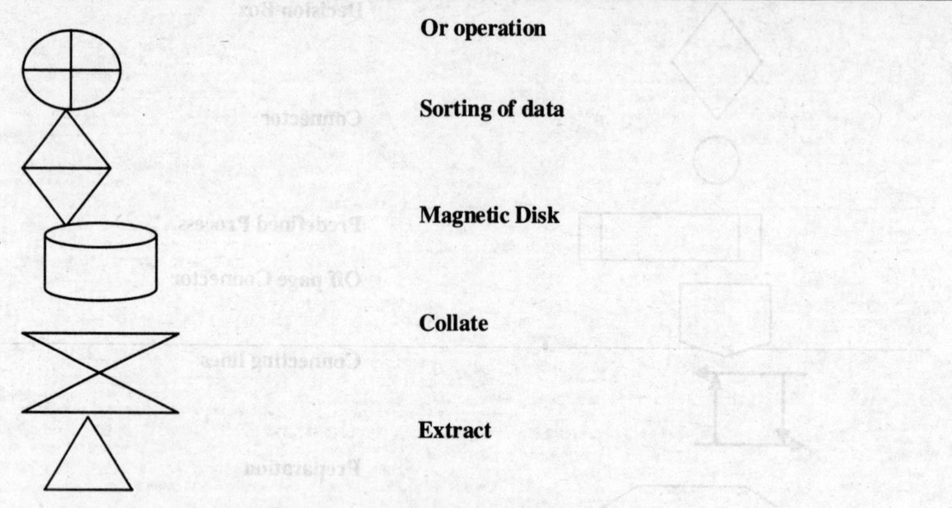

Figure 1.25 Set of advanced flowchart symbols.

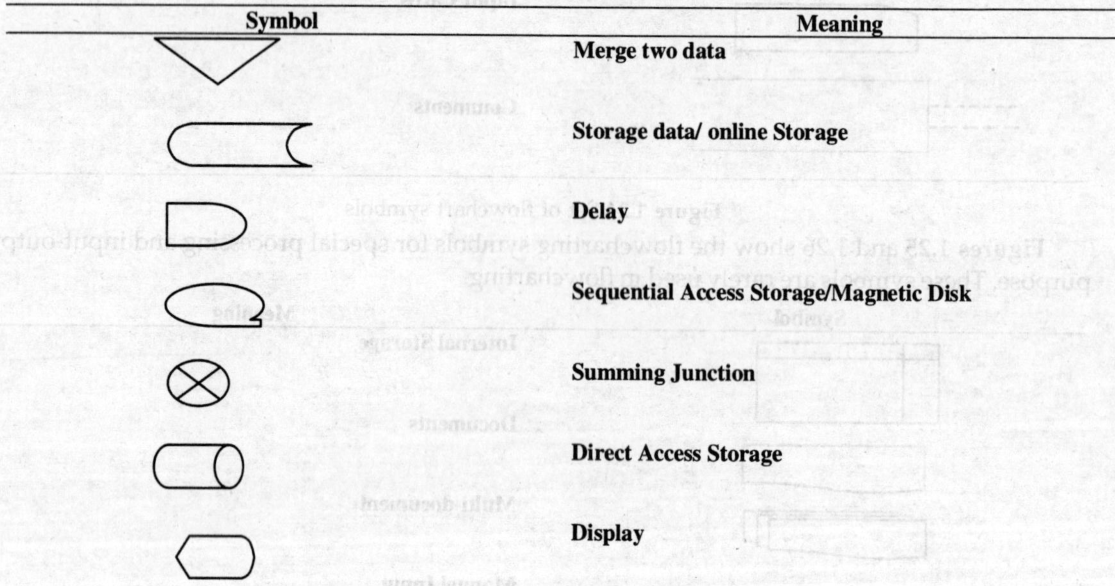

Figure 1.26 Set of advanced flowchart symbols.

1.22.1 Advantages of flowcharts

1. Each symbol of flowchart denotes an instruction in a program.
2. Since flowchart is the pictorial representation of the program steps so it becomes easy to understand the problem, as it is easy to explain anything with the help of pictures instead of printed words.
3. It gives the clear picture of flow of data in any program. Before coding begins, the flowchart assists the programmer to determine the type of logic control to be used in a program.
4. It is easy to detect an error with the help of flowchart.

5. It can be compared in future that if all the steps have been included or not.
6. Flowchart serves as a guiding document for program writing or coding.

1.22.2 Conventions of flowcharts

1. Each symbol of flowchart denotes a particular type of operation.
2. A note is written inside each symbol to indicate the specific function to be performed.
3. Flowcharts are read from top to bottom and left to right.
4. Sequence of operations is performed until a terminate symbol designates the end of the run.
5. Crossed lines do not imply any logical relationship.
6. Where two incoming lines join one outgoing line, they should not join at the same point.
7. Annotation should be included within the symbol to process decision file and input, output giving an indication of the action decision file or document used.
8. Identification of the symbols on a flowchart is aided by numbering the most left top symbols sequentially from 1, so that each symbol can be referred uniquely. Connectors and terminators need to be numbered.
9. Flowcharts are not case-sensitive, so instructions inside the symbols can be written in any case.

1.22.3 Limitations of flowcharts

1. Drawing of flowcharts is a very time consuming process and laborious too especially for large complex problems.
2. Redrawing of flowcharts is even more difficult and time consuming. It is very difficult to include any new step in the existing flowchart. Only redrawing of the flowchart is the only solution.
3. There are no standards which specify the detail that should be included in any flowchart.
4. If an algorithm has complex branches and loops, flowcharts become very difficult to draw.
5. Some times flowcharts could not be in as detail as desired.

Example 1.4: Write an algorithm for the problem of finding the roots of a quadratic equation $ax^2 + bx + c = 0$. Using the formula $\frac{-b \pm \sqrt{b^2 - 4ac}}{2a}$ or $\frac{-b \pm \sqrt{D}}{2a}$ where $D = b^2$. Draw flowchart for this algorithm

Answer: Algorithm is as follows:

1. Start
2. Read the numeric values for a, b, and c.
3. Calculate the value of D using the formula D = $b^2 - 4ac$.
4. if D> 0
   (a) Calculate one root using the formula $R_1 = \frac{-b + \sqrt{D}}{2a}$.
   (b) Calculate another root using the formula $R2 = \frac{-b - \sqrt{D}}{2a}$.
   (c) Display "roots are real and distinct".

(d) Display "Root 1 = ", R_1.
(e) Display "Root 2 = ", R_2.
(f) Exit

5. If D=0, then
   (a) Calculate one root using the formula $R_1 = \frac{-b}{2a}$.
   (b) Display "roots are real and equal".
   (c) Display "Root 1 = ", R_1.
   (d) Display "Root 2 = ", R_1
   (e) Exit
6. If D=0, then
   (a) Calculate one term using the formula $T_1 = \frac{-b}{2a}$.
   (b) Calculate another term T_2 using the formula $T_2 = \frac{\sqrt{(b^2 - 4ac)(-1)}}{2a}$ or $T_2 = \frac{\sqrt{D(-1)}}{2a}$
   (c) Display "roots are imaginary".
   (d) Display "Root 1 = ", $T_1 + iT_2$.
   (e) Display "Root 2 = ", $+T_1 + iT_2$.
   (f) Exit
7. Stop

Details of the flowchart are shown in **Figure 1.27**.

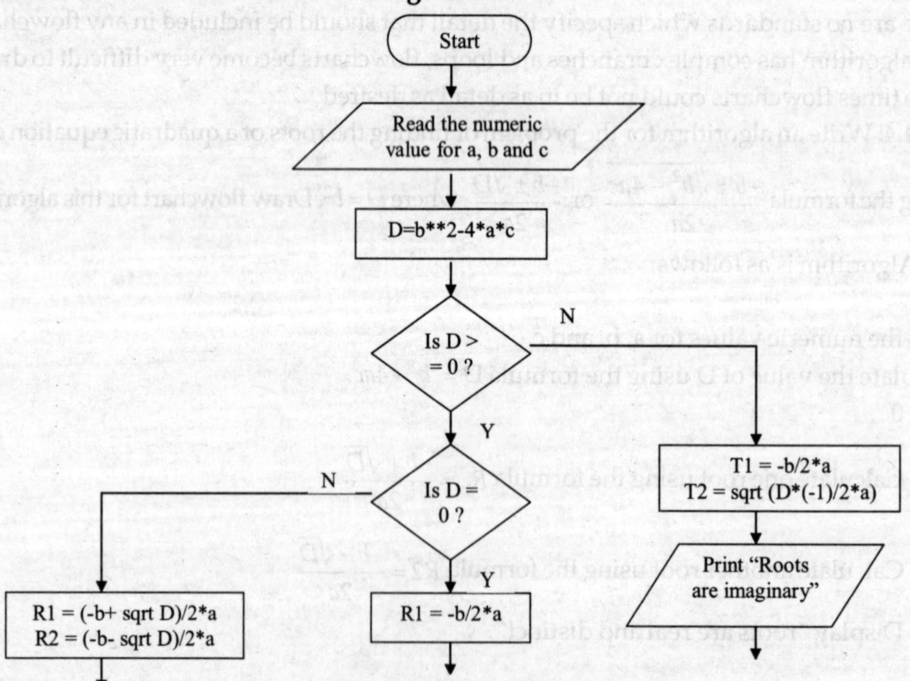

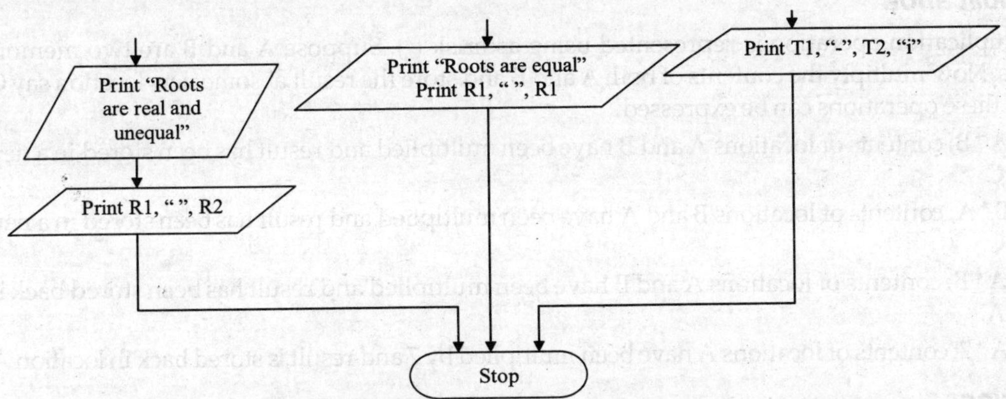

Figure 1.27 Flowchart for quadratic equation

Flowcharts are designed to facilitate encoding. Following section expresses the representation of different mathematical and logical expressions in flowcharts.

1.22.4 Expressions in flowcharts

This section explains how different type of expressions are formed and expressed in flowcharts. These expressions could be mathematical as well as logical. Also how to initialize the memory location or variables or symbols is another consideration. How to input feed in the values and what is the way of printing or displaying the output.

In flowcharting the memory locations are given a symbolic name and through out the flowchart these symbolic names are used to represent various quantities and figures. Same is done in programs. These symbolic names are known as variables also. One variable can hold one value at a time. As many quantities will be required as input or as temporary processing elements or as output in the flowchart as much will be the variables in that variable.

1. Addition

Addition operation is represented using the symbol (+). Suppose A and B are two memory locations. Add the contents of location A & location B and place the result of this addition in location either A & B or in a new memory location say C. We write these steps while drawing the flowchart as,

C = A + B; Adds the contents of location A & location B and put result in a memory location C.

A = A + B; Adds the contents of A & B and result is stored back to location A.

B = A + B; contents of locations A & B are added and result is stored back to location B.

2. Subtraction

Subtraction operation is represented using the symbol (-). Suppose A and B are two memory locations. Suppose some operations are to be performed on, the contents of there locations. Say, subtract the contents of B from the contents of location A and store the result in B. Then subtract the contents of A from B and store the result in new location C. After that subtract the contents of B from A and store the result in A. Then these will be written in form of mathematical expressions as:

B = A - B; Subtracts the contents of location B from location A and put result back in location B.

C = B - A; Subtracts the contents of location A from contents of location B and store the result in a new location C.

A = A - B; Subtracts the contents of location B from location A and put result back in location A.

3. Multiplication

Multiplication operation is represented using asterisk (*). Suppose A and B are two memory locations. Now multiply the contents of both A and B and store the result at some new location say C. See how these operations can be expressed.

C = A * B; contents of locations A and B have been multiplied and result has been stored in a new location C.

C = B * A; contents of locations B and A have been multiplied and result has been stored in a new location C.

A = A * B; contents of locations A and B have been multiplied and result has been stored back in location A.

A = A * 7; contents of locations A have been multiplied by 7 and result is stored back in location A.

4. Division

Symbols "/" are used to represent the operation of division. A/B means that contents of memory location A has been divided by the contents of memory location B. See some expressions are

C = B / A; Divide the contents of locations B by contents of location A and store the result in a new location C.

A = A / B; Divide the contents of locations B by contents of location A and store the result in location C.

A = A/7; Divide contents of location A by number 7 and store the result back in location A.

C = *10*/B; Divide 10 by contents of location B and store the result in a new location C.

5. Transfer

Transfer means copying the contents of one memory location into another memory location. Operator or symbol used for this purpose is "=", i.e., equal to symbol. Suppose A and B are two memory locations. When contents of memory location B are to be placed in memory location A it is written as- A=B. Similarly, for initialization, i.e., if some initial value is to be stored to some memory location say 17 is to be stored at C, then it is written as C = 17.

6. Comparison

We often confront with the cases where comparison of contents of two locations is required. The operators which are used to represent comparisons are <, >, =, <=, >=, <>. These operators are known as relational operators also. Suppose A and B are two memory locations. Consider the following expressions and their interpretations.

A > B; It means contents of A is greater than the contents of B.

B ≤ A; contents of B is less than or equal to A.

A = B; contents of A ia equal to B.

A ≠ B; contents of A is not equal to B.

7. Print

Print expressions are the output expressions and are required to represent the printing of outputs in flowcharts. Suppose B is a memory location with value A then if A is to be printed, then expressions could be either Display B or Print B. If some value say 15 is to be printed, then expressions could be either Display 15 or Print 15. If suppose some character string says "this is a test string" is to be printed then the expressions could be either Display "this is a test string" or print "this is a test string".

8. Feed

Feeding expressions are the input expressions, i.e., expressions showing the input of values to some locations. If value is to be read into the memory location say B, then expressions could be

Input B or Read B or Read the value of B.

All of the three above written statements will mean that enter some value for memory location B.

Example 1.5: Problem is to determine the highest marks obtained by the students in an Examination and the roll no. of the student securing the highest marks. (Assume that only one student has got the highest marks). Write the necessary steps for writing the program to solve the problem.

Answer: Detailed Problem Statement is

We start with the first step of solving this problem that is its detailed statement. We have to write a program which will determine the highest marks obtained by the students in B. Tech 1st year examination.

The input to the programs will be

1. The roll number of a student.
2. The marks obtained by a student.

   This process of inputting their roll numbers and marks obtained will be repeated for all the students of the class.

The output to be received from the program is

1. The name of that student who secured the highest marks
2. His/her percentage in class.

The algorithm of problem is

1. Start
2. Read the roll number and marks of number 1 student. This is the highest marks found so far as marks of only one student have been read.
3. Is there any more students in the class?
4. If yes, then go to step 5. If not, then go to step 8.
5. Read next roll number and its marks. Compare the marks of this student (roll no.) previous roll number with the highest marks found so far.
6. If marks read in step 5 is greater than the highest marks found so far, then erase the previously noted highest marks, and replace it by the marks read in step 5. Also replace the roll number with the new roll number. In this situation other than this, that is, if marks of step 5 are less than the highest marks, then do nothing.
7. Repeat the step 3 thru 6 till all the roll numbers of class have been entered.
8. Calculate the percentage.
9. Print the roll number of the student with highest marks and percentage of the student.
10. Stop.

Shown in **Figure 1.28** is the flowchart for this problem. In this we have used few symbols to represent the memory locations for storing the data. These symbols and their meaning and use are

ROLLNO	store the roll no of a student
MARKS	store the marks of that student
MAXMARKS	store the maximum marks
MAXROLLNO	store the roll no of student who secured maximum marks

All the marks and roll numbers will be input at these locations one by one overwriting the previous one.

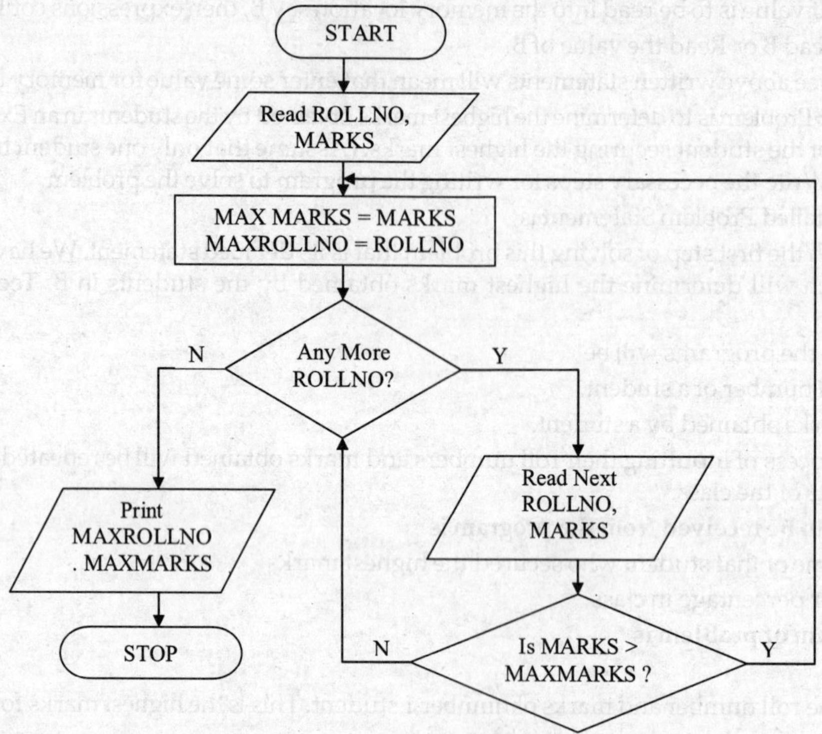

FIgure 1.28 Flowchart for markssheet problem Example 1.5.

1.22.5 Types of logic used in flowchart

There are different logic structures available which are used in the flowchart to represent any construct for iterations of programming language. These constructs are

1. Sequence
2. Selection
3. Iteration

Example 1.6: (i) Prepare the flowchart to calculate the simple interest for the given amount (P) for the given number of years (N) using the formula PNR/100 taking the rate of interest R=13% if P < 10,000 and R = 14% if P >= 10,000.

(ii) Modify the above flowchart to calculate and print the new amount also.

Answer: (i) See **Figure 1.29**.

(ii) We introduce one more arithmetic operation P = P+SI in processing box just before the **Print** box and modify the print expression of **Print** box as **"Print 51, POI** {**Figure 1.30**}.

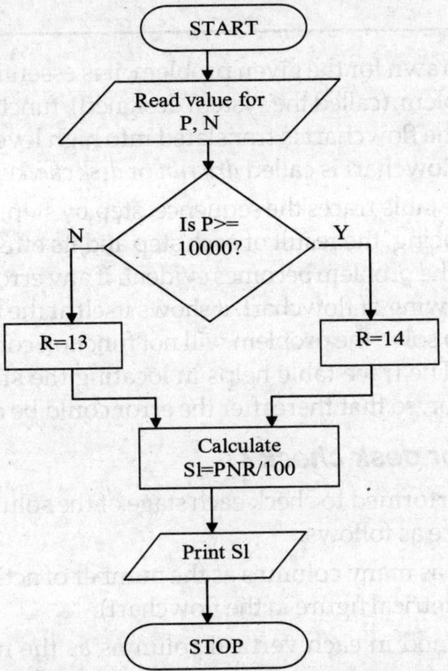

FIgure 1.29 Flowchart for Example 1.6(i)

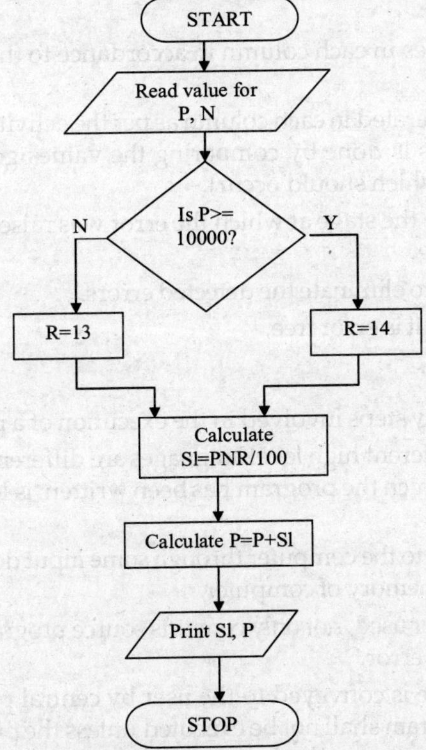

FIgure 1.30 Flowchart for Example 1.6(ii)

1.23 TRACE TABLE

After the flowchart has been drawn for the given problem, it is essential to check that the method and plan deployed to solve the problem, (called the system designed), functions correctly and produces the desired objective. Thereafter, the flowchart is translated into high level language to be run on the computer. The manual test of the flowchart is called *dry run* or *desk check.*

As the name suggests, the trace table traces the sequence, step by step, which leads to the solution of the problem. In the process of tracing, the result of each step and its effect on the next step becomes clear. The logic involved in solving the problem becomes evident. If any error at any stage is discovered, while framing the algorithm, or drawing of flowchart, it shows itself at the time of dry run. In presence of any error, the system designed to solve the problem will not function correctly and will produce the incorrect results during dry run. The trace table helps in locating the stage at which the error has occurred and also the nature of error, so that thereafter the error could be eliminated.

How to perform the dry run or desk check?

The dry run or desk check is performed to check each stage of the solution developed to solve the problem. The steps involved in it are as follows:

(a) Draw the table containing as many columns as the number of activities in the flowchart (i.e., one column for each geometrical figure in the flowchart).

(b) Write the activity performed in each vertical columns as the number of activities in the flowchart (i.e., one column for each geometrical figure in the flowchart).

(c) Consider a suitable numerical value, for the variable as required, in the flowchart within the prescribed range.

(d) Keep on writing the values in each column in accordance to the activity mentioned above each column.

(e) Check that the values generated in each column as per the activity mentioned in it are correct and are as expected (this is done by comparing the values generated according to each activity with the values which should occur).

(f) In case of any error locate the stage at which the error was raised and identify the nature of error.

(g) Take adequate measures to eliminate the detected errors.

(h) Recheck the flowchart till it is error free.

How a program is executed?

The following are the necessary steps involved in the execution of a program.

(a) Since the compilers of different high level languages are different hence the compiler for the high level language, in which the program has been written, is loaded in the memory of the computer.

(b) The source program is fed to the computer through some input device. The control unit stores the program in the main memory of computer.

(c) The compiler or interpreter used, not only converts source program in machine code but also check each line for syntax error.

(d) The syntax error message is conveyed to the user by central processing unit through the output devices. The program shall not be executed unless the program is made completely error-free.

(e) Memory locations are allotted to each variable, by the name of each variable itself, in the main memory.

(f) The result of the executed program is communicated to the user, in high level language, through the output devices.

1.23.1 Decision Table

Though earlier discussed flowcharts give a clear idea of direction of flow of data but it has a disadvantage. This is, the flowcharts become more complicated and difficult to understand if there are many different decisions to be taken in program. Also a flowchart may run for more than one page. So at times following and understanding a flowchart becomes more difficult. Because of these disadvantages, in such complex cases instead of flowcharts there is another algorithm development and documentation aid that is the decision table. A *decision table* depicts in a tabular form the set of conditions to be tested and the sequence of actions to be performed to solve a problem. This aid is useful in solving the problems, which require a large number of decisions.

STUB	*ENTRY*
CONDITION	**RULE NUMBER**
ACTION	

Figure 1.31 General layout of Direction table

Decision table is a table defining the problem and the actions to be taken. It is a single representation of conditions and actions. **Figure1.31** shows the general layout of any decision table. A decision table consists of two main partitions- STUB and ENTRY.

The stub part is divided into an upper quadrant called the conditional stub and a lower quadrant called the action stub. The entry part is also divided into two quadrants. The upper quadrant is called the condition entry and a lower quadrant is called the action entry. The *condition stub* contains in the question form, the condition that may exist. The *action stub* contains outlines in the narrative form, the action to be taken to meet each condition. The condition entry provides the answers to the questions that are asked in the condition stub quadrant. The action entry indicates the appropriate action resulting from the answers to the conditions in the condition entry quadrant. We now consider an example to understand the way of writing the entries in a decision table.

Example 1.7: In a marketing firm, commission is given based on the sales. If sales are less than 5000.00, then there is no commission. If sales are more than or equal to 5000. 00 but less than 10000 then commission is 2%. If sales is greater than or equal to 10000 but less than 50000 then commission is 4%. If sales is greater than 50000. 00 the discount is 6%.

Answer: Now we draw a decision table for it. In this case, the conditions are

If sales are less than 5000.00

If sales are less than 10000.00

If sales is less than 50000.00

If sales is greater then 50000.00

From **Figure 1.32**, we note certain things. First of all, we see that the answers have been denoted by Y & N and blank column & row denotes that the corresponding condition has not been tested. The check mark (X) denotes the action. Each column indicates a rule. For example, rule 3 is, "IF sale is less than 50000 and greater than 10000/- then allow 4% discount".

STUB		ENTRY					
		1	2	3	4	5	6
(Condition)							
	Sale >= 50000?	Y	N	N	N	N	N
	Sale < 50000?		Y	Y	Y	Y	Y
IF	Sale >= 10000?			Y	N	N	N
	Sale < 10000?				Y	Y	Y
	Sale >= 5000?					Y	N
	Sale < 5000?						Y
(Action)							
	Allow 6% discount	X					
THEN	Allow 4% discount		X	X			
	Allow 2% discount				X		
	No discount allowed						X

Figure 1.32 Decision Table for Example 1.7

Example 1.8: Student results are declared using the following rules: There are two subjects in the examination called main and ancillary. If a student gets 50 % or more in the main subject and 40% in the ancillary he/she is passed. If he/she gets less than 50% in the main subject, he/she must get 50% or more in the ancillary to pass. However, the minimum pass marks are 40% in the main subject. If a student gets 60% or more in the main subject, he/she is allowed to repeat ancillary subject if the ancillary subject is less than 40%. However, there are a group of students in the class who are granted special consideration. Their percentage is 40% in main and 40% in ancillary. If they get less than 40% in the ancillary, they are allowed to repeat that subject, if they obtain 40% or more in the main subject.

Answer: The decision table for this problem is shown in **Figure 1.33**.

Conditions	Rule1	Rule2	Rule3	Rule4	Rule5	Else
Main marks %age	≥50	≥40	≥60	≥40	≥40	
Ancillary marks %age	≥40	≥50	< 40	≥40	< 40	
Special status	No	No	No	Yes	Yes	
Actions						
Pass	x	x	-	x	-	-
Repeat	-	-	x	-	x	-
Fail	-	-	-	-	-	x

Figure 1.33 Decision Table for Example 1.8.

1.23.2 Rules for drawing decision table

The rules that should be following while constructing the decision table are as follows:

1. A decision should have a same.
2. The logic of the table is independent of the sequence in which condition rules are written.
3. Duplication of the terms must be eliminated.

1.23.3 Advantages of decision table

Decision tables are best suited for dealing with complex branching routines such as complex links of inventory control or calculating purchasing discounts, sales commissions, etc. These tables are easier to construct than flowcharts if several conditions are to be tested and decisions to be taken. Also, it is easier to follow the table when a particular condition is met just by coming down the column.

1.24 DATA STRUCTURES

A programmer is concerned with developing and implementing algorithms for a variety of tasks. As tasks become more complex, algorithm development is facilitated by structuring or organizing data in specialized ways. There is no best data structure for all tasks; suitable data structures must be selected for the specific task. Some data structures are provided by programming languages; others must be derived by the programmer from available data types and structures. A **data structure** is a *logical* or *mathematical* way of storing data in a computer so that it can be used efficiently. Often a carefully chosen data structure will allow a more efficient operation. Choice of a particular data structure model depends on two considerations: it must be rich enough in structure to mirror the actual relationships of the data in the real world. On the other hand, the structure should be simple enough that one can effectively process the data when necessary. In other words data structure is a collection of data elements whose organization is characterized by assessing operations that are used to store and retrieve the individual data elements; the implementation of the composite data members in an abstract data type. A abstract data type can be defined as a data type whose properties are specified independently of any particular implementation. The data structures are classified in the following two categories

- **Linear data structures**: For example, Arrays, Linked Lists, Stacks, and Queues.
- **Nonlinear data structures**: For example, Trees (like B Trees, B^+ Trees, B* Trees, etc.), and Graph.

1.24.1 Linear Data Structures

In the linear data structures processing of data items is possible in linear fashion, i.e., data can be processed one by one sequentially. Linear data structures includes the following types of data structures:

- Array
- Linked list
- Stack and Queues

1.24.1.1 Arrays

This is the simplest type of data structure, is a linear (one-dimensional) array. By a linear array, we mean a list of finite number **n** of similar data elements referenced respectively by a set of **n** consecutive numbers, usually **1, 2, 3 ... n.** If we choose the name **V** for the array, then the elements of **V** are denoted by parenthesis notation such as V(1), V(2), V(3) … V(N) or by bracket notation V[1], V[2], V[3] … V[n] or by subscript notation $V_1, V_2, V_3 \dots V_n$

1.24.1.2 Linked List

A linked list can be defined as collection of nodes. A node has two fields, information and address fieldthat contains the address of the next node, i.e., pointer to the next node. For example, **Figure 1.34** represents a linked in memory.

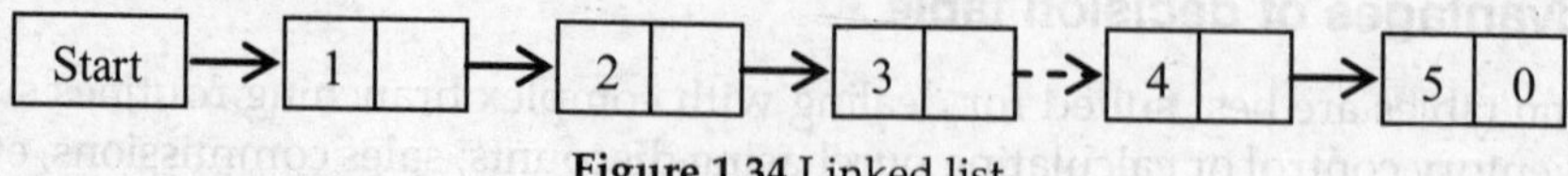

Figure 1.34 Linked list

1.24.1.3 Stack and Queues

A stack, also called a last-in first-out (LIFO) system, is a linear list in which insertions and deletions can take place at one end, called the **TOP**. This structure is similar in its operation to a stack of discs on a peg system shown in **Figure 1.35**.

A queue, also called a first-in first-out (FIFO) system, is linear list in which deletions can take place at one end of the list, the **front** of the list and insertions can take place only at the other end of the list, the **rear** of the list. This structure operates in much same way as a line of people waiting for railway reservation ticket at booking window.

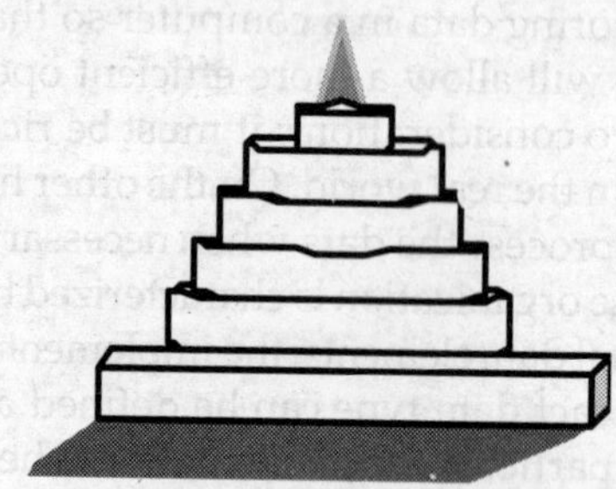

Figure 1.35 Stack of discs on a peg

1.24.2 Nonlinear Data Structures

A data structure in which insertion and deletion are not possible in a linear fashion is called nonlinear data structure. In this category of data structure, we will discuss the following:

- Tree
- Graph

1.24.2.1 Tree

Data frequently contain a hierarchical relationship between various elements. The data structure, which reflects this relationship, is called a rooted tree graph or simply a tree. For example, **Figure 1.36** discusses a tree structure of student personnel record.

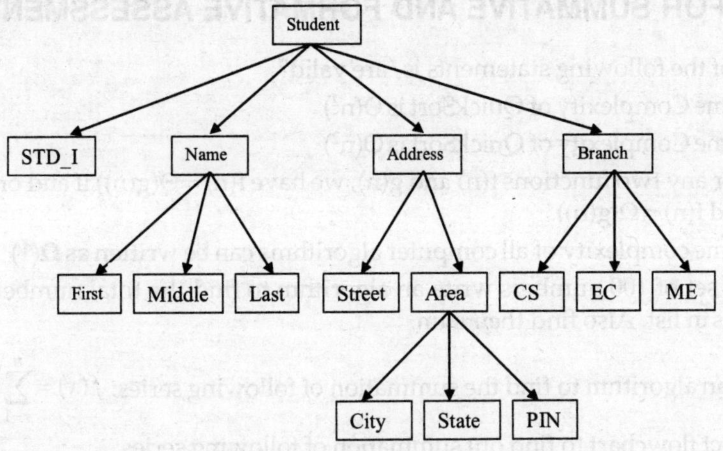

Figure 1.36 Tree

1.24.2.2 Graph

This is a data structure that sometimes contains a relationship between pairs of elements, which is not necessarily hierarchical in nature. For example, suppose airline flies only between the cities connected by line in **Figure 1.39**.

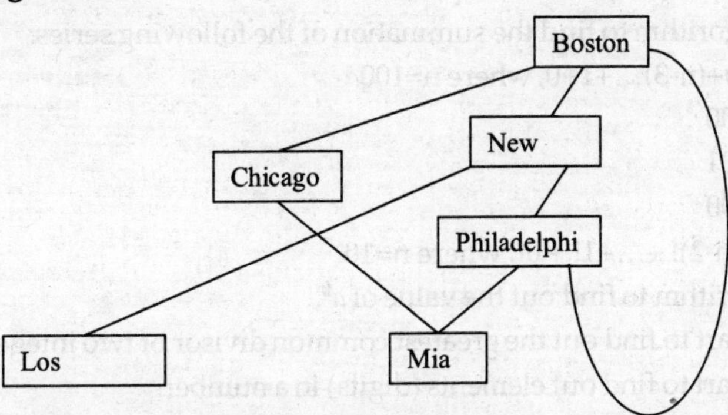

Figure 1.39 Airline flights

1.25 DATA STRUCTURE OPERATIONS

The data appearing in our data structures are processes by means of certain operation. In fact, the particular data structure that one chooses for a given situation depends largely on the frequency with which specific operations are performed. The following operations play major role in the processing of data:

(a) Traversing
(b) Searching
(c) Inserting
(d) Deleting
(e) Sorting
(f) Merging

The details of these operations will be discussed in the subsequent chapters.

FOR SUMMATIVE AND FORMATIVE ASSESSMENT

1.1 Which of the following statements is/are valid?
   (a) Time Complexity of QuickSort is $\Theta(n^2)$
   (b) Time Complexity of QuickSort is $O(n^2)$
   (c) For any two functions f(n) and g(n), we have $f(n) = \Theta(g(n))$ if and only if $f(n) = O(g(n))$ and $f(n) = \Omega(g(n))$.
   (d) Time complexity of all computer algorithms can be written as $\Omega(1)$

1.2 Given a set of 100 numbers write an algorithm to find the total number of even and odd numbers in list. Also find their sum.

1.3 Design an algorithm to find the summation of following series: $f(x)=\sum_{r=1}^{n} x^r$

1.4 Construct flowchart to find out summation of following series:

$$f(x)=1+\frac{x^2}{2}+\frac{x^4}{4}+\frac{x^6}{6}+\ldots+\frac{x^n}{n}.$$

1.5 Construct flowchart to find out summation of the following series:
   (a) n+(n-1)+(n-2)+(n-3)…+1+0, where n=100
   (b) n! + (n-1)! + (n-2)! +…+1! + 0!, where n=10

1.6 Design an algorithm to find the summation of the following series:
   (a) n+(n-1)+(n-2)+(n-3)…+1+0, where n=100
   (b) 1+2+3+…+100
   (c) 1+3+5+…+101
   (d) 0+2+4+…+200
   (e) n! + (n-1)! + (n-2)! +…+1! + 0!, where n=10

1.7 Write an algorithm to find out the value of a^b.

1.8 Draw flowchart to find out the greatest common divisor of two integer numbers.

1.9 Draw flowchart to find out elements (digits) in a number.

1.10 A Company manufactures three product engines, pumps and fans. It gives a discount of 20 percent on orders for engines if the order is worth Rs. 10000 or more. The same discount of 20 percent or more on fan orders of value 5000 or more and on pump orders value Rs. 7000 or more. On all other orders, they do not give any discount. Prepare a decision table and flowchart.

1.11 What are the differences between pointers to constants and constant to pointers? Discuss with the help of suitable examples.

1.12 Write a function that counts number of vowels in a given text.

1.13 Write a function that works like petrol pump counter, it increases character counter by one when a key is pressed, when finds a blank it increases the word counter by one and when it finds a dot after that a blank then it increases the sentence counter by one.

1.14 Write a function that counts number of words in a given text and also counts the words of different types.

1.15 Write a function that inserts a sub-string in a string some where in the middle.

1.16 Write a complete program to access number of students in a class using pointers to structure.

1.17 Write a complete program to implement a structure for the following fields:

- Name
- Father's Name
- Enrollment Number
- Roll Number
- Date of Birth
- Date of joining the college
- Address

And also provide the provision to sort the list on any desired field e.g., on Name, Enrollment Number, etc.

1.18 Write a function, which reads a string and transfers its reverse to another pointer variable.

1.19 Write a program for inventory control, which should contain the following options:

- Add record
- Delete record
- Update record
- Print record
- List record (Random access)

You can choose different fields by your own.

1.20 The following is the list entries with level number in a student's record
1 Student 2 Number 2 Name 3 Last 3 First 3 Middle 2 Sex 2 Birth Day 3 Day 3 Month 3 Year 2 SAT 3 C-Programming 3 Viva Voce

(a) Draw the corresponding hierarchical structure
(b) Which of the items are elementary items?
(c) Write a function that implements

1.21 Write a complete program to access number of students in a class using pointers to object members.

1.22 Discuss the function with the help of suitable examples. Write functions that compute values of $A\pi R^3/4$ where parameters are used as:

- Integer
- Float
- Double

1.23 What do you understand by aggregate data types? Discuss with the help of suitable examples.

1.24 The harmonic mean defined by $h = \frac{n}{\sum_{i=1}^{n} 1/a_i}$ is sometimes used as a mean of central tendency.

Develop a program that computes the harmonic mean of **n** data values.

1.25 Write a program that works like a binary calculator for the flowing operations:

(a) Addition
(b) Subtraction
(c) Multiplication

(d) Division
(e) Modulo operation
(f) Remainder

1.26 Design an algorithm that reads in **n** single digits and converts them into a single integer. For example, the algorithm should convert the set of 5 digits {2, 7, 4, 9 and 3} to the integer 27493. Finally implement the designed algorithm.

1.27 The binomial theorem of basic algebra indicates that the coefficient ^nC_r of the rth power of x in the expansion of $(1 + x)^n$ is given by $^nC_r = \frac{n!}{r!(n-r)!}$. Draw flowchart that evaluates all coefficient of **x** for a given value of **n**, Also design an algorithm and implement the designed algorithm.

1.28 Write an algorithm to find out the value of x^y, where x and y are two positive integers.

1.29 Draw flowchart to find out the greatest common divisor of two integer numbers.

1.30 Draw flowchart to find out digits of a number.

1.31 A Company manufactures three product engines, pumps and fans. It gives a discount of 25 percent on orders for engines, if the order is worth Rs. 10,000 or more. The same discount or more on fan orders of value 5000 or more and on pump orders value Rs. 7000 or more. On all other orders, they do not give any discount. Prepare flowchart for this decision problem.

1.32 Define the features of C language.

1.33 Define the algorithm. What is the need of algorithms in computer world?

1.34 Why flowchart is much expressive as compared to the algorithm?

1.35 Given the values of three variables x, y and z, write a program to compute and display the value of a, where $a = x/(y-z)$. Execute the program for the following values:

(a) x = 125, y = 85, z = 25
(b) x = 150, y = 70, z = 70

1.36 Given two integers 20 and 10, write a program that uses a function add( ) to add these two numbers and sub( ) to find the difference of these two numbers and then display the sum and difference in the following form: .

20 + 10 = 30
20 – 10 = 10

1.37 Prove that: 2n + 1 d" 2^n for all n e" 3.

1.38 What are two problems with arrays? Discuss.

1.39 What are two criteria usually used to measure algorithm's efficiency? Discuss.

These are sets of simple multiple choice questions, provided entirely for your self-assessment, and are based on the most fundamental aspects of data structure and algorithms. The level of the questions is no more than that of what one would encounter in an introductory Programming and Data Structures.

Quiz-1 (Basics of Data Structures & Programming Language 'C')

1. A variable P is called pointer if
   (a) P contains the address of an element in DATA(a)
   (b) P points to the address of first element in DATA
   (c) P can store only memory addresses
   (d) P contain the DATA and the address of DATA
2. Each data item in a record may be a group item composed of sub-items; those items which are indecomposable are called
   (a) elementary items (b) atoms
   (c) scalars (d) all of above
3. The difference between linear array and a record is
   (a) An array is suitable for homogeneous data but the data items in a record may have different data type
   (b) In a record, there may not be a natural ordering in opposed to linear array.
   (c) A record form a hierarchical structure but a lienear array does not
   (d) All of above
4. Two main measures for the efficiency of an algorithm are
   (a) Processor and memory (b) Complexity and capacity
   (c) Time and space (d) Data and space
5. The time factor when determining the efficiency of algorithm is measured by
   (a) Counting microseconds (b) Counting the number of key operations
   (c) Counting the number of statements (d) Counting the kilobytes of algorithm
6. The space factor when determining the efficiency of algorithm is measured by
   (a) Counting the maximum memory needed by the algorithm
   (b) Counting the minimum memory needed by the algorithm
   (c) Counting the average memory needed by the algorithm
   (d) Counting the maximum disk space needed by the algorithm
7. Which of the following case does not exist in complexity theory
   (a) Best case (b) Worst case
   (c) Average case (d) Null case
8. The indirect change of the values of a variable in one module by another module is called
   (a) internal change (b) inter-module change
   (c) side effect (d) side-module update
9. The largest and the second largest number from a set of n distinct numbers can be found in
   (a) O (n) (b) O (2n)
   (c) O (n^2) (d) O (log n)
10. What is the output of the below code snippet?

```
#include<stdio.h>
main()
{
```

```
for()printf("Hello");
}
```

(a) Infinite loop (b) Prints "Hello" once
(c) No output (d) Compile error

11. **Which operator is used to continue the definition of macro in the next line?**
(a) # (b) ##
(c) $ (d) \

12. **Which of the following functions disconnects the stream from the file pointer.**
(a) fremove() (b) fclose()
(c) remove() (d) file pointer to be set to NULL

13. C Language developed at _________?
(a) AT & T's Bell Laboratories of USA in 1972
(b) AT & T's Bell Laboratories of USA in 1970
(c) Sun Microsystems in 1973
(d) Cambridge University in 1972

14. C was primarily developed as
(a) System programming language
(b) General purpose language
(c) Data processing language
(d) None of the above

15. **What will be printed after execution of the following program code?**

```
# include<stdio.h>
main()
{
printf("\\n ab");
printf("\\b si");
printf("\\r ha");
}
```

(a) absiha (b) asiha
(c) haasi (d) hai
(e) None of these

16. **If integer needs two bytes of storage, then maximum value of an unsigned integer is**
(a) $2^{16} - 1$ (b) $2^{15} - 1$
(c) 2^{16} (d) 2^{15}
(e) None of these

17. **What is the correct value to return to the operating system upon the successful completion of a program?**
(a) 1 (b) –1
(c) 0 (d) Program do no return a value
(e) 2

18. What is the difference between a declaration and a definition of a variable?
    (a) Both can occur multiple times, but a declaration must occur first.
    (b) A definition occurs once, but a declaration may occur many times.
    (c) Both can occur multiple times, but a definition must occur first.
    (d) A declaration occurs once, but a definition may occur many times.
    (e) There is no difference between them.
19. "My salary was increased by 15%" Select the statement, which will exactly reproduce the line of text above.
    (a) printf("My salary was increased by 15/%!");
    (b) printf("My salary was increased by 15%!");
    (c) printf("My salary was increased by 15'%'!");
    (d) printf("My salary was increased by 15%%");
    (e) printf("My salary was increased by 15'%'!");
20. Assuming a short is two bytes long, what will be printed by the above code?
    short testarray[4][3] = { {1}, {2,3}, {4,5,6}};
    printf("\n %d", sizeof(testarray));
    (a) 6 (b) 7
    (c) 12 (d) 24

❑

CHAPTER 2

Recursion

Recursive definitions of data types are extremely common in Computer Science. It is the name given to a technique for defining a function in terms of itself. With the help of recursion, the process of execution is not speeded; rather it defines the process in a simple way to understand. They have the advantage that they give great insight into *how* many basic operations may be performed. First, we will look at the use of recursion as a method for describing/specifying something.

Now we will discuss some kind of examples which are related to recursion.

Royalty: A person is royal if he/she is a monarch, or is descended from a royal person.

Citizenship: A person is a Indian citizen if he/she is born in India, or has acquired citizenship after immigrating to India, or has a parent who is a Indian citizen.

Mathematical Examples

Functions are very often defined recursively. The classic example is the factorial function

factorial(0) = 1

factorial(n) = n * factorial(n-1) [for n>0]

This definition is concise and very easy to understand and to use. Let us compute factorial(4).

```
factorial(4) = 4 * factorial(3)
 = 4 * ( 3 * factorial(2) )
 = 4 * ( 3 * ( 2 * factorial(1) ))
 = 4 * ( 3 * ( 2 * (1*factorial(0) )))
 = 4 * ( 3 * ( 2 * (1 * 1 ) ))
 = 24
```

In general, a recursive definition is made up of two parts. There is a base case that tells us directly what the answer is, and there is a recursive case that defines the answer in terms of the answer to some other, related problem. In factorial, the base case is factorial(0)=1, this directly tells us the answer; the recursive case is factorial(n) = n * factorial(n-1). This does not directly tell us the answer, but tells how to construct the answer for factorial(n) on the basis of the answer to the related problem, factorial(n-1).

The Royalty and Citizenship definitions are just the same - there is a base case, which directly determines royalty or citizenship, and a recursive case, which defines the royalty/citizenship of one person in terms of the royalty/citizenship of some other person.

Another classical example is the Fibonacci function:

```
fibonacci(0) = 1
fibonacci(1) = 1
fibonacci(n) = fibonacci(n-1) + fibonacci(n-2) [for n>1]
```

This definition is a little different than the previous ones because

- It has two base cases, not just one; in fact, we can have as many as we like.
- In the recursive case, there are two recursive calls, not just one. There can be as many as we like.

Let's compute fibonacci(4) to see how the definition works:

```
fibonacci(4)
= fibonacci(3)+ fibonacci(2)
= (fibonacci(2) + fibonacci(1)) + (fibonacci(1) + fibonacci(0))
= ((fibonacci(1) + fibonacci(0)) + 1) + (1 + 1)
= (1 + 1) + 1) + (1 + 1)
= 5
```

Computing Examples

Under this section we will consider two problems stack and arithmetic expressions, first we consider stack after that arithmetic expression.

Stack

A stack is *anything* on which we can perform the operations POP, PUSH, etc. as specified. This is a perfectly valid definition and a very useful one too, because it leaves us entirely free to impose any shape or structure on a stack that we like (as long as we can still perform the operations). There is also a structural definition that defines a stack in terms of its 'structure':

- A stack is either EMPTY
- or it consists of two parts: (1) a **top** value and (2) a **remainder**, which is a stack.

This follows normal pattern for a recursive definition. There is a base case, which tells us directly that EMPTY is a valid value for a stack to have. Then there is the recursive case, which tells us how to determine if a value is a valid stack by looking at its two parts and checking that they have appropriate values.

For example, consider the value S = (7, (29, (11, EMPTY))). We can use the above definition to recognize that this is a valid stack. S has two parts, we will regard the first part (7) as its **top**, and the second part as its remainder = (29, (11, EMPTY)). According to the definition, S is a valid stack providing that this remainder is a valid stack. Is it?

Well, it has two parts; its **top** (first part) is 29, and its second part, or **remainder**, is (11, EMPTY). So this will be a valid stack value providing that this remainder is a valid stack. We apply the definition to this remainder. (11, EMPTY) has two parts, top = 11, and remainder = EMPTY, and it is a valid stack providing that its remainder is a valid stack.

The base case allows us to immediately recognize that EMPTY is a valid stack. And this allows us to conclude that (11, EMPTY) is a valid stack. This, in turn, allows to conclude that (29, (11, EMPTY)) is a valid stack, and this, finally, allows us to conclude that original stack, S = (7, (29, (11, EMPTY))) is indeed a valid stack.

For example, the recursive definition of stack suggests that we could implement stacks, with a **pair**, i.e., a record/structure having two parts, one of type **value**, and other is stack. With this implementation, we can pop a stack S, just by returning its remainder, POP (S) = S. remainder, and we can PUSH value V onto stack S just by creating the pair (V, S). We can see that the definition itself has given us very strong guidance in implementing the basic operations on the data type {Chapter 6}.

Arithmetic Expression

All programming languages allow us to write arithmetic expressions such as 5*(2+3). How can we define the concept of arithmetic expression? The only way, really, is to do it recursively. An arithmetic expression is any of the following:

1. a numeric constant
2. an identifier (of a numeric type variable or constant)
3. an *arithmetic expression* enclosed in parentheses
4. two *arithmetic expressions* separated by a binary arithmetic operator.

Definitions such as this are used universally to define the syntax of programming languages, and the first step in any compiler is to use these definitions to uncover the basic building blocks and organization of a program. This process is called parsing, and the result is a parse tree. The process is actually very similar to the one we just used when we verified that S was valid stack. We repeatedly apply the definitions to break a given value into parts, and then check the validity of each of the parts. The base cases give us direct answers about the validity of certain values. For example, we can use the above definition to parse this input:

```
5 * (2 + 3)
```

Apply rule 4. This breaks the given input into 3 parts, 5, *, (2+3) and imposes these constraints on them:

(a) 5 must be an arithmetic expression

(b) * must be a binary arithmetic operator

(c) (2 + 3) must be an arithmetic expression

Once these have been verified, we know that our original input is a valid arithmetic expression. We verify (a) by application of rule 1, and (b) by looking up * in a list of known binary arithmetic operators. All that remains, in order to show that our original input is a valid expression, is to verify (c). Verifying (c) requires several steps:

- First, apply rule 3: This says that (2 + 3) is an arithmetic expression only if 2 + 3 is an arithmetic expression.
- To verify that 2+3 is a valid expression, we apply rule 4. This breaks 2+3 into 3 parts, 2, +, and 3 and imposes these constraints:

  (d) 2 must be an arithmetic expression

  (e) + must be a binary arithmetic operator

  (f) 3 must be an arithmetic expression
- We verify (d) and (f) by rule 1, and (e) by looking up + in a list of known binary arithmetic operators. Thus, we have verified all the conditions necessary to show that our initial input is a valid expression. This process not only gives us a 'yes/no' answer, the trace of the verification steps shows us the structure of the expression. This is called the parse tree of the expression {**Figure** 2.1}.

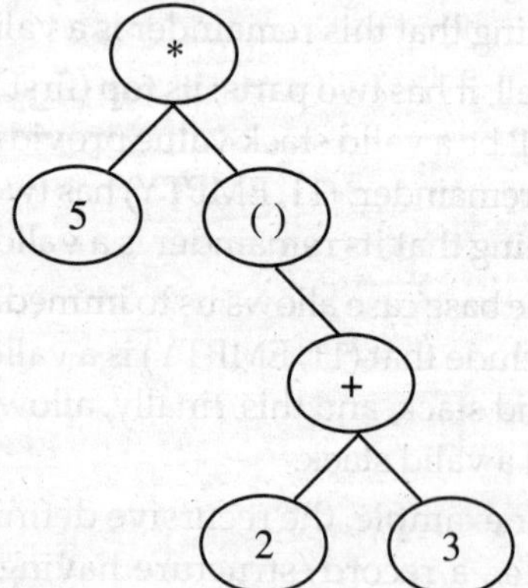

Figure 2.1 Parse tree

2.1 USING RECURSION TO SOLVE PROBLEMS

Recursion is a common form of the general-purpose problem-solving technique called "divide and conquer". The principle of divide-and-conquer, is that we solve a given problem P in 3 steps:

1. Divide P into several subproblems, $P_1, P_2, ... P_n$.
2. Solve, however we can, each of the subproblems to get solutions $S_1 ... S_n$.
3. Use $S_1 ... S_n$ to construct a solution to the original problem, P.

This is often recursive, because in order to solve one or more of the subproblems, we might use this very same strategy. For instance, we might solve P_1 be subdividing it into P_1a, P_1b..., solving each one of them, and putting together their solutions to get the solution S_1 to problem P_1.

2.1.1 An Everyday Example

To give a simple example, suppose we want to solve this problem:

P = carry a pile of 50 books from our office to car.

Well, one can't even lift such a big pile, never mind carry it. So we split the original pile into 3 piles: P_1 contains 10 books, P_2 contains 15 books, P_3 contains 25 books.

Our plan, of course, is to carry each pile to the car separately, and then put them back together into one big pile once they are all there. This is a recursive divide-and-conquer strategy; we have divided the original problem P into 3 problems *of the same kind*. Now suppose we can directly solve P_1 and P_2 - they are small enough that we can carry them to the car. So, P_1 and P_2 are now sitting out there by the car. Once we get P_3 there, we will pile them up again. But P_3 is too big to be carried. We apply the same strategy recursively: divide P_3 into smaller problems, solve them, and combine the results to make the solution for P_3. We divide P_3 into two piles, P_3a has 11 books, P_3b has 14, and carries these separately to the car. Then we put P_3a back onto P_3b to form the pile P_3 there at the car. Now we have solved all the subproblems: P_1, P_2, P_3 are sitting at the car. We stack them into one big pile, and presto, we have solved the original problem. This may seem like a rather hokey example, but it illustrates very well the principles of divide-and-conquer. Let us see how we can use the very same ideas to solve mathematical and computer science problems.

2.1.2 A Mathematical Example

Find an algorithm for raising a number X to the power N, where N is a positive integer. We may use *only* two operations: multiplication, subtraction. We would like to multiply N copies of X all at once, but, like the piles of books, we do not have an operation that directly allows us to do that: we can only multiply two numbers at a time. In other words, the problems we can solve directly are these:

- raise X to the power 1: answer = X.
- raise X to the power 2: answer = X * X.

Any other problem we have to solve indirectly, by breaking it down into smaller and smaller problems until we have reduced it to one of these base cases.

So, if N > 2, we split the original problem into two subproblems:

- P_1: raise X to the power I. The answer to this is S_1.
- P_2: raise X to the power N-I. The answer to this is S_2.
- To get the final answer, S, combine S_1 and S_2: $S = S_1 * S_2$.

How do we solve P_1 and P_2? They are problems of exactly the same type as original problem, so we can apply to them exactly the same strategy that we applied to the original problem. We check to see if we can solve them directly, if I=1 or I=2 we can solve P_1 directly; if N-I=1 or N-I=2 we can solve P_2 directly. The problems we cannot solve directly, we solve recursively, as just described. An interesting feature of this strategy is that it works no matter how we split up N. To see the strategy in action consider raising 3 to the power 7, 7 is too big, we cannot directly solve this problem, so we divide it into:

- P_1: raise 3 to the power 2. (choose I=2, no particular reason)
- P_2: raise 3 to the power 5.

We can directly solve P_1, the answer is $S_1 = 9$. But P_2 we have to further decompose:

- $P_{2.1}$: raise 3 to the power 1. (choose I=1, no particular reason)
- $P_{2.2}$: raise 3 to the power 4. Again, $P_{2.1}$ can be directly solved, $S_{2.1} = 3$, but $P_{2.2}$ must be further decomposed:
- $P_{2.2.1}$: raise 3 to the power 2.
- $P_{2.2.1}$: raise 3 to the power 2.

These both can be directly solved; $S_{2.2.1} = S_{2.2.1} = 9$. These are *combined* to give $S_{2.2} = 9*9 = 81$.

Now that we have the solutions to $P_{2,1}$ and $P_{2.2}$ we combine them to get the solution to P_2, $S_2 = 3*81 = 243$.

Now we have solutions for P_1 and P_2, we combine them to get the final solution, $S = S_1*S_2 = 9*243 = 2187$.

This strategy would work no matter how we chose to subdivide the problem: any choice of I will give the correct answer. However, some choices of I compute the final answer *faster* than others. Which do we think is faster: choosing I=1 (every time) or I=2? The computation will be faster if we choose I=2 because there will be half the number of recursive calls, and therefore half the overhead. This is true of most recursive strategies: they usually work correctly for many different ways of decomposing the problem, but some ways are much more efficient than others. In our first example, we also were free to divide the pile of books into as many piles and whatever sizes we liked. But it obviously would be very inefficient to carry one book at a time.

2.1.3. Data Structures Examples

Many problems involving data structures are naturally solved recursively. This is because most of the data structures are *collections* of components and they can easily be divided into *sub*-collections that can be independently processed, just as, in first example, we divided the pile of books into smaller piles that could be carried to the car separately. For example, suppose we want to add up the numbers stored in array X between positions FIRST and LAST. We can solve this directly in two very simple cases:

`FIRST=LAST:`

there is one number to be added, the answer is X[FIRST].

`FIRST+1=LAST:`

there are 2 numbers to be added, the answer is X[FIRST] + X[LAST].

Otherwise, there are too many numbers to be added all at once, so we divide the problem into two subproblems by dividing the array into two parts:

- P_1: add up the numbers in X between positions FIRST and M; the answer is S_1.
- P_2: add up the numbers in X between positions M+1 and LAST; the answer is S_2.

The final answer is obtained by combining S_1 and S_2 in an appropriate way. In order to get the sum of all the numbers in the array, we add together the two partial sums: $S = S_1 + S_2$. The exact way we divide up the array does not affect the correctness of this strategy: M can be any value at all, FIRST<M<LAST.

The structure of the collection dictates which the easiest ways to divide up the collection are. As arrays are very flexible, it is easy to divide them into a *front* and a *back* at any division point we care to choose. Other data structures are easily divided only in certain ways.

For example, suppose we want to add up all the numbers in a stack. We will base our solution on the recursive definition of stack we saw earlier: a stack is Empty, or has 2 parts, Top and Remainder. We can directly add up all the numbers in an Empty stack. There are none, and by convention, the sum of *no* numbers is 0. To add up the numbers in a non-empty stack, we will divide the stack into two parts, add up the parts separately, and combine the results. This is exactly what we did for arrays, but now we have to think, what is an easy way to divide a stack into two parts?

The definition of stack gives us an immediate answer: a stack naturally decomposes into a Top element (which is a number, not a stack), and a Remainder, which is a stack. So we can decompose the problem of adding up the numbers in a nonempty stack into these two subproblems:

- P_1: add up all the numbers in the Top part. This is not a recursive call, because Top is not a stack. In fact, Top is just a number, so the solution to this subproblem is just the top value itself. S_1=Top value.
- P_2: add up all the numbers in Remainder. This is a recursive call, because Remainder is a stack. The solution is S_1.

Now, combine S_1 and S_2 in the appropriate way to construct the final solution: S= $S_1 + S_2$, or, S=Top value + S_2. Of course, there is nothing special about adding. The very same strategy would work if we wanted to multiply together all the values in a collection, to find the largest value, to print out the elements, to count the number of elements, and so on. Suppose we wished to *sort* the values in array X between positions FIRST and LAST. We can solve this directly in two very simple cases:

`FIRST=LAST:`

there is one number to be sorted, nothing needs to be done.

`FIRST+1=LAST:`

there are 2 numbers to be sorted; compare them and, if they are out of order, swap them.

Otherwise, there are too many numbers to be sorted all at once, so we divide the problem into two subproblems by dividing the array into two parts:

- P_1: sort the numbers in X between positions FIRST and M; the answer is S_1.
- P_2: sort the numbers in X between positions M+1 and LAST; the answer is S_2.

The final answer is obtained by combining S_1 and S_2 in an appropriate way. The method for combining them is called merging, and it is a simple, efficient process. As before, the exact way we divide up the array does not affect the correctness of this strategy: M can be any value at all, FIRST<M<LAST. Certain values of M correspond to well-known sorting algorithms:

`M = 1`

`gives rise to the sorting algorithm called insertion sort.`

`M = the midpoint between FIRST and LAST`

`gives rise to the MergeSort algorithm.`

Both are correct, but their efficiency is very different: MergeSort is extremely fast (optimal in fact), whereas insertion sort is very slow.

2.1.4 Recursion as A Programming Technique

Let us now turn to the final way in which we might use or encounter recursion in computer science. Almost all-programming languages allow recursive functions call, i.e., they allow a function to call itself. And some languages allow recursive definitions of data structures. This means we can directly implement the recursive definitions and recursive algorithms that we have just been discussing. For example, the definition of the factorial function is,

```
factorial(0) = 1
factorial(n) = n * factorial(n-1) [ for n > 0 ].
```

can be written in C without the slightest change is executed as shown in **Figure** 2.2:

```
int factorial(int n)
{
    if (n == 0) return 1 ;
    else return n * factorial(n-1) ;
}
```

Similarly, our strategy for adding up the values in array can be implemented directly in C. Here is the strategy:

- if FIRST=LAST, the answer is X[FIRST].
- if FIRST+1=LAST, the answer is X[FIRST] + X[LAST]
- Otherwise, choose any M between FIRST and LAST, and
- add up the numbers in X between positions FIRST and M; the answer is S_1;
- add up the numbers in X between positions M+1 and LAST; the answer is S_2
- the final answer is $S_1 + S_2$.

Here is the C code:

```
int addup(int first, int last, int x[])
{
    int s1, s2, m ;
    if (first == last) return x[first];
    else if (first+1 == last) return x[first] + x[last];
    else
   {
    m = first + 1 ;
    s1 = addup( first, m, x);
    s2 = addup( m+1, last, x);
    return s1 + s2;
   }
}
```

The main benefits of using recursion as a programming technique are these:

- invariably recursive functions are clearer, simpler, shorter, and easier to understand than their non-recursive counterparts.
- the program directly reflects the abstract solution strategy (algorithm).

From a practical software engineering point of view these are important benefits, greatly enhancing the cost of maintaining the software. There is a third benefit that will become clear later when we move to trees {Chapter 7}. Recursive solutions can very often be translated or rewritten as iterative solutions: we all know iterative solutions for adding up the values in an array, for sorting and searching, and for processing linear data structures like arrays and stacks. However, when we are faced with a *non-linear* data structure, such as a tree, there is no obvious alternative to recursion.

The main disadvantage of programming recursively is that, while it makes it easier to write simple and elegant programs, it also makes it easier to write inefficient ones. Before looking at the efficiency question in detail, let me first point out one other difficulty that sometimes arises when programming with recursion. To illustrate this problem, consider the following program for computing the fibonacci function.

```
int s1, s2 ;

int fibonacci (int n)
{
 if (n == 0) return 1;
 else if (n == 1) return 1;
 else
 {
 s1 = fibonacci(n-1);
 s2 = fibonacci(n-2);
 return s1 + s2;
 }
}
```

The main thing to note here is that the variables that will hold the intermediate results, s1 and s2, have been declared as global variables. This is a mistake. Although the function looks just fine, its correctness crucially depends on having *local* variables for storing all the intermediate results. It will not correctly compute the fibonacci function for n=4 or larger. However, if we move the declaration of s1 and s2 inside the function, it works perfectly.

This sort of bug is *very* hard to find, and bugs like this are almost certain to arise whenever we use global variables to store intermediate results of a recursive function. This sort of bug does not seem to arise if iteration is used instead of recursion. However, this is not an argument against recursion: it is an argument against using global variables. We should always follow this rule: *Always declare variables in the function where they are needed.* Now, let us return to the question of efficiency. Recursion is based upon calling the same function over and over, whereas iteration simply 'jumps back' to the beginning of the loop {**Figure** 2.3}. A function call {**Figure** 2.4} is often more expensive than a jump. The overheads that may be associated with a function call are:

Space

Every invocation of a function call may require space for parameters and local variables, and for an indication of where to return when the function is finished. Typically this space (allocation record) is allocated on the stack and is released automatically when the function returns. Thus, a recursive algorithm may need space proportional to the number of nested calls to the same function.

Time

The operations involved in calling a function - allocating, and later releasing, local memory, copying values into the local memory for the parameters, branching to/returning from the function - all contribute to the time overhead.

If a function has very large local memory requirements, it would be very costly to program it recursively. But even if there is very little overhead in a single function call, recursive functions often call themselves many times, which can magnify a small individual overhead into a very large cumulative overhead. For example, the factorial function

```
int factorial(int n)
{
  if (n == 0) return 1;
  else return n * factorial(n-1);
}
```

There is very little overhead in calling this function, as it has only one word of local memory, for the parameter n. However, when we try to compute factorial (20), there will end up being 21 words of memory allocated - one for each invocation of the function:

```
factorial(20) ⇒ allocate 1 word of memory,
 call factorial(19) ⇒ allocate 1 word of memory,
 call factorial(18) ⇒ allocate 1 word of memory,
 ...
 call factorial(2) ⇒ allocate 1 word of memory,
 call factorial(1) ⇒ allocate 1 word of memory,
  call factorial(0) ⇒ allocate 1 word of memory,

at this point 21 words of memory and 21 activation records have been allocated.
  return 1. ⇒ release 1 word of memory.

 return 1*1. ⇒ release 1 word of memory.
 return 2*1. ⇒ release 1 word of memory.
```

The other reason that recursive programs may turn out to be inefficient is the simple fact that, when we use recursion to solve problems we are interested exclusively with correctness, and not at all with efficiency. Consequently, our simple, elegant recursive algorithms may be inherently inefficient. Therefore, it is essential, after we have solved the problem, to critically examine our solution and attempt to improve on it; both by removing sources of inefficiency and by refining its elegance. The fibonacci algorithm is a very striking example: if we directly coded it in C it is an *exponential* algorithm, meaning that in order to compute fibonacci(n) it would require about 2^n additions. Yet there is a very simple iterative version that requires only about n additions to compute fibonacci(n). This algorithm too can be expressed as a straightforward recursive computation.

The program segment **FACT.C** illustrates the definition of factorial discussed above.

```
/* Factorial of integer number */
/* FACT.C */
# include<stdio.h>
int n;
long int Factorial( int );
void Display( int);
/* The definition of the Factorial() function */
```

```
long int Factorial( int n)
{
   if( n == 0)
      return(1);
   else
      return(n * Factorial( n -1 ));
}

/* Output Function */
void Display(int n)
{
   printf("\n Factorial of : %d = %ld", n, Factorial(n));
}

/* main function */
void main()
{
   int n ;
   printf("\n Input the number of which you want to find factorial: ");
   scanf("%d", &n);
   Factorial( n );
   Display( n );
}
```

In the above program segment, the function **Factorial()** is called with argument 0 value. Then function returns 1, otherwise it returns **n*Factorial(n-1)**. To calculate the value of the expression, the Factorial**()** is called with **n-1.** This process continues until **n** equals to 0. This process is demonstrated in **Figure 2.2**.

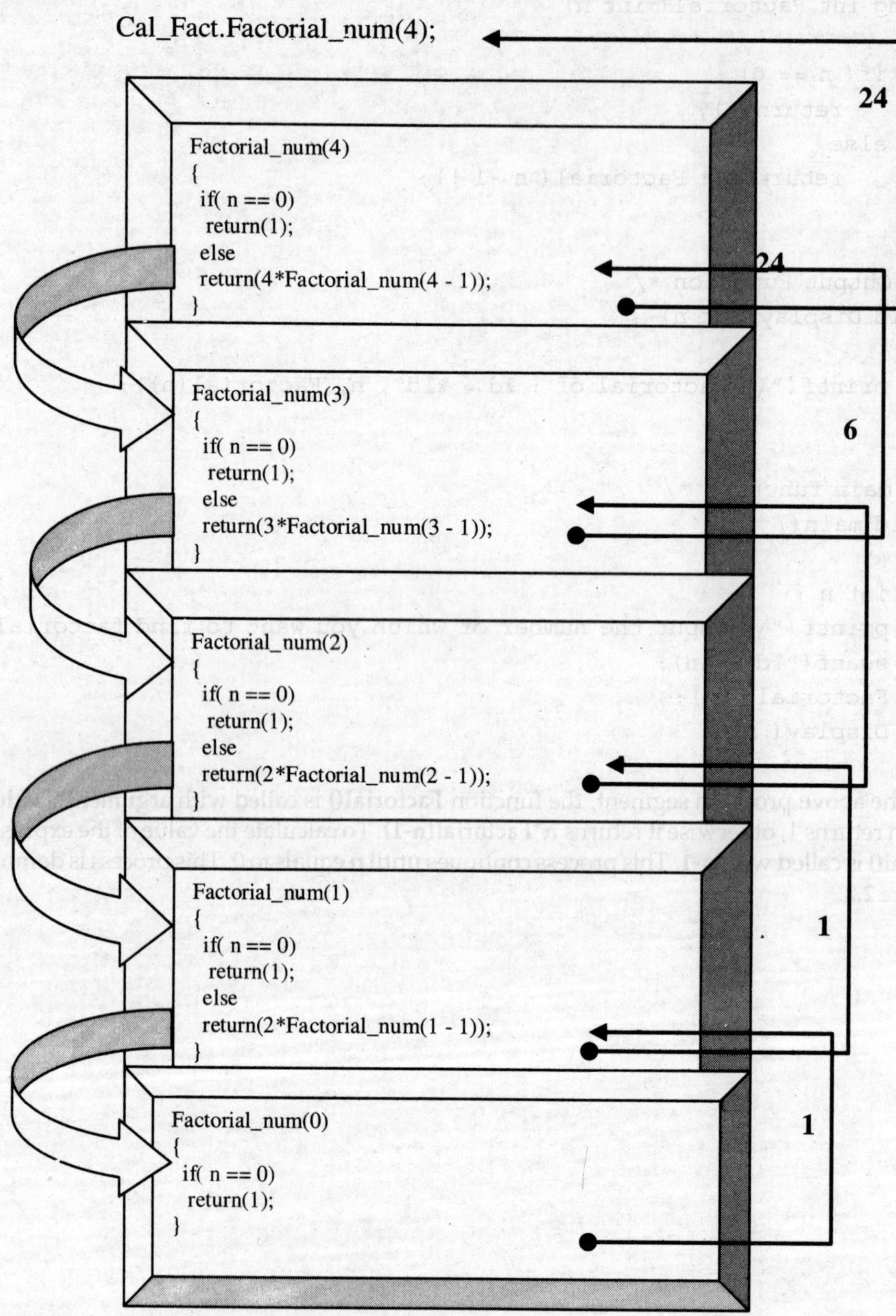

Figure 2.2 Sequence of function calls and the value returned

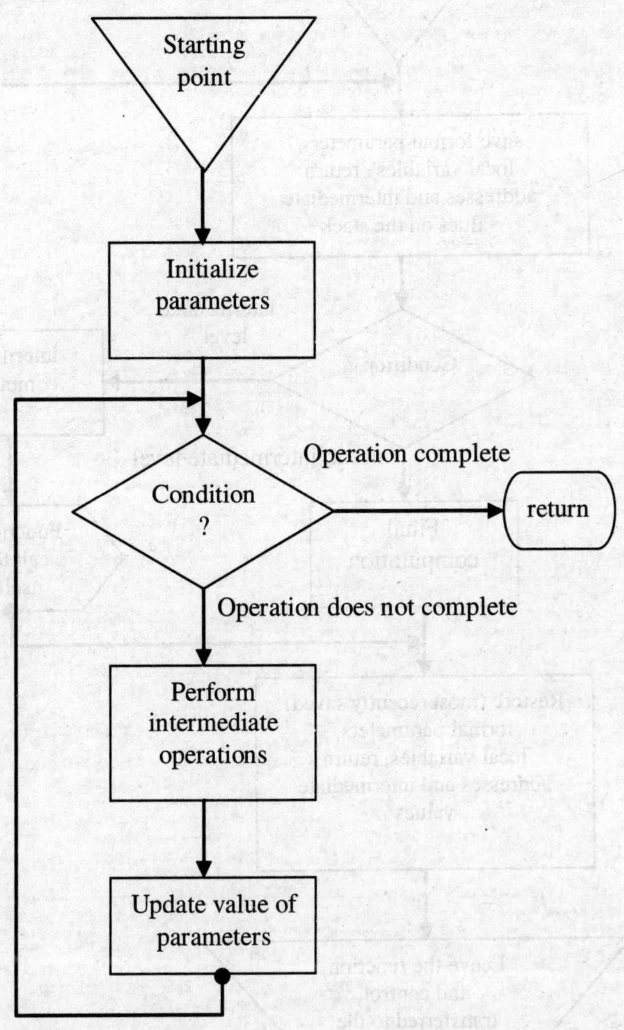

Figure 2.3 Iterative method

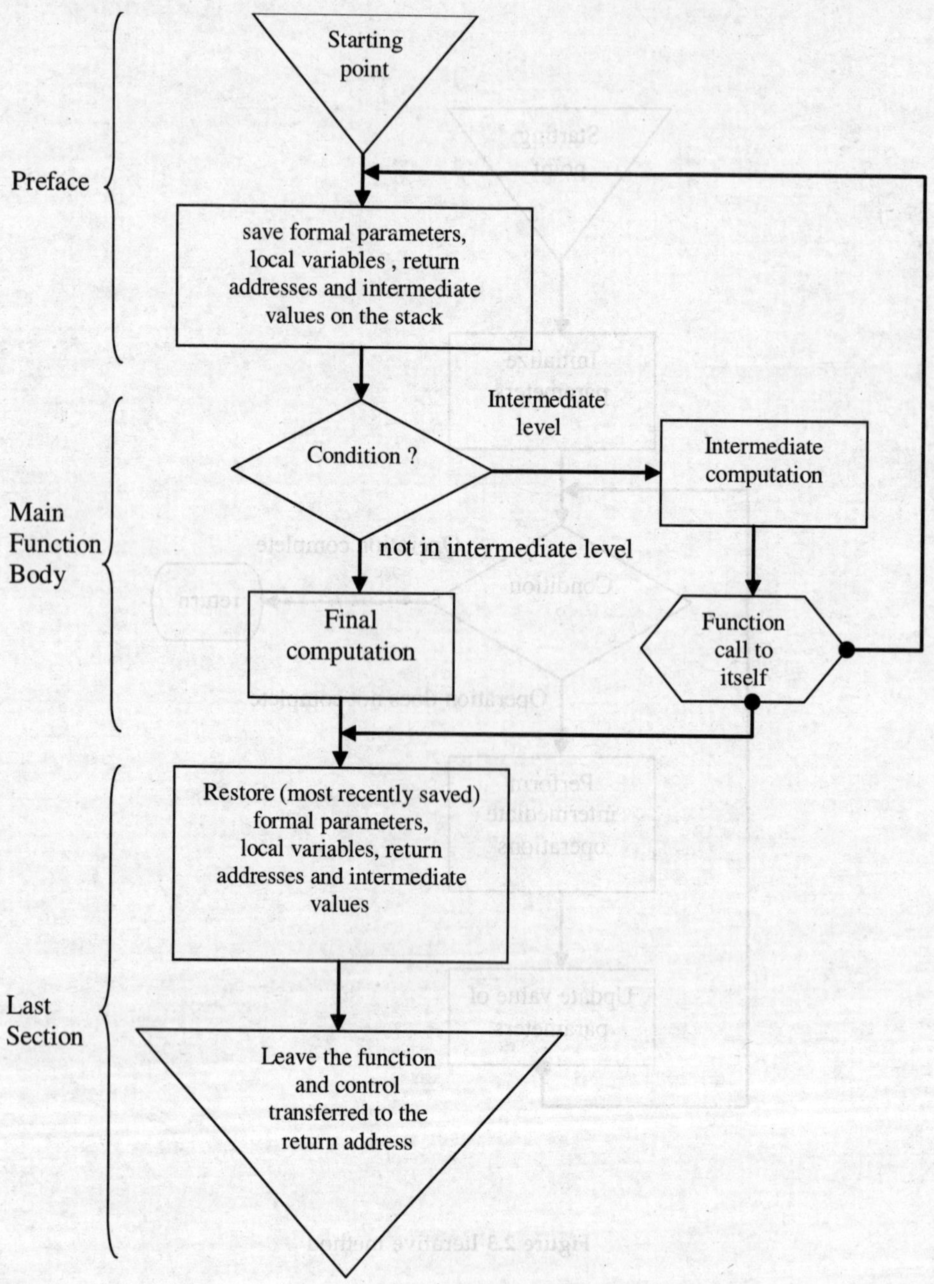

Figure 2.4 Recursive process

2.2 TYPES OF RECURSION

Recursion is of two types:

- Preemptive recursive function for example, factorial algorithm (discussed earlier).

- Non-preemptive recursive function for example, *Ackermann*'s function, a function with two arguments, which can be assigned any positive integer such as 0, 1, 2, 3,…, etc. The function is defined in **Figure** 2.5.

$$\text{Ack\_fun(M,N)} = \begin{cases} N+1 & \text{If } M=0 \quad \text{(a)} \\ \text{Ack\_fun(M - 1 , 1)} & \text{If } N=0 \quad \text{(b)} \\ \text{Ack\_fun(M -1 , Ack\_fun(M, N-1))} & \text{Otherwise.} \quad \text{(c)} \end{cases}$$

Figure 2.5. Ackermann's recursive algorithm

The following steps show, how one can find the value **Ack_fun(1, 3)?**

(i) Ack_fun(1,3) = Ack_fun(1-1,Ack_fun(1,3-1)) = Ack_fun(0,Ack_fun(1,2))
(ii) Ack_fun(1,2) = Ack_fun(1-1,Ack_fun(1,2-1)) = Ack_fun(0,Ack_fun(1,1))
(iii) Ack_fun(1,1) = Ack_fun(1-1,Ack_fun(1,1-1)) = Ack_fun(0,Ack_fun(1,0))
(iv) Ack_fun(1,0) = Ack_fun(1-1,1) = Ack_fun(0,1)
(v) Ack_fun(0,1) = N+1 = 1 + 1 = 2 **Here value of N is 1**
(vi) Ack_fun(1,0) = 2
(vii) Ack_fun(1,1) = (0,2) Consider step 3 to 6
(viii) Ack_fun(0,2) = 2 + 1 = 3 **Here value of N is 2**
(ix) Ack_fun(1,1) = Ack_fun(0,2) Consider step 3 to 8
(x) Ack_fun(1,2) = Ack_fun(0,3)
(xi) Ack_fun(0,3) = 3 + 1 = 4 **Here value of N is 3**
(xii) Ack_fun(1,2) = 4
(xiii) Ack_fun(1,3) = Ack_fun(0,4)
(xiv) Ack_fun(0,4_ = 4 + 1 = 5 **Here value of N is 4**
(xv) Ack_fun(1,3) = 5 Result

Recursion occurs in *Ackermann*'s function, because the function **Ack_fun()** becomes an argument in a call of function **Ack_fun()**. This is a very typical case of recursion. Preemptive recursive algorithm can be easily implemented with the help of iterative method {**Figure** (2.3)}. The pictorial representation of recursive process is given in **Figure 2.4**.

2.3 EXPONENTIAL POWER

In the similar way one can easily compute the positive (integer) exponential power of a number, i.e., a^b. The recursive definition is defined in **Figure** 2.6.

$$\textbf{power\_f(a, b)} = \begin{cases} 1 & \text{If } b = 0 \\ a * \text{power\_f}(a, b+1) & \text{If } b > 0 \end{cases}$$

Figure 2.6. Recursive definition of a^b

In the similar way one can easily compute the negative (integer) exponential power of a number, i.e., $\mathbf{a^{-b}}$. The recursive definition is:

$$\text{power\_f(a,b)} = \begin{cases} 1 & \text{If } b = 0 \\ a*\text{power\_f}(a,-b+1) & \text{If } b < 0 \end{cases}$$

Figure 2.7. Recursive definition of a^{-b}

Here, we have taken **mantissa = a** and **exponent = - b**. The power is negative so the returned value of the function is taken as inverse of the **returned value of the function.** The recursive programs for the two definitions are shown in **Figure 2.6** and **Figure 2.7** are illustrated in the program segment **POWER.C**.

```
/* Power Function */
/* POWER.C */

# include<stdio.h>

double power_f(double, float );

/* Definition of the function power_f() */

double power_f(double a, float b)
{
    if( b == 0)
    {
        return 1;
    }else if ( b< 0)
    {
        return( (a * power_f(a,b+1)));
    }else
        return( a* power_f(a,b-1));
}

/* Function main */

void main()
{
    double mantissa;
    float exponent;

    printf("\n Input the Mantissa: ");
    scanf("%lf", &mantissa);
    printf("\n Input the exponent: ");
    scanf("%f", &exponent);
    if( exponent < 0)
        printf("\n maintissa ^ exponent: %lf", 1/ power_f(mantissa,
exponent));
    else printf("\n maintissa ^ exponent: %lf", power_f(mantissa, exponent));
}
```

In the similar way one can easily compute the positive (fractional) exponential power of a number, i.e., $\mathbf{a}^{b}$. The recursive definition is given in **Figure** 2.8.

$$power\_f(a,b) = \begin{cases} 1 & \text{If } b = 0.0 \\ a * power\_f(a, b - i, i) & \text{If } b > 0.0 \end{cases}$$

Figure 2.8. Recursive definition of a^b

For computing the negative (fractional) exponential power of a number, i.e., $\mathbf{a^{-b}}$, the recursive definition is given in **Figure** 2.9.

$$power\_f(a,b) = \begin{cases} 1 & \text{If } b = 0.0 \\ a * power\_f(a, -b + i, i) & \text{If } b < 0.0 \end{cases}$$

Figure 2.9. Recursive definition of a^b

To see, how the definitions shown in **Figure 2.8** and **Figure 2.9** work, consider the following program segment **(POWER1.C).**

In this program segment, **i** have been taken as a counter and its value is calculated by passing 10 as **mantissa**. The number of digits after the decimal point is passed as **exponent**. For example, if the digits after the decimal point are four then we pass 4 to the recursion function for calculating the value of **i**. After getting the value of **i,** the exponential power of the number is calculated. If the exponent is positive then returned value of the function will be the value of the exponential power the number else we take the inverse of the returned value of the function as the exponential power of the number. Here, in this function we input exponent parameter value as a string because it is easier to find the number of digits before and after the decimal point by using string.

```
/* Power Function */
/* POWER1.C */

# include<stdio.h>
# include<math.h>
double power_fract(double, float, float );
void expo();

/* The definition of the power_fract() function */
double power_fract(double a, float b, float i)
{
    if( b == 0)
    {
        return 1;
    }
    else if ( b< 0)
    {
        return( (a * power_fract(a,b + i,i)));
    }

    else
```

```
      return( a* power_fract(a,b - i,i));
  }

  /* The definition of the expo() function */
  void expo()
  {
     char str[50];
     char *pstr;
     char temp;
     int count = 0;
     char ch;
     int i = 0;
     float counter;
     float exponent;
     float mantissa;
     printf("\n Input the Mantissa: ");
     scanf("%f", &mantissa);
     printf(" Input the Exponent: ");
     fflush(stdin);

     ch = getchar();

     while( ch != '\n')
     {
        if((ch == '-') || (ch == '+'))
           count++;
        if( ch == '.')
           temp = ch;
        str[i] = ch;
        ch = getchar();
        i ++;
        count ++;
     }
     str[i]='\0';
     printf("\n\n Number of digits including '.' = %d", count);
     count = i;
     if (temp == '.')
     {
        i = 1;
        pstr = &str[0];
        while(*pstr != '.')
```

```
    {
        pstr++;
        i ++;
    }
  }
  printf("\n Number of digits including sign & period(.) character =
%d",i);
  count = count - i;
  printf("\n Number of digits after decimal point = %d", count);
  exponent = atof(str);
  counter = 1/power_fract(10, -count,1);
  printf("\n Increment/Decrement counter = %i", counter);
  printf("\n\n Mantissa = %f", mantissa);
  printf("\n Exponent = %f", exponent);

  if(exponent < 0)
 printf("\n\n    mantissa   ^    exponent    =    %lf",    1/
power_fract(mantissa,exponent,counter));
  else
 printf("\n\n    mantissa    ^     exponent     =     %lf",
power_fract(mantissa,exponent,counter));
 }

 // Function main
 void main()
 {
  expo();
 }
```

2.4 FIBONACCI NUMBERS (REVISITED)

This is another problem, which can be easily solved with the help of recursion. The recursive definition of the Fibonacci number generator function is defined in **Figure** 2.10.

$$\text{fibo\_number (n)} = \begin{cases} 0 & \text{If } n = 0 \text{ or } n = 1 \\ 1 & \text{If } n = 2 \\ \text{fibo\_number(n-1)} + \text{fibo\_number(n-2)} & \text{If } n > 2 \end{cases}$$

Figure 2.10 Recursive definition of Fibonacci generator function

The fibonacci sequence is as follows, **0, 1, 1, 2, 3, 5, 8, 13, 21, 21, 34, 55,** etc. This list is generated from the definition shown in the **Figure 2.10.**

If we consider $\mathbf{F_0 = 0}$ and $\mathbf{F_1 = 1}$, then $\mathbf{F_2 = F_1 + F_0 = 1 + 0 = 1}$, similarly $\mathbf{F_3 = F_2 + F_1 = 1 + 1 = 2}$, $\mathbf{F_4 = F_3 + F_2 = 2 + 1 = 3}$ and so on. Thus, it is clear that each succeeding term is the sum of the two preceding terms. The **fibo_number ()** function generates one Fibonacci number at a time. So in the main program a while loop is implemented, which calls the **fibo_number ()** function until the value of **i** is less than the value of **n.** The program segment **FIBO.C** illustrates this idea.

```
/* Fibonacci Numbers */
/* FIBO.C */

# include<stdio.h>

long fibo_number(int );

/* Definition of the function Fibonacci number generator */

long fibo_number( int n)
{
    int r;
    if(( n == 1) || ( n == 0))
        return 0;
    else
        if(n == 2)
            return 1;
        else
            return (fibo_number(n-1) + fibo_number(n-2));

}

/* main function */

void main()
{
    int n;
    int i =0;
    printf("\n Input the number for Fibonacci series, you want to generate:
");
    scanf("%d", &n);
    printf("\n Fibonacci Series is as follows: \n");

    while(i < n)
    {
        ++i;
        printf(" %d", fibo_number(i));
    }
}
```

2.5 GREATEST COMMON DIVISOR

A more complex recursive example is to find the greatest common divisor of two positive integers with the help of **Euclid**'s algorithm. The definition of **Euclid**'s algorithm is as follows:

$$\text{Greatest\_Comm\_Div}(n, m) = \begin{cases} \text{Greatest\_Comm\_Div}(m, n) & \text{If } n < m \\ m & \text{If } n \geq m \text{ and } n \bmod m = 0 \\ \text{Greatest\_Comm\_Div}(m, n \bmod m) & \text{Otherwise} \end{cases}$$

Figure 2.11 Greatest common divisor algorithm

The greatest common divisor algorithm is implemented in the program segment **GCD.C.**

```
/* Greatest Common Divisor */
/* GCD.C */
# include<stdio.h>

int Greatest_Comm_Div(int , int);

/* Definition of the Greatest Comman Divisor Function */
int Greatest_Comm_Div( int n, int m)
{
    if(( n >= m) && (( n % m) == 0))
        return(m);
    else
        Greatest_Comm_Div(m,(n % m));
}

/* main function */
void main()
{
    int n, m;
    int result;
    printf("\n Input the first integer number: ");
    scanf("%d", &n);

    printf("\n Input the second integer number: ");
    scanf("%d", &m);

    result = Greatest_Comm_Div(n, m);
    printf("\n Greatest Comman Diviser of : %d and %d is = %d", n, m,
result);
}
```

2.6 THE TOWERS OF HANOI

The Tower of Hanoi is a famous recursive problem, which is based on three pegs and a set of discs of graduated sizes. Suppose three pegs, labeled **X**, **Y** and **Z** are given and on peg **X** there are finite number of discs **n** in increasing (size) order, i.e., biggest one at the bottom and smallest one at the top. The problem is to move discs from peg **X** to peg **Z** using peg **Y** whenever it is required. The rules, which we have to take into account before moving a disc, are:

(i) Only one disc may be moved at a time.

(ii) Only the top disc on any peg may be moved to any other peg.

(iii) A larger disc can not be placed on a smaller one.

Pictorial view of Tower of Hanoi is given in **Figure 2.12. Figure 2.12** shows that there are 4 discs on peg **X**. The solution of the Tower of Hanoi for **n = 4** discs are shown in **Table 2.1**. The solution of this problem is very simple, if there are only two discs to move. First disc $\mathbf{D_1}$ is moved to peg **Y**, then disc $\mathbf{D_2}$ is moved to peg **Z**. Finally the disc $\mathbf{D_1}$ is moved from peg **Y** to peg **Z**. **Figure 2.13 (a)** illustrates the problem with two discs and **Figure 2.13 (b-c-d)** describes its solution.

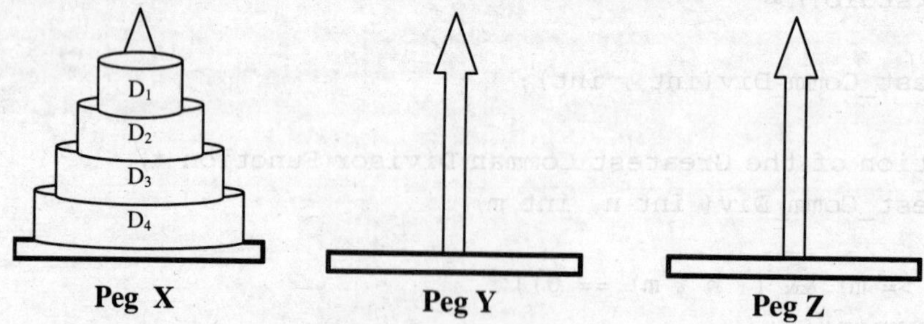

Figure 2.12 Tower of Hanoi Problem

Table 2.1 Disc Movement in Tower of Hanoi For 4 Discs

```
Input the number of disc : 4
Tower of Hanoi for 4 DISC
Move Disk from X to YMove Disk from X to Z
Move Disk from Y to Z
Move Disk from X to Y
Move Disk from Z to X
Move Disk from Z to Y
Move Disk from X to Y
Move Disk from X to Z
Move Disk from Y to Z
Move Disk from Y to X
Move Disk from Z to X
Move Disk from Y to Z
Move Disk from X to Y
Move Disk from X to Z
Move Disk from Y to Z
```

With four discs the problem becomes more complex and complicated. After analyzing the problem it is found that in order to move the largest disc from peg **X** to peg **Z**, we must do the following:

If n = 1 then move the disc from the peg X to peg Z

If n > 1 then the following moves are to be performed: as per **Table 2.1**

The above analysis may indicate that the implementation of this problem is very typical. However, this is not so as illustrated with the help of the **HANOI.C**. This code segment produces result as shown in **Table 2.1**.

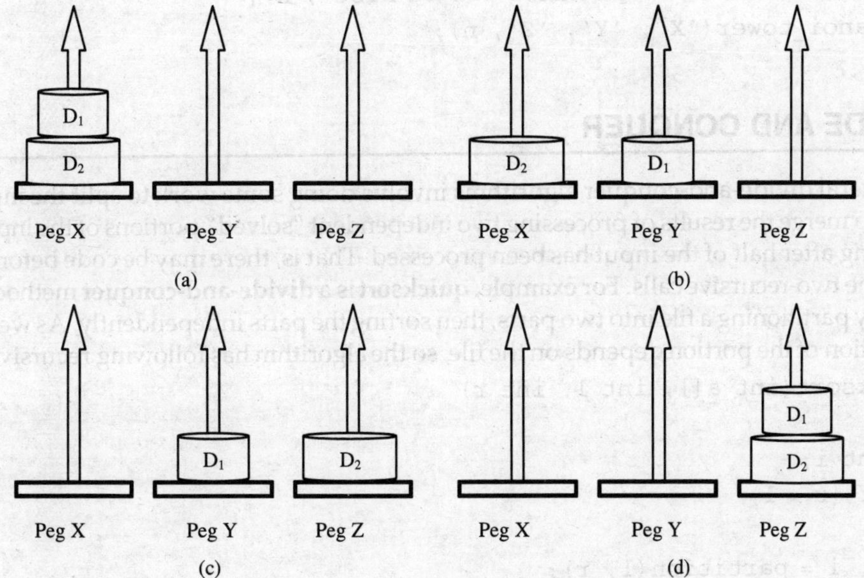

Figure 2.13 Tower of Hanoi with Two Discs

```
/* Tower of Hanoi problem*/
/* HANOI.C */
# include<stdio.h>
void hanoi_tower(char , char , char , int );
/* Definition of the Tower Of Hanoi generator function */
void hanoi_tower(char peg1, char peg2, char peg3, int n)
{
   if( n <= 0)
      printf("\n Illegal entry ");
   if(n == 1)
      printf("\n Move Disk from %c to %c", peg1, peg3);
   else{
      hanoi_tower(peg1, peg3, peg2, n-1);
      hanoi_tower(peg1, peg2, peg3, 1);
      hanoi_tower(peg2, peg1, peg3, n-1);
   }
}
```

```
/* main function */
void main()
{
    int n;
    printf("\n Input the number of disc: ");
    scanf("%d", &n);
    printf("\n Tower of Hanoi for %d DISC", n);
    hanoi_tower('X', 'Y', 'Z', n);
}
```

2.7 DIVIDE AND CONQUER

In general divide-and-conquer algorithms involve doing some work to split the input into two pieces or to merge the results of processing two independent "solved" portions of the input or to help things along after half of the input has been processed. That is, there may be code before, after or in between the two-recursive calls. For example, **quicksort** is a **divide-and-conquer** method for sorting. It works by partitioning a file into two parts, then sorting the parts independently. As we will see, the exact position of the portion depends on the file, so the algorithm has following recursive structure:

```
Quicksort(int a[], int l, int r)
{
    int i;
    if (r > l)
    {
        i = partition(l, r);
        Quicksort(a, l, i-1);
        Quicksort (a, i+1, r);
    }
}
```

The parameters **l** and **r** the sub-file within the original file that is to be sorted; the call **Quicksort(1, n)** sorts the whole file.

The crux of the method is the partition procedure, which rearrange the array to make the following three considerations hold:

(i) The element **a[i]** is in its final place are less than or equal to some **i**.
(ii) All the elements in **a[1], ..., a[i-1]** are less than or equal to **a[i]**.
(iii) All the elements in **a[i+1], ..., a[r]** are greater than or equal to **a[i]**.

This can be simply and easily implemented through the general strategy. First, arbitrarily choose **a[r]** to be the element that will go into its final position, next, scan from the left end of the array until an element greater than **a[r]** is found and scan from right end of the elements which stopped the scans are obviously out of place in the partitioned array, so exchange them. Continuing in this way ensures that all array elements to the left of the left pointer are less than **a[r]** and all array elements to the right of the right pointer are greater than **a[r]**. When nearly complete all that remains is to exchange **a[r]** with the leftmost element of the right sub-file. **Figure 2.14(a)** shows how our sample file of keys is partitioned with this method. The rightmost element, E, is chosen as the partitioning element. First, the scan from the left stops at the S, then the scan from the right stops at A **Figure 2.14(b)** and then these two are exchanged. Next, the scan from left stops at the O, then the scan from the right stops at E **Figure 2.14(c)**, then these two are exchanged. Next, the pointers cross. The scan from the left stops at the R and the scan from the right stops at the E. The proper move at this point is to exchanged the E at the right with the R, leaving the partitioned file as shown in **Figure2.14(e)**.

Sorting the two sub-files on either side of the partitioning element (recursively) finishes the sort. Consider the following program that gives full implementation of the method:

```
Quicksort( int a[] , int l, int r)
{
   int v, i, j, t;
   if(r > l)
   {
      v = a[r];
      i = l-1;
      j = r;
   for(; ;)
      {
         while (a[++i] < v);
         while(a[--j] > v);
         if(i >= j)
         break;
         t = a[i];
         a[i] = a[j];
         a[j] = t;
      }
      t = a[i];
      a[i] = a[r];
      a[r] = t;
      Quicksort(a, l, i-1);
      Quicksort(a, i+1, r);
   }
}
```

In this implementation, the variable **v** holds the current value of the partitioning element, **a[r]** and **i** and **j** are the left and right scans pointers, respectively. The partitioning loop is implemented as an infinite loop, with a break out when the pointer cross.

A	S	O	R	T	I	N	G	E	X	A	M	P	L	E

(a)

A	S									A	M	P	L	E

(b)

A	A	O						E	X	A	M	P	L	E

(c)

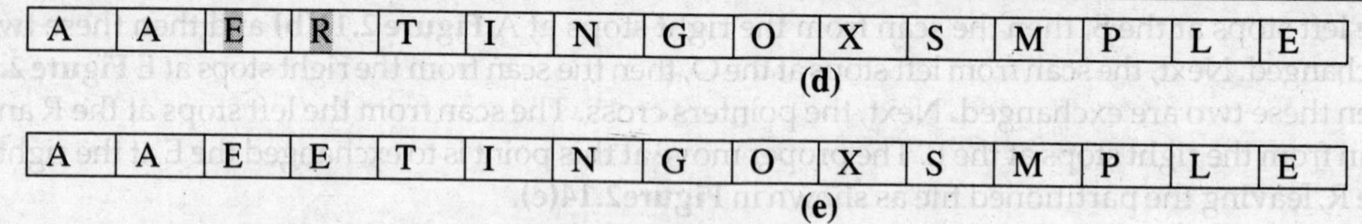

A	A	E	R	T	I	N	G	O	X	S	M	P	L	E

(d)

A	A	E	E	T	I	N	G	O	X	S	M	P	L	E

(e)

Figure 2.14 Partitioning

A problem that can be separated into two sub-problems that can be handled separately is more than half solved by that separation. This simple principle can be applied in an amazing variety of ways. The divide and conquer is one of them. For example, consider the problem of finding maximum and minimum of a list of integers simultaneously. The solution of the problem is implemented below **(DIV_ITER.C)**:

```
/* FIND MAXIMUM AND MINIMUM USING ITERATIVE METHOD */
/* DIV_ITER.C */
# include<stdio.h>
void max_min(int *, int, int , int );
/* Definition of the function max_min() */
void max_min(int l[], int n, int max, int min)
{
   int i;
   max = min = l[0];
   for(i = 1; i < n; i++)
   {
      if(l[i] > max)
         max = l[i];
      if(l[i] < min)
         min = l[i];
   }
   printf("\n Maxmum = %d", max);
   printf("\n Minimum = %d", min);
}
/* main function */
void main()
{
   int i, list[100];
   int n, max, min;
   printf("\n Number of elements in the list :");
   scanf("%d", &n);
   printf("\n Input elements of the list:");
   for(i =0; i < n; i++)
      scanf("%d", &list[i]);
   max_min(list, n, max, min);
}
```

In the above program segment, the function **max_min ()** performs **2*(n –1)** comparisons. The recursive definition for **divide and conquer** for the above problem is given in **Figure 2.15** and **DIV_CON.C** implements this algorithm.

```
div_con(l, n, max, min)

 where l → Represents the list of elements
 n ® Represents the number of elements in the list
   max → It has to found
   min → It has to found

Step 1: If n = 1 do Step 2
Step 2: min = max = l[0]
Step 3: If n = 2 then
(i)    max = l[0]
(ii)   min = l[1]
Else
(iii)  max = l[1]
(iv)   min = l[0]

 Else
   Divide the list in two sections and find recursively the min and max
of each half. Assign min the smaller of two mins and max the larger of the
two maxs.
```

Figure 2.15 Algorithm for Divide and Conquer

```
/* Divide and Conquer */
/* Find minimum and maximum from a given series of numbers */
/* by using above said policy */
/* DIV_CON.C */
# include<stdio.h>
# define size 100

int min1, max1;
void div_con(int *, int, int *, int *);

/* definition of the function div_con() */
void div_con( int list[], int n, int *min, int *max)
{
   if( n == 1)
      *min = *max = list[0];
   else if( n == 2){
         if(list[0] < list[1])
```

```
            {
               *min = list[0];
               *max = list[1];
            }else{
               *min = list[1];
               *max = list[0];
            }
         }else{
            div_con(list, n/2, min, max);
            div_con(list+ n/2, n - n/2, &min1, &max1);
            if( min1 < *min)
               *min = min1;
            if( max1 > *max)
               *max = max1;
         }
   }

   /* Function main */

   void main()
   {
      int i;
      int *min, *max;
      int list[size];
      int number;
      printf("\n Input the number of elements in the list :");
      scanf(" %d", &number);
      printf("\n Input the list of elements:\n");
      for(i = 0; i < number; i++)
      {
         scanf("%d", &list[i]);
      }
      printf("\n Min and Max are :");
      div_con( list, number, min, max);
      printf("\n Mimimum = %d", *min);
      printf("\n Maximum = %d", *max);
   }
```

2.8 FUNCTION OVERHEAD

When we define functions in a program, C pushes the return address, parameters and local variables onto the stack. When the function completes, C discards (pops) the stack space that contain the local variables then uses the return value to resume the program's execution at the correct location. The use of the stack lets the program invoke and pass information to the functions consumes processing time. The amount of time required pushing and popping stack information is function overhead. For example, go through the program segment **FUNCTOVR.C**, in this first for loop requires approximately 8 seconds to sum 1 to 1,00, 000, 000. The second loop for the same range of data with the help of function takes approximately 54 seconds on 133 MHz machine **SCO UNIX** machine for same number of running processes.

```
/* FUNCTOVR.C */
#include <stdio.h>
#include <time.h>

float add_em(long int a, float b)
 {
 float result;
 result = a + b;
 return(result);
 }

 // Function main
 void main(void)
 {
 long int i;
 float result = 0;
 time_t start_time, stop_time;
 printf("Working...\n");
 time(&start_time);

 for (i = 1; i <= 100000000L; i++)
 result += i;

 time(&stop_time);
 printf("Using loop: %d seconds\n", stop_time - start_time);

 printf("Working...\n");
 time(&start_time);

 for (i = 1; i <= 100000000L; i++)
   result = add_em(i, result);

 time(&stop_time);
 printf("Using function: %d seconds\n", stop_time - start_time);
 }
```

```
Working...
Using loop: 8 seconds
Working...
Using function: 54 seconds
```

2.9 EFFICIENT RECURSION

Recursion is such an elegant and powerful technique that a lot of effort has been invested in creating compilers that can optimize it and make its use competitive with iteration.

Iteration as a special case of recursion

The first insight is that iteration is a special case of recursion.

```
void do_loop () { do { ... } while (e); }
```

is equivalent to:

```
void do_loop () { ... ; if (e) do_loop(); }
```

A compiler can recognize instances of this form of recursion and turn them into loops or simple jumps, e.g.:

```
void do_loop () { start: ...; if (e) goto start; }
```

Notice that this optimization also removes the space overhead associated with function calls.

Tail Calls

The second insight concerns *tail* calls. A call is said to be a tail call if it is the last thing that needs to be executed in a particular invocation of the function where it occurs. For example:

```
void zig (int n) { ... ; if (e) zag(n-1); }
```

The call to zag is a tail call because, if it happens - i.e., if (e) evaluates to true - then it is the last thing that needs to be executed in the current invocation of **zig**.

What it so special about tail calls? Simply this: if **zag** is the last thing to be executed in **zig**, surely **zig** won't need its local variables while **zag** is executing, and it won't need them after **zag** returns since there won't be anything left to do. Therefore, we can release the local space allocated to **zig** *before* calling zag.

Thus, tail recursive algorithms can be optimized to execute in *constant* space - a tail recursive algorithm is one where the recursive steps are all tail calls. The most natural version of an algorithm is *not* tail recursive. Consider the factorial function:

```
int factorial(int n)
{ return (n == 0) ? 1 : n * factorial(n-1); }
```

The recursive call to factorial is not tail recursive: the last thing that needs to be done is the multiplication, not the call. Therefore, factorial executes in space proportional to n (linear space). It is often not too difficult to turn a non tail-recursive algorithm into a tail-recursive one. Typically, adding extra parameters to the definition does this: these parameters serve to accumulate intermediate results. For example, the definition of factorial can be augmented with an 'accumulator':

```
int factorial(int n,int accu)
{
  return (n == 0) ? accu : factorial(n-1,n*accu);
}
```

Or we can keep the same interface as before and use an auxiliary definition:

```
int fact_aux (int n,int accu)
{
  return (n == 0) ? accu : fact_aux(n-1,n*accu);
}

int factorial(int n)
{
  return fact_aux(n,1);
}
```

A modern optimizing compiler will turn this version into machine code equivalent to the iterative version. How do we know that this second version is correct? We prove it by *induction.* Note that there is a strong connection between recursion and induction. They are really two aspects of the same fundamental idea.

Notice that, for n>0, fact_aux(n,a) = fact_aux(n-1,n*a). On the right-hand side of the equation, the first argument has decreased by 1. As long as n is sufficiently large, we can iterate the process:

```
fact_aux(n,a) = fact_aux(n-1,n*a)
 = fact_aux(n-2,(n-1)*n*a)
 = fact_aux(n-3,(n-2)*(n-1)*n*a)
 ...
 = fact_aux(n-k,(n-k+1)*...*(n-2)*(n-1)*n*a)
in particular for k=n, we have:
fact_aux(n,a) = fact_aux(0,1*2*...*(n-2)*(n-1)*n*a)
 = 1*2*...*(n-2)*(n-1)*n*a
```

because when its 1st argument is 0, fact_aux simply returns its 2nd argument. By definition of factorial:

```
factorial(n) = fact_aux(n,1) = 1*2*...*(n-2)*(n-1)*n*1
```

This result is precisely 'n!'.

Optimizing the Fibonacci algorithm

The fibonacci function is defined by the following equations:

- fib(0) = 1
- fib(1) = 1
- fib(n) = fib(n-2) + fib(n-1), if n>1

which we can directly implement by:

```
int fib(int n)
{
  return (n == 0 || n == 1) ? 1 : fib(n-2)+fib(n-1);
}
```

Unfortunately, there are two sources of inefficiency. Firstly, this algorithm is not tail recursive. Secondly, it spends a lot of time re-computing the same values over and over again. To wit, in order to compute fib(n):

- First we compute fib(n-2), which in particular involves computing fib(n-3).
- Then we compute fib(n-1), which requires re-computing both fib(n-2) and fib(n-3).

We can improve the algorithm as follows: we notice that the computation of fib(n-2) involves computing fib(n-3); therefore, if we could only save these two results, we could subsequently just add them together to produce fib(n-1). This is the basis for the first optimization. We are going to introduce the auxiliary function fib2() which is exactly like fib, but returns a compound value containing the two aforementioned results: i.e., fib2(n) contains both fib(n) and fib(n-1). Then, we shall write the function fib1, which computes the same value as fib(), but does it more efficiently by calling fib2().

```
typedef struct { int first, second; } Pair;
Pair fib2 (int n)
{
 if (n == 0) { Pair p = {1,0}; return p; }
 else {
 Pair p1 = fib2(n-1);
 Pair p2;

 p2.first = p1.first + p1.second;
 p2.second = p1.first;

 return p2;
 }
}

int fib1 (int n)
{
   return fib2(n).first;
}
```

How do we know this code is correct? First we verify the two base cases:

- fib1(0) = 1 = fib(0)
- fib1(1) = 1 = fib(1)

Then we proceed by induction, and show that for n>1

- fib2(n) = {fib(n),fib(n-1)}
- therefore: fib1(n) = fib2(n).first = fib(n)

The above improvement no longer spends time recomputing the same values. However, it is not tail recursive and consequently consumes stack space. It is possible to do better by using a *bottom-up* algorithm instead of a *top-down* algorithm. This time, we need to introduce 2 accumulators - they correspond to the pair of values of our first improvement.

```
 int fib3(int n, int i, int j)
 {
   return (n==0)?i:fib3(n-1,i+j,i);
 }
 int fib1(int n)
```

```
    {
       return fib3(n,1,0);
    }
```

How do we know this code is correct? Again, we proceed by induction:

- fib1(n) = fib3(n,1,0) = fib3(n-k,fib(k),fib(k-1))
- in particular for k=n: fib1(n) = fib3(0,fib(n),fib(n-1)) = fib(n)

We find that the recursive algorithm above is essentially equivalent to the following iterative version:

```
    int fib1(int n)
    {
       int fib, fib_prev, fib_next, i;

    for (fib=1, fib_prev=0, i=0; i<n; fib_next = fib+fib_prev, fib_prev = fib,
fib = fib_next, i++);
       return fib;
    }
```

Therefore, the lesson is not that recursion is intrinsically inefficient, but rather that there are efficient algorithms as well as inefficient ones. We need to be able to analyze our algorithms to get a ballpark estimate of their efficiency. We can directly implement any of the recursive algorithms that are reasonably efficient.

One final note about programming using recursion, we mentioned that most programming languages permit recursive function calls, but we might occasionally be using a language that does not. This does not mean that there is no way to use recursive algorithms. Most recursive algorithms can be translated, by a fairly mechanical procedure, into iterative algorithms. Sometimes this is very straightforward - for example, most compilers detect a special form of recursion, called tail recursion, and automatically translate into iteration without ones knowing. Sometimes, the translation is more involved: for example, it might require introducing an explicit stack with which to 'fake' the effect of recursive calls.

FOR SUMMATIVE AND FORMATIVE ASSESSMENT

2.1 Explain the functionality of following functions

```
int fun1(int x, int y)
{
   if(x == 0)
      return y;
   else
      return fun1(x - 1,  x + y);
}
```

2.2 What will be the output of the following program segment, if one gives input GARHWAL?

```
/* RECURSION TO REVERSE A STRING */
/* STRING_R.C */
# include<stdio.h>
```

```
void recurs_string(char * );

// Definition of the recurs_string() function
void recurs_string(char *string)
{
    if (*string)
    {
        recurs_string(string+1);
        putchar(*string);
    }
}

void main(void)
{
    char str[100];
    printf("\n Input a string: ");
    gets(str);
    printf("\n Reverse of the string: ", str);
    printf("\n Reverse string is: ");
    recurs_string(str);
}
```

2.3 What does the following function represent? Implement the function in C.

$$F(n)=\frac{1}{\sqrt{5}}*\left[\left[\frac{1+\sqrt{5}}{2}\right]^{n-1}-\left[\frac{1-\sqrt{5}}{2}\right]^{n-1}\right]$$

2.4 The function F(n, r) can be defined recursively as F(n – 1, r) + F(n – 1, r – 1). Write a recursive program to compute F(n, r). What is the base case?

2.5 Design an algorithm, which concatenates two strings using recursion.

2.6 Write a recursive function, which takes a floating number as input and displays real and integer part separately.

2.7 Compute the value of **A (4, 3)** using ***Ackermann's*** function.

2.8 Write a program, which takes an integer number as input and displays reverse of the number on the screen. Use recursion to implement the problem.

2.9 Suppose **x** and **y** represent positive integer numbers and a function **F** is defined as

$$F(x, y)=\begin{cases}0 & \text{if } x<y\\ F(x-y, y)+1 & \text{if } y\le x\end{cases}$$

(i) Find the value of **F (4, 5).**

(ii) Explain the working of this function.

2.10 Suppose **n** is a positive integer number and a function **Lambda(n)** is defined as

$$\text{Lambda}(n)=\begin{cases}0 & \text{if } n=1\\ \text{Lambda}(n/2) & \text{if } y>1\end{cases}$$

(i) Find the value of **Lambda (50).**

(ii) Explain the working of this function.

2.11 Suppose **LIST** is an integer array with **m** elements and let **F** is an integer function defined by

$$F(j) = F(LIST, m, j) = \begin{cases} 0 & \text{if } j = 0 \\ F(j-1) + LIST[j] & \text{if } 0 < j \le m \\ F(j-1) & \text{if } j > m \end{cases}$$

Find **F (5)** for each of the following list

(i) m = 8 LIST: 3,7, -2, 5, 6, -4, 2, 7

(ii) m = 3 LIST: 8, 7, 10

2.12 Let **m** be an integer and suppose **L(m)** is defined as

$$L(m) = \begin{cases} 3*m & \text{if } m < 5 \\ 2*L(m-5) + 7 & \text{otherwise} \end{cases}$$

Discuss for **m = 10.**

2.13 Consider the problem of calculating a **binomial coefficient** (BC). The binomial coefficient refers to the kth coefficient of the polynomial resulting from the expansion of a binomial term of the form **A+B** raised to the nth power.

$$(A+B)^n = \frac{A^n}{0!} + \frac{(n*A^{n-1}B)}{1!} + \frac{(n*(n-1)*A^{n-2}*B^2)}{2!} + \frac{(n*(n-1)*(n-2)*A^{n-3}*B^3)}{3!}$$

An explicit formula for the coefficient of the kth term of that nth term degree polynomials is

$$BC(n,k) = \frac{n*(n-1)*(n-2)*...*(n-k+1)}{k!}$$

or

$$BC(n,k) = \frac{n!}{k!(n-k)!}$$

n!

Note that we can expand this formula to

$$BC(n,k) = \frac{(n-1)*(n-2)*\ ...\ *(n-k)}{k!} + \frac{(n-1)*(n-2)*\ ...\ *(n-k+1)}{(k-1)!}$$

Equivalently, BC(n, k) = BC(n – 1, k) + BC(n – 1, k – 1)

Note that when n = k then BC(k, k) = 1 and that BC(n, 0) = 1 for any value of **n.**

(i) Write a recursive function based on the above identities for calculating the kth binomial coefficient of the polynomial of degree **n** given by $(A+B)^n$.

(ii) Illustrate how the contents of the run-time stack change as program for calculating BC(n, k) computes BC(4, 3).

2.14 What is need of stack in implementing a recursive function?

2.15 Write a recursive function that trims all blanks from the front and rear of a string of text.

2.16 Write a recursive function to convert decimal integers to their radix r representation by successive divisions.

2.17 Write a recursive function to compute the square root of a number.

2.18 Write a recursive function to compute the summation of the contents of an array.

2.19 Write a recursive function to compute the multiplication of the contents of an array.

2.20 Write a recursive function to reverse a string and write a recursive function to reverse the words in a string, i.e., "cat is running" becomes "running is cat".

Quiz-2(Recursion)

1. Infinite recursion leads to

   (a) Overflow of run-time stack (b) Underflow of registers usage

   (c) Overflow of I/O cycles (d) Underflow of run-time stack

2. What would be returned by the following recursive function after we call test (0, 3)

```
int test (int a, int b)
{
 if (a==b) return (1);
 else if (a>b) return(0);
 else return (a+test(a+1, b));
}
```

   (a) 1 (b) 2

   (c) 3 (d) 4

3. Recursive procedures are implemented by using ____ data structure.

   (a) queues. (b) stacks.

   (c) linked lists. (d) strings.

4. What is the output of the following code?

```
# include<stdio.h>
main()
{
 printf("%d", doSomething(2,3));
}

int doSomething(int a, int (b)
{
if (b==1)
return a;
else
return a + doSomething(a,b-1);
}
```

   (a) 4 (b) 2

   (c) 3 (d) 6

5. What's happen if base condition is not defined in recursion ?
   (a) Stack underflow (b) Stack Overflow
   (c) None of these (d) Both a and b
6. What's the output of the following code?

```
# include<stdio.h>
main()
{
printf("%d",rec(4567));
}

int rec(int num){
return (num) ? num%10 + rec(num/10):0;
}
```

   (a) 4 (b) 12
   (c) 22 (d) 21
7. What will be the output of **func(3,8)**.

```
# include<stdio.h>
main()
{
   printf("\n Return value is : %d",func(3,8));
}

int func(int a, int b)
{
if(b==0)
return 0;
if(b==1)
return a;
return a + func(a,b-1);
}
```

   (a) 11 (b) 24
   (c) 22 (d) 21
8. What will be the output of **fun1(3,3)**.

```
# include<stdio.h>
main()
{
 printf("\n Return value is : %d",fun1(3,3));
}
int fun1(int x, int y)
{
 if(x == 0)
```

```
return y;
else
return fun1(x - 1, x + y);
}
```

(a) 9 (b) 24
(c) 22 (d) 21

9. Consider the following recursive C function. Let *len* be the length of the string s and *num* be the number of characters printed on the screen, give the relation between *num* and *len* where *len* is always greater than 0. Then what will be printed?

```
#include<stdio.h>

void abc(char *s)
{
```

```
Note:
s[0] is 1 time printed
s[1] is 2 times printed
s[2] is 4 times printed
s[i] is printed 2^i times
s[strlen(s)-1] is printed 2^(strlen(s)-1) times
total = 1+2+....+2^(strlen(s)-1)
 = (2^strlen(s)) - 1
```

```
if(s[0] == '\0')
return;

abc(s + 1);
abc(s + 1);
printf("%c", s[0]);
}

int main()
{
abc("xyz");
return 0;
}
```

(a) x (b) xyz
(c) xyzxyzx (d) zzyzzyx

10. Guess the output of following program.

```
# include<stdio.h>

int fun(int a[],int n)
```

```
{
 int x;
 if(n == 1)
 return a[0];
 else
 x = fun(a, n-1);
 if(x > a[n-1])
 return x;
 else
 return a[n-1];
}

int main()
{
 int arr[] = {12, 10, 30, 50, 100};
 printf(" %d ", fun(arr, 5));
 getchar();
 return 0;
}
```

(a) 12 (b) 10
(c) 30 (d) 100

❑

CHAPTER

3

String Manipulation and Pattern Matching

Today computers are being frequently used in processing numbers, character data, records, arithmetic calculations, etc. In small organizations as well as in multinational companies word processing is widely used. Small shops to big one use the word processing. In computer science, **pattern matching** is the act of checking a given sequence of tokens for the presence of the constituents of some **pattern**. In contrast to **pattern** recognition, the **match** usually has to be exact. The **patterns** generally have the form of either sequences or tree structures. For example, if we have following text information,

"TWINKLE, TWINKLE LITTLE STAR
HOW I WONDER WHAT YOU ARE
UP ABOVE THE WORLD SO HIGH
LIKE A DIAMOND IN THE SKY
WHEN THE BURNING SUN IS SET
AND THE GRASS WITH DUE IS WET
THEN YOU SHOW YOUR LITTLE LIGHT
TWINKLE TWINKLE ALL THE NIGHT"

And suppose we want to search pattern/word "**TWINKLE**" in this text. Then each word in the text is compared or matched with "**TWINKLE**". If a match is found then the counter may be incremented else next word is read from the text to match with "**TWINKLE**". This process is repeated until end of the text is reached. In the above text we find that "**TWINKLE**" word appears at four places. Pattern matching algorithms are discussed latter on. For the time being we define some of the terms which are commonly used in word processing:

- String processing.
- String manipulation.
- Text editing, etc.

A ***Word*** is defined as a collection of characters. In other words one can define a word as concatenation of characters. For example, **We have a very powerful language, i.e., "C"**. Here, in this sentence there are 8 words. A group of words is called **string**. The sentence may be considered as a string or group of sub-strings. A single word is also treated as a string. Before starting discussion on strings, basic elements of the strings are discussed. The basic elements of the string are the character sets which are given in **Table 3.1**.

The significance of NULL character or the blank character varies from language to language. In C/**C++** language it is represented as '\0' and called NULL string marker or terminator of string. In other words a string is defined as a finite sequence of zero, one or more characters. The number of characters in a string is called its length. For example, "C language is very powerful."

This string contains five words and its size is twenty-eight characters long. Generally, a word or group of words or a sentence is put within double quotes ("") to represent a string. A string of zero length is called NULL string. For example, " " is a NULL string of zero length. For the above discussion consider the program segment **STRING1.C**.

Table 3.1 Character set

Type of character set	Associated values
Alphabets	a to z lower case, A to Z upper case
Numeric	0 to 9
Special characters	{ } ( ) [ ] " ' , . < > _ (underscore) & $? : ; # NULL ('\0')
Arithmetic Operator	+ - * / ++ --
Logical Operators	|| && !
Relational Operators	< <= > >= == !=
Bitwise Operators	| & ^ ~ >> <<

```
/* STRING1.C**/
# include<stdio.h>

void main()
{
    char null_string[] = "\0";
    char blank_string[] = " ";
    char string[] = "The C is a powerful language";
    printf("\n %s", null_string);
    printf("\n %s", blank_string);
    printf("\n %s", string);
}
```

This program segment produces "The C is a powerful language" as an output. From this result, it is clear that the two strings are not printed indicating that those are blank.

3.1 STRUCTURE OF STRING STORAGE

The strings are stored in three ways,

- Fixed length (Array type structure).
- Variable length but maximum size is fixed during running time (Pointer type structure).
- Linked list structure.

3.1.1 Fixed Length

In this structure each record is of fixed size, i.e., each record contains the same number of characters. Consider the monitor of a computer or **TURBO-C/C++/vi** editor. In the case of monitor and **vi** editor its size is 80 columns where as in the case of **Turbo/C/C++** editor its size is 256 characters. If one inputs the information with the help of keyboard using **TURBO-C/C++** editor then the editor contains standard size 256 characters. Suppose one defines an array in the following format:

```
char screen[256];
```

Here, it is possible to input a string of 256 characters into the array screen. This type of storage of strings is of fixed length. If one wants to store 128 strings of each having 128 characters then the program segment **STRING2.C** can be used to implement the same:

```
/** STRING2.C **/
# include<stdio.h>
void main()
{
    char s[128][128];
    int i, j;
    char ch;
    int n,m;
    j = 0;
    i = 0;
    printf("Enter size of information in line: ");
    scanf("%d", &n);
    fflush(stdin);
    while(n)
    {
        ch = getchar();
        s[i][j] = ch ;
        j++;
        if(ch == '\n'){
            s[i][j]='\0';
            printf("\n");
            j = 0;
            i++;
            n--;
        }
    }
    s[i][j]='\0';
    m = i;
    printf("\nm ->%d ", m);

    /** Display section **/
    printf("\n");
    for( i = 0 ; i < m ; i++)
    {
        printf("\n %s\n ", s[i]);
    }
}
```

Figure 3.1 discusses how the strings are stored in the computer memory? The major advantages of using fixed length storage techniques are:

- Easy to access information
- Easy to update records or information
- Easy to insert new additional information

The main problems associated with fixed storage techniques are:

- When one wants to update a record of larger size than the room fixed for storage (Update operation not possible).
- If one wants to update a record, which is longer than that of new one, then the record may be misspelled, if care is not taken properly.
- If most of the space of a record is blank then more time is required to update/access the records.

Figure 3.1 Fixed length string storage

Consider the program segment **STRING3.C** which illustrates the above discussion.

```
/** STRING3.C **/
# include<stdio.h>
int i, choice;
char ch;
void display (int, char day[7][20]);
void update_fun (int, char day[7][20]);
void draw_back ( int, char day[7][20]);

/* Output function */
void display (int n, char weak_days[7][20])
{
   printf("\n ***************************");
   printf("\n RECORD No. INFORMATION");
   printf("\n ***************************");
   for(i = 0 ; i < n ; i++)
   {
```

```
        printf("\n %d      %s", i, weak_days[i]);
    }
    printf("\n ***************************");
    printf("\nPress a key");
    getchar();
}

/* Update function */
void update_fun(int n, char weak_days[7][20])
{
    printf("\nInput the record number to which want to update: ");
    scanf("%d", &choice);

    printf("\nYou want to update it : %s", weak_days[choice]);
    printf("\n Input the new value : ");
    scanf("%s", weak_days[choice]);
}

/* Draw back function */
void draw_back(int n, char weak_days[7][20])
{
    printf("\n Draw back section Update");
    printf("\n ************************");
    printf("\nInput the record number to which want to update: ");
    scanf("%d", &choice);
    fflush(stdin);
    printf("\n You want to update it : %s", weak_days[choice]);
    printf("\nInput the new value : ");
    gets(weak_days[choice]);
    ch = getchar();
    i = 0 ;
    while(ch != '\n')
    {
        weak_days[choice][i++] = ch ;
        ch = getchar();
    }
}

/* Function main */
void main()
{
```

```
    char weak_days[7][20]= {
                        "MONDAY",
                        "TUESDAY",
                        "WEDNESDAY",
                        "THURSDAY",
                        "FRIDAY",
                        "SATURDAY",
                        "SUNDAY"
                };
    int n = 7;
    printf("\n Information List ");
    display(n, weak_days);
    update_fun(n, weak_days);
    printf("\n List after update operation\n");
    display(n, weak_days);
    draw_back (n, weak_days);
    printf("\n List after Draw back operation\n");
    display(n, weak_days);
}
```

```
Information List
***************************
RECORD No. INFORMATION
***************************
0 MONDAY
1 TUESDAY
2 WEDNESDAY
3 THURSDAY
4 FRIDAY
5 SATURDAY
6 SUNDAY
***************************
Press a key
Input the record number to which want to update: 4
You want to update it : FRIDAY
Input the new value : Friday
List after update operation

***************************
RECORD No. INFORMATION
***************************
0 MONDAY
```

```
 1 TUESDAY
 2 WEDNESDAY
 3 THURSDAY
 4 Friday
 5 SATURDAY
 6 SUNDAY
 ***************************
Press a key
 Draw back section Update
 *************************
Input the reccrd number to which want to update: 0
You want to update it : MONDAY
Input the new value : Mon
List after Draw back operation

 ***************************
 RECORD No. INFORMATION
 ***************************
 0 MonDAY
 1 TUESDAY
 2 WEDNESDAY
 3 THURSDAY
 4 Friday
 5 SATURDAY
 6 SUNDAY
 ***************************
Press a key
```

3.1.2 Variable Length Fixed Maximum

When size of a string is known, according that size the space for the string is fixed into computer memory. The strings occupy space in the memory from beginning that is from the base address of the array on word. Here, the space occupies by string, assigned according to its size, so that the updating is being easy. This implementation varies from language to language. Let, we want to implement it through **C**, to implement it pointers are used, we define it as:

```
char *string[128];
```

This definition declares a group of 128 strings of variable length. In other words we can say that the string variable reserves space for 128 strings and size of each string being infinite. The actual size of the string depends upon the type of computer being used. It is required to input the size of the string first before starting to input the string itself. It ensures that the required storage space for the string is properly allocated. In **TURBO C/C++** and **UNIX/LINUX C/C++** storage space is automatically allocated as we start inputting the information. Pressing return key marks end of string. For the above discussion consider the following example (**STRING4.C**):

```
/** STRING4.C **/

# include<stdio.h>
# include<malloc.h>
void gets1 (char **, int );
void display ( char **, int);
void input (char **, int );

/* gets1() function to read a string */

void gets1(char **s, int i )
{
   int j;
   char ch;
   ch = getchar();
   while(ch != '\n')
   {
      s[i][j] = ch ;
      ch = getchar();
      j++;
   }
   s[i][j]='\0';
}

/* Output funtion */

void display(char **str, int n)
{
   int i;
   printf("\n Entered strings are follows");
   printf("\n****************************");
   for(i = 0 ; i < n; i++ )
   {
      printf("\n %s", str[i]);
   }
   printf("\n Press a key");
   getchar();
}

/* Input function */

void input( char **str, int n)
```

```
{
    int i;
    int size;

    for ( i = 0 ; i < n ; i++ )
    {
        fflush(stdin);
        printf("\n Enter Approximate size of string->");
        scanf("%d", &size);
        fflush(stdin);
        str[i] = (char *) malloc(size);
        printf("\n Input the string: ");
        gets1(str,i);
    }
}

/* Function main */

void main()
{
    int n;
    char *str[50];
    printf("\n Input number of strings want to process:");
    scanf("%d", &n);
    input(str, n);
    display(str, n);
}
```

Figure 3.2 illustrates how the strings are attached to the pointers? The update operation on these types of stored strings is also simple. In this case string may shrink or expand, but the programmer does these operations (shrink/expand) because allocation of memory spaces is done on the request of the programmer. For this discussion consider the following example (**STRING5.C**).

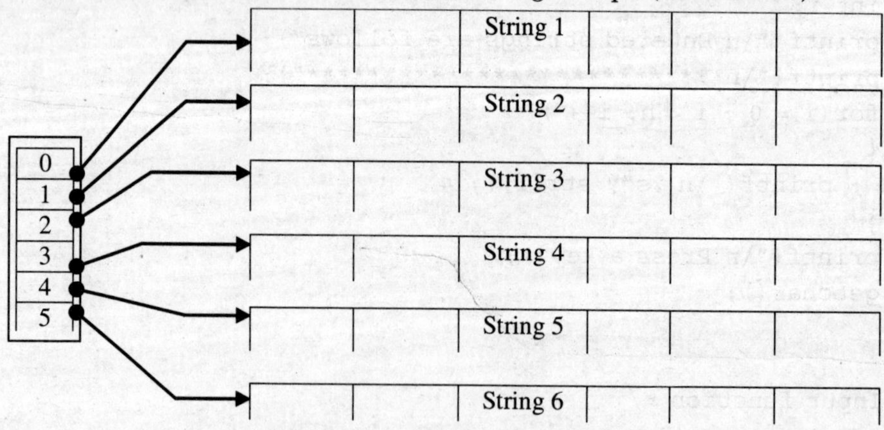

Figure 3.2 Pointer attachment to the strings

```
/** STRING5.C **/
# include<stdio.h>
# include<string.h>
# include<malloc.h>
# include<stdlib.h>

void main()
{
   char *buffer;
   char string[] = "language";
   char *s;
   char s1[8];
   int size ;
   int i, j;
   int length;
   int l ;
   int position ;
   int back1, back2 ;
   FILE *fp ;

   fp = fopen("TEST","r");
   if( fp == NULL )
   {
      printf(" FILE \n");
      perror("ERROR : ");
      exit(0);
   }

   fseek(fp, 0L, SEEK_END);
   size = ftell(fp);
   printf("SIZE OF INFORMATION: %d", size);
   printf("\n Press a key");
   getchar();
   buffer = (char *) malloc(size);
   fseek(fp,0L,0);
   fread(buffer, size, 1, fp) ;
   printf("\n");
   buffer[size]='\0';
   printf("\n %s", buffer);
   fclose(fp);
   fflush(stdin);
   printf("\n Input the Pattern: ");
```

```
gets(string);
length = strlen(string);
s = ( char *) malloc(length);
printf("Length => %d", length);
back1 = length;
back2 = size ;
getchar();

i = 0 ;
j = 0 ;
l = 0 ;
position = 0 ;

while(size)
{
   size --;
   while(length)
   {
      position ++ ;
      if ( buffer[i] == string[j])
      {
         if ((position >= back2) || (position < 0))
            exit(0);
         s[j] = buffer[i];
         l ++ ;
         i ++ ;
         size --;
         j ++ ;
         length --;
         if( l == back1)
         {
           s[j] = '\0';
           printf("\n Pattern is found\n");
        printf(" Length of pattern: %d and Pattern is : %s ", l, s);
           printf("\n Starting Position -> %d", (position-1));
           printf("\n Press a key");
           getchar();
           l= 0 ;
           j = 0 ;
           for(i = (position - back1); i < position ; i++)
           {
              s1[j] = buffer[i] ;
              j++;
```

```
                }
                s1[j] = '\0';
                printf("\nThe old pattern is as follows ");
                printf("\n*****************************\n");
                puts(s1);
                fflush(stdin);
                printf("\n Enter New Pattern : ");
                gets(s1);
                printf("\nThe pattern replacement in progress");
                printf("\n*****************************\n");
                j = 0 ;
                for(i = (position - strlen(s1)); i < position ; i++)
                {
                    buffer[i] = s1[j];
                    putchar(buffer[i]);
                    getchar();
                    j++;
                }
                printf("\n After replacing the pattern");
                printf("\n *****************************\n");
                printf("\n %s", buffer);
            }
        }else{
            i++;
            j = 0;
            l = 0;
            size -- ;
            length = back1;
        }
    }
    length = back1 ;
  }
  fclose(fp);
}
```

Figure 3.3 shows the above implementation.

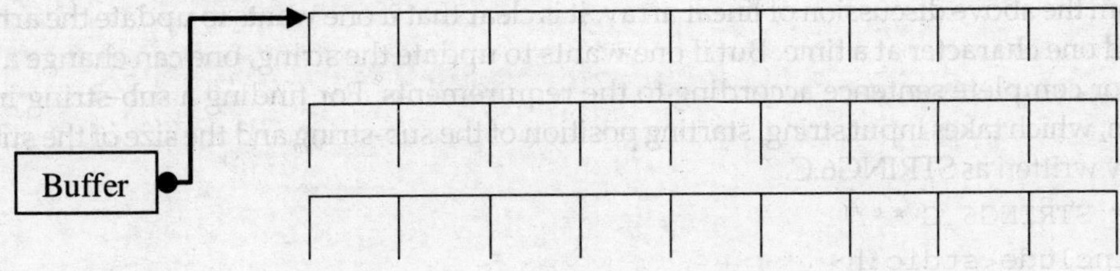

Figure 3.3 Representation of strings in memory

3.1.3 Linked List Storage

The major use of the computers is in data/information processing. Towards this word processing is one of the task performed by many organizations. Computers in word processing work perform the following operations.

- Deletion (Word, sentence, line, string, sub-string, block, paragraphs, etc.).
- Insertion (Word, sentence, line, paragraph, etc.).
- Changing spelling of word (Updating).
- Formatting paragraph (Text).

If we use fixed length memory storage (arrays) to perform the above operations, it is not always possible. For this purpose linked list type of storage structure is used.

3.2 STRING OPERATIONS

A string is simply a linear array of characters but there is a basic difference between linear array and string. A linear array may be treated as a continuous stream of characters where as string can be defined as a collection of sub-strings for example, **Figure 3.4** represents a linear array of 26 characters. This array may be treated as a single string of 26 characters, where size of the array is 26 characters and in **Figure 3.5** array represents a linear array of 17 integers. This is a linear array but it is not a string.

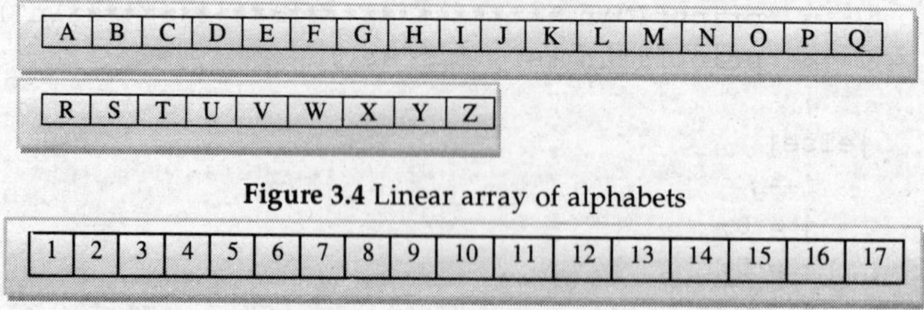

Figure 3.4 Linear array of alphabets

Figure 3.5 Array of integers

Figure 3.4 and **Figure 3.5** illustrate the linear representation of the array. Consider the following example, "**Drastic change in environment**". This is a string of 29 characters or in other words we can say that this is a string formed by four sub-strings. The sub-strings are as follows:

```
"Drastic"
"change"
"in"
"environment"
```

From the above discussion of linear array, it is clear that if one wants to update the array, it can be updated one character at a time. But if one wants to update the string, one can change a word (sub-string) or complete sentence according to the requirements. For finding a sub-string in a string, a function, which takes input string, starting position of the sub-string and the size of the sub-string can be easily written as STRING6.C.

```
/** STRING6.C **/
# include<stdio.h>
# include<malloc.h>
```

```
char *sub_string(char *, int , int );

void main()
{
   char string[] = "MY FATHER IS PRINCIPAL OF G.B.P.E.C";
   char *substr;
   substr = ( char *) malloc(9);
   printf("\n INPUT PATTERN IS ");
   printf("\n **************** \n");
   printf("\n %s", string);
   printf("\n\n PATTERN FOUND ");
   printf("\n ************* \n");
   substr = sub_string(string, 13, 9);
   printf("\n %s", substr);
   printf("\n Press a key");
   getchar();
}

/* This function finds the pattern */
char *sub_string(char *string, int strpos, int size )
{
   char *substring;
   int i = 0 ;
   substring = ( char *) malloc(size);
   while(size)
   {
      substring[i] = string[strpos];
      strpos ++;
      i ++;
      size --;
   }
   substring[i] = '\0';
   return(substring);
}
```

```
INPUT PATTERN IS
****************
 PRINCIPAL

PATTERN FOUND
****************
 PRINCIPAL

Press a key
```

3.2.1 Indexing (Pattern Matching)

Finding the position where a string pattern first appears in a given string text is called **indexing**. The syntax for indexing operation is as follows:

```
index(text, pattern)
```

If a pattern does not appear in the text, the function **index()** returns the value 0. For example, if a text contains the text (string)

```
"MY FATHER IS PRINCIPAL OF G.B.P.E.C."
then
index (text,"THE") has value 0.
index(text,"MY" ) has value 1.
index(text,"TO" ) has value 0.
index(text,"PRINCIPAL") has value 14.
```

How can **index()** be function written? For example, the program segment **STRING7.C** illustrates the development procedure.

```
/** STRING7.C **/
/** In this program segment the text **/
/** provided through file **/
# include<stdio.h>
# include<string.h>
# include<malloc.h>
# include<stdlib.h>
int index(char *buffer, char *string);

/** Global Parameters **/
char *buffer;
char string[] = "language";
char *s;
char s1[8];
int size ;
int i, j;
int length;
int l ;
int position ;
int back1, back2 ;
/** end **/
void main()
{
    FILE *fp;
    char file[13];
    printf("\nEnter Text File ");
    gets(file);
```

```
    fp = fopen(file,"r");
    if( fp == NULL )
    {
       puts(file);
       perror("ERROR : ");
       exit(0);
    }
    fseek(fp, 0L, SEEK_END);
    size = ftell(fp);
    printf("\n SIZE OF FILE: %d", size);
    printf("\n Press a key");
    getchar();
    buffer = (char *) malloc(size+1);
    fseek(fp,0L,0);
    fread(buffer, size, 1, fp);
    buffer[size+1] = '\0';
    printf("\n Enter The Pattern ");
    fflush(stdin);
    gets(string);
    printf("TEXT PROVIDED IS AS FOLLOWS \n");
    printf("****************************\n\n");
    printf(buffer);
    printf("\n Press a key");
    getchar();
    fclose(fp);
    printf("\n Index value: %d", index(buffer, string));
}
/* Index function */
int index(char *buffer, char *string)
{
    length = strlen(string);
    s = ( char *) malloc(length);
    printf("Length: %d", length);
    back1 = length ;
    back2 = size ;
    i = 0 ;
    j = 0 ;
    l = 0 ;
    position = 0 ;
    while(size!= 0)
    {
```

```
        size --;
        while(length)
        {
           position ++ ;
           if ( buffer[i] == string[j])
           {
              s[j] = buffer[i];
              l ++ ;
              i ++ ;
              j ++ ;
              length --;
              if( l == back1)
              {
                 s[j] = '\0';
                 printf("\nPattern is found");
                 printf("\nSize of Pattern: %d", l);
                 printf("\n Pattern is : %s", s);
              printf("\n Pattern Found at %d", position-back1);
                 free(s);
                 return(position-back1);
              }
           }else
           {
              i++;
              j = 0;
              l = 0;
              length = back1;
           }
        }
     }
     free(buffer);
  }
```

```
Enter text file: TEST
SIZE OF FILE : 344
Press a key
Enter pattern: LITTLE
TEXT PROVIDED IS AS FOLLOWS
***************************
TWINKLE, TWINKLE LITTLE STAR
HOW I WONDER WHAT YOU ARE
UP ABOVE THE WORLD SO HIGH
```

```
LIKE A DIAMOND IN THE SKY
WHEN THE BURNING SUN IS SET
AND THE GRASS WITH DUE IS WET
THEN YOU SHOW YOUR LITTLE LIGHT
TWINKLE, TWINKLE ALL THE NIGHT

Press a key

Length => 6
Pattern is found
Size of Pattern: 6
Pattern is : LITTLE
Pattern Found at 29

Press a key
```

The discussion can also be implemented with the help of **LO_NO.C** and **LOCAT.C** program segment.

```
/* Find locations of a substring in a string */
/* LO_NO.C */
# include<stdio.h>
# include<string.h>

int index_str1,index_str2,k;
int c[100];

int str(char *, char *, int *);
int Number_occ(char *, char *, int *);

/* Function str that finds locations of the sub-string */
int str(char *s1, char *s2, int c[])
{
    int count = 0;
    int l =0;
    for(index_str1 = 0; s1[index_str1]; index_str1++)
     for(index_str2=index_str1, k = 0; s1[index_str2] ==
s2[k]&&s1[index_str1]; index_str2++, k++)
        if(!s2[k+1])
        {
           count ++;
           c[l++] = index_str1;
        }
```

```
    return(count);
  }

  /* Function main */
  void main()
  {
    char *s;
    int c[100];
    int location ;
    char s1[]="Ram Bahadur Bahadur Patel";
    char s2[] ="Baha";
    int i, loc;
    int count;

    count = str (s1, s2,c);

    printf("\n Number of occurences = %d", count);

    for(i = 0;i < count; i++)
    {
      location = c[i];
      s = &s2[0];
      printf("\n Starting location = %d|", location+1);
      while(*(s++))
      {
        putchar(s1[location++]);
      }
    }
  }

  /* Find location of a substring first start in a string */
  /* LOCAT.C */
  # include<stdio.h>

  int index_str1,index_str2,k;
  int str(char *, char *);

  /* Function str that finds first location of the sub-string */

  int str(char *s1, char *s2)
  {
```

```
    for(index_str1 = 0; s1[index_str1]; index_str1++)
    for(index_str2=index_str1, k =0; s1[index_str2] == s2[k]; index_str2++,
k++)
        if( !s2[k+1])
        {
            return(index_str1);
        }
    return(NULL);
}

/* Function main */

void main()
{
    char *s;
    char s1[]="Ram Bahadur Patel";
    char s2[] ="Baha";
    int location = str (s1, s2);
    s = s2;
    printf("\n Location = %d", location);
    while(*(s++))
    {
        putchar(s1[location++]);
    }
}
```

3.2.2 Concatenation

Suppose we have two-string $\mathbf{s}_1$ and $\mathbf{s}_2$ then concatenation of $\mathbf{s}_1$ and $\mathbf{s}_2$ denoted by $\mathbf{s}_1+\mathbf{s}_2$, is linking together two strings. The concatenation function varies from language to language. In C language it is **strcat ()**, in **BASIC** $\mathbf{s}_1+\mathbf{s}_2$ and in **SNOBOL** it is $\mathbf{s}_1\ \mathbf{s}_2$.

If s_1 = "RAM"
s_2 = "LAKHAN"

then $s_1 + s_2$ = "RAMLAKHAN"

The above discussion can be implemented as follows (**STRING8.C**):

```
/** STRING8.C **/

# include<stdio.h>
# include<string.h>
void concatenate( char *, char *, char *);
```

```
void main()
{
   char str1[128];
   char str2[128];
   char output_str[257];

   printf(" Input the first string: ");
   gets(str1);
   printf("\nInput the second string: ");
   gets(str2);

   concatenate(str1, str2, output_str);
   puts(output_str);
}

/* This function concatenate two strings */
void concatenate( char *s1, char *s2, char *rs)
{
   while(*s1)
   {
      *rs++ = *s1++ ;
   }

   while(*s2)
   {
      *rs++ = *s2++ ;
   }
   *rs = '\0';
}
```

3.2.3 Length

The number of characters in a string is called its length. For example, the string "**ENGINEERING**" has length 11. The function **length ()** is given below to find the length of a string.

```
int length(char *p)
{
int len = 0 ;
while(*p++)
{
   len ++;
}
return (len) ;
}
```

In the above function a string is passed. The function **length ()** processes the string character by character and finds the length of the string. The program segment **STRING9.C** illustrates the idea.

```
/* Length function */
/* STRING9.C */
# include<stdio.h>
# include<string.h>

int length(char *p);

/* Definition of the length function */

int length(char *p)
{
   int len = 0 ;
   while(*p++)
   {
      len ++;
   }
   return (len) ;
}

/* Function main */

void main()
{
   char string[60];
   printf(" Input the string : ");
   gets(string);
   printf("Length of Input String = %i", length(string));
   getchar();
}
```

```
Input the string : NO ALTERNATIVE OF HARD WORK
Length of Input String = 27
```

3.3 APPLICATION OF STRING OR TEXT PROCESSING

There are many applications of the string processing, but there are two main areas where the string processing is widely used. These are:

- TEXT EDITING
- TEXT FORMATTING

3.3.1 Text Editing

General functions that are required in text editor are as follows:

- Insertion (Insert a string, word and paragraph in given text).
- Deletion (Delete a string, word, a line and paragraph from a given text).
- Update (a word, sub-string, string and a line, etc.).
- Replacement (Replacing a string, sub-string, line, paragraph etc. by another in the text).

3.3.1.1 Insertion

Suppose in a given text one is interested in insertion of a string at some location (position). Then the syntax of insertion function will be:

```
insertion ( text , position, string )
```

For example, if there is a text "**COMPUTER ENGINEERING**" and one wants to insert string "**SCIENCE**" in between "**COMPUTER**" and "**ENGINEERING**" then it can be written as:

```
insertion("COMPUTER ENGINEERING", 10, "SCIENCE")
```

The output produced by this function is:

"COMPUTER SCIENCE ENGINEERING"

Similarly, one can insert "**AND**" between "**SCIENCE**" and **ENGINEERING**".

```
insertion("COMPUTER SCIENCE ENGINEERING", 18 , "AND")
```

The output comes as:

"COMPUTER SCIENCE AND ENGINEERING"

The program segment **STRING10.C** illustrates the procedure.

```
/** STRING10.C **/
# include<stdio.h>
# include<string.h>
# include<malloc.h>
# include<ctype.h>

void insertion ( char *, int , char *, char *);

/* Function insert */
void insertion ( char *text , int position, char *s, char *p)
{
   char ch ;
   while(position)
   {
      *p++ = *text++ ;
      position--;
   }
   while(*s)
   {
      *p++ = *s++ ;
```

```
    }
    printf("\n After insertion of the pattern\n ");
    printf("there needs blank at right side of the pattern(y): ");
    ch = getchar() ;
    ch = toupper(ch);

    if (ch == 'Y')
        *p++ = ' ';
    while(*text)
    {
        *p++ = *text++ ;
    }
    *p = '\0';
}

/* Function main */

void main()
{
    char *point ;
    char text[128]="COMPUTER SCIENCE ENGINEERING";
    char s[4] ="AND";
    int position = 17 ;
    point =(char*) malloc(128);
    printf("\n*********************************\n");
    printf(" TEXT AND PATTERN ARE AS FOLLOWS\n");
    printf("\n*********************************\n");
    printf("\n %s", text);
    printf("\n%s", s);
    printf("\n*********************************\n");
    insertion ( text, position, s, point);
    printf("\n*********************************\n");
    printf("\n %s", point);
    printf("\n*********************************\n");
    printf("\n Press a key");
    getchar();
}
```

```
TEXT AND PATTERN ARE AS FOLLOWS
*********************************************************
COMPUTER SCIENCE ENGINEERING
```

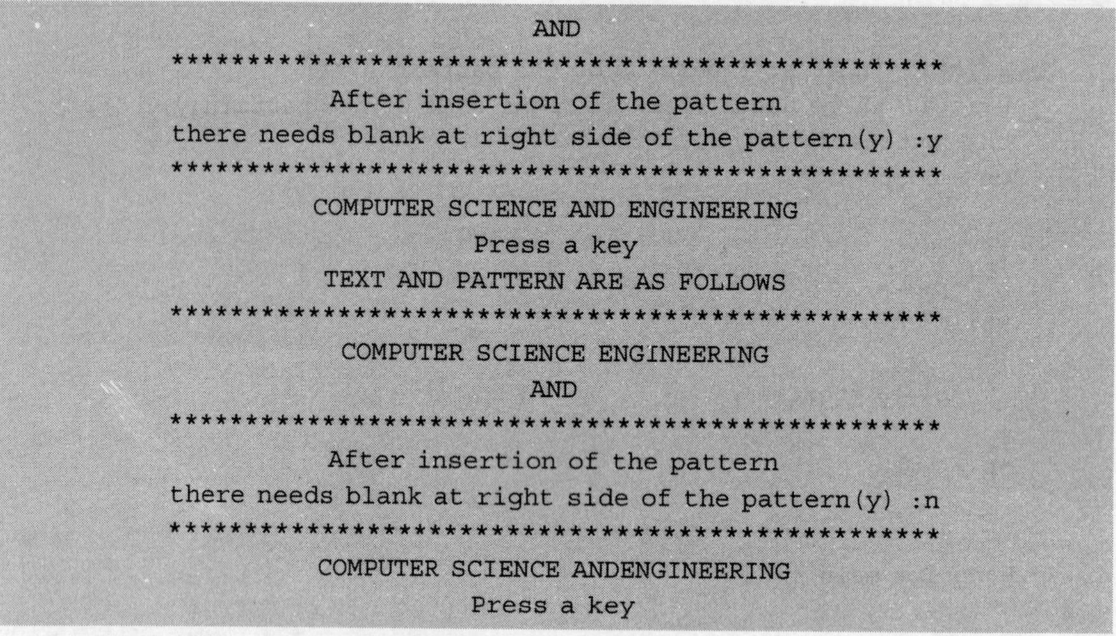

```
                                AND
 ***************************************************
                  After insertion of the pattern
 there needs blank at right side of the pattern(y) :y
 ***************************************************
                  COMPUTER SCIENCE AND ENGINEERING
                             Press a key
                  TEXT AND PATTERN ARE AS FOLLOWS
 ***************************************************
                   COMPUTER SCIENCE ENGINEERING
                                AND
 ***************************************************
                  After insertion of the pattern
 there needs blank at right side of the pattern(y) :n
 ***************************************************
                  COMPUTER SCIENCE ANDENGINEERING
                             Press a key
```

The above program segment creates a temporary array in the memory. Copy the content of the text up to the position where we want to insert the sub-string, then copy sub-string into temporary array. In the last rest of the text is copied into the temporary array. The algorithm is shown in the **Figure 3.6**.

3.3.1.2 Deletion

Suppose in a given text one wants to delete a sub-string **S,** which begins from position **K** and has a length **L** that is possible with the help of following syntax.

`deletion(text, position, length)`

For example, if there is a text

"COMPUTER SCIENCE AND ENGINEERING"

and one wants to remove sub-string "AND", then

deletion("COMPUTER SCIENCE AND ENGINEERING", 18, 3)

will produce the following output

"COMPUTER SCIENCE ENGINEERING"

```
Step1: [Initialization]
          i = 0
          j = 0
Step2: while position ≠ 0 repeat
          (a) temp [i] = text[i]
          (b) i = i + 1
Step3: m = i - 1
Step4: Repeat while ( j ≠ length (string))
          (a) temp [i] = string[j]
```

```
            (b) i = i + 1
            (c) j = j + 1
   Step5: l = length (text) - position
   Step6: while ( l ≠ 0) repeat
   (a) temp [i] = text[m]
            (b) i = i + 1
            (c) m = m + 1
   Step7: exit.
```

Figure 3.6 Insertion algorithm

The following steps are required to implement the deletion operation:

- Copy from starting position of the text to the given position into **temp** string variable.
- Copy text from the **(length (text) - position -length (string) + 1)** until end of the text, into **temp** string variable.

The deletion function can be developed as illustrated in the program segment **STRING11.C.**

```
/** STRING11.C **/
# include<stdio.h>
# include<string.h>
# include<malloc.h>

void deletion ( char *, int , int , char * );

/* Function delete */
void deletion (char *text, int position, int length, char *p)
{
   while(position)
   {
      *p++ = *text++ ; /* copying the pattern */
      position--;
   }
   while(length)
   {
      *text++; /* skipping the pattern */
      length --;
   }

   *p++ = ' ';
   while(*text)
   {
      *p++ = *text++ ; /* copying the rest of text */
   }
```

```
    *p = '\0';
  }

  /* Function main */
  void main()
  {
     char *point ;
     char text[128]="COMPUTER SCIENCE AND ENGINEERING";
     int length = 3 ;
     int position = 17 ;

     point = (char *) malloc(128);

     printf("\n TEXT IS AS FOLLOWS ");
     printf("\n********************************\n");
     printf("\n %s", text);
     printf("\n********************************\n");
     deletion (text, position, length , point);
     printf("\nOUTPUT AFTER DELETION OF PATTERN");
     printf("\n********************************\n");
     printf("\n %s", point);
     printf("\n********************************\n");
     printf("\n Press a key");
     getchar();
  }
```

```
TEXT IS AS FOLLOWS
****************************************
COMPUTER SCIENCE AND ENGINEERING

OUTPUT AFTER DELETION OF PATTERN
****************************************
COMPUTER SCIENCE ENGINEERING

Press a key
```

The program **DELET.C** also shows the above discussion in different way. The algorithm is shown in **Figure 3.7**.

```
/* Delete a substring from a string */
/* DELET.C */
# include<stdio.h>
# include<string.h>
```

```
int index_str1,index_str2,k;
int c[100];

int str_del_loc(char *, char *, int *);

/* Function str_del_loc that finds location of the sub-string and delete. */

int str_del_loc(char *s1, char *s2, int c[])
{
    int j, count = 0;
    int i, l =0;
    for(index_str1 = 0; s1[index_str1]; index_str1++)
        for(index_str2=index_str1, k = 0; s1[index_str2] ==
s2[k]&&s1[index_str1]; index_str2++, k++)
            if( !s2[k+1])
            {
                count ++;
                c[l++] = index_str1;
                for(j = index_str1, i = strlen(s2)+index_str1; s1[i]; j++,
i++)
                    s1[j] = s1[i];
                s1[j] = NULL;
                printf("\n After delete operation the output %s", s1);
            }
    return(count);
}

/* Function main */

void main()
{
    char *s;
    int c[100];
    char s1[]="Ram Bahadur Bahadur Patel";
    char s2[] ="Baha";
    int count;
    count = str_del_loc (s1, s2,c);
    printf("\n Number of occurences = %d", count);
}
```

```
After delete operation the output
Ram dur Bahadur Patel
After delete operation the output
Ram dur dur Patel
Number of occurrences =2
```

If one wants to delete first occurrence of a pattern in a given text then the same can be achieved with one modification in the above algorithm. The modification involves the replacement of **length$_1$** by **length(pattern)** if the **length$_1$** is not equal to **length(pattern)**. If one wants to delete every occurrences of a pattern in a given text then **index()** function can be used to find the different occurrences of a pattern. After finding the position **delete()** function is called to delete the pattern.

3.3.1.3 Pattern Matching (Replacement)

Suppose one wants to replace the first occurrence of a **pattern$_1$** by **pattern$_2$** in a given text then it is possible with the help of following syntax:

`replacement(text, pattern`$_1$`, pattern`$_2$`)`

For example, suppose one wants to replace "**and**" pattern by "**AND**" in the given text.

"COMPUTER SCIENCE and ENGINEERING"

replacement("COMPUTER SCIENCE and ENGINEERING", "and", "AND")

```
deletion(text, position, length1)
Step 1: [Initialization]
        i = position
        j = length1
        k = 0
Step 2: Repeat while( i ≠ 0 )
        (a) temp[k] = text[k]
        (b) i = i - 1
        (c) k = k + 1
Step 3: i = position + length1
        j = length(text) - i + 1
Step 4: Repeat while( j ≠ 0 )
        (a) temp[k] = text[i]
        (b) k = k + 1
        (c) j = j - 1
        (d) i = i + 1
Step 5: Exit.
```

Figure 3.7 Deletion algorithm

The output of the above function is

"COMPUTER SCIENCE AND ENGINEERING"

This operation can be implemented with the help of following steps:

- Index the text for **pattern$_1$** and record the position.
- Delete the **pattern$_1$**
- Copy content of text from beginning to the position (recorded in step 1) into the **temp** string variable.
- Add **pattern$_2$** to **temp.**
- Copy contents of the text from the **position + 1** into the **temp.**

The above steps are coded in program format as illustrated in the program segment **STRING12.C.**

```
/** STRING12.C **/
# include<stdio.h>
# include<string.h>
# include<malloc.h>
# include<stdlib.h>

/** Global parameters **/

char *buffer;
char pattern1[9];
char pattern2[9];
char *s;
char s1[8];
int size ;
int i, j;
int length;
int l ;
int position ;
int back1, back2 ;

void replacement(char *, char *, char * );

void replacement(char *buffer, char *pattern1, char *pattern2 )
{
   length = strlen(pattern1);
   s = ( char *) malloc(length);
   printf("Length => %d", length);
   back1 = length ;
   back2 = size ;
   getchar();

   i = 0 ;
   j = 0 ;
   l = 0 ;
   position = 0 ;

   while(size)
   {
      size --;
      while(length)
      {
```

```
        position ++ ;
        if ( buffer[i] == pattern1[j])
        {
           if ((position >= back2) || (position < 0))
              exit(0);
           s[j] = buffer[i];
           l ++ ;
           i ++ ;
           size --;
           j ++ ;
           length --;
           if( l == back1)
           {
              s[j] = '\0';
              printf("\nPATTERN IS FOUND");
              printf("\n***************\n");
              printf(" LENGTH OF PATTERN: %d ",l);
              printf("\n PATTERN IS: %s", s);
              printf("\n Starting Position = %d", (position-l));
              printf("\n Press a key");
              getchar();
              l= 0 ;
              j = 0 ;
              printf("\n PATTERN REPLACEMENT IN PROGRESS");
              printf("\n*****************************\n");
              for(i = (position - strlen(pattern2)); i < position ;
              i++)
              {
                 buffer[i] = pattern2[j];
                 putchar(buffer[i]);
                 j++;
                 getchar();
              }

              printf("\nSEE AFTER FIRST PATTERN REPLACEMENT ");
              printf("\n***************************\n");
              printf("\n %s", buffer);
              printf("\n Press a key");
              getchar();
           } /* end of if */
        } /* end of if */
```

```
        else{
            i++;
            j = 0;
            l = 0;
            size -- ;
            length = back1;
        }

    } /* end first while */

    length = back1 ;
  } /* end of second while */
}

void main()
{
  FILE *fp ;
  fp = fopen(TEST","r");
  if( fp == NULL )
  {
    printf(" FILE \n");
    perror("ERROR : ");
    exit(0);
  }
  fseek(fp, 0L, SEEK_END);
  size = ftell(fp);
  printf("SIZE OF FILE: %d ", size);
  printf("\n Press a key");
  getchar();
  buffer = (char *) malloc(size);
  fseek(fp,0L,0);
  fread(buffer, size, 1, fp) ;
  buffer[size+1] = '\0';
  printf("\n %s", buffer);
  printf("\nPress a key");
  getchar();
  fclose(fp);
  fflush(stdin);
  printf("\n ENTER PATTERN TO WHICH WANT TO REPLACE: ");
  gets(pattern1);
  fflush(stdin);
```

```
    printf("\n ENTER NEW PATTERN: ");
    gets(pattern2);
    replacement(buffer, pattern1, pattern2);
    printf("\n %s", buffer);
    printf("\nPress a key");
    getchar();
}
```

```
SIZE OF FILE : 344
Press a key
```

```
TWINKLE, TWINKLE LITTLE STAR
HOW I WONDER WHAT YOU ARE
UP ABOVE THE WORLD SO HIGH
LIKE A DIAMOND IN THE SKY
WHEN THE BURNING SUN IS SET
AND THE GRASS WITH DUE IS WET
THEN YOU SHOW YOUR LITTLE LIGHT
TWINKLE, TWINKLE ALL THE NIGHT
Press a key
ENTER PATTERN TO WHICH WANT TO REPLACE: LITTLE
ENTER NEW PATTERN : little
Length => 6
PATTERN IS FOUND
******************
LENGTH OF PATTERN: 6
PATTERN IS : LITTLE
Starting Position = 29
Press a key
PATTERN REPLACEMENT IN PROGRESS
****************************************
little
SEE AFTER FIRST PATTERN REPLACEMENT
****************************************
TWINKLE, TWINKLE little STAR
HOW I WONDER WHAT YOU ARE
UP ABOVE THE WORLD SO HIGH
LIKE A DIAMOND IN THE SKY
WHEN THE BURNING SUN IS SET
AND THE GRASS WITH DUE IS WET
THEN YOU SHOW YOUR LITTLE LIGHT
TWINKLE, TWINKLE ALL THE NIGHT
```

```
Press a key
PATTERN IS FOUND
******************
LENGTH OF PATTERN : 6
PATTERN IS : LITTLE

Starting Position -> 274
Press a key
PATTERN REPLACEMENT IN PROGRESS
*************************************
SEE AFTER FIRST PATTERN REPLACEMENT
****************************************
TWINKLE, TWINKLE little STAR
HOW I WONDER WHAT YOU ARE
UP ABOVE THE WORLD SO HIGH
LIKE A DIAMOND IN THE SKY
WHEN THE BURNING SUN IS SET
AND THE GRASS WITH DUE IS WET
THEN YOU SHOW YOUR little LIGHT
TWINKLE, TWINKLE ALL THE NIGHT
Press a key
```

The program segment **REPLACE.C** also shows the above discussion in some different ways.

```
/* Replace a sub-string in a string */
/* REPLACE.C*/
# include<stdio.h>
# include<string.h>
int index_str1,index_str2,k;
int c[100];
int str_rep(char *, char *, int *);

/* Function str that finds first location of the sub-string */
int str_rep(char *s1, char *s2, int c[])
{
   int count = 0;
   int l =0;
   int j, i = 0;
   char s3[]= -Jaunpur-;
   for(index_str1 = 0; s1[index_str1]; index_str1++)
   for(index_str2=index_str1, k = 0; s1[index_str2] ==
s2[k]&&s1[index_str1]; index_str2++, k++)
      if(!s2[k+1])
      {
```

```
            count ++;
            c[l++] = index_str1;
            for(j = index_str1; j < strlen(s3)+index_str1; j++)
               s1[j] = s3[i++];
            printf("\n %s ", s1);
         }
   return(count);
}

/* Function main */

void main()
{
   char *s;
   int c[100];
   char s1[]="Ram Bahadur Bahadur Patel";
   char s2[] ="Bahadur";
   int count;
   str_rep(s1, s2,c);
}
```

3.3.2 Text Formatting

Text formatting comprises of many related functions. These functions vary from word processor (editor) to word processor. The objectives of these functions are same in the every word processor. The common text formatting functions are listed below:

- Formatting a paragraph.
- Setting left margin.
- Setting right margin.
- Left justified.
- Right justified, etc.

3.4 MARKOV ALGORITHM

The *Markov* algorithm named after the Russian mathematician *A. Markov*, is a formal system for string manipulation that was originally developed to support a theory of computation. First language to support string-processing concept was **COMIT.** After this language another language **SNOBOL** used this concept. At present **C, PASCAL** and **C++** all are supporting *Markov* algorithm for string processing.

The main strategy in a *Markov* algorithm is that it takes an input string **x** and through a number of production rules in the algorithm it transforms **x** to an output string **y**. When we pass **s** string through a number of production rules, the string may shrink or expand in length. For example, the following program segment produces an output string **"STRING MANIPULATION AND PATTERN MATCHING"**.

```
# include<stdio.h>
void main()
{
 printf(-STRING MANIPULATION AND PATTERN MATCHING-);
}
```

The size of this source code is 108 bytes when we compile this source code through **C** compiler the size of output object code become 454 bytes.

3.4.1 Basic Concept

Let **A** is a finite nonempty set of symbols, i.e.,

A = {a, b, c, ..., z}

The concatenation of two alphabetic characters form a sequence of characters for example, if **a** and **b** are two characters, then their concatenation will produce **ab**, a sequence of characters. The concatenation operation is also possible on sequence of characters. The concatenation of **ab** with **ab** will produce **abab**. If we consider **o** as a concatenation operator then the concatenation of **ab** to **ab** can be written as **ab o ab** and it produces **abab** as an output. Thus, we can define a string over an alphabet set **A** as a

- A letter from the alphabet set **A**.
- A sequence of letters derived from the concatenations from the alphabet set **A.**

For example, consider the alphabet set A = {a, b, c}. The string derived from this alphabet set is as follows:

"abc" string of 3 characters.

"aaaaaa" string of 6 characters.

"aabbcc" string of 6 characters.

"a" string of 1 character.

"b" string of 1 character.

"c" string of 1 character.

similarly,

$A \circ A = A^2$ represents all strings length two.

$A \circ A \circ A = A^3$ represents all strings of length three.

$A \circ A \circ A \circ \ldots \circ A = A^n$ represents all strings of length **n.**

Closure of **A** denoted by $\mathbf{A^+}$ and is defined as follows:

$A^+ = A^1 U A^2 \text{ U } A^3 U \text{ } A^4 \text{ U } \ldots$

If $\wedge$ is empty string or **NULL** string then

$A^* = \wedge U A^1 U \text{ } A^2 \text{ U } A^3 \text{ U } A^4 \text{ U } \ldots$

$= \wedge \text{ U } A^+$

$\wedge$ is called the identify elements in the algebra formed by the set $\mathbf{A^*}$.

The followings are some properties of strings, for any string **y**

3.4.2 Identity Property

y o ∧ = ∧ o y = y

3.4.3 Associative Property

(x o y) o z = x o (y o z) = x o y o z where **x, y, z** belongs to A*

3.4.4 Production

The production is a statement of the form **a** → **b**, where **a** and **b** represents string in **A***, where **A** does not contain the symbol arrow (→) and period (.). In the above production **a** is called antecedent and **b** is called consequent. A production **a** → **b** is applicable to a string **c**, if **c** belongs to **A*** and there is at least one occurrence of **a** in **c**, otherwise production is not applicable. If production is applicable then the first occurrence of **a** in **c** is replaced by **b**. For example, let "**abababbcabbc**" is a input string and **bc** → **c** is production rule. If we apply this production rule on the above input string, the output comes like:

```
abababcabbc First Step
ababacabbc Second Step
ababacabc Third Step
ababacac Fourth Step
```

If we consider the production rule **bd** → **a**, it is not applicable to the above input string.

3.4.5 Termination

Markov algorithm terminates in one of the following ways:

·Last production is not applicable.

·A terminal production is applicable.

A terminal production is a statement of the form **a** → **b**, where **a** and **b** represents string in **A*** and the period operator immediately follows the consequent. For example:

P_1: bc → c

P_2: ba → a

P_3: aa → a

P_4: ac → a

P_5: ad → d

On the alphabet set **A** = {a, b, c } and input string is "abababbcabbcd".

Applying the above production rules on the input string provided in the problem the discussion is given in **Table 3.1**.

Table 3.1 Example

Let w = abababbcabbcd	
=> aababbcabbcd	By P_2
=> aaabbcabbcd	By P_2
=> aabbcabbcd	By P_3
=> abbcabbcd	By P_3
=> abcabbcd	By P_1

```
=> acabbcd          By P1
=> acabcd           By P1
=> acacd            By P1
=> aacd             By P4
=> aad              By P4
=> ad               By P3
=> a                By P5
```

3.4.6 Algorithm

Markov algorithm is illustrated in **Figure 3.8.** Let $\mathbf{P_1}$, $\mathbf{P_2}$, $\mathbf{P_3}$ ... $\mathbf{P_n}$ are production rules that are applicable to input string **u** which belongs to $\mathbf{A}^*$. The variable k and l are indices and $\mathbf{u}_k$ denotes the result after application of the $\mathbf{k}^{th}$ transformation or production rule to the input string **u**. The algorithm illustrated in **Figure 3.8** is discussed in the program segment **STRING13.C**

```
Step 1 : [Initialize intermediate string index]
 k = 0
Step 2 : [Initialize production index]
    l = 1
Step 3 : If Pl is applicable then apply production Pl
 k = k + 1
step 4 : If Pl is terminal production then output uk and Exit
 Else
 l = 1
 Else
 l = l + 1
Step 5 : Output uk and Exit
```

Figure 3.8 Markov algorithm

```
/** STRING13.C **/
# include<stdio.h>
# include<string.h>
# include<malloc.h>
# include<stdlib.h>

void markov(char *, char *, char * );

/** Global parameters **/

char *buffer;
char ch;
char pattern1[9];
char pattern2[9];
char *s;
```

```
char s1[8];
int size ;
int i, j;
int length;
int l ;
int position ;
int back1, back2 ;

void main()
{
  FILE *fp ;

    fp = fopen("TEST","r");
    if( fp == NULL )
    {
        printf(" FILE \n");
        perror("ERROR : ");
        exit(0);
    }
    fseek(fp, 0L, SEEK_END);
    size = ftell(fp);
    printf("SIZE OF FILE: %d", size);
    printf("\n Press a key\n");
    getchar();
    buffer = (char *) malloc(size+1);
    fseek(fp,0L,0);
    fread(buffer, size, 1, fp) ;
    buffer[size] = '\0' ;
    printf("%s", buffer);
    getchar();
    fclose(fp);

    do{
        fflush(stdin);
        printf("Enter choice n for break ");
        ch = getchar();
        fflush(stdin);
        printf("\n ENTER PATTERN TO WHICH WANT TO REPLACE: ");
        gets(pattern1);
        fflush(stdin);
        printf("\n ENTER NEW PATTERN : ");
        gets(pattern2);
```

```
        markov(buffer, pattern1, pattern2);
    } while( ch !='n');
}

void markov(char *buffer, char *pattern1, char *pattern2)
{
    int k, b;
    char *temp ;
    length = strlen(pattern1);
    s = ( char *) malloc(length);
    printf("\n Length = %d", length);
    back1 = length ;
    back2 = size ;
    getchar();

    i = 0 ;
    j = 0 ;
    l = 0 ;
    position = 0 ;

    while(size)
    {
        size --;
        while(length)
        {
            position ++ ;
            if ( buffer[i] == pattern1[j])
            {
                if ((position >= back2) || (position < 0))
                    exit(0);
                s[j] = buffer[i];
                l ++ ;
                i ++ ;
                size --;
                j ++ ;
                length --;
                if( l == back1)
                {
                    s[j] = '\0';
                    printf("\nPATTERN IS FOUND");
                    printf("\n****************\n");
                    printf(" LENGTH OF PATTERN = %d", l);
```

```
            printf("\n PATTERN IS : %s", s);
            printf("\n Starting Position = %i", (position-1));

            /* REPLACEMENT SECTION */

            k = 0;
            for( k = 0 ; k < (position-1) ; k++ )
            {
               temp[k] = buffer[k] ;
            }
            j = 0 ;
            b = (k+ strlen(pattern2));

            for ( ; k < b ; k ++)
            {
               temp[k] = pattern2[j] ;
               j++ ;
            }
            temp[k] = '\0';
            getchar();

            b = k ;
            k = position + 1;

            for ( ; k < back2 ; k ++)
            {
               temp[b] = buffer[k] ;
               b++ ;
            }
            temp[b] = '\0';
            buffer = temp ;

            /* END OF REPLACEMENT SECTION */

            l= 0 ;
            j = 0 ;
            printf("\nPATTERN REPLACEMENT IN PROGRESS");
            printf("\n****************************\n");
            printf("\nSEE AFTER FIRST PATTERN REPLACEMENT ");
            printf("\n*****************************n");
            printf("%s", buffer);

         } /* end of if */
      } /* end of if */
```

```
            else{
                i++;
                j = 0;
                l = 0;
                size -- ;
                length = back1;
            }
        } /* end first while */

        length = back1 ;
    } /* end of second while */
}
```

FOR SUMMATIVE AND FORMATIVE ASSESSMENT

3.1 Design a general *Markov* algorithm which takes an input the following text:

"Cobbler, Cobbler Mend My Shoe"

and produces output

"My Shoe Cobbler, Cobbler Mend"

Write **C** program to implement the designed algorithm.

3.2 Write an algorithm and **C** program to implement right justifies text-processing function.

3.3 How to print duplicate characters from String? Discuss.

3.4 Consider the integer numbers **1 2 3 4 5 6 7 8 ... n** develop an algorithm to find the output

1 2 3 4 5 6.... n-2 n-1 n n-1 n-2 ... 6 5 4 3 2 1.

3.5 Design an algorithm, which trims off all the blank characters except the single one between two words for example, if the input string or text is as follows:

" TOM ALTER HAS TWO APPLES"

then the output must come:

"TOM ALTER HAS TWO APPLES"

Implement this algorithm in **C**.

3.6 Design an algorithm, which finds number of words, lines and characters in a given text. Implement the algorithm in **C**.

3.7 Design an algorithm which counts different types of words occurred in a given text. Implement the algorithm in **C**. The output is to be displayed in tabular form.

3.7 Design an algorithm which searches a word in a given text and replaces the word by another word if it is found.

3.8 Design an algorithm which generates all possible words of four characters, formed from alphabet set

A = {a, b, c ... z}

Implement it in **C**.

3.9 Implement the **lexical analyzer** phase of any compiler.

3.10 Design an algorithm that counts the number of paragraphs in a short story. Implement the designed algorithm.

3.11 Find the string stored in **Figure 3.9.**

3.12 Write a program which reads a word and then counts the number of times the word in a given paragraph.

3.13 Write a program which interchanges the jth and k^{th} paragraphs.

3.14 Write a sub-program **insert (Text, New, k),** which inserts a string **New** into **Text** beginning at **Text [k].**

3.15 Write a sub-program **output(Text, k)** which prints the character string **Text** in lines with at most **k** characters. No words should be divided in the middle and appear on two lines, so some lines may contain trailing blank spaces. Each paragraph should begin with its own line and be indented using 6 blank spaces.

Start: 5

Free: 10

Index	Info	Link
1	UNIT	11
2	HE P	8
3		
4	S	\0
5	WE T	2
6	THE	1
7		3
8	EOPL	12
9	TATE	4
10		7
11	EDS	9
12	E OF	6

Figure 3.9 List in memory

3.9 Show two ways to concatenate the following two strings together to get the string "Hi, mom.":

(a) String hi = "Hi, ";

(b) String mom = "mom.";

3.17 Write a program that computes initials from full name and displays them.

3.18 An anagram is a word or a phrase made by transposing the letters of another word or phrase; for example, "parliament" is an anagram of "partial men," and "software" is an anagram of "swear oft." Write a program that figures out whether one string is an anagram of another string. The program should ignore white space and punctuation.

3.19 How to program to print first non repeated character from String?

3.20 How to check if a String contains only digits?

3.21 Write an algorithm to remove given characters from String? Implement the designed algorithm.

3.22 Write a program to find longest palindrome in a string?

3.23 Write a program to check if a String contains another String, e.g., indexOf()?

3.24 How to check if a String is valid shuffle of two Strings?

❑

CHAPTER

4 Arrays

This chapter discusses the common data structure known as the array. Arrays are basic building blocks for more complex data structures. Nearly every kind of complex structure can be represented indirectly using an array. A data structure is said to be linear if its elements form a linear sequence, i.e., elements are organized one after another. In this chapter we will see about linear data structure arrays. The operations possible on arrays like insertion, deletion, searching, sorting, matrix operations, multidimensional arrays, sparse matrix, etc.

4.1 ONE DIMENSIONAL ARRAY

An array is set of values of similar type. Array elements share common name and array elements are stored in sequential memory locations. Means the data elements in an array are represented in linear manner, i.e., there is linear relationship among the elements and these elements are stored in consecutive memory locations and this is why an array is known as linear data structure. To refer to the elements of the array, we use indexes accordingly. Array indexing starts from "zero". That is an array is a finite, ordered set of homogeneous elements. The ordering property means that the first, second, third, ..., nth element of an array can be identified. The elements of an array are homogeneous, i.e., they all have the same data type. In other words, an array is a compound data type which allows a collection of data of the same type to be grouped into a single object. As with any data type, to understand how to use an array, one must know how such a structure can be declared, how data may be stored and accessed in the structure, and what operations may be performed using this new type. Predetermination of an array size is must except in the case of giving values at the time of declaring an array.

For example, one array might be comprised of elements that are all strings; another might be comprised of elements that are all integers. The elements of an array may also each be arrays. Arrays are also commonly referred to as tables. The simplest form of array is a one-dimensional array, or vector. A one-dimensional array named EMPLOYEE_REC, which consists of n records, as shown in **Figure** 4.1.

EMPLOYEE_REC[1]	EMPLOYEE_REC[20]	....	EMPLOYEE_REC[I]	....	EMPLOYEE_REC[n]

Figure 4.1 One Dimensional Array representation

The subscript, or index, of an element designates its position in the array's ordering. In the notation used here, a particular element is identified by the name of the array followed by the element's subscript enclosed in parentheses, i.e., EMPLOYEE_REC[i]. Other possible notations to designate the element of array EMPLOYEE_REC with subscript *i* include EMPLOYEE_REC[i], EMPLOYEE_REC(i) and EMPLOYEE_REC_i. Note that only the array itself is given a name. Elements of an array are referred to by their subscripts, i.e., by their relative positions in the array. This naming convention enables the programmer to write algorithms that loop through the elements of an array, rather than having to name each of the elements distinctly.

More formally, the one-dimensional array A can be defined as with elements of data structure of data type T having subscripts extending from L through U is

```
A[L: U] = {A[i]: for i= L, L + 1, . . . , U - 1, U, }
```

where each element A[i] is a data structure of data type T.

The number of elements in an array is called its range. The range of array A[L: U] is U - L + 1. The range of array B[1 : N] is N.

Note: The notation A[L: U] indicates that A's subscript value ranges from L through U. This notation can also be represented as A[U], but limitation of this notation is that lower limit always represents 0 or 1 depending upon the language in which are going to implement it. For clarity we have considered A[L: U] notation.

For example, a one-dimensional array might contain the temperatures recorded in a city for every hour during a 24-hour period. These elements are ordered by their corresponding time of the day. All elements are of the same kind, each is a temperature.

The minimum allowable value of an array's subscript is called its lower bound and the maximum allowable value is called its upper bound. In the formal definition of an array, L is the lower-bound and U is the upper-bound of A's subscript range. In the temperature record example, a natural lower bound is 1 and upper bound is 24. Call the array TEMP. TEMP[l] is the temperature recorded at hour 1, for $1 \leq i \leq 24$.

Another example of a one-dimensional array is a table of average state incomes. Name the array AVG_INCOME. The element AVG_INCOME[i] is the average incomes of the ith state, where the states are ordered sequentially, say alphabetically. Thus, AVG-INCOME[l] is the average income of Arunachal Pradesh and AVG_INCOME[28] is the average income of Uttar Pradesh for states of the India.

For some applications it is more natural to use a lower bound that is not equal to 1. For example, temperatures of an experiment that are recorded every ten seconds from time zero might more conveniently be stored in an array with lower bound 0. The lower bound may even be negative. This is commonly the case for arrays that store data to be displayed graphically, such as on an axis of points ranging from -100 to + 100.

The most common programming languages all use the same approach to declaration of variables that are arrays. Three things need to be specified to declare an array: (i) the array name, (ii) the subscript range, and (iii) the type of data structure for the array elements. The general syntax to define an array is:

```
Data type array name [size];
```

The above syntax is equivalent to **C, C++, Visual C** and **Visual C++.** For example, if we want to define an array, which has 100 elements then the declaration will be:

int Number [100];

In the above example **Number** is an array name with size 100. The data type that is used to declare **Number** is integer type. The array **Number** can store maximum of 100 integer data. The size of an array is also called its length. The subscripts of an array are also called index. The index set consists of integers **0, 1, 2, 3 ... n - 1**, if we are using the languages said above. The index set **1, 2, 3 ... n** is used by **PASCAL, FORTRAN, BASIC** and **PL/I.** The elements of the array **Number** may be denoted by the subscripted variables as:

$Number_1$, $Number_2$, $Number_3$ ... $Number_n$

In **FORTRAN, BASIC** and **PL/I** languages the elements can be represented as:

Number (1), Number (2), Number (3) ... Number (n)

But in **C, C++, Visual C/C++** and **PASCAL** languages the above notations are written as:

Number [1], Number [2], Number [3] ... Number [n]

For example, if we have an array **N** with storage capacity of 14 elements and having 10 elements that is:

N [14] ={11, 22, 33, 44, 55, 66, 77, 88, 99, 00}

The illustration of array **N** is shown in **Figure 4.2.**

The length of an array can be evaluated as:

Length = Upper limit – Lower limit + 1

That is

Length = UL – LL + 1

For an array **N [100]** the length of the array can be evaluated as:

UL = 100

LL = 1

Length = UL – LL + 1

⇒ 100 – 1 + 1

⇒ 100

From the above example, it is clear that **N** will store maximum of 100 elements only.

Few points we are required to remember which are as follows.

Advantages

- Easy to implement.
- It allows random accessing of elements, i.e., any element of the array can be randomly accessed using indexes.
- Suitable when the numbers of elements are predefined or already known.

Disadvantages

- Larger array may lead to high memory wastage, if we add only few elements in it
- Inserting and deleting elements at and from random position requires shifting of preceding and succeeding elements, i.e., we need to traverse throughout the array.
- Size of array is fixed so the elements beyond the size cannot be added.

4.2 ONE DIMENSIONAL ARRAY IN MEMORY

There is very simple way to find the address or location of array elements by using pointer operator (&) in **C, C++** and **Visual C/C++**. If one is interested in address of array's elements, he/she can evaluate in the following fashion. The base address or starting address of an array is denoted by **Base (N).** Thus, the address of an element of an array **N** evaluated by,

Loc (N[k]) = Base(N) +w*(k - Lower limit),

where, **w** represents number of words per memory cell for the array **N**, and k is the current index for which address is requested. The details about memory presentation will be discussed in section {4.10}.

For example, if we have an array **A** with 14 elements then they can represent as:

```
A[14] = {99,88,77,66,55,44,33,22,11,100,200,300,400,500}
```

The memory representation of the array **A** is illustrated in **Figure 4.2**.

ADDRESS	INFO
0x1334ff dc	99
0x1334ffde	88
0x1334ffe0	77
0x1334ffe2	66
0x1334ffe4	55
0x1334ffe6	44
0x1334ffe8	33
0x1334ffea	22
0x1334ffec	11
0x1334ffee	100
0x1334fff0	200
0x1334fff2	300
0x1334fff4	400
0x1334fff6	500

Figure 4.2 Array in memory

4.3 TRAVERSING ONE DIMENSIONAL ARRAY

Suppose we have an array **M** that is collection of integer data type in the computer memory. If we visit each element in **M** then this visiting process is called traversing. The traversing algorithm is illustrated in **Figure 4.3.** For example, if we have an array as illustrated in **Figure 4.4**, from this illustration it is found that:

```
L_B = 0 (Lower bound)
U_B = 12 (Upper bound)
Counter = L_B = 0
Linear_array [Counter] = 100
Counter = Counter +1 = 0+1 = 1
Linear_array [Counter] = 200
```

Step 1: [Initialization]
    Counter = L_B
Step 2: [Perform visiting]
    Repeat while Counter ≤ U_B
    (i) Process to Linear_array [Counter]
    (ii) Counter = Counter + 1
Step 3: Exit

Figure 4.3 Traversing algorithm

INDEX	INFO
0	100
1	200
2	300
3	400
4	500
5	600
6	700
7	800
8	900
9	11
10	22
11	33
12	44

Figure 4.4 Array in memory

This process continues and stops when the value 44 and **Counter** becomes 12. If one wants to find number of elements in an array, the following algorithm illustrates the idea:

```
(i)   [Initialization]
        Number = 0
(ii)  [Count information in the array]
        Repeat for Counter = L_B, L_B+1 ... U_B
        Process Linear_array [Counter]
        Number = Number +1
(iii) Exit
```

The program segment **ARRAY_T.C** implements the traversing algorithm shown in **Figure 4.3.**

```
/* Traversing a linear array */
/* ARRAY_T.C */
# include<stdio.h>
/* prototypes of the function used */
void traversing_array(int *, int, int);
void input(int *, int, int);

/* Definition of the function*/
void traversing_array(int linear_array[], int l_b, int u_b)
{
   int counter;
   for(counter = l_b; counter<=u_b; counter++)
   {
      printf("\n Element at position: %d is %d ", counter,
      linear_array[counter]);
   }
}

/* Definition of the function*/
void input(int array[], int l_b, int u_b)
{
   int counter;
   for(counter = l_b; counter<= u_b; counter++)
   {
      printf("\n Input value for the: %d: ", counter);
      scanf("%d", &array[counter]);
   }
}

/* Definition of the function */
void main()
{
```

```
    int a[100];
    int lb, ub;
    printf("\n Input the Lower limit of the array:");
    scanf("%d", &lb);
    printf("\n Input the Upper limit of the array:");
    scanf("%d", &ub);
    input(a, lb, ub);
    traversing_array(a,lb,ub); /* traversing the list */
}
```

4.4 INSERTION IN ONE DIMENSIONAL ARRAY

It can be visualized that for inserting an element in one-dimensional array, one has to shift all the elements one position down For example, if we have an array of items as illustrated in **Figure 4.5,** where array represents "**COMPTER SCIENCE**". But the actual information, which is to be stored is "**COMPUTER SCIENCE**". Now we have to insert '**U**' in the array at the proper place so that we get the desired string. By inspecting the array, we find that '**U**' is missing at position 5. Before inserting '**U**' in the array, we have to move each element of the array from position 5 to 12 one position down. The operations performed are:

```
    Temp = 14 [Represents position of last element the array]. The total number
of elemets with array is 15.
    Array [15] = Array [Temp] = E
    Array [Temp] = Array [Temp-1] = C
    Array [Temp-1] = Array [Temp-2] = N
    Array [Temp-2] = Array [Temp-3] = E
    Array [Temp-3] = Array [Temp-4] = I
    Array [Temp-4] = Array [Temp-5] = C
    Array [Temp-5] = Array [Temp-6] = S
    Array [Temp-6] = Array [Temp-7] = ' '
    Array [Temp-7] = Array [Temp-8] = R
    Array [Temp-8] = Array [Temp-9] = E
    Array [Temp-9] = Array [Temp-10] = T
    Array [Temp-10] = U [Newly inserted element]
```

The size of the array is also changed from 15 to 16. After insertion the array becomes like **Figure 4.6.** Consider another example, suppose we have an array **LIST** with 15 rooms as illustrated in **Figure 4.7.** Let we want to insert integer 255 in the list at position 10. The insertion is not possible because there is no free room in **LIST**. Thus, before making an insertion into an array one should first of all check for the available room in the array. For it, there is very simple way subtracting occupied space from maximum size of an array one can get the number of available rooms. The insertion algorithm is illustrated in **Figure 4.8** and its implementation is illustrated by **ARRAY_I.C** program segment.

INDEX	INFO
0	C
1	O
2	M
3	P
4	T
5	E
6	R
7	
8	S
9	C
10	I
11	E
12	N
13	C
14	E
15	
16	
17	

Figure 4.5 Array before insertion

INDEX	INFO
0	C
1	O
2	M
3	P
4	U
5	T
6	E
7	R
8	
9	S
10	C
11	I
12	E
13	N
14	C
15	E
16	
17	

Figure 4.6 Array U after inserting

INDEX	INFO
0	11
1	22
2	33
3	44
4	55
5	66
6	77
7	88
8	99
9	100
10	111
11	122
12	133
13	144
14	155

Figure 4.7 Array with no free room

```
Step 1: [Initialization]
 Temp = Number [Number of elements in the list, i.e., least of occupied space]
Step 2: [Scan the list for the position of the new element]
   Repeat while Temp ≥ Position
   [Move the last element one position down]
(i)    Array [Temp+1] = Array [Temp]
(ii)   Temp = Temp - 1
Step 3: [Insert the element]
   Array [Position] = Element
Step 4: [Change number of information by one]
   Number = Number + 1
Step 5: Return (Number)
```

Figure 4.8 Insertion algorithm

```
/* INSERTING AN ELEMENT INTO LINEAR ARRAY AT SPECIFIED POSITION */
/* ARRAY_I.C */
# include<stdio.h>
/* Function prototypes */
int insert_array(char *, int, int, char);
```

```
void input(char *, int );
void display(char *, int );
/* Definition of the function */
int insert_array(char array[], int number, int position, char element)
{
    int temp = number;
    while( temp >= position)
    {
        array[temp+1] = array[temp];
        temp --;
    }

    array[position] = element;
    number = number +1 ;
    return(number);
}

/* INPUT FUNCTION TO READ DATA */
void input(char array[], int number)
{
    int i;
    for(i = 1; i<= number ; i++)
    {
        fflush(stdin);
        printf("\n Input value for: %d: ", i);
        scanf("%c", &array[i]);
    }
}

/* OUTPUT FUNCTION TO PRINT ON THE CONSOLE */
void display(char array[], int number)
{
    int i;
    for(i = 1; i<= number; i++)
    {
        printf("\n Value at the position: %d: %c ", i, array[i]);
    }
}

/* main function */
void main()
```

```
{
    int number;
    char array[100];
    int position;
    char element;
    fflush(stdin);
    printf("\n Input the number of element into the LIST: ");
    scanf("%d", &number);
    fflush(stdin);
    input(array, number);
    printf("\n Entered list as follows:\n");
    fflush(stdin);
    display(array,number);
    fflush(stdin);
    printf("\n Input the position where you want to add a new data:");
    scanf("%d", &position);
    fflush(stdin);
    printf("\n Input the value for the position:");
    scanf("%c", &element);
    number = insert_array(array,number,position,element);
    display(array,number);
}
```

4.5 DELETION FROM ONE DIMENSIONAL ARRAY

Deleting an element or information from the end of an array is simple but deleting an element from some other position is difficult and requires moving all the element up-word to fill-up the gap into the array. Before deleting an element from an array one should go through the following points:

- Delete an element if it is known then find whether it is in the array or not.
- Searched it in the array.
- Delete the element.
- Update the array.

For example, suppose we have list of 10 employee **EMPLOY** as illustrated in **Figure 4.9**. If **Mr. JONES** leaves the organization, so it is required to update the employee list. To update the employee list following steps are made:

```
Position of Mr. JONES in the list is 5th

EMPLOY [4] = EMPLOY [5] = CHAIPPEL
EMPLOY [5] = EMPLOY [6] = BOTHOM
EMPLOY [6] = EMPLOY [7] = DESMOND
EMPLOY [7] = EMPLOY [8] = LARA
EMPLOY [8] = EMPLOY [9] = RACHITA
EMPLOY [10] = NULL
```

INDEX	INFO
0	DON
1	TOM
2	HITLER
3	CHARLES
4	JONES
5	CHAIPPEL
6	BOTHOM
7	DESMOND
8	LARA
9	RACHITA

Figure 4.9 List of employee EMPLOY

INDEX	INFO
0	DON
1	TOM
2	HITLER
3	CHARLES
4	CHAIPPEL
5	BOTHOM
6	DESMOND
7	LARA
8	RACHITA
9	

Figure 4.10 List of employee after leaving JONES EMPLOY

The resulting employee list is illustrated in **Figure 4.10.** The deletion algorithm illustrated in **Figure 4.11** and implemented as **ARRAY_D.C.**

```
Step 1: [Initialization]
Element = Array [Position] [Keep information of deleted item]
Step 2: [Make copy of the position]
   Temp = Position
Step 3: [Update the list, Number represents number of items in the list]
   Repeat while Temp ≤ Number - 1
 (i)     Array [Temp] = Array [Temp + 1]
 (ii)    Temp = Temp + 1
Step 4: [Decrease size of information in the list by one]
   Number = Number - 1
Step 5: Return (Number)
```

Figure 4.11 Deletion algorithm

```
/* DELETING FROM A LINEAR ARRAY AT SPECIFIED POSITION */
/* ARRAY_D.C */
# include<stdio.h>
# define s 20

char employ[s][s];
/* Prototpyes of the functions used */
int delete_array(char employ[s][s], int, int, char *);
void input(char emply[s][s], int );
void display(char employ[s][s], int );

/* Definition of the function */
int delete_array(char employ[s][s], int number, int position, char
element[])
```

```
{
    int temp = position;
    element = employ[position];
    printf("\n Information which we have to delete: %s", element);
    while( temp <= number-1)
    {
        *employ [temp] = *employ[temp+1];
        temp ++;
    }
    number = number - 1 ;
    return(number);
}

void input(char employ[s][s], int number)
{
    int i;
    for(i = 1; i<= number ; i++)
    {
        fflush(stdin);
        printf("\n Input value for: %d: ", i);
        gets(employ[i]);
    }
}

void display(char employ[s][s], int number)
{
    int i;
    for(i = 1; i<= number; i++)
    {
        printf("\n Value at the position: %d: %s", i, employ[i]);
    }
}

/* main function */
void main()
{
    int number;
    int position;
    char element[s];
    printf("\n Input the number of elements in the array:");
```

```
    scanf("%d", &number);
    fflush(stdin);
    input(employ, number);
    printf("\n Entered list is as follows:\n");
    display(employ, number);
    fflush(stdin);
    printf("\n Input the position from where you want delete an element:");
    scanf("%d", &position);
    number = delete_array(employ, number, position, element);
    display(employ,number);
}
```

If in a list same information is existing more than one place then the repeated information is called duplicate. The removal of such duplicates is very necessary in some applications. Because, if some one is accessing an information from a list but does not know about its duplication and modifying the such information in one place the inconsistency takes place.

For example, suppose we have a list of 15 elements as illustrated in **Figure 4.12.** It is clear that 11 exists at 4 places, 77 at 3 and 88 at 2 places. Suppose we want to remove duplicates from the list. First of all we consider the first element in the list and start scanning for the next occurrences of it. If it is found at position P in the list then each element is moved one position upward. For example, if we have list as show in **Figure 4.12** and 11 is found at position 8. Now from 9th position onwards move one position upward each element of the array. The operation is as follows:

```
Position = 8 [FROM 0 TO 7]
LIST [7] = LIST [8] = 100
LIST [8] = LIST [9] = 22
LIST [9] = LIST [10] = 11
LIST [ 10] LIST [11] = 77
LIST [11] = LIST [12] = 88
LIST [12] = LIST [13] = 77
LIST [13] = LIST [14] = 11
LIST [14] = NULL
```

After first iteration the list becomes as shown in **Figure 4.13**. Again we start scanning for the next occurrence of 11 in the list. By scanning the list, we find the next occurrence of 11 at position 10.

```
LIST [9] = LIST [10] = 77
LIST [10] = LIST [11] = 88
LIST [11] = LIST [12] = 77
LIST [12] = LIST [13] = 11
```

After second iteration the resulting list is as shown in **Figure 4.14.** After third iteration resulting list is shown as in **Figure 4.15.** Now choose second element in the list and repeat the above process and it is continued till all the duplicates are removed from the list. Final list after elimination of all the duplicates is illustrated in **Figure 4.16.** The algorithm to remove duplicates from a list is given in **Figure 4.17**. The program segment **DUPL_A.C** implements the duplicate removal algorithm.

INDEX	INFO
0	11
1	13
2	14
3	44
4	99
5	88
6	77
7	11
8	100
9	22
10	11
11	77
12	88
13	77
14	11
15	

Figure 4.12 List of information

INDEX	INFO
0	11
1	13
2	14
3	44
4	99
5	88
6	77
7	100
8	22
9	11
10	77
11	88
12	77
13	11
14	
15	

Figure 4.13 List after eliminating 11 at position 8

INDEX	INFO
0	11
1	13
2	14
3	44
4	99
5	88
6	77
7	100
8	22
9	77
10	88
11	77
12	11
13	
14	
15	

Figure 4.14 List after eliminating 11 at position 10

INDEX	INFO
0	11
1	13
2	14
3	44
4	99
5	88
6	77
7	100
8	22
9	77
10	88
11	77
12	
13	
14	
15	

Figure 4.15 List after eliminating 11 at position 13

INDEX	INFO
0	11
1	13
2	14
3	44
4	99
5	88
6	77
7	100
8	22
9	
10	
11	
12	
13	
14	
15	

Figure 4.16 List after eliminating all the duplicates

```
Step 1: [Initialization] Duplicate = N [Number of elements in the list]
Step 2: [Set flag] Status = 0
Step 3: [Check and remove duplicates]
        Repeat through Step 8 for I = 0, 1, 2 ...N - 2
Step 4: Repeat through Step 8 for J = I+1, I+2 ...N - 1
Step 5: If Array [I] = Array [J]
        N = N - 1
Step 6: Repeat for K = J, J+1 ... N - 1
        Array [K] = Array [K+1]
Step 7: [Set flag] Status = 1
Step 8: J = J - 1
Step 9: If Status = 0
        Output No duplicate is found
Step 10:[Find total duplicates in the list]
        Duplicate = Duplicate - N
Step 11: [Return the total duplicates in the list]
        Return (Duplicate)
```

Figure 4.17 Duplicate removal algorithm

```
/* DELETING DUPLICATES FROM A LINEAR ARRAY*/
/* DUPL_A.C */
# include<stdio.h>

int status ;
int dup;
/* Prototypes for the function used */
int duplicate_array(int *, int);
void input(int *, int );
void display(int *, int );

/* Definition of the function */
int duplicate_array(int array[], int number)
{
    int i, j, k;
    status = 0;
    dup = number;

    for(i = 0; i< number-1; i++)
        for(j = i+1; j< number; j++)
        {
            if(array[i] == array[j])
            {
```

```
                number = number - 1 ;
                for(k = j; k<number; k++)
                    array[k] = array[k+1];
                status = 1;
                j = j - 1;
            }
        }
    if( status ==0)
        printf("\n No duplicate is found");
    return(dup-number);
}

/* Input function to read data */
void input(int array[], int number)
{
    int i;
    for(i = 0; i< number ; i++)
    {
        printf("Input value for: %d: ", i+1);
        scanf("%d", &array[i]);
    }
}

/* Output function */
void display(int array[], int number)
{
    int i;
    for(i = 0; i< number; i++)
    {
        printf("\n Value at the position: %d: %d", i+1, array[i]);
    }
}

/* main function */
void main()
{
    int number;
    int array[100];
    int n;
    printf("\n Input the number of elements in the list: ");
    scanf("%d", &number);
    input(array, number);
    printf("\n Entered list is as follows:\n");
    display(array, number);
    n = duplicate_array(array,number);
```

```
    printf("\nNumber of duplicate elements in the list are: %d", n);
    printf("\n After removing duplicates from the list, the list is as
follows:");
    display(array, number-n);
  }
```

4.6 SEARCHING

Suppose a specific **INFO** information is given in an array. Searching refers to the operation of finding the location of the **INFO** in an array or output some message if **INFO** does not exist in the array. The search is said to be successful if **INFO** appears in the array else it is called unsuccessful. Some times it is required to add **INFO** in the array if it does not exist.

For example, suppose we have a list of employees **EMPLOY** as illustrated in **Figure 4.18**. Mr. **JONES** joins the institute and it is required to update the database **EMPLOY**. Before any insertion into the list, it is required to scan the list of employees to find some other employee with the same name. If in the list there is no other employee with name **JONES**, insert the name Mr. **JONES** into the list. After inserting Mr. **JONES** in the employee list the new list is illustrated in **Figure 4.19**.

INDEX	INFO
0	MORE
1	DAVID
2	TOM
3	THOMPSON
4	ARVIND
5	SANATH
6	MAJID
7	KIRAN
8	DEEPAK
9	MISHTHU
10	
11	
12	
13	
14	
15	

Figure 4.18 List employee EMPLOY

INDEX	INFO
0	MORE
1	DAVID
2	TOM
3	THOMPSON
4	ARVIND
5	SANATH
6	MAJID
7	KIRAN
8	DEEPAK
9	MISHTHU
10	JONES
11	
12	
13	
14	
15	

Fig 4.19 List employee EMPLOY after adding Mr. JONES

INDEX	INFO
0	22
1	99
2	10
3	1
4	100
5	200
6	999
7	88
8	77
9	
10	
11	
12	
13	
14	
15	

Figure 4.20 List of integers in memory

For more discussion on sorting, searching, and merging, please go through **chapter sorting and searching.**

Some times it is required to find maximum and minimum element in a list. For example, if we have a list of 9 elements as illustrated in **Figure 4.20**, and then by inspection one can easily say 999 is maximum and 1 minimum element in the list. When a list becomes very large it is very difficult to perform such type of operation by inspection. By inspection one can say that 7th element is the largest and 4th element is the smallest in the given list. But the actual operation that is performed by a computer is quite different and can be described as follows:

Big = Small = List [0] = 22

List [1] > Big that is 99 > 22, the value of **Big** requires to be change.

Big = List [1] = 99

List [1] > Small that is 99 > 22, the value of **Small** will remain unchanged.

List [2] < Big that is 10 < 99, the value of **Big** will remain unchanged.

List [2] < Small that is 10 < 22, the value of **Small** requires to be change.

Small = List [2] = 10

List [3] < Big that is 1 < 99, the value of **Big** will remain unchanged.

List [3] < Small that is 1 < 10, the value of **Small** requires to change.

Small = List [3] = 1

If we will continue this process at the end of process we will get

Small = 1 Smallest element in the list

Big = 999 Largest element in the list

The algorithm to find out smallest and largest in a list is illustrated in **Figure 4.21**. The program segment **S_L_S_A.C** implements the above discussion.

```
Step 1: [Initialization]
         Temp = 0
Step 2: [Consider the first element of the list as Big and Small]
        Big = Small = List [0]
Step 3: [Check whether the size of the list is 1]
        If (N = 1) then
        Big = Small = List [0]
Step 4: [Check whether the size of the list is 2]
        If (N = 2) then
        If (List [0] < List [1]) then
        Big = List [1]
        Small = List [0]
        Else
Big = List [0]
       Small = List [1]
Step 5: [This step is performed if the number of elements in the list is
         more than 2]
Big = Small = List [0]
       Repeat while Temp ≤ N
       If List [Temp] > Big
       Big = List [Temp]
       Else if List [Temp] < Small
       Small = List [Temp]
Step 6: Temp = Temp + 1
Step 7: Output Small and Big
Step 8: Exit
```

Figure 4.21 Algorithm to find Smallest and Largest

```
/* SEARCHING FOR LARGEST AND SMALLEST ELEMENTS IN A LINEAR ARRAY */
/* S_L_S_A.C */
# include<stdio.h>
int s;
int small, big, temp;
/* Prototypes of the used functions */
int search_array(int *, int);
void input(int *, int );
void display(int *, int );
/* Definition of the function */
int search_array(int array[], int number)
{
    big = small = array[0];
    temp = 0;
    while(temp < number)
    {
        if(array[temp] > big)
        {
            big = array[temp] ;
        }else if(array[temp] < small)
        {
            small = array[temp];
        }
        temp ++;
    }
    s = small;
    return(big);
}

/* Input function */
void input(int array[], int number)
{
    int i;
    for(i = 0; i< number ; i++)
    {
        printf("Input value for : %d: ",i+1);
        scanf("%d", &array[i]);
    }
}

/* Output function */
```

```
void display(int array[], int number)
{
    int i;
    for(i = 0; i < number; i++)
    {
        printf("\n Value at the position: %d: %d", i+1, array[i]);
    }
}
/* main function */
void main()
{
    int number,big;
    int array[100];
    printf("\n Input the number of elements in the list:");
    scanf("%d", &number);
    input(array, number);
    printf("\n Entered list is as follows:\n");
    display(array,number);
    big = search_array(array,number);
    printf("\n Largest number in the array is : %d", big);
    printf("\n Smallest number in the array is : %d", s);
}
```

4.7 MULTI DIMENSIONAL ARRAYS

A two-dimensional array is an array in which each element is itself an array. An array named B which consists of *m* elements, each of which is an array of *n* elements can be depicted as an mxn table, as shown in **Figure 4.22**.

	1	2	...	j	...	n
1						
2						
...						
i						
...						
m						

Figure 4.22 mxn array representations

Now it is necessary to specify two subscript values in order to identify an individual element of a two-dimensional array. By convention, the first subscript refers to a row of the array, while the second subscript refers to a column of the array B[i][j] is the element of B that is in the ith row and j^{th} column of array B. This phenomenon is shown in **Figure 4.23**.

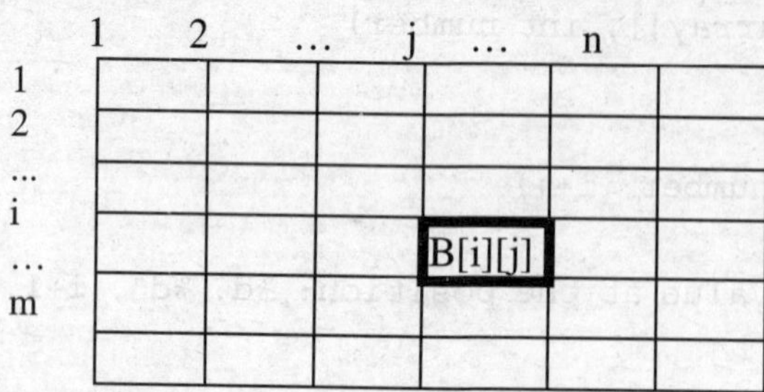

Figure 4.23 Element B[i][j] in two-dimensional array

More formally, the two-dimensional array B with individual elements of data type T having row subscripts extending from i to m and column subscripts ranging from j to n is

```
B[1 :m][1: n] = {B[i][j] | for i = 1, . . . , m and j = 1, . . . , n}
```

where each B[i,j] is a data structure of data type T.

Array B is said to be of dimensions mxn. There are n elements in each row and m elements in each column of B; thus the total number of elements in array B is m*n. In general, a two-dimensional array B with its first subscript having lower bound L_1 and upper bound U_1 and its second subscript having lower bound L_2 and upper bound U_2 is defined as

$$B[L_1: U_1][L_2: U_2] = \{B[i][j]\} \text{ for } L_1 \le i \le U_1 \text{ and } L_2 \le j \le U_2\}$$

where each B[i][j] is a data structure of data type T.

The number of elements in a row of B is $U_2 - L_2 + 1$ and the number of elements in a column of B is $U_I - L_I + 1$. Thus, the total number of elements in array B is $[U_2 — L_2 + 1]*[U_1 – L_1 + 1]$.

Two-dimensional arrays are quite common. For example, the Chamber of Commerce of a city might keep track of the number of hours of fair weather in each day of the year. These data can be stored in an array with dimensions 365 by 24. Call the array W. Values of W could be determined by

W[i][j] = 1 if it is fair during the jth hour of the ith day of the year 0 otherwise, i.e., if it snows, rains, sleets, drizzles, etc, during the jth hour of the ith day of the year. All elements of the array are of the same kind; each is a Boolean.

Another example of a two-dimensional array is one that contains data about the grades of students in a class on the eight semester examinations. This array, called GRADE, would have dimensions m by 8, where m is the number of students. Then GRADE[i][j] is the grade achieved by the ith student on the jth examination. The value of must be between 1 and m inclusive; j must be between 1 and 8 inclusive. Each element of the array is a grade; they could all be integers, or all be fixed-point numbers with two decimal places, or all be characters, depending on the convention adopted.

Suppose **Mat** is a two dimensional **Row x Col** array. The first dimension of **Mat** contains the index set **0, 1, 2 ... Row-1** with lower bound **0** and upper bound **Row – 1** and the second dimension contains the index set **0, 1, 2 ... Col - 1** with lower bound **0** and upper bound **Col – 1**. This array is **Row x Col**.

Some programming languages allow one to define multidimensional arrays in which the lower bounds is 1 and rather than 0. However, the index set for each dimension still consists of the consecutive integers from lower bound to the upper bound of the dimension. The length of a given dimension can be obtained by

Length = Upper bound – Lower bound + 1

For example, if we have an array {**Figure 4.24**}. The length of each dimension may be

Row = Upper bound – Lower bound + 1

$\Rightarrow$ $10 - 6 + 1$

$\Rightarrow$ 5

Col = Upper bound – Lower bound – 1

$\Rightarrow$ $15 - 10 + 1$

$\Rightarrow$ 6

The size of the array shown in **Figure 4.24** will be

$\Rightarrow$ Row * Col

$\Rightarrow$ $5 * 6$

$\Rightarrow$ 30

Column → / Row ↓	10	11	12	13	14	15
6	1	2	3	4	5	6
7	7	8	9	10	11	12
8	13	14	15	16	17	18
9	19	20	21	22	23	24
10	25	26	27	28	29	30

Figure 4.24 Two dimensional array in memory

4.7.1 Cross-section

A cross-section of a two-dimensional array is obtained by holding one of the subscripts constant while varying the other through its entire range of values. The notation that is commonly used to denote a cross-section is an asterisk [*] for the subscript value that is to be allowed to take on its entire range of values. For example, B[* ,4] refers to the fourth column of the array B pictured at the beginning of this section, i.e., B[* ,4] = {B[1][4], B[2][4], B[3][4], . . . , B[m][4]}.

Similarly, B[i, *] is the ith row of the array B. For example, W[47,*] is the row of W values recording the weather conditions on the 47th day of the year. Similarly GRADE[*,3] is the column of GRADE values for recording examination grades for all students on the third examination. A cross-section of a two-dimensional array is essentially a slice taken from the array.

4.7.2 Transpose

The transpose of a two-dimensional array is obtained by reversing the subscript positions. The transpose of an mxn array is an nxm array. The transpose of array B is commonly denoted B^T. The transpose of the array B pictured at the beginning of this section is shown in **Figure** 4.25. By definition, $B[i][j] = B^T[j][i]$. For example, $B[3][8] = B^T[8][3]$. The element in row 3, column 8 of array B is the same as the element in row 8, column 3 of the transpose of array B.

	1	2	…	j	…	m
1						
2						
…						
i						
…						
n						

Figure 4.25 Transpose of the array in Figure 4.22.

4.7.3 Representation of Two Dimensional Arrays In Memory

Let **Mat** be a two-dimensional **Row x Col** array. Although **Mat** is represented as a rectangular array of elements with **Row** rows and **Col** columns, the array will be represented in the memory by a block of **Row x Col** sequential memory locations. The **Mat** array may be stored in the memory in one of the following way:

(i) Column by column that is in column major order

(ii) Row by row that is in row major order

Figure 4.26 illustrates the different memory representation of a two-dimensional array **Mat. Figure 4.27** illustrates two-dimensional array in memory. Details about memory representation are given in section {4.10}.

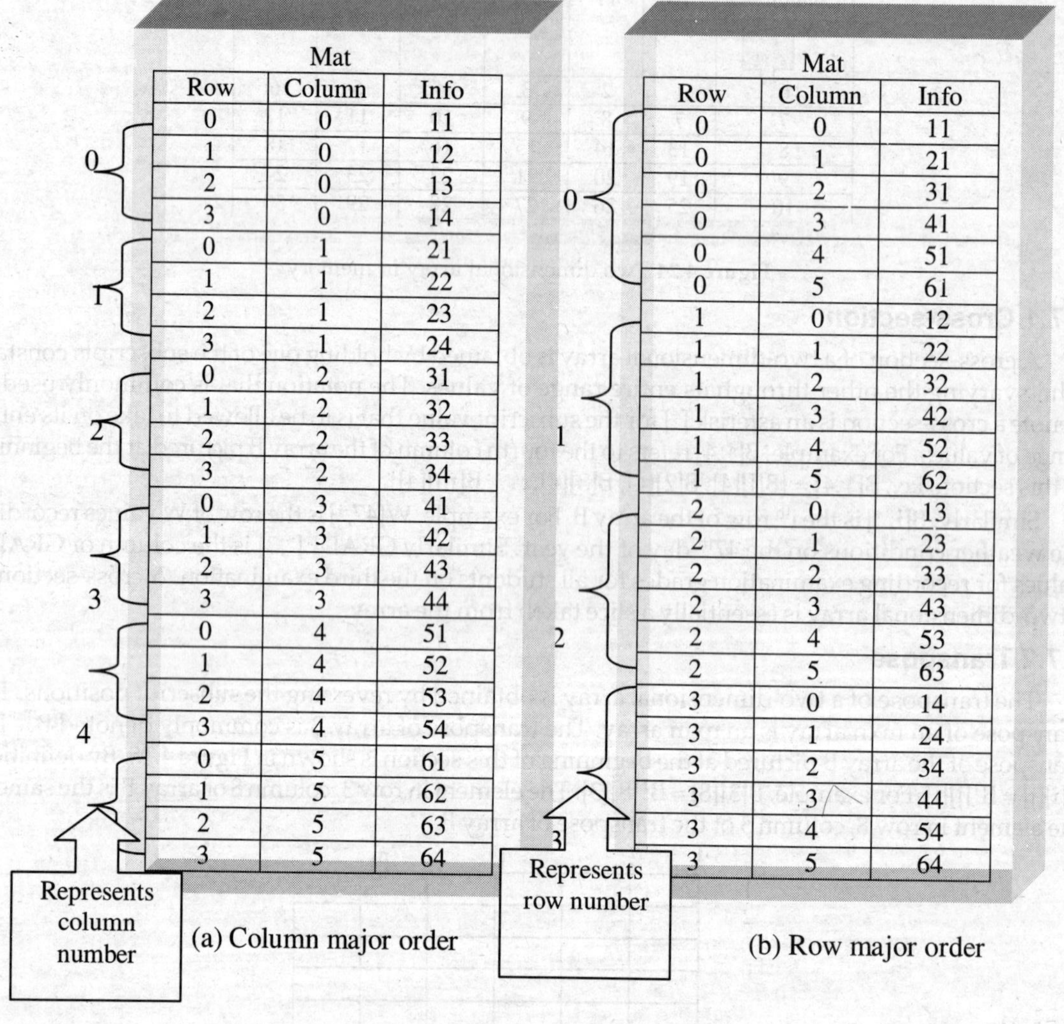

Row	Column	Info
0	0	11
1	0	12
2	0	13
3	0	14
0	1	21
1	1	22
2	1	23
3	1	24
0	2	31
1	2	32
2	2	33
3	2	34
0	3	41
1	3	42
2	3	43
3	3	44
0	4	51
1	4	52
2	4	53
3	4	54
0	5	61
1	5	62
2	5	63
3	5	64

(a) Column major order

Row	Column	Info
0	0	11
0	1	21
0	2	31
0	3	41
0	4	51
0	5	61
1	0	12
1	1	22
1	2	32
1	3	42
1	4	52
1	5	62
2	0	13
2	1	23
2	2	33
2	3	43
2	4	53
2	5	63
3	0	14
3	1	24
3	2	34
3	3	44
3	4	54
3	5	64

(b) Row major order

Figure 4.26 Two-dimensional arrays in memory

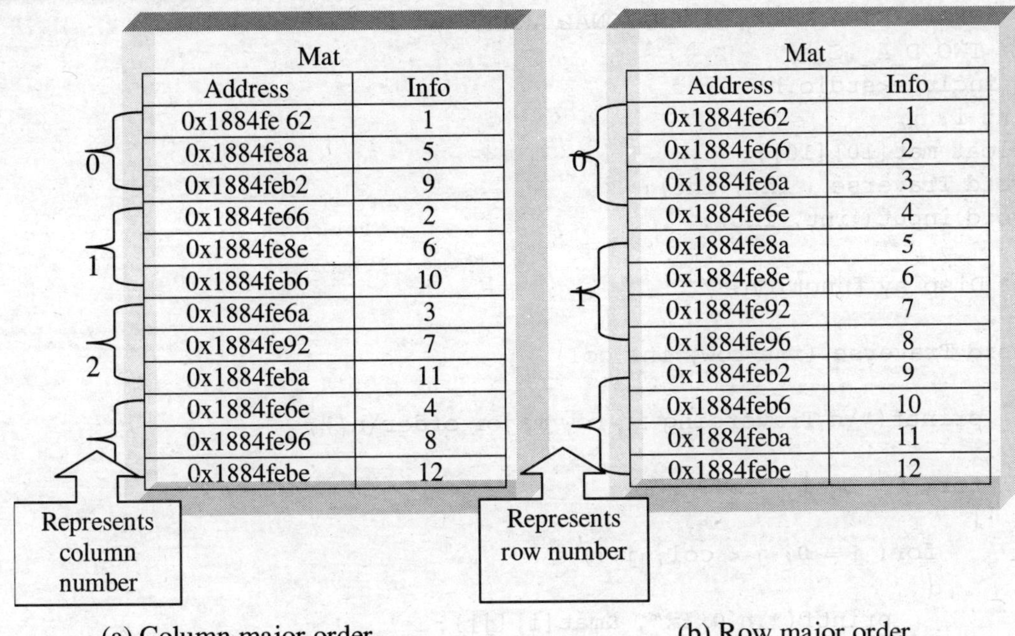

(a) Column major order (b) Row major order

Figure 4.27 Two-dimensional array in memory

4.7.4 Traversing Two Dimensional Arrays

Traversing of a two-dimensional array can be classified into two categories, depending upon the two types of representation:

(i) Column major order

(ii) Row major order

Note that the traversing in above two techniques is different. The program segment **TWO_D_A_.C** implements the two traversing algorithms (**Figure 4.28**, and **4.29**).

```
Step 1: [Perform traversing]
   Repeat for I = 0, 1, 2 ... Row - 1
   Repeat for J = 0, 1, 2 ... Col - 1
   Process to Mat [I][J]
Step 2: Exit
```

Figure 4.28 Algorithm to traverse a two-dimensional array in row major order

```
Step 1: [Perform traversing]
   Repeat for J = 0, 1, 2 ... Col - 1
   Repeat for I = 0, 1, 2 ... Row - 1
   Process to Mat [I][J]
Step 2: Exit
```

Figure 4.29 Algorithm to traverse a two dimensional array in column major order

```
/* TRAVERSING A TWO DIMENSIONAL ARRAY */
/* TWO_D_A_.C */
# include<stdio.h>
int i, j;
float mat[10][10];
void Traverse ( int, int);
void input( int, int);

/* Display function */

void Traverse (int row, int col)
{
    printf("\n Traversing in row major order\n");

    for( i = 0; i < row; i++)
    {
        for( j = 0; j < col; j++)
        {
            printf("\n 0x%x", &mat[i][j]);
            printf(" %f", mat[i][j]);
        }
        printf("\n");
    }

    printf("\n Traversing in column major order\n");
    for(j = 0; j < col; j++)
    {
        for(i = 0; i < row; i++)
        {
            printf("\n 0x%x", &mat[i][j]);
            printf(" %f", mat[i][j]);
        }
        printf("\n");
    }
    printf("\n Traversing in row major order\n");
    for(i = 0; i < row; i++)
    {
        for(j = 0; j < col; j++)
        {
            printf(" mat[%d][%d] = ", i, j);
            printf("%f", mat[i][j]);
        }
        printf("\n");
    }
    printf("\n Traversing in column major order\n");
```

```
    for(j = 0; j < col; j++)
    {
        for(i = 0; i < row; i++)
        {
            printf(" mat[%d][%d] = ", i, j);
            printf("%f", mat[i][j]);
        }
        printf("\n");
    }
}

/* Input function */
void input(int row, int col)
{
    for(i = 0 ; i< row; i++)
    {
        for(j = 0 ; j<col; j++)
        {
            printf("\nInput Value for : %d: %d: ",i+1, j+1);
            scanf("%f", &mat[i][j]);
        }
    }
}

/* main function */
void main()
{
    int r,c;
    printf("\n Input the number of rows:");
    scanf("%d", &r);
    printf(" Input the number of cols:");
    scanf("%d", &c);
    input(r, c);
    Traverse(r, c);
}
```

4.8 ALGEBRA OF MATRICES

Under this section we will study some algebraic operations, which are possible on arrays. We will consider the operations that are based on two-dimensional arrays that is matrix. Here we will discuss only multiplication of two matrices. Other operations on matrices are left as exercise to the readers. The product of two matrices **A** and **B** is possible if the number of columns in **A** is equal to the number of rows in **B** or number of rows in **A** is equal to the number of columns in **B**. Let **A** = $[a_{ij}]$ be an **m x n** matrix and **B** = $[b_{jk}]$ be an **n x p** matrix. Then the product **A.B** of these matrices is of the order of **m x p** say **C** = $[c_{ik}]$, where

$$c_{ik} = a_{i1}.b_{1k}+a_{i2}.b_{2k}+ \ldots + a_{in}.b_{nk}$$

$$c_{ik} = \sum_{k=1}^{n} a_{ij}.b_{jk}$$

For example, suppose we have two matrices **A** and **B** then by multiplying rows of first matrix and columns of second matrix we will get

$$A = \begin{pmatrix} 1 & -2 & 3 \\ 2 & 3 & -1 \\ -3 & 1 & 2 \end{pmatrix} B = \begin{pmatrix} 1 & 0 & 2 \\ 0 & 1 & 2 \\ 1 & 2 & 0 \end{pmatrix}$$

$$A.B = \begin{pmatrix} 1*1+ -2*0 + 3*1 & 1*0+-2*1+3*2\ 1* & 2+-2*2+3*0 \\ 2*1+3*0+-1*1 & 2*0+3*1+-1*2 & 2*2+3*2+-1*0 \\ 3*1+1*0+2*1 & -3*0+1*1+2*2 & -3*2+1*2+2*0 \end{pmatrix}$$

$$A.B = \begin{pmatrix} 1-0+3 & 0-2+6 & 2-4+0 \\ 2+0-1 & 0+3-2 & 4+6-0 \\ 3+0+2 & -0+1+4 & -6+2+0 \end{pmatrix}$$

$$A.B = \begin{pmatrix} 4 & 4 & -2 \\ 1 & 1 & 10 \\ 1 & 5 & -4 \end{pmatrix}$$

```
Step 1: [Check condition of multiplicity]
    If Col1 = Row2 [When we are taking column of first matrix and multiplying
it with rows of second matrix]

    Repeat for I = 0, 1, 2 ... Row1 - 1
    Repeat for J = 0, 1, 2 ... Col2 - 1
    Mat_res[I][J] = 0
    Repeat for K= 0, 1, 2 ... Col1 - 1
    Mat_res[I][J] = Mat_res[I][J]+Mat1[I][K]*Mat2[K][J]
    Else if Row1 = Col2 [When we are taking rows of first matrix and
multiplying it with the columns of the second matrix]

  Repeat for I = 0, 1, 2 ... Col1 - 1
    Repeat for J = 0, 1, 2 ... Row2 - 1
    Mat_res[I][J] = 0
    Repeat for K= 0, 1, 2 ... Col2 - 1
    Mat_res[I][J] = Mat_res[I][J]+Mat1[I][K]*Mat2[K][J]
    Else
  Output "Multiplication is not possible" and Exit
  Step 2: Exit
```

Figure 4.30 Algorithm to multiply two matrices

The program segment **MULT_MAT.C** implements the algorithm shown In **Figure 4.30**, i.e., multiplication performed on two matrices.

```
/* Multiply Two Matrices */
/* MULT_MAT.C */
# include<stdio.h>
# include<stdlib.h>
# define row 10
# define col 10

int i, j;
int row1, col1;
int row2, col2;
float mat1[row][col];
float mat2[row][col];
float mat_res[row][col];
void mat_mult( float mat1[row][col], int, int,
float mat2[row][col], int, int,
float mat_res[row][col]);

void display(float mat[row][col], int, int);
void input(float mat[row][col], int, int);

/* function to multiply two matrices */
void mat_mult( float mat1[row][col], int row1, int col1,
float mat2[row][col], int row2, int col2,
float mat_res[row][col])
{
   int i, j, k;
   if(col1 == row2)
   {
      printf("\n Multiplication is possible and Result is as follows\n");

      for(i =0; i<row1; i++)
         for(j=0; j<col2; j++)
         {
            mat_res[i][j] = 0;
            for(k = 0; k < col1; k ++)
            {
               mat_res[i][j] += mat1[i][k] * mat2[k][j];

            }
         }
```

```
        display(mat_res, row1, col2);
      }

      else
         printf("\n Multiplication is not possible");
      exit(0);
   }

   /* Output function */
   void display(float mat[row][col], int r, int c )
   {
      for( i = 0; i < r; i++)
      {
         for( j = 0; j < c; j++)
         {
            printf(" %f", mat[i][j]);
         }
         printf("\n");
      }
   }

   /* Input function */
   void input(float mat[row][col], int r, int c)
   {
      for( i = 0 ; i< r; i++)
      {
         for( j = 0 ; j<c; j++)
         {
            printf("Input Value for : %d: %d: ", i+1, j+1);
            scanf("%f", &mat[i][j]);
         }
      }
   }

   /* main function */
   void main()
   {
      int row1, col1;
      int row2, col2;
      float mat1[row][col];
      float mat2[row][col];
      float mat_res[row][col];
```

```
    printf("\n Input the row of the matrix->1:");
    scanf("%d", &row1);
    printf("\n Input the column of the matrix->1:");
    scanf("%d", &col1);
    printf("\n Input data for matrix-> 1\n");
    input(mat1, row1, col1);
    printf("\n Input the row of the matrix ->2:");
    scanf("%d", &row2);
    printf("\n Input the column of the matrix->2:");
    scanf("%d", &col2);
    printf("\n Input data for matrix-> 2\n");
    input(mat2, row2, col2);
    printf("\n Entered Matrix First is as follows:\n");
    display(mat1,row1,col1);
    printf("\n Entered Matrix Two is as follows:\n");
    display(mat2, row2, col2);
    mat_mult(mat1 ,row1 ,col1, mat2, row2, col2, mat_res);
}
```

4.9 GENERAL MULTIDIMENSIONAL ARRAYS

An array can be defined to be three-dimensional, four-dimensional, n-dimensional. The concepts of subscript range and number of elements can be directly extended from one- and two-dimensional arrays to these higher-order arrays. In general, an n-dimensional array requires that the values of n subscripts be specified in order to identify an individual element of the array. An n-dimensional array A could be identified as

$A[L_1: U_1][L_2: U_2] \dots [L_N: U_N]$.

An individual element of array A could then be specified by $A[i_1, i_2, \dots, i_n]$ where each subscript i_k is within the appropriate bounds $L_k \le i_k \le U_k$, for each k = 1, 2, . . . , n. The total number of elements in array A is $\prod_{k=1}^{n} [U_k - L_k + 1]$ which could alternatively be written as $[U_1 - L_1 + 1] * [U_2 - L_2 + 1] * \dots * [U_n - L_n + 1]$.

An example of a three-dimensional array is one containing data about the number of students in each of a university's six classifications of students [freshman, sophomore, junior, senior, graduate, unclassified], by sex, for all of a university's ten colleges. Such an array might be called **COLLEGE_CT** and could be of dimensions 6 by 2 by 10. Alternatively, it could be of dimensions 10, by 6 by 2, or 10 by 2 by 6, or 2 by 6 by 10, etc., as long as the reader knows what the meaning of each dimension is. The value of element **COLLEGE_CT**[*i*][*j*][*k*] is an integer, representing the number of students in class [i] of sex [j] for college[k] . To be valid,[i] must be 1, 2, 3, 4, 5 or 6;[j] must be 1 or 2;[k] must be between 1 and 10 inclusive. It is difficult to draw pictures of arrays with more than three dimensions. A cross-section of a multi-dimensional array is formed by holding one or more subscript values constant and varying each of the other subscripts through its entire range of values. For example, **COLLEGE_CT**[5][*][3] is the "row" of **COLLEGE_CT** containing the number of students in the fifth class (graduate) of college 3, for both sexes. **COLLEGE_CT** [*][*][3] is the "plane" of **COLLEGE_CT** containing the number of students in college 3, for each class and both sexes.

The memory representation of multidimensional arrays is illustrated in **Figure 4.31** and **Figure 4.32**. The program segment **D9.C** illustrates a 9 subscript array.

```
/* D9.C */
# include<stdio.h>
# define r 2
void main()
{
   int m[r][r][r][r][r][r][r][r][r];
   int a, b, c, d, e, f, g, h, i;

/* Input section */
for (a = 0; a < r; a++)
   for (b = 0; b < r; b++)
    for (c = 0; c < r; c++)

for (d = 0; d < r; d++)
   for (e = 0; e < r; e++)
    for (f = 0; f < r; f++)
for (g = 0; g < r; g++)
   for (h = 0; h < r; h++)
    for (i = 0; i < r; i++)
   m[a][b][c][d][e][f][g][h][i] = a+b+c+d+e+f+g+h+i;

/* Output section row major order */
   printf("\n ADDRESS   ARRAY M WITH INDEX VALUE \n");
   for (a = 0; a < r; a++)
    for (b = 0; b < r; b++)
     for (c = 0; c < r; c++)
   for (d = 0; d < r; d++)
    for (e = 0; e < r; e++)
     for (f = 0; f < r; f++)
   for (g = 0; g < r; g++)
    for (h = 0; h < r; h++)
    for (i = 0; i < r; i++)
    {
    printf("\n 0x%x", &m[a][b][c][d][e][f][g][h][i]);
    printf(" m[%d][%d][%d][%d][%d][%d][%d][%d][%d] = %d",a, b, c, d, e, f,
              g, h, i, m[a][b][c][d][e][f][g][h][i]);
    }

/* Column major order */
   printf("\n ADDRESS   ARRAY M WITH INDEX VALUE \n");
   for (i = 0; i < r; i++)
```

```
    for (h = 0; h < r; h++)
     for (g = 0; g < r; g++)
  for (f = 0; f < r; f++)
    for (e = 0; e < r; e++)
     for (d = 0; d < r; d++)
  for (c = 0; c < r; c++)
    for (b = 0; b < r; b++)
     for (a = 0; a < r; a++)
     {
     printf("\n 0x%x", &m[a][b][c][d][e][f][g][h][i]);
     printf(" m[%d][%d][%d][%d][%d][%d][%d][%d][%d] = %d",a, b, c, d, e, f,
          g, h, i, m[a][b][c][d][e][f][g][h][i]);
     }
  }
```

If one runs the above program segment the output comes like:

ADDRESS	INFO	m[a][b][c][d][e][f][g][h][i]
0x1ebbfbe8	0	m[0][0][0][0][0][0][0][0][0]
0x1ebbfbea	1	m[0][0][0][0][0][0][0][0][1]
0x1ebbfbec	1	m[0][0][0][0][0][0][0][1][0]
0x1ebbfbee	2	m[0][0][0][0][0][0][0][1][1]
0x1ebbfbf0	1	m[0][0][0][0][0][0][1][0][0]
0x1ebbffe0	7	m[1][1][1][1][1][1][1][0][0]
0x1ebbffe2	8	m[1][0][1][1][1][1][1][0][1]
0x1ebbffe4	8	m[1][1][1][1][1][1][1][1][0]
0x1ebbffe6	9	m[1][1][1][1][1][1][1][1][1]

Figure 4.31 Row major order representation of a 9x9 array in memory

ADDRESS	INFO	m[a][b][c][d][e][f][g][h][i]
0x1ebbfbe8	0	m[0][0][0][0][0][0][0][0][0]
0x1ebbfde8	1	m[1][0][0][0][0][0][0][0][0]
0x1ebbfce8	1	m[0][1][0][0][0][0][0][0][0]
0x1ebbfee8	2	m[1][1][0][0][0][0][0][0][0]
0x1ebbfc68	1	m[0][0][1][0][0][0][0][0][0]
0x1ebbfce6	7	m[0][0][1][1][1][1][1][1][1]
0x1ebbfee6	8	m[1][0][1][1][1][1][1][1][1]
0x1ebbfde6	8	m[0][1][1][1][1][1][1][1][1]
0x1ebbffe6	9	m[1][1][1][1][1][1][1][1][1]

Figure 4.32 Column major order representation of a 9x9 array in memory

4.10 MAPPINGS TO STORAGE

As with other data structures, there are several ways to represent arrays in memory. These representation schemes can be evaluated on the basis of four characteristics: (i) the simplicity of element access, (ii) ease of traversal along various paths, (iii) storage efficiency, and (iv) ease of growth. It is not possible to optimize all four of these factors simultaneously.

4.10.1 ONE-DIMENSIONAL ARRAYS

Lower Bound: One

Let us initially consider storage mappings for a one-dimensional array named **EMP_NO** with subscript lower bound 1 and subscript upper bound n. One way to store this array is so that the physical order of elements is the same as the logical order of elements. Storage for element **EMP_NO**[i + 1] will be adjacent to storage for element **EMP_NO**[i], for i = 1, . . . , n – 1. In order to calculate the starting address (i.e., the location) of element **EMP_NO**[i], it is necessary to know

1. The starting address of the storage space allocated to the array.
2. The size of each element in the array.

Denote by B the array's starting address also known as its base address. Assume that each element of the array occupies[w] bytes. Then the location of the ith element of the array is

$$B + [i - 1]*w \qquad ...(4.1)$$

Because[i+1] elements, each of size[w] is physically precede the ith element. The compiler needs to be able to determine element locations, they can be of use to a programmer using a memory dump to debug.

Let us now extend eq. 2-1 to find the location of the ith element of an array which has its subscript lower bound not equal to one. For instance, consider the array declared A1 [4: 10]. Taking a specific case, the starting address of A1[6] is B + [6 - 4] * w, because 6 - 4 (i.e., 2) elements precede A1[6]. For an array declared A2[-2:2], the location of A2[l] is B + [1 - [-2]] * w, because 1 - [- 2], or three, elements [A2[- 2], A2[-1], and A2[0]] precede A2[1]. In general, the element ARRAY[l] of the array defined as ARRAY [L: U] is at location

$$B + [i - L] * w \qquad (4.2)$$

This formula is correct whether the lower-bound L is positive, negative or zero.

4.10.2 MULTI-DIMENSIONAL ARRAYS

Row-major Order: Because computer memory is linear, a multi-dimensional array must be linearized as it is mapped to storage. One alternative for linearization is to store first the first row of the array, then the second row of the array, then the third row, and so forth. For example, the array defined by RATE [1 : 4][1: 6], which logically appears as shown in **Figure 4.33**, appears physically in row-major order as shown in **Figure 4.34**.

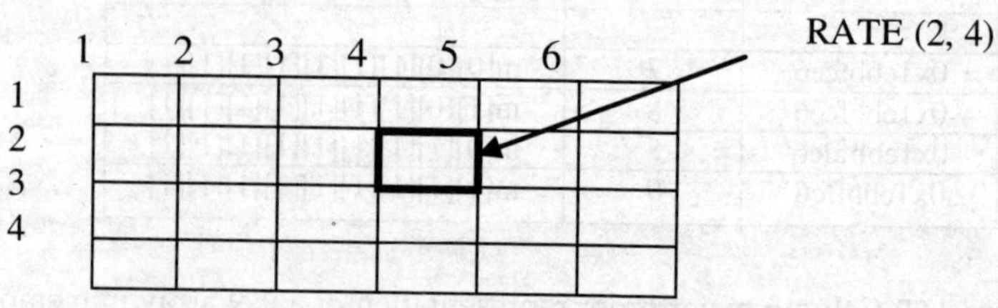

Figure 4.33 A two-dimensional array representation

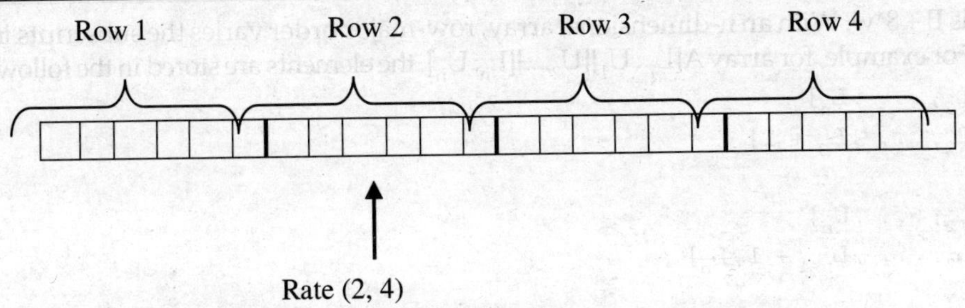

Figure 4.34 Array Figure 4.33 linearized in row-major order.

This is the storage-allocation scheme used for arrays declared in most implementations of Pascal, C, C++, and VC++. Assuming that B is the array's base address and that each element of the array is of size w, the starting address of the element RATE[i][j] is

```
B + (i - 1)*6*w + (j - 1)*w
```

because there are i - 1 rows, each of length 6 * w, which precede the row that element RATE[i][j] is in, and there are j - 1 elements, each of length w, which precede element RATE[i][j] in row i. Element RATE[2,4] is located at (B + 9*w). Generalizing, the element ARRAY[i][j] of array defined by ARRAY[L_1 :U_1][L_2: U_2] is at location:

$$B + (i - L_1)*(U_2 - L_2 + 1)*w + (j - L_2)*w \qquad ...(4.3)$$

because there are $i - L_1$ rows, each of length $(U_2 - L_2 + 1)*w$, which precede the row that element ARRAY[i][j] is in, and there are $j - L_2$ elements, each of length w, which precede element ARRAY[i][j] in row i. Illustrating this, the array defined by A[- 2: 2][4: 6] can be depicted logically as shown in **Figure 4.35**.

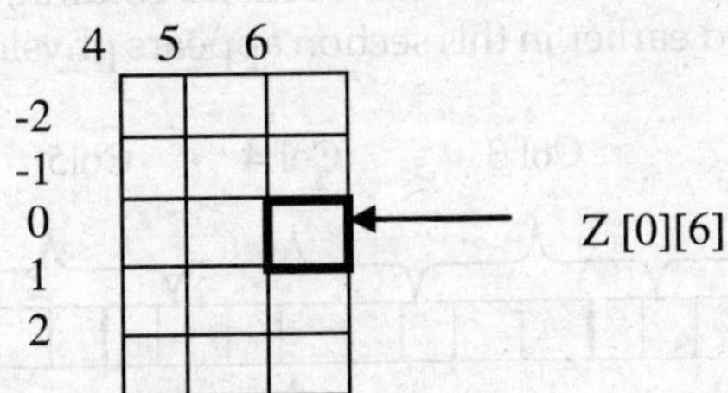

Figure 4.35 Two dimensional arrays

This array appears physically in row-major order as shown in **Figure 4.36**.

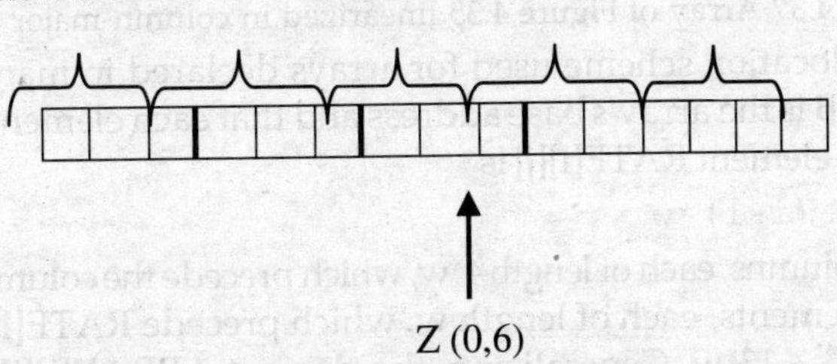

Figure 4.36 Array of Figure 4.35 linearized in row-major order.

There are two rows [row -2 and row -1], each of length 3 * w, preceding row 0. In row 0, there are 2 (i.e., 6 – 4) elements, each of length w, preceding element A[0][6], i.e., the starting location of A[0][,6] is

```
B + (0 - (-2))*(6 - 4 + 1)*w + (6 - 4)*w,
```

which is B + 8*w. With an n-dimensional array, row-major order varies the subscripts in right-to-Left order. For example, for array $A[L_1 : U_1][U_2,...][L_n: U_n]$, the elements are stored in the following order:

$A[L_1, L_2, ..., L_n]$
$A[L_1, L_2, ..., L_N + 1]$
...
$A[L_1, L_2, ..., U_n]$
$A[L_1, L_2, ..., L_{n-1} + 1, L_n]$
...
$A[L_1, L_2, ..., L_{n-1} + 1, U_n]$
...
$A[L_1, L_2, ..., L_{n-1}, U_n]$
...
$A[U_1, L_2, ..., L_{n-1}, L_n]$
$A[U_1, L_2, ..., L_{n-1}, L_n +$
...
$A[U_1, L_2, ..., U_{n-1}, U_n]$
...
$A[U_1, U_2, ..., U_n]$

Column-major Order

Another alternative for linearization of a two-dimensional array is to store the elements in column-major order, i.e., store first the first column, then the second column, then the third column, and so forth. The RATE array mentioned earlier in this section appears physically in column-major order as shown in **Figure 4.37**.

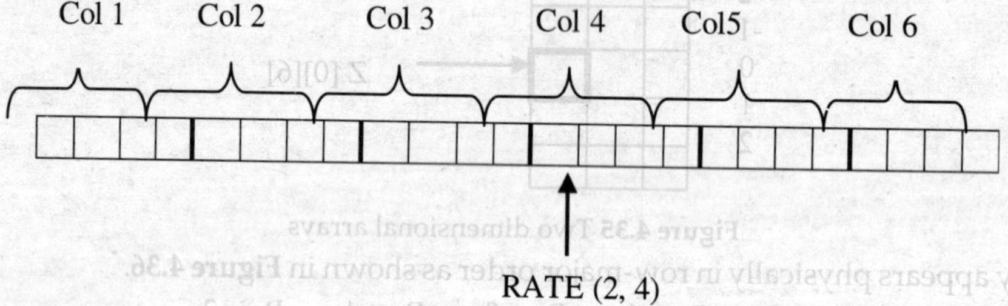

Figure 4.37 Array of Figure 4.35 linearized in column-major order.

This is the storage allocation scheme used for arrays declared in many implementations of C language. Assuming that B is the array's base address and that each element of the array is of size w, the starting address of the element RATE[i][j] is

```
B + (j - 1)*4*w + (i-1)*w
```

because there are j-1 columns, each of length 4*w, which precede the column that element RATE[i][j] is in, and there are i - 1 elements, each of length w, which precede RATE[i][j] in column j. Element RATE[2][4] is located at B + 13*w. Generalizing, the element ARRAY[i][j] of the array defined by $ARRAY[L: U_1][L_2: U_2]$, with column-major storage, is at location

$$B + (j - L_2)*(U_1 - L_1 + 1)*w + (i - L_1)*w \quad ...(4.4)$$

Compare this equation to eq. 4.3.

With an n-dimensional array, column-major order varies the subscripts in left-to--right order. For example, for array $A[L_1 : U_1][U_2, ...,][L_n : U_N]$, the elements are stored in the following order:

```
A[L1,L2,... ,Ln]
A[L1+1,L2,... ,Ln]
...
A[U1,L2,... ,Ln]
A[L1,L2+1,... ,Ln]
A[L1+1,L2+1,... ,Ln]
...
A[U1,L2+1,... ,Ln]
...
A[L1,L2,... ,Ln+1]
A[L1+1,L2,... ,Ln+1]
...
A[U1,L2,... ,Ln+1]
...
A[L1,L2,... ,Un]
...
A[L1,U2,... ,Un]
...
A[U1,U2,... ,Un]
```

In order to determine whether it is more advantageous to store an array in column-major order or in row-major order, it is necessary to know in what order the array elements are to be referenced. In fact, the available programming languages do not give the programmer a choice of array storage technique. Rather, especially in a virtual memory environment, the programmer should make a concerted effort to tailor the pattern of array element references to the storage pattern. For example, consider a procedure to calculate .the average value of the elements in a 50-by-225 array named A. With column-major storage, the following reference pattern should be used,

```
total = 0;
for (j = 1; j< 225 ; j++)
for (i = 1; i<50; i++)
total = total + a[i][j];
```

This algorithm adds all the elements of one column before proceeding to the next. On the other hand, with row-major storage, which is more common for C, the following reference pattern is preferable. The algorithm adds all the elements of one row before proceeding to the next.

```
total = 0;
for (i = 1; i<50; i++)

for (j = 1; j< 225 ; j++)
total = total + a[i][j];
```

When it is necessary to pass arrays between any language routines, it is extremely important that the programmer be aware of the combination of linearization techniques used.

4.11 TRIANGULAR ARRAYS

A triangular array may be either upper-triangular, as shown in **Figure 4.38**, or lower -triangular, as shown in **Figure 4.39**, where all elements below [or above] the diagonal are zero. An array is called strictly upper- (or lower) triangular if the elements of the diagonal are also zero.

$$\begin{pmatrix} x & x & x & x & x \\ 0 & x & x & x & x \\ 0 & 0 & x & x & x \\ 0 & 0 & 0 & x & x \\ 0 & 0 & 0 & 0 & x \\ 0 & 0 & 0 & 0 & 0 \end{pmatrix}$$

Figure 4.38 Upper-triangular array

$$\begin{pmatrix} 0 & 0 & 0 & 0 & 0 \\ x & 0 & 0 & 0 & 0 \\ x & x & 0 & 0 & 0 \\ x & x & x & 0 & 0 \\ x & x & x & x & 0 \\ x & x & x & x & x \end{pmatrix}$$

Figure 4.39 Lower-triangular array

In a lower-triangular array with n rows, the maximum number of nonzero elements in the ith row is[i]. The total number of nonzero elements thus is no more than $\sum_{i=1}^{n} i = \frac{n(n+1)}{2}$. This expression is also true for an upper-triangular array with n rows. For large[n] , it would be desirable not to have to store all of the array's zero-valued elements.

4.11.1 Linearization

One approach to this problem is to linearize the array and store only the elements of the nonzero triangular portion. Let us store the upper-triangular array T by rows in a one-dimensional array named S with subscript bounds 1 through $\frac{n(n+1)}{2}$. Element T[1][1l] is stored as element S[1],element T[1][2] is stored as element S[2], and so forth up to element T[1][n] which is stored as element S[n]. Then element T[2][2] is stored as S[n+1], because T[2][1] is zero. Element T[n][n] is stored as S[n(n+1)/n]. In general, where in S is T[i][j] stored? Note that $i \le j$ for all elements in the nonzero part of T.

4.11.2 Sharing Space

Sometimes a program requires the use of more than one triangular array. If two of these arrays are of essentially the same dimensions, then it is a relatively straightforward task to store them in a manner that conserves space. Assume that array A is upper-triangular and n by n, and that array B is lower-triangular and n - 1 by n - 1. Then A and B can be stored together in an n-by-n array C. Elements C[i][j]] where $i > j$ are elements of A, and elements C[i][j] where $i > j$ are elements of B. In fact, element A[i][j] is stored as C[i][j] for $i \le j$, and element B[i][j] is stored as C[i + 1][j] for $i \ge j$.

Let array A be upper-triangular, let array B be lower-triangular, and let both be N by n. Then array C must be n by n+1 in order to contain both A and B. Here element A[i][j] is stored as C[i][j+1] for $i \le j$ and B[i][j] is stored as C[i][j] for $i \ge j$.

Consider now the case in which two upper-triangular arrays, say A and AA, both of which are n by n, are to share the same array space. One approach is to transpose one of the triangular arrays, say AA, such that instead of being upper-triangular, it appears to be lower-triangular i.e., array AA is transposed to form array AA^T, and element AA[i][j] becomes element AA^T[j][i]. Then A and AA^T can be stored together in an array C with dimension n-by-[n + 1] as shown in the preceding paragraph. Element A[i][j] is stored as C[1][j + 1], and element AA[i][j] is stored as C[j][i].

One problem with all of these linearization techniques arises when elements are made nonzero in the lower part of an upper-triangular array. The array then is no longer upper triangular. If it shares the space of a square array with a lower-triangular array, there will be an obvious conflict. One solution is to not allow an upper-triangular array to be updated if that would cause the array no longer to be upper-triangular. Another approach is to recognize the change in array characteristics and move it to its own space.

4.12 SPARSE ARRAYS

Another special type of array which arises commonly in applications is a sparse array. It is actually difficult to draw the dividing line between those arrays that are sparse and those that are not; loosely, an array is called sparse if it has a relatively high density of zero elements. For instance, the array in **Figure 4.40**, which has 8 nonzero elements out of 80, is sparse; it is 90% zero.

$$\begin{pmatrix} 0 & 0 & 0 & 0 & 1 & 0 & 0 & 2 & 0 & 0 \\ 0 & 1 & 0 & 0 & 0 & 0 & 0 & 0 & 0 & 0 \\ 1 & 0 & 0 & 0 & 0 & 0 & 0 & 0 & 0 & 0 \\ 0 & 0 & 0 & 0 & 0 & 0 & 0 & 0 & 0 & 0 \\ 0 & 0 & 0 & 4 & 0 & 0 & 0 & 0 & 0 & 0 \\ 0 & 0 & 0 & 0 & 0 & 0 & 0 & 2 & 0 & 0 \\ 0 & 0 & 0 & 0 & 0 & 0 & 0 & 0 & 0 & 0 \\ 2 & 1 & 0 & 0 & 0 & 0 & 0 & 0 & 0 & 0 \end{pmatrix}$$

Figure 4.40 Sparse array

4.12.1 Vector Representation

Each nonzero element in a two-dimensional sparse array can be represented as a triple with the format [row-subscript, column-subscript, value]. These triples then can be ordered by increasing row-subscript major and column-subscript minor, and can be stored as a vector. For example, using this approach, the 8-by-10 sparse array shown in **Figure 4.40** is represented by vector V, shown in **Figure 4.41**.

	row	column	value
V[1]:	1,	5,	1
V[2]:	1,	8,	2
V[3]:	2,	2,	1
V[4]:	3,	1,	1
V[5]:	5,	4,	4
V[6]:	6,	S,	2
V[7]:	8,	1,	2
V[8]:	8,	2,	1

Figure 4.41 Vector representation of the sparse array of **Figure 4.40**

This storage mapping uses more space to represent any particular nonzero element but avoids representing the zero elements. If the sparse array were one-dimensional, each nonzero element would be represented by a pair. In general, each nonzero element of an n-dimensional array is represented by an entry with n + 1 values.

Operations on the vector representation of the two-decimal sparse array must use the row and column information to determine where each value resides. One inconvenience with this form of representation is handling addition of nonzero elements to the array or changing previously nonzero elements to have zero value. The problem is not in changing the element's value, but in maintaining the order of nonzero elements in the representation vector. For example, if the above array were updated so that the element with subscripts [1][8] were to have value zero, then vector elements V[3] through V[8] should be shifted to become elements V[2] through V[7]. Similarly, if the element with subscripts [4][6] were to be updated to have value 9, then vector elements V[5] through V[8] would need to be shifted to become elements V[6] through V[9] and V[5] would be the triple [4][6][9].

4.12.2 Sparse Matrices

Matrices with a relatively high proportion of zero entries are called sparse matrices. Two general types of n-square sparse matrices, which occur in various applications, are shown in **Figure 4.42**. The second matrix where all entries above the main diagonal are zero or equivalently where nonzero entries can only occur on or below the main diagonal is called a lower triangular matrix. The first matrix where nonzero entries can only occur on the diagonal or on elements immediately above or below the diagonal is called a tri-diagonal matrix. The natural method of representing matrices in memory as two-dimensional arrays may not be suitable for sparse matrices. That is, one may save space by storing only those entries, which may be nonzero. This can be explained with the help of suitable example, consider the matrix given below:

M [6][7] =

0	0	6	0	9	0	0
2	0	0	7	8	0	4
10	0	0	0	0	0	0
0	0	12	0	0	0	0
0	0	0	0	0	0	0
0	0	0	3	0	0	5

of the 42 elements in this 6x7 matrix only 10 are nonzero. These are
M[1][3] = 6, M[1][5] = 9, M[2][1] = 2, M[2][4] = 7, M[2][5] = 8, M[2][7] = 4
M[3][1] = 10, M[4][3] = 12, M[6][4] = 3, M[6][7] = 5

4	-3					
5	-5	6				
	0	6	-9			
		-4	3	-7		
			2	-8	0	
				5	-7	9
					8	10

(a) Tri-diagonal matrix

4						
3	-5					
1	0	6				
-7	8	-4	3			
5	-5	0	2	-8		
1	4	-9	-8	0	-7	
6	-8	4	-56	1	8	10

(b) Triangular matrix

Figure 4.42 Sparse matrices

One of the basic methods for storing such a sparse matrix is to store nonzero elements in a one-dimensional array and to identify each array element with row and column indices as shown in **Figure 4.43**. The ith element of vector **V** is the matrix element with row and column indices **Row[i]** and **Col[i]**. Note that the matrix elements are stored in row major order with zero elements removed. A more efficient representation in terms of storage requirements and access time to the rows of the matrix is shown in **Figure 4.44**. The Row vector is changed so that its ith element is the index to the first of the column indices for the element in row **i** of the matrix. We assume that the **Row** and **Col** vectors consist of half words. The representations of matrix **M** in **Figure 4.43** and **Figure 4.44** have cut storage requirements by more than one half. For large matrices the conservation of storage is very significant.

Index	Row	Col	V
1	1	3	6
2	1	5	9
3	2	1	2
4	2	4	7
5	2	5	8
6	2	7	4
7	3	1	10
8	4	3	12
9	6	4	3
10	6	7	5

Figure 4.43 Sequential representation of sparse matrix

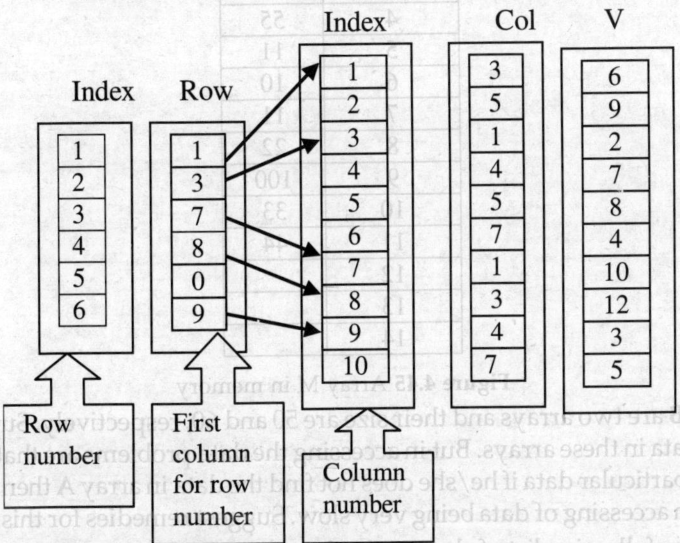

Figure 4.44 Sequential representation of sparse matrix

The sequential allocation scheme for sparse matrices is also of value, in that matrix operations can be executed faster than possible with a conventional two-dimensional array representation, particularly when matrices are large. A general algorithm for adding two sparse matrices is as follows:

1. Repeat through step 8 until all rows have been processed
2. Obtain current row indices for matrix **M** and **N**
3. Obtain starting position in vectors of next row in matrix **M** and **N**
4. Repeat through step 6 until either the end of matrix **M**'s or **N**'s row is reached
5. If elements exist in the same column in matrix **M** and **N** then sum elements and move on the next column in matrix **M** and **N** else if matrix **M** column number is less than matrix **N**'s column number then move on to the next column in matrix M else move on to next column of matrix **N**

6. Add new element to matrix **R**
7. If the end of matrix **M**'s row has not been reached then add remaining elements in row to matrix **R**
8. If the end of matrix **N**'s row has not been reached then add remaining elements in row to matrix **R**

FOR SUMMATIVE AND FORMATIVE ASSESSMENT

4.1 Suppose we have an array **M** as illustrated in **Figure 4.45.** If one deletes 11 and insert 22 at place of 11 then find the number of moves performed to complete operations. If final array required in sorted order then how many moves are required to complete the insertion and deletion operations.

INDEX	INFO
0	99
1	88
2	77
3	66
4	55
5	11
6	10
7	11
8	22
9	100
10	33
11	44
12	
13	
14	

Figure 4.45 Array M in memory

4.2 Let **A** and **B** are two arrays and their size are 50 and 60, respectively. Suppose one wants to keep 100 data in these arrays. But in accessing the data problems are that when one makes a search for particular data if he/she does not find the data in array **A** then goes into array **B** in this fashion accessing of data being very slow. Suggest remedies for this problem.

4.3 Consider the following list of elements and generate PASCAL triangle.
LIST: 0, 1, 2, 3, 4, 5, 6, 7, 8, 9, 10, 15, 20, 21, 28, 35, 36, 56, 70, 84, 126.

4.4 Suppose one wants to create students record of a class with following information:
- Name
- Father's name
- Branch
- Class
- Roll number
- Enrollment number

How will one maintain records of 20 students with the help of arrays?

4.5 Evaluate the following polynomial with the help of ***Horner's*** method.

$$P(x) = a_1x^n + a_2x^{n-1} + a_3x^{n-2} + \dots + a_{n+1}.$$

4.6 Write an algorithm to concatenate two arrays **A** and **B**. Implement the designed algorithm.

4.7 Find inverse of the following matrices:

(a) $A = \begin{pmatrix} 1 & 2 & 3 \\ 2 & 4 & 7 \\ 3 & 6 & 10 \end{pmatrix}$ (b) $A = \begin{pmatrix} 1 & 2 & 1 \\ 1 & 0 & 2 \\ 2 & 1 & -3 \end{pmatrix}$

4.8 Consider the matrix

$$A = \begin{pmatrix} 1 & 2 & 3 & 4 & 5 & 6 & 7 \\ 8 & 9 & 10 & 11 & 12 & 13 & 14 \\ 15 & 16 & 17 & 18 & 19 & 20 & 21 \end{pmatrix}$$

Write a program that finds upper and lower half of the matrix.

4.9 An input alphabet consists of the following twenty nine symbols:
ZERO, ONE, TWO, THREE, FOUR, FIVE, SIX, SEVEN, EIGHT, NINE, TEN, ELEVEN, TWELVE, THIRTEEN, FOURTEEN, FIFTEEN, SIXTEEN, SEVENTEEN, EIGHTEEN, NINTEEN, TWENTY, THIRTY, FORTY, FIFTY, SIXTY, SEVENTY, EIGHTY, NINETY, HUNDRED.
Write an algorithm that accepts as input the English language representation for example "**ONE HUNDRED THIRTY**" of any number from 0 to 999 and outputs the equivalent decimal number (130 in this case). Implement the designed algorithm.

4.10 What do you understand trace of a matrix? Design an algorithm.

4.11 A dynamic declared array **A** is defined with row subscripts varying from **0** to **n-1** and column subscripts varying from 0 to 5. Show the storage mapping function to map **A** into memory assuming row-major order storage.

4.12 How to find the missing number in integer array of 1 to 100? Write a program to find it.

4.13 Assume that 8-byte of storage are required to hold each element of the following **A** array:
int A[10][18];
Assuming further that storage for the array begins at byte 4000 in memory, show the actual address of the element values **A [8][4]**.

4.14 Consider the three-dimensional array **D** whose subscript limits are
$1 \le i \le 3, 1 \le j \le 3, 0 \le k \le 1$
Give the addressing function for the element **D[i][j][k]** where the storage representation is in column major order.

4.15 Consider the linear array **A[5:100]**, **B[-5:20]** and **C[20]**
(i) Find the number of elements in each array.
(ii) Suppose **base(A) = 0x800** and **w = 4** per words per memory cell for **A**. Find the address of **A[10]** and **A[85]**

4.16 Suppose a company keeps a linear array **year[1940:1985]** such that **year[k]** contains the number of employees born in year **k**. Write a function for each of the following tasks:
(i) Find years in which no employee was born.
(ii) To find the number of employees who will be at least **L** year old at the end of the year. Read the systems date for the current date; take care of **Y2K** problem.

4.17 Consider the alphabetized linear arrays List in **Figure 4.46**.
   (i) Find the number of elements that must be moved if Scotch, David and Sanath are inserted into List at the three different times.
   (ii) How many elements are moved if three names are inserted at the same time?
   (iii) How does the Telephone Company handle insertions in a telephone directory?
   (iv) Write a function for each of the above tasks.

4.18 Let **M** is a **n x n** matrix. Write a function which finds
   (i) The number of zero elements in **M**
   (ii) The summation of the diagonal elements
   (iii) The products of the diagonal elements

4.19 How to find repeated numbers in an array if it contains multiple duplicate? Write an algorithm for the same and implement it.

4.20 An array contains 100 integers number. Write a module which
   (i) Finds all pairs of elements whose sum is 50.
   (ii) Finds even and odd, +ve and –ve numbers.

Index	Name
1	Ajay Jadeja
2	Anil Kumble
3	Chndra Shekhar
4	Donald
5	Edwords
6	Gopal
7	Hunter
8	Imran
9	Klein
10	Lewis
11	More
12	Richards
13	Sachin
14	Vinod Kambli

Figure 4.46 List in memory

Quiz-3(Arrays)

1. Which of the following data structure is linear type?
   (a) Array (b) Tree
   (c) Graphs (d) Hierarchy
2. The logical or mathematical model of a particular organization of data is called a ....
   (a) Data structure (b) Data arrangement
   (c) Data configuration (d) Data formation
3. Linear arrays are also called ....
   (a) Straight line array (b) One-dimensional array
   (c) Vertical array (d) Horizontal array

4. Arrays are best data structures ....
   (a) For relatively permanent collections of dat(a)
   (b) For the size of the structure and the data in the structure are constantly changing
   (c) For both of above situation
   (d) For none of the above
5. Which of the following data structures are indexed structures?
   (a) Linear arrays (b) Linked lists
   (c) Graphs (d) Trees
6. A .... does not keep track of address of every element in the list.
   (a) Stack (b) String
   (c) Linear array (d) Queue
7. The memory address of the first element of an array is called
   (a) floor address (b) foundation address
   (c) first address (d) base address
8. The memory address of fifth element of an array can be calculated by the formula
   (a) LOC(Array[5]=Base(Array)+w(5-lower bound), where w is the number of words per memory cell for the array
   (b) LOC(Array[5])=Base(Array[5])+(5-lower bound), where w is the number of words per memory cell for the array
   (c) LOC(Array[5])=Base(Array[4])+(5-Upper bound), where w is the number of words per memory cell for the array
   (d) None of above
9. Two dimensional arrays are also called
   (a) tables arrays (b) matrix arrays
   (c) both of above (d) none of above
10. Which of the following data structure can't store the non-homogeneous data elements?
    (a) Arrays (b) Records
    (c) Pointers (d) None
11. Each array declaration need not give, implicitly or explicitly, the information about
    (a) the name of array
    (b) the data type of array
    (c) the first data from the set to be stored
    (d) the index set of the array
12. The elements of an array are stored successively in memory cells because
    (a) by this way computer can keep track only the address of the first element and the addresses of other elements can be calculated
    (b) the architecture of computer memory does not allow arrays to store other than serially
    (c) both of above
    (d) none of above

13. The complexity of the average case of an algorithm is
    (a) Much more complicated to analyze than that of worst case
    (b) Much simpler to analyze than that of worst case
    (c) Sometimes more complicated and some other times simpler than that of worst case
    (d) None or above
14. Comment on the following statement:
    int (*a)[7];
    (a) An array "a" of pointers.
    (b) A pointer "a" to an array.
    (c) A ragged array.
    (d) None of the mentioned
15. Comment on the 2 arrays regarding P and Q:
    int *a1[8];
    int *(a3[8]);
    P. Array of pointers
    Q. Pointer to an array
    (a) a1 is P, a2 is Q
    (b) a1 is P, a2 is P
    (c) a1 is Q, a2 is P
    (d) a1 is Q, a2 is Q

❑

CHAPTER

5 Linked List

In this chapter we will discuss linear data structure linked list. We will consider simple linked, doubly linked, header and circular header linked. Finally we will conclude this chapter with an application of simple linked list, i.e., polynomial implementation. If we use fixed length memory storage (arrays) it is not always possible to perform above tasks. A linked list allocation storage method can result in efficient use of computer memory and time. Linked list is useful because:

- **Unpredictable storage requirements**: The exact amount of data storage space required by a program in these areas often depends on the data being processed and consequently this requirement cannot be easily determined at the time of writing a program.
- **Extensive manipulation of the stored data**: Programs in these areas require the operations such as insertion and deletion to perform frequent operations on the data.

5.1 LINKED LIST

A linked list is defined as a collection of nodes. Each node has two parts:

- Information
- Pointer to next node

Information part may consist of one or more than one fields. In other words a linked list consists of series of structures, which are not necessarily contiguous. Each structure contains one or more than one contiguous information fields and a pointer to a structure containing its successor. The last node of the list contains **NULL ('\0' or 0)** in the pointer field. The pointer contains the address of the location where next information is stored. For example, **Figure 5.1** illustrates a linked list structure with 5 nodes, each node is containing one information field. A linked list also contains a list pointer variable called **start,** which contains the address of the first node in the list. Hence, there is an arrow drawn from **start** to the first node in the linked list. If there is no node in the list, it is called **NULL** list or empty list.

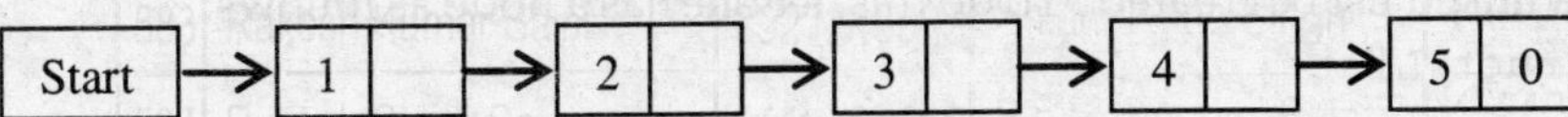

Figure 5.1 Linked list

To create a linked list, the following steps are required:

(a) Declare the structure that defines the list entries.

(b) Declare the variables **start** and ***ptr (or *start** and ***ptr)**

(c) Assign **next [start] = NULL** when start is declared without pointer operator (or **start = NULL** if **start** is declared as ***start**) to signify an empty list.

(d) Find each list entry

 (i) Find end of the list so that **next [ptr]** (it represents the address of the next node pointed to by ptr) is **NULL.**

 (ii) Allocate memory for the new entry by assigning it to **next [ptr]**.

(iii) Assign node the value of **next[ptr]**.

(iv) Assign the information member values to node.

(v) Assign **next[ptr]** the value **NULL** to indicate the end of the list.

We have discussed that a linked list is a collection of the nodes (structure) of the same type and hence it can be defined as:

```
struct Node
{
        Data type Information;
        struct Node *Next ;
} start;
```

The above definition of the structure (Node) is equivalent to the following figure:

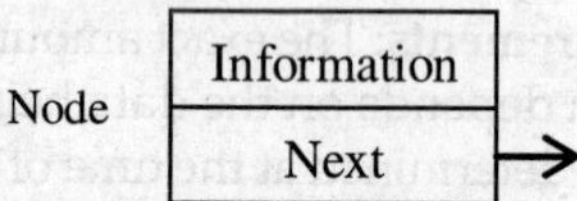

A node may contain any number of information fields. The general declaration of a node is:

```
struct Tag Name
   {
        Data Type1 Field1 ;
        Data Type2 Field2 ;
        Data Type3 Field3 ;
       ...
        Data Type n Field n ;
        struct Tag Name *Next ;
   };
```

The above syntax may be represented as:

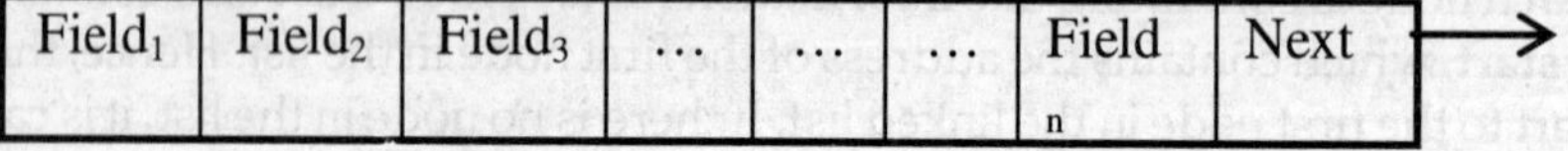

How can a linked list be created? To do this, let one has a node as follows:

```
struct List
{
        char Data ;
        struct List *Next ;
};
```

Let one wants to create a linked list that contains four nodes, the nodes are **Node$_1$**, **Node$_2$**, **Node$_3$** and **Node$_4$**. These nodes are defined as

```
struct List node1, node2, node3, node4;
```

Figure 5.2 illustrates the allocation of memory spaces to the nodes **Node$_1$**, **Node$_2$**, **Node$_3$** and **Node$_4$**.

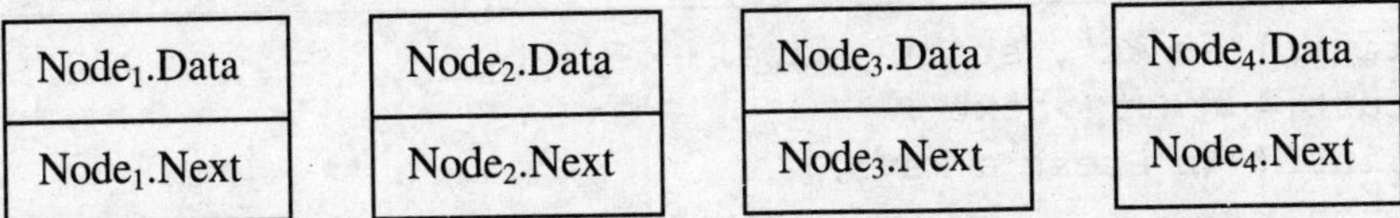

Figure 5.2 Allocation of memory space to individual node

If one wants to create a link between these four nodes, the following arrangement is required.

- $Node_1$.Next = &$Node_2$;
  Assign the address of the **$Node_2$** to **$Node_1$.Next**, which establishes a link between **$Node_1$** and **$Node_2$**
- $Node_2$.Next = &$Node_3$;
  Assign the address of the **$Node_3$** to **$Node_2$.Next**, which establishes a link between **$Node_2$** and **$Node_3$**
- $Node_3$.Next = &$Node_4$;
  Assign the address of the **$Node_4$** to **$Node_3$.Next,** which establishes a link between **$Node_3$** and **$Node_4$**.

By repeating the above process, one can create a linked list of desired size. Example 5.1 demonstrates simple linked list code.

Example 5.1: Write C code which creates a simple linked list.

Answer: The program segment **LINK.C** implements the above discussion.

```
/* LINK.C */
/* This program segment defines linked list having a character type node */
# include<stdio.h>
# include<malloc.h>
  struct List
  {
          char data ;
          struct List *next ;
  } ;

  typedef  struct List Linked;
  void main()
  {
      Linked *start, node1, node2 , node3 , node4;
      int i ;
      start = (struct List *) malloc(sizeof(Linked));
      start = &node1;
      node1.data = 'A' ;
      node1.next = &node2;
      node2.data = 'B' ;
      node2.next = &node3;
      node3.data = 'C' ;
      node3.next = &node4;
      node4.data = 'D' ;
  for( i = 0 ; i < 4 ; i++ ){
```

```
        printf("\n %c", start->data);
        start = start->next ;
        printf("\n Press a key");
        getchar() ;
    }
}
```

The program segment **LINK.C** illustrates that four nodes exist in the memory as illustrated in **Figure 5.3.**

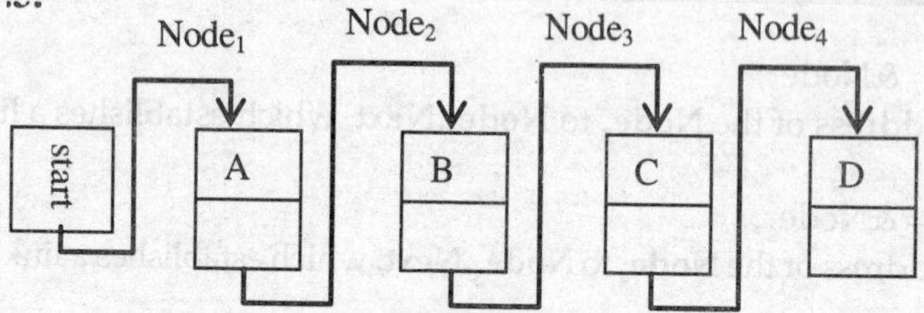

Figure 5.3 Existence of nodes in memory

If one wants to create a linked list of desired size, one can does the same using algorithm shown in Figure 5.4. Example 5.2 implements this algorithm.

```
Step 1: [Initially list is empty]
   Start = NULL
Step 2: [Allocate space to newly created node]
Node = Create a node
Step 3: [Assign address of first node to start variable]
   Start =Node
Step 4: [Assign value to the information part of the node]
   Info [Node] = Data
Step 5: [Allocate space to newly created node]
Next[ Node]= Create a node
Step 6: Repeat thru Step 4 till the desired number of nodes.
Step 7: [Assign NULL to the address part for signaling end of the list]
   Next [Node] = NULL
Step 8: [Return the created node]
   Return (Start)
```

Figure 5.4 Linked list creation algorithm

Example 5.2: Write C code to create a linked of any size.

Answer: Following program segment (LINK_C.C) implements algorithms defines above. Run this program segment and see the way it is executing the implementation.

```
/* CREATING SIMPLE LINKED LIST */
/* LINK_C.C */
#include <stdio.h>
#include <malloc.h>

struct link_list
{
```

```
    int data;
    struct link_list *next;
  };
  typedef struct  link_list node;
  node *start;
  int num;

  void  create(node *);
  void  display(node *);
  /* Function main */
  void main()
  {
    /* Assign memory to single(struct) type variables */
    start = (node *) malloc(sizeof(node));
    create(start);
    printf("\n created list is as follows:\n");
    display(start);
    getch();
  }

  /* function create */
  void create(node *ptr)
  {
    char ch;

    num = 0;
    printf("\n Enter E for Exit any other key to continue: ");
    ch = getchar();
    if(ch=='e'){
    free(ptr);
    exit(0);
    }
    do{
       printf("\n Input the values of the node : %d: ", (num+1));
       scanf("%d", &ptr->data);
       fflush(stdin);
       printf("\n want to continue(y/n)->: ");
       ch = getchar();
       if(ch=='y')
       {
          ptr->next = (node *) malloc(sizeof(node));
          ptr = ptr->next;
       }
       num ++;
     }while(ch=='y');
```

```
    ptr->next=NULL;
    printf("\n Total nodes = %d", num);
}

/* function display */
void display(node *ptr)
{
    while (ptr!=NULL)
    {
        printf(" %d",  ptr->data);
        ptr = ptr->next;
    }
}
```

5.2 TRAVERSING A LINKED LIST

It is a methodology in which each node is processed exactly once. When a list is stored in computer memory as a linked list, our aim is to traverse the list starting from the first node to the end of the list. Consider a pointer type variable **Current_node** that points to the node currently being processed. Accordingly, **Next[Current_node]** points to the next node that is to be processed as shown in Figure 5.5. Thus, the statement

```
Current_node = Next [Current_node];
```

moves the pointer to the next node in the list.

The steps involved in the processing of linked list nodes are shown in **Figure 5.6**. The variable **start** points to the first entry in the list. The code **ptr = strart** assigns the address of the first entry to **ptr**. Likewise, as we will recall, the end of the list is indicated by **NULL**; the loop simply tests the current value of **ptr** to see if it is **NULL**. If **ptr** is not **NULL**, the loop displays the entry's value and assigns **ptr** the address of the next list entry. Suppose we have a list that contains **9** elements (integer) numbers: 11, 22, 33, 44, 55, 66, 77, 88, 99. The links of each element are shown in **Figure 5.7.** When we apply the steps of algorithm shown in Figure 5.6 for processing each element in list, we see the following operations.

Current_node = 2 and start = 2

Info [2] = 11 Next [2] = 5
Info [5] = 55 Next [5] = 6
Info [6] = 44 Next [6] = 12
Info [12] = 80 Next [12] = 1
Info [1] = 22 Next [1] = 9
Info [9] = 33 Next [9] = 4
Info [4] = 66 Next [4] = 8
Info [8] = 99 Next [8] = 7
Info [7] = 88 Next [7] = '\0'

Thus, the processed list is: 11, 55, 44, 80, 22, 33, 66, 99, 88. Implementation of the above discussion is shown in Example 5.3.

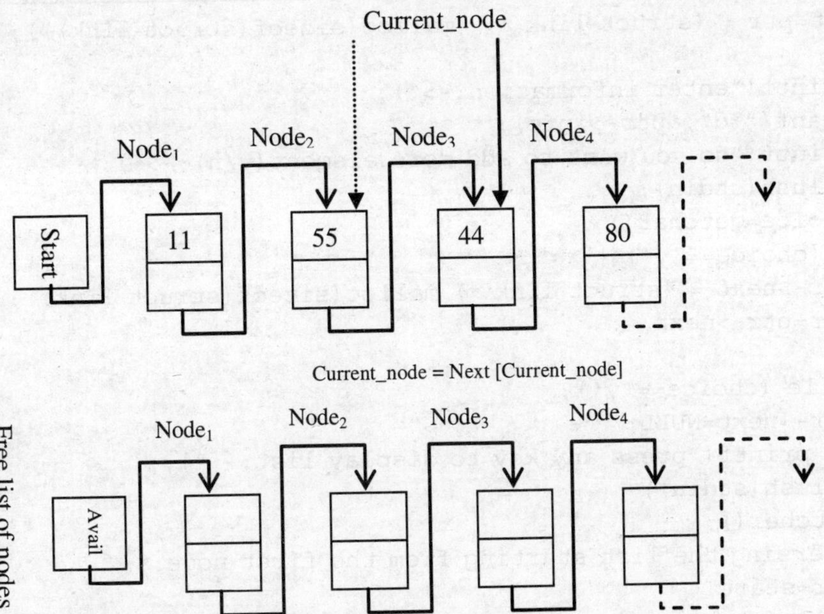

Figure 5.5 Traversing a linked list

```
Step 1: [Initialize pointer variable current_node]
   Current_node = start
Step 2: [Perform the traversing operation]
   Repeat thru Step 3 while Current_node ≠ NULL
   Process  Info [Current_node]
Step 3: [Move pointer to next node]
   Current_node = Next [Current_node]
Step 4: Exit
```

Figure 5.6 Algorithm to traverse each node in a linked list

Example 5.3: Write C code to process every node in a linked list.

Answer: See the following program segment.

```
/* TRVERSE.C */

#include <stdio.h>
#include <malloc.h>
struct link{
int info;
struct link *next;
} *start, *ptr;

void main(void){
   char choice;
   start = NULL; /* Empty list */
   ptr = start;     /* Point to the start of the list */
```

```
start=ptr = (struct link *) (malloc(sizeof(struct link)));
do{
  printf("enter information:->");
  scanf("%d",&ptr->info);
  printf("do you want to add more element(y/n):->");
  fflush(stdin);
  choice=getchar();
  if(choice=='y'){
  ptr->next = (struct link *) malloc(sizeof(struct link));
  ptr=ptr->next;
  }
 }while (choice=='y');
  ptr->next=NULL;
     printf("press any key to display list:->");
  fflush(stdin);
  getchar();
/* Traversing the list starting from the first node.*/
  ptr=start;
  while(ptr){
 printf("\n %d", ptr->info);
 ptr = ptr->next;
 }
 getchar();
}
```

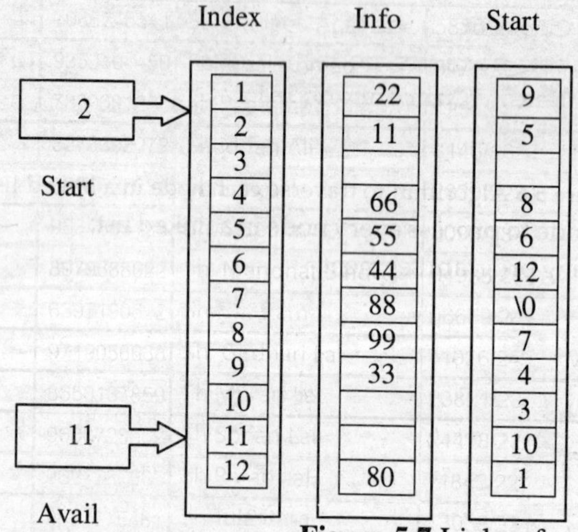

Figure 5.7 Links of nodes

5.3 INSERTION IN A LINKED LIST

There are many applications where it is desirable to maintain an ordered linear list. The ordering may be in increasing or decreasing order of the information field. Such an ordering often results more efficient processes in many cases. If one wants to insert some information into a linked list, following points must be remembered before performing the required operation:

1. Create a new node or remove a node from the availability stack or free memory space.
2. Setting the field of the new node means allocating required memory space to newly created node.
3. If the linked list is empty, return the address of a new node.
4. If the node precedes all others in the list, insert the node at front of the list and return its address.
5. Repeat thru Step 6 while information contents of the new node.
6. Obtain the next node in the linked list.
7. Insert the new node in the linked list and return address of its first node.

Suppose we have a list as illustrated in **Figure 5.5** and want to perform insertion operation on the list. The insertion operations which are possible on this list are classified into the following three categories:

- Insert as a first node
- Insert as a last node
- Insert as a node at any place in a list

5.3.1 Insertion as a First Node

Let the **start** pointer hold the address of the first node. If we want to insert new1 node into the list as a first node then **next[new$_1$]** variable holds the address of the first node of the list (previously existing). If **Figure 5.5** illustrates a list before insertion operation then after insertion the list becomes as shown in **Figure 5.8.**

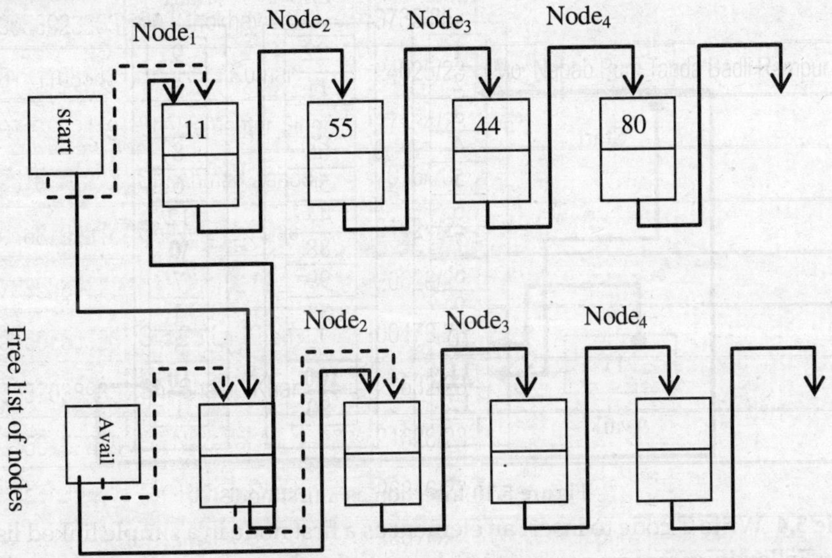

Figure 5.8 Insertion as a first node

The above discussion can be summarized in the form of an algorithm which is shown in Figure 5.9.

For example, consider the list shown in **Figure 5.7.** Then after inserting 100 in this list as a first node, the list is as illustrated in **Figure 5.10.** In the C language, in the statement form above discussion can be written as:

ptr = start; /* receive address of the first node in the list */
new1 = (struct link) **malloc (sizeof (struct link));** /* create a node */

/* assign address of the previously first node to the next of the new1 */
new1->next = ptr;
new1->data = some_value;
start = new1; /* assign address of the new1 to node to start pointer */
Go through the Example 5.4 which is implementing the above statements.

```
Step 1: [Allocate free space]
   New1= Create new node
Step 2: [Check for free space]
If New1= NULL output "OVERFLOW" and Exit
Step 3: [Read value of information part of a new node]
   Info [New1] = Value
Step 4: [Link address part of the currently created node with the address
of start]
   Next [New1] = Start
Step 5: [Now assign address of newly created node to the start]
   Start = New1
Step 6: Exit
```

Figure 5.9 Algorithm to insert a node at the begging of a list

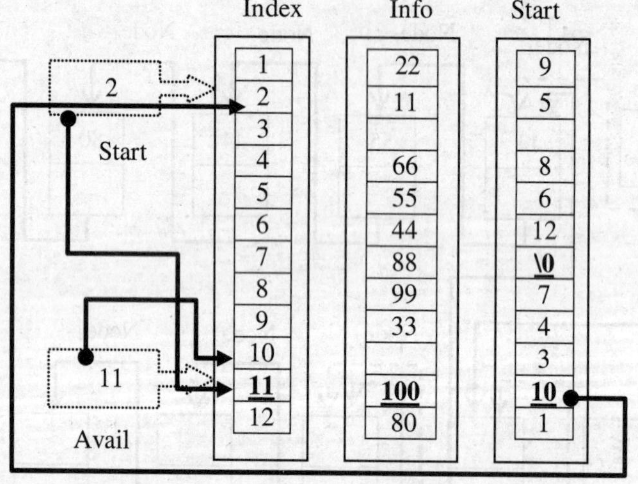

Figure 5.10 Insertion as a first node

Example 5.4: Write C code to insert an element as a first node in a simple linked list.
Answer: Following program segment implements the above discussion.

```
/* INSERT A NODE INTO A SIMPLE LINKED LIST AT THE BEGINNING */
/* LINK_IF.C */
# include <stdio.h>
# include <malloc.h>
```

```
struct link_list
{
   int info;
   struct link_list *next;
};
typedef struct link_list node;
int i,num;
node *start;
void insert(node *);
void create(node *);
void display(node *);

/* Function main */
void main()
{
   start = (node *) malloc(sizeof(node));
   create(start);
   display(start);
   insert(start);
   display(start);
   getch();
}
/* Function create a linked list */
void create(node *ptr)
{
   char ch;
   num = 0;
   printf("\n Enter E for Exit any other key to continue: ");
   ch = getchar();
   if(ch=='e'){
   free(ptr);
   exit(0);
   }
   do{
      printf("\n Input the values of the node : %d: ", (num+1));
      scanf("%d", &ptr->info);
      fflush(stdin);
      printf("\n want to continue(y/n)->: ");
      ch = getchar();
      if(ch=='y')
      {
      ptr->next = (node *) malloc(sizeof(node));
      ptr = ptr->next;
      }
      num ++;
```

```
    }while(ch=='y');
    ptr->next=NULL;
    printf("\n Total nodes = %d", num);
}

/* function display */
void display(node *ptr)
{
    while (ptr!=NULL)
    {
        printf("\n %d",  ptr->info);
        ptr = ptr->next;
    }
}

/* Inserting a node */
void insert (node *ptr)
{
    node *new1;
    new1 = (node *) malloc(sizeof(node));
    printf("\n Enter element you want to insert :");
    scanf("%d", &new1->info);
    if ( start == NULL)  /* check for empty list */
    {
        new1->next=NULL;
        start=new1;
    }else{
        new1->next=start;
        start=new1;
    }
}
```

5.3.2 Insertion As A Last Node

The easiest way to add an entry is to append it at the end of the list. To append an item to a linked list, we loop through the list until find the element whose next member points to **NULL**. The code segment, which is used to perform this task, is:

```
ptr = start;
while (ptr->next)
    ptr = ptr->next;
```

When **ptr->next** points to **NULL**, it gives the end of the list. So we can allocate memory for the entry as given below:

```
ptr->next = malloc(required size);
```

Next we assign the desired entry values and assign the new entry's next field to point to **NULL**.

```
ptr = ptr->next;
ptr->member = some_value;
ptr->next = NULL;
```

If **Figure 5.5** illustrates a list before insertion operation then the list after inserting a node at the end of the list, it becomes as illustrated in **Figure 5.11.** The step involved to insert any information (node) in a list at its end is shown in **Figure 5.12**.

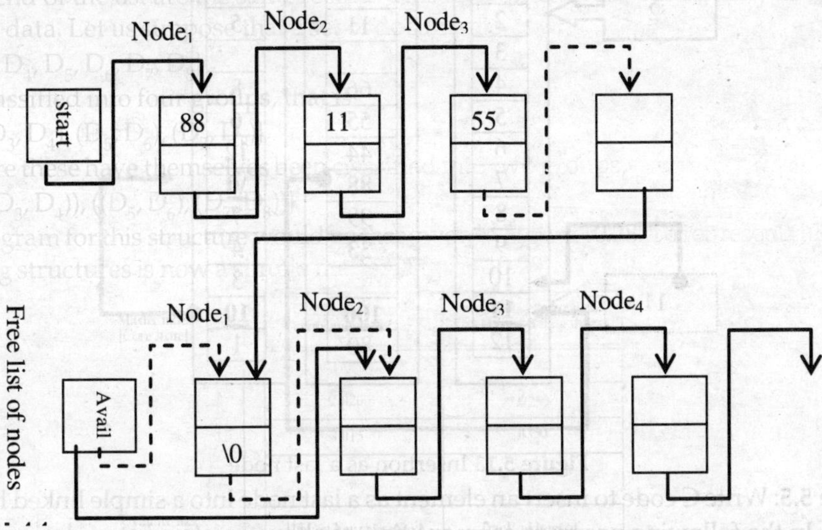

Figure 5.11 Insertion as a last node

```
    Step 1: [Allocate free space]
        New1 = Create new node
    Step 2: [Check for free space]
    If New1 = NULL output "OVERFLOW" and Exit
    Step 3: [Read value of information part of a new node and set next pointer
of New1 to NULL]
        Info [New1] = Value
    Next[New1] = NULL
    Step 4: [Move the pointer to the end of the list]
        Repeat while Next[Ptr] ¹ NULL
        Ptr = Next [Ptr]
    Step 4: [Link currently created node with the last node of the list]
        Next [Ptr] = New1
    Step 5: Exit
```

Figure 5.12 Algorithm to insert a node at the end of a list

For example, if we have a list shown in **Figure 5.7** then after inserting 100 in this list as a last node, resulting list is shown in **Figure 5.13.** Example 5.5 demonstrates the insertion of a node as a last node in a given list.

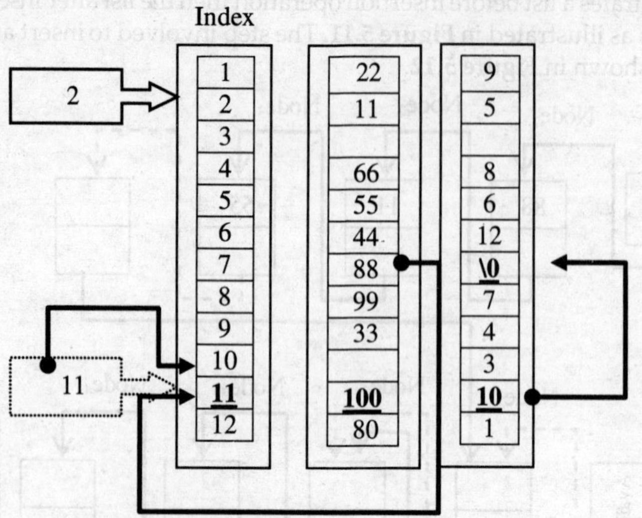

Figure 5.13 Insertion as a last node

Example 5.5: Write C code to insert an element as a last node into a simple linked list.

Answer: In the following program segment first of all we create a list of desired size then an insertion of last is done.

```
/*  INSERT A NODE INTO A SIMPLE LINKED LIST AT THE END OF THE LIST */
/* LINK_IL.C */
# include <stdio.h>
# include <malloc.h>

struct link_list
{
    int info;
    struct link_list *next;
};
typedef struct link_list node;

void insert(node *);
void create(node *);
void display(node *);

int num;
node *start=NULL;

/* Function main */
void main()
{
    start = (node *) malloc(sizeof(node));
    create(start);
```

```
    display(start);
    insert(start);
    display(start);
    getch();
}
/* Function create a linked list */
void create(node *ptr)
{
    char ch;

    num = 0;
    printf("\n Enter E for Exit any other key to continue: ");
    ch = getchar();
    if(ch=='e'){
    free(ptr);
    exit(0);
    }
    do
    {
        printf("\n Input the values of the node: %d: ", (num+1));
        scanf("%d", &ptr->info);
        fflush(stdin);
        printf("\n want to continue(y/n)->: ");
        ch = getchar();
        if(ch=='y')
        {
        ptr->next = (node *) malloc(sizeof(node));
        ptr = ptr->next;
        }
        num ++;
    }while(ch=='y');
    ptr->next=NULL;
    printf("\n Total nodes = %d", num);
}

/* function display */
void display(node *ptr)
{
    while (ptr!=NULL)
    {
    printf("\n %d", ptr->info);
    ptr = ptr->next;
    }
}
```

```
/* Inserting a node */
void insert (node *ptr)
{
    int x;
    node *new1;
    new1 = (node *) malloc(sizeof(node));
    printf("\n Enter element you want to insert :");
    scanf("%d", &new1->info);
    if ( start == NULL)  /* check for empty list */
    {
      new1->next=NULL;
      start=new1;
     }else{
       while(ptr->next!=NULL)
       ptr=ptr->next;
       new1->next=NULL;
       ptr->next=new1;
     }
}
```

5.3.3 Insertion of a Node at Specific Location

In some cases, one might want to place elements at specific locations in a list. For example, if we want to create a linked list that contains the sorted names of files in the current directory, program needs to place each file name into the list at the correct position. To insert an item at a specific place (location) in a list, the program will normally track the **starting node, current node** and the **previous** of the current node. To achieve this we scan the list from the beginning and move up to the desired node where we want to insert the new node. Here, we create a new node and insert it into the list and restructure the complete list.

From the following steps it is clear that when one wants to insert a node into a linked list, one should know the node number/node information where he/she wants to insert a new node in the list. If one does not know the node number/node information it is not easy job to insert a new node into the list. If one goes through trial and error method may insert the new node in the list but it requires much more time. In trial and error method if one input a new node number but that particular node does not exists in the list that may create problems. Some times it may crash the list. When a program needs to insert a new element, it will perform the following processing:

```
new1 = malloc(sizeof(struct link);
previous->next = new1;
new1->member = some_value;
new1->next = ptr;
```

If **Figure 5.5** illustrates a list before insertion operation then the list after inserting a node into a list it becomes as illustrated in **Figure 5.14.** For example, consider the list shown in **Figure 5.7**. Then after inserting 100 in this list at a specific place, the list becomes as shown in **Figure 5.15.** From the result it is clear that insertion operation simply places new node between node 1 and 2. The next field of node 1 is now linked with newly inserted node and next field of newly inserted node is linked with node 2. Thus, new node that was inserted occupies the place of 2nd node.

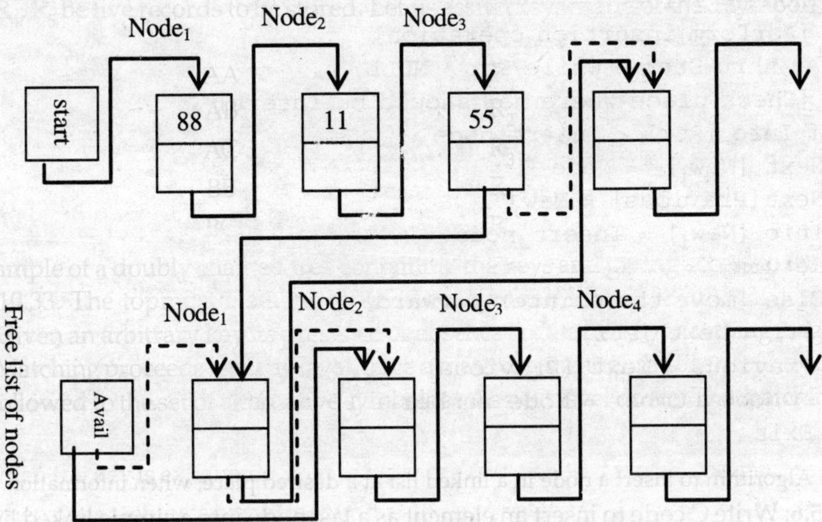

Figure 5.14 Pointer Links for Insertion of a node at a specific place

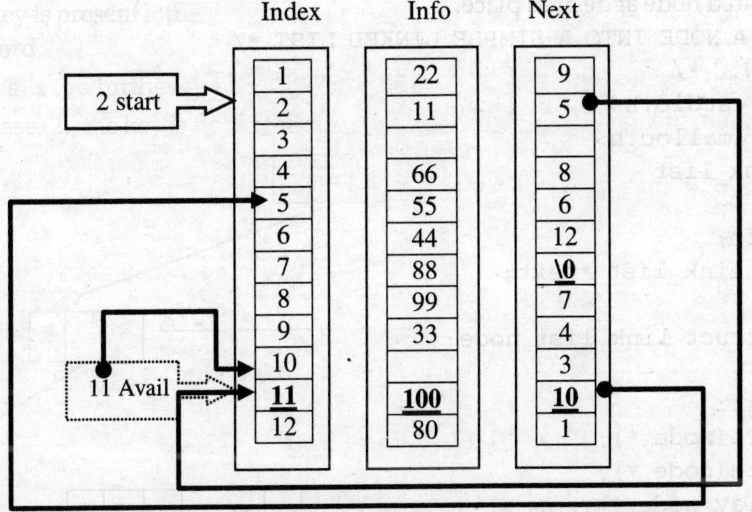

Figure 5.15 Insertion of a node at a specific place

The program segment **LINK_IN.C** demonstrates the same operation as discussed in **Figure 5.14** and implements the algorithm shown in **Figure 5.16**. Example 5.6 demonstrates the insertion of node at desired place in a given list.

```
Step 1: [Creat a new node and check for availability of space]
   New1 = creat a new node
   If New1 = NULL output "OVERFLOW" and Exit
Step 2: [Initialization]
   Node_number = 0
   Ptr= Start [Points to first node of the list]
Step 3: [Read information of new node number]
```

```
  Insert_node = Value
Step 4: [Perform insertion operation]
    Repeat thru Step 6 while Ptr ¹ NULL
Step 5: [Check place where new should be insert]
        If Info [Ptr] < Insert_node
         Next [New1]  = Node
         Next[Previous] = New1
         Info [New1] = Insert_node
         Return
         Else [move the pointer forward]
          Ptr = Next [Ptr]
          Previous = Next [Previous]
Step 6:    Node_number = Node_number + 1
Step 7: Exit
```

Figure 5.16 Algorithm to insert a node in a linked list at a desired place, when information is known

Example 5.6: Write C code to insert an element as a last node into a simple linked list.

Answer: In the following program segment, first of all we create list of desired size then an insertion of a desired node at desired place.

```
/* INSERT A NODE INTO A SIMPLE LINKED LIST */
/* LINK_IN.C */
# include <stdio.h>
# include <malloc.h>
struct link_list
{
    int info;
    struct link_list *next;
};
typedef struct link_list node;
int i,num;
node *start;
void insert(node *);
void create(node *);
void display(node *);

/* Function main */
void main()
{
    start = (node *) malloc(sizeof(node));
    create(start);
    display(start);
    insert(start);
    display(start);
    getch();
}
```

```
/* Function create a linked list */
void create(node *ptr)
{
    char ch;
    num = 0;
    printf("\n Enter E for Exit any other key to continue: ");
    ch = getchar();
    if(ch=='e'){
    free(ptr);
    exit(0);
    }
    do
    {
        printf("\n Input the values of the node : %d: ", (num+1));
        scanf("%d", &ptr->info);
        fflush(stdin);
        printf("\n want to continue(y/n)->: ");
        ch = getchar();
        if(ch=='y'){
        ptr->next = (node *) malloc(sizeof(node));
        ptr = ptr->next;
        }
        num ++;
    }while(ch=='y');
    ptr->next=NULL;
    printf("\n Total nodes = %d", num);
}

/* function display */
void display(node *ptr)
{
    while (ptr!=NULL)
    {
        printf("\n %d", ptr->info);
        ptr = ptr->next;
    }
}
void insert (node *ptr)
{
    node *new1;
    int i,node_no;
    new1 = (node *) malloc(sizeof(node));
    printf("\n Enter node number you want to insert:");
    printf("\n Value should be less are equalto the");
    printf("\n Enter node no.:-> ");
```

```
    scanf("%d", &node_no);
    printf("\n Enter element you want to insert :");
    scanf("%d", &new1->info);

    if(node_no==1){
    new1->next=start;
    start=new1;
    }
    else if(node_no==num)
    {
    while(ptr->next!=NULL)
     ptr=ptr->next;
     ptr->next=new1;
     new1->next=NULL;
    }else
    {
    for(i=1;i<node_no-1;i++)
    ptr=ptr->next;
    new1->next=ptr->next;
    ptr->next=new1;
    }
}
```

5.4 DELETION IN A LINKED LIST

If one is interested in deletion of a node from a linear linked list, before performing the deletion, one should take into account following points:

1. If the linked list is empty, the deletion is not possible and the output should display **Underflow** message.
2. Consider the Step 3 while end of the list has not been reached or the node has not been found.
3. Obtain the next node in the list and record its predecessor. Check for the existence of the node for which information is given.
4. If the end of the list has been reached, "**node not found**" message can be displayed.
5. Delete the node from the list.
6. Return the node to the free area.

The deletion operation is classified into the following three categories:

- Deletion of first node
- Deletion of last node
- Deletion of desired node from any place in the list

5.4.1 Deletion of First Node

Suppose we have a linked list as shown in **Figure 5.17** and want to delete first node. Then accomplish the following operations:

- Make link of **start** pointer to the second node in the list.
- Free the space associated with first node.

- Operating system then collects the free space and makes link for currently freed node with available free space.

The **start** pointer points to first element in the list. The value associated with it is stored into **ptr** variable. If the value of this node is **NULL,** it means that the list is empty and messages **UNDERFLOW** is displayed and function exits. If the list is not empty, the address of the next node is assigned to **start** pointer and the list becomes as shown in **Figure 5.18**. When we free the space associated with a node, it is attached to the free list. This discussion can be formulated in order in which it is performed. These steps show the property of the operation done by a statement.

```
ptr = start; /* Points to the first element of the list */
/*This statement makes link of start to link of the next node that is linked
with second node*/
start = ptr ->next;
free (ptr);
```

Steps involved in deletion of first node from a linked list are shown in **Figure 5.19**.

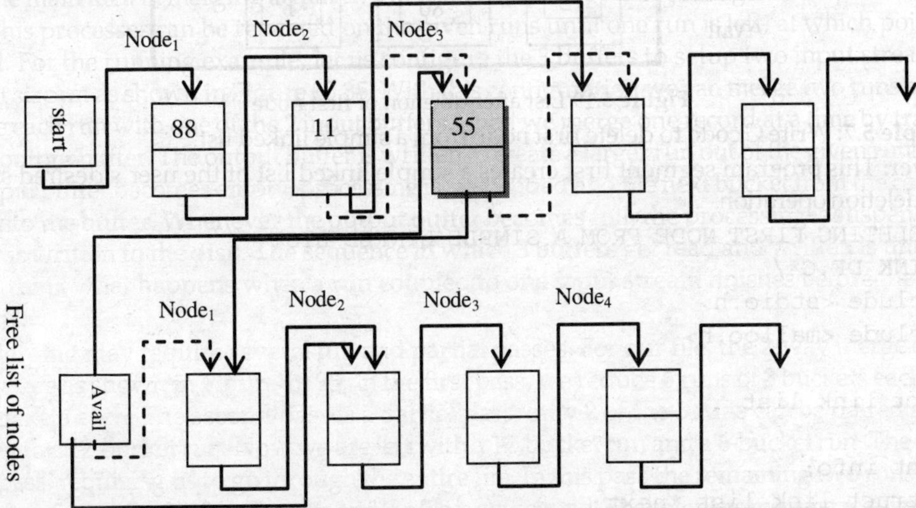

Figure 5.17 List with deletion operation

```
Step 1: [Initialization]
   Ptr = Start [Points to the first node in the list]
Step 2: [Perform deletion operation]
   If Ptr = NULL
   Output "UNDERFLOW" and Exit
   Else if (Next[Ptr]= NULL)  [Delete first node]
   Start=NULL
Free space associated with Ptr
Else
   Start = Next [Ptr] [Move pointer to next node in the list]
   Free space associated with Ptr
Step 3: Exit
```

Figure 5.18 Algorithm for deletion of first node from a linked list

For example, if we have list as shown in Figure 5.7 then after deleting first node from the list it becomes like list shown in **Figure 5.19.** Example 5.7 demonstrates the above discussion.

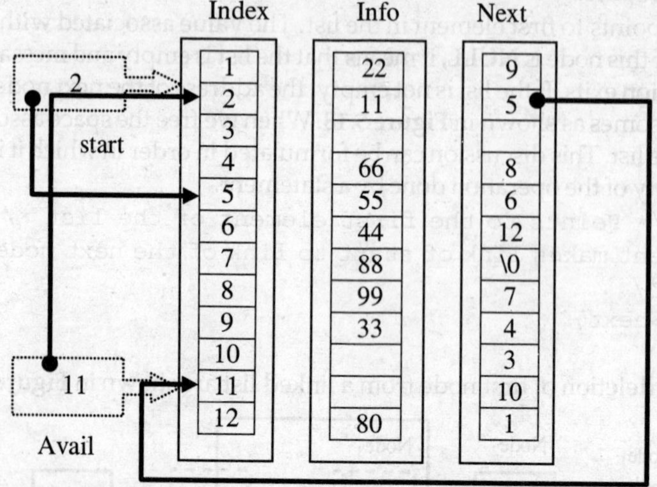

Figure 5.19 List after deletion of first node

Example 5.7: Write C code to delete first node from a simple linked list.

Answer: This program segment first creates a simple linked list of the user's desired size then performs deletion operation.

```
/* DELETING FIRST NODE FROM A SIMPLE LINKED LIST */
/* LINK_DF.C*/
# include <stdio.h>
# include <malloc.h>

struct link_list
{
   int info;
   struct link_list *next;
};
typedef struct link_list node;
int num;
node *start=NULL;
void create(node *);
void deleete(node *);
void display(node *);

/* Function main */
void main()
{
   start = (node *) malloc(sizeof(node));
   create(start);
   printf("\n created list is as follow:");
```

```
    display(start);
    deleete(start);
    printf("\n new list is as follow:");
    display(start);
    getch();
  }
  /* Function create a linked list */
  void create(node *ptr)
  {
    char ch;
    num = 0;
    printf("\n Enter E for Exit any other key to continue: ");
    ch = getchar();
    if(ch=='e'){
    free(ptr);
    exit(0);
    }
    do{
       printf("\n Input the values of the node : %d: ", (num+1));
       scanf("%d", &ptr->info);
       fflush(stdin);
       printf("\n want to continue(y/n)->: ");
       ch = getchar();
       if(ch=='y'){
       ptr->next = (node *) malloc(sizeof(node));
       ptr = ptr->next;
       }
       num ++;
    }while(ch=='y');
    ptr->next=NULL;
    printf("\n Total nodes = %d", num);
  }
  void deleete(node *ptr)
  {
    if ( ptr == NULL)
       printf("\n List is empty\n");
    else if(ptr->next==NULL)
  {
       start=NULL;
       free(ptr);
  }    else  {
       start=ptr->next;
       free(ptr);
  }
  }
```

```
/* function display */
void display(node *ptr)
{
    while (ptr!=NULL)
    {
        printf("\n %d", ptr->info);
        ptr = ptr->next;
    }
}
```

5.4.2 Deletion of Last Node

The simple method to delete last node of a linked list is described as follows. First count the number of nodes in the list. Scan the list from beginning to end of the list will effectively counts the number of nodes in the list. Let it contains **n** nodes. Now second time once again we scan the list from beginning to **n-1** nodes of the list. At last we free the last node. The deletion mechanism is similar to the previous one. Suppose we have a list as shown in **Figure 5.7**. Then after deletion of last node the list becomes as illustrated in **Figure 5.20.** The code segment, which is used to perform this task, is:

```
ptr = start;
while (ptr->next)
    ptr = ptr->next;
```

Figure 5.7 represents a linked list of which each node has integer number as an information. If we want to traverse the list we can easily traverse the list from starting end to end of the list. **Figure 5.20** illustrates the deletion operation.

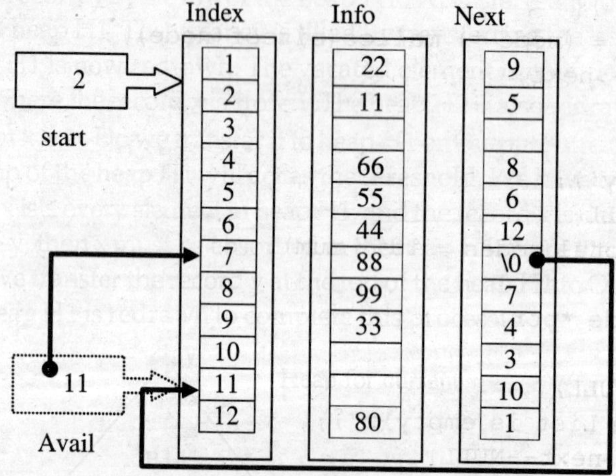

Figure 5.20 List after deletion of last node

Example 5.8 implements the algorithm illustrated in Figure 5.21.

```
Step 1: [Initialization]
    Previous = Ptr = Start [Points to the first node in the list]
Step 2: [Check list is empty or not]
    If Ptr = NULL
    Output "UNDERFLOW" and Exit
```

```
Step 3: [Scan the list to count the number of nodes in the list]
    Repeat while Next[Ptr] ≠ NULL
    Previous = Ptr
    Ptr = Next [Ptr]
Step 4: [Check if last node is arising]
    Next [Previous] = NULL
    Free (Ptr)
Step 5: Exit
```

Figure 5.21 Algorithm to delete last node

Example 12.8: Write C code to delete last node from a simple linked list.

Answer: This program segment first creates a simple linked list of the user's desired size then performs deletion operation.

```
/* DELETING LAST NODE FROM A SIMPLE LINKED LIST */
/* LINK_DL.C */
# include <stdio.h>
# include <malloc.h>
struct link_list
{
    int info;
    struct link_list *next;
};
typedef struct link_list node;
int num;
node *start=NULL;
void create(node *);
void deleete(node *);
void display(node *);

/* Function main */

void main()
{
    start = (node *) malloc(sizeof(node));
    create(start);
    printf("\n created list is as follows:");
    display(start);
    deleete(start);
    printf("\n new list is as follows:");
    display(start);
    getch();
}
/* Function create a linked list */
void create(node *ptr)
{
```

```
        char ch;

        num = 0;
        printf("\n Enter E for Exit any other key to continue: ");
        ch = getchar();
        if(ch=='e')
        {
        free(ptr);
        exit(0);
        }
        do{
            printf("\n Input the values of the node : %d: ", (num+1));
            scanf("%d", &ptr->info);
            fflush(stdin);
            printf("\n want to continue(y/n)->: ");
            ch = getchar();
            if(ch=='y')
            {
            ptr->next = (node *) malloc(sizeof(node));
            ptr = ptr->next;
            }
            num ++;
        }while(ch=='y');
        ptr->next=NULL;
        printf("\n Total nodes = %d", num);
    }
    void deleete(node *ptr)
    {
        node *prev=ptr;
        if ( ptr == NULL)
          printf("\n List is empty\n");
            else if(ptr->next==NULL)
            {
              start=NULL;
              free(ptr);
            } else{
          while(ptr->next!=NULL)
          {
           prev=ptr;
           ptr=ptr->next;
          }
          prev->next=NULL;
          free(ptr);
    }
    }
```

```
/* function display */
void display(node *ptr)
{
    while (ptr!=NULL)
    {
        printf("\n %d", ptr->info);
        ptr = ptr->next;
    }
}
```

5.4.3 Deletion of a Desired Node

Suppose we want to delete a desired node from a linked list. In this section we have assumed that we know the node number, which we want to delete. First of all we provide node number to which we want to delete. We scan the list up to that node. If the node exists in the list, we move the pointer to that particular node, free the node and adjust the pointer to make the list in linked form (The pointer of the previous node of this node will now point to the successor of this node). Before deletion operation we must check whether the list is empty or not. If the list is empty a message **UNDERFLOW** is displayed and the program terminates.

When we have given information which is in a given linked list and we want to remove that information from the list. For this purpose we have to perform search operation for the information, if it is found delete the information containing node from the list. Suppose we have a linked list as illustrated in **Figure 5.22** and we have to delete information **33**, whether it is present in the given list or not and if it is present then at which or how many places.

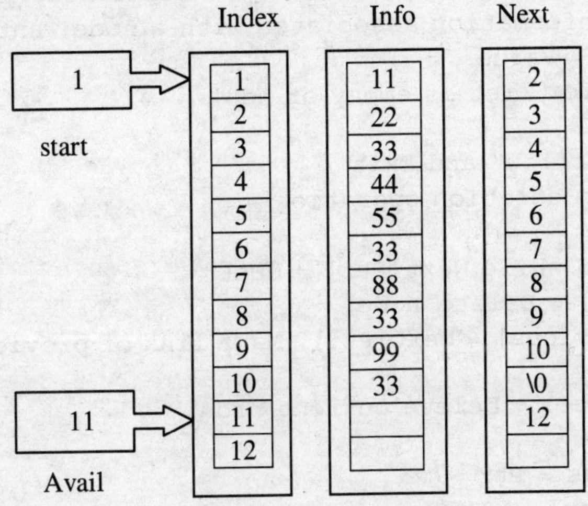

Figure 5.22 List in memory

See the following how we search the information in the list.

Let Search = 33

Node = 1,Info [1] <> Search that is 11 <> 33 Search is unsuccessful

Next [1] = 2,Info [2] <> Search that is 22 <> 33 Search is unsuccessful

Next [2] = 3,Info [3] = Search That is 33 = 33 Search is successful and position = 3

For deleting the node 3 simply set the next pointer of node 2 to the next pointer of node 3, i.e., Next[2]=Next[3] and free (Node 3)

Next [3] = 4,Info [4] <> Search that is 44 <> 33 Search is unsuccessful
Next [4] = 5,Info [5] <> Search that is 55<> 33 Search is unsuccessful
Next [5] = 6,Info [6] = Search that is 33 = 33 Search is successful and position = 6

For deleting the node 6 simply set the next pointer of node 5 to the next pointer of node 6, i.e., Next[5]=Next[6] and free (Node 6)

Next [6] = 7,Info [7] <> Search that is 88 <> 33 Search is unsuccessful
Next [7] = 8,Info [8] = Search that is 33 = 33 Search is successful and position = 8

For deleting the node 8 simply set the next pointer of node 7 to the next pointer of node 8, i.e., Next[7]=Next[8] and free (Node 8)

Next [8] = 9,Info [9] <> Search that is 99 <> 33 Search is unsuccessful
Next [9] = 10, Info [10] = Search that is 33 = 33 Search is successful and position = 10

For deleting the node 10 simply set the next pointer of node 9 to the next pointer of node 10, i.e., Next[9]=Next[10], i.e., NULL here and free (Node 10)

From the above result it is clear that **33** is found in the linked list at four places. **Example 5.9** creates a linked list of desired size. The program then searches the list for the node containing the desired information which we want to delete, and finally delete the node from the list. Steps involved in the operation are summarized in Figure 5.23.

```
Step 1: [Initialization]
    Previous = Ptr = Start [Points to the first node in the linked list]
Step 2: [Read information associated with a node want to delete]
    Delete_node = Value
Step 3: [Check for list is empty or not]
    If Ptr = NULL
    Output "Underflow" and Exit
Step 4: [Perform deletion operation]
    Flag = 0
    Repeat thru 5 while Next[Ptr] ≠ NULL
    If Info [Ptr] = Delete_node
(a)     Next [Previous] = Next[Ptr] [Make link of previous node to the next
node]
(b)     Delete (Ptr)  [Delete current node]
(c)     Exit
Step 5:  Previous = Ptr
    Ptr = Next[Ptr]
Step 6: [Check status value]
    If  (Flag=0) Start= NULL
Step 7: Return  Start
```

Figure 5.23 Deletion algorithm when information associated with a field of a node is known

Example 5.9: Write C code to delete desired node from a simple linked list.

Answer: This program segment first creates a simple linked list of the user's desired size then performs deletion operation.

```
/* DELETING A NODE FROM A SIMPLE LINKED LIST */
/* WHEN INFORMATION OF A NODE IS GIVEN */
/* LINK_DIN.C */
# include <stdio.h>
# include <malloc.h>

struct link_list
{
    int info;
    struct link_list *next;
};
typedef struct link_list node;
int num;
node *start=NULL;
void create(node *);
void Delete(node *);
void display(node *);

/* Function main */

void main()
{
    start = (node *) malloc(sizeof(node));
    create(start);
    printf("\n created list is as follow:");
    display(start);
    Delete(start);
    printf("\n new list is as follow:");
    display(start);
    getch();
}
/* Function create a linked list */
void create(node *ptr)
{
    char ch;
    clrscr();
    num = 0;
    printf("\n Enter E for Exit any other key to continue: ");
    ch = getchar();
    if(ch=='e')
    {
        free(ptr);
        exit(0);
    }
    do{
```

```
        printf("\n Input the values of the node : %d: ", (num+1));
        scanf("%d", &ptr->info);
        fflush(stdin);
        printf("\n want to continue(y/n)->: ");
        ch = getchar();
        if(ch=='y')
        {
        ptr->next = (node *) malloc(sizeof(node));
        ptr = ptr->next;
        }
        num ++;
    }while(ch=='y');
    ptr->next=NULL;
    printf("\n Total nodes = %d", num);
}
void Delete(node *ptr)
{
    node *prev;
    int x;
    if ( ptr == NULL)
      {
        printf("\n List is empty\n");
        exit(0);
      }
    printf("Enter element you want to delete:->");
    scanf("%d",&x);
    while(ptr->info!=x && ptr!=NULL)
    {
     prev=ptr;
     ptr=ptr->next;
    }
    if(ptr==NULL)
     printf("element you want to delete does not exist:");
    else
    {
     if(prev->info==x)
     prev=prev->next;
     else if(ptr->next==NULL)
     prev->next=NULL;
     else
     prev->next=ptr->next;
     free(ptr);
    }
}
```

```
/* function display */
void display(node *ptr)
{
   while (ptr!=NULL)
   {
      printf("\n %d", ptr->info);
      ptr = ptr->next;
   }
}
```

5.5 DOUBLY LINKED LIST

A singly linked list is so named because each list element contains a pointer to the next element. We have seen that, to insert elements in a singly linked list, program has to maintain pointers to the current and previous nodes.

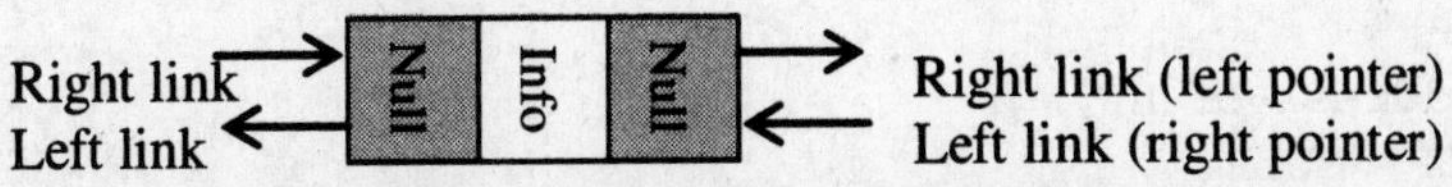

Figure 5.24 Node with two links

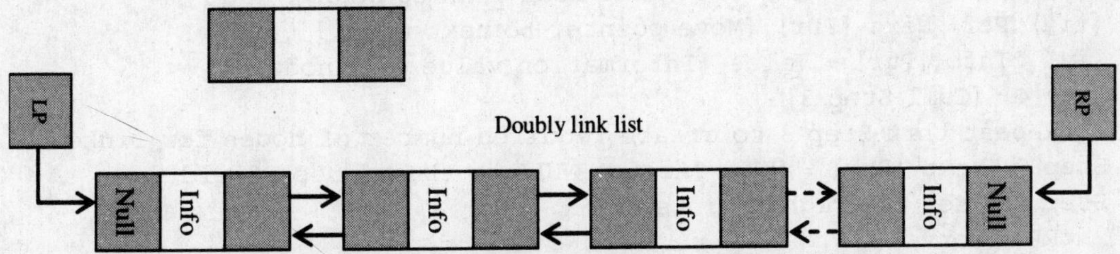

Figure 5.25 Doubly linked list

In linear linked list structure, traversing is possible only in one direction. Some times it is required to traverse the list in either direction, i.e., forward or backward. This increases the performance and efficiency of the algorithm. So traversing of linked list in both the directions requires nodes having the links as illustrated in **Figure 5.24.** The links are used to denote the predecessor and successor of a node. The link denoting the predecessor of a node is called the left link and that denoting its successor is right link. A list with this type of arrangement is called doubly linked list as shown in **Figure 5.25.** Now it is possible to define a doubly linked list used as a collection of nodes, each node having three fields:

- Pointer to previous node (Pointer to predecessor)
- Information field
- Pointer to next node (Pointer to successor)

Figure 5.24 illustrates that the left link of the left most node and the right link of the right most node are **NULL**. The **NULL** indicates the end of the list in each direction. How can one create a node of doubly linked? For this consider the following declaration:

```
struct Tag name
{
        Data type₁ information field ₁;
        Data type₂ Information field ₂;
            ...
        Data typeₙ information field ₙ;
        struct  Tag name *previous;
        struct Tag name  *next;
};
```

This definition represents a node. If the previous and next of left pointer (LP) and right pointer (RP) pointers are null then there will be single node in the list. If both pointers (LP and RP) points to the **NULL**, indicating that that list is **NULL** or empty. Algorithm to build a doubly linked list is given in **Figure 5.26**.

```
Step 1: [Initialization of LP and  RP ponters]
    (i)    LP = NULL
    (ii)   RP = NULL
Step 3: [Assign address of LP variable to Ptr and set previous of LP pointer NULL]
    Ptr = Address of LP,
Previous[LP]=NULL
Step 3: [Make left and right links of a node]
(i)     Next [Ptr] = Ptr [Make right link to Node].
(ii)    Previous [Ptr] = Ptr [Make left link to Node].
(iii)   Ptr= Next [Ptr] [Move pointer to next node].
(iv)    Info [Ptr] = Value [Information value of a node].
Step 4: [Call Step 3]
    Repeat thru Step 3 to create required number of nodes for linked list
Step 5: Next [Ptr] = NULL [Assign NULL to the address field]
Step 6: [set the right pointer]
    RP = Ptr
Step 5: End
```

Figure 5.26 Doubly linked list creation algorithm

The notations that are used in the algorithm are

LP (left pointer, i.e., right link stands for structure type pointer variable pointing to the left most node

RP (right pointer, i.e., left link stands for structure type pointer variable pointing to the right most node

Next → structure type pointer variable- pointing to the next node in the list

Previous → structure type pointer variable pointing to previous node in the list

Ptr → structure type pointer variable used to traverse the list

From first step of algorithm it is clear that LP and RP both points to the **NULL**, indicating that list is **NULL**. The program segment **DBLINK.C** creates a doubly linked list.

```
/* CREATING A SIMPLE DOUBLY LINKED LIST */
/* DBLINK.C */
# include <stdio.h>
# include <malloc.h>
struct Dlink_list
{
   struct Dlink_list *previous;
   int info;
   struct Dlink_list *next;
};
typedef struct Dlink_list Dnode;

/* Global declaration */
int num ;
Dnode *lp=NULL,*rp=NULL;

/* Prototypes of various functions */
void Create(Dnode *);
void display_left (Dnode *);
void display_right (Dnode *);
/* Function main */
void main()
{
   lp = (Dnode *) malloc(sizeof(Dnode));
   Create(lp);
   display_left(lp);
   display_right(rp);
   getch();
}

/* Function create */
void Create(Dnode *ptr)
{
   char ch;
   clrscr();
   num = 0;
   lp->previous = NULL;
   printf("\n Enter E for Exit any other key for continue: ");
   ch = getchar();
   if(ch=='e')
   {
   free(lp);
   exit(0);
   }
```

```
    do
    {
        printf("\n Input the values of the node : %d: ", (num+1));
        scanf("%d", &ptr->info);
        fflush(stdin);
        printf("\n want to continue(y/n)->: ");
        ch = getchar();
        if(ch=='y')
        {
        ptr->next = (Dnode *) malloc(sizeof(Dnode));
        ptr->next->previous = ptr;
        ptr = ptr->next;
        }
        num ++;
    }while(ch=='y');
    ptr->next=NULL;
    rp=ptr; /* Assign the address of rightmost node to rp */
    printf("\n Total nodes = %d", num);
}

/* Function Display left to right */
void display_left (Dnode *ptr)
{
    while(ptr!=NULL)  /* Traverse up to end of the list */
    {
        printf("\n 0x%x", ptr);
        printf(" %d", ptr->info);
        ptr = ptr->next;
    }
}
/* Function Display right to left */
void display_right (Dnode *ptr)
{
    while(ptr!=NULL)  /* Traverse up to end of the list */
    {
        printf("\n 0x%x", ptr);
        printf(" %d", ptr->info);
        ptr = ptr->previous;
    }
}
```

5.5.1 Traversing a Doubly Linked List

Traversing a doubly linked list means scanning (processing) each node exactly once either in forward or backward direction or in both the directions, i.e., the program can traverse the list from left to right or right to left. Therefore, two **NULL** pointers are maintained. When traversing the list from left to right, it identifies the end of the list when **next[ptr]** is **NULL**. Likewise, when traversing the list from right to left, the end of the list is indicated when **previous[ptr]** is **NULL**. For example, the program **DOUBLE_L.C** creates a doubly linked list and display information associated with each node in forward and backward. **Figure 5.27** illustrates an algorithm for traversing doubly linked in forward and backward directions. According to the requirement of applications one can easily edit this algorithm.

```
Step 1: [Initialization]
   Ptr = LP [Points to the left most node in the list]
Step 2: [Traverse the list in forward direction]
   Repeat while Next [Ptr] ≠ NULL
   Process Info [Ptr]
Step 3: [Traverse the list in backward direction]
   Ptr = RP [Points to the right most node in the list]
   Repeat while Previous [Ptr] ≠ NULL
   Process Info [Ptr]
Step 4: Exit
```

Figure 5.27 Algorithm for traversing a doubly linked list

Figure 5.28 clearly indicates that, first of all, it is required to assign address of very first node to the variable **Ptr** with the help of **LP** and **RP** variable. Now we move pointer forward or backword to access the information associated with each node, such as

Ptr = LP = 1
Info [1] = 11 Next [1] = 2
Info [2] = 22 Next [2] = 3
Info [3] = 33 Next [3] = 4
Info [4] = 44 Next [4] = 5
Info [5] = 55 Next [5] = 6
Info [6] = 66 Next [6] = 7
Info [7] = 77 Next [7] = 8
Info [8] = 88 Next [8] = 9
Info [9] = 99 Next [9] = **NULL**

Similarly in backward direction traversing can be performed as

Ptr = RP = 9
Info [9] = 99 Previous [9] = 8
Info [8] = 88 Previous [8] = 7
Info [7] = 77 Previous [7] = 6
Info [6] = 66 Previous [6] = 5
Info [5] = 55 Previous [5] = 4
Info [4] = 44 Previous [4] = 3
Info [3] = 33 Previous [3] = 2
Info [2] = 22 Previous [2] = 1
Info [1] = 11 Previous [1] = **NULL**

	Index	Info	Next	Previous
LP (1) →	1	11	2	NULL
	2	22	3	1
	3	33	4	2
	4	44	5	3
	5	55	6	4
	6	66	7	5
	7	77	8	6
	8	88	9	7
RP (9) →	9	99	NULL	8

Figure 5.28 Traversing doubly linked list

The program segment **DBLINK.C** illustrates the algorithm shown in **Figure 5.27.** Using the program segment **Double_L.C** one can easily verify the results shown above.

```
/* Doubly linked list */
/* This program segment creates a doubly linked list then prints in forward
and backword */
/* Double_L.c */
# include <stdio.h>
# include <malloc.h>

struct Dlink_list
{
   struct Dlink_list *previous;
   int info;
   struct Dlink_list *next;
};
typedef struct Dlink_list Dnode;
/* Global declaration */
int num ;
Dnode *lp=NULL,*rp=NULL;

/* Prototype declaration */
void Doubly_Link_Create(Dnode *);
void display (Dnode *);
```

```
/* Function main */
void main()
{
   lp = (Dnode *) malloc(sizeof(Dnode));
   Doubly_Link_Create(lp);
   printf("\n Created doubly linked list is as follows\n");
   display(lp);
   getch();
}

/* Function creates a doubly linked list */
void Doubly_Link_Create(Dnode *ptr)
{
   char ch;

   num = 0;
   lp->previous = NULL;
   printf("\n Enter E for Exit any other key for continue: ");
   ch = getchar();
   if(ch=='e')
   {
   free(ptr);
   exit(0);
   }
   do
   {
      printf("\n Input the values of the node : %d: ", (num+1));
      scanf("%d", &ptr->info);
      fflush(stdin);
      printf("\n want to continue(y/n)->: ");
      ch = getchar();
      if(ch=='y')
      {
      ptr->next = (Dnode *) malloc(sizeof(Dnode));
      ptr->next->previous = ptr;
      ptr = ptr->next;
      }
      num ++;
   }while(ch=='y');
   ptr->next=NULL;
   printf("\n Total nodes = %d", num);
   rp=ptr;
}
/* Display the list */
void display (Dnode *ptr)
```

```
{
   while(ptr!=NULL)
     {
       printf("\n 0x%x", ptr);
       printf(" %d", ptr->info);
       ptr = ptr->next;
     }
   ptr=rp;
   while(ptr!=NULL)
     {
       printf("\n 0x%x", ptr);
       printf(" %d", ptr->info);
       ptr = ptr->previous;
     }
}
```

5.5.2 Insertion in A Doubly Linked List

Before making insertion operation, one should go through the following steps to get the idea:

1. Obtain a new node and set its fields.
2. If the linked list is empty, insert the node in the list and update the previous and next pointers of the list.
3. If the node is to be inserted at the front of the list, insert the node and update the previous pointer of the list.
4. Insert the node in the list at desired place.

Insertion into a doubly linked list is possible and classified into three categories.

- Insertion as a first node (Left of the left most nodes in the list)
- Insertion as last node (Right of the right most node in the list)
- Insertion at any place

5.5.2.1 Inserting First Node (LEFT TO THE LEFT MOST NODE IN A LIST)

Given a doubly linked list whose left most and right most nodes addresses are given by the pointer variables **LP** and **RP**, respectively. It is required to insert a node whose address is given by the pointer variable **new**$_1$. The information field of a node is denoted by the variable **info**. Suppose we have a doubly linked list as shown in **Figure 5.29,** the insertion operation may be performed as illustrated in **Figure 5.30**.

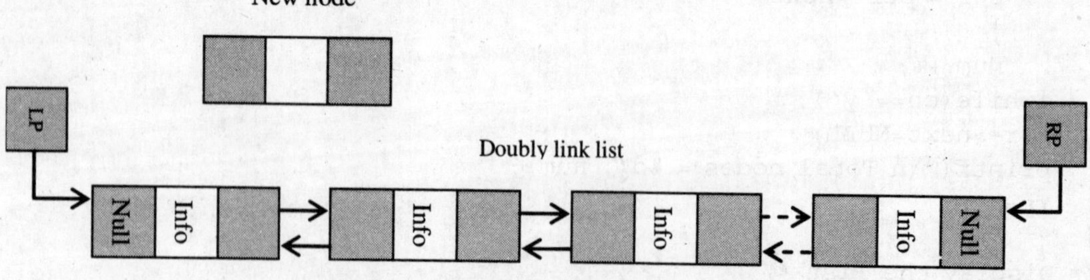

Figure 5.29 Doubly linked list before insertion

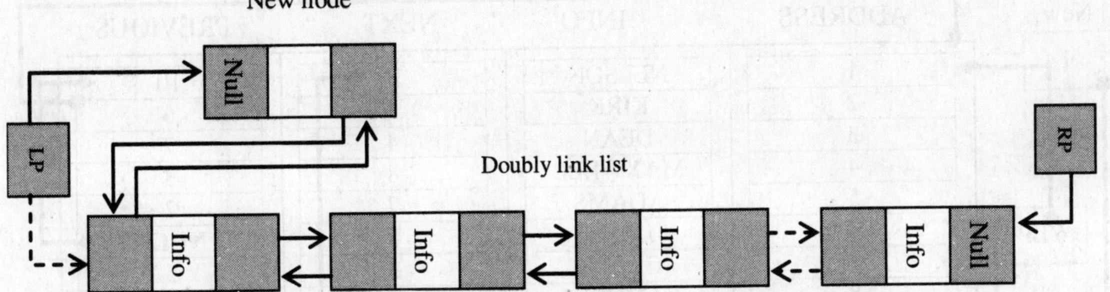

Figure 5.30 Doubly linked list after inserting a node at left most position

For example, if we have a linked list as shown in **Figure 5.31**, the insertion to the left of the left most node in the list may be performed as

```
Ptr = Next[LP] = 2 [Index value]
info [new1] = NELSON
info [1] = NELSON
next [new1] = Ptr
next [1] = 2
previous [new1] = previous [Ptr] = NULL
previous [1] = previous [2] = NULL
previous [Ptr] = new1
previous [2] = new1 = 1
```

Now from the above discussion, it is clear that after insertion of a node to the left of the left most node in the list, the list shown in **Figure 5.31** becomes as shown in **Figure 5.32**. The program segment **DBL_IF.C** implements the algorithm discussed in **Figure 5.33**.

New_1	ADDRESS	INFO	NEXT	PREVIOUS
1	1		10	10
	2	KIRK	5	6
	3	DEAN	4	7
	4	MAXWELL	8	3
	5	ADAMS	7	2
6 LP	6	LANE	2	**NULL**
	7	GREEN	3	5
	8	SAMUELS	9	4
9 RP	9	FIELDS	**NULL**	8
	10		11	11
	11			

Figure 5.31 List before inserting a node

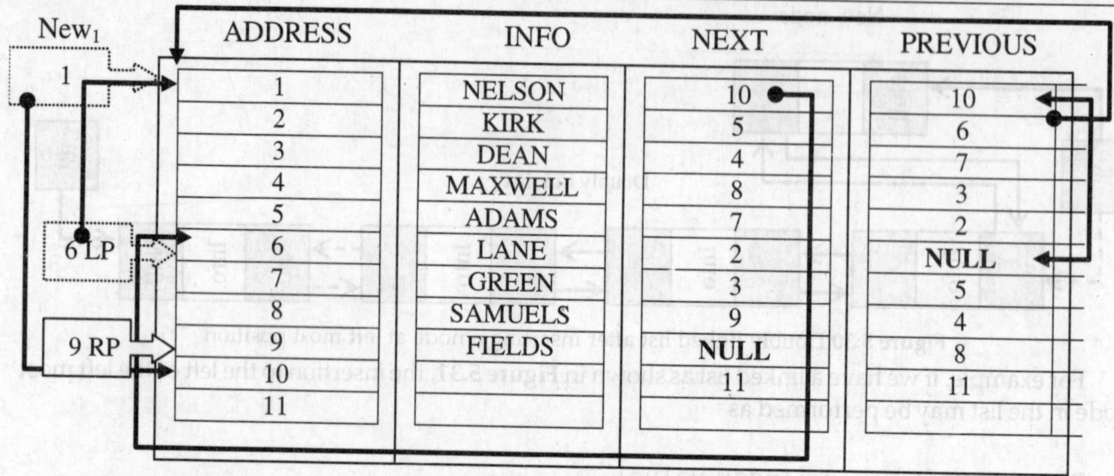

Figure 5.32 List after inserting a node

```
Step 1: [Initialization]
    Ptr = LP [Points to the left most node in the list]
Step 2: [Check whether list is empty or not]
    If Ptr = NULL
    Output "List is empty insert as a first in the list"
Step 3: [Create new node]
    New1 = Allocate space [create new node]
Step 4: [Input value about newly created node]
    Info [New1] = Value
Step 5: [Make link of newly created node with first node in the list]
    Next [New1]
    Previous [New1] = Previous [Ptr]
    Next [Previous [Ptr]] = New1
    Previous [Ptr] = New1
Step 6: Exit
```

Figure 5.33 Algorithm to insert left to the left most node in a list

```
/* INSERTING AS FIRST NODE IN THE DOUBLY LINKED LIST */
/*  DBL_IF.C */
# include <stdio.h>
# include <malloc.h>

struct Dlink_list
{
    struct Dlink_list *previous;
    int info;
    struct Dlink_list *next;
};
typedef struct Dlink_list Dnode;
```

```
/* Global declaration */
int num ;
Dnode *lp=NULL,*rp=NULL;

/* Prototypes of various functions */
void Create(Dnode *);
void display (Dnode *);
void Insert (Dnode *);

/* Function main */
void main()
{
   lp = (Dnode *) malloc(sizeof(Dnode));
   Create(lp);
   printf("\n Created doubly linked list is as follows\n");
   display(lp);
   Insert(lp);
   printf("\n After deletion of a node linked list is as follows\n");
   display(lp);
   getch();
}

/* Function create */
void Create(Dnode *ptr)
{
   char ch;

   num = 0;
   lp->previous = NULL;
   printf("\n Enter E for Exit any other key for continue: ");
   ch = getchar();
   if(ch=='e'){
   free(lp);
   exit(0);
   }
   do{
      printf("\n Input the values of the node : %d: ", (num+1));
      scanf("%d", &ptr->info);
      fflush(stdin);
      printf("\n want to continue(y/n)->: ");
      ch = getchar();
      if(ch=='y'){
      ptr->next = (Dnode *) malloc(sizeof(Dnode));
      ptr->next->previous = ptr;
      ptr = ptr->next;
```

```
    }
    num ++;
  }while(ch=='y');
  ptr->next=NULL;
  rp=ptr;    /* Assign the address of rightmost node to rp pointer */
  printf("\n Total nodes = %d", num);
}

/* Function insert */
void Insert (Dnode *ptr)
{
  Dnode *new1;
  new1 = (Dnode *) malloc(sizeof(Dnode));
  printf("\n Input the values of the node :");
  scanf("%d", &new1->info);
  if ( ptr == NULL)  /* for empty list */
   {
    new1->previous=NULL;
    new1->next=NULL;
    lp=new1;
   }else {    /* for list containing some node */
    new1->next=lp;
    lp->previous=new1;
    new1->previous=NULL;
    lp=new1;
   }
}

/* Display the list */
void display (Dnode *ptr)
{
  while(ptr!=NULL)  /* Traverse up to end of the list */
   {
    printf("\n 0x%x", ptr);
    printf(" %d", ptr->info);
    ptr = ptr->next;
   }
}
```

5.5.2.2 Inserting A Node At The End (A node to the right of the right most node in a list)

Suppose we want to insert a node into a doubly linked list at the right of the right most node, it is required to skip all the nodes from beginning, i.e., from the left most node to the right most node where one gets **NULL**. Another way of insertion is add new node after RP (RP contains the address of the right of the right most node). At this point a node is inserted. To insert a newly created node, following arrangement is required:

- Copy the **NULL** value at the next pointer value of the newly created node.
- Copy the **RP** pointer value of the last node to the previous pointer value of a newly created node.
- Make arrangements like **Figure 5.35**, i.e., adjust pointers accordingly.
- Copy address of the newly created node to the next pointer value of node.

Note: In C/C++ language, equivalent of **Figure 5.35** can be implemented as:
ptr->previous->next = new1;

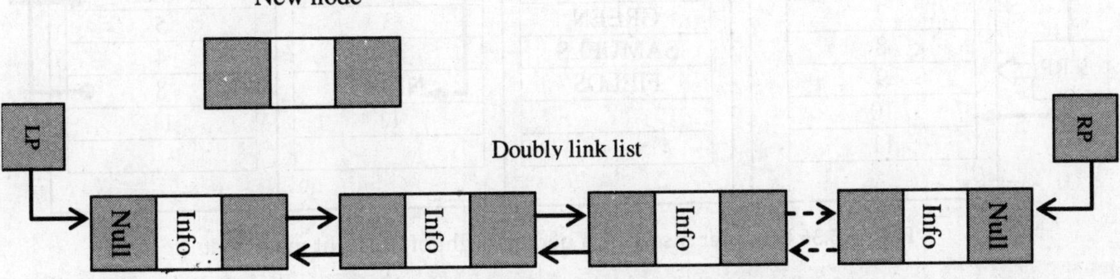

Figure 5.34 Doubly linked list before insertion

Suppose we have a doubly linked list as shown in **Figure 5.34**, then after insertion of a node at the right of right most node generates the list as shown in **Figure 5.35**.

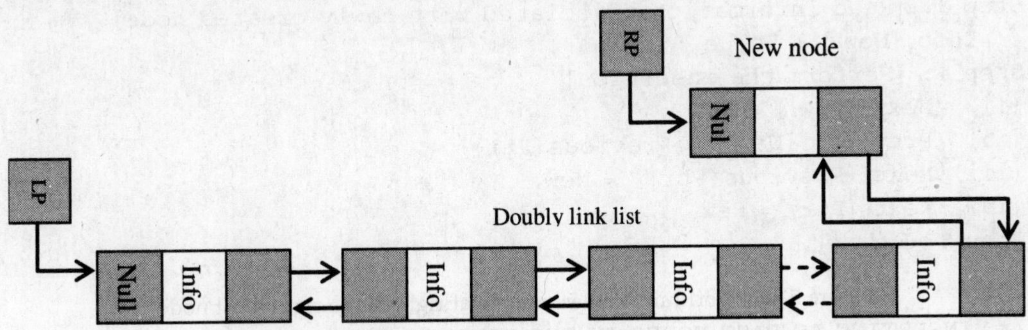

Figure 5.35 Doubly linked list after insertion of a right most node

For example, if we have a doubly linked list as shown in **Figure 5.31**, then the insertion of a node at the right of the right most node can be performed as shown in **Figure 5.36**.

$$\begin{aligned}&\texttt{Next [New}_1\texttt{] = Next [RP] = NULL}\\&\texttt{Next [11] = Next [10] = NULL}\\&\texttt{Previous [11] = Previous [10]}\\&\texttt{Next [10] = Next [10] = New}_1\texttt{ = 11}\end{aligned}$$

The algorithm to insert a node at the right of the right most is given in the **Figure 5.38**. Program segment **DBL_IL.C** illustrates the insertion algorithm given in **Figure 5.38**.

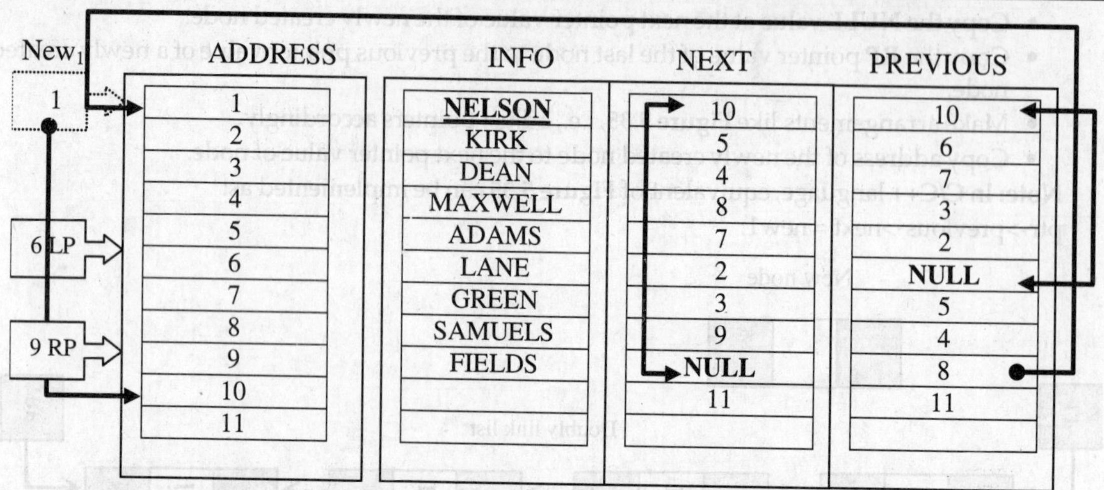

Figure 5.36 List after inserting a node at right of the right most node

```
Step 1: [Initialization]
   Ptr = RP
Step 2: [Create a new node]
   New1 = Create a node
Step 3: [Read information associated with newly created node]
   Info [New1] = Value
Step 4: [Perform the insertion]
(i)    Next [new1] = Ptr
(ii)   Previous [New1] = Previous[Ptr]
(iii) Next [Previous[Ptr]] = New1
(iv)   Next [Ptr] = New1
Step 5: Exit
```

Figure 5.38 Algorithm to insert a node at right of the right most node

```
/*  INSERTING AS LAST NODES IN THE DOUBLY LINKED LIST */
/*  DBL_IL.C */
# include <stdio.h>
# include <malloc.h>

struct Dlink_list
{
    struct Dlink_list *previous;
    int info;
    struct Dlink_list *next;
};
typedef struct Dlink_list Dnode;

/* Global declaration */
int num ;
```

```
Dnode *lp=NULL,*rp=NULL;
/* Prototypes of various functions */
void Create(Dnode *);
void display (Dnode *);
void Insert (Dnode *);

/* Function main */
void main()
{
   lp = (Dnode *) malloc(sizeof(Dnode));
   Create(lp);
   printf("\n Created doubly linked list is as follows\n");
   display(lp);
   Insert(lp);
   printf("\n After deletion of a node linked list is as follows\n");
   display(lp);
   getch();
}

/* Function creates a doubly linked list */
void Create(Dnode *ptr)
{
   char ch;

   num = 0;
   lp->previous = NULL;
   printf("\n Enter E for Exit any other key for continue: ");
   ch = getchar();
   if(ch=='e'){
   free(lp);
   exit(0);
   }
   do{
      printf("\n Input the values of the node : %d: ", (num+1));
      scanf("%d", &ptr->info);
      fflush(stdin);
      printf("\n want to continue(y/n)->: ");
      ch = getchar();
      if(ch=='y')
      {
      ptr->next = (Dnode *) malloc(sizeof(Dnode));
      ptr->next->previous = ptr;
      ptr = ptr->next;
      }
      num ++;
```

```
    }while(ch=='y');
    ptr->next=NULL;
    rp=ptr;   /* Assign the address of rightmost node to rp pointer */
    printf("\n Total nodes = %d", num);
}

/* Function insert */
void Insert (Dnode *ptr)
{
    Dnode *new1;
    new1 = (Dnode *) malloc(sizeof(Dnode));
    printf("\n Input the values of the node :");
    scanf("%d", &new1->info);
    if ( ptr == NULL) /* for empty list */
      {
       new1->previous=NULL;
       new1->next=NULL;
       lp=new1;
      }else {   /* for list containing some node */
       rp->next=new1;
       new1->previous=rp;
       new1->next=NULL;
       rp=new1;
      }
}

/* Display the list */
void display (Dnode *ptr)
{
    while(ptr!=NULL)  /* Traverse up to end of the list */
      {
       printf("\n 0x%x", ptr);
       printf(" %d", ptr->info);
       ptr = ptr->next;
      }
}
```

5.5.2.3 Inserting A Node At Desired Place

The insertion procedure is same as discussed earlier pointer arrangement after making an insertion at a desired place is shown in **Figure 5.39**. For the implementation of discussion, consider the program segment **DOUBL_I.C.**

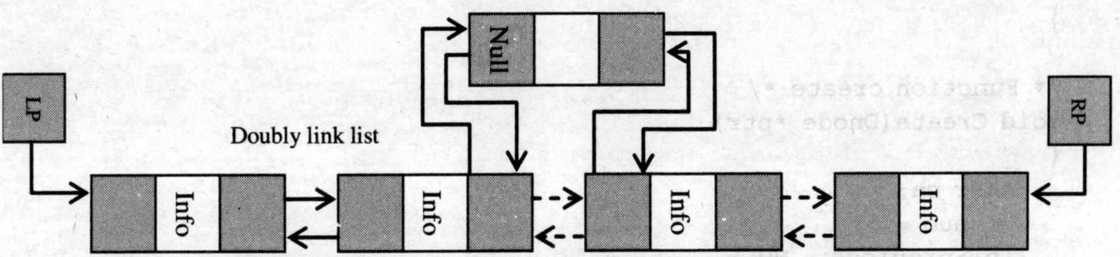

Figure 5.39 Doubly linked list after inserting a node at desired position

```
/* Inserting a nodes in double linked list at desired location */
/* Double_i.c */
# include <stdio.h>
# include <malloc.h>

struct Dlink_list
{
    struct Dlink_list *previous;
    int info;
    struct Dlink_list *next;
};
typedef struct Dlink_list Dnode;

/* Global declaration */
int num ;
Dnode *lp=NULL,*rp=NULL;

/* Prototype declaration */
void Create(Dnode *);
void display (Dnode *);
void Insert_before (Dnode *);
void Insert_after (Dnode *);

/* Function main */
void main()
{
    lp = (Dnode *) malloc(sizeof(Dnode));
    Create(lp);
    printf("\n Created doubly linked list is as follows\n");
    display(lp);
    Insert_before(lp);
    printf("\n After inesertion of a node linked list is as follows\n");
    display(lp);
    Insert_after(lp);
    printf("\n After inesertion of a node linked list is as follows\n");
```

```
    display(lp);
    getch();
}

/* Function create */
void Create(Dnode *ptr)
{
    char ch;
       num = 0;
    lp->previous = NULL;
    printf("\n Enter E for Exit any other key for continue: ");
    ch = getchar();
    if(ch=='e')
    {
    free(ptr);
    exit(0);
    }
    do{
       printf("\n Input the values of the node : %d: ", (num+1));
       scanf("%d", &ptr->info);
       fflush(stdin);
       printf("\n want to continue(y/n)->: ");
       ch = getchar();
       if(ch=='y'){
       ptr->next = (Dnode *) malloc(sizeof(Dnode));
       ptr->next->previous = ptr;
       ptr = ptr->next;
       }
       num ++;
    }while(ch=='y');
    ptr->next=NULL;
    printf("\n Total nodes = %d", num);
    rp=ptr;   /* Assign the address of rightmost node to rp pointer */
}

/* Function insert_before */
void Insert_before (Dnode *ptr)
{
    int x;
    Dnode *new1;
    new1 = (Dnode *) malloc(sizeof(Dnode));
    printf("\n Enter the element before which you want to insert :");
    scanf("%d", &x);
    while(ptr->info!=x&&ptr!=NULL)  /* Traverse list to locate the node */
      ptr=ptr->next;
```

```
    if(ptr==NULL) {
        printf("\n The element before which you want to insert does not
exist:");
        exit(0);
        }
    printf("\n Enter the element you want to insert :");
    scanf("%d", &new1->info);
    if(ptr==lp)   /* insertion before first node */
    {
    new1->next=ptr;
    new1->previous=NULL;
    ptr->previous=new1;
    lp=new1;
    } else {
    ptr->previous->next=new1;
    new1->previous=ptr->previous;
    new1->next=ptr;
    ptr->previous=new1;
    }
    num++;
}
/* Function insert_after */
void Insert_after(Dnode *ptr)
{
    int x;
    Dnode *new1;
    new1 = (Dnode *) malloc(sizeof(Dnode));
    printf("\n Enter the element after which you want to insert :");
    scanf("%d", &x);
    while(ptr->info!=x&&ptr!=NULL)  /* Traverse list to locate the node */
     ptr=ptr->next;
    if(ptr==NULL) {
        printf("\n The element after which you want to insert does not
exist:");
        exit(0);
        }
    printf("\n Enter the element you want to insert :");
    scanf("%d", &new1->info);
    ptr->next->previous=new1;
    new1->next=ptr->next;
    ptr->next=new1;
    new1->previous=ptr;
}
/* Function Display */
void display (Dnode *ptr)
```

```
{
    while(ptr!=NULL)  /* Traverse up to end of the list */
      {
        printf("\n 0x%x", ptr);
        printf(" %d", ptr->info);
        ptr = ptr->next;
      }
}
```

5.5.3 Deletion in a Doubly Linked List

In the case of deletion, there are several possibilities. If the list contains a single node, a deletion may result in an empty list with the previous and next pointer value for left most and right most pointers set to **NULL**. The node being deleted could be the left most node of the list. In this case, the pointer variable **previous** must be changed. Same situation arises when one is interested in deleting at the right most node of the list. The following points are taken care of at the time of deletion:

- If the list is empty, flash **UNDERFLOW** message.
- If a single node exits in the list, set the left and right pointers of the list as **NULL**. Else if the left most node in the list is to be deleted, delete the node and update the left pointer of the list.
- Else if the right most node in the list is to be deleted, delete the node and update the right pointer to the list. Else delete the node from the desired place of the list.
- Restore the deleted node to the free area.

From the above discussion, it is clear that the deletion operation can be classified into three categories:

- Delete the left most node
- Delete the right most node
- Delete any desired node (based on information, node number, etc.)

5.5.3.1 Deletion of Left Most Node

Suppose we have a doubly linked list as illustrated in **Figure 5.40**, then after deleting left most node from the list, it becomes as illustrated in **Figure 5.41**. The algorithm to delete left most node from a doubly linked list is illustrated in **Figure 5.42**. The program segment **DBL_DF.C** implements the discussion. Suppose, we have a doubly linked list as shown in **Figure 5.43** then the deletion operation is done like the illustration shown in **Figure 5.44**.

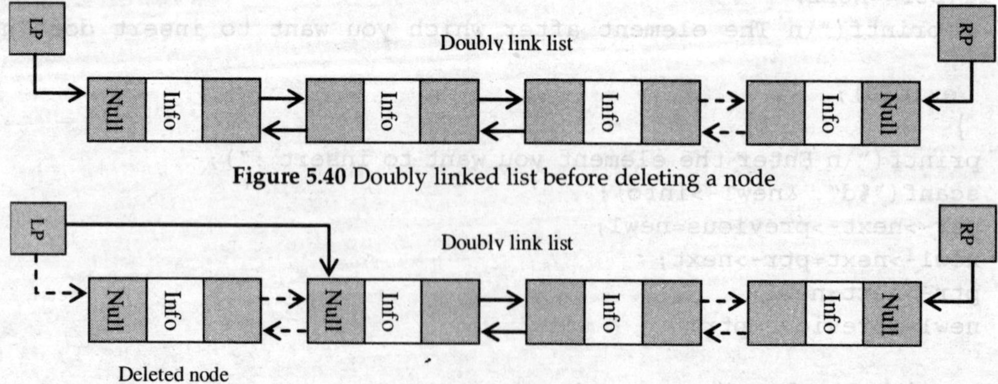

Figure 5.40 Doubly linked list before deleting a node

Figure 5.41 List after deleting left of the left most node

```
Step 1: [Initialization]
   Ptr = LP [Points to the left to the left most node in the list]
Step 2: [Check the list]
   If Ptr ≠ NULL
   Output "UNDERFLOW" and Exit
Step 3: [Perform deletion]
   Next [Previous [Ptr]] = Next [Ptr]
   Previous [Next [Ptr]] = Previous [Ptr]
   Delete (Ptr)
Step 4: Exit
```

Figure 5.42 Deletion algorithm for a doubly linked list (left mode node)

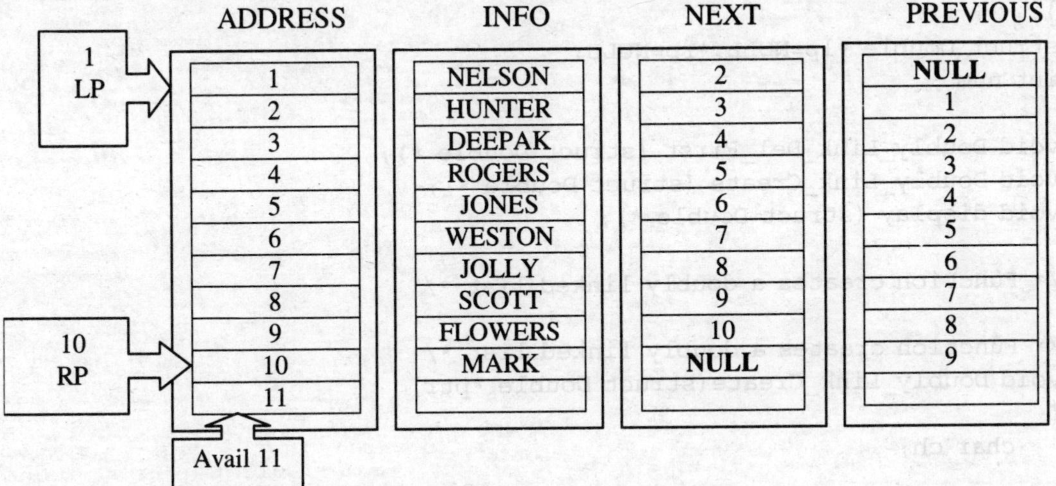

Figure 5.43 List before deleting a node

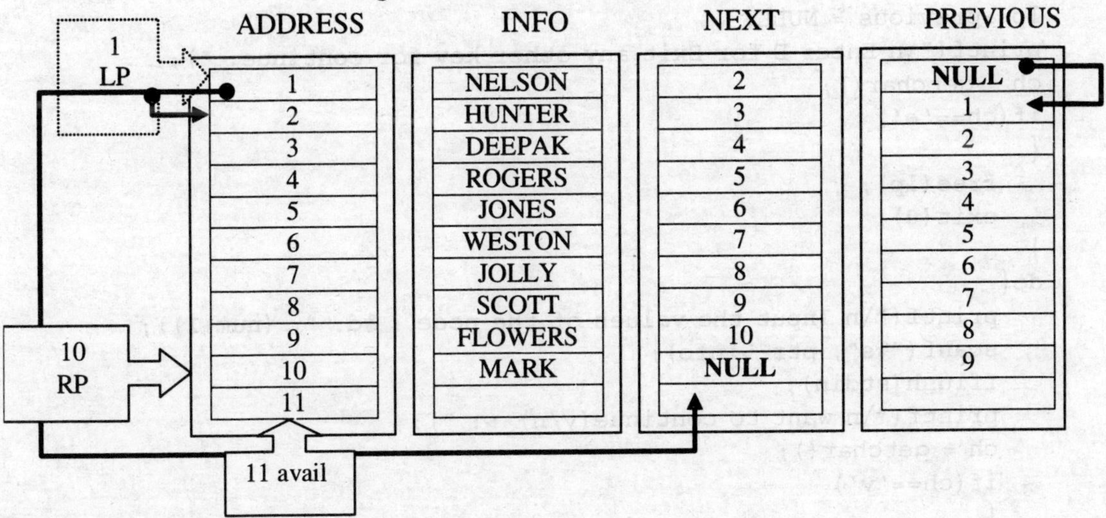

Figure 5.44 List after deleting left most node

```
/* DELETE LEFT OF THE LEFT MOST NODE FROM A SIMPLE DOUBLY LINKED LIST */
/* DBL_DF.C */

# include <stdio.h>
# include <malloc.h>

struct Double
{

   struct Double *next;
   char info[20];
   struct Double *previous;
};
struct Double *lp=NULL,*rp=NULL;
int num ;

void Doubly_Link_Del_First (struct Double *);
void Doubly_Link_Create (struct Double *);
void display (struct Double *);

/* Function creates a doubly linked list */

/* Function creates a doubly linked list */
void Doubly_Link_Create(struct Double *ptr)
{
   char ch;

   num = 0;
   lp->previous = NULL;
   printf("\n Enter E for Exit any other key for continue: ");
   ch = getchar();
   if(ch=='e')
   {
      free(lp);
      exit(0);
   }
   do{
      printf("\n Input the values of the node : %d: ", (num+1));
      scanf("%s", ptr->info);
      fflush(stdin);
      printf("\n want to continue(y/n)->: ");
      ch = getchar();
      if(ch=='y')
      {
```

```
        ptr->next = (struct Double *) malloc(sizeof(struct Double));
        ptr->next->previous = ptr;
        ptr = ptr->next;
      }
      num ++;
   }while(ch=='y');
   ptr->next=NULL;
   printf("\n Total nodes = %d", num);
}

/* Function delete */
void Doubly_Link_Del_First (struct Double *ptr)
{
   if ( ptr == NULL)
     printf("\n List is empty\n");
   else if(lp==rp)
   {
      lp=rp=NULL;
      free(ptr);
   }else{
        ptr=lp;
        lp=ptr->next;
        lp->previous=NULL;
        free(ptr);
   }
}
/* Display the list */
void display(struct Double *ptr)
{
   while (ptr!=NULL)
   {
      printf("\n 0x%x", ptr);
      printf(" %s", ptr->info);
      ptr = ptr->next;
   }
}

/* Function main */

void main()
{
   lp = (struct Double *) malloc(sizeof(struct Double));
   Doubly_Link_Create (lp);
   printf("\n Created linked list is as follows\n");
   display (lp);
```

```
    Doubly_Link_Del_First (lp);
    printf("\n After deletion of first node list is as follows\n");
    display(lp);
}
```

5.5.3.2 Deletion of Right Most Node

Suppose we have doubly linked list as illustrated in **Figure 5.40** and we have to delete right of the right most node from the list. To achieve the purpose, consider **Figure 5.45**. **Figure 5.46** represents a doubly linked list before deletion of a node and **Figure 5.47** represents necessary arrangement for deletion of right of the right most node from the list. The deletion algorithm is discussed in **Figure 5.48**. The program segment **DBL_DL.C** implements the discussion.

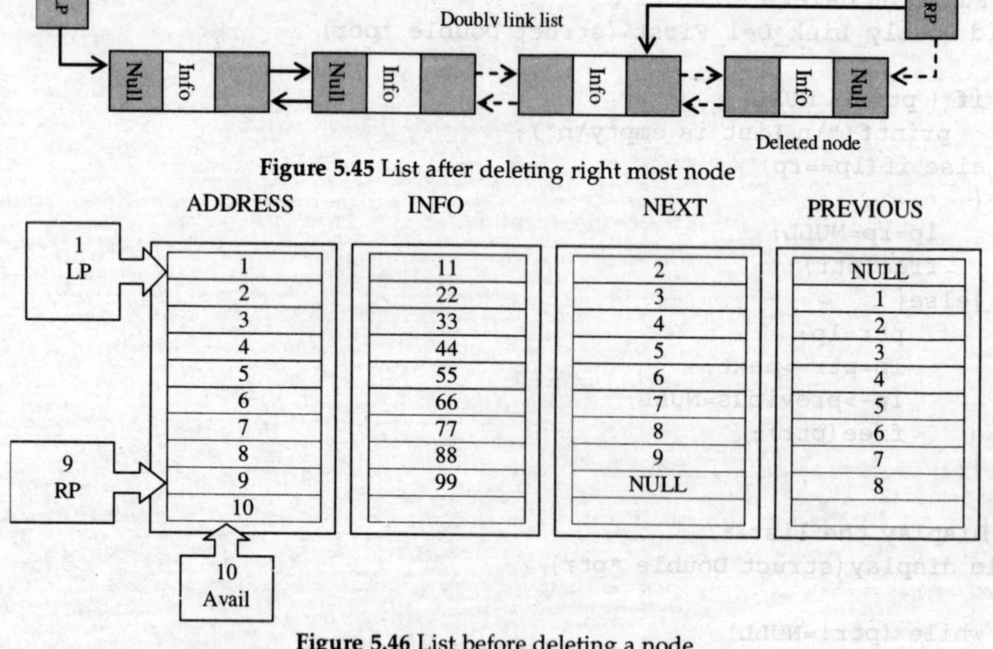

Figure 5.45 List after deleting right most node

Figure 5.46 List before deleting a node

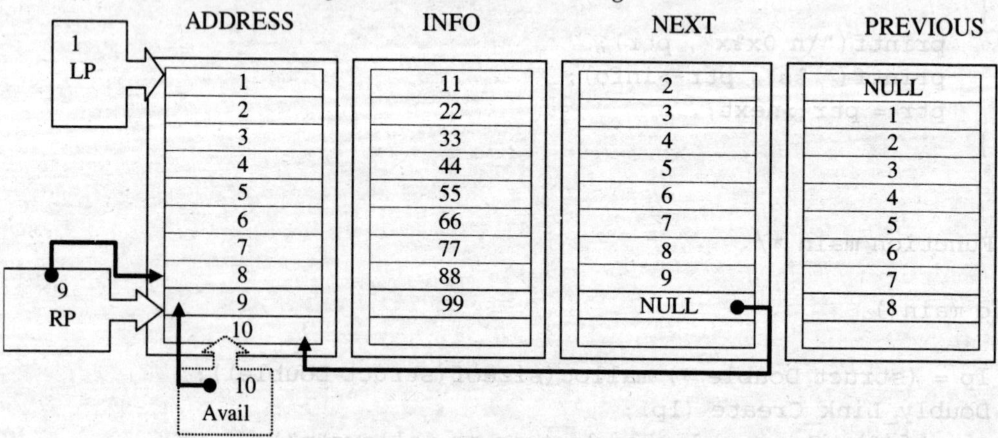

Figure 5.47 List after deleting right of right most node

```
Step 1: [Initialization]
   Ptr = RP
Step 2: [Check the list]
   If Ptr = NULL
   Output "Underflow" and Exit
Step 3: [Delete the node]
(i)   Next [Previous [Ptr]]= Next {Ptr]
(ii)  Previous [Next [Ptr]] = Previous [Ptr]
(iii) Delete (Ptr)
Step 6: Exit
```

Figure 5.48 Algorithm to delete right most node

```
/* DELETE LAST NODE FROM A SIMPLE DOUBLY LINKED LIST*/
/* DBL_DL.C */
# include <stdio.h>
# include <malloc.h>

struct Dlink_list
{
   struct Dlink_list *previous;
   int info;
   struct Dlink_list *next;
};
typedef struct Dlink_list Dnode;

/* Global declaration */
int num ;
Dnode *lp=NULL,*rp=NULL;

/* Prototypes of various functions */
void Create(Dnode *);
void display (Dnode *);
void Delete (Dnode *);

/* Function main */
void main()
{
   lp = (Dnode *) malloc(sizeof(Dnode));
   Create(lp);
   printf("\n Created doubly linked list is as follows\n");
   display(lp);
   Delete(lp);
   printf("\n After deletion of a node linked list is as follows\n");
   display(lp);
   getch();
}
```

```
/* Function create */
void Create(Dnode *ptr)
{
    char ch;
    num = 0;
    lp->previous = NULL;
    printf("\n Enter E for Exit any other key for continue: ");
    ch = getchar();
    if(ch=='e'){
    free(lp);
    exit(0);
    }
    do{
        printf("\n Input the values of the node : %d: ", (num+1));
        scanf("%d", &ptr->info);
        fflush(stdin);
        printf("\n want to continue(y/n)->: ");
        ch = getchar();
        if(ch=='y')
        {
        ptr->next = (Dnode *) malloc(sizeof(Dnode));
        ptr->next->previous = ptr;
        ptr = ptr->next;
        }
        num ++;
    }while(ch=='y');
    ptr->next=NULL;
    rp=ptr;
    printf("\n Total nodes = %d", num);
}


/* Function delete */
void Delete (Dnode *ptr)
{
    if ( lp == NULL)   /* for empty list */
      printf("\n List is empty\n");
    else if(lp==rp)    /* for list containing single node */
        {
    lp=rp=NULL;
    free(ptr);
      }else {            /* for list containing more than one node */
      ptr=rp;
```

```
        rp=ptr->previous;
        rp->next=NULL;
        free(ptr);
      }
}

/* Functio Display */
void display (Dnode *ptr)
{
    while(ptr!=NULL)  /* Traverse up to end of the list */
      {
        printf("\n 0x%x", ptr);
        printf(" %d", ptr->info);
        ptr = ptr->next;
      }
}
```

5.5.3.3 Deletion of A Desired Node

Suppose a doubly linked list is shown in **Figure 5.40**, and we want to delete a desired node from this list. For this, first of all we have to move next pointer to the desired node and then finally delete that node. **Figure 5.49** illustrates the above discussion and the program segment **DBL_D.C** implements the discussion. For example, if **Figure 5.50** represents a list and **Figure 5.51** shows necessary arrangement for deletion of a desired node. The deletion algorithm is given in **Figure 5.52**.

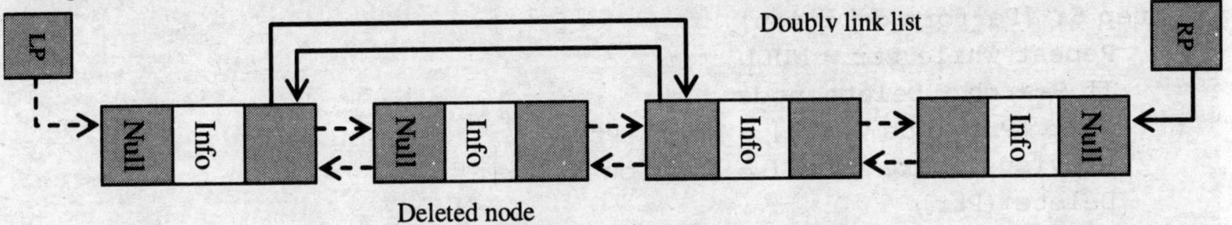

Figure 5.49 List after deleting desired node

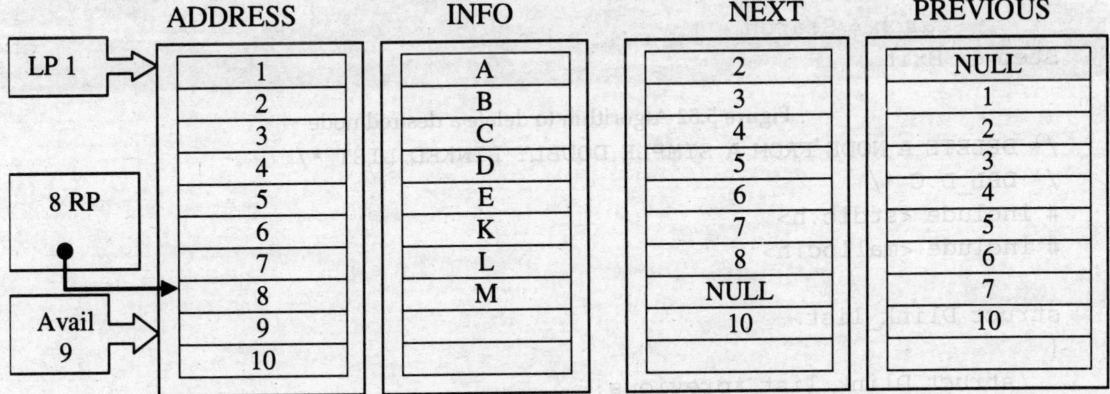

Figure 5.50 List before deleting a node

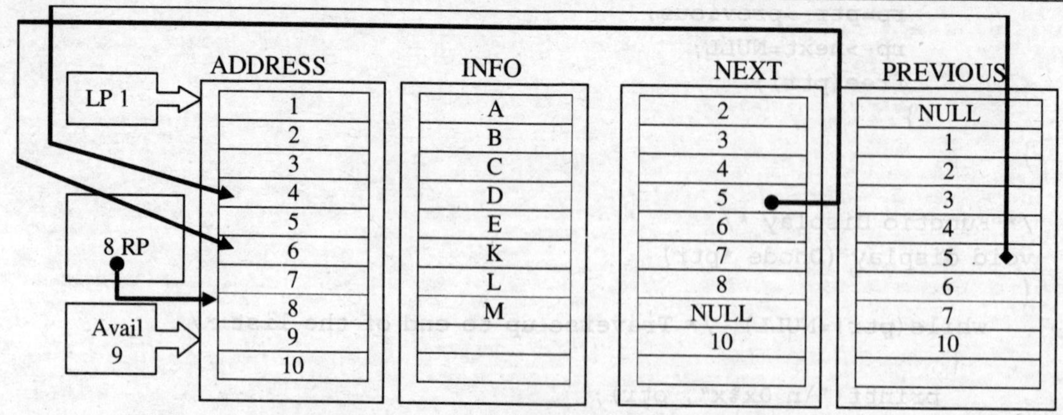

Figure 5.51 List before deleting 5th node

```
Step 1: [Initialization]
    Ptr = LP [Starting from left most pointer]
Step 2: [Check the list]
    If Ptr = NULL
    Output "Underflow" and exit
Step 3: [Set the counter]
    Search = 0
Step 4: [Input the node number to which you want to delete]
    Node_delete = Value
Step 5: [Perform deletion]
    Repeat while Ptr ≠ NULL
    If Search = Delete_node
    Next [Previous [Ptr]] = Next [Ptr]
    Previous [Next [Ptr]] = Previous [Ptr]
    Delete (Ptr)
    Else
        Ptr = Next [Ptr]
        Search = Search + 1
Step 6: Exit
```

Figure 5.52 Algorithm to delete a desired node

```
/* DELETE A NODE FROM A SIMPLE DOUBLY LINKED LIST */
/* DBL_D.C */
# include <stdio.h>
# include <malloc.h>

struct Dlink_list
{
    struct Dlink_list *previous;
    int info;
    struct Dlink_list *next;
```

```
};
typedef struct Dlink_list Dnode;

/* Global declaration */
int num ;
Dnode *lp=NULL,*rp=NULL;

/* Prototypes of various functions */
void Create(Dnode *);
void display (Dnode *);
void Delete (Dnode *);

/* Function main */
void main()
{
   lp = (Dnode *) malloc(sizeof(Dnode));
   Create(lp);
   printf("\n Created doubly linked list is as follows\n");
   display(lp);
   Delete(lp);
   printf("\n After deletion of a node linked list is as follows\n");
   display(lp);
   getch();
}

/* Function create */
void Create(Dnode *ptr)
{
   char ch;
   num = 0;
   lp->previous = NULL;
   printf("\n Enter E for Exit any other key for continue: ");
   ch = getchar();
   if(ch=='e'){
   free(lp);
   exit(0);
   }
   do{
      printf("\n Input the values of the node : %d: ", (num+1));
      scanf("%d", &ptr->info);
      fflush(stdin);
      printf("\n want to continue(y/n)->: ");
      ch = getchar();
      if(ch=='y')
      {
```

```
        ptr->next = (Dnode *) malloc(sizeof(Dnode));
        ptr->next->previous = ptr;
        ptr = ptr->next;
        }
        num ++;
     }while(ch=='y');
    ptr->next=NULL;
    rp=ptr;
    printf("\n Total nodes = %d", num);
}

/* Function delete */
void Delete (Dnode *ptr)
{
    int node_no;
    int search_counter = 1;
    Dnode *prev=NULL;
    printf("\n Input the node number you want delete: ");
    scanf("%d", &node_no);  if ( lp == NULL)  /* Check for empty list */
    {
      printf("\n List is empty\n");
       exit(0);
    }
    while(search_counter<node_no)  /* Locate the element */
    {
        prev=ptr;
        ptr=ptr->next;
        search_counter++;
    }
    if(ptr==NULL){
      printf("\n node does not exist");
      exit(0);
    }
    if(ptr->previous==NULL)   /*if it is first node */
    {
        lp=ptr->next;
        lp->previous=NULL;
        free(ptr);
    }else if(ptr->next==NULL)  /*if it is last node */
     {
      rp=ptr->previous;
      rp->next=NULL;
      free(ptr);
    }else{
      prev->next=ptr->next;
```

```
        ptr->next->previous=prev;
        free(ptr); /* delete node */
      }
  }

  /* Function display */
  void display (Dnode *ptr)
  {
    while(ptr!=NULL)  /* Traverse up to end of the list */
      {
        printf("\n 0x%x", ptr);
        printf(" %d", ptr->info);
        ptr = ptr->next;
      }
  }
```

When node number is given and we want to delete a node then the program segment **DBL_D.C** is useful. When information of a node is given and we want to delete the node then we need to modify this program segment.

5.6 MERGING TWO LISTS

Suppose we have two doubly linked lists as illustrated in **Figures 5.53** and **5.54**. We have to insert each element of the second list into the first so that the resulting list maintains the sorted order. To accomplish this task first we will remove first node from the second list and find its proper place in the first list. When we find proper place for the first element removed from the second list, we insert it into the first list. Next we remove second element from the second list, and once again we start scanning from the very first node of the first list. When we find the proper place for the removed element from the second list, we insert into the first list. This process continues till the end of second list.

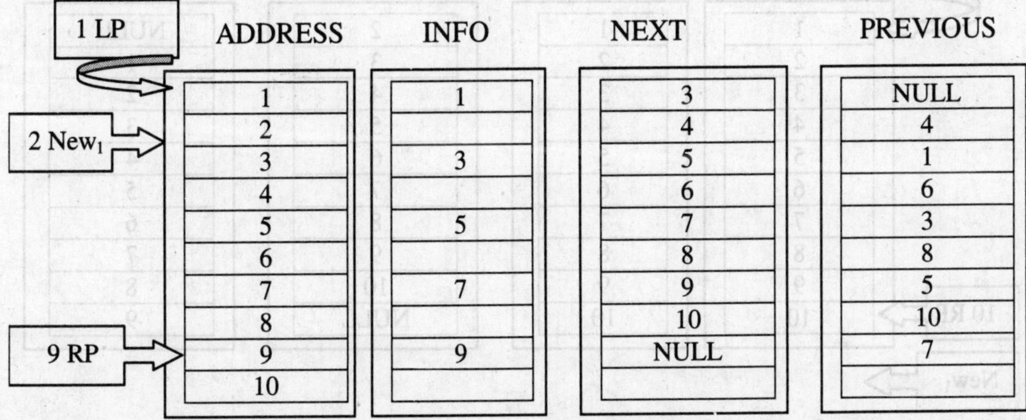

Figure 5.53 List before insertion operation

For example, first element of the second list in **Figure 5.54** is 2. We remove this element from the list and scan the first list for the proper place for it. We find that the first element takes place in between first and second elements of the list. The resulting list is illustrated in **Figure 5.55**. If one continues this process, he/she gets final list as illustrated in **Figure 5.56**. Algorithm for merging two lists is given in **Figure 5.57**.

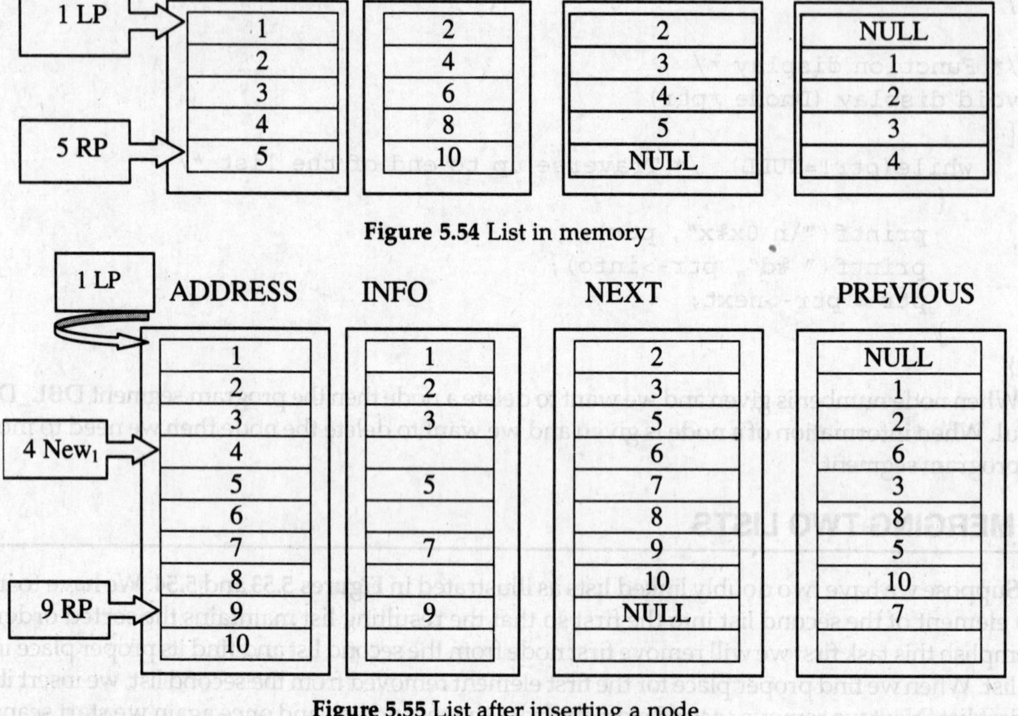

Figure 5.54 List in memory

Figure 5.55 List after inserting a node

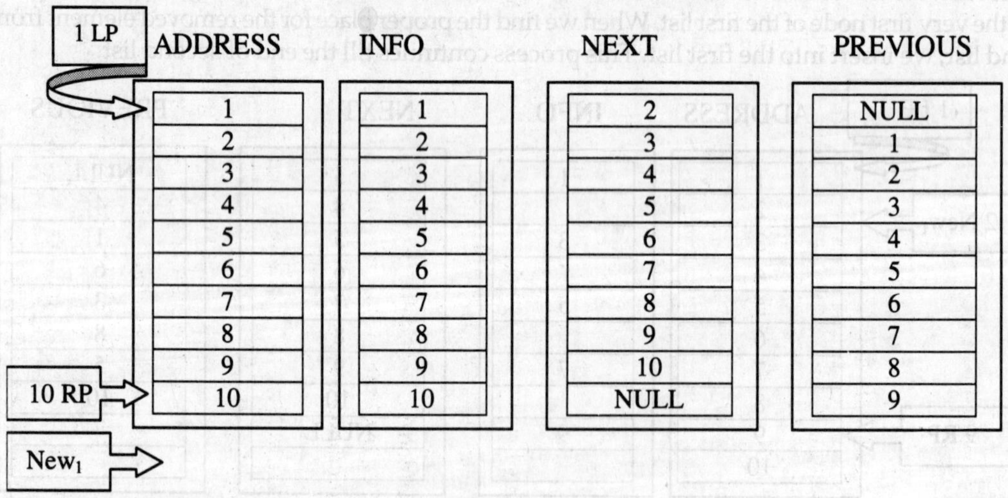

Figure 5.56 List after inserting some nodes

```
Merge (list1, list2) /* This function merges two doubly linked list in
sorted order */
LP1 = left pointer of List 1, LP2 left pointer of List 2, LP left pointer
of produced list.
  Step 1: [check for the NULL of List 1]
    If (LP1 = NULL) LP= LP2
  Step 2: [check for the NULL of List 2]
    If (LP2 = NULL) LP= LP1
  Step 3: Else [Initial node of List generated]
    LP = list = create a node
  Step 4: [Set the next and previous pointer to the NULL
    Previous[LP] = Next[LP]=NULL
  Step 5: while (list1  ≠ NULL and list 2  ≠  NULL) repeat thru Step 10
  Step 6: if(Info[list1] <= Info[list2]
    Info[list] = Info[list1]
    List1 = Next[list1]
  Setp 7 Else
    Info[list] = Info[list2]
    list2 = Next[list2]
  Step 8:  Next[list] = create a node [ Create next node of the produced
list]
  Step 9: Previous[Nextplist] = list
  Step 10: list = Next[list]
  Step 11: if(list1= NULL)
    While (list 2  ≠  NULL) repeat thru Step (e)
    (a)  Info[list] = Info[list2]
    (b)  list2 = Next[list2]
    (c)  Next[list] = create a node [ Create next node of the produced list]
    (d)  Previous[Nextplist] = list
    (e)  list = Next[list]
    else
  While (list 1  ≠  NULL) repeat thru Step (e)
    (a)  Info[list] = Info[list1]
    (b)  list1 = Next[list1]
    (c)  Next[list] = create a node [ Create next node of the produced list]
    (d)  Previous[Nextplist] = list
    (e)  list = Next[list]
  Setp 12: Previous[Nextplist] = NULL
  Step 13 Exit

  Repeat through thru Step (vii) while Node ≠ NULL and Found ≠ 0
  (i)  if Info [Ptr] = Info [New1]

  (a)  Next [Temp] = Ptr
  (b)  Previous [Temp] = Previous [Ptr]
```

```
(c)  Next [Previous[Ptr] = Temp
(d)  Previous [Ptr] = Temp
(e)  Found = 1
     Else
      Ptr = Next [Ptr]
(ii) if Found ≠ 0
(iii)    if Info [Ptr] > Info [Temp]
(a)  Next [Temp] = Ptr
(b)  Previous [Temp] = Previous [Ptr]
(c)  Next [Previous[Ptr]] = Temp
Else
(a)  Next [Temp] = NULL
(b)  Previous [Temp] = Ptr
(c)  Next [Ptr] = Temp
Step 3: Exit
```

Figure 5.57 Algorithm to merge a two list

The program segment **DBL_MRG.C** implements the above discussion in better way.

```
/* MERGING TWO DOUBLY LINKED LISTS (ASCENDING ORDER) */
/* DBL_MRG.C */
# include <stdio.h>
# include <malloc.h>

struct Dlink_list
{
   struct Dlink_list *previous;
   int info;
   struct Dlink_list *next;
};
typedef struct Dlink_list Dnode;

/* Global declaration */
int num ;
Dnode *lp1=NULL,*lp2=NULL,*lp=NULL;
Dnode *list1=NULL,*list2=NULL,*list=NULL,*new1;

/* Prototypes of various functions */
void Create(Dnode *);
void display (Dnode *);
void Merge (Dnode *,Dnode *);

/* Function main */
void main()
{
   lp1 = (Dnode *) malloc(sizeof(Dnode));
```

```
    lp2 = (Dnode *) malloc(sizeof(Dnode));
    Create(lp1);
    printf("\n first list is as follows\n");
    display(lp1);
    Create(lp2);
    printf("\n second list is as follows\n");
    display(lp2);
    Merge(lp1,lp2);
    printf("\n After inesertion of a node linked list is as follows\n");
    display(lp);
    getch();
  }
  /* Function create */
  void Create(Dnode *ptr)
  {
    char ch;

    num = 0;
    ptr->previous = NULL; /* set previous pointer of ptr to NULL */
    printf("\n Enter E for Exit any other key for continue: ");
    ch = getchar();
    if(ch=='e')
    {
    free(ptr);
    exit(0);
    }
    printf("\n Enter first list: ");
    do{
      printf("\n Input the values of the node : %d: ", (num+1));
      scanf("%d", &ptr->info);
      fflush(stdin);
      printf("\n want to continue(y/n)->: ");
      ch = getchar();
      if(ch=='y'){
      ptr->next = (Dnode *) malloc(sizeof(Dnode));
      ptr->next->previous = ptr;
      ptr = ptr->next;
      }
      num ++;
    }while(ch=='y');
    ptr->next=NULL;
    printf("\n Total nodes = %d", num);
    printf("\n Enter second list:");
```

```
}

/* Function insert */
void Merge (Dnode *list1 ,Dnode *list2)
{

    if (lp1 == NULL)  /* if list1 is empty */
      lp=lp2;      /* resultant list will be list2 */
    else if(lp2==NULL) /* if list2 is empty */
      lp=lp1;      /* resultant list will be list1 */
    else{
        lp=list = (Dnode *) malloc(sizeof(Dnode));
        lp->previous=lp->next=NULL; /* set previous and next pointer of LP
to NULL */
        while(list1!=NULL&&list2!=NULL)
        {
          if(list1->info<=list2->info)
          {
            list->info=list1->info;
            list1=list1->next;
          }else {
            list->info=list2->info;
            list2=list2->next;
          }
        list->next = (Dnode *) malloc(sizeof(Dnode));
        list->next->previous=list;
        list=list->next;
          }
         if(list1==NULL)
           while(list2!=NULL) /* copy the remaining element of list2 */
           {
           list->info=list2->info;
           list2=list2->next;
           list->next = (Dnode *) malloc(sizeof(Dnode));
           list->next->previous=list;
           list=list->next;
           }else
        while(list1!=NULL) /* copy the remaining element of list2 */
        {
           list->info=list1->info;
           list1=list1->next;
           list->next = (Dnode *) malloc(sizeof(Dnode));
           list->next->previous=list;
           list=list->next;
        }
```

```
        list->previous->next=NULL;
        free(list);
    }
}
/* Display the list */
void display (Dnode *ptr)
{
    while(ptr!=NULL)    /* Traverse up to end of the list */
    {
        printf("\n 0x%x", ptr);
        printf(" %d", ptr->info);
        ptr = ptr->next;
    }
}
```

5.7 HEADER LINKED LIST

A header node is a special node that is found at the front of the list. A list, which contains this type of node, is called the header-linked list. This type of list is useful when information other than that found in each node is needed. For example, suppose there is an application in which the number of items in a list is often calculated. Usually a list is always traversed to find the length of the list. However, if the current length is maintained in an additional header node this information can be easily obtained. The following are two widely used header linked lists.

(i) Grounded header linked list
(ii) Circular header linked list

5.7.1 Grounded Header Linked List

A grounded header linked list is one whose last node contains the **NULL** pointer. **Figure 5.58** illustrates header-linked list. In the header linked list the **Start** pointer always points to the header node. **Next [Start] = NULL** indicates that a grounded header linked list is empty. The operations that are possible on this type of linked list are (a) Insertion (b) Deletion and (c) Traversing which are similar to the simple linked list discussed earlier.

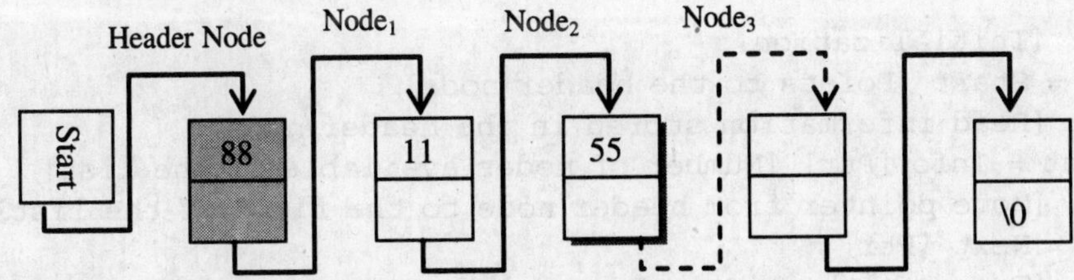

Figure 5.58 Grounded header linked list

Algorithm to build a header-linked list is illustrated in **Figure 5.59**. Algorithm to traverse a header-linked list is illustrated in **Figure 5.60**. For example, if we have a header linked as illustrated in **Figure 5.61** and want to traverse this list. Here in this list header node contains 10 and the list contains 10 elements. Then traversing can be performed as follows:

Ptr = Start = 1

Count = Info [Ptr] = Info [1] = 10 Header node value
Now moving pointer from header to very first node of the list
Ptr = Next [Ptr]
Next [1] = 2 Info [2] =11
Next [2] = 3 Info [3] = 22
Next [3] = 4 Info [4] = 33
Next [4] = 5 Info [5] = 44
Next [5] = 6 Info [6] = 55
Next [6] = 8 Info [8] = 66
Next [8] = 9 Info [9] = 77
Next [9] = 10 Info [10] = 88
Next [10] = 11 Info [11] = 99
Next [11] = 12 Info [12] = 100
Next [12] = NULL that is end of the list

```
Step 1: [Initialization]
   Ptr = Start [Points to header node]
Step 2: [Create header node]
   Next [Ptr] = Create a node
Step 3: [Initialize counter]
   I = 0
Step 4: [Create linked list]
   Repeat while choice < n
(i)    Next [Ptr] = Create  new node
(ii)   Ptr = Next [Ptr] [Make link of the current node to the next node]
(iii)  Info [Ptr] = Value [Read information of the node]
(iv)   Next [Ptr] = NULL [Assign NULL to the next node value]
(v)    I = I + 1[Increment the counter]
Step 5: [Copy totals number of nodes in the list into the header node]
(i)    Ptr = Start
(ii)   Info [Ptr] = I
Step 6: Exit
```

Figure 5.59 Algorithm to build a header linked list

```
Step 1: [Initialization]
   Ptr = Start [Points to the header node]
Step 2: [Read information stored in the header node]
   Count = Info [Ptr] [Number of nodes available in the list]
Step 3: [Move pointer from header node to the first of the list]
   Ptr = Next [Ptr]
Step 4: [Traverse the list]
   Repeat while Count ≠ 0
(i)    Process Info [Ptr]
(ii)   Ptr = Next [Ptr]
(iii)  Count = Count - 1
Step 5: Exit
```

Figure 5.60 Algorithm to traverse a header linked list

We have shown insertion of an element in the list given in **Figure 5.61** and final generated list is presented in **Figure 5.62**. The program segment **LINK_CH.C** illustrates **creation, insertion** and **traversing** of the header-linked list. This program segment implements the algorithms discussed in **Figures 5.59, 5.60,** and **5.63**.

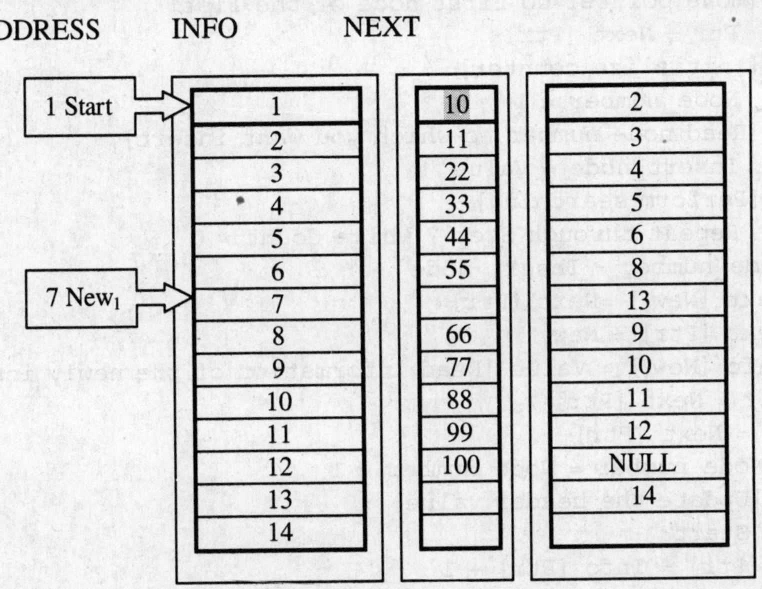

Figure 5.61 Header linked list in memory

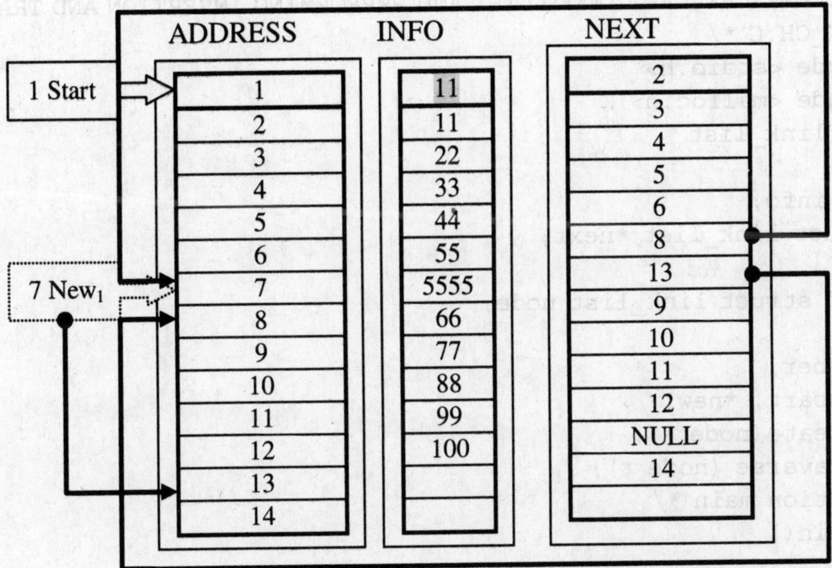

Figure 5.62 Header linked list after inserting a node

```
Step 1: [Initialization]
        Ptr = Start
Step 2: [Process the header node]
        Count = Info [Ptr]
Step 3: [Move pointer to first node of the list]
        Ptr = Next [Ptr]
Step 4: [Initialize counter]
        Node_number = 1
Step 5: [Read node number to which you want insert]
        Insert_node = Value
Step 6: [Perform searching]
        Repeat through Step 7 while Count ≠ 0
   If Node_number = Insert_node
(i)    Next [New1] =Next [Ptr]
(ii)   Next [Ptr] = New1
(iii)  Info [New1] = Value [Read information of the newly inserted node]
(iv)   Ptr = Next [Ptr]
Else Ptr = Next [Ptr]
Step 7: Node_number = Node_number + 1
Step 8: [Update the header value]
   Ptr = Start
   Info [Ptr] = Info [Ptr] + 1
Step 9: Exit
```

Figure 5.63 Algorithm to insert a node in a header linked list

```
/* CREATING A HEADER LINKED LIST AND PERFORMING INSERTION AND TRAVERSING*/
/* LINK_CH.C */
# include <stdio.h>
# include <malloc.h>
struct link_list
{
   int info;
   struct link_list *next;
};
typedef struct link_list node;
int i;
int number;
node *start, *new1;
void create(node *);
void traverse (node *);
/* Function main */
void main()
{
   start = (node *) malloc(sizeof(node));
   create (start);
```

```
    printf("\n created list is as follows:\n");
    traverse (start);
    getch();
  }
  /* function create */
  void create(node *ptr)
  {
    char ch;
    start->info = 0;
    printf("\n Enter E for Exit any other key for continue: ");
    ch = getchar();
    if(ch=='e'){
    free(ptr);
    exit(0);
    }
    ptr->next = (node *) malloc(sizeof(node));
    ptr=ptr->next;
    do{
       printf("\n Input the values of the node : %d: ", (start->info+1));
       scanf("%d", &ptr->info);
       fflush(stdin);
       printf("\n want to continue(y/n)->: ");
       ch = getchar();
       if(ch=='y'){
       ptr->next = (node *) malloc(sizeof(node));
       ptr = ptr->next;
       }
       start->info ++;
    }while(ch=='y');
    ptr->next=NULL;
    printf("\n Total nodes = %d", start->info);
  }
  /* function display */
  void traverse(node *ptr)
  {
    ptr=ptr->next;
    while (ptr!=NULL)
    {
       printf(" %d", ptr->info);
       ptr = ptr->next;
    }
  }
```

5.7.2 Circular Header Linked List

A linked list in which last node points to the header node is called circular header linked list. The chains do not indicate first or last nodes. In this case, external pointers provide a frame of reference because last node of a circular header linked list does not contain the **NULL** pointer as shown in **Figure 5.64**. Possible operations on a circular header linked list are: (a) Insertion (b) Deletion and (c) Traversing.

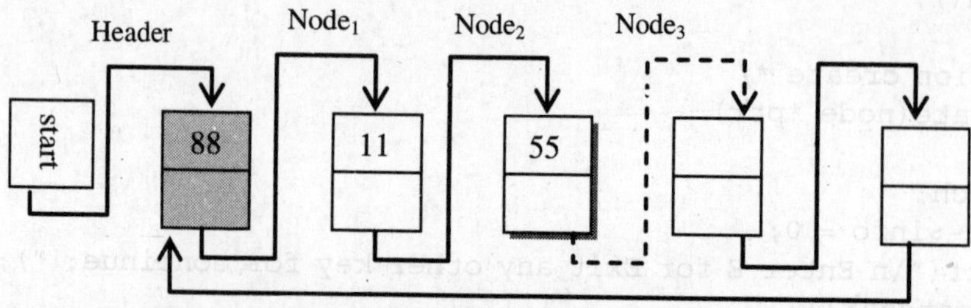

Figure 5.64 Circular header linked list

```
Step 1: [Initialization]
Node = Start [Points to header node]
Step 2: [Create header node]
   Next [Ptr] = Create header node
Step 3: [Initialize counter]
   I = 0
Step 4: [Create linked list]
   Repeat while choice < e
(vi)   Next [Ptr] = Create  new node
(vii)  Ptr = Next [Ptr] [Make link of the current node to the next node]
(viii)    Info [Ptr] = Value [Read information of the node]
(ix)   I = I + 1[Increment the counter]
Step 5: [If the end of the creation link last of the list to the header node]
   If choice = e
    Next [Ptr] = Start
Step 6: [Fill information in the header node]
   Ptr = Start
Info [Ptr] = I
Step 7: Exit
```

Figure 5.65 Algorithm to build a circular header linked list

```
Step 1: [Initialization]
   Ptr = Start [Points to the header node]
Step 2: [Read information stored in the header node]
   Count = Info [Ptr] [Number of nodes available in the list]
Step 3: [Move pointer from header node to the first of the list]
   Ptr = Next [Ptr]
Step 4: [Traverse the list]
   Repeat while Ptr ≠ Start
(iv)   Process  Info [Ptr]
(v)    Ptr = Next [Ptr]
(vi)   Count = Count - 1
Step 5: Exit
```

Figure 5.66 Algorithm to traverse a circular header linked list

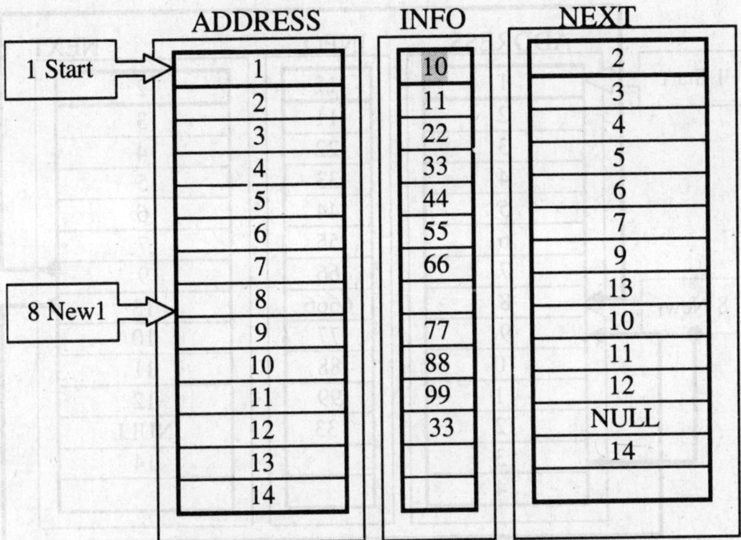

Figure 5.67 Circular header linked list in memory

Algorithm to traverse a circular header-linked list is illustrated in **Figure 5.66**. If we have a header linked as illustrated in **Figure 5.67** and wants to traverse this list. Here, header node has information 10 meaning by the list contains the 10 elements. The traversing is as follows:

```
Ptr = Start = 1
Count = Info [Ptr] = Info [1] = 10 Header node value
Now moving pointer from header to very first node of the list
Ptr = Next [Ptr]
Next [1] = 2 Info [2] =11
Next [2] = 3 Info [3] = 22
Next [3] = 4 Info [4] = 33
Next [4] = 5 Info [5] = 44
Next [5] = 6 Info [6] = 55
Next [6] = 7 Info [8] = 66
Next [7] = 9 Info [9] = 77
Next [9] = 10 Info [10] = 88
Next [10] = 11 Info [11] = 99
Next [11] = 12 Info [12] = 33
Next [12] = NULL that is end of the list
```

From the list shown in **Figure 5.67**, it is clear that the first available space in the list is at position 8. When one wants to insert a node in the list the newly inserted node in the list firstly occupies this available space. When one inserts a node, first of all it is required to make link of the first free space with the node after that one wants to insert the node. Then make link of this newly inserted node with the next node in the list that was previously linked with previous node before inserting the new one. For example, in the **Figure 5.67** first we link the available (Newly inserted that is 8th node) node with the 9th node in the list and the make link of this (Newly inserted) with node that was previously linked with the 8th node that is make link with 7th node. The resulting list is illustrated in **Figure 5.68**.

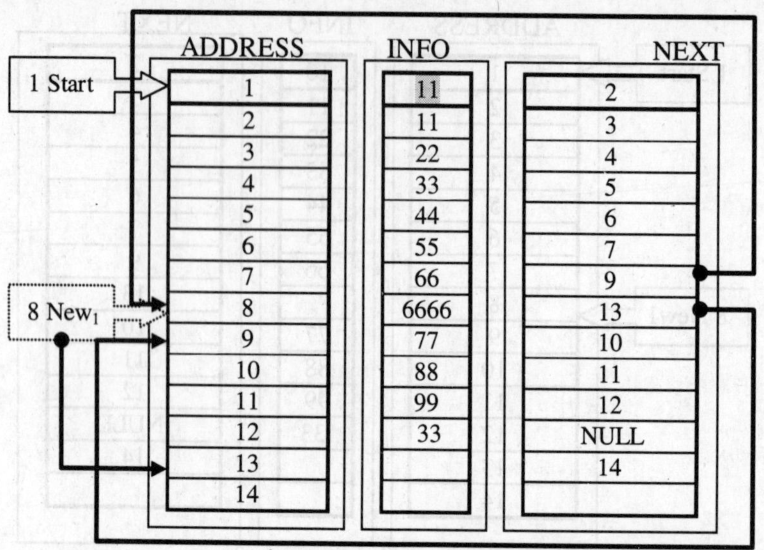

Figure 5.68 Circular header linked list after inserting a node

The program segment **CIRCLIST.C** illustrates the **creation, traversing** and **insertion** operation of a circular linked. This program segment implements algorithms discussed in **Figures 5.65, 5.66** and **5.69.**

```
Step 1: [Initialization]
   Ptr = Start
Step 2: [Process the header node]
   Count = Info [Ptr]
Step 3: [Move pointer to first node of the list]
   Ptr = Next [Ptr]
Step 4: [Initialize counter]
   Node_number = 1
Step 5: [Read node number to which you want insert]
   Insert_node = Value
Step 6: [Perform searching]
   Repeat through Step 7 while Ptr ≠ Start
    If Node_number = Insert_node
(a)    Next [New1] =Next [Ptr]
(b)    Next [Ptr] = New1
(c)    Info [New1] = Value [Read information of the newly inserted node]
Else
   Ptr = Next [Ptr]
Step 7: Node_number = Node_number + 1
Step 8: [Update the header node]
   Ptr = Start
   Info [Ptr] = Info [Ptr] + 1
Step 9: Exit
```

Figure 5.69 Algorithm to insert a node in a header linked list

```
/* CREATING CIRCULAR LINKED LIST WITH HEADER NODE */
/* CIRCLIST.C */
# include <stdio.h>
# include <malloc.h>
struct link_list
{
   int info;
   struct link_list *next;
};
typedef struct link_list node;

/* Global declaration */
int i;
int number;
node *start, *new1;
/* Prototypes of various functions */
void create(node *);
void display (node *);

/* Function main */
void main()
{
    start = (node *) malloc(sizeof(node));

    create (start);
    printf("\n created list is as follows:\n");
    display (start);
    getch();
}

/* function create */
void create(node *ptr)
{
    char ch;
    start->info = 0; /* Set header node */
    printf("\n Enter E for Exit any other key for continue: ");
    ch = getchar();
    if(ch=='e'){
    free(ptr);
    exit(0);
    }
    ptr->next = (node *) malloc(sizeof(node)); /* Create a new node */
    ptr=ptr->next;
    do{
        printf("\n Input the values of the node : %d: ", (start->info+1));
```

```
        scanf("%d", &ptr->info);
        fflush(stdin);
        printf("\n want to continue(y/n)->: ");
        ch = getchar();
        if(ch=='y')
        {
        ptr->next = (node *) malloc(sizeof(node));
        ptr = ptr->next;
        }
        start->info ++;
    }while(ch=='y');
    ptr->next=NULL;
    printf("\n Total nodes = %d", start->info);
}

/* function display */
void display(node *ptr)
{
    ptr=ptr->next;
    while (ptr!=NULL)  /* Traverse up to end of the list */
    {
        printf(" %d", ptr->info);
        ptr = ptr->next;
    }
}
```

5.8 APPLICATION OF HEADER LINKED LIST

In this section we will consider polynomial and possible operations on polynomial such as Addition of it.

5.8.1 Polynomials

The header-linked lists are frequently used to maintain the polynomials in memory. The header node is used to represents the zero polynomial. For example, suppose we have

$F(x) = 5x^5 - 3x^3 + 2x^2 + x^1 + 10x^0$

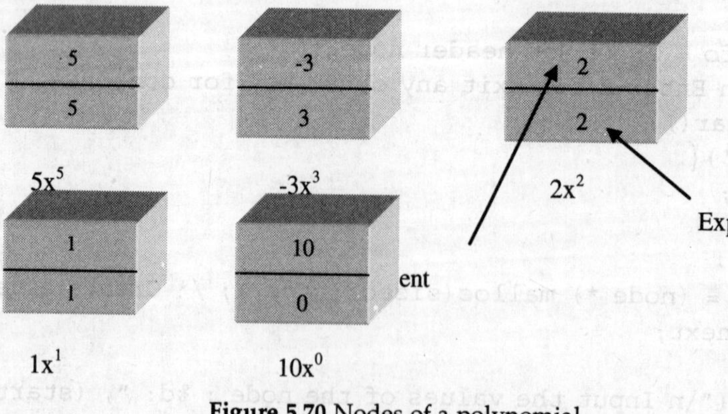

Figure 5.70 Nodes of a polynomial

From the polynomial represented by **F (x)** it is clear that this polynomial contains two things coefficient and exponent, where **x** is a formal parameter. Hence, we can say that a polynomial is sum of terms and each of which consists of a coefficient and an exponent. The computer implementation requires implementing polynomials as a list of pairs of coefficient and exponent. Each of these pairs will constitute a structure, so a polynomial will be represented as a list of structures. If one wants to represent **F (x)** with the help of linked list then the list will contain 5 nodes. The individual nodes are illustrated in **Figure 5.70**. When we link each node represented in **Figure 5.70**, we get a linked list structure that represents polynomial **F (x). Figure 5.71** illustrates the polynomial **F (x)**.

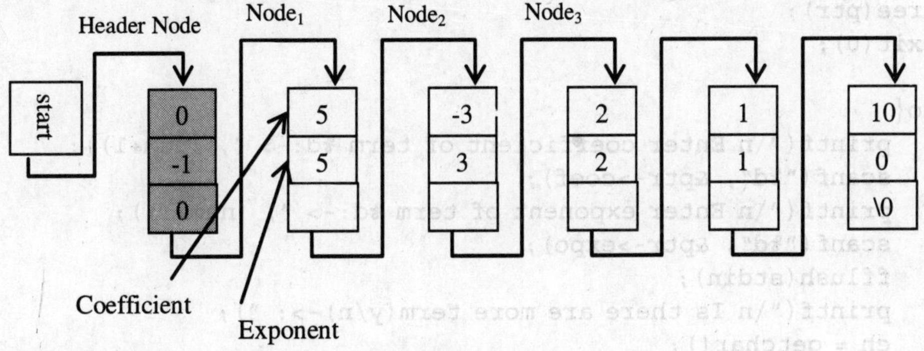

Figure 5.71 Polynomial

The program segment **POLY.C** illustrates the polynomial creation procedures.

```
/* POLY NOMIAL WITH HELP OF LINKED LIST */
/* POLY.C */
# include <stdio.h>
# include <malloc.h>
struct polynode
{
   int coef;
   int expo;
   struct polynomial *next;
};
typedef struct polynode node;
node *start;
//void insertion(node *);
void read_poly(node *);
void display(node *);
/* Function main */
void main()
{
   start= (node *) malloc(sizeof(node));
   read_poly(start);
   display(start);
   getch();
}
/* Function create a ploynomial list */
```

```
void read_poly(node *ptr)
{
  char ch;
  int num=0;
  printf("\n Enter E for Exit any other key for continue: ");
  ch = getchar();
  if(ch=='e'){
  start=NULL;
  free(ptr);
  exit(0);
  }
  do{
    printf("\n Enter coefficient of term %d:-> ", (num+1));
    scanf("%d", &ptr->coef);
    printf("\n Enter exponent of term %d:-> ", (num+1));
    scanf("%d", &ptr->expo);
    fflush(stdin);
    printf("\n Is there are more term(y/n)->: ");
    ch = getchar();
    if(ch=='y'){
    ptr->next = (node *) malloc(sizeof(node));
    ptr = ptr->next;
    }
    num ++;
  }while(ch=='y');
  ptr->next=NULL;
  printf("\n Total term = %d", num);
}

/* Display the polynomial */
void display(node *ptr)
{
  int num=0;
  if(start==NULL)
  printf("Polynomial is Nil");
  while (ptr!=NULL)
  {
    printf("\n coefficient of term %d:-> ", (num+1));
    printf("%d", ptr->coef);
    printf("\n exponent of term %d:-> ", (num+1));
    printf("%d", ptr->expo);
    num++;
    ptr = ptr->next;
  }
}
```

5.8.2 Addition of Polynomials

To add two polynomials we need to scan them once. If we find terms with the same exponent in the two polynomials, then we add the coefficients, otherwise, we copy the term of larger exponent into the sum and go on. When we reach at the end of one of the polynomial, then remaining part of the other is copied into the sum. Suppose we have two polynomials as illustrated in **Figures 5.72** and **5.73** and we have to perform addition of these polynomials.

When we scan first node of the two polynomials, we find that exponential power of first node in the second polynomial is greater than that of first node of the first polynomial. Here the exponent of the first node of the second polynomial is greater, hence we have to copy first node of the second polynomial into the sum. Then we consider the first node of the first polynomial and once again first node value of first polynomial is compared with the second node value of the second polynomial. Here the first node exponent value of the first polynomial is greater than second node exponent value the second polynomial. We copy the first node of the first polynomial into the sum. Now consider the second node of the first polynomial and it compared with the second node of the second polynomial. Here the exponent value of the second node of the second list greater than the second node of the first polynomial, hence we copy the second node of the second list into sum. Now we consider the third node exponent of the second polynomial and compare it with second node exponent value of the first polynomial. We find that both are equal, hence perform addition of their coefficient and copied into the sum. This process is continuing till all the nodes of both the polynomials are exhausted. For example, after adding the above two polynomial, we get the polynomial illustrated in **Figure 5.74**.

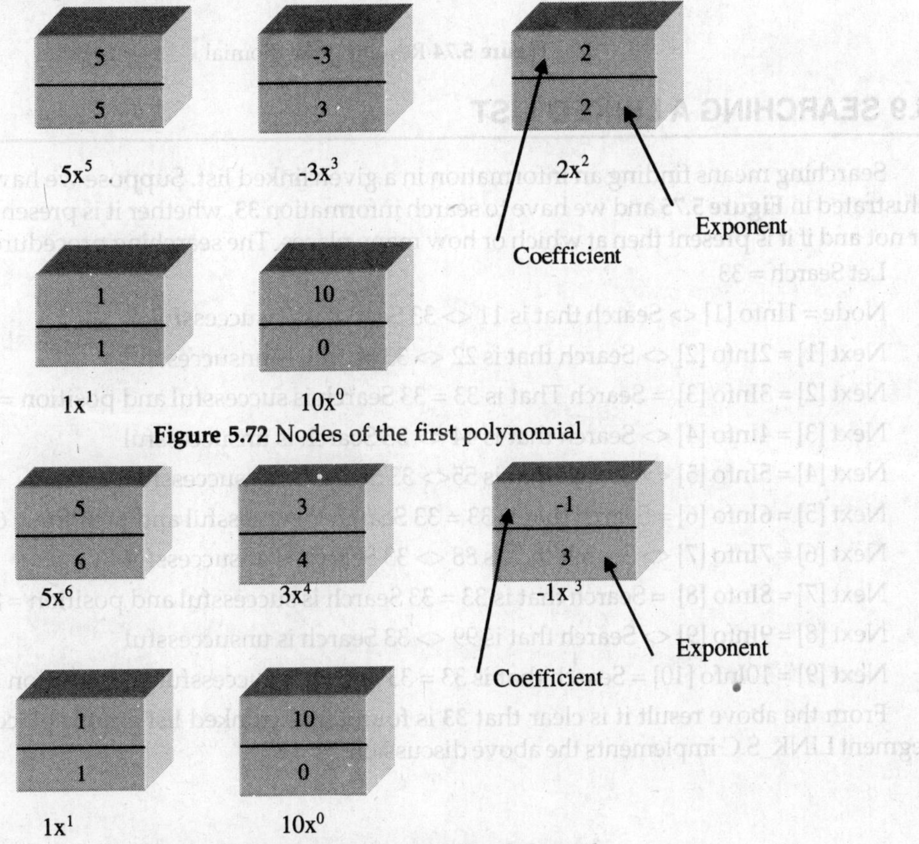

Figure 5.72 Nodes of the first polynomial

Figure 5.73 Nodes of the second polynomial

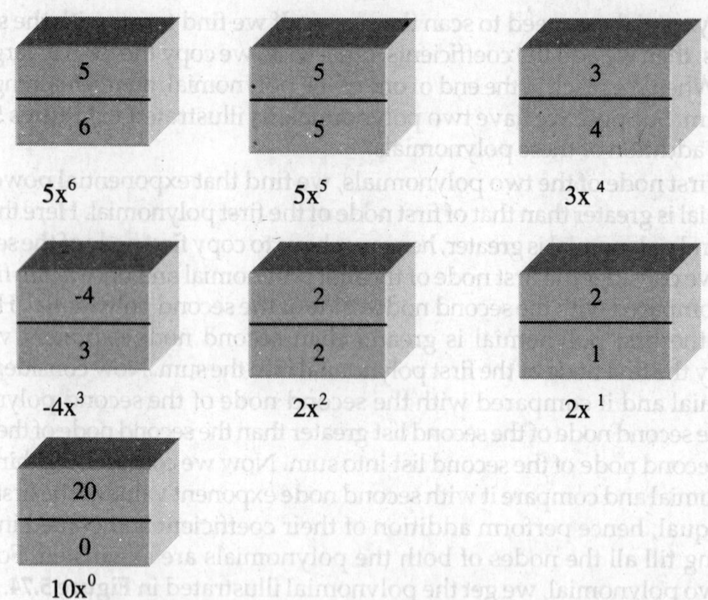

Figure 5.74 Resulting polynomial

5.9 SEARCHING A LINKED LIST

Searching means finding an information in a given linked list. Suppose we have a linked list as illustrated in **Figure 5.75** and we have to search information **33**, whether it is present in the given list or not and if it is present then at which or how many places. The searching procedure is given below:

Let Search = 33

Node = 1Info [1] <> Search that is 11 <> 33 Search is unsuccessful

Next [1] = 2Info [2] <> Search that is 22 <> 33 Search is unsuccessful

Next [2] = 3Info [3] = Search That is 33 = 33 Search is successful and position = 3

Next [3] = 4Info [4] <> Search that is 44 <> 33 Search is unsuccessful

Next [4] = 5Info [5] <> Search that is 55<> 33 Search is unsuccessful

Next [5] = 6Info [6] = Search that is 33 = 33 Search is successful and position = 6

Next [6] = 7Info [7] <> Search that is 88 <> 33 Search is unsuccessful

Next [7] = 8Info [8] = Search that is 33 = 33 Search is successful and position = 8

Next [8] = 9Info [9] <> Search that is 99 <> 33 Search is unsuccessful

Next [9] = 10Info [10] = Search that is 33 = 33 Search is successful and position = 10

From the above result it is clear that **33** is found in the linked list at four places. The program segment LINK_S.C implements the above discussion.

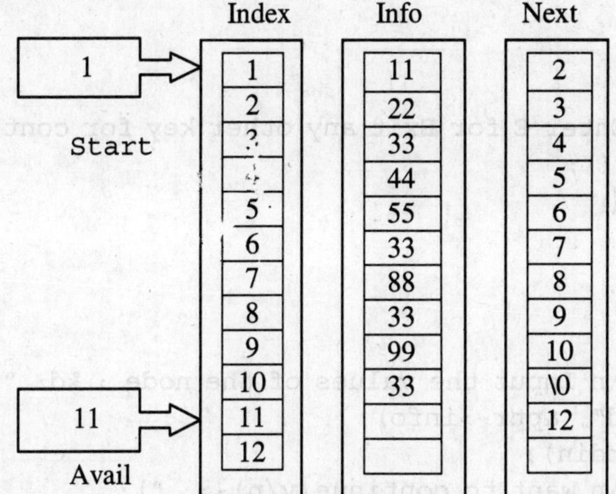

Figure 5.75. List in memory

```
/* SEARCH A NODE INTO A SIMPLE LINKED LIST WITH INFORMATION IS KNOWN */
/* LINK_S.C */
# include <stdio.h>
# include <malloc.h>

struct link_list
{
   int info;
   struct link_list *next;
};
typedef struct link_list node;
int i,num;
node *start;
void search(node *);
void create(node *);
void display(node *);

/* Function main */

void main()
{
   start = (node *) malloc(sizeof(node));
   create(start);
   display(start);
   search(start);
   getch();
}
/* Function create a linked list */
void create(node *ptr)
{
```

```
    char ch;
    clrscr();
    num = 0;
    printf("\n Enter E for Exit any other key for continue: ");
    ch = getchar();
    if(ch=='e'){
    free(ptr);
    exit(0);
    }
    do{
        printf("\n Input the values of the node : %d: ", (num+1));
        scanf("%d", &ptr->info);
        fflush(stdin);
        printf("\n want to continue(y/n)->: ");
        ch = getchar();
        if(ch=='y'){
        ptr->next = (node *) malloc(sizeof(node));
        ptr = ptr->next;
        }
        num ++;
    }while(ch=='y');
    ptr->next=NULL;
    printf("\n Total nodes = %d", num);
}

/* function display */
void display(node *ptr)
{
    while (ptr!=NULL)
    {
        printf("\n %d", ptr->info);
        ptr = ptr->next;
    }
}
/* Searching a value */
void search(node *ptr)
{
    int node_number = 1;
    int search_node;
    printf("\n Enter information of a node you want to search:");
    scanf("%d", &search_node);
    if (start == NULL)
        printf("\n List is empty");

    while(ptr!=NULL && search_node != ptr->info)
```

```
{
ptr=ptr->next;
node_number++;
}
if(ptr==NULL){
printf("\n Search is unsuccessful");
printf("\n Information does not found in the list:");
}
else
{
 printf("\n Search is successful");
printf("\n Information to which we want search is: %d", search_node);
 printf("\n Position from beginning of the list: %d", node_number);
}
}
```

5.10 SORTING A LINKED LIST

Some times it is also required to sort a list in ascending or descending order. The program segment **LINKSORT.C** implements ascending order technique, by some modifications one can change it for descending order technique (details of sorting and searching techniques are given in Chapter 9).

```
/* SORTING A LINKED LIST IN ASCENDING ORDER */
/* LINKSORT.C */
#include <stdio.h>
#include <malloc.h>

struct  link_list
{
   int data;
   struct link_list *next;
};
typedef struct  link_list node;
node *start;
int num;

void  create(node *);
void  sort(node *);
void  display(node *);
/* Function main */
void main()
{
   /* Assign memory to single(struct) type variables */
   start = (node *) malloc(sizeof(node));
   create(start);
   printf("\n created list is as follows:\n");
```

```
    display(start);
    sort(start);
    printf("\n sorted is as follows:\n");
    display(start);
    getch();
}

/* function create */
void create(node *ptr)
{
    char ch;
    clrscr();
    num = 0;
    printf("\n Enter E for Exit any other key for continue: ");
    ch = getchar();
    if(ch=='e'){
    free(ptr);
    exit(0);
    }
    do{
        printf("\n Input the values of the node : %d: ", (num+1));
        scanf("%d", &ptr->data);
        fflush(stdin);
        printf("\n want to continue(y/n)->: ");
        ch = getchar();
        if(ch=='y')
        {
        ptr->next = (node *) malloc(sizeof(node));
        ptr = ptr->next;
        }
        num ++;
    }while(ch=='y');
    ptr->next=NULL;
    printf("\n Total nodes = %d", num);
}

/* function display */
void display(node *ptr)
{
    while (ptr!=NULL)
    {
        printf(" %d", ptr->data);
        ptr = ptr->next;
    }
}
```

```
/* SORTING THE LINK LIST START FROM HERE */
void sort(node *ptr)
{
 node *counter;
 for(; ptr->next != NULL; ptr = ptr->next)
  {
   for(counter = ptr->next; counter != NULL; counter = counter->next)
    {
    if(ptr->data > counter->data)
    {
      int temp = ptr->data;
      ptr->data = counter->data;
      counter->data = temp;
     }
   }
  }
}
```

If we want to create a linked list that contains the sorted names of files in the current directory, program needs to place each file name into the list at the correct position. The program **FILELIST.C** creates a linked list that contains the names of the current directory files. It uses the function **readdir()** to read directory entries. It then allocates the memory to hold an entry and copies to the list entry, the corresponding file name. After all the files have been added to the list the program loops through the list and display list entry.

```
/* FILELIST.C */
#include <stdio.h>
#include <dirent.h>
#include <malloc.h>
#include <string.h>
#include <stdlib.h>

void main(int argc, char *argv[])
{
   DIR *directory_pointer;
   struct dirent *entry;

   struct FileList {
      char filename[64];
      struct FileList *next;
   } start, *node;

   if ((directory_pointer = opendir(argv[1])) == NULL)
      printf("Error opening %s\n", argv[1]);
   else
   {
      start.next = NULL;
```

```
        node = &start;

        while (entry = readdir(directory_pointer))
        {
          node->next = (struct FileList *) malloc(sizeof(struct FileList));
          if (node == NULL)
          {
             printf("Insufficient memory to store list\n");
             exit(1);
          }
          node = node->next;
      strcpy(node->filename, entry->d_name);
          node->next = NULL;
        }

        closedir(directory_pointer);
        node = &start;
        while (node)
        {
          printf("%s\n", node->filename);
          node = node->next;
        }

    }
}
```

Some times it is also required to merge two lists. This can be done with the help of program segment **LINKCAT.C.**

```
/* CONCATENATE TWO LINKED LIST */
/* LINKCAT.C */
#include <stdio.h>
#include <malloc.h>

struct  link_list
{
   int data;
   struct link_list *next;
};
typedef struct  link_list node;
node *list1, *list2, *list3;
int num;
void  create(node *);
void  concate(node *, node *, node *);
void  display(node *);
/* Function main */
void main()
```

```
{
    /* Assign memory to single(struct) type variables */
    list1 = (node *)malloc(sizeof(node));
    list2 = (node *)malloc(sizeof(node));
    list3 = (node *)malloc(sizeof(node));
    create(list1);
    printf("\n Original list ONE is as follows:\n");
    display(list1);
    create(list2);
    printf("\n Original list TWO is as follows:\n");
    display(list2);
    concate(list1, list2, list3);
    printf("\n concatenated list is as follows:\n");
    display(list3);
    getch();
}

/* function create */
void create(node *ptr)
{
    char ch;
    clrscr();
    num = 0;
    printf("\n Enter E for Exit any other key for continue: ");
    ch = getchar();
    if(ch=='e'){
    free(ptr);
    exit(0);
    }
    do{
        printf("\n Input the values of the node : %d: ", (num+1));
        scanf("%d", &ptr->data);
        fflush(stdin);
        printf("\n want to continue(y/n)->: ");
        ch = getchar();
        if(ch=='y'){
        ptr->next = (node *) malloc(sizeof(node));
        ptr = ptr->next;
        }
        num ++;
    }while(ch=='y');
    ptr->next=NULL;
    printf("\n Total nodes = %d", num);
}
```

```
/* function display */
void display(node *ptr)
{
    while (ptr!=NULL)
    {
        printf(" %d", ptr->data);
        ptr = ptr->next;
    }
}

/* function concatenate */
void concate(node *list1, node *list2, node *list3)
{

    /* Copying first list */
    while(list1!= NULL)
    {
        list3->data = list1->data;
        list1 = list1->next;
        list3->next = (node* ) malloc(sizeof(node));
        list3 = list3->next;
    }

    /* Copying second list  */
    while(list2->next!=NULL)
    {
        list3->data = list2->data;
        list2 = list2->next;
        list3->next = (node*)malloc(sizeof(node));
        list3 = list3->next;
    }
    list3->data = list2->data;
    list3->next = NULL;
}
```

5.11 INTERSECTION OF TWO LINKED LIST

Two linked lists list1 and list2 are joined at a particular node, called the point of intersection of two linked lists. Find the point of intersection, i.e. the first node after which both lists have same nodes. Desired order is O(m + n), Time Complexity and O(1) Space Complexity, where m and n are size of two list, respectiviley. These, statements can be coded as algorithm which is shown in Figure 5.33.

```
    Step 1:  Find length of list1 - use a ptr1 node starting from head of list1
and move till last node.
    Step 2: Find length of list2 - use a ptr2 node starting from head of list2
and move till last node.
```

```
Step 3: If ptr1 and ptr2 are different, it means that linked lists are
        non-intersecting. Return null.
Example: list1: 1-2-3-4 , list2: 5-6-7-8, last nodes are different.
Step 4: Else set variables diff, ptr1 and ptr2 as:
   a). ptr1 (a list node) to head node of larger list.
   b). ptr2 (a list node) to head node of smaller list.
   c). diff (an integer) to difference of lengths of larger to smaller
lists i.e.—> absolute difference of the lengths.
Step 5: Move forward ptr1 by diff number of nodes.
Step 6: Now lists starting from ptr1 and ptr2 have same number of nodes
        and intersect at a particular node. Therefore, both ptr1 and
        ptr2 are equidistant from the intersection node.
Step 7: Starting from ptr1 and ptr2 simultaneously, move node by node
        till a common node is reached. This node is the intersection of
        the 2 lists.
```

Figure 5.76 Intersention of Two Lists

FOR SUMMATIVE AND FORMATIVE ASSESSMENT

5.1 Discuss the advantages, if any, of a two-way linked list over a one-way linked list for each of the following operations:

(i) Traversing the list to process each node

(ii) Deleting a node whose location is given

(iii) Searching an unsorted list for a given element

(iv) Searching a sorted list for a given element

(v) Inserting a node before the node with a given location

(vi) Inserting a node after the node with a given location

5.2 Write an algorithm, which deletes the last node from the **LIST.** Suppose **LIST** is a header list in memory.

5.3 Find the polynomials **POLY$_1$** and **POLY$_2$** stored in **Figure 5.77**.

5.4 Consider the **Figure 5.78** and find the following:

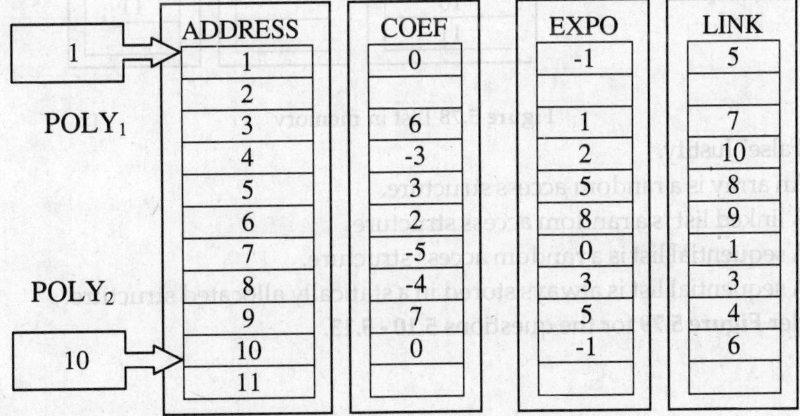

ADDRESS	COEF	EXPO	LINK
1	0	-1	5
2			
3	6	1	7
4	-3	2	10
5	3	5	8
6	2	8	9
7	-5	0	1
8	-4	3	3
9	7	5	4
10	0	-1	6
11			

Figure 5.77 Polynomials in memory

(i) Sequence of characters in the list.

(ii) Suppose **A** then **L** are deleted from the list and then **G** is inserted at the beginning of the list. Find the final structure.

(iii) Suppose **L** then **A** are deleted from the list and then **G** is inserted at the beginning of the list. Find the final structure.

(iv) Suppose **G** is inserted at the beginning of the list and then **A** and then **L** are deleted from the list. Find the final structure.

5.5 Write a program that takes as input an integer number, split the number in its digits and stores the digits in a linked list structure.

5.6 Suppose **LIST** is a linked list in memory consists of numerical values. Write a procedure for each of the following:

(i) Finding the minimum **Min** of the values in **LIST**.

(ii) Finding the average of the values in **LIST**.

(iii) Finding the summation of the elements.

5.7 Write a procedure, which interchanges the **kth** and **k+1st** elements in a list without affecting any other values.

5.8 (a) Explain the difference between a sequential and linked list representation of a list.

(b) Give an example of a problem for which a linked list would be the better solution.

(c) Give an example of a problem for which a sequential list would be the better solution.

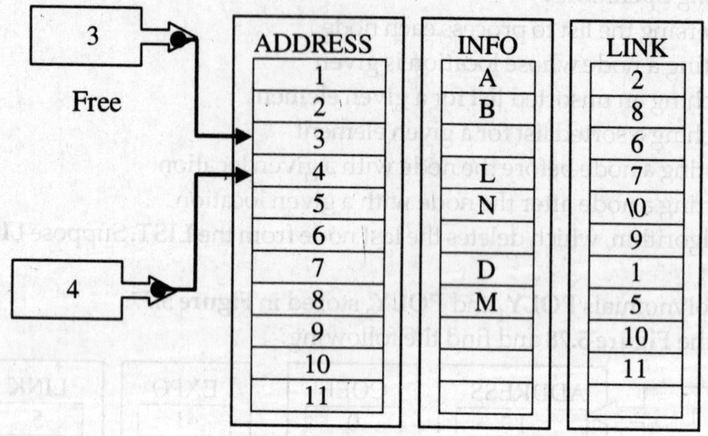

Figure 5.78 List in memory

5.9 True/False? Justify.

(i) An array is a random access structure.

(ii) A linked list is a random access structure.

(iii) A sequential list is a random access structure.

(iv) A sequential list is always stored in a statically allocated structure.

Consider **Figure 5.79** for the questions **5.10 - 5.13**.

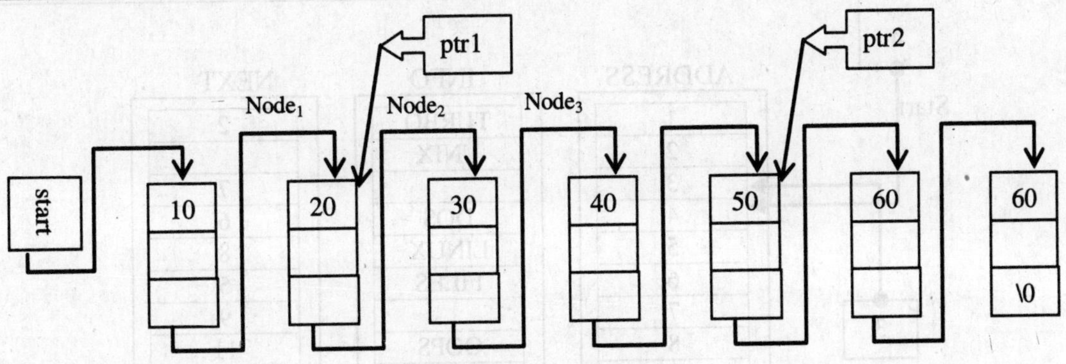

Figure 5.79 List in memory

5.10 Illustrate the following expressions:

(i) ptr1 -> info (ii) ptr2->next->info

(iii) start->next->next->info

5.11 Are the following expressions true/false?

(i) start->next = ptr1; (ii) ptr1 ->next ->info == 40;

(iii) ptr2->next == NULL; (iv) start-> info = 10;

5.12 Discuss whether the syntax of the each of the following statements are valid or invalid.

(i) start->next = ptr1->next; (ii) start->next = *(ptr2->next);

(iii) *start = ptr2; (iv) ptr2=ptr1->next->info;

(v) ptr1->info = ptr2->info; (vi) ptr2 = ptr2->next->next;

5.13 Write one statement to do each of the following:-

(i) Make **start** point to the node containing 30.

(ii) Make **ptr2** point to the last node in the list

(iii) Make **start** point to an empty list.

(iv) Set the **info** member of the node containing 30 to 40.

5.14 Consider the linked list shown in **Figure 5.80.**

(a) Find the alphabetical list of strings.

(b) Suppose **LINUX** is deleted and then **C** and **SQL** are inserted into the list. Find the final structure.

5.15 Suppose we have following list of months: January, February, March, April, May, June, July, August, September, October, November, and December. Create a linked structure to sort months in their alphabetical order.

5.16 Suppose **LIST** is in memory and contains duplicate information. Write an algorithm that removes all the duplicates.

5.17 Write a function that removes the first element of a linked list and adds it to the end of the list without changing any value in information field. [It is required to change only **Start** and **Next** field values.]

5.18 Let **LIST** be a linked list in memory. Write a function that

(a) Adds a given information (That is k) to each element in **LIST**.

(b) Finds the number **N** of times a given element occurs in **LIST**.

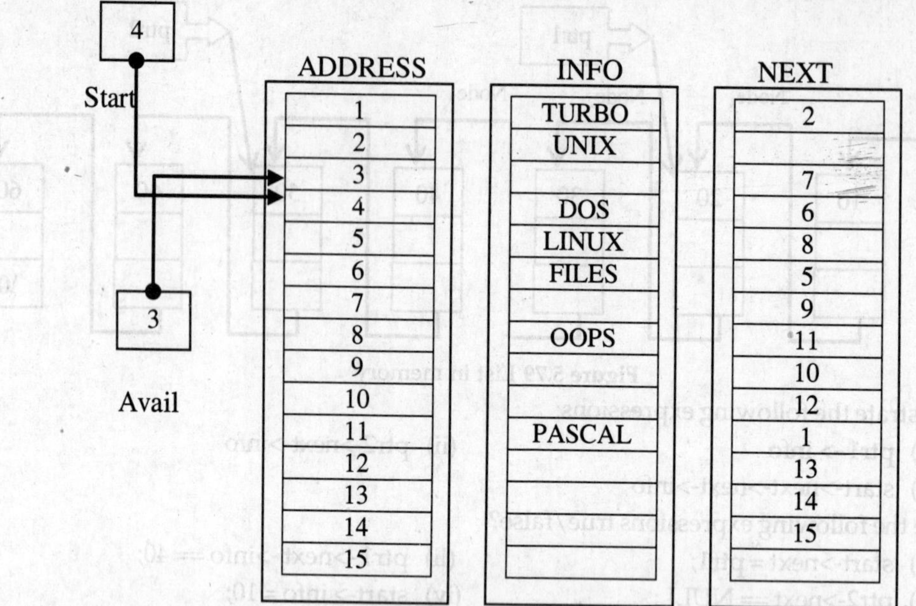

Figure 5.80 List in memory

5.19 Suppose **LIST** is in memory. Write an algorithm, which reverse the list.

5.20 Write an algorithm, which sort files of a directory in alphabetical order and implement the same using linear linked list. Suppose **ls** is a **UNIX** command. The **ls** command lists all the files in a directory. Write an algorithm, which represents implementation of **ls** command. Implement the designed algorithm using **C**.

5.21 Write a function to delete a node from a circular linked list.

5.22 Write a function that concatenates two circular linked lists, producing a circular linked list.

5.23 Write a function that split a circular linked list into three circular linked lists.

5.24 Write a function that creates a two-way header linked list.

5.25 Write a function that creates a two-way circular linked list.

5.26 Write a function that splits a circular two way linked list in two two-way circulars linked list.

5.27 Write a function that multiplies two polynomials.

5.28 Write a function that multiplies a polynomial with a monomial.

Quiz-4 (Linked List)

1. Each node in a linked list has two pairs of............ and ....
   (a) Link field and information field
   (b) Link field and avail field
   (c) Avail field and information field
   (d) Address field and link field
2. Which of the following is two way list?
   (a) grounded header list
   (b) circular header list
   (c) linked list with header and trailer nodes
   (d) none of above

3. In a circular linked list
   (a) Components are all linked together in some sequential manner.
   (b) There is no beginning and no end.
   (c) Components are arranged hierarchically.
   (d) Forward and backward traversal within the list is permitted.
4. A linear collection of data elements where the linear node is given by means of pointer is called?
   (a) Linked list (b) Node list
   (c) Primitive list (d) None
5. Which of the following operations is performed more efficiently by doubly linked list than by singly linked list?
   (a) Deleting a node whose location in given
   (b) Searching of an unsorted list for a given item
   (c) Inverting a node after the node with given location
   (d) Traversing a list to process each node
6. Consider an implementation of unsorted singly linked list. Suppose it has its representation with a head and tail pointer. Given the representation, which of the following operation can be implemented in O(1) time?
   (i) Insertion at the front of the linked list
   (ii) Insertion at the end of the linked list
   (iii) Deletion of the front node of the linked list
   (iv) Deletion of the last node of the linked list
   (a) i and ii (b) i and iii
   (c) i, ii and iii (d) i, ii and iv
7. Consider an implementation of unsorted singly linked list. Suppose it has its representation with a head pointer only. Given the representation, which of the following operation can be implemented in O(1) time?
   (i) Insertion at the front of the linked list
   (ii) Insertion at the end of the linked list
   (iii) Deletion of the front node of the linked list
   (iv) Deletion of the last node of the linked list
   (a) i and ii (b) i and iii
   (c) i, ii and iii (d) i, ii and iv
8. Consider an implementation of unsorted doubly linked list. Suppose it has its representation with a head pointer and tail pointer. Given the representation, which of the following operation can be implemented in O(1) time?
   (i) Insertion at the front of the linked list
   (ii) Insertion at the end of the linked list
   (iii) Deletion of the front node of the linked list
   (iv) Deletion of the end node of the linked list
   (a) i and ii (b) i and iii
   (c) i, ii and iii (d) i, ii, iii and iv

9. Consider an implementation of unsorted doubly linked list. Suppose it has its representation with a head pointer only. Given the representation, which of the following operation can be implemented in O(1) time?
   (i) Insertion at the front of the linked list
   (ii) Insertion at the end of the linked list
   (iii) Deletion of the front node of the linked list
   (iv) Deletion of the end node of the linked list
   (a) i and ii (b) i and iii
   (c) i, ii and iii (d) i, ii, iii and iv
10. Consider an implementation of unsorted circular linked list. Suppose it has its representation with a head pointer only. Given the representation, which of the following operation can be implemented in O(1) time?
   (i) Insertion at the front of the linked list
   (ii) Insertion at the end of the linked list
   (iii) Deletion of the front node of the linked list
   (iv) Deletion of the end node of the linked list
   (a) i and ii (b) i and iii
   (c) i, ii, iii and iv (d) None
11. Consider an implementation of unsorted circular doubly linked list. Suppose it has its representation with a head pointer only. Given the representation, which of the following operation can be implemented in O(1) time?
   (i) Insertion at the front of the linked list
   (ii) insertion at the end of the linked list
   (iii) Deletion of the front node of the linked list
   (iv) Deletion of the end node of the linked list
   (a) i and ii (b) i and iii
   (c) i, ii and iii (d) i, ii, iii and iv
12. What would be the asymptotic time complexity to add a node at the end of singly linked list, if the pointer is initially pointing to the head of the list?
   (a) O(1) (b) O(n)
   (c) θ (n) (d) θ (1)
13. What would be the asymptotic time complexity to add an element in the linked list?
   (a) O(1) (b) O(n)
   (c) O(n^2) (d) None
14. What would be the asymptotic time complexity to find an element in the linked list?
   (a) O(1) (b) O(n)
   (c) O(n^2) (d) None
15. The concatenation of two list can performed in O(1) time. Which of the following variation of linked list can be used?
   (a) Singly linked list (b) Doubly linked list
   (c) Circular doubly linked list (d) Array implementation of list

16. A variant of linked list in which last node of the list points to the first node of the list is?
    (a) Singly linked list (b) Doubly linked list
    (c) Circular linked list (d) Multiply linked list
17. What kind of linked list is best to answer question like "What is the item at position n?"
    (a) Singly linked list (b) Doubly linked list
    (c) Circular linked list (d) Array implementation of linked list
18. A variation of linked list is circular linked list, in which the last node in the list points to first node of the list. One problem with this type of list is?
    (a) It waste memory space since the pointer head already points to the first node and thus the list node does not need to point to the first node.
    (b) It is not possible to add a node at the end of the list.
    (c) It is difficult to traverse the list as the pointer of the last node is now not NULL
    (d) All of above
19. In circular linked list, insertion of node requires modification of?
    (a) One pointer (b) Two pointer
    (c) Three pointer (d) None
20. Which of the following statements about linked list data structure is/are TRUE?
    (a) Addition and deletion of an item to/ from the linked list require modification of the existing pointers
    (b) The linked list pointers do not provide an efficient way to search an item in the linked list
    (c) Linked list pointers always maintain the list in ascending order
    (d) The linked list data structure provides an efficient way to find kth element in the list

❑

CHAPTER

6

Stack and Queues

In this chapter we will see about stacks and queues. First we will see the basic stack operations and their implementation. After that queues will be considered.

6.1 STACK

A stack is defined formally as a list (a linear data structure) in which all insertions and deletions are made at one end called the top of stack (**TOS**). The fundamental operations, which are possible on a stack, are:

- Push ⟶ Insertion
- Pop ⟶ Deletion
- Peep ⟶ Extract information
- Update ⟶ Update information associated at some location in the stack

The most recently pushed element can be checked prior to performing a push operation. A stack is based on the **last-in first-out (LIFO)** algorithm in which insertion and deletion operations is performed at one end of a stack. Also, the information can only be removed in the opposite order in which it was added to the stack. The most accessible information in a stack is at the top of the stack and least accessible information is at the bottom of the stack.

For example, consider a stack of plates placed on the counter in a cafeteria. During the dinner time customers take plates from the top of the stack and waiter puts the washed plates on the top of the stack. The plate that is put most recently on the stack is the first one to be taken off. The plate at the bottom is the last one to be used. This discussion can further be understood with the help of **Figure 6.1.**

Another example of a stack is a collection of disk system on a peg as illustrated in **Figure 6.2.** In this system the last disk to be placed on the stack is the first to leave. Repeated insertion and deletion operations permit the disks to be arranged in the various orders.

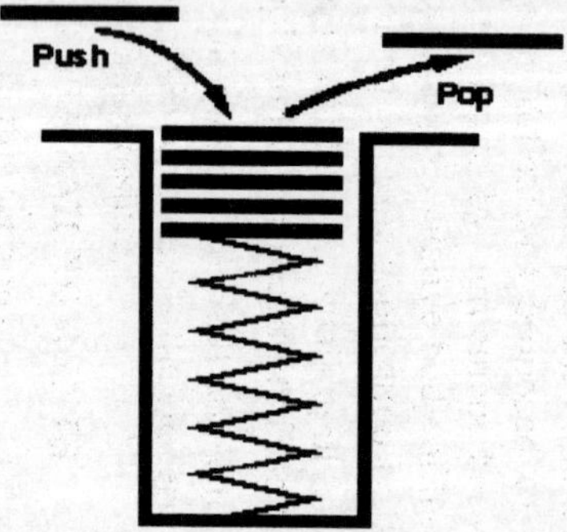

Figure 6.1 Plates at the counter in a cafeteria

Figure 6.2 Disks on a peg

6.2 REPRESENTATION OF STACK

There are various ways to represent a stack, such as railway shunting method, vertical vector method and horizontal vector method {See **Figure 6.3, Figure 6.4** and **Figure 6.5**}. A pointer **TOS** keeps track of the top most information in the stack. Initially when the stack is empty, **TOS** has a value zero (if implementing through C/C++ this may be –1) and when the stack contains single information **TOS** has a value one and so on. Before an item is pushed onto the stack, the pointer is incremented by one. The pointer is decrement by one each time a deletion is made from the stack.

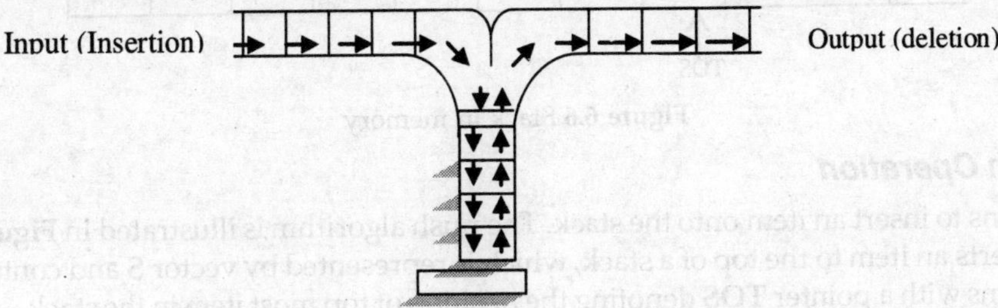

Figure 6.3 Railway shunting system representation

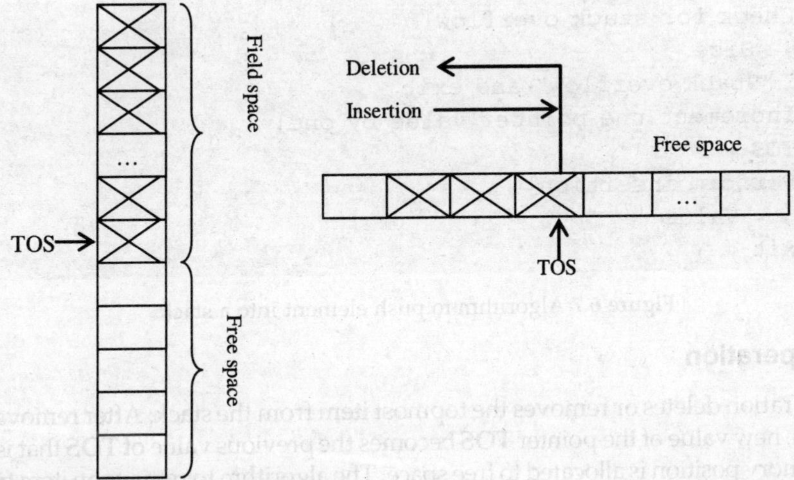

Figure 6.4 Vertical representation of stack **Figure 6.5** Horizontal representation of stack

6.3 IMPLEMENTATION OF STACK

We have already discussed that a stack is a list and hence any of the list implementation techniques may be used to implement a stack. Two common implementations are:

- Pointer (Linked list)
- Array

6.3.1 Array's Implementation

The array implementation technique is very simple and easy to implement. But there is one potential hazard that we need to declare the size of an array before start the operation. Generally this is not a big problem as in typical applications, if there are quite few stack operations, the actual number of elements in the stack at any time never gets too large. It is usually easy to declare the array to be large enough without wasting too much memory spaces. Associated with each stack there is a **TOS** that is 0 (–1 for C/C++) for an empty stack. For example, let **Figure 6.6** represents a stack of 100 items. Now, we will discuss the basic stack operations one by one.

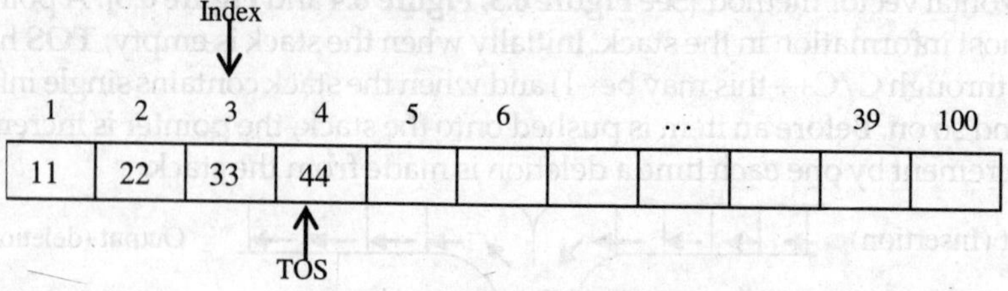

Figure 6.6 Stack in memory

6.3.1.1 Push Operation

Push means to insert an item onto the stack. The push algorithm is illustrated in **Figure 6.7**. This algorithm inserts an item to the top of a stack, which is represented by vector **S** and containing **Size** number of items with a pointer **TOS** denoting the position of top most item in the stack.

```
Step 1: [Check for stack overflow]
    If TOS ≥ Size
    Output "Stack overflow" and exit
Step 2: [Increment the pointer value by one]
    TOS = TOS + 1
Step 3: [Perform insertion]
    S [TOS] = Value
Step 4: Exit
```

Figure 6.7 Algorithm to push element into a stack

6.3.1.2 Pop Operation

The pop operation deletes or removes the topmost item from the stack. After removal of topmost item information, new value of the pointer **TOS** becomes the previous value of **TOS** that is **TOS = TOS - 1** and freed memory position is allocated to free space. The algorithm to remove an item from the stack is illustrated in **Figure 6.8.** The program segment **STACK_A.C** implements algorithms illustrated in **Figure 6.7** and **Figure 6.8.** And the program segment **STACK_L.C** implements the same algorithms with the help of linked list.

```
Step 1 [Check whether the stack is empty]
    If TOS = 0
    Output "Stack underflow" and exit
Step 2: [Remove the TOS information]
    Value = S [TOS]
    TOS = TOS - 1
Step 3: [Return the former information of the stack]
    Return (Value)
```

Figure 6.8 Algorithm to POP an Element from a Stack

```
/* IMPLEMENTATION OF THE STACK USING ARRAYS */
/* STACK_A.C */
# include<stdio.h>
# include<string.h>
# include<ctype.h>
# define size 100
int top = -1;
int flag = 0;
int stack[size];
void push(int *, int);
int pop(int *);
void display(int *);

/* Definition of the push function */
void push(int s[], int d)
{
   if(top ==(size-1))
      flag = 0;
   else{
      flag = 1;
      ++top;
      s[top] = d;
   }
}

/* Definition of the pop function */
int pop(int s[])
{
   int popped_element;
   if(top == -1)
   {
      popped_element = 0;
      flag = 0;
   }else{
      flag = 1;
      popped_element = s[top];
      --top;
   }
   return (popped_element);
}

/* Definition of the display function */
void display(int s[])
{
   int i;
```

```
    if(top == -1)
    {
       printf("\n Stack is empty");
    }else{
       for(i = top; i >= 0; --i)
          printf("\n %d", s[i] );
    }
}

/* Function main */
void main()
{
   int data;
   char choice;
   int q = 0;
   int top = -1;
   do{
      printf(" \nPush->i Pop->p Quit->q:");
      printf("\nInput the choice : ");
      do{
         choice = getchar();
         choice =tolower(choice);
      }while(strchr("ipq",choice)==NULL);
      printf("Your choice is: %c",choice);

      switch(choice)
      {
      case 'i' :
         printf("\n Input the element to push:");
         scanf("%d", &data);
         push(stack, data);
         if(flag)
         {
            printf("\n After inserting ");
            display(stack);
            if(top == (size-1))
               printf("\n Stack is full");
         }else
            printf("\n Stack overflow after pushing");
         break;
      case 'p' :
         data = pop(stack);
         if(flag)
         {
            printf("\n Data is popped: %d", data);
```

```
            printf("\n Rest data in stack is as follows:\n");
            display(stack);
         }else
            printf("\n Stack underflow" );
         break;
      case 'q':
         q = 1;
      }
   } while(!q);
}

/* STACK IMPLEMENTATION USING LINKED LIST */
/* STACK_L.C */
# include<stdio.h>
# include<malloc.h>
struct link
{
   int info;
   struct link *next;
} *start;
void display(struct link *);
struct link *push(struct link *);
struct link *pop(struct link *);
int main_menu();
void display(struct link *rec)
{
   while(rec != NULL)
   {
      printf(" %d ",rec->info);
      rec = rec->next;
   }
}
struct link * push(struct link *rec)
{
   struct link *new_rec;
   printf("\n Input the new value for next location of the stack:");
   new_rec = (struct link *)malloc(sizeof(struct link));
   scanf("%d", &new_rec->info);
   new_rec->next = rec;
   rec = new_rec;
   return(rec);
}
struct link * pop(struct link *rec)
{
   struct link *temp;
```

```
    if(rec == NULL)
    {
       printf("\n Stack is empty");
    }else{
       temp = rec->next;
       free(rec);
       rec = temp;
       printf("\n After pop operation the stack is as follows:\n");
       display(rec);
       if(rec == NULL)
          printf("\n Stack is empty");
    }
    return(rec);
}
int main_menu ()
{
    int choice;
    do
    {
       printf("\n 1<-Push ");
       printf("\n 2<-Pop");
       printf("\n 3<-Quit");
       printf("\n Input your choice :");
       scanf("%d", &choice);
       if(choice <1 || choice >3)
          printf("\n Incorrect choice-> Try once again");
    } while(choice <1 || choice >3);
    return(choice);
}

/* main function */
void main()
{
    struct link *start ;
    int choice;
    start = NULL;
    do{
       choice = main_menu();
       switch(choice)
       {
       case 1:
          start = push(start);
          printf("\n After push operation stack is as follows:\n");
          display(start);
          break;
```

```
        case 2:
           start = pop(start);
           break;
        default :
           printf("\n End of session");
        }
    } while(choice != 3);
}
```

6.3.1.3 Peep Operation

If one is interested only about an information stored at some location in a stack then peep operation is required. In this operation we simply move the pointer to the desired location and then fetch the information associated with that location. This operation actually requires two stacks S and BS. S is actual stack and BS is called backup stack. This operation requires copy all those elements in a backup stack (BS) from the original stack (S) up to just above the actual element to be fetched. After getting the required element, original stack is reconstructed. The algorithm for the peep operation is illustrated in **Figure 6.9.** The program segment **PEEPCH.C** implements the algorithm given in **Figure 6.9.** This algorithm requires location of the element to which we want to access. This index value is subtracted from the TOS and information associated with this resulting value is fetched.

```
Peep_stack(S, TOS, loc)
Where S: Stack,
TOS: Top of the stack,
loc: location for the interested information
BS: Back stack is equal to size of actual stack
Step 1: [Check for the stack overflow]
   If TOS - loc = 0
      Output "Stack overflow" and exit
Else
   k=1 {temporary index]
For j=TOS to LOC-1 repeat thru (b)
(a)   BS[k] = S[j] [copying element of the stack till the
peeped element is located]
(b)    k=k+1
Step 2[Get the located information]
   Element=S[loc]
Step 3 [Reconstruct the original stack]
   For k=k-1 to 1 repeat thru (b)
(a)   loc=loc+1
(b)   S[loc]=BS[k]
Step 3: [Return the locth element from the top of the stack]
   Return (element])
```

Figure 6.9 Algorithm Peep an element from form a stack

```
/* PEEP OPERATION ON THE STACK USING ARRAYS */
/* PEEPCH.C */
```

```
# include<stdio.h>
# include<string.h>
# include<ctype.h>
# define size 100

int top = -1;
int flag = 0;
int stack[100];
int BackStack[100];
int data;
void push(int *, int);
int peep(int *);
void display(int *);
/* Definition of the push function */
void push(int s[], int d)
{
    if(top ==(size-1))
        flag = 0;
    else{
        flag = 1;

        ++top;
        s[top] = d;
    }
}

/* Definition of the peep function */
int peep(int s[])
{
    int loc, k, j;
    int peeped_element;
    printf("\n Number of elements in the stack: %d", top+1);
    printf("\n Location start from '0'Input the position number to which
you want to access: ");
    scanf("%d", &loc);
    if((top - loc + 1) < 0)
    {
        peeped_element = 0;
        printf("\n Value of entered location: %d", loc);
    }else{
        k=0;
        for(j=top; j>=loc; --j)
  {
  BackStack[++k]=stack[j];
```

```
stack[j]=0;
printf("\n Elements moved to BackStack: %d ", BackStack[k]);
}

   peeped_element = s[j]; /* peeped element */

printf("\n input the new value: %d", peeped_element);
s[j]=peeped_element+10;
/* reconstruct the stack after peep */

     for(j=k; j>=-1; --j)
 {
 stack[loc++]=BackStack[j];
 printf("\n Elements moved back to Stack: %d ", BackStack[j]);
 }
 }
   return (peeped_element);
}

/* Definition of the display function */
void display(int s[])
{
   int i;
   if(top == -1)
   {
      printf("Stack is empty");
   }else{
      for(i = top; i>=0; --i)
         printf(" %d ", s[i]);
   }
}

/* Function main */

int main()
{
   int data;
   char choice;
   int q, top;
   q = 0;
   top = -1;
   do{
      printf(" \nPush->i Peep->p Quit->q:");
      printf("\nInput the choice : ");
      do{
```

```
            choice = getchar();
            choice =tolower(choice);
        }while(strchr("ipq",choice)==NULL);
        printf("Your choice is: ", choice);
        switch(choice){
        case 'i' :
            printf("\n Input the element to push into the stack:");
            scanf("%d", &data);
            push(stack, data);
            if(flag){
                printf("\n Stack Contents After inserting ");
                display(stack);
                if(top == (size-1))
                    printf("\n Stack is full");
            }else
                printf("\n Stack overflow after pushing");
            break;
        case 'p' :
            data = peep(stack);
            if(flag){
                printf("\n Data is peeped: %d", data);
                printf("\n Stack is as follows:\n");
                display(stack);
            }else
                printf("\n Stack underflow");
            break;
        case 'q':
            q = 1;
        }
    } while(!q);
    return 0;
}
```

6.3.1.4 Update Operation

Update operation is required when the content of some location in a stack is to be changed. Suppose one wants to update information at the locth location in the stack **S**. In this operation we simply move the pointer to the desired location and then fetch the information associated with that location. This operation actually requires two stacks S and BS. S is actual stack and BS is called backup stack. This operation requires copy all those elements in a backup stack (BS) from the original stack (S) up to just above the actual element to be updated. After getting the required element, original stack is reconstructed. The update algorithm is illustrated in **Figure 6.10.** The program segment **UPDATE.C** illustrates the algorithm given in **Figure 6.10.**

```
Update_stack(S, TOS, loc)
Where S: Stack,
TOS: Top of the stack,
loc: location for the interested information
BS: Back stack is equal to size of actual stack
Step 1: [Check for the stack overflow]
    If TOS - loc = 0
        Output "Stack overflow" and exit
        Else
           k=1 {temporary index]
        For j=TOS to LOC-1 repeat thru (b)
        (a)BS[k] = S[j] [copying element of the stack till the peeped
           element is located]
        (b)k=k+1
Step 2[ Get the located information]
        Element = get the new value
S[loc] = Element

Step 3 [Reconstruct the original stack]
        For k=k-1 to 1 repeat thru (b)
        (a)loc=loc+1
        (b)S[loc]=BS[k]
Step 3: [Return the locth element from the top of the stack]
        Return (Element])
```

Figure 6.10 Algorithm to Update value of an element in a stack

```
/* /* UPDATE OPERATION ON THE STACK USING ARRAYS */
/* update.C */
# include<stdio.h>
# include<string.h>
# include<ctype.h>
# define size 100

int top = -1;
int flag = 0;
int stack[100];
int BackStack[100];
int data;
void push(int *, int);
int update1(int *);
void display(int *);

/* Definition of the push function */
void push(int s[], int d)
{
```

```
    if(top ==(size-1))
        flag = 0;
    else{
        flag = 1;

        ++top;
        s[top] = d;
    }
}

/* Definition of the peep function */
int update1(int s[])
{
    int loc, k, j;
    int update_element;
    printf("\n Number of elements in the stack: %d", top+1);
    printf("\n Location start from '0'Input the position number to which
you want to access: ");
    scanf("%d", &loc);
    if((top - loc + 1) < 0)
    {
        update_element = 0;
        printf("\n Value of entered location: %d", loc);
    }else{
        k=0;
        for(j=top; j>=loc; —j)
 {
 BackStack[++k]=stack[j];
 stack[j]=0;
 printf("\n Elements moved to BackStack: %d ", BackStack[k]);
 }

    update_element = s[j]; /* Update element */

 printf("\n Input the new value for: %d: ", update_element);
 scanf("%d", &update_element);
 s[j]=update_element; /* Update element */
 /* reconstruct the stack after peep */

     for(j=k; j>=-1; --j)
 {
 stack[loc++]=BackStack[j];
 printf("\n Elements moved back to Stack: %d ", BackStack[j]);
 }
 }
```

```
    return (update_element);
}

/* Definition of the display function */
void display(int s[])
{
    int i;
    if(top == -1)
    {
        printf("Stack is empty");
    }else{
        for(i = top; i>=0; --i)
            printf(" %d ", s[i]);
    }
}

/* Function main */

int main()
{
    int data;
    char choice;
    int q, top;
    q = 0;
    top = -1;
    do{
        printf(" \n Push->i update->u Quit->q:");
        printf("\n Input the choice : ");
        do{
            choice = getchar();
            choice =tolower(choice);
        }while(strchr("iuq",choice)==NULL);
        printf("Your choice is: ", choice);
        switch(choice){
        case 'i' :
            printf("\n Input the element to push into the stack:");
            scanf("%d", &data);
            push(stack, data);
            if(flag){
                printf("\n Stack Contents After inserting ");
                display(stack);
                if(top == (size-1))
                    printf("\n Stack is full");
            }else
                printf("\n Stack overflow after pushing");
```

```
            break;
        case 'u' :
            data = update1(stack);
            if(flag){
                printf("\n Data is updated: %d", data);
                printf("\n Stack is as follows:\n");
                display(stack);
            }else
                printf("\n Stack underflow");
            break;
        case 'q':
            q = 1;
        }
    } while(!q);
    return 0;
}
```

6.4 POLISH NOTATION

The process of writing the operators of an expression either before their operands or after them is called the **Polish** notation in honour of its discoverer, the **Polish** mathematician ***Jan Luksiewicz.*** The fundamental property of **Polish** notation is that the order in which the operations are to be performed is completely determined by the positions of the operators and operands in the expression. Accordingly, one never needs parenthesis when writing expression in **Polish** notation. The **Polish** notations are classified into three categories. These are:

- Infix
- Prefix
- Postfix

When the operators exist between two operands then the expression is called **infix** expression. For example, let **a + b * c** is an expression, by inspection we find that the operator **+** exists between the operands **a** and **b**, and operator * exists between the operands **b** and **c**, hence we can say that **a + b * c** is an infix expression.

When the operators are written before their operands then the resulting expression is called the prefix Polish notation. Suppose we want to change the infix expression **a + b * c** into it's prefix form. First of all we consider the precedence of the operators present in the infix expression. Here in the given infix expression there are two operands + and *. The precedence of the * is higher than that of the +. The steps which are required to change infix expression **a + b * c** into it's equivalent prefix form are as follows:

```
Step 1: a + * b c    [Putting * before operands b and c]
Step 2: + a * b c [Putting + before operands a and b]
```

When the operators come after their operands the resulting expression is called the reverse Polish notation or postfix expression.

For example, suppose **a + b * c** is an infix expression then after changing this expression into postfix form we get **a b c * +**. Thus, we can say that post expression is not a mirror image of prefix expression but a different one. Another example, the transformation of infix expression "**z + (y * x - (w / v - u) * t)*s**" into its postfix form is as follows:

z + (y * x – (w / v ↑ u) * t) * s

z + (y * x – (w / vu ↑) * t) * s

z + (y * x – (w vu ↑/)* t) * s

z + (y * x – w vu ↑ / t *) * s

z + (yx* – w vu ↑ / t *) * s

z + (y x * w vu ↑/ t * –) * s

z + y x * w vu ↑ / t * – s *

z + y x * w vu ↑ / t * – s * + [Resulting postfix expression]

The steps shown above to translate infix expression into postfix expression can be implemented with the help of stack. For this we insert '(' at the end of the infix expression then we label each and every elements of the infix expression.

Attached parenthesis

z	+	(	y	*	x	–	(	w	/	v	^	u	)	*	t	)	*	s	) ⇩
1	2	3	4	5	6	7	8	9	10	11	12	13	14	15	16	17	18	19	20 ⇦ Label

The stack implementation of the above infix expression is illustrated in **Table 6.1.**

6.4.1 Uses of Stack

The stack is a region of memory within which programs temporarily store data as they execute. For example, when a program sends parameters to a function, the parameters are placed on the stack. When the function completes, the items from the stack are popped. Similarly, when the function passes local variables the values of these local variables are stored on the stack during the execution of the function. When the subprogram completes the variables are discarded.

What happens in the computer system, when subprograms are called? The system must remember the place where the call was made so that it can return there when the subprogram completes. It must also remember all the local variables, **CPU** registers, jump addresses and intermediate results, so that the information is not lost when the subprogram is working on. We can think of all this information as one large structure a temporary storage area for each subprogram.

Table 6.1 Stack implementation of infix expression z + (y * x – (w / v ^ u) * t) * s

LABEL NUMBER	SYMBOL SCANNED	STACK	EXPRESSION
1	z	(	z
2	+	(+	z
3	(	(+ (	z
4	y	(+ (	z y

5	*	(+(*	z y
6	x	(+(*	z y x
7	-	(+(-	z y x *
8	(	(+(-(	z y x *
9	w	(+(-(	z y x * w
10	/	(+(-(/	z y x * w
11	v	(+(-(/	z y x * w v
12	^	(+(-(/^	z y x * w v
13	u	(+(-(/^	z y x * w v u
14	)	(+(-	z y x * w v u ^ /
15	*	(+(- *	z y x * w v u ^ /
16	t	(+(- *	z y x * w v u ^ /t
17	)	(+	z y x * w v u ^ /t * -
18	*	(+ *	z y x * w v u ^ /t * -
19	s	(+ *	z y x * w v u ^ /t * - s

For example, suppose we have three subprograms **X, Y** and **Z**. Let **X** invokes **Y** and **Y** invokes **Z** then **Y** will not finish it's work until **Z** has finished and returned. Similarly **X** is the first to execute work, but is last to be finished. Thus, the sequence by which subprograms' activity proceed are summed up as the property **LIFO**. Assigning temporary storage areas for subprograms, by the machine is similar to the property of stack. The above discussion is illustrated in **Figure 6.11**. The program segment **POSTFIX.C** implements the algorithm illustrated in **Figure 6.12**.

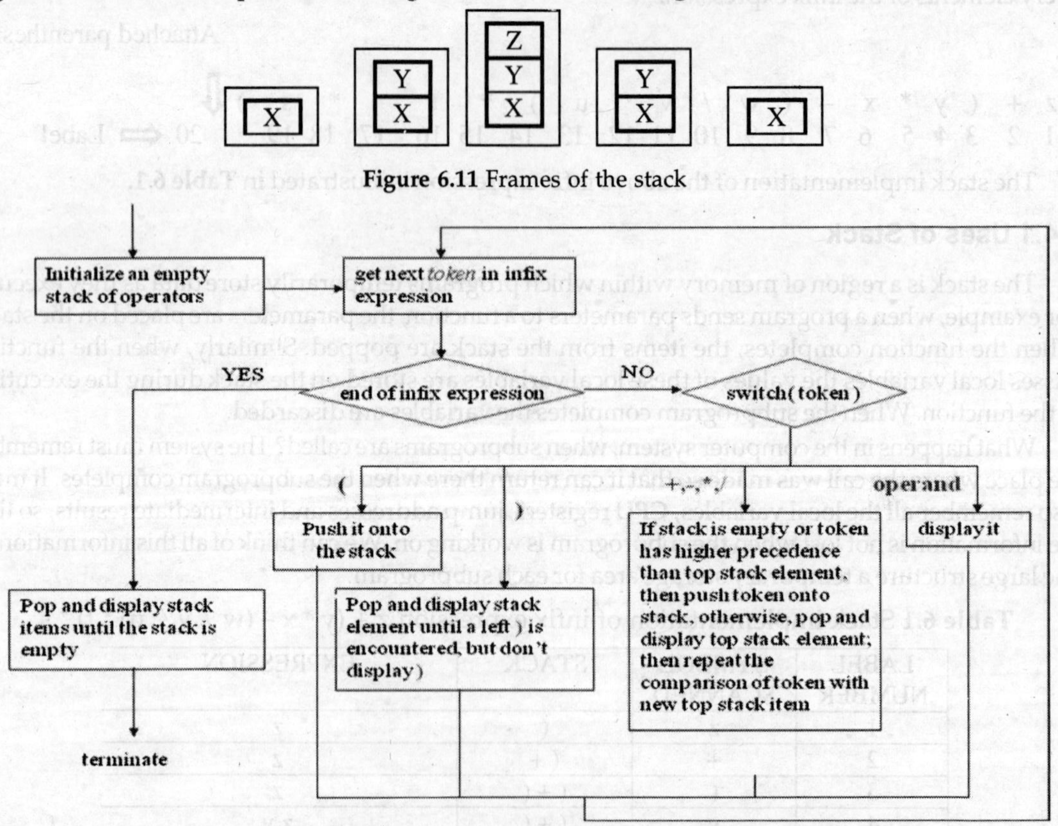

Figure 6.11 Frames of the stack

Figure 6.12 Algorithm to convert an infix expression into Polish postfix form

Initialize the stack. Scan the leftmost symbol in the given infix expression and denote it as the current input symbol. Repeat through while infix expression. Remove and output all stack symbols whose precedence values are greater than or equal to the precedence of the current input symbol. Push the current input symbols onto the stack. Scan the leftmost symbol in the infix expression and let it be the current input symbol. These steps can be easily represented with the help of flowchart {Figure 6.12}.

```
/* POSTFIX.C */
# include<stdio.h>
# include<string.h>
# include<ctype.h>
# include<stdlib.h>
# define Arnold '\0'
# define Blank ' '
# define Tab '\t'
#define Maxlen 64
static char infix [Maxlen+1], stack[Maxlen], postfix[Maxlen+1];
# define Empty (-1) /* empty stack */
static int top;

/* symbol types */
#define Operator (-10)
# define Operand (-20)
# define LeftParen (-30)
# define RightParen (-40)

static char *symbols = "()+-%*/";

/* Symbol precedence */
# define LeftParenPrec 0 /* ( */
# define AddPrec 1 /* + */
# define SubPrec 1 /* - */
# define MultPrec 2 /* * */
# define DivPrec 2 /* / */
# define RemPrec 2 /* % */
# define None 999 /* all else */

/* prototypes of the function used */
void read_input(void);
void infix_to_postfix(void);
void write_output(void);
void push(char symbol);
char pop (void);
int get_type(char );
int get_prec(char );
int white_space(char );
```

```
void full_stack();
void empty_stack();

void main()
{
    char ans[2];
    do{
        top = Empty; /* reset stack */
        read_input();
        infix_to_postfix();
        write_output();

        /* Selection */
        printf("\n\n Another (y/n)");
        gets(ans);
    } while (toupper(ans[0]) == 'Y');
}

/* function infix to postfix conversion */
void infix_to_postfix(void)
{
    int i,p, len, type, precedence;
    char next ;
    /* i for infix, p for postfix */
    i = p = 0;
    len = strlen(infix);
    /* loop through input string */
    while(i < len)
    {
        /* ignore white space in infix expression */
        if( !white_space(infix[i]))
        {
          type = get_type(infix[i]);
          switch(type)
          {
            /* push left parenthesis onto stack */
          case LeftParen:
            push(infix[i]);
            break;
            /* pop stack until matching left paren */
          case RightParen:
            while((next = pop()) != '(')
                postfix[p++] = next;
            break;
          case Operand: postfix[p++] = infix[i];
```

```
            break;
         /* Pop stack until first operator of higher precedence and then
stack this operator */
         case Operator:
            precedence = get_prec(infix[i]);
            /* Anything on stack to pop */
            while(top > Empty && precedence<= get_prec(stack[top]))
               postfix[p++] = pop();
            push(infix[i]);
            break;
         }
      }
      i++; /* next symbol in infix expression */
   }

   /* pop any remaining operators */
   while(top > Empty )
      postfix[p++] = pop();
   postfix[p] = Arnold ; /* ensure a string */
}

/* Function to find operator type */
int get_type(char symbol )
{
   switch(symbol)
   {
   case '(' :
      return (LeftParen);
   case ')':
      return (RightParen);
   case '+':
   case '-':
   case '%':
   case '*':
   case '/':
      return (Operator);
   default:
      return (Operand);
   }
}

/* Find precedence of the operator */
int get_prec(char symbol )
{
   switch(symbol)
```

```
    {
    case '+':
        return (AddPrec);
    case '-':
        return (SubPrec);
    case '*':
        return (MultPrec);
    case '/':
        return (DivPrec);
    case '%':
        return (RemPrec);
    case '(':
        return (LeftParenPrec);
    default:
        return (None);
    }
}

/* Function push */
void push(char symbol)
{
    /* check for overflow */
    if(top > Maxlen)
        full_stack();
    else
        stack[++top] = symbol;
}

/* Function pop */
char pop(void)
{
    /* check for underflow */
    if (top <= Empty )
        empty_stack();
    else
        return (stack[top--]);
}

/* Exit in case of overflow */
void full_stack(void )
{
    printf("\n Full Stsck ... exiting. \n");
    exit(1);
}
```

```
/* Exit in case of underflow */
void empty_stack(void)
{
   printf("\n Empty Stack ... exiting \n");
   exit(2);
}
void read_input(void)
{
   printf("\n Infix (up to %d chars): ", Maxlen);
   gets(infix);
}

/* Output function */
void write_output(void)
{
   printf("\n Infix: %s", infix);
   printf("\n Postfix: %s \n",postfix);
}

/* function white space checking */
int white_space(char symbol)
{
   return( symbol == Blank || symbol == Tab || symbol == Arnold);
}
```

6.4.1.1 Evaluation of The Postfix Expression

Let **E** is an arithmetic expression written in Polish postfix notation. We add a right parenthesis ')' at the end of **E**. Now we scan **E** from left to right. If an operand is encountered it is put onto the stack. If an operator **op** is encountered then we remove the two top elements of stack, let **x** is the top element and **y** is the next top element, we evaluate **x op y** and place the result back on the stack. We repeat this process until we get last element of the stack that is right parenthesis ')'. A[1...n] - a legal arithmetic expression in postfix notation. E is a stack of evaluated parts of the expression and Output is Top of stack. These steps are summarized as follows.

```
For i=1 to n do
        If A[i] is not an operator
                                then PUSH(E,A[i])
                                else POP(E,x)
                                    POP(E,y)
                                    PUSH(E,y A[i] X) (remember: A[i] is operator)

endFor
POP(E, Solution)
```

For example, suppose the expression **E** is as follows:

E: 2 3 10 + * 8 2 / -

The equivalent infix expression is

I: 2 * (3 + 10) – 8 / 2

E:	2	3	10	+	*	8	2	/	-	)
Label:	1	2	3	4	5	6	7	8	9	10

The evaluation procedure is given **Table 6.2**. Implementation code for postfix expression is given below.

Table 6.2 Evaluation of Expression with help of Stack

LABEL NUMBER	SYMBOL SCANNED	STACK CONTENTS
1	2	2
2	3	2 3
3	10	2 3 10
4	+	2 13
5	*	26
6	8	26 8
7	2	26 8 2
8	/	26 4
9	-	22
10	)	

```
/* PostFix.C */
#include<stdio.h>
#define SIZE 10

int TOP=SIZE;
int stack[SIZE];

/* Prototypes of the function used */
void push(int);
int pop();

void main()
{
 char postfix[100],c;
 int i=0,r1,r2,r,x;
 printf("Enter the exp with variables:");
 scanf("%s",postfix);
 while((c=postfix[i])!='\0')
 {
 switch(c)
 {
    case'+':
        r1=pop();
        r2=pop();
        r=r2+r1;
```

```
      push(r);
      break;
   case'-':
      r1=pop();
      r2=pop();
      r=r2-r1;
      push(r);
      break;
   case'*':
      r1=pop();
      r2=pop();
      r=r2*r1;
      push(r);
      break;
   case'/':
      r1=pop();
      r2=pop();
      r=r2/r1;
      push(r);
      break;
   default: printf("Enter the value of variable: %c ",c);
      scanf("%d",&x);
      push(x);
  }

    i++;
  }
    r=pop();
    printf("result of exp:->%d",r);
    getch();
  }
  void push(int x)
  {
  if(TOP==0)
    printf("stack is full");
  else{
    TOP=TOP-1;
    stack[TOP]=x;
  }
  }
  int pop()
  {
  int x;
  if(TOP==SIZE)
  printf("stack is empty");
```

```
  else{
    x=stack[TOP];
    TOP=TOP+1;
  }
  return(x);
  }
```

See another to implement the evaluation of the postfix expression. For example Let the given expression be "2 3 1 * + 9 -". We scan all elements one by one. The actual operation made are as follows.

1. Scan '2', it's a number, so push it to stack. Stack contains '2'
2. Scan '3', again a number, push it to stack, stack now contains '2 3' (from bottom to top)
3. Scan '1', again a number, push it to stack, stack now contains '2 3 1'
4. Scan '*', it's an operator, pop two operands from stack, apply the * operator on operands, we get 3*1 which results in 3. We push the result '3' to stack. Stack now becomes '2 3'.
5. Scan '+', it's an operator, pop two operands from stack, apply the + operator on operands, we get 3 + 2 which results in 5. We push the result '5' to stack. Stack now becomes '5'.
6. Scan '9', it's a number, we push it to the stack. Stack now becomes '5 9'.
7. Scan '-', it's an operator, pop two operands from stack, apply the – operator on operands, we get 5 – 9 which results in -4. We push the result '-4' to stack. Stack now becomes '-4'.
8. There are no more elements to scan, we return the top element from stack (which is the only element left in stack).

```
// C program to evaluate value of a postfix expression
#include <stdio.h>
#include <string.h>
#include <ctype.h>
#include <stdlib.h>

// Stack type
struct Stack
{
 int top;
 unsigned capacity;
 int* array;
};

// Stack Operations
struct Stack* createStack( unsigned capacity )
{
 struct Stack* stack = (struct Stack*) malloc(sizeof(struct Stack));

 if (!stack) return NULL;

 stack->top = -1;
 stack->capacity = capacity;
 stack->array = (int*) malloc(stack->capacity * sizeof(int));
```

```
  if (!stack->array) return NULL;
    return stack;
 }

 int isEmpty(struct Stack* stack)
 {
  return stack->top == -1 ;
 }

 char peek(struct Stack* stack)
 {
  return stack->array[stack->top];
 }

 char pop(struct Stack* stack)
 {
  if (!isEmpty(stack))
  return stack->array[stack->top--] ;
  return '$';
 }

 void push(struct Stack* stack, char op)
 {
  stack->array[++stack->top] = op;
 }

  // The main function that returns value of a given postfix expression
  int evaluatePostfix(char* exp)
  {
   // Create a stack of capacity equal to expression size
   struct Stack* stack = createStack(strlen(exp));
   int i;

   // See if stack was created successfully
   if (!stack) return -1;

   // Scan all characters one by one
   for (i = 0; exp[i]; ++i)
   {
   // If the scanned character is an operand or number,
   // push it to the stack.
   if (isdigit(exp[i]))
   push(stack, exp[i] - '0');

   // If the scanned character is an operator, pop two
```

```
// elements from stack apply the operator
else {
int val1 = pop(stack);
int val2 = pop(stack);
switch (exp[i])
{
case '+': push(stack, val2 + val1); break;
case '-': push(stack, val2 - val1); break;
case '*': push(stack, val2 * val1); break;
case '/': push(stack, val2/val1); break;
}
}
}
return pop(stack);
}

// Driver program to test above functions
int main()
{
char exp[] = "231*+9-"; // expression for discussion only.
printf("Ïnput the postfix expreession:");
gets(exp);
printf ("Value of %s is %d", exp, evaluatePostfix(exp));
return 0;
}
```

6.5 QUEUES

This is a linear data structure used to represent a linear list and permits deletion to be performed at one end of the list and the insertion at the other. The information in such a list is processed in the same order as it was received, i.e., on **first-come-first-serve** basis **(FCFS)**.

An example of queue is time-sharing computer system where many users share the system simultaneously. The procedure, which is used to design such type of system, is **Round Robin Technique.** The railway reservation counter is also an example of queue where the people collect their tickets on the **first-come-first-serve** basis.

6.5.1 Implementation of Queues

Two common ways in which queues may be implemented are as follows:

- Arrays
- Pointers (One way linear linked list)

A queue has two pointers **front** and **rear**, pointing to the front and rear elements of the queue, respectively. Consider a queue **Q** consisting of **n** elements and an element **Value,** which we have to insert into the **Q**. The value NULL (0) of front pointer implies an empty queue. **Figure 6.13** illustrates a queue and **Figure 6.14** illustrates a queue with the help of vector.

For example, suppose **Q** has 40 elements. But at present there are only 4 elements in the queue. **Figure 6.15** illustrates the **Q**.

When we remove one element from the **Q** we get the resulting **Q** as illustrated in **Figure 6.16** and when we further insert one element in **Q** we get the result as illustrated in **Figure 6.17.** It is observed from **Figure 6.16** that when an element is removed from **Q** the value of **front** pointer is increased by 1, i.e., front = front + 1.Similarly, when an element is added to **Q** the value of the **rear** pointer is increased by 1 that is rear = rear + 1.

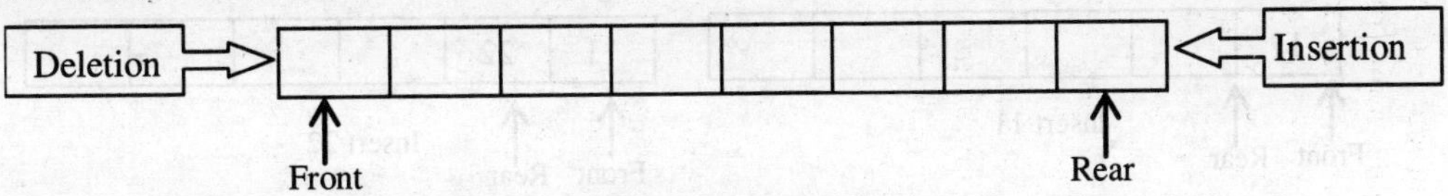

Deletion → [| | | | | | | |] ← Insertion

Front ↑ ↑ Rear

Figure 6.13 Queue

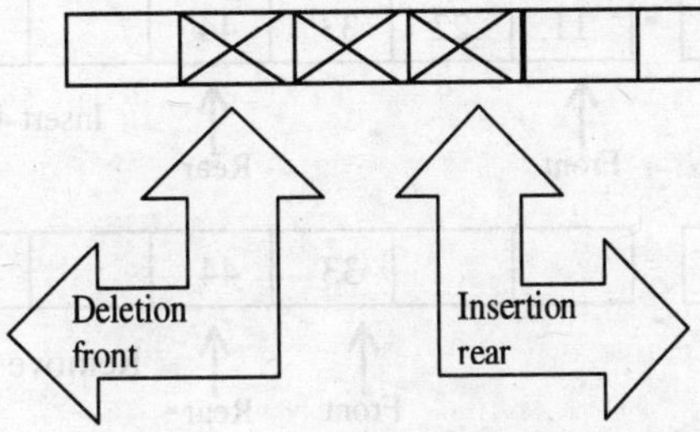

Deletion front

Insertion rear

Figure 6.14 Vector representation of a queue

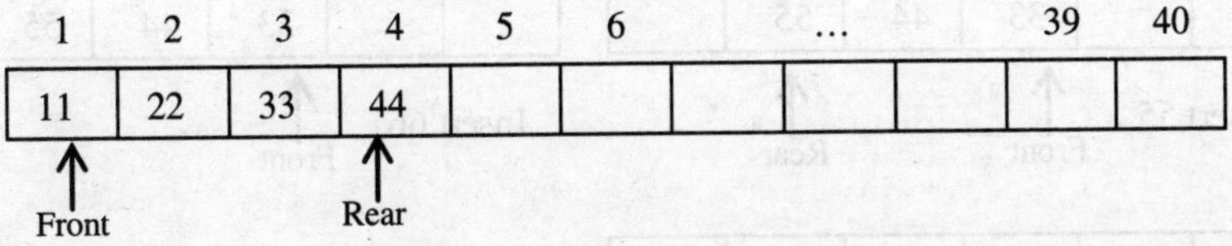

1	2	3	4	5	6		...		39	40
11	22	33	44							

Front ↑ (1) Rear ↑ (4)

Figure 6.15 Queue Q in memory

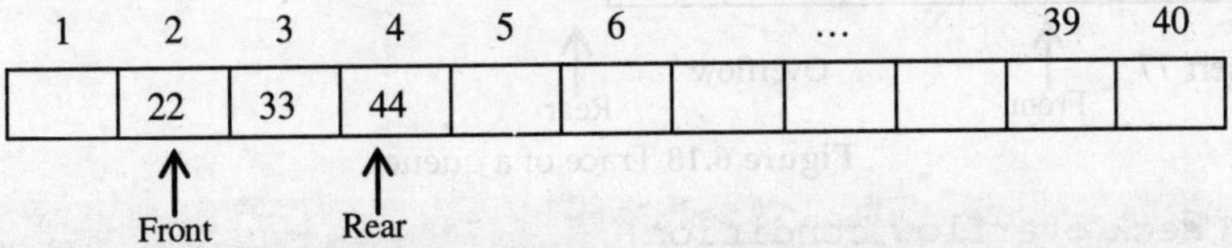

1	2	3	4	5	6		...		39	40
	22	33	44							

Front ↑ (2) Rear ↑ (4)

Figure 6.16 Queue Q after deleting first element

When we continue insertion of elements in **Q** then after a stage we have **rear = 40**, i.e., the **rear** pointer points to end of the array. Now suppose we still want to insert an element into the queue then this can be done by moving entire queue to the beginning of the array, changing **front** and **rear** pointers value accordingly and then inserting an element into the queue. But for an array, such operation is time consuming and expensive. Here, circular queue comes as a solution, which we shall discuss in section {6.6}. For example, consider a queue, which has 6 rooms. Initially the queue is empty. It is required to insert integers 11, 22, 33, 44, remove 11 and 22 and then insert 55, 66 and 77. **Figure 6.18** illustrates trace of the above problem. **Figure 6.19** and **Figure 6.20** illustrate the insertion and deletion algorithms, respectively.

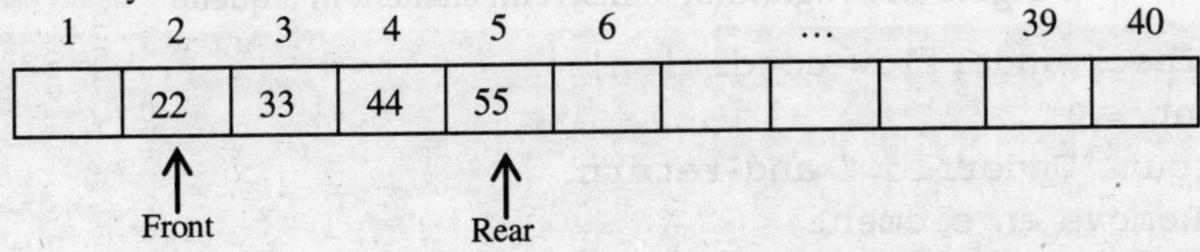

Figure 6.17 Queue Q after inserting one element

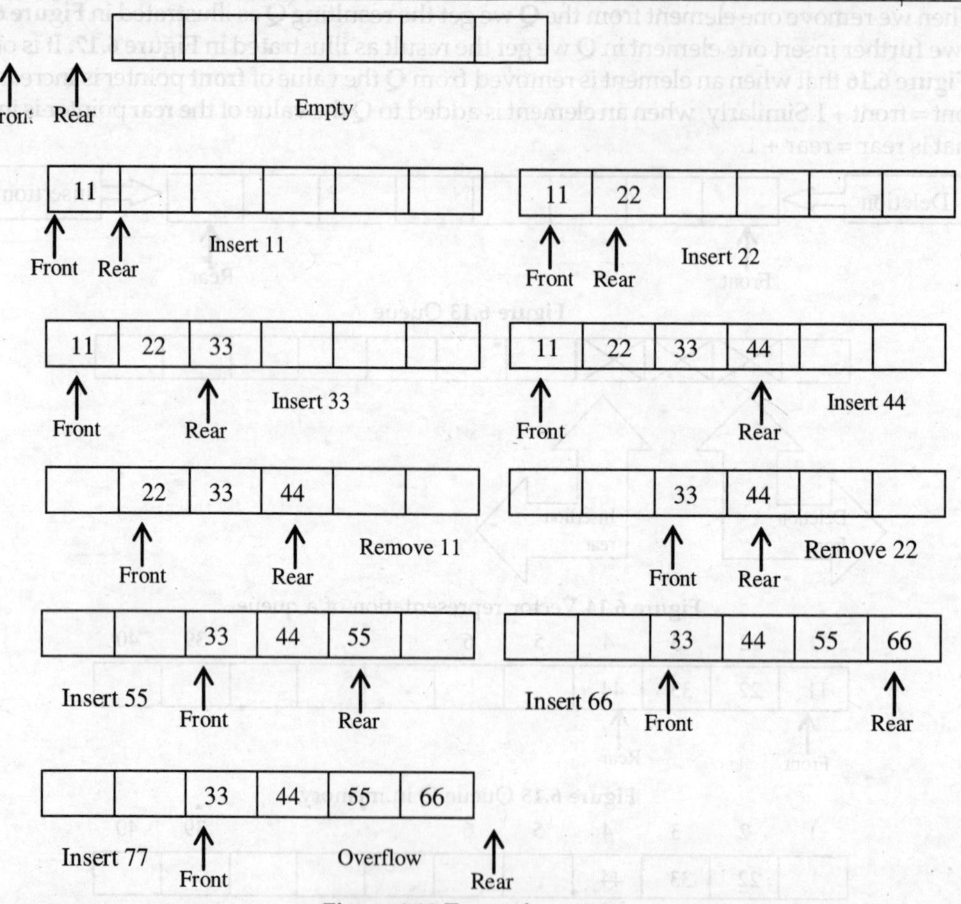

Figure 6.18 Trace of a queue

```
Step 1: [Check overflow condition]
   If (rear ³ size) Output "Overflow" and return
Step 2: [Increment rear pointer]
   rear = rear + 1
step 3: [Insert an element]
   Q [rear] = value
Step 4: [Set the front pointer]
   If (front = 0)
front = 1
Step 5: return
```

Figure 6.19 Algorithm to insert an element in a queue

```
Step 1: [Check underflow condition]
   If front = 0
      Output "Underflow" and return
Step 2: [Remove an element]
   value = Q [front]
```

```
Step 3: [Check for empty queue]
    If front = rear
    front = 0
    rear = 0
    Else
        front = front + 1
Step 4: Return (value)
```

Figure 6.20 Deletion algorithm for queue

When we try to insert integer 77 overflow occur even though the first two rooms are free. The program segment **QUEUE_A.C** implements the algorithm given in **Figure 6.19** and **Figure 6.120**.

```
/* INSERTION AND DELETION IN A QUEUE ARRAY IMPLEMENTATION */
/* Queue_A.C */
# include<stdio.h>
# include<string.h>
# include<ctype.h>
# include<stdlib.h>
# define size 10
int rear, front;
int ch;
int q[size];
int rear = 0;
int front = 0;
void Insert_queue();
void Delete_queue();
void Display_queue();
/* Function to create queue */
void Insert_queue()
{
    printf("\n Input the element :");
    scanf("%d", &ch);
    if(rear < size){
        rear ++;
        q[rear] = ch ;
        if(front == 0)
            front = 1;
    }else
        printf("\n Queue is overflow");
}
/* Function to perform delete operation */
void Delete_queue()
{
    if (front == 0){
        printf("\n Underflow");
        return ;
```

```
    }else{
        ch = q[front];
        printf("\n Element deleted : %d", ch);
    }
    if(front == rear){
        front = 0;
        rear = 0;
    }else
        front = front + 1;
}
/* Output function */
void Display_queue() //char q[])
{
    int i;
    if (front == 0)
        return;
    for(i = front ; i <= rear; i++)
        printf(" %d ", q[i]);
}
/* Function main */
void main()
{
    int k = 0;
    char choice;
    do{
        printf("\n Insert->i Delete->d Quit->q:");
        printf("\n Input the choice : ");
        do{
            choice = getchar();
            choice = tolower(choice);
        }while(strchr("idq", choice)==NULL);
        printf("Your choice is: %c ", choice);
        switch(choice){
        case 'i' :
            Insert_queue();
            printf("\n Queue after inserting ");
            Display_queue();
            break;
        case 'd' :
            Delete_queue();
            printf("\n Queue content after deletion is as follows:\n");
            Display_queue();
            break;
        case 'q':
```

```
        k = 1;
      }
    } while(!k);
  }
```

6.6 CIRCULAR QUEUES

Let we have an array **Q** that contains **n** elements in which **Q[1]** comes after **Q[n]** in the array. When this technique is used to construct a queue then the queue is called circular queue. In other word we can say that a queue is called circular when the last room comes just before the first room. **Figure 6.21** illustrates a circular queue.

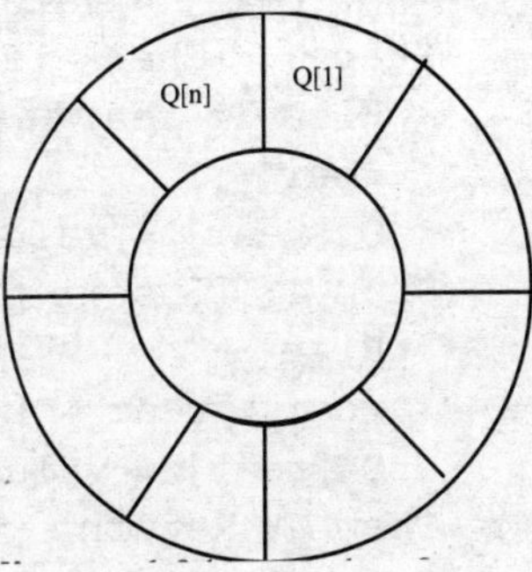

Figure 6.21 Circular Queue

In a circular queue when **rear = n,** if we insert an element then this element is assigned to **Q [1]**, i.e., instead of increasing rear to **n + 1,** we reset **rear** to 1. Similarly, if **front = n** and an element of the queue is removed, we reset **front** to 1 instead of **n + 1**. If a queue contains only one element that is **front = rear** ≠ NULL and if the element is removed then the **front** and **rear** pointers are now assigned NULL to indicate that the queue is empty.

Suppose we have a circular queue with 6 rooms that is **n = 6**. Insert 99, 88, 66, 55 and 44 remove 99 and 88 then insert 33, 22 and 11. The trace of this operation is illustrated in **Figure 6.22**.

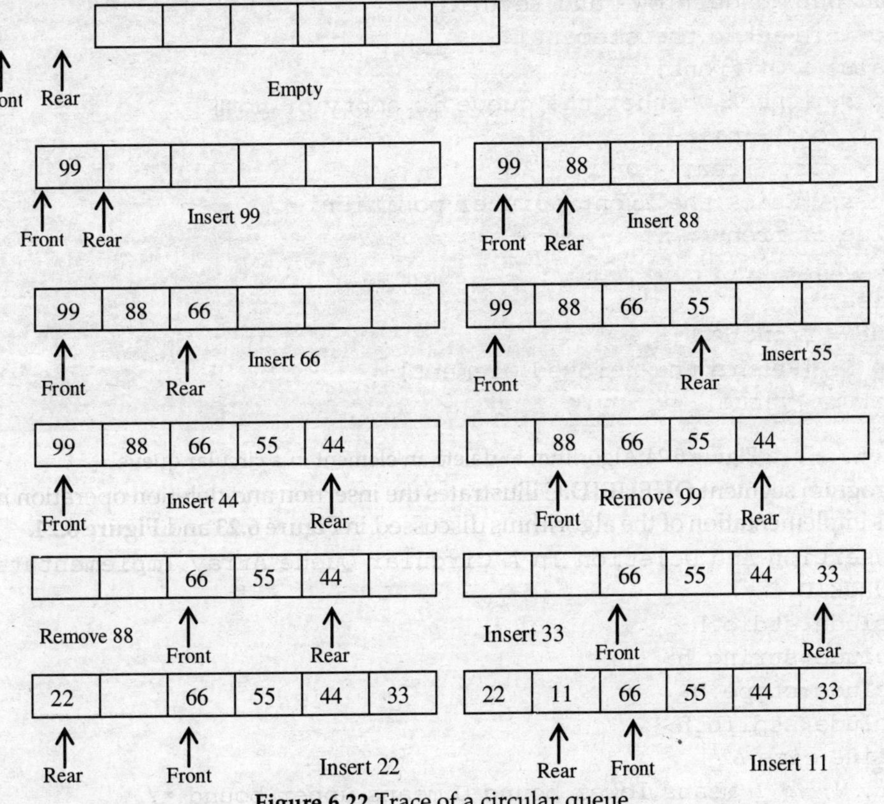

Figure 6.22 Trace of a circular queue

```
   Step 1: [Check for the overflow]
     If (front = 1 and rear = n) or (front=rear+1) Output "Overflow" and
return
   Step 2: [Insert element in the queue]
     Else if front = rear=0
     front = rear = 1
     Q [rear] = value
   Step 3: [Check if the rear at the end of the queue]
     Else if rear = n
     rear = 1
     Q [rear] = value
   Step 4: [insert the element]
     Else
     rear = rear + 1
     Q [rear] = value
   Step 5: Return
```

Figure 6.23 Algorithm to insert an element in a circular queue

```
   Step 1: [Check for underflow]
     If front = 0
      Output "Underflow" and return
   Step 2: [Backup the element]
     value = Q [front]
   Step 3: [Check whether the queue is empty or not]
     If front = rear
        front = rear = 0
   Step 4: [Check the front pointer position]
     Else if front = n
      front = 1
     Else
   front = front + 1
   Step 5: [Return the removed element]
     Return[value]
```

Figure 6.24 Algorithm to delete an element in a circular queue

The program segment **QUEUEID.C** illustrates the insertion and deletion operation in a circular queue. It is implementation of the algorithms discussed in **Figure 6.23** and **Figure 6.24.**

```
/* Insertion And Deletion In A Circular Queue Array Implementation */
/* QUEUEID.C */
# include<stdio.h>
# include<string.h>
# include<ctype.h>
# include<stdlib.h>
# define size 6
int L, U; /* L means lower bound U means upper bound */
```

```
int rear, front;
int ch;
int q[size];
int rear = -1;
int front = -1;
void Insert_queue();
void Delete_queue();
void Display_queue();
/* Function to create queue */
void Insert_queue()
{
   if ((front == 0) && (rear == size-1))
   {
      printf("\n Overflow");
      rear = 1;
      return;
   }else
      if (front < 0) /* Insert first element */
      {
         front = 0;
         rear = 0;
         printf("\nInput the element :");
         scanf("%d", &ch);
         q[rear] = ch ;
      }else if (rear == size-1){
            rear = 0;
            printf("\n Input the element :");
            scanf("%d", &ch);
            q[rear] = ch ;
         }else{
            rear ++;
            printf("\n Input the element :");
            scanf("%d", &ch);
            q[rear] = ch ;
         }
}

/* Function to perform delete operation */
void Delete_queue()
{
   if (front < 0)
   {
      printf("\nUnderflow");
      return ;
   }
```

```
        ch = q[front];
        q[front] = NULL;
        printf("\n Element deleted :", ch);
        if(front == rear)
        {
            front = -1;
            rear = -1;
        }else if ( front == size-1)
        {
            front = 0;
        }else{
            front++ ;
        }
    }
    /* Output function */
    void Display_queue()
    {
        int i;
        if (front < 0)
            return;
        if ( rear >= front)
        {
            for(i = front; i <= rear; i++)
            {
                printf("\n i = %d", i);
                printf(" %d ", q[i]);
            }
        }else{
            for(i = front; i < size; i++)
            {
                printf("\n i = %d", i);
                printf(" %d", q[i]);
            }
            for(i = 0; i <= rear; i++)
            {
                printf("\n i = %d", i);
                printf(" %d ", q[i]);
            }
        }
    }
    /* Function main */
    void main()
    {
        int k = 0;
        char choice;
```

```
    do
    {
        printf("\nInsert->i Delete->d Quit->q:");
        printf("\nInput the choice : ");
        do
        {
            choice = getchar();
            choice = tolower(choice);
        }while(strchr("idq",choice)==NULL);
        printf("Your choice is: %c", choice);
    switch(choice)
        {
        case 'i' :
            Insert_queue();
            printf("\nQueue after inserting ");
            Display_queue();
            break;
        case 'd' :
            Delete_queue();
            printf("\nQueue content after deletion is as follows:\n");
            Display_queue();
            break;
        case 'q':
            k = 1;
        }
    } while(!k);
}
```

6.7 DOUBLE ENDED QUEUE

Double-ended queue is an abstract data type similar to an ordinary queue, except that it allows to insertion and deletion from both the ends. Double-ended queue is also known as **deque**. **Figure 6.25** represents a **deque**. We know that in stack insertions and deletions are possible only at one end **LIFO**, while in a queue insertion at one end and deletion at other end, i.e., operation in queue is performed in **FIFO** or **FCFS** basis. Thus, we can say that **deque** is more superior representation of linear list as compared to stack and simple queue. Other than the **deque** illustrated in **Figure 6.25** there are other two forms of **deque**.

- Input restricted **deque** [Insertion at one end]
- Output restricted **deque** [Deletion at one end]

Figure 6.26 illustrates a **deque** and **Figure 6.27** with input restricted **deque**. The insertion algorithm for **deque** is illustrated in **Figure 6.28.** Similarly, one can design input restricted and output restricted algorithms for **deque**.

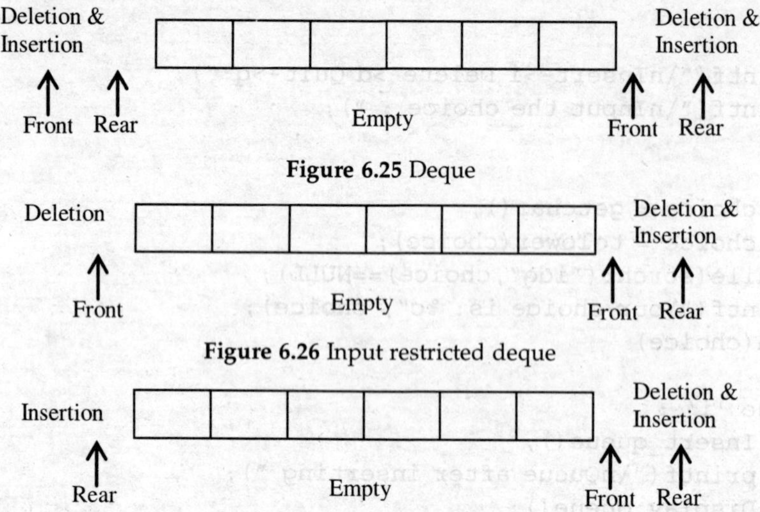

Figure 6.25 Deque

Figure 6.26 Input restricted deque

Figure 6.27 Output restricted deque

```
Step 1: [Check overflow condition]
    If ((rear = n) and (front = 1))
    Output "Overflow" and Return
Step 2: [Check front pointer value]
    If front > 0
    front = front - 1
    Else Return
Step 3: [Insert element at the front end]
    Q [front] = value
Step 4: [Check rear pointer value]
    If rear < n
    rear = rear + 1
    Else Return
Step 5: [Insert element at the rear end]
    Q [rear] = value
Step 6: Return
```

Figure 6.28 Algorithm for insertion in deque

6.8 PRIORITY QUEUES

A queue in which it is possible to insert or remove an element at any position depending on some priority is called priority queue. **Figure 6.30** illustrates a priority queue of jobs waiting to use printer on a local area network (**LAN**) system. Priorities of 1, 2, 3 and 4 have been attached to the jobs of supervisors, teachers, students and outside users, respectively. Therefore, if a job is initiated with priority **p**, it is inserted immediately at the end of the queue of other jobs with priority **p**, for **p** = 1, 2, 3 and 4. Here in the present example jobs are always removed from the front of the queue.

In general way, we can say that a priority queue is a series of queues representing situations in which it is known a priori what priorities are associated with queue elements. **Figure 6.31** illustrates how the single priority queue can be visualized as four separate queues; each follows a **FIFO** behaviour. The elements in the second queue are removed only when the first queue is empty, elements from the third queue are removed only when the first and second queues are empty elements from the third queue are removed only when the first and second queues are empty and so on. This separation of a single priority queue into a series of queues also suggests an efficient storage representation of a priority queue. When the elements are added, they are always added at the end of one of the queues as determined by priority. If one uses a single sequential storage structure for the priority queue then insertion may mean that the new element must be placed in the middle of the queue. This requires the movement of several elements. Thus, we can say that it is better to split a priority queue in several queues, each having its own storage structure.

S_1	S_2	...	S_{i-1}	T_1	T_2	...	T_{j-1}	ST_1	ST_2	...	ST_{k-1}	O_1	O_2	...	O_{l-1}
1	1	...	1	2	2	...	2	3	3	...	3	4	4	...	4

S i_{-1} T $_{j-1}$ ST $_{k-1}$ O $_{l-1}$

Figure 6.30 Priority queue

```
Step 1: [Check for underflow]
        If front = 0 and rear = 0
        Output "Underflow" and Return
Step 2: [Backup the element at front end]
        If front >0
        value = Q [front]
            Return (value)
Step 3: [Check queue for empty]
        If front = rear
        front = rear = 0
        Else
front = front + 1
Step 4:-> [Backup the element at the rear end]
        If rear > 0
        value = q [ rear]
            Return (value)
Step 5: [Check queue for empty]
        If front = rear
        front = rear = 0
    Else
    rear = rear - 1
Step 6: Return
```

Figure 6.29 Deletion algorithm for deque

Let telephone department contains the list of telephone holders in alphabetical order. Suppose some new users we have to add into the list at their proper place. It means we have to insert new users some where in middle, it will require more and more processing time if the list is very large. The remedies for it to divide the list into 26 sub-lists then the processing time will be automatically reduced. If it is required to sort the list use radix technique for efficient processing, **Figure 6.32** illustrates such type of representation.

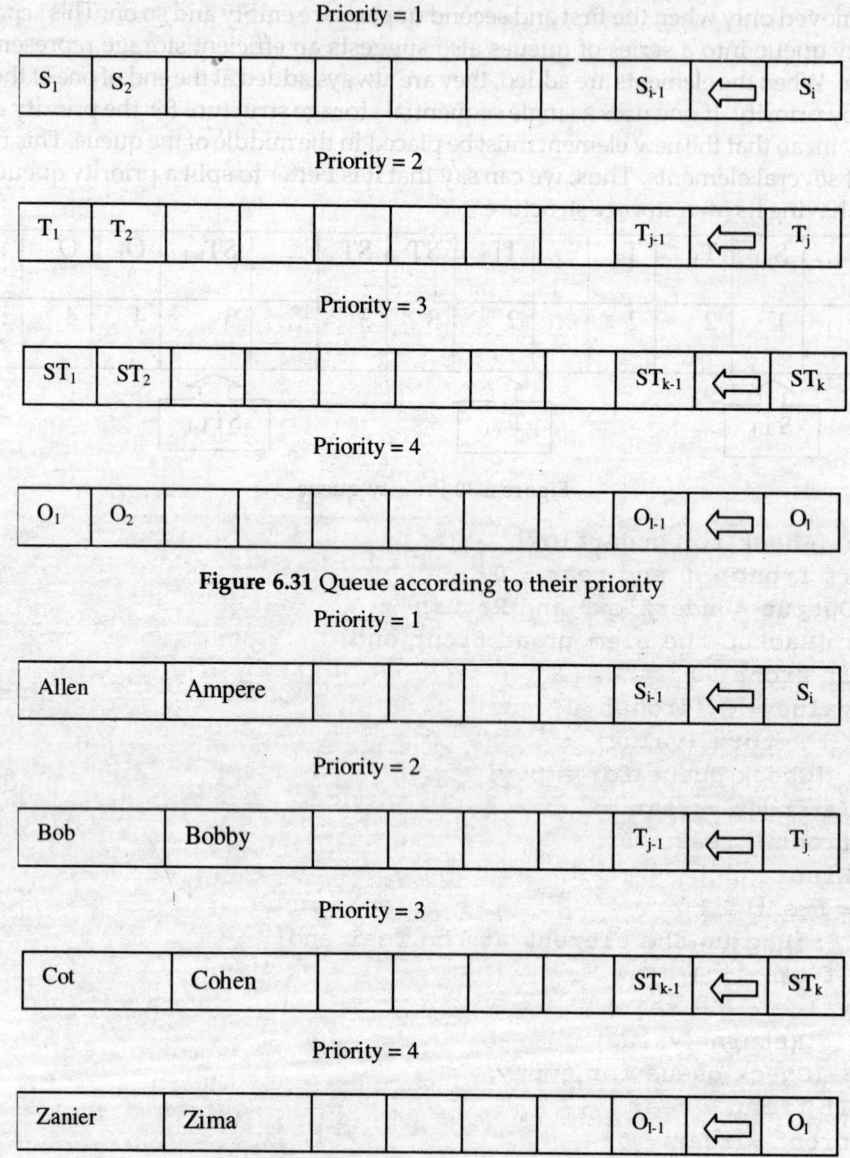

Figure 6.31 Queue according to their priority

Figure 6.32 Alphabetized list of telephone holders

FOR SUMMATIVE AND FORMATIVE ASSESSMENT

6.1 Translate the following infix expression into its equivalent postfix expression:

(i) (x-y) * ((z+v) / f) (ii) ((a+b)/d- ((e-f) + g)

(iii) 12/3*6+6-6+8/2

6.2 Evaluate the following expressions:

(i) 10+3 - 2 – 8/2 * 6 – 7 (ii) 12-2 -3+10/2+4*2

(iii) 3+4/2+5-3*4+3

6.3 Translate the following infix expression into its equivalent prefix expression:

(i) (a+b) -c – d / e * f – g (ii) a – b - c + d / e + f *g

(iii) c+d/e+a-b*c

6.4 Translate each expression into infix notation and then evaluate.

(i) 5, 3, +, 2, *, 6, 9, 7, -, /, - (ii) 6, 10, +, 12, 8, -, *, 8, 2,-, 4, -, +

6.5 Consider the following queue where **QUEUE** is allocated 10 rooms:

Front = 2, Rear = 6

QUEUE: ________, Pauri, Bombay, Delhi, Chennai, Lucknow, ________, ________, ________, ________.

Describe the **QUEUE**, including **Front** and **Rear**, as the following operations take place:

Ahmadabad is added

(i) Two cities are deleted (ii) Varanasi is added

(iii) Bangalore is added (iv) Goa is added

(v) Four cities are deleted (vi) Hyderabad is added

6.6 Consider the following deque where **DEQUE** is allocated 10 rooms:

Left = 3, Right = 6

DEQUE: ________, ________, Tokyo, Now York, London, Masco, ________, ________, ________, ________.

Describe the **DEQUE** including **Left** and **Right** as following operations take place:

(i) Athens is added on the left (ii) India is added on the right

(iii) Bombay is added on the right (iv) Two cities are deleted from the left

(v) California is added on the right (vi) UAE is added on the left

(vii) Two cities are deleted from the right

6.7 Suppose a queue is maintained by a circular array **QUEUE** with **n = 20** rooms. Find the number of elements in the **QUEUE**, if

(i) Front = 6 and Rear = 14

(ii) Front = 20 and Rear = 6

(iii) Front = 5, Rear = 15 and then two elements are deleted.

6.8 Consider the following **Stack** of fibonacci numbers:

Stack: 0, 1, 1, 2, 3, 5, ______, ______, ______, ______.

(a) Describe the **Stack** when the following operation take place:

(i) pop(Stack, 5) (ii) push(Stack, Num)

(iii) push(Stack, Num (iv) pop(Stack, Num

(b) Describe the stack if the operation **pop(Stack, Num)** deletes 3.

6.9 Suppose the following **Stack** of names is in memory, where **Stack** is allocated **n = 10** rooms:

TOP = 7

Stack: DON, RACHITA, MISTHI, TOM ALTER, NAFIZ, JEF, DONO MANN, ______, ______, ______.

Find output of the following codes:

(a) pop(Stack, Name1)
pop(Stack, Name2)
push(Stack, Name3)

(c) Do while (TOP ^{1} 0)
pop (Stack, Name)
[End of loop]

6.10 Write a program that uses a stack to read an integer and print all its prime divisors in ascending order. For example, with integer 2100 the output should be, 2, 2, 3, 5, 5, 7.

6.11 Write an algorithm that translates an infix expression into Polish prefix notation. Implement the designed algorithm with the help of stack.

6.12 Is it possible to implement a queue with the help of two stacks?

6.13 Implement a queue with the help of doubly linked list.

6.14 Implement a **deque** with the help of an array.

6.15 Implement a **deque** with the help of linear linked list.

6.16 Design an algorithm for a input restricted **deque**. Implement the designed algorithm.

6.17 Design an algorithm for a output restricted **deque.** Implement the designed algorithm.

6.18 Consider the grammar G = (V_N, V_T, S, P) where

V_N = {<S>}
V_T = {a, b, c}
P = {<S> ::= a<S>a
<S> ::= b <S> b
<S> ::= c }

Implement it with the help of stack.

6.19 Two stacks are given as illustrated in **Figure 6.33;** join these stacks in such a way that the efficiency of stacks should not be affected.

6.20 Implement the following factorial algorithm with the help of stack:

$$\text{fact}(n) = \begin{cases} 1 & \text{if } n = 0 \text{ or } n = 1 \\ n * \text{fact}(n-1) & \text{if } n > 1 \end{cases}$$

6.21 What is the practical use of circular queue? Give at least two examples and implement one of them.

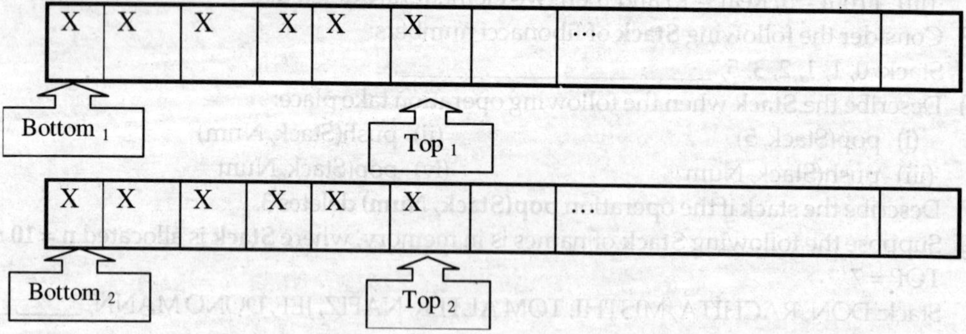

Figure 6.33 Stacks in memory

6.22 How to efficiently implement k stacks in a single array? Discuss the procedure.

Quiz-5 (Stack and Queues)

1. .... form of access is used to add and remove nodes from a queue.
   (a) LIFO, Last In First Out (b) FIFO, First In First Out
   (c) Both a and b (d) None of these
2. In linked list representation of stack .... holds the elements of the stack.
   (a) INFO fields (b) TOP fields
   (c) LINK fields (d) NULL fields
3. .... form of access is used to add remove nodes from a stack.
   (a) LIFO (b) FIFO
   (c) Both A and B (d) None of these
4. In the linked list representation of the stack .... behaves as the top pointer variable of stack.
   (a) Stop pointer (b) Begin pointer
   (c) Start pointer (d) Avail pointer
5. New nodes are added to the .... of the queue.
   (a) Front (b) Back
   (c) Middle (d) Both A and B
6. In linked list representation of stack the null pointer of the last node in the list signals ....
   (a) Beginning of the stack (b) Bottom of the stack
   (c) Middle of the stack (d) In between some value
7. What happens when you push a new node onto a stack?
   (a) The new node is placed at the front of the linked list
   (b) The new node is placed at the back of the linked list
   (c) The new node is placed at the middle of the linked list
   (d) No Changes happens
8. In conversion from prefix to postfix using stack data-structure, if operators and operands are pushed and popped exactly once, then the run-time complexity is "
   (a) O(1) (b) O(n)
   (c) O(log n) (d) $O(n^2)$
9. Which of the following name does not relate to stacks?
   (a) FIFO lists (b) LIFO lists
   (c) Piles (d) Push down lists
10. The retrieval of items in a stack is .... operation.
    (a) push (b) pop
    (c) retrieval (d) access
11. The term push and pop is related to
    (a) Array (b) Lists
    (c) Stacks (d) Trees
12. Which is the pointer associated with the stack?
    (a) FIRST (b) FRONT
    (c) TOS (d) REAR
13. The elements are removal from a stack in .... order.
    (a) Reverse (b) Hierarchical
    (c) Alternative (d) Sequential

14. ...... is the term used to insert an element into stack.
   (a) Push (b) Pull
   (c) Pop (d) Pump
15. Stack follows the strategy of ....
   (a) LIFO (b) FIFO
   (c) LRU (d) RANDOM
16. .... is the term used to delete an element from the stack.
   (a) Push (b) Pull
   (c) Pop (d) Pump
17. What is the value of the postfix expression 6 3 2 4 + - *:
   (a) Something between -15 and -100 (b) Something between -5 and -15
   (c) Something between 5 and -5 (d) Something between 5 and 15
   (e) Something between 15 and 100
18. A pointer variable which contains the location at the top element of the stack is called .....
   (a) Tos (b) Last
   (c) Final (d) End
19. Items in a priority queue are entered in a ______ order
   (a) random (b) order of priority
   (c) as and when they come (d) none of the above
20. Program with highest run-time complexity is
   (a) Tower of Hanoi (b) Fibonacci Series
   (c) Prime Number Series (d) None of the above

❑

CHAPTER

7 Trees

In this chapter we will explore one of the non-linear data-structure trees: binary tree, Complete Binary tree, Expression tree, Search tree, B-tree, AVL tree, Read-Black Tree, Threaded binary Tree, etc. Operations possible on tree like insertion, deletion and searching also presented in this chapter.

7.1 INTRODUCTION

Tree is a type of data structure in which each element is attached to one or more elements directly *beneath* it. The connections between elements are called branches (means data is organized as branches). Trees are often called *inverted trees* because they are normally drawn with the *root* at the top. The elements at the very bottom of an inverted tree (that is, those that have no elements below them) are called *leaves*. In tree structures, a branch is a single line of the tree that ends with a *leaf*. Inverted trees are the data structures used to represent hierarchical file structures. In this case, the leaves are files and the other elements above the leaves are directories. Another example where a tree structure is commonly used is the investigation of genealogies. We are familiar with one very common genealogical chart that is used to represent tree structure is lineage chart and is illustrated in **Figure 7.1**.

The lineage chart represents ancestors and in this example **Mc Dowel** has two children **Scot** and **Leacha**. **Don** and **Mac** are children of **Scot** and **Scot** is son of **Mc Dowel** thus we can say that **Mc Dowel** is grandfather of **Don** and **Mac**. Similarly, **Don** has two child **Jackery** and **Tom**. **Jackery**'s and **Tom**'s great grandfather is **Mc Dowel**. By nature we know that a lineage chart is normally two-way branching, though this does not allow for inbreeding. When inbreeding occurs a tree structure is no longer valid unless we insist that each occurrence of breeding be separately listed. If one describes the family history of vegetables, fruits (like mango, apple, orange, etc.), flowers or animals, inbreeding occurs frequently.

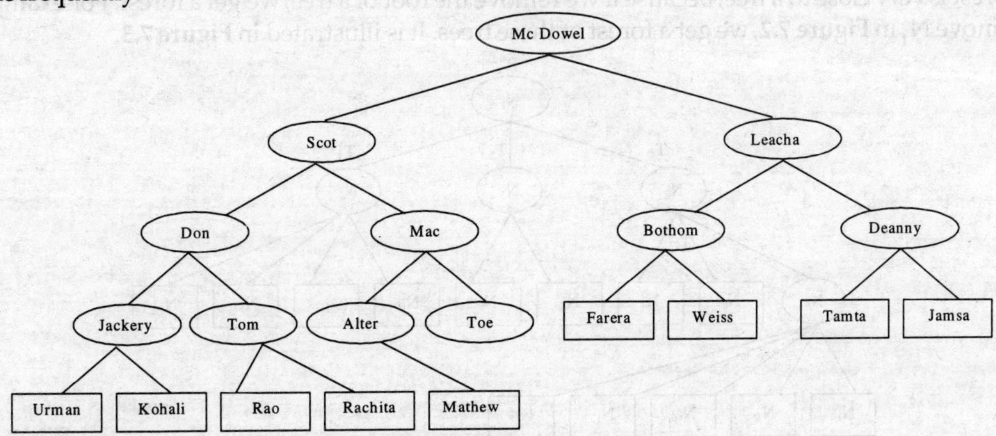

Figure 7.1 Lineage Chart

A tree **T** is defined as a finite set of one or more nodes such that

- There is a special node called the root **R**.
- The remaining nodes are divided into $\mathbf{n} \geq \mathbf{0}$ disjoint sets $\mathbf{T_1}, \mathbf{T_2}, \mathbf{T_3} \ldots \mathbf{T_n}$, where each of these sets is a tree. $\mathbf{T_1}, \mathbf{T_2}, \mathbf{T_3} \ldots \mathbf{T_n}$ is called the sub-trees of the root.

For example, if we consider **Figure 7.1** then we can say that **Mc Dowel** is father and **Scot** and **Leacha** are two son of **Mc Dowel**. In other words we can say that **Mc Dowel** is root and the tree has two sub-trees whose roots are **Scot** and **Leacha**. The condition that $\mathbf{T_1}, \mathbf{T_2}, \mathbf{T_3} \ldots \mathbf{T_n}$ be disjoint sets prevents sub-trees from connecting with each other (No cross breeding) thus it follows that every element in a tree is the root of some sub-tree of the whole.

In other words one may define a tree as a collection of nodes and each node is linked with another node with the help of a branch. The nodes are connected in such a way that there are no loops and there is a special node called the root. For example, consider the tree in **Figure 7.2**, which has 18 nodes. The root node $\mathbf{N_1}$ has three sub-trees $\mathbf{T_1}, \mathbf{T_2}, \mathbf{T_3}$ and $\mathbf{N_2}, \mathbf{N_3}, \mathbf{N_4}$ being roots of the sub-trees shown in **Figure 7.3.** The number of sub-trees of a node is called its degree, root $\mathbf{N_1}$ has degree 3. Similarly, node $\mathbf{N_5}$ has degree 5 and node $\mathbf{N_{14}}$ has degree zero. A node with degree zero is called leaf. $\mathbf{N_6}, \mathbf{N_7}, \mathbf{N_8}, \mathbf{N_9}, \mathbf{N_{10}}, \mathbf{N_{11}}, \mathbf{N_{12}}, \mathbf{N_{13}}, \mathbf{N_{14}}, \mathbf{N_{15}}, \mathbf{N_{16}}, \mathbf{N_{17}}, \mathbf{N_{18}}$ are leaf nodes. The leaf nodes are also called terminal nodes and rest of the nodes in a tree are called non-terminal. If **x** is root node and its sub-trees are $\mathbf{T_1}, \mathbf{T_2}$ and $\mathbf{T_3}$ and roots of sub-trees are $\mathbf{R_1}, \mathbf{R_2}, \mathbf{R_3}$ then $\mathbf{R_1}, \mathbf{R_2}, \mathbf{R_3}$ are called children of **x**. In turn **x** is called the parent of $\mathbf{R_1}, \mathbf{R_2}$ and $\mathbf{R_3}$. Children of same parent are called siblings. In **Figure 7.2** $\mathbf{N_1}$ is parent of $\mathbf{N_2}, \mathbf{N_3}$ and $\mathbf{N_4}$ hence $\mathbf{N_2}, \mathbf{N_3}$ and $\mathbf{N_4}$ are siblings. The degree of a tree is the highest degree of a node in the tree. The tree of **Figure 7.2** has degree 5. The ancestors of a node are all the nodes along the path from the root to that node. The ancestors of $\mathbf{N_{14}}$ are $\mathbf{N_5}, \mathbf{N_2}$ and $\mathbf{N_1}$. The descents of a node are all the nodes along the path from node to terminal node. The descents of $\mathbf{N_1}$ are $\mathbf{N_2}, \mathbf{N_5}$ and $\mathbf{N_{14}}$. Similarly, observing into the tree **T** shown in **Figure 7.2** one can have other descents of $\mathbf{N_1}$.

Each node in a tree is assigned a level number as follows- The root node **R** of the tree is assigned a level number 0, and a node is assigned a level number, which is one more than the level number of its parent (Root). The nodes which are at the same level numbers, are said to be of the same generation. The maximum number of access operations required to reach the desired node (record) is called the depth. It is the maximum number of nodes in a branch. This turns out to be one more than the largest level number of the tree.

A forest is a set of $\mathbf{n} \geq 0$ disjoint trees, where **n** represents number of nodes in the tree. The meaning of a forest is very close to a tree, because if we remove the root of a tree, we get a forest. For example, if we remove $\mathbf{N_1}$ in **Figure 7.2**, we get a forest of three trees. It is illustrated in **Figure 7.3**.

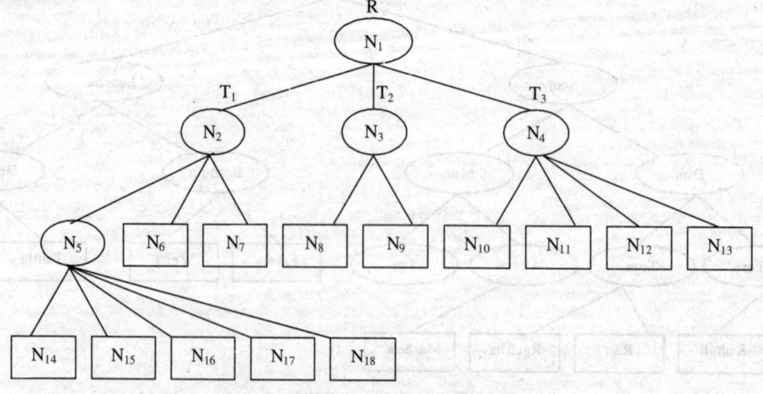

Figure 7.2 Tree T with 18 nodes

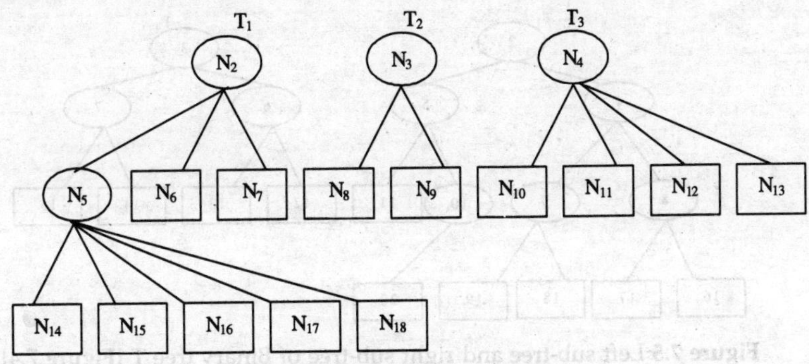

Figure 7.3 Forest of Trees

7.2 BINARY TREE

A binary tree is an important type of data structure, which is very useful. It is a method of placing and locating files (called records or keys or data) in a database, especially when all the data are known to be in random access memory. The algorithm finds data by repeatedly dividing the number of ultimately accessible records in half until only one remains. A tree is a binary tree if each node of it can have at the most two branches. In other words we can say that if every node of a tree can have at most degree two, then this is called a binary tree. In a binary tree left and right sub-trees distinguish sub-trees of a node. The number of leaves in a binary tree is always a power of 2. The number of access operations required to reach the desired record is called the depth of the tree.

A binary tree **T** is a finite set of nodes, which is either empty or consists of special node called root **R** and two disjoint binary trees T_1 and T_2 (which are called the left sub-tree and right sub-tree, respectively). If T_1 is non-empty then the root of T_1 is called the left successor of **R**. If T_2 is non-empty then the root of T_2 is known as right successor of **R**. Each node contains a "left" pointer, a "right" pointer, and a data element. The "root" pointer points to the topmost node in the tree. The left and right pointers recursively point to smaller "subtrees" on either side. A null pointer represents a binary tree with no elements, i.e., the empty tree.

For example, **Figure 7.4** illustrates a binary tree T that consists of 20 nodes and the value of each node is equivalent to its node number. Root is 1, its left successor is 2 and right successor is 3. Similarly, left successor of 2 is 4 and right successor is 5. Thus, we can say that the left sub-tree of root node 1 is equivalent to T_1 in **Figure 7.5** and the right sub-tree is equivalent to T_2 in **Figure 7.5**.

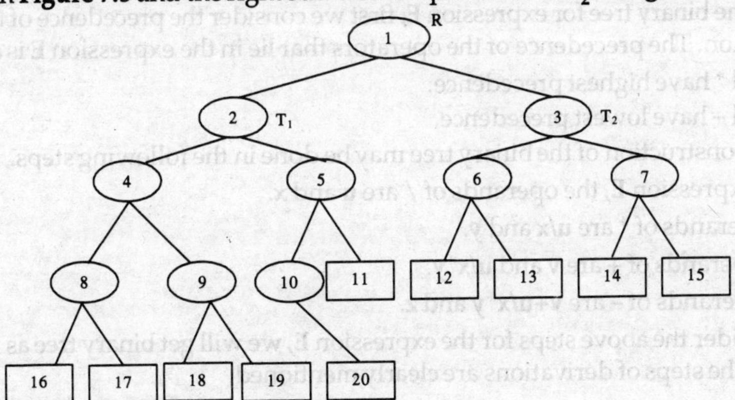

Figure 7.4 Binary tree

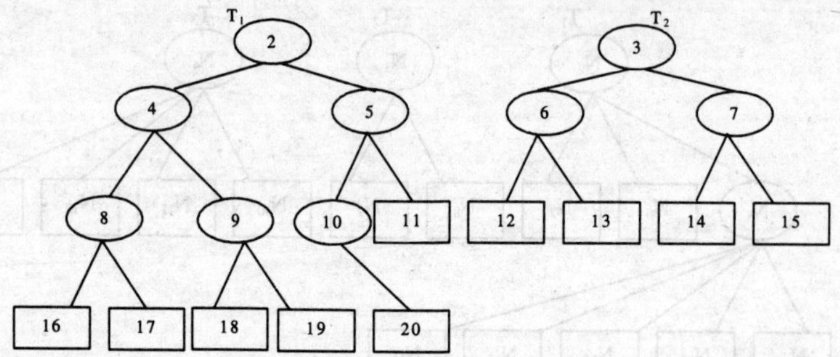

Figure 7.5 Left sub-tree and right sub-tree of Binary tree T {**Figure** 7.4}

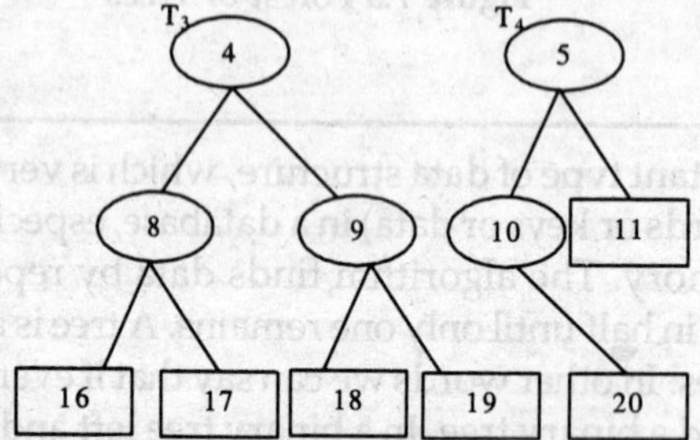

Figure 7.6 Left sub-tree and right sub-tree of Binary tree T_1 {**Figure** 7.5}

The above definition of binary tree T is recursive since T is defined in terms of the binary sub-trees T_1 and T_2. Similarly, we can define T_1 in terms of its sub-trees T_3 and T_4 as illustrated in **Figure 7.6.** This means, in particular every node of T contains left and right sub-trees. If **N** is terminal node then both of its left and right sub-trees are empty.

An expression tree is a binary tree which is used to represent a mathematical expression. Expression trees are used to represent arithmetic expressions: specifically the combinations of operators, operands, and order of evaluation. In an expression tree, every operator and operand has its own node in the tree, operators are always stored in internal nodes and operands are always stored in leaves, i.e., in an expression tree, the parent nodes are the operators, and the children are the operands. In a binary expression tree, every operator node has exactly two children.

For example, consider the expression **E** = v + u / x * y – z, which is shown in **Figure 7.7**. Before constructing the binary tree for expression **E,** first we consider the precedence of the operators that lie in the expression. The precedence of the operators that lie in the expression **E** is as follows:

(i) / and * have highest precedence.

(ii) + and – have lowest precedence.

Now the construction of the binary tree may be done in the following steps.

(i)In the expression **E**, the operands of / are **u** and **x**.

(ii)The operands of * are **u/x** and **y**.

(iii)The operands of **+** are **v** and **u/x*y**.

(iv)The operands of – are **v+u/x*y** and **z.**

If we consider the above steps for the expression **E**, we will get binary tree as illustrated in **Figure 7.7**, where all the steps of derivations are clearly mentioned.

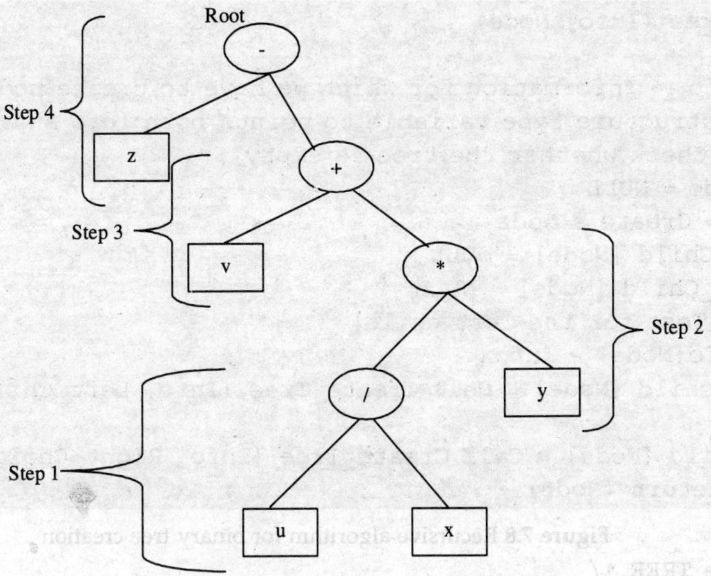

Figure 7.7 Binary tree for the expression E

To evaluate a tree (or subtree) we can use the following recursive algorithm. BTree is structure having three fields- left pointer, right pointer and information field.

```
double evaluate(BTree *node)
if value[node] is a number
  then return value[node]
otherwise
  if value[node] is the + operator
    then return evaluate(left[node]) + evaluate(right[node])
  else if value[node] is the - operator
    then return evaluate(left[node]) - evaluate(right[node])
  else if value[node] is the * operator
    then return evaluate(left[node]) * evaluate(right[node])
  else if value[node] is the / operator
    then return evaluate(left[node]) / evaluate(right[node])
  else
    generate an error message (invalid operator)
    and return a default value
```

The binary tree creation algorithm is illustrated in **Figure 7.8.** This is a recursive algorithm that creates a binary tree by inserting the desired information. After insertion of the information at proper place in the tree, next information is inserted into the binary tree in the second step. This process is continued till last information is inserted. The recursive algorithm of **Figure 7.8** is implemented in the program segment **CREAT_T.C.** Program segment **CREAT_BT.C** illustrates the algorithm discussed in **Figure 7.9.**

```
Create_Tree (Info, Node)

Where Info → Information for which we have to create node.
Node  → structure type variable to points both left and right child.
Step 1: [Check whether the tree is empty]
   If Node = NULL
   Node = Create a Node
   Left_Child [Node] = NULL
   Right_Child [Node] = NULL
Step 2: [Test for the left child]
   If Info[Node] ≥ Info
   Left_child [Node] = Call Create_Tree (Info, Left_Child [Node])
   Else
Right_child [Node] = Call Create_Tree (Info, Right_Child [Node])
Step 3: Return (Node)
```

Figure 7.8 Recursive algorithm for binary tree creation

```
/* Create TREE */
/* CREAT_T.C */
# include<stdio.h>
# include<malloc.h>

struct NODE
{
   int Info;
   struct NODE *Left_Child;
   struct NODE *Right_Child;
};

struct NODE *Create_Tree (int , struct NODE *);
void Output(struct NODE *, int );

/* Function to create a tree */

struct NODE * Create_Tree (int Info, struct NODE *Node)
{
   if (Node == NULL)
   {
      Node = (struct NODE *) malloc( sizeof(struct NODE ));
      Node->Info = Info;
      Node->Left_Child = NULL;
      Node->Right_Child = NULL;
      return (Node);
   }
   /* Test for the left child */
```

```
    if (Node->Info >= Info )
        Node->Left_Child = Create_Tree (Info, Node->Left_Child);
    else
        /* Set all the rest of the elements as right child */
        Node->Right_Child = Create_Tree (Info, Node->Right_Child);
    return(Node);
}

/* Output function */
void  Output(struct NODE *T, int Level)
{
    int i;
    if (T)
    {
        Output(T->Right_Child, Level+1);
        printf("\n ");
        for (i = 0; i < Level; i++)
            printf("   ");
        printf("%d", T->Info);
        printf("\n");
        Output(T->Left_Child, Level+1);
    }
}

/* Function main */
void main()
{
    int Info ;
    char choice;
    struct NODE *T = (struct NODE *) malloc(sizeof(struct NODE *));
    T = NULL;
    printf("\n Input choice 'b' to break:");
    choice = getchar();
    while(choice != 'b')
    {
        printf("\n Input information of the node: ");
        scanf("%d", &Info);
        T = Create_Tree (Info, T);
        printf("\n Tree is ");
        Output(T, 1);
        printf("\n Input choice 'b' to break:");
        choice = getchar();
    }
}
```

```
/* Create Binary TREE */
/* CREAT_BT.C */
# include<stdio.h>
# include<malloc.h>
struct NODE
{
   int Info;
   struct NODE *Left_Child;
   struct NODE *Right_Child;
};

struct NODE *Binary_Tree (char *, int, int);
void Output(struct NODE *, int );

/* Function to insert an element into tree */
struct  NODE *  Binary_Tree (char *List, int Lower, int Upper)
{
   struct NODE *Node;
   int Mid = (Lower + Upper)/2;
   Node = (struct NODE *) malloc(sizeof(struct NODE));
   Node->Info = List [Mid];
   if ( Lower>= Upper)
   {
      Node->Left_Child = NULL;
      Node->Right_Child = NULL;
      return (Node);
   }

   if (Lower <= Mid - 1)
      Node->Left_Child = Binary_Tree (List, Lower, Mid - 1);
   else
      Node->Left_Child = NULL;
   if (Mid + 1 <= Upper)
      Node->Right_Child = Binary_Tree (List, Mid + 1, Upper);
   else
      Node->Right_Child = NULL;
   return(Node);
}

/* Output function */
void Output(struct NODE *T, int Level)
{
   int i;
   if (T)
   {
```

```
        Output(T->Right_Child, Level+1);
        printf("\n");
        for (i = 0; i < Level; i++)
            printf("   ");
        printf("%c", T->Info);
        Output(T->Left_Child, Level+1);
    }
}

/* Function main */
void main()
{
    char List[100];
    int Number = 0;
    char Info ;
    char choice;
    struct NODE *T = (struct NODE *) malloc(sizeof(struct NODE));
    T = NULL;
    printf("\n Input choice 'b' to break:");
    choice = getchar();
    while(choice != 'b')
    {
        printf("\n Input information of the node: ");
        scanf("%c", &Info);
        List[Number++] = Info;
        fflush(stdin);
        printf("\n Input choice 'b' to break:");
        choice = getchar();
    }
    Number --;
    printf("\n Number of elements in the lsit is %d", Number);
    T = Binary_Tree(List, 0, Number);
    Output(T,1);
}
```

Now see the stack based implementation of the CREAT_BTS.C code. Readers will find this stack based implementation is more simpler than recursive. Due to simplicity of the code we are not going to discuss the algorithm.

```
/* Create Binary TREE */
/* CREAT_BTS.C */

# include<stdio.h>
# include<malloc.h>
#define SIZE 10

struct tree
```

```
{
    struct tree *left_child;
    int info;
    struct tree *right_child;
};
typedef struct tree Tnode;

Tnode *root=NULL,*ptr,*par,*New;
int top=SIZE;
Tnode *stack[SIZE];
void create(Tnode *);
void display(Tnode *,int);
void push(Tnode *);
Tnode *pop();

void main()
{
    char x,choice;
    create(root);
    printf("created tree is as follow:");
    display(root,1);
    getchar();
}

void create(Tnode *ptr)
  {
     int x;
     char choice;
    do
    {
    New= (Tnode *) malloc(sizeof(Tnode));
    printf("Enter element:->");
    scanf("%d",&x);
    New->info=x;
    New->left_child=NULL;
    New->right_child=NULL;
    /* attach new node in to its correct position */

    if(root==NULL)  /* insert at root */
     root=New;
    else
    {
     /* locate the leaf node */
     ptr=root;
     while(ptr!=NULL)
```

```
      {
        if(x==ptr->info)
          {
       printf("already present");
       exit(0);
          }
        par=ptr;
        if(x<ptr->info)
          ptr=ptr->left_child;
        else
          ptr=ptr->right_child;
       }
     if(x<par->info)  /* insert as left child */
          par->left_child=New;
     else
          par->right_child=New;  /* insert as right child */

    }
   printf("more element:->");
   fflush(stdin);
   choice=getchar();
   }while(choice=='y');
}

void display(Tnode *ptr, int Level)
 {
   int i;
   if (ptr!=NULL)
   {
   display(root,1);
   /* pre_order tree traversal  */
   printf("\n pre order traversal is:->");
   ptr=root;
   while(ptr!=NULL)
   {
      printf("%d  ",ptr->info);   /* process the root */
      if(ptr->right_child!=NULL)  /* push the right sub tree on stack */
      push(ptr->right_child);
     if(ptr->left_child!=NULL)    /* move to left subtree */
      ptr=ptr->left_child;
      else
      ptr=pop();
    }
   getchar();
 }
```

```
void push(Tnode *x)
  {
   if(top==0)
  printf("stack is full");
   else
  {
  top=top-1;
  stack[top]=x;
  }
  }
Tnode *pop()
 {
  Tnode *x;
  if(top==SIZE){
   printf("\n tree has been traversed");
   exit(0);
  } else
   {
 x=stack[top];
 top=top+1;
   }
  return(x);
 }
```

```
Binary_Tree (List, Lower, Upper)
Where List → Represents list of elements that forms a binary tree.
   Lower → Represents lower limit of the list that is lower index value of
the list.
Upper → Represents upper limit of the list that is upper index value.
Step 1: [Find middle of the list]
(i)   Mid = (Lower + Upper) / 2 [Integer division]
(ii)  Info [Node] = List [Mid]
Step 2: If Lower ≥ Upper
(i)   Left_Child [Node] = NULL
(ii)  Right_Child [Node] = NULL
   (iii) Return (Node)
Step 3: If Lower  ≤ Mid - 1
   Left_Child = Call Binary_Tree (List, Lower, Mid - 1)
   Else
Left_Child [Node] = NULL
Step 4: If Upper ≥ Mid + 1
   Right_Child = Call Binary_Tree (List, Mid+1, Upper)
   Else
Right_Child [Node] =  NULL
Step 5: Return (Node)
```

Figure 7.9 Algorithm to create binary tree

7.3 COMPLETE BINARY TREE

It is a binary tree in which every level, except possibly the deepest, is completely filled, i.e, each node of tree can have at the most two children. A complete binary tree has at level L, 2^L nodes, at every depth L < n and between 2^n and 2^{n+1}-1 nodes altogether. It can be efficiently implemented as an array, where a node at index **i** has children at indexes **2i** and **2i+1** and a parent at index **i/2**, with one-based indexing. If child index is greater than the number of nodes, the child does not exist. For example:

- If L = 0, then $2^0 = 1$ implies that there is only one node in the tree that is a root. And number of nodes in the tree is $n = 2^0 = 1$
- If L = 1, then $2^1 = 2$ implies that there are two nodes in the tree at level 1 as a left and right successor. And total number of nodes will be $n= 2^0 + 2^1 = 3$
- If L = 2, then $2^2 = 4$ implies that there are four nodes in the tree at the level 2. And total number nodes in tree are $n = 2^0+2^1+2^2 = 7$.

Similarly If L = 3, then $2^3 = 8$ implies that there are eight nodes in the tree at this level and total number of nodes in tree will be 15. Thus, we can say that a tree **T** is said to be complete if all its levels except the last have the maximum number of possible nodes; and if all the nodes at last level appear to be left as far as possible. For example, **Figure 7.10** illustrates a complete binary tree. If we look into **Figure 7.10,** we find that at level 0 there is only one node; at level 1 there are two nodes and at level 2 there are four nodes, etc.

If we assume that $\mathbf{v_1 = 1}$ is a root and its left sub-tree's root is $\mathbf{v_2 = 2*v_1 = 2*1 = 2}$ and right sub-tree's root is $\mathbf{v_3 = 2*v_1 + 1 = 2*1 + 1 = 3}$ and we consider the 4th nodes' value is 4 then its left sub-tree value is = 4*2 = 8, and right sub-tree's value is 4*2 + 1 = 9 and so on. In the next paragraph we will discuss complexity of binary tree in respect to node insertion and for deletion both.

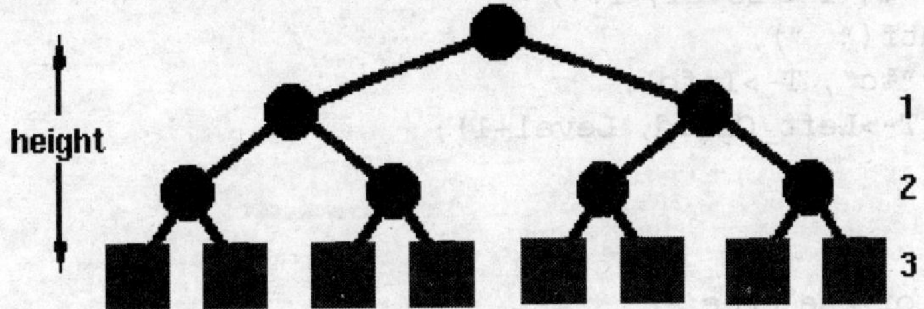

Figure 7.10 A complete tree

This forms a complete tree, whose height is defined as the number of links from the root to the deepest leaf. First, we need to work out how many nodes, **n**, we have in such a tree of height, **h**. Now,

$$\mathbf{n = 1 + 2^1 + 2^2 + ... + 2^h}$$

from this we have,

$\mathbf{n = 2^{h+1} - 1}$ or $2^{h+1} = n+1$ taking log of both sides we get $h+1 = \log_2(n+1)$ which is approximately $\mathbf{h = floor(\log_2 n)}$.

Examination shows that in the worst case, **h**+1 or **ceiling($\log_2$n)** comparisons are needed to find an item. This is the same as for binary search {will be discussed in the latter sections}. However, addition of an item in the binary tree also requires **ceiling($\log_2$n)** comparisons to determine where to add an item. Actually adding the item takes a constant number of operations, so we say that a binary tree requires **O($\log_2$ n)** operations for both adding and finding an item - a considerable improvement over binary search for a dynamic structure which often requires addition of new items. Deletion is also an **O($\log_2$ n)** operation. For example, consider the following program segment that implements the above discussion.

```
/* Finding Depth of Binary Tree */
/* DEPTH_BT.C */
# include<stdio.h>
# include<malloc.h>
struct NODE
{
   char Info;
   struct NODE *Left_Child;
   struct NODE *Right_Child;
};
int depth = 0;
void Output (struct NODE *, int );
int Depth (struct NODE *, int );
struct NODE *Create_Tree (char , struct NODE *);
/* Output function */
void Output(struct NODE *T, int Level)
{
   int i;
   if (T)
   {
      Output(T->Right_Child, Level+1);
      printf("\n");
      for (i = 0; i < Level; i++)
         printf("  ");
      printf("%c", T->Info);
      Output(T->Left_Child, Level+1);
   }
}

/* Find depth of the tree */
int Depth (struct NODE *Node, int Level)
{
   if (Node != NULL)
   {
      if (Level > depth)
         depth = Level;
      Depth (Node->Left_Child, Level + 1);
      Depth (Node->Right_Child, Level + 1);
   }
   return (depth);
}

/*  Create binary tree */
struct NODE *  Create_Tree (char Info, struct NODE *Node)
{
```

```
    if (Node == NULL)
    {
        Node = (struct NODE *) malloc(sizeof(struct NODE));
        Node->Info = Info;
        Node->Left_Child = NULL;
        Node->Right_Child = NULL;
        return (Node);
    }

    /* Test for the left child */
    if (Info < Node->Info)
        Node->Left_Child = Create_Tree (Info, Node->Left_Child);
    else
        /* Test for the right child */
        if (Info > Node->Info)
            Node->Right_Child = Create_Tree (Info, Node->Right_Child);

    return(Node);
}

/* Function main */
void main()
{
    int Number = 0;
    char Info ;
    char choice;
    int depth;
    struct NODE *T = (struct NODE *) malloc(sizeof(struct NODE));
    T = NULL;
    printf("\n Input choice 'b' to break:");
    choice = getchar();

    while(choice != 'b')
    {
        fflush(stdin);
        printf("\n Input information of the node: ");
        scanf("%c", &Info);
        T = Create_Tree(Info, T);
        Number++;
        fflush(stdin);
        printf("\n Input choice 'b' to break:");
        choice = getchar();
    }
    printf("\n Number of elements in the tree is %d", Number);
    printf("\n Tree is \n");
    Output(T, 1);
```

```
    depth = Depth(T, 0);
    printf("\n Depth of the above tree is:  %d", depth);
}
```

7.4 EXTENDED BINARY TREE OR 2-TREE

An *extended binary tree* is a transformation of any binary tree into a complete binary tree. This transformation consists of replacing every null subtree of the original tree with "special nodes." The nodes from the original tree are then *internal nodes*, while the "special nodes" are *external nodes*. Every internal node in the extended tree has exactly two children, and every external node is a leaf. The result is a complete binary tree. In other words a binary tree is called extended or 2-tree if each node **N** has either 0 or 2 degree. In this case, the nodes with degree 2 are called internal and nodes with degree 0 are called terminal (or external or leaf) nodes. The 2-trees are used to represent algebraic expression and shown in **Figure 7.7**.

7.5 REPRESENTATION OF BINARY TREE

It is often required to maintain binary trees in the computer memory. There are two traditional popular techniques that are used to maintain binary trees in the memory. These are:

- Sequential representation
- Linked list representation

7.5.1 Sequential Representation

A sequential representation of a binary tree requires numbering of nodes; starting with nodes on level 0, then on level 1and so on. The nodes are numbered from left to right. As we have already discussed that numbering of nodes gives a complete binary tree. The nodes of the binary tree are maintained in a one-dimensional array. For example, consider the binary tree **T** illustrated in **Figure 7.11**.

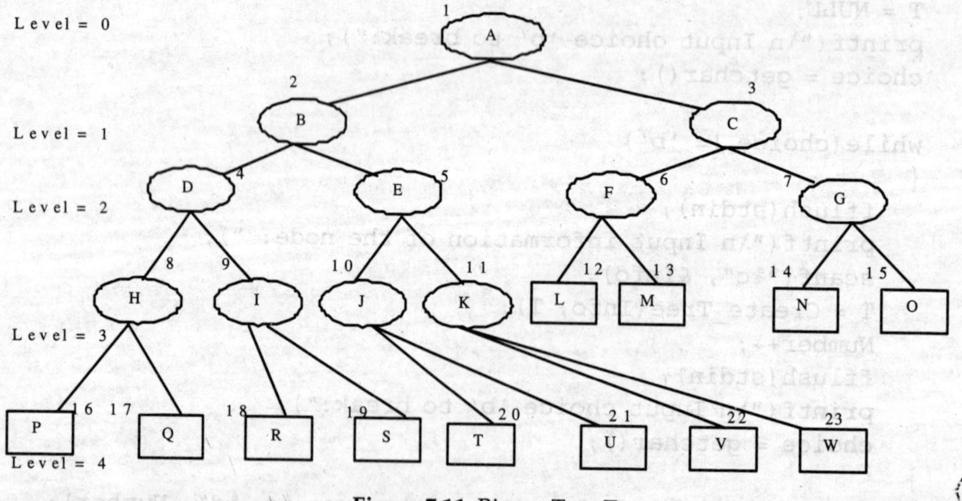

Figure 7.11 Binary Tree T

In **Figure 7.11** the root node is numbered as 1, then its left child as 2 and the right child as 3. Now node 2 is the parent and its left child is numbered 4 and right child is numbered 5. The node 3 is right child of node 1 (Root) and is parent of nodes 6 and 7. The nodes at level 2 are 4, 5, 6 and 7 will be treated as children of nodes at level 1, and parent of the nodes at level 3 and so on. If we consider **Figure 7.12,** we find that the root node occupies room at index 1(Node numbered 1). The left child of node 1 will occupy room at index 2, and right child at index 3. Similarly, left child of node 2 at index 4 and right child at index 5, left child of node 3 at index 6 and right child at index 7 occupy rooms, and so on. If we have any node numbered **i** then its left child will occupy room at index **2i** and right child at **2i+1**.

The above representation of binary tree can also be applied to the complete binary tree. It is an ideal representation for complete binary tree and in this case no space is wasted. However, for other binary trees most of the memory space remains unutilized. For example, if we have a skewed binary tree then more than 50% of the space is unutilized, if it is implemented through the arrays {**Figure 7.13**}. The sequential representation of the tree shown in **Figure 7.13** is illustrated in **Figure 7.14**. From this figure we find that out of 30 spaces, the tree thereby wasting about 70% memory occupies only 9.

Other problems arise during the insertion and deletion of new node when information is to be inserted/deleted in the middle of the tree, because it requires much more movement of the nodes, requires renumbering of nodes.

Linear_T

INDEX	INFO
1	A
2	B
3	C
4	D
5	E
6	F
7	G
8	H
9	I
10	J
11	K
12	L
13	M
14	N
15	O
16	P
17	Q
18	R
19	S
20	T
21	U
22	V
23	W
24	
25	
26	
27	
28	
29	

Figure 7.12 Sequential representation of tree T illustrated in **Figure 7.11**

Linear_Skewed_Tree

INDEX	INFO
1	A
2	B
3	G
4	C
5	
6	H
7	
8	
9	D
10	
11	
12	
13	I
14	
15	
16	
17	
18	E
19	
20	
21	
22	
23	
24	
25	
26	J
27	
28	
29	
30	

Figure 7.14 Sequential representation of tree illustrated in **Figure 7.13**

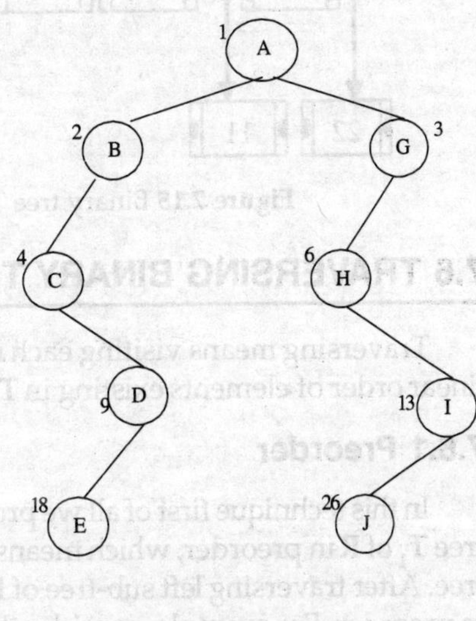

Figure 7.13 Skewed tree

7.5.2 Linked List Representation

The problem associated with the sequential representation of binary tree can be overcome through the use of the linked list representation. In this representation each node requires three fields, one for the link of the left child, second field for representing the information associated with the node and the third field is used to represent the link of the right child. For example, **Figure 7.15** illustrates a binary tree, each node having three fields and is represented in computer memory as shown in **Figure 7.16**.

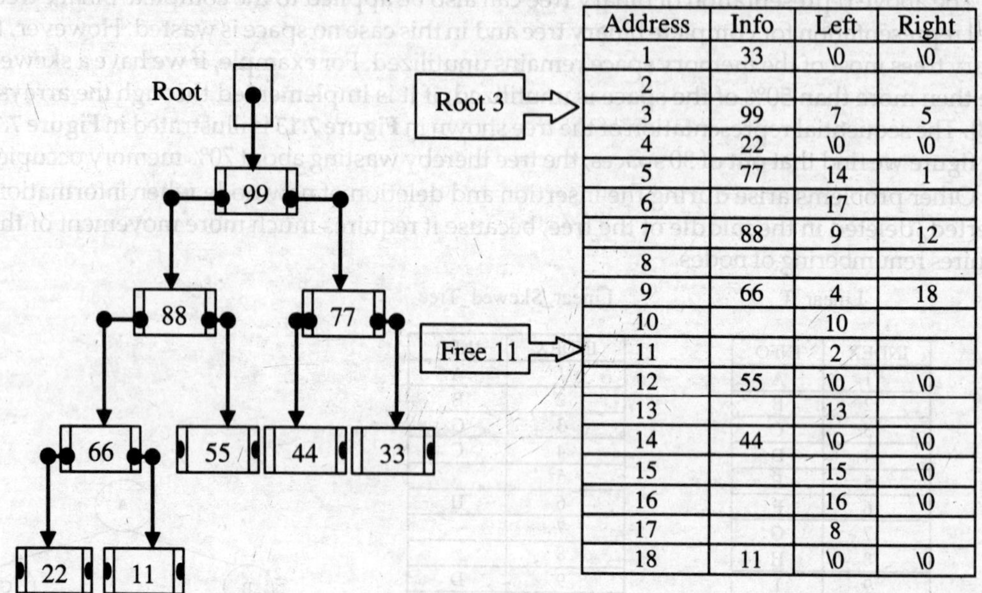

Address	Info	Left	Right
1	33	\0	\0
2			
3	99	7	5
4	22	\0	\0
5	77	14	1
6		17	
7	88	9	12
8			
9	66	4	18
10		10	
11		2	
12	55	\0	\0
13		13	
14	44	\0	\0
15		15	\0
16		16	\0
17		8	
18	11	\0	\0

Figure 7.15 Binary tree T

Figure 7.16 Linked list representation of Binary tree T

7.6 TRAVERSING BINARY TREE

Traversing means visiting each node exactly once. A full traversal of a binary tree **T** produces a linear order of elements existing in **T**. There are three basic ways for traversing a binary tree.

7.6.1 Preorder

In this technique first of all we process the root **R** of the binary tree **T**. Then we traverse the left sub-tree T_1 of **R** in preorder, which means that we traverse root of the sub-tree T_1 first and then its left sub-tree. After traversing left sub-tree of **R**, then we take over right sub-tree of **R** and process all the nodes in preorder. For example, consider the binary tree shown in **Figure 7.17**.

According to the above discussion first of all we consider the root node **A**; then consider its left sub-tree as illustrated in **Figure 7.18**. Now we process root of sub-tree T_1 (node B) then its left sub-tree T_3 that is a terminal node **D**. Now consider the right sub-tree of T_1 (T_4). The root of T_4 is **E** and left sub-tree of T_4 is T_9 that is a terminal node **F**. Thus, the processing of all the nodes of the left sub-tree T_1 is finished. Now we will take over right sub-tree T_2 of **R** as illustrated in **Figure 7.18**. We will process all the nodes of the T_2 in same way as we have processed the nodes of sub-tree T_1. After completion of the preorder traversing of the binary tree we get the linear list of the nodes as A, B, D, E, F, C, G, H, J, L, M, K, O. This process is illustrated in **Figure 7.19**. Algorithm for the preorder traversal of a binary tree is shown in **Figure 7.20**.

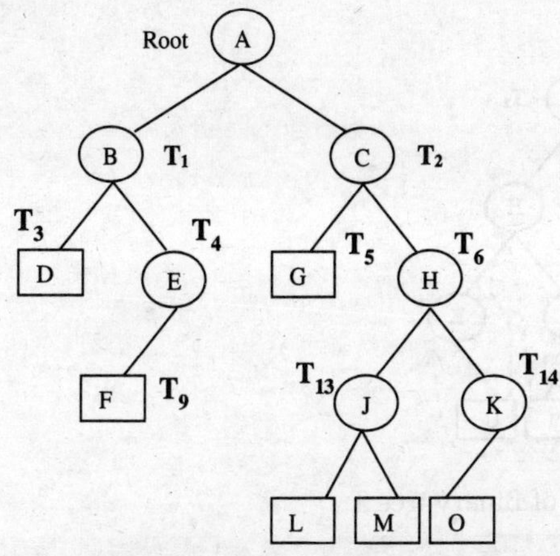

Figure 7.17 Binary tree T with 13 nodes

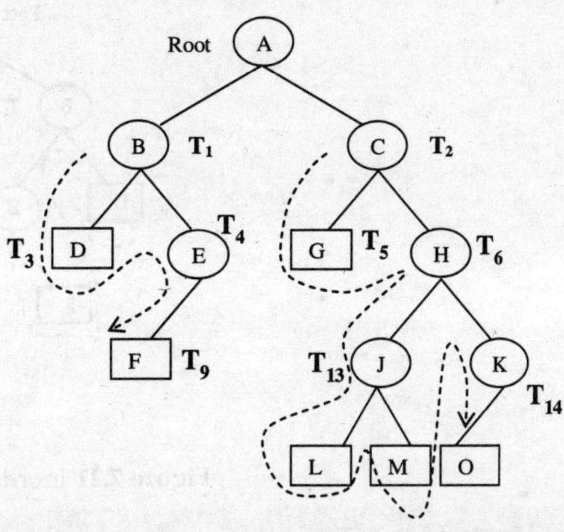

Figure 7.18 Preorder travsersal of left Sub-tree T_1 and right sub-tree T_2 of **Figure** 7.17

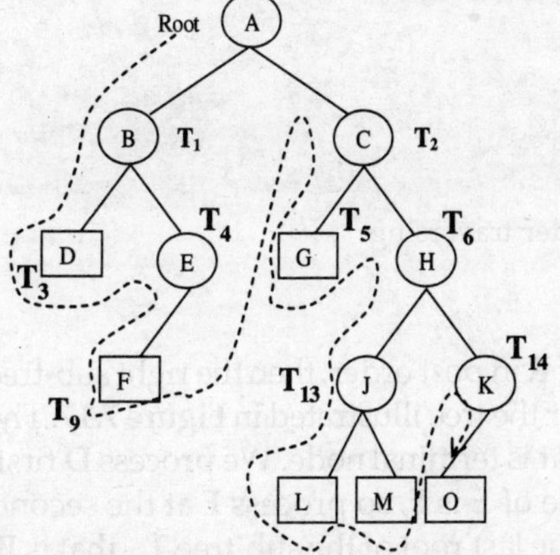

Figure 7.19 Preorder traversal of Binary tree T

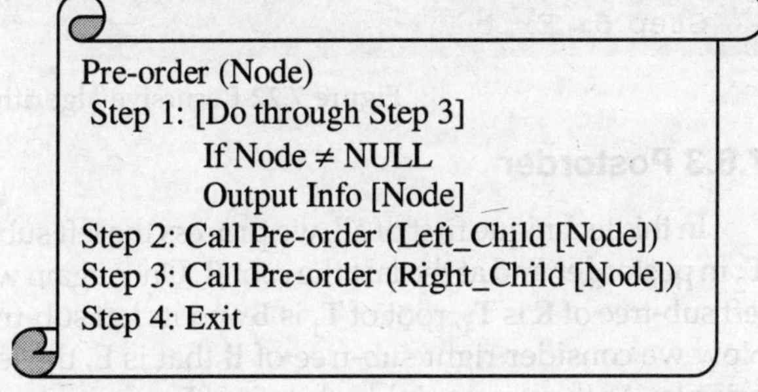

Pre-order (Node)
Step 1: [Do through Step 3]
If Node ≠ NULL
Output Info [Node]
Step 2: Call Pre-order (Left_Child [Node])
Step 3: Call Pre-order (Right_Child [Node])
Step 4: Exit

Figure 7.20 Recursive algorithm of preorder traversing

7.6.2 Inorder

In the inorder traversing technique first of all we process the left sub-tree T_1 of the root **R** in the in-order. Then process the root **R** and at the last we process the right sub-tree T_2 of **R.** In **Figure 7.17, A** is root and its left sub-tree is T_1. The root of T_1 is **B** and its left sub-tree **D** is a terminal node. We first process node **D** then root of **D** (B) and the last the right sub-tree of **B** (E). The left sub-tree of **E** is **F** that is terminal node. We first process **F** and then right sub-tree of **E**. There is no right sub-tree, hence we process **E**. Thus, all the nodes of left sub-tree are processed and resulting list is as follows: D B F E. Secondly we process root **R** and then process right sub-tree T_2 in the similar fashion as T_1. List of processed nodes is as follows: G C L J M H O K. When we combine list of elements of left sub-tree T_1, root **R** and elements of right sub-tree T_2 we get the list of all the elements in the binary tree T: D B F E A G C L J M H O K. The above discussion is straightforward if one consider the tree in **Figure 7.21**. The algorithm to traverse a tree in inorder is illustrated in **Figure 7.22**.

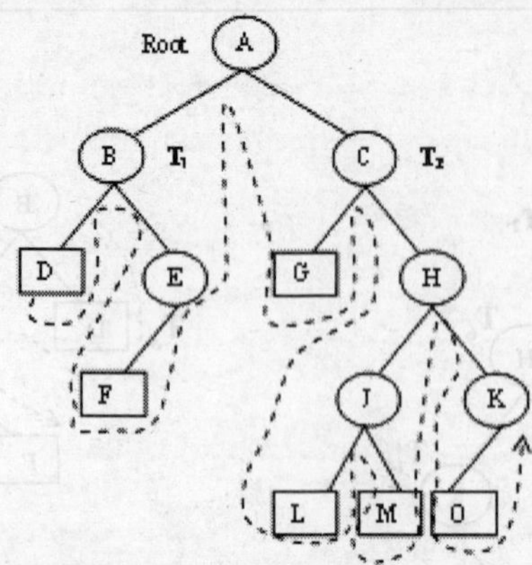

Figure 7.21 Inorder traversing of Binary tree T

```
In-order (Node)
 Step 1: [Do through Step 4]
    If Node ≠ NULL
Step 2: Call In-order (Left_Child [Node])
Step 3: Output Info [Node]
Step 4: Call In-order (Right_Child [Node])
Step 5: Exit
```

Figure 7.22 Recursive algorithm of inorder traversing

7.6.3 Postorder

In this technique first of all, we process the left sub-tree T_1 of **R** in post order, then the right sub-tree T_2 in postorder and at the last the root **R**. Once again we consider the tree illustrated in **Figure 7.17**. The left sub-tree of **R** is T_1, root of T_1 is **B** and its left sub-tree is **D** that is terminal node. We process **D** first. Now we consider right sub-tree of **B** that is **E**, the left sub-tree of **E** is **F**, so process **F** at the second priority. As there is no right sub-tree of **E** we process **E** and at the last root of the sub-tree T_1, that is **B**. The resulting list of elements after traversing the left sub-tree in postorder is as follows: D F E B. In the

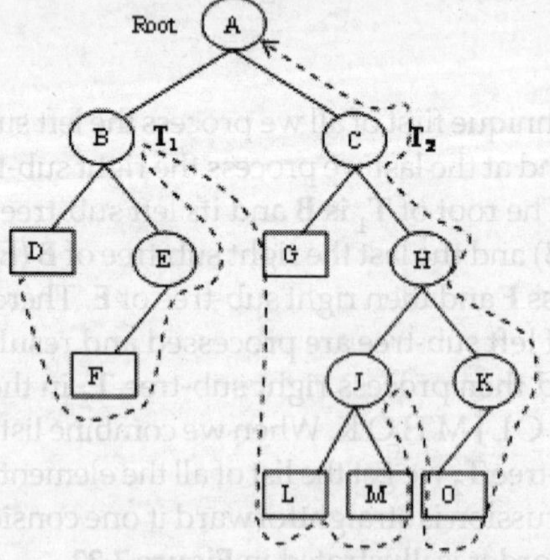

Figure 7.23 Postorder traversing of Binary tree T

same fashion we process all the nodes of the right sub-tree T_2. The list of elements after processing right sub-tree in postorder is as follows: G L M J O K H C. The final list of elements after traversing binary tree illustrated in **Figure 7.17** is as follows: D F E B G L M J O K H C **A**. Process of postorder traversal is shown in **Figure 7.23**. The postorder traversing algorithm is illustrated in **Figure 7.24**. The program segment **BT_TRAV.C** implements these traversing algorithms.

```
Post-order (Node)
Step 1: [Do through Step 4]
   If Node ≠ NULL
Step 2: Call Post-order (Left_Child [Node])
Step 3: Call Post-order (Right_Child [Node])
Step 4: Output Info [Node]
Step 5: Exit
```

Figure 7.24 Recursive algorithm of postorder traversing

```
/* Binary tree traversal */
/* BT_TRAV.C */
# include<stdio.h>
struct NODE
{
   char Info;
   struct NODE *Left_Child;
   struct NODE *Right_Child;
};
struct NODE *Binary_Tree (char *, int, int);
void Output(struct NODE *, int );
void Pre_order(struct NODE *);
void In_order(struct NODE *);
void Post_order(struct NODE *);

/* Function to create an binary tree */
struct NODE *  Binary_Tree (char *List, int Lower, int Upper)
{
   struct NODE *Node;
   int Mid = (Lower + Upper)/2;
   Node = (struct NODE*) malloc(sizeof(struct NODE));
   Node->Info = List [Mid];
   if ( Lower>= Upper)
   {
      Node->Left_Child = NULL;
      Node->Right_Child = NULL;
      return (Node);
   }
   if (Lower <= Mid - 1)
      Node->Left_Child = Binary_Tree (List, Lower, Mid - 1);
   else
```

```
      Node->Left_Child = NULL;
   if (Mid + 1 <= Upper)
      Node->Right_Child = Binary_Tree (List, Mid + 1, Upper);
   else
      Node->Right_Child = NULL;
   return(Node);
}

/* Output function */
void Output(struct NODE *T, int Level)
{
   int i;
   if (T)
   {
      Output(T->Right_Child, Level+1);
      printf("\n");
      for (i = 0; i < Level; i++)
         printf("   ");
      printf(" %c", T->Info);
      Output(T->Left_Child, Level+1);
   }
}

/* Pre-order traversal */
void Pre_order (struct NODE *Node)
{
   if (Node)
   {
      printf(" %c", Node->Info);
      Pre_order(Node->Left_Child);
      Pre_order(Node->Right_Child);
   }
}

/* Inorder traversal */
void In_order (struct NODE *Node)
{
   if (Node)
   {
      In_order(Node->Left_Child);
      printf(" %c", Node->Info);
      In_order(Node->Right_Child);
   }
}
```

```
/* Postorder traversal */
void Post_order (struct NODE *Node)
{
   if (Node)
   {
      Post_order(Node->Left_Child);
      Post_order(Node->Right_Child);
      printf(" %c", Node->Info);
   }
}

/*  Function main */
void main()
{
   char List[100];
   int Number = 0;
   char Info;
   char choice;
   struct NODE *T = (struct NODE *) malloc(sizeof(struct NODE));
   T = NULL;
   printf("\n Input choice 'b' to break:");
   choice = getchar();
   fflush(stdin);
   while(choice != 'b')
   {
      printf("\n Input information of the node: ");
      scanf("%c", &Info);
      List[Number++] = Info;
      fflush(stdin);
      printf("\n Input choice 'b' to break:");
      choice = getchar();
      fflush(stdin);
   }
   Number --;
   printf("\n Number of elements in the list is %d", Number);
   T = Binary_Tree(List, 0, Number);
   Output(T,1);
   printf("\n Pre-order traversal\n");
   Pre_order (T);
   printf("\n Inorder traversal\n");
   In_order (T);
   printf("\n Postorder traversal\n");
   Post_order (T);
}
```

Binary tree is very useful to represent expression tree and it is discussed earlier. The internal nodes of a binary tree represents operators and external (leaf) nodes represents operands. It means with the help of tree travseral algorithms it is possible to convert an expression into postfix, prefix or infix expressions. For example, consider the expression tree shown in **Figure 7.25**. If traverse this tree in different mode, we are getting the result as follows:

preoder traversal: -+/846*2-98

inorder traversal: 8/4+6-2*9-8

Postoder traversal: 84/6+298-*-

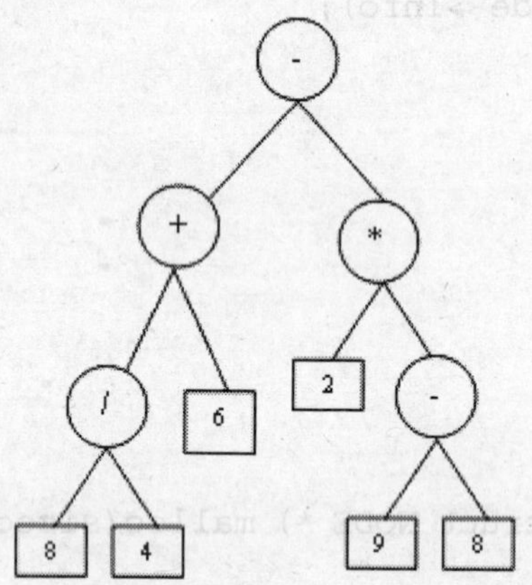

Figure 7.25 Expression Tree

Now see the stack based implementation of the Binary tree traversal algorithms in next program segments for the BT_TRAV.C code. Readers will find this stack based implementation is more simpler than recursive. Due to simplicity of the code we are not going to discuss the algorithm.

```
/* PRE_ORDER Tree traversal */
/* Pre_ORDR.C */
# include<stdio.h>
# include<malloc.h>
#define SIZE 10

struct tree
{
    struct tree *left_child;
    int info;
    struct tree *right_child;
};
typedef struct tree Tnode;

/* Prototype Declaration*/
void push(Tnode *);
Tnode *pop();

/*Global variable declaration*/
```

```
Tnode *root=NULL,*ptr,*par,*New;
int top=SIZE;
Tnode *stack[SIZE];
Tnode *temp;

void main()
  {
   char x,choice;

   do
    {
    /* create  new node */
    New= (Tnode *) malloc(sizeof(Tnode));
    printf("Enter element:->");
    scanf("%d",&x);
    New->info=x;
    New->left_child=NULL;
    New->right_child=NULL;
    /* attach new node in to its correct position */

    if(root==NULL)  /* insert at root */
      {
      root=New;
      }
    else
    {
     /* locate the leaf node */
     ptr=root;
     while(ptr!=NULL)
       {
        if(x==ptr->info)
          {
      printf("already present");
      exit(0);
          }
        par=ptr;
        if(x<ptr->info)
          ptr=ptr->left_child;
        else
          ptr=ptr->right_child;
       }
      if(x<par->info)  /* insert as left child */
          par->left_child=New;
      else
          par->right_child=New;  /* insert as right child */
```

```
    }
  printf("more element:->");
  fflush(stdin);
  choice=getchar();
  }while(choice=='y');

  /* pre_order tree traversal  */

  printf("\n preorder traversal is:->");
  ptr=root;
  while(ptr!=NULL)
    {
     printf("%d  ",ptr->info);    /* process the root */
     if(ptr->right_child!=NULL)  /* push the right sub tree on stack */
     push(ptr->right_child);
     if(ptr->left_child!=NULL)    /* move to left subtree */
     ptr=ptr->left_child;
     else
       {
     temp=pop();
     ptr=temp;
       }
    }
  getchar();
  }

void push(Tnode *x)
  {
   if(top==0)
  printf("stack is full");
   else
  {
  top=top-1;
  stack[top]=x;
  }
  }

Tnode *pop()
 {
  Tnode *x;
  if(top==SIZE)  /*tree has been traversed*/
    {
  printf("\n tree has been traversed");
  return NULL;
    }
```

```
    x=stack[top];
    top=top+1;
     return(x);
   }

/* IN_ORDER Tree traversal */
/* In_ ORDR.C */

# include<stdio.h>
# include<malloc.h>
#define SIZE 10

struct tree
{
   struct tree *left_child;
   int info;
   struct tree *right_child;
};
typedef struct tree Tnode;
/*Prototype declaration*/
void push(Tnode *);
Tnode *pop();

/*Global variable declaration*/
Tnode *root=NULL,*ptr,*par,*New;
int top=SIZE;
Tnode *stack[SIZE];
Tnode *temp;

void main()
{
   char x,choice;

   do
   {
   /* create  new node */
   New= (Tnode *) malloc(sizeof(Tnode));
   printf("Enter element:->");
   scanf("%d",&x);
   New->info=x;
   New->left_child=NULL;
   New->right_child=NULL;
   /* attach new node in to its correct position */

   if(root==NULL)  /* insert at root */
```

```
    {
     root=New;
    }
   else
   {
    /* locate the leaf node */
    ptr=root;
    while(ptr!=NULL)
     {
      if(x==ptr->info)
       {
     printf("already present");
     exit(0);
       }
      par=ptr;
      if(x<ptr->info)
        ptr=ptr->left_child;
      else
        ptr=ptr->right_child;
     }
     if(x<par->info)  /* insert as left child */
        par->left_child=New;
     else
        par->right_child=New;  /* insert as right child */

   }
   printf("more element:->");
   fflush(stdin);
   choice=getchar();
   }while(choice=='y');
 /* in_order tree traversal  */
   printf("\n inorder traversal is:->");
   ptr=root;
 IN_BEGIN: while(ptr!=NULL)
      {
     push(ptr);              /* push the root of sub tree on stack */
     ptr=ptr->left_child;    /* move to left subtree */
      }
      temp=pop();
      ptr=temp;
   while(ptr!=NULL)
    {
      printf("%d ",ptr->info); /* process the root */
      if(ptr->right_child!=NULL)
     {
```

```
      ptr=ptr->right_child;
      goto IN_BEGIN;
      }
      temp=pop();
      ptr=temp;
    }
   getchar();
}

void push(Tnode *x)
  {
   if(top==0)
   printf("stack is full");
   else
   {
   top=top-1;
   stack[top]=x;
   }
   }

Tnode *pop()
  {
   Tnode *x;
   if(top==SIZE)  /*tree has been traversed*/
     {
   printf("\n tree has been traversed");
   return NULL;
     }
   else
     {
   x=stack[top];
   top=top+1;
     }
    return(x);
  }

/* POST_ORDER Tree traversal */
/* Pos_ ORDR.C */

# include<stdio.h>
# include<malloc.h>
#define SIZE 10

struct tree
{
```

```
    struct tree *left_child;
    int info;
    struct tree *right_child;
  };
  typedef struct tree Tnode;

  struct stack
  {
   int flag;
   Tnode *sub_tree;
  };
  typedef struct stack stk;

  Tnode *root=NULL,*ptr,*par,*New;
  int top=SIZE;
  stk stack[SIZE];
  stk temp;
  void push(int,Tnode *);
  stk pop();

  void main()
  {
      char x,choice;

      do
      {
      /* create new node */
      New= (Tnode *) malloc(sizeof(Tnode));
      printf("Enter element:->");
      scanf("%d",&x);
      New->info=x;
      New->left_child=NULL;
      New->right_child=NULL;
      /* attach new node in to its correct position */

      if(root==NULL)  /* insert at root */
        {
        root=New;
        }
      else
      {
       /* locate the leaf node */
      ptr=root;
      while(ptr!=NULL)
        {
```

```
         if(x==ptr->info)
           {
         printf("already present");
         exit(0);
           }
         par=ptr;
         if(x<ptr->info)
           ptr=ptr->left_child;
         else
           ptr=ptr->right_child;
        }
       if(x<par->info)  /* insert as left child */
           par->left_child=New;
       else
           par->right_child=New;  /* insert as right child */

     }
     printf("more element:->");
     fflush(stdin);
     choice=getchar();
     }while(choice=='y');

     printf("\n postorder traversal is:->");
     ptr=root;
 POST_BEGIN:  while(ptr!=NULL)
        {
          /* push the right sub tree on stack */
           push(0,ptr);
           if(ptr->right_child!=NULL)    /* move to left subtree */
             push(1,(ptr->right_child));
           ptr=ptr->left_child;
          }
         temp=pop();
         while(temp.flag==0)
           {
            ptr=temp.sub_tree;
            printf("%d ",ptr->info);   /* process the root */
             temp=pop();
            }
          if(temp.flag==1)
            {
             ptr=temp.sub_tree;
             goto POST_BEGIN;
            }
```

```
        getchar();
    }

void push(int f,Tnode *x)
    {
     if(top==0)
    printf("stack is full");
     else
    {
    top=top-1;
    stack[top].flag=f;
    stack[top].sub_tree=x;
    }
    }

stk pop()
{
    stk x;
    if(top==SIZE)  /*tree has been traversed*/
      exit(0);
    else
      {
   x=stack[top];
   top=top+1;
      }
     return(x);
  }
```

7.7 MINIMUM WEIGHTED PATH LENGTH ALGORITHMS

Suppose we have **n** values $\mathbf{w_1, w_2, w_3, ..., w_n}$ and want to find out the extended binary trees with **n** external (terminal) nodes, and to associate the values $\mathbf{w_1, w_2, w_3, ..., w_n}$ with these nodes in such a way that the sum $\sum \mathbf{w_i l_i}$ is minimized, where $\mathbf{l_i}$ is the length of path from the root and the sum is taken over all external nodes. For example, if we have following list of elements then the complete binary trees for the list are shown in **Figure 7.26,** where rectangle are used to represent external nodes. The list is 11, 13, 14, 15, 16 and the weighted path length for the binary tree illustrated in **Figure 7.26 (a)** is

$$\sum_{i=1}^{n} w_i l_i$$

$$\sum_{i=1}^{5} w_i l_i$$

$$= 11*3+13*3+14*3+15*3+16*1$$

$$= 33+39+42+45+16$$

$$= 175$$

the weighted path length for the binary tree illustrated in **Figure 7.26(b)** is:

$$\sum_{i=1}^{5} w_i l_i$$
$$= 11*3+13*3+14*2+15*2+16*2$$
$$= 33+39+28+30+32$$
$$= 162$$

From the above two results it is clear that a perfectly balanced tree does not give the minimum weighted path length. But a complete binary tree gives a minimum weighted path length only when all the weights of terminal nodes are 1, i.e., $w_1 = w_2 = w_3 = \ldots = w_n = 1$.

To find a tree with minimum weighted path length, an algorithm was developed by **D. Huffman.** In this algorithm first of all we find two weight's $\mathbf{w_1}$ and $\mathbf{w_2}$ of lowest value and then solve the problem for **n-1** weights $\mathbf{w_1+w_2, w_3, w_4, \ldots, w_n}$, and replace the nodes as illustrated in **Figure 7.27**. For example, find the optimal tree for the weight list given below:

List: 1, 2, 4, 6, 10, 12, 16, 18, 22, 28, 30, 36, 40

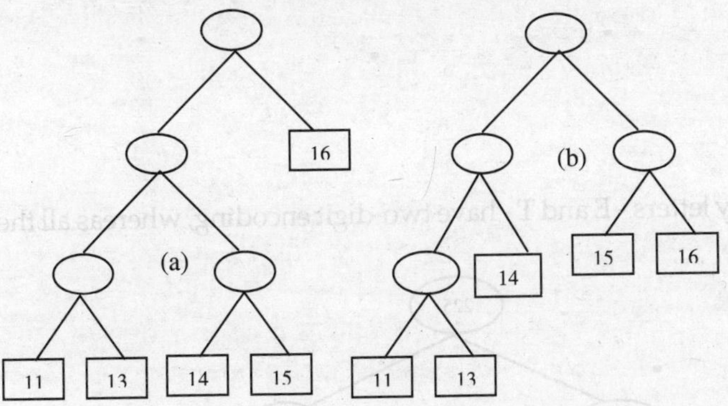

Figure 7.26 Complete binary tree

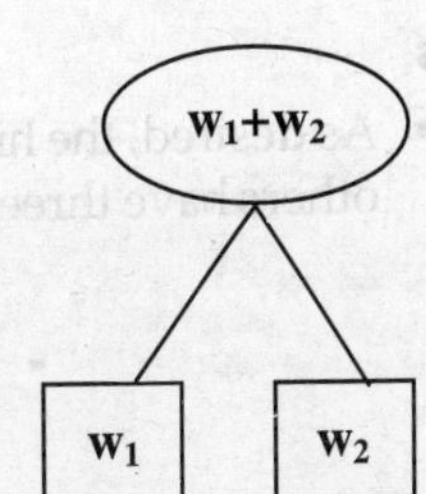

Figure 7.27 Huffman Algorithm

If we look into the above list we find that 1 and 2 are least values. First of all we combine 1 and 2 and look for the solution weights 1 + 2, 4, 6, 10, 12, 16, 18, 22, 28, 30, 36, 40, then we combine (1+2) = 3 and 4 that is 3+4 = 7 and look for the solution. 7, 6, 10, 12, 16, 18, 22, 28, 30, 36, 40 then combine 7 and 6 and so on. The detail solution for the given list is illustrated in **Figure 7.28**. Now the problem is how this can be used to construct **Huffman** tree? **Figure 7.29** helps to illustrate this.

1	2	4	6	10	12	16	18	22	28	30	36	40
	3	4	6	10	12	16	18	22	28	30	36	40
		7	6	10	12	16	18	22	28	30	36	40
			13	10	12	16	18	22	28	30	36	40
			13		22	16	18	22	28	30	36	40
					22	29	18	22	28	30	36	40
						29	40	22	28	30	36	40
						29	40		50	30	36	40
							40		50	59	36	40
									50	59	76	40
										59	76	90
											135	90
												225

Figure 7.28 Discussion of D. Huffman algorithm

7.8 HUFFMAN ENCODING

This is problem of finding the minimum length bit string, which can be used to encode a string of symbols. One application is text compression: What is the smallest number of bits (hence the minimum size of file) which can be used to store an arbitrary piece of text?

Huffman's scheme uses a table of frequency of occurrence for each symbol (or character) in the input. This table may be derived from the input itself or from data, which is representative of the input. For instance, the frequency of occurrence of letters in normal English might be derived from processing a large number of text documents and then used for encoding all text documents. Then we need to assign a variable-length bit string to each character that unambiguously represents that character. This means that the encoding for each character must have a unique prefix. If the characters to be encoded are arranged in a binary tree as shown in **Figure 7.30**. An encoding for each character is found by following the tree from the route to the character in the leaf: the encoding is the string of symbols on each branch followed. For example:

String Encoding
TEA 10 00 010
SEA 011 00 010
TEN 10 00 110

Notes

- As desired, the highest frequency letters - E and T - have two-digit encoding, whereas all the others have three-digit encoding.

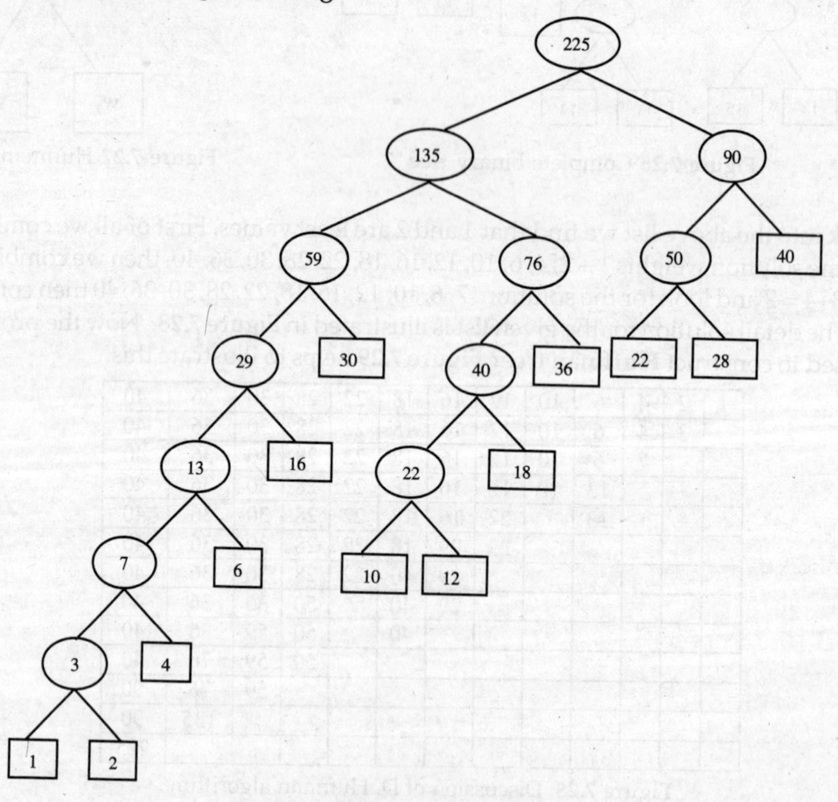

Figure 7.29 Resulting Huffman tree

- Encoding would be done with a lookup table.
- A divide-and-conquer approach might have us asking which characters should appear in the left and right sub-trees and trying to build the tree from the top down. As with the optimal binary search tree, this will lead to an exponential time algorithm.
- A greedy approach places **n** characters in **n** sub-trees and starts by combining the two least weight nodes into a tree which is assigned the sum of the two leaf node weights as the weight for its root node. The time complexity of the Huffman algorithm is **O(nlog$_2$ n)**. Using a heap to store the weight of each tree, each iteration requires **O(log$_2$ n)** time to determine the cheapest weight and insert the new weight. There are **O(n)** iterations, one for each item.

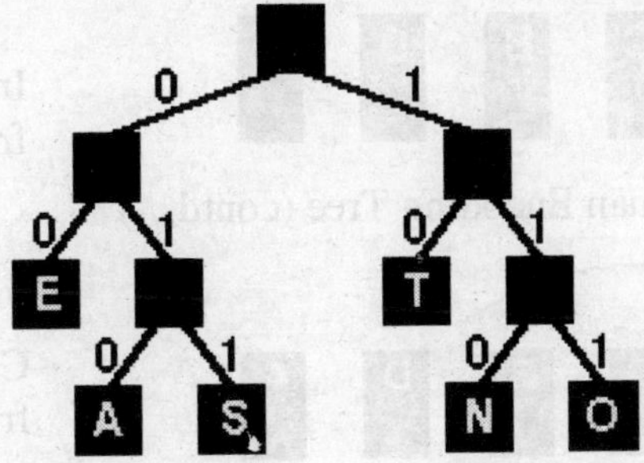

Figure 7.30 Encoding tree for **ETASNO**

7.8.1 Decoding Huffman-encoded Data

How do we **decode** a Huffman-encoded bit string? With these variable length strings, it is not possible to break up an encoded string of bits into characters. The decoding procedure is deceptively simple. Starting with the first bit in the stream, one then uses successive bits from the stream to determine whether to go left or right in the decoding tree. When we reach a leaf of the tree, we have decoded a character, so we place that character onto the (uncompressed) output stream. The next bit in the input stream is the first bit of the next character. Process of decoding a character is shown in **Figure 7.31**.

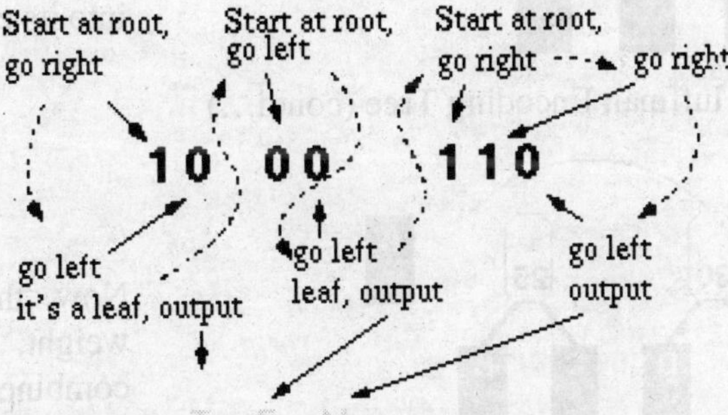

Figure 7.31 Decoding information stream

7.8.2 Transmission and storage of Huffman-encoded Data

If a system is continually dealing with data in which the symbols have similar frequencies of occurrence, then both encoders and decoders can use a standard encoding table/decoding tree. However, even text data from various sources will have quite different characteristics. For example, ordinary English text will have generally have 'e' at the root of the tree, with short encoding for 'a' and 't', whereas C programs would generally have ';' at the root, with short encoding for other punctuation marks such as '(' and ')' (depending on the number and length of comments). If the data has variable frequencies, then for optimal encoding, we have to generate an encoding tree for each data set and store or transmit the encoding with the data. The extra cost of transmitting the encoding tree means that we will not gain an overall benefit unless the data stream to be encoded is quite long - so that the savings through compression more than compensate for the cost of the transmitting the encoding tree also. **Figure 7.32(a-f)** show how a Huffman encoding tree is built using a straightforward greedy algorithm, which combines the two smallest-weight trees at every step.

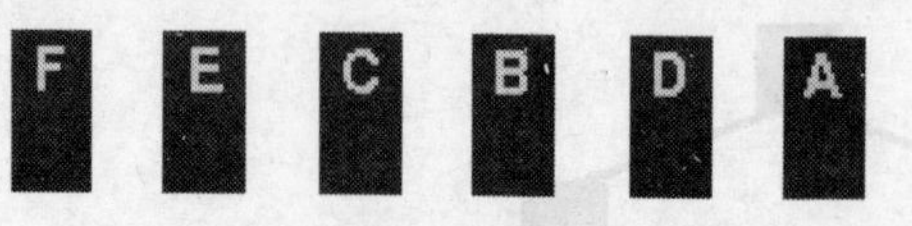

Initial data sorted by frequency

Figure 7.32(a) Huffman Encoding Tree (contd...)

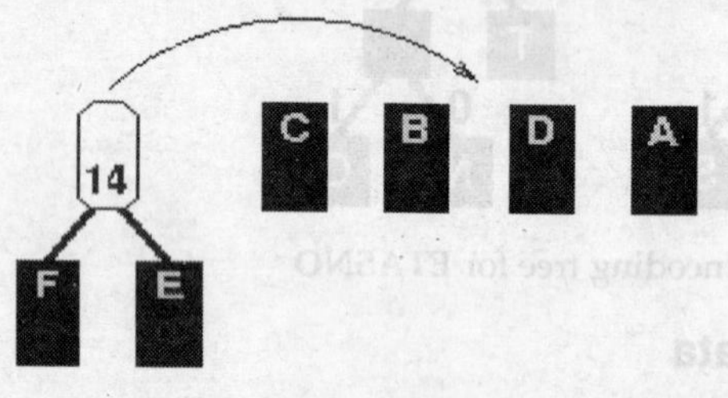

Combine the two lowest frequencies, F and E, to form a sub-tree of weight 14. Move it into its correct place.

Figure 7.32(b) Huffman Encoding Tree (contd...)

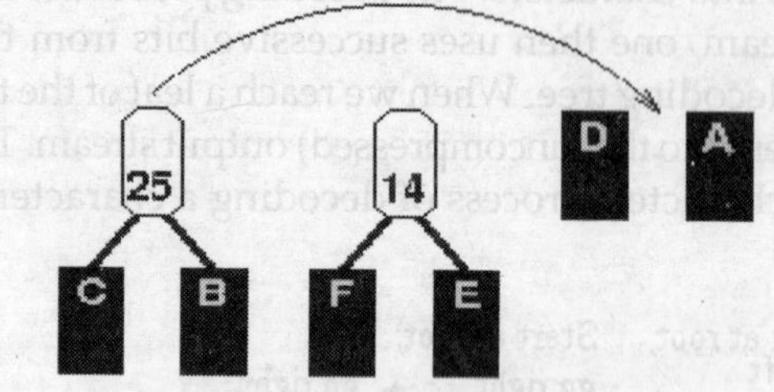

Again combine the two lowest frequencies, C and B, to form a sub-tree of weight 25. Move it into its correct place.

Figure 7.32(c) Huffman Encoding Tree (contd...)

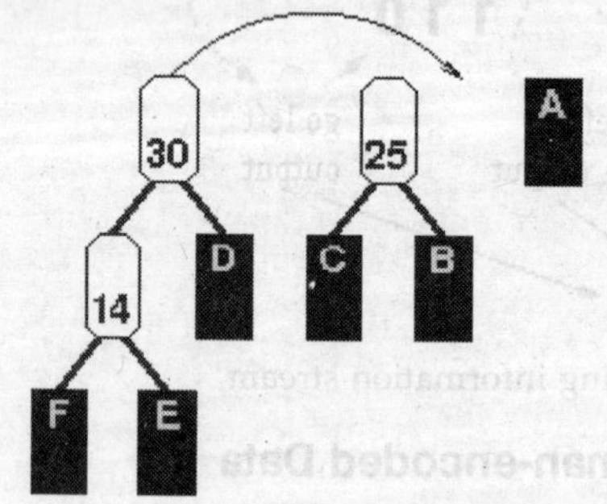

Now the sub-tree with weight, 14, and D are combined to make a tree of weight, 30. Move it to its correct place.

Figure 7.32(d) Huffman Encoding Tree (contd...)

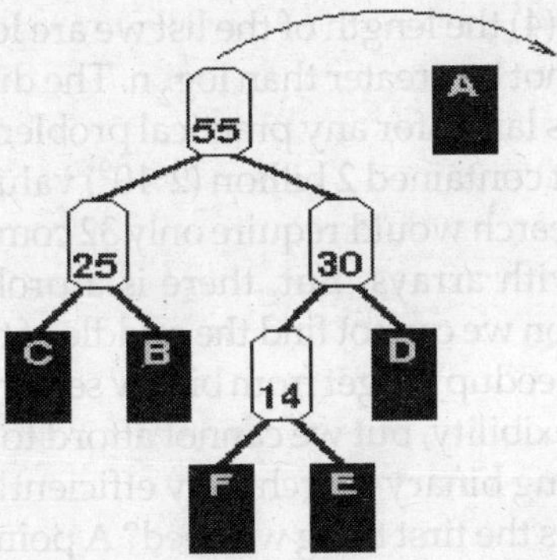

Now the two lowest weights are held by the "25" and "30" sub-trees, so combine them to make one of weight, 55. Move it after the A.

Figure 7.32(e) Huffman Encoding Tree (contd...)

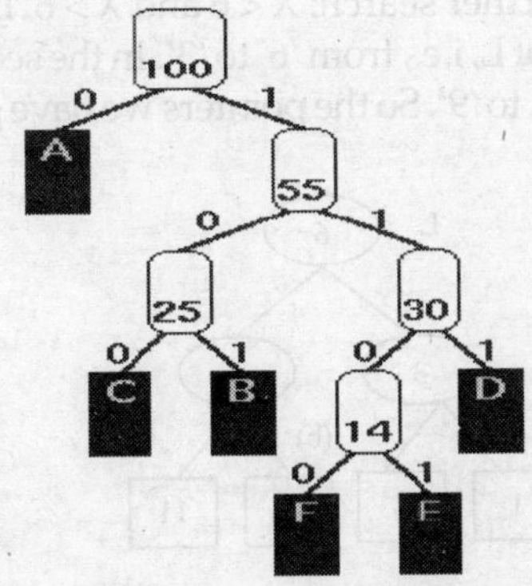

Finally, combine the A and the "55" sub-tree to produce the final tree.
The encoding table is:

A 0
C 100
B 101
F 1100
E 1101
D 111

Figure 7.32(f) Huffman Code Tree

Figure 7.32 Huffman Encoding

7.9 BINARY SEARCH TREE (BST)

Before discussing the binary search tree, we first need to understand the idea of binary search. Suppose we have a list L and in this list we are searching for a value X. If L has no special properties, if it might be any old list, then there is no better way to search it than to start at the beginning and go through the list one step at a time comparing each element to X in turn. This is called *linear* search - the time it takes (on average, and in the worst case) is *linear*, or O(n), in the length of the list. But if L is a sorted list, there is a much faster way to search for X:

1. Compare X to the middle value (M) in L.
2. if X = M we are done.
3. if X < M we continue search, but we can confine search to the first half of L and entirely ignore the second half of L.
4. if X > M we continue, but confine ourselves to the second half of L.

For example, consider the list, L = 1, 3, 4, 6, 8, 9, 11 for X = 4 and do the following:

- Compare X to 6. It is smaller. Repeat with L = 1, 3, 4.
- Compare X to 3. It is bigger. Repeat with L = 4.
- Compare X to 4. It is equal. We are done, we found X.

This is called *Binary Search,* each iteration of (1)-(4) the length of the list we are looking in gets cut in half. Therefore, the total number of iterations cannot be greater than $\log_2 n$. The difference between $O(\log_2 n)$ and O(n) is extremely significant when n is large: for any practical problem it is crucial that we avoid O(n) searches. For example, suppose a list contained 2 billion ($2*10^9$) values. Linear search would involve about a billion comparisons; binary search would require only 32 comparisons. Binary search works perfectly if lists are implemented with arrays. But, there is a problem with *linked* implementations of lists. With a linked implementation we cannot find the middle of the list in constant time: it takes linear time and this takes away all the speedup we get from binary search. We need linked implementations for their memory efficiency and flexibility, but we cannot afford to do linear search. Let us design a linked structure specifically for doing binary search very efficiently. It will contain exactly the pointers needed for binary search. What is the first thing we need? A pointer to the middle element.

Using our previous example (L→ 6), what should the node '6' point to? Well, when we compare X to 6 there are two possible outcomes that involve further search: X < 6 and X > 6. In the first case we need a pointer from '6' to the middle of the front half of L, i.e., from '6' to '3'. In the second case we need a pointer from '6' to the middle of the last half of L, i.e., to '9'. So the pointers we have got so far is shown in **Figure 7.33**.

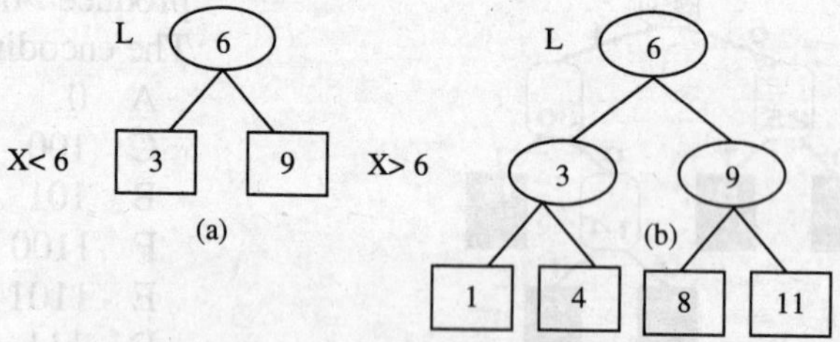

Figure 7.33 (a) Binary tree (b) Resulting structure

What pointers do we need emanating out of '3'? Again there are two, one for each possible outcome of comparing X to 3 that requires further search. If X < 3 we need a pointer to the middle of the portion of L less than 3. If X > 3 we need a pointer to be careful here this pointer should not be to the middle of the portion of L bigger than 3. We have already eliminated all the elements bigger than or equal to 6. So, this pointer should point to the middle of the portion of the list between 3 and 6, similarly for 9. So here is our final data structure **Figure 7.33**. As we can see this structure is a binary tree. But is not an arbitrary binary tree; it has two special properties:

1. Every element in a node's left subtree is smaller than the node's value
2. Every element in a node's right subtree is bigger than the node's value

These hold for every node in the tree. A binary tree with these properties is called a *Binary Search Tree.* In other words we can say that a binary search tree is a binary tree that is either empty or in which each node possesses a key that satisfies the following conditions:

(i) All keys (if any) in the left sub-tree of the root precede the key in the root.

(ii) The key in the root precedes all keys (if any) in its right sub-tree.

(iii) The left and right sub-trees of the root are again search trees.

To search for the target, we first compare it with the key at the root of the tree. If it is not same, we go to either the left sub-tree or right sub-tree as appropriate and repeat the search in that sub-tree. What condition will terminate the execution? Clearly if we find the key, the function succeeds. If not, then we continue searching until we find an empty sub-tree.

In a binary search tree we can *search* for a value in $O(\log_2 n)$ time, where n is the number of nodes in the tree. The algorithm is exactly the binary search algorithm, but translated in terms of root and subtrees:

1. Compare X to the *root* (i.e., *middle value*) (M) in L.
2. If X = M we are done.
3. If X < M we recursively search for X in L's *left subtree*.
4. If X > M we recursively search for X in L's *right subtree*.

It is not mentioned what happens if the subtree is empty (does not exist). Obviously when this happens, we are finished and X is known not to be in the tree. For example, search for 5 in **Figure 7.33**. The properties defining a BST, mean that it is very easy to *traverse* the tree in increasing (or in decreasing order). To traverse a BST in increasing order here is what we must do? From the node containing the value N:

1. Process all values smaller than N, i.e., traverse N's *left* subtree.
2. Process N itself.
3. Process all values bigger than N, i.e., traverse N's *right* subtree.

This is just ordinary left-to-right *inoder* traversal. How would we traverse the BST in decreasing order? Answer is Right to Left *inoder* traversal.

7.9.1 Insertion In Binary Search Tree

BSTs are binary trees, so all the operations we have defined for binary trees will be applicable to BSTs. However, one of our tree operations does not *preserve* the special properties of a BST. The problematic operation is joining. When we divide a list sort individual sub-list and join them we face a problem - we have the same problem, for the same reasons, when we join two BSTs: the result may not be a BST.

The solution for sorted lists was to recognize that there is always has a unique correct position in a sorted list for any new value. The same is true for a BST - if one give me a BST and a value, there is a *unique* position for that new value in the BST - assuming that we are not allowed/willing to re-arrange the existing values. If the existing values must stay where they are, we have no choice about where to put a new value. If it is smaller than the root value, it must go in the left subtree; if larger it must go in the right subtree. This reasoning applies recursively until we reach a node where the required subtree does not exist. And that is where we place the new value. Now question where to place '2' in the tree of **Figure 7.33**. It must go in 6's left subtree, 3's left subtree, 1's right subtree. 1 has no right subtree, so we make a singleton with '2' and it becomes 1's right subtree. Other problems are where to place '7'? '10'?

Here is the general pseudocode for BSTINSERT(V,T) (assume V is not in T):

```
BSTINSERT(V,T)
{
        if T is empty
        then T = create_singleton(V)
        else if V > rootvalue(T)
            then if T's right subtree exists
                then BSTINSERT(V,T's right subtree)
                else T's right subtree = create_singleton(V)
            else if T's left subtree exists
                then BSTINSERT(V,T's left subtree)
```

```
else T's left subtree = create_singleton(V)
}
```

We see that this is exactly the same as the search for V in T is performed as described above, except for

1. the processing we do in the base case (empty tree or subtree)
2. the assumption that V is not in the tree for insertion.

Things can go wrong if we allow the user to insert a value directly into a subtree. If we try to insert 99 into the subtree rooted at 3, it would end up in the wrong part of the whole tree (it ought to be in '6's right subtree, but the user started the process out in its left subtree). So we must add a precondition: argument T must not be a subtree. But then, strictly speaking, this procedure may not call itself recursively, because this violates the precondition. What we actually need is a procedure called insert in subtree, which is not available to the user and which does not have this precondition.

There is one final operation on BSTs to discuss. And that is, how to delete a value from a BST. Although we have not included delete as a primitive operation on general binary trees. Furthermore delete is particularly important for BSTs because delete is a standard operation on Collections and the primary use of BSTs is as a very efficient way to implement Collections. It is not perfectly obvious *how* we can delete a node from a BST and have the resulting tree still have the special properties of a BST.

7.9.2 Deletion From a Binary Search Tree

Of course, if we are trying to delete a leaf, there is no problem. We just delete it and rest of the tree is exactly as it was, so it is still a BST. There is another simple situation: suppose the node we are deleting has only one subtree. In the three of **Figure 7.34(a)**, '3' has only 1 subtree.

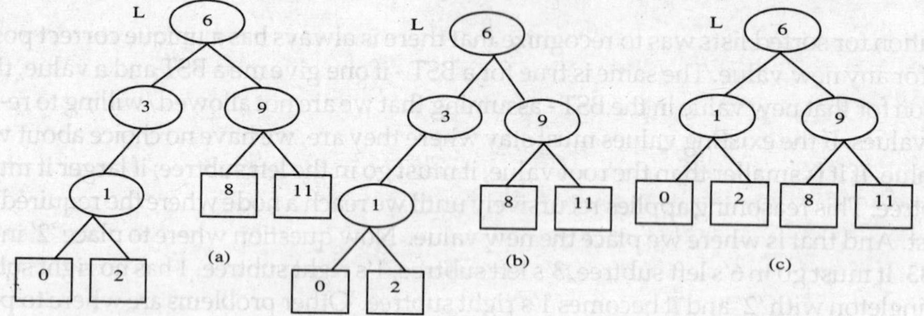

(a) Binary tree (b) After deletion of 3 form (c) Final resulting tree

Figure 7.34 Deletion in Binry Search Tree

To delete a node with 1 subtree, we just 'link past' the node, i.e., connect the parent of the node directly to the node's only subtree. This always works, whether the one subtree is on the left or on the right. Deleting '3' gives **Figure 7.34**(b). Final resulting tree is shown in **Figure 7.34(c)**.

Finally, let us consider the only remaining case: how to delete a node having two subtrees. For example, how to delete '6' {**Figure** 7.35(a)}? We had like to do this with minimum amount of work and disruption to the structure of the tree.

The standard solution is based on this idea: we leave the node containing '6' exactly where it is, but we get rid of the value 6 and find another value to store in the '6' node. This value is taken from a node below the '6's node, and it is *that* node that is actually removed from the tree. So, here is the plan.

Starting with **Figure** 7.35(a). Erase 6, but keep its node is given in **Figure** 7.35(b).

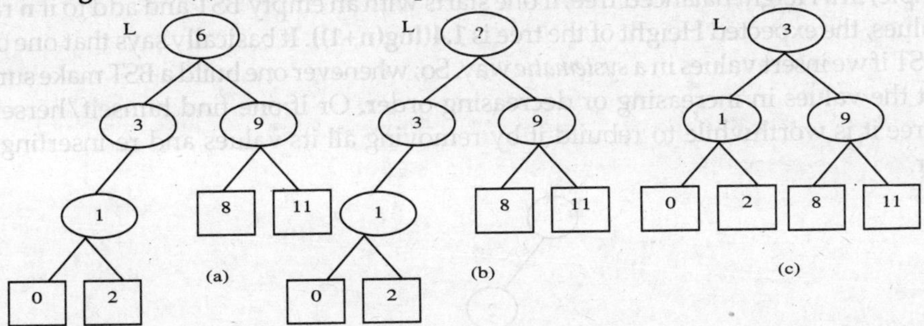

Figure 7.35 (a) Binary tree (b) Binary tree after removal of 6 (c) Binary tree after deleting a node having left and right subtree.

Now, what value can we move into the vacated node and have a binary search tree? Well, here's how to figure it out. If we choose value X, then:

1. every element in the left subtree must be smaller than X.
2. every element in the right subtree must be bigger than X.

Let us suppose we are going to get X from the left subtree. (2) is guaranteed because every element in the left subtree is smaller than every element in the right subtree. What about (1)? If X is coming from the left subtree, (1) says that there is a unique choice for X - we must choose X to be the largest value in the left subtree. In **Figure** 7.35(a), 3 is the largest value in the left subtree. So if we put 3 in the vacated node and delete it from its current position we will have a BST with 6 deleted {**Figure** 7.35(c)}. So our general algorithm is: to delete N, if it has two subtrees, replace the value in N with the largest value in its left subtree and then delete the node with the largest value from its left subtree. It should be noted that the largest value in the left subtree will never have two subtrees. Why? Because if it is the largest value, it cannot have a *right* subtree. Finally, there is nothing special about the left subtree. We could do the same thing with the right subtree: just use the *smallest* value in the right subtree.

7.9.3 Binary Search Trees: A Problem

To finish off the discussion of binary search trees, we would like to return to the issue that originally motivated them - we wanted a data structure that could be searched in O($\log_2$ n) time, where n is the number of values in the data structure. Do BSTs actually meet this requirement? In other words, is it true that we can find any value X in any BST in O($\log_2$) n time? What does one think? Yes, no?

Well, while one think about that, here is something that *is* certainly true. The time to search in a BST is definitely limited by the *height* (or depth) of the tree. Each step in the search goes down one level, so in the absolute worst case, we will have to go all the way from the root to the deepest leaf inorder to find X, or to find out that X is not in the tree. So, we can say with certainty that search is O(Height). But we want to know, is search O($\log_2$ n)? Well, since we know search is O(Height), this is really asking is Height O($\log_2$ n), is it always the case that the height of a BST is proportional to the logarithm of the number of nodes? Unfortunately, the answer to all the questions is *no*. There are BSTs in which Height and number of Nodes are *equal*. In these trees, searching is O(n), linear time, not log time. It is obvious once as shown in **Figure 7.36**.

This is called a Degenerate tree, or linear tree. In it, no node has two subtrees, every node has 1 (except the lone leaf who has 0). Obviously this is nothing more than a sorted *linked list*, which was where all our problems began. So, are not we are back where we started? Not quite. Most BSTs are not degenerate: in most of them Height is proportional to log(# nodes), and we get efficient search.

For example, in a Height balanced tree, if one starts with an empty BST and add to it **n** randomly generated values, the expected Height of the tree is **1.4(log(n+1))**. It basically says that one only get a degenerate BST if we insert values in a *systematic* way. So, whenever one build a BST make sure he/she do not insert the values in increasing or decreasing order. Or if one find himself/herself with a degenerate tree it is worthwhile to rebuild it by removing all its values and re-inserting them in random order.

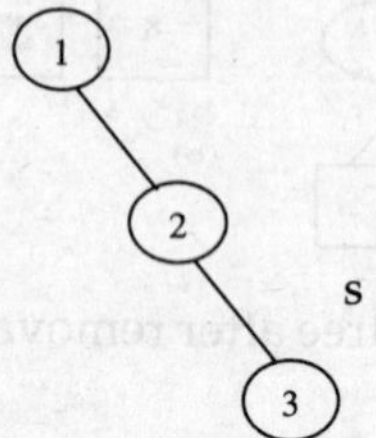

Figure 7.36 Degenerated tree

There is another approach to keeping Height related to log(# nodes), based on the observation that in all degenerate BSTs, there is a node that has one subtree that is much deeper than the other in **Figure 7.36**, the right subtree of '1' is much taller than the left subtree. What would happen if we absolutely required that the subtrees be the same height (within 1)? Answer is Height would always be O(log(# nodes)), so search would always be O(log n).

Note: # is used for number and (log n) must be treated as ($\log_2$ n). Now look at the implementation code of the binary search tree discuss till now, which is as follows:

```
/* binary search tree: bst.c */
#include <stdio.h>
#include <stdlib.h>
#define compLT(a,b) (a < b)
#define compEQ(a,b) (a == b)

/* implementation dependents declarations */
typedef enum {
    STATUS_OK,
    STATUS_MEM_EXHAUSTED,
    STATUS_DUPLICATE_KEY,
    STATUS_KEY_NOT_FOUND
} statusEnum;

typedef int keyType;            /* type of key */

/* user data stored in tree */
typedef struct {
    int stuff;                  /* optional related data */
} recType;

typedef struct nodeTag
{
```

```
    struct nodeTag *left;         /* left child */
    struct nodeTag *right;        /* right child */
    struct nodeTag *parent;       /* parent */
    keyType key;                  /* key used for searching */
    recType rec;                  /* user data */
} nodeType;

nodeType *root = NULL;            /* root of binary tree */

statusEnum insert(keyType key, recType *rec)
{
    nodeType *x, *current, *parent;
   /*********************************************
    * allocate node for data and insert in tree  *
    *********************************************/
    /* find future parent */
    current = root;
    parent = 0;
    while (current)
   {
        if (compEQ(key, current->key))
            return STATUS_DUPLICATE_KEY;
        parent = current;
        current = compLT(key, current->key) ?
            current->left : current->right;
    }

    /* setup new node */
    if ((x = malloc (sizeof(*x))) == 0)
    {
        return STATUS_MEM_EXHAUSTED;
    }
    x->parent = parent;
    x->left = NULL;
    x->right = NULL;
    x->key = key;
    x->rec = *rec;

    /* insert x in tree */
    if(parent)
        if(compLT(x->key, parent->key))
            parent->left = x;
        else
            parent->right = x;
    else
```

```
        root = x;
    return STATUS_OK;
}

statusEnum delete(keyType key) {
    nodeType *x, *y, *z;

   /***************************
    *  delete node from tree  *
    ***************************/

    /* find node in tree */
    z = root;
    while(z != NULL)
    {
        if(compEQ(key, z->key))
            break;
        else
            z = compLT(key, z->key) ? z->left : z->right;
    }
    if (!z) return STATUS_KEY_NOT_FOUND;

    /* find tree successor */
    if (z->left == NULL || z->right == NULL)
        y = z;
    else
   {
        y = z->right;
        while (y->left != NULL) y = y->left;
   }

    /* x is y's only child */
    if (y->left != NULL)
        x = y->left;
    else
        x = y->right;

    /* remove y from the parent chain */
    if (x) x->parent = y->parent;
    if (y->parent)
        if (y == y->parent->left)
            y->parent->left = x;
        else
            y->parent->right = x;
    else
```

```
        root = x;
    /* if z and y are not the same, replace z with y. */
    if (y != z)
    {
        y->left = z->left;
        if (y->left) y->left->parent = y;
        y->right = z->right;
        if (y->right) y->right->parent = y;
        y->parent = z->parent;
        if (z->parent)
            if (z == z->parent->left)
                z->parent->left = y;
            else
                z->parent->right = y;
        else
            root = y;
        free (z);
    } else
    {
        free (y);
    }
    return STATUS_OK;
}

statusEnum find(keyType key, recType *rec)
{
    /*******************************
     *  find node containing data  *
     *******************************/
    nodeType *current = root;
    while(current != NULL)
    {
        if(compEQ(key, current->key))
        {
            *rec = current->rec;
            return STATUS_OK;
        } else
        {
            current = compLT(key, current->key) ?
                current->left : current->right;
        }
    }
    return STATUS_KEY_NOT_FOUND;
}

int main(int argc, char **argv)
```

```
{
    int i, maxnum, random;
    recType *rec;
    keyType *key;
    statusEnum status;
    maxnum = atoi(argv[1]);
    random = argc > 2;

    if ((rec = malloc(maxnum * sizeof(recType))) == 0)
    {
        fprintf (stderr, "insufficient memory (rec)\n");
        exit(1);
    }
    if ((key = malloc(maxnum * sizeof(keyType))) == 0)
    {
        fprintf (stderr, "insufficient memory (key)\n");
        exit(1);
    }

    if (random) { /* random */
        /* fill "key" with unique random numbers */
        for (i = 0; i < maxnum; i++) key[i] = rand();
        printf ("ran bt, %d items\n", maxnum);
    }else
    {
        for (i=0; i<maxnum; i++)
  key[i] = i;
        printf ("seq bt, %d items\n", maxnum);
    }

    for (i = 0; i < maxnum; i++)
    {
        status = insert(key[i], &rec[i]);
        if (status) printf("pt1, i=%d: %d\n", i, status);
    }
    for (i = maxnum-1; i >= 0; i--)
    {
        status = find(key[i], &rec[i]);
        if (status) printf("pt2, i=%d: %d\n", i, status);
    }
    for (i = maxnum-1; i >= 0; i--)
    {
        status = delete(key[i]);
        if (status) printf("pt3, i=%d: %d\n", i, status);
    }
    return 0;
```

}

To run the above program segment use the command-line: bst 5000 /* 5000 sequential, and bin 2000 r */ /* 2000 random. */

Stack based implementation of the code is given in **BST_DEL.C**.

Suppose we want to delete node **a** at location **Loc** and **a** does not have two children. The pointer **Parent** gives the location of the parent of **a**. If **Parent = NULL** then **a** is the root node. The pointer **Dnode** gives the location of the only child of **a. Dnode = NULL** indicates that **a** has no children. This discussion is illustrated in **Figure 7.37(a)**.

Other algorithm, that deletes node **a** (**a** has two children) at location **Loc.** The pointer **Parent** gives the location of the parent of **a. Parent = NULL,** indicates that **a** is the root node. The pointer **Temp** (Successor) gives the location of the inorder successor of **a**, and **Parent_Succ** gives the location of the parent of the inorder successor. The algorithm is illustrated in **Figure 7.37(b).**

```
DELE (Loc, Parent)
Step 1: [Initialization]
  If Left_Child[Loc] = NULL Then
 Dnode = Right_Child[Loc]
 Else   Dnode = Left_Child [Loc]
Step 2: If Parent ≠ NULL Then
          If Loc = Left_Child [Parent]
   Then Left_Child [Parent] = Dnode
   Else Right_Child [Parent] = Dnode
   Else Root = Dnode
Step 3: Return
```

Figure 7.37(a) Deletion in binary search tree phase 1

```
Delete_Node (Parent, Loc)
Step 1:    (i)  Temp = Right_Child [Loc]
(ii)  Parent_Succ = Loc
Step 2: Repeat while Left_Child [Temp] ¹ NULL
(i)    Parent_Succ = Temp
(ii)   Temp = Left_Child [Temp]
(iii)  Successor = Parent
(iv)   Parent_Successor = Save
Step 3: Call DELE (Temp, Parent_Succ)
Step 4:  If Parent ≠ NULL Then
      If Loc = Left_Child[Parent] Then
      Left_Child[Parent] = Temp
       Else  Left_Child[Temp] = Left_Child[Loc]
         Right_Child[Successor] = Right_Child[Loc]
Step 4: Return
```

Figure 7.37(b) Deletion in Binary search tree phase 2

```
Search_Node (Node, Info)
Step 1: [Initialize]
    Flag = 0
Step 2: Repeat three Step 3 while Node ≠ NULL
Step 3: If Info [Node] = Info
    Flag = 1
    Return (Flag)
    else if Info < Info [Node]
    Node = Left_Child[Node]
    Else  Node = Right_Child[Node]
Step 4: Return (Flag)
```

Test the value returned by the function **Search_Node ()**, if it is zero then element is not found in the tree else it is found.

Figure 7.37(c) Binary search algorithm

```
DELETE_NODE (Info, Parent, Loc)
Step 1: Call Search_Node (Info, Parent, Loc) [Figure (7.31)]
Step 2: If Loc = NULL
   Output" Information does exists in the tree" and  Exit
   Else If Left_Child[Loc] ¹ NULL and
 Right_Child[Loc] ≠ NULL
Call Delete_Node (Parent, Loc)
Call DELE(Parent, Loc)
```

Figure 7.37(d) Deletion in binary search tree

```
/* Deletion in Binary Search Tree */
/* BST_DEL.C */
# include<stdio.h>
# include<malloc.h>
# define SIZE 10

struct tree
{
   struct tree *left_child;
   int info;
   struct tree *right_child;
};
typedef struct tree Tnode;


Tnode *root=NULL,*ptr=NULL,*New=NULL;
Tnode *loc=NULL,*par=NULL;
int top=SIZE;
Tnode *stack[SIZE];

void create(Tnode *);
```

```
Tnode *search(int);
void display(Tnode *);
void Del_First_Case(void);
void Del_Second_Case(void);
void push(Tnode *);
Tnode *pop();

void main()
 {
  char choice;
  int x;

  create(root);
  display(root);
  printf("\n enter element to be deleted:->");
  scanf("%d",&x);
  loc=search(x);
  if(loc==NULL)
   {
    printf("element to be deleted not present");
    exit(0);
   }
  if(loc->left_child!=NULL && loc->right_child!=NULL)
   Del_Second_Case();
  else
   Del_First_Case();
  display(root);
  getchar();
 }


void create(Tnode *ptr)
 {
  char choice;
  int x;
  do
    {
   New= (Tnode *) malloc(sizeof(Tnode));
   printf("Enter element:->");
   scanf("%d",&x);
   New->info=x;
   New->left_child=NULL;
   New->right_child=NULL;
   /* attach new node in to its correct position */
```

```
    if(root==NULL)  /* insert at root */
     {
     root=New;
     }
    else
    {
     /* locate the leaf node */
     ptr=root;
     while(ptr!=NULL)
      {
       if(x==ptr->info)
      printf("\n already present");
       par=ptr;
       if(x<ptr->info)
         ptr=ptr->left_child;
       else
         ptr=ptr->right_child;
      }
     if(x<par->info)  /* insert as left child */
         par->left_child=New;
     else
         par->right_child=New;  /* insert as right child */

    }
    printf("more element:->");
    fflush(stdin);
    choice=getchar();
    }while(choice=='y');
}

/* pre_order tree traversal  */
void display(Tnode *ptr)
 {
   Tnode *temp;
   printf("\n pre order traversal is:->");
   ptr=root;
   while(ptr!=NULL)
    {
      printf("%d  ",ptr->info);     /* process the root */
      if(ptr->right_child!=NULL)   /* push the right sub tree on stack */
      push(ptr->right_child);
      if(ptr->left_child!=NULL)    /* move to left subtree */
      ptr=ptr->left_child;
      else
       {
```

```
      temp=pop();
      ptr=temp;
        }
     }

   }

  Tnode *search(int x)
   {
    if(root==NULL)
     { loc=par=NULL;return(loc);}
    if(x==root->info)
     {loc=root;par=NULL;return(loc);}
    else
      {
     if(x<root->info)
      {ptr=root->left_child;par=root;}
     else
      {ptr=root->right_child;par=root;}
     while(ptr!=NULL && ptr->info!=x)
      {
       if(x<ptr->info)
        {par=ptr;ptr=ptr->left_child;}
       else
         {par=ptr;ptr=ptr->right_child;}
      }
       if(ptr->info!=x)
        loc=ptr;
       else
        loc=NULL;
      return(loc);
      }
   }
  void Del_Second_Case()
   {
     Tnode *ptr,*suc,*parsuc;
     ptr=loc->right_child;
     par=loc;
     while(ptr->left_child!=NULL)
       par=ptr;ptr=ptr->left_child;
     suc=ptr;parsuc=par;
     loc=suc;par=parsuc;
     Del_First_Case();
     if(par!=NULL)
       {
```

```
      if(loc==par->left_child)
    par->left_child=suc;
      else
    par->right_child=suc;
     }
   else
     root=suc;
   suc->left_child=loc->left_child;
   suc->right_child=loc->right_child;
 }

void Del_First_Case()
 {
    Tnode *chld;
     if(loc->left_child==NULL && loc->right_child==NULL)
       chld=NULL;
     else if(loc->left_child!=NULL)
       chld=loc->left_child;
     else
       chld=loc->right_child;
     if(par!=NULL)
       {
        if(loc==par->left_child)
       par->left_child=chld;
        else
       par->right_child=chld;
       }
    else
      root=chld;
 }

void push(Tnode *x)
  {
    if(top==0)
   printf("stack is full");
    else
   {
   top=top-1;
   stack[top]=x;
   }
   }

Tnode *pop()
  {
```

```
    Tnode *x;
    if(top==SIZE)  /*tree has been traversed*/
      {
    printf("tree has been traversed");
    return NULL;
      }
    x=stack[top];
   top=top+1;
     return(x);
  }
```

7.10 BALANCED BINARY TREE

We have seen that the efficiency of many important operations on trees is related to the Height of the tree - for example searching, inserting, and deleting in a BST are all O(Height). In general, the relation between Height (h) and the number of nodes (n) in a tree can vary from h = n (degenerate tree) to h = $\log_2$ n. One way to improve efficieny is to force trees to be height-balanced. A tree is *perfectly* height-balanced if the left and right subtrees of any node are at the same height as shown in **Figure 7.38**.

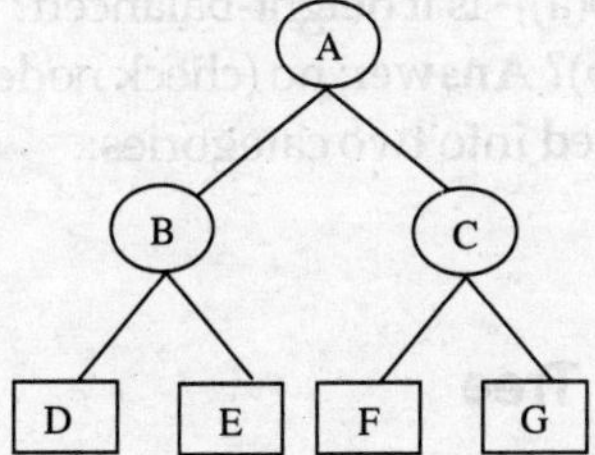

Figure 7.38 Perfectly height balanced binary tree

It is clear that at every level there are twice as many nodes as at the previous level, so we do indeed get h = O($\log_2$ n). However, perfect height balance is very rare: it is only possible if there are exactly 2^{h-1} nodes. As a practical alternative, we use trees that are almost perfectly height balanced. We will say that a tree is height-balanced if the heights of the left and right subtree's of each node are within difference of 1 {**Figure 7.39(a)**}.

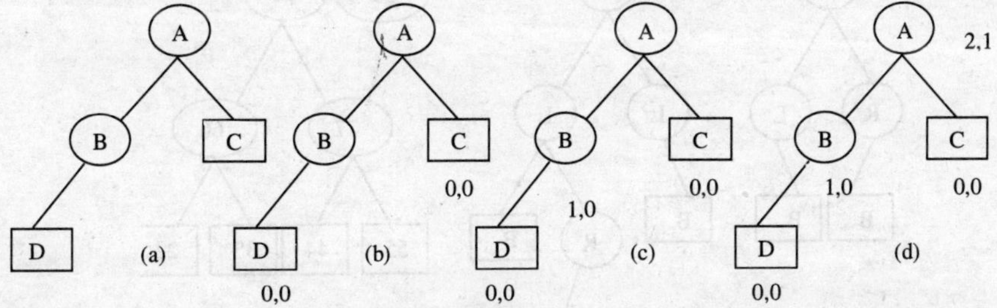

(a) Height balanced binary tree (b) Computing Height of a tree (c) Computing Height of a tree (d) Computing Height of a tree

Figure 7.39 Computing Height of Binary Tree

We will say tree in **Figure** 7.39(a) is height-balanced. How can we tell if a tree is height-balanced? We have to check every node. The fastest way is to start at the leaves and work towards upward (root). When we reach a node, we will know the heights of its two subtrees; from that one can tell whether it is height-balanced and also compute the node's height (for use by its parent). For example, in the tree shown in **Figure** 7.39(a). C and D are leaves. Their subtrees are all height 0 so C and D are both perfectly balanced. Having finished D we can compute the heights of B's subtrees {**Figure** 7.39(b)}. B is not perfectly balanced, but the heights of its subtrees differ only by 1, so B is regarded as height-balanced {**Figure** 7.39(c)}. Now we can compute the balance of A. Like B, A's two subtrees {**Figure** 7.39(d)} differ by 1 in height. We have now looked at every node; every one is height-balanced, so the tree as a whole is considered to be height-balanced.

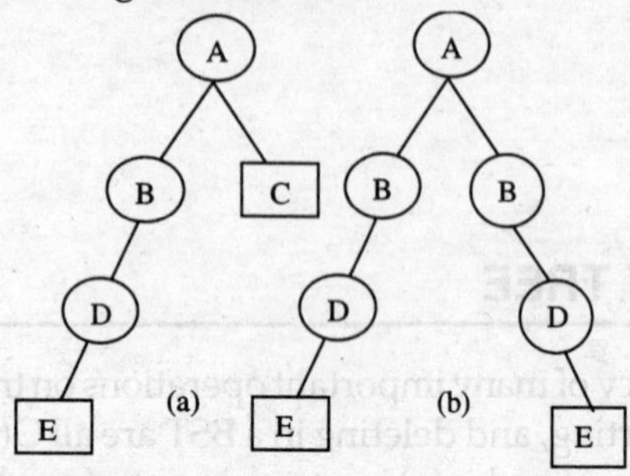

(a) Binary tree (b) Binary tree

Figure 7.40 Computing Height of Binary Tree

What about this tree {**Figure** 7.40(a)}- is it height-balanced? **Answer**: no.

Finally, what about **Figure** 7.40(b)? **Answer**: no (check node B).

Balanced binary trees are classified into two categories:

- Height Balanced
- Weight Balanced

7.10.1 Height Balanced Binary Tree

Two Russian mathematicians, **G. M. ADELSON-VELSKII** and **E.M. LANDIS**, gave a technique in 1962. It is feasible to balance the height of binary trees using this technique and the resulting tree is

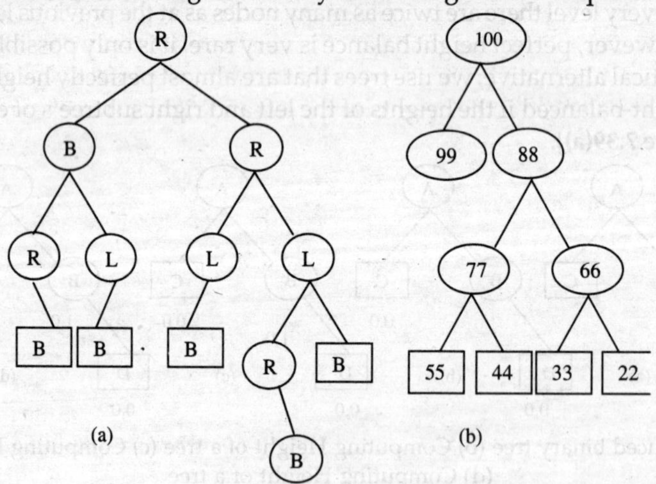

(a) Balanced (b) Unbalanced

Figure 7.41 Binary Tree

called **AVL** trees in their honour. With the help of **AVL** trees searching, insertions and deletions in a tree with **n** nodes achieved in time of order **O (n),** even in the worst case. The height of an **AVL** tree with **n** nodes can never exceed by **1.44 $\log_2$n** and thus the behaviour of an **AVL** tree could not be much below that of a random binary search tree. The actual length of a search is near to **$\log_2$n** and thus **the** behaviour of **AVL** trees are closed to ideal balanced binary tree.

A tree is called **AVL** tree (Balanced binary tree), if each node possesses one of the following properties:

1. A node is called left heavy, if the longest path in its left sub-tree is one longer than the longest path of its right sub-tree.
2. A node is called right heavy, if the longest path in the right sub-tree is one longer than **the** longest path in its left sub-tree.
3. A node is called balanced, if the longest paths in both the right and left sub-trees are equal. For example, **Figure 7.41(a)** illustrates a balanced binary tree.

A node in a binary tree that does not contain the above properties is said to be unbalanced. **For** example, **Figure 7.41(b)** illustrates an unbalanced binary tree. If one inserts a new node into a balanced binary tree at the leaf, then the possible changes in the status of a node on the path (balanced indicator), which can occur are as follows:

Condition 1: The node was either left or right heavy and has now become balanced.

Condition 2: The node was balanced and has now become left or right heavy.

Condition 3: The node was heavy and the new node has been inserted in the heavy sub-tree, thus creating an unbalanced sub-tree, such a node is called a critical node.

If we apply first condition to current node, then the balance indicators of all the ancestor nodes of this node remain unchanged, since the length of the longest path in the sub-tree remains unchanged. When second condition is applied to a current node, then the balance indicators of the ancestors will change. If the third condition applies to a current node, then the binary tree becomes unbalanced and the node has become critical. For example, **Figure 7.42** illustrates the above discussion.

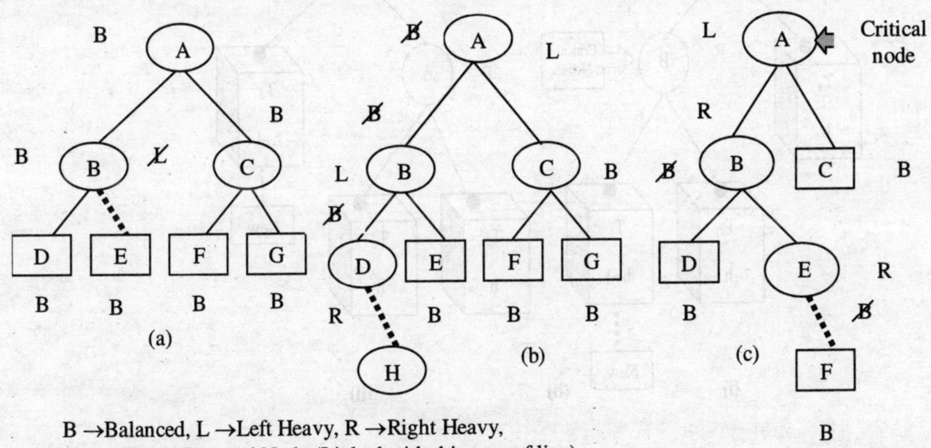

(a) Condition 1st (b) Condition 2nd (c) Condition 3rd

Figure 7.42 Balancing Binary Tree

Now we discuss re-balancing of a tree when a critical node has been encountered. There are two broad cases, which can arise, each of which can be further sub-divided into two similar sub-cases. A general representation of case 1st is illustrated in **Figure 7.43(a-b),** where the 3-D boxes labeled T_1, T_2, T_3, T_4, etc. represent sub-trees and the node attached with dotted line is the node being inserted. The expression shown in the rectangles shows the height of that sub-tree. In **Figure 7.43(a),** since node **A** is critical, node **B** must be balanced before inserting a node. It is also possible that **B** becomes heavy in the same direction that **A** was heavy. This discussion is illustrated in **Figure 7.43(c-d).** The 2nd case, which is illustrated in **Figure 7.44,** is much like the first one, except that node **B** becomes heavy in the opposite direction to that in which **A** was heavy. It is clear that node **C** must have been balanced prior to insertion.

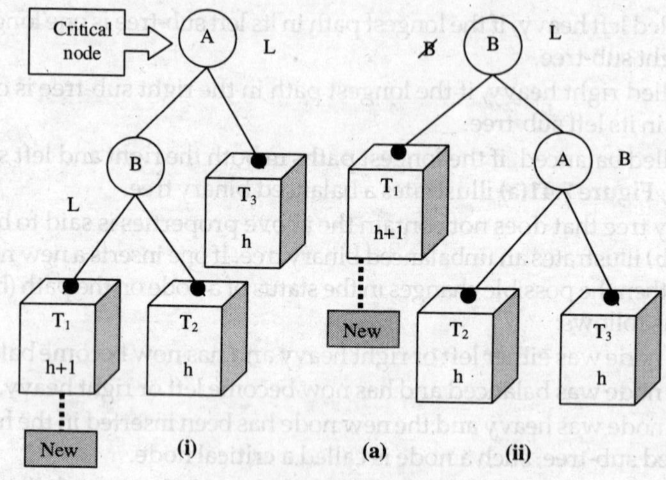

(a) AVL Tree (contd...)

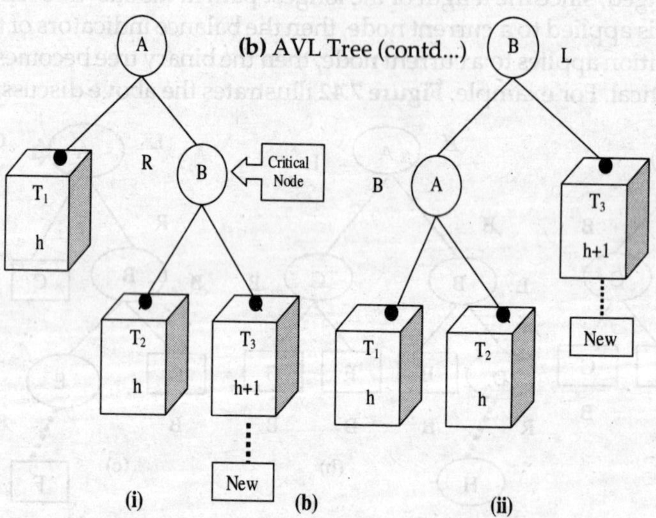

(b) AVL Tree (contd...)

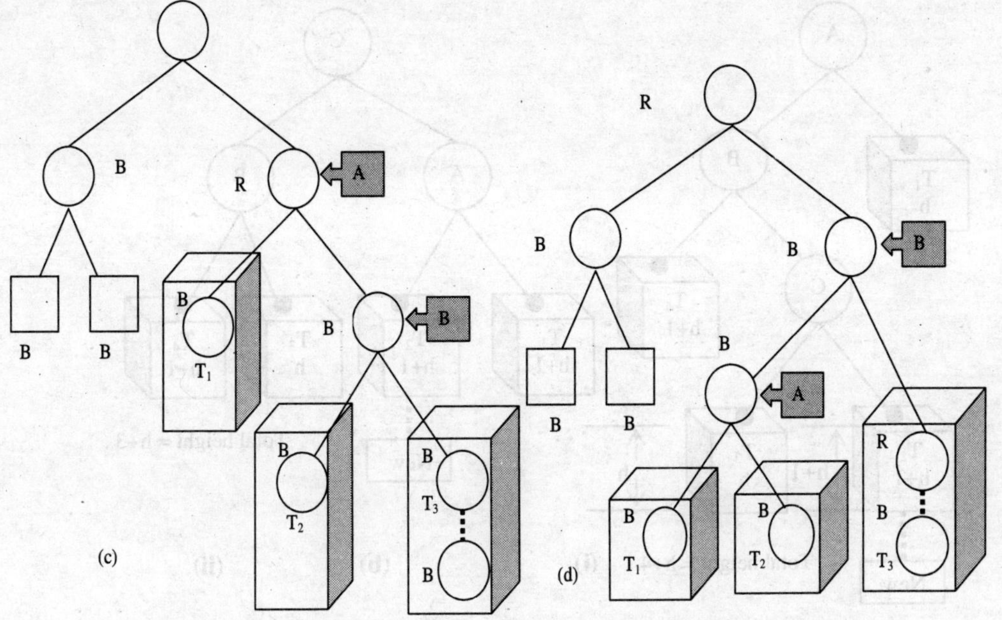

(c) Before balancing condition 1st **(d)** AVL Tree After balancing

Figure 7.43 AVL Tee 1st Case

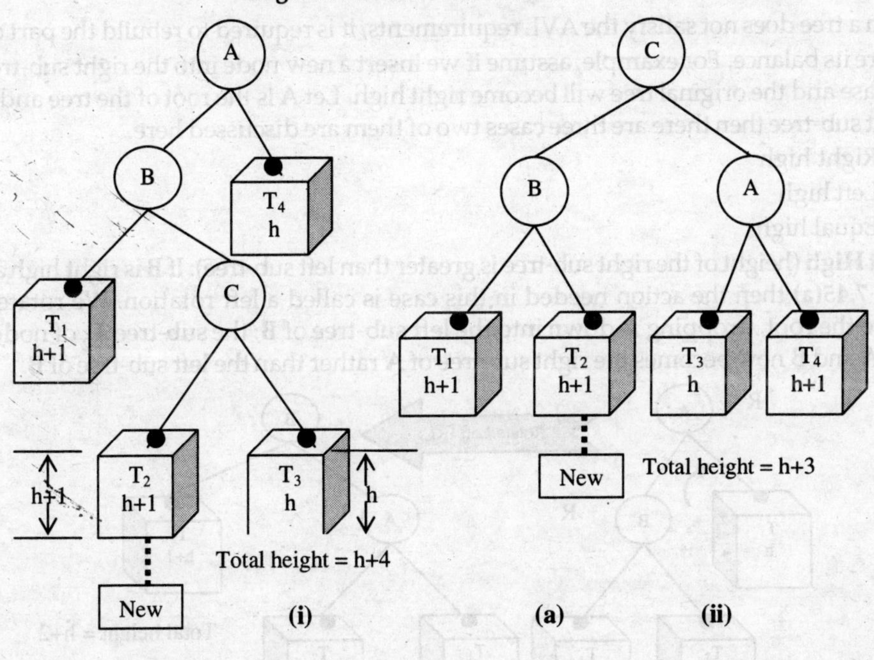

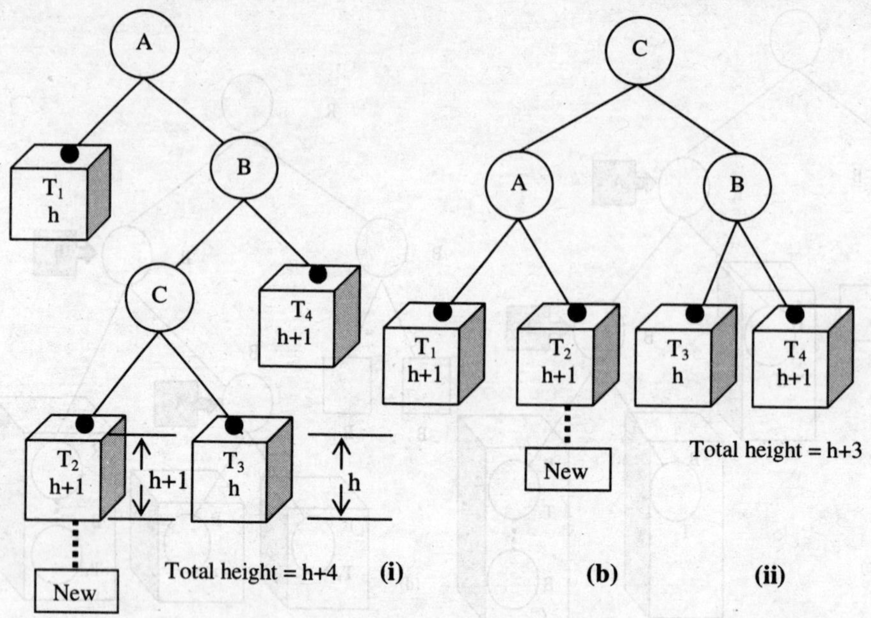

Figure 7.44. AVL Tree 2nd case

7.10.2 Balancing AVL Tree

When a tree does not satisfy the AVL requirements, it is required to rebuild the part of the tree to restore its balance. For example, assume if we insert a new node into the right sub-tree, its height will increase and the original tree will become right high. Let **A** is the root of the tree and **B** is the root of its right sub-tree then there are three cases two of them are discussed here.

- Right high
- Left high
- Equal high

Right High (height of the right sub-tree is greater than left sub-tree): If **B** is right high as illustrated in **Figure 7.45(a)** then the action needed in this case is called a left rotation. We rotate the node **B** upward to the root, dropping **A** down into the left sub-tree of **B**; the sub-tree $\mathbf{T_2}$ of nodes with keys between **A** and **B** now becomes the right sub-tree of **A** rather than the left sub-tree of **B**.

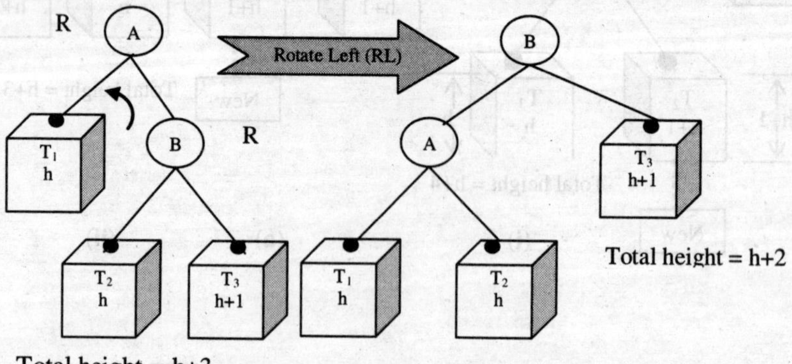

(a) Restoring balance by left rotation

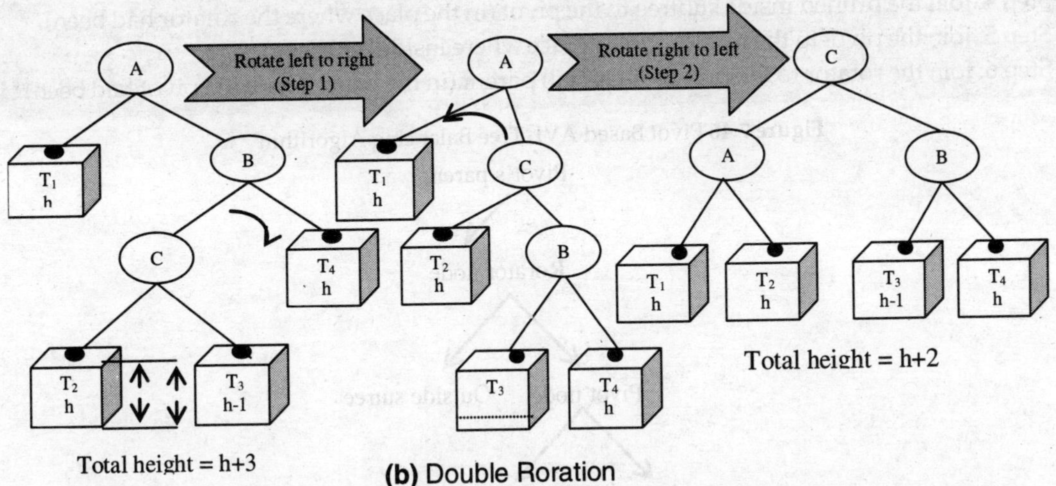

(b) Double Roration

Figure 7.45 AVL Tree Balancing

Left High (height of left sub-tree is greater than right sub-tree): When the balance factor of **B** is left high then it is required to move two levels to the node **C** that roots the left sub-tree of **B**, to find the new root. This process is called the double rotation, because the transformation can be obtained in two steps, first rotating the sub-tree with root **B** to the right so that **C** becomes its root and then rotating the tree with root **A** to the left (moving **C** up to become the new root). In this case, new balance factors for **A** and **B** depend on the previous balance factor of **C** as illustrated in **Figure 7.45(b)**.

Pivot based balancing

The pivot node is the deepest node at which there is an imbalance. The rotator node is the root of the pivot's taller subtree. There may be more nodes above the pivot's parent. Step 3 prunes the rotator's 'inside' subtree, i.e., the one on the pivot's side. Which of the rotator's subtrees is the inside subtree, which is the outside? It depends on whether the rotator is the left or right child of the pivot. If the rotator is the right child (as in this picture), the inside subtree is its left subtree and the outside subtree is its right subtree. On the other hand, if the rotator is the left child the inside subtree is its right subtree and the outside subtree is its left subtree. Following the steps shown in **Figure 7.46**, the result of the rotation is: the rotator has rotated up, the pivot has rotated down on the other side, and the inside subtree has jumped across to join the pivot. For example, one operation is shown in the following illustration.

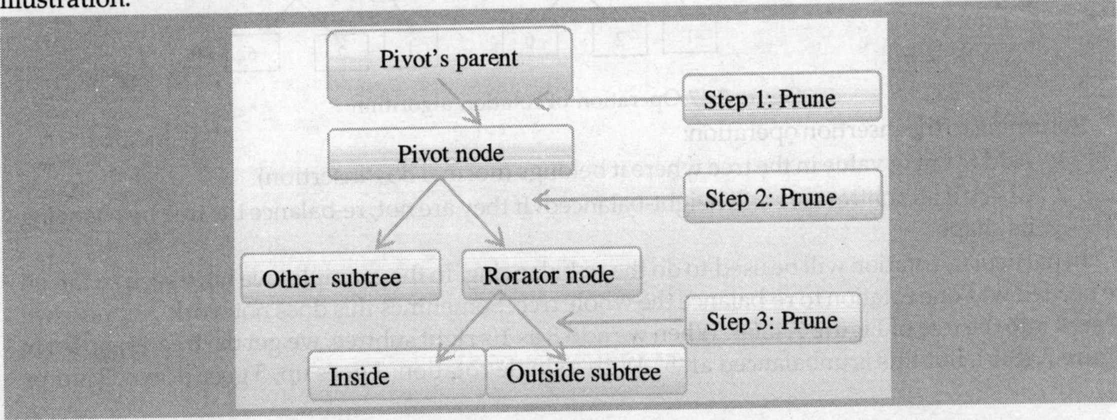

Step 4: Join the pruned inside subtree to the pivot (in the place where the rotator had been).
Step 5: Join the pivot to the rotator (in the place where inside had been).
Step 6: Join the rotator to the pivot's (original) parent (in the place where the pivot had been).

Figure 7.46 Pivot Based AVL Tree Balancing Algorithm

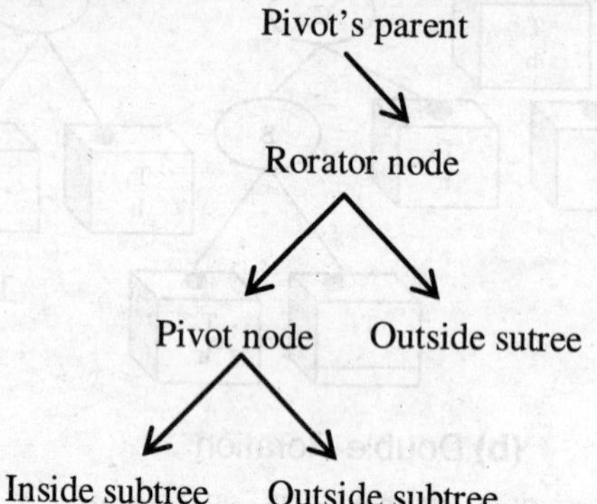

Figure 7.47 Operation of rotation algorithm

For example, consider the tree in **Figure 7.47(a)**. After steps 1-3, the tree is the same but the parts that will be re-arranged have been pruned from the main tree {**Figure 7.47(a)**} and from one another {**Figure 7.47(b)**}.

Step 4: Join the pruned *inside* subtree to the *pivot* {**Figure** 7.47 (c)}.

Step 5: Join the *pivot* to the rotator (in the place where *inside* had been) {**Figure** 7.47(d)}.

Step 6: Join the rotator to the *pivot*'s (original) *parent* {**Figure** 7.47 (e)}.

The result of the rotation in this example is: '1' rotates up, '5' rotates down on the other side, and '2' jumps across to join '5'.

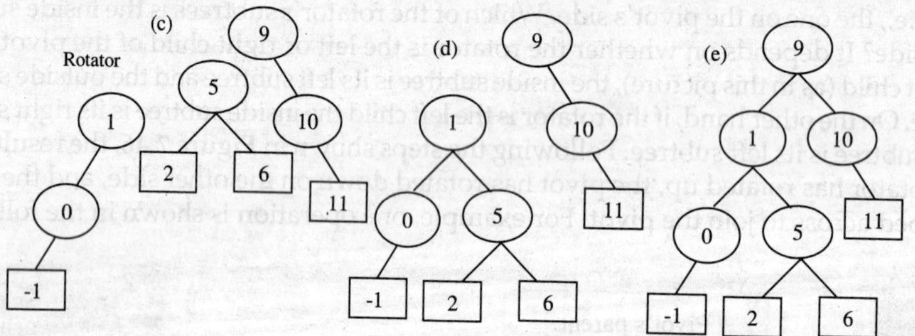

Figure 7.47 Operation of rotation algorithm

Returning to the insertion operation:

1. Add the new value in the tree where it belongs (normal BST insertion).
2. Check if all subtrees are still height-balanced. If they are not, re-balance the tree by changing its shape.

In particular, rotation will be used to do the re-balancing. In the examples we have seen so far, all we needed was one rotation to re-balance the whole tree. Sometimes this does not work. Suppose we insert 3 into the tree of **Figure 7.48(a)**. When we add 3 as 1's right subtree, we get the tree as shown in **Figure 7.48(b)**. But this is unbalanced at '5'. With a single rotation: 1 goes up, 5 goes down, 3 jumps across, and we get **Figure 7.48(c).** Which is just as bad as what we started with. What has gone wrong? Let us look closely at how a rotation changes the level of two subtrees - the inside and outside subtrees in the general algorithm (in **Figure** 7.48(b), '3' is the inside subtree, outside is empty). A rotation causes inside to jump across to the other side - but it stays at the same level. Outside stays on the same side, but it goes up one level. If there is a height-imbalance and outside is taller than inside then a rotation will correct the imbalance. But if inside is taller than outside, the rotation will not fix the imbalance, it will just move it to the other side. So, before doing the rotation we need to do something to ensure that the outside subtree is taller than the inside one. What can we do? If inside is taller then rotate its root to the outside. Going back to **Figure** 7.48(a), '1' is the rotator, '3' is the inside subtree. It is taller than the outside subtree (which is empty), so we rotate '3' up, and '1' down (to the outside), etc. giving **Figure** 10.48(d), and now we do the main rotation (3 up, 5 down) and get **Figure** 10.48(e).

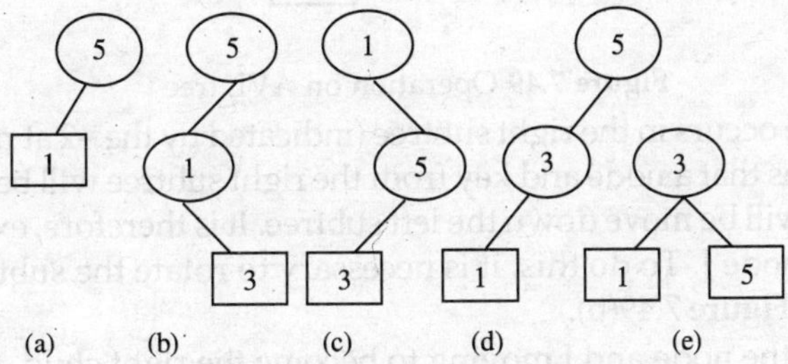

Figure 7.48 Insertion in tree

Balancing AVL Using Balance Factor: See another flovour for balancing an AVL tree, this method is simper than earlier discussed. The result of the prescribed operations is to maintain the tree so that **at any node 1 is the maximum difference between the longest path to a leaf node and the shortest path to a leaf node.** Two possible situations arise (four if the mirror situations are counted) upon insertion of a key into the tree.

Rotation 1: Consider the tree in **Figure** 7.49(a) into which the node H has just been inserted. Without the node H, the tree meets the AVL requirement that the maximum difference between the left subtree and the right subtree be 1. With the node H inserted, the tree becomes out of balance. The numbers beside each node indicate the difference in the lengths of the subtrees. The numbers are positive and negative to reflect the algebraic result of subtracting the length of the left subtree from the length of the right subtree. In other words, a positive number indicates that the right subtree is deeper than the left subtree; a negative number indicates that the left subtree is deeper than the right.

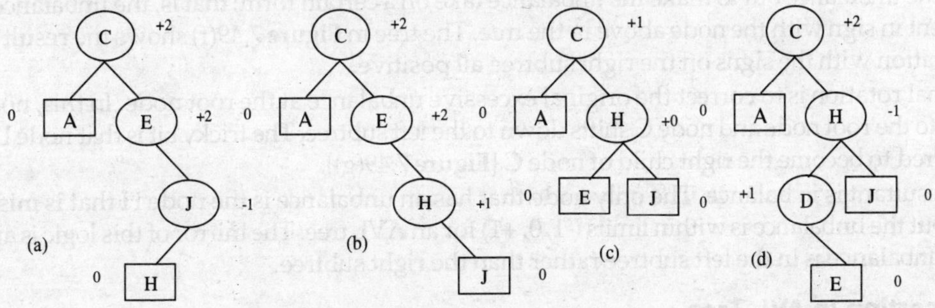

Figure 7.49 Operation on AVL tree (continue)

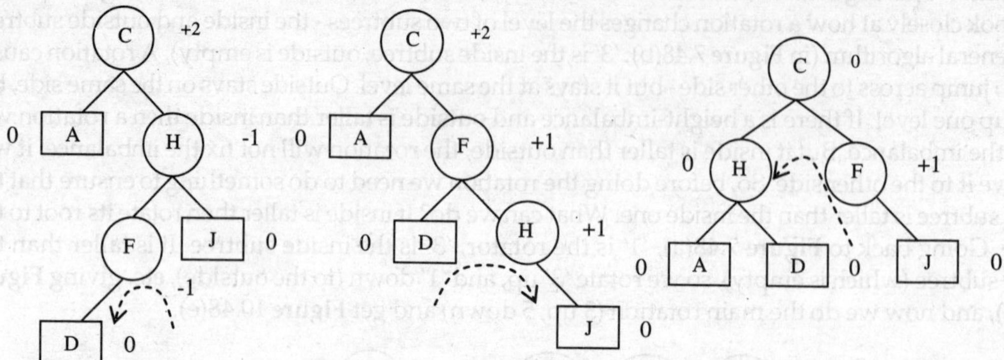

Figure 7.49 Operation on AVL tree

Because the unbalance occurs in the right subtree (indicated by the +2 at node E), a rotation to the left is indicated. This means that a node and key from the right subtree will be moved up the tree and the current node and key will be move down the left subtree. It is therefore, expedient to first create a unbalance to the right at node J. To do this, it is necessary to rotate the subtree to the right. Such a rotation produces the tree **Figure** 7.49(b).

With H replacing J at the node and J moving to become the right child, the unbalance is on the right. It must be pointed out that the unbalance of +1 is not an out-of-balance condition that must be corrected; the unbalance at node E is an out-of-balance condition that must be corrected. It is corrected with a rotation to the left. That is, H replaces E, E becomes the left child of H, and J remains the right child of H {**Figure** 7.49(c).}

The example above {**Figure** 7.49(b)} is applied to the right subtree because the unbalance was on the right. Should the unbalance occur on the left, the same procedures would be employed except the directions of the rotations would be reversed.

Rotation 2: Consider the tree in **Figure** 7.49(d) into which node F had just been inserted. The new node causes an unbalance at the root (node C). Because the unbalance at the root is positive, preliminary rotations will be necessary to make the unbalance at node H a positive unbalance. And before the unbalance at node H can be changed, the unbalance at node D must be made consistent (made negative) with the unbalance at node H. The tree in **Figure** 7.49(e) shows the result of this first preliminary rotation.

Next, the second preliminary rotation takes place around node H. Remember the goal of this is not to correct the unbalance but to make the unbalance take on a certain form; that is, the unbalance must be consistent in sign with the node above in the tree. The tree in **Figure** 7.49(f) shows the result of this second rotation with the signs on the right subtree all positive.

The final rotation is to correct the original excessive unbalance at the root node. In this, node F is promoted to the root node and node C shifts down to the left subtree. The tricky bit is that node D must be transferred to become the right child of node C {**Figure** 7.49(g)}.

This resultant is in balance. The only node that has an unbalance is the node H that is missing a left child, but the unbalance is within limits (-1, 0, +1) for an AVL tree. The mirror of this logic is applied when the unbalance is in the left subtree rather than the right subtree.

7.10.3 Insertion In AVL Tree

We can insert a new node into an AVL tree by first using the usual binary tree insertion technique, comparing the key of the new node with that in the root and inserting the new node into the left or right sub-trees accurately. It often turns out that the new node can be inserted without changing the height of the sub-tree, in that case neither the height nor the balance factor of the root is changed. Even when the height of a sub-tree increases, it may be the shorter sub-tree that has grown up, so that only the balance factor of the root will be changed. The only case that can cause difficulty occurs when the new node is added to a sub-tree of the root that is strictly taller than the other sub-tree and the height is increased. This would cause one sub-tree to have height 2 more than other, where as the AVL condition restricts one height difference to be never more than one.

General Insertion Algorithm

1. Do as a normal BST insertion
2. If the tree is balanced, done, otherwise do 3-4.
3. Starting at the newly inserted node, work way up the tree until find the first node whose subtrees' heights differ by 2. This node is the *pivot*, the root of its taller subtree is the *rotator*.
4. It is necessarily the case that the new value was inserted in one of the *rotator*'s subtrees. If it was inserted in the *rotator*'s *outside* subtree, then this subtree will be taller than *inside*, and a single rotation (of the *rotator*) will correct the imbalance. Otherwise, one must first rotate the root of the rotator's inside subtree up into the rotator's position (the rotator does down the other side), and then rotate the node that replaced the rotator up into the pivot's position.

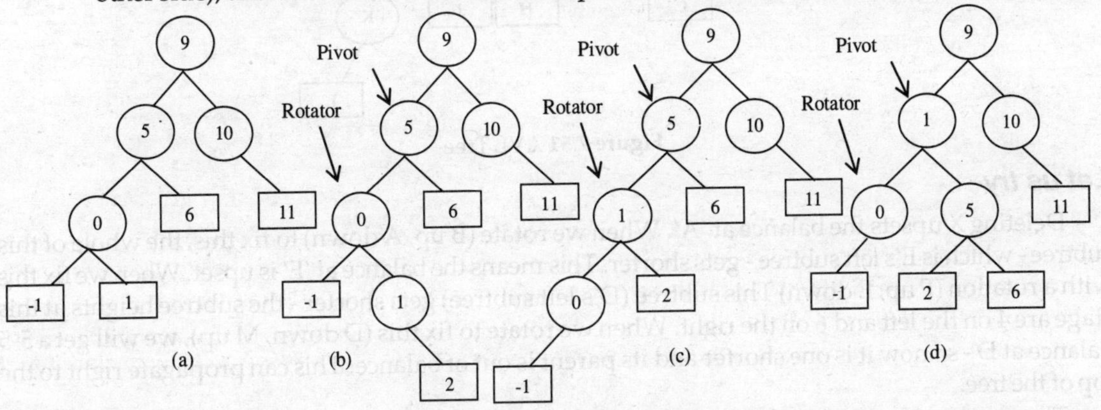

Figure 7.50 Insertion in AVL Tree

For example, consider the tree in **Figure** 7.50(a) and insert 2 into this tree then we get tree as shown in **Figure** 7.50(b). The pivot is the lowest node whose subtree's heights differ by 2. The rotator is the root of the pivot's taller subtree (the one in which the new value was inserted). The new value is in the rotator's inside subtree. Therefore, we must rotate this subtree before correcting the imbalance.

Note: If the rotator's inside subtree was already shorter than its outside subtree we should just skip the 'setup' step that follows and go straight to the last step.

This rotation does not change the imbalance at all; all it does it make the rotator's outside subtree taller than its inside one. The pivot node does not change and the rotator is the same node as before (different value) {**Figure** 7.50(c)}. When the rotator's outside subtree is taller, a single rotation of the rotator will correct the height imbalance in the whole tree {**Figure** 10.50 (d)}. Add 4 or 7 to the tree shown in **Figure** 7.50(d) and see the effect of algorithm discussed above.

7.10.4 Deletion of a Node from an AVL Tree

The inverse of the insertion operation is the deletion operation: given a value X and an AVL tree T, delete the node containing X and rebalance the resulting tree, if necessary. It turns out that deletion is considerably more complex than insertion. To illustrate the additional complexity, recall that to insert a new value into an AVL tree, we never need to do more than 2 rotations inorder to restore the tree's balance. We can use rotations to restore the balance when we do a deletion too, but in some cases we may have to do a rotation at every level of the tree (O($\log_2 n$) rotations in the worst case). Here is a tree {**Figure** 7.51} that causes this worse case number of rotations (we are deleting X). At every node the left subtree is one shorter than the right subtree (numbers shown are height of subtrees {**Figure** 7.51}.

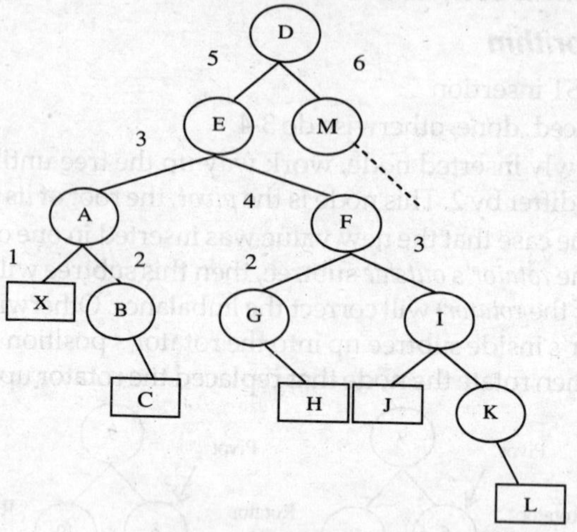

Figure 7.51 AVL Tree

Let us try-

Deleting X upsets the balance at 'A'. When we rotate (B up, A down) to fix this, the whole of this subtree - which is E's left subtree - gets shorter. This means the balance at 'E' is upset. When we fix this with a rotation (F up, E down) This subtree (D's left subtree) gets shorter - the subtree heights at this stage are 4 on the left and 6 on the right. When we rotate to fix this (D down, M up), we will get a 5-5 balance at D - so now it is one shorter and its parent is out of balance. This can propagate right to the top of the tree.

The program segment **INSERT.C** implements general insertion algorithm for binary tree. This program segment insert a node in a binary tree and it does not completely follow the algorithm discussed here. According to need it is required to update this program segment. The program segment AVL_Tree.C implements the complete AVL tree operations discussed above.

```
/* Insertion in a Binary Tree */
/* INSERT.C */
# include<stdio.h>

struct NODE
{
    char Info;
    struct NODE *Left_Child;
    struct NODE *Right_Child;
};

int flag = 0;
```

```
struct NODE *Binary_Tree (char *, int, int);
void Output(struct NODE *, int );
struct NODE *Insert_Node(struct NODE *, char);/* Function to create an
binary tree */
struct NODE * Binary_Tree (char *List, int Lower, int Upper)
{
   struct NODE *Node;
   int Mid = (Lower + Upper)/2;
   Node = (struct NODE*) malloc(sizeof(struct NODE));
   Node->Info = List [Mid];
   if ( Lower>= Upper)
   {
      Node->Left_Child = NULL;
      Node->Right_Child = NULL;
      return (Node);
   }
   if (Lower <= Mid - 1)
      Node->Left_Child = Binary_Tree (List, Lower, Mid - 1);
   else
      Node->Left_Child = NULL;
   if (Mid + 1 <= Upper)
      Node->Right_Child = Binary_Tree (List, Mid + 1, Upper);
   else
      Node->Right_Child = NULL;
   return(Node);
}

/* Output function */
void Output(struct NODE *T, int Level)
{
   int i;
   if (T)
   {
      Output(T->Right_Child, Level+1);
      printf("\n");
      for (i = 0; i < Level; i++)
         printf(" ");
      printf("%c", T->Info);
      Output(T->Left_Child, Level+1);
   }
}
/* Insert a node in the tree */
struct NODE * Insert_Node(struct NODE *Node, char Info)
{
   if (Node == NULL)
```

```
    {
        Node = (struct NODE *) malloc(sizeof(struct NODE));
        Node->Info = Info;
        Node->Left_Child = NULL;
        Node->Right_Child = NULL;
        return (Node);
    }

    /* Test for the left child */
    if (Node->Info >= Info )
        Node->Left_Child = Insert_Node (Node->Left_Child, Info);
    else
        /* Set all the rest of the elements as right child */
        Node->Right_Child = Insert_Node (Node->Right_Child, Info);
    return(Node);
}
/* Function main */
void main()
{
    char List[100];
    int Number = 0;
    char Info ;
    char choice;
    struct NODE *T = (struct NODE*) malloc (sizeof(struct NODE));
    T = NULL;
    printf("\n Input choice 'b' to break:");
    choice = getchar();
    while(choice != 'b')
    {
        fflush(stdin);
        printf("\n Input information of the node: ");
        scanf("%c", &Info);
        List[Number++] = Info;
        fflush(stdin);
        printf("\n Input choice 'b' to break:");
        choice = getchar();
    }
    Number --;
    printf("\n Number of elements in the list is %d", Number+1);
    T = Binary_Tree(List, 0, Number);
    printf("\n Tree is \n");
    Output(T,1);
    fflush(stdin);
    printf("\n Input the information of the node to which want to insert:
");
```

```
    scanf("%c", &Info);
    T = Insert_Node(T, Info);
    printf("\n Tree is \n");
    Output(T, 1);
}
```

7.10.5 The Height of An AVL Tree

What is the maximum height that an AVL tree with **n** nodes can have? Instead of this we can ask what is the minimum number of nodes that an AVL tree of height **h** can have. If $\mathbf{F_h}$ is such a tree, and the left and right sub-trees of its root are $\mathbf{F_l}$ and $\mathbf{F_r}$, then one of $\mathbf{F_l}$ or $\mathbf{F_r}$ must have height **h-1**, say, $\mathbf{F_l}$, and the other has height either **h-1** or **h-2**. Since, $\mathbf{F_h}$ has the minimum number of nodes among AVL trees of height **h**, it follows that $\mathbf{F_l}$ must have the minimum number of nodes among AVL trees of height **h-1**. $\mathbf{F_l}$ is of the form $\mathbf{F_{h-1}}$, and $\mathbf{F_r}$ must have height **h-2** with minimum number of nodes simply that $\mathbf{F_r}$ is of the form $\mathbf{F_{h-2}}$.

Trees that are built upon the above rules, are therefore as sparse as possible for AVL trees and are called **Fibonacci** trees. The first few trees of this category are illustrated in **Figure 7.52**. If $|F_r|$ is the number of nodes in a tree F_r, then by recurrence relation $|F_h| = |F_{h-1}| + 1$, where $|F_0| = 1$ and $|F_1|$, by adding 1 to both sides, we find that $|F_h| + 1|$ satisfy the **Fibonacci** number generator

function that is: $|F_h|+1 \approx \frac{1}{\sqrt{5}}\left(\frac{1+\sqrt{5}}{2}\right)^{h+3}$

Taking logarithms of both sides and discarding small terms we get the approximate result

$$h \approx 1.44 \log_2 |F_h|$$

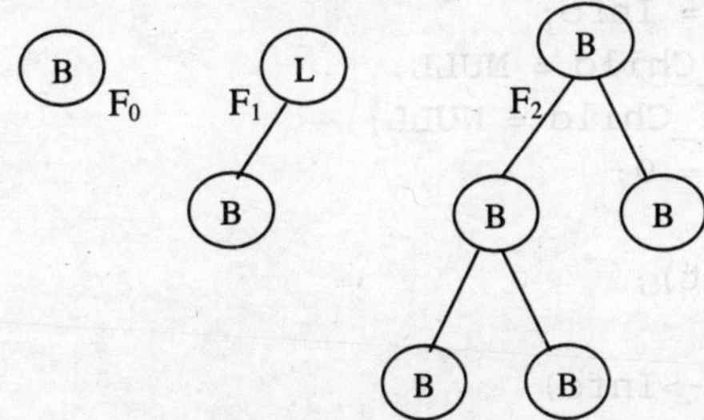

Figure 7.52 Fibonacci Trees

From the above result it is clear that the sparsest possible AVL tree with **n** nodes has approximate height $\mathbf{1.44 \log_2 n}$. A perfectly balanced binary tree with **n** nodes has height $\mathbf{\log_2 n}$ and a degenerate tree has height as large as **n**. Hence the algorithms for manipulating AVL trees require more than 44% time than the optimum. But in practice, AVL trees do much well than this. It is shown that for **Fibonacci** trees, which are the worst case for AVL trees, the average search time is only 4% more than the optimum. Most AVL trees are not nearly as sparse as **Fibonacci** trees and therefore it is reasonable to accept that average search times for average AVL trees are very close to the optimum. The average comparisons are:$\log_2 n + 0.25$, where **n** is large.

```
/* Create AVL Binary TREE */
/* AVL_TREE.C */
# include<stdio.h>
# include<malloc.h>
```

```
# define F 0
# define T 1
struct NODE
{
    char Info;
    int Flag;
    struct NODE *Left_Child;
    struct NODE *Right_Child;
};
struct NODE *Binary_Tree (char, struct NODE *, int *);
void Output(struct NODE *, int );
struct NODE *Balance_Right_Heavy(struct NODE *, int *);
struct NODE *Balance_Left_Heavy(struct NODE *, int *);
struct NODE *DELETE(struct NODE *, struct NODE *, int *);
struct NODE *Delete_Element(struct NODE *, char , int *);
/* Function to insert an element into tree */
struct NODE * Binary_Tree (char Info, struct NODE *Parent, int *H)
{
    struct NODE *Node1;
    struct NODE *Node2;
    if(!Parent)
    {
        Parent = (struct NODE *) malloc(sizeof(struct NODE));
        Parent->Info = Info;
        Parent->Left_Child = NULL;
        Parent->Right_Child = NULL;
        Parent->Flag = 0;
        *H = T;
        return (Parent);
    }
    if(Info < Parent->Info)
    {
        Parent->Left_Child = Binary_Tree(Info, Parent->Left_Child, H);
        if(*H)
        /* Left branch has grown higher */
        {
            switch(Parent->Flag)
            {
            case 1: /* Right heavy */
                Parent->Flag = 0;
                *H = F;
                break;
            case 0: /* Balanced tree */
                Parent->Flag = -1;
```

```
            break;
        case -1: /* Left heavy */
            Node1 = Parent->Left_Child;
            if(Node1->Flag == -1)
            {
                printf("\n Left to Left Rotation\n");
                Parent->Left_Child= Node1->Right_Child;
                Node1->Right_Child = Parent;
                Parent->Flag = 0;
                Parent = Node1;
            }else
            {
                printf("\n Left to right rotation\n");
                Node2 = Node1->Right_Child;
                Node1->Right_Child = Node2->Left_Child;
                Node2->Left_Child = Node1;
                Parent->Left_Child = Node2->Right_Child;
                Node2->Right_Child = Parent;
                if(Node2->Flag == -1)
                    Parent->Flag = 1;
                else
                    Parent->Flag = 0;
                if(Node2->Flag == 1)
                    Node1->Flag = -1;
                else
                    Node1->Flag = 0;
                Parent = Node2;
            }

            Parent->Flag = 0;
            *H = F;
        }
    }
}
if(Info > Parent->Info)
{
    Parent->Right_Child = Binary_Tree(Info, Parent->Right_Child, H);
    if(*H)
    /* Right branch has grown higher */
    {
        switch(Parent->Flag)
        {
        case -1: /* Left heavy */
            Parent->Flag = 0;
            *H = F;
```

```
        break;
    case 0: /* Balanced tree */
        Parent->Flag = 1;
        break;

    case 1: /* Right heavy */
        Node1 = Parent->Right_Child;
        if(Node1->Flag == 1)
        {
            printf("\n Right to Right Rotation\n");
            Parent->Right_Child= Node1->Left_Child;
            Node1->Left_Child = Parent;
            Parent->Flag = 0;
            Parent = Node1;
        }
        else
        {
            printf("\n Right to Left Rotation\n");
            Node2 = Node1->Left_Child;
            Node1->Left_Child = Node2->Right_Child;
            Node2->Right_Child = Node1;
            Parent->Right_Child = Node2->Left_Child;
            Node2->Left_Child = Parent;

            if(Node2->Flag == 1)
                Parent->Flag = -1;
            else
                Parent->Flag = 0;
            if(Node2->Flag == -1)
                Node1->Flag = 1;
            else
                Node1->Flag = 0;
            Parent = Node2;
        }
        Parent->Flag = 0;
        *H = F;
    }
  }
 }
 return(Parent);
}

/* Output function */
void Output(struct NODE *Tree,int Level)
{
```

```
    int i;
    if (Tree)
    {
        Output(Tree->Right_Child, Level+1);
        printf("\n");
        for (i = 0; i < Level; i++)
            printf(" ");
        printf("%c", Tree->Info);
        Output(Tree->Left_Child, Level+1);
    }
}

/* Balancing Right Heavy */
struct NODE * Balance_Right_Heavy(struct NODE *Parent, int *H)
{
    struct NODE *Node1, *Node2;
    switch(Parent->Flag)
    {
    case -1:
        Parent->Flag = 0;
        break;

    case 0:
        Parent->Flag = 1;
        *H= F;
        break;
    case 1: /* Rebalance */
        Node1 = Parent->Right_Child;
        if(Node1->Flag >= 0)
        {
            printf("\n Right to Right Rotation\n");
            Parent->Right_Child= Node1->Left_Child;
            Node1->Left_Child = Parent;
            if(Node1->Flag == 0)
            {
                Parent->Flag = 1;
                Node1->Flag = -1;
                *H = F;
            }
            else
            {
                Parent->Flag = Node1->Flag = 0;
            }
            Parent = Node1;
        }
```

```
        else
        {
            printf("\n Right to Left Rotation\n");
            Node2 = Node1->Left_Child;
            Node1->Left_Child = Node2->Right_Child;
            Node2->Right_Child = Node1;
            Parent->Right_Child = Node2->Left_Child;
            Node2->Left_Child = Parent;
            if(Node2->Flag == 1)
                Parent->Flag = -1;
            else
                Parent->Flag = 0;
            if(Node2->Flag == -1)
                Node1->Flag = 1;
            else
                Node1->Flag = 0;
            Parent = Node2;
            Node2->Flag = 0;
        }
    }
    return(Parent);
}

/* Balancing Left Heavy */
struct NODE * Balance_Left_Heavy(struct NODE *Parent, int *H)
{
    struct NODE *Node1, *Node2;

    switch(Parent->Flag)
    {
    case 1:
        Parent->Flag = 0;
        break;
    case 0:
        Parent->Flag = -1;
        *H= F;
        break;
    case -1: /* Rebalance */
        Node1 = Parent->Left_Child;
        if(Node1->Flag <= 0)
        {
            printf("\n Left to Left Rotation\n");
            Parent->Left_Child= Node1->Right_Child;
            Node1->Right_Child = Parent;
```

```
        if(Node1->Flag == 0)
        {
            Parent->Flag = -1;
            Node1->Flag = 1;
            *H = F;
        }else
        {
            Parent->Flag = Node1->Flag = 0;
        }
        Parent = Node1;
    }
    else
    {
        printf("\n Left to Right Rotation\n");
        Node2 = Node1->Right_Child;
        Node1->Right_Child = Node2->Left_Child;
        Node2->Left_Child = Node1;
        Parent->Left_Child = Node2->Right_Child;
        Node2->Right_Child = Parent;
        if(Node2->Flag == -1)
            Parent->Flag = 1;
        else
            Parent->Flag = 0;
        if(Node2->Flag == 1)
            Node1->Flag = -1;
        else
            Node1->Flag = 0;
        Parent = Node2;
        Node2->Flag = 0;
    }
  }
  return(Parent);
}

/* Replace the node at which key is found with last right key of a left child
*/
struct NODE * DELETE(struct NODE *R, struct NODE *Temp, int *H)
{
    struct NODE *Dnode = R;
    if( R->Right_Child != NULL)
    {
        R->Right_Child = DELETE(R->Right_Child, Temp, H);
        if(*H)
            R = Balance_Left_Heavy(R, H);
    }
```

```
      else
      {
         Dnode = R;
         Temp->Info = R->Info;
         R = R->Left_Child;
         free(Dnode);
         *H = T;
      }
      return(R);
   }
   /* Delete the key element from the tree */
   struct NODE * Delete_Element(struct NODE *Parent, char Info, int *H)
   {
      struct NODE *Temp;
      if(!Parent)
      {
         printf("\n Information does not exist");
         return(Parent);
      }
      else
      {
         if (Info < Parent->Info )
         {
         Parent->Left_Child = Delete_Element(Parent->Left_Child, Info, H);
            if(*H)
               Parent = Balance_Right_Heavy(Parent, H);
         }
         else
            if(Info > Parent->Info)
            {
         Parent->Right_Child = Delete_Element(Parent->Right_Child, Info,
H);
               if(*H)
                  Parent = Balance_Left_Heavy(Parent, H);
            }
            else
            {
               Temp= Parent;
               if(Temp->Right_Child == NULL)
               {
                  Parent = Temp->Left_Child;
                  *H = T;
                  free(Temp);
               }
```

```
              else
                  if(Temp->Left_Child == NULL)
                  {
                      Parent = Temp->Right_Child;
                      *H = T;
                      free(Temp);
                  }else{
          Temp->Left_Child = DELETE(Temp->Left_Child, Temp, H);
                      if(*H)
                  Parent = Balance_Right_Heavy(Parent, H);
                  }
          }
      }
      return(Parent);
  }

  /* Function main */
  void main()
  {
      int H;
      char Info ;
      char choice;
      struct NODE *Tree = (struct NODE *)malloc(sizeof(struct NODE));
      Tree = NULL;
      printf("\n Input choice 'b' to break:");
      choice = getchar();
      while(choice != 'b')
      {
          fflush(stdin);
          printf("\n Input information of the node: ");
          scanf("%c", &Info);
          Tree = Binary_Tree(Info, Tree, &H);
          printf("\n Tree is:\n");
          Output(Tree, 1);
          fflush(stdin);
          printf("\n Input choice 'b' to break:");
          choice = getchar();
      }
      fflush(stdin);
      while(1)
      {
          printf("\n Input choice 'b' to break:");
          printf("\n Input the key value want to deletedir:");
          scanf("%c", &Info);
          if (Info == 'b')
```

```
            break;
        Tree = Delete_Element(Tree, Info, &H);
        printf("\n Tree is:\n");
        Output(Tree, 1);
    }
}
```

The AVL tree is significant because it introduced the concept of using prescribed algorithms to achieve balance in tree structures. Central to these algorithms is the **rotation**, wherein a child is promoted to its parent node and the parent is demoted to the other child position. This concept will form the basis for B-trees, which are the heart of the indexed sequential file management system.

7.11 PAGED BINARY TREE

Although the AVL tree solved the problem of unbalances in the binary tree, it did not solve the problem caused by seeking for each node individually. If each node is stored separately, the average number of seeks in a search is the same as the number of comparisons in a binary search (9.5 in a 1000 record search). This performance is still unacceptable. The concept of blocking was tried because it produces dramatic improvements in earlier situations involving unacceptable amounts of seeking.

In this problem context blocking became the paged binary tree as shown in **Figure 7.53**. A page is a physical record in which several nodes are stored, i.e., a parent and several levels of descendents are stored on a page. Descendents from the lowest level on given page are identified with pointers to pages containing those descendents. By storing several connected nodes in one physical record, multiple nodes may be retrieved with a single seek and overall search performance is greatly improved.

If all of the keys are available at the time tree is first built, the structure requires no maintenance. On the other hand, with a dynamic file in which the keys are presented in random order, the maintenance problem is significant. Rotations that are confined to a single page are not a problem, but rotations that cross page boundaries pose big problems, especially when entire subtrees must be transferred from one page to another. In these cases, changes may be needed in not only the adjacent page, but also in all of the descendent pages. Paged binary trees solved one problem but reintroduced another. The history of file structures is filled with similar cases. If, for each disk read, only a binary node is retrieved, it would waste most of the data read from the disk. The paged binary trees attempt to address the problem by locating multiple binary nodes on the same disk page. The main design problem with the paged binary trees is how to group binary nodes (or keys) in pages to make disk access and tree maintenance efficient. The number of disk accesses (i.e., page reads) required for the paged version of a completely full balanced tree is, $\log_{k+1}(n+1)$, where, **n**= the number of keys in the tree and **k** = the number of keys in a page (k = 1, 3, 7, 15, 31, ...)

Page level	Number of keys on this page level
1	k
2	$(k+1) . k$ (i.e., (k+1) pages, k keys per page)
3	$(k+1)^2 . k$ (i.e., $(k+1)^2$ pages, k keys per page)
4	$(k+1)^3 .k$ (i.e., $(k+1)^3$ pages, k keys per page)
...	...
m	$(k+1)^{m-1} . k$ (i.e., $(k+1)^{m-1}$ pages, k keys per page)

Sum up all the keys in each page level.

$$k + (k+1)k + (k+1)^2k + (k+1)^3k + \ldots + (k+1)^{m-1}k = n$$

$$k\,(1 + (k+1) + (k+1)^2 + (k+1)^3 + \ldots + (k+1)^{m-1}) = n$$

$$k\,((k+1)^m - 1)\,/\,((k+1) - 1) = n$$

$$(k+1)^m = n + 1$$

Solving for m, we have

$$m = \log_{k+1}(n+1)$$

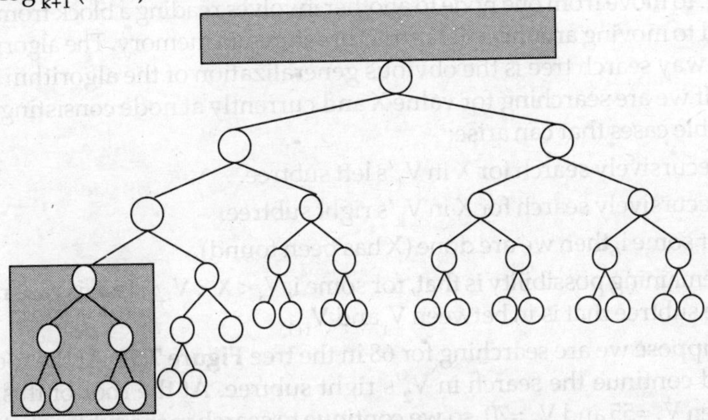

Figure 7.53 Tree with multiple pages

7.12 M-WAY SEARCH TREES

A binary search tree has one value in each node and two subtrees. This notion easily generalizes to an m-way search tree, which has (m-1) values per node and m subtrees. m is called the degree of the tree. A binary search tree, therefore, has degree 2. In fact, it is not necessary for every node to contain exactly (m-1) values and have exactly m subtrees. In an m-way subtree a node can have anywhere from 1 to (m-1) values, and the number of (non-empty) subtrees can range from 0 (for a leaf) to 1+(the number of values). m is thus a fixed upper limit on how much data can be stored in a node.

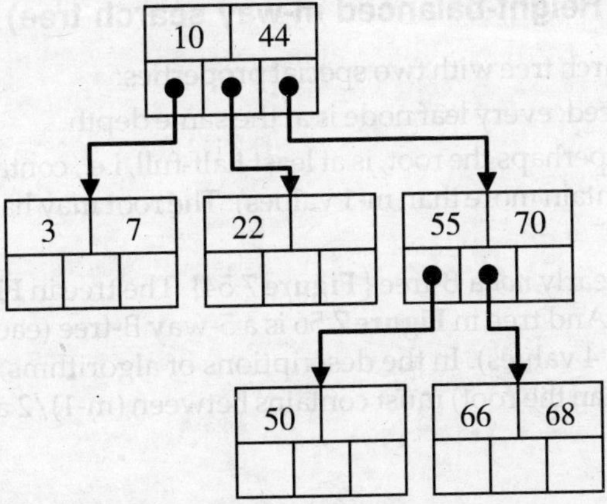

Figure 7.54 3-way Search Tree

The values in a node are stored in ascending order, $V_1 < V_2 < ... V_k$ ($k \le m$-1) and the subtrees are placed between adjacent values, with one additional subtree at each end. We can thus associate with each value a 'left' and 'right' subtree, with the right subtree of V_i being the same as the left subtree of V_{i+1}. All the values in V_1's left subtree are less than V_1; all the values in V_k's right subtree are greater than V_k; and all the values in the subtree between V_i and V_{i+1} are greater than V_i and less than V_{i+1}. For example, tree in **Figure** 7.54 is a 3-way search tree.

It will be convenient to illustrate m-way trees using a small value of m. But bear in mind that in practice m is usually very large. Each node corresponds to a physical block on disk, and m represents the maximum number of data items that can be stored in a single block. m is maximized inorder to speedup processing: to move from one node to another involves reading a block from disk - a very slow operation compared to moving around a data structure stored in memory. The algorithm for searching for a value in an m-way search tree is the obvious generalization of the algorithm for searching in a binary search tree. If we are searching for value X and currently at node consisting of values $V_1 ... V_k$, there are four possible cases that can arise:

1. If $X < V_1$, recursively search for X in V_1's left subtree.
2. If $X > V_k$, recursively search for X in V_k's right subtree.
3. If $X = V_i$, for some i, then we are done (X has been found).
4. The only remaining possibility is that, for some i, $V_i < X < V_{i+1}$. In this case recursively search for X in the subtree that is in between V_i and V_{i+1}.

For example, suppose we are searching for 68 in the tree **Figure 7.54**. At the root, case (2) would apply, so we would continue the search in V_2's right subtree. At the root of this subtree, case (4) applies, 68 is between V_1=55 and V_2=70, so we continue to search in the subtree between them. Now case (3) applies, 68= V_2, so we are done. If we want search for 69, exactly the same processing will be required down to the last node. At that point, case (2) is applied, but the subtree we want to search in is empty. Therefore, we conclude that 69 is not in the tree.

Other algorithms for binary search trees - insertion and deletion - generalize in a similar way. As with binary search trees, inserting values in ascending order will result in a degenerate m-way search tree, i.e., a tree whose height is O(n) instead of O($\log_2$ n). This is a problem because all the important operations are O(height), and it is aim to make them O($\log_2$ n). One solution to this problem is to *force* the tree to be height-balanced as discussed in the previous sections; we will examine it in detail for m-way search trees.

7.12.1 B-tree (Perfectly Height-balanced m-way search tree)

A B-tree is an m-way search tree with two special properties:

1. It is perfectly balanced: every leaf node is at the same depth.
2. Every node, except perhaps the root, is at least half-full, i.e., contains m/2 or more values (of course, it cannot contain more than m-1 values). The root may have any number of values (1 to m-1).

A 3-way search tree is clearly *not* a B-tree { **Figure** 7.54}. The tree in **Figure** 7.55 is a 3-way B-tree containing the same values. And tree in **Figure** 7.56 is a 5-way B-tree (each node other than the root must contain between 2 and 4 values). In the descriptions of algorithms, we assume that m is odd; therefore each node (other than the root) must contains between (m-1)/2 and m-1 values.

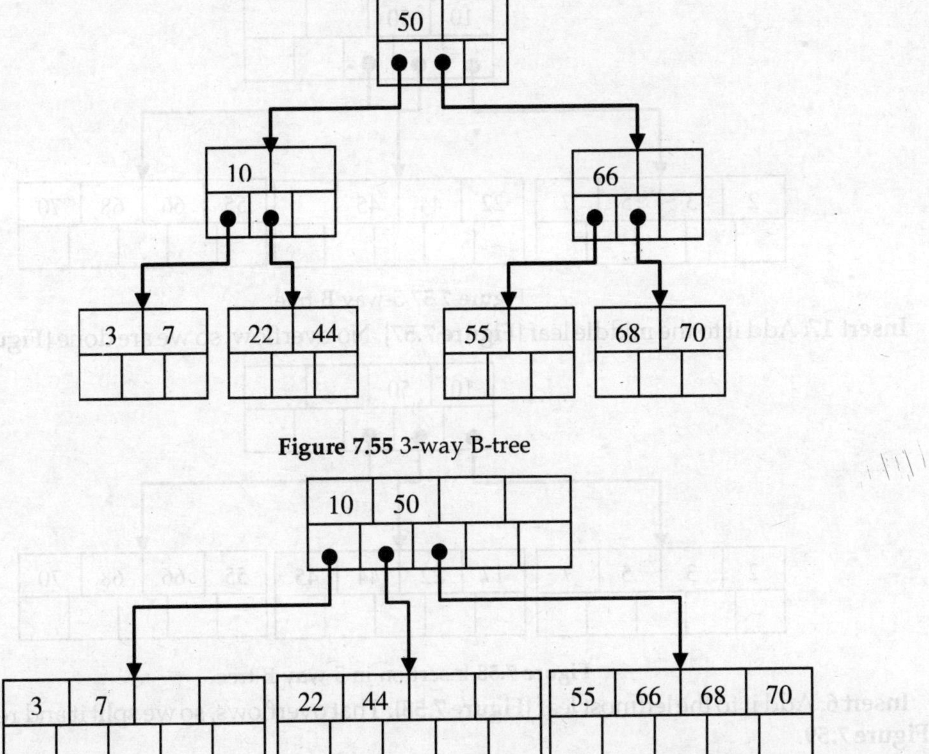

Figure 7.55 3-way B-tree

Figure 7.56 5-way B-tree

Insertion into a B-Tree

To insert value X into a B-tree, there are 3 steps:

1.Using the search procedure for m-way trees (described earlier) find the leaf node to which X should be added.

2.Add X to this node in the appropriate place among the values already there. Being a leaf node there are no subtrees to worry about.

3.If there are m-1 or fewer values in the node after adding X, then we are finished. If there are m nodes after adding X, we say the node has *overflowed*. To repair this, we split the node into three parts:

Left: the first (m-1)/2 values

Middle: the middle value (position 1+((m-1)/2)

Right: the last (m-1)/2 values

Note that Left and Right have just enough values to be made into individual nodes. That's what we do, they become the left and right children of Middle, which we add in the appropriate place in this node's parent. But what if there is no room in the parent? If it overflows we do the same thing again: split it into Left-Middle-Right, make Left and Right into new nodes and add Middle (with Left and Right as its children) to the node above. We continue doing this until no overflow occurs, or until the root itself overflows. If the root overflows, we split it, as usual, and create a new root node with Middle as its only value and Left and Right as its children (as usual).

For example, let us do a sequence of insertions into B-tree **Figure** 7.57 (m=5, so each node other than the root must contain between 2 and 4 values).

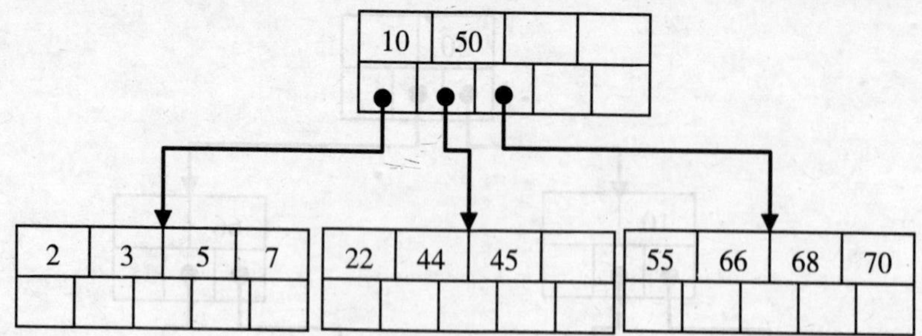

Figure 7.57 5-way B-tree

Insert 17: Add it to the middle leaf {**Figure 7.57**}. No overflow, so we are done {**Figure 7.58**}.

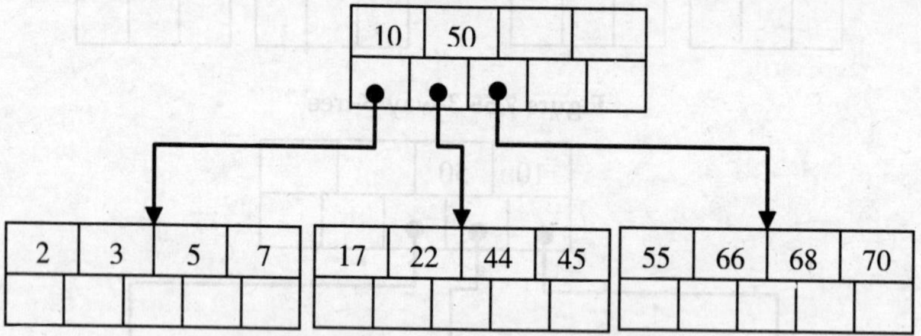

Figure 7.58 Insertion in 5-way B-tree

Insert 6: Add it to the leftmost leaf {**Figure 7.58**}. That overflows, so we split it and resulting tree is in **Figure 7.59**.

- Left = [2 3]
- Middle = 5
- Right = [6 7]

Left and Right become nodes; Middle is added to the node above with Left and Right as its children. The node above (the root in this small example) does not overflow, so we are done.

Insert 21: Add it to the middle leaf {**Figure 7.59**}. That overflows, so we split it the resulting tree is in **Figure 7.60.**

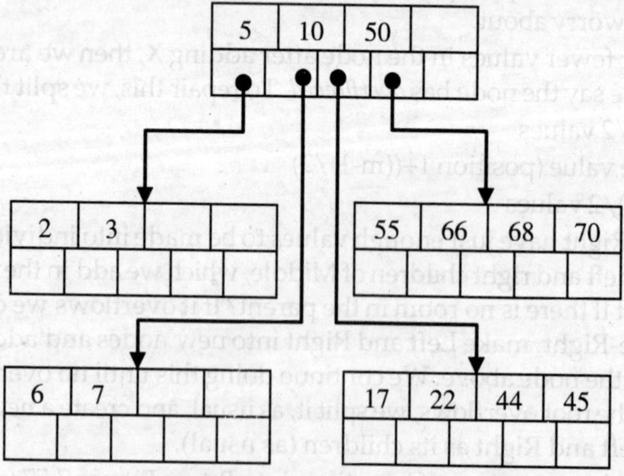

Figure 7.59 Insertion in 5-way B-tree

- left = [17 21]
- Middle = 22
- Right = [44 45]

Left and Right become nodes; Middle is added to the node above with Left and Right as its children. The node above (the root in this small example) does not overflow, so we are done.

Insert 67: Add it to the rightmost leaf {**Figure 7.60**}. That overflows, so we split it:

- Left = [55 66]
- Middle = 67
- Right = [68 70]

Left and Right become nodes; Middle is added to the node above with Left and Right as its children {**Figure** 7.61}.

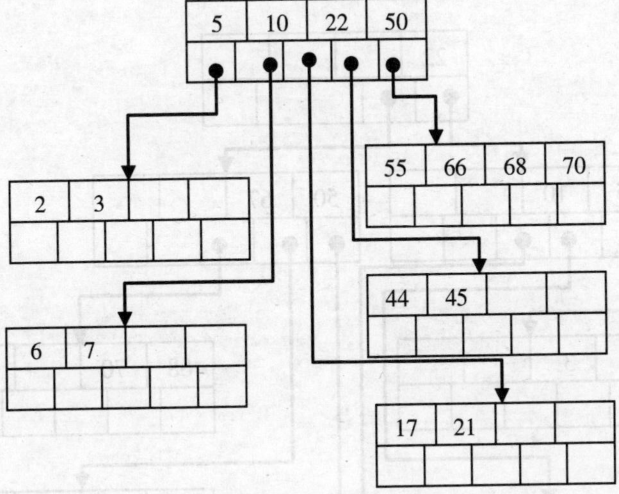

Figure 7.60 5-way B-tree after insertion of 21 in Figure 7.59

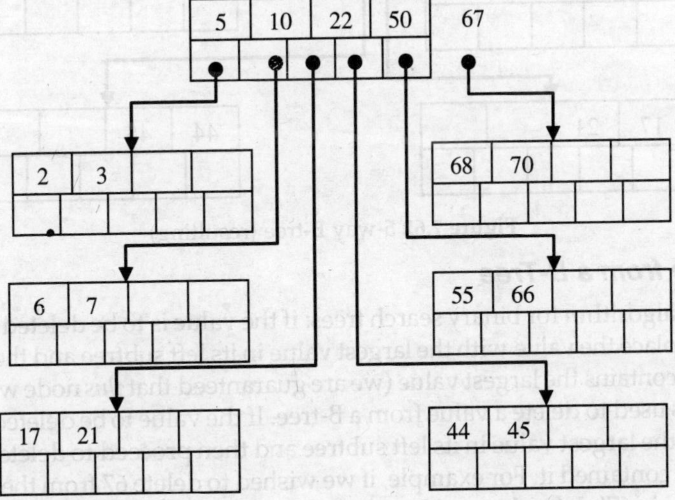

Figure 7.61 5-way B-tree after insertion of 67 in Figure 7.60

But now the node above does overflow {**Figure 5.61**}. So, it is splitting in exactly the same manner:

- Left = [5 10] (along with their children)
- Middle = 22
- Right = [50 67] (along with their children)

Left and Right become nodes, the children of Middle. If this is not the root, Middle is added to the node above and the process repeated. If there is no node above, as in this example, a new root is created with Middle as its only value.

The tree-insertion algorithms we have previously seen add new nodes at the bottom of the tree, and then have to worry about whether doing so creates an imbalance. The B-tree insertion algorithm is just the opposite: it adds new nodes at the *top* of the tree (a new node is allocated only when the root splits). B-trees grow at the root, not at the leaves. Because of this, there is never any doubt that the tree is always perfectly height balanced: when a new node is added, all existing nodes become one level deeper in the tree.

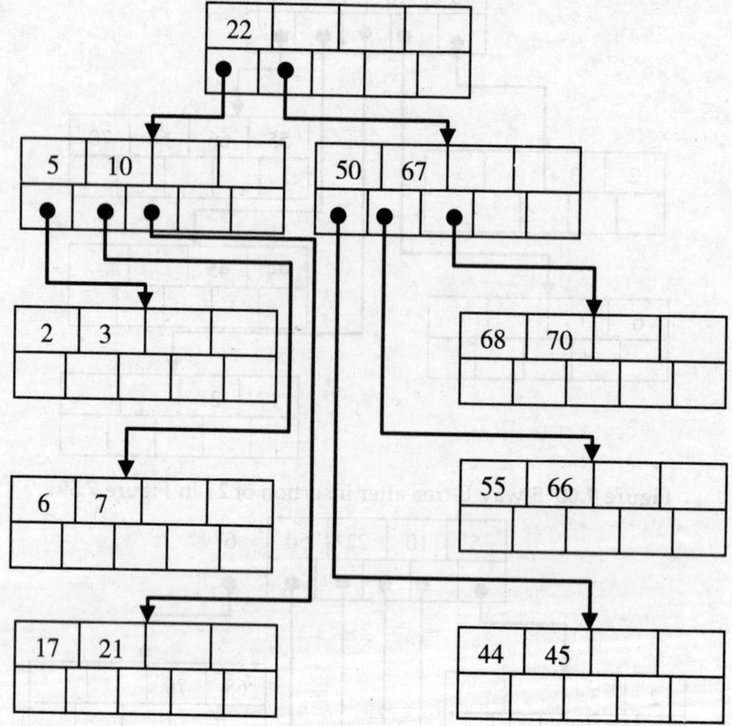

Figure 7.62 5-way B-tree (resulting)

Deleting a Value from a B-Tree

Recall deletion algorithm for binary search trees: if the value is to be deleted from a node having two subtrees, we replace the value with the largest value in its left subtree and then delete the node in the left subtree that contains the largest value (we are guaranteed that *this* node will be easy to delete). A similar strategy is used to delete a value from a B-tree. If the value to be deleted does not occur in a leaf, replace it with the largest value in its left subtree and then proceed to delete that value from the node that originally contained it. For example, if we wished to delete 67 from the tree **Figure** 7.62, we find the largest value in 67's left subtree, 66, replace 67 with 66, and then delete the occurrence of 66 in the left subtree. In a B-tree, the largest value in any value's left subtree is guaranteed to be in leaf. Therefore, wherever the value to be deleted initially resides, the following deletion algorithm always begins at a leaf. To delete value X from a B-tree, starting at a leaf node, there are 2 steps:

1. Remove X from the current node. Being a leaf node there are no subtrees to worry about.
2. Removing X might cause the node containing it to have *too few* values.
   Recall that we require the root to have at least 1 value in it and all other nodes to have at least (m-1)/2 values in them. If the node has too few values, we say it has *underflowed*.
   If underflow does not occur, then we are finished the deletion process. If it does occur, it must be fixed. The process for fixing a root is slightly different than the process for fixing the other nodes, and will be discussed afterwards.

How do we fix a non-root node that has underflowed? Let us take as a specific example, deleting 6 from the B-tree (of degree 5) in **Figure 7.63**.

Removing 6 causes the node into underflow, as it now contains just one value 7. For fixing this is to try to borrow values from a neighbouring node. We join together the current node and its more populous neighbour to form a combined node - and we must also include in the combined node the value in the parent node that is in between these two nodes. In **Figure** 7.63, we join node [7] with its more populous neighbour [17 22 44 45] and put '10' in between them, to create [6 7 10 17 22 44 45]. How many values might there be in this combined node?

Case 1: The parent node contributes 1 value.

Case 2: The node that underflowed contributes exactly (m-1)/2-1 values.

Case 3: The neighbouring node contributes somewhere between (m-1)/2 and (m-1) values.

The treatment of the combined node is different depending on whether the neighbouring contributes exactly (m-1)/2 values or more than this number.

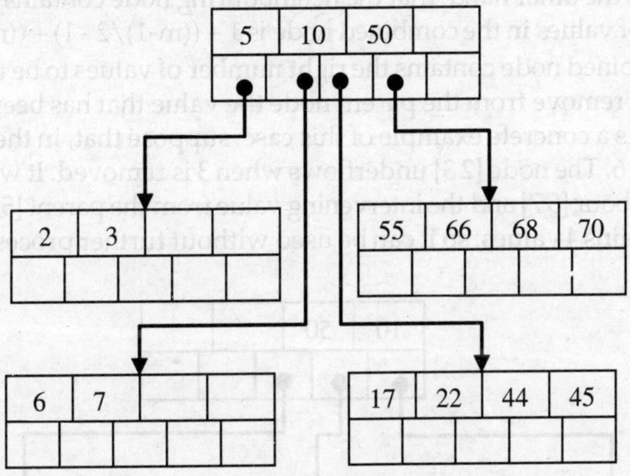

Figure 7.63 5-way B-tree

Case 1: Suppose that the neighbouring node contains more than (m-1)/2 values. In this case, the total number of values in the combined node is strictly greater than 1 + ((m-1)/2 - 1) + ((m-1)/2), i.e., it is strictly greater than (m-1). So it must contain m values or more.

We split the combined node into three pieces: Left, Middle, and Right, where Middle is a single value in the very middle of the combined node. Because the combined node has m values or more, Left and Right are guaranteed to have (m-1)/2 values each, and therefore are legitimate nodes. We replace the value we borrowed from the parent with Middle and we use Left and Right as its two children. In this case the parent's size does not change, so we are completely finished.

This is what happens when deleting 6 from the tree of **Figure** 7.63. The combined node [6 7 10 17 22 44 45] contains more than 3 values, so we split it into:

- Left = [6 7 10]
- Middle = 17
- Right = [22 44 45]

Then put Middle into the parent node (in the position where the '10' had been) with Left and Right as its children {**Figure** 7.64}.

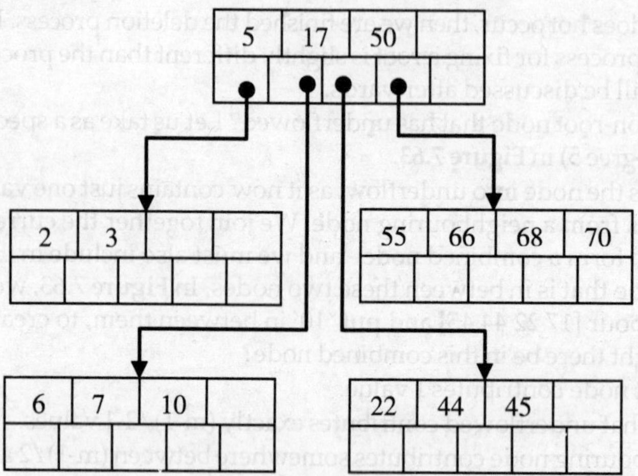

Figure 7.64 5-way B-tree

Case 2: Suppose, on the other hand, that the neighbouring node contains exactly (m-1)/2 values. Then the total number of values in the combined node is 1 + ((m-1)/2 - 1) + ((m-1)/2) = (m-1)

In this case the combined node contains the right number of values to be treated as a node. So we make it into a node and remove from the parent node the value that has been incorporated into the new, combined node. As a concrete example of this case, suppose that, in the tree of **Figure** 7.63, we had deleted 3 instead of 6. The node [2 3] underflows when 3 is removed. It would be combined with its more populous neighbour [6 7] and the intervening value from the parent [5] to create the combined node [2 5 6 7]. This contains 4 values, so it can be used without further processing. The result would be **Figure** 7.65.

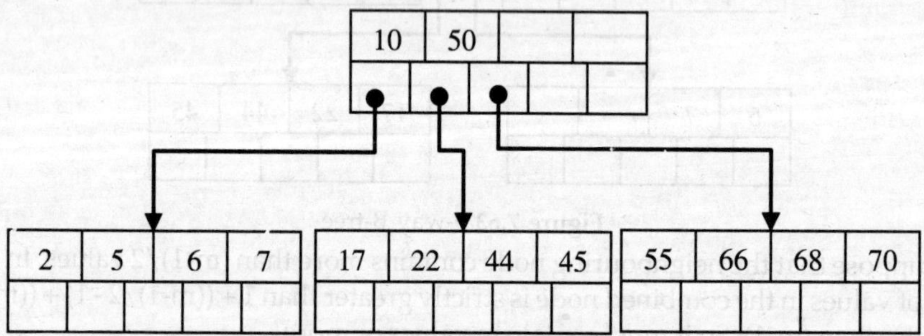

Figure 7.65 5-way B-tree

It is very important to note that the parent node now has one fewer value. This might cause *it* to underflow - imagine that 5 had been the *only* value in the parent node. If the parent node underflows, it is treated in exactly the same way - combined with *its* more populous neighbor, etc. The underflow processing repeats at successive levels until no underflow occurs or until the root underflows (the processing for root-underflow is described next).

Now let us consider the root. For the root to underflow, it must have originally contained just one value, which now has been removed. If the root is also a leaf, then there is no problem: in this case the tree has become completely empty. If the root is not a leaf, it must originally have had two subtrees (because it originally contained one value). How could it possibly underflow?

The deletion process always starts at a leaf and therefore, the only way the root may have its value removed is through the Case 2 processing just described: the root's two children have been combined, along with the root's only value to form a single node. But if the root's two children are now a single node, then *that node* can be used as the new root, and the current root (which has underflowed) can simply be deleted. To illustrate this, suppose we delete 7 from this B-tree (m=5) {**Figure** 7.66}.

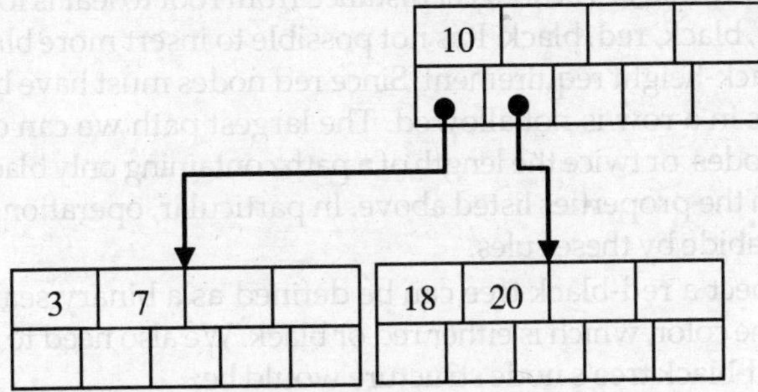

Figure 7.66 5-way B-tree

The node [3 7] would underflow, and the combined node [3 10 18 20] would be created. This has 4 values, which is acceptable when m=5. So it is kept as a node, and '10' is removed from the parent node - the root. This is the only circumstance in which underflow can occur in a root that is not a leaf. The situation is **Figure** 7.67. Clearly, the current root node, now empty, can be deleted and its child used as the new root.

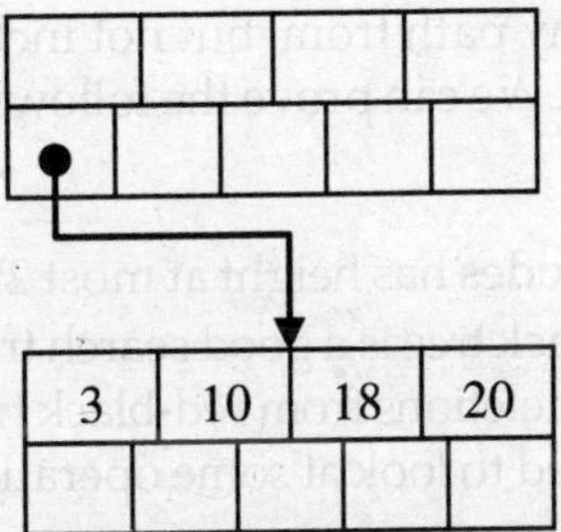

Figure 7.67 5-way B-tree

A variation of the B-tree, known as a **B+-tree** {detailed description is in **chapter 11**} considers all the keys in nodes except the leaves as dummies. All keys are duplicated in the leaves. This has the advantage that is all the leaves are linked together sequentially; the entire tree may be scanned without visiting the higher nodes at all.

7.13 RED-BLACK TREE

Binary search trees work best when they are balanced or the path length from root to any leaf is within some bounds. The red-black tree algorithm is a method for balancing trees. The name derives from the fact that each node is colored red or black, and the color of the node is instrumental in determining the balance of the tree. During insertion and deletion operations, nodes may be rotated to maintain tree balance. Both average and worst-case search time is **O**($\log_2$ n). A red-black tree is a balanced binary search tree {**Figure** 7.68} with the following properties:

1. Every node is colored red or black.
2. Every leaf is a NULL node, and is colored black.
3. If a node is red, then both its children are black.
4. Every simple path from a node to a descendant leaf contains the same number of black nodes.

The number of black nodes on a path from root to leaf is known as the black-height of a tree. These properties guarantee that any path from the root to a leaf is no more than twice as long as any other. To see why this is true, consider a tree with a black height of two. The shortest distance from root to leaf is two, where both nodes are black. The longest distance from root to leaf is four, where the nodes are colored (root to leaf): red, black, red, black. It is not possible to insert more black nodes as this would violate property 4, the black-height requirement. Since red nodes must have black children (property 3), having two red nodes in a row is not allowed. The largest path we can construct consists of an alternation of red-black nodes, or twice the length of a path containing only black nodes. All operations on the tree must maintain the properties listed above. In particular, operations, which insert or delete items from the tree must abide by these rules.

In programming aspect a red-black tree can be defined as a binary search tree with one extra attribute for each node: the color, which is either red or black. We also need to keep track of the parent of each node, so that a red-black tree's node structure would be:

```
struct t_red_black_node
{
enum { red, black } colour;
void *item;
struct t_red_black_node *left, *right, *parent;
};
```

The number of black nodes on any path from, but not including, a node **x** to a leaf is called the black-height of a node, denoted **bh(x)**. We can prove the following lemma:

Lemma

A red-black tree with **n** internal nodes has height at most **2**$\log_2$ **(n+1)**.

This demonstrates why the red-black tree is a good search tree: it can always be searched in **O(**$\log_2$ **n)** time. As with heaps, additions and deletions from red-black trees destroy the red-black property, so we need to restore it. To do this we need to look at some operations on red-black trees.

Rotations

A rotation is a local operation in a search tree that preserves inorder traversal key ordering.

Note that in both trees, an inorder traversal yields:

```
A x B y C
```

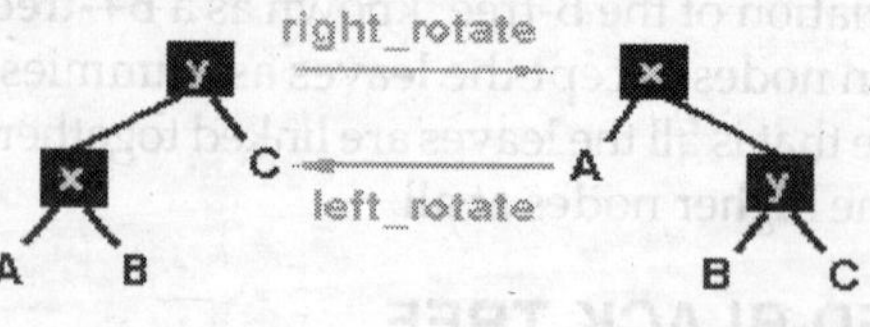

The left_rotate operation may be encoded:

```
left_rotate( Tree T, node x ) {
 node y;
```

```
y = x->right;
/* Turn y's left sub-tree into x's right sub-tree */
x->right = y->left;
if ( y->left != NULL )
y->left->parent = x;
/* y's new parent was x's parent */
y->parent = x->parent;
/* Set the parent to point to y instead of x */
/* First see whether we're at the root */
if ( x->parent == NULL ) T->root = y;
else
if ( x == (x->parent)->left )
/* x was on the left of its parent */
x->parent->left = y;
else
/* x must have been on the right */
x->parent->right = y;
/* Finally, put x on y's left */
y->left = x;
x->parent = y;
}
```

Insertion

To insert a node, we search the tree for an insertion point, and add the node to the tree. A new node replaces an existing NULL node at the bottom of the tree, and has two NULL nodes as children. In the implementation, a NULL node is simply a pointer to a common sentinel node {**Figure** 7.69} that is colored black. After insertion, the new node is colored red. Then the parent of the node is examined to determine if the red-black tree properties have been violated. If necessary, we recolor the node and do rotations to balance the tree.

By inserting a red node with two NULL children, we have preserved black-height property (property 4). However, property 3 may be violated. This property states that both children of a red node must be black. Although both children of the new node are black (they are NULL), consider the case where the parent of the new node is red. Inserting a red node under a red parent would violate this property. There are two cases to consider (Note the detailed is marked with **Figures** {7.70-7.77}:

- **Red parent, red uncle: Figure 7.71** illustrates a red-red violation. Node 4 (marked x) is the newly inserted node, with both parent and uncle colored red. A simple re-coloring removes the red-red violation {**Figure** 7.72}. After re-coloring, the grandparent (node 7) must be checked for validity, as its parent may be red. Note that this has the effect of propagating a red node up the tree. On completion, the root of the tree is marked black. If it was originally red, then this has the effect of increasing the black-height of the tree.
- **Red parent, black uncle: Figure 7.73** illustrates a red-red violation, where the uncle is colored black. Here the nodes may be rotated, with the subtrees adjusted as shown {**Figure** 7.74-7.76}. At this point the algorithm may terminate as there are no red-red conflicts and the top of the subtree is colored black. Note that if node **x** was originally a right child, a left rotation would be done first, making the node a left child.

Each adjustment made while inserting a node causes us to travel up the tree one step. At most 1 rotation (2 if the node is a right child) will be done, as the algorithm terminates in this case. The technique for deletion is similar.

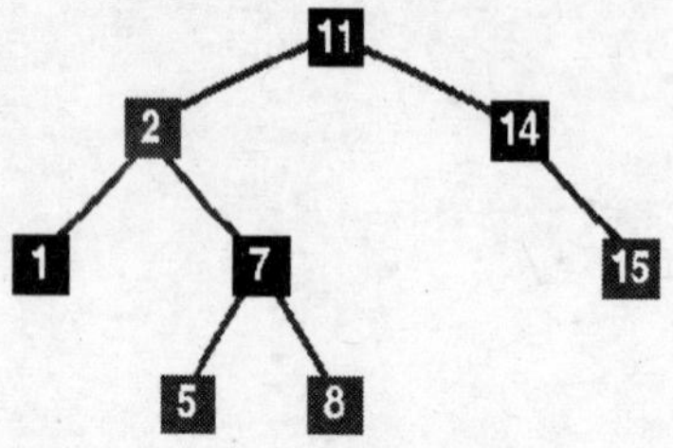

A basic red-black tree

Figure 7.68. Red-Black Tree

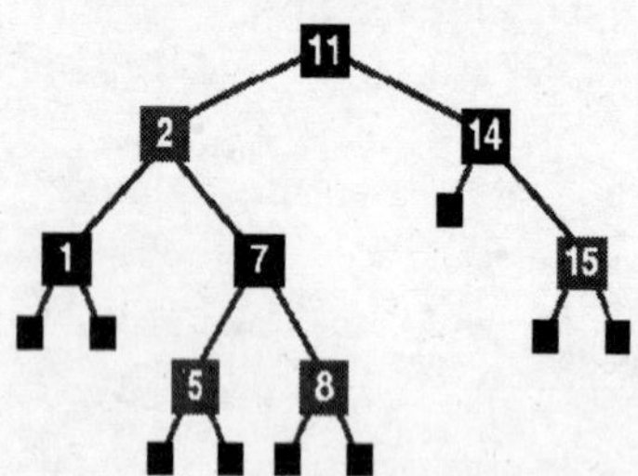

Basic red-black tree with the sentinel nodes added. Implementations of the red-black tree algorithms will usually include the sentinel nodes as a convenient means of flagging that we have reached a leaf node.
They are the NULL black nodes of property 2.

Figure 7.69. Red-Black Tree

Insertion algorithm is somewhat complex and involves a number of cases. Note that we start by inserting the new node, x, in the tree just as we would for any other binary tree, using the rb_insert function. This new node is labeled red, and possibly destroys the red-black property. The main loop moves up the tree, restoring the red-black property.

```
rb_insert( Tree T, node x ) {
  /* Insert in the tree in the usual way */
  tree_insert( T, x );
  /* Now restore the red-black property */
  x->colour = red;
  while ( (x != T->root) && (x->parent->colour == red) ) {
  if ( x->parent == x->parent->parent->left ) {
  /* If x's parent is a left, y is x's right 'uncle' */
  y = x->parent->parent->right;
  if ( y->colour == red ) {
  /* case 1 - change the colours */
  x->parent->colour = black;
  y->colour = black;
  x->parent->parent->colour = red;
  /* Move x up the tree */
  x = x->parent->parent;
  }
  else {
  /* y is a black node */
  if ( x == x->parent->right ) {
```

```
/* and x is to the right */
/* case 2 - move x up and rotate */
x = x->parent;
left_rotate( T, x );
}
/* case 3 */
x->parent->colour = black;
x->parent->parent->colour = red;
right_rotate( T, x->parent->parent );
}
}
else {
/* repeat the "if" part with right and left
exchanged */
}
/* Colour the root black */
T->root->colour = black;
}
```

Examination of the code reveals only one loop. In that loop, the node at the root of the sub-tree whose red-black property we are trying to restore, x, may be moved up the tree at least one level in each iteration of the loop. Since the tree originally has **O($\log_2$ n)** height, there are **O($\log_2$ n)** iterations. The rb_insert routine also has **O($\log_2$ n)** complexity, so overall the rb_insert routine also has **O($\log_2$ n)** complexity. Trees which remain **balanced** - and thus guarantee **O($\log_2$ n)** search times - in a dynamic environment or more importantly, since any tree can be re-balanced - but at considerable cost can be re-balanced in **O($\log_2$ n)** time.

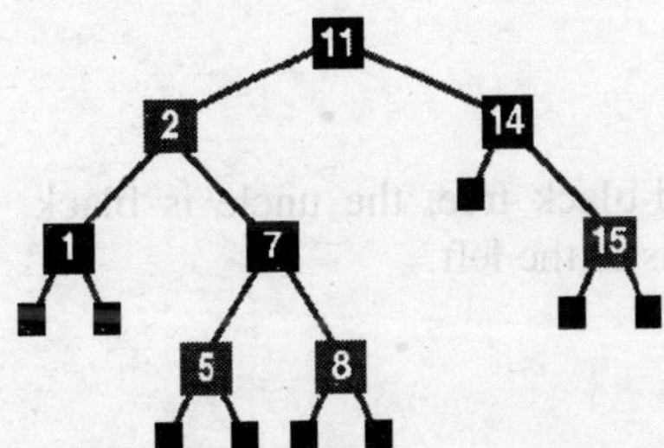

Figure 7.70. Red-Black Tree

Here's the original tree. Note that in Fig. 7.71 to 7.77 the black sentinel nodes have been omitted.

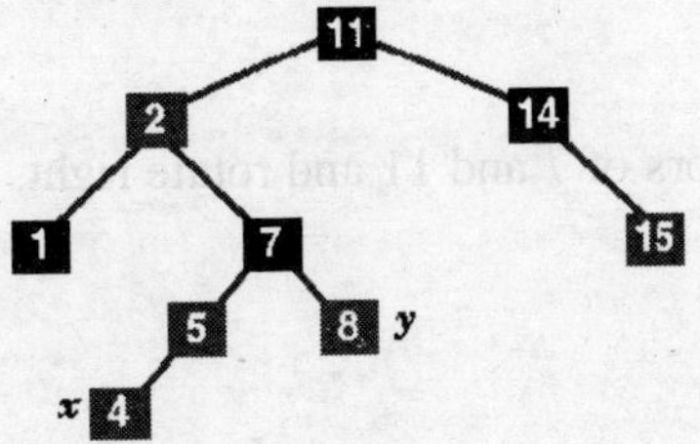

Figure 7.71. Red-Black Tree

The tree insert routine has just been called to insert node "4" into the tree. This is no longer a red-black tree - there are two successive red nodes on the path 11 - 2 - 7 - 5 – 4. Mark the new node, x, and it's uncle, y. y is red, so we have case 1. [Note – light grey colour node is red node]

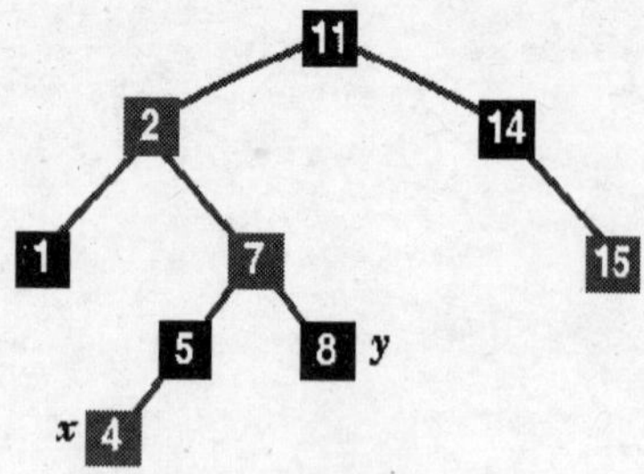

Change the colors of nodes 5, 7 and 8.

Figure 7.72. Red-Black Tree

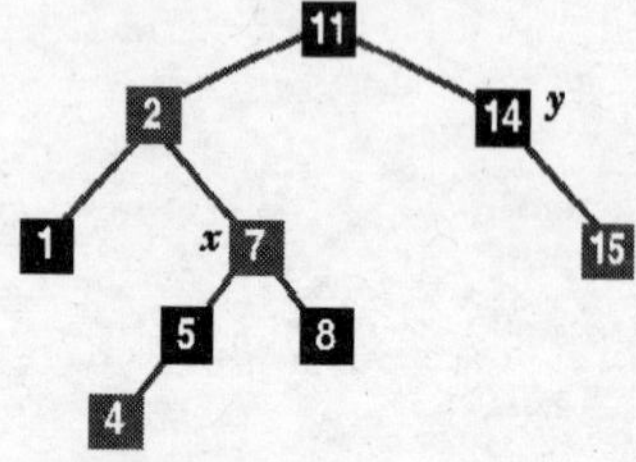

Move x up to its grandparent, 7. x's parent (2) is still red, so this is not a red-black tree yet. Mark the uncle, y. In this case, the uncle is black, so we have case 2.

Figure 7.73. Red-Black Tree

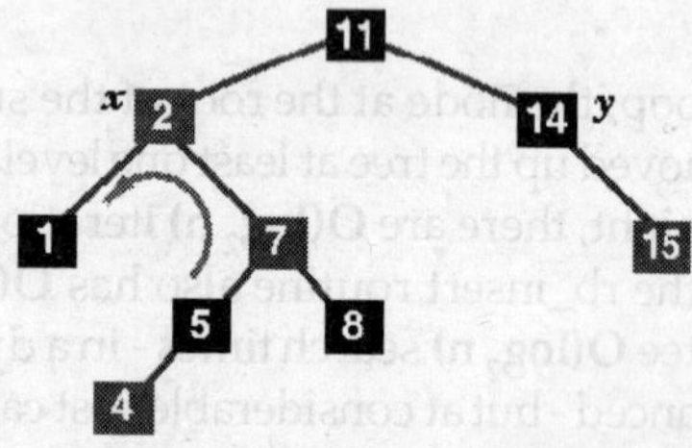

Move x up and rotate left.

Figure 7.74. Red-Black Tree

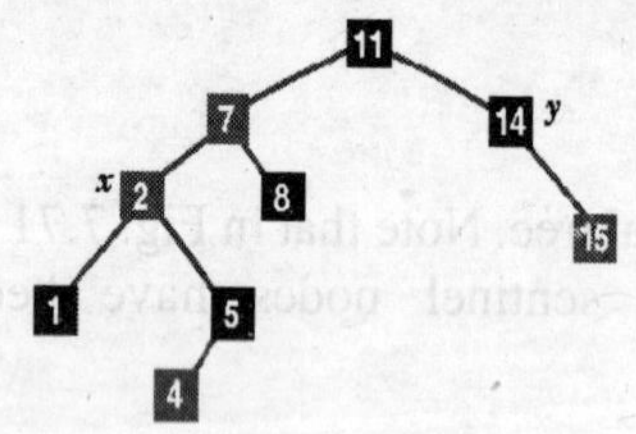

Still not a red-black tree, the uncle is black, but x's parent is to the left.

Figure 7.75. Red-Black Tree

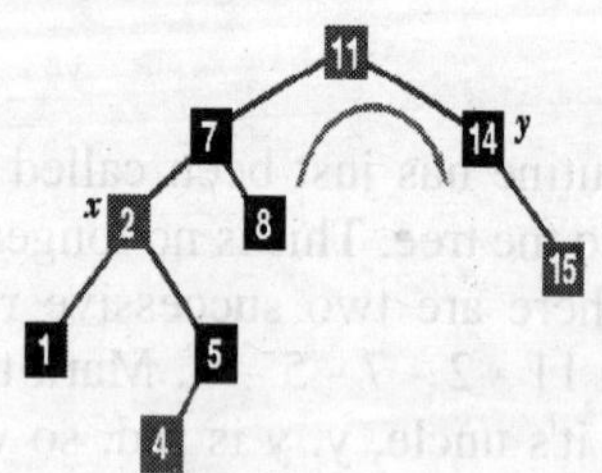

Change the colors of 7 and 11 and rotate right.

Figure 7.76. Red-Black Tree

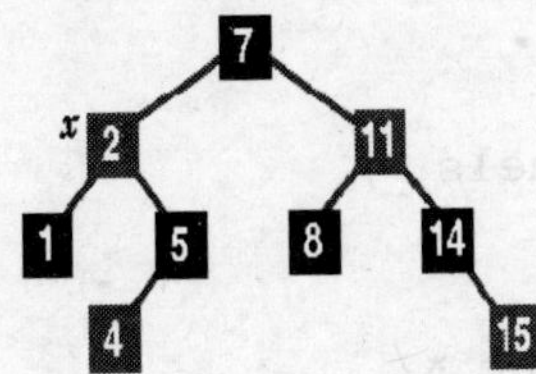

This is now a red-black tree, $O(\log_2 n)$ time.

Figure 7.77. Red-Black Tree

The implementation code is as follows:

```
/* Red-Black Tree */
/* RBTree.c */
#include <stdio.h>
#include <stdlib.h>
#include <string.h>
#include <stdarg.h>

/* implementation dependend declarations */
typedef enum {
 STATUS_OK,
 STATUS_MEM_EXHAUSTED,
 STATUS_DUPLICATE_KEY,
 STATUS_KEY_NOT_FOUND
} statusEnum;

typedef int keyType; /* type of key */

/* user data stored in tree */
typedef struct {
 int stuff; /* optional related data */
} recType;

#define compLT(a,b) (a < b)
#define compEQ(a,b) (a == b)

/* implementation independent declarations */
/* Red-Black tree description */
typedef enum { BLACK, RED } nodeColor;

typedef struct nodeTag {
 struct nodeTag *left; /* left child */
 struct nodeTag *right; /* right child */
 struct nodeTag *parent; /* parent */
 nodeColor color; /* node color (BLACK, RED) */
 keyType key; /* key used for searching */
 recType rec; /* user data */
```

```
} nodeType;

#define NIL &sentinel /* all leafs are sentinels */
nodeType sentinel = { NIL, NIL, 0, BLACK, 0};

nodeType *root = NIL; /* root of Red-Black tree */

void rotateLeft(nodeType *x) {

 /***************************
 * rotate node x to left *
 ***************************/

 nodeType *y = x->right;

 /* establish x->right link */
 x->right = y->left;
 if (y->left != NIL) y->left->parent = x;

 /* establish y->parent link */
 if (y != NIL) y->parent = x->parent;
 if (x->parent) {
 if (x == x->parent->left)
 x->parent->left = y;
 else
 x->parent->right = y;
 } else {
 root = y;
 }

 /* link x and y */
 y->left = x;
 if (x != NIL) x->parent = y;
}

void rotateRight(nodeType *x) {

 /****************************
 * rotate node x to right *
 ****************************/

 nodeType *y = x->left;

 /* establish x->left link */
 x->left = y->right;
```

```
    if (y->right != NIL) y->right->parent = x;

    /* establish y->parent link */
    if (y != NIL) y->parent = x->parent;
    if (x->parent) {
    if (x == x->parent->right)
    x->parent->right = y;
    else
    x->parent->left = y;
    } else {
    root = y;
    }

    /* link x and y */
    y->right = x;
    if (x != NIL) x->parent = y;
}

void insertFixup(nodeType *x) {

    /*************************************
     * maintain Red-Black tree balance *
     * after inserting node x *
     *************************************/

    /* check Red-Black properties */
    while (x != root && x->parent->color == RED) {
    /* we have a violation */
    if (x->parent == x->parent->parent->left) {
    nodeType *y = x->parent->parent->right;
    if (y->color == RED) {

    /* uncle is RED */
    x->parent->color = BLACK;
    y->color = BLACK;
    x->parent->parent->color = RED;
    x = x->parent->parent;
    } else {

    /* uncle is BLACK */
    if (x == x->parent->right) {
    /* make x a left child */
    x = x->parent;
    rotateLeft(x);
    }
```

```
/* recolor and rotate */
x->parent->color = BLACK;
x->parent->parent->color = RED;
rotateRight(x->parent->parent);
}
} else {

/* mirror image of above code */
nodeType *y = x->parent->parent->left;
if (y->color == RED) {

/* uncle is RED */
x->parent->color = BLACK;
y->color = BLACK;
x->parent->parent->color = RED;
x = x->parent->parent;
} else {

/* uncle is BLACK */
if (x == x->parent->left) {
x = x->parent;
rotateRight(x);
}
x->parent->color = BLACK;
x->parent->parent->color = RED;
rotateLeft(x->parent->parent);
}
}
}
root->color = BLACK;
}

statusEnum insert(keyType key, recType *rec) {
nodeType *current, *parent, *x;

/*********************************************
* allocate node for data and insert in tree *
*********************************************/

/* find future parent */
current = root;
parent = 0;
while (current != NIL) {
if (compEQ(key, current->key))
return STATUS_DUPLICATE_KEY;
```

```
parent = current;
current = compLT(key, current->key) ?
current->left : current->right;
}

/* setup new node */
if ((x = malloc (sizeof(*x))) == 0)
return STATUS_MEM_EXHAUSTED;
x->parent = parent;
x->left = NIL;
x->right = NIL;
x->color = RED;
x->key = key;
x->rec = *rec;

/* insert node in tree */
if(parent) {
if(compLT(key, parent->key))
parent->left = x;
else
parent->right = x;
} else {
root = x;
}

insertFixup(x);

return STATUS_OK;
}

void deleteFixup(nodeType *x) {

/*************************************
* maintain Red-Black tree balance *
* after deleting node x *
*************************************/

while (x != root && x->color == BLACK) {
if (x == x->parent->left) {
nodeType *w = x->parent->right;
if (w->color == RED) {
w->color = BLACK;
x->parent->color = RED;
rotateLeft (x->parent);
w = x->parent->right;
```

```
}
if (w->left->color == BLACK && w->right->color == BLACK) {
w->color = RED;
x = x->parent;
} else {
if (w->right->color == BLACK) {
w->left->color = BLACK;
w->color = RED;
rotateRight (w);
w = x->parent->right;
}
w->color = x->parent->color;
x->parent->color = BLACK;
w->right->color = BLACK;
rotateLeft (x->parent);
x = root;
}
} else {
nodeType *w = x->parent->left;
if (w->color == RED) {
w->color = BLACK;
x->parent->color = RED;
rotateRight (x->parent);
w = x->parent->left;
}
if (w->right->color == BLACK && w->left->color == BLACK) {
w->color = RED;
x = x->parent;
} else {
if (w->left->color == BLACK) {
w->right->color = BLACK;
w->color = RED;
rotateLeft (w);
w = x->parent->left;
}
w->color = x->parent->color;
x->parent->color = BLACK;
w->left->color = BLACK;
rotateRight (x->parent);
x = root;
}
}
}
x->color = BLACK;
}
```

```
statusEnum delete(keyType key) {
nodeType *x, *y, *z;

/*****************************
* delete node z from tree *
*****************************/

/* find node in tree */
z = root;
while(z != NIL) {
if(compEQ(key, z->key))
break;
else
z = compLT(key, z->key) ? z->left : z->right;
}
if (z == NIL) return STATUS_KEY_NOT_FOUND;

if (z->left == NIL || z->right == NIL) {
/* y has a NIL node as a child */
y = z;
} else {
/* find tree successor with a NIL node as a child */
y = z->right;
while (y->left != NIL) y = y->left;
}

/* x is y's only child */
if (y->left != NIL)
x = y->left;
else
x = y->right;

/* remove y from the parent chain */
x->parent = y->parent;
if (y->parent)
if (y == y->parent->left)
y->parent->left = x;
else
y->parent->right = x;
else
root = x;

if (y != z) {
z->key = y->key;
z->rec = y->rec;
}
```

```
  if (y->color == BLACK)
  deleteFixup (x);

  free (y);
  return STATUS_OK;
 }

statusEnum find(keyType key, recType *rec) {

  /******************************
  * find node containing data *
  *******************************/

  nodeType *current = root;
  while(current != NIL) {
  if(compEQ(key, current->key)) {
  *rec = current->rec;
  return STATUS_OK;
  } else {
  current = compLT (key, current->key) ?
  current->left : current->right;
  }
  }
  return STATUS_KEY_NOT_FOUND;
 }

void main(int argc, char **argv) {
 int maxnum, ct, n;
 recType rec;
 keyType key;
 statusEnum status;
 maxnum = atoi(argv[1]);
 printf("maxnum = %d\n", maxnum);
 for (ct = maxnum; ct; ct--) {
 key = rand() % 9 + 1;
 if ((status = find(key, &rec)) == STATUS_OK) {
 status = delete(key);
 if (status) printf("fail: status = %d\n", status);
 } else {
 status = insert(key, &rec);
 if (status) printf("fail: status = %d\n", status);
 }
 }
}
```

7.14 THREADED BINARY TREE

Because of the importance of linked binary trees, it is worth while to develop non-recursive algorithms to manipulate them, and to study the time and space requirement of these algorithms. We shall find that, by changing the NULL links in a binary tree to special links called threads, it is possible to perform traversals, insertions and deletions without using either a stack or recursion. A binary tree with **n** nodes, when **n >0** has exactly **n+1** NULL links. A **threaded binary tree** defined as follows: "A **binary tree** is **threaded** by making all right child pointers that would normally be null point to the inorder successor of the node (if it exists), and all left child pointers that would normally be null point to the inorder predecessor of the node."

In a right-threaded binary tree each NULL right link (RLink) is replaced by a special link to the successor of that node under inorder traversal, called a right thread. Using right threads we shall find that it easy to perform an inorder traversal of the binary tree, since we need to follow either an ordinary link or a thread to find the next node to visit. If one wants to define left thread, it is required to replace each NULL left link (LLink) by a special link to the predecessor of the node under inorder traversal. Then the resulting tree is called a fully threaded binary tree. **Figure 7.78(a)** illustrates a fully threaded binary tree other forms of threaded tree are shown in **Figure 7.78(b-c)**.

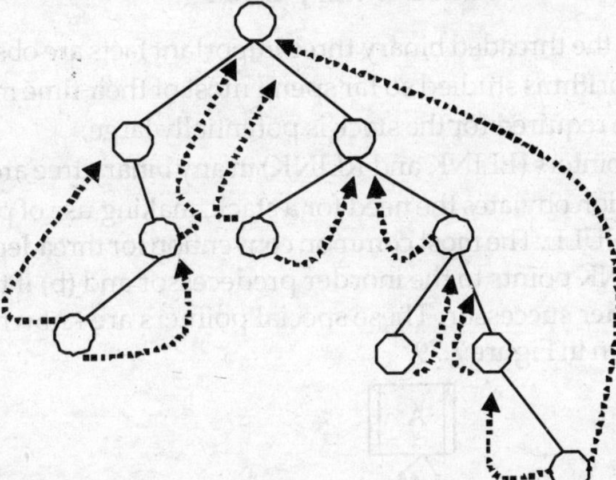

Figure 7.78(a) A **threaded tree**, with the special threading links shown by dashed arrows (Fully threaded tree binary tree (Two-way))

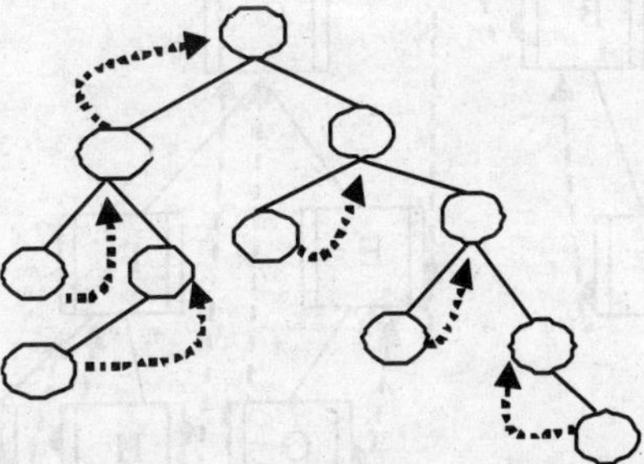

Figure 7.78(b) A **threaded tree**, with the special threading links shown by dashed arrows (**One way threaded tree binary tree)**

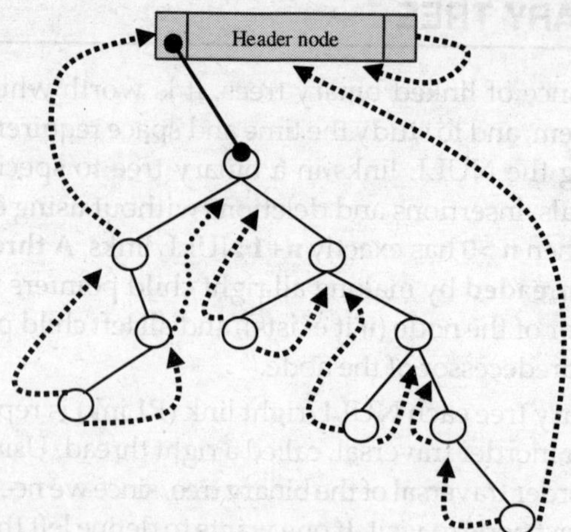

Figure 7.78(c) A **threaded tree**, with the special threading links shown by dashed arrows (Two-way threading with header node)

7.14.1 Representation of Threaded binary trees

From the definition of the threaded binary three important facts are observed which are as under:

(a) the traversal algorithms studied so far spend most of their time manipulating a stack;

(b) the storage space required for the stack is potentially large;

(c) the majority of pointers (LLINK and RLINK) in any binary tree are NULL.

Threaded representation obviates the need for a stack, making use of pointer fields which would otherwise have the value NULL. The most common convention for threaded representation is (a) if the left subtree is empty, LLINK points to the inorder predecessor and (b) if the right subtree is empty, RLINK points to the inorder successor. These special pointers are known as threads. Consider the threaded binary tree shown in Figure 7.79.

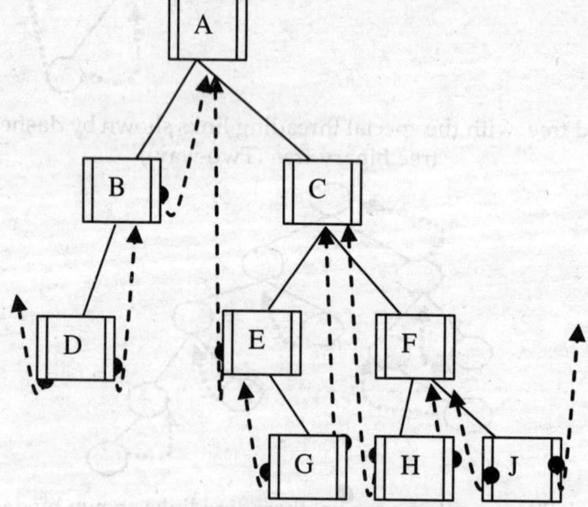

Fugure 7.79. Threaded Binary Tree

But any program examining the tree must be able to distinguish between a branch and a thread. So we introduce two additional fields into each node giving us, for threaded trees, nodes of the following form:

LTAG	LLINK	INFO	RTAG	RLINK

LTAG and RTAG obviously need be only one-bit fields. Because of word-length considerations, these fields will often not make any difference to the amount of storage used per node; the convention adopted, for instance, might be to use negated pointer values to indicate threads. The following convention may be used:

if LTAG = 0, LLINK points to the left child;
if LTAG = 1, LLINK points to the inorder predecessor;
if RTAG = 0, RLINK points to the right child;
if RTAG = 1, RLINK points to the inorder successor.

But this is only one of a number of ways of threading a tree. For example, a common method is right-threading, where each node has four fields (LLINK, INFO, RTAG, and RLINK). LLINK is NULL if the left subtree is empty, and RTAG and RLINK are as above. In the representation of a threaded binary tree, it is convenient to use a special node HEAD — the "list" head — which is always present, even for an empty tree, when its value is:

Conventionally, HEAD.RLINK = HEAD and HEAD.RTAG = 0 for any threaded binary tree. The tree shown earlier would therefore be represented as shown in Figure 7.80 as:

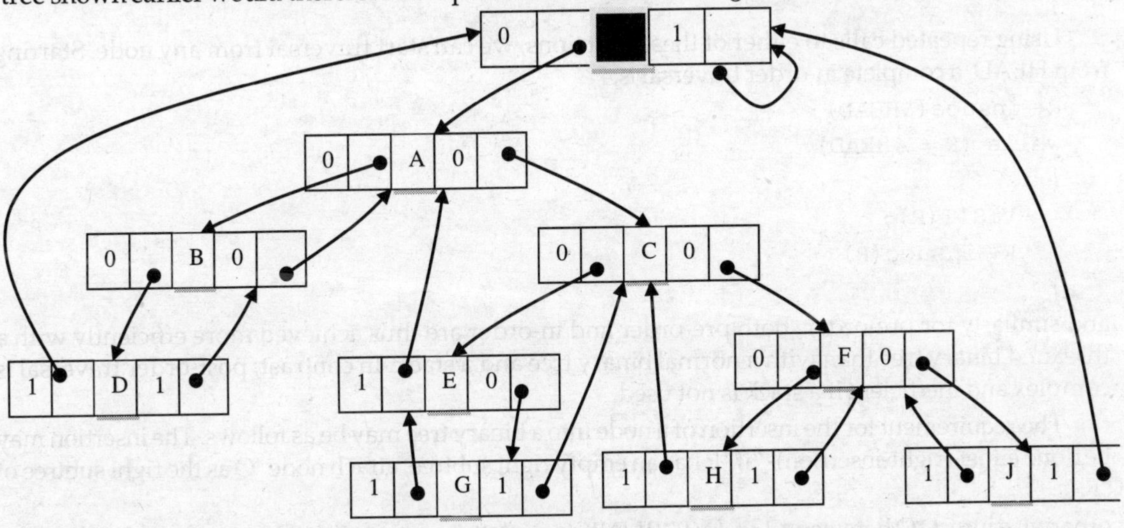

Figure 7.80. Threaded Binary Tree representation

Without having to use a stack, it is a simple matter to traverse a threaded binary tree in inorder. Further, given a pointer P to any node in the tree, we can find its inorder successor directly as follows:

```
Pointer insucc(Pointer P)
{
```

```
if (P→RTAG = 1)
return P→RLINK;
else{
    P←P→RLINK;
while (P→LTAG = 0)
P←P→LLINK;
return P;
}
}
```

Similarly, a function to produce the pre-order successor:

```
Pointer presucc(Pointer P)
{
if (P→LTAG = 0)
return P→LLINK;
else{
while (P→RTAG = 1)
    P←P→RLINK;
return P→RLINK;
}
}
```

Using repeated calls to either of these functions, we can start traversal from any node. Starting from HEAD, a complete in-order traversal is:

```
R←insucc(&HEAD);
while (R = &HEAD)
{
    VISIT(R);
    R←insucc(R);
}
```

and similarly for pre-order. Both pre-order and in-order are thus achieved more efficiently with a threaded binary tree than with a normal binary tree and a stack. In contrast, post-order traversal is complex and inefficient if a stack is not used.

The requirement for the insertion of a node into a binary tree may be as follows. The insertion may be done either (right-insertion)- "if *P has an empty right subtree, attach node *Q as the right subtree of *P;

otherwise insert *Q between *P and *(P'!RLINK)," or (left-insertion) "if *P has an empty left subtree, attach node *Q as the left subtree of *P; otherwise insert *Q between *P and *(P'!LLINK)." For example inserting *Q between *P and *R will be interpreted as the first of the following alternatives rather than the second:

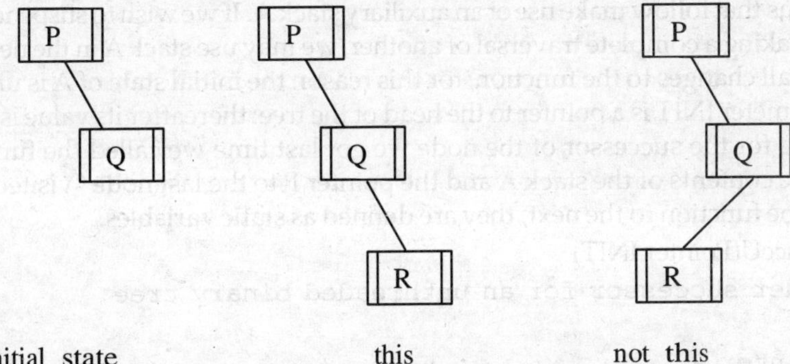

Initial state this not this

The insertion operations are almost trivial for an unthreaded binary tree. For a threaded tree they turn out to be reasonably straightforward. The following is for right-insertion:

```
Q→RLINK←P'!RLINK;
Q→RTAG←P'!RTAG;
Q→LLINK←P;
Q→LTAG←1;
P→RLINK←Q;
P→RTAG←0;
if (Q→RTAG = 0)
insucc(Q)→LLINK  ! Q;
```

In many machine representations RLINK/RTAG can be set by a single machine instruction, making this an efficient process provided the in-order successor function insucc(Q) is not called; and this function will never be called when Q is inserted as a leaf (which it usually is during initial set-up). A similar algorithm can be defined for left-insertion.

For a threaded binary tree, it is possible to find the pre-order or in-order successor of any given node without performing a complete tree traversal. For an unthreaded tree, the functions presuccU(P) and insuccU(P) must rely on previous traversal history in a stack (unless they are to be wildly inefficient), and clearly the parameter P is redundant since what we must ask for is the successor of the node we got last time. This leads to the conclusion that, for unthreaded trees, the successor functions are really calls to co-routines (or co-functions) — with resumption of the calling pro- gram substituted for VISIT. However, it can be convenient to think of these successor functions as subroutines (or functions) and this can be realized by:

(a) providing every binary tree with a list-head, rather than a tree pointer
(b) adopting the convention that, for an unthreaded tree, the head node is of the form:

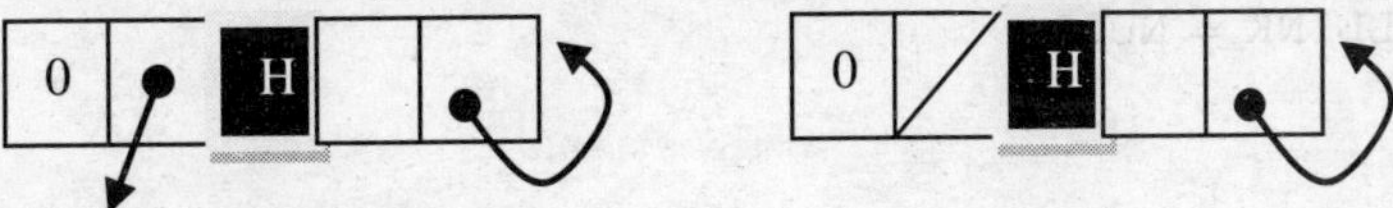

Root of the tree for an empty tree

(c) calling the function first to find the successor of the head (which, in both cases, will give the first node in the appropriate traversal order)
(d) ensuring that the calling program recognizes the end of the traversal by being given the value HEAD by the function. (If it does not recognize this, another traversal will begin when the function is next called.)

The algorithms that follow make use of an auxiliary stack A. If we wish to suspend traversal of one tree while undertaking a complete traversal of another, we may use stack A in the nested traversal by making some small changes to the function; for this reason the initial state of A is undefined. On the first call, the parameter INIT is a pointer to the head of the tree; thereafter its value is NULL, since we are simply asking for the successor of the node we got last time we called the function. Since it is necessary that the contents of the stack A and the pointer P to the last node "visited" are preserved from one call of the function to the next, they are defined as static variables.

```
Pointer presuccU(Pointer INIT)
// pre-order successor for an unthreaded binary tree
{
static Pointer P;
static Pointer_stack A;
if (INIT = NULL)
P ← INIT;
if (P→LLINK = NULL)
{
    STACK(A,P);
P ← P→LLINK;
}else{
    while (P→RLINK = NULL)
P ← UNSTACK(A);
P ← P→RLINK;
}
return P;
}
Pointer insuccU(Pointer INIT) /* in-order successor for an unthreaded binary tree */
{
static Pointer P;
static Pointer_stack A;
if (INIT = NULL) P ← INIT;
if (P→RLINK = NULL)
P  ! UNSTACK(A);
else{
P ← P→RLINK;
while (P→LLINK = NULL)
{
STACK(A,P);
P ← P→LLINK;
}
 }
return P;
}
```

To erase a binary tree: In these algorithms, the nodes of the tree are returned one by one to the storage pool. The reasons for selecting the in-order traversal sequence for this purpose should be clear:

```
/* For an unthreaded tree */
Q ← insuccU(&HEAD);
while (Q ≠ &HEAD){
R ← insuccU(NULL);
    RELEASE(Q);
 Q ← R;
}
HEAD.LLINK ← NULL;
```

```
/* For a threaded tree */

Q ← insucc(&HEAD);
while (Q ≠ &HEAD)
{
       R ← insucc(Q);
       RELEASE(Q);
Q← R;
}
HEAD.LLINK ← &HEAD;
HEAD.LTAG ← 1;
```

To thread an unthreaded binary tree: Assume that the layout of each node is that appropriate to a threaded tree, i.e., the LTAG and RTAG fields are present in all nodes including HEAD, but that in the initial (unthreaded) version, these fields are not used, and a node with an empty left or right subtree has LLINK = NULL or RLINK = NULL (except for HEAD.RLINK).

```
void ThreadTree(Node HEAD)
{
   Pointer Q, R;
Q ← &HEAD:
R ← insuccU(&HEAD);
InsertThread(Q, R);
while (R ≠ &HEAD)
{
   Q ← R;
   R ← insuccU(NULL);
   InsertThread(Q, R);
}
}

void InsertThread(Pointer q, Pointer r){
if (q→RLINK = NULL)
{
   q→RLINK ← r;
   q→RTAG ← 1;
   r→LTAG ← 0;
```

```
}else if(r→LLINK = NULL)
{  r→LLINK ← q;
   r→LTAG ← 1;
   q→RTAG ← 0;
}
}
```

7.15 RELATION BETWEEN LEAF NODES AND NON LEAF NODES IN A BINARY TREE

A Binary tree has n nodes. Let n1 be the number of nodes of degree one, n0 be the number of nodes of degree 0, leaf nodes are the ones which have degree 0 and n2 be the number of nodes of degree 2. Root node is one example of a degree 2 node if it has left and right sub-trees. Thus, the total number of nodes in the tree may be computed as

$n = n0 + n1 + n2$ ... ... (1)

If we count the number of edges in a binary tree, we see that every node except the root has an incoming edge into it. If E is the number of edges, then $n = E + 1$, i.e., number of edges in a binary tree is one less than the total number of nodes. It is found that each n0 node is not contributing any edge, each n1 node contributes one edge, and each n2 node contributes 2 edges to the total number of edges, E. Thus,

$E = 0*n0 + 1*n1 + 2*n2$

$E = n1 + 2n2$

We know that $n = E + 1$

$n = n1 + 2n2 + 1$ ...(2)

Using equations (1) and (2), we get

$n0 + n1 + n2 = n1 + 2n2 + 1$, i.e., $n0 = n2 + 1$

Note: The number of leaf nodes in a binary tree is one more than the number of degree 2 nodes.

For example in binary tree shown in Figure 7.81(a) total number of nodes are 6 {1, 2, 3, 4, 5, 6}. Number of internal nodes are 3 {1, 2, 3}, number of leaf nodes, i.e., nodes with 0 degree are 3 {4, 5, 6}. Number of nodes with degree 1 are 1 {2} and number of nodes with degree 2 are 2 {1, 3}. Total number of edges is 5.

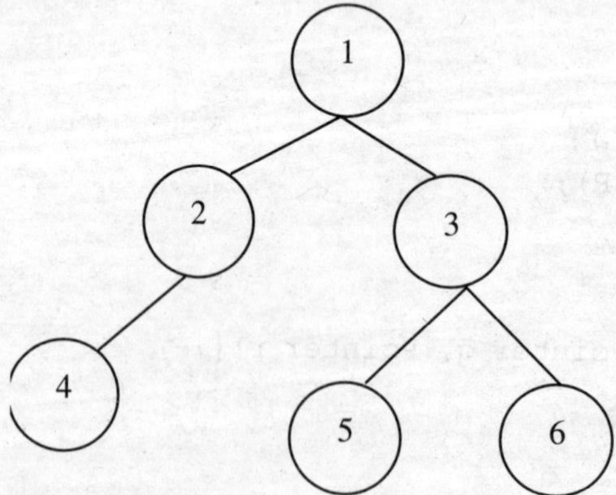

Figure 7.81(a). Binary Tree

In the above binary there are 6 nodes in total, n = 6. We know that n = n0 + n1 + n2, i.e., n = 3 + 1 + 2 also we know that n = E + 1. E is the total number of edges, E = 5, every node has one incoming edge except the root node. Thus, E = n1 + 2n2. In the figure number of nodes with degree 1, i.e., n1 = 1 means only node {2} , which contributes an edge. Number of nodes with degree 2 are 2 {1, 3}, i.e., n2 = 2 nodes {1, 3}and n0 =3, i.e., {4,5,6} doesn't contribute any edge.

E = 1 + 2 * 2 = 5

n = E+ 1 = 6

n0 = n2 + 1 = 2 + 1 = 3

Similarly, in a ternary tree we have n = n0 + n1 + n2 + n3 ... (3)

In equation (3) n3 is the number of nodes of degree 3. If we count the number of edges in a ternary tree, we see that every node except the root has an incoming edge into it. If E is the number of edges, then n = E + 1, i.e. number of edges in a ternary tree is one less than the total number of nodes. If we proceed in the same pattern to count the number of nodes as their degree it is found that each n0 node contributes no edge, each n1 node contributes one edge, each n2 node contributes 2 edges, and each n3 node contributes 3 edges to the total number of edges, E. Thus, E = 0*n0 + 1 * n1 + 2* n2 + 3* n3 , i.e., E = n1 + 2n2 + 3n3. We know that n = E + 1, hence,

n = n1 + 2n2 + 3n3 + 1 ...(4)

from equations (3) and (4), we get

n0 + n1 + n2 +n3= n1 + 2n2 + 3n3 + 1

n0 = n2 + 2n3 + 1 ... (5)

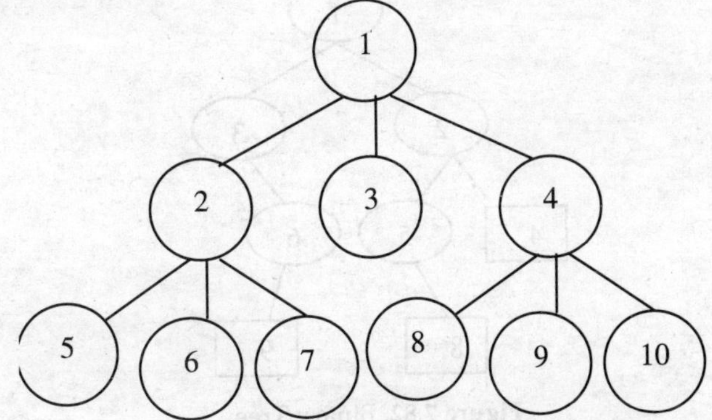

Figure 7.81(b). Ternary Tree

In ternary tree with height 2 at level 0 there is one node, at level 1 there are 1*3 nodes, at level 2 there are 3*3 nodes but in Figure 7.81(b), there are only 2*3 nodes. The maximum number of nodes in ternary tree with height 2 are-1+1*3+3*3+9*3+27*3+.... But in tree Figure 7.81(b) we have 10 nodes. The number of leaf nodes in a ternary tree of n nodes, with each node having 0 or 3 children is n0 = n2 + 2n3 + 1., n2 = 0, n1 = 0 as there are only nodes having degree 0 or degree 3 then n0 = 2n3 + 1. We know that n = n0 + n1 + n2 + n3, thus n = (2n3 + 1) + 0 + 0 + n3, when simplify we get n3 = (n - 1) / 3 and n0 = 2n3 + 1 = 2 ((n-1)/3) + 1 = (2n + 1) / 3 .

In an m-ary tree we have n = n0 + n1 + n2 + n3 + ... +n_m quation 5 can be generalized to n0 = n2 + 2n3 + 3n4 +... + (m-1)n_m + 1. The number of leaf nodes in an m-ary tree of n nodes, with each node having 0 or m children is n1= 0, n2 = 0, n3 = 0, ..., n_{m-1} = 0 as there are only nodes having degree 0 or m then n0 = 0 + 0 + 0 + ... (m-1)n_m + 1 when simplified we get the following n0 = (m-1)n_m + 1. We know that

$n = n0 + n1 + n2 + n3 + \ldots + n_m$
$n = ((m-1)n_m + 1) + 0 + 0 + \ldots + n_m$
$n = m*n_m + 1$
$n_m = (n - 1) / m$
then $n0 = (m-1)n_m + 1 = ((m-1)(n-1) / m) + 1 = (m*n - m - n + m + 1) / m$
$n0 = (m*n - n + 1) / m$

The number of nodes n in a full binary tree, is at least n=2h+1and at most $n=2^{hhhhh+1}-1$, where h is the height of the tree. A tree consisting of only a root node has a height of 0. The number of leaf nodes n0 in a perfect binary tree, is n0=(n+1)/2 because the number $n - n_0 = \sum_{k-0}^{\log(n_0)-1}(2^k) = 2^k - 1 = n_0 - 1$, internal nodes. This means that a perfect binary tree with n0 leaves has n=2n0 – 1 nodes. In a **perfect** full binary tree, $n0=2^h$ thus $n=2^{hhhhh+1}-1$. The maximum possible number of null links (i.e., absent children of the nodes) in a **complete** binary tree of *n* nodes is (*n*+1), where only 1 node exists in bottom-most level to the far left.

7.16 VIEW OF NODES IN BINARY TREE

Given a binary tree, print the values of nodes which would be present in right view of binary tree. A node will be in the right-view if it is the right-most node at its level (imagine level order traversal). For example, consider binary tree in Figure 7.82.

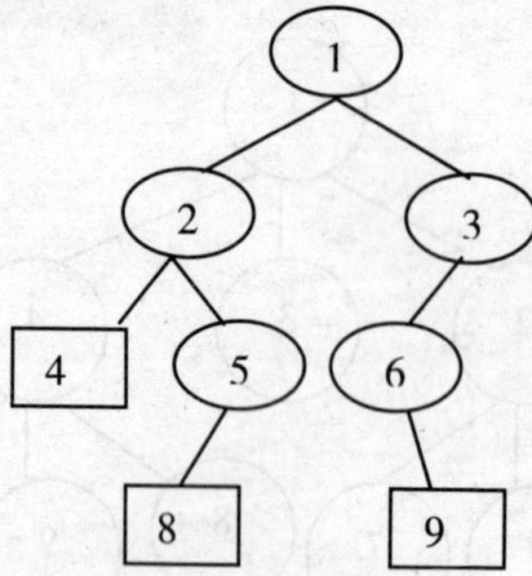

Figure 7.82. Binary Tree

In the above tree,
node 1 is right-most node for level 0.
node 3 is right-most node for level 1.
node 6 is right-most node for level 2.
node 9 is right-most node for level 3.
And therefore right view for this tree is 1,3,6,9

Similarly, for a given binary tree, print the values of nodes which would be present in left view of binary tree. A node will be in the left-view if it is the left-most node at its level (imagine level order traversal). For example, consider binary tree in Figure 7.82.

In the above tree,
node 1 is left-most node for level 0.
node 2 is left-most node for level 1.
node 4 is left-most node for level 2.

node 8 is left-most node for level 3.

And therefore left view for this tree is 1,2,4,8.

Other is also required to be considered, for example for given a binary tree, print the values of nodes which would be present in bottom of view of binary tree. One is not allowed to use level order traversal. Print the node values starting from left-most end. A node will be in the bottom-view if it is the bottommost node at its horizontal distance from the root. Horizontal distance of root from itself is 0. Horizontal distance of right child of root node is 1 and horizontal distance of left child of root node is -1. Horizontal distance of node 'n' from root = horizontal distance of its parent from root + 1, if node 'n' is right child of its parent. Horizontal distance of node 'n' from root = horizontal distance of its parent from root - 1, if node 'n' is left child of its parent. If more than one nodes are at the same horizontal distance and are the bottom-most nodes for that horizontal distance, then one can choose to include either of the nodes in the bottom view. For the following tree {Figure 7.83(a)}:

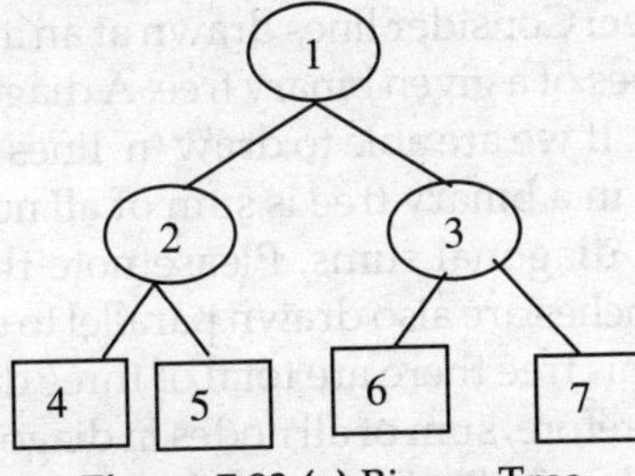

Figure 7.83 (a) Binary Tree

Horizontal distance of 1 = +0
Horizontal distance of 2 = -1
Horizontal distance of 3 = +1
Horizontal distance of 4 = -2
Horizontal distance of 5 = +0
Horizontal distance of 6 = +0
Horizontal distance of 7 = +2
and the bottom view would be 4, 2, 6, 3, 7.

Please note that though there are three nodes(nodes 1,5,6) with horizontal distance of 0, only node 6 is in bottom view because it is at the bottom-most level of all three nodes. Note that we could have chosen to keep node 5 instead of node 6 in bottom view since it is also at the bottom-most layer. For the following tree {Figure 7.83(b)}.:

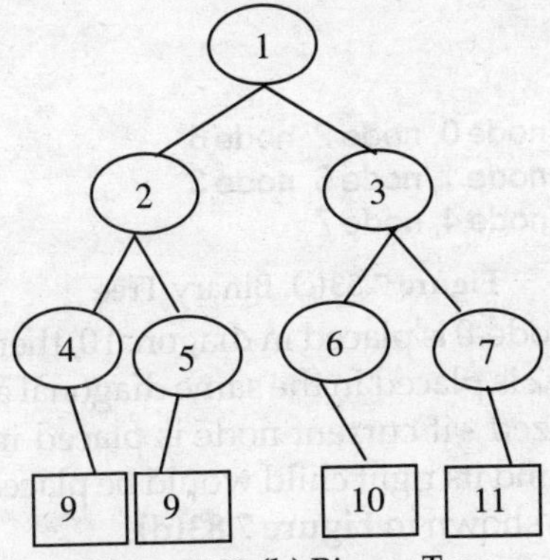

Figure 7.83 (b) Binary Tree

Horizontal distance of 1 = +0
Horizontal distance of 2 = -1
Horizontal distance of 3 = +1
Horizontal distance of 4 = -2
Horizontal distance of 5 = +0
Horizontal distance of 6 = +0
Horizontal distance of 7 = +2
Horizontal distance of 8 = -1 (right child of 4)
Horizontal distance of 9 = -1 (left child of 5)
Horizontal distance of 10 = +1 (right child of 6)
Horizontal distance of 11 = +3 (right child of 7)

and the bottom view would be 4, 9, 6, 10, 7, 11

Diagonal property of binary tree: Consider lines drawn at an angle of 135 degrees(that is slope = -1) which cut through the left branches of a given binary tree. A diagonal is formed by nodes which lie between two such consecutive lines. If we are able to draw 'n' lines then the complete tree is divided into 'n+1' diagonals. Diagonal sum in a binary tree is sum of all node's values lying between these lines. Given a binary tree, print all diagonal sums. Please note that all right branches are drawn parallel to each other and all left branches are also drawn parallel to each other. For example, consider the binary tree in Figure 7.83(c). In this tree there are total of three diagonals. Diagonal-0 has 3 nodes in it: node-0, node-2 and node-6. Therefore, sum of all nodes in diagonal-0 is 8. Similarly, sum of nodes in diagonal-1 is 9(node-1, node-5 and node-3). And sum of nodes in diagonal-2 is 11(node-4, node-7).

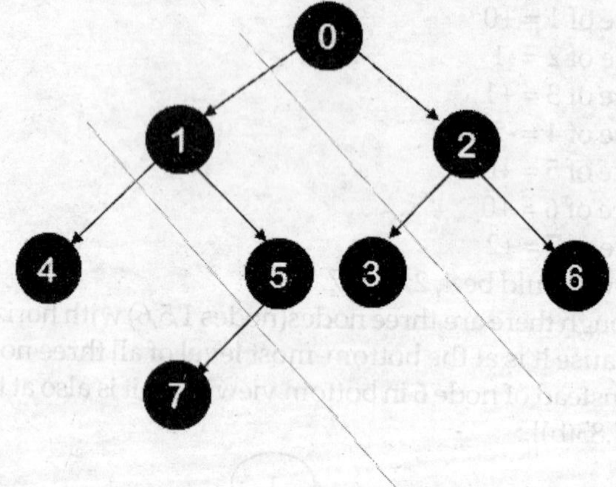

Diagonal-0 : node 0, node 2, node 6
Diagonal-1 : node 1, node 5, node 3
Diagonal-2 : node 4, node 7

Figure 7.83(c). Binary Tree

As is marked in the tree, root node-0 is placed in diagonal 0, then its left child node-1 is placed in diagonal 1 and its right child node-2 is placed in the same diagonal as node-0 that is diagonal 0. This observation can be easily generalized - if current node is placed in diagonal 'd' then its left child would be placed in diagonal 'd+1' and its right child would be placed in the same diagonal as that of current node that is diagonal 'd' as shown in **Figure 7.83(d)**.

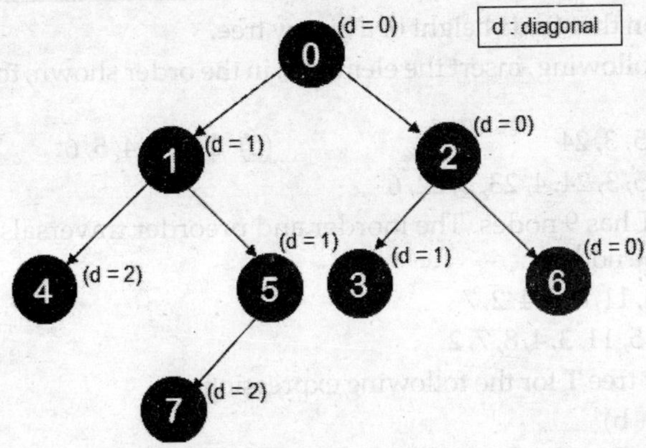

Figure 7.83(d). Binary Tree

Now using above insight, we can easily find the diagonal in which a node is placed in and then add that node's value to that diagonal. We traverse the complete tree using inorder traversal starting from the root node. During this traversal, we pass the 'current Diagonal' to each node indicating which diagonal that current node is placed in. We start by passing 'current Diagonal holds value '0' for the root node. ach node passes down 'current Diagonal + 1' to its left child and 'current Diagonal ' to its right child. Now using this 'current Diagonal' value, we add current node to appropriate diagonal's sum. To store diagonal sum for each diagonal separately, use Hash Maping with its key as diagonal number and value as sum of nodes in that diagonal see **Figure 7.83(d)**.

Time complexity of this algorithm is O(n) since each node would be visited once. Space complexity in the worst case would be O(n). Worst case space complexity occurs for the skewed tree where right child for each node is null. Average case space complexity of this algorithm would be O(log(n)).

FOR SUMMATIVE AND FORMATIVE ASSESSMENT

7.1 How many binary trees are possible with four nodes?

7.2 Determine the order in which the vertices of the following binary trees will be visited under:

(i) Preorder (ii) Inorder

(iii) Post order

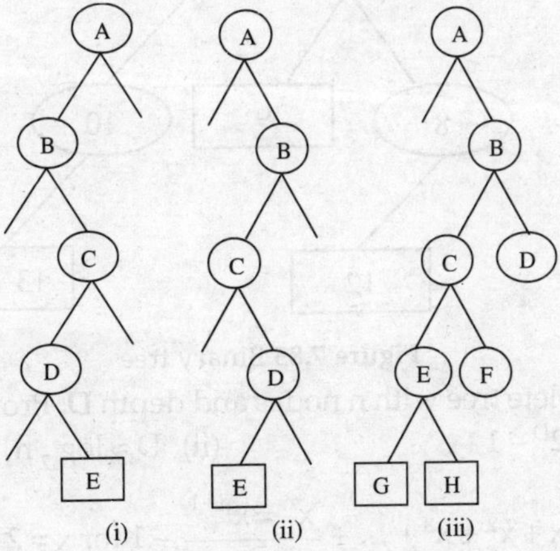

Figure 7.84 Binary trees

7.3 Write a function that finds height of a binary tree.

7.4 In each of the following, insert the elements, in the order shown, to build them into an AVL tree.

(i) 1, 26, 2, 25, 3, 24 (ii) 1, 2, 3, 4, 5, 6

(iii) 1, 26, 2, 25, 3, 24, 4, 23, 5, 22, 6

7.5 A binary tree **T** has 9 nodes. The inorder and preorder traversals of **T** yield the following sequences of the nodes:

In-order: 5, 1, 3, 11, 6, 8, 4, 2, 7

Pre-order: 6, 1, 5, 11, 3, 4, 8, 7, 2

7.6 Find the binary tree **T** for the following expression

$E = (3x - y)(5a + b)^4$

7.7 Find all the possible non-similar trees **T** where

(i) T is a binary tree with 3 nodes

(ii) T is a 2-tree with 4 external nodes

7.8 Suppose the following list of numbers is inserted in inorder into an empty binary search tree. Draw the resulting binary tree.

10, 18, 4, 7, 20, 5, 13, 8, 16, 1, 6, 17

7.9 Consider the tree illustrated in **Figure 7.85** find the tree after

(i) the node 13 is deleted and

(ii) The node 4 is also deleted.

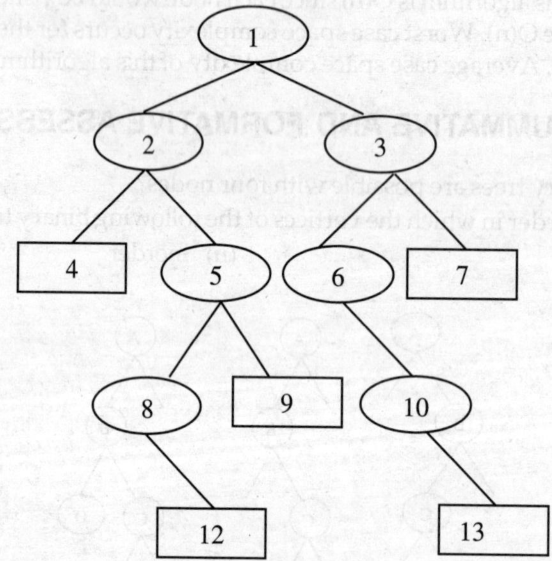

Figure 7.85 Binary tree

7.10 Suppose **T** is a complete tree with **n** nodes and depth **D**. Prove that

(i) $2^{D-1} - 1 < n \le 2^D - 1$ (ii) $D \approx \log_2 n$

Use the relation $1 + x + x^2 + x^3 + \ldots + \frac{x^n = x^{n+1}}{x-1} - 1$ for $x = 2$

7.11 Write a program that implements the list of employees of CCET Company. Write a recursive function that searches an employee record using binary search. Sort the list of employees' record in alphabetical order.

7.12 Suppose a binary tree **T** is in memory. Write a function that deletes all the terminal nodes from **T**.

7.13 Suppose a binary tree **T** is in memory. Write a function that finds number of terminal nodes in **T**.

7.14 Suppose a binary tree **T** is in memory. Write a function that finds duplicate elements.

7.15 Suppose a binary **T** is in memory. Write a function that deletes duplicate elements from **T**.

7.16 Write a function that counts number of nodes in a binary tree.

7.17 Suppose 8 weights 16, 32, 6, 18, 19, 20, 3, 8 are given. Find a 2-tree **T** with the given weights and a minimum weighted path length.

7.18 Write a function that finds minimum weighted path length (use Huffman technique) for a binary tree.

7.19 Draw the binary expression tree that represents the following postfix expression:

x y + c / d *

7.20 Write a recursive function to print the postfix representation of binary tree.

7.21 Find the **prefix, infix** and **postfix** notation of binary trees shown in Figures 7.86 and 7.87 (supply parenthesis for infix notation)

7.22 Evaluate th binary expression tree in **Figure 7.86,** where

x = 3 u = 10
y = 2 v = 30
z = 10 w = 2

7.23 Evaluate the binary expression tree in **Figure 7.87,** where

x = 6 u = 10
y = 4 v = 30
w = 2

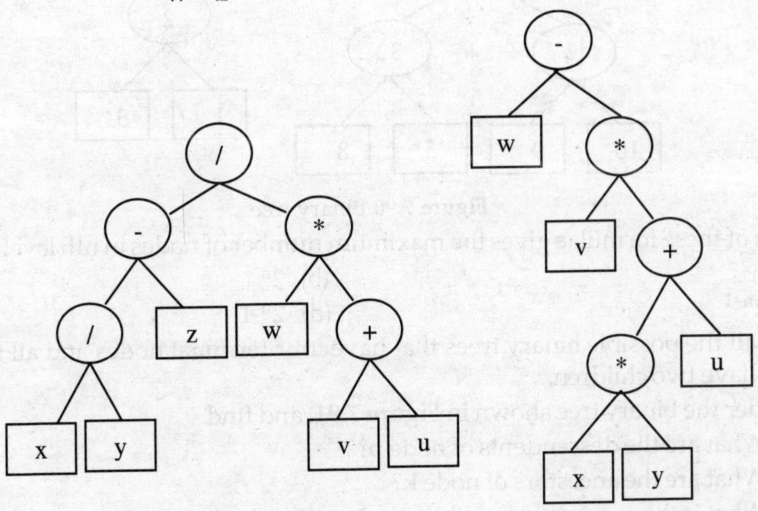

Figure 7.86 Binary tree **Figure 7.87** Binary tree

7.23 Draw the binary tree that represents the following prefix expression:
+*x y/- z v w

7.24 Draw the binary tree that represents the following infix expression:
(((x-y) +z) / ((u-v) * w)) +t

7.25 State whether the following trees are [**Figure** 7.88, **Figure** 7.89 and **Figure** 7.90]
(i) Complete (ii) Full
(iii) Heap

7.26 What is the maximum number of levels that a binary search tree with 100 nodes can have?

7.27 What is the minimum number of levels that a binary search tree with 100 nodes can have?

7.28 Which of these from gives the maximum total number of nodes in a tree that has **n** levels?
(i) n^2-1 (ii) 2^n
(iii) 2^n-1 (iv) 2^{n+1}

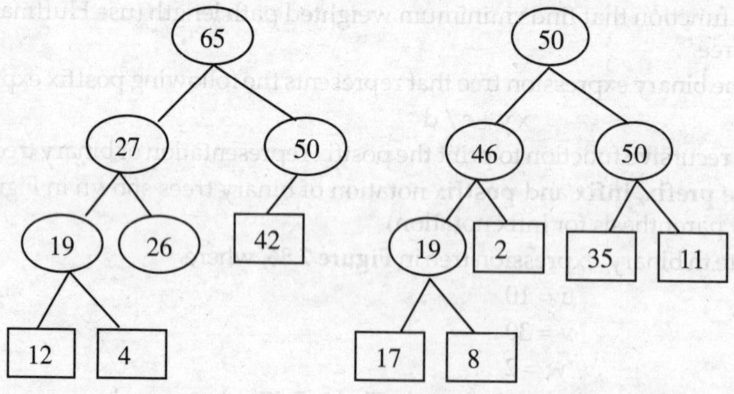

Figure 7.89 Binary tree

Figure 7.88 Binary tree

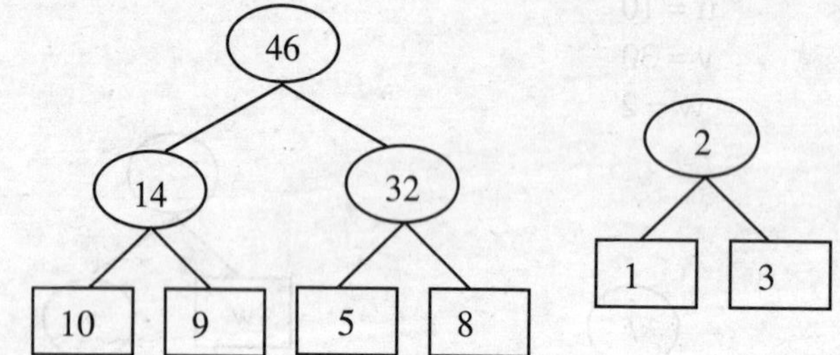

Figure 7.90 Binary tree

7.29 Which of these formulae gives the maximum number of nodes in nth level of a binary tree?
(a) n^2 (b) 2^n
(c) 2^{n+1} (d) 2^n-1

7.30 Draw all the possible binary trees that have four terminal nodes and all the non-terminal nodes have two children.

7.31 Consider the binary tree shown in **Figure 7.91.** and find
(i) What are the descendents of node **p**?
(ii) What are the ancestors of node **k**?
(iii) What is the maximum possible number of nodes in the tree at the level of node **w**?

7.32 Draw binary search tree whose elements are inserted in the following order:

50, 72, 96, 94, 107, 26, 12, 11, 9, 2, 10, 25, 51, 16, 17, 95

7.33 Construct the **min** and **max** heap for the following data:

50, 72, 96, 94, 107, 26, 12, 11, 9, 2, 10, 25, 51, 16, 17, 95

7.34 Examine the binary search tree given in **Figure 7.92** and discuss the following:

(i) If an item is to be inserted whose key value is less than the key value in node 1 but greater than the key value in node 5, where would it be inserted?

(ii) If node 1 is to be deleted, the value in which node could be used to replace it?

(iii) 44, 22, 77, 55, 11, 66, 88, 33 is a traversal of the tree in which order?

(iv) 11, 22, 44, 55, 77, 33, 66, 88 is a traversal of the tree in which order?

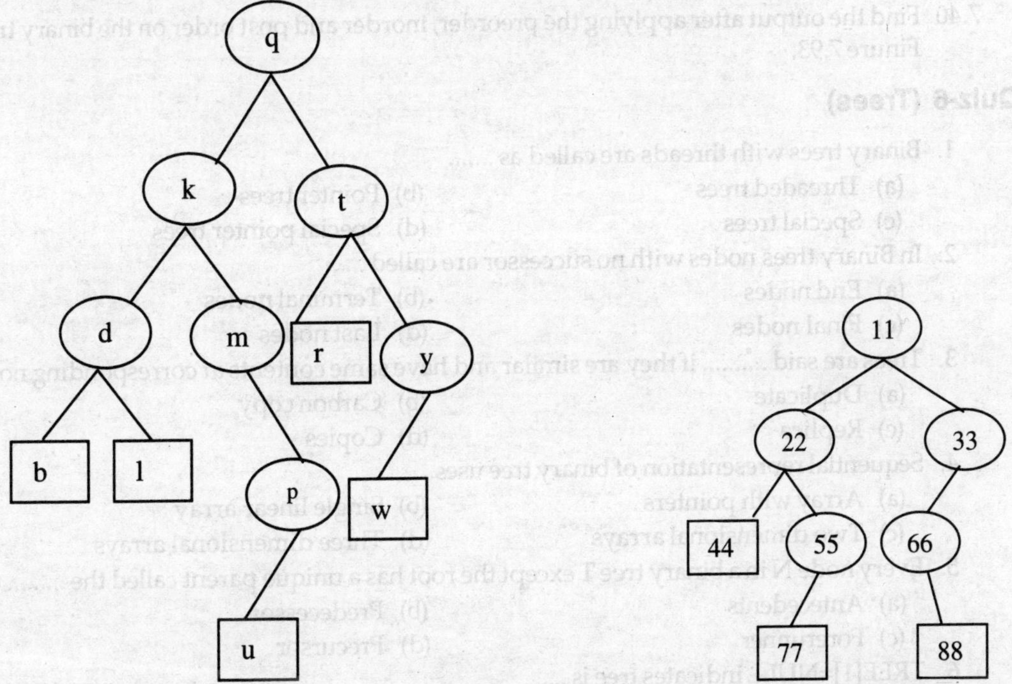

Figure 7.91 Binary tree

Figure 7.92 Binary Tree

7.35 The number of leaf nodes in a binary tree of n nodes, with each node having 0 or 2 children is?

7.36 How many binary trees will be formed with 10 nodes?

7.37 A tree has 2n vertices of degree 1, 3n vertices of degree 2, and n vertices of degree 3. Determine the number of vertices and edges in the tree.

7.38 The number of leaf nodes in a ternary tree of n nodes, with each node having 0 or 3 children is?

7.39 Evaluate arithmetic expression given in binary tree of Figure 7.93. Consider the values of x, y, z, u, v, w-11,22,13,54,5,6, respectively.

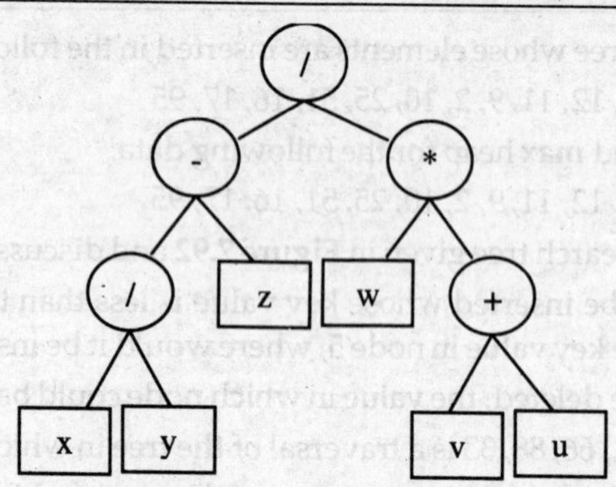

Figure 7.93 Expression Tree

7.40 Find the output after applying the preorder, inorder and post order on the binary tree given Finure 7.93.

Quiz-6 (Trees)

1. Binary trees with threads are called as ....
   (a) Threaded trees (b) Pointer trees
   (c) Special trees (d) Special pointer trees
2. In Binary trees nodes with no successor are called ......
   (a) End nodes (b) Terminal nodes
   (c) Final nodes (d) Last nodes
3. Trees are said .... if they are similar and have same contents at corresponding nodes.
   (a) Duplicate (b) Carbon copy
   (c) Replica (d) Copies
4. Sequential representation of binary tree uses ....
   (a) Array with pointers (b) Single linear array
   (c) Two dimensional arrays (d) Three dimensional arrays
5. Every node N in a binary tree T except the root has a unique parent called the .... of N.
   (a) Antecedents (b) Predecessor
   (c) Forerunner (d) Precursor
6. TREE[1]=NULL indicates tree is ....
   (a) Overflow (b) Underflow
   (c) Empty (d) Full
7. A binary tree whose every node has either zero or two children is called ....
   (a) complete binary tree (b) binary search tree
   (c) extended binary tree (d) data structure
8. Linked representation of binary tree needs .... parallel arrays.
   (a) 4 (b) 2
   (c) 3 (d) 5
9. The depth of complete binary tree is given by ......
   (a) $Dn = n \log_2 n$ (b) $Dn= n \log_2 n+1$
   (c) $Dn = \log_2 n$ (d) $Dn = \log_2 n+1$

10. When inorder traversing a tree resulted E A C K F H D B G; the preorder traversal would return
    (a) FAEKCDBHG (b) FAEKCDHGB
    (c) EAFKHDCBG (d) FEAKDCHBG
11. Which indicates preorder traversal?
    (a) Left sub-tree, Right sub-tree and root
    (b) Right sub-tree, Left sub-tree and root
    (c) Root, Left sub-tree, Right sub-tree
    (d) Right sub-tree, root, Left sub-tree
12. In an extended-binary tree nodes with 2 children are called ....
    (a) Interior node (b) Domestic node
    (c) Internal node (d) Inner node
13. The balance factor for an AVL tree is either
    (a) 0,1 or –1 (b) –2,–1 or 0
    (c) 0,1 or 2 (d) All the above
14. A binary search tree whose left subtree and right subtree differ in hight by at most 1 unit is called ......
    (a) AVL tree (b) Red-black tree
    (c) Lemma tree (d) None of the above
15. AVL trees have LL, LR, RR, RL rotations to balance the tree to maintain the balance factor (LR : Insert node in Right sub tree of Left sub tree of node A, etc). Among rotations the following are single and double rotations
    (a) LL, RL and LR, RR (b) LL, RR and LR, RL
    (c) LR, RR and LL, RL (d) LR, RL and LR, RL
16. AVL trees have a faster ________________
    (a) Insertion (b) Deletion
    (c) Updation (d) Retrieval
17. What is the peculiarity of red black trees?
    (a) In red-black trees, the root does not contain data.
    (b) In red-black trees, the leaf nodes are not relevant and do not contain data.
    (c) In red-black trees, the leaf nodes are relevant but do not contain data.
    (d) Both a and c above
18. A ______________ tree is tree where for each parent node, there is only one associated child node
    (a) balanced binary tree (b) rooted complete binary tree
    (c) complete binary tree (d) degenerate tree
19. In ______________ tree, the heights of two child subtree of any node differ by at most one
    (a) Binary tree (b) Red black tree
    (c) Splay tree (d) AVL tree
20. Which of the following ways below is an inorder traversal?
    (a) Root->left sub tree->right sub tree (b) Root-> right sub tree ->left sub tree
    (c) right sub tree->left sub tree->Root (d) left sub tree->right sub tree->Root

❑

CHAPTER

8

Graphs

This chapter investigates another nonlinear data structures **Graph.** In this chapter we will discuss the representation of graphs, operations on them and algorithms such Breadth first search and Depth first search, Dijkstra, Floyd, Warshall's, Spanning tree, Kruskal Algorithm, etc, certain applications of graphs, including topological sorting is also covered.

8.1 BASIC CONCEPTS AND DEFINITIONS

A graph **G** is defined as a set of two tuples that is **G = (V, E),** where **V** represents set of vertices and **E** represents the set of edges of **G.** There exists a mapping from the set of edges to a set of pairs of elements of **V.** For example, **Figure 8.1** illustrates the different type of graphs.

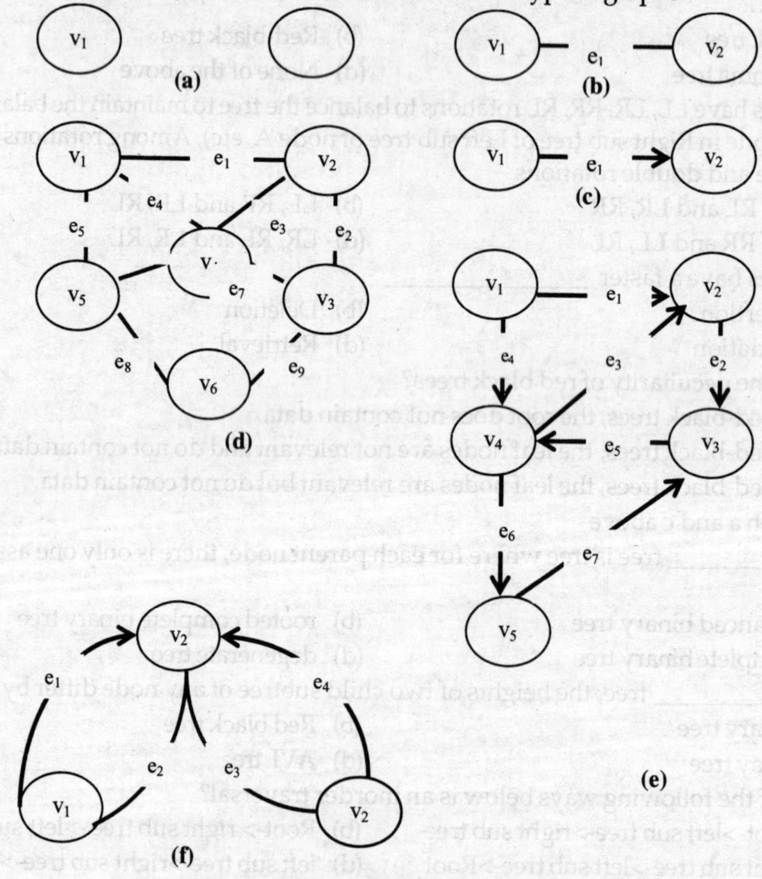

Figure 8.1 Different types of graph

From **Figure 8.1** it is clear that part (a) consists of 2 vertices each one is stand-alone; (b) contains an undirected graph having one edge and two vertices. Similarly (c) consists of two vertices and one edge and it is directed graph; (d) illustrates an undirected graph with 6 vertices and 9 edges; (e) is a directed graph with 5 vertices and 7 edges. **Figure 8.1(f)** consists of 3 vertices and 4 edges in which 2 edges are directed and two are undirected (no direction for two edges is to be shown as it is mixed graph).

Thus, we can say that in a graph **G = (V, E),** an edge that is directed from one vertex to another is called a directed edge, while an edge which has no specific direction is called an undirected edge. A graph in which every edge is directed is called a directed graph or a digraph. A graph in which every edge is undirected is called undirected graph. If some of the edges are directed and some are undirected in a graph, then the graph is called a mixed graph. **Figure 8.1(f)** represents a mixed graph.

Suppose **Figure 8.2** represents road map of Delhi State. By observing into this figure one can say that some roads are one way while others are two-ways. If some one is at Palam and wants to go to New Delhi Railway Station then he/she can't go there directly from Palam to New Delhi Railway Station. For this purpose, he/she must follow the path Palam-Old Delhi – New Delhi Railway Station or Palam – Sahadara - Old Delhi - New Delhi Railway Station. There are more than two routes from Palam to New Delhi Railway Station. **Figure 8.2** represents a mixed graph.

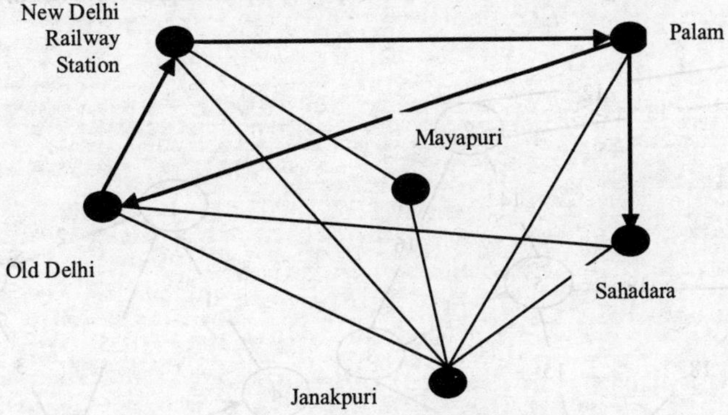

Figure 8.2 Road map of Delhi

Let **G = (V, E)** be a graph and **e** ∈ **E** be a directed edge associated with ordered pair of vertices **(v_1, v_2)**. Then the edge **e** is said to be initiating from the vertex **v_1** and terminating at the vertex **v_2**. Thus, vertex **v_1** and **v_2** are also called the initial and terminal vertices of the edge **e**, e ∈ **E,** which joins the vertices **v_1** and **v_2** in graph **G**. It is an incident to the vertices **v_1** and **v_2**. An edge of a graph that joins a vertex is called **sling**. The direction of the loop is of no significance; hence it can be considered either a directed or undirected edge.

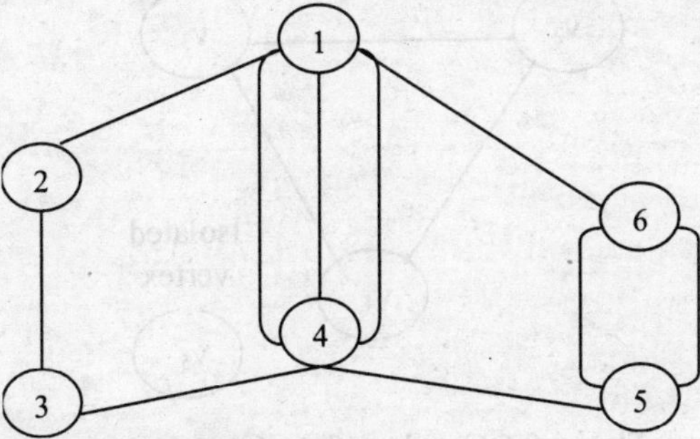

Figure 8.3 Undirected graph.

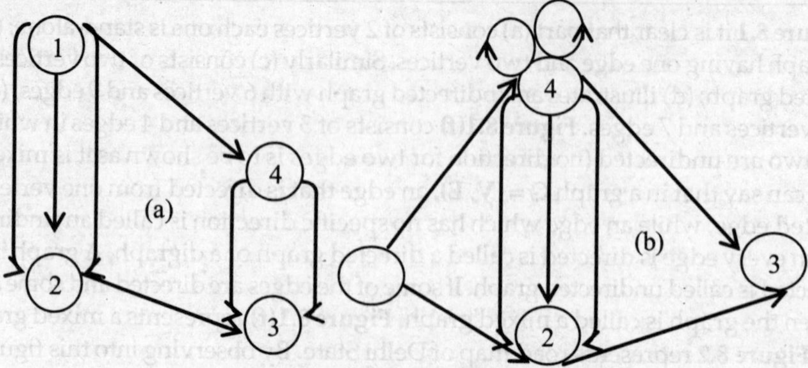

Figure 8.4 Directed graph

When in a graph, two or more than two edges are used to join two vertices, such edges are called parallel edges and the graph is called multi-graph. In **Figure 8.3** there are three parallel edge between the vertices 1 and 4, and two parallel edge between vertices 6 and 5. If there is only one edge between a pair of vertices then such a graph is called a simple graph. **Figure 8.1(a- e)** is example of simple graphs.

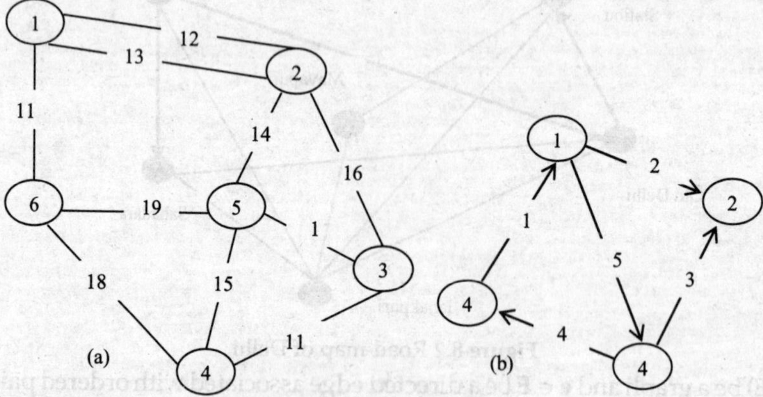

Figure 8.5 Weighted graphs (a) Undirected weighted graph (b) Directed weighted graph

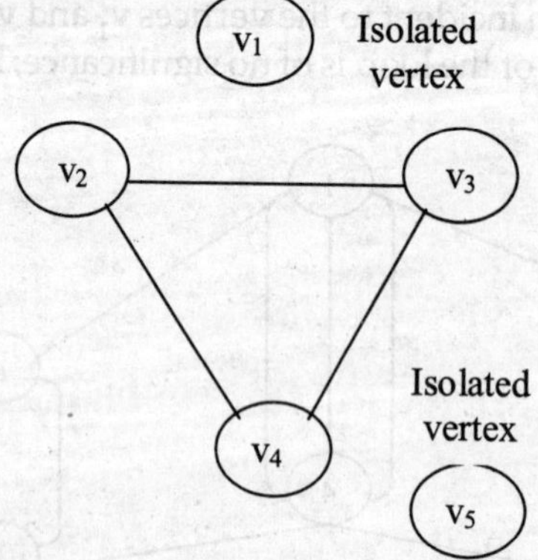

Figure 8.6 Graph with isolated vertices

In a graph there may exist two or more directed edges between two vertices. Parallel loops are also possible in a graph as illustrated in **Figure 8.4(b).** A graph with edge value is called weighted graph as shown in **Figure 8.5.** In a graph a vertex which is not adjacent to any other vertices in the graph is called an isolated vertex. A graph containing only isolated vertices is called **null** graph or in other words a graph without an edge is called a null graph. **Figure 8.6** illustrates a graph with isolated vertices $\mathbf{v_1}$ and $\mathbf{v_5}$ and graph is shown in **Figure 8.7** is null graph.

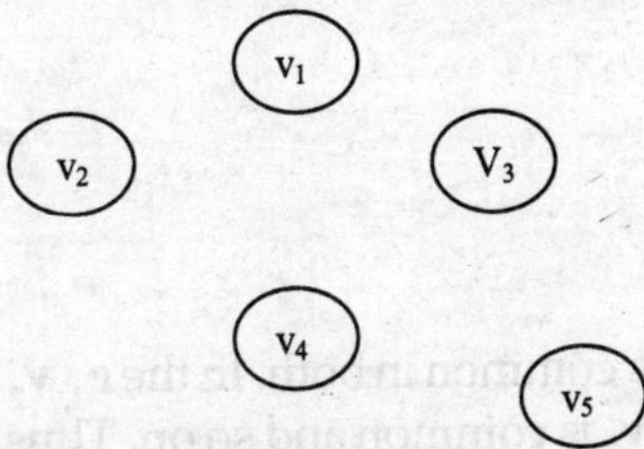

Figure 8.7 Null graph

In a directed graph for any vertex **v** the number of edges which have **v** as their initial vertex is called the **out-degree** of **v.** The number of edges, which have **v** as their terminal vertex, is called the **in-degree** of **v.** The sum of the out-degree and in-degree of a vertex is called its total degree. In case of an undirected graph, the total degree or the degree of a vertex **v** is equal to the number of edges incident with **v.** The total degree of a loop is 2 and that of an isolated vertex is 0. Take a simple graph **G = (V, E).** Consider a sequence of edges of **G** such that the terminal vertex of an edge in the sequence is the initial vertex of the next edge if any in the sequence. Suppose we have a set of edges

$E = \{(v_{i1}, v_{i2}), (v_{i2}, v_{i3}), (v_{i3}, v_{i4}), \ldots, (v_{ik-2}, v_{ik-1}), (v_{ik-1}, v_{ik})\}$,

Here in v_{i1} i stands for initial vertex and it may be $1 \le i \le n$, where n is number of vertices in graph.

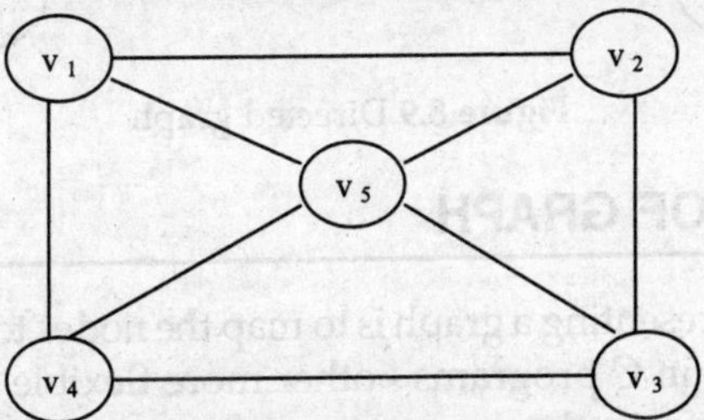

Figure 8.8 Undirected graph

Then the set of vertices **V** will contain all the vertices existing in the set **E,** that is

$V = \{v_{i1}, v_{i2}, v_{i3}, v_{i4} \ldots v_{ik-2}, v_{ik-1}, v_{ik}\}$

Let we have a graph as illustrated in **Figure 8.8,** then from the above description, we have

$E = \{(v_1, v_2), (v_1, v_4), (v_1, v_5), (v_2, v_1), (v_2, v_3), (v_2, v_5), (v_3, v_2), (v_3, v_4),$
$(v_3, v_5), (v_4, v_1), (v_4, v_3), (v_4, v_5), (v_5, v_1), (v_5, v_2), (v_5, v_3), (v_5, v_4)\}$

$V = \{v_1, v_2, v_3, v_4, v_5\}$

If we consider **Figure 8.9** then we have

$E = \{(v_1, v_2), (v_1, v_4), (v_2, v_3), (v_3, v_5), (v_3, v_4), (v_3, v_5), (v_4, v_5), (v_5, v_1)\}$

$V = \{v_1, v_2, v_3, v_4, v_5\}$

8.2 PATH

A sequence of edges of a digraph such that the terminal vertex of an edge sequences in the initial vertex of the next edge if exists is called the path. For example, let we have

$E = \{(v_1, v_2), (v_2, v_3), (v_3, v_4), (v_4, v_5), (v_5, v_1)\}$

If we consider the elements of **E**, we find that **E** is a set of 5 tuples, that is

$e_1 = (v_1, v_2)$
$e_2 = (v_2, v_3)$
$e_3 = (v_3, v_4)$
$e_4 = (v_4, v_5)$
$e_5 = (v_5, v_1)$

From $\mathbf{e_1}$ and $\mathbf{e_2}$ we find that $\mathbf{v_2}$ is common in both. In the $\mathbf{e_1}$, $\mathbf{v_2}$ is the terminal vertex and it is initial vertex of $\mathbf{e_2}$. Similarly, in $\mathbf{e_2}$ and $\mathbf{e_3}$, $\mathbf{v_3}$ is common and so on. Thus, we can say that there is a cycle, i.e., there exists a circular path. The circular path is illustrated in **Figure 8.9** with the help of dark line.

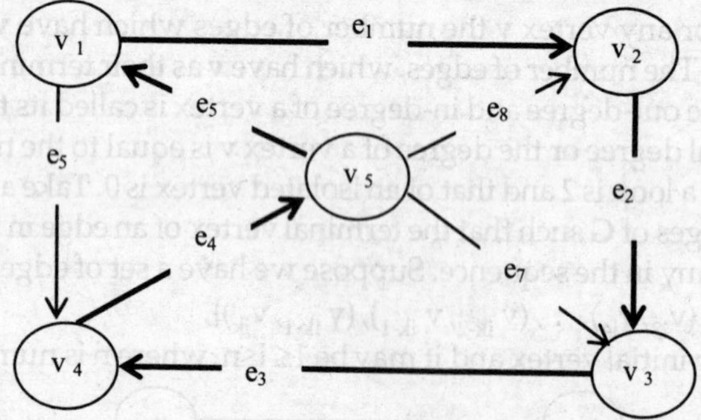

Figure 8.9 Directed graph

8.3 REPRESENTATION OF GRAPH

Usually the first step in representing a graph is to map the nodes to a set of contiguous integers. (0, |**V**|-1) is the most convenient in C programs - other more flexible languages allowing us greater choice. The mapping can be performed using any type of search structure: binary trees, **m**-way trees, hash tables, etc. There is two popular ways that are used to maintain a graph in a computer memory. These are:

- Sequential
- Linked list

8.3.1 Sequential Representation

The graphs can be represented as matrices in sequential representation. There are two most common matrices. These are:

- Adjacency
- Incidence

The adjacency matrix is a sequence matrix with one row and one column for each vertex. The values of the matrix are either 0 or 1. A value of 1 for row **i** and column **j** implies that edge $\mathbf{e_{ij}}$ exists between $\mathbf{v_i}$ and $\mathbf{v_j}$ vertices. A value of 0 implies that there is no edge between vertex $\mathbf{v_i}$ and $\mathbf{v_j}$. In other words we can say that if graph **G** consists of $\mathbf{v_1, v_2, v_3 \ldots v_n}$ vertices then the adjacency matrix $\mathbf{A = [a_{ij}]}$ of the graph **G** is the **n x n** matrix and can be defined as:

$$a_{ij} = \begin{cases} 1 & \text{If } v_i \text{ is adjacent to } v_j \text{ (that is if there is an edge between } v_i \text{ and } v_j) \\ 0 & \text{If there is no edge between } v_i \text{ and } v_j \end{cases}$$

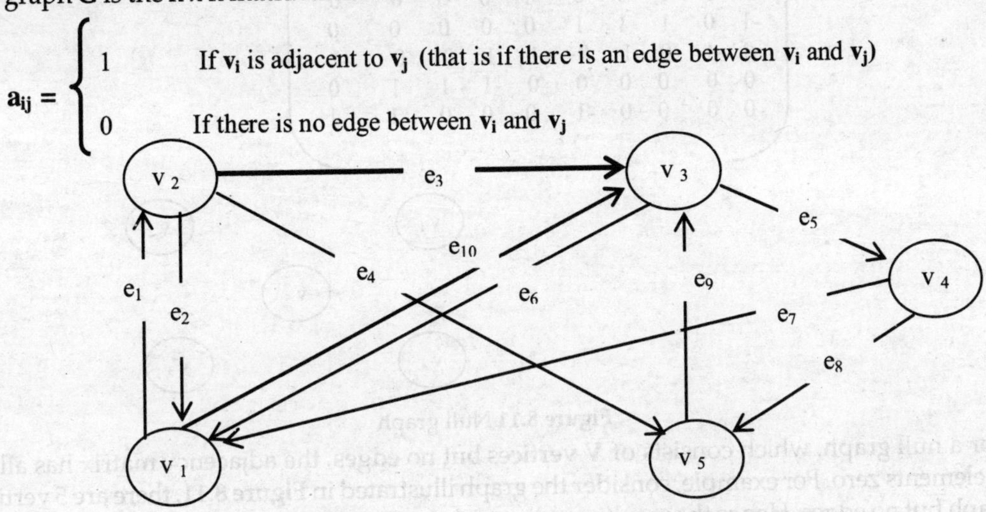

Figure 8.10 5 Vertices and 10 edges of a directed graph

Such a matrix **A**, which contains entries of only 0 or 1, is called a bit matrix or a Boolean. For example, consider the graph **G** illustrated in **Figure 8.10**, which consists of 5 vertices and 10 edges. The set of vertices is as follows:

$V = \{v_1, v_2, v_3, v_4, v_5\}$

and the set of edges is:

$E = \{(v_1, v_2), (v_1, v_3), (v_2, v_1), (v_2, v_3), (v_2, v_5), (v_3, v_1), (v_3, v_4), (v_4, v_1), (v_4, v_5), (v_5, v_3)\}$

The adjacency matrix **A** for **G** is as follows:

$$A = \begin{array}{c} \\ v_1 \\ v_2 \\ v_3 \\ v_4 \\ v_5 \end{array} \begin{array}{c} \begin{array}{ccccc} v_1 & v_2 & v_3 & v_4 & v_5 \end{array} \\ \begin{pmatrix} 0 & 1 & 1 & 0 & 0 \\ 1 & 0 & 1 & 0 & 1 \\ 1 & 0 & 0 & 1 & 0 \\ 1 & 0 & 0 & 0 & 1 \\ 0 & 0 & 1 & 0 & 0 \end{pmatrix} \end{array}$$

From the matrix **A**, it is clear that number of 1's in an adjacency matrix is equal to the number of edges in the graph. When one is constructing an adjacency matrix for a graph, one must follows the following points:

- Adjacency matrix **A** does not depend on the ordering of the vertex of a graph **G**, that is different ordering of the vertices may result in a different adjacency matrix. One can obtain the same matrix by interchanging rows and columns.
- If graph **G** is undirected then the adjacency matrix of **G** will be symmetric, i.e., $[a_{ij}] = [a_{ji}]$ for every **i** and **j**.

The incidence matrix consists of a row for every vertex and a column for every edge. The values of the matrix are –1, 0 or 1. If the kth edge is (v_i, v_j), the kth column has a value 1 in the ith row, -1 in the jth row and 0 elsewhere. For example, the incidence matrix **I** for the graph illustrated in **Figure 8.10** is as follows:

$$I = \begin{pmatrix} 1 & 1 & -1 & 0 & 0 & -1 & 0 & -1 & 0 & 0 \\ -1 & 0 & 1 & 1 & 1 & 0 & 0 & 0 & 0 & 0 \\ 0 & -1 & 0 & -1 & 0 & 1 & 1 & 0 & 0 & -1 \\ 0 & 0 & 0 & 0 & 0 & 0 & -1 & 1 & 1 & 0 \\ 0 & 0 & 0 & 0 & -1 & 0 & 0 & 0 & -1 & 1 \end{pmatrix}$$

Figure 8.11 Null graph

For a null graph, which consists of **V** vertices but no edges, the adjacency matrix has all of its entire elements zero. For example, consider the graph illustrated in **Figure 8.11**, there are 5 vertices in the graph but no edges. Hence the resulting adjacency matrix will be

$$A = \begin{array}{c} \\ V_1 \\ V_2 \\ V_3 \\ V_4 \\ V_5 \end{array} \begin{array}{c} \begin{array}{ccccc} V_1 & V_2 & V_3 & V_4 & V_5 \end{array} \\ \begin{pmatrix} 0 & 0 & 0 & 0 & 0 \\ 0 & 0 & 0 & 0 & 0 \\ 0 & 0 & 0 & 0 & 0 \\ 0 & 0 & 0 & 0 & 0 \\ 0 & 0 & 0 & 0 & 0 \end{pmatrix} \end{array}$$

Figure 8.12 Graph in which loop at each vertex

If there are loops at each vertex but no edges in the graph, then the adjacency matrix is the unit matrix. For example, consider the graph illustrated in **Figure 8.12.** The adjacency matrix for this graph will be:

$$U = \begin{array}{c} \\ V_1 \\ V_2 \\ V_3 \\ V_4 \\ V_5 \end{array} \begin{array}{c} \begin{array}{ccccc} V_1 & V_2 & V_3 & V_4 & V_5 \end{array} \\ \begin{pmatrix} 1 & 0 & 0 & 0 & 0 \\ 0 & 1 & 0 & 0 & 0 \\ 0 & 0 & 1 & 0 & 0 \\ 0 & 0 & 0 & 1 & 0 \\ 0 & 0 & 0 & 0 & 1 \end{pmatrix} \end{array}$$

Let us now consider the powers of an adjacency matrix. As we know that an entry of 1 in the ith row and j^{th} column of adjacency list **A** shows existence of an edge of (v_i, v_j), that is, a path of length 1 from v_i to v_j. Let us denote the elements of A^2 by

$$a_{ij}^2$$

then

$$a_{ij}^2 = \sum a_{ik} a_{kj}$$

For any fixed value of **k**; $a_{ik}\ a_{kj} = 1$ if and only if both a_{ik} and a_{kj} are equal to **1**; that is (v_i, v_k) and (v_k, v_j) are the edges of the graph. For each such **k** we get a contribution of 1 in the sum. Which implies that there is a path from v_i to v_j of length 2. Therefore, a_{ij}^2 is equal to the number of different paths of length 2 from v_i to v_j. Similarly, the diagonal element a_{ii}^2 shows the number of cycles of length 2 at the vertex v_i for **i = 1, 2, 3 … n.**

In the similar way, we can show that the element in the ith row and j^{th} column of A^3 gives the number of paths of length 3 from v_i to v_j. Hence in general we can say that the element in the ith row and j^{th} column A^n $(n > 1)$ is equal to the number of paths of length **n** from v_i to v_j. For example, consider the graph **G** illustrated in **Figure 8.10.** The adjacency matrix **A** for **G** is as follows:

$$A = \begin{array}{c} \\ v_1 \\ v_2 \\ v_3 \\ v_4 \\ v_5 \end{array} \begin{array}{c} \begin{array}{ccccc} v_1 & v_2 & v_3 & v_4 & v_5 \end{array} \\ \begin{pmatrix} 0 & 1 & 1 & 0 & 0 \\ 1 & 0 & 1 & 0 & 1 \\ 1 & 0 & 0 & 1 & 0 \\ 1 & 0 & 0 & 0 & 1 \\ 0 & 0 & 1 & 0 & 0 \end{pmatrix} \end{array}$$

Now consider A^1, A^2, A^3, A^4 and A^5 if **A** is the adjacency matrix of the graph **G** illustrated in **Figure 8.10.** The A^1 is same as adjacency matrix **A** and other powers are as follows:

$$A^1 = \begin{pmatrix} 0 & 1 & 1 & 0 & 0 \\ 1 & 0 & 1 & 0 & 1 \\ 1 & 0 & 0 & 1 & 0 \\ 1 & 0 & 0 & 0 & 1 \\ 0 & 0 & 1 & 0 & 0 \end{pmatrix} \quad A^2 = \begin{pmatrix} 2 & 0 & 1 & 1 & 1 \\ 1 & 1 & 2 & 1 & 0 \\ 1 & 1 & 1 & 0 & 1 \\ 0 & 1 & 2 & 0 & 0 \\ 1 & 0 & 0 & 1 & 0 \end{pmatrix}$$

$$A^3 = \begin{pmatrix} 2 & 2 & 3 & 1 & 1 \\ 4 & 1 & 2 & 2 & 2 \\ 2 & 1 & 3 & 1 & 1 \\ 3 & 0 & 1 & 2 & 1 \\ 1 & 1 & 1 & 0 & 1 \end{pmatrix} A^4 = \begin{pmatrix} 6 & 2 & 5 & 3 & 3 \\ 5 & 4 & 7 & 2 & 3 \\ 5 & 2 & 4 & 3 & 2 \\ 3 & 3 & 4 & 1 & 2 \\ 2 & 1 & 3 & 1 & 1 \end{pmatrix} A^5 = \begin{pmatrix} 10 & 6 & 11 & 5 & 5 \\ 13 & 5 & 12 & 7 & 6 \\ 9 & 5 & 9 & 4 & 5 \\ 8 & 3 & 8 & 4 & 4 \\ 5 & 2 & 4 & 3 & 2 \end{pmatrix}$$

Now we define the matrix B_r as follows:

$B_r = A^1 + A^2 + A^3 + A^4 + A^5 + \ldots + A^r$

Then the ith row and j^{th} column entry of the matrix B_r gives the number of the paths of length **r** or less than **r** from vertex v_i to v_j.

Let **G = (V, E)** be a simple directed graph with **n** vertices $v_1, v_2, v_3 \ldots v_n$. Then path matrix or the reachability matrix of **G** is the **n x n** matrix $P = p_{ij}$ defined as:

$$p_{ij} = \begin{cases} 1 & \text{If there is a path from } v_i \text{ to } v_j \\ 0 & \text{Otherwise} \end{cases}$$

If there is path from v_i to v_j then there must be a simple path, path without loop, etc–from v_i to v_j when $v_i \neq v_j$ or there must be a cycle from v_i to v_j when $v_i = v_j$. Since **G** has **n** vertices, such a simple path must have length **n – 1** or less or such a cycle must have length **n** or less. The path matrix can be calculated from the matrix $\mathbf{B_n}$ by choosing $\mathbf{p_{ij} = 1}$ if the elements in the ith row and j[th] column of $\mathbf{B_n}$ is nonzero and $\mathbf{p_{ij} = 0}$, otherwise. From this method one can easily calculate path matrix. For example, once again consider the graph illustrated in **Figure 8.10**, the adjacency matrix and powers of adjacency matrix of this graph, i.e., calculated $\mathbf{A^2}$, $\mathbf{A^3}$, $\mathbf{A^4}$ and $\mathbf{A^5}$. We have

$$B_5 = A^1 + A^2 + A^3 + A^4 + A^5$$

$$B_5 = \begin{pmatrix} 20 & 11 & 21 & 10 & 10 \\ 24 & 11 & 24 & 12 & 12 \\ 19 & 9 & 17 & 9 & 9 \\ 15 & 7 & 15 & 7 & 8 \\ 9 & 4 & 9 & 5 & 4 \end{pmatrix}$$

The path matrix for **G** will be:

$$P = \begin{pmatrix} 1 & 1 & 1 & 1 & 1 \\ 1 & 1 & 1 & 1 & 1 \\ 1 & 1 & 1 & 1 & 1 \\ 1 & 1 & 1 & 1 & 1 \\ 1 & 1 & 1 & 1 & 1 \end{pmatrix}$$

When space is a problem, bit maps can be used for the adjacency matrix. In this case, an abstract data type (ADT) for the adjacency matrix improves the clarity of a code immensely by hiding the bit twiddling that this space saving requires. In undirected graphs, only one half of the matrix needs to be stored, but you will need to calculate the element addresses explicitly yourself. Again an ADT can hide this complexity from a user. If the graph is dense, i.e., most of the nodes are connected by edges, then the $\mathbf{O(|V|^2)}$ cost of initializing an adjacency matrix is matched by the cost of inputting and setting the edges. However, if the graph is sparse, i.e., $\mathbf{|E|}$ is closer to $\mathbf{|V|}$, then an adjacency list representation may be more efficient.

8.4 SHORTEST PATH ALGORITHMS

Graphs may be used to represent the highway structure, communication lines, heavy structures in Civil Engineering, etc. of a city, state or country. The vertices representing highway cities or Telecommunication towers (Transmitters) or heavy structures load centered (column) edges representing for highway sections or Telecommunication link lines and or heavy structure supporting walls. The edges may be assigned weights, which might be either distance between the two cities and average time to spend along that section of highway. If we have a map as shown in Figure 8.13 and a pilot wishing to drive from city **A** to city **B** would be interested in getting the answers of the following questions:

- Is there a path from **A** to **B**?
- If there is more than one path from **A** to **B**, which is the shortest one?

Similarly, in the case of the Telecommunication the edges can be assigned weights, which might be either distance between the two transmitters area or pulse rate to transmit messages along the line of communication. A customer wishing to send a message from city **A** to city **B** may ask about pulse rate and distance. For getting answer of such type of problems there are several algorithms which are discussed next.

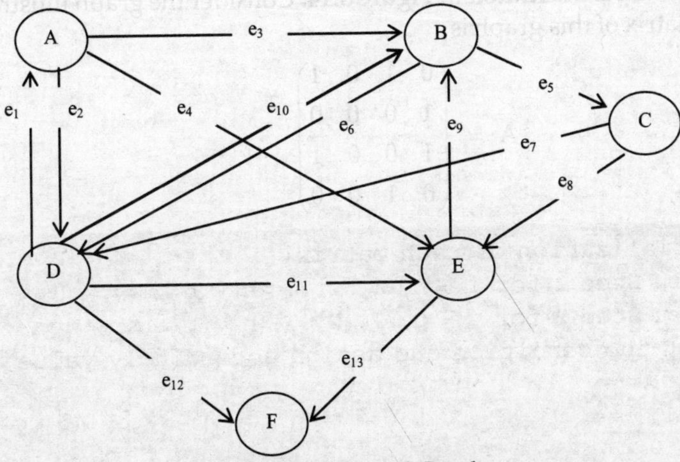

Figure 8.13 Directed Graph

8.4.1 Warshall's Algorithm

Let **G = (V, E)** is a multi-graph with **n** vertices $\mathbf{v_1, v_2 \ldots v_n}$. Suppose we want to find the path matrix **P** of the graph, **G. Warshall** gave an algorithm for this purpose which is efficient to find the path between two vertices in a graph. He had defined **n+1, n x n** matrices $\mathbf{P_0, P_1, P_2 \ldots P_n}$, such as:

$$P_k\,[i][j] = \begin{cases} 1 & \text{If there is simple path from } \mathbf{v_i} \text{ to } \mathbf{v_j}\text{, which does not use any other vertices except possibly } \mathbf{v_1, v_2 \ldots v_k}. \\ 0 & \text{Otherwise} \end{cases}$$

For example:

$P_0\,[i][j] = 1$, if there is an edge from $\mathbf{v_i}$ to $\mathbf{v_j}$.

$P_1\,[i][j] = 1$, if there is a path from $\mathbf{v_i}$ to $\mathbf{v_j}$ which does not use any other vertex except possibly $\mathbf{v_1}$.

$P_2\,[i][j] = 1$, if there is a path from $\mathbf{v_i}$ to $\mathbf{v_j}$ which does not use any other vertices except possibly $\mathbf{v_1}$ and $\mathbf{v_2}$.

From the above discussion it is clear that matrix $\mathbf{P_0}$ is equivalent to adjacency matrix **A** of the graph **G**. Since **G** consists of **n** vertices, the last matrix $\mathbf{P_n = P}$ becomes the path matrix of **G. Warshall** said that $\mathbf{P_k}$ **[i][j] = 1** can occur only when one of the following two cases occurs:

- There exists an edge between $\mathbf{v_i}$ and $\mathbf{v_j}$ which does not use any other vertex except possibly $\mathbf{v_1, v_2 \ldots v_{k-1}}$, hence

```
P_k-1 [i] [j] = 1
```

- There exists an edge between v_i and v_k and an edge between v_k and v_j where each edge does not use any other vertex except possibly $v_1, v_2 \ldots v_{k-1}$, hence
  P_{k-1} [i][k] = 1 and P_{k-1} [k][j] = 1

One can obtain the elements of matrix $\mathbf{P_k}$ with the help of the following formula:

P_k [i][j] = P_{k-1} [i][j] V (P_{k-1} [i][k] ∧ P_{k-1} [k][j])

where

∧ → Means logical AND operations (For example: $1 \wedge 1 = 1$ and $1 \wedge 0 = 0$)

V → Means logical OR operations (For example: 1 V 1 = 1, 1 V 0 = 1 and 0 V 0 = 0)

Warshall's algorithm is illustrated in **Figure 8.14.** Consider the graph illustrated in **Figure 8.15** and the adjacency matrix of this graph is

$$A = \begin{pmatrix} 0 & 1 & 0 & 1 \\ 1 & 0 & 0 & 0 \\ 1 & 0 & 0 & 1 \\ 0 & 1 & 0 & 0 \end{pmatrix}$$

```
Step 1: [Initialization of path matrix]
    Repeat thru Step 2 for i = 0, 1, 2 ... n - 1
    Repeat thru Step 2 for j = 0, 1, 2 ... n - 1
  Step 2: [Test the condition and assign accordingly value to path matrix
accordingly]
     If (a [i][j] == 0)
     p[i][j] = 0
     Else
     p [i][j] = 1
 Step 3: [Evaluate path matrix]
  Repeat thru Step 4 for k = 0, 1, 2... n - 1
    Repeat thru Step 4 for i = 0, 1, 2 ... n - 1
    Repeat thru Step 4 for j = 0, 1, 2 ... n - 1
 Step 4: p[i][j] = p[i][j] V ( p[i][k] ∧ p[k][j])
 Step 5: Exit
```

Figure 8.14 Warshall's algorithm of path matrix

If we apply the above **Warshall**'s technique we find the path matrix **P** that is as follows:

$$P = \begin{pmatrix} 1 & 1 & 0 & 1 \\ 1 & 1 & 0 & 1 \\ 1 & 1 & 0 & 1 \\ 1 & 1 & 0 & 1 \end{pmatrix}$$

If we apply general procedure to find path matrix, we get the same result. For example, for the graph illustrated in **Figure 8.15.** Consider the following steps:

$$A = \begin{pmatrix} 0 & 1 & 0 & 1 \\ 1 & 0 & 0 & 0 \\ 1 & 0 & 0 & 1 \\ 0 & 1 & 0 & 0 \end{pmatrix}$$

$$A = \begin{pmatrix} 0 & 1 & 0 & 1 \\ 1 & 0 & 0 & 0 \\ 1 & 0 & 0 & 1 \\ 0 & 1 & 0 & 0 \end{pmatrix}$$

$$A^2 = A \times A = \begin{pmatrix} 1 & 1 & 0 & 0 \\ 0 & 1 & 0 & 1 \\ 1 & 2 & 0 & 1 \\ 1 & 0 & 0 & 0 \end{pmatrix}$$

$$A^3 = A \times A \times A = \begin{pmatrix} 1 & 1 & 0 & 1 \\ 1 & 1 & 0 & 0 \\ 2 & 2 & 0 & 1 \\ 0 & 1 & 0 & 1 \end{pmatrix}$$

$$A^4 = A \times A \times A \times A = \begin{pmatrix} 1 & 2 & 0 & 1 \\ 1 & 1 & 0 & 1 \\ 2 & 3 & 0 & 2 \\ 1 & 1 & 0 & 0 \end{pmatrix}$$

Path matrix can be evaluated with the help of general formula:

$$P = A \vee A^2 \vee A^3 \vee A^4$$

If we apply the above formula to find path matrix, we get the following resultant matrix. Thus, we can say that the general technique to find path matrix requires much more theoretical work and it is slow in comparison to **Warshall**'s algorithm even if we implement it on computer.

$$P = \begin{pmatrix} 1 & 1 & 0 & 1 \\ 1 & 1 & 0 & 1 \\ 1 & 1 & 0 & 1 \\ 1 & 1 & 0 & 1 \end{pmatrix}$$

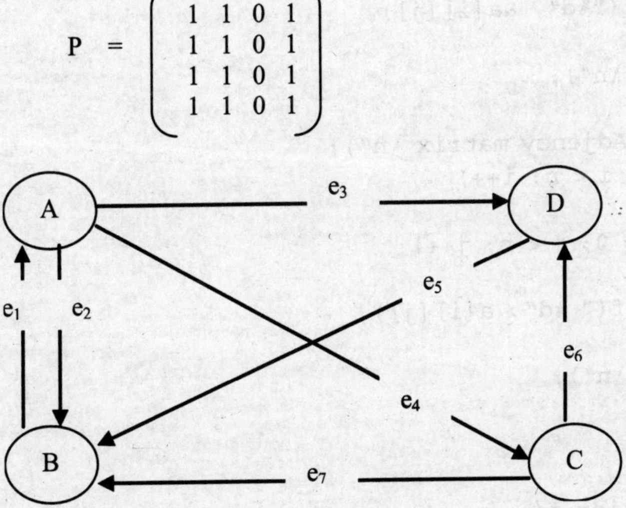

Figure 8.15 Directed Graph

The program segment **WARSHALL.C** illustrates the algorithm given in **Figure 8.14.** The result of this program segment can be tested with the help of **Figure 8.15.**

```
/* SHORTEST PATH */
/* WARSHALL.C */

# include<stdio.h>
# define size 10

int a [size][size];
int p [size][size];
int i,k,j;
int n;

void Input ();
void Warshall ();
void Output ();

/* Input function */

void Input()
{
    printf("\n Input the number of vertices: ");
    scanf("%d", &n);
    printf("\n Input adjency matrix\n");
    for ( i = 0; i < n; i++)
    {
        for ( j = 0; j < n; j++)
        {
            scanf("%d", &a[i][j]);
        }
        printf("\n");
    }
    printf("\n Adjency matrix \n");
    for ( i = 0; i < n; i++)
    {
        for ( j = 0; j < n; j++)
        {
            printf(" %d", a[i][j]);
        }
        printf("\n");
    }
}

/* Output function */
void Output()
```

```
{
    for ( i = 0; i < n; i++)
    {
        for ( j = 0; j < n; j++)
        {
            printf(" %d", p [i][j]);
        }
        printf("\n");
    }
}

/* Shortest path function */

void Warshall ()
{
    /* Initialization of matrix m */

    for ( i = 0; i < n; i++)
    {
        for ( j = 0; j < n; j++)
        {
            if (a[i][j] == 0)
                p [i][j] = 0;
            else
                p[i][j] = 1;
        }
    }

    /* Shortest Path evaluation start from here */

    for( k = 0; k < n; k++)
    {
        for ( i = 0; i < n; i++)
        {
            for ( j = 0; j < n; j++)
            {
                p[i][j] = p[i][j] | ( p[i][k] & p[k][j]);
            }
        }
    }
}

/* Function main */

void main()
```

```
{
    Input ();
    Warshall ();
    printf("\n Path matrix:\n");
    Output ();
}
```

```
Input the number of vertices: 4
Input adjacency matrix
0 1 0 1
1 0 0 0
1 0 0 1
0 1 0 0
Adjacency matrix
0 1 0 1
1 0 0 0
1 0 0 1
0 1 0 0

Path matrix:
1 1 0 1
1 1 0 1
1 1 0 1
1 1 0 1
```

8.4.2 Warshall's Modified Algorithm

Warshall's algorithm can be modified to obtain a matrix which gives the length of the shortest paths between the vertices of a graph **G**. For example, suppose **A** is adjacency matrix of **G**, replace all those elements of **A** which are zero by infinity (∞ or by a very-very large number), which now indicates that there is no edge between the vertices. In this technique we obtain a set of matrices $\mathbf{M_0}$, $\mathbf{M_1}$, $\mathbf{M_2}$ ... $\mathbf{M_n}$, with the help of following formula:

$$M_k [i][j] = \text{Min} (M_{k-1} [i][j], M_{k-1} [i][k] + M_{k-1} [k][j])$$

The input matrix is same as adjacency matrix **A** except that each 0 is replaced by infinity (∞ or by a very-very large number). The final resulting matrix $\mathbf{M_n}$ will be the desired shortest path matrix. For example, consider the graph illustrated in **Figure 8.16.** The adjacency matrix for this graph is:

$$A = \begin{pmatrix} 0 & 1 & 0 & 1 \\ 1 & 0 & 0 & 0 \\ 1 & 1 & 0 & 1 \\ 0 & 1 & 0 & 0 \end{pmatrix}$$

$$M_0 = \begin{pmatrix} 9999 & 1 & 9999 & 1 \\ 1 & 9999 & 9999 & 9999 \\ 1 & 1 & 9999 & 1 \\ 9999 & 1 & 9999 & 9999 \end{pmatrix}$$

Step0

$$M_1 = \begin{pmatrix} 9999 & 1 & 9999 & 1 \\ 1 & 2 & 9999 & 2 \\ 1 & 1 & 9999 & 1 \\ 9999 & 1 & 9999 & 9999 \end{pmatrix}$$

Step1

$$M_2 = \begin{pmatrix} 2 & 1 & 9999 & 1 \\ 1 & 2 & 9999 & 2 \\ 1 & 1 & 9999 & 1 \\ 2 & 1 & 9999 & 3 \end{pmatrix}$$

Step2

$$M_3 = \begin{pmatrix} 2 & 1 & 9999 & 1 \\ 1 & 2 & 9999 & 2 \\ 1 & 1 & 9999 & 1 \\ 2 & 1 & 9999 & 3 \end{pmatrix}$$

Step3

$$M_4 = \begin{pmatrix} 2 & 1 & 9999 & 1 \\ 1 & 2 & 9999 & 2 \\ 1 & 1 & 9999 & 1 \\ 2 & 1 & 9999 & 3 \end{pmatrix}$$

Figure 8.16 A graph with equal wrights

M_4 is the shortest path matrix for the graph illustrated in **Figure 8.16.**

If graph **G** is a weight graph, we can find its weight matrix and apply the above procedure to find the shortest path matrix if the length of the edges is the weights. If the weight of each edge is the cost then the shortest path matrix gives the minimal cost matrix. For example, let the graph **G** illustrated in **Figure 8.17.**

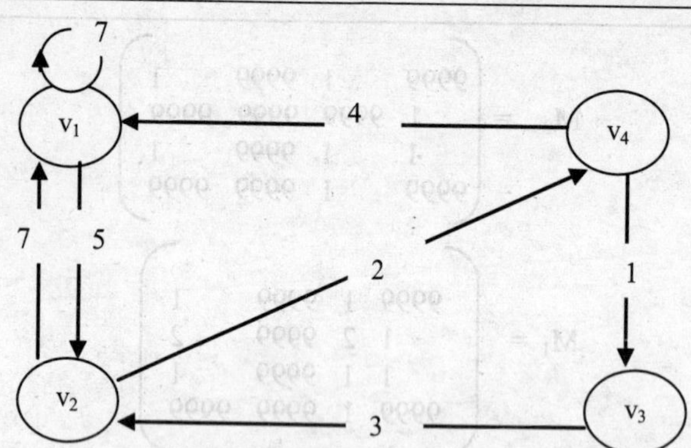

Figure 8.17 A graph with ring (cycle)

The adjacency matrix **A** for **G** is as follows.

$$A = \begin{pmatrix} 7 & 5 & 0 & 0 \\ 7 & 0 & 0 & 2 \\ 0 & 3 & 0 & 0 \\ 4 & 0 & 1 & 0 \end{pmatrix}$$

Matrix after replacing all 0′s elements by a large value

$$M_0 = \begin{pmatrix} 7 & 5 & 9999 & 9999 \\ 7 & 9999 & 9999 & 2 \\ 9999 & 3 & 9999 & 9999 \\ 4 & 9999 & 1 & 9999 \end{pmatrix}$$

Step0

$$M_1 = \begin{pmatrix} 7 & 5 & 9999 & 9999 \\ 7 & 12 & 9999 & 2 \\ 9999 & 3 & 9999 & 9999 \\ 4 & 9 & 1 & 9999 \end{pmatrix}$$

Step1

$$M_2 = \begin{pmatrix} 7 & 5 & 9999 & 7 \\ 7 & 12 & 9999 & 2 \\ 10 & 3 & 9999 & 5 \\ 4 & 9 & 1 & 11 \end{pmatrix}$$

Step2

$$M_3 = \begin{pmatrix} 7 & 5 & 9999 & 7 \\ 7 & 12 & 9999 & 2 \\ 10 & 3 & 9999 & 5 \\ 4 & 4 & 1 & 6 \end{pmatrix}$$

Step3

$$M_4 = \begin{pmatrix} 7 & 5 & 8 & 7 \\ 6 & 6 & 3 & 2 \\ 9 & 3 & 6 & 5 \\ 4 & 4 & 1 & 6 \end{pmatrix}$$

M_4 represents shortest path matrix for the graph illustrated in **Figure 8.17**.

```
Step 1: [Initialize matrix m]
Repeat thru step 2 for i = 0, 1, 2, 3 ... n - 1
       Repeat thru step 2 for j = 0, 1, 2, 3 ... n - 1
Step 2: [Test the condition and assign the required value to matrix m]
       If (a[i][j] = 0)
       m [i][j] = Infinity
       Else
      m[i][j] = a [i][j]
Step 3: [Shortest Path evaluation]
       Repeat thru step 4 for k = 0, 1, 2, 3 ... n - 1
       Repeat thru step 4 for i = 0, 1, 2, 3 ... n - 1
       Repeat thru step 4 for j = 0, 1, 2, 3 ... n - 1
Step 4: If (m [i][j] < (m [i][k] + m [k][j]))
       m [i][j] = m [i][j]
       Else
       m [i][j] = m [i][k] + m [k][j]
Step 5: Exit
```

Figure 8.18 Modified Warshall's algorithm

The program segment **SPATH.C** illustrates the algorithm given in **Figure 8.18** and result is tested for graph illustrated in **Figure 8.16** and **Figure 8.17**.

```
/* SHORTEST PATH */
/* SPATH.C */
 # include<stdio.h>
 # define size 10
 # define infinity 9999

    int a[size][size];
      int m[size][size];
      int i,k,j;
      int n;
    void Input ();
      void Short ();
      void Output ();
 /* Input function */

 void Input()
 {
 printf("\n Input the number of vetices: ");
 scanf("%d", &n);
 printf("\n Input adjacency matrix\n");
 for (i = 0; i < n; i++) {
    for (j = 0; j < n; j++)
    {
```

```
        scanf("%d", &a[i][j]);
        }
        printf("\n");
        }
        printf("\n Adjacency matrix \n");
       for ( i = 0; i < n; i++) {
        for ( j = 0; j < n; j++) {
        printf(" %i", a[i][j]);
        }
        printf("\n");
        }
    }

    /* Output function */

    void Output()
    {
    for ( i = 0; i < n; i++) {
        for ( j = 0; j < n; j++) {
        printf(" %d", m[i][j]);
        }
        printf("\n");
        }
    }

    /* Shortest path function */

    void Short ()
    {
    /* Initialization of matrix m */

    for ( i = 0; i < n; i++) {
        for ( j = 0; j < n; j++) {
        if (a[i][j] == 0)
        m[i][j] = infinity;
        else
        m[i][j] = a[i][j];
        }
        }
      printf("\n Adjacency matrix after replacing zeros by very large value");
      Output();

   /* Shortest path evaluation start from here */
    for ( k = 0; k < n; k++){
    for ( i = 0; i < n; i++) {
```

```
    for ( j = 0; j < n; j++) {
    if ( m [i][j] <= m [i][k] + m [k][j] )
    m [i][j] = m [i][j];
    else
    m [i][j] = m[i][k] + m [k][j];
    }
    }
    printf("\n STEP %d \n", k);
    Output();
  }
  }

/* Function main */

 void main()
 {
    Input();
    Short();
    printf("\n Shortest path matrix is as follows\n");
    Output();
 }
```

```
Input the number of vertices: 4
Input adjacency matrix
  0   1   0   1
  1   0   0   0
  1   1   0   1
  0   1   0   0

Adjacency matrix
  0   1   0   1
  1   0   0   0
  1   1   0   1
  0   1   0   0
Matrix after replacing zeros by large value

  9999       1   9999       1
     1    9999   9999    9999
     1       1   9999       1
  9999       1   9999    9999

STEP0
  9999   1   9999       1
     1   2   9999       2
     1   1   9999       1
  9999   1   9999    9999
```

```
STEP1
   2   1   9999   1
   1   2   9999   2
   1   1   9999   1
   2   1   9999   3

STEP2
   2   1   9999   1
   1   2   9999   2
   1   1   9999   1
   2   1   9999   3

STEP3
   2   1   9999   1
   1   2   9999   2
   1   1   9999   1
   2   1   9999   3

Shortest path matrix is as follows
   2   1   9999   1
   1   2   9999   2
   1   1   9999   1
   2   1   9999   3
```

```
Input the number of vertices: 4
 Input adjacency matrix
  7 5 0 0
  7 0 0 2
  0 3 0 0
  4 0 1 0

Adjacency matrix
  7 5 0 0
  7 0 0 2
  0 3 0 0
  4 0 1 0
Matrix after replacing zeros by large value

     7     5 9999 9999
     7  9999 9999    2
  9999     3 9999 9999
     4  9999    1 9999

STEP0
     7    5 9999 9999
     7   12 9999    2
  9999    3 9999 9999
     4    9    1 9999
```

```
STEP1
   7   5  9999  7
   7  12  9999   2
  10   3  9999   5
   4   9      1 11

STEP2
   7   5  9999  7
   7  12  9999  2
  10   3  9999  5
   4   4      1  6

STEP3
 7  5  8  7
 6  6  3  2
 9  3  6  5
 4  4  1  6

Shortest path matrix is as follows
 7  5  8  7
 6  6  3  2
 9  3  6  5
 4  4  1  6
```

8.4.3 Dijkstra's Technique

This technique is used to determine the shortest path between two arbitrary vertices in a graph. Let, weight **w** (v_i, v_j) is associated with every edge (v_i, v_j) in a given graph **G**. Furthermore, the weights are such that the total weight from vertex v_i to the vertex v_k via vertex v_j is $w(v_i, v_j) + w(v_j, v_k)$. Using this technique, the weight from a vertex v_s (starting of the path) to vertex v_t (the end of the path) in the graph **G** for a given a path $(v_s, v_1), (v_1, v_2), (v_2, v_3) \ldots (v_i, v_t)$ is given by $w(v_s, v_1) + w(v_1, v_2) + w(v_2, v_3) + \ldots + w(v_i, v_t)$. In a graph there are many possible paths between v_s and v_t.

Dijkstra's method is a very popular and efficient one to find every path from starting to terminal vertices. If there is an edge between two vertices, then the weight of this edge is its length. If several edges exist however, use the shortest length edge. If no edge actually exists set the length to infinity. Edge (v_i, v_j) does not necessarily have the same length as edge (v_j, v_i). This allows different routes between two vertices that take different paths depending on the direction of travel.

Dijkstra's technique is based on assigning labels to each vertex. The label is equal to the distance (weight) from the starting vertex to that vertex. Obviously, the starting vertex v_s has a label 0. A label can be in one of two states-temporary or permanent. A permanent label that lies along the shortest path while a temporary label is one that has uncertainty as to whether the label is along the shortest path.

```
Step 1: Assign a temporary label level(vi) = ∞ to all vertices except vs.
Step 2: [Mark vs as permanent by assigning 0 label to it]
  level(vs) = 0
Step 3: [Assign value of vs to vr where vr is last vertex to be made
permanent]
```

```
        v_r = v_s
    Step 4:
        if level(v_i) > level(v_k) + w (v_k, v_i)
        level(v_i) = level(v_k) + w (v_k, v_i)
    Step 5: v_r = v_i

    Step 6: If v_t has temporary label, repeat Step 4 to Step 5, otherwise the
value of v_t is permanent·label and is equal to the shortest path v_s to v_t.
    Step 6: Exit
```

Figure 8.19 Dijkstra's Algorithm

This technique gradually changes the temporary labels to permanent labels until the end vertex has a permanent label. At each step, the aim is to make the temporary labels shorter by finding paths to the associated vertices using the shortest paths to the permanent labeled vertices. After this the temporary label with the smallest value is made permanent. This process eliminates one temporary vertex at each step, ensuring that the shortest path from v_s to v_t will eventually be found.

For example, consider the graph **G** illustrated in **Figure 8.20** and the weight matrix of **G** is as follows:

W =

	v_1	v_2	v_3	v_4
v_1	0	5	0	4
v_2	7	0	0	2
v_3	0	3	0	0
v_4	0	0	1	0

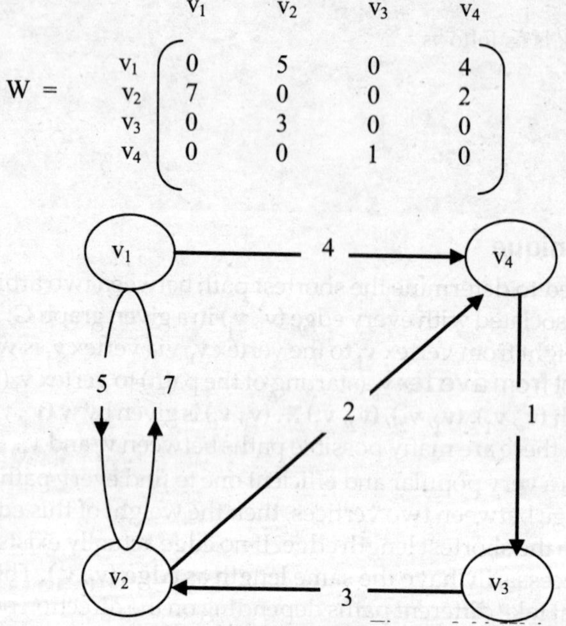

Figure 8.20 Weighted graph

If we replace the elements, which have 0 with 9999 (very large value) except diagonal elements, we get a distance matrix **D**.

D =

	v_1	v_2	v_3	v_4
v_1	0	5	9999	4
v_2	7	0	9999	2
v_3	9999	3	0	9999
v_4	9999	9999	1	0

Now, we have to travel from v_1 to v_4 in the graph **G** illustrated in **Figure 8.20**. There are two possible route (a) from vertex v_1 to v_4 (direct) and (b) vertex v_1 to v_2 and then from v_2 to v_4. The distances for the two possible routes are 4 and 7 represented?

Step 1, Step 2 and Step 3: Assign labels as follows and set $v_r = v_s = v_1$.

	v_s	v_2	v_3	v_t
Label:	0	9999	9999	9999
Permanent:	Y	N	N	N

Step 4 and Step 5: Redefine temporary labels as follows:

Label (v_2) = min (9999, 0 + 5) = 5
Label (v_3) = min (9999, 0 + 9999) = 9999
Label (v_t) = min (9999, 0 + 4) = 4
Make Label (v_2) permanent, $v_r = v_2$

	v_s	v_2	v_3	v_t
Label:	0	5	9999	9999
Permanent:	Y	Y	N	N

Step 6: Repeat Step 4 and Step 5, redefine the temporary labels as follows:

Label (v_3) = min (9999, 7 + 0) = 7
Label (v_t) = min (4, 7+2) = 4
Make Label (v_3) permanent set $v_r = v_3$

	v_s	v_2	v_3	v_t
Label:	0	5	7	9999
Permanent:	Y	Y	Y	N

Step 6: Repeat Step 4 and Step 5, redefine

Label (v_t) = min (4, 0+9999) = 4
Make Label (v_t) permanent set $v_r = v_t$

	v_s	v_2	v_3	v_t
Label:	0	5	7	4
Permanent:	Y	Y	Y	Y

Step 6: Label (v_t) is permanent. The shortest path length is 4.

The program segment **DIJKSTRA.C** implements **DIJKSTRA**'s algorithm.

```
/* DIJKSTRA METHOD */
/* DIJKSTRA.C*/

# include<stdio.h>

# define size 20
# define P 1
# define T 0
# define infinity 9999

struct Label
{
   int predecessor;
   int length;
   int flag;
};

int k, min, count;
struct Label state[size];
int visit_path[size];

int Short_Path(int a[size][size], int , int , int,
int path [size], int *);
void Input(int , int a[size][size]);
void Output(int , int a[size][size]);

/* Shortest path computing function */
int Short_Path(int a[size][size], int n, int s, int t,
int path[size], int *dist)
{
   int i;
   int t1, t2;
   *dist = 0;

   for(i = 1; i <= n; i ++)
   {
      state[i].predecessor = 0;
      state[i].length = infinity ;
      state[i].flag = T;
   }
   /* Make source vertex permanent */
   state[s].predecessor = 0;
   state[s].length = 0;
   state[s].flag = P;
```

```
    /* Start from source vertex */

    k = s;
    do
    {
        /* Check all the paths from kth vertex and find their distance from
k vertex */
        for ( i = 1; i <= n; i++)
        {
            if ((a[k][i] > 0) && (state[i].flag == T))
            {
                if ((state[k].length + a[k][i]) < state[i].length)
                {
                    state[i].predecessor = k;
                    state[i].length = state[k].length + a[k][i];
                }
            }
        }
        min = infinity;
        k = 0;
        for ( i =1; i <= n; i++)
        {
            if ((state[i].flag == T) && (state[i].length < min))
            {
                min = state[i].length;
                k = i;
            }
        }
        if ( k==0)
            return (0);
        state[k].flag = P;
    } while(k != t);

    /* Store optimal path */
    k = t;
    count = 1;
    do
    {

        visit_path[count] = k;
        count ++;
        k = state[k].predecessor;
    } while(k!= 0);

  /* Reverse the vertices since algorithm stores path in reverse direction */
```

```
    count --;
    for ( i = 1; i <= count ; i++)
        path[i] = visit_path[count-i+1];

    for ( i = 1; i < count ; i ++)
    {
        t1 = path[i];
        t2 = path [i+1];
        *dist += a[t1] [t2];
    }
    return (count);
}

/* Input function */
void Input(int n, int a[size] [size])
{
    int i, j;
    printf("\n Input adjacency matrix \n");
    for(i =0; i < n; i++)
    {
        for(j =0; j < n; j++)
        {
            scanf("%d", &a[i] [j]);
        }
        printf("\n");
    }
}

/* Output function */
void Output(int n, int a[size] [size])
{
    int i, j;
    printf("\n Adjacency matrix \n");
    for(i =0; i < n; i++)
    {
        for(j =0; j < n; j++)
        {
            printf(" %d", a[i] [j]);
        }
        printf("\n");
    }
}

/* Function main */
void main()
```

```
{
    int a[size][size];
    int path [size];
    int org, dest, dist;
    int count, i, n;
    printf("\n Input the number of vertices in the graph: ");
    scanf("%d", &n);
    Input(n,a);
    Output(n,a);
    printf("\n Input strating vertex: ");
    scanf("%d", &org);
    printf("\n Input destination: ");
    scanf("%d", &dest);
    count = Short_Path(a, n, org, dest, path, &dist);
    if (dist)
    {
        printf("\n Shortest path: %d", path[1]);
        for (i = 2; i<=count; i++);
        printf(" => %d", path[i]);
        printf("\n Minimum distance = %i", dist);
    }
    else
        printf("\n Path does not exist \n");
}
```

Input the number of vertices in the graph: 4
Input adjacency matrix

0 1 0 1
1 0 1 0
0 1 0 1
1 0 1 0

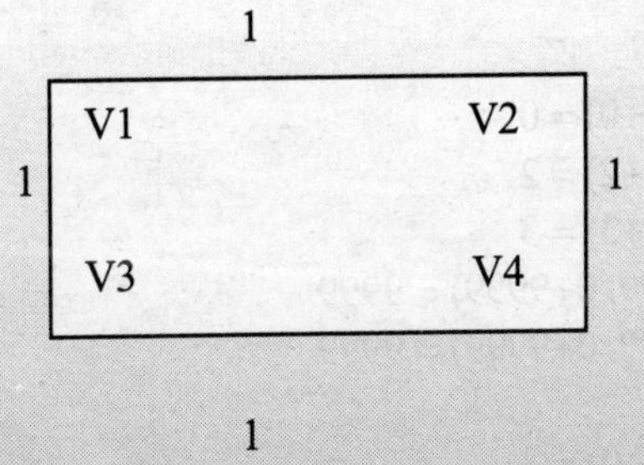

Adjacency matrix

0 1 0 1
1 0 1 0
0 1 0 1
1 0 1 0
Input starting vertex: 1

Input destination: 3
Shortest path:
1 => 0 =>2 => 3
Minimum distance = 2

8.4.4 Floyd's Technique

Floyd's technique starts by numbering each vertex from $\mathbf{v}_1$ to $\mathbf{v}_n$ and uses the weight matrix (Distance matrix or adjacency matrix) first to find the shortest paths that are either direct or use vertex $\mathbf{v}_1$ as an intermediate vertex. Then it finds the shortest path that uses vertex $\mathbf{v}_1$ or vertex $\mathbf{v}_2$ as intermediate vertices. This process continues until the shortest paths are found that are either direct or use some or all of the vertex $\mathbf{v}_1$ to $\mathbf{v}_n$ as intermediate vertices.

The intermediate results are stored in an **n x n** matrix **r**, where element $\mathbf{r}_k$ **[i][j]** represents the shortest path between vertices $\mathbf{v}_i$ and $\mathbf{v}_j$, **when the vertices** $\mathbf{v}_1$ to $\mathbf{v}_k$ are used as intermediate vertices. The element $\mathbf{r}_{k+1}$ **[i][j]** is either $\mathbf{r}_k$ **[i][j]** or $\mathbf{r}_k$ **[i][k]** + $\mathbf{r}_k$ **[k][j]. Figure 8.21** illustrates the algorithm for **Floyd**'s technique.

For example, consider the graph **G** illustrated in **Figure 8.22**. The adjacency (weight) matrix for this graph is as follows:

$$W = \begin{pmatrix} 0 & 2 & 3 & 0 & 0 \\ 2 & 0 & 1 & 0 & 5 \\ 3 & 0 & 0 & 1 & 0 \\ 1 & 0 & 0 & 0 & 2 \\ 0 & 0 & 3 & 0 & 0 \end{pmatrix}$$

Step 2 and Step 3:

Replacing zero elements by very large value (9999) except diagonal elements, we get distance matrix D.

$$D = \begin{pmatrix} 0 & 2 & 3 & 9999 & 9999 \\ 2 & 0 & 1 & 9999 & 5 \\ 3 & 9999 & 0 & 1 & 9999 \\ 1 & 9999 & 9999 & 0 & 2 \\ 9999 & 9999 & 3 & 9999 & 0 \end{pmatrix}$$

Step 4 and Step 5:

r_0 (0, 0) = min (0, 0+0) = 0
r_0 (0, 1) = min (2, 0+2) = 2
r_0 (0, 2) = min (3, 0+3) = 3
r_0 (0, 3) = min (9999, 0+9999) = 9999
r_0 (0, 4) = min (9999, 0+9999) = 9999

r_0 (1, 0) = min (2, 2+0) = 2
r_0 (1, 1) = min (0, 0+2) = 0
r_0 (1, 2) = min (1, 1+2) = 1
r_0 (1, 3) = min (5, 2+9999) = 5
r_0 (1, 4) = min (5, 2+5) = 5

r_0 (2, 0) = min (3, 3+0) = 3
r_0 (2, 1) = min (9999, 3+9999) = 9999
r_0 (2, 2) = min (0, 3+0) = 0

$r_0(2, 3) = \min(1, 3+9999) = 1$

$r_0(2, 4) = \min(9999, 3+1) = 4$

If we continue the above process we get the final shortest distance matrix $\mathbf{r_n}$. The program segment **FLOYD.C** is the implementation of the algorithm given in **Figure 8.21**.

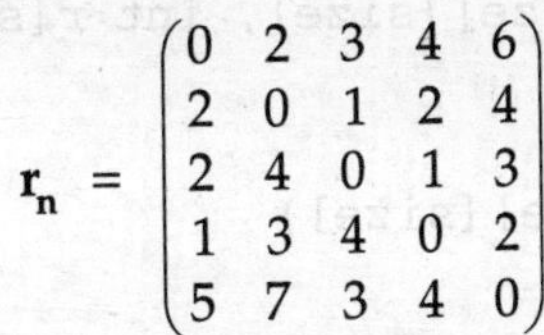

$$\mathbf{r_n} = \begin{pmatrix} 0 & 2 & 3 & 4 & 6 \\ 2 & 0 & 1 & 2 & 4 \\ 2 & 4 & 0 & 1 & 3 \\ 1 & 3 & 4 & 0 & 2 \\ 5 & 7 & 3 & 4 & 0 \end{pmatrix}$$

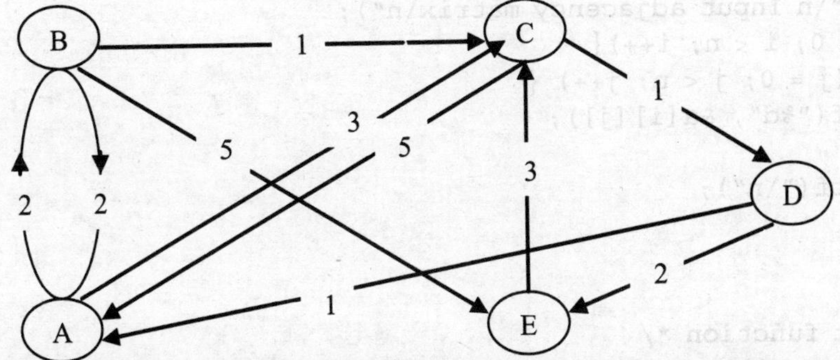

Figure 8.22 Air route between 5 highly populated cities in INDIA

```
Step 1: [Set diagonal elements of adjacency matrix to zero]
   Repeat for i = 0, 1, 2, 3 ... n - 1
    a [i][i] = 0
Step 2: [Replace zero elements by a very large value and
store the resulting matrix into r]
   Repeat thru Step 3 for i = 0, 1, 2, 3 ... n - 1
   Repeat thru Step 3 for j = 0, 1, 2, 3 ... n - 1
Step 3: If (a [i][j] = 0 and (i ¹ j))
   r [i][j] = Infinity
   Else
   r [i][j] = a [i][j]
Step 4:  Repeat thru Step 5 for k = 0, 1, 2, 3 ... n - 1
   Repeat thru Step 5 for i = 0, 1, 2, 3 ... n - 1
   Repeat thru Step 5 for j = 0, 1, 2, 3 ... n - 1
Step 5: If ((r [i][k] + r[k][j] )< r [i][j])
 r [i][j] = r [i][k] + r[k][j]
Step 6: Exit
```

Figure 8.21 Floyd's algorithm

```
/* FLYOD'S METHOD */
/* FLYOD.C */
 # include<stdio.h>
 # define Infinity 9999
```

```
# define size 20
   int i,k,j;
   void Input(int , int a[size][size]);
   void Output(int , int a[size][size]);
   void Flyod(int , int a[size][size], int r[size][size]);

/* Input function */
void Input(int n, int a[size][size])
{
int i, j;
printf("\n Input adjacency matrix\n");
for (i = 0; i < n; i++){
   for (j = 0; j < n; j++) {
   scanf("%d", &a[i][j]);
   }
   printf("\n");
}
}

/* Output function */
void Output (int n, int a[size][size])
{
int i, j;
for (i =0; i < n; i++)
{
   for (j =0; j < n; j++)
   {
   printf(" %d", a[i][j]);
   }
   printf("\n");
}
}

/* Shortest path evaluation function */
void Flyod(int n, int a[size][size], int r[size][size])
{
   for (i = 0; i < n; i ++)
   a[i][i] = 0;    /* Set diagonal elements zero */
   printf("\n After setting diagonal elements to zero \n");
   Output(n, a);
   for (i = 0; i < n; i++)
   {
   for (j = 0; j < n; j++)
   {
```

```
        if ((a[i][j] == 0) && (i != j))
         r[i][j] = Infinity;
         else
         r[i][j] = a[i][j];
      }
      }
     printf("\n Replacing zeros by very large value \n");
     Output(n, r);
     for (k = 0; k < n; k++)
     {
     for (i = 0; i < n; i++)
     {
     for (j = 0; j < n; j++)
     {
        if (r[i][k] + r[k][j]< r[i][j])
        {
        printf("\n r[%d][%d] = %d ", i, k, r[i][k]);
        printf("\n r[%d][%d] = %d ", k, j, r[k][j]);
        printf("\n r[%d][%d] = %d ", i, j, r[i][j]);
        r[i][j] = r[i][k] + r[k][j];
        printf("\n r[%d][%d] = r[%d][%d] + r[%d][%d] = %d ", i, j, i, k, k,
j,
  r[i][j]);
        }
        else
        {
        r[i][j] = r[i][j];
        printf("\n r[%d][%d] = r[%d][%d] = %d ", i, j, i, j, r[i][j]);
        }
     }
     printf("\n");
     }
     printf("\n Step %d \n", k);
     Output (n,r);
     }
  }

 /* Function main */

  void main()
  {
     int a[size][size];
     int r[size][size];
     int n;
     printf("\n Input number of vertices in the graph: ");
```

```
    scanf("%d", &n);
    Input(n,a);
    printf("\n Adjacency matrix\n");
   Output(n,a);
   Flyod(n,a,r);
   printf("\n Shortest path matrix \n");
    Output(n,r);
}
```

```
Input number of vertices in the graph: 4
Input adjacency matrix
0 1 0 1
1 0 1 0
0 1 0 1
1 0 1 0
Adjacency matrix
0 1 0 1
1 0 1 0
0 1 0 1
1 0 1 0
After setting diagonal elements to zero
0 1 0 1
1 0 1 0
0 1 0 1
1 0 1 0
Replacing zeros by very large value
0 1 9999 1
1 0 1 9999
9999 1 0 1
1 9999 1 0
Step 1
0 1 2 1
1 0 1 2
2 1 0 1
1 2 1 0
Step 2
0 1 2 1
1 0 1 2
2 1 0 1
1 2 1 0
Step 3
0 1 2 1
1 0 1 2
2 1 0 1
1 2 1 0
```

```
Shortest path matrix
0 1 2 1
1 0 1 2
2 1 0 1
1 2 1 0
```

```
Input number of vertices in the graph: 5
Input adjacency matrix
0 2 3 0 0
2 0 1 0 5
3 0 0 1 0
1 0 0 0 2
0 0 3 0 0

Adjacency matrix
0 2 3 0 0
2 0 1 0 5
3 0 0 1 0
1 0 0 0 2
0 0 3 0 0

After setting diagonal elements to zero
0 2 3 0 0
2 0 1 0 5
3 0 0 1 0
1 0 0 0 2
0 0 3 0 0
Replacing zeros by very large value [by 9999 except diagonal elements]
   0     2     3  9999  9999
   2     0     1  9999     5
   3  9999     0     1  9999
   1  9999  9999     0     2
9999  9999     3  9999     0

Step 0 [Resulting matrix after first iteration]
   0     2  3  9999  9999
   2     0  1  9999     5
   3     5  0     1  9999
   1     3  4     0     2
9999  9999  3  9999     0

Step 1[Resulting matrix after second iteration]
   0     2  3  9999   7
   2     0  1  9999   5
   3     5  0     1  10
   1     3  4     0   2
9999  9999  3  9999   0
Step 2 [Resulting matrix after 3rd iteration]
0 2 3 4  7
2 0 1 2  5
3 5 0 1 10
1 3 4 0  2
6 8 3 4  0
```

Step 3 [Resulting matrix after 4th iteration]

```
0 2 3 4 6
2 0 1 2 4
2 4 0 1 3
1 3 4 0 2
5 7 3 4 0
```

Step 4 [Resulting matrix after 5th and last iteration]

```
0 2 3 4 6
2 0 1 2 4
2 4 0 1 3
1 3 4 0 2
5 7 3 4 0
```

Shortest path matrix [*RESULT*]

```
0 2 3 4 6
2 0 1 2 4
2 4 0 1 3
1 3 4 0 2
5 7 3 4 0
```

8.5 ADJACENCY LIST

Let **G = (V, E)** is a graph with **n** vertices. This graph can be represented by **n x n** adjacency matrix. The **n** linked lists represent the **n** rows of the adjacency matrix **A** and there is one linked list for each vertex in **G**. The vertices in the list **L** represent the vertices that are adjacent to the vertex **L,** each vertex represented by two fields: **Vertex** and **Link.** The **Vertex** fields contain the indices of the vertices adjacent to vertex L. The adjacency list for the graph illustrated in **Figure 8.23** is given in **Figure 8.24.** The adjacency matrix for **G** is as follows:

$$A = \begin{array}{c} \\ v_1 \\ v_2 \\ v_3 \\ v_4 \\ v_5 \\ v_6 \end{array} \begin{pmatrix} v_1 & v_2 & v_3 & v_4 & v_5 & v_6 \\ 0 & 1 & 0 & 0 & 1 & 0 \\ 0 & 0 & 1 & 1 & 1 & 0 \\ 0 & 0 & 0 & 0 & 1 & 0 \\ 1 & 0 & 1 & 0 & 0 & 1 \\ 0 & 0 & 0 & 0 & 0 & 0 \\ 0 & 1 & 0 & 0 & 1 & 0 \end{pmatrix}$$

The number of distinct unordered pairs **(v_i, v_j)** with **$v_i \neq v_j$** in a graph with **n** vertices is **n (n – 1) / 2.** This is the maximum number of edges in any **n** vertex undirected graph. An **n** vertex undirected graph with exactly **n (n – 1) /2** edges is said to be complete. In the case of a directed graph having **n** vertices the maximum number of edges is **n (n – 1).**

8.6 GRAPH TRAVERSAL

Sometimes it is required to examine all the vertices in a graph in some systemic orders, as we have seen in the case of binary trees where we use pre-order, post-order or in-order to examine the vertices. For examining all the vertices we start from the root in case of in-order traversal for a tree and for post and preorder traversal is done by starting from leaf, while in the graph we start examination from an arbitrary vertex. There are two popular techniques for examination of the graphs. These are, (a) Depth first search (DFS), and (b) Breadth first search (BFS).

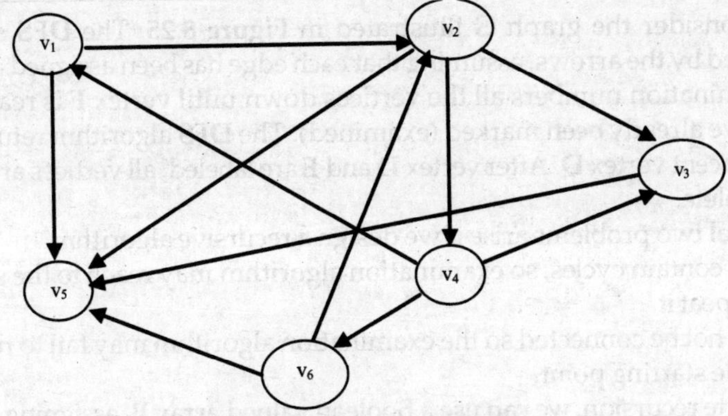

Figure 8.23 Directed graph

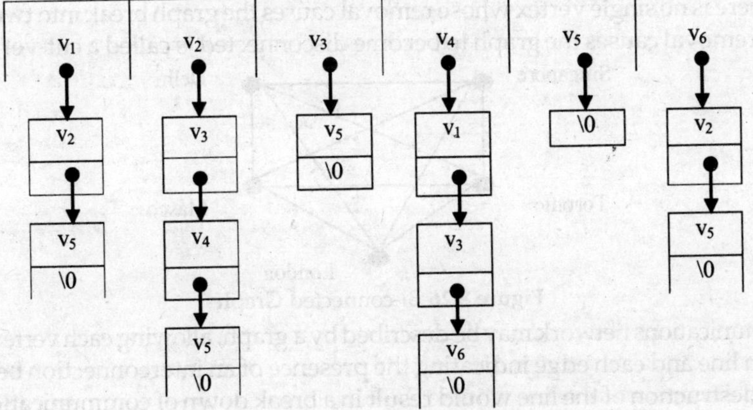

Figure 8.24 Adjacency lists for the graph G

8.6.1 Depth First Search (DFS)

This is similar to pre-order examination of an order tree. Suppose the examination has just examined a vertex $\mathbf{v_i}$ and let $\mathbf{w_1}, \mathbf{w_2}, \mathbf{w_3} \ldots \mathbf{w_k}$, be the vertices adjacent to $\mathbf{v_i}$. We next examine $\mathbf{w_1}$ and keep $\mathbf{w_2}, \mathbf{w_3} \ldots \mathbf{w_k}$ waiting. After examining $\mathbf{w_1}$ we examine all the vertices to which it is adjacent to before returning to examine $\mathbf{w_2}, \mathbf{w_3} \ldots \mathbf{w_k}$.

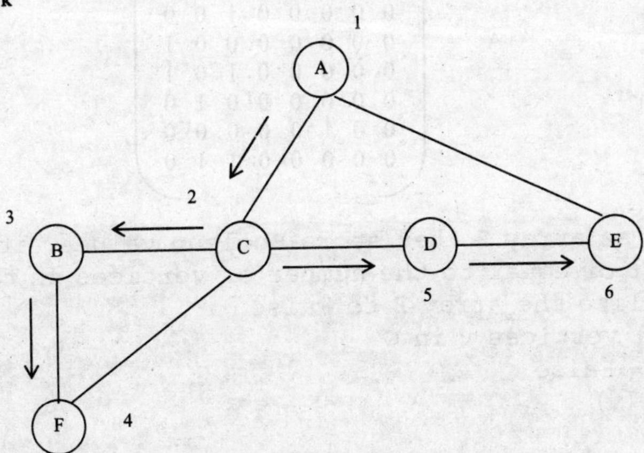

Figure 8.25 Graph with root direction

For example, consider the graph **G** illustrated in **Figure 8.25**. The **DFS** strategy results the examination indicated by the arrows, assuming that each edge has been assigned a value of 1. Starting at vertex **A** the examination numbers all the vertices down until vertex **F** is reached, where all the adjacent vertices have already been marked (examined). The **DFS** algorithm returns to **C**, which still has an unlabeled adjacent vertex **D**. After vertex **D** and **E** are labeled, all vertices are numbered and the examination is complete.

In graph traversal two problems arise if we design a recursive algorithm.

- Graph may contain cycles, so examination algorithm may reach to the same vertex second time and repeat it.
- Graph may not be connected so the examination algorithm may fail to reach all the vertices from a single starting point.

To prevent infinite recursion, we can use a Boolean valued array **B**, assigning **B [v] = True**, before the recursion begins and check the value of **B [w]** before processing **w**. A graph is called a bi-connected {**Figure 8.26**} if there is no single vertex whose removal causes the graph break into two or more pieces. A vertex whose removal causes the graph to become disconnected is called a cut-vertex.

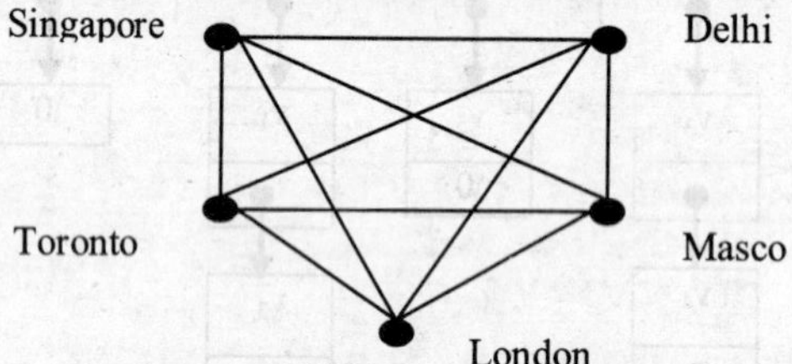

Figure 8.26 Bi-connected Graph

A vital communications network may be described by a graph, allowing each vertex to representing a communication line and each edge indicating the presence of an interconnection between the lines. For a cut-vertex destruction of the line would result in a break down of communications. If the graph is bi-connected the removal of one line (vertex) would not affect the communication, since there will still be other links. The **DFS** algorithm is illustrated in **Figure 8.27** and the program segment **DFS.C** implements this algorithm. The result of the program segment tested on the graph **G** is illustrated in **Figure 8.30.** The adjacency matrix **A** of the graph is as follows:

$$A = \begin{pmatrix} 0 & 1 & 1 & 0 & 0 & 0 & 0 & 0 \\ 0 & 0 & 0 & 1 & 1 & 0 & 0 & 0 \\ 0 & 0 & 0 & 0 & 0 & 1 & 0 & 0 \\ 0 & 0 & 0 & 0 & 0 & 0 & 0 & 1 \\ 0 & 0 & 0 & 0 & 0 & 1 & 0 & 1 \\ 0 & 0 & 0 & 0 & 0 & 0 & 1 & 0 \\ 0 & 0 & 1 & 0 & 0 & 0 & 0 & 0 \\ 0 & 0 & 0 & 0 & 0 & 1 & 1 & 0 \end{pmatrix}$$

```
Step 1: Define an array B that store Boolean values, its size should be
        greater or equal to the number of vertices in the graph G.
Step 2: Initialize the array B to False.
Step 3: For all vertices v in G
       If B[v] = False
       Process (v)
Step 4: Exit
```

Figure 8.27 Depth first search algorithm

```
/* DEPTH FIRST SEARCH TECHNIQUE */
/* DFS.C */
# include<stdio.h>
# define size 20
# define T 1
# define F 0

struct Edge
{
   int terminal;
   struct Edge *next;
};
struct Vertex
{
   int visit;
   int vertex_no;
   char info;
   int path_length;
   struct Edge *Edge_Ptr;
};

void Table(int , int matrix [size][size], struct Vertex vert[size]);
struct Edge *Insert_Vertex (int , struct Edge *);
void DFS ( int , int *dist, struct Vertex vert [size]);
void Input(int, int a [size][size]);
void Output(int, int a [size][size]);

struct Edge * Insert_Vertex (int vertex_no, struct Edge *first)
{
   struct Edge *new1, *current;
   new1 = (struct Edge *) malloc(sizeof(struct Edge));
   new1->terminal = vertex_no;
   new1->next = NULL;
   if (!first)
      return (new1);
   for (current = first; current->next; current = current->next);
   current->next = new1;
   return (first);
}

/* Initializing entries */
void Table(int vertex_num, int matrix [size][size], struct Vertex
vert[size])
{
   int i, j;
```

```
    for (i = 0; i < vertex_num; i++)
    {
        vert [i].visit = F;
        vert [i].vertex_no = i+1;
        vert [i].info = 'A'+ i;
        vert [i].path_length = 0;
        vert [i].Edge_Ptr = NULL;
    }

    for (i =0; i < vertex_num ; i++)
        for (j =0; j < vertex_num ; j++)
            if (matrix [i][j] > 0)
                vert [i].Edge_Ptr = Insert_Vertex (j, vert [i].Edge_Ptr);
}

/* Computing path length */
void DFS ( int index, int *dist, struct Vertex vert [size])
{
    struct Edge *Link;
    vert [index].visit = T;
    vert [index].path_length = *dist;
    *dist += 1;
    for ( Link = vert [index].Edge_Ptr; Link; Link = Link->next)
        if (vert [Link->terminal].visit == F)
            DFS (Link->terminal, dist, vert);
}

/* Input function to read adjacency matrix */
void Input(int number, int a [size][size])
{
    int i, j;
    printf("\n Input the adjacency matrix \n");
    for (i =0; i < number; i++)
    {
        for (j=0; j < number; j ++)
        {
            scanf("%d", &a [i][j]);
        }
        printf("\n");
    }
}

/* Output function */
void Output(int number, int a [size][size])
{
```

```
    int i, j;
    printf("\n Adjacency matrix \n");
    for (i = 0; i < number; i++)
    {
        for (j = 0; j < number; j ++)
        {
            printf(" %d", a [i][j]);
        }
        printf("\n");
    }
}

/* Function main */
void main()
{
    int i;
    int number, index, dist;
    int a [size][size];
    struct Vertex vert [size];
    struct Edge *List;
    printf("\n Input the number of vertices in the graph: ");
    scanf("%d", &number);
    Input(number, a);
    Output(number, a);
    Table(number, a, vert);
    printf("\n Input the starting vertex 0- %d:", number-1);
    scanf("%d", &index);
    dist = 0;
    DFS (index, &dist, vert);
    printf("\n Path length of the vertex from %c", vert[index].info);
    printf("\n Vertex Length Vertex Connectivity \n ");
    for (i = 0; i < number; i++)
    {
        printf("\n %c   %d ", vert[i].info, vert[i].path_length);
        for (List= vert[i].Edge_Ptr; List; List = List->next)
        {
            printf(" ");
            putchar(List->terminal+'A');
        }
    }
}
```

```
Input the number of vertices in the graph: 8
 Input the adjacency matrix

 0  1  1  0  0  0  0  0
 0  0  0  1  1  0  0  0
 0  0  0  0  0  1  0  0
 0  0  0  0  0  0  0  1
 0  0  0  0  0  1  0  1
 0  0  0  0  0  0  1  0
 0  0  1  0  0  0  0  0
 0  0  0  0  0  1  1  0

Adjacency matrix

 0  1  1  0  0  0  0  0
 0  0  0  1  1  0  0  0
 0  0  0  0  0  1  0  0
 0  0  0  0  0  0  0  1
 0  0  0  0  0  1  0  1
 0  0  0  0  0  0  1  0
 0  0  1  0  0  0  0  0
 0  0  0  0  0  1  1  0
Input the starting vertex 0-7: 0
 Path length of the vertex from A
 Vertex Length Vertex Connectivity

  A    0 B C
  B    1 D E
  C    6 F
  D    2 H
  E    7 F H
  F    4 G
  G    5 C
  H    3 F G
```

8.6.2 Breadth First Search (BFS)

Breadth first examination (search) of a graph is similar to level-by-level examination of an ordered tree. If the examination has just visited a vertex **v**, then it visits all the vertices adjacent to **v** by putting the vertices adjacent to those in a waiting queue to be examined, after all vertices adjacent to **v** have been visited.

For example, consider the undirected graph **G** illustrated in **Figure 8.28.** A breadth first examination beginning at vertex **A** of the graph **G** would first visit **A** and then **B** and **C**. Next visits **D, E, F** and **G** will be visited and finally **H**. The adjacency lists of **G** are shown in **Figure 8.29.** The directed graph **G** and the adjacency lists corresponding to this graph are illustrated in **Figure 8.30** and **Figure 8.31,** respectively.

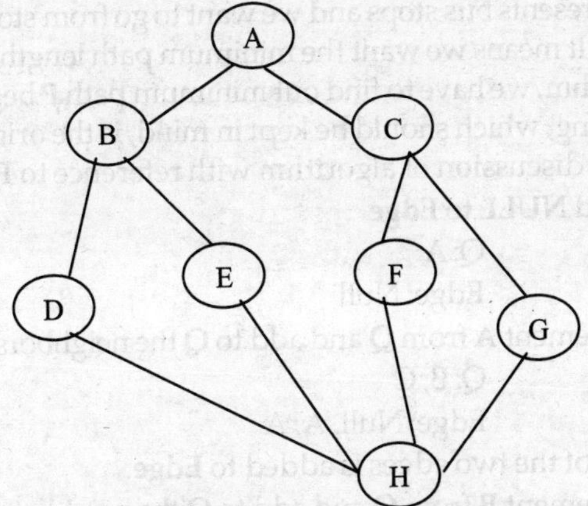

Figure 8.28 Undirected graph

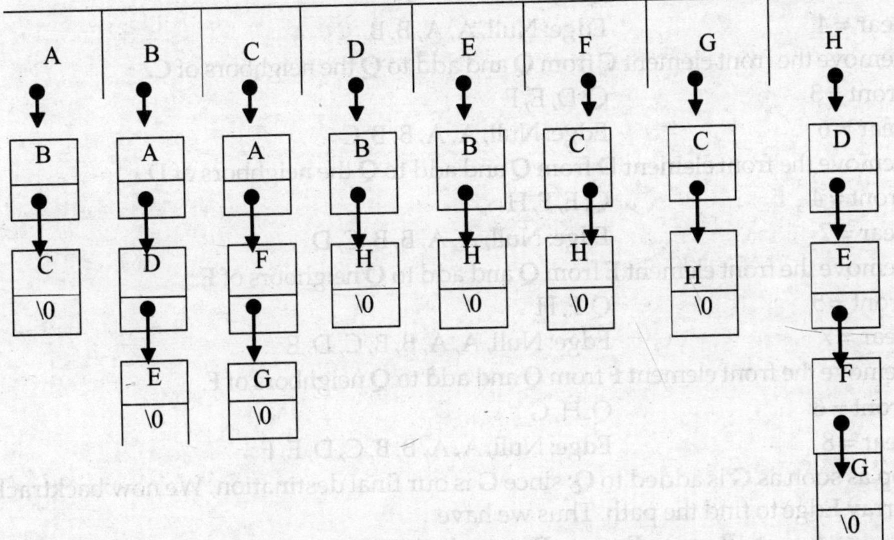

Figure 8.29 Adjacency lists for the graph G

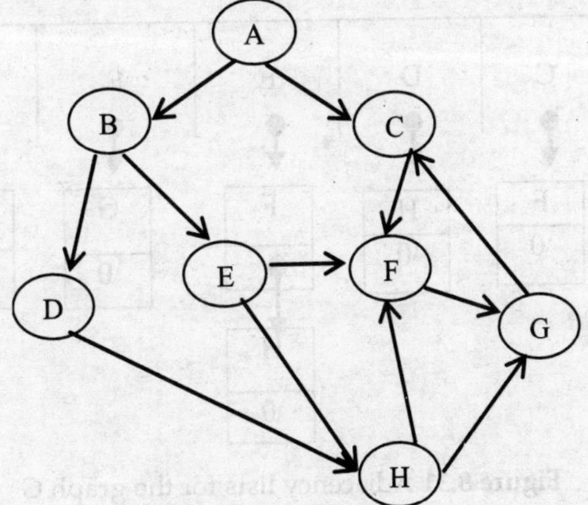

Figure 8.30 Directed graph

Suppose **Figure 8.30** represents bus stops and we want to go from stop **A** to stop **G** with minimum number of stops in between. It means we want the minimum path length **P** from **A** to **G.** With the help of breadth first search algorithm, we have to find out minimum path **P** beginning at **A** and ending at **G.** During the execution one thing, which should be kept in mind, is the origin of each edge. Let we have two arrays **Edge** and **Q**. The discussion of algorithm with reference to **Figure 8.30** is as follows:

(i) Add **A** to **Q** and add **NULL** to **Edge**

Front = 0 Q: A
Rear = 0 Edge: Null

(ii) Remove the front element **A** from **Q** and add to **Q** the neighbors of **A**

Front = 1 Q: B, C
Rear = 2 Edge: Null, A, A

Here origin of each of the two edges is added to **Edge.**

(iii) Remove the front element **B** from **Q** and add to **Q** the neighbors of **B.**

Front = 2 Q: C, D, E
Rear = 4 Edge: Null, A, A, B, B

(iv) Remove the front element **C** from **Q** and add to **Q** the neighbors of **C.**

Front = 3 Q: D, E, F
Rear = 6 Edge: Null, A, A, B, B, C

(v) Remove the front element **D** from **Q** and add to **Q** the neighbors of **D.**

Front = 4 Q: E, F, H
Rear = 7 Edge: Null, A, A, B, B, C, D

(vi) Remove the front element **E** from **Q** and add to **Q** neighbors of **E.**

Front = 5 Q: F, H
Rear = 7 Edge: Null, A, A, B, B, C, D, E

(vii) Remove the front element **F** from **Q** and add to **Q** neighbors of **F.**

Front = 6 Q: H, G
Rear = 8 Edge: Null, A, A, B, B, C, D, E, F

We stop as soon as **G** is added to **Q**; since **G** is our final destination, We now backtrack from **G,** using the array Edge to find the path. Thus we have

A ⟶ B ⟶ E ⟶ F is required path.

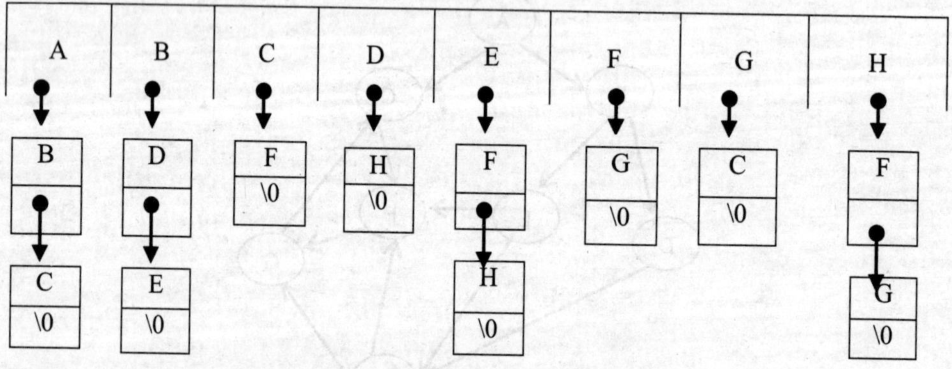

Figure 8.31 Adjacency lists for the graph G

```
Step 1: Initialize all the vertices by setting Flag = 1
Step 2: Put the starting vertex A in Q and change its status to the waiting
        state by setting Flag = 0
Step 3: Repeat thru Step 5 while Q is not NULL.
Step 4: Remove the front vertex v of Q. Process v and set the status of v
        to the processed status by setting Flag = -1
Step 5: Add to the rear of Q all the neighbors of v that are in the ready
        state by setting Flag = 1, and change their status to the waiting
        state by setting Flag = 0
Step 6: Exit
```

Figure 8.32 Breadth first search algorithm

The program segment **BFS.C** illustrates the algorithm given in **Figure 8.32**. The program segment is tested on the graph illustrated in **Figure 8.30**. The adjacency matrix of this graph is as follows:

$$A = \begin{pmatrix} 0 & 1 & 1 & 0 & 0 & 0 & 0 & 0 \\ 0 & 0 & 0 & 1 & 1 & 0 & 0 & 0 \\ 0 & 0 & 0 & 0 & 0 & 1 & 0 & 0 \\ 0 & 0 & 0 & 0 & 0 & 0 & 0 & 1 \\ 0 & 0 & 0 & 0 & 0 & 1 & 0 & 1 \\ 0 & 0 & 0 & 0 & 0 & 0 & 1 & 0 \\ 0 & 0 & 1 & 0 & 0 & 0 & 0 & 0 \\ 0 & 0 & 0 & 0 & 0 & 1 & 1 & 0 \end{pmatrix}$$

```
/* BREADTH FIRST SEARCH TECHNIQUE */
/* BFS.C */
# include<stdio.h>
# define size 20
# define T 1
# define F 0
struct Edge
{
   int terminal;
   struct Edge *next;
};
struct Vertex
{
   int visit;
   int vertex_no;
   char info;
   int path_length;
   struct Edge *Edge_Ptr;
};
struct Q
{
   int info;
```

```
    struct Q *next;
};
void Table(int , int matrix [size][size], struct Vertex vert[size]);
struct Edge *Insert_Vertex (int , struct Edge *);
void BFS ( int , struct Vertex vert [size]);
void Input(int, int mat [size][size]);
void Output(int number, int mat [size][size]);
struct Q *Insert_Queue(int vertex_no, struct Q *first);
struct Q *Delete_Queue(int *vertex_no, struct Q *first);
/* Insert vertex into connectivity list */
struct Edge * Insert_Vertex (int vertex_no, struct Edge *first)
{
    struct Edge *new1, *current;
    new1 = (struct Edge *) malloc(sizeof(struct Edge));
    new1->terminal = vertex_no;
    new1->next = NULL;
    if (!first)
        return (new1);
    for (current = first; current->next; current = current->next);
    current->next = new1;
    return (first);
}

/* Insert vertices into queue */
struct Q * Insert_Queue(int vertex_no, struct Q *first)
{
    struct Q *new1, *current;
    new1 =(struct Q *) malloc(sizeof(struct Q));
    new1->info = vertex_no;
    new1->next = NULL;
    if (!first)
        return (new1);
    for (current = first; current->next; current = current->next);
    current->next = new1;
    return (first);
}
struct Q * Delete_Queue(int *vertex_no, struct Q *first)
{
    struct Q *previous;
    if (!first)
        return (NULL);
    *vertex_no = first->info;
    previous = first;
    first = first->next;
    free(previous);
```

```
    return (first);
  }
  /* Initializing entries */
  void Table(int vertex_num, int matrix [size][size], struct Vertex
vert[size])
  {
    int i, j;
    for (i = 0; i < vertex_num; i++)
    {
      vert [i].visit = F;
      vert [i].vertex_no = i+1;
      vert [i].info = 'A'+ i;
      vert [i].path_length = 0;
      vert [i].Edge_Ptr = NULL;
    }
    for (i =0; i < vertex_num ; i++)
      for (j =0; j < vertex_num ; j++)
        if (matrix [i][j] > 0 )
          vert [i].Edge_Ptr = Insert_Vertex (j, vert [i].Edge_Ptr);
  }
  /* Computing path length */
  void BFS ( int index, struct Vertex vert [size])
  {
    struct Q *queue = NULL;
    struct Edge *Link;
    vert [index].visit = T;
    queue = Insert_Queue(index, queue);
    while(queue)
    {
      queue = Delete_Queue(&index, queue);
      for ( Link = vert [index].Edge_Ptr; Link; Link = Link->next)
      {
        if (vert [Link->terminal].visit == F)
        {
          vert[Link->terminal].visit = T;
        vert[Link->terminal].path_length=vert[index].path_length+1;
          queue = Insert_Queue(Link->terminal, queue);
        }
      }
    }
  }
  /* Input function to read adjacency matrix */
  void Input(int number, int mat [size][size])
  {
    int i, j;
```

```
    printf("\n Input the adjacency matrix \n");
    for (i =0; i < number; i++)
    {
        for(j=0; j < number; j ++)
        {
            scanf("%d", &mat [i][j]);
        }
        printf("\n");
    }
}
/* Output function to display adjacency matrix */
void Output(int number, int mat [size][size])
{
    int i, j;
    printf("\n Adjacency matrix \n");
    for (i =0; i < number; i++)
    {
        for (j=0; j < number; j ++)
        {
            printf(" %d", mat [i][j]);
        }
        printf("\n");
    }
}

/* Function main */
void main()
{
    int i, number, index;
    int mat [size][size];
    struct Vertex vert [size];
    struct Edge *List;
    printf("\n Input the number of vertices in the graph: ");
    scanf("%d", &number);
    Input(number, mat);
    Output(number, mat);
    Table(number, mat, vert);
    printf("\n Input the starting vertex 0- %d :",number-1);
    scanf("%d", &index);
    BFS (index, vert);
    printf("\n Path length of the vertex from %c", vert[index].info);
    printf("\n Vertex Length Vertex Connectivity \n ");
    for (i = 0; i < number; i++)
    {
```

```
        printf("\n %c %d ",vert[i].info, vert[i].path_length);
        for (List= vert[i].Edge_Ptr; List; List = List->next)
        {
            printf(" ");
            putchar(List->terminal+'A');
        }
    }
}
```

```
Input the number of vertices in the graph: 8
 Input the adjacency matrix
   0 1 1 0 0 0 0 0
   0 0 0 1 1 0 0 0
   0 0 0 0 0 1 0 0
   0 0 0 0 0 0 0 1
   0 0 0 0 0 1 0 1
   0 0 0 0 0 0 1 0
   0 0 1 0 0 0 0 0
   0 0 0 0 0 1 1 0
 Adjacency matrix
   0 1 1 0 0 0 0 0
   0 0 0 1 1 0 0 0
   0 0 0 0 0 1 0 0
   0 0 0 0 0 0 0 1
   0 0 0 0 0 1 0 1
   0 0 0 0 0 0 1 0
   0 0 1 0 0 0 0 0
   0 0 0 0 0 1 1 0
 Input the starting vertex 0-7: 4
 Path length of the vertex from E
 Vertex Length Vertex Connectivity
   A      0      B C
   B      0      D E
   C      3      F
   D      0      H
   E      0      F H
   F      1      G
   G      2      C
   H      1      F G
```

8.7 TOPOLOGICAL SORTING

If **G** is a directed graph with no directed cycles then a topological order **T** is a sequential listing of all the vertices in **G,** such that for all vertices **v**, **w** ∈ **G**, if there is an edge from **v** to **w**, then **v** precedes **w** in the sequential listing. Consider the graph illustrated in **Figure 8.33.** The topological order is equivalent to this as illustrated in **Figure 8.34** and **Figure 8.35.**

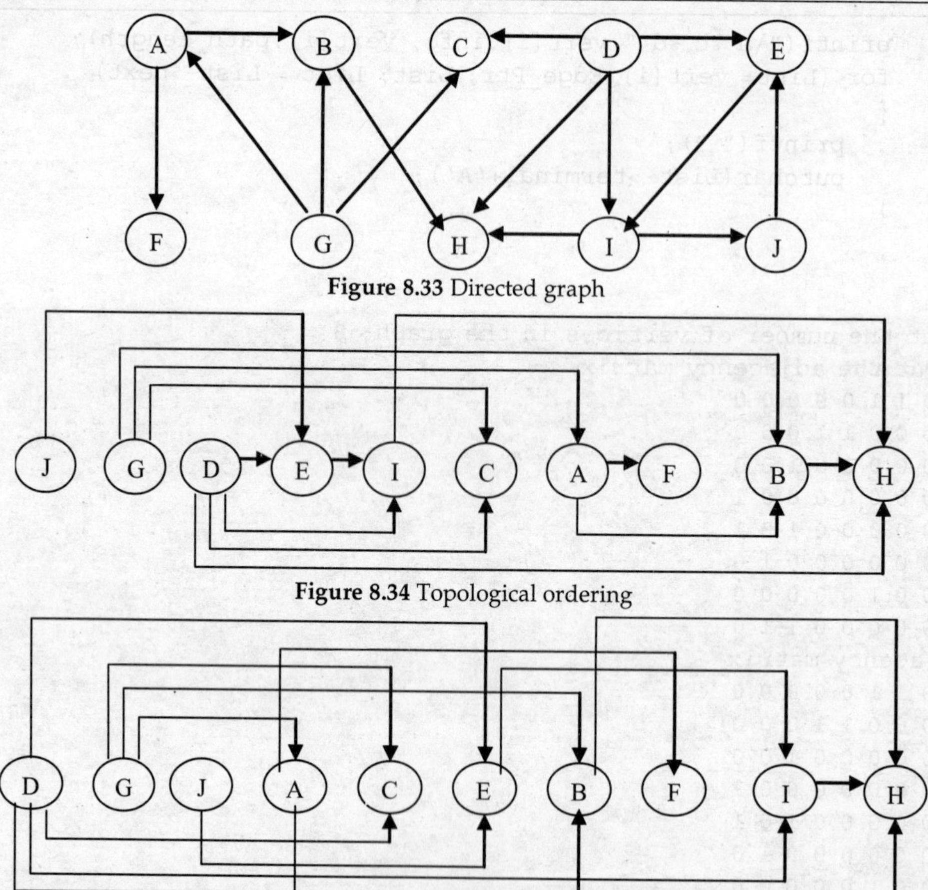

Figure 8.33 Directed graph

Figure 8.34 Topological ordering

Figure 8.35 Topological ordering

The main idea behind the algorithm to find a topological order **T** of a graph without cycles is that any vertex **v** with zero in-degree (i.e., without any predecessors) may be selected as the first element in the order **T**. We repeat the following steps until the graph **G** is empty:

- Find a vertex **v** with zero in-degree.
- Remove vertex **v** and its edges from the graph **G**.

The detail of the algorithm is illustrated in **Figure 8.36** and the development of the program is left as an exercise to the readers.

```
Step 1: Find the in-degree of each vertex v of G.
Step 2: Put in a queue all the vertices with zero degree.
Step 3: Repeat thru Step 5 while the queue is not NULL.
Step 4: Remove front vertex v of the queue.
Step 5: Repeat thru Sub-step (ii) for each neighbor w of the vertex v.
   (i)    Decrease the in-degree of w by 1 [Remove the edge from v to w]
   (ii)   If in-degree of w is zero, then add w to the rear of the queue.
Step 6: Exit
```

Figure 8.36 Topological Algorithm

8.8 MINIMUM SPANNING TREE (MST)

Suppose we have a group of islands that we wish to link with bridges so that it is possible to travel from one island to any other in the group. Further suppose that (as usual) our government wishes to spend the absolute minimum amount on this project (because other factors like the cost of using, maintaining, etc. these bridges will probably be the responsibility of some future government). The engineers are able to produce a cost for a bridge linking each possible pair of islands. The set of bridges, which will enable one to travel from any island to any other at minimum capital cost to the government, is the **minimum spanning tree**.

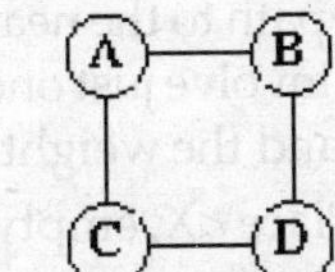

Figure 8.37 Graph

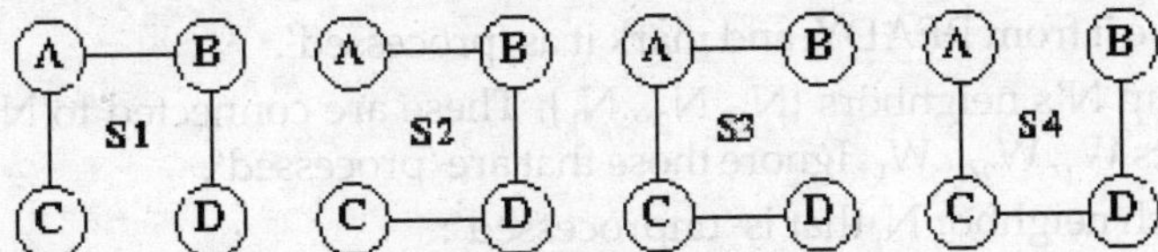

Figure 8.38 Spanning Trees

A spanning tree of a connected graph G is a connected subgraph of G having no cycles. Every connected graph has a spanning tree. For example, graph of **Figure 8.37** has *four* distinct spanning trees {**Figure 8.38**}.

In general, it is possible to construct multiple spanning trees for a graph, **G**. Recall that the *weight* of a subgraph to be sum of all the edge weights in the subgraph. Different spanning trees have different weights; the *minimum spanning tree* is the spanning tree with the minimum weight. For example, weights added to the graph in **Figure 8.37** for finding the minimum-spanning tree, the obtained graph is represented in **Figure 8.39**. If a cost, $\mathbf{c_{ij}}$, {weights} is associated with each edge, $\mathbf{e_{ij} = (v_i, v_j)}$, then the minimum spanning tree is the set of edges, $\mathbf{E_{span}}$, forming a spanning tree, such that: $\mathbf{C = sum(c_{ij} \mid}$ all $\mathbf{e_{ij}}$ in $\mathbf{E_{span}}$) is a minimum. After adding the weights calculation of the spanning trees are as follows:

- spanning tree S1 has weight 3+2+4 = 9
- spanning tree S2 has weight 2+4+1 = 7
- spanning tree S3 has weight 3+2+1 = 6
- spanning tree S4 has weight 3+4+1 = 8

S3 is the minimum spanning tree of this graph.

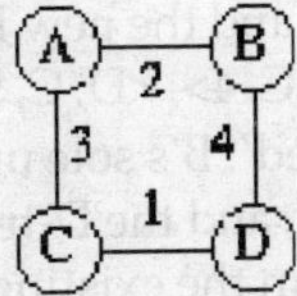

Figure 8.39 Weighted Graph

8.8.1 Algorithm For Computing a Minimum Spanning Tree

This algorithm is extremely similar to shortest path algorithm. In the shortest path algorithm, the key ideas is to pick from READY {List of nodes} the node that is closest to the starting point: to do this we needed to store extra information on the READY list along with each node - in particular we need to store the length of the shortest known path to the node from the starting point (we also stored the path itself).

In Minimum spanning tree (MST), the key idea is very similar: pick from READY the node that is closest to the spanning tree we have built so far. To do this we need to store extra information on the READY list along with each node: the length of the shortest known path to the node from any node in the tree built so far. We note that the shortest path to the nearest node (N) will always be a single edge, so to store the 'path' leading to N will always involve just one other node (one that already in the MST), so along with N we will just store this node and the weight of the edge connecting them.

1. Pick any node X as starting point. Place <X, empty path, 0> on READY.
2. pick the triple <N,P,L> on READY such that L is minimum.
    - Process it. (print "N is connected to P in the MST")
    - Remove it from READY, and mark it as 'processed'.
    - Look up N's neighbors {N_1, N_2...N_k}. These are connected to N by edges that have weights W_1, W_2,...W_k. Ignore those that are 'processed'.
      For each neighbor N_i that is 'unprocessed':
        - create the triple <N_i,N,W_i>
        - add this triple to READY - if there is already a triple for N_i on READY, only add the new one (and delete the old one) if its path length (weight) is smaller.
3. repeat 2 until READY is empty.

For example, consider graph in **Figure 8.40** and find the MST, the steps of the algorithm discussed above takes place in the following ways:

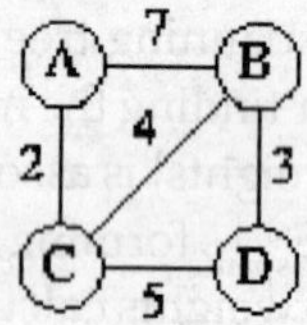

Figure 8.40 Weighted Graph

- Step 1: READY = [<A, A, 0>]
- Step 2: Process A, mark it 'processed'. READY = [< B, A, 7>, <C, A, 2 >]
- Step 2: Process C, mark it 'processed'. C's unprocessed neighbors are B and D. Make up a triple for each of them: <B,C,4> <D,C,5>. Add these to READY if the node name is not already there, or if it is there but the new triple has a smaller path length (weight). In this case, we add the new D triple because D is new, and the new B triple because it has a smaller weight than the one on READY. READY = [<B, C, 4>, <D, C, 5>]
- Step 2: Process B, mark it 'processed'. B's sole unprocessed neighbor is D. Create the triple <D, B, 3>. This is added to READY, and the D-triple on READY is deleted, because the new triple has a smaller path length than the existing one.
- Step 2: Process D, mark it 'processed'. D has no unprocessed neighbors. READY =[] {i.e., empty}.

The output produced by this algorithm is:

- C is connected to A in the MST.
- B is connected to C in the MST.
- D is connected to B in the MST.

It should be clear that if we swapped the weights of the edges connecting D to B and C, then D would be connected to C in the minimum spanning tree.

8.9 KRUSKAL'S ALGORITHM

This algorithm creates a forest of trees. Initially the forest consists of N single node trees (and no edges). At each step, we add one (the cheapest one) edge so that it joins two trees together. If it forms a cycle, it would simply link two nodes that were already part of a single connected tree, so that this edge would not be needed. The algorithm can be defined as:

```
Forest MinimumSpanningTree( Graph g, int n, double **costs )
{
    Forest T;
    Queue q;
    Edge e;
    T = ConsForest( g );
    q = ConsEdgeQueue( g, costs );
    for(i=0;i<(n-1);i++)
  {
    do
    {
    e = ExtractCheapestEdge( q );
    } while ( !Cycle( e, T ) );
    AddEdge( T, e );
    }
  return T;
}
```

The steps are:

1. The forest is constructed - with each node in a separate tree.
2. The edges are placed in a priority queue.
3. Until we have added **n**-1 edges,
    1. Extract the cheapest edge from the queue,
    2. If it forms a cycle, reject it,
    3. Else add it to the forest. Adding it to the forest will join two trees together.

Every step joins two trees in the forest together, so that at the end, there will be only one tree in T. We can use a heap for the priority queue. The trick here is to detect cycles. For this, we need a union-find structure. To understand the union-find structure, we need to look at a **partition** of a set. A partition is a set of sets of elements of a set.

- Every element of the set belongs to one of the sets in the partition.
- No element of the set belongs to more than one of the sub-sets. or
- Every element of a set belongs to one and only one of the sets of a partition.

The forest of trees is a partition of the original set of nodes. Initially all the sub-sets have exactly one node in them. As the algorithm progresses, we form a union of two of the trees (sub-sets), until eventually the partition has only one sub-set containing all the nodes.

A partition of a set may be thought of as a set of equivalence classes. Each sub-set of the partition contains a set of equivalent elements (the nodes connected into one of the trees of the forest). This notion is the key to the cycle detection algorithm. For each sub-set, we denote one element as the representative of that sub-set or equivalence class. Each element in the sub-set is, somehow, equivalent and represented by the nominated representative.

As we add elements to a tree, we arrange that all the elements point to their representative. As we form a union of two sets, we simply arrange that the representative of one of the sets now points to any one of the elements of the other set.

So, the test for a cycle reduces to. For the two nodes at the ends of the candidate edge, find their representatives. If the two representatives are the same, the two nodes are already in a connected tree and adding this edge would form a cycle. The search for the representative simply follows a chain of links.

Each node will need a representative pointer. Initially, each node is its own representative, so the pointer is set to NULL. As the initial pairs of nodes are joined to form a tree, the representative pointer of one of the nodes is made to point to the other, which becomes the representative of the tree. As trees are joined, the representative pointer of the representative of one of them is set to point to any element of the other. (Obviously, representative searches will be somewhat faster if one of the representatives is made to point directly to the other). For example, consider a graph G = (V, E), where **V** is the set of vertices and the set of edges, E = **{(v_i, v_j)}**, where $\mathbf{v_i}$ and $\mathbf{v_j}$ are in **V**. Then the steps of Kruskal algorithm can be defined as:

Initialize the forest		$\mathbf{O(\|V\|)}$
Sort the edges		$\mathbf{O(\|E\|log\|E\|)}$
Until we have added |V|-1 edges	$\mathbf{O(\|V\|)}$ x	
Check whether an edge forms a cycle	$\mathbf{O(\|V\|)}$ =	$\mathbf{O(\|V\|^2)}$
Total		$\mathbf{O(\|V\|+\|E\|log\|E\|+\|V\|^2)}$
Since $\mathbf{\|E\|=O(\|V\|^2)}$		$\mathbf{O(\|V\|^2log\|V\|)}$

Thus, we may refer to Kruskal's algorithm as an $\mathbf{O(n^2 \log n)}$ algorithm, where **n** is the number of vertices. However, note that if |**E**| is similar to |**V**|, then the complexity is $\mathbf{O(n^2)}$. **Figure 8.41** demonstrates Kruskal's algorithm.

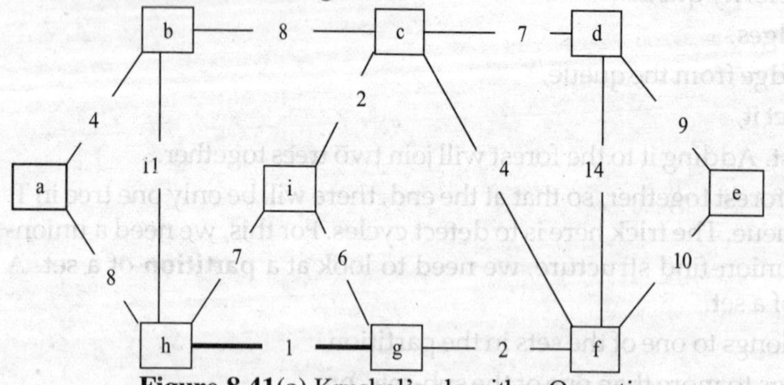

gh is shortest. Either g or h could be the representative, g chosen arbitrarily.

Figure 8.41(a) Kruskal's algorithm Operation

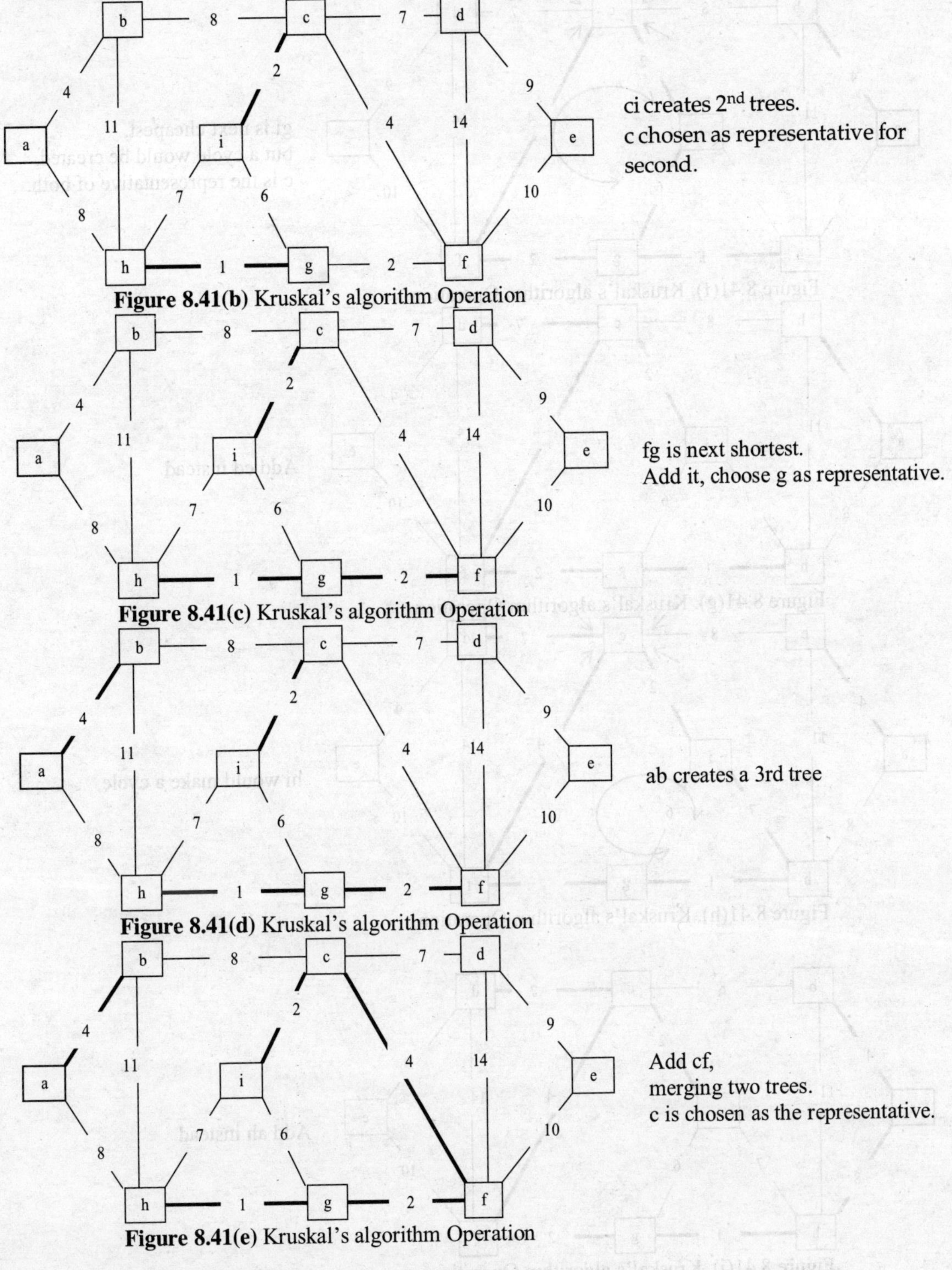

Figure 8.41(b) Kruskal's algorithm Operation

Figure 8.41(c) Kruskal's algorithm Operation

Figure 8.41(d) Kruskal's algorithm Operation

Figure 8.41(e) Kruskal's algorithm Operation

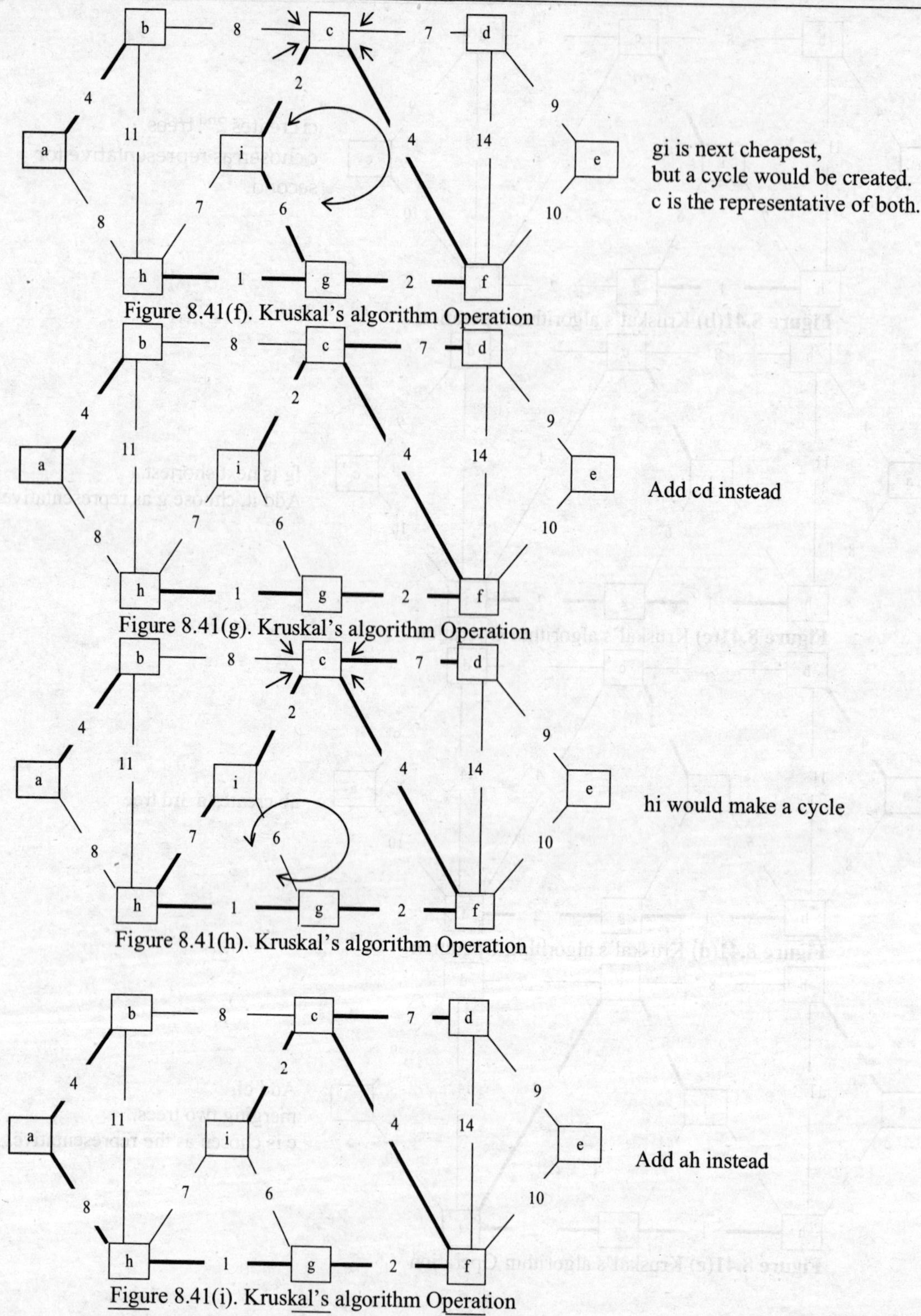

Figure 8.41(f). Kruskal's algorithm Operation

Figure 8.41(g). Kruskal's algorithm Operation

Figure 8.41(h). Kruskal's algorithm Operation

Figure 8.41(i). Kruskal's algorithm Operation

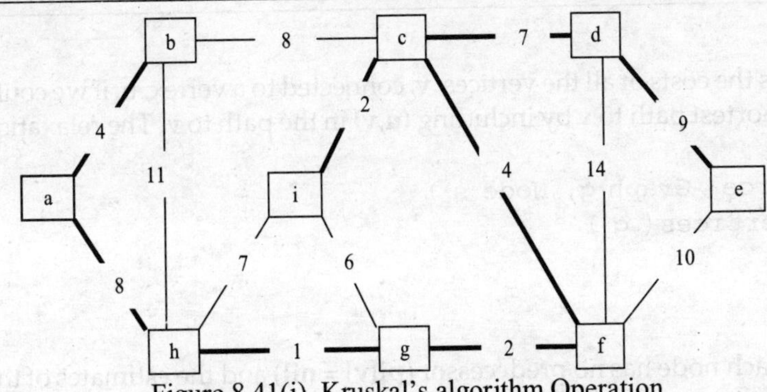

bc would create a cycle. Add de instead to complete the spanning tree - all trees joined, c is sole representative.

Figure 8.41(j). Kruskal's algorithm Operation

8.10 DJIKSTRA'S ALGORITHM (REVISITED)

Now we will discuss Djikstra's algorithm in respect to spanning. It solves the problem of finding the shortest path from a point in a graph (the source) to a destination. It turns out that one can find the shortest paths from a given source to all points in a graph in the same time, hence this problem is sometimes called the single-source shortest paths problem.

This problem is related to the spanning tree one. The graph representing all the paths from one vertex to all the others must be a spanning tree - it must include all the vertices. There will also be no cycles, as a cycle would define more than one path from the selected vertex to at least one other vertex. For a graph, **G = (V, E),** where, **V** is a set of vertices and **E** is a set of edges. Dijkstra's algorithm keeps two sets of vertices: **S**- The set of vertices whose shortest paths from the source have already been determined and **V-S:** The remaining vertices. The other data structures needed are: **d-** Array of best estimates of shortest path to each vertex, and **pi** an array for each vertex as shown in **Figure 8.42**. The predecessor list is an array of indices, one for each vertex of a graph. Each vertex's entry contains the index of its predecessor in a path through the graph. The basic mode of operation is:

1. Initialize **d** and **pi**,
2. Set **S** to empty,
3. While there are still vertices in **V-S**,
   (i) Sort the vertices in **V-S** according to the current best estimate of their distance from the source,
   (ii) Add **u**, the closest vertex in **V-S**, to **S**,
   (iii) **Relax** all the vertices still in **V-S** connected to **u**

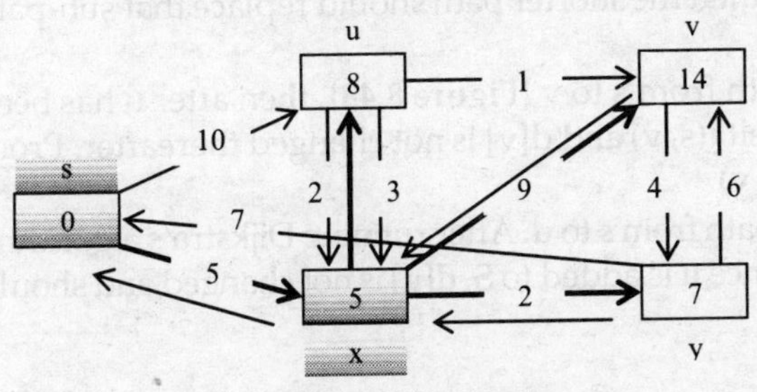

Figure 8.42 Graph

In this example {**Figure 8.42**}, the arrows show the predecessor relations, so the predecessor list would be:

Vertex	**Predecessor pi**
s	s*
u	x
v	x
x	s
y	x

*Any convention to indicate a vertex with no predecessor will do: it can point to itself, as here, or be set to -1.

Relaxation

The **relaxation** process updates the costs of all the vertices, **v**, connected to a vertex, **u**, if we could improve the best estimate of the shortest path to **v** by including **(u,v)** in the path to **v**. The relaxation procedure proceeds as follows:

```
initialise_single_source( Graph g, Node s )
for each vertex v in Vertices( g )
g.d[v] = infinity
g.pi[v] = nil
g.d[s] = 0;
```

This sets up the graph so that each node has no predecessor (**pi[v] = nil**) and the estimates of the cost (distance) of each node from the source (**d[v]**) are infinite, except for the source node itself (**d[s] = 0**).

We have also introduced a further way to store a graph (or part of a graph - as this structure can only store a spanning tree), the **predecessor sub-graph** - the list of predecessors of each node, **pi[j], 1 ≤ j ≤ |V|**. The edges in the predecessor sub-graph are **(pi[v], v)**. The relaxation procedure checks whether the current best estimate of the shortest distance to **v** (**d[v]**) can be improved by going through **u** (i.e., by making **u** the predecessor of **v**):

```
relax( Node u, Node v, double w[][] )
    if d[v] > d[u] + w[u,v] then
        d[v] = d[u] + w[u,v]
            pi[v] = u
```

The algorithm itself is now:

```
shortest_paths( Graph g, Node s )
initialise_single_source( g, s )
S = { 0 } /* Make S empty */
Q = Vertices( g ) /* Put the vertices in a Permanent Q */
while not Empty(Q)
u = ExtractCheapest( Q );
AddNode( S, u ); /* Add u to S */
for each vertex v in Adjacent( u )
relax( u, v, w )
```

We use a proof by contradiction. But first, we assert the following Lemma:

Lemma 1: Shortest paths are composed of shortest paths. The proof of this is based on the notion that if there was a shorter path than any sub-path, then the shorter path should replace that sub-path to make the whole path shorter.

Lemma 2: If s →→...→ u → v is a shortest path from s to v {**Figure 8.43**}, then after u has been added to S and relax(u, v, w) called, then d[v] = delta(s, v) and d[v] is not changed thereafter. Proof follows from the fact that at all times d[v] ≥ delta(s, v).

delta(s, u) denotes the distance of the shortest path from **s** to **u**. After running Dijkstra's algorithm, we assert that **d[u] = delta(s,u)** for all **u**. Note that once **u** is added to **S**, **d[u]** is not changed and should be **delta(s,u)**.

Proof by contradiction

Suppose that **u** is the first vertex added to S for which d[u] ≠ delta(s,u). We note:

1. u cannot be s, because d[s] = 0.

2. There must be a path from s to u. If there were not, d[u] would be infinity.
3. Since there is a path, there must be a shortest path.

Let s -(p1) → x → y -(p2) → u be the shortest path from s to u. Where x is within S and y is the first vertex not within S {**Figure 8.43**}. When x is inserted into S, d[x] = delta(s, x) (since we hypothesize that u is the first vertex for which this is not true). Edge (x, y) was relaxed at that time, so that

d[y] = delta(s, y) ≤ delta(s, u) ≤ d[u]. Now both y and u are in V-S when u is chosen, so d[u] ≤ d[y]. Thus, the two inequalities must be equalities, d[y] = delta(s,y) = delta(s,u) = d[u]. So d[u] = delta(s,u) contradicting hypothesis. Thus, when each u is inserted, d[u] = delta(s,u). **Figure 8.44** illustrates the operation of Dijkstra's Algorithm.

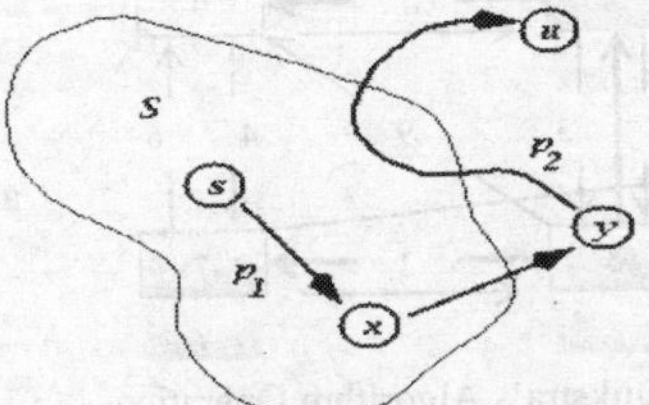

Figure 8.43 Graph

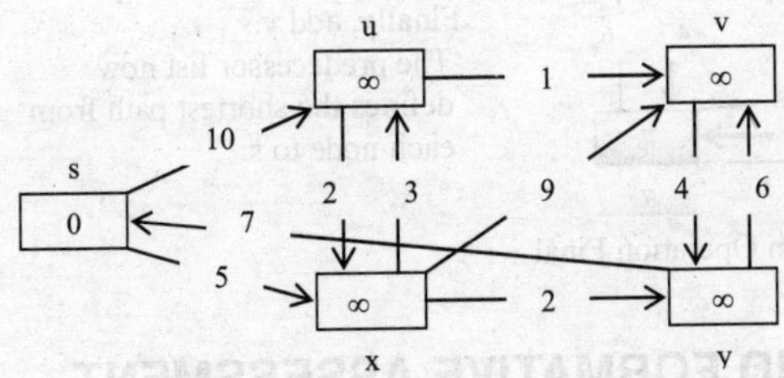

Initial graph
All nodes have infinite cost except the source

Figure 8.44(a) Initial Graph

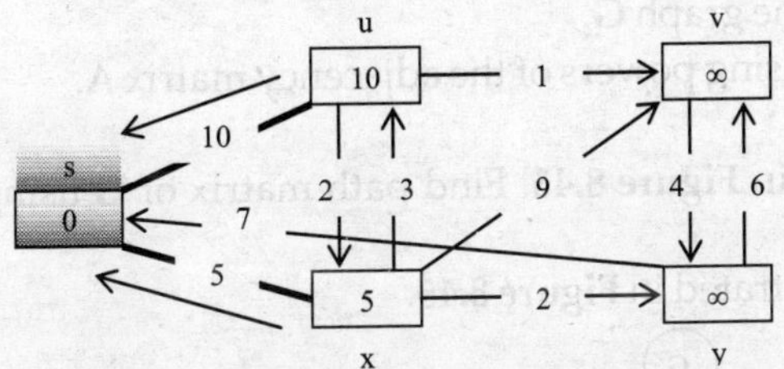

Choose the closest node to s.
As we initialized d[s] to 0, it is s.
Add it to S
Relax all nodes adjacent to s.
Update predecessor (thin lines parallel to thick lines) for all nodes are updated.

Figure 8.44(b) Dijkstra's Algorithm Operation

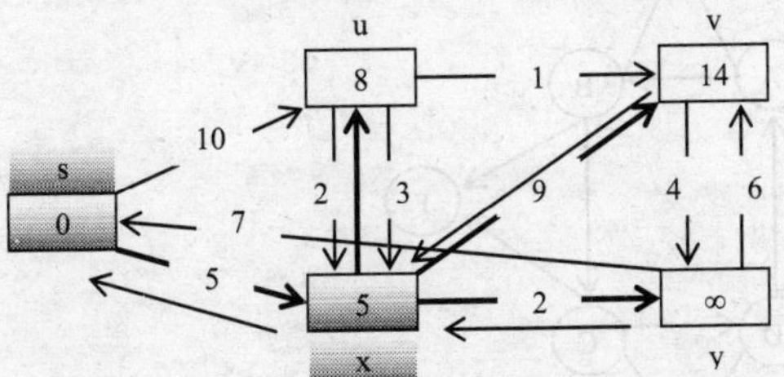

Choose the closest node, x
Relax all nodes adjacent to x
Update predecessors for u, v and y.

Figure 8.44(c) Dijkstra's Algorithm Operation

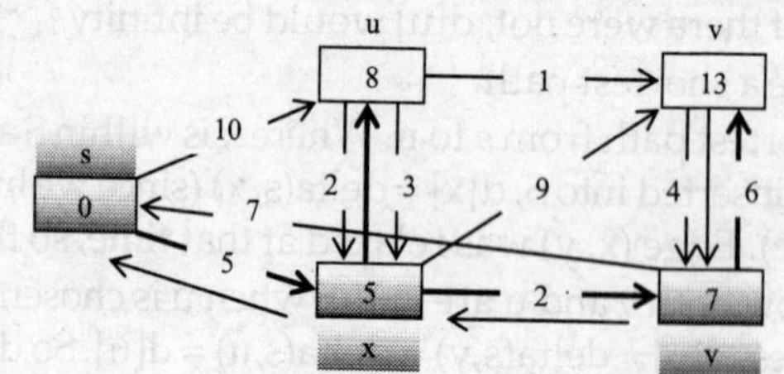

Now y is the closest, add it to S.
Relax v and adjust its predecessor.

Figure 8.44(d) Dijkstra's Algorithm Operation

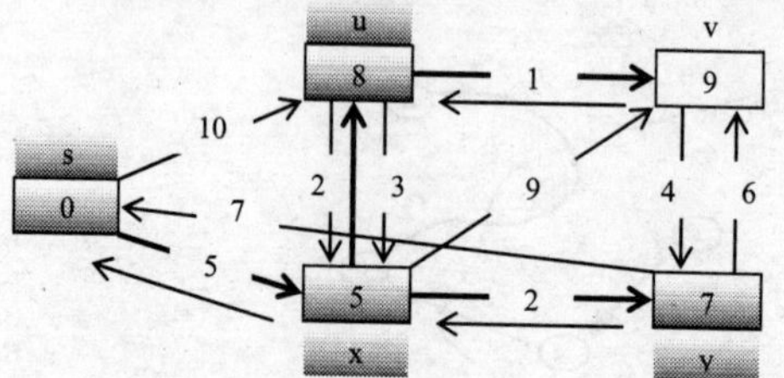

u is now closest, choose it and adjust its neighbour, v.

Figure 8.44(e) Dijkstra's Algorithm Operation

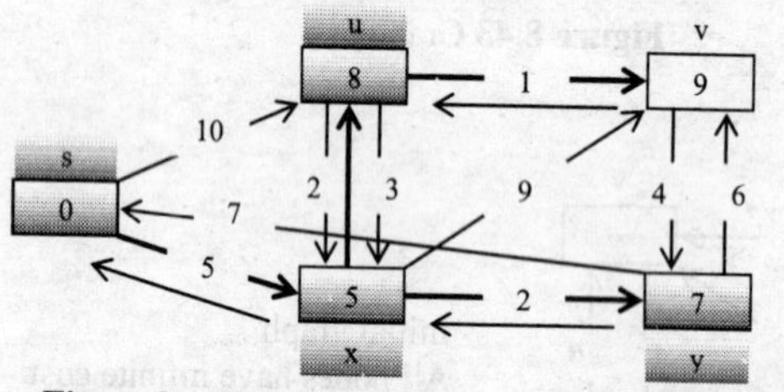

Finally, add v.
The predecessor list now defines the shortest path from each node to s.

Figure 8.44(f) Dijkstra's Algorithm Operation Final Result

FOR SUMMATIVE AND FORMATIVE ASSESSMENT

8.1 Consider the graph **G** illustrated in **Figure 8.45**.
   (i) Find adjacency matrix **A** of the graph **G**.
   (ii) Find the path matrix **P** of **G** using powers of the adjacency matrix **A**.
   (iii) Is this graph bi-connected?

8.2 Consider the graph **G** illustrated in **Figure 8.45**. Find path matrix of **G** using **Warshall**'s algorithm.

8.3 Find the depth of the graph **G** illustrated in **Figure 8.45**.

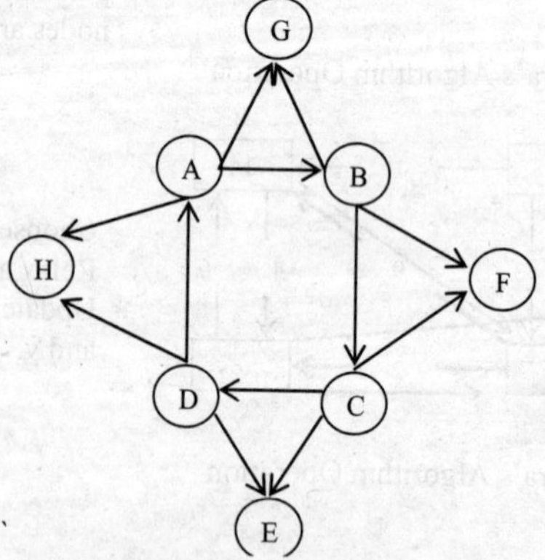

Figure 8.45 Directed graph

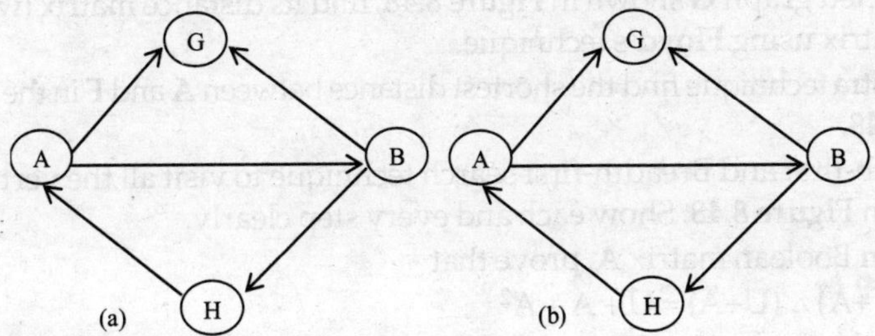

Figure 8.46 Directed Graph

8.4 Is the graph illustrated in **Figure 8.46** complete? Comment.

8.5 Consider the graph G illustrated in **Figure 8.47.** Find the shortest path matrix using **Warshall's** modified algorithm.

8.6 Suppose a weighted graph **G** is stored in computer memory by a vertex array **V** and a weighted matrix **W** such as:

V => vertex array

A	*B*	*C*	*D*	*E*	*F*	*G*

W => Weight matrix

7	0	0	0	3	0	4
0	9	7	0	0	3	3
1	0	10	0	2	0	0
2	0	3	11	4	0	7
8	9	10	11	12	0	1
0	9	8	3	0	13	0
0	0	1	7	0	0	14

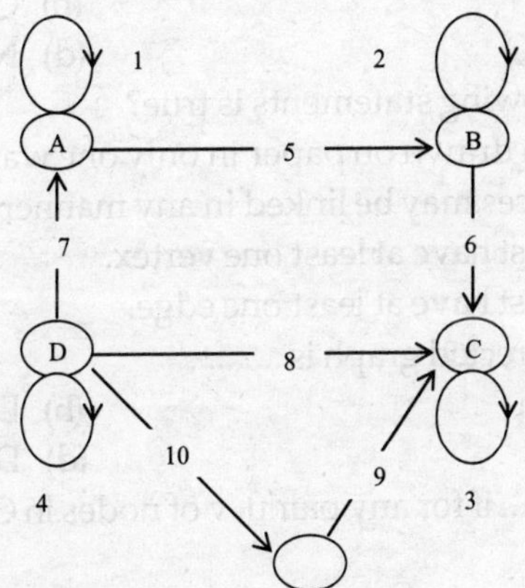

Figure 8.47 Cyclic Graph

8.7 Draw the complete undirected graph for the five vertices. Prove the number of edges in an **n** vertex graph is **n (n – 1)/2.**

8.8 For an undirected graph **G** with **n** vertices and **e** edges show that $\sum_{i=1}^{n} d_i = 2 * e$ where d_i is in-degree of the vertex **i**.

8.9 For the directed graph **G** shown in **Figure 8.48,** find its distance matrix (weight) and shortest distance matrix using **Floyd**'s technique.

8.10 Using **Dijkstra** technique find the shortest distance between **A** and **F** in the graph **G** illustrated in **Figure 8.48.**

8.11 Apply Depth-first and Breadth-first search technique to visit all the vertices in the graph **G** illustrated in **Figure 8.48**. Show each and every step clearly.

8.12 For any **n x n** Boolean matrix **A,** prove that

$(U+A)^2 = (U+A) \wedge (U+A) = U + A + A^2$

where **U** is the **n x n** identity matrix and A^2 = **A L A**. Also prove that for any positive integer r.

$(U+A)^r = U + A + A^2 + \ldots + A^r$

8.13 For what kind of graph is the topological sorting defined?

8.14 Explain the difference between Depth-first and Breadth-first traversing techniques of a graph.

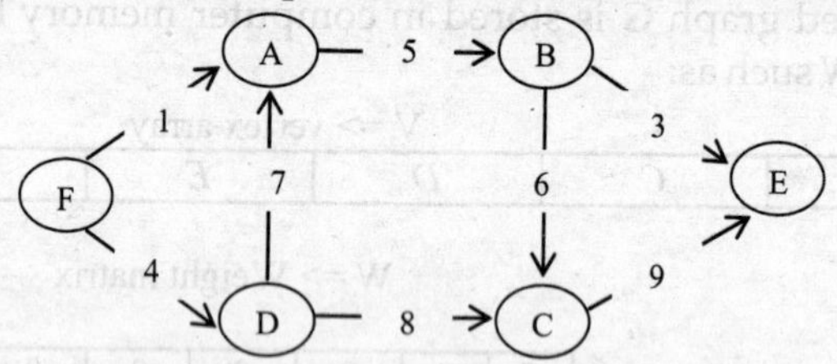

Figure 8.48 Directed and Weighted Graph

Quiz-7 (Graphs)

1. Which of the following statements is/are TRUE for an undirected graph?
   P: Number of odd degree vertices is even
   Q: Sum of degrees of all vertices is even
   (a) P Only (b) Q Only
   (c) Both P and Q (d) Neither P nor Q
2. Which of the following statements is true?
   (a) A graph can drawn on paper in only one way.
   (b) Graph vertices may be linked in any manner.
   (c) A graph must have at least one vertex.
   (d) A graph must have at least one edge.
3. Other name for directed graph is ....
   (a) Direct graph (b) Digraph
   (c) Dir-graph (d) Digraph
4. Graph G is .... if for any pair u, v of nodes in G there is a path from u to v or path from v to u.
   (a) Laterally connected (b) Widely Connected
   (c) Unliterally connected (d) Literally connected
5. A connected graph T without any cycles is called ....
   (a) free graph (b) no cycle graph
   (c) non cycle graph (d) circular graph

6. A connected graph T without any cycles is called a ....
   (a) A tree graph
   (b) Free tree
   (c) A tree d
   (d) All of the above
7. In a graph if E=(u,v) means ......
   (a) u is adjacent to v but v is not adjacent to u
   (b) e begins at u and ends at v
   (c) u is processor and v is successor
   (d) both b and c
8. In a graph if e=[u,v], Then u and v are called ....
   (a) End points of e
   (b) Adjacent nodes
   (c) Neighbours
   (d) All of the above
9. The Floyd-Warshall all-pairs shortest path algorithm for finding the shortest distances between nodes in a graph is an example of:
   (a) A Dynamic Programming formulation.
   (b) A Greedy Algorithm
   (c) A recursion based divide and conquer technique.
   (d) Non of the above
10. What is the expected number of ɔperations needed to loop through all the edges terminating at a particular vertex given an adjacency matrix representation of the graph? (Assume n vertices are in the graph and m edges terminate at the desired node.)
    (a) O(m)
    (b) O(n)
    (c) O(m²)
    (d) O(n²)
11. A union find data-structure is commonly applied while implementing:
    (a) A depth-first search traversal of a graph.
    (b) A breadth-first search traversal of a graph.
    (c) Computing the minimum spanning tree of a graph using the Kruskal algorithm.
    (d) Computing the all-pairs shortest path in a graph.
12. Suppose a directed graph representing all the flights that an airline flies. What algorithm might be used to find the best sequence of connections from one city to another?
    (a) Breadth first search.
    (b) Depth first search.
    (d) A cycle-finding algorithm.
    (d) A shortest-path algorithm.
13. If G is a directed graph with 20 vertices, how many Boolean values will be needed to represent G using an adjacency matrix?
    (a) 20
    (b) 40
    (c) 200
    (d) 400
14. How many linked lists are used to represent a graph with n nodes and m edges, when using an edge list representation,
    (a) m
    (b) n
    (c) m + n
    (d) m*n
15. What is the expected number of operations needed to loop through all the edges terminating at a particular vertex given an adjacency matrix representation of the graph? (Assume n vertices are in the graph and m edges terminate at the desired node.)
    (a) O(m)
    (b) O(n)
    (c) O(m²)
    (d) O(n²)

16. Let G be a graph with n vertices and m edges. What is the tightest upper bound on the running time on Depth First Search of G? Assume that the graph is represented using adjacency matrix.
    (a) O(n) (b) O(m+n)
    (c) $O(n^2)$ (d) O(mn)
17. Which of the following statements is/are TRUE for an undirected graph?
    P: Number of odd degree vertices is even
    Q: Sum of degrees of all vertices is even
    (a) P Only (b) Q Only
    (c) Both P and Q (d) Neither P nor Q
18. The number of edges in a simple, n-vertex, complete graph is
    (a) n*(n-2) (b) n*(n-1)
    (c) n*(n-1)/2 (d) n*(n-1)*(n-2)
19. An undirected graph G has n nodes. Its adjacency matrix is given by an n × n square matrix whose (i) diagonal elements are 0's and (ii) non-diagonal elements are 1's. which one of the following is TRUE?
    (a) Graph G has no minimum spanning tree (MST)
    (b) Graph G has a unique MST of cost n-1
    (c) Graph G has multiple distinct MSTs, each of cost n-1
    (d) Graph G has multiple spanning trees of different costs
20. A directed graph is .... if there is a path from each vertex to every other vertex in the digraph.
    (a) Weakly connected (b) Strongly Connected
    (c) Tightly Connected (d) Linearly Connected

❑

CHAPTER

9

Searching and Sorting

One of the fundamental problems of computer science is ordering a list of records. Computer systems are often used to store large amounts of data from which individual records must be retrieved according to some search criterion. Thus, the efficient storage of data to facilitate fast searching is an important issue. Sorting is one of the most important operations performed by computers. There is a plethora of solutions to this problem, known as sorting algorithms. Some sorting algorithms are simple and intuitive, such as the bubble sort. Others, such as the quick sort is extremely complicated, but produce lightening-fast results. In the days of magnetic tape storage before modern databases, it was almost certainly the most common operation performed by computers as most database updating was done by sorting transactions and merging them with a master file. It is still important for presentation of data extracted from databases: most people prefer to get reports sorted into some relevant order before wading through pages of data. We shall investigate the performance of some searching and sorting algorithms and the data structures, which they use. First we will take searching techniques, then sorting and in the last hashing.

9.1 LINEAR SEARCH

This is the simplest technique to find out an element in an unsorted list. Linear searching is a way to find if a certain element (number, string, etc.) is in a specified array or list. The array can be in any order, or be completely jumbled and this search will find the element if it is there. If the element is found we can return the **index** where the element is located in the array. If the element is not found we can return -1. We can assume no array will ever have a negative number as an index. Our approach will be to check every element in the array to see if it is what we are looking for. We will use a loop to cycle through the array.

Let we have an unsorted list **l** which consists of **n** elements and want to search the value of a particular element in the list, as illustrated in **Figure 9.1**. In this technique the value of the **key** is compared with the first element of the list, if match is found then the search is terminated. Otherwise next element from the list is fetched and compared with the **key** and this process is continued till the **key** is found or list is completely exhausted. For example, **Figure 9.2** represents the list of elements in the memory, having 6 elements 22, 33, 66, 05, 44, 89 and we want to search for **key** = 05. **Figure 9.2** illustrates the idea. Let us examine how long it will take to find an item matching a key in the list. We are interested in:

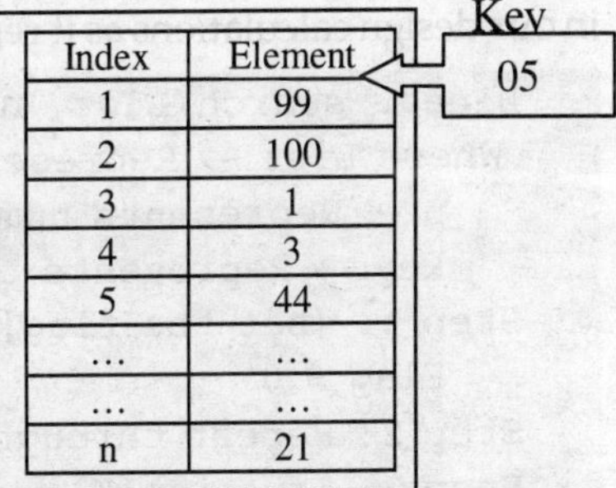

Figure 9.1 Linear list l in memory

- the average time
- the worst case time and
- the best possible time.

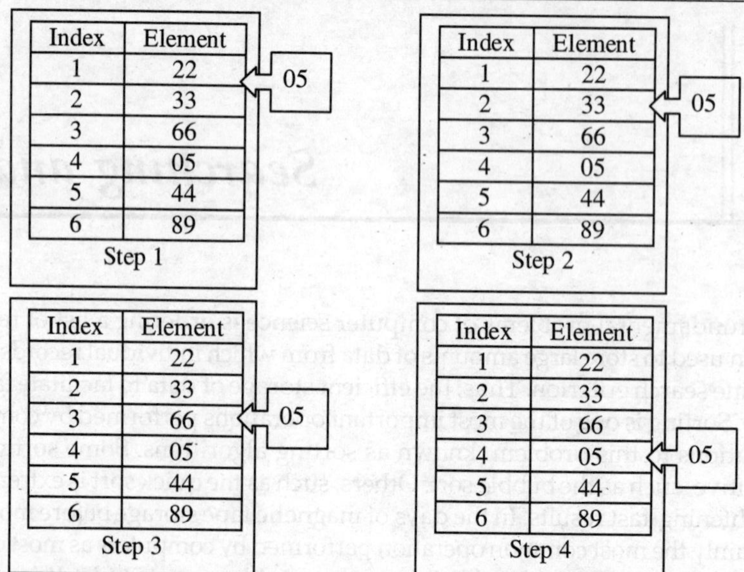

Figure 9.2 Searching for key = 05

However, we will generally be most concerned with the worst case time as calculations based on worst-case times can lead to guaranteed performance predictions. Conveniently, the worst-case times are generally easier to calculate than average times. If there are **n** items in our collection - whether it is stored as an array or as a linked list - then it is obvious that in the worst case, when there is no item in the collection with the desired key, then **n** comparisons of the key with keys of the items in the collection will have to be made. To simplify analysis and comparison of algorithms, we look for a dominant operation and count the number of times that dominant operation has to be performed. In the case of searching, the dominant operation is the comparison, since the search requires **n** comparisons in the worst case; we say this is an **O (n)** algorithm. The best case - in which the first comparison returns a match - requires a single comparison and is **O (1)**. The average time depends on the probability that the key will be found in the collection - this is something that we would not expect to know in the majority of cases. Thus, in this case, as in most others, estimation of the average time is of little utility. If the performance of the system is vital, i.e., it is part of a life-critical system, then we must use the worst case in our design calculations as it represents the best guaranteed performance.

```
Linear_search(List, n, key)
 Where List → Represents the list of elements,
   n → Represents number of elements in the list and
   key → Represents the value to be searched in the list
Step 1: [set the flag]
   Flag = 0
Step 2: Repeat through Step 3 for K = 1, 2, 3 ... n
Step 3: If (List[K] = key)
(i)    Flag = 1
(ii)   Output " search is successful" and element is found at location K
Step 4: If (Flag = 0) output "Search in unsuccessful" and Exit
Step 5: Exit
```

Figure 9.3 Algorithm for Linear Search

In the linear search algorithm {Figure 9.3}, there are **n** key comparisons in worst case and **n/2** in average case. The time taken in the average and the worst case is proportional to **n,** i.e., **O (n).** These results are based on the assumption that the probability of finding an element or record in the list is same as for any other element or record. Let $\mathbf{P_i}$ is the probability of finding an element or record $\mathbf{E_i}$ ($1 \leq i \leq n$) in the list. The average length of search for **n** elements or records is given by:

$$E(n) = 1 * P_1 + 2 * P_2 + 3 * P_3 + ... + n * P_n$$
$$= (1 + 2 + 3 + ... + n)P_a$$

where $P = 1 = P_1 + P_2 + P_3 + ... + P_n$

If average probability then and putting this value of into the equation we get the final result.

$$= (1 + 2 + 3 + ... n)P_a$$
$$= P_a * [n(n+1)/2]$$
$$= 1/n * [n(n+1)/2]$$
$$= (n+1)/2, i.e., O(n)$$

The algorithm for linear search is given in **Figure 9.3** and program segment **LSEARCH.C** implements the above discussion.

```
/* LINEAR SEARCH */
/* lsearch.c */
# include<stdio.h>
int flag = 0;
int list[200];

void linear_search(int * , int , int );
void display(int *, int);

/* This function implements the linear search algorithm */
void linear_search(int list[], int n, int key)
{
   int k;
   flag = 1;
   for(k = 0; k< n; k++)
   {
      if(list[k] == key)
      {
         printf("\n Search is successful \n");
         printf("\n Element: %i Found at Location: %i", key,k+1);
         flag = 1 ;
      }
   }
   if (flag==0)
      printf("\n Search is unsuccessful");
}

/* Output function display the data list */
void display(int list[], int n)
```

```
{
    int i;
    for(i = 0 ; i < n ; i++)
    {
        printf(" %d", list[i]);
    }
}

void main()
{
    int number, key, list[200];
    int i;
    printf("Input the number of elements in the list:");
    scanf("%d", &number);
    for(i = 0 ; i < number; i++)
    {
        list[i] = rand() %100; /* Generates data list */
    }
    printf("\n Input Element to be searched");
    scanf("%d", &key);

    printf("\n Entered list is as follows:\n");
    display(list, number);
    /* invoking function to search the key */
    linear_search(list, number, key);
    printf("\n In the following list\n");
    display(list, number);
}
```

9.2 BINARY SEARCH

Binary search works for sorted lists and is a very efficient searching technique. The binary search is like looking up a phone number in the directory or looking up a word in the dictionary. For looking a word in the dictionary, we start from the middle in the dictionary as shown in Figure 9.4. If the word that we are looking for comes before words on the page, it shows that the word should be before this page. So we look in the first half. Otherwise, we search for the word in the second half of the dictionary. Suppose the word is in the first half of the dictionary, we consider first half for looking the word. We have no need to look into the second half of the dictionary. Thus, the data to be searched becomes half in a step. Now we divide this portion into two halves and look for the word. Here we again come to know that the word is in the first half or in the second half of this portion. The same step is repeated with the part that contains the required word. Finally, we come to the page where the required word exists. We see that in the binary search, the data to be searched becomes half in each step. And we find the entry very fast. The number of maximum steps needed to find an entry is *log n*, where *n* is the total number of entries. Now if we have 1000000 entries, the maximum number of attempts (steps) required to find out the entry will be 20 (i.e. log 1000000). The binary search finds an element in the sorted array in *log n* time. If we have 1000000 elements in the array, the log 1000000 will be 20, i.e., very small as compared to 1000000. Thus, binary search is very fast. It is used to find the location of a given element or record in a list. Other information associated with the element can also be fetched if required. To find the location of a file in the computer directory one can use this searching technique. If we are on the Internet then it is not an easy task using linear search to find out the information about some records or files. For this one prefers Binary searching technique.

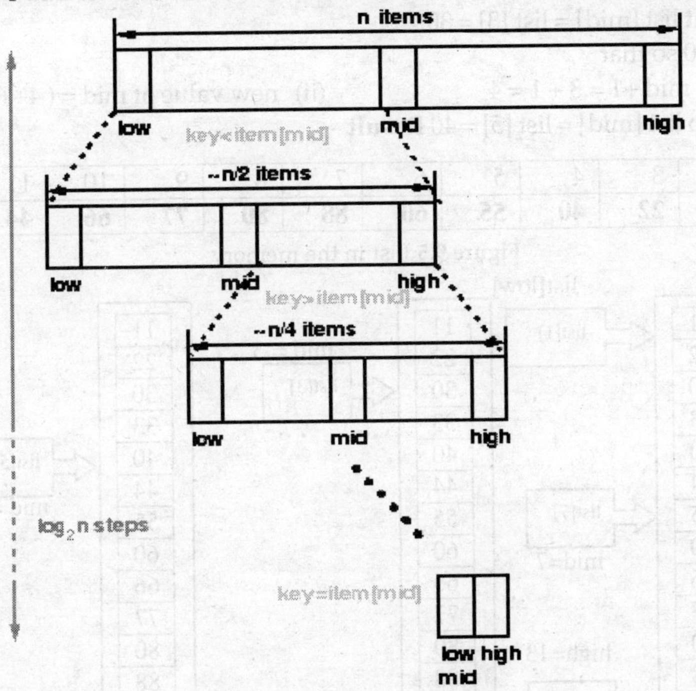

Figure 9.4 Binary Search Steps

However, if we place items in a list and sort them in either ascending or descending order on the key first, then we can obtain much better performance with an algorithm called binary search. It is a technique for searching an ordered list in which we first check the middle item and - based on that comparison – "discard" half the data. The same procedure is then applied to the remaining half of the list until a match is found or there are no more items left.

In binary search, we first compare the key with the item in the middle position of the list, i.e., {Figure 9.4}. If there is a match, we can return immediately. If the key is less than the middle key, then the item sought must lie in the lower half of the list; if it is greater then the item sought must lie in the upper half of the list. So, we repeat the procedure on the lower (or upper) half of the list.

Let **low** represents lower limit of the **list**, **high** upper and **mid** is average of **low** and **high** that is middle of the lower and upper limits, i.e., **mid = (low + high)/2.** We compare the middle element with **key** to be searched. If the value of middle element is greater than **key**, then **key** will exist in lower half of the list, take **high = mid – 1** and find new value of **mid**, i.e., mid = (low + high)/2, otherwise, **key** will exist in upper half and take low = mid + 1 and mid = (low + high)/2. This process continues until the entire list is exhausted or **key** is searched.

For example, consider the list given in **Figure 9.5.** This list contains 13 elements, i.e., from 01 – 13, suppose we want to search for **key = 40**. The list is unsorted so that it is required to sort the list before starting the searching. The sorted list is given in **Figure 9.6(a)** and final result is shown in **Figure 9.6(c)**. How does the binary search technique work? It is shown in the following steps.

1. Initially
   (i) list[low] = list[1] = 11 (ii) list[high] = list [13] = 99
   (iii) mid = (low + high)/2 = (1+13)/2 = 7 (iv) list [mid] = list[7] = 55
2. Since 40 < 55 means element < list [mid] so that
   (i) high = mid-1 (ii) now new value of mid = (1+6)/2 = 3
   (iii) so that list [mid] = list [3] = 30
3. Since 40> 30 so that
   (i) low = mid +1 = 3 + 1 = 4 (ii) new value of mid = (4+ 6)/2 = 5
   (iii) and so list [mid] = list [5] = 40 **Result**

index	1	2	3	4	5	6	7	8	9	10	11	12	13
	99	**11**	**22**	**40**	**55**	**60**	**88**	**80**	**77**	**66**	**44**	**33**	**30**

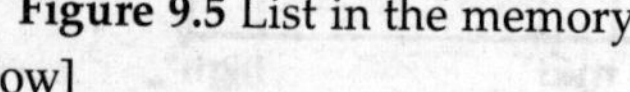

Figure 9.5 List in the memory

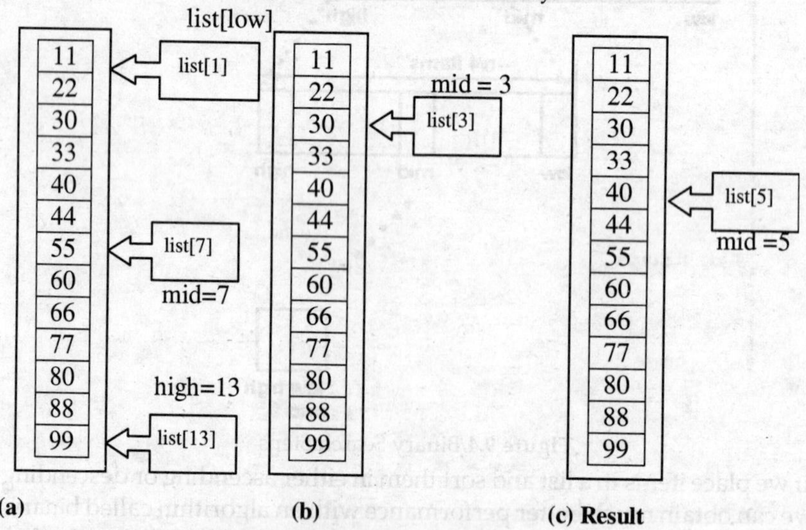

Figure 9.6 Binary search operations

Next we are interested in insertion and deletion of an item in a given list using binary search at/ from the proper place. In the worst case, insertion may require **n** operations to insert into a sorted list.

1. We can find the place in the list where the new item belongs using binary search in **O(log n)** operations.
2. However, we have to shuffle all the following items up one place to make room for the new one. In the worst case, the new item is the first in the list, requiring **n** move operations for the shuffle.

A similar analysis will show that deletion is also an **O(n)** operation. If our collection is static, i.e., it does not change very often - if at all - then we may not be concerned with the time required to change its contents: we may be prepared for the initial build of the collection and the occasional insertion and deletion to take some time. In return, we will be able to use a simple data structure (an array) which has little memory overhead. However, if our collection is large and dynamic, i.e., items are being added and deleted continually, then we can obtain considerably better performance using a data structure called a **tree**.

```
Binary_search(list , key, n)
Where
 key → To which we have to search in the list, low → lower limit and
 high → upper limit, n → Represents number of elements in the list
 list →Represents list of the elements, flag → is set or reset.
Step 1: [Initialize]
   low = 1
   high = n
   flag = 0
Step 2: Repeat through Step 4 while (low £ high)
Step 3: mid = (low high)/2
Step 4: if(key < list[mid])
then high = mid -1
   else if (element > list[mid] )
   then low = mid + 1
   else if ( key = list[mid] )
   Output "Search is successful" and location of the element is mid
   flag = 1
   return (mid)
Step 5: if( flag=0) output" Search is unsuccessful",
   return (mid)
```

Figure 9.7 Algorithm for Binary Search

The above discussion can be formulated in the form of algorithm and is given in **Figure 9.7.** Each step of the algorithm divides the block of items being searched in half. We can divide a set of **n** items in half at most **$\log_2$ n** times. Thus, the running time of a binary search is proportional to **$\log_2$ n** and we say this is a **O($\log_2$ n)** algorithm. Binary search requires a more complex program than linear search and thus, for small **n** it may run slower than the simple linear search. However, for large **n**,

$$\lim_{n\to\infty} \frac{\log n}{n} = 0$$

Thus, at large **n**, **$\log_2$ n** is much smaller than **n**, consequently an **O($\log_2$ n)** algorithm is much faster than an **O(n)**. This illustration is shown in **Figure 9.8**. The implementation of this algorithm is given in BINARY.C.

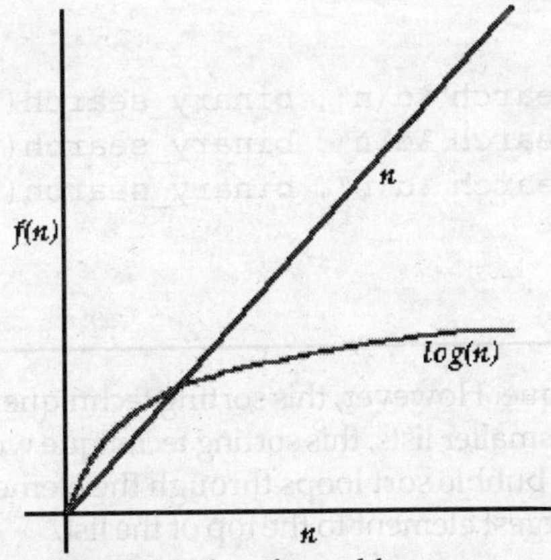

Figure 9.8 Plot of n and $\log_2$ n vs. n

```
/* binary.c */
#include <stdio.h>
/* thisfunction implements the binary search algorithm */
int binary_search(int list[], int key, int n)
{
   int flag = 0;
   int high = n-1, low = 0, mid;
   mid = (high + low) / 2;

   printf("\n\n Looking for %d \n", key);

   while ((! flag) && (high >= low))
   {
      printf(" Low %d Mid %d High %d \n", low, mid, high);

      if (key == list[mid])
         flag = 1;
      else if (key < list[mid])
         high = mid - 1;
      else
         low = mid + 1;

      mid = (high + low) / 2;
   }
   return((flag) ? mid: -1);
}

void main(void)
{
   int list[100], i;

   for (i = 0; i < 100; i++)
      list[i] = i+20;

   printf("Result of search %d\n", binary_search(list, 33, 100));
   printf("Result of search %d\n", binary_search(list, 75, 100));
   printf("Result of search %d\n", binary_search(list, 1001, 100));
}
```

9.3 BUBBLE SORT

It is very simple sorting technique. However, this sorting technique is not efficient in comparison to other sorting techniques. But for smaller lists, this sorting technique works fine. Suppose we sort the elements in descending order, the bubble sort loops through the elements in the list comparing the adjacent element and moves the largest element to the top of the list.

The bubble sort algorithm is given in **Figure 9.10.** From this algorithm it is clear that the bubble sort places the smallest element in the proper position and selects the second element and searches for the second smallest element. **Figure 9.9** illustrates the complete operation performed on 5-element list.

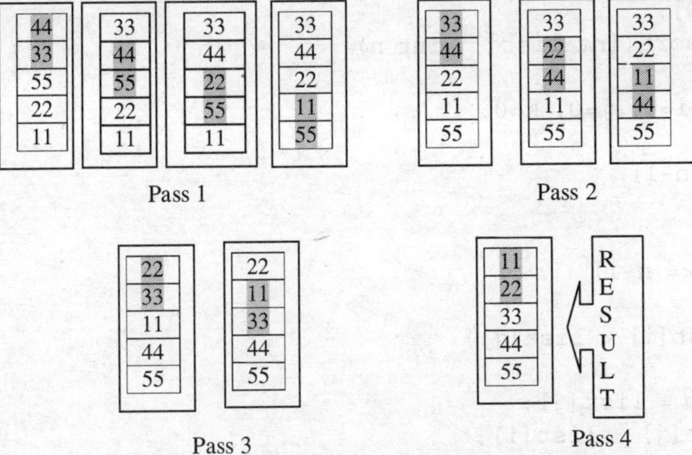

Figure 9.9 Operation of Bubble Sort

As we can see, the algorithm consists of two nested loops. The index j in the inner loop travels up the list, comparing ith entry with j=(i+1)th entry in the list (i.e., at i and j=i+1), while the outer loop causes the inner loop to make repeated passes through the list. After the first pass, the largest element is guaranteed to be at the end of the list, after the second pass, the second largest element is in position, and so on. That is why the upper bound in the inner loop (n-i) decreases with each pass: we do not have to revisit the end of the list. Total number of comparisons for all the passes is:

$$E(n) = \sum_{i=1}^{n} n-i$$
$$= (n-1)+(n-2)+(n-3)+...+2+1$$
$$= n(n-1)/2$$
$$= O(n^2)-O(n/2), i.e., O(n^2)$$

The program segment **BUBBLE.C** implements the algorithm given in **Figure 9.10**.

```
Bubble_sort (n, list)
Where : n → Represents the number of elements in the list
 l → Represents the list of elements
Step 1: [Initialize]
    i = 1
Step 2: Repeat thru Step 7 while (i < n)
Step 3: j = i+1
Step 4: Repeat thru Step 6 while (j ≤ n)
Step 5: if list[i] < list[j]
(i)    temp = list[j]
(ii)   list[j] = list[i]
(iii)  list[i] = temp
Step 6: j=j+1
Step 7: i=i+1
Step 8: Exit
```

Figure 9.10 Algorithm for Bubble Sort

```
/* bubble.c */
#include <stdio.h>
#include <stdlib.h>
//int list[30];
void bubble_sort(int list[], int n)
{
    int temp, i=0, j=0, k=0;

    while(i < n-1)
    {
     j = i+1;
     while (j <= n-1)
     {
        if (list[i] < list[j])
        {
            temp = list[j];
            list[j] = list[i];
            list[i] = temp;
        }
     j++;
     }
     printf(" \n Result after %d pass \n", i);
     for (k = 0; k < n; k++)
     printf(" %d ", list[k]);
    i++;
    }
}

void main(void)
{
    int list[30], i, n;
    printf(" Input the number of elements in the list");
    scanf(" %d", &n);
    printf("\n Unsorted list is as follows\n");
    for (i = 0; i < n; i++)
    {
        list[i] = rand()%100;
    }

    for (i = 0; i < n; i++)
        printf(" %d ", list[i]);
    bubble_sort(list, n);
    printf("\n Sorted list is as follows\n");
    for (i = 0; i < n; i++)
        printf(" %d ", list[i]);
}
```

If one is interested in sorting the strings may choose the following program segment. In this program segment we have modified the bubble sort algorithm and replaced while loop with for loop.

```
/* BUBBLE SORT FOR SORTING STRINGS */
/* BUB_STR.C */
# include <stdlib.h>
# include <string.h>
# include <malloc.h>
# include <stdio.h>
void bubble_sort(char *list[], int );
void display(char *list[], int);

void bubble_sort(char *list[], int n)
{
  char *temp;
  int i, j;
  for (i = 0; i < n-1; i++)
  {
    for (j = i+1; j <= n-1; j++)
    {
      if (strcmp(list[i], list[j]) < 0)
      {
        temp =(char *) malloc(sizeof(list[i]));
        temp = list[j];
        list[j] = list[i];
        list[i] = temp;
      }
    }
    printf(" \n List after pass: %d", i+1);
    display(list, n);
  }
}
void display(char *list[], int n)
{
  int i;
  for(i = 0 ; i < n; i++)
  {
    printf(" %s ", list[i]);
  }
}

void main(void)
{
  int n;
  char *list[100] = {"MONDAY", "TUESDAY", "WEDNESDAY", "FRIDAY",
"SATARDAY"};
```

```
    n = 5;
    printf("\n Input list is as follows:");
    display(list, n);
    bubble_sort(list, n);
    printf("\n Sorted list is as follows:\n");
    display(list, n);
}
```

9.4 INSERTION SORT

The insertion sort works just like its name suggests - it inserts each item into its proper place in the final list. It is one of the simplest methods to sort a list of record. An example of an insertion sort occurs in everyday life while playing cards. To sort the cards in one's hand one extract a card, shift the remaining cards, and then insert the extracted card in the correct place. This process is repeated until all the cards are in the correct sequence.

The simplest implementation of this requires two list structures - the source list and the list into which sorted items are inserted. To save memory, most implementations use an in-place sort that works by moving the current item past the already sorted items and repeatedly swapping it with the preceding item until it is in place.

Suppose **list** is the list of **n** elements. The insertion sort technique scans the **list** from **list[1]** to **list[n]**, inserting each element into its proper position in the previously sorted sub-list **list[1], list[2] ... list[i-1]**. The discussion of the algorithm given in **Figure 9.12** can be explained with the help of the following steps:

Step = 1	-0	7	3	4	1	8	2	6	5
Step = 2	-0	3	7	4	1	8	2	6	5
Step = 3	-0	3	4	7	1	8	2	6	5
Step = 4	-0	1	3	4	7	8	2	6	5
Step = 5	-0	1	3	4	7	8	2	6	5
Step = 6	-0	1	2	3	4	7	8	6	5
Step = 7	-0	1	2	3	4	6	7	8	5
Step = 8	-0	1	2	3	4	5	6	7	8

Figure 9.11 Insertion sort

```
Insertion_sort (list, n)
Where list → Represents the list of elements.
n → Represents number of elements in the list.
Step 1: [Initialize]
list[0] = -0
Step 2: Repeat thru Step 5 for i = 2, 3, 4 ... n
Step 3: (i) temp = list[i]
(ii) pointer = i - 1
Step 4: while(temp < list[pointer])
(i)   list[pointer + 1] = list[pointer]
(ii)  pointer = pointer - 1
Step 5: list[pointer] = temp
Step 6: Exit
```

Figure 9.12 Algorithm for Insertion sort

For smaller values of **n** this algorithm is useful. The inner loop of the algorithm performs **i-1** comparisons. Hence:

$$\begin{aligned} E(n) &= \sum_{i=2}^{n} i-1 \\ &= 1+2+3+4+\ldots+n-1 \\ &= n(n-1)/2 \\ &= O(n^2) \end{aligned}$$

For average case the inner loop performs comparisons.

$$\begin{aligned} E(n) &= \sum_{i=2}^{n} (i-1)/2 \\ &= (1+2+3+4+\ldots+n-1)/2 \\ &= n(n-1)/4 \\ &= O(n^2) \end{aligned}$$

The insertion sort is a good middle-of-the-road choice for sorting lists of a few thousand items or less. The algorithm is significantly simpler than the shell sort, with only a small trade-off in efficiency. At the same time, the insertion sort is over twice as fast as the bubble sort and almost 40% faster than the selection sort. The insertion sort should not be used for sorting lists larger than a couple thousand items or repetitive sorting of lists larger than a couple hundred items.

Figure 9.11 illustrates the algorithm given in **Figure 9.12.** The program segment **INSERT.C** implements the above discussion.

```
/* Insertion sort */
/* INSERT.C */
# include<stdio.h>
# include<stdlib.h>
void insertion_sort(int *, int);
void display(int*, int);

void insertion_sort(int list[], int n)
{
   int pointer, temp;
   int i, k;

   list[0] = -0;
   for(i = 1 ; i <= n; i++)
   {
      pointer = i -1;
      temp = list[i];
      while(temp < list[pointer])
      {
         list[pointer+1] = list[pointer];
         pointer --;
      }
      list[pointer+1] = temp;
      printf("Step = %d", i);
```

```
        for(k = 0; k <= n; k++)
            printf(" %d", list[k]);
        printf("\n");
    }
}

void display(int list[], int n)
{
int i;
    printf("\n Sorted list is as follows\n");
    for(i = 1; i <= n; i++)
        printf(" %d", list[i]);
}

void main()
{
    int number = 10;
    int list[100];
    int i;
    printf("\n Input Number of elements in the list: ");
    scanf("%d", &number);
    printf("\n Unsorted list is as follows \n");

    for(i = 1; i <= number; i++)
    {
        list[i] = rand() %100;
        printf(" %d", rand() %100);
    }
    printf("\n");

    printf("\n Step wise result is as follows \n\n");
    insertion_sort(list,number);
    display(list, number);
}
```

Another way of implementation of above technique is given below:

```
/* INSERTION SORT */
/* INSERS.C */
# include<stdio.h>
# include<stdlib.h>
int key;
int insertion_sort(int *);
/* prototype */
void display(int *, int);
```

```
/* Definition of the insertion sort function */
int insertion_sort(int list[])
{
   int i = 0;
   int j, k ;
   printf("\nElement to be inserted Break condition is -0 : ");
   scanf("%d", &key);
   printf("\n Selected Element is: %d", key);
   while(key != -0 ) /* -0 is break condition */
   {
      k = i - 1;
      while((key< list[k]) && (k >= 0))
      {
         list[k+1] = list[k];
         --k;
      }
      list[k+1] = key ;
      printf("\n List after inserting an element");
      for(j = 0 ; j<=i; j++)
         printf(" %d", list[j]);
      printf("\n Element to be inserted Break condition is -0: ");
      scanf("%d", &key);
      printf("\n Selected Element is: %d", key);
      i ++;
   }
   return i;
}

/* End of the insertion sort function */
/* Definition of the function */
void display(int list[], int n)
{
   int j;
   printf("\n Final sorted list is as follows:\n");
   for(j = 0 ; j < n ; j++)
      printf(" %d", list[j]);
}
/* End of the display function */
void main()
{
   int list[200];
   int n ;
   n = insertion_sort(list);
   display(list,n);
}
```

Next we are considering an insertion algorithm where we are taking an empty list. In this alsoirthm an extra empty list holds the sorted list. This algorithm is as follow:

n- represent the number of element in this list to sorted.

L1[n] is the list of element, L2[n] empty list,

```
L2 [1] =0 { initialize the list L2
for( i=2, 3, 4, ..., n
j=i-1
while(L1[i]<L2[j])
    (a)L2[j+1]=L2[j]
    (b)j=j-1
L2[j+1]=L1[i]
```

For example, suppose list L1=9, 4, 6, 7, 3. List L2 [1]= -0, initialized. When i=1,then j=0. Now i=2 then j=1. When applying this algorithm we are getting

L1[2]=9, L2[1]=0, i.e., 9>0 last step of the algorithm update the L2. Now L2 contains elements: 0, 9. Next increment the value of i=3, j=i-1=2. L1[3]=4, L2[2]=9. Here 4<9 means update the value of L2 and index j, i.e., L[2+1]=L2[j]=9, j=j-1=2-1=1. Now insert the value of L1[3] into the L2 at its proper location, i.e., L2[j+1]=L1[3]=4. Now list is: 0, 4, 9.If we continue this process we get finally sorted list: 0, 3, 4, 6, 7, 9. Te above algorithm is implemented in the following code segment.

```
/* Insert algorithm where we are trying to perform sorting operation on a new list.
# include<stdio.h>
    void  insert(int *, int *, int);
    int L1[5]={9,4,6,7, 3};
    int L2[5],i, j;
    int n=5;

int main()
{

    insert(L1, L2, n);
 for(int k=0; k<5; k++)
 printf("\n %d", L2[k]);
 return 0;
}

void insert (int L1[], int L2[], int n)
 {
    L2[0]=-0;
    for(i=0; i<5; i++){
 j=i-1;
 while(L1[i]<L2[j]){
    L2[j+1]=L2[j];
    j=j-1;
 }
 L2[j+1]=L1[i];
    }
}
```

9.5 QUICK SORT

Quicksort has a couple of other differences from merge sort. Quicksort works in place. And its worst-case running time is as bad as selection sort's and insertion sort's: $\Theta(n^2)$). But its average-case running time is as good as merge sort's: $\Theta(n\lg n)$. So why think about quicksort when merge sort is at least as good? That's because the constant factor hidden in the big-Θ notation for quicksort is quite good. In practice, quicksort outperforms than merge sort, and it also significantly outperforms than insertion and selection sort algorithms.

Quick sort is a highly efficient sorting algorithm and is based on partitioning of array of data into smaller arrays. A large array is partitioned into two arrays one of which holds values smaller than specified value say pivot based on which the partition is made and another array holds values greater than pivot value. It then calls itself recursively twice to sort the resulting two subarray. Here is how quicksort uses divide-and-conquer. As with merge sort, think of sorting a subarray array[left...right], where initially the subarray is array[0...n-1].

1. **Divide** by choosing any element in the subarray array[left…right]. Call this element the **pivot**. Rearrange the elements in array[left...right] so that all other elements in array[left..right] that are less than or equal to the pivot are to its left and all elements in array[left..right] are to the pivot's right. We call this procedure **partitioning**. At this point, it doesn't matter what order the elements to the left of the pivot are in relative to each other, and the same holds for the elements to the right of the pivot. We just care that each element is somewhere on the correct side of the pivot.

   As a matter of practice, we will always choose the rightmost element in the subarray, array[right], as the pivot. So, for example, if the subarray consists of [9, 7, 5, 11, 12, 2, 14, 3, 10, 6], then we choose 6 as the pivot. After partitioning, the subarray might look like [5, 2, 3, 6, 12, 7, 14, 9, 10, 11]. Let **q** be the index of where the pivot ends up.

2. **Conquer** by recursively sorting the subarrays array[left...q-1] (all elements to the left of the pivot, which must be less than or equal to the pivot) and array[q+1...right] (all elements to the right of the pivot, which must be greater than the pivot).

3. **Combine** by doing nothing. Once the conquer step recursively sorts, we are done. Why? All elements to the left of the pivot, in array[left...q-1], are less than or equal to the pivot and are sorted, and all elements to the right of the pivot, in array[q+1..right], are greater than the pivot and are sorted. The elements in array[left…right] can't help but be sorted!

   See the example shown in Figure 9.13. After recursively sorting the subarrays to the left and right of the pivot, the subarray to the left of the pivot is [2, 3, 5], and the subarray to the right of the pivot is [7, 9, 10, 11, 12, 14]. So the subarray has [2, 3, 5], followed by 6, followed by [7, 9, 10, 11, 12, 14]. The subarray is sorted.

The base cases are subarrays of fewer than two elements, just as in merge sort. In merge sort, we never see a subarray with no elements, but we can in quicksort, if the other elements in the subarray are all less than the pivot or all greater than the pivot.

Let's go back to the conquer step and walk through the recursive sorting of the subarrays. After the first partition, we have subarrays of [5, 2, 3] and [12, 7, 14, 9, 10, 11], with 6 as the pivot.

To sort the subarray [5, 2, 3], we choose 3 as the pivot. After partitioning, we have [2, 3, 5]. The subarray [2], to the left of the pivot, is a base case when we recurse, as is the subarray [5], to the right of the pivot.

To sort the subarray [12, 7, 14, 9, 10, 11], we choose 11 as the pivot, resulting in [7, 9, 10] to the left of the pivot and [14, 12] to the right. After these subarrays are sorted, we have [7, 9, 10], followed by 11, followed by [12, 14].

Here is how the entire quicksort algorithm unfolds. Array locations in blue have been pivots in previous recursive calls, and so the values in these locations will not be examined or moved again. It is assumed that l-left and r-right:

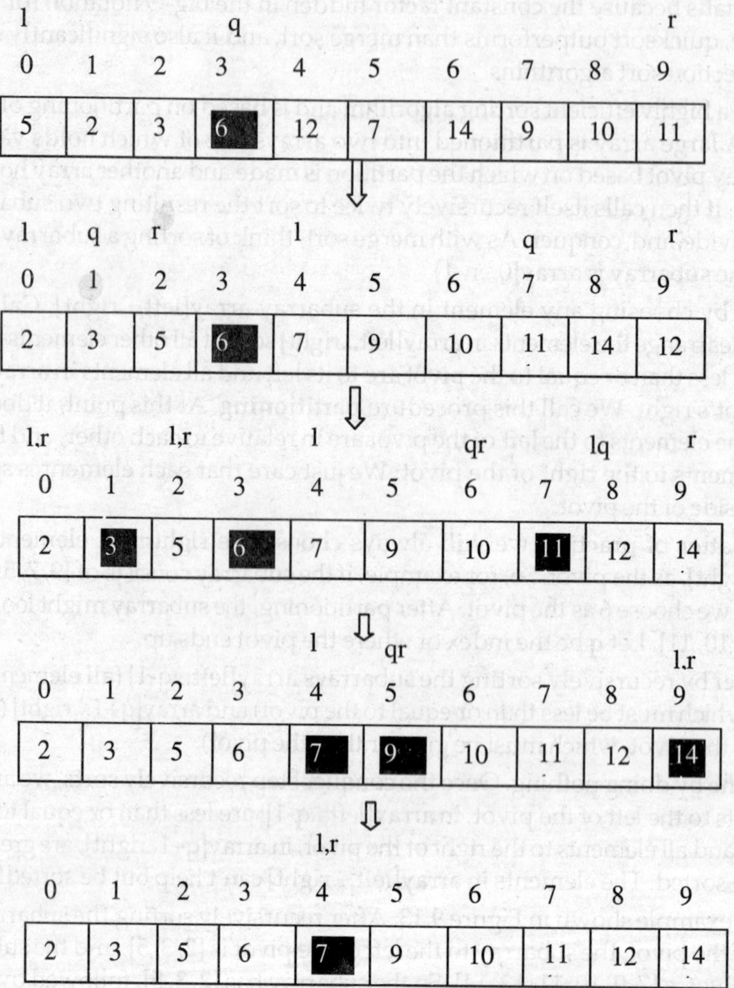

Figure 9.13. Example QuckSort Algorithm

Based on our understanding of partitioning in quicksort, the following steps are summarizing the partitioning.

1. Choose the highest index value has pivot
2. Take two variables to point left and right of the list excluding pivot
3. left points to the low index
4. right points to the high
5. while value at left is less than pivot move right
6. while value at right is greater than pivot move left

7. if both step 5 and step 6 do not match swap left and right
8. if left e" right, the point where they met is new pivot

The pseudocode for the above steps are derived in Figure 14(a).

```
partitionFunc(left, right, pivot)
Where A → Represents the list of elements.
left → Represents the position of the first element in the list (Only at the starting point, it's value changes during the execution of the function).
right → Represents the position of the last element in the list(Only at starting point the value of it's changes during the execution of the function).
leftPointer = left -1
rightPointer = right
while True do
while A[++leftPointer] < pivot do
end while
while rightPointer > 0 && A[--rightPointer] > pivot do
end while
if (leftPointer >= rightPointer)
break
else
swap (leftPointer, rightPointer)
end if
end while
swap (leftPointer, right)
return leftPointer
```

Figure 9.14(a) Algorithm of Partition for Quick Sort

Using pivot algorithm recursively, we end-up with smaller possible partitions. Each partition then processed for quick sort. We define recursive steps of algorithm for quicksort as below –

1. Make the right-most index value pivot
2. partition the array using pivot value
3. quicksort left partition recursively
4. quicksort right partition recursively

To get more into it, let see the pseudocode for quick sort algorithm which is given in Figure 14(b).

```
procedure quickSort(left, right)
Where left → Represents the position of the first element in the list (Only at the starting point, it's value changes during the execution of the function).
right → Represents the position of the last element in the list(Only at starting point the value of it's changes during the execution of the function).
A → Represents the list of elements.
if right-left <= 0
return
else
pivot = A[right]
```

```
partition = partitionFunc(left, right, pivot)
quickSort(left,partition-1)
 quickSort(partition+1,right)
 end if
end procedure
```

Figure 9.14(b) Algorithm of Quick Sort

The efficiency of the algorithm is majorly impacted by which element is chosen as the pivot point. The worst-case efficiency of the quick sort, $O(n^2)$, occurs when the list is sorted and the left-most element is chosen. Randomly choosing a pivot point rather than using the left-most element is recommended if the data to be sorted is not random. As long as the pivot point is chosen randomly, the quick sort has an algorithmic complexity of $O(n \log n)$. The following program segment implements the quick sort technique (QUICK.C).

```
/* quick.c*/
#include <stdio.h>
#include <stdbool.h>
#define MAX 10

int intArray[MAX] = {9,7,5,11,12,2,14,3,10,6};

void printline(int count)
{
 int i;
        for(i = 0;i <count-1;i++){
           printf("=");
        }
        printf("=\n");
}

void display(){
 int i;
 printf("[");

  // navigate through all items
 for(i = 0;i<MAX;i++){
 printf("%d ",intArray[i]);
 }
    printf("]\n");
}

void swap(int num1, int num2){
 int temp = intArray[num1];
 intArray[num1] = intArray[num2];
 intArray[num2] = temp;
}
```

```
int partition(int left, int right, int pivot){
 int leftPointer = left -1;
 int rightPointer = right;

 while(true){

 while(intArray[++leftPointer] < pivot){
 //do nothing
 }

 while(rightPointer > 0 && intArray[--rightPointer] > pivot){
 //do nothing
 }

 if(leftPointer >= rightPointer){
 break;
 }else{
 printf(" item swapped :%d,%d\n",
 intArray[leftPointer],intArray[rightPointer]);
 swap(leftPointer,rightPointer);
 }

 }

 printf(" pivot swapped :%d,%d\n", intArray[leftPointer],intArray[right]);
 swap(leftPointer,right);
 printf("Updated Array: ");
 display();
 return leftPointer;
}

void quickSort(int left, int right)
{
   if(right-left <= 0){
    return;
 }else {
 int pivot = intArray[right];
 int partitionPoint = partition(left, right, pivot);
 quickSort(left,partitionPoint-1);
 quickSort(partitionPoint+1,right);
 }
}

main()
{
```

```
    printf("Input Array: ");
    display();
    printline(50);
    quickSort(0,MAX-1);
    printf("Output Array: ");
    display();
    printline(50);
}
```

```
Input Array: [9 7 5 11 12 2 14 3 10 6 ]
========================================
 item swapped :9,3
 item swapped :7,2
 pivot swapped :11,6
Updated Array: [3 2 5 6 12 7 14 9 10 11 ]
 pivot swapped :5,5
Updated Array: [3 2 5 6 12 7 14 9 10 11 ]
 pivot swapped :3,2
Updated Array: [2 3 5 6 12 7 14 9 10 11 ]
 item swapped :12,10
 item swapped :14,9
 pivot swapped :14,11
Updated Array: [2 3 5 6 10 7 9 11 12 14 ]
 item swapped :10,7
 pivot swapped :10,9
Updated Array: [2 3 5 6 7 9 10 11 12 14 ]
 pivot swapped :14,14
Updated Array: [2 3 5 6 7 9 10 11 12 14 ]
Output Array: [2 3 5 6 7 9 10 11 12 14 ]
========================================
```

9.6 SELECTION SORT

The selection sort starts from first element and searches the entire list until it finds the minimum value. The sort places the minimum value in the first place, selects the second element and searches for the second smallest element. This process continues until the complete list is sorted. This operation is implemented in **selects.c**.

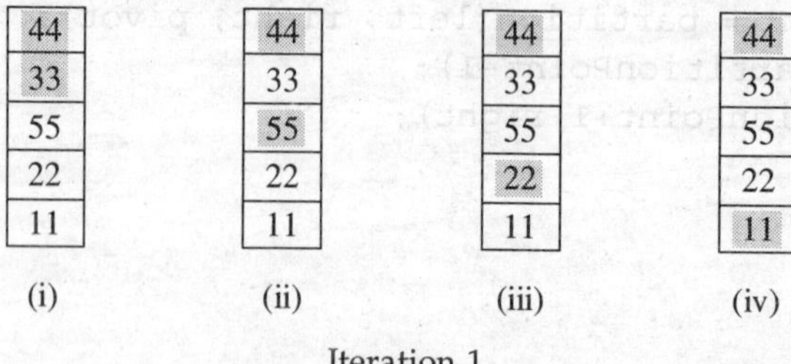

Iteration 1

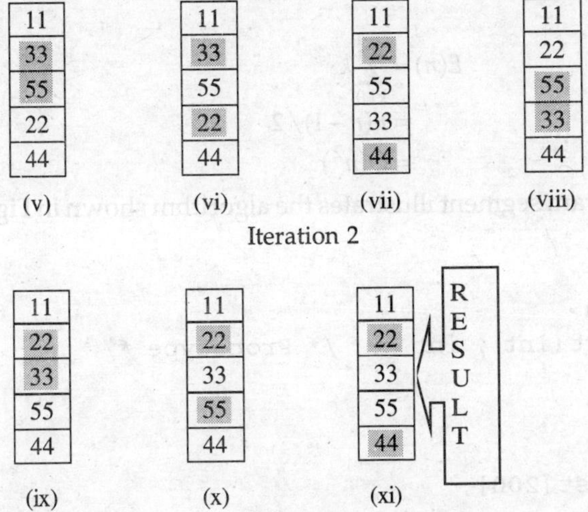

Figure 9.15 Selection Sort Implementation

For example, suppose we have a list, which contains the elements: 44, 33, 55, 22 and 11. If we want to sort this list using the selection sort technique, the details of this technique are illustrated in **Figure 9.15.** In this figure parts **(i), (ii), (iii)** and **(iv)** are generated during the first iteration, similarly **(v), (vi)** and **(vi)** in the second iteration and in the third iteration **(vii), (ix)** and **(x)** are produced.

```
Selection_sort (n, list)
Where list → Represents the list of elements
   n → Represents size of the list
Step 1: Repeat thru Step 5 for index =1, 2, 3, ..., n-1
Step 2: min= index
Step 3: Repeat thru Step 4 for k = index+1, 2, 3,... n-1
Step 4: if (list[min] > list [k]
   min = k
Step 5: if (min ≠ index)
(i)   temp = list[index]
(ii)  list[index] = list[min]
(iii) list[min] = temp
Step 6: Exit
```

Figure 9.16 Algorithm of Selection Sort

From the algorithm given in **Figure 9.16**, it is clear that the algorithm consumes most of its time in the inner loop. During the pass **current** of the outer loop **size – current** elements are examined to find the smallest remaining elements. This requires **size – current – 1** comparisons. The number of comparisons for all passes is:

$$E(n) = \sum_{index=0}^{n-1} n - index - 1$$

Let k = n – index – 1

k = n – 1 at index = 0

k = 0 at index = n - 1

$$E(n) = \sum_{k=0}^{n-1} k$$
$$= n(n-1)/2$$
$$= O(n^2)$$

The **SELECTS.C** program segment illustrates the algorithm shown in **Figure 9.16**.

```
/* SELECTION SORT */
/* SELECTS.C */
# include<stdio.h>
int selection_sort(int , int *); /* Prototype */

void main()
{
    int number, list[200];
    int i;
    printf("Input the number of elements in the list:");
    scanf("%d", &number);
    printf("\n Number of elements in the list is: %d", number);
    printf("\nInput the elements of the list\n");
    for(i = 0 ; i < number ; i++)
        scanf("%d", &list[i]);
    selection_sort( number, list);
}

/* Definition of function */
int selection_sort(int n, int l[])
{
    int min ;
    int k, index;
    for(index = 0; index< n - 1 ; index++)
    {
        min = index ;
        for(k = index + 1; k < n ; k ++)
        {
            if(l[min] > l[k])
                min = k ;
        }
        if( min != index){
            int temp = l [index];
            l[index] = l[min];
            l[min] = temp ;
        }
    }
```

```
    printf("\n Entered list is as follows:\n");
    for( index = 0 ; index < n; index++)
        printf(" %d", l[index]);
    return 0;
}
```

9.7 SHELL SORT

The shell sort is named after its developer **Donald Shell.** The sort technique works by comparing the list elements that are separated by a specific distance, i.e., a **gap** until the elements compared with the current **gap** are in order. Two then divides **gap** and the process continues. When the **gap** is reached to 0 and no changes are possible, the list is sorted. For example, consider a list, which contains the elements: 11, 88, 22, 77, 33, 66, 44, 55.

Iteration 1:

n = 8 /* where n is number of elements in the list */

gap = n/2 = 8/2 = 4

and initial value of swap = 0

After completion of the first iteration the value of **swap** becomes 1, hence further execution with **gap = 4** is possible. Now, after second iteration, the value of **swap** is 0, so further execution is not possible. Consider **Figure 9.17 (a)**, which illustrates the related steps.

Iteration 2:

gap = gap /2 = 4/2 = 2

With the help of **gap = 2** execution starts, after completion of the first iteration we get value of **swap = 1**, hence further execution with **gap = 2** is possible. Execution once again resumes and after completion of execution, the value of **swap** becomes 0. The value of **swap** is 0 so that further execution is not possible. Consider **Figure 9.17(b)**, which illustrate the associated steps.

Iteration 3:

gap = gap / 2 = 2/2 = 1

With the help of **gap = 1** execution starts, after completion of the first iteration we get value of **swap = 1**, hence further execution with **gap = 1** is possible. Execution once again resumes and after completion of execution the value of **swap** remains 1, once again the same process is repeated and after third execution the value of **swap** becomes 0. The value of **swap** is 0 so that further execution is not possible. Consider **Figure 9.17 ((c), (d) and (e))**, which illustrates each step clearly.

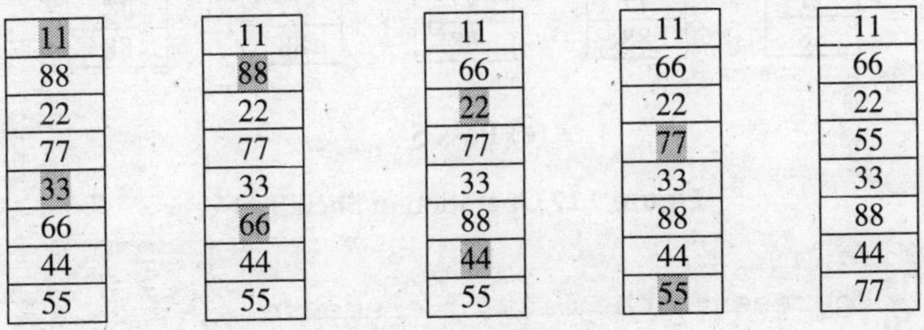

11	11	11	11	11
88	88	66	66	66
22	22	22	22	22
77	77	77	77	55
33	33	33	33	33
66	66	88	88	88
44	44	44	44	44
55	55	55	55	77

(a) Pass 1

11	11	11	11	11	11	11
66	66	55	55	55	55	55
22	22	22	22	22	22	22
55	55	66	66	66	66	66
33	33	33	33	33	33	33
88	88	88	88	88	88	77
44	44	44	44	44	44	44
77	77	77	77	77	77	88

(b) Pass 2

11	11	11	11	11	11	11
55	55	22	22	22	22	22
22	22	55	55	55	55	55
66	66	66	66	33	33	33
33	33	33	33	66	66	66
77	77	77	77	77	77	44
44	44	44	44	44	44	77
88	88	88	88	88	88	88

(c) Pass 3

11	11	11	11	11	11	11
22	22	22	22	22	22	22
55	55	55	33	33	33	33
33	33	33	55	55	55	55
66	66	66	66	66	44	44
44	44	44	44	44	66	66
77	77	77	77	77	77	77
88	88	88	88	88	88	88

(d) Pass 4

11	11	11	11	11	11	11
22	22	22	22	22	22	22
33	33	33	33	33	33	33
55	55	55	55	44	44	44
44	44	44	44	55	55	55
66	66	66	66	66	66	66
77	77	77	77	77	77	77
88	88	88	88	88	88	88

Result

(e) Pass 5

Figure 9.17 Operation of Shell Sort

```
Shell_sort(list, n)
Where list → Represents the list of elements
   n → Represents the size of the list
Step 1: [Initialize]
```

```
   gap = n / 2
Step 2: Repeat thru Step 6 while (gap = gap / 2)
Step 3: swap = 0
Step 4: Repeat thru Step 6 while (swap)
Step 5: Repeat thru Step 6 for i = 0, 1, 2, 3 ... i < (n - gap )
Step 6: if (list [i] > list[ i+ gap ] )
        (i)    temp = list [i]
        (ii)   list [i] = list [i + gap ]
        (iii) list [i + gap ] = temp
        (iv)   swap = 1
[End of for loop]
[End of inner while loop]
[End of outer while loop]
Step 7: output list elements (sorted)
Step 8: Exit
```

Figure 9.18 Shell sort algorithm

The algorithm for shell sort is given in **Figure 9.16**. It is difficult to predict the time requirements of the shell sort since it is hard to show the effect of one pass on another. It should be obvious that is the above method calculating **gap** is used, the number of passes will be approximately **($\log_2$ gap)** since bubbling when **gap = 1** will complete the sort. Empirical studies have shown that the shell approximately takes **B*n*($\log_2$ n)^2** units of time for an **n** element array. The constant of proportionality **B** is fairly small so for small **n** the shell sort will perform the radix exchange sort. When **n** is very large then the number of moves is in the range of **n $^{1.5}$** to **1.6 n $^{1.5}$**. The following program segment implements the above discussion (**SHELL.C**):

```
/* shell.c -shell sort */

#include <stdio.h>
#include <stdlib.h>
void display(int *, int );
void shell_sort(int *, int );

/* function for shell sort */
void shell_sort(int list[], int n)
{
   int temp, gap, i, swap=0;
   gap = n / 2;
   do {
      do {
         swap = 0;
         for (i = 0; i < n - gap; i++)
            if (list[i] > list[i + gap])
            {
               temp = list[i];
               list[i] = list[i + gap];
```

```
                list[i + gap] = temp;
                swap = 1;
            }
        printf("\n List after pass \n");
        display(list, n);
        } while (swap);
    } while (gap = gap / 2);
}
/* Output Function */
void display(int list[], int n)
{
    int k;
    for(k = 0; k < n; k++)
        printf(" %d ", list[k]);
}

void main(void)
{
    int list[50], i, n;
    printf("\n Input Number of Data Elements: ");
    scanf("%d", &n);
    printf("\n Randomly Generated Unsorted list is as follows \n");
    for (i= 0; i < n; i++)
    {
        list[i] = rand() % 100;
        printf(" %d", list[i]);
    }
    shell_sort(list, n);
    printf("\n Sorted list is as follows \n");
    for (i = 0; i < n; i++)
        printf("%d ", list[i]);
}
```

9.8 MERGE SORT

Suppose **list_a** is a list with **n** elements and **list_b** with **m** elements. The operation that combines the elements of **list_a** and **list_b** into a single **result_list** list with **r = n+m** elements is called merging. If the elements of **list_a** and **list_b** are in sorted order then we may get a **result_list** in sorted order. If the **list_a** and **list_b** are not in sorted order we can make them in sorted order and then both the lists can be merged. It is also possible that first merging of **list_a** and **list_b** is done and then sort the merged **result_list.** In the later case execution time will be less.

For example, suppose we have two rows of policemen sorted by increasing heights and let we want to merge them into a single sorted row. Choosing at the head of their respective rows forms the new row. When one of these rows has no more policemen, the remaining policemen line up at the end of the combined row. Let we have two lists as shown in **Figure 9.19.** The top row of **Figure 9.19** to **Figure 9.21** represents index of the lists.

1	2	3	4
77	44	55	66

(a) list 1

1	2	3	4	5
99	11	22	33	88

(b) list2

Figure 9.19 Two list of elements

From **Figure 9.19** it is clear that the two lists are unsorted. Before merging, it is required to sort the list individually. The sorted lists are given in **Figure 9.20.**

1	2	3	4
44	55	66	77

(a) list 1

1	2	3	4	5
11	22	33	88	99

(b) list 2

Figure 9.20 List after sorting their elements

	1	2	3	4	5	6	7	8	9
Step 1	11								
Step 2	11	22							
Step 3	11	22	33						
Step 4	11	22	33	44					
Step 5	11	22	33	44	55				
Step 6	11	22	33	44	55	66			
Step 7	11	22	33	44	55	66	77		
Step 8	11	22	33	44	55	66	77	88	
Step 9	11	22	33	44	55	66	77	88	99

Figure 9.21 Illustration of Merging and Sorting

The algorithm for the merge sort is given in **Figure 9.22.** From the algorithm given **Figure 9.22** it is clear that the total number of comparisons performed is **r = n + m** at the most so:

E(r) = r = n + m, i.e., O(r)

The program segment **MERGES.C** implements the above discussion.

```
/* SIMPLE MERGE SORT */
/* MERGES.C */
# include<stdio.h>

int merge_sort( int , int *, int , int *, int * );
int bubble_sort(int , int *);

/* Definition of function */

bubble_sort(int n, int list[])
{
   int flag = 1 ;
   int i, j, k, temp;
   for(j = 0 ; j< n - 1; j++)
   {
      for(k = 0 ; k< n - j - 1 ; k++)
      {
         if(list[k] > list[k+1])
         {
            temp = list[k];
            list[k] = list[k+1];
            list[k+1] = temp ;
            flag = 0;
         }
      }
      if(flag)
         break ;
      else
         flag = 1;
   }
   printf("\n Entered list as follows in");
   printf("\n Ascending order: ");
   for(i = 0 ; i < n ; i++)
      printf(" %d", list[i]);
   return 0 ;
}

/* Definition of function */

merge_sort( int n, int list_a[], int m ,
```

```
   int list_b[], int result_list[] )
   {
      int i = 0;
      int j = 0;
      int k = 0;
      int ch, l;

      /* Repeat the process until the elements of list_a and list_b are
exhausted */

      while((i < n) &&(j<m))
      {
         if(list_a[i] < list_b[j])
         {
            result_list[k] = list_a[i];
            i++;
            k++;
         } /* end of if statement */
         else
            if(list_a[i] > list_b[j])
            {
               result_list[k] = list_b[j];
               j++;
               k++;
            } /* end of if statement */
            else{
               result_list[k] = list_a[i];
               i++;
               j++;
               k++;
            } /* end of else statement */
         printf("\n");
         for(ch = 0; ch < k; ch++)
            printf(" %d", result_list[ch]);

      } /* end of while statement */

      /* checks if size of list_a larger than list_b
       copy rest of the elements of list_a into result_list */

      if(i <n )
      {
         for(l = i ; l <n ; l++)
         {
            result_list[k] = list_a[i];
```

```
            i++;
            k++;
            printf("\n");
            for(ch = 0; ch < k; ch++)
               printf(" %d", result_list[ch]);
        }
    }  else if(j < m)
              /* checks if size of list_b larger than list_a copy rest of the
              elements of list_b into result_list */

        {
          for(l = j; l<m; l++)
          {
             result_list[k] = list_b[j];
             j++;
             k++;
             printf("\n");
             for(ch = 0; ch < k; ch++)
                printf(" %d", result_list[ch]);
          }
        }
    return (k);
}

/* function main */

void main()
{
    int list_a[100],list_b[100];
    int result[200];
    int n, m, k, i;

    printf("\n Input the number of elements of list_a: ");
    scanf("%d", &n);

    for(i = 0; i<n ; i++)
    {
       printf("\n Input the element: %d: ", i+1);
       scanf("%d", &list_a[i]);
    }
```

```
    /* Sort the elements of list_a */

    bubble_sort(n, list_a);
    /* End of sorting */

    printf("\n Input the number of elements of list_b:");
    scanf("%d", &m);
    for(i = 0 ; i< m ; i++)
    {
       printf("\n Input the element: %d: ", i+1);
       scanf("%d", &list_b[i]);
    }

    /* Sort the elements of list_b */

    bubble_sort(m, list_b);

    /* End of sorting */

    k = merge_sort( n, list_a, m , list_b, result);
    printf("\n Duplicates are : %d", m+n-k);
    printf("\n");

    printf("\n Sorted list is as follows:\n");
    for(i = 0 ; i< k ; i++)
    {
       printf(" %d", result[i]);
    }
}
```

Now we will simplify the algorithm discussed in **Figure 9.22.** The simplified algorithm discussed in **Figure 9.23**. Assumptions, which are taken into account: Given two ordered sub-tables stored in a **list** with **First, Second** and **Third** (**First** through **Second -1** elements and **Second** through the **Third** elements represents the first and second tables, respectively), this algorithm performs a simple merge. **Temp** is a temporary array variable used in the merging process. The variables **I** and **J** denote the cursor associated with the first and second sub-tables, respectively. The **L** is the index variable associated with the array **Temp**. Performance of this algorithm is also **O (n)** and is equivalent to the algorithm given in **Figure 9.22.**

The algorithm given in **Figure 9.23** can also be generalized to merge **k** sorted tables into a single sorted table. Such merging operation is called multiple merging or **k-way** merging. Multiple merging can also be accomplished by performing a single merge repeatedly. For example, if we have 16 tables to merge, we can first merge them in pairs using algorithm simple merge {**Figure 9.23**}. The result of this first step yields eight tables, which again merged in pairs to give four tables. This process is repeated until a single table is obtained. Result of this example, four separate passes is required to yield a single table. In general, **k** separate passes are required to merge 2^k separate tables into a single table. This technique can also be applied for sorting. Given a table containing **n** records, one merely considers this table to be a set of **n** tables, each with a single record. Obviously, a table, which contains a single record, is sorted.

```
Merge_sort(n, list_a, m, list_b, result)
Where n → Represents number of elements in first list (list_a)
    list_a → Represents the list of elements(first list)
    m → Represents number of elements in the second list(list_b)
    list_b → Represents the list of elements(second list)
Step 1: [initialize]
    i = 0
    j = 0
    k = 0
Step 2: Repeat step 3 while((i < n ) and ( j < m))
Step3: if(list_a[i] < list_b[j])
        (i)   result_list[k] = list_a[i]
        (ii)  i = i + 1
        (iii) k = k + 1
else if(list_a[i] > list_b[j])
        (iv)  result_list[k] = list_b[j]
        (v)   j = j + 1
        (vi)  k = k + 1

else [ Means elements of both the list are equal and insert only one of them
into the result_list]
        (vii) result_list[k] = list_a[i]
        (viii)    i = i + 1
        (ix)  j = j + 1
        (x)   k = k + 1
Step4: if( i < n) [size of list_a is larger than the list_b]
Step 5: Repeat thru Step 5 for l =i, i+1, i+2, ..., n-1
        (i)    result_list[k] = list_a[i]
        (ii)   i = i + 1
        (iii) k = k + 1
Step 6: [Size of lits_b is larger than list)a]
 else if( j < m )
Step 7: Repeat thru Step 7 for l = j, j+1, j + 2 ...  m -1
        (i)    result_list[k] = list[j]
        (ii)   j = j + 1
        (iii) k = k + 1
Step 8: return
```

Figure 9.22 Algorithm of Merge sort

```
Simple_Merge(list, First, Second, Third)
Step 1: [Initialization]
   I = First
   J = Second
   L = 0
Step 2: [Compare corresponding elements and the output smallest one]
   If list[I] ≤ list [J]
   Then
      L = L+1
      Temp [L] = list[I]
      I = I + 1
Else
   L = L + 1
   Temp [L] = list[J]
   J = J + 1
Step 3 : [Copy the remaining element in output list]
   If I ≥ Second
   Then     Repeat while J ≤ Third
         L = L + 1
         Temp[L] = list[J]
         J = J + 1
   Else     Repeat while I < Second
         L = L + 1
         Temp[L] = list [J]
         I = I + 1
Step 4: [Copy elements in the temporary list into original list]
   Repeat for I = 1, 2, 3 ... L
      list[First -1 + I] = Temp[I]
Step 5: Return
```

Figure 9.23 Simple merge algorithm (Simplified form of the algorithm given in Figure 9.22

For example, suppose a **list** with **n** elements **list** [1], **list** [2], **list** [3] ... **list** [n] is in memory, having 14 elements: 66, 33, 40, 22, 55, 88, 60, 11, 80, 20, 50, 44, 77, 30. Each pass of the merge sort algorithm will start at the beginning of the **list** and merge pairs of sorted sub-arrays as shown in **Figure 9.24**. **The** merge sort algorithm for sorting a **list** has the following important property. After pass **k**, the **list** will be partitioned into sorted sub-lists where each sub-list, except possibly the last, will contain exactly **L** **= 2^k^** elements. Hence the algorithm requires at most $\log_2 n$ pass to sort an n-element **list**. The merge **sort** algorithm is given in **Figure 9.25.** The assumptions are: **list** is an array, **Start** (Top) is first element positions in the list, **Finish** (bottom) is the last element position, **Size** denotes the current size of the sub-table to be sorted and **Mid** denotes the position of the middle element of that sub-table.

Values	Pass 1	Pass 2	Pass 3	Pass 4
66	33	22	11	11
33	66	33	22	20
40	22	40	33	22
22	40	66	40	30
55	55	11	55	33
88	88	55	60	40
60	11	60	66	44
11	60	88	88	50
80	20	20	20	55
20	80	44	30	60
50	44	50	44	66
44	50	80	50	77
77	30	30	77	80
30	77	77	80	88

Figure 9.24 Merge sort

The above informal description of merge sort will now be translated into a formal algorithm, which will be divided into two parts. The first part will be a merge pass algorithm, which is given in **Figure 9.26** to execute a single pass of the algorithm and the second part will repeatedly apply merge pass until **list** is sorted. The merge pass algorithm applies to an n-element **list** consists of a sequence of sorted sub-**lists**. Moreover, each sub-list consists of **L** elements except that the last sub-list may have fewer than **L** elements. Dividing **N** by **2*L**, we obtain the quotient **Q**, which tells the number of pairs of **L** element sorted sub-lists, i.e.,

$$Q = N/(2*L)$$

Setting **S = 2*L*Q,** we get the total number **(S)** of elements in the **Q** pairs of sub-lists. Hence **R = N – S** denotes the number of remaining elements. The procedure first merges the initial **Q** pairs of L-element sub-lists then the procedure takes care of the case where there is an odd number of sub-lists (when $R \leq L$) or where the last sub-list has fewer than **L** elements. The merge sort algorithm is given in **Figure 9.27**.

Let **f (n)** denotes the number of comparisons needed to sort an n-element **list** using the merge sort algorithm. Recall that the algorithm requires at most $\mathbf{\log_2 n}$ pass. Moreover each pass merges a total of **n** elements and by the discussion on the complexity of merging each pass will require at most **n** comparisons. Accordingly, for both the worst case and average case:

$f(n) \leq n \log_2 n$

Observe that this algorithm has the same order as heap sort and the same average as quick sort. The main drawback of merge sort is that it requires an auxiliary array with **n** elements. Each of the other sorting algorithms we have studied requires only a finite number of extra locations, which is independent of **n**. The summarized result is as follows:

Algorithm	Worst case	Average case	Extra memory
Merge sort	$n \log_2 n = O(n \log_2 n)$	$n \log_2 n = O(n \log_2 n)$	O(n)

```
Two_Way_Merge_Sort (list, Start, Finish)

Step 1: [Compute the size of the current sub-table]
   Size = Finish - Start + 1
Step 2: [Test base condition for sub-tables of size one]
   If Size ≤ 1
   Then
      Return
Step 3: [Calculate midpoint position of current sub-table]
   Mid = Start + Size/2 - 1
Step 4: [Recursively sort the first sub-table]
   Call Two_Way_Merge_Sort (list, Start, Mid)
Step 6: [Recursively sort the second sub-table]
   Call Two_Way_Merge_Sort (list, Mid +1, Finish)
Step 7: Call Simple_Merge (list, Start, Mid+1, Finish)
Step 8: Return
```

Figure 9.25 Merge sort algorithm

```
Merge_Sort(list, M, N )
Step 1: [Compute Middle index value]
Mid = M + N/2
Step 2: [Test Non equality of M and N]
   If (M ≠ N)
   Call Merge_Pass (list, M, Mid)
   Call Merge_Pass (list, Mid+1, N)
   Call Merge_Sort(list, M, Mid, N)
Step 3: Return
```

Figure 9.27 Merge sort algorithm

```
Merge_Pass (list, Top, Size, Bottom)
Step 1: [Initialization]
F = Top
   S = Size +1
   T = Top
Step 2: [Start merging from here]
Repeat thru Step 3 while (F ≤ Size) and (S ≤ Bottom)
      If (list [F] ≤ list [S])
      Then
         Temp[T] = list [F]
         F = F + 1
      Else
         Temp[T] = list [S]
         S = S + 1
Step 3:  T = T+ 1
```

```
Step 4:   If (F ≤ Size) Then
    Repeat for F = F, F+1, F+2 ... Size
        Temp[T] = list [F]
        T = T + 1
    Else
     Repeat for S = S, S+1, S+2 ... Bottom
        Temp[T]= list [S]
        T = T + 1
Step 5:
    Repeat for Upper = Top, Top+1, Top +2 ... Bottom
    list [Upper]=Temp[Upper]
Step 6: Return
```

Figure 9.26 Merge pass algorithm

The algorithm in **Figure 9.23** and **Figure 9.25** are almost same. Program segment **MERGE.C** implements the above discussion of the merge sort technique.

```
/* MERGE SORT */
/* merge.c */
# include<stdio.h>
# include<stdlib.h>

void merge_sort(float *, int , int , int );
void merge_pass(float *, int , int );

/* Definition of the function */

void merge_sort(float list[], int top, int n, int bottom)
{
    float temp[1000];
    int f = top;
    int s = n +1 ;
    int t = top ;
    int upper;
    while(( f <= n)&&(s <=bottom))
    {
        if(list[f] <= list[s])
        {
            temp[t] = list[f] ;
            f ++;
        }else{
            temp[t] = list[s] ;
            s ++;
        }

        t ++;
    }
```

```
    if(f <=n)
    {
       for(f = f ; f<=n; f++)
       {
          temp[t] = list[f];
          t++;
       }
    }else{
       for(s = s ; s<= bottom ; s++)
       {
          temp[t]=list[s];
          t++;
       }
    }

    for(upper = top; upper <= bottom ; upper++)
    {
       list[upper]=temp[upper];
    }

 }

 /* Definition of the function */
 void merge_pass( float append[], int m, int n )
 {
    if( m!= n)
    {
       int mid = (m+n)/2;
       merge_pass( append, m, mid );
       merge_pass( append, mid+1, n );
       merge_sort( append, m, mid, n );
    }
 }

 /* main function */
 void main()
 {
    float list[1000];
    int i, n;
    printf("Input the number of element in the list ");
    scanf("%d", &n);
    for(i = 0 ; i < n ; i++)
    {
       list[i] = (float) (rand() %100);
    }
```

```
    printf("\n Entered list as follows:\n");
    for( i = 0 ; i<n ; i++)
        printf(" %d ", (int) list[i]);
    i = 0 ;
    merge_pass(list, i, n-1);

    printf("\n Merge sorted list is as follows:\n");
    for( i = 0 ; i<n ; i++)
        printf(" %d", (int) list[i]);
}
```

9.9 HEAP SORT

Heap is based on the notion of a **complete tree,** formally a binary tree is **completely full** if it is of height, h, and has 2^{h+1}-1 nodes. A binary tree of height, h, is complete iff

(a) it is empty or

(b) its left subtree is complete of height h-1 and its right subtree is completely full of height h-2 or

(c) its left subtree is completely full of height h-1 and its right subtree is complete of height h-1.

A complete tree is filled from the left: all the leaves are on

(a) the same level or

(b) two adjacent ones and

(c) all nodes at the lowest level are as far to the left as possible.

A binary tree has the **heap property** iff

(a) it is empty or

(b) the key in the root is larger than that in either child and both subtrees have the heap property.

A heap can be used as a priority queue: the highest priority item is at the root and is trivially extracted. But if the root is deleted, we are left with two sub-trees and we must efficiently re-create a single tree with the heap property. The value of the heap structure is that we can both extract the highest priority item and insert a new one in **O($\log_2$ n)** time.

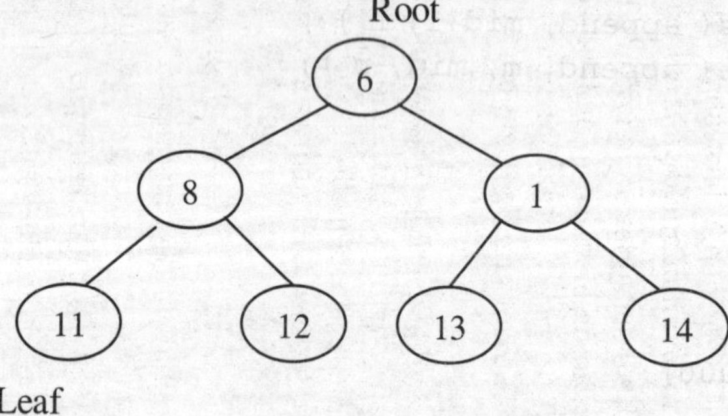

Figure 9.28 Heap (Min-heap)

A heap is an ordered balanced binary tree (complete binary tree) in which the value of the node at the root of any sub-tree is less than or equal to the value of either of its children. This inherent ordering implies that only valued items may be placed in the heap. In general a heap represents a table of **n** elements or records satisfying the following property:

$N_j \geq N_i$ for $2 \leq j \leq n$ and $i = \lfloor j / 2 \rfloor$

A heap satisfying the above definition is called a min-heap. For example, **Figure 9.28** illustrates a min-heap.

If the value at the node **N** is greater than or equal to the value at each of the children of **N** then heap is called a max-heap {**Figure 9.29**}. In general a heap represents a table of **n** elements or records satisfying the following property:

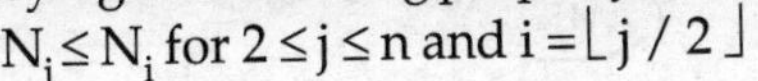

$N_j \le N_i$ for $2 \le j \le n$ and $i = \lfloor j / 2 \rfloor$

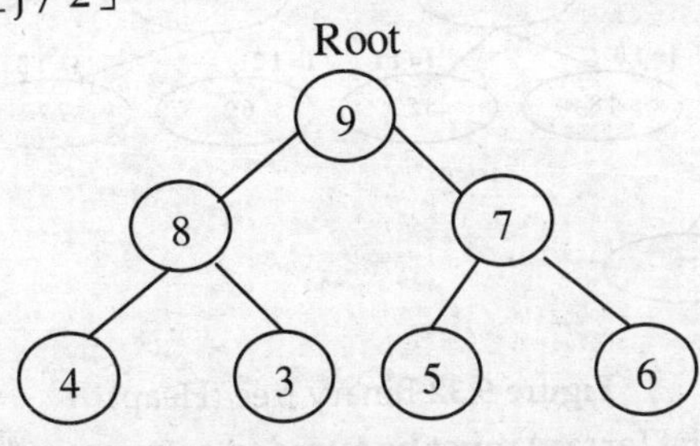

Leaf **Figure 9.29** Heap (Max-heap)

Figure 9.29 Heap (Max-heap)

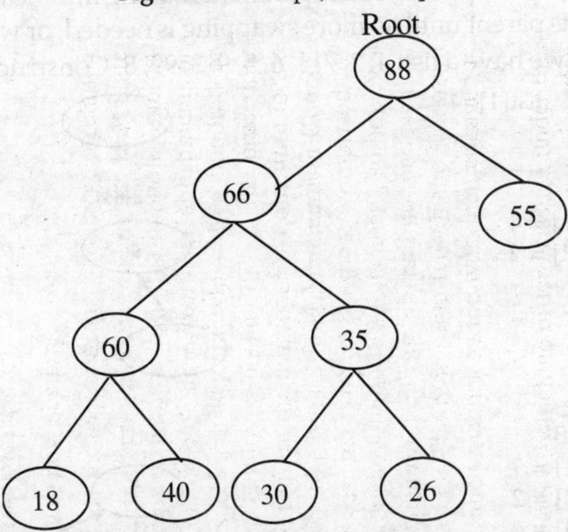

Figure 9.30 Tree but not a heap

In a balanced tree the number of links traversed between the root of the tree and any leaf node will differ by only one. Due to this restriction the tree shown in **Figure 9.30** is not a heap. The binary tree is allocated sequentially such that the indices of the left and right children (if exist) of elements **i** are **2i** and **2i + 1,** respectively. Similarly, the index of the parent of element **i** (if exists) is **i / 2**. In other words, let the root of any sub-tree be at position **i** in the list then left child will be at position **2i** and the right child will be at position **2i + 1**. For example, if we have the list shown in **Figure 9.31** then **Figure 9.32** represents a heap equivalent to this list.

1	2	3	4	5	6	7	8	9	10	11	12	13	14	15	16	17	18
97	88	95	66	55	95	48	60	45	48	55	62	77	25	38	18	40	38

Figure 9.31 List in the memory

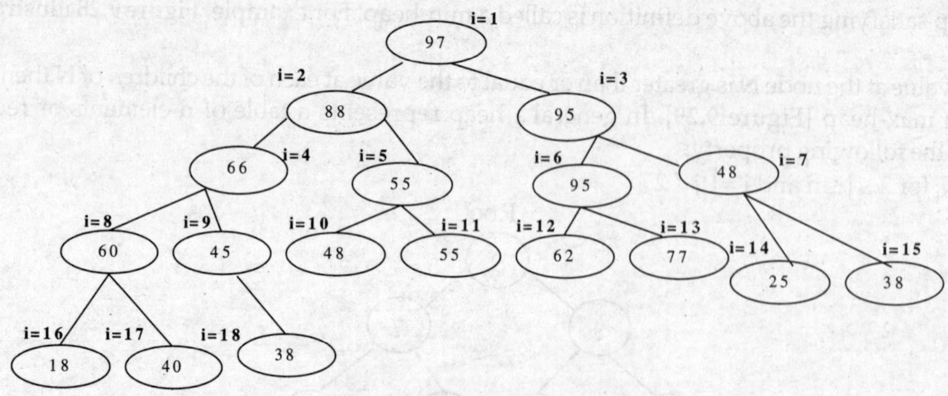

Figure 9.32 Binary tree (Heap)

Don't Forget: Holes in the list (array) must be avoided so as new elements can be added. They are always added at the end of the list (array). If the value of new element is less than its parent's value then the new element must be swapped with its parent (if making min-heap). This process continues with the new element and its parent until no more swapping is needed, or we are at the root of the tree.

For example, suppose we have a list: 4, 2, 7, 1, 6, 5, 9, 3, 99, 8. Construction of heap is as follows:

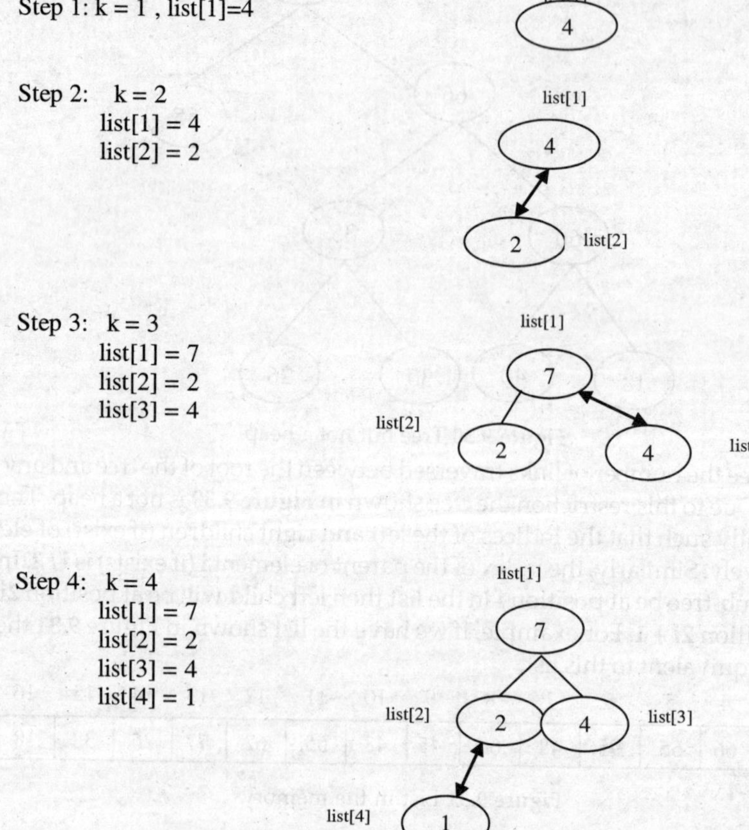

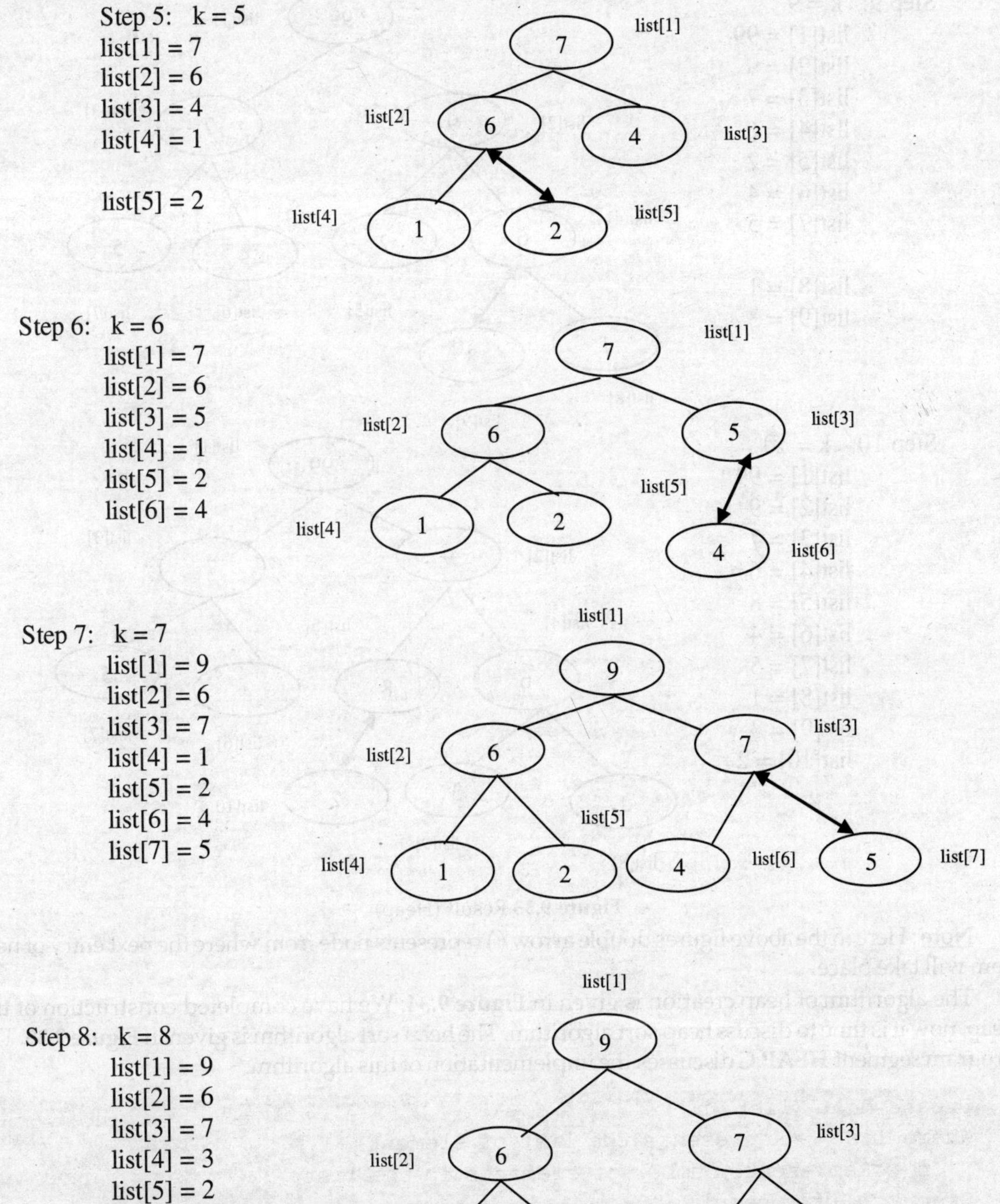
Step 5: k = 5
list[1] = 7
list[2] = 6
list[3] = 4
list[4] = 1
list[5] = 2
Step 6: k = 6
list[1] = 7
list[2] = 6
list[3] = 5
list[4] = 1
list[5] = 2
list[6] = 4
Step 7: k = 7
list[1] = 9
list[2] = 6
list[3] = 7
list[4] = 1
list[5] = 2
list[6] = 4
list[7] = 5
Step 8: k = 8
list[1] = 9
list[2] = 6
list[3] = 7
list[4] = 3
list[5] = 2
list[6] = 4
list[7] = 5
list[8] = 1

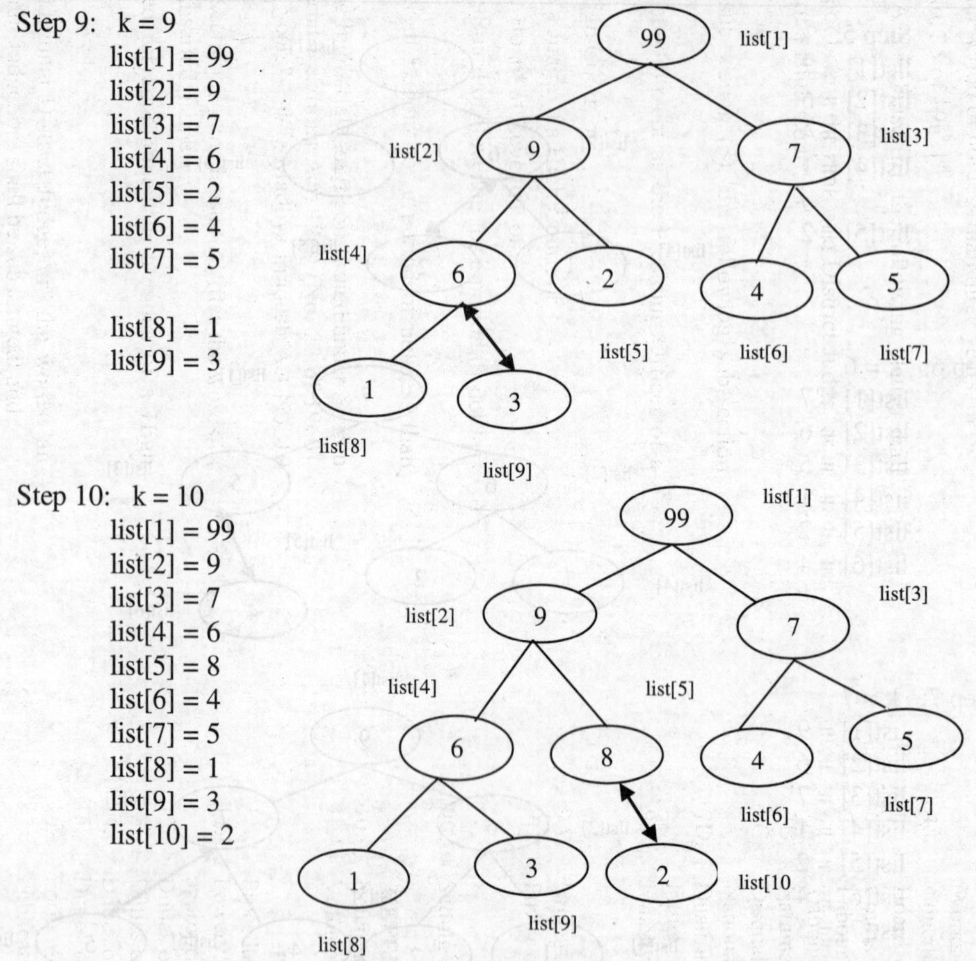

Figure 9.33 Result (Heap)

<u>**Note**</u> : Here in the above figures double arrow ( ) represents node from where the next entry of new item will take place.

The algorithm of heap creation is given in **Figure 9.34.** We have completed construction of the heap, now it is time to discuss heap sort algorithm. The heap sort algorithm is given in **Figure 9.35.** The program segment **HEAP.C** discusses the implementation of this algorithm.

```
Create_heap (list, n)
Where list → Represents the list of elements
   n → Represents number of elements in the list
Step 1: [Build heap]
   Repeat thru Step 7 for k = 2, 3, 4 ... n
Step 2: [Initialize]
         (i)    i = k
         (ii)   temp = list[k]
```

```
Step 3: [Obtain parent of new element]
   i = i / 2
Step 4: [Place new element in the existing heap]
   Repeat thru Step 6 while( i > 1) and (temp > list[j])
Step 5: [Interchange elements]
   list[i] = list[j]
Step 6: [Obtain next parent]
      (i)   i = j
      (ii)  j = i / 2
      (iii) if( j < 1) then j = 1
Step 7: [Copy new element value into its proper place]
   list[i] = temp
Step 8: Return
```

Figure 9.34 Algorithm of Heap construction

```
Heap_sort(list, n)
Where list → Represents the list of elements.
   n → Represents the number of elements in the list.
Step 1: [Create initial heap]
   Call create_heap(list,n)
Step 2: [Start sort]
   Repeat thru Step 10 for k = n, n-1 ... 2
Step 3: [Exchange elements]
   list [1] = list[k]
Step 4:
         (i)   temp = list[1]
         (ii)  i = 1
         (iii) j = 2
Step 5: [find index of largest child of new element]
   If (j + 1 < k) then If (list[j+1] > list[j]) then j = j + 1
Step 6: [Reconstruct the new heap]
   Repeat thru Step 10 while (j ≤ k -1) and (list[j] > temp)
Step 7: [Interchange element]
   list[i] = list[j]
Step 8: [ Obtain left child]
         (i)   i = j
         (ii)  j = 2 * i
Step 9: [Obtain index of next largest child]
   If j +1 < k
   If (list[j+1] > list[j]) then j = j +1 else if (j > n) then j =1
Step 10:  [Copy element into its proper place]
   list[j] = temp
Step 11: Exit
```

Figure 9.35 Heap sort algorithm

```
/* HEAP SORT */
/* HEAP.C */
# include<stdio.h>
void heap_sort(int *, int );
void create_heap(int *, int);
void display(int *, int);

/*  Definition of the function */

void create_heap(int list[], int n )
{
   int k, j, i, temp;

   for(k = 2 ; k <= n; ++k)
   {
      i = k ;
      temp = list[k];
      j = i / 2 ;

      while((i > 1) && (temp > list[j]))
      {
         list[i] = list[j];
         i = j ;
         j = i / 2 ;
         if ( j < 1 )
            j = 1 ;
      }

      list[i] = temp ;
   }
}

/* End of heap creation function */

/* Definition of the function */
void heap_sort(int list[], int n)
{
   int k, temp, value, j, i, p;
   int step = 1;
   for(k = n ; k >= 2; --k)
   {
      temp = list[1] ;
      list[1] = list[k];
      list[k] = temp ;
      i = 1 ;
```

```
        value = list[1];
        j = 2 ;

        if((j+1) < k)
           if(list[j+1] > list[j])
              j ++;
        while((j <= ( k-1)) && (list[j] > value))
        {
           list[i] = list[j];
           i = j ;
           j = 2*i ;
           if((j+1) < k)
              if(list[j+1] > list[j])
                 j++;
              else
                 if( j > n)
                    j = n ;
           list[i] = value;
        } /* end of while statement */

        printf("\n Step = %d ", step);
        step++;
        for(p = 1; p <= n; p++)
           printf(" %d", list[p]);
     } /* end for loop */
   }

   /* Display function */
   void display(int list[], int n)
   {
      int i;
      for(i = 1 ; i <= n; ++ i)
      {
         printf(" %d", list[i]);
      }
   }

   /* Function main */
   void main()
   {
      int list[100];
      int i, n ;

      printf("\n Size of the list:");
      scanf(" %d", &n);
```

```
    for(i = 1 ; i <= n ; ++i)
    {
       list[i] = rand() % 100;
    }
    printf("\n Entered list is as follows:\n");
    display(list, n);
    create_heap(list, n);
    printf("\n Heap\n");
    display(list, n);
    printf("\n\n");

    heap_sort(list,n);

    printf("\n\n Sorted list is as follows :\n\n");
    display(list,n);
}
```

9.10 RADIX SORT

Radix sort is a technique, which is usually used when a large list of names is to be sorted alphabetically. Using this sorting technique one can classify the list of names into 26 groups. The list is first sorted on the first letter of each name, i.e., the names are arranged in 26 classes where the first class consists of those names that begin with alphabet '**A**', the second class consists of those names that begin with alphabet '**B**' and so on. During the second pass each class is alphabetized according to the second letter of the name and so on. For example, if no name contains more than 20 characters then the sort requires 20 passes. The radix sort is a technique, which is used by a card sorter. A card sorter contains 13 receiving pockets labeled as

9, 8, 7, 6, 5, 4, 3, 2, 1, 0, 11, 12, R

Here **R** represents reject, if any card comes in this pocket.

Each pocket other than **R** corresponds to a row on a card in which a hole can be punched. Decimal numbers where the radix is 10 are punched in the obvious way and hence use only the first 10 pockets on the sorter. The sorter uses a radix reverse digit sort on numbers. For example, suppose a card sorter is given a collection of cards where each card contains four-digit number punched in columns 1-4. The cards are first sorted according to the unit's digit. In the second pass, the cards are sorted according to the tens digit. In the third pass the cards are sorted according to the hundreds digit. In the fourth and last pass, the cards are sorted according to the thousands digit. For example, suppose cards are punched as shown in **Figure 9.36**.

1	2	3	4	5	6	7
4348	2143	4361	5423	4538	2128	5438

Figure 9.36 Punched card data

Input	Pocket 0	Pocket 1	Pocket 2	Pocket 3	Pocket 4	Pocket 5	Pocket 6	Pocket 7	Pocket 8	*Pocket 9*
4348									4348	
2143				2143						
4361		4361								
5423				5423						
4538									4538	
2128									2128	
5438									*5438*	

Figure 9.36(a) Pass 1 sort units digit

(i) Pass 1 → The unit digits are sorted into pockets. The cards are collected pocket by pocket from pocket 9 to pocket 0. The cards are now re-input to the sorter.

(ii) Pass 2 → The tens digits are sorted into pockets. Again cards are collected pocket by pocket and re-input to the sorter.

(iii) Pass 3 → The 100th digits are sorted into pockets. Again cards are collected pocket by pocket and re-input to the sorter.

(iv) Pass 4 → The 1000's digits are sorted into pocket. Again cards are sorted pocket by pocket.

When the cards are collected after 4th pass, the numbers are in the sorted order.

Input	Pocket 0	Pocket 1	Pocket 2	Pocket 3	Pocket 4	Pocket 5	Pocket 6	Pocket 7	Pocket 8	Pocket 9
4348					4348					
4538				4538						
2128			2128							
5438				5438						
2143					2143					
5423			5423							
4361							4361			

Figure 9.36(b) Pass 2 sort on 10th digit

Input	Pocket 0	Pocket 1	Pocket 2	Pocket 3	Pocket 4	Pocket 5	Pocket 6	Pocket 7	Pocket 8	Pocket 9
4361				4361						
4348				4338						
2143		2143								
4538						4538				
5438					5438					
2128		2128								
5423					5423					

Figure 9.36 (c) Pass 3 sort on 100th digit

Input	Pocket 0	Pocket 1	Pocket 2	Pocket 3	Pocket 4	Pocket 5	Pocket 6	Pocket 7	Pocket 8	Pocket 9
4538					4538					
5438						5438				
5423						5423				
4361					4361					
4348					4348					
2143			2143							
2128			2128							

Figure 9.36 (d) Pass 4 sort on 1000's digit

Now collecting the values of pockets from 9th to 0th then we get the list of array as shown in Figure 9.37.

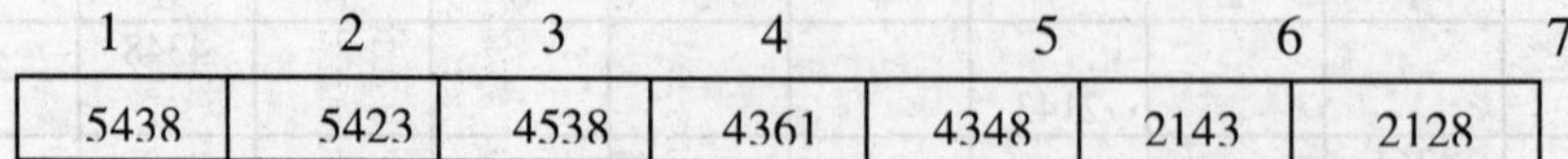

Figure 9.37 Sorted list using radix sort

Input	Pocket 0	Pocket 1	Pocket 2	Pocket 3	Pocket 4	Pocket 5	Pocket 6	Pocket 7	Pocket 8	Pocket 9
4348									4348	
2143				2143						
4361		4361								
5423				5423						
4538									4538	
2128									2128	
5438									5438	

Figure 9.37(a) Pass 1 sort units digit

Input	Pocket 0	Pocket 1	Pocket 2	Pocket 3	Pocket 4	Pocket 5	Pocket 6	Pocket 7	Pocket 8	Pocket 9
4361							4361			
2143					2143					
5423			5423							
4348					4348					
4538				4538						
2128			2128							
5438				5438						

Figure 9.37(b) Pass 2 sort on 10th digit

Input	Pocket 0	Pocket 1	Pocket 2	Pocket 3	Pocket 4	Pocket 5	Pocket 6	Pocket 7	Pocket 8	Pocket 9
5423					5423					
2128		2128								
4538						4538				
5438					5438					
2143		2143								
4348				4348						
4361				4361						

Figure 9.37 (c) Pass 3 sort on 100th digit

Input	Pocket 0	Pocket 1	Pocket 2	Pocket 3	Pocket 4	Pocket 5	Pocket 6	Pocket 7	Pocket 8	Pocket 9
2128			2128							
2143			2143							
4348					4348					
4361					4361					
5423						5423				
5438						5438				
4538					4538					

Figure 9.37 (d) Pass 4 sort on 1000's digit

From the result shown in **Figure 9.37,** it is clear that the list is sorted in descending order. If during the sorting operation one collects the pocket from 0th to 9th the result will come in ascending order. For example, **Figure 9.37 (a-d)** illustrates the preceding statement. Now collecting the values of pockets from 0th to 9th , we get the list of array as shown in **Figure 9.38.**

1	2	3	4	5	6	7
2128	2143	4348	4361	4538	5423	5438

Figure 9.38 Sorted list using radix sort

The result shown in **Figure 9.38** denotes that the list is sorted in ascending order. The pen paper method, which is shown in **Figure 9.37(a-d)** can be implemented on a computer. The sequential allocation of techniques is not practical in representing the pockets, since we do not know how many elements or records will occupy a particular pocket during a certain pass. The linked list allocation is used to resolve this uncertainty. Each pocket can be represented as a linked list **FIFO** queue. At the end of each pass, these queues can be easily combined in the proper order. If the maximum number of digits in an element is **m**, then **m** successive passes from the unit digit to the most significant digits are required in order to sort the number.

In general we can define an algorithm for radix sort as follows:

Step 1: Repeat thru Step 6 for each digit in the key.

Step 2: Initialize the pockets.

Step 3: Repeat thru Step 5 until end of the linked list.

Step 4: Obtain the next digit of the key.

Step 5: Insert the element in appropriate pocket.

Step 6: Combine the pockets to form a new linked list.

Suppose **rec** represents a list of **n** elements, i.e., $\textbf{rec}_1$, $\textbf{rec}_2 \ldots \textbf{rec}_n$ and **d** denote the radix (For decimal number system, which is 10, for alphabets it is 26, for binary it is 2, for octal number system it is 8, etc.) and each element $\textbf{rec}_i$ is represented by means of **m** digits. The detailed analysis of the radixsort algorithm is given in the next section; see analysis in brief before going to next section.

$rec_i = d_{i1}\, d_{i2}\, d_{i3} \ldots d_{im}.$

The radix sort algorithm requires **m** pass - the number of digits in each element. Pass **j** will compare each $\mathbf{d}_{ij}$ with each of the **d** digits. Hence, total number of comparisons (and in turn efficiency) is:

E (n) = d*m*n [Maximum value possible that is possible]

Where **d** and **m** are independent of **n.**

(i) Worst case : If n = m the $E(n) = d*n*n = d*n^2 = O(n^2)$

(ii) Best case : $m = \log_d n$

$$E(n) = d*(\log_d n)*n$$
$$= O(n \log_d n)$$

Analysis of Radix Sort

Assume that the keys of the items that we wish to sort lie in a small fixed range and there is only one item with each value of the key. Then we can sort with the following algorithm:

1. Set up an array of bins (pockets) - one for each value of the key - in order,
2. Examine each item and use the value of the key to place it in the appropriate bin.
3. Examine each bin to see whether there is an item in it.

Now collection is sorted and it only took **n** operations, so this is an **O(n)** operation. However, note that it will only work under very restricted conditions. To understand these restrictions, let us be a little more precise about the specification of the problem and assume that there are **m** values of the key. To recover the sorted collection, we need to examine each bin. This adds a third step to the algorithm above, which requires **m** operations. So, the algorithm's time becomes: $T(n) = c_1 n + c_2 m$, and it is strictly **O(n + m)**. Now if $m \leq n$, this is clearly **O(n)**. However if $m \geq n$, then it is **O(m)**. For example, if we wish to sort 10^4 32-bit integers, then $m = 2^{32}$ and we need 2^{32} operations (and a rather large memory).

For $n = 10^4$:

nlogn $\sim 10^4 \times 13 \sim 2^{13} \times 2^4 \sim 2^{17}$

So quicksort or heapsort would clearly be preferred. If there are duplicates, then each bin can be replaced by a linked list. The third step of the above algorithm then becomes:

3. Link all the lists into one list.

We can add an item to a linked list in **O(1)** time. There are **n** items requiring **O(n)** time. Linking a list to another list simply involves making the tail of one list point to the other, so it is **O(1)**. Linking **m** such lists obviously takes **O(m)** time, so the algorithm is still **O(n+m)**. In contrast to the other sorts, which sort in place and don't require additional memory, bin sort requires additional memory for the bins and is a good example of trading space for performance. Having highlighted this constraint, there is a version of bin sort, which can sort in place.

```
#define EMPTY   -1 /* Some convenient flag */
void bin_sort( int *a, int n )
{
        int i;
        /* Pre-condition: for 0<=i<n : 0 <= a[i] < n */
        for(i=0;i<n;i++)
        if ( a[i] != i )
        SWAP( a[i], a[a[i]] );
}
```

Note: Although memory tends to be cheap in modern processors - so that we would normally use memory rather profligately to obtain performance, memory consumes power and in some circumstances, e.g., computers in spacecraft, power might be a higher constraint than performance.

However, this assumes that there are **n** distinct keys in the range 0... **n**-1. In addition to this restriction, the SWAP operation is relatively expensive, so that this version trades space for time. The bin sorting strategy may appear rather limited, but it can be generalized into a strategy known as radix sorting. For example, assume that we have **n** integers in the range $(0, n^2)$ to be sorted. For a bin sort, $m = n^2$, and we would have an $O(n+m) = O(n^2)$ algorithm. Sort them in two phases:

1. Using **n** bins, place a_i into bin a_i mod **n**,
2. Repeat the process using **n** bins, placing a_i into bin floor(a_i/n), being careful to append to the end of each bin.

This results in a sorted list. As an example, consider the list of integers illustrated in **Figure 9.37** after final iteration list is given in **Figure 9.38.** We can apply this process to numbers of any size expressed to any suitable base or radix. We can further observe that it is not necessary to use the same radix in each phase, suppose that the sorting key is a sequence of fields, each with bounded range, e.g., the key is a date using the structure:

```
typedef struct t_date
{
 int day;
 int month;
 int year;
} date;
```

If the ranges for day and month are limited in the obvious way, and the range for year is suitably constrained, e.g. $1900 < \text{year} \le 2000$, then we can apply the same procedure except that we will employ a different number of bins in each phase. In all cases, we will sort first using the least significant "digit" (where "digit" means a field with a limited range), then using the next significant "digit", placing each item after all the items already in the bin, and so on. Assume that the key of the item to be sorted has **k** fields, $\mathbf{f_i} \mid \mathbf{i = 0...}k - 1$, and that each $\mathbf{f_i}$ has $\mathbf{s_i}$ discrete values, then a generalized radix sort procedure can be written:

radixsort(A, n) {
  for(i=0;i<k;i++) {
    for(j=0;j<si;j++) bin[j] = EMPTY;
	$O(s_i)$

for(j=0;j<n;j++) {
      move A_i
      to the end of bin[A_i->f_i]
      }
	$O(n)$

for(j=0;j<s_i;j++)
      concatenate bin[j] onto the end of A;
    }
}
	$O(s_i)$

Total	$\sum_{i=1}^{k} O(s_i + n) = O\left(kn + \sum_{i=1}^{k} s_i \right) = O\left(n + \sum_{i=1}^{=k} s_i \right)$

If the keys are integers in (0, $\mathbf{b}^{\mathbf{k}}$-1), for some constant **k**, then the keys can be viewed as **k**-digit base-**b** integers. Thus, $\mathbf{s_i} = \mathbf{b}$ for all **i** and the time complexity becomes **O(n+kb)** or **O(n)**. This result depends on **k** being constant. If **k** is allowed to increase with **n**, then we have a different picture. For example, it takes $\log_2 \mathbf{n}$ binary digits to represent an integer <**n**. If the key length were allowed to increase with **n**, so that **k** = log **n**, then we would have:

$$\sum_{i=1}^{k} O(s_i + n) = O\left(n \log n + \sum_{i=1}^{\log n} 2 \right) = O(n \log n + 2 \log n) = O(n \log n)$$

Another way of looking at this, if the range of the key is restricted to (0, $\mathbf{b}^{\mathbf{k}}$-1), then we will be able to use the radixsort approach effectively and if we allow duplicate keys when $\mathbf{n} > \mathbf{b}^{\mathbf{k}}$. However, if we need to have unique keys, then **k** must increase to at least $\log_b \mathbf{n}$. Thus, as **n** increases, we need to have log **n** phases, each taking **O(n)** time, and the radix sort is the same as quick sort. The implementation of radix is as follows:

```
/* Header file used by radix sort with the help of binsort. */
/* Bins.h: Possible bin array for RadixSort */
#define TYPE int
```

```
typedef struct t_bins *Bins;
Bins ConsBins( int n_bins, int items_per_bin );
/* Construct an array of n_bins bins, each with items_per_bin spaces */

int AddItem( Bins b, TYPE item, int bin_index );
/* Add item to bin bin_index, Pre: b != NULL && item != NULL && bin_index
>= 0 && bin_index < n_bins */

TYPE *MergeBins( Bins b, TYPE *list );
/* Merge the bins by copying all the elements in bins into list, return a
pointer to list */

void DeleteBins( Bins b ); /* Destructor frees all space used by b */

/* This is bin sort algorithm implementation, which will be used by the
radix sort */
/* Bins.c: Possible bin array for RadixSort */
#include <stdlib.h>
#include <stdio.h>
#include <assert.h>
#include "Bins.h"

struct t_bins
{
 int n_bins, max_items;
 int *bin_cnt;
 TYPE **bin_pts;
 };

/* Construct an array of n_bins bins, each with items_per_bin spaces */
Bins ConsBins( int n_bins, int items_per_bin )
{
Bins b;
    int i;
#ifdef ONE_LARGE
    int max;
    TYPE *bins;
#endif
/* fprintf(stdout, "ConsBins %d/%d ", n_bins, items_per_bin ); fflush(
stdout ); */
    b = (Bins)malloc( sizeof( struct t_bins ) );
    if ( b != NULL )
{
        b->n_bins = n_bins;
b->max_items = items_per_bin;
```

```
b->bin_pts = (TYPE **)malloc( n_bins*sizeof(TYPE *) );
b->bin_cnt = (int *)calloc( n_bins, sizeof(int) );
if ( b->bin_pts != NULL )
{
#ifdef ONE_LARGE
 /* Allocate a single large bin */
 max = n_bins*items_per_bin*sizeof(TYPE);
 bins = malloc( max );
         if( bins == NULL )
{
 printf("ConsBins: insuff mem %d bytes needed\n", max );
 return NULL;
}
/* Divide it into n_bins, each holding items_per_bin items */
for(i=0;i<n_bins;i++)
{
 b->bin_pts[i] = bins;
 bins += (items_per_bin);
}
#else
/* Allocate n_bins individual bins */
for(i=0;i<n_bins;i++)
{
b->bin_pts[i] = (TYPE *)malloc( items_per_bin*sizeof(TYPE) );
 if( b->bin_pts[i] == NULL ) {
 printf("ConsBins: insuff mem after %d bins\n", i );
 b = NULL; break;
 }
         }
#endif
       }
    }
 else
{
fprintf( stdout, "Insuff mem\n");
   }
   return b;
}

int AddItem( Bins b, TYPE item, int bin_index )
{
/* Add item to bin bin_index
 Pre: b != NULL && item != NULL &&
 bin_index >= 0 && bin_index < n_bins
*/
```

```
int k;
assert( b != NULL );
assert( bin_index >= 0 );
assert( bin_index < b->n_bins );
k = b->bin_cnt[bin_index];
assert( (k>=0) && (k<b->max_items) );
assert( (b->bin_pts[bin_index]) != NULL );
(b->bin_pts[bin_index])[k] = item;
b->bin_cnt[bin_index]++;
return 1;
}

TYPE *MergeBins( Bins b, TYPE *list )
{
/* Merge the bins by copying all the elements in bins 1..n_bins-1
   into list
return a pointer to list
(This pointer can be used in the next phase!) */
int j, k;
TYPE *lp;
assert( b != NULL );
assert( list != NULL );

lp = list;
for( j = 0; j<b->n_bins; j++ )
{
   for(k=0;k<b->bin_cnt[j];k++)
{
*lp++ = (b->bin_pts[j])[k];
}
   }
   return list;
}

void FreeUnusedBins( Bins b )
{
/* Free bins 1 .. n_bins-1 in preparation for next phase */
   int k;
assert( b != NULL );
#ifdef ONE_LARGE
free( b->bin_pts[0] );
#else
for(k=0;k<b->n_bins;k++)
{
assert( b->bin_pts[k] != NULL );
```

```
 free( b->bin_pts[k] );
   }
#endif
free( b->bin_pts );
 }

void DeleteBins( Bins b )
{
/* Destructor .. frees all space used by b */
 assert( b != NULL );
 FreeUnusedBins( b );
 free( b->bin_cnt );
 free( b );
 }

/* Radix sort header file */
/* RadixSort.h - a single method which sorts arrays of items with keys that
can be split into groups of bits - useful for unsigned integers or characters
*/

#ifndef TRUE
#define TRUE 1
#define FALSE  0
#endif
#ifndef RADIX_SORT_H
#define RADIX_SORT_H

int SetRadices( int n_bits, int n_radices );
/* Set the radices to sort numbers with n_bits using n_radices phases */

int *RSort( int *ip, int n ); * Sort n numbers in array ip, using RadixSort */
#endif

/* Radix main code */
/* RadSort.c - a single method which sorts arrays of items with keys that
can be split into groups of bits - useful for unsigned integers or characters
*/

#include <stdlib.h>
#include <stdio.h>
#include <assert.h>
#include <time.h>
#include <math.h>
#include "Bins.c"
#include "RadSort.h"
```

```
/* These parameters control the whole operation, they are set up once by a
call to SetRadices They do not need to be reset unless the radices change */
    static int *n_bins;
    static unsigned int mask;
    static int *shifts;
    static int n_phases;

    int SetRadices( int n_bits, int n_radices )
    {
        int i, tot_bits, bits_per_phase;

        /* Calculate how many bits in each phase */
        bits_per_phase = n_bits/n_radices;
        if( (n_radices*bits_per_phase) < n_bits )
    {
            bits_per_phase++;
        }
        /* Set up the mask */
        mask = (1<<bits_per_phase) - 1;

        /* Now set up the count of the number of bins and the shifts appropriate
for each
     phase */
        n_bins = malloc( n_radices*sizeof(int) );
        shifts = malloc( n_radices*sizeof(int) );
        tot_bits = 0;
        for(i=0;i<n_radices;i++)
    {
            shifts[i] = tot_bits;
            tot_bits += bits_per_phase;
            /* Last phase may not need so many bins */
            if ( tot_bits > n_bits )
    {
                bits_per_phase = n_bits - tot_bits + bits_per_phase;
            }
            n_bins[i] = 1<<bits_per_phase;
        }
        n_phases = n_radices;
        printf("Bits %d, radices %d, mask %x\n", n_bits, n_phases, mask );
        for(i=0;i<n_phases;i++)
    {
            printf("%d: sh %d bins %d, ", i, shifts[i], n_bins[i] );
        }
        printf("\n");
        return TRUE;
```

```
}

/* Function to return bin number to use for phase */
/* int bin_number( int x, int phase )
{
  return (x>>shifts[phase])&mask;
} */
/* Implemented as a macro for speed! */
#define bin_number(x,phase) ((x>>shifts[phase])&mask)
int *RSort( int *ip, int n )
{
  Bins b1, b2;
  int i, bn, phase;
  b2 = NULL;
  for(phase=0;phase<n_phases;phase++)
  {
    b1 = ConsBins( n_bins[phase], n );
    for(i=0;i<n;i++)
  {
        bn = bin_number( ip[i], phase );
        AddItem( b1, ip[i], bn );
    }
    ip = MergeBins( b1, ip );
    DeleteBins( b1 );
  }
  return ip;
}

int VerifySort( int *ip, int n )
{
  int k;
  for(k=0;k<(n-1);k++)
  {
    if ( ip[k+1]<ip[k] )
  {
        printf("Order error %d: %d s/b < %d\n",
            k, ip[k], ip[k+1] );
        return FALSE;
    }
  }
  return TRUE;
}
```

In the above program segment it is shown how radixsort algorithm sorts arrays of integers on various radices: the number of bits used for each radix can be set with the call to SetRadices. The Bins struct is used in each phase to collect the items as they are sorted. ConsBins is called to set up a set of bins: each bin must be large enough to accommodate the whole array, so RadixSort can be very expensive in its memory usage. Linked list implementation is left to the radix as an exercise.

9.11 RADIX EXCHANGE SORT

A considerably better distributive sort is the radix exchange sort, which is applicable when the keys are expressed in binary. Sorting is accomplished by considering groups with the same (M) first bits and ordering that group with respect to the (M+1st) bit. The ordering of a group on a given bit is accomplished by scanning down from the top of the group for a one bit and up from bottom for a zero bit, these two are exchanged and the sort continues. This algorithm requires the program to keep up with a large number of groups and coded in bad form, could require an additional table **n** long. However, with optimal coding it is possible to keep track of the groups by simply monitoring the top of the table and a list of break points, one for each bit of the keyword. Thus, with 5-bit words a table of only 32 entries is required. For example, consider radix exchange sort shown in **Figure 9.39**.

If the sort algorithm is programmed to quick sorting when a group contains only one item then the time required for the radix exchange sort is proportional to **nlog n** as compared to **n log$_p$k** (where **k** is the maximum key size and **p** is the radix) for the radix sort. Note that the radix exchange sort does not require extra table space for buckets.

Highlighted data show the interchange made there, Order of collection is C1, C2, C3, C4, C5, C6, C7, C8, C9, C10, C11 and C12, i.e., 01, 02, 05, 09, 11, 13, 16, 19, 21, 26, 27, 31.

Decimal	Pass 1	Pass 2	Pass 3	Pass 4	Pass 5	
19	10011	01011	00010	00010	00001	C1
13	01101	01101	00001	00001	00010	C2
05	00101	00101	00101	00101	C3	
27	11011	01001	01001	01001	01001	C4
01	00001	00001	01101	01011	01011	C5
26	11010	00010	01011	01101	C6	
31	11111	11111	10101	10011	10000	C7
16	10000	10000	10000	10000	10011	C8
02	00010	11010	10011	10101	C9	
09	01001	11011	11011	11011	11011	11010 C10
11	01011	10011	11010	11010	11010	11011 C11
21	10101	10101	11111	11111	C12	

Figure 9.39 Radix exchange sort

9.12 SKIP LISTS

Dictionaries are data structures that support *search*, *insert*, and *delete* operations. One of the most effective representations is a *hash table*. Typically, a simple function is applied to the key to determine its place in the dictionary. There are *binary trees* and *red-black trees* both these *tree* methods use a technique similar to the binary search algorithm to minimize the number of comparisons during search and update operations on the dictionary. The *skip list* illustrates a simple approach that utilizes random numbers to construct a dictionary. Skip lists are linked lists that allow one to skip to the correct node. The performance bottleneck inherent in a sequential scan is avoided, while insertion and deletion remain relatively efficient. Average search time is O(log n). Worst-case search time is O(n), but is extremely unlikely. The indexing scheme employed in a skip list is similar in nature to the method used to lookup names in an address book. To lookup a name, we index to the tab representing the first character of the desired entry. In **Figure 9.40,** for example, the top-most list represents a simple linked list with no tabs. Adding tabs (middle figure) facilitates the search. In this case, level-1 pointers are traversed. Once the correct segment of the list is found, level-0 pointers are traversed to find the specific entry.

The indexing scheme may be extended as shown in the bottom figure, where we now have an index to the index. To locate an item, level-2 pointers are traversed until the correct segment of the list is identified. Subsequently, level-1 and level-0 pointers are traversed.

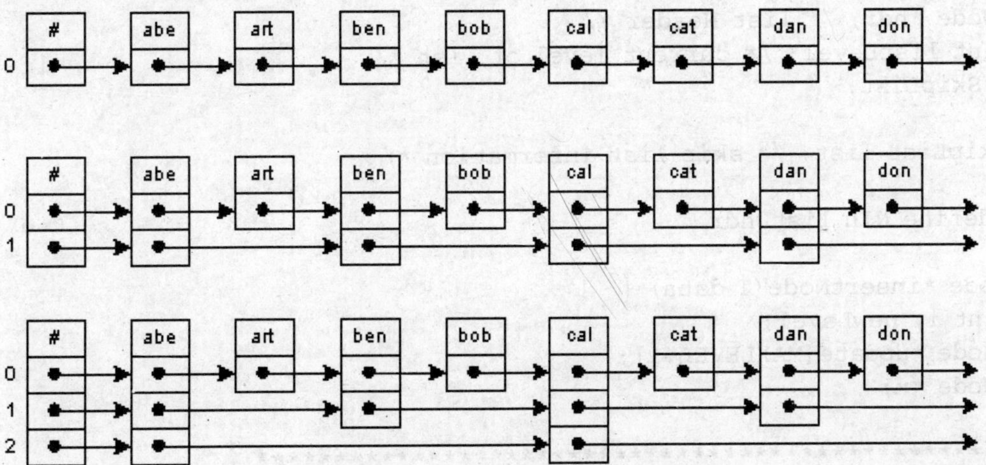

Figure 9.40 Skip List Construction

During insertion the number of pointers required for a new node must be determined. This is easily resolved using a probabilistic technique. A random number generator is used to toss a computer coin. When inserting a new node, the coin is tossed to determine if it should be level-1. If one wins, the coin is tossed again to determine if the node should be level-2. Another wins, and the coin is tossed to determine if the node should be level-3. This process repeats until one loses. If only one level (level-0) is implemented, the data structure is a simple linked-list with **O**(n) search time. However, if sufficient levels are implemented, the skip list may be viewed as a tree with the root at the highest level, and search time is **O**(log n).

The skip list algorithm has a probabilistic component, and thus probabilistic bounds on the time required to execute. However, these bounds are quite tight in normal circumstances. For example, to search a list containing 1000 items, the probability that search time will be 5 times the average is about 1 in 1,000,000,000,000,000,000. The above discussion is illustrated in **SkipList.C**

```
/* SkipList.c */
#include <stdio.h>
#include <stdlib.h>

/* define data-type and compare operators here */
typedef int T; /* type of item to be stored */
#define compLT(a,b) (a < b)
```

```
#define compEQ(a,b) (a == b)

/* levels range from (0 .. MAXLEVEL) */
#define MAXLEVEL 15

typedef struct Node_ {
 T data; /* user's data */
  struct Node_ *forward[1]; /* skip list forward pointer */
} Node;

typedef struct {
 Node *hdr; /* list Header */
 int listLevel; /* current level of list */
} SkipList;

SkipList list; /* skip list information */

#define NIL list.hdr

Node *insertNode(T data) {
 int i, newLevel;
 Node *update[MAXLEVEL+1];
 Node *x;

 /********************************************
 * allocate node for data and insert in list *
 ********************************************/

 /* find where data belongs */
 x = list.hdr;
 for (i = list.listLevel; i >= 0; i--) {
   while (x->forward[i] != NIL && compLT(x->forward[i]->data, data))
   x = x->forward[i];
    update[i] = x;
 }
 x = x->forward[0];
 if (x != NIL && compEQ(x->data, data)) return(x);

 /* determine level */
 for (newLevel = 0; rand() < RAND_MAX/2 && newLevel < MAXLEVEL; newLevel++);

 if (newLevel > list.listLevel) {
   for (i = list.listLevel + 1; i <= newLevel; i++)
    update[i] = NIL;
```

```
    list.listLevel = newLevel;
  }

  /* make new node */
  if ((x = (Node *) malloc(sizeof(Node) + newLevel*sizeof(Node *))) == 0)
{
    printf ("insufficient memory (insertNode)\n");
    exit(1);
  }
  x->data = data;

  /* update forward links */
  for (i = 0; i <= newLevel; i++) {
    x->forward[i] = update[i]->forward[i];
    update[i]->forward[i] = x;
  }
  return(x);
  }

void deleteNode(T data) {
  int i;
  Node *update[MAXLEVEL+1], *x;

  /*****************************************
  * delete node containing data from list *
  *****************************************/

  /* find where data belongs */
  x = list.hdr;
  for (i = list.listLevel; i >= 0; i--) {
    while (x->forward[i] != NIL
     && compLT(x->forward[i]->data, data))
     x = x->forward[i];
    update[i] = x;
  }
  x = x->forward[0];
  if (x == NIL || !compEQ(x->data, data)) return;

  /* adjust forward pointers */
  for (i = 0; i <= list.listLevel; i++) {
    if (update[i]->forward[i] != x) break;
    update[i]->forward[i] = x->forward[i];
  }

  free (x);
```

```
    /* adjust header level */
    while ((list.listLevel > 0) && (list.hdr->forward[list.listLevel] ==
NIL))
      list.listLevel--;
    }

   Node *findNode(T data) {
    int i;
    Node *x = list.hdr;

    /*******************************
    * find node containing data *
    *******************************/

    for (i = list.listLevel; i >= 0; i--) {
      while (x->forward[i] != NIL && compLT(x->forward[i]->data, data))
       x = x->forward[i];
    }
    x = x->forward[0];
    if (x != NIL && compEQ(x->data, data)) return (x);
    return(0);
   }

   void initList() {
    int i;

    /**************************
    * initialize skip list *
    **************************/

    if ((list.hdr = (Node *) malloc(sizeof(Node) + MAXLEVEL*sizeof(Node *)))
== 0) {
      printf ("insufficient memory (initList)\n");
      exit(1);
    }
    for (i = 0; i <= MAXLEVEL; i++)
      list.hdr->forward[i] = NIL;
    list.listLevel = 0;
   }
   /* Function main */
   int main()
   {
    int i, *a, maxnum, random;
    printf(" Input Data ");
    scanf("%d", &maxnum);
```

```
    printf("Input type of operation 2 or 1 for sequential more than 2 for
random: ");
    scanf("%d",&random);
    random = random > 2; /* This statement decides whether we interested in
sequential or random */
    initList();

    if ((a = malloc(maxnum * sizeof(*a))) == 0) {
    fprintf (stderr, "insufficient memory (a)\n");
    exit(1);
    }

    if (random) {
    /* fill "a" with unique random numbers */
    for (i = 0; i < maxnum; i++) a[i] = rand();
    printf ("ran, %d items\n", maxnum);
    } else {
    for (i = 0; i < maxnum; i++) a[i] = i;
    printf ("seq, %d items\n", maxnum);
    }

    for (i = 0; i < maxnum; i++) {
    insertNode(a[i]);
    }

    for (i = maxnum-1; i >= 0; i--) {
    findNode(a[i]);
    }

    for (i = maxnum-1; i >= 0; i--) {
    deleteNode(a[i]);
    }
    return 0;
    }
```

In the above program segment **typedef T** and comparison operators **compLT** and **compEQ** should be altered to reflect the data stored in the list. In addition, **MAXLEVEL** should be set based on the maximum size of the dataset.

To initialize, **initList** is called. The list header is allocated and initialized. To indicate an empty list, all levels are set to point to the header. Function **insertNode** allocates a new node, searches for the correct insertion point, and inserts it in the list. While searching, the **update** array maintains pointers to the upper-level nodes encountered. This information is subsequently used to establish correct links for the newly inserted node. The **newLevel** is determined using a random number generator, and the node allocated. The forward links are then established using information from the **update** array. Function **deleteNode** deletes and frees a node, and is implemented in a similar manner. Function **findNode** searches the list for a particular value.

9.13 HASHING

So far, we have succeeded in paring down **O (n)** search to **O (n $\log_2$ n)** by keeping the list sorted sequentially with respect to the key value, i.e., the key in the first element is less than or equal to the key in the second element, which is less than the key in the third and so on. Can we do better than that? Is it possible to design a search of O (1), i.e., one that has a constant search time, no matter where the element is in the list? While worst-case time is **O**(n).

Hash Function: Assuming n data items, the hash table size should be large enough to accommodate a reasonable number of entries. As seen in **Table 9.1**, a small table size substantially increases the average time to find a key. A hash table may be viewed as a collection of linked lists {**Figure 9.41**}. As the table becomes larger, the number of lists increases, and the average number of nodes on each list decreases. If the table size is 1, then the table is really a single linked list of length n. Assuming a perfect hash function, a table size of 2 has two lists of length n/2. If the table size is 100, then we have 100 lists of length n/100. This considerably reduces the length of the list to be searched. There is considerable leeway in the choice of table size.

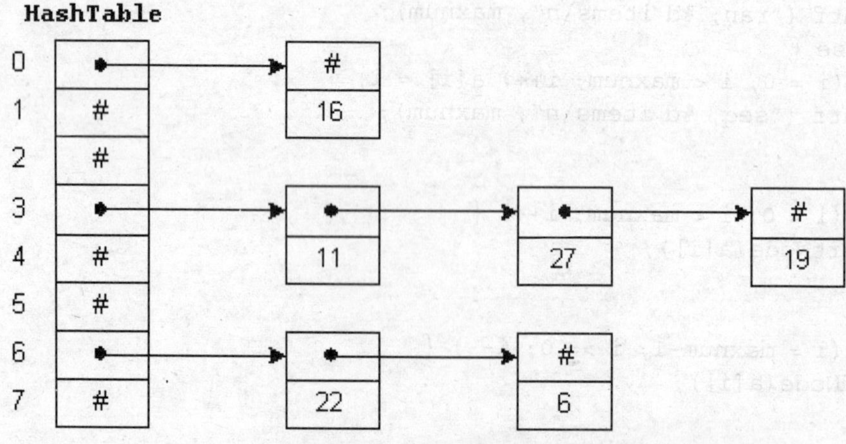

Figure 9.41 A Hash Table

Consider another example, list of students of Panjab University. Each of the 100 students has an ID number in the range 0 to 99 and we want to access the student records by the key **STD_ID**. If we store the elements in an array that is indexed from 0 to 99, we can directly access any student's record through the array index. There is a one-to-one correspondence between the element keys and the array index, in effect the array index functions as the key of each element.

In practice, however, this perfect relationship between the key value and the location of an element is not easy to establish or maintain. Consider similar case, Panjab University that uses its students five-digit ID number as the primary key. Now the range of key values is from 00000 to 99999. Obviously it is impractical to set up an array of 100000 elements of which only 100 are needed, just to make sure that each student's element is in a perfectly unique and predictable location. What if we keep the array size down to the size that we actually need (array of 100 elements) and just use the last two digits of the key to identify each student? For instance, the element of student 53374 is in **Student_Record[74]** and the element if the student 81235 is in **Student_Record[35]**. Note that the elements are not sorted according to the value of the key as they were in our earlier discussion, the position of the student 81235's record precedes that of student 53374 in the array, even though the value of its key is larger. Instead, the elements are sorted with respect to some function of the key value. This function is called a **hash function** and the search technique we are using is called hashing. In the case of the student list above, the hash function is (key%100). 100 divides **STD_ID** the key and the remainder is used as an index into the array of students. The discussion is illustrated in **Figure 9.42**. This function assumes that the array is indexed from 0 to 99 (MAX_INFO = 100). The function to perform the conversion of key values to indexes is very simple. The hash function is defined as

```
int Hash(int Key)
{
    return (Key%100);
}
```

Table 9.1 Hashing

size	time	size	time
1	869	128	9
2	432	256	6
4	214	512	4
8	106	1024	4
16	54	2048	3
32	28	4096	3
64	15	8192	3

This function returns integer value between 0 and **MAX_INFO – 1**. Thus, we can say that a **hash** function used to manipulate the key of an element is a list to identify its location in the list. And **hashing** technique used for searching and accessing elements in a list in a relatively constant amount of time by manipulating the key to identify its location in the list. This hash function has two uses. As we have seen, it is used as a method of accessing the list element. The result of the hash function tells one where to look for a particular element-information we need to access, modify or delete the element. For example, consider the following function that demonstrates the accessing of information from a list.

```
struct Student * Access_Record(int Key, struct Student Student_Record[])
{
    int location;
    location = Hash(Key);
    return(Student_Record[location]);
}
```

There is second use of the hash function. It determines where in the array to store the element. If the student list elements were inserted into the list using an insert operation- into sequential array rooms or into rooms with their relative order determined by the key value- we could not use the hash function to retrieve them. We have to create a version of insert operation that puts each new record into the correct room according to the hash function. Here is a simple version of **Insert_Record()**, which assumes that the array room at the index returned from the hash function is not in use.

```
struct Student * Insert_Record(int Key, struct Student Student_Record[], struct Student Info)
{
    int location;
    location = Hash(Key);
    Student_Record[location] = Info;
    Length ++;
}
```

Figure 9.43 illustrates an array, whose elements-records for the students with key values (unique ID numbers) 12704, 31300, 49001, 52202 and 65606-were added using **Insert_Record()** function. Note that this function does not fill the array positions sequentially. Because we have not yet inserted any elements whose keys produce the hash values 3 and 5, the array rooms 3 and 5 are logically "empty". In **Figure 9.43 (b)**, the same student records have been inserted into sorted list using linear insertion operation.

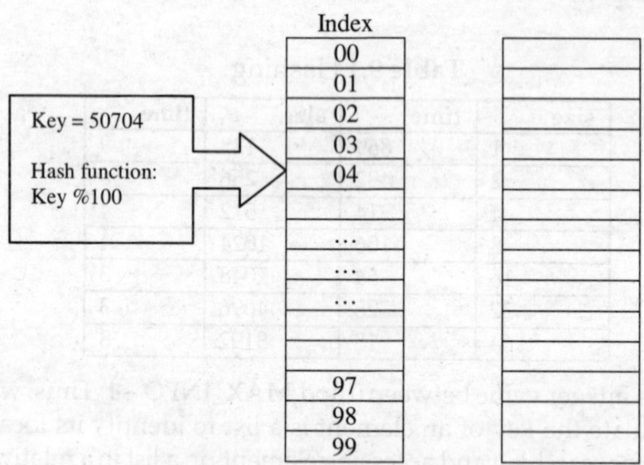

Figure 9.42 Using a hash function to determine the location of the element in an array.

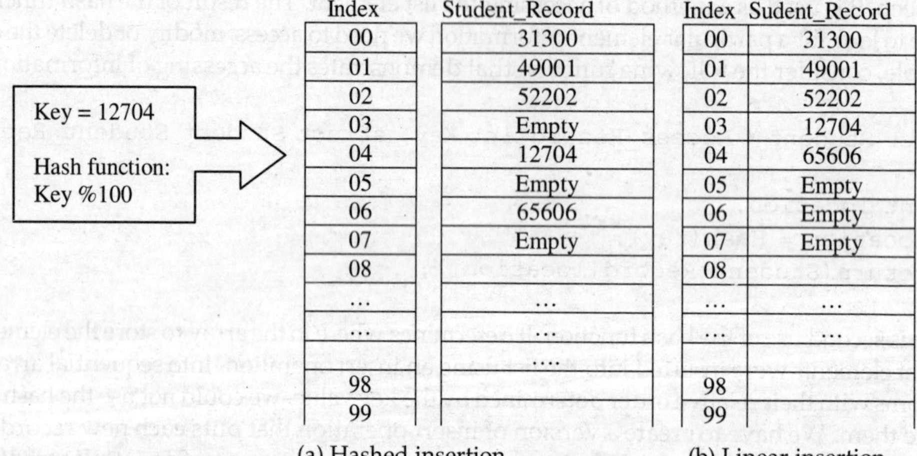

Figure 9.43 Comparing hashed and sequential lists of identical elements

Classification of Hash Function: A hash table is simply an array that is addressed via a hash function. For example, in **Figure 9.41**, **HashTable** is an array with 8 elements. Each element is a pointer to a linked list of numeric data. The hash function for this example simply divides the data key by 8, and uses the remainder as an index into the table. This yields a number from 0 to 7. Since the range of indices for **HashTable** is 0 to 7, we are guaranteed that the index is valid.

To insert a new item in the table, we hash the key to determine which list the item goes on, and then insert the item at the beginning of the list. For example, to insert 11, we divide 11 by 8 giving a remainder of 3. Thus, 11 goes on the list starting at **HashTable[3]**. To find a number, we hash the number and chain down the correct list to see if it is in the table. To delete a number, we find the number and remove the node from the linked list.

Entries in the hash table are dynamically allocated and entered on a linked list associated with each hash table entry. This technique is known as chaining. An alternative method, where all entries are stored in the hash table itself, is known as direct or open addressing and may be found in the references. If the hash function is uniform, or equally distributes the data keys among the hash table indices, then hashing effectively subdivides the list to be searched. Worst-case behavior occurs when all keys hash to the same index. Then we simply have a single linked list that must be sequentially searched. Consequently, it is important to choose a good hash function. Several methods may be used to hash key values. To illustrate the techniques, we will assume unsigned char is 8-bits, unsigned short int is 16-bits and unsigned long int is 32-bits.

- **Division method (tablesize = prime).** This technique was used in the proceeding example. A **HashValue**, from 0 to (**HashTableSize - 1**), is computed by dividing the key value by the size of the hash table and taking the remainder. For example:

```
typedef int HashIndexType;
HashIndexType Hash(int Key)
{
 return Key % HashTableSize;
}
```

  Selecting an appropriate **HashTableSize** is important to the success of this method. For example, a **HashTableSize** of two would yield even hash values for even **Keys**, and odd hash values for odd **Keys**. This is an undesirable property, as all keys would hash to the same value if they happened to be even. If **HashTableSize** is a power of two, then the hash function simply selects a subset of the **Key** bits as the table index. To obtain a more random scattering, **HashTableSize** should be a prime number not too close to a power of two.

- **Multiplication method (tablesize = 2^n).** The multiplication method may be used for a **HashTableSize** that is a power of 2. The **Key** is multiplied by a constant, and then the necessary bits are extracted to index into the table. Knuth recommends using the fractional part of the product of the key and the golden ratio, or (sqrt(5) - 1)/2. For example, assuming a word size of 8 bits, the golden ratio is multiplied by 2^8 to obtain 158. The product of the 8-bit key and 158 results in a 16-bit integer. For a table size of 2^5 the 5 most significant bits of the least significant word are extracted for the hash value. The following definitions may be used for the multiplication method:

```
/* 8-bit index */
typedef unsigned char HashIndexType;
static const HashIndexType K = 158;

/* 16-bit index */
typedef unsigned short int HashIndexType;
static const HashIndexType K = 40503;

/* 32-bit index */
typedef unsigned long int HashIndexType;
```

```
static const HashIndexType K = 2654435769;

/* w=bitwidth(HashIndexType), size of table=2^m */
static const int S = w - m;
HashIndexType HashValue = (HashIndexType)(K * Key) >> S;
```

For example, if **HashTableSize** is 1024 (2^{10}), then a 16-bit index is sufficient and **S** would be assigned a value of 16 - 10 = 6. Thus, we have:

```
typedef unsigned short int HashIndexType;
HashIndexType Hash(int Key) {
 static const HashIndexType K = 40503;
 static const int S = 6;
 return (HashIndexType)(K * Key) >> S;
}
```

- **Variable string addition method (tablesize = 256).** To hash a variable-length string, each character is added, modulo 256, to a total. A **HashValue**, range 0-255, is computed.

```
typedef unsigned char HashIndexType;
HashIndexType Hash(char *str) {
 HashIndexType h = 0;
 while (*str) h += *str++;
 return h;
}
```

- **Variable string exclusive-or method (tablesize = 256).** This method is similar to the addition method, but successfully distinguishes similar words and anagrams. To obtain a hash value in the range 0-255, all bytes in the string are exclusive-or'd together. However, in the process of doing each exclusive-or, a random component is introduced.

```
typedef unsigned char HashIndexType;
unsigned char Rand8[256];
HashIndexType Hash(char *str) {
 unsigned char h = 0;
 while (*str) h = Rand8[h ^ *str++];
 return h;
}
```

Rand8 is a table of 256 8-bit unique random numbers. The exact ordering is not critical. The exclusive-or method has its basis in cryptography, and is quite effective.

- **Variable string exclusive-or method (tablesize ≤ 65536).** If we hash the string twice, we may derive a hash value for an arbitrary table size up to 65536. The second time the string is hashed, one is added to the first character. Then the two 8-bit hash values are concatenated together to form a 16-bit hash value.

```
typedef unsigned short int HashIndexType;
unsigned char Rand8[256];

HashIndexType Hash(char *str) {
 HashIndexType h;
 unsigned char h1, h2;
 if (*str == 0) return 0;
```

```
    h1 = *str; h2 = *str + 1;
    str++;
    while (*str) {
    h1 = Rand8[h1 ^ *str];
    h2 = Rand8[h2 ^ *str];
    str++;
    }

    /* h is in range 0...65535 */
    h = ((HashIndexType)h1 << 8)|(HashIndexType)h2;
    /* use division method to scale */
    return h % HashTableSize
}
```

9.13.1 Collisions

By now we are probably objecting to this scheme on the grounds that it does not guarantee unique hash locations. ID number 01234 and ID number 91234 both hash to the same location, **Student_Record[34]**. The problem of avoiding these collisions is the challenge in designing a good hash function. A good hash function minimizes collisions by spreading the elements uniformly throughout the array. But minimization of collision is very difficult job. Assuming that there are some collisions, where we want to store the elements that cause them? We will briefly describe several collisions handling methods.

9.13.2 Linear Probing

A simple approach to resolving collisions is to store the colliding record (element) into the next available space. This technique is known as linear probing. Suppose in **Figure 9.44** we want to add the student record (element) with the key ID number 77003. The function returns 3. But there already is a record stored in this array room, the record for student 50003. We increment location to 4 and examine the next array room. **Student_Record[4]** is also in use, so we increment location again. This time we find a room, i.e., empty, so we store the new record into **Student_Record[5]**.

Linear probing resolves hash collision by sequential searching a hash table beginning at the location returned by the hash function. What happens if the key hashes to the last index in the array and that space is in use? We can consider array as a circular structure and continue looking for an empty room at the beginning of the array {Consider chapter 6 for circular queue}.

How do we know whether an array room is empty? We can initialize the array room to contain a special empty information, i.e., NULL ('\0') or if all students have nonnegative **STD_ID** keys, we can use –1 as the key value for an empty room. Now it is easy to tell if the room is free. We compare the value in the position to the empty value.

Here we define **Insert_Record()** function in another way, i.e., that use linear probing to find a place to store a new record. It assumes that there is room in the array for another record, i.e., a check has been made for is array full before the function is called.

```
struct Student * Insert_Record(int Key, struct Student Student_Record[],
struct Student Info)
{
    int location;
    location = Hash(Key);
```

```
while (Student_Record[location] != EmptyInfo)
{
    location = (location+1) % MAX_INFO;
}
  Student_Record[location = Info;
  Length ++;
}
```

To search for a record using this collision-handing technique, we perform the hash function on the key, then compare the desired key to the actual key in the record at the designated location. If the keys do not match, we use linear probing, beginning at the next room in array. Now we will give another version of **Access_Record ()** function that uses this approach. If the record is not found in the list, the outgoing parameter found is false and no record is return by the function.

```
struct Student * Access_Record(int Key, struct Student Student_Record[])
{
  int location;
  int Start_Loc;
  Flag = true;
  Start_Loc = Hash(Key);
  location = Start_Loc;

do
{
  if(Student_Record[location] !=Info || Student_Record[location]
  EmptyInfo)
  Flag = false;
  else  location = (location+1) % MAX_INFO;
} while(location != Start_Loc && Flag);
  Found = (Student_Record[location] == Info);
  If (found)
    Info = Student_Record[location];
}
```

9.13.3 Deletion

Collisions, however, complicate the matter. We can find the element using the same search approach as we used for **Access_Record()**. But when we locate the record in the hash table, we cannot merely replace the info with **EmptyInfo.** A review of **Access_Record ()** above shows the problem. In the loop, the detection of an empty room ends the search. If **Remove_Info()** "empties" the room occupied by a deleted record, we may terminate a subsequent search prematurely.

For example, in **Figure 9.44,** suppose we remove the record with key 77003 by setting the array room 5 to **Empty_Info**. A subsequent search for the record with the key 42504 would begin at the hash location 4. The record in this room is not the one we are looking for, so we increment the hash location to 5. This room, which formerly was occupied by the record that we removed, is now empty, so we terminate the search. We have not really finished searching; however, the record that we are looking for is the next room.

One solution to this problem is to create a third constant value, **Removed_Record**, to use in rooms that were occupied by the deleted records. If a room contains **Removed_Record** it means that this room is currently free, but the room was previously occupied.

Order of insertion	Index	Student_Record
	00	Empty
	01	Record with key = 14001
	02	Empty
14001	03	Record with key = 50003
00104	04	Record with key = 00104
50003	05	Record with key = 77003
77003	06	Record with key = 42504
42504	07	Empty
33099	08	Empty
	....	....
....	....	....
....	....	....
	98	
	99	

Figure 9.44 Hash table with linear probing

With this change we must modify both the insertion and accessing function operation, function to process rooms correctly. The insertion technique treats a room with **Removed_Record** and **Empty_Info** the same, the search for an available room for the new record ends. The **Empty_Info** halts the search in function **Access_Record()** but **Removed_Record** does not.

This solution corrects the search problem but generates another: after many deletions, the search path to a record may travel through many array rooms with **Removed_Record**. This may cause the efficiency of retrieving a record to deteriorate. These problems illustrate that hash tables, in the forms that we have studied thus far, are not the most effective data structure for implementing lists whose elements may be deleted.

9.13.4 Clustering

One problem with linear probing is that its results in a situation called clustering. A good hash function results in a uniform distribution of indexes throughout the array's index range. Initially, therefore, records are inserted throughout the array, each room equally likely to be filled. Over time, however, after a number of collisions have been resolved, the distribution of records in the array becomes less and less uniform. The records tend to cluster together, as multiple keys begin to complete for a single hash function. For example, consider the hash table given in **Figure 9.44,** only a record whose key produces the hash value 8 would be inserted into array room 8. However, any records with keys that produce the hash values 3, 4, 5, 6 or 7 would be inserted into array room 7. That is array room 7 is five times as likely as array room 8 to be filled. Clustering results in inconsistent efficiency of insertion and retrieval operations.

9.13.5 Rehashing

The technique of linear probing discussed here is an example of collision resolution by rehashing. If the hash function produces a collision, the hash value is used as the input to rehash function to compute a new hash value. In the previous section, we added 1 to hash value that is we used the rehash function:

```
(Hash value + 1) % 100
```

For rehashing with linear probing we can use any function

```
(Hash value + constant) % array_size
```

as long as **constant** and **array_size** are relatively prime- that is the largest number that divides both of them evenly is 1. For instance, given the 100-rooms array in **Figure 9.45**, we might use the constant 3 in the rehash function:

```
(Hash value + 3) % 100
```

Note 100 is not a prime number, 3 and 100 are relatively prime; they have no common factor larger than 1.

Suppose that we want to add a record with the key 14001 to the hash table in **Figure 9.45**. The original hash function (Key %100) returns the hash value 1, but this array room is in use, it contains the record with key value 44001. To determine the next array room to try, we apply the rehash function using the results of the first hash function an input: (1+3) %100 = 4. The array room at index 4 is also in use, so we reapply the rehash function until we get an available room. Each time, we use the value computed from the previous rehash as input to the rehash function. The second rehash gives (4+3)%100 = 7; this room is in use. Third rehash gives (7+3)%100 = 10; the array room at index 10 is empty, so the new record is inserted there. Why the constant and array rooms must be relatively prime? For example, consider the rehash function

```
(Hash value +2) %100
```

We want to add the record with the key 14001 to the hash table shown in **Figure 9.45,** the original hash function, Key %100, returns the hash value 1. This arrays room is already occupied. We resolve the collision by applying the rehash function above, examining successive odd-numbered indexes until a free room is found. What happens if all of the rooms with odd-numbered indexes are already in use? The search would fail-even though there are free rooms with even-numbered indexes. This rehash function does not cover the full index range of the array. However, if the constant and the number of array rooms are relatively prime, e.g. 3 and 100, the function produces successive rehashes that eventually cover every index in the array. Rehash functions that use linear probing do not eliminate clustering. For example, in **Figure 9.45,** any record with a key value that produces the hash value 1, 4, 7 or 10 would be inserted into the room at index 10.

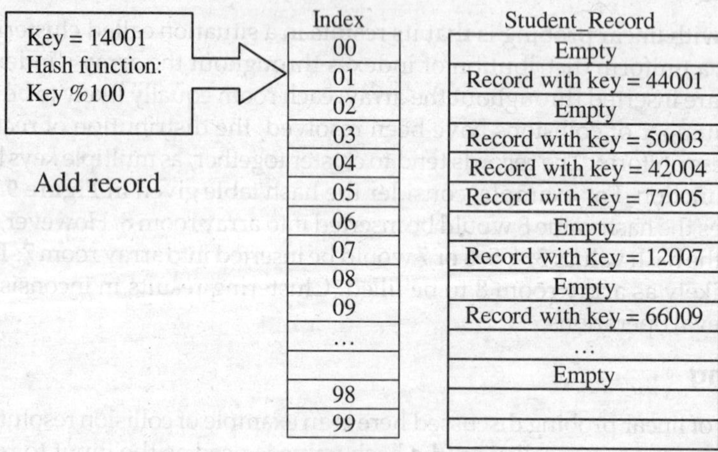

Figure 9.45 Handling collisions with rehashing

In linear probing, we add a constant usually 1, in each successive application of the rehash function. Another approach, called quadratic probing, makes the result of rehashing dependent on how many times the rehash function has been applied. In the ith rehash, the function is

$$(Hash\_Value + i^2) \% array\_size$$

The first rehash adds 1 to **Hash_Value**, the second rehash adds 4, the third rehash adds 9 and so on. Quadratic probing reduces clustering, but it does not necessarily examine every room in the array. For example, if **array_size** is a power of 2 (e.g. 256, 512, 1024 or 2448), relatively few array rooms are examined. However, if **array_size** is a prime number of the **4*some_integer + 3,** quadratic probing does examine every room in the array. A third approach uses a pseudo-random generator to determine the increment to **Hash_Value** in each application of the rehash function. Random probing is excellent for eliminating clustering, but it tends to be slower than the other techniques we have discussed.

9.13.6 Bucket And Chaining

Another alternative for handling collisions is to allow multiple element keys to hash to the same location. One solution is to let each computed hash location contain rooms for multiple elements, rather than just a single element. Each of these multi-element locations is called bucket. **Figure 9.46** illustrates a hash table with buckets that can contain three elements each. Using this approach, we can allow collisions to produce duplicate entries at the same hash location, up to a point. When the bucket becomes full, we must again deal with handling collisions.

Another solution, which avoids this problem, is to use the hash value not as the actual location of the element, but as the index into an array of pointers. Each pointer accesses a chain of elements that share the same hash location. **Figure 9.47** illustrates this solution to the problem of collisions. Rather than rehashing, we simply allow both elements to share hash location 3. The entry in the array at this location contains a pointer to a linked list that includes both elements. To search for a given element, one first applies the hash function to the key and then searches the chain for the element. Searching is not eliminated, but it is limited to elements that actually share a hash location. In contrast, with linear probing one may have to search through many additional elements if the rooms following the hash location are filled with elements from collisions on other hash locations.

Key = 77003 Hash function: Key %100

Add record

Index	Student_Record		
00	Empty	Empty	Empty
01	Record with key = 14001	Record with key = 54011	Record with key = 57021
02	Empty	Empty	Empty
03	Record with key = 50003	Add new record	Empty
04	Record with key = 00104	Record with key = 43004	Record with key = 48004
05	Empty	Empty	Empty
06	Empty	Empty	Empty
07	Record with key = 12007	Record with key = 12015	Record with key = 13008
08	Empty	Empty	Empty
09			
...	...	...	...
98	Empty	Empty	Empty
99			

Figure 9.46 Handling collisions with hashing with buckets

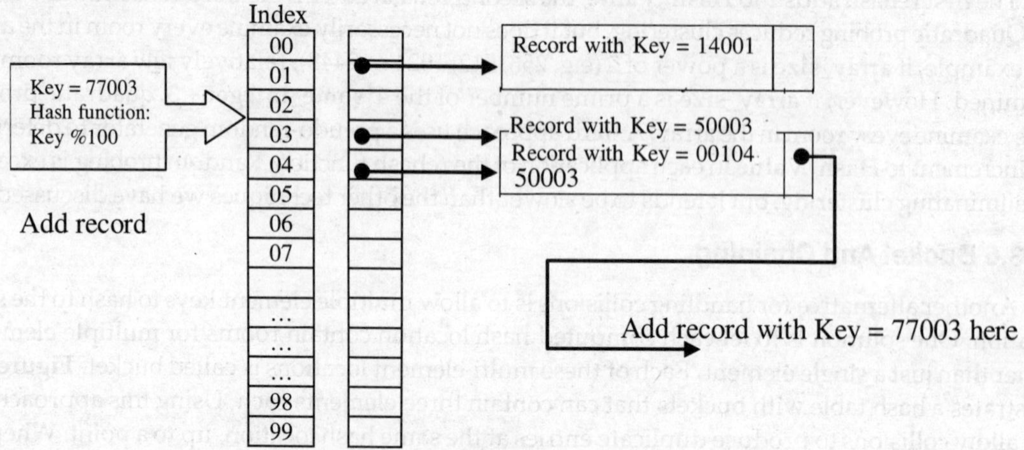

Figure 9.47 Handling collisions by hashing with chaining

9.13.7 Selecting Good Hash Function

One way to minimize collisions is to use data structure that has more space than is actually needed for the number of elements, in order to increase the range of the hash function. In practice it desirable to have the array size somewhat larger than the number of elements required, in order reducing the number of collisions. Selecting the table size involves a space vs. time tradeoff. The larger the range of hash locations, the less likely it is that two keys hash to the same location. However, allocating an array that contains a large number of empty rooms wastes space.

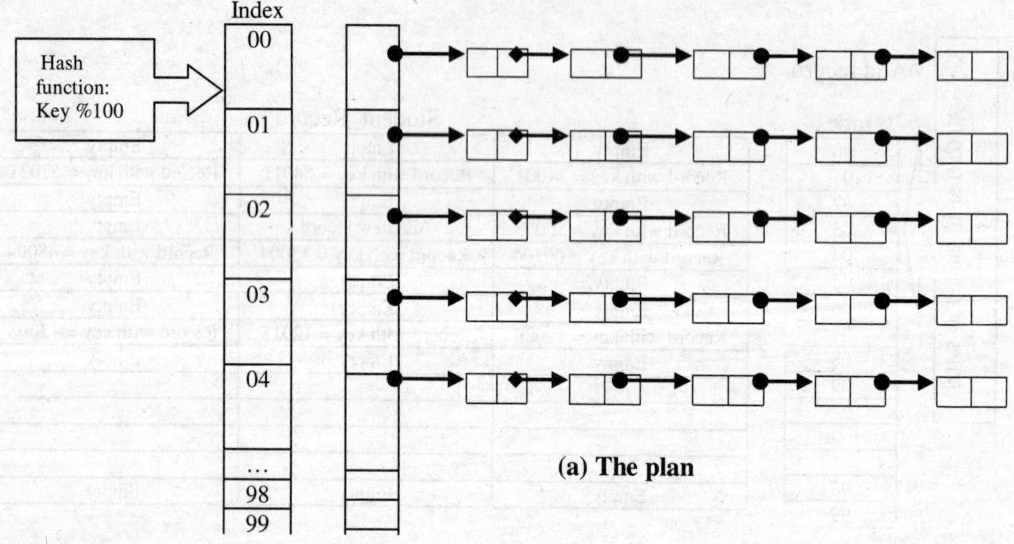

Average 5 records / chain , 5 records x100 chains = 500 Students, expected search O(5)

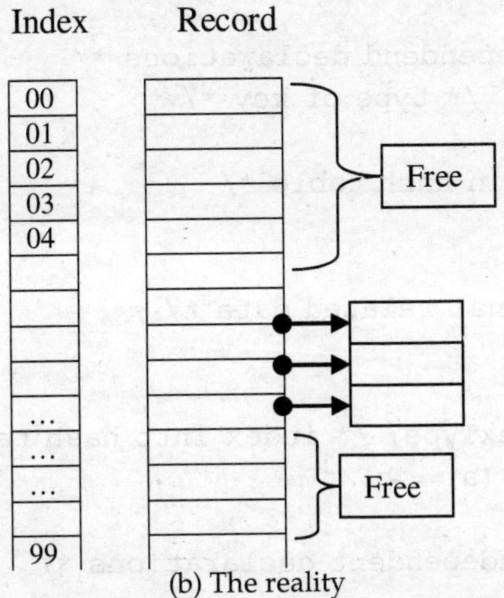

(b) The reality

Figure 9.48 Hash scheme to handle student record

More important, one can design his/her own hash function to minimize collisions. The goal is to distribute the elements as uniformly as possible throughout the array. Therefore one wants his/her hash function to produce unique values as often as possible. Once we admit collisions, we must introduce some sort of searching, either through array or chain searching or through rehashing. The access to each element is no longer direct and the search is no longer **O (1)**. In fact, if the collisions cause very disproportionate chains, the worst case may be almost **O (n)**.

To avoid such a situation one needs to know something about the statistical distribution of keys. Imagine HNB Garhwal University whose student records are sorted according to a university ID six digits long. There are 500 students and we decide to use a chained approach to handling collisions. We set up 100 chains and use the hash function

```
STD_ID % 100
```

That is, we use the last two digits of the six-digit ID number as index. The planned hash scheme is shown in **Figure 9.48(a). Figure 9.48(b)** shows what happened when the hash scheme was implemented. How could the distribution of the elements have come out so skewed? It turns out that the university's ID number is a concatenation of three fields:

Unique number   Dept number   Year enrolled (e.g. 17)

The hash scheme depended solely on the year student enrolled to produce hash values. Because the university was founded in 1917, all the elements were crowed very disproportionately into a small subset of the hash locations. A search for a student element, in this case is **O (n).** Although this is an exaggerated example, it illustrates the need to understand as completely as possible the domain and predicted values of keys in a hash scheme. The implementation of the above discuss is given in the program segment **Hash.c**.

```
/* hash table */
/* Hash.C*/
#include <stdio.h>
```

```
#include <stdlib.h>
/* implementation dependend declarations */
typedef int keyType; /* type of key */

/* user data stored in hash table */
typedef struct
{
 int stuff; /* optional related data */
} recType;

typedef int hashIndexType; /* index into hash table */
#define compEQ(a,b) (a == b)

/* implementation independent declarations */
typedef enum
{
 STATUS_OK,
 STATUS_MEM_EXHAUSTED,
 STATUS_KEY_NOT_FOUND
} statusEnum;

typedef struct nodeTag
{
 struct nodeTag *next; /* next node */
 keyType key; /* key */
 recType rec; /* user data */
} nodeType;

nodeType **hashTable;
int hashTableSize;

hashIndexType hash(keyType key)
{
 /*********************************
 * hash function applied to data *
 *********************************/
 return (key % hashTableSize);
}

statusEnum insert(keyType key, recType *rec)
{
 nodeType *p, *p0;
 hashIndexType bucket;
```

```
/*********************************************
* allocate node for data and insert in table *
*********************************************/
/* insert node at beginning of list */

bucket = hash(key);
if ((p = malloc(sizeof(nodeType))) == 0)
return STATUS_MEM_EXHAUSTED;
p0 = hashTable[bucket];
hashTable[bucket] = p;
p->next = p0;
p->key = key;
p->rec = *rec;
return STATUS_OK;
}

statusEnum delete(keyType key)
{
nodeType *p0, *p;
hashIndexType bucket;

/********************************************
* delete node containing data from table *
********************************************/

/* find node */
p0 = 0;
bucket = hash(key);
p = hashTable[bucket];
while (p && !compEQ(p->key, key)) {
p0 = p;
p = p->next;
}
if (!p) return STATUS_KEY_NOT_FOUND;

/* p designates node to delete, remove it from list */
if (p0)
/* not first node, p0 points to previous node */
p0->next = p->next;
else
/* first node on chain */
hashTable[bucket] = p->next;

free (p);
return STATUS_OK;
}
```

```
statusEnum find(keyType key, recType *rec)
{
 nodeType *p;

 /******************************
 * find node containing data    *
 ******************************/

 p = hashTable[hash(key)];
 while (p && !compEQ(p->key, key))
 p = p->next;
 *rec = p->rec;
 return STATUS_OK;
}
/* Function main */
int main()
{
 int i, maxnum, random;
 recType *rec;
 keyType *key;
 statusEnum err;
 printf("Input maximum number");
 scanf("%d", &maxnum);
 printf("Input Table Size");
 scanf("%d",&hashTableSize);
 printf("Input option greater than 3 for random otherwise sequential: ");
 scanf("%d", &random);
 random = random > 3;

 if ((rec = malloc(maxnum * sizeof(recType))) == 0){
 fprintf (stderr, "out of memory (rec)\n");
 exit(1);
 }
 if ((key = malloc(maxnum * sizeof(keyType))) == 0) {
 fprintf (stderr, "out of memory (key)\n");
 exit(1);
 }

 if ((hashTable = malloc(hashTableSize * sizeof(nodeType *))) == 0) {
 fprintf (stderr, "out of memory (hashTable)\n");
 exit(1);
 }

 if (random) { /* random */
 /* fill "key" with unique random numbers */
```

```
for (i = 0; i < maxnum; i++) key[i] = rand();
printf ("ran ht, %d items, %d hashTable\n", maxnum, hashTableSize);
} else   {
for (i=0; i<maxnum; i++) key[i] = i;
printf ("seq ht, %d items, %d hashTable\n", maxnum, hashTableSize);
}

for (i = 0; i < maxnum; i++) {
err = insert(key[i], &rec[i]);
if (err) printf("pt1, i=%d\n", i);
}

for (i = maxnum-1; i >= 0; i--){
err = find(key[i], &rec[i]);
if (err) printf("pt2, i=%d\n", i);
}

for (i = maxnum-1; i >= 0; i--) {
err = delete(key[i]);
if (err) printf("pt3, i=%d\n", i);
}
return 0;
}
```

Note: In the above program segment **typedef T** and comparison operator **compEQ** should be altered to reflect the data stored in the table. The **hashTableSize** must be determined and the **hashTable** allocated. The division method was used in the **hash** function. Function **insertNode** allocates a new node and inserts it in the table. Function **deleteNode** deletes and frees a node from the table. Function **findNode** searches the table for a particular value.

9.14 EXTERNAL SORTING

One method for sorting a file is to load the file into memory, sort the data in memory, then write the results. When the file cannot be loaded into memory due to resource limitations, an *external sort* is applicable. We will implement an external sort using *replacement selection* to establish initial runs, followed by a *polyphase merge sort* to merge the runs into one sorted file.

For clarity, we will assume that data is on one or more reels of magnetic tape. **Figure 9.49** illustrates a 3-way polyphase merge. Initially, in phase A, all data is on tapes T1 and T2. Assume that the beginning of each tape is at the bottom of the frame. There are two sequential runs of data on T1: 4-8, and 6-7. Tape T2 has one run: 5-9. At phase B, we have merged the first run from tapes T1 (4-8) and T2 (5-9) into a longer run on tape T3 (4-5-8-9). Phase C is simply renames the tapes, so we may repeat the merge again. In phase D we repeat the merge, with the final output on tape T3.

Several interesting details have been omitted from the previous illustration. For example, how were the initial runs created? And, notice that they merged *perfectly*, with no extra runs on any tapes? Before we explain the method used for constructing initial runs, let me digress for a bit.

In 1202, Leonardo Fibonacci presented the following exercise in his *Liber Abbaci* (Book of the Abacus): "How many pairs of rabbits can be produced from a single pair in a year's time?" We may assume that each pair produces a new pair of offspring every month, each pair becomes fertile at the age of one month, and that rabbits never die. After one month, there will be 2 pairs of rabbits; after two months there will be 3; the following month the original pair and the pair born during the first month will both usher in a new pair, and there will be 5 in all; and so on. This series, where each number is the sum of the two preceding numbers, is known as the Fibonacci sequence: 0, 1, 1, 2, 3, 5, 8, 13, 21, 34, 55, 89, ...

Curiously, the Fibonacci series has found widespread application to everything from the arrangement of flowers on plants to studying the efficiency of Euclid's algorithm. And, as we might suspect, the Fibonacci series has something to do with establishing initial runs for external sorts.

Recall that we initially had one run on tape T2, and 2 runs on tape T1. Note that the numbers {1,2} are two sequential numbers in the Fibonacci series. After first merge, we had one run on T1 and one run on T2. Note that the numbers {1,1} are two sequential numbers in the Fibonacci series, only one *notch* down. We could predict, in fact, that if we had 13 runs on T2, and 21 runs on T1 {13, 21}, we would be left with 8 runs on T1 and 13 runs on T3 {8,13} after one pass. Successive passes would result in run counts of {5,8}, {3,5}, {2,3}, {1,1}, and {0,1}, for a total of 7 passes. This arrangement is ideal, and will result in the minimum number of passes. Should data actually be on tape, this is a big savings, as tapes must be mounted and rewound for each pass. For more than 2 tapes, *higher-order* Fibonacci numbers are used.

Phase	T1	T2	T3
A	7 6 8 4	 9 5	
B	 7 6		9 8 5 4
C	9 8 5 4	 7 6	
D			9 8 7 6 5 4

Figure 9.49 Merge Sort

Initially, all the data is on one tape. The tape is read, and runs are distributed to other tapes in the system. After the initial runs are created, they are merged as described above. One method we could use to create initial runs is to read a batch of records into memory, sort the records, and write them out. This process would continue until we had exhausted the input tape. An alternative algorithm, *replacement selection*, allows for longer runs. A buffer is allocated in memory to act as a holding place for several records. Initially, the buffer is filled. Then, the following steps are repeated until the input is exhausted:

1. Select the record with the smallest key that is ≥ the key of the last record written.
2. If all keys are smaller than the key of the last record written, then we have reached the end of a run. Select the record with the smallest key for the first record of the next run.
3. Write the selected record.
4. Replace the selected record with a new record from input.

Figure 9.50 illustrates replacement selection for a small file. The beginning of the file is to the right of each frame. To keep things simple, we have allocated a 2-record buffer. Typically, such a buffer would hold thousands of records. We load the buffer in step B, and write the record with the smallest key (6) in step C. This is replaced with the next record (key 8). We select the smallest key ≥ 6 in step D. This is key 7. After writing key 7, we replace it with key 4. This process repeats until step F, where our last key written was 8, and all keys are less than 8. At this point, we terminate the run, and start another.

This strategy simply utilizes an intermediate buffer to hold values until the appropriate time for output. Using random numbers as input, the average length of a run is twice the length of the buffer. However, if the data is somewhat ordered, runs can be extremely long. Thus, this method is more effective than doing partial sorts.

When selecting the next output record, we need to find the smallest key ≥ the last key written. One way to do this is to scan the entire list, searching for the appropriate key. However, when the buffer holds thousands of records, execution time becomes prohibitive. An alternative method is to use a binary tree structure, so that we only compare **log n** items. The above discussion is implemented in the program segment **EXTMRG.C**.

Step	Input	Buffer	Output
A	5-3-4-8-6-7		
B	5-3-4-8	6-7	
C	5-3-4	8-7	6
D	5-3	8-4	7-6
E	5	3-4	8-7-6
F		5-4	3 | 8-7-6
G		5	4-3 | 8-7-6
H			5-4-3 | 8-7-6

Figure 9.50 Replacement Selection

```
/* merge sort and external sort */
/* EXTMRG.C */
#include <stdio.h>
#include <stdlib.h>
#include <string.h>

/****************************
 * Implementation dependent *
 ****************************/

/* template for workfiles (8.3 format) */
#define FNAME "_sort%03d.dat"
#define LNAME 13

/* comparison operators */
#define compLT(x,y) (x < y)
#define compGT(x,y) (x > y)

/* define the record to be sorted here */
#define LRECL 100
typedef int keyType;
typedef struct recTypeTag {
 keyType key; /* sort key for record */
 #if LRECL
 char data[LRECL-sizeof(keyType)]; /* other fields */
 #endif
} recType;
```

```
/*******************************
 * implementation independent *
 *******************************/
typedef enum {false, true} bool;

typedef struct tmpFileTag {
 FILE *fp; /* file pointer */
 char name[LNAME]; /* filename */
 recType rec; /* last record read */
 int dummy; /* number of dummy runs */
 bool eof; /* end-of-file flag */
 bool eor; /* end-of-run flag */
 bool valid; /* true if rec is valid */
 int fib; /* ideal fibonacci number */
} tmpFileType;

static tmpFileType **file; /* array of file info for tmp files */
static int nTmpFiles; /* number of tmp files */
static char ifName[13]; /* input filename */
static char ofName[13]; /* output filename */

static int level; /* level of runs */
static int nNodes; /* number of nodes for selection tree */

void deleteTmpFiles(void) {
 int i;

 /* delete merge files and free resources */
 if (file) {
 for (i = 0; i < nTmpFiles; i++) {
 if (file[i]) {
 if (file[i]->fp) fclose(file[i]->fp);
 if (*file[i]->name) remove(file[i]->name);
 free (file[i]);
 }
 }
 free (file);
 }
}

void termTmpFiles(int rc) {

 /* cleanup files */
 remove(ofName);
```

```
    if (rc == 0) {
    int fileT;

    /* file[T] contains results */
    fileT = nTmpFiles - 1;
    fclose(file[fileT]->fp); file[fileT]->fp = NULL;
    if (rename(file[fileT]->name, ofName)) {
    perror("io1");
    deleteTmpFiles();
    exit(1);
    }
    *file[fileT]->name = 0;
    }
    deleteTmpFiles();
}

void cleanExit(int rc) {

    /* cleanup tmp files and exit */
    termTmpFiles(rc);
    exit(rc);
}

void *safeMalloc(size_t size) {
    void *p;

    /* safely allocate memory and initialize to zero */
    if ((p = calloc(1, size)) == NULL) {
    printf("error: malloc failed, size = %d\n", size);
    cleanExit(1);
    }
    return p;
}

void initTmpFiles(void) {
    int i;
    tmpFileType *fileInfo;

    /* initialize merge files */
    if (nTmpFiles < 3) nTmpFiles = 3;
    file = safeMalloc(nTmpFiles * sizeof(tmpFileType*));
    fileInfo = safeMalloc(nTmpFiles * sizeof(tmpFileType));
    for (i = 0; i < nTmpFiles; i++) {
    file[i] = fileInfo + i;
    sprintf(file[i]->name, FNAME, i);
```

```
if ((file[i]->fp = fopen(file[i]->name, "w+b")) == NULL) {
perror("io2");
cleanExit(1);
}
}
}

recType *readRec(void) {

typedef struct iNodeTag { /* internal node */
struct iNodeTag *parent;/* parent of internal node */
struct eNodeTag *loser; /* external loser */
} iNodeType;

typedef struct eNodeTag { /* external node */
struct iNodeTag *parent;/* parent of external node */
recType rec; /* input record */
int run; /* run number */
bool valid; /* input record is valid */
} eNodeType;

typedef struct nodeTag {
iNodeType i; /* internal node */
eNodeType e; /* external node */
} nodeType;

static nodeType *node; /* array of selection tree nodes */
static eNodeType *win; /* new winner */
static FILE *ifp; /* input file */
static bool eof; /* true if end-of-file, input */
static int maxRun; /* maximum run number */
static int curRun; /* current run number */
iNodeType *p; /* pointer to internal nodes */
static bool lastKeyValid; /* true if lastKey is valid */
static keyType lastKey; /* last key written */

/* read next record using replacement selection */

/* check for first call */
if (node == NULL) {
int i;

if (nNodes < 2) nNodes = 2;
node = safeMalloc(nNodes * sizeof(nodeType));
for (i = 0; i < nNodes; i++) {
```

```
node[i].i.loser = &node[i].e;
node[i].i.parent = &node[i/2].i;
node[i].e.parent = &node[(nNodes + i)/2].i;
node[i].e.run = 0;
node[i].e.valid = false;
}
win = &node[0].e;
lastKeyValid = false;

if ((ifp = fopen(ifName, "rb")) == NULL) {
   printf("error: unable to open a file: %s\n", ifName);
cleanExit(1);
}
}

while (1) {

/* replace previous winner with new record */
if (!eof) {
if (fread(&win->rec, sizeof(recType), 1, ifp) == 1) {
if ((!lastKeyValid || compLT(win->rec.key, lastKey))
&& (++win->run > maxRun))
maxRun = win->run;
win->valid = true;
} else if (feof(ifp)) {
fclose(ifp);
eof = true;
win->valid = false;
win->run = maxRun + 1;
} else {
perror("io4");
cleanExit(1);
}
} else {
win->valid = false;
win->run = maxRun + 1;
}

/* adjust loser and winner pointers */
p = win->parent;
do {
bool swap;
swap = false;
if (p->loser->run < win->run) {
swap = true;
```

```
} else if (p->loser->run == win->run) {
if (p->loser->valid && win->valid) {
if (compLT(p->loser->rec.key, win->rec.key))
swap = true;
} else {
swap = true;
}
}
if (swap) {
/* p should be winner */
eNodeType *t;

t = p->loser;
p->loser = win;
win = t;
}
p = p->parent;
} while (p != &node[0].i);

/* end of run? */
if (win->run != curRun) {
/* win->run = curRun + 1 */
if (win->run > maxRun) {
/* end of output */
free(node);
return NULL;
}
curRun = win->run;
}

/* output top of tree */
if (win->run) {
lastKey = win->rec.key;
lastKeyValid = true;
return &win->rec;
}
}
}

void makeRuns(void) {
recType *win; /* winner */
int fileT; /* last file */
int fileP; /* next to last file */
int j; /* selects file[j] */
```

```
/* Make initial runs using replacement selection.
* Runs are written using a Fibonacci distintbution.
*/

/* initialize file structures */
fileT = nTmpFiles - 1;
fileP = fileT - 1;
for (j = 0; j < fileT; j++) {
file[j]->fib = 1;
file[j]->dummy = 1;
}
file[fileT]->fib = 0;
file[fileT]->dummy = 0;

level = 1;
j = 0;


win = readRec();
while (win) {
bool anyrun;

anyrun = false;
for (j = 0; win && j <= fileP; j++) {
bool run;

run = false;
if (file[j]->valid) {
if (!compLT(win->key, file[j]->rec.key)) {
/* append to an existing run */
run = true;
} else if (file[j]->dummy) {
/* start a new run */
file[j]->dummy--;
run = true;
}
} else {
/* first run in file */
file[j]->dummy--;
run = true;
}

if (run) {
anyrun = true;
/* flush run */
```

```
while(1) {
 if (fwrite(win, sizeof(recType), 1, file[j]->fp) != 1) {
 perror("io3");
 cleanExit(1);
 }
 file[j]->rec.key = win->key;
 file[j]->valid = true;
 if ((win = readRec()) == NULL) break;
 if (compLT(win->key, file[j]->rec.key)) break;
 }
 }
 }

 /* if no room for runs, up a level */
 if (!anyrun) {
 int t;
 level++;
 t = file[0]->fib;
 for (j = 0; j <= fileP; j++) {
 file[j]->dummy = t + file[j+1]->fib - file[j]->fib;
 file[j]->fib = t + file[j+1]->fib;
 }
 }
 }
}

void rewindFile(int j) {
 /* rewind file[j] and read in first record */
 file[j]->eor = false;
 file[j]->eof = false;
 rewind(file[j]->fp);
 if (fread(&file[j]->rec, sizeof(recType), 1, file[j]->fp) != 1) {
 if (feof(file[j]->fp)) {
 file[j]->eor = true;
 file[j]->eof = true;
 } else {
 perror("io5");
 cleanExit(1);
 }
 }
}

void mergeSort(void) {
 int fileT;
 int fileP;
```

```
int j;
tmpFileType *tfile;

/* polyphase merge sort */

fileT = nTmpFiles - 1;
fileP = fileT - 1;

/* prime the files */
for (j = 0; j < fileT; j++) {
rewindFile(j);
}

/* each pass through loop merges one run */
while (level) {
while(1) {
bool allDummies;
bool anyRuns;

/* scan for runs */
allDummies = true;
anyRuns = false;
for (j = 0; j <= fileP; j++) {
if (!file[j]->dummy) {
allDummies = false;
if (!file[j]->eof) anyRuns = true;
}
}

if (anyRuns) {
int k;
keyType lastKey;

/* merge 1 run file[0]..file[P] ->file[T] */

while(1) {
/* each pass thru loop writes 1 record to file[fileT] */

/* find smallest key */
k = -1;
for (j = 0; j <= fileP; j++) {
if (file[j]->eor) continue;
if (file[j]->dummy) continue;
if (k < 0 ||
(k != j && compGT(file[k]->rec.key, file[j]->rec.key)))
```

```
k = j;
}
if (k < 0) break;

/* write record[k] to file[fileT] */
if (fwrite(&file[k]->rec, sizeof(recType), 1,
file[fileT]->fp) != 1) {
perror("io6");
cleanExit(1);
}

/* replace record[k] */
lastKey = file[k]->rec.key;
if (fread(&file[k]->rec, sizeof(recType), 1,
file[k]->fp) == 1) {
/* check for end of run on file[s] */
if (compLT(file[k]->rec.key, lastKey))
file[k]->eor = true;
} else if (feof(file[k]->fp)) {
file[k]->eof = true;
file[k]->eor = true;
} else {
perror("io7");
cleanExit(1);
}
}

/* fixup dummies */
for (j = 0; j <= fileP; j++) {
if (file[j]->dummy) file[j]->dummy--;
if (!file[j]->eof) file[j]->eor = false;
}

} else if (allDummies) {
for (j = 0; j <= fileP; j++)
file[j]->dummy--;
file[fileT]->dummy++;
}

/* end of run */
if (file[fileP]->eof && !file[fileP]->dummy) {
/* completed a fibonocci-level */
level--;
if (!level) {
/* we're done, file[fileT] contains data */
```

```
return;
}

/* fileP is exhausted, reopen as new */
fclose(file[fileP]->fp);
if ((file[fileP]->fp = fopen(file[fileP]->name, "w+b"))
== NULL) {
perror("io8");
cleanExit(1);
}
file[fileP]->eof = false;
file[fileP]->eor = false;

rewindFile(fileT);

/* f[0],f[1]...,f[fileT] <- f[fileT],f[0]...,f[T-1] */
tfile = file[fileT];
memmove(file + 1, file, fileT * sizeof(tmpFileType*));
file[0] = tfile;

/* start new runs */
for (j = 0; j <= fileP; j++)
if (!file[j]->eof) file[j]->eor = false;
}
}

}
}


void extSort(void) {
initTmpFiles();
makeRuns();
mergeSort();
termTmpFiles(0);
}

/* Main Function */
int main()
{
printf("Provide Input file name");
gets(ifName);
printf("Provide Output file name");
gets(ofName);
printf("Input number of files");
```

```
    scanf("%d",&nTmpFiles);
    printf("Input number of nodes");
    scanf("%d",&nNodes);
    printf("extSort: nFiles=%d, nNodes=%d, lrecl=%d\n", nTmpFiles, nNodes,
sizeof(recType));

    extSort(); /* invoking function */
    return 0;
}
```

In the above program **makeRuns()** calls **readRec()** to read the next record. Function **readRec()** employs the replacement selection algorithm (utilizing a binary tree) to fetch the next record and **makeRuns()** distributes the records in a Fibonacci distribution. If the number of runs is not a perfect Fibonacci number, *dummy* runs are simulated at the beginning of each file. Function **mergeSort()** is then called to do a polyphase merge sort on the runs. The above program segment desires data inform collection of records stored in a file that will trated as input file. This prpgram segment is also depends on the user choice for temporary file used during the sorting.

FOR SUMMATIVE AND FORMATIVE ASSESSMENT

9.1 Suppose **String** is the following list of 14 alphabetic characters: D A T A S T R U C T U R E S. Suppose the characters in **String** are to be sorted alphabetically. Use the quick sort algorithm to find the position of the first character **D**.

9.2 Suppose **Name** consists of the following list of names with **n = 5**. The list is: Tom, Boy, Jadeja, Sachin, Sanath. Find the number **C** of comparisons to sort **Name** using radix sort.

9.3 Suppose **S** consists of the following **n = 6** letters, A B E H C L. Find the number of comparisons to sort **S** using shell sort.

9.4 Sort the following lists in ascending order using selection sort:
   (*i*) 66, 77, 11, 88, 99, 22, 33, 44, 55, 77, 03, 04, 05
   (*ii*) S, T, R, U, C, T, U, R, E, S, D, A, T, A

9.5 Sort the following lists in ascending order using insertion sort:
   (*i*) 66, 77, 11, 88, 99, 22, 33, 44, 55, 77, 03, 04, 05
   (*ii*) S, T, R, U, C, T, U, R, E, S, D, A, T, A

9.6 Using the bubble sort algorithm, find the number **C** of comparisons and the number **I** of interchanges which alphabetize the **n= 10** letters in **STRUCTURES.**

9.7 Find the contents of the array **A** shown in **Figure 9.51** after 3rd and 7th iterations if sorting is done by
   (i) bubble sort
   (ii) shell sort
   (iii) insertion sort
   (iv) selection sort
   (v) merge sort

53	17	20	33	28	14	29	15	77	24

Figure 9.51 List in memory

9.8 Show how the values in the array **A** shown in **Figure 9.51** would have to be rearranged to satisfy **min** and **max** heap property. Sort the array using heap sort algorithm.

9.9 Sort the array **A** shown in **Figure 9.51** using merge sort.

9.10 How many comparisons would be needed to sort a list of 50 elements using radix sort
(i) in worst case (ii) in the best case

9.11 A sorting function is called to sort a list of 50 integers that have been read from a data file. If all 50 values are zero what would be the execution requirement (in terms of big O) if the sort used was
(i) quick sort (ii) bubble sort
(iii) selection sort (iv) heap sort
(v) insertion sort (vi) merge sort

9.12 How many comparisons are required to sort a list of 50 elements using selection sort, if the original list values were already sorted?
(i) 5000 (ii) 4950
(iii) 49 (iv) non of these

9.13 A merge sort is used to sort a list of 1000 test scores in the descending order. Which of the following statement is true?
(i) The sort is fasted if the original test scores are in order from smallest to largest.
(ii) The sort is fasted if the original test scores are in completely in random order.
(iii) The sort is fasted if the original test scores are in order from largest to smallest.
(iv) The sort is same, no matter what the order of the original elements.

9.14 Which of the following sorts will take longest time to execute and which will take the shortest time?
(i) merge sort (ii) heap sort
(iii) selection sort (iv) shell sort
(v) quick sort (vi) insertion sort

9.15 Fill in table shown in **Figure 9.52,** showing the number of comparisons needed either to find the value or to determine that the value is not in the list, given the following values: 26, 15, 27, 12, 33, 95, 9, 5, 99, 14

Value	Unsorted	Sorted, sequential search	Sorted, binary search	Binary search tree
15				
17				
14				
5				
99				
100				
0				

Figure 9.52 Table

9.16 Apply selection sort algorithm to sort files in a directory?
9.17 Does the tree shown in **Figure 9.53** represent a heap or not? Discuss.
9.18 Implement selection sort algorithm for a linked list. What is its complexity?
9.19 Implement bubble sort for doubly linked list. What is its complexity?
9.20 Implement the insertion sort for a linked list. What is time complexity of this sort?
9.21 Implement merge sort algorithm to merge two linked lists. Sort the concatenated list. What is its time complexity?
9.22 Implement radix sort algorithm to sort files in a directory.

9.23 Implement radix sort algorithm that sorts a list of **n** cells with values from 0 to **n-1** in place. Write a general radix sort algorithm for sorting strings using doubly linked list.

9.24 Create a heap for the list of elements shown in **Figure 9.54**.

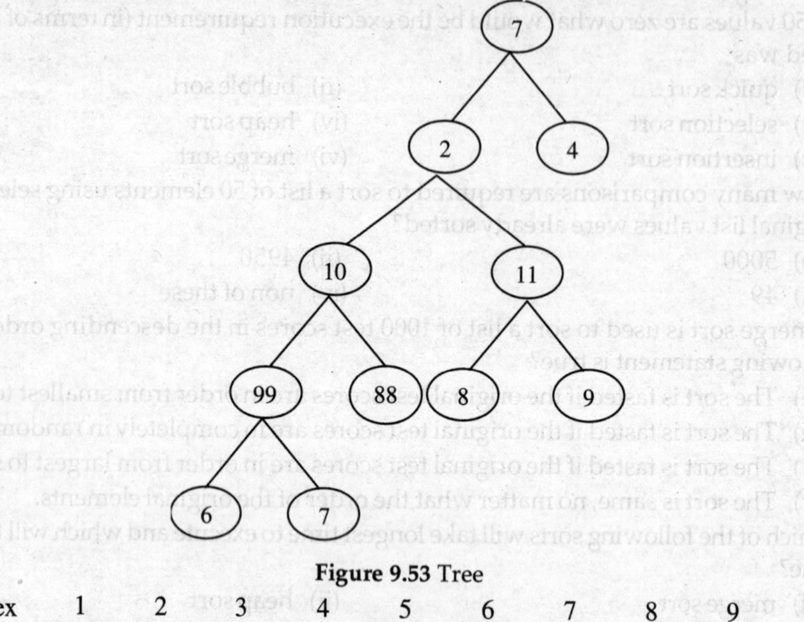

Figure 9.53 Tree

Index	1	2	3	4	5	6	7	8	9	10
Values	97	22	43	100	34	97	81	10	44	41

Figure 9.54 List of elements in memory

Quiz-8(Searching and Sorting)

1. Which of these is the Worst-case time complexity of Quick Sort - and cannot be expressed in lower order terms?
   (a) O(n) (b) O(n log n)
   (c) $\theta(n^2)$ (d) θ (log n)
2. Which of these is the worst case time complexity of Merge Sort - and cannot be expressed in lower order terms?
   (a) O(n) (b) O(n log n)
   (c) $O(n^2)$ (d) O(log n)
3. Which of these is the average case time complexity of Merge Sort - and cannot be expressed in lower order terms?
   (a) O(n) (b) O(n log n)
   (c) $O(n^2)$ (d) O(log n)
4. Which of these is the time complexity involved in building a heap of n elements - and cannot be expressed in lower order terms?
   (a) O(n) (b) O(n log n)
   (c) $O(n^2)$ (d) O(log n)

5. Which of these is the worst case time complexity for looking up a key in a binary search tree - and cannot be expressed in lower order terms?
   (a) O(n) (b) O(n log n)
   (c) $O(n^2)$ (d) O(log n)
6. A sorting algorithm which can prove to be a best time algorithm in one case and a worst time algorithm at other time?
   (a) Selection Sort (b) Heap Sort
   (c) Quick Sort (d) All of the above
7. Which of the following is not the required condition for binary search algorithm?
   (a) The list must be sorted
   (b) There should be the direct access to the middle element in any sublist
   (c) There must be mechanism to delete and/or insert elements in list
   (d) none of above
8. Which of the following is not a limitation of binary search algorithm?
   (a) must use a sorted array
   (b) requirement of sorted array is expensive when a lot of insertion and deletions are needed
   (c) there must be a mechanism to access middle element directly
   (d) binary search algorithm is not efficient when the data elements are more than 1000.
9. Binary search algorithm cannot be applied to
   (a) sorted linked list (b) sorted binary trees
   (c) sorted linear array (d) pointer array
10. The Worst case occur in linear search algorithm when
    (a) Item is somewhere in the middle of the array
    (b) Item is not in the array at all
    (c) Item is the last element in the array
    (d) Item is the last element in the array or is not there at all
11. The Average case occur in linear search algorithm
    (a) When Item is somewhere in the middle of the array
    (b) When Item is not in the array at all
    (c) When Item is the last element in the array
    (d) When Item is the last element in the array or is not there at all
12. The complexity of the average case of an algorithm is
    (a) Much more complicated to analyze than that of worst case
    (b) Much more simpler to analyze than that of worst case
    (c) Sometimes more complicated and some other times simpler than that of worst case
    (d) None or above
13. The complexity of linear search algorithm is
    (a) O(n) (b) O(log n)
    (c) O(n2) (d) O(n log n)
14. The complexity of Binary search algorithm is
    (a) O(n) (b) O(logn)
    (c) O(n2) (d) O(n log n)

15. The complexity of Bubble sort algorithm is
    (a) O(n) (b) O(log n)
    (c) $O(n^2)$ (d) O(n log n)
16. The complexity of merge sort algorithm is
    (a) O(n) (b) O(log n)
    (c) O(n2) (d) O(n log n)
17. We have an array of n elements. Suppose we implement quicksort by always choosing the central element of the array as the pivot. Then the tightest upper bound for the worst case performance is
    (a) $O(n^2)$ (b) O(nLogn)
    (c) È(nLogn) (d) $O(n^3)$
18. If the array is already sorted, which of these algorithms will exhibit the best performance
    (a) Merge Sort (b) Insertion Sort
    (c) Quick Sort (d) Heap Sort
19. Quick sort algorithm is an example of
    (a) Greedy approach (b) Improved binary search
    (c) Dynamic Programming (d) Divide and conquer
20. A pivot element to partition unsorted list is used in
    (a) Merge Sort (b) Quick Sort
    (c) Insertion Sort (d) Selection Sort

❑

CHAPTER 10 File Structure

File structures are devoted to minimizing response time while minimizing the cost of doing so. Because response time depends on the capabilities of computer hardware, the history of file structures parallels the development of computer hardware. Early computers were expensive and ferrite core main memory was especially so; on the other hand, secondary storage in the form of magnetic tape and punch cards was not particularly costly but was limited to sequential access. As a result, most research of that period was devoted to efficient use of the limited main memory; the results of this study are found in the field of data structures and algorithms. The impact of file structures did not emerge until the introduction of direct access storage devices in the mid-to-late 1950's.

The first direct access devices were magnetic drums but magnetic disk devices entered business data processing with the introduction of IBM's RAMAC in 1956. At a lease price of $620 per month (about one-third of the price of a new Ford sedan at that time) for five megabytes, this was certainly a resource to be used carefully. Conserving this precious space became the motivation for studying file structures, in addition, recognition that a meaningful amount of this precious space was being wasted on duplicate information across several files led to the interest in the database concept.

The development of multitasking operating systems furthered the motivation for efficient file structures. Disk drives were and still are much slower than CPU and main memory processes. Folk and Zoellick (1992) place the difference as 250,000 to 1. In a shared resource environment, for example, the disk drive in a multitasking operating system or the file server in a network, every additional disk access by one process slows not only that process but all other processes in that environment. This fact, along with the inherent sluggishness of disk drives became the motivation for studying file structures with a view towards minimizing disk accesses.

The development of COBOL in 1960 gave practicality to the desire to move applications from one computing platform to another without rewriting the code. To support this goal, the emphasis in file processing turned from the physical to the logical, with the fit to the hardware being left to the operating system. Thus, programmers lost some of their ability to seek efficiency by fitting a program's file structures and processing algorithms to attributes of the physical storage device. This tradeoff has never been reconciled; however, depending on the circumstances, some choices are better than others at preserving portability while achieving an improvement in response time.

In today's world of distributed data, networks, Internets, and the World Wide Web, shared access to data storage are even greater than in a multitasking operating system. The progress in disk drive and CPU speeds has enabled more users to expect interactive access to even more data. Thus, the motivation for efficient access has become even greater, and although the motivation for conserving storage has diminished somewhat, the fact that often the data must be transmitted through crowded networks maintains the motivation to avoid storing or transmitting unnecessary bytes.

At first, secondary storage was purely sequential, punched cards and magnetic tape. Thus, algorithms for sorting and sequential processing were a focus of research right from the beginning. Sorting in restricted main memory with relatively slow processors was a continuing challenge. The development of the heap sort in 1964 by J. W. J. Williams overcame some of the problems that arose from very large files on slow secondary storage devices. Dwyer's (1981) description of the balance line algorithm formalized designs that had been used since the 1960's, and the balance line algorithm continues to provide the basis for most multiple file sequential processing.

The introduction of direct access storage devices brought a new realm of problems. In the early 1960's, the network database management system (Bachman, 1964) promised to provide some relief to direct access problems and, if properly designed to the problems of duplicate data, e.g., wasted storage and inconsistencies. But the problem of efficient direct access to user-managed files survived until the early 1970's with the publication by Bayer and Mc Creight (1972) of a description of B-tree indexes.

Dr. E.F. Codd published the foundation for relational databases in 1970, and work was continued throughout the 1970's to develop the concept. However, it wasn't until the early 1980's when progress in processor and storage speed made their performance acceptable that commercial relational database management systems appeared. In parallel with the work on relational databases, hashing schemes for direct access were explored during the 1970's, and Fagin, Nievergelt, Pippenger, and Strong published their description of extendible hashing in 1979.

We will first present the basic concepts of files used in most operating systems including UNIX, MS-DOS, and Windows and then explain MS-DOS file system (FAT file system) and UNIX i-node file system.

10.1 WHY FILE STRUCTURES?

Data is an important asset of an organization. It is often said that in contemporary computer systems hardware has a short life; software has a relatively longer life; but it is data, which has the longest life. Here we are interested in files of records. We will assume that all records within a given file have the same format and size. The implicit assumption will be that the number of records in a file is very large and that the file cannot fit in the main memory. This necessitates a multilevel hierarchical memory organization. We have assumed a bi-level memory organization. At the upper level there is the main memory, which is used for processing the information. The most important assumption is that at the lower level there is a disk (typically a magnetic disk), and this is where a file is stored. A disk is essentially a random access device allowing retrieval of a record in an amount of time that is independent of where the record is stored. This random access capability of disks make them suitable for creating sophisticated structures. Because tapes are sequential in nature they are not appropriate for contemporary file structures. Therefore, we will not consider tapes as the storage media for files. Tapes are currently cheaper than disks, and therefore should not be ruled out for use in some systems for storage of immense amounts of data. An introduction of tapes would give rise to a tri-level memory hierarchy, with the main memory at the top level, magnetic disks at the middle level, and tape at the lowest level. Read and write optical disks are also becoming a viable option for mass storage due to their capacity and speed, these are also cheaper than tape. So, it is replacing the tape.

Therefore, it would be natural to place them at the lowest level in a tri-level memory hierarchy. As stated above, our discussion will be limited to two levels of memory hierarchy. Typically, files of records are invisible to the end user of contemporary computer systems, but they are an important component of a database system. Therefore, when the term user is used context of a file, this user could be a database system. For database developers and manufacturers a clear understanding of files is important.

Of paramount importance are the performance issues surrounding files. Let us assume that files are dynamic in nature. A file, once created, is updated continually; new records are added and existing records are modified and deleted. However, the most significant operation on files is retrieval of one or more records. If retrieval of records is not necessary, records can simply be dumped into a log as a sequence of updates (perhaps on a tape and compact disk). The user is pre-occupied with the assumption that records are stored only to be retrieved in the future. To introduce the concept of a file and a file structure, it should first be known that a file has two distinct aspects: logical and physical; we refer to them simply as the logical file and the physical file. A logical file is simply a set of records.

The bi-level memory makes the concepts of retrievals and updates more interesting and dictates that we provide an integrated solution to them. Different physical representations called file structures are possible for a file. A physical file refers to the state of a file in the disk. The desire to obtain good performance in a system with bi-level memory hierarchy demands that the records of a logical file be stored in a physical file in containers called buckets.

Because files are continually updated, file structures must allow physical files to be elastic so that they can grow (and shrink) dynamically. Obviously, the growth of a physical file should be graceful without necessitating abrupt disruptions in performance. File elasticity is achieved through chaining and splitting. Chaining is a simple idea and it can be used in any file structure. It allows containers to be more elastic by allowing buckets to be chained. Chaining is generally a good short-term measure to make a file elastic. A rule of thumb is that chaining makes updates quicker at the cost of retrievals. Chaining makes a file locally elastic and continues to deteriorate the performance for records in the locality where chaining is used. Clearly, chaining by itself is not enough to provide needed elasticity to a file.

Splitting is the fundamental tool for making a file elastic. Splitting provides a good long-term measure to expand a file. Splitting is perhaps the most useful idea in file structures; different ways of splitting lead to different file structures. It would not be a gross exaggeration to say that splitting is the most important primitive operation on physical files. However, chaining is not always dispensable in favor of splitting. For example, an important splitting technique, called linear splitting requires the file to be locally elastic, an environment that can be facilitated by chaining.

10.2 GOALS OF FILE STRUCTURES

Every step away from the physical attributes of the computer system toward a purely logical view allows the programmer to focus on the business problem and ignore the hardware's characteristics and to employ third- and fourth-generation languages that improve programmer productivity. The shift away from the physical toward the logical also improves portability. This shift does introduce inefficiencies and reduces response time. The goals for study of files structures is to develop an understanding of the alternatives so that application systems can be developed that minimizes response time, reduce the amount of data transmitted unnecessarily, and reduce wasted secondary storage. Moreover, these should be accomplished without resorting to unnecessarily complex processing algorithms that might hamper subsequent software maintenance activities. And further, design decisions should not unnecessarily compromise portability.

10.3 FILE SYSTEMS

After a disk is formatted, it is ready to store data. Because the sector oriented disk organization by FAT is the most popular mean to utilize disk space, we will assume sector-oriented organization is used. In theory, to do any disk data input/output, a programmer needs only the following two low-level disk input/output (I/O) functions:

- ReadSector (SectorAddress);
- WriteSector (SectorAddress);

These low-level functions usually are supported in the disk device driver and they give the programmer complete control of disk storage usage. As a result, disk performance can be optimized to meet specific data requirements of an application. To take advantage of power of this approach, however, the programmer has to do lots of work. For example, he/she needs to map the application data structures to the sector organization, manage disk space allocation, and design efficient disk I/O methods. These tasks which require the knowledge of disk devices and operating system internals, are not for the majority of programmers, who usually have a tight project schedule and have no low-level system programming skills. Another problem with this approach is that it is very difficult to share a disk space among applications. Since this approach allows programmers to call the sector read/write functions as they see fit, there is no central coordination of the sector space usage. Without a central coordination, an application could not know whether a particular sector is used or free. To remedy the problems just mentioned, a system software layer between a low-level sector view and a high-level application program data abstraction is definitely needed.

In most operating systems, there is a subsystem called file system, which is designed to make use of secondary storage devices in a convenient and orderly manner. Although a file system can be implemented on various storage devices, it is most commonly implemented on disks. For this reason, we will mainly discuss file systems implemented on disks, which appropriately called disk file systems. Since disk file systems are so common, the term file system is often used to refer to a disk file system. But, keep in mind that there are other non-disk file systems, viz., ISO 9660 CD-ROM file system and RAM file systems (also called RAM disks.) A file system is usually a part of or installed on top of an operating system (like UNIX or Windows). The design objectives of a file system include the following:

- Providing higher-level abstraction of data (vs. bits or bytes stored in sectors)
- Allowing many users to use the same disk I/O each user can use disk space allocated to him/her securely.
- Having high disk space utilization
- Having good disk I/O performance

10.3.1 Basic Concepts of Files and File Systems

A file can be defined loosely as a collection of related data and a file system is a software module that provides file-related services. To maximize the flexibility of file usage, the interpretation of data stored in a file should be completely up to the file's user or creator. A file may contain a computer program, an experiment data set, a word-processor document, a list of customer names and addresses, a digital image, or a digital movie. The list of types of data contained in files is virtually endless. As a result, the file system should not impose a data interpretation mechanism, which might unnecessarily limit its applications. We know that a byte is the most basic unit of data. Other types of data such as names and numbers can be built from sequences of bytes. Therefore, a simple and useful definition of files is that a file is **a sequence of bytes**. In fact, this definition of files is used in UNIX and Windows.

10.3.1.1 File System Services

Before we discuss the design of a file system, a logical question to ask is, what file services it should provide and what the design criteria should be considered to implement these services. The desired file services can be divided into three categories:

1. File data storage and retrieval: In this category of services, the file system needs to know where to store the data on disk and how to locate and retrieve them on demand as fast as possible.

2. File naming and file attributes maintenance: How is a file named? The file name is the means for human users to tell the file system which file they want. Additionally, there are other file attributes needed. Here, file attributes refer to those file properties (not the data), which may be of interests to the users. Many file attributes could be supported in a file system. The following list gives some of the most common attributes supported.
   - owner or creator
   - file type
   - creation date and time
   - last access (read or write) data and time
   - protection (who can use a file and how)
   - size
3. File system application program interface (API): A file system API allows programmers to write applications for end users to use the file system services. **Figure** 10.1 illustrates this file system API application.

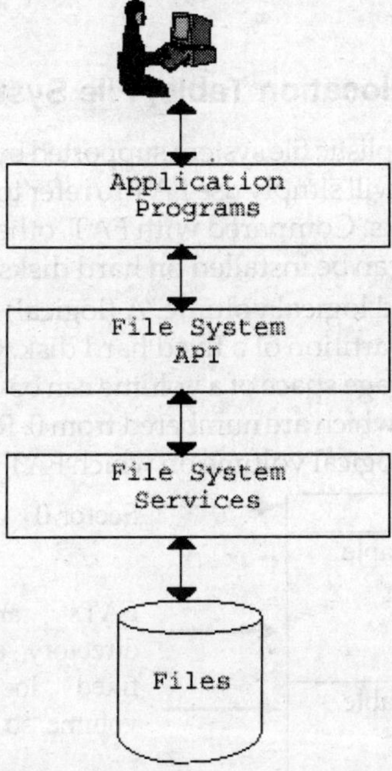

Figure 10.1 System file Organization

10.3.1.2 Disk Space Allocation

There are several ways to allocate disk space to files. The smallest unit of disk space allocation is a sector. This entails that even if a file only needs a few bytes of disk space, it still needs one sector. As a result, most space in that sector is unused or wasted. This problem of space-waste internal to a sector is called **internal fragmentation**. A large file may use thousands of sectors and in that case, the internal fragmentation is negligible with respect to the total space actually used.

As part of normal file operations, new data are constantly inserted into and data are deleted from a file. Consequently, the sectors used by a file may scatter all over the disk surface after the file has been used for a long period of time. We say that a file is fragmented if the sectors used by the file scatter all over the disk. The sequential processing of a fragmented file (i.e., to read or write from the beginning to the end of the file) is very inefficient. To improve the performance of sequential processing, some file systems may use lager allocation units or even user-defined units. In Windows, a cluster is a fixed number of "physically" consecutive sectors. In UNIX, a block has similar meaning as a cluster in Windows. An extent is a user-defined unit that could range from several consecutive sectors to several consecutive cylinders. Either a cluster or an extent can be used as the disk allocation unit.

Since making data of a file stored in close proximity on disk can improve the performance of sequential processing, a larger disk allocation unit has the advantage of better file processing performance. The penalty of this performance improvement, of course, is larger internal fragmentation.

Suppose that the block (or cluster) is used as the disk allocation unit. Then, the file system needs to have a mechanism to keep track of what blocks are used (i.e., allocated to which files) and what blocks are free. In general, there are two approaches to keep track of disk space allocation and usage. The first is to use a single table, commonly called File Allocation Table (FAT), for that purpose. The second approach is to use a table to keep track of all free blocks and a separate area per file to keep track of all blocks allocated to a file. The MS-DOS FAT file system uses the first approach, whereas the UNIX file system uses the second approach.

10.3.2 The MS-DOS FAT (File Allocation Table) File System

The FAT file system is the most simplistic file system supported by MS-DOS, Windows 9x, Windows NT, and OS/2 operating systems. We will simply use FAT to refer to the FAT file. FAT can be installed on hard disks as well as on floppy disks. Compared with FAT, other more sophisticated file systems such as the Windows NT file system can be installed on hard disks, but not on floppy disks.

FAT can be installed on a so-called logical volume. A (logical) volume can be an entire physical unit (such as a floppy disk) or only a partition of a fixed hard disk. On PC, a volume is referenced by a drive letter: A:, B:, C:, D:, etc. The storage space of a volume can be conveniently viewed as organized into a consecutive sequence of sectors, which are numbered from 0. Recall that a sector usually contains 512 bytes worth of data. The map of a logical volume on which FAT is installed is given in **Figure** 10.2.

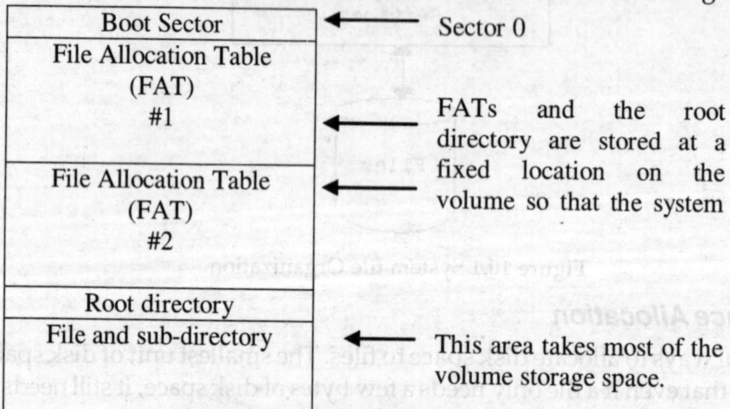

Figure 10.2 Map of a FAT Volume.

At heart of FAT volume is the FAT, which essentially contains a set of linked lists, each of which links all the clusters allocated to a file. As such, the integrity of the file allocation table is very critical to the stored data. If the FAT is damaged, it may be very difficult to recover the disk data. Therefore, it is very important to back up vital disk data from time to time.

10.3.2.1 File Allocation Table (FAT)

In FAT volume, several copies of FAT may be stored for reliability purpose, which is stored at a known location on the disk and contains disk space allocation information. Conceptually speaking, the table is a linear array of entries, one per cluster. For the sake of discussion, assume that the clusters on the disk are numbered in an ascending order starting from 1 and the table entries are also indexed starting with 1. The nth entry in the array can contain any one of the three values representing three possible states of the nth cluster.

These three possible values are:

- a valid cluster number, which is the number of the next cluster in the chain of clusters that are allocated to a file.
- an EOF mark - a special value that tells FAT this cluster is the last cluster allocated to a file.
- a FREE mark - a special value that says this cluster is free.

In FAT, the size of clusters and the size of the table entries depend on the size of the disk volume used. Table 10.1 shows this dependency.

Table 10.1 FAT Structure

Volume size (MB)	**Table entry size**	**Sectors per cluster**	**Cluster size**
0 – 15	12 bits	8	4K
16 – 127	16 bits	4	2K
128 – 255	16 bits	8	4K
256 – 511	16 bits	16	8K
512 – 1023	16 bits	32	16K
1024 – 2048	16 bits	64	32K

Given this FAT structure, how can FAT read a given file, from the beginning to the end of the file? First of all, FAT needs to know where to start the read. As we can see from the FAT structure, it does not have the information regarding where is the first cluster of a given file. In fact, FAT uses a directory system to supports a hierarchical file naming mechanism. A directory is a file (i.e., contains a sequence of bytes) with a special structure. Conceptually, a directory contains 32-byte directory entries, where each entry contains information (or attributes) about a file in FAT. In a directory entry, it contains the starting cluster number of the file. Given this starting cluster number, FAT can locate the first cluster allocated to the file and then using the file allocation table, it can allocate all subsequent clusters allocated to the file as needed.

10.3.2.2 The Tree-Structured Directory System

Users of a file system usually reference files in the file system by descriptive, user-defined names. The name of a file is chosen by the file creator to make the intended use of the file clear. What file naming rules are used in a file system? Given a file name, how does a file system locate the file attributes as well as file data? We discuss next how FAT deals with these questions.

FAT File and directory Naming Conventions: FAT employs a tree-structured directory system to support a hierarchical file naming system. FAT uses 8.3 file naming convention and all file names must be created with the ASCII character set. Specifically, the name of a file or directory can be up to eight characters long {DOS}, then a period (.) separator, and up to three character extension. The name must start with either a letter (i.e., a-z and A-Z) or number and can contain any printable ASCII characters except for the following:

. " \ / [ ] : ; | = , and space

If any of these characters are used, unexpected results may occur. File names are not case-sensitive. This means uppercase and lowercase letters have the same meanings. For example, the following file names all reference to the same file:

```
mydata.dat  MYDATA.DAT  MyData.dat  myDATA.DAT
```

As a matter of fact, FAT always converts lowercase letters in a file name to uppercase letters. The following names are reserved:

```
CON, AUX, COM1, COM2, COM3, COM4, LPT1, LPT2, LPT3, PRN, NUL
```

FAT supports two file specification methods: the absolute pathnames and the relative pathnames. A pathname is file names separated by the special character '\'. The following give examples of these two file specification methods:

```
Absolute pathnames
C:\MSoffice\word\document\my.doc
Relative pathnames (i.e., relative to the current working directory)
mydoc.coc
document\my.doc
```

FAT Directory Structure: FAT uses the root directory and as many sub-directories as needed to implement the hierarchical file naming system. The root directory has a fixed size and contains 255 directory entries. As a result, we can create up to 255 files, including regular files and sub-directories, in the root directory. A (sub-) directory contains a variable number of directory entries. A directory entry is 32-byte long and contains file attribute information of the file and attribute bytes information {Table 10.2 and 10.3}.

Table 10.2 File Attribute Structure.

Byte offset (in HEX)	Field description
00	File name (8 characters)
08	File extension (3 characters)
0B	File attributes (1 byte)
0C	Reserved
16	Time created or last updated (2 bytes)
18	Date created or last updated (2 bytes)
1A	Starting cluster (2 bytes)
1C	File size in bytes (4 bytes)

When a disk volume is formatted, the user can assign a volume label to the volume. This volume label can have up to 11 characters long. A volume label is stored as a special type of entry in the volume's root directory.

Advantages of FAT

- Support "un-delete"
- Simple (i.e., little system overhead)
- Efficient for volumes of 200MB or less

Disadvantages of FAT

- 8.3 file naming (but Windows 95 and Windows NT support long filenames under FAT)
- Single-user file system (no protection)
- Reliability is compromised by single-sector failures

Table 10.3 File Attribute Bytes Information.

Bit position	Meaning (if set, i.e., if bit is 1)
0	Read-only (i.e., write or delete will fail)
1	Hidden-file (excluded from normal search)
2	System-file (excluded from normal search)
3	Volume label (can exist only in the root directory)
4	Sub-directory
5	Archive bit (set whenever file is modified)
6	Reserved
7	Reserved

10.3.3 The UNIX File System

The UNIX File System is given in **Figure** 10.3 and File Mode is illustrated in **Figure** 10.4. The unit of disk space allocation unit is blocks each disk volume (i.e., partition) is divided into five areas.

1. Boot area: Loading and executing this block can start up the UNIX operating system.
2. Super block: This block specifies the boundaries of the next three areas on the volume, contains the head of the free list of blocks, etc.
3. The i-node area: This area contains a fixed number of i-nodes, each of which contains information about a file.
4. File data area (data blocks)
5. Swap area (for operating system use)

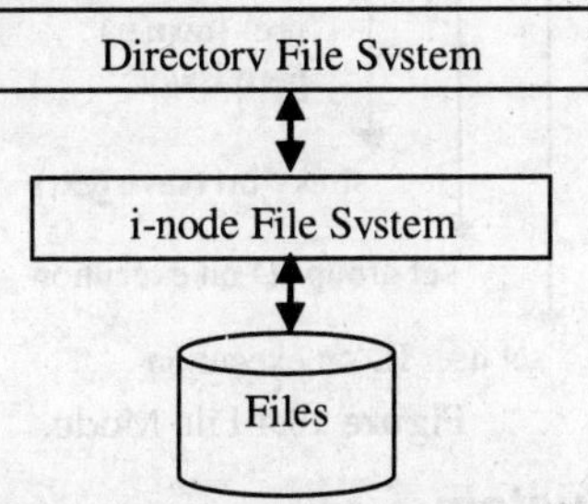

Figure 10.3 UNIX File System.

10.3.3.1 The i-node File System (Flat File System)

The i-node area contains a fixed number of i-nodes, each of which contains file attributes and pointers to data blocks of a file. In this sense, a file is represented by an i-node. In other words, if an i-node is given, the file system knows exactly everything about the file represented by the i-node. The i-nodes in the i-node area are numbered sequentially from 0 to n-1, where n is the number of i-nodes in the i-node area. These numbers are called i-numbers. The i-nodes of i-numbers 0 and 1 are reserved. The remaining i-nodes are used for files or directories (i.e., sub-directories). An i-node contains the following fields (as defined in the system header file **inode.**h):

1. File owner identifier (the command **chown** can be used to change the owner.)
2. File type
    1. regular directory
    2. character or block special (device drivers)
    3. FIFO (pipes)

3. File mode word: The file-mode word contains file permissions among others. The UNIX command
   $ chmod [ugoa][+-] [rwxst]
   can be used to changed the permissions. Only the owner of a file or the super-user can change the file mode of the file {**Figure** 10.4}.
4. File last accessed (i.e., opened) time
   File last modified time
   Modified time of this i-node
5. File size in bytes (32 bits)
   Number of (hard) links to the file
   Thirteen data block addresses or pointers
   1-9 direct block pointers
   10 indirect block pointer
   11 double indirect block pointer
   12 triple indirect block pointer

The file mode word is shown in shown in **Figure 10.4**.

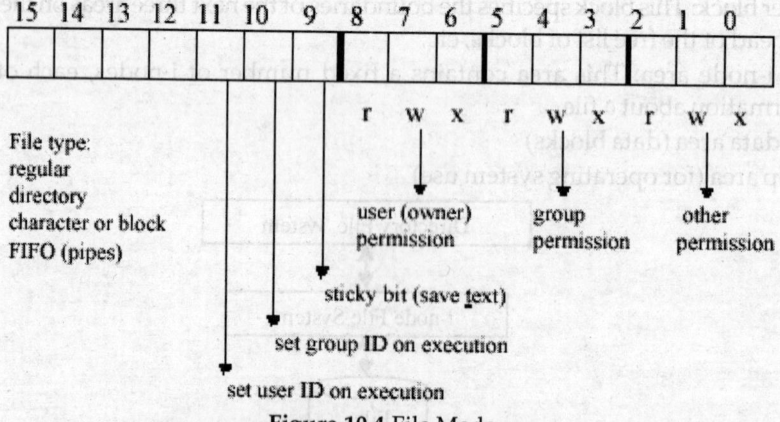

Figure 10.4 File Mode.

10.3.3.2 The Directory File System

There are two approaches to providing a file naming system: flat naming space and hierarchical naming space. The UNIX directory file system provides a hierarchical file naming system for the files referenced internally by i-nodes. The root directory is represented by the i-node of i-number 2. Conceptually, a UNIX directory contains directory entries, each of which contains two fields: file name and i number. For example, the root directory may contain entries as shown in **Table 10.4**.

Table 10.4 Root Directory Contents

File name	i number
.	2
..	2
usr	201
bin	45
etc	38
lost+found+etc	67
…	

Each directory entry maps a file name to an i-number (hence to an i-node). In other words, the named file is represented by the mapped i-node. For example, in the above example, the named file **bin** is the file represented by i-node 45. The system can read i-node 45 to find out everything (file type, file permissions, file data, etc.) about the file called **bin**. As such, a directory entry is also called a hard link (to an i-node file) in UNIX jargon. The file, **bin**, is a directory, which contains "links" to the files contained in the directory.

Now we will introduce some basic concepts in the following sections, which are considered during the discussion of over all file structure.

10.4 FILE STRUCTURE ANALYSIS CONCEPT

There is one important distinction that must be made at the outset when discussing file structures. And that is the difference between the logical and physical organization of the data. On the whole a file structure specifies the logical structure of the data, that is the relationships that exist between data items independently of the way in which these relationships may actually be realized within any computer. The physical organization is much more concerned with optimizing the use of the storage medium, when a particular logical structure is stored on, or in it. Typically for every unit of physical store there will be a number of units of the logical structure (probably records) to be stored in it. For example, if we want to store a tree structure on a magnetic disk, the physical organization must be concerned with the best way of packing the nodes of the tree on the disk given the access characteristics of the disk.

10.4.1 User's view of a file: the logical file

In many business applications, there is a common need to store information about people and things, specifically about those properties relevant to the applications at hand. Examples include:

- An insurance company needs to have information about its customers, claims, and its own employees.
- A library needs to have information about its users and books.
- A video rental store needs to have information about its customers and movie titles in stock.
- A university needs to have information about its students, faculty, staffs, degrees offered, courses and classes taught in each semester, etc.

Of all these applications mentioned above, we could identify a very important common characteristic of the data. The kind of data required for an application domain to keep track of information about each person (or thing) has rather uniform structure and only the data values vary from person to person. For a university, it may require the following data for its students who are getting fellowship:

Name (last, middle initial, and first)
Enrollment number
Department
Amount of fellowship

In C we can define this collection of data as a C struct like this:

```
struct Student
{
    char name[30];
    int ID;
    int Dept;
```

```
    int Fship;
    };
```

Some observations:

1. There are many alternatives C structures for the required student information. For example, to store the student name we can define three string fields: FirstName, Minit, and LastName (instead of just one Name field). This structure selection decision is an important problem in information processing, called record (or database) design.
2. Different applications have different data requirement characteristics. In general, we can classify data requirement characteristics into the following categories:
   - Simple data structure with relatively small volume of data (e.g., personal data)
   - Simple data structure with large volume of data (e.g., business applications data)
   - Complex data structure with relatively small volume of data (e.g., Computer-Aided Design data)
   - Complex data structure with large volume of data (e.g., Geographical Information Systems)

A record can be defined as a set of fields, each of which describes a certain aspect of a person or thing relevant to a particular application. For example, the record

Adam, 151, 54, 15K

describes the student's name, enrollment number, Department number, and amount of fellowship (Fship) he/she is getting. Note: here we use comma (,) to separate fields to make it easy to read.

A record type is a set of records of the same record structure. The record structure determines how many fields in a record and field structures. A field structure, in turn, determines syntax as well as semantics of the possible values that are allowed in a field. It is important to understand the different roles of records, record structures, and field structures play in information processing. While a record contains the data specific to a person or thing, the record structure tells the user how to read or interpret the data. Both the record structure and records must be stored in the computer for automatic and correct information processing.

A record may contain several fields called attributes. At the logical level a file is a set of records. As stated above, we are assuming that all records in a file have the same attributes and size.

Example 4.1. Table 10.5 shows an std file, which consists of records of students who are entitled for the fellowship (Fship). Each record contains four attributes.

Table 10.5 User's view of std (Name, ID, Dept, Fship) file.

Name	ID	Dept	Fship
Anna	151	54	15K
Art	306	52	15K
Ben	200	32	22K
Chi	310	36	21K
Chin	101	26	20K
Don	311	15	15K
Joe	312	30	14K
John	305	40	15K
Mary	165	25	11K
Paul	160	15	26K
Pete	300	38	16K
Roy	180	28	23K

- Name: Name of a student is up to 30 characters. We assume that no two students have the same name.
- ID: Student Enrollment number, an integer in the range 101...9999. We also assume that no two students have the same ID. (Primary key)
- Dept: An integer between 10 and 99.
- Fship: A dollar value up to 50.

We assume that the Name, ID, Branch and Result require 30, 4, 2, and 2 bytes, respectively. Therefore, each record requires 38 bytes.

The logical operations that can be performed on files are categorized into two categories and for the **std** file, illustrations of operations are given in **Example 4.2**:

- Update operations: This operation allows one to insert, modify, and delete records.
- Retrieval operations: This operation allows one to retrieve records.

Example 4.2. The following is an assortment of operations that one may perform on **std** file.

(a) Given the name of a student, find the record.
(b) Find who belongs in Dept 15.
(c) Insert a new record.
(d) Give a raise to a student.
(e) Delete a student's record.
(f) Correct the Name of a student.

10.4.2 Keys

The selection of a key field for a record can sometimes be troubling. Studying the purpose of a key field can provide insights to the attributes of a good key. The first purpose of a primary key is to serve as an identifier for a particular record. The value of the primary key be **unique** for each record. At worst, duplication will cause the data for one record to overwrite the data for another record. At best, duplication leads to confusion and a requirement for human intervention, which is unacceptable in unattended batch processing.

Another characteristic of a key value is related to uniqueness that is a key value should not be capable of multiple interpretations. This characteristic is called being **unambiguous**. To that end, rules are formed about the key values, e.g., alphabetic characters must be upper case, alphabetic characters may be either case, numeric must be in display mode, blanks are not allowed, etc. A key value that meets all of the rules established for a given file is said to be in canonical form. One of the tasks of the programmer is to provide editing routines that will insure a key value is in canonical form before record access is attempted.

Further, to avoid unnecessary file maintenance (resorting files, rearranging records, resorting indexes, or rearranging index entries) the key value should be **unchanging**. Not only does a changing key result in undesirable file maintenance, it will also hamper data mining and longitudinal studies of business activities that use archival records.

To meet the goals above, it has often been found that real-world data cannot serve as a key. In those cases, the programmer must create a field and assign arbitrary, unique, unambiguous, unchanging, data-less values to that field. An in-house part numbering system based on the relative key of the record associated with a given part would be an example of a data-less value.

The purpose of a file structure is to support efficient execution of update and retrieval operations. The user operations on files often involve attributes and their values, for example, "who belongs in department 15" and "give a fellowship raise to a student named John." An attribute or a set of attributes needing a good performance is loosely termed a key. We often have a key in mind and use k as a variable to denote a value of such key. Given a key value k, we use <u>k</u> to denote any record whose key value is k. The file structures are building around keys. More formal definitions of two different kinds of keys are given below.

A unique key (or simply a key) is a minimal set of attributes that uniquely identifies a record. For std file, we note that Name is a (unique) key because for a given name there is only one record. For example, in std file of **Table 10.5**, Name = Chi identifies the record (Chi; 310; 36; 21K). Using our notation, this record can also be denoted, as <u>Chi</u>. ID is also a unique key. ID value of 305 identifies the record (John; 305; 40; 15K), also denoted as <u>305</u>. Clearly, Dept is not a unique key. Note that {Name, ID} also uniquely identify a record, but we do not consider {Name, ID} as a unique key because it is not minimal.

A non-unique key is any set of attributes. A non-unique key does not necessarily identify a record uniquely. For example, Dept is a non-unique key. Dept = 15 gives us two records. Note that in the context where Dept is being considered as a key, each of the two records can be denoted as <u>15</u>. Similarly, Fship is a non-unique key. Another non-unique key is {Dept, Fship} because it is possible that two or more students belong in the same department and have the same Fship.

Suppose K is a unique or a non-unique key, and k is a K-value, then all records that have k as their key values are called K-synonyms, or simply synonyms if K is clear from the context. If K is a unique key, K-synonyms are unique. On the other hand, if K is a non-unique key, a given key value can lead to multiple synonyms. For example in Result file of Table 10.5, records of Don and Paul are Dept-synonyms because both Don and Paul belong in department 15.

10.4.3 System architecture

As stated earlier, we assume that we are dealing with computer systems with two levels of memory. At the upper level we have the main memory, and at the lower level we have the disk. This does not rule out systems with multiple levels of memory hierarchy. For example, the main memory may have a cache above it. But in such a situation we would consider the main memory + cache combination as the main memory and we would still assume a two-level memory hierarchy.

It turns out that disks are much slower than the main memory. Accessing a disk has a large overhead associated with it. For this reason fetching only a few bytes at a time is not a good idea. It leads to the concept of a block in operating systems. The size of a block is fixed by the operating system and is treated as the smallest unit for all input and output. For example, the block size in VAX/VMS is 512 bytes (0.5 KB).

Bucket: Since a block has a fixed size, the concept of a block too rigid. Files naturally lead to the concept of a bucket. A bucket consists of multiple blocks. We will assume that the size of a bucket is fixed for a given file. Therefore, a bucket can hold a fixed maximum number of records; this maximum number of records is termed the bucket capacity. Clearly, for a given state of a file, the number of records may vary from bucket to bucket, but all the buckets have the same maximum size. In other words, bucket capacity is a file level parameter. It is obviously desirable that a bucket be stored in contiguous sectors; let's assume that this is the case. The time needed to transfer the contents of a bucket is denoted as b. Note that s and l are fixed for a disk and that they do not vary from bucket to bucket even across different files on the same disk. On the other hand, transfer time depends upon the physical size of a bucket. The access time, T, for a bucket is given by the equation below. Here s is the seek time, l is the latency, and b is the time needed to transfer the bucket.

$$T = s + l + b$$

Buffers: Let us assume that a file is too large to fit into the main memory. This means that we can only bring small portions of the file into the main memory at a time. To facilitate this we must use a certain amount of space in the main memory, called the buffer space, which acts as a window to the file. The buffer space is a premium resource, so we choose its size conservatively. In order to fix terminology for a given file, a single buffer must have the same size as a bucket for that file. Therefore, the buffer space consists of an integral number of buffers. We will use the symbols a and b, sometimes with subscripts, to denote addresses of buffers.

Example 4.3. Let's suppose that a block consists of 512 bytes. Now if there is a file where a record consists of 200 bytes, 2 records fit in a block. In this situation 400 bytes in a block are occupied but 112 bytes remain unused. This would waste about 21.8% space in the block. Note that this is a true wastage, as this space will never be used. For the same file, if the bucket size is fixed at 2 blocks, a bucket would have 1024 bytes and capacity would be 5. The wastage would now be reduced to 2.3%, which may be acceptable.

Example 4.4. As another example, what if the size of a record is 764 bytes? We cannot fit a record in a 512 byte block and it has to be splitted across block boundaries. We may choose a bucket size of 3 blocks capable of holding 2 records. In this case we would waste less than 1% space. **Figure** 10.5 shows a simplified model of the computer system. This model basically captures the fact that the memory is a two-level hierarchy, and that all I/O operations use buckets as units of information.

Example 4.5. In the context of the student file of Example 4.1, we assume that the system block consists of 64 bytes. (This does not imply existence of any real system with such a small block size.) As in Example 4.1 we will continue to assume that the size of a student record is 38 bytes. Throughout chapter the student file will be given a bucket size of 128 bytes, spanning 2 blocks. Therefore, the bucket capacity is 3, and a bucket can hold 0 to 3 records. Note that 14 bytes are wasted in every bucket. We must also note that the block size of 64 bytes is rather small, and again this does not imply existence of any real system with such a block size. The reason for choosing a small block size is to keep the bucket size small, thereby give good, short examples.

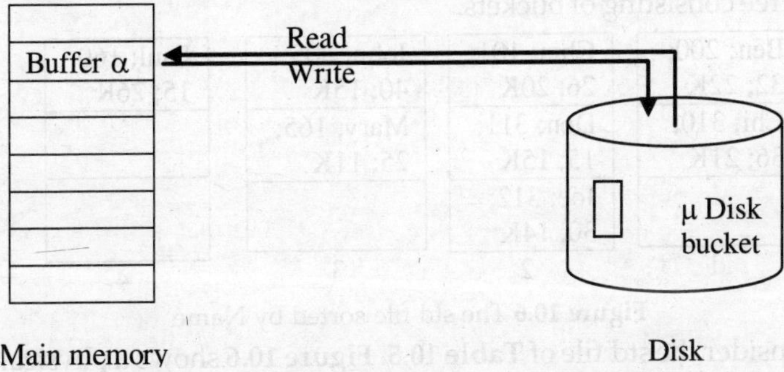

Figure 10.5 Model of a Computer System

Wastage at bucket boundaries: As the bucket is unit of I/O, in order to access a record from the disk, we have to access the whole bucket in which the record resides. We do not split a record across a bucket boundary, so some wastage at bucket boundaries becomes inevitable.

Example 4.6. To eliminate wastage at bucket boundaries, the file of Example 4.3 must have buckets containing 25 blocks each. a bucket will have to contain 25 blocks. To perform any operations on this file would require at least 25 blocks of main memory, which seems rather excessive. So when choosing a bucket size for a given file, we must try to reduce the wastage due to boundary alignment; but it is not goal to eliminate it. With reasonable reductions, wastage due to boundary alignment can be disregarded.

Space utilization: As stated above wastage at bucket boundaries is inevitable, but we neglect it. Independent of this fact, it is common in contemporary file structures not to fully utilize the capacity of a bucket. For example, in a B^+-tree, an important file structure; on average a bucket may be 70% full. Note that this underutilization is in addition to the wastage due to boundary alignment. The idea is to store fewer than maximum number of records in a bucket, so that it can absorb insertions without demanding frequent changes in the structure of the file. In order to maintain a good time performance, modern file structures, as a rule underutilize disk space.

Assume a fixed file in a given context with the total number of records in the file is denoted as n and the number of buckets in the file denoted as N with bucket capacity c. The space utilization, denoted as u, is defined as the ratio of number of the records actually in the file and the number of slots for records in the buckets allocated for the file. Hence, the space utilization is given by the following equation. Note that space utilization is independent of the wastage at bucket boundaries.

```
u = n/(N * c)
```

Example 4.7. We are given a file with 5000 records, with each record consisting of 200 bytes. The bucket size is 1024 bytes. Currently, 1200 buckets are being used in the file. Bucket capacity $c = \lfloor 1024/200 \rfloor = 5$. Note that if we utilized the capacity of every bucket, the file would only need $5000/c = 1000$ buckets. Space utilization is $5000/(1200 \times 5) = 5000/6000 = 83.3\%$. The average number of records in a bucket = 5 ´ 0.833 = 4.17. Note that in the above example 24 bytes, or 2.3% space, is wasted in every bucket. This is true wastage; it will not be used under any circumstances. Wastage at the bucket boundaries is inevitable, but it is not an important issue. In contrast, space utilization is an important parameter in file structures.

10.4.4 Physical files

A (user) file is stored by the system as a physical file. A physical file consists of buckets of the same size. A file structure is an organization for a physical file. In this chapter we will study several interesting file structures. A simple file structure is an array of buckets. Another example of a file structure is a search tree consisting of buckets.

0	1	2	3	4	5
Anna;151; 54; 15K	Ben; 200; 32; 22K	Chin; 101; 26; 20K	John; 305; 40; 15K	Paul; 160; 15; 26K	Pete; 300; 38; 16K
Art; 306; 52; 15K	Chi; 310; 36; 21K	Don; 311; 15; 15K	Mary; 165; 25; 11K		Roy; 180; 28; 23K
		Joe; 312; 30; 14K			

Figure 10.6 The std file sorted by Name

Example 4.8. Consider the std file of **Table 10.5**. **Figure 10.6** shows a physical file that is used to store the std file. The file structure here is simple: it is a sorted array of buckets. There are 6 buckets with addresses 0…5. Note that the file is physically sorted by Name. This is perhaps one of the simplest (not necessarily a good) file structure.

10.4.5 Primary vs. Secondary Structure

As stated before, all keys do not necessarily give good performance. Therefore, certain keys are chosen by a user to be more important than others. Formally such keys are said to be designated. Designation of a key normally implies that there is a file structure supporting fast access for that key. Let us revisit the std file of Table 10.5. Note that IDs are much like social security numbers, and they are not assigned in the alphabetical order of names. If a file is sorted by Name, then it is not sorted by ID, and vice-versa. If we want to find a student record by ID, the file sorted by Name, as in **Figure** 10.6, is of no help. We simply have to scan through the file one bucket at a time.

How can we speed the searches by ID? One obvious answer is to keep the file sorted by ID. But then the file would not be sorted by Name and searches by name would become expensive. Can we have good performances for both Name and ID? One choice is to maintain two copies of the std file, one sorted by Name and the other sorted by ID. Such duplication is not desirable because in addition to doubling the storage requirement, it increases the cost of updates and also increases potential for inconsistencies between the two copies. Note that we do not rule out duplication of records under some circumstances. For example, in a distributed system some replication of records may be considered desirable. Information about bank accounts at a particular bank may be replicated at the main office. Note such replication is necessary due to reasons other than the desire to support multiple keys.

A primary structure is one that pins the bucket where a record is stored. Suppose that every record is stored only once on a disk; a moment's thought would reveal that a given file could not have two primary structures. In this example, if we wish to keep the file sorted by Name, we cannot keep it sorted by ID. However, we can create (ID, bucket pointer) pairs for every record of the given file. Then we can store these pairs in another file and keep the file sorted by ID. A (primary key, primary bucket pointer) pair is called a secondary record, and a structure for secondary record is called a secondary structure. Note that if the number of secondary records is very large, therefore, a secondary structure is also a data structure for the disk. The buckets in a secondary structure are called secondary buckets.

0				
101	151	160	165	
2	0	4	3	

1				
180	200	300	305	306
5	1	5	3	0

2				
310	311	312		
1	2	2		

(a) Secondary index on std file by ID

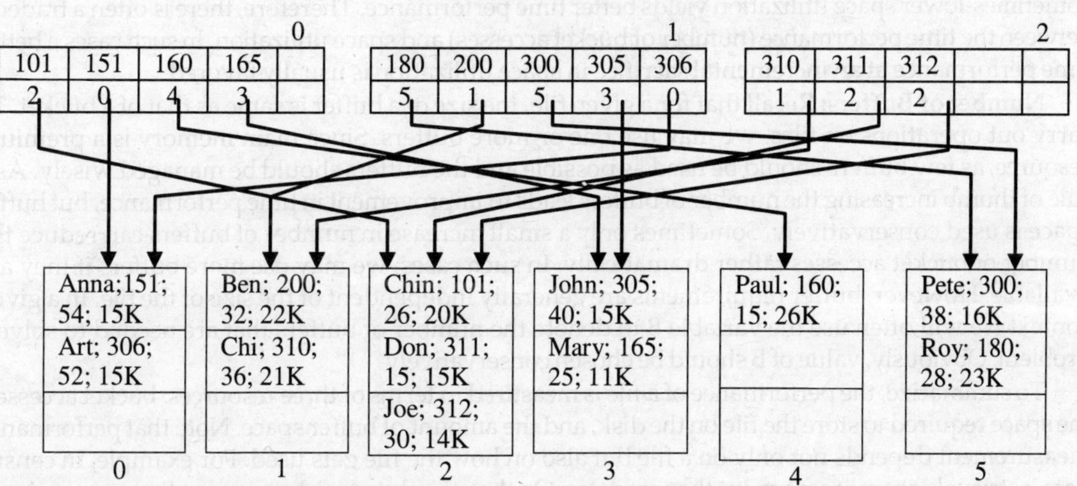

Figure 10.7 Primary and Secondary index view

Example 4.9. The file in **Figure** 10.6 is a primary structure for the std file, allowing fast retrievals by Name. Now ID adds a secondary structure to facilitate fast retrievals. Thus, the secondary record is a pair of the form (ID, bucket#). For the state of the std file as in **Figure** 10.6, the secondary records are (101,2), (151,0), (160,4), (165,4), (180,5), (200,1), (300,5), (305,3), (306,0), (310,1), (311,2), (312,2).

We assume that a primary bucket pointer consists of 2 bytes. In Example 4.1 it was assumed that an ID value requires 4 bytes. Therefore, a secondary record requires 6 bytes. Recall from Example 4.1

that a block consists of **38** bytes. The capacity of a secondary bucket is then 5 records. The secondary file, sorted by ID, is as shown in **Figure** 10.7(a). **Figure** 10.7(b) shows how to logically visualize the primary index and secondary indices on the std. It is clear that only one primary structure is possible, but any numbers of secondary structures are possible. Note that unique versus non-unique keys on one hand and primary structure versus secondary structures on the other, are mutually independent concepts. In summary, we can have one primary structure with respect to a unique key or with respect to a non-unique key. In contrast we can have any number of secondary structures with respect to unique and non-unique keys.

10.4.6 File Performance

Now let us see resources needed in handling of files as well as the relative importance of these resources.

Number of Disk Accesses: Disk accesses are slow; by comparison, we assume that processing is fast. Therefore, unless stated otherwise, the number of bucket accesses measures time performance. It is obvious that the cost of retrieving a record is at least 1 (1 bucket access); this case arises when we know the address of the bucket where the record is stored. Yet we often do not know the address of the bucket where the record is stored. If there is no structure on the file, then in the worst case we have to read all buckets in the file. The objective of file structures is to keep bucket accesses to a minimum.

The cost of inserting a record is at least 2 because the bucket where the record is to be stored is first read into a buffer. This buffer may contain several records. If the bucket is not full, the record to be inserted is appropriately placed into the buffer and the bucket is written back to the disk. If the retrieved bucket is full the insertion is more expensive.

Disk Space Required: Disk space is the amount of space required to store the file on the disk. Obviously, in isolation of other considerations, full space utilization would be desirable. However, sometimes-lower space utilization yields better time performance. Therefore, there is often a tradeoff between the time performance (number of bucket accesses) and space utilization. In such cases a better time performance at an incremental sacrifice in space utilization is usually favored.

Number of Buffers: Recall that for a given file, the size of a buffer is same as that of a bucket. To carry out operations on files, we may use one or more buffers. Since main memory is a premium resource, as few buffers should be used as possible and the buffers should be managed wisely. As a rule of thumb increasing the number of buffers leads to improvement in time performance, but buffer space is used conservatively. Sometimes only a small increase in number of buffers can reduce the number of bucket accesses rather dramatically. In such cases, we may use more buffers if they are available. However, buffer requirements are generally independent of the size of the file. In a given context we will often use the variable B to denote the number of buffers that are needed to solve a problem. Obviously, value of B should be chosen conservatively.

To summarize, the performance of a file is measured in terms of three resources: bucket accesses, the space required to store the file on the disk, and the amount of buffer space. Note that performance measurement depends not only on a file but also on how the file gets used. For example, in census data, retrievals are more frequent than updates. On the other hand, airline reservations are updated rather frequently.

Example 4.10. Now let us revisit the operations of Example 4.2 for the std file sorted by Name. Although **Figure** 10.6 shows a possible state of the file, in what follows we assume that the file contains N buckets, where N is very large.

(a) Given the name of a student, find the record: Because the file is sorted by Name, use binary search, needing $\lceil \log_2 N \rceil$ bucket accesses. Note: if the file is not sorted, in the worst case the cost of this query would be N.

(b) Find who belongs in Dept = 15? The cost of this query is N, because the fact that the file is sorted by Name does not help us. The only way to answer this query is to scan through all the buckets of the file.

(c) Insert a new record. First do a binary search to find the bucket where the record may be stored. If that bucket has fewer than 3 records, store the record in that bucket. Cost in this case? $\lceil \log_2 N \rceil + 1$. What if the bucket is full? To keep the file sorted, we may need to move some records. For each bucket that changes, we need 2 bucket accesses, 1 for reading and 1 for writing.

(d) Give a raise to a student. We first search for the std record, change the Fship value and write the bucket containing the record back. The cost is $\lceil \log_2 N \rceil + 1$.

(e) Delete a student's record. A quick way is to search for the record and simply remove it from the bucket. Cost = $\lceil \log_2 N \rceil + 1$. However, this is not a totally satisfactory solution because the storage used by the deleted record has not been reclaimed.

(f) Correct the Name of a student. We cannot handle this in the same way as a raise because if the name is corrected the record may destroy the sorted-ness of the file. This operation can be handled by deletion of the student record followed by an insertion of the record with the correct values.

10.4.7 File Structure Implementation

A file is not directly accessible to the CPU. In order to process a record residing on the disk it has to be brought into the main memory. We will assume that a file consists of a sequence of buckets. We will use the symbols μ and ν, possibly with subscripts, to denote disk-bucket addresses, and α and β, possibly with subscripts, to denote buffers. The following operations are then available to us:

- read μ in α
- write α to μ

The read operation "read μ in α" brings the contents of the disk bucket μ into a buffer α, and the write operation "write α to μ" stores contents of α buffer α onto the disk bucket μ. Note that the bucket addresses μ and ν are at the file level. A disk can contain several files, and therefore it is necessary to map the bucket addresses to actual addresses on the disk. Throughout this chapter we assume that such a mapping is handled by the system. We do not take the cost of such mapping into account.

10.4.8 File Expansion

As records are inserted into a file, the file expands. This expansion is accomplished either by bucket expansion, address expansion, or a combination of the two. Similarly, as records are deleted from the file, the file contracts, such contraction is accomplished by bucket contraction or address contraction. File expansion is discussed below; file contraction is similar.

Bucket Expansion (Chaining): Note that the term bucket expansion is not to be taken literally. We have stated that for a given file a bucket has a fixed size. Therefore, in a literal sense a bucket neither expands nor contracts. Instead, we can chain a new bucket to an existing one, the advantage being that there is no need to create an independent address for the newly added bucket. The new bucket is reached by following a pointer from the old one. Clearly, this gives rise to the concept of a chain of buckets. A chain is a physical realization of an expandable bucket. The disadvantage of chaining is that it costs us an additional bucket access to follow every pointer. **Figure** 10.8 shows chaining (and also its graphical representation).

Two buckets are contiguous if in going from the first to the next there is no seek or latency. Storing a file as a sequence of contiguous buckets can eliminate latency. A cascade is defined to be a sequence of contiguous buckets. Thus, accessing an entire cascade consisting of m buckets requires one seek, one latency, and mb transfer time. In other words, the access time for a cascade consisting of m buckets is s + l + mb. The concept of a cascade presented here is not to be taken literally. What happens if a cascade needs to be larger than a cylinder, say three cylinders? We assume that cylinders are fairly large. More specifically, we assume that the time required for a single seek is negligible compared to the transfer time for a whole cylinder. Therefore, three cascades stored on portions of three cylinders can be considered as a single cascade. This allows us to imagine that a whole file, however large, can be stored as a single cascade. On the other hand, we cannot assume that every file is stored as a cascade. Moreover, even if a file is stored as a cascade, the physical order of the buckets, i.e., the order in which they appear in the cascade, may not be useful in a given situation. If a file is stored as a cascade, a traversal of the file in a physical order can be done in the time approximated by the transfer time for all the buckets of the file.

Address Expansion (Splitting): Making fewer disk accesses to accomplish a task is the single most important goal of file structures. Chaining can be used to expand a file quickly, but its long-term effect is expensive because it increases the cost of retrievals and updates. For a long-term maintenance of good performance, expansion of the address space is of critical importance. Splitting is a fundamental tool that is widely used in contemporary file structures. It allows a file to grow a few buckets (chains) at a time. As shown in **Figure** 10.9(a), the context is that we are given a full bucket μ, and we want to insert an additional record into it. The bucket μ is splitted into two buckets, μ, and a new bucket, ν. The existing records and the record being inserted are distributed in buckets μ and ν {**Figure** 10.9(b)}.

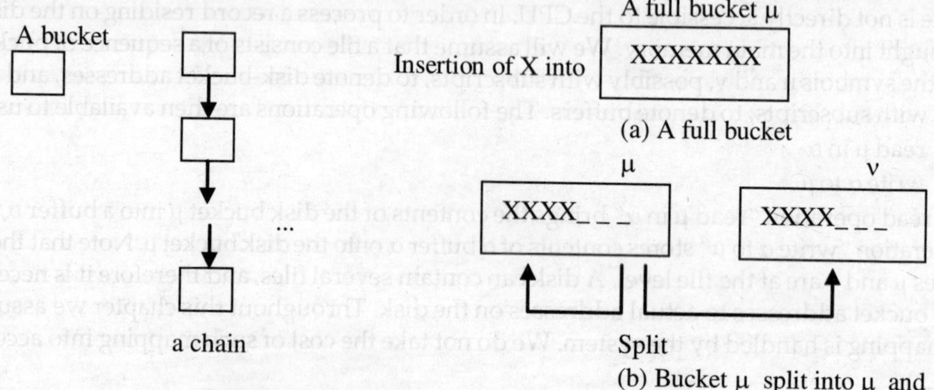

Figure 10.8 Chaining

Figure 10.9 Splitting

Splitting requires two buckets of buffer. One-bucket access brings a bucket μ to the buffer. The split then composed in the two buffers. Finally the buffers are written to disk buckets μ and ν. Thus, the cost of insertion using a single split is 3, compared to 2, the cost of an ordinary insertion in a non-full bucket.

To summarize, the main concept is that the new bucket ν is not chained to μ; rather, ν is integrated into a file structure so that ν becomes as accessible as μ. This is a basic idea, which has to be adopted with some twists in the context of a given file structure. It is important to note that the split improves performance of future insertions in m and ν.

10.5 SECONDARY STORAGE DEVICES

Good design is always responsive to the constraints of the medium and to the environment. This is as true for file structure design as it is for carvings in wood and stone. Given ability to create, open and close files and to seek, read and write we can perform the fundamental operations of the file construction. Now we need to look at the nature and limitations of the devices and systems used to store and retrieve files in order to prepare ourselves for design.

If files were stored just in memory, there is no separate discipline called file structures. The general study of data structures gives us all the tools we need to build file applications, but secondary storage devices very different from memory. One difference is that accesses to secondary storage take much more time than do accesses to memory. An even more important difference, measured in terms of design impact, is that not all accesses are equal. Good file structure design uses knowledge of disk and tape performance to arrange data in ways that minimize access costs. In this section we examine the characteristics of secondary storage devices. We begin with a look at the major media used in the storage and processing of files, magnetic tape and magnetic disks.

10.5.1 Disk Storage

Early disk storage units were quite expensive, and this expense served as motivation to develop file structures that conserved disk space while enabling efficient direct access. Today, disk storage is the preferred medium for secondary storage. Disk storage has several characteristics to recommend it: it is secure, requiring no handling provides both sequential and direct access to records; and it is reasonable in cost.

While tape storage is relatively simple, disk storage can be complex. While sequential access on disk is no more complex than on tape, direct access may involve complex file structures. Efficient use of these structures requires an understanding of the physical medium and the operating system components that perform the actual reading and writing of data on the disk.

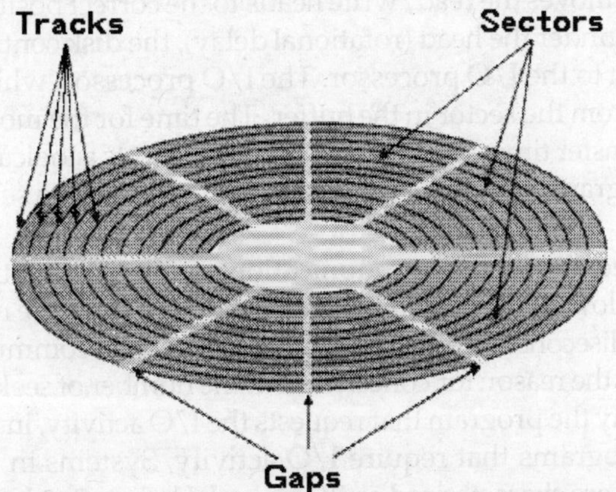

Figure 10.10 Surface of disk showing tracks and sectors.

Consider the disk platter. Regardless of physical diameter, the surface will be organized into rings of recording media called tracks. Vinyl phonograph platters have a single recording grove that spirals into the center from the outside of the surface. Magnetic disk platters are different; they have many tracks on a single surface, and the tracks are separated. Some disk drives have the tracks subdivided into sectors when the drive is formatted; other disk drives do not use sectors, but rather employ a blocking scheme to subdivide tracks. Perhaps the easiest arrangement to understand is the sectored disk.

Figure 10.10 shows a sectored arrangement with gaps between the sectors to allow the system's electronics time to perform data transfer. The image does not do justice to the capabilities of modern media. On even rather low-tech media such as 3.5 inch floppy disks, there are 40 tracks per side and 18 sectors per track; on close-tolerance hard drives there may be more than 800 tracks per side.

On disk, the divergence of the physical storage from the logical needs of the program becomes complete. Data is read and written in sectors or blocks, depending on which is used. The operating system determines when the physical reading or writing takes place based on its own assessment of logical reads and writes from the program and the data it knows already resides in buffers. **Buffers** are random access memory that the operating system uses as an intermediate collection point for data before it is written to disk or as a staging area for data that has been read from disk before it is turned over to the user's program. Buffers are sized to match the size of the sector or block that is used on the disk.

Consider what happens when the program issues a read instruction. First the operating system calls the file manager (a subprogram of the operating system) and turns the instruction over to the file manager. The file manager checks the file allocation table (FAT) for the availability of the file and checks to see if the instruction is consistent with its opening status. It also checks on file type, file ownership, and the user's permissions to access the file. Next the file manager checks to see where the next record is located from the file pointer. The file manager then checks to see if the sector containing the requested record is in one of the I/O buffers. If the requested record is in one of the buffers, it is transferred to the program without further ado.

Suppose that the sector containing the requested record is not in one of the buffers. The file manager would now issue an instruction to the I/O processor giving the cylinder, track and sector address and the buffer location in which to deposit the data from the sector. At this point, the I/O processor would query the disk controller if the drive is ready for reading. If the drive is ready for reading, the disk controller instructs the drive to move its heads to the correct position, cylinder, track, and sector. After the drive moves the read/write heads to the correct position (seek time) and waits for the correct sector to move under the head (rotational delay), the disk controller receives the data from the sector and passes it on to the I/O processor. The I/O processor, which holds the address of the buffer, deposits the data from the sector in the buffer. The time for the movement of the data from the disk to the buffer is the transfer time. The file manager now selects a logical record from the buffer and passes that data to the program by moving the data to the memory area set aside for the program's file description.

In the events described above, the communication among most of the participants occurred at nanosecond speeds. The slowest process in the entire sequence was the movement of the heads; this movement occurred at millisecond speeds. The ratio of seek time to communication time is in the range of 250,000 to 1. This ratio is the reason for concern about the number of seeks that I/O activities require. Not only does seeking delay the program that requests the I/O activity, in a multitasking environment it also delays all other programs that require I/O activity. Systems in which CPU operations are delayed by I/O operations are characterized as **I/O bound**. Unfortunately, most computer systems fall into that characterization. As a result, almost all of our efforts are aimed at achieving access to all of the needed data in a single seek.

10.5.1.1 Buffer Management

From the description above, one can see that the use of a buffer by the operating system is central to input and output operations. In fact, operating system often use several buffers in I/O operations. Consider again the output scenario described above. After the CPU fills one buffer according to program instructions, it must suspend any other output activity until the I/O processor completes its operations (probably including a seek). During this relatively long time, the CPU can do nothing more. What if the operating system had two buffers to use? While the I/O processor was sending one buffer's contents to the disk, the CPU could be filling the other buffer in response to program instructions. When the I/

O processor finishes with the first buffer, it begins processing the contents of the second buffer, and the first buffer is given to the CPU to fill. This process of exchanging buffers between CPU and I/O processor is called **double buffering**.

In the example above, both buffers were being used for output. It is not unusual for a system to employ two or more buffers, dividing the roles of the buffers among input and output. Consider all of the seeking that would result if only one buffer were assigned to a program that is reading from and writing to disk. First the system would have to seek to get the sector (or block) containing the desired record. After the correct record were passed to the program, a write statement would result in another seek to get the sector (or block) into which the output must be placed. Then after the successful write, another seek would be needed to get the sector (or block) from which the next record were required. In the case of sequential access, the fact that the correct sector might have been in the buffer previously does not help because it would have been replaced with the output sector (or block). To avoid this unnecessary seeking, most operating systems allocate at least two buffers to a file, one for input and one for output.

One scheme to overcome the buffer bottleneck is to employ buffer pooling. In this arrangement, the operating system maintains a pool of buffers. When a program performs an I/O operation, the operating system first checks all of the buffers to see if the affected sector (or block) might already be in memory. If it is, the needs of the program are accommodated without further ado. If the required sector is not in memory, then one of the buffers from the pool is selected to serve the I/O operation. Generally, a least-recently-used criterion is employed to determine exactly which buffer will be selected.

10.5.1.2 Hard Disk Drives

Compared with the time it takes to access an item in memory, disk accesses are always expensive. However, not all disk accesses are equally expensive. This has to do with the way a disk drive works. Disk drive belonging to a class of devices, i.e., magnetic disk known as direct access storage devices (DASDs) because they make it possible to access data directly. DASDs are contrasted with serial devices, the other major class of secondary storage devices. Magnetic disks come in many forms. So called hard disks offer high capacity and low cost per bit. Hard disks are most common disk used in every file processing.

Drives with multiple platters require a more sophisticated organization. The reason for this arises from the hardware itself. Consider a multiple-platter disk drive shown in **Figure 10.11**. It shows four platters mounted on a central spindle, which revolves and turns the platters. The read/write heads are mounted on a boom that moves the heads in and out to position the heads over a specified track. This movement is the portion of disk access that takes milliseconds of time. No data is recorded on the topmost surface nor on the bottommost surface. These surfaces serve as a cover to prevent dust, smoke, and other particles from resting on a recording surface. The underside of the top platter is surface 1, the top of the second platter is surface 2, the underside of the second platter is surface 3, and so on. In the image, the drive has six surfaces.

The heads in the image are positioned at the outer edge of the platters, which would be over track 1. To simplify the record keeping, the collection of all of the tracks that are available without any other movement of the boom is called a cylinder. In the image, the cylinder that is available is cylinder 1. The specific track that is being accessed in referred to by the number of the recording surface on which it is located. Movement of the boom and activation of the heads is accomplished by the disk controller. The sequence of events to access data in cylinder 2 on surface 3 would be to move the boom into cylinder 2 and then by electronic switching activate the head for the underside of the second platter.

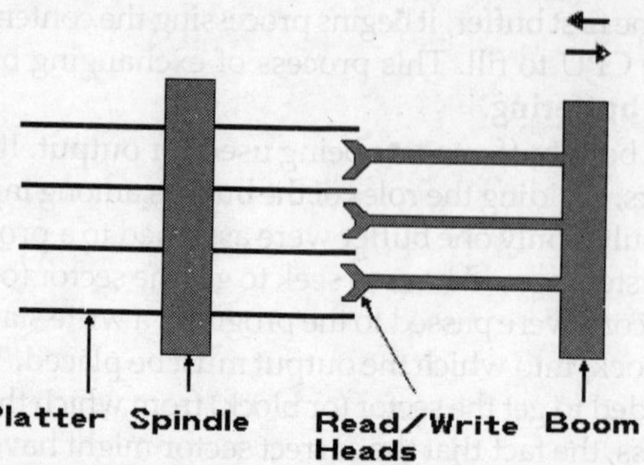

Figure10.11 Schematic illustration of disk drive

The information stored on a disk is stored on the surface of one or more platters. The arrangement is such that the information is stored in successive tracks on the surface of the disk. Each track is often divided into a number of the sectors. A sector is the smallest addressable portion of a disk. When a read statement calls for a particular byte from a disk file, the computer operating system finds the correct surface, track and sector, reads the entire sector into a special area in memory called buffer and then finds the requested byte within that buffer. Disk drive typically has a number of platters. The tracks that are directly above and below one another form a cylinder {**Figure** 10.12}. The significance of the cylinder is that all of the information on a single cylinder can be accessed without moving the arm that holds the read / write heads. Moving this arm is called seeking. This arm movement is usually the slowest part of reading information from a disk.

10.5.1.3 Reducing Seeking

The use of multiple buffers was discussed as one way of reducing seeking. On hard disk drives, there are other approaches to reduce seeking. If space is assigned to files one sector at a time, the possibility that the next sector may be in a different cylinder increases (more seeking). Rather than leaving such an assignment to chance, would it not be better to assign multiple contiguous sectors to the file when it needs more space? This approach is called clustering. A **cluster** is a group of contiguous sectors on a track. The size of the cluster is set when the drive is configured. Large clusters reduce seeking but increase the chance of wasted space (clusters are not shared); therefore, the selection of a cluster size is a tradeoff between wasted space and response time.

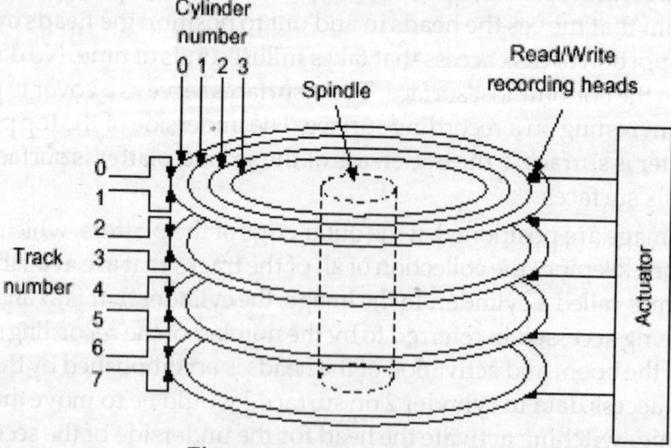

Figure 10.12 Magnetic Disk

If the use of clusters can reduce seeking, why not go a step further and assign contiguous clusters? The answer is that such an approach exists. When a file needs additional space, the file manager attempts to assign space that is contiguous with the last cluster in the file. It is possible that a file manager may be able to put the entire file on contiguous clusters; in this case the file would have **one extent**. If a file were assigned to two groups of contiguous clusters, the file would have two extents. An extent is simply one or more contiguous clusters. The number of extents that a file has is an indication of how scattered it is on the drive and how much seeking is involved in processing the file sequentially. A file manager may use clusters on a properly configured drive and not employ extents; the use of extents depends on the developer of the file management system.

10.5.1.4 Disk Capacity

The capacity of a drive is almost always given by the documentation that accompanies it. However, one may be asked to work on an unfamiliar machine for which the documentation is not available. There is almost always a facility in the operating system that will give both the capacity of a given drive and the amount of free space available.

A disk or disk pack is a collection of platters. Each surface of platter consists of a number of concentric rings called tracks {**Figure** 10.13a}. Data are encoded on each track in a serial representation. In a typical disk, each platter has two surfaces, so the number of tracks per cylinder is twice the number of platters. The number of cylinders is the same as the number of tracks on single surface and each track has the same capacity. Hence capacity of a disk is a function of the number of cylinders, the number of tracks per cylinder and the capacity of a track. The capacity of a track (TC) is the number of bytes that can be stored in a track and density of tracks toward the center is greater than those nearer the periphery {**Figure** 10.13b}.

A cylinder is the set of all tracks with the same number in a pack of disks. The track at the top-most surface is referred to track 0. To address a specific track, two parameters are needed:

1. Cylinder number
2. Track number

Since a cylinder consists of a group of tracks, a track consists of a group of sectors and a sector consists of a group of bytes, it is easy to compute track, cylinder and drive capacities.

Track capacity (TC) = number of sectors per track * bytes per sector

Cylinder capacity = number of tracks per cylinder (TPC) * track capacity (TC)

Drive Capacity (DC) = number of cylinder (NC) * cylinder capacity = NC* TPC * TC

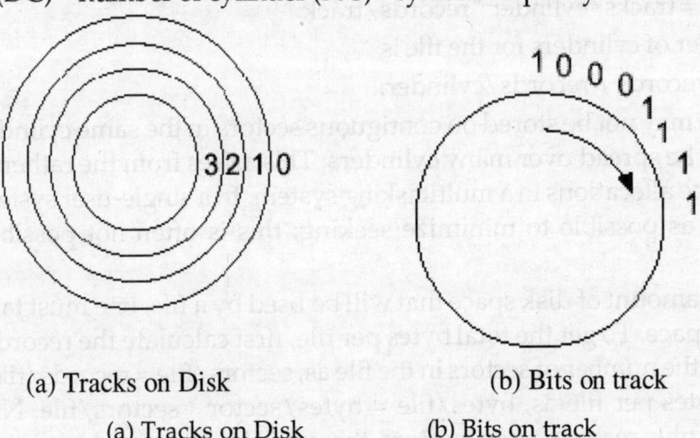

(a) Tracks on Disk (b) Bits on track

Figure 10.13 Dist Track and Bits Storage

For example, if we have the number of bytes in a file, we can use these relationships to compute the amount of disk space the file is likely to be required. Suppose for instance, that we have to store a file with 50,000 fixed length data records on a "typical" 2.1GB small computer disk with the following information:

Number of bytes per sector = 512

Number of sectors per track = 63

Number of tracks per cylinder = 16

Number of cylinders = 4096

How many cylinders does the file require if each data record requires 256 bytes? Since each sector hold two records, the file requires 50000/2 = 25000 sectors. Once cylinder can hold 63*16 = 1008 sectors, so the number of cylinders required is approximately 25000/1008 = 24.8 cylinder.

Calculation of the amount of space that a given file will use is a slightly different matter. Assuming that a fixed-length record is used, first determine how many records there are. Next, calculate the number of records that will fit in a sector. In these calculations, the assumption is that records will not be splitted across sectors; that is, there may be an amount of unusable space in each sector. This arises because of the need to avoid two seeks to retrieve a record. If records are allowed to span sectors, there arises the problem of the record that begins on one sector and ends on another, and thus requires two seeks to retrieve the record. To avoid this problem, individual records can be padded with characters to make the record length an integral power of 2. As a result, the number of such records that fit into a 512 byte sector becomes an integer. The calculation becomes

records/sector = bytes/sector / bytes/record.

Should padding each record result in unacceptable waste of space, the programmer may elect to establish a sector-sized "record" for the program, including in it the largest number of whole logical records possible and using filler for the remainder of the sector. To see one example where this second approach might be desirable, consider the situation of fixed-length records of 100 bytes. Only 12 bytes are wasted with the second approach; 112 bytes are wasted with the "record padding" approach. In either case, the programmer should know the number of records per sector for the next calculation.

Calculate the number of records per track as

records/track = sectors/track * records/sector.

Next, calculate the number or records per cylinder as

records/cylinder = tracks/cylinder * records/track.

Finally, the number of cylinders for the file is

cylinders = total records / records/cylinder.

Of course, the file may not be stored on contiguous sectors in the same cylinder. It is much more likely that the file will be spread over many cylinders. This arises from the rather random pattern of disk accesses and space allocations in a multitasking system. In a single-user system, it is desirable to use as few cylinders as possible to minimize seeking; this is often not possible in a multi-user, multitasking system.

To determine the amount of disk space that will be used by a file, one must take into account the amount of unusable space. To get the total bytes per file, first calculate the records per sector just as above. Then calculate the number of sectors in the file as, sectors/file = records/file / records/sector. Next calculate the bytes per file as, bytes/file = bytes/sector * sectors/file. Naturally, if the file management system splits records across sectors, there will be no unused space in the sector and the calculations can all be done in terms of bytes.

10.5.1.5 Blocked Disks

Up to this point, all of the discussion has been directed toward sectored drives. Many drives are not sectored, but are blocked similarly to blocking on tape, and some file management systems treat sectored drives as if they were a blocked drive, making the translation from sectors to blocks transparent to the user. Regardless of the implementation, blocks are handled as physical records with all of the data for a block being read or written in one operation. This eliminates the problem of logical records spanning sector boundaries.

The **non-data overhead** on a blocked drive is usually greater than that for a sectored drive. This non-data overhead is made up of **count sub-blocks** that contain information about the size of the data block and other parameters of use to the file management system. If the records are organized by key, there may also be a **key sub-block** that contains the key for the last data record in the data block; this allows the disk controller to search the track for a block containing a given key. There is also an **inter-block gap** (IBG: like that on a tape drive) that must be accounted for.

The result of this non-data overhead is to make large blocks preferable to small blocks because larger blocks lead to fewer blocks and consequently less non-data overhead. There may be, however, some choices of block size that are better than others. A track has a fixed length and blocks never span tracks; therefore, the optimum block size is the largest one (with its non-data overhead) that fits the track and leaves the least unused space at the end of the track. The programmer must explore these possibilities before setting a block size. Now we will see different blocking constraints in brief.

- The size of the block and the blocking factor is user-defined.
- The number of blocks can vary from track to track.
- Most IBM's devices are block addressable and are classified into two categories:
  A. Count data format
  B. Count-key data format

A. Count data format: The structure of a track {**Figure** 10.14(a)} briefly can be described as follows:

(a) IM (Index Marker): Indicates the physical beginning of a track. It is Electro-magnetically detected.

(b) HA (Home Address): Contains information about a track:
  (i) Cylinder number
  (ii) Head number (Track number)
  (iii) Physical address of this track
  (iv) A flag indicating whether this track is a defective or operative and whether it is a primary or an alternate track
  (v) A 2-byte field used for a cyclic check, i.e., used for error checking

(c) Base Block or Track Descriptor Block: First physical block {**Figure** 10.14(b)}, contains system information, not user data
  (i) Count area: Indicates address of an alternate track if this track is defective. A key length sub field which is equal to 0.
  (ii) Data area
    - 10 bytes long
    - Contains information about how much unused space is in a track
    - A 2-byte sub field for cyclic check

(d) Interblock Gaps (IBG): Size varies according to the block size and the number of blocks per track {**Figure** 10.14(c)}. Count data and count-key data formats differ in the structure of the data blocks. The meaning of different sections is as follows:

1. A (Address marker): A is 2-byte field which indicates physical beginning of the data block
2. ISBG (Intersubblock gap): Permits the switching of the operation of the R/W head from read to write and vice versa.
3. Count area
   (i) Cylinder number
   (ii) Head number (Track number)
   (iii) Block number
   (iv) Key length field
   => 0 : count data
   => Key length: count-key
   (v) Data length field indicates the length of the data area.
   (vi) Flag field : its contents are the same as that of the flag field in the count area.
   (vii) Cyclic check : 2 bytes
   (viii) Physical address of the block
4. Data area: The area in which user data is stored. Data block overhead (BOS): Includes the fields A, Count area and ISBG's, total = 185 bytes.

B. Count-key Data Format: The presence of key area field in the data blocks {**Figure** 10.14(d)}.

(a) A (Address marker): Beginning of a block
(b) Count area: The only difference is that the key length is set to the length of the key in bytes
(c) Key area; The key of the last record of the following data area:

- Non-embedded format {**Figure** 10.14(e)}: The key of each record is attached to the beginning of that record.
- Embedded format{**Figure** 10.14(f)}: Records are arranged in the same way as the count data format.
- The block overhead for count-key data format is larger than that for count data format.
- The overhead of embedded key format per data block:
  $(267 + k) + k = 267 + 2k$
  where
  k : Length of the key
  The overhead of non-embedded key format:
  $(267 + k) + k + BF * k = 267 + (BF + 2) * k$
  where
  BF: Blocking Factor

Note:

- The IBG's have no fixed size. Their size is a function of both factors:
  1. Block size
  2. Specific device
- From now on, the IBG size will be ignored

Parity Checking: It is the disk controller's responsibility to perform parity checking. Cyclic Check Redundancy is also used. The cyclic check redundancy occupies 2 bytes. The Error Correction Code has 4 bytes. If during a READ the cyclic check fails, the error correction code is used to aid in the correction of the error.

Clusters and Extents: A cluster is a collection of contiguous (physically adjacent) blocks. Cluster size is number of blocks in the cluster. An extent is a collection of contiguous tracks and/or cylinders.

Volume Table of Contents (VTOC) and File Labels {Figure 10.14(g)}: A disk is identified via its volume label. VTOC is usually resides in the first track of the first cylinder. It is the disk directory. The physical location and organization of all physical files residing on this disk. As different from tapes, disks can be updated and inserted "in place", i.e., the block must have empty "slots".

Loading Density and Storage Requirements: Loading density is defined as the ratio of the storage area utilized by user data and the storage data allocated to user data. And the effective Blocking Factor (EBF) is defined as the number of fixed-length records that must be stored in each block, i.e., $EBF = \lfloor BF * LD \rfloor$, where BF: Blocking Factor and LD: Loading Density. The NBLK (Number of Blocks Required)- is defined as the ratio of number of records (NR) and EBF, i.e., $NBLK = \lceil NR/EBF \rceil$. The BS (Block Size) is defined as multiplication of block factor (BF) and record size (RS), i.e., $BS = BF * RS$. It should be noted that we have not considered the block overhead. The NT (Number of tracks) is defined as the ratio of number of tracks (TC) and block size (BS) which divides NBLK, i.e., $NT = \lceil NBLK / \lfloor (TC/BS) \rfloor \rceil$. And NC (Number of Cylinders) is defined as the ratio of number of tracks (TC) and number of tracks per cylinder (TPC), i.e., $NC = \lceil NT/TPC \rceil$. It is assumed that each file is stored in a new cylinder and the block overhead is ignored.

Blocking can produce savings in time and storage efficiency; however, the programmer must resolve issues of size and organization on the disk. As emphasized in earlier sections, the ability to fit the logical to the physical can improve performance. On downside, blocking schemes prevent coordinating I/O operations with the physical movement of the disk, which is sometimes done on sectored drives.

The modern disk drive is a marvel of engineering and miniaturization. Nevertheless, it remains the bottleneck for most file processing operations because of its relatively slow operation. The use of multiple buffers and overlapping I/O and processing operations is one way to reduce the bottleneck. The use of clusters on sectored drives or large blocks on blocked drives reduces the total number of accesses when processing files sequentially.

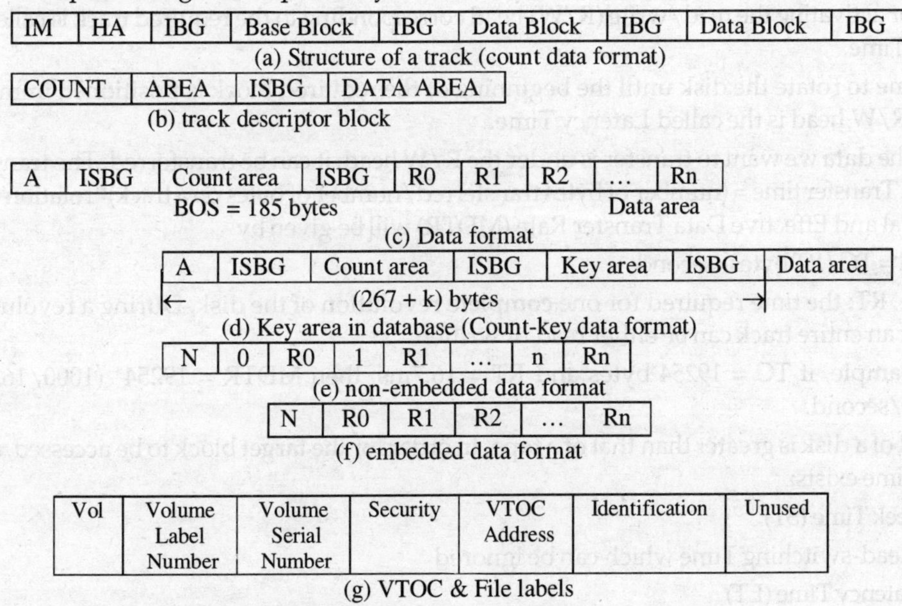

Figure 10.14 Parameters of blocking factor of Disk

10.5.1.6 Disk Access

The cost of physical disk access is made up of three distinct actions: **seek time(ST), rotational delay (RD)** and **transfer time (TT)**. These will be discussed in turn below.

Seek time is the time it takes to move the disk heads from one track to another. This is a mechanical movement and is therefore relatively slow. On a modern hard disk drive this time may be as low as 8 to 10 milliseconds, on older drives this may be as much as 40 milliseconds. In either event, the time is by far the slowest phase of disk access.

Rotational delay is the time it takes for the desired sector or block to arrive under the read/write heads. It is a function of the rotation speed of the drive (3600 rpm for older hard drives and many floppy drives, 7200 rpm for most hard drives but for recent drives this is 10,000 rpm) and is usually given an average value equal to one half the time for a full revolution. On a 7200 rpm drive, this value would be about 4 milliseconds. While this is a considerable portion of total access time, there is little that can be done about it, because it depends on the fixed speed on the drive and on the chance position of the desired data relative to the head, once the head is in place.

Transfer time is a function of the amount of data transferred and the time it takes for the heads to pass over that data. Consider the transfer of one sector on an 18-sectors-per-track drive. The time for rotation over 18 sectors at 7200 rpm is 8.33 milliseconds. The transfer of one sector takes one eighteenth of that, or 0.416 milliseconds. This is the smallest value in the whole access equation.

10.5.1.7 Data Transfer Rate

The time required for moving the actuator from the current cylinder to the required one. The amount of time spent in seeking during a disk access depends, on how far the actuator has to move. If we accessing a file sequentially and the file is packed into several consecutive cylinders, seeking needs to be done only after all the tracks on a cylinder have been processed and then the read/write head needs to move the width of only one track. At the extreme, if we are alternatively accessing sectors from two files that are stored at opposite extremes on a disk, seeking is very expensive. The time required for activating the read/write (R/W) head corresponding to the required track is called Head-Switching Time.

The time to rotate the disk until the beginning of the required block is positioned immediately under the R/W head is the called Latency Time.

Once the data we want to transfer is under the R/W head, it can be transferred. The transfer time is given by, Transfer time = (number of bytes transferred/number of bytes on a track)* rotation time and the Maximal and Effective Data Transfer Rate (MDTR) will be given by

MDTR = TC/RT bytes/second

Where, RT: the time required for one complete revolution of the disk. During a revolution, the contents of an entire track can be either read or written.

For example, if TC = 19254 bytes and RT = 16.7ms, then MDTR = 19254* (1000/16.7) = 1.1 megabytes/second.

MDTR of a disk is greater than that of a tape. In order for the target block to be accessed, a certain overhead time exists:

1. Seek Time (ST)
2. Head-switching Time which can be ignored
3. Latency Time (LT)

The target block consists of two portions:

1. System data such as information identifying the block, its length, i.e., Block Overhead with size (BOS).
2. User data: They are referred to as the data subblock and its size is DBS

The total time (TT) required getting the target block:

TT = ST + LT + (BOS + DBS) / MDTR

Note: ST + LT ⇒ overhead

The time spent directly reading the data subblock, t = DBS/MDTR

Effective Data Transfer Rate (EDTR) can be estimated with the following formula:

EDTR = (t/TT)* MDTR = DBS / {(ST + LT) + (BOS+DBS)/MDTR}

Example: IBM 3350 Disk

ST = 25 ms

LT = 16.7/2 ms = 8.3 ms

DBS = 2000 bytes

BOS = 185 bytes

MDTR = TC/RT = 19254 bytes/16.7 ms = 1.1 MB/sec

EDTR = 2000/{(25/1000) + (8.3/1000) + (2000+185)/{(19254 *1000)/16.7}
= 2000*1000/(25 + 8.3 + 1.9)
= 56818 bytes/sec

The dominant quantity in the delay is the seek time. To reduce seek time, some manufacturers produce fixed head disks which have a R/W head per track.

Now we will discuss how the average seek time can affect the data transfer rate. The following assumption can be considered before going for the estimation of the average seek time in reading/writing an information from/to disk:

- The exact value of ST is important for the determination of EDTR
- The time required to travel a distance **d** is not linear
- The average ST is used as the ST
- Assume that the accesses are distributed randomly, and the disk has n cylinders

The average or expected value of the ST **s** can calculated with help of following formula:

$$s = \sum_{j=0}^{n-1} s[j] * p[j] \qquad ...(1)$$

where

s[j] : ST for a seek of length j

p[j] : probability that length of seek = j

- Assume that the R/W head is positioned over cylinder k currently
- A seek of length l is possible towards the center of the disk iff

$$k \le (n-1) - l$$

A seek is possible towards the outer surface of the disk **iff**

$$k \ge 1$$

the cylinder positions are shown in **Figure** 10.15.

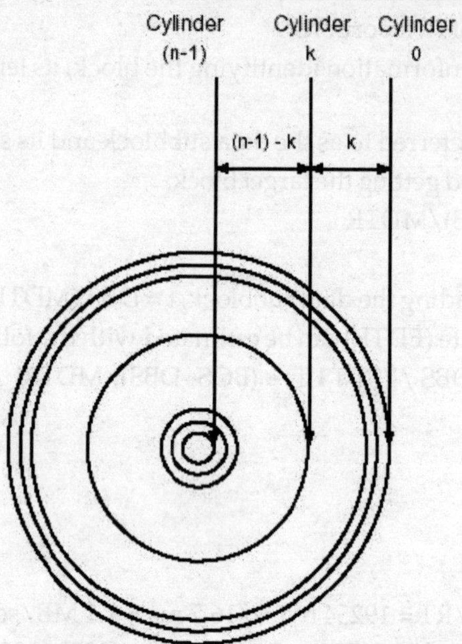

Figure 10.15 Cylinders of a Magnetic Disk

The probability of a seek of length **l**:

$$p[l] = \sum_{t=0}^{(n-1)-l} r[t] + \sum_{q=l}^{n-1} r[q] \qquad \ldots(2)$$

where :

r[t] : Probability of a seek of length **l** from the current cylinder **t** to the inside of the disk

r[q] : Probability of a seek of length **l** from the current cylinder **q** to the outside of the disk

Assume that r[t] = r[q] for all **t** and **q** between 0 and **n-1**the R/W head movement is shown in **Table 10.6.**

Table 10.6 Head movement

Number of other cylinders	Current cylinder the R/W head may go
0	n-1
1	n-1
2	n-1
...	...
n-1	n-1
Total : n	

Therefore,

$$r[t] = \frac{1}{n(n-1)}$$

$$p[l] = \sum_{t=0}^{(n-1)-l} r[t] + \sum_{q=l}^{n-1} r[q]$$

$$= \sum_{t=0}^{(n-1)-l} \frac{1}{n(n-1)} + \sum_{q=l}^{n-1} \frac{1}{n(n-1)}$$

$$= \frac{1}{n(n-1)} \sum_{t=0}^{(n-1)-l} 1 + \sum_{q=l}^{n-1} 1$$

$$= \frac{1}{n(n-1)} [((n-1)-l+1)+((n-1)-l+1)]$$

$$= \frac{2(n-l)}{n(n-1)}$$

Since s[0]= 0, and putting value of p[l] in (1), we get

$$s = \sum_{j=1}^{n-1} \left[s[j] * \frac{2(n-j)}{n(n-1)} \right]$$

$$= \frac{2}{n(n-1)} \sum_{j=1}^{n-1} [s[j]*(n-j)]$$

10.5.2 Tape Storage

Magnetic tape is compact external storage device. It is made of a plastic material coated with a ferrite substance, which is easily magnetized. The physical appearance of the tape is similar to the tape used for sound recording although computer magnetic tape is wider. Several thousand feet of tape are wound on one reel and information is encoded on the tape character by character. A number of channels or tracks run the length of the tape, one channel being required for each bit position in the binary coded representation of a character.

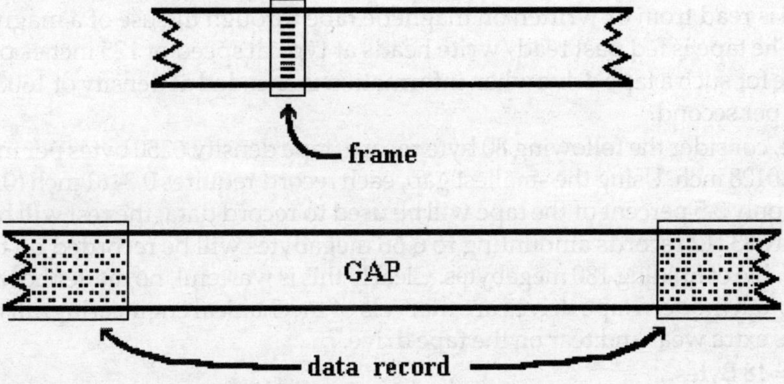

Figure 10.16 Magnetic tape

Magnetic tape {**Figure** 10.16} has two noteworthy characteristics: it is cheap, and it is durable. Its main drawback is that it may be read only sequentially. It continues in use today primarily as a medium for archival data; however, there remain applications that are based on tape storage. Tape storage is useful to introduce basic structures. It is simple in structure, easy to understand, and a good starting point for the study of fixed-length records with fixed-length fields. This combination is by far the most frequently used file structures, both in file systems and in database management systems.

Tape storage is also a good first example of divergence of the logical form of the data from the physical storage medium.

Consider the common reel of one-half inch magnetic tape. The length of the tape is 2400 feet, and its recording density is 6250 bytes per inch. This suggests a capacity of approximately 180 megabytes. Running lengthwise on the tape are nine parallel tracks {**Figure** 10.17}, eight for recording data bits and one for parity checking. At any point on the tape (called a frame {**Figure** 10.16}) a single byte may be recorded. When data is recorded on the tape, a gap is left between the physical data groups or records. This gap is used to stop and start the tape drive, to allow the tape to get up to correct recording or reading speed. The size of this gap will be from one-third to three-fourths of an inch, depending on the drive.

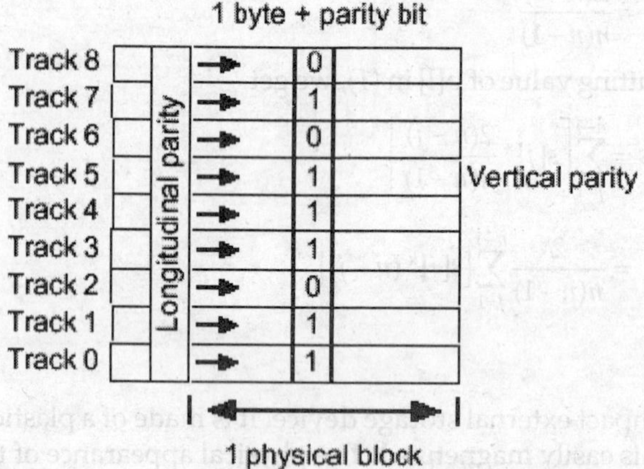

Figure 10.17 Tape channel one channel for one bit of information

It is possible to encode several hundred characters on one inch of magnetic tape; common encoding densities are 800 and 1600 bytes per inch. On a 3600 feet reel of tape which stores 1600 bytes per inch, a maximum of 1600 bytes/inch*12inches/foot*3600feet = 69120000 bytes can be stored.

Information is read from or written on magnetic tape through the use of a magnetic tape drive {**Figure** 10.18}. The tape is fed past read/write heads at typical speed of 125 inches per second. The data transfer rate for such a tape drive when information is encoded at density of 1600 bytes per inch is, 200,000 bytes per second.

For example, consider the following 80 byte record, tape density 6250 bytes per inch, that record would require 0.0128 inch. Using the smallest gap, each record requires 0.3461 inch (0.0128 + 0.3333). This means that only 3.5 percent of the tape will be used to record data; the rest will be gap space. In other words, only 83212 records amounting to 6.66 megabytes will be recorded on this tape that is theoretically capable of holding 180 megabytes. Clearly this is wasteful, no matter how cheap the tape is. Further, although modern tape drives are marvels of mechanical engineering, all of the stopping and starting puts extra wear and tear on the tape drive.

Last_Name= 18 Bytes,
First_Name = 13 Bytes
SOC_Sec_No = 9 Bytes
Address = 21 Bytes
City = 12 Bytes
State = 2 Bytes
Zip = 5

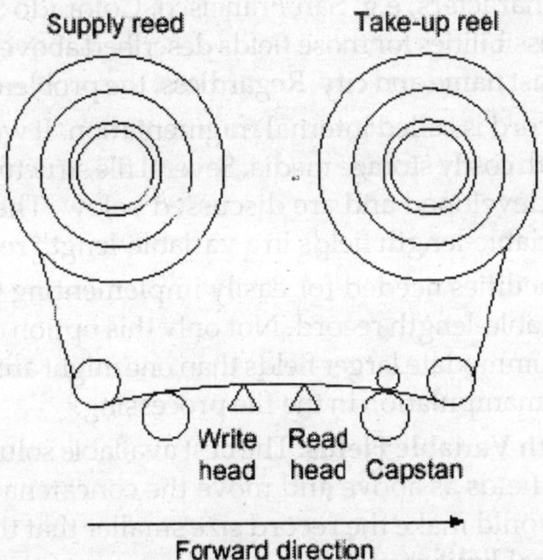

Figure 10.8 Tape Drive

The answer is the ability to "BLOCK" records, that is, to treat a number of logical records as a single physical record. The result is that a gap is placed between the blocks and not between successive logical records. When the operating system reads a blocked file, it reads a block at a time into the system's memory area for the file. After the block is read, the system passes the first logical record to the program; it then passes successive logical records to the program as read commands are issued; when all of the block's data is used, a physical read will be executed to retrieve the next block. This will continue until the end of the file or until no more reads are attempted.

Continuing with the 80 byte record example, consider the effect of placing 100 records in each block. With a blocking factor of 1, 100 records would take 34.61 inches; with a blocking factor of 100, 100 records take 1.61 inches (0.0128 * 100 + 0.33). This is 4.65 percent of the unblocked size. The cost of this gain is the amount of memory used for system buffers; in this case the buffer must be 8000 bytes.

The blocking factor must be set when the file is created. In modern operating systems, the blocking factor is often left to assume default settings that are determined by system programmers based on the characteristics of the storage devices. Should an application programmer need to set a blocking factor for an application file? The programmer should consult a system technician when making that decision.

Fixed-Length Records: The first and easiest file structure is the fixed-length record made up of fixed-length fields. In this structure, each field is allotted enough space to hold the maximum length of value that will occur. In a given instance, if the value for a field is less than the space allotted, the remainder of the space is padded, usually with blanks for alphanumeric fields and zeros for numeric fields. Fields that have no value are filled with blanks or zeros as appropriate. The total space allotted to all of the fields described for a record becomes the record size, thus making up a fixed-length record.

Variable Length Records: In the example above, blocking eliminates a large amount of wasted space between the records. It is possible to imagine sets of realistic data values that would result in considerable wasted space in the fields, particularly the alphanumeric fields. Consider the amount of unused space in the case of Adam Black of 9428 Cass St. in Omaha, Nebraska. In the last name there are 13 bytes unused, in the first name there are 9 bytes used, in the address there are 9 bytes unused, and in the city there are 7 bytes unused. This is a total of 38 bytes, nearly half of the allotted space. This did not arise because of overly generous allocations; indeed, hyphenated surnames often exceed 18 characters, e.g., Farnsworth-Livingston, Rothlisberher-Castillo, and Shaughnessy-Cornell, and many city names will not fit in 12 characters, e.g. San Francisco, Colorado Springs, and Daytona Beach. Thorough evaluation of the possibilities for those fields described above might cause one to shift a few characters from first name to last name and city. Regardless, the problem of wasted space will remain.

Wasted space within a record is called internal fragmentation. It was a considerable problem for early programmers dealing with costly storage media. Several file structures that reduced or eliminated internal fragmentation were developed and are discussed below. The best of these from a storage utilization point of view is variable-length fields in a variable-length record.

Java provides all of the facilities needed for easily implementing the best space saving option: variable-length fields in a variable-length record. Not only this option eliminate the wasted space, it also allows the program to accommodate larger fields than one might anticipate. This solution requires more programming and data manipulation in the file processing.

Fixed-Length Records with Variable Fields: The best available solution to internal fragmentation was to create variable-length fields as above and move the concatenated result into a fixed-length record. Some programmers would make the record size smaller that the sum of the maximum field sizes and depend on the central limit theorem to keep the sum of the actual field sizes within the smaller record size. Statistical analysis of several hundred randomly selected records would provide a mean and standard deviation for the actual byte counts of the variable-length fields. Setting the basic record size to the sum of the fixed-length-field lengths plus the mean of the variable-length fields would leave half of the records too large to fit in the area provided. Those records could be stored in a separate overflow file with a record size equal to the sum of the fixed-length-field lengths plus the mean of the variable-length fields plus standard deviations. Setting the basic record size to the mean record size may not be the optimum in terms of saving space (this would arise from sampling error); depending on the exact distribution of the lengths of the variable-length fields, some adjustment of the basic record size to a larger value might produce a greater space savings.

The fixed-length record with a variable number of fixed-length fields must not be discounted completely. It will emerge in later sections on hashing as a technique for reducing multiple accesses to storage, a much more important consideration today than saving space.

10.5.2.1 Tape Utilization

When a tape is not reading/writing information, it is in a stopped position. When the processor issues a command to read/write, the tape must be accelerated to a constant speed. Following the completion of a read/write command, the tape is de-accelerated to a stop position. During either an acceleration or de-acceleration phase, a certain length of tape is passed over. This section of tape is neither read nor written upon. It appears between successive records {block} and is called an inter-record gap (inter block gap: IBG) {**Figure** 10.19}. An inter-record gap varies from ½ to ¾ inch, depending on the nature of tape unit. The greater the number of inter-record gaps, the smaller the storage capacity of the tape. For example, suppose records consisting of 800 bytes each are written one at a time on a tape having a density of 1600 bytes per inch. If ½ inch inter-record gaps result then only ½ of the tape is used for storing data.

Figure 10.19 Record layout for magnetic tape

To circumvent this problem, records are often grouped in blocks. If records are blocked one write command can transfer a number of consecutive records to the tape without requiring inter-record gaps between them. The utilization (U) factor can be formulated as:

$$U = \frac{BS}{BS + IGS} = \frac{1}{1+\frac{IGS}{BS}}$$

where

BS : Block size

IGS : Inter-block gap size

Following points affect the utilization factor:

- If IGS/BS => 0, U = 1
- Inter-block size IGS should be made minimum. But IGS is machine dependent
- Larger block size BS
  - — Larger blocking factor BF
  - — Fewer number of physical blocks
  - — Fewer number of reads/writes for the whole tape
  - — Larger Input and Output Buffers
  - — BS affects utilization
- Rate of increase in utilization decreases as BS increases

10.5.2.2 Effective Data Transfer Rate (EDTR)

The average time taken to read/write a record is inversely proportional to the blocking factor, since fewer gaps must be spanned and more records can be read/written per command. To utilize tape storage efficiently and to minimize read and write time, it appears that the blocking factor should be arbitrarily large.

Maximum data transfer rate (MDTR) = Speed * Density

Before formulating the effective data transfer rate we required to consider the following assumptions:

- Bytes of user data that can be transferred in a second
- Time to start and stop tape and in IBG
- T : total time to transfer a block

  T = r + ss + gt

  where

  r : time to transfer the data

  ss : time to start and stop the tape

  gt : time spent in inter-block gaps
- f : fraction of T user data is actually transferred

$$f = \frac{r}{T} = \frac{r}{r + ss + gt}$$

$$BS = \frac{r}{1000} * MDTR$$

$$r = \frac{BS * 1000}{MDTR}$$

$$gt = \frac{IGS * D}{MDTR}$$

$$EDTR = f * MDTR$$

$$EDTR = \frac{BS * 1000 * MDTR}{BS * 1000 + ss * MDTR + CS * D * 1000}$$

Note: EDTR increases when BS increases and D : Density

10.5.2.3 File Structure on Tape

Header records are often used in file handling. These records have their own size and layout that has nothing to do with the layout of the data record. They are used to store values that the system or the application program will need to process the data in the file. As a result, header records are usually read immediately after the file is opened to obtain the information that will govern further processing. To support this immediate access, a header record will be the first record (at the head of) the file, hence the name. What kinds of information are stored there?

- Date of last update
- Successful update flag
- Number of records
- Pointers to overflow areas
- Pointer to the first available (deleted) record
- Descriptions and names of fields (self describing files)
- Color palette information (graphics files)
- Dimensions (graphics files)

In an indexed file, the header record usually holds a pointer to the root of the index and to the first data block for sequential access. Naturally, processing routines must hold provisions to update these values if they change. How a file exists on the tape is shown in **Figure** 10.20. A small discussion of the different section of the file having information is as follows:

VOL	VOLUME LABEL NUMBER	VOLUME SERIAL NUMBER	SECURITY	UNUSED	IDENTIFIC ATION	UNUSED

Figure 10.20 File information on a tape

Volume, Header, Trailer Labels

- A volume label is an 80-byte block which resides immediately after the load mark point.
- Volume label number: A number between 1 and 8 that indicates the relative position within the current volume set. It occupies byte position 3.
- Volume serial number: A 6-byte numeric field, which is a unique identification code. It occupies byte positions 4 through 9.
- Security: It occupies byte position 11.
- Identification: It contains the owner's name and the identification. It occupies byte positions 41 through 50.
- The blocks of an individual file are delimited by two labels.

Header label and Trailer label

Structure of this situation is shown in **Figure** 10.21.

HEADER	IBG	BLOCK	IBG	...	BLOCK	IBG	TRAILER

Figure 10.21 Header, Label and Trailer of tape file

- Each label is an 80-byte block.
- Label identifier: It is used to indicate the type of label. It occupies the first 3 bytes of the label.
  - (a) HDR : for header.
  - (b) EOF (end of file) or EOV (end of volume) : for trailer.
- File label number: It is set to 1.
- File identifier: A 17-byte field that uniquely identifies the entire file.
- File serial number: A 6-byte field that indicates the file/volume relationship.
- Volume sequence number: A 4-byte field that indicates the order of the volume in a multiple set.
- File sequence number: A 4-byte field that indicates the numeric sequence of a file within a multi-volume set.
- File security field: A 1-byte field, which is set to 0 if no security protection is required. Otherwise, it is set to 1.
- Block count: It is a 6-byte field used in trailers, only to record the number of blocks written onto the tape from the last header label to the current trailer label.

Advantages and Disadvantages of Tapes

Tape storage allows only sequential access. It is still an important medium for archival storage and some legacy applications. Storing multiple logical records as a single physical record is called blocking. Blocking is a significant concept for efficient tape storage, and blocking, perhaps called other names, will also be used to implement rapid direct access techniques. Variable numbers of fixed-length fields in a fixed-length record may be employed to achieve rapid data retrieval at a cost Variable-length fields in a fixed-length record may be employed to reduce internal fragmentation, but this reduction will be at a cost of handling two files at once and not all wasted space will be eliminated.

- The only file structure is physical sequential structure
- A record cannot be updated in place
- Low cost
- The most efficient way of transferring data
- Facilitating off-line storage

10.6 FILE ORGANIZATION

Given a set of attributes A and a set of values V, then a record R is a subset of the Cartesian product A x V in which each attribute has one and only one value {here we have defined record with the help of set theory}. Thus, R is a set of ordered pairs of the form (an attribute, its value). For example, the record for a document, which has been processed by an automatic content analysis algorithm, would be

$$R = \{(K_1, x_1), (K_2, x_2), \ldots, (K_m, x_m)\}$$

The K_i's are keywords functioning as attributes and the value x_i can be thought of as a numerical weight. Frequently documents are simply characterized by the absence or presence of keywords, in which case we write

$$R = \{Kt_1, Kt_2, \ldots, Kt_i\}$$

where Kt_i is present if $xt_i = 1$ and is absent otherwise.

Records are collected into logical units called files. They enable one to refer to a set of records by name, the file name. The records within a file are often organized according to relationships between the records. This logical organization is known as a file structure (or data structure).

It is difficult in describing file structures to keep the logical features separate from the physical ones. The latter are characteristics forced upon by the recording media (e.g., tape, disk). Some features can be defined abstractly (with little gain) but are more easily understood when illustrated concretely. One such feature is a field. In any implementation of a record, the attribute values are usually positional, that is the identity of an attribute is given by the position of its attribute value within the record. Therefore, the data within a record is registered sequentially and has a definite beginning and end. The record is said to be divided into fields and the nth field carries the nth attribute value. Pictorially we have an example of a record with associated fields in **Figure** 10.22.

R =

K_1	K_2
K_3	
K_4	
P_1	P_2
P_3	P_4

Figure 10.22 An example of a record with associated fields

The fields are not necessarily constant in length. To find the value of the attribute K_4, we first find the address of the record R (which is actually the address of the start of the record) and read the data in the 4th field. In the same figure we have also shown some fields labeled P_i. They are addresses of other records, and are commonly called pointers. Now we have extended the definition of a record to a set of attribute value pairs and pointers. Each pointer is usually associated with a particular attribute value pair. For example, {**Figure** 10.23} pointers could be used to link all records for which the value x_1 (of attribute K_1) is a, similarly for x_2 equal to b, etc.

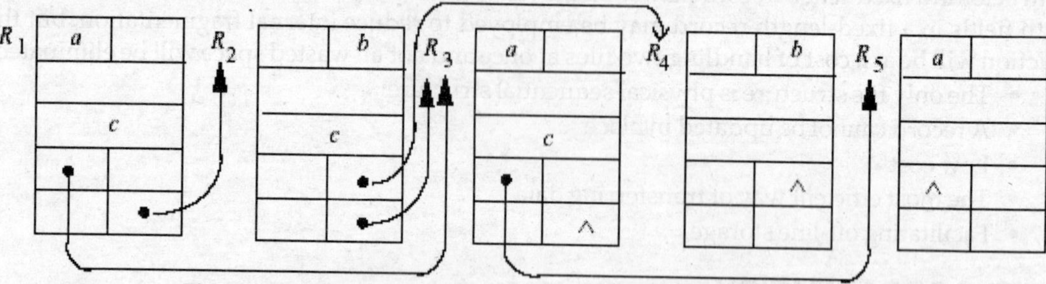

Figure 10.23 A demonstration of the use of pointers to link records

To indicate that a record is the last record pointed to in a list of records we use the null pointer {∧}. The pointer associated with attribute K in record R will be called a K-pointer. An attribute (keyword) that is used in this way to organize a file is called a key. To unify the discussion of file structures we need some further concepts. We define a list L of records with respect to a keyword K, or more briefly a K-list as a set of records containing K such that:

1. The K-pointers are distinct;
2. Each non-null K-pointer in L gives the address of a record within L;
3. There is a unique record in L not pointed to by any record containing K; it is called the beginning of the list; and
4. There is a unique record in L containing the null K-pointer; it is the end of the list.

From previous example:

K_1-list : R_1, R_2, R_3
K_2-list : R_2, R_4
K_4-list : R_3, R_5

Finally, we need the definition of a directory of a file. Let F be a file whose records contain just m different keywords $K_1, K_2, \ldots, K_m$. Let n_i be the number of records containing the keyword K_i, and h_i be the number of K_i-lists in F. Furthermore, we denote by a_{ij} the beginning address of the jth K_j-list. Then the directory is the set of sequences

$(K_i, n_i, h_i, a_{i1}, a_{i2}, \ldots, a_ih_i)$ $i = 1, 2, \ldots, m$

10.6.1 Indexes

Hashing satisfies direct access needs in static files; on the other hand, a hashed static file is not easy to process sequentially. It is true that one could set a counter and increment it to cover the whole file, but the order of the records is unpredictable and the empty spaces (needed to give a low load factor and good direct access performance) result in 30 to 40 percent of accesses producing blanks. This is unacceptable performance, especially in large files.

What if a table is set up that holds the key values? If the file is needed in key sequence, the table can be sorted and the records can be retrieved in key order. While this solution is certainly doable, consider the cost of sorting the table and consider the multiple seeks that will be required to process the entire file. In fact, a desirable hashing algorithm is one that spreads the records out over the entire address space, thereby making the need to seek to retrieve the next record in key sequence even more likely. Contrast the multiple seeks of this approach with the single seek needed to retrieve multiple records in a blocked sequential file.

The table described in the paragraph above is an example of the simplest of indexes. If a key is in the table, the record associated with the key is in the file somewhere. Some indexes would include the relative key (relative record number), but this is unnecessary in this case. If a given record was positioned in the file using a hashing algorithm, then that same algorithm can be used to retrieve it. A point to be made here is that if the file must be reorganized because of growth, the index does not have to be changed. The file may be reorganized and a revised hashing algorithm implemented and used to populate the file, but this simple index may be left alone.

An **index** then is a table that directly or indirectly allows one to access a record specified by a key. Although an index does not answer the problem of sequential access to a relative file, the above discussion does suggest an answer to another problem, that of direct access on secondary or alternate keys. Make a table of the values of the secondary keys along with their associated primary key. If the table is maintained in secondary key order, binary searching can quickly produce the primary key and hashing can produce the relative record number of the data record. The primary key value is maintained in the secondary index for the same reason that no relative record number was kept above, to avoid unnecessary maintenance. No help for the sequential access problem, but an answer to another problem that arises frequently.

But this is intended to suggest that simple indexes are not necessarily the answer to all processing problems. As will be seen in later sections, more complex indexes are a compromise that delivers tolerable direct access performance along with sequential access in key order. But for now, using the starting point above, a static hashed file, no acceptable solution has been found to the problem of direct access and key-ordered sequential access.

The history of indexes did not begin with the hashed file. The history of indexes began with a sequential file that was too large to load into main memory and with a desire for direct access. Obviously, if the whole file can be loaded into memory, load it and search it for the desired record Using byte-addressing techniques available in assembly language or a middle-level language like C, indexing approaches can be developed using simple sequential files on disk. Some of the following discussion is intended only to demonstrate concepts; some parts may be useful in specific circumstances.

We are now in a position to give a unified treatment of sequential files, inverted files, index-sequential files and multi-list files.

10.6.2 Sequential Files

A sequential file is the most primitive of all file structures. It has no directory and no linking pointers. The records are generally organized in lexicographic order on the value of some key. In other words, a particular attribute is chosen whose value will determine the order of the records. Sometimes when the attribute value is constant for a large number of records a second key is chosen to give an order when the first key fails to discriminate. The implementation of this file structure requires the use of a sorting routine. Its main advantages are:

(a) It is easy to implement;

(b) It provides fast access to the next record using lexicographic order.

Its disadvantages are:

1. It is difficult to update when inserting a new record may require moving a large proportion of the file;
2. Random access is extremely slow.

Sometimes a file is considered to be sequentially organized despite the fact that it is not ordered according to any key. Perhaps the date of acquisition is considered to be the key value; the newest entries are added to the end of the file and therefore pose no difficulty to update.

10.6.3 Inverted Files

An inverted file is a file structure in which every list contains only one record. Remember that a list is defined with respect to a keyword K, so every K-list contains only one record. This implies that the directory will be such that $n_i = h_i$ for all i, that is, the number of records containing K_i will equal the number of K_i-lists. So the directory will have an address for each record containing K_i. For document retrieval this means that for given keyword we can immediately locate the addresses of all the documents containing that keyword. For the previous example let us assume that a non-black entry in the field corresponding to an attribute indicates the presence of a keyword and a black entry its absence. Then the directory will point to the file in the way shown in **Figure** 10.24. The definition of inverted files does not require that the addresses in the directory be in any order. However, to facilitate operations such as conjunction (and) and disjunction (or) on any two inverted lists, the addresses are normally kept in record number order. This means that 'and' and 'or' operations can be performed with one pass through both lists. The penalty we pay is of course that the inverted file becomes slower to update.

10.6.4 Index-Sequential Files

An index-sequential file is an inverted file in which for every keyword K_i, we have $n_i = h_i = 1$ and $a_{11} < a_{21} \ldots < a_{m1}$. This situation can only arise if each record has just one unique keyword, or one unique attribute-value. In practice, this set of records may be order sequentially by a key. Each key value appears in the directory with the associated address of its record. An obvious interpretation of a key of this kind would be the record number. In the example shown in Figure 10.25 none of the attributes would do the job except the record number. Diagrammatically the index-sequential file would therefore appear as shown in **Figure** 10.25. We have deliberately written R_i instead of K_i to emphasize the nature of the key.

An index-sequential file is usually thought of as a sequential file with a hierarchy of indices. This does not contradict the previous definition; it merely describes the way in which the directory is implemented. It is not surprising therefore that the indexes ('index' = 'directory' here) are often oriented to the characteristics of the storage medium. For example {**Figure** 10.26}, there might be three levels of indexing: track, cylinder and master. Each entry in the track index will contain enough information to locate the start of the track, and the key of the last record in the track, which is also normally the highest value on that track. There is a track index for each cylinder. Each entry in the cylinder index gives the last record on each cylinder and the address of the track index for that cylinder. If the cylinder index itself is stored on tracks, then the master index will give the highest key referenced for each track of the cylinder index and the starting address of that track.

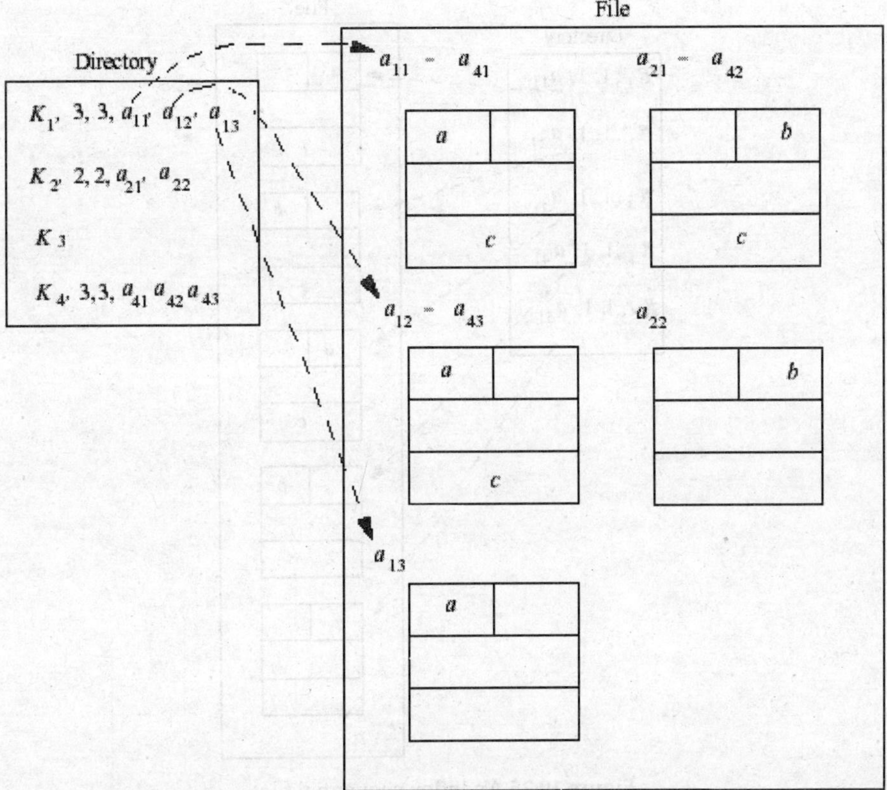

Figure 10.24 An inverted file

The possibility of overflow during an updating process is not considered. Normally provision is made in the directory to administer an overflow area. This of course increases the number of bookkeeping entries in each entry of the index.

10.6.5 Multi-Lists

A multi-list is really only a slightly modified inverted file. There is one list per keyword, i.e., h_i = 1. The records containing a particular keyword K_i are chained together to form the K_i-list and the start of the K_i -list is given in the directory, as illustrated in **Figure** 10.27. Since there is no K_3-list, the field reserved for its pointer could well have been omitted. So could any blank pointer field, so long as no ambiguity arises as to which pointer belongs to which keyword. One way of ensuring this, particularly if the data values (attribute-values) are fixed format, is to have the pointer not pointing to the beginning of the record but pointing to the location of the next pointer in the chain.

The multi-list is designed to overcome the difficulties of updating an inverted file. The addresses in the directory of an inverted file are normally kept in record-number order. But, when the time comes to add a new record to the file, this sequence must be maintained, and inserting the new address can be expensive. No such problem arises with the multi-list, we update the appropriate K-lists by simply chaining in the new record. The penalty we pay for this is of course the increase in search time. This is in fact typicalfor the many of the file structures. Inherent in their design is a tradeoff between search time and update time.

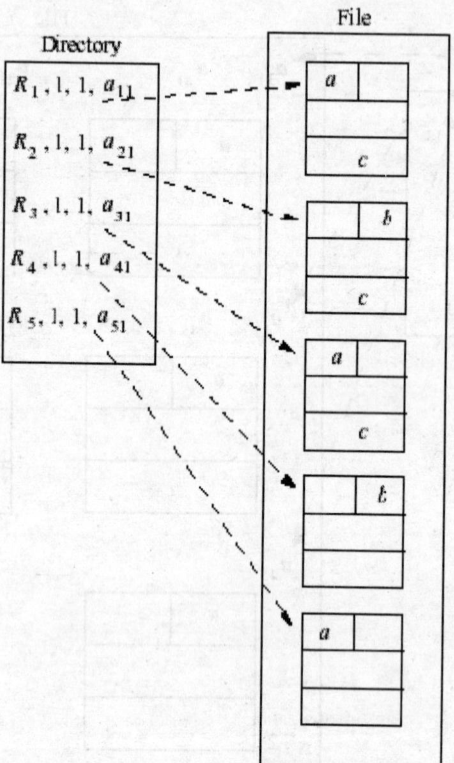

Figure 10.25 An index-sequential file

10.6.6 Cellular Multi-Lists

A further modification of the multi-list is inspired by the fact that many storage media are divided into pages, which can be retrieved one at a time. A K-list may cross several page boundaries, which means that several pages may have to be accessed to retrieve one record. A modified multi-list structure, which avoids this, is called a cellular multi-list. The K-lists are limited so that they will not cross the page (cell) boundaries. At this point the full power of the notation introduced before comes into play. The directory for a cellular multi-list will be the set of sequences

$(K_i, n_i, h_i, a_{i1}, \ldots, a_i h_i)$ $i = 1, 2, \ldots, m$

where the h_i have been picked to ensure that a K_i-list does not cross a page boundary. In an implementation, just as in the implementation of an index-sequential file, further information will be stored with each address to enable the right page to be located for each key value.

10.6.7 Ring Structures

A ring is simply a linear list that closes upon itself. In terms of the definition of a K-list, the beginning and end of the list are the same record. This data structure is particularly useful to show classification of data. Let us suppose that a set of documents

$\{D_1, D_2, D_3, D_4, D_5, D_6, D_7, D_8\}$

has been classified into four groups, that is

$\{(D_1, D_2), (D_3, D_4), (D_5, D_6), (D_7, D_8)\}$

Furthermore these have themselves been classified into two groups,

$\{((D_1, D_2), (D_3, D_4)), ((D_5, D_6), (D_7, D_8))\}$

The dendrogram for this structure would be that given in **Figure** 10.28. To represent this in storage by means of ring structures is now a simple matter {**Figure** 10.29}.

Master index [Core store]

Cylinder and track containing index	Highest key referenced for corresponding index
1.010	0150
2.020	0250
3.015	0350

Cylinder index [Cylinder 1, track 010]

Highest key referenced for corresponding index	Track address of record index
0050	015
0150	030

Track index [Cylinder 1, track 030]

Highest key in track	Start of track
0080	090
00100	091

Data area

Track	Key	Data
090	0060	
	0065	
	0070	
	0080	
091	0085	
	0090	
	0095	
	0100	

Figure 10.26 An example of an implementation of an index-sequential file

The D_i indicates a description (representation) of a document. Notice how the rings at a lower level are contained in those at a higher level. The field marked C_i normally contains some identifying information with respect to the ring it subsumes. For example, C_1 in some way identifies the class of documents $\{D_1, D_8\}$. Were we to group documents according to the keywords they shared, then for each keyword we would have a group of documents, namely, those which had that keyword in common. C_i would then be the field containing the keyword uniting that particular group. The rings would of course overlap {**Figure** 10.30}, as in this example:

$D_1 = \{K_1, K_2\}$
$D_2 = \{K_2, K_3\}$
$D_3 = \{K_1, K_4\}$

The usefulness of this kind of structure will become more apparent when we discuss searching of classifications. If each ring has associated with it a record which contains identifying information for its members, then a search strategy searching a structure such as this will first look at C_i (or K_i in the second example) to determine whether to proceed or abandon the search.

A simple list representation of the classification

$((D_1, D_2), (D_3, D_4)),((D_5, D_6), (D_7, D_8))$

is given in **Figure** 10.31. Each sublist in this structure has associated with it a record containing only two pointers. (We can assume that D_i is really a pointer to document D_i.) The function of the pointers should be clear from the diagram. The main thing to note, however, is that the record associated with a list does not contain any identifying information.

A modification of the implementation of a list structure like this, which makes it resemble a set of ring structures, is to make the right hand pointer of the last element of a sublist point back to the head of the sublist. Each sublist has become effectively a ring structure. We now have what is commonly called a threaded list {**Figure** 10.32}. The representation we have given is a slight oversimplification in that we need to flag which elements are data elements (giving access to the documents D_i) and which elements are just pointer elements.

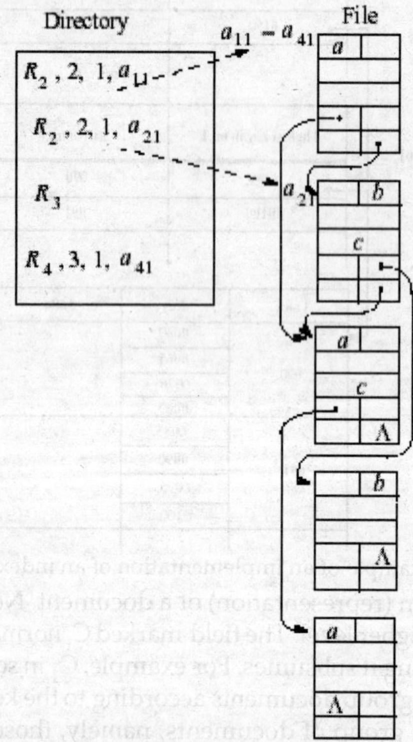

Figure 10.27 A multi-list

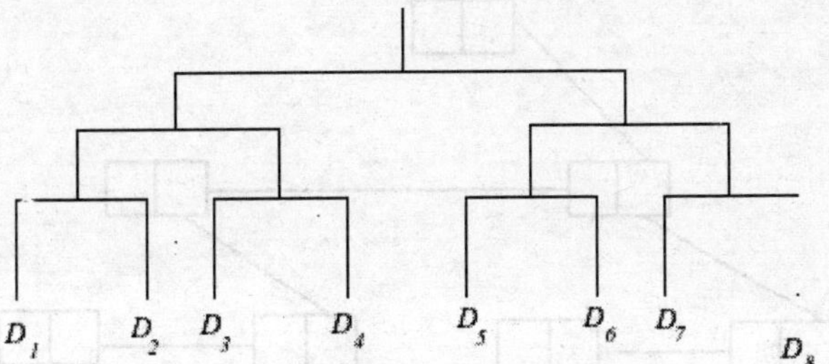

Figure 10.28 A dendrogram

The major advantage associated with a threaded list is that it can be traversed without the aid of a stack. Normally when traversing a conventional list structure the return addresses are stacked, whereas in the threaded list they have been incorporated in the data structure.

One disadvantage associated with the use of list and ring structures for representing classifications is that they can only be entered at the 'top'. An additional index giving entry to the structure at each of the data elements increases the update speed considerably.

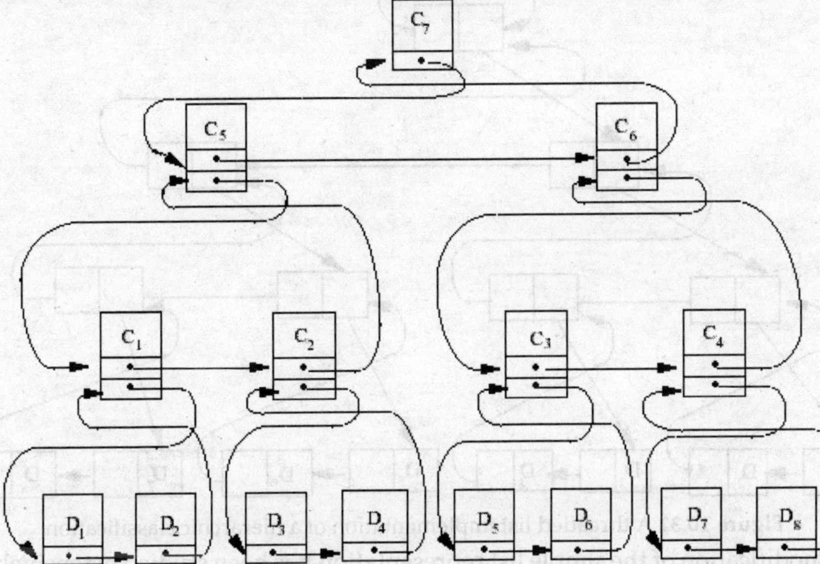

Figure 10.29 An implementation of a dendrogram via ring structures

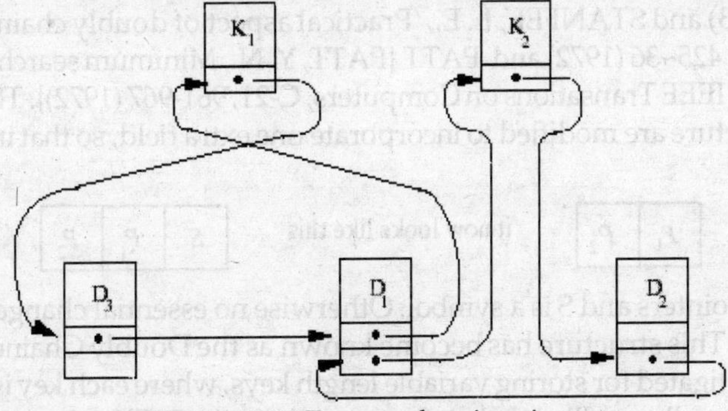

Figure 10.30 Two overlapping rings

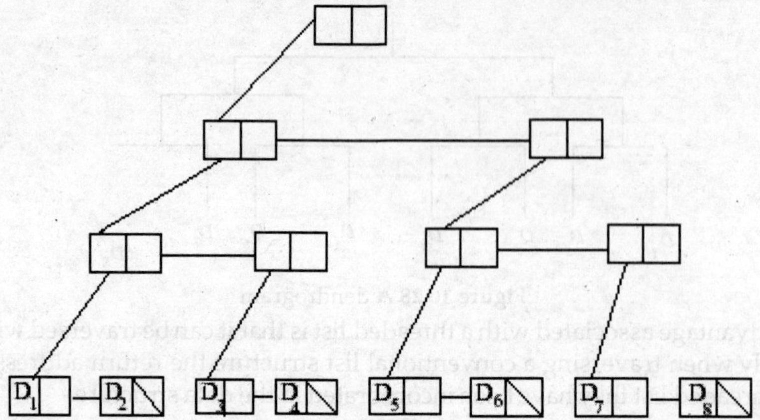

Figure 10.31 A list structure implementation of a hierarchical classification

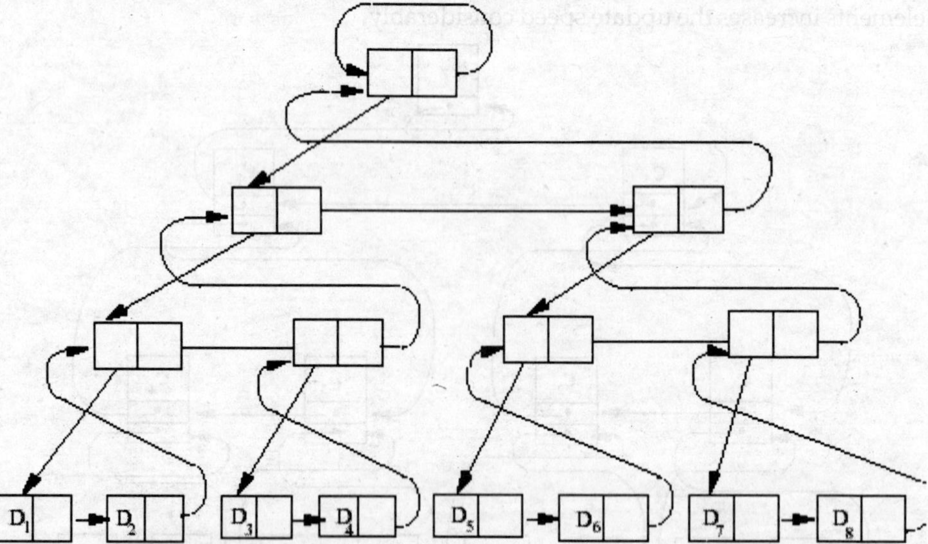

Figure 10.32 A threaded list implementation of a hierarchic classification

Another modification of the simple list representation has been studied extensively by Stanfel { STANFEL, L. E., 'Optimal trees for a class of information retrieval problems', Information Storage and Retrieval, 9, 43-59 (1973) and STANFEL, L. E., 'Practical aspect of doubly chained trees for retrieval', Journal of the ACM, 19, 425~36 (1972} and PATT {PATT, Y. N., Minimum search tree structure for data partitioned into pages', IEEE Transations on Computers, C-21, 961-967 (1972)}. The individual elements (or cells) of the list structure are modified to incorporate one extra field, so that instead of each element looking like this

P_1	P_2

it now looks like this

S	P_1	P_2

where the P_is are pointers and S is a symbol. Otherwise no essential change has been made to the simple representation. This structure has become known as the Doubly Chained Tree. Its properties have mainly been investigated for storing variable length keys, where each key is made up by selecting symbols from a finite (usually small) alphabet. For example, let {A,B,C} be the set of key symbols and let

R_1, R_2, R_3, R_4, R_5 be five records to be stored. Let us assign keys made of the 3 symbols, to the record as follows:

AA	R_1
AB	R_2
AC	R_3
BB	R_4
BC	R_5

An example of a doubly chained tree containing the keys and giving access to the records is given in **Figure** 10.33. The topmost element contains no symbol; it merely functions as the start of the structure. Given an arbitrary key its presence or absence is detected by matching it against keys in the structure. Matching proceeds level by level, once a matching symbol has been found at one level, the P_1 pointer is followed to the set of alternative symbols at the next level down. The matching will terminate either:

1. when the key is exhausted, that is, no more key symbols are left to match; or
2. when no matching symbol is found at the current level.

For case (1):

(a) the key is present if the P_1 pointer in the same cell as the last matching symbol now points to a record;

(b) P_1 points to a further symbol, that is, the key 'falls short' and is therefore not in the structure.

Also for case (2), the key is not in the structure, but now there is a mismatch.

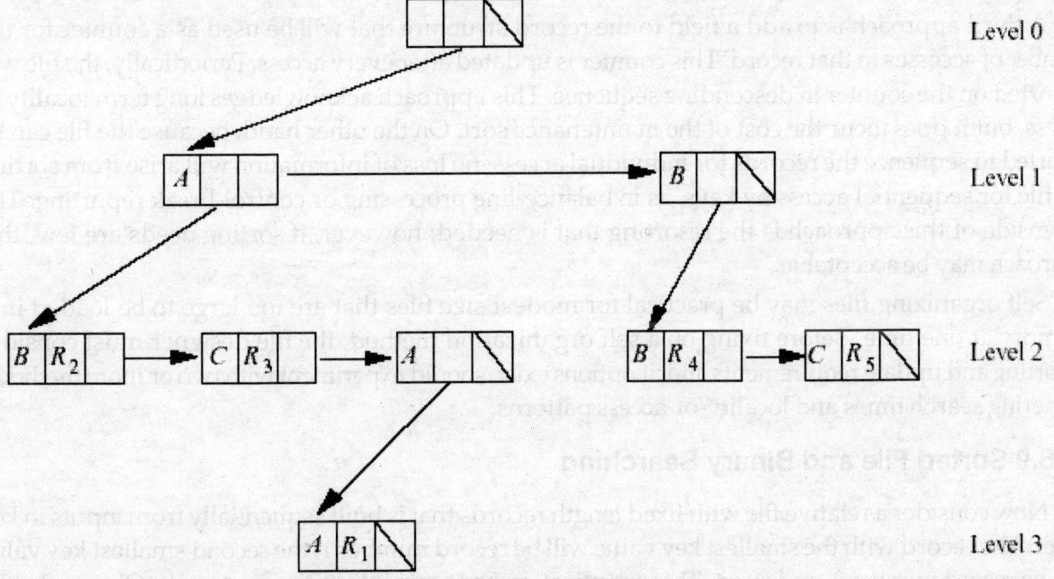

Figure 10.33 An example of a doubly chained tree

10.6.8 Self-Organizing Files

For example, consider a relative file with fixed length records that is built sequentially using unordered inputs, i.e., the position of a given record in the file is unrelated to any key field. Each record will have a relative record number; the first record in the file will be 1, the second, 2, and so on. Such a file is clearly not very useful. To find any specific record requires a sequential search, and processing the file in key sequence is impossible. Perhaps the file can be organized so that frequently accessed records are located near the beginning of the file. Self-organizing access algorithms try to achieve this, and the amount of additional code required is small. One approach is to exchange the record that has been located with one at the beginning of the file. A simple counter in a header record can be used to keep track of the most recently exchanged record and use the subsequent record in the next exchange. The downside of this approach is that when an infrequently used record is moved to the front of the file, it extends the search for all records after it. This approach does recognize a phenomenon called **locality of access**, which is the name for a tendency for accesses to a given record to be clustered together in time. Thus, the most recently accessed record will be near the beginning of the file where it may be easily found on subsequent accesses. This approach will not allow the file to be sorted for balance-line processing or control-break reporting without destroying the useful positioning in the file.

A different and simpler approach is to simply exchange the record that has been located with the record immediately ahead of it every time the record is accessed. Frequently accessed records tend to move to the front of the file. Handling new records poses a problem. Moving a new record to the front of the file will displace a record that has earned a place at the beginning of the file through regular and frequent access and that will probably continue to merit such a position; however, beginning of file positioning does exploit locality of access. Positioning the new record at the end of file does not exploit locality of access. Another problem is that this approach, like the previous one, will not allow the file to be sorted for balance-line processing or control-break reporting.

A third approach is to add a field to the record structure that will be used as a counter for the number of accesses to that record. This counter is updated after every access. Periodically, the file will be sorted on the counter in descending sequence. This approach acknowledges long term locality of access, but it does incur the cost of the maintenance sort. On the other hand, because the file can be resorted to sequence the records for individual access, no loss of information will arise from sorting the file for sequential access by keys, as in balance-line processing or control-break reporting. The downside of this approach is the resorting that is needed; however, if sorting needs are few, this approach may be acceptable.

Self organizing files may be practical for modest size files that are too large to be loaded into memory at one time. Before fixing on a self organization method, the file designer must consider reporting and update requirements and, if options exist, should experiment with two or more methods, gathering search times and locality-of-access patterns.

10.6.9 Sorted File and Binary Searching

Now consider a relative file with fixed length records that is built sequentially from inputs in key order. The record with the smallest key value will be record number 1, the second smallest key value will be record number 2, and so on. This organization has some interesting prospects. Obviously, the file may be processed sequentially in key order. If the total number of records are known, say from a count in a header record, a binary search of the file may be made for a given record. But will this be acceptable performance? Binary searches require, on average, log n - 1 comparison in a successful search, where the logarithm is base 2 and n is the number of records in the file being searched. This would mean that a 10,000 record file would require 12 accesses in the average successful search. An unsuccessful search requires log n + 1 comparisons, which means that a search in a 10,000 record file for a record that did not exist would require 13 accesses. Either case is probably unacceptable.

Another problem arises from the need to maintain the file in sorted sequence. In a dynamic file, the cost of keeping the file in order can be considerable. Searching for the position to place the new record would require the same number of accesses as an unsuccessful search. Then all of the records with larger keys would have to be moved one position toward the end of file, beginning at the end and working record at a time toward the position identified by the binary search, on average n / 2 reads and writes! This is too long time to add a record interactively.

10.6.10 Entry-Sequenced Files And An Index

What if the file is not sorted? What if it is entry sequenced as postulated above with sequential searching? At this point, the index enters the picture. The key for each record is placed in the table along with its relative record number. The table is placed in a separate file and loaded into memory when the data file is opened. The table is kept in key sequence so that it may be searched quickly using a binary search. When a given record is wanted, its key is located in the table using a binary search and its relative record number is used to retrieve the record from the file.

Although adding a record to the data file is not a problem (simply place it at the end of the file), putting its key and relative record number into the proper place in the table is a problem. If the index table fits in main memory, then inserting a new record is simply a variant of the insertion sort. But if the index is too large to fit into memory at once, getting a new key into place may involve several loading of parts of the table, depending on how big the index is. Even though this may be acceptable, accessing the file in key sequence still requires multiple seeks and makes performance for a balance line algorithm or a control-break report unacceptable.

For direct access, an index to an entry-sequenced file may be useful if disk space is at a premium and a hashed file is unacceptable because of the space requirements. This approach is considered especially when the index will fit into memory. If the index will not fit into memory at one time and requires more than two segments, the complexity of the algorithm and the multiple seeks required to add new keys probably mitigate against this approach.

If sequential access in key order is needed, working through a simple index is not appropriate because of the excessive seeking that will be required. The file must be sorted to provide acceptable performance, but sorting the file must not disturb the order of the records in the original file or the index will be useless. Control-break logic may be employed in an output procedure to produce reports. On the other hand, the requirement to sort the file for every report may generate an unacceptable processing load.

Finally, the balance line algorithm cannot be used for updating a file with a simple index; updates must be made through direct access, which may cause unacceptable levels of seeking. In all, there is a lot against the simple-index-to-an-entry-sequenced-file approach. And it must be remembered that this approach had the simplest maintenance requirements, and the approaches that kept the data file in key order had maintenance requirements that were unacceptable.

10.7 EXTERNAL SORTING (REVISITED)

In this section we will consider sorting of records on a physical file, simply referred to as a file. As usual, we will assume that the file is very large and it cannot fit into the main memory. Using a small number of buffers, a few buckets of the file can be accessed at a time for internal processing required for the sorting. This type of sorting is called external sorting. External sorting is different from internal sorting, where the whole file can be stored in the main memory at once. Final implementation of the external sorting algorithm is given at the end of this section.

In order to fix notation, we will also assume that sorting will be done in ascending order (≤) of key values. For the sake of simplicity, we will implicitly assume that all buckets in the file are full, that is, the space utilization is 100%. Note that a key may consist of several attributes, and it may be a unique or a non-unique key. We will only consider the discrete model of the disk. We assume that the file contains N buckets and B buffers are available to sort it. To understand external sorting, we need to introduce the concept of a run. A run is a sorted segment of the file. Consider the following example.

Example 7.1. Consider the std file of Table 10.5. This file is sorted by Name, but not sorted by ID. Suppose we use ID as our key. Then the sequence of records in the file is 151, 306, 200, 310, 101, 311, 312, 305, 165, 160, 300, 180. The sequence consists of the following 7 runs (separated by semicolons): 151, 306; 200, 310; 101, 311, 312; 305; 165; 160, 300; 180.

We face a problem that we may not be aware of the runs that are contained in a given file. For example, we may be given a file that happens to be completely sorted. If we are not aware of this, even to realize that the file is sorted, the least we have to do, is read all buckets in the file once, costing us N disk accesses. In order to recognize this problem, we introduce the terms real run and certified run. A real run refers to a run that is present in a file, irrespective of whether we are aware of it or not. On the other hand, a certified run is a sorted segment that we know is a run. When we are given a file without any information about distribution of keys, we may assume that keys are completely out of order, that is, every record forms a run. Thus, the number of certified runs is same as the number of records in the file. The file in Example 7.1 contains 7 real runs and 12 certified runs. The goal of sorting is to reduce the number of certified runs to 1. We will first present the basic underlying method of external sorting.

10.7.1 Basic Underlying Method Of Sorting

Essentially, external sorting is done in two phases: creation of runs, followed by merging. In the phase for creation of runs, segments of the file are brought into the main memory and sorted using an internal sort. At the end of this phase, each segment becomes a run. In the merge phase, the runs are continually merged together to form larger runs until the whole file becomes a single run. The two phases are illustrated through the example given below.

Example 7.2. Consider a file containing 1800 records. Assume that 100 records fit in 1 bucket. Therefore, the file contains 1800/100 = 18 buckets. Assume that B = 3, that is, we are given 3 buffers to sort this file.

Phase 1: Creation of runs

For creation of runs, it is appropriate to use all the B buffers that are available to us. These buffers are used to read a segment of B buckets from the file, sort it into the main memory, thereby making and certifying it as a single run, and write the segment back to the file. For sorting the file in Example 7.2, we are given B = 3 buffers. We configure all 3 buffers for reading and writing. The buffer configuration is shown in **Figure** 10.34(a). In accordance with this buffer configuration, we may view the file to consist of 6 segments of 3 buckets each. This view of the file is shown in **Figure** 10.34(b).

We read the first 3-bucket segment into the buffers, sort the data in these buffers as a single run using an internal sort, and finally write the 3 buffers on the disk. If we do not care about disturbing the original file, we can write the 3-bucket segment in its original location. In other words, the old 3-bucket segment gets overwritten as a 3-bucket run. This procedure is repeated for the remaining 5 segments. In this way we obtain 6 runs of 3 buckets each, which completes the run creation phase.

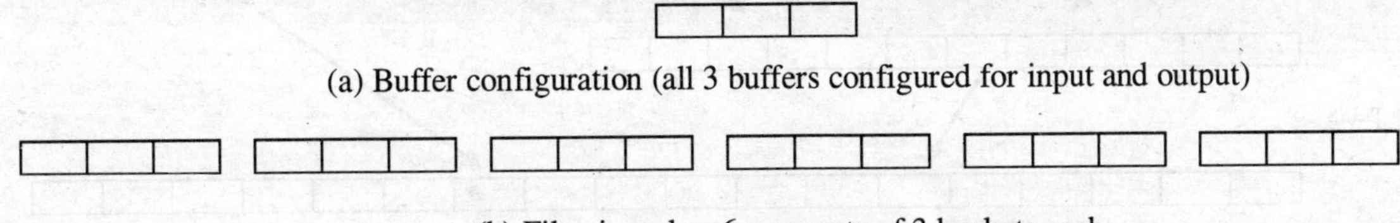

(a) Buffer configuration (all 3 buffers configured for input and output)

(b) File viewed as 6 segments of 3 buckets each

Figure 10.34 Creation of runs for the file of Example 7.1

Phase 2: Merging

The main idea in merging is that two or more runs can be merged together to produce one larger run. This processes can be repeated on the given runs until one run is left, at which point the file is sorted. For the running example, let us configure the 3 buffers to setup two input streams and one output stream as shown in **Figure** 10.35. With this configuration we can merge two runs at a time. We couple each run with one of the 2 input buffers. Then we merge one record at a time by transferring it to the output buffer. The output buffer is written to create a larger run out of the given runs. Whenever one input buffer becomes empty, processing is suspended and the next bucket from the coupled run is read into the buffer. Whenever the output buffer becomes full, the processing is suspended and the buffer is written to the disk. The sequence in which 3 buffers get read and written is unpredictable. (Also, think what happens when a run coupled to one input stream finishes before the other input stream?)

Merging may require several full and partial passes. For our file, the 2-way merge consists of a binary tree as shown in **Figure** 10.35. In the first pass, we reduce 6 runs of 3 buckets each into 3 runs of 6 buckets each. The second pass is a partial pass; only 2 of the 3 runs can be paired and merged leading to a 12-bucket run. Now we are left with a 12-bucket run and a 6-bucket run. The third pass is a full pass, requiring us to go through the entire file. In this pass the remaining two runs are merged together to form a single 18-bucket run and the file is now sorted. The complete merging requires 2.67 passes.

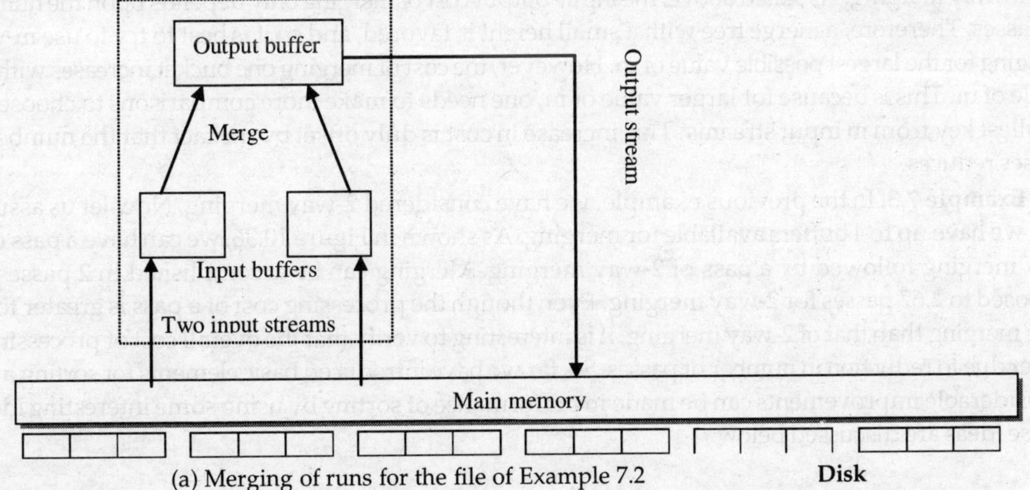

(a) Merging of runs for the file of Example 7.2 **Disk**

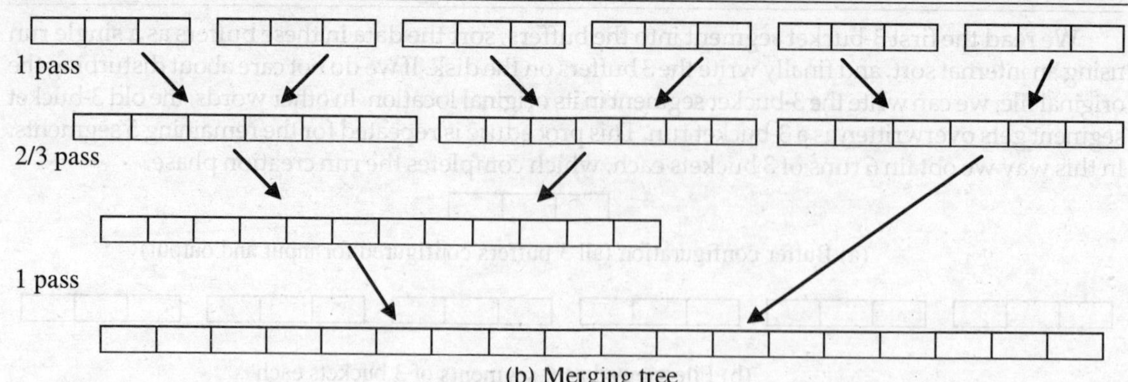

(b) Merging tree

Figure 10.35 Merging

The concept of a pass: A pass consists of reading all buckets, processing all buckets in some appropriate manner, and writing all buckets. Every pass leads to a refinement in the order of records, reducing the number of runs. For a file with N buckets, it is clear that the number of disk accesses for a pass is 2N. On the other hand, the cost of processing in a given pass depends upon the nature of processing required in that pass. In the above example, 1 pass is needed for creation of runs, and then 2.67 passes are needed to do 2-way merging until the file is completely sorted. Therefore, we can say, "the total cost of sorting is 3.67 passes." This figure, 3.67 passes, completely characterizes the number of disk accesses, which is $3.67 \times 2 \times 18 = 132$. The cost of processing per pass during creation of runs and during merging is different because the nature of processing is different. Note that during the partial run, the activity is same as a full pass, except that only two-thirds of the file is handled. The cost, measured at the rate of per bucket, is the same for partial and full passes. Therefore, the number of passes needed to sort a file is a good measure of performance of sorting, especially the disk accesses.

We have stated that we do not formally quantify cost of processing and disk accesses, but we offer some insights into how to reduce such costs. Because the number of disk accesses in a pass is constant (2N), a rule of thumb is to reduce the number of passes that are needed to sort a file. We hope that even if reducing number of passes increases the cost of processing for some passes, the overall cost of processing will still decrease.

m-way merging: As stated above, the input-output cost of merging only depends upon the number of passes. Therefore, a merge tree with a small height is favored, and so it is best to try to use m-way merging for the largest possible value of m. However, the cost of merging one bucket increases with the value of m. This is because for larger value of m, one needs to make more comparisons to choose the smallest key from m input streams. This increase in cost is duly offset by the fact that the number of passes reduces.

Example 7.3. In the previous example, we have considered 2-way merging. Now let us assume that we have up to 4 buffers available for merging. As shown in **Figure** 10.36, we can have a pass of 3-way merging followed by a pass of 2-way merging. Merging can be accomplished in 2 passes, as opposed to 2.67 passes for 2-way merging. Even though the processing cost of a pass is greater for 3-way merging than that of 2-way merging, it is interesting to verify that the overall cost of processing is lower due to reduction in number of passes. So, far we have introduced basic elements for sorting a file. Considerable improvements can be made in performance of sorting by using some interesting ideas. These ideas are discussed below.

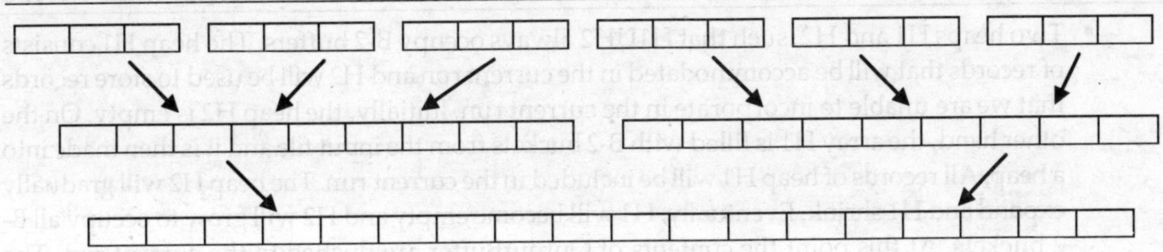

Figure 10.36 Merge tree for Example 7.3

10.7.2 Creating Large Runs

We have already seen that with B buffers, we can create runs that consist of B buckets. By using a clever technique, we can create runs that are twice as long on average. Although, this does not reduce the cost of creating runs, but it yields fewer runs. The reduced number of runs helps in reducing the cost of merging because fewer passes are needed. It pays no attention to the real runs, the runs that are already present in a file. Instead, independently of the state of the file, it reads fixed length segments of records from the file, sorts them and certifies them as runs. Even if the file happens to be sorted to begin with, the fact that it is sorted is never realized.

It is not unreasonable to expect that the certified runs should contain the original real runs. Runs should be expanded and they should not be fragmented. It is natural to expect that the amount of expansion of runs will depend upon the available memory. Using the B buffers that are available to us, by using the technique in the previous section we can create runs that consist of B buckets. Now we give an interesting technique that is known to create runs consisting of 2B buckets on average for random data. In addition, the technique will guarantee that existing runs will not shrink in size.

In order to understand the main idea, we concentrate upon creation of a single run which we will term as the current run. Since we want to be able to expand the current run, we have to read more data from the input file. Since the available memory, consisting of B buffers, cannot expand, we must be willing to write a part of the current run in the output file. Since we are only allowed a single pass, the portion of the output run that has been written to the disk will not be read again. This leads to two observations. First, we should be conservative about what we write to the disk: smallest possible values belonging to the current run should be written. Second, the largest value that has been written into the current run becomes a threshold. If an input record has a smaller key value than the threshold, it is obvious that this record cannot be accommodated in the current run and should be deferred to a future run. Since we want everything to be finished in one pass, the record has to be stored in the memory. As we input and process more records, the records that cannot be incorporated in the current run will increase in number. This means that the memory available for composing the current run will decrease and sooner or later it will completely diminish. At this time we have written all the records in the current run and the memory is now filled with the record belonging to the next run. Now, we can start composing the next run by repeating the above process again.

Now we describe how the idea outlined above can be implemented. Heaps (priority queues with the smallest key at the top) are appropriate for such implementation. As shown in **Figure** 10.37, the B buffers that are given to us, are partitioned into four logical compartments described below:

- InputBuffer, a buffer for continual streaming of input of raw data, one bucket at a time
- OutputBuffer, a buffer for continual streaming of output to the current run, one bucket at a time

- Two heaps H1 and H2, such that H1UH2 always occupy B-2 buffers. The heap H1 consists of records that will be accommodated in the current run and H2 will be used to store records that we are unable to incorporate in the current run. Initially, the heap H2 is empty. On the other hand, the array H1 is filled with B-2 buckets from the input file and it is then made into a heap. All records of heap H1 will be included in the current run. The heap H2 will gradually expand and H1 shrink. Eventually, H1 will become empty and H2 will grow to occupy all B-2 buckets. At this point the contents of OutputBuffer are flushed to the current run. The current run is now completed and it is time to start the next run. Simply interchanging the roles of the heaps H1 and H2 does this.

The above description makes it clear how the buffers are configured and it outlines the overall strategy. What remains to be seen is how records are transferred from InputBuffer to heap H1, heap H2, and Output-Buffer. Note that at any given moment we have H2 < OutputBuffer < H1. This is meant to express that every key in H2 is smaller than every key in OutputBuffer, and every key in OutputBuffer is smaller than every key in H1.

Imagine that currently we are composing a run and some records in the run have already been output. As shown in **Figure** 10.37, suppose we are considering a record x in InputBuffer that is waiting to be processed. Suppose that w is the last record deposited to OutputBuffer. Then, w represents a threshold for determining what belongs to the current run and what does not. A record with the key value smaller than w will have to wait for the next run; otherwise it can be accommodated in the current run.

In other words, if x < w, the record x should be transferred to the heap H2. In order to do this, heap H2 has to be expanded by one element. Therefore, the heap H1 has to be shrunk by one element. To accomplish this, the record y at the top of the heap H1 is transferred to OutputBuffer. This creates a vacancy at the top of heap H1. The vacancy is filled by transferring the last element of heap H1 to the top of H1. The heap H1 is now redrawn. The vacated element is now claimed as the last element of heap H2 and this is where the record x is stored. The heap H2 is also redrawn to complete the process.

Now assume that x ≥ w. Do we transfer it to heap H1 or OutputBuffer? To decide this y, the key of the record y at the top of the heap H1 will act as the threshold. We have two possibilities. Either x ≤ y or x > y. If x ≤ y, then x is ≤ every element in heap H1, and the record x is deposited in OutputBuffer. On the other hand, if x > y, then x must be absorbed in the heap H1. Since we cannot expand H1 in order to accommodate x, we transfer the record y at the top of the heap H1 to OutputBuffer. The vacancy is filled by x and the heap H1 is redrawn to complete this process.

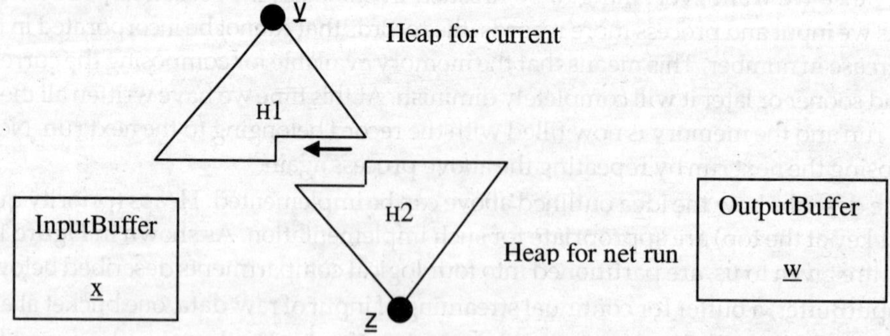

Figure 10.37 Organization of B buffers for creating large runs

In order to implement the heaps, an array of B–2 buffers may be used. Each end of the array can be used for top of a heap. The heap elements are stored inward in the array in opposite directions. The bottoms of the two heaps are consecutive elements of the array. As one heap shrinks the other heap easily absorbs the vacancy. At the end of a pass, the roles of the two arrays are swapped.

Because of the fact that the H1 and H2 occupy only B–2 buckets and not B buckets, the technique as described above will create runs that are on average 2(B–2) buckets long. (This fact is not trivial.) Further improvements can be made at the start of run creation so that the runs are 2B buckets long on average.

10.7.3 Fast m-Way Merging

The second improvement is to make m-way merging faster. Ordinarily, choosing the smallest number in m input streams requires us to make m–1 comparisons. This can be reduced to $\log_2 m$ comparisons using a clever data structure called tree of losers. This would save processing time that is of critical importance in sorting. It allows one to do m-way merging with a larger value of m which reduces the number of passes needed during the merging phase.

In m-way merging there are m input streams and one output stream. In such merging m+1 buffers are required, one for m input streams and one for the output stream. One has to continually determine the smallest of m keys of the records at the front of the input stream and transfer the record to the output stream. Ordinarily, this would require m–1 comparisons. However, while making m–1 comparisons, we not only determine the smallest key, but also come across some information about the relative magnitude among other keys. The tree of losers helps us "remember" such information; the next smallest of m keys can be determined in only $\log_2 2k$ comparisons rather than m–1 comparisons. The tree of losers is a binary tree. Its leaves are the records waiting to be processed in the m input streams.

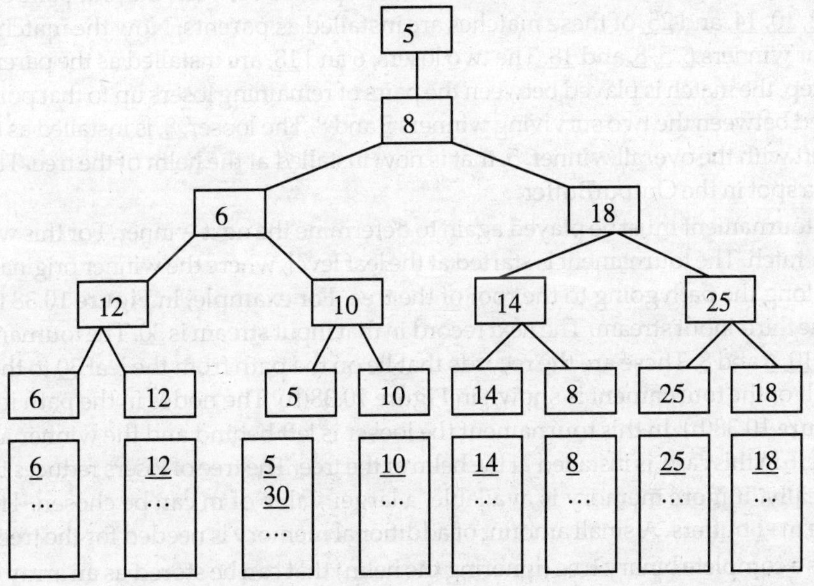

(a) The first tournament

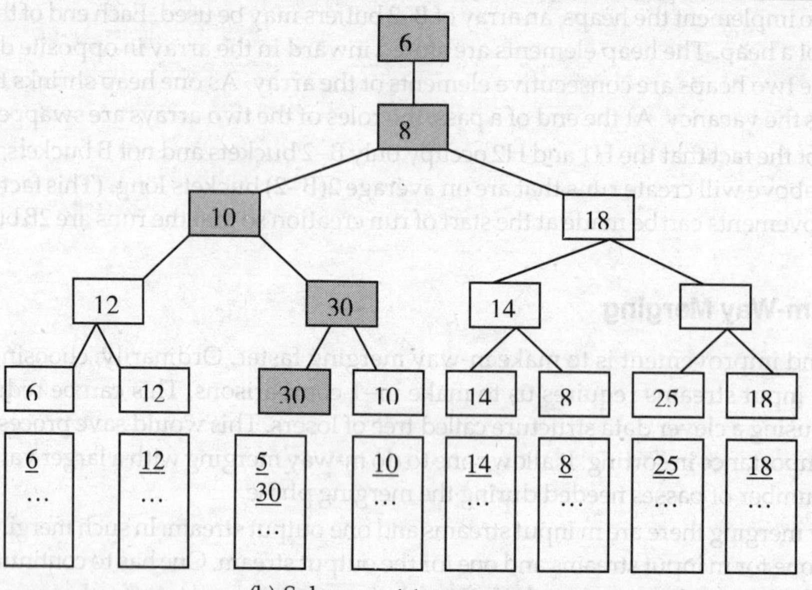

(b) Subsequent tournaments

Figure 10.38 m-way merging with tree of losers

To draw the tree, the keys of pairs of records are compared. We refer to such comparison as a match between the two records. The record with the smaller key is said to win the match. **Figure** 10.38(a) shows 8-way merging with tree of losers. The tree corresponds to a tournament with the objective of determining the overall winner. The leaves of the tree are the eight records, 6, 12, 5, 10, 14, 8, 25, and 18, from the front of each input stream. The matches are first played between the four pairs of records. The four losers, 12, 10, 14, and 25, of these matches are installed as parents. Now the matches are played among the four winners 6, 5, 8, and 18. The two losers, 6 and 18, are installed as the parents at the next level. In any step, the match is played between the pairs of remaining losers up to that point. So, the last match is played between the two surviving winners 5 and 8. The looser, 8, is installed as the root of the tree. We are left with the overall winner, 5, that is now installed at the helm of the tree. The helm of the tree is simply a spot in the OutputBuffer.

Now, the tournament must be played again to determine the next winner. For this we do not have to start from scratch. The tournament is started at the leaf level, where the winner originated from, and played only along the path going to the root of the tree. For example, in **Figure** 10.38 the winner, 5, comes from the third input stream. The next record in that input stream is 30. The tournament will now be among 30, 10, 6 and 8. These are the records that lie on the path from the leaf 30 to the root 8 of the tree. The result of the tournament is shown in **Figure** 10.38(b). The nodes in the path in question are shaded in **Figure** 10.38(b). In this tournament the looser is left behind and the winner advances. The overall winner, 6 in this case, is installed at the helm of the tree. The tree of losers reduces the processing time dramatically. If more memory is available, a larger value of m can be chosen. The memory is needed for the m+1 buffers. A small amount of additional memory is needed for the tree.

The tree is a complete binary tree (ignoring the helm) that can be stored as an array of nodes. The child and parent pointers can be computed and need not be stored explicitly in these nodes. Moreover, it is not necessary to store records in these nodes; the pointers to the records suffice. In our example we implicitly assumed that m in m-way merging is a power of 2.

10.7.4 Pipeline Merging: Minimizing Elapsed Time

The third improvement is pipeline processing. Here, input, processing and output are all done in parallel. Although, it does not save the processing time or the number of disk accesses, it does reduce the time between start and end of sorting by keeping the system dedicated and fully utilized to the task of sorting.

We will assume that the system permits disk access and processing can be done in parallel. At this point we will pursue an interesting case when a system has two parallel disks and the system is dedicated to our task of merging. We will assume that for m-way merging, m has been chosen such that the time to process one bucket is same as its access time. Thus, we can do merging in a pipeline by performing the following three operations in parallel: read a bucket, process the bucket, and write the bucket. This gives rise to pipeline as shown in **Figure** 10.39. Therefore, we define a pipeline operation to be an operation of the form ⟨read α1, process α2, write α3⟩.

Note that the operation "process α2" refers to merging records from m input buffers to fill one output buffer α2. Thus, in this operation m+1 buffers are involved in the processing. A buffer can be involved in only one operation at a time: it can be read, it can be processed, or it can be written. In other words the cost of a pipeline operation is the sum of the costs of its three component operations. However, a pipeline operation allows all three-component operations to be performed in parallel, thereby minimizing the elapsed time.

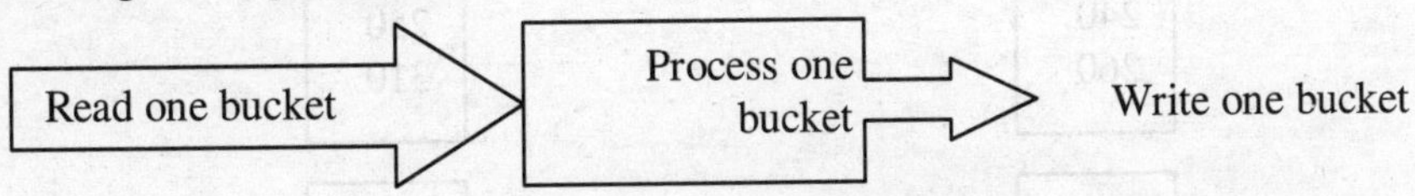

Figure 10.39 Pipeline merging

A buffer cannot be involved in input/output (I/O) and processing at the same time. Therefore, support of uninterrupted m-way merging would require 2k+2 buffers. The behavior of the output stream is simple, and out of the 2k+2 buffers, 2 buffers can be permanently coupled to the output stream. The buffer configuration for the input buffers is interesting and will be discussed next.

A simple strategy, termed static buffer configuration, is to couple 2 input buffers permanently to each input stream. Example 7.4 shows that the static buffer configuration does not guarantee uninterrupted pipeline.

The alternative is to use a dynamic buffer configuration. This configuration maintains the 2k input buffers in a pool. A buffer is coupled dynamically to a strategically chosen input stream. It might happen that at a given time some input streams have more buffers coupled to them than others, but it can be shown that the dynamic buffer configuration guarantees uninterrupted pipeline merging.

Example 7.4. In this example we show that static buffer configuration does not guarantee uninterrupted pipeline merging. Suppose that for 2-way merging (m =2) we are given 2k+2 = 6 buffers.

Suppose that the 6 buffers are numbered α1, α2, α3, α4, β1, and β2. For 2-way merging we need 2 input streams and 1 output stream. As shown in **Figure** 10.40, we couple buffers α1 and α2 to input stream 1, α3 and α4 to input stream 2, and β1 and β2 to the output stream. A bucket consists of 2 records. **Figure** 10.40 also shows 2 runs given to us.

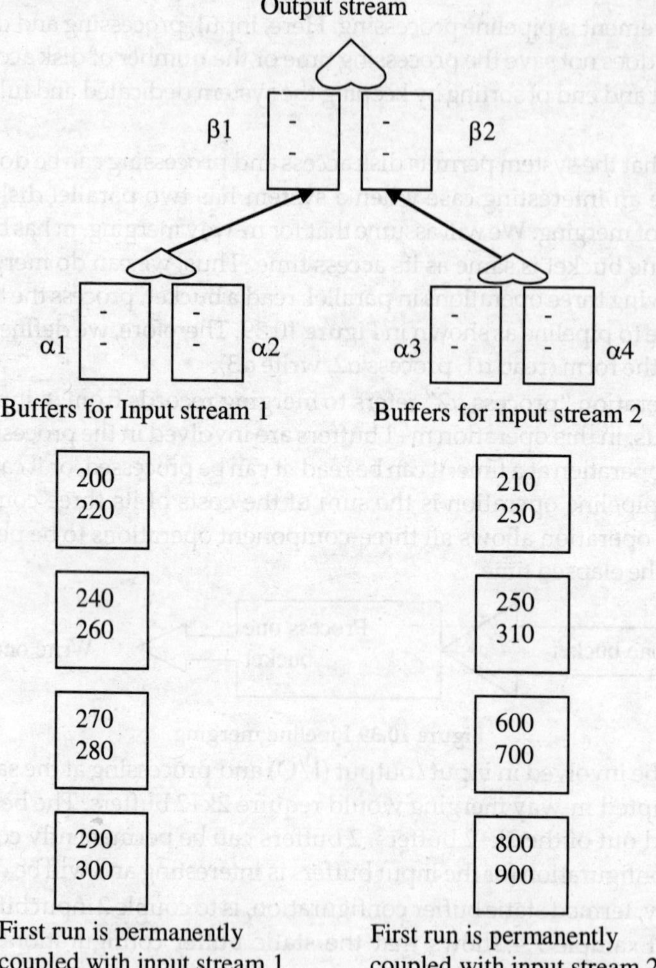

Figure 10.40 Merging setup with static buffer configuration

The implementation of external sorting algorithm is as follows:

```
/* merge sort and external sort */
/* ExtMrg.C */

#include <stdio.h>
#include <stdlib.h>
#include <string.h>

/****************************
 * implementation dependent *
 ****************************/

/* template for workfiles (8.3 format) */
```

```
#define FNAME "_sort%03d.dat"
#define LNAME 13
/* comparison operators */
#define compLT(x,y) (x < y)
#define compGT(x,y) (x > y)

/* define the record to be sorted here */
#define LRECL 100
typedef int keyType;
typedef struct recTypeTag
{
   keyType key;                          /* sort key for record */
   #if LRECL
      char data[LRECL-sizeof(keyType)];     /* other fields */
   #endif
} recType;

/******************************
 * implementation independent *
 ******************************/

typedef enum {false, true} bool;

typedef struct tmpFileTag
{
   FILE *fp;                 /* file pointer */
   char name[LNAME];          /* filename */
   recType rec;              /* last record read */
   int dummy;                /* number of dummy runs */
   bool eof;                 /* end-of-file flag */
   bool eor;                 /* end-of-run flag */
   bool valid;               /* true if rec is valid */
   int fib;                  /* ideal fibonacci number */
} tmpFileType;

static tmpFileType **file;     /* array of file info for tmp files */
static int nTmpFiles;          /* number of tmp files */
static char *ifName;           /* input filename */
static char *ofName;           /* output filename */

static int level;              /* level of runs */
static int nNodes;             /* number of nodes for selection tree */

void deleteTmpFiles(void) {
```

```
    int i;
    /* delete merge files and free resources */
    if (file) {
        for (i = 0; i < nTmpFiles; i++) {
            if (file[i]) {
                if (file[i]->fp) fclose(file[i]->fp);
                if (*file[i]->name) remove(file[i]->name);
                free (file[i]);
            }
        }
        free (file);
    }
}

void termTmpFiles(int rc) {

    /* cleanup files */
    remove(ofName);
    if (rc == 0) {
        int fileT;

        /* file[T] contains results */
        fileT = nTmpFiles - 1;
        fclose(file[fileT]->fp); file[fileT]->fp = NULL;
        if (rename(file[fileT]->name, ofName)) {
            perror("io1");
            deleteTmpFiles();
            exit(1);
        }
        *file[fileT]->name = 0;
    }
    deleteTmpFiles();
}

void cleanExit(int rc) {

    /* cleanup tmp files and exit */
    termTmpFiles(rc);
    exit(rc);
}

void *safeMalloc(size_t size) {
    void *p;

    /* safely allocate memory and initialize to zero */
```

```
    if ((p = calloc(1, size)) == NULL) {
        printf("error: malloc failed, size = %d\n", size);
        cleanExit(1);
    }
    return p;
}

void initTmpFiles(void) {
    int i;
    tmpFileType *fileInfo;

    /* initialize merge files */
    if (nTmpFiles < 3) nTmpFiles = 3;
    file = safeMalloc(nTmpFiles * sizeof(tmpFileType*));
    fileInfo = safeMalloc(nTmpFiles * sizeof(tmpFileType));
    for (i = 0; i < nTmpFiles; i++) {
        file[i] = fileInfo + i;
        sprintf(file[i]->name, FNAME, i);
        if ((file[i]->fp = fopen(file[i]->name, "w+b")) == NULL) {
            perror("io2");
            cleanExit(1);
        }
    }
}

recType *readRec(void) {

    typedef struct iNodeTag {  /* internal node */
        struct iNodeTag *parent;/* parent of internal node */
        struct eNodeTag *loser; /* external loser */
    } iNodeType;

    typedef struct eNodeTag {   /* external node */
        struct iNodeTag *parent;/* parent of external node */
        recType rec;            /* input record */
        int run;               /* run number */
        bool valid;             /* input record is valid */
    } eNodeType;

    typedef struct nodeTag {
        iNodeType i;            /* internal node */
        eNodeType e;            /* external node */
    } nodeType;

    static nodeType *node;     /* array of selection tree nodes */
```

```
static eNodeType *win;      /* new winner */
static FILE *ifp;           /* input file */
static bool eof;            /* true if end-of-file, input */
static int maxRun;          /* maximum run number */
static int curRun;          /* current run number */
iNodeType *p;               /* pointer to internal nodes */
static bool lastKeyValid;   /* true if lastKey is valid */
static keyType lastKey;     /* last key written */

/* read next record using replacement selection */

/* check for first call */
if (node == NULL) {
   int i;

   if (nNodes < 2) nNodes = 2;
   node = safeMalloc(nNodes * sizeof(nodeType));
   for (i = 0; i < nNodes; i++) {
      node[i].i.loser = &node[i].e;
      node[i].i.parent = &node[i/2].i;
      node[i].e.parent = &node[(nNodes + i)/2].i;
      node[i].e.run = 0;
      node[i].e.valid = false;
   }
   win = &node[0].e;
   lastKeyValid = false;

   if ((ifp = fopen(ifName, "rb")) == NULL) {
      printf("error: file %s, unable to open\n", ifName);
      cleanExit(1);
   }
}

while (1) {

   /* replace previous winner with new record */
   if (!eof) {
      if (fread(&win->rec, sizeof(recType), 1, ifp) == 1) {
         if ((!lastKeyValid || compLT(win->rec.key, lastKey))
         && (++win->run > maxRun))
            maxRun = win->run;
         win->valid = true;
      } else if (feof(ifp)) {
         fclose(ifp);
         eof = true;
```

```
            win->valid = false;
            win->run = maxRun + 1;
        } else {
            perror("io4");
            cleanExit(1);
        }
    } else {
        win->valid = false;
        win->run = maxRun + 1;
    }

    /* adjust loser and winner pointers */
    p = win->parent;
    do {
        bool swap;
        swap = false;
        if (p->loser->run < win->run) {
            swap = true;
        } else if (p->loser->run == win->run) {
            if (p->loser->valid && win->valid) {
                if (compLT(p->loser->rec.key, win->rec.key))
                    swap = true;
            } else {
                swap = true;
            }
        }
        if (swap) {
            /* p should be winner */
            eNodeType *t;

            t = p->loser;
            p->loser = win;
            win = t;
        }
        p = p->parent;
    } while (p != &node[0].i);

    /* end of run? */
    if (win->run != curRun) {
        /* win->run = curRun + 1 */
        if (win->run > maxRun) {
            /* end of output */
            free(node);
            return NULL;
        }
```

```
            curRun = win->run;
        }

        /* output top of tree */
        if (win->run) {
            lastKey = win->rec.key;
            lastKeyValid = true;
            return &win->rec;
        }
    }
}

void makeRuns(void) {
    recType *win;       /* winner */
    int fileT;          /* last file */
    int fileP;          /* next to last file */
    int j;              /* selects file[j] */

    /* Make initial runs using replacement selection.
     * Runs are written using a Fibonacci distintbution.
     */

    /* initialize file structures */
    fileT = nTmpFiles - 1;
    fileP = fileT - 1;
    for (j = 0; j < fileT; j++) {
        file[j]->fib = 1;
        file[j]->dummy = 1;
    }
    file[fileT]->fib = 0;
    file[fileT]->dummy = 0;

    level = 1;
    j = 0;


    win = readRec();
    while (win) {
        bool anyrun;

        anyrun = false;
        for (j = 0; win && j <= fileP; j++) {
            bool run;
```

```
            run = false;
            if (file[j]->valid) {
                if (!compLT(win->key, file[j]->rec.key)) {
                    /* append to an existing run */
                    run = true;
                } else if (file[j]->dummy) {
                    /* start a new run */
                    file[j]->dummy--;
                    run = true;
                }
            } else {
                /* first run in file */
                file[j]->dummy--;
                run = true;
            }

            if (run) {
                anyrun = true;

                /* flush run */
                while(1) {
                    if (fwrite(win, sizeof(recType), 1, file[j]->fp) != 1) {
                        perror("io3");
                        cleanExit(1);
                    }
                    file[j]->rec.key = win->key;
                    file[j]->valid = true;
                    if ((win = readRec()) == NULL) break;
                    if (compLT(win->key, file[j]->rec.key)) break;
                }
            }
        }

        /* if no room for runs, up a level */
        if (!anyrun) {
            int t;
            level++;
            t = file[0]->fib;
            for (j = 0; j <= fileP; j++) {
                file[j]->dummy = t + file[j+1]->fib - file[j]->fib;
                file[j]->fib = t + file[j+1]->fib;
            }
        }
    }
}
```

```
void rewindFile(int j) {
   /* rewind file[j] and read in first record */
   file[j]->eor = false;
   file[j]->eof = false;
   rewind(file[j]->fp);
   if (fread(&file[j]->rec, sizeof(recType), 1, file[j]->fp) != 1) {
      if (feof(file[j]->fp)) {
         file[j]->eor = true;
         file[j]->eof = true;
      } else {
         perror("io5");
         cleanExit(1);
      }
   }
}

void mergeSort(void) {
   int fileT;
   int fileP;
   int j;
   tmpFileType *tfile;

   /* polyphase merge sort */

   fileT = nTmpFiles - 1;
   fileP = fileT - 1;

   /* prime the files */
   for (j = 0; j < fileT; j++) {
      rewindFile(j);
   }

   /* each pass through loop merges one run */
   while (level) {
      while(1) {
         bool allDummies;
         bool anyRuns;

         /* scan for runs */
         allDummies = true;
         anyRuns = false;
         for (j = 0; j <= fileP; j++) {
            if (!file[j]->dummy) {
               allDummies = false;
```

```
            if (!file[j]->eof) anyRuns = true;
        }
    }

    if (anyRuns) {
        int k;
        keyType lastKey;

        /* merge 1 run file[0]..file[P] -> file[T] */

        while(1) {
            /* each pass thru loop writes 1 record to file[fileT] */

            /* find smallest key */
            k = -1;
            for (j = 0; j <= fileP; j++) {
                if (file[j]->eor) continue;
                if (file[j]->dummy) continue;
                if (k < 0 ||
              (k != j && compGT(file[k]->rec.key, file[j]->rec.key)))
                    k = j;
            }
            if (k < 0) break;

            /* write record[k] to file[fileT] */
            if (fwrite(&file[k]->rec, sizeof(recType), 1,
                    file[fileT]->fp) != 1) {
                perror("io6");
                cleanExit(1);
            }

            /* replace record[k] */
            lastKey = file[k]->rec.key;
            if (fread(&file[k]->rec, sizeof(recType), 1,
                    file[k]->fp) == 1) {
                /* check for end of run on file[s] */
                if (compLT(file[k]->rec.key, lastKey))
                    file[k]->eor = true;
            } else if (feof(file[k]->fp)) {
                file[k]->eof = true;
                file[k]->eor = true;
            } else {
                perror("io7");
                cleanExit(1);
```

```
            }
        }

        /* fixup dummies */
        for (j = 0; j <= fileP; j++) {
            if (file[j]->dummy) file[j]->dummy--;
            if (!file[j]->eof) file[j]->eor = false;
        }

    } else if (allDummies) {
        for (j = 0; j <= fileP; j++)
            file[j]->dummy--;
        file[fileT]->dummy++;
    }

    /* end of run */
    if (file[fileP]->eof && !file[fileP]->dummy) {
        /* completed a fibonocci-level */
        level--;
        if (!level) {
            /* we are done, file[fileT] contains data */
            return;
        }

        /* fileP is exhausted, reopen as new */
        fclose(file[fileP]->fp);
        if ((file[fileP]->fp = fopen(file[fileP]->name, "w+b"))
                == NULL) {
            perror("io8");
            cleanExit(1);
        }
        file[fileP]->eof = false;
        file[fileP]->eor = false;

        rewindFile(fileT);

        /* f[0],f[1], ...,f[fileT] <= f[fileT],f[0]...,f[T-1] */
        tfile = file[fileT];
        memmove(file + 1, file, fileT * sizeof(tmpFileType*));
        file[0] = tfile;

        /* start new runs */
        for (j = 0; j <= fileP; j++)
            if (!file[j]->eof) file[j]->eor = false;
    }
```

```
    }
}
}

void extSort(void) {
    initTmpFiles();
    makeRuns();
    mergeSort();
    termTmpFiles(0);
}

int main(int argc, char *argv[]) {

    if (argc != 5) {
        printf("%s ifName ofName nTmpFiles nNodes\n", argv[0]);
        cleanExit(1);
    }

    ifName = argv[1];
    ofName = argv[2];
    nTmpFiles = atoi(argv[3]);
    nNodes = atoi(argv[4]);

    printf("extSort: nFiles=%d, nNodes=%d, lrecl=%d\n",
        nTmpFiles, nNodes, sizeof(recType));

    extSort();
    return 0;
}
```

How this program can be run for this use syntax of the command: **ExtMrg ifName ofName nTmpFiles nNodes**, e.g., **ExtMrg in.dat out.dat 5 2000**, this command reads **in.dat**, sorts using 5 files and 2000 nodes, output to **out.dat**

10.8 Hashing (Revisited)

Hashing concentrates upon direct access of a single record: we are given a key value k, and want to retrieve the record k. In the best case the cost of such a retrieval is 1 bucket access. The ideal goal of hashing is to achieve the best-case performance. To achieve the ideal performance, it seems natural to try to compute the address of the bucket containing k. Because the key value is a clue to the address, the needed address is a function, called a hash function, $k \rightarrow H(k)$. Key space is defined to be the set of all possible keys, and address space is defined to be the set of all bucket (chain) addresses of the file where records are stored.

Example 8.1. Consider a file containing student records at a Punjab University having, 25000 students. Suppose with certain space utilization in mind, we expect to store 5 records on average per bucket. Then we expect about 5000 buckets in the file. At such a university, it is common to use a social security number as a key, let us suppose this is the case. There are a total of 1 billion different social security numbers possible. Therefore, in this example the size of the key space and address space are 1000000000 and 5000, respectively.

We can make a reasonable assumption that the size of the key space is much larger than the size of the address space. Under this assumption, a hash function cannot be one to one. In other words, a hash function maps more records to a bucket than the capacity of the bucket. A collision is a condition arising when a new record being inserted, hashes to a bucket that is already full. Clearly, collisions will arise, and we need a procedure, called collision resolution, to handle them. Therefore, hashing typically consists of (i) a hash function $k \rightarrow H(k)$, and (ii) a procedure to resolve collisions. Below are two simple examples of hashing.

Example 8.2. Consider records whose keys are in the range 101...999. Suppose we have a file with 5 buckets with addresses 0...4 such that each bucket can hold up to 2 records. Records within a bucket are not necessarily stored in a sorted order. The total capacity of the file is 10 records. Suppose hashing consists of the following:

Hash function: H1(k) = k mod 5

Collision resolution: To resolve the collisions, we try bucket k+1 mod 5, k+2 mod 5, k+3 mod 5, ··· until we find a bucket containing an empty slot.

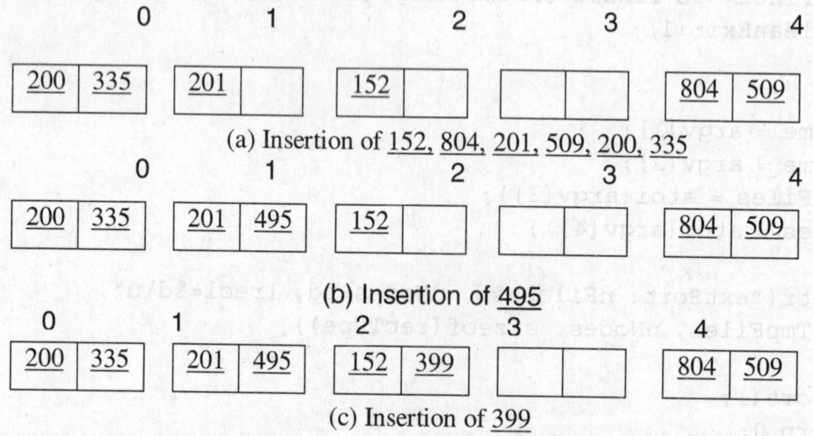

Figure 10.41 Hash file of Example 8.2.

Suppose we have the following sequence of insertions: 152, 804, 201, 509, 200, 335, 495, and 399. 152 mod 5 = 2. Hence 152 can be stored in bucket #2. Similarly, 804 can be stored in #4, 201 can be stored in bucket #1, 509 in #4, 200 in #0, and 335 also in #0. There are no collisions so far. The state of the file at this point is as shown in **Figure** 10.41(a).

The record 495 hashes to bucket #0, and thus there is a collision. According to our collision resolution method, we try the next bucket, which is bucket #1. Since that bucket has an empty slot, we store 495 there. Note that the cost of insertion of 495 is 3 bucket accesses (read #0, read #1, write #1). The state of the file is now as shown in **Figure** 10.41(b).

It remains to insert 399, which hashes to bucket #4. Since bucket #4 is full, we have a collision. In order to resolve the collision, we try (399+1) mod 5 = bucket #0. We again have a collision. Next we try bucket #1 and have yet another collision. Finally we try bucket #2, find an empty slot, and insert 399 in that bucket. Note that the cost of this insertion is 5. The final state of the file is now as shown in **Figure** 10.41(c).

Let us consider the cost of retrieval. What is the cost of retrieval of 200, 399, and 555? Clearly, the cost of retrieving 200 is 1. To retrieve 399, we read the sequence of buckets #4, #0, #1, and #2. Therefore, the cost is 4 bucket accesses. The record 555 is not in the file. However, this is realized only after retrieving the entire file.

Example 8.3. In this example we are considering hashing with chaining. We assume that the records within a chain appear in a sorted order. We use the hash function H2(k) = k mod 3. Collisions are simply resolved by chaining additional buckets. The result of inserting the records of Example 8.2 is shown in **Figure** 10.42.

Example 8.2 illustrates a potential problem with hashing: as the space utilization increases, the performance deteriorates. In an extreme (but likely) situation, what if we want to store more than 10 records in the file? One solution is to use chaining. But chaining is an incremental and short-term solution in the life of a growing file. A good solution requires the address space to be expanded, with or without chaining. One way to achieve this is to use a new hashing function with a larger address space and rehash the entire file. But such a solution would require an enormous amount of time for large files.

We need a solution that allows us to enlarge the address space gracefully – affecting a small number of buckets. We will use variants of splitting to give solutions to this problem in the next section.

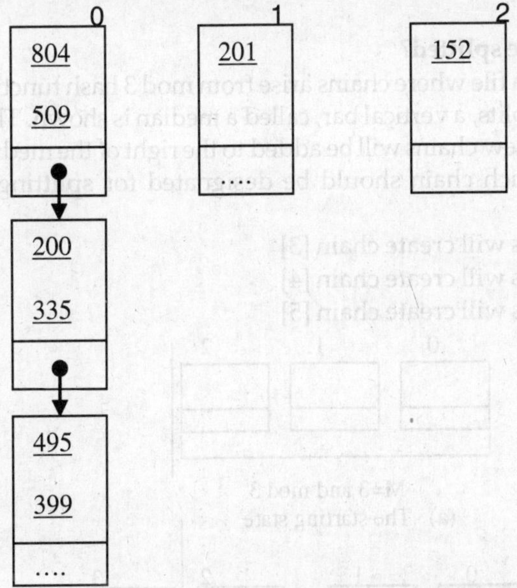

Figure 10.42 Hash file of Example 8.3

10.8.1 Linear Hashing

Linear hashing uses a mod function to generate chain addresses. An illustration of hashing using a mod function was given in Example 8.3. In this example, the address space {0,1,2} is fixed. Therefore, it has the shortcoming that as a file expands, the chains become longer. Linear hashing provides a way to control chains from growing too large on average. Linear hashing accomplishes this by expanding the address space gracefully, one chain at a time. This graceful expansion is achieved by using chain splitting.

Suppose we have a file, F, which uses the mod M hash function to determine chain addresses. The file has a static address space consisting of chains with addresses 0, 1, ···, M–1. The contents of [m], the chain #m, are as follows:

[m] = {k in F: k mod M = m}

Example 8.4 Suppose M = 3. Then there are three chains [0], [1], and [2]. In particular, the chain [1] may consists of [1] = {106, 217, 151, 415, 379}.

How can we enlarge the address space for this file? To do this we use chain splitting and ask the following questions.

(a) How can a chain split? (b) Which chain should split?
(c) When should a chain split?

How can a chain split?

How do we split a chain [m] evenly into two chains using a mod function? Because we want to expand the address space, the argument for a mod function does not have to be M. The answer to the above question is simple: use mod 2M to rehash the records in [m]. On average, mod 2M will hash half of the records to chain [m], and the other half to chain [M+m]. This is the main idea behind linear hashing.

Example 8.5. Continuing Example 8.4, we see that 2M = 6. By rehashing the keys in chain [1] we obtain chains [1] and [4]. The contents of these two chains are shown below.

[1] = {217, 151, 379, 415}
[4] = {106}

Which chain should be splitted?

Figure 10.43(a) shows a file where chains arise from mod 3 hash function. To separate new chains to be generated by future splits, a vertical bar, called a median is shown. The existing chains are on the left of the median, and the new chains will be added to the right of the median. The median is given the numerical value of 3. Which chain should be designated for splitting? There are the following possibilities:

- split chain [0]: this will create chain [3]
- split chain [1]: this will create chain [4]
- split chain [2]: this will create chain [5]

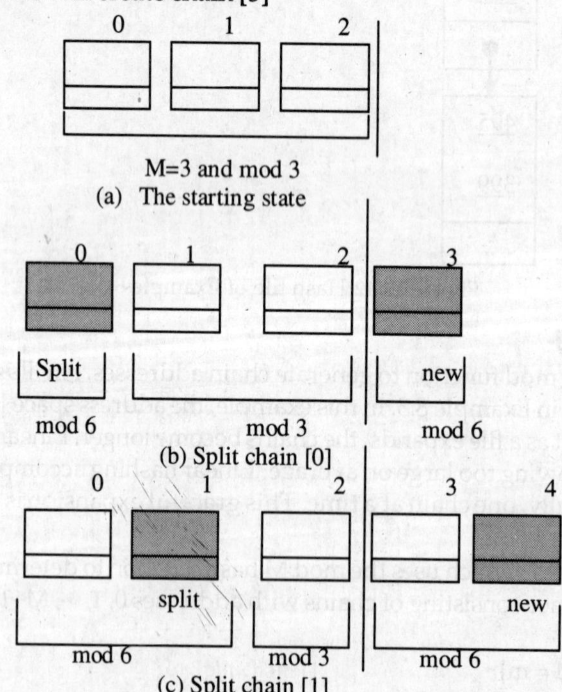

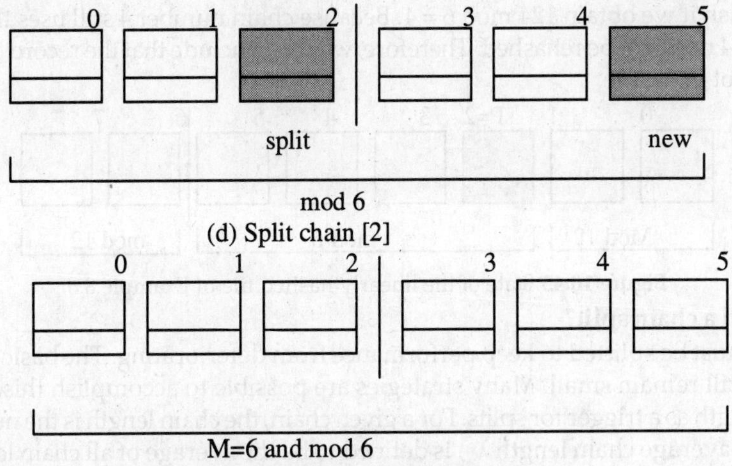

Figure 10.43 Splitting in linear hashing

Linear hashing gets its name from the fact that chains are designated linearly for splitting. In the above situation, we would first split chain [0], next chain [1], and then chain [2]. Note that this is independent of where the insertions are taking place.

As shown in **Figure** 10.43(b), chain [0] is splitted first. This split first creates a new chain [3]. Next, the records in chain [0] are rehashed using mod 6. This figure also shows the chains covered by mod 3 and mod 6 hash functions. Then, chain [1] is splitted into chains [1] and [4] {**Figure** 10.43(c)}. The third split creates the new chain [5], as shown in **Figure** 10.43(d). At this point we have 6 chains, and all of them are covered by mod 6. This completes one cycle, essentially doubling M from 3 to 6. The new state of the file is shown in **Figure** 10.43(e). Now we can repeat the same procedure as above. During the next cycle, 6 splits will be made and the address space will double to 0…11.

An important feature of linear splitting is that it does not create gaps between existing chains and the new chains. This feature prevents address space from becoming complicated or unnecessarily large. The address space increases gracefully, one chain at a time. It is easy to characterize the configuration of a linearly hashed file. With sP denoting the chain designated to be splitted next, and M as the current value of the median, the state of a linearly hashed file is as shown in **Figure** 10.44.

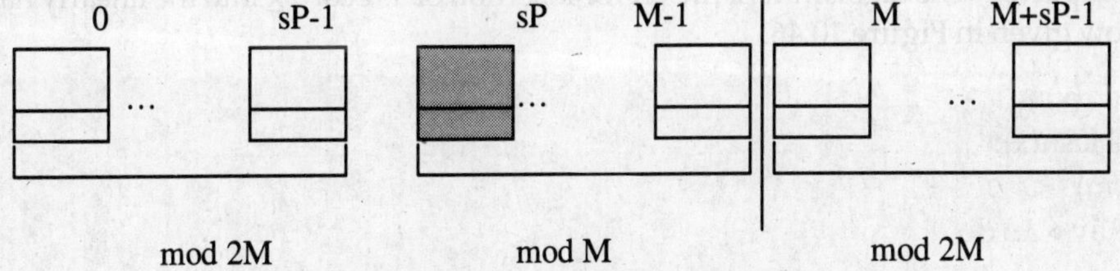

Figure 10.44 State of a linearly hashed file

Example 8.6. To understand the parameters sP and M associated with a linearly hashed file, suppose M = 6 and sP = 2. This means that in the current cycle of splitting, chains [0] and [1] has been splitted. Therefore, the state of the file is shown in **Figure** 10.45.

Now consider the record 319. We have 319 mod 6 = 1. Thus, we suspect that 319 is in chain [1]. But chain [1] has been splitted using mod 12. Thus, we must rehash the key: 319 mod 12 gives us 7. This means the record 319 is either in chain [7] or the record is not in the file. As another example consider

124. When we hash it we obtain 124 mod 6 = 4. Because chain number 4 still uses the hash function mod 6, the key 124 need not be rehashed. Therefore, we can conclude that the record 124 is either in [4] or the record is not in the file.

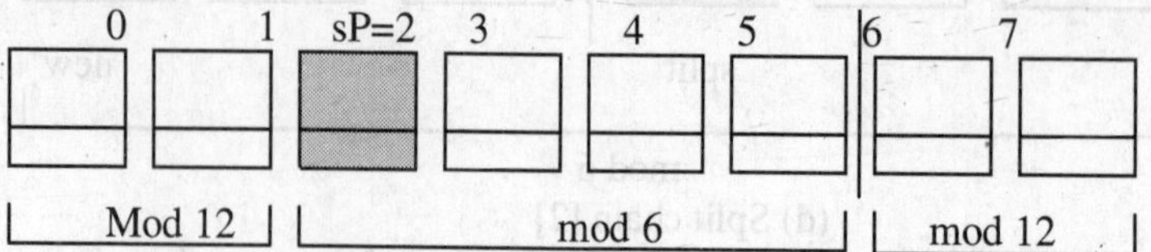

Figure 10.45 State of the linearly hashed file of Example 8.6

When should a chain split?

The chains must be splitted to keep performance from deteriorating. The basic idea is to ensure that the chains will remain small. Many strategies are possible to accomplish this. Let us consider average chain length as a trigger for splits. For a given chain, the chain length is the number of buckets in the chain. The average chain length λ_{av} is defined to be the average of all chain lengths in the file. Next we set acceptable lower and upper bounds, λ_l and λ_u, for λ_{av}. In other words, $\lambda_l \le \lambda_{av} \le \lambda_u$ are the acceptable limits. A split occurs when λ_{av} exceeds λ_u, and a collapse occurs when λ_{av} drops below λ_l.

10.8.1.1 An Algorithm For Insertion

In context of linear hashing the parameters M and sP help us determine the configuration of a linearly hashed file. These parameters tell us how and which chain to split. We also have introduced the parameters λ_l and λ_u, which trigger splitting. Note that the number of home buckets in the file is same as the number of chains, and that number is M+sP. Therefore, $\lambda_{av} = N/(M+sP)$, where N is the number of buckets in the file. The parameters M, sP, λ_l, λ_u and N are stored in a header of the linearly hashed file. With the help of these parameters, the state of the file can be determined and performance can be controlled. We treat all these parameters as global variables. Before giving the algorithm for insertion of a record in a linearly hashed file, we need to list some auxiliary functions used in the main algorithm.

- LHash hashes a key. Example 8.6 motivates this: LHash (k){m ← k mod M; if m < sP then m ← k mod 2M; return m;}.
- split(m) splits the chain [m] into chains [m] and [M+m].
- add(k, m) adds the record k into chain [m]. We assume that the chain [m] remains sorted and compacted. The algorithm LHInsert for insertion of a record x into the linearly hashed file is now given in **Figure** 10.46.

```
LHInsert(x);
m ← LHash(x);
add(x, m)
while λav > λu do
{
split(sP);
If sP < M – 1, then sP ← sP + 1;
else {M ← 2M; sP ← 0;},
}
end LHInsert;
```

Figure 10.46 LHInsert, an algorithm for insertion

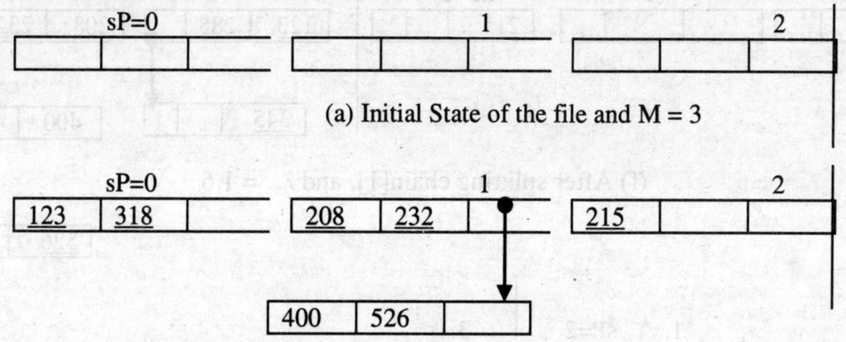

(a) Initial State of the file and M = 3

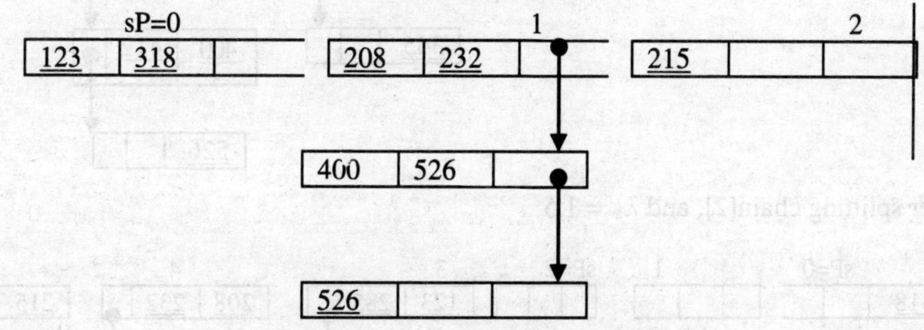

(b) First seven insertions, $\lambda_{av} = 1.33$

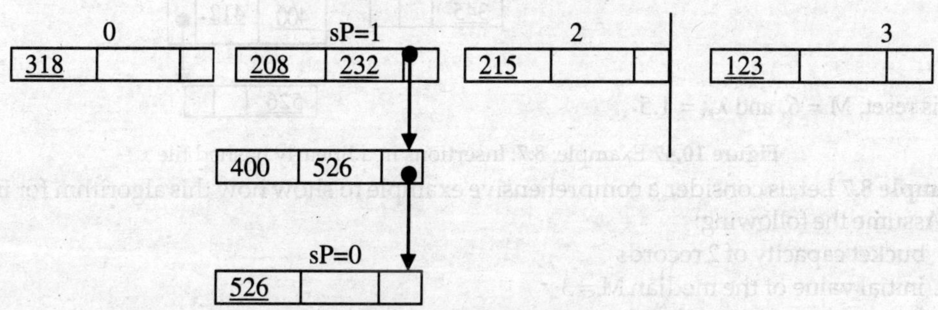

(c) After addition of 412, $\lambda_{av} = 1.67$

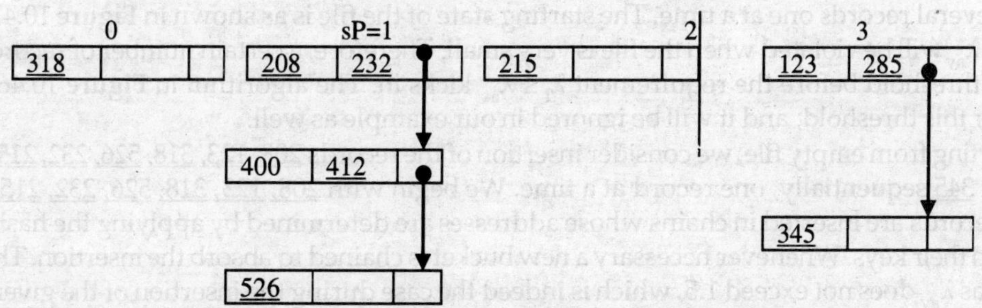

(d) After chain [0] is splitted, $\lambda_{av} = 1.5$

Figure 10.47 Example: 8.4: Insertions in a linearly hashed file (contd...)

(e) After adding 285 and 345 and $\lambda_{av} = 1.75$

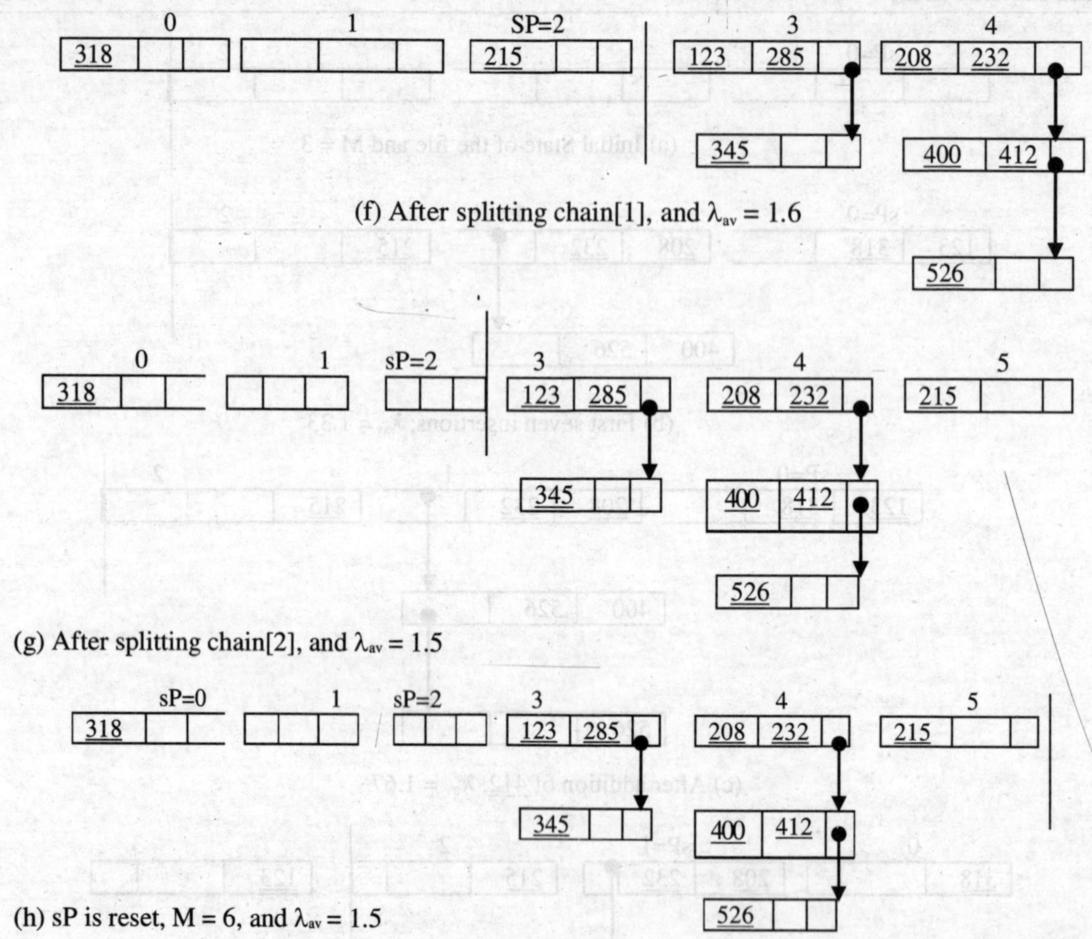

Figure 10.47 Example: 8.7: Insertions in a linearly hashed file

Example 8.7 Let us consider a comprehensive example to show how this algorithm for insertion works. Assume the following:

- bucket capacity of 2 records
- initial value of the median M = 3
- lower average chain length $\lambda_l = 1.25$
- upper average chain length $\lambda_u = 1.5$

The average chain length λ_{av} is required to satisfy $1.25 \leq \lambda_{av} \leq 1.5$. We start with an empty file and insert several records one at a time. The starting state of the file is as shown in **Figure** 10.47(a). Note that $\lambda_l \leq \lambda_{av}$ will be violated when the file is very small. Therefore, a certain number of records may be set as a threshold before the requirement $\lambda_l \leq \lambda_{av}$ kicks in. The algorithm in **Figure** 10.46 does not consider this threshold, and it will be ignored in our example as well.

Starting from empty file, we consider insertion of the records 208, 123, 318, 526, 232, 215, 400, 412, 285 and 345 sequentially, one record at a time. We begin with 208, 123, 318, 526, 232, 215, and 400. These records are inserted in chains whose addresses are determined by applying the hash function mod 3 to their keys. Whenever necessary a new bucket is chained to absorb the insertion. This is done as long as λ_{av} does not exceed 1.5, which is indeed the case during the insertion of the given records.

The state of the file after these insertions is shown in **Figure** 10.47(b). We note that the average chain lengths are 1, 2, and 1, and their average λ_{av} is (1+2+1)/3 = 1.33, which is still in bounds.

Now we insert 412. As shown in **Figure** 10.47(c), the record 412 goes in chain [1]. The average length of this chain becomes 3. The average chain length λ_{av} becomes (1+3+1)/3 = 1.67, which is not acceptable. Therefore, it is time to split chain [0]. The contents of the file after the split are shown in **Figure** 10.47(d). After the split we have four chains and λ_{av} = (1+3+1+1)/4 = 1.5, which is acceptable.

Now we insert 285 and 345. As in **Figure** 10.47(e), addition of these keys causes a bucket to be added to chain [3] violating the condition on λ_{av}. Therefore, chain [1] is splitted, the result after splitting is shown in **Figure** 10.47(f). The condition for λ_{av} is still violated. Therefore, chain [2] is splitted, the result after splitting chain [2] is shown in **Figure** 10.47(g). This completes one round of splitting. The parameter sP is reset to 0, and median M is set to 6, λ_{av} is now acceptable. The final state of the file is shown in **Figure** 10.47(h).

10.8.2 Dynamic Hashing

In its pure form, dynamic hashing can guarantee 1 bucket access per retrieval. This performance is achieved by permanently replicating a directory in the main memory. The directory is organized in a search tree-like structure called trie, where the leaves contain the pointers to the data buckets. If 2 bucket accesses are acceptable, the permanent main memory overhead can be circumvented by suppressing the replication of the directory, but bringing it into the main memory only on demand. In this case the main memory overhead due to the directory can be reduced by partitioning the directory into smaller subdirectories and only bringing the needed subdirectory into main memory on demand. If a guaranteed performance for all retrievals is not required and good average performance is enough, the main memory overhead due to directory or subdirectories can be minimized. This is achieved by using a form of linear splitting.

10.8.2.1 Virtual Addressing

A virtual address, is a string of bits b1b2···bp, where $p \geq 0$. Note that when p = 0, the address reduces to the null string, denoted Λ. All variations of dynamic hashing mentioned above use virtual addresses. We postulate nodes in the main memory, called external nodes, which will be represented as ●. Avirtual address is the physical address of an external node, and an external node holds the physical address of a bucket.

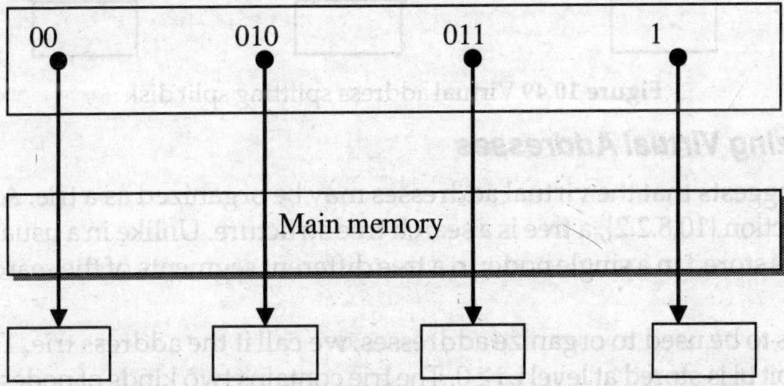

Figure 10.48 Virtual addressing of buckets

Example 8.8. Figure 10.48 shows a file with buckets whose virtual addresses are 00, 010, 011 and 1. As there are four virtual addresses, there are four external nodes, pointing to four buckets in a file. In later sections we will present a scenario under which the illustrated virtual addresses may arise.

Using virtual addressing gives us the freedom to generate addresses dynamically in a flexible manner without having to worry about the physical addresses of the buckets. Note that the lengths of virtual addresses can vary from bucket to bucket.

10.8.2.2 Virtual Address Splitting

The concept of splitting in virtual addressing is as elementary as possible: a virtual address can be splitted by simply adding a bit to it. In other words, the virtual address b1b2···bp is splitted into two addresses b1b2···bp0 and b1b2···bp1, as shown in **Figure** 10.49. Splitting a virtual address implies splitting a bucket as well. In fact, at any given time, there is a one-to-one correspondence between the virtual addresses in use, the external nodes and the buckets in a file. Therefore, we extend the term splitting to apply to any one of these entities interchangeably.

Example 8.9. The virtual address space {00, 010, 011, 1} of Example 8.8 can arise in the following manner. Initially the virtual address space is empty. At that point we have one bucket in the system, pointed to by one external node whose address is Λ, the empty string of bits. The first split expands the virtual address space to {Λ0, Λ1} = {0,1}. By splitting 0, the address space expands to {00, 01, 1}. Finally, when 01 is splitted, we obtain the address space {00, 010, 011, 1}.

Note that Example 8.9 presents only one scenario leading to the given address space. In general, splits and collapses are interleaved and other scenarios are possible as well.

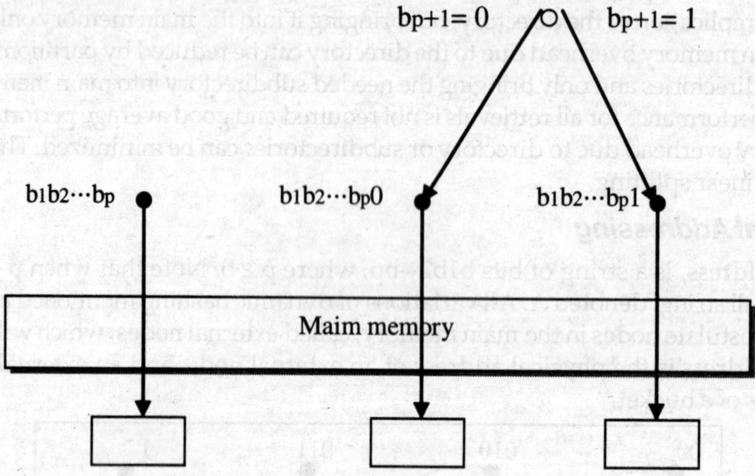

Figure 10.49 Virtual address splitting split disk

10.8.2.3 Organizing Virtual Addresses

Figure 10.49 suggests that the virtual addresses may be organized as a trie. As mentioned in the beginning of the Section {10.8.2.2}, a tree is a search tree structure. Unlike in a usual search tree where a given search key is stored in a single node; in a tree different segments of the search key are stored at different levels.

Since the tree is to be used to organize addresses, we call it the address trie. The address trie is a binary tree, where bit bi is stored at level i, i ≥ 0. The trie contains two kinds of nodes, external nodes (●) and internal nodes (●). As stated before, an external node holds the physical address of a bucket. Internal nodes are only for internal navigation within the trie. A structure for virtual addresses is termed a directory. In Section {10.8.2.6}, we will see that a directory may contain more than one address trie.

Example 8.10. Figure 10.50 shows the address trie for the virtual addresses 00, 010, 011, and 1. It also shows buckets pointed to by the external nodes in the trie. In Example 8.11 we will present a scenario-giving rise to this trie. First we need to discuss how dynamic hashing maps the records.

10.8.2.4 Mapping Records To Buckets

Let us assume that a hash function V(k) is given. For a key value k it gives us the virtual address of the record k. The virtual address can be as long as necessary. We denote the ith bit of V(k) as V(k, i). These bits can be generated by a pseudorandom function described in Example 8.11.

Example 8.11. In this example we have assumed that a bucket can hold up to two records. Starting from an empty file, we want to insert records 128, 305, 803, and 234. We assumed that the virtual addresses of the four keys are as shown in **Figure** 10.51. The steps required to insert the given records are as shown in **Figure** 10.52. **Figure** 10.52(a) shows how an empty file can be initialized. At the start, the address trie has only one node, which is an external node with virtual address Λ, the null string. This node points to an empty bucket. Note that the allocation of an empty bucket may be withheld until there is at least one record in it; however, our default assumption is that a bucket is always allocated, even if it is empty. It is clear that the first two records 128 and 305 can be inserted without any problem. This does not require any bits. The result of these insertions is shown in **Figure** 10.52(b).

Insertion of 803 causes an overflow. Therefore, the only external node is splitted into two nodes. At this point we have two virtual addresses: 0 and 1. Because V(128) = 1···, 128 is hashed to bucket 1. The first bits of V(305) and V(803) are 0, therefore 305 and 803 are hashed to bucket 0. This outcome is shown in **Figure** 10.52(c).

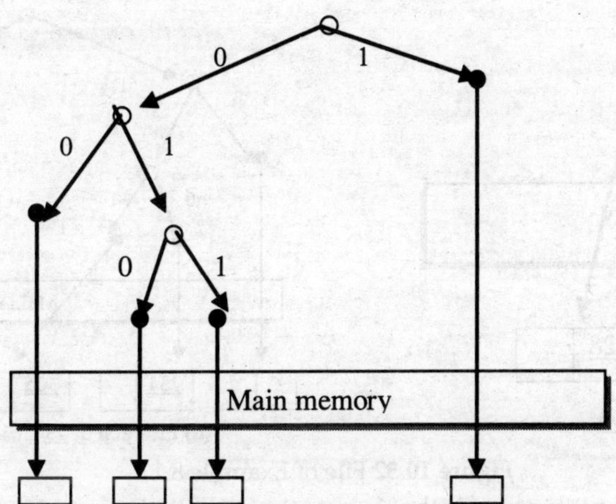

Figure 10.50 Virtual addresses organized as a trie

k	V(k)
128	1···
305	011···
803	011···
234	010···

Figure 10.51 Virtual addresses for keys of Example 8.11

Insertion of 234 is interesting. As V(234) = 0···, the bucket 0 overflows. When we split virtual address 0, we get the new addresses 00 and 01. It turns out that the first two bits for the records 305, 802 and 234 are still equal, namely 01. Therefore we next split the address 01 into addresses 010 and 011. The insertion finally leads to the state of the file as shown in **Figure** 10.52(d).

10.8.2.5 Design Of Nodes In The Address Trie

A null pointer indicates an empty bucket and, as stated earlier, an empty bucket need not be allocated. Despite this recall our default assumption that a bucket is always allocated, even if it is empty. Suppose an address trie points to N buckets. Then the address tree contains N external nodes and N–1 internal nodes. Therefore, the main memory overhead is 1 external node + (approximately) 1 internal node per bucket.

The formats of external and internal nodes are shown in **Figure** 10.53. In an external node we can store a bucket pointer, while an internal node contains two pointers. A pointer may point to an internal node or an external node, and to indicate which one, a tag is added to each pointer.

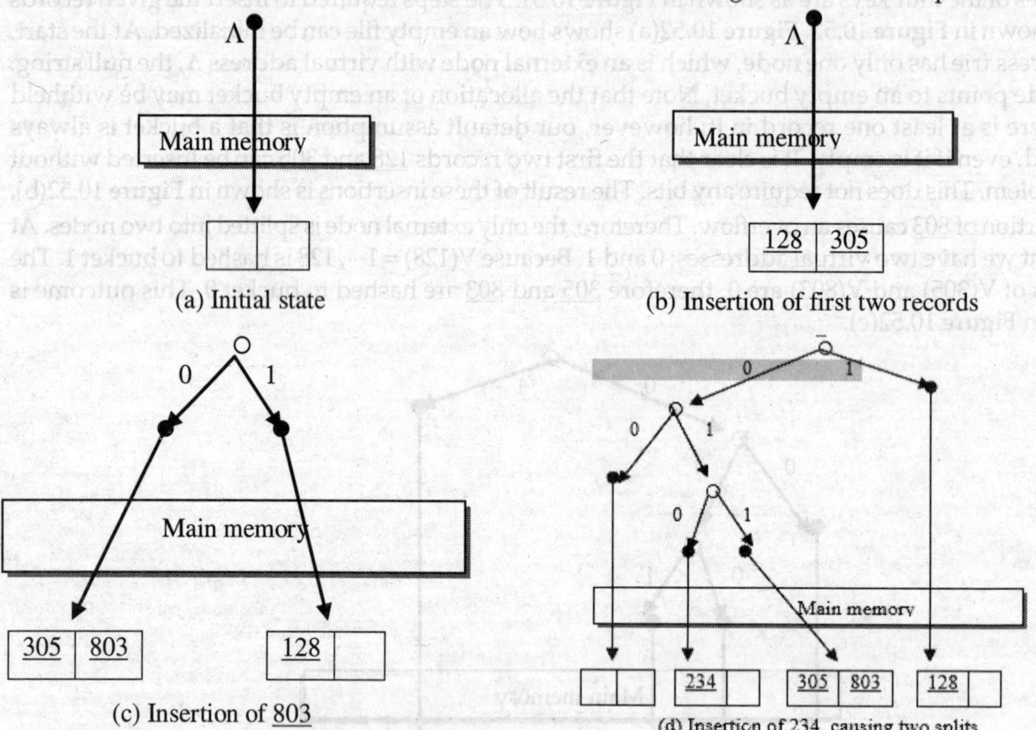

Figure 10.52 File of Example 8.11

Example 8.12. Suppose we have a file that is expected to contain up to 10,000 buckets. We compute the main memory requirements for the address tree.

The physical bucket addresses are integers in the range 0...9999. Therefore, the size of an address is 14 bits. This is also the size of an external node. There are 10000 external nodes, so these external nodes require 140000 bits.

Because the address tree contains 10000 external nodes and 9999 {approximated value is 10000 can chosen it} internal nodes, 14-bit internal pointers suffice for each type of node. An internal node contains two tags and two pointers. Therefore, the size of an internal node is 1+14+1+14 = 30 bits. Thus, internal nodes require 300000 bits. The total main memory requirement is then 440000 bits = 55000 bytes = 53.71 Kilobytes.

10.8.2.6 Multiple Address Tries

A nice feature of dynamic hashing as presented above is that it guarantees 1 bucket access for retrievals. The tradeoff is the main memory required to replicate the address trie. If necessary, the replication of an address trie in the main memory can be suppressed, and the trie can be brought into the main memory on demand. Assuming that the address trie can be retrieved in 1 bucket access, dynamic hashing guarantees 2 bucket accesses for retrievals. If necessary, the size of an address trie can be reduced by using several address tries instead of one. For m address tries 0 to m–1, we can use k mod m to determine the address trie for the record k.

Bucket pointer

(a) Format of an external node

Tag	Tag
Left child	Right child

(b) Format of an internal node

Figure 10.53 Formats of external and internal nodes

Example 8.13. Consider the file {128, 305, 803, 234}. Suppose we want to partition the directory into three address tries. To do this we can use mod 3 to determine a trie. There are three tries, T0, T1 and T2, because 128 mod 3 = 2, 128 is stored in T2. Similarly, 305 and 803 are also stored in T2, and 234 are stored in T0. The state of the file is shown in **Figure** 10.54.

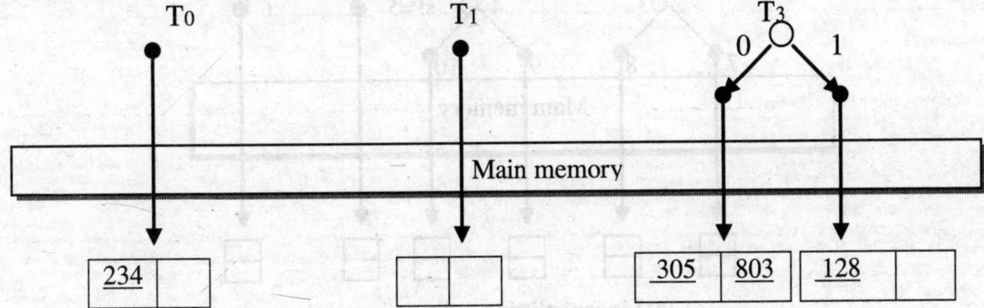

Figure 10.54 A file with multiple addresses tries

10.8.2.7 Linear Splitting

The growth pattern of an address trie is unpredictable. If we can control the pattern, internal pointers can sometimes be computed, eliminating the need to store them explicitly.

Perhaps the simplest pattern for a trie is as a complete binary tree, in a complete binary tree, nodes at a given level are generated from left to right, and all nodes at that level are generated before going to the next level {**Figure** 10.55(a)}. Having such a trie implies linear splitting. Since the address trie is a complete binary tree, the internal pointers can be computed. This makes the internal nodes redundant and they need not be stored. Thus, the trie reduces to an array of external nodes. The memory overhead is 1 external node per bucket, if we start the numbering of nodes in the trie from 0, then the range of indices for the external nodes is 5...10. Note that if there have been x splits, the indices of the external nodes are in the range x...2x, this range is completely characterized by the number of splits.

Example 8.14. In the address trie of **Figure** 10.55(a) the external nodes are stored in an array whose indices are in the range 5..10. Suppose we are given a key value of 356, and want to retrieve the record 356. Suppose further that the virtual address for 356, V(256) is 0100···. There are no internal nodes, but in order to pretend to navigate, we start at the root of the trie, which is the 0th node. Now we use bits 0, 1, 0, etc. from the virtual address, which means go left, right, left, and so on. Left of 0 is 1, right of 1 is 4, and left of 4 is 9. The index 9 is in the range 5...10. Therefore, the address of the record 356 is in the external node appearing in the array at index location 9.

When we use linear splitting, we cannot guarantee a uniform performance for all retrievals because we have to use chains. We may use the average chain length λ^+ as a trigger for splitting.

Example 8.15 Suppose we have a file with 3000 records, buckets with capacity of 2 records, and a single address trie where linear splitting is used. Suppose that the average chain length $\lambda = 3$. This means that on average a chain can hold up to 6 records. This amounts to splitting at every sixth insertion. The file then contains $\lceil 3000/6 \rceil = 500$ chains, and assuming no collapses, it has gone through 499 splits.

As is evident by now, the dynamic hashing is an interesting technique. In its pure form, it can give an excellent, guaranteed, uniform performance for all retrievals, it has the problem of the size of the directory growing linearly with the size of the file. Although we may use several address tries to slow the linear growth per trie, the number of tries is not dynamic.

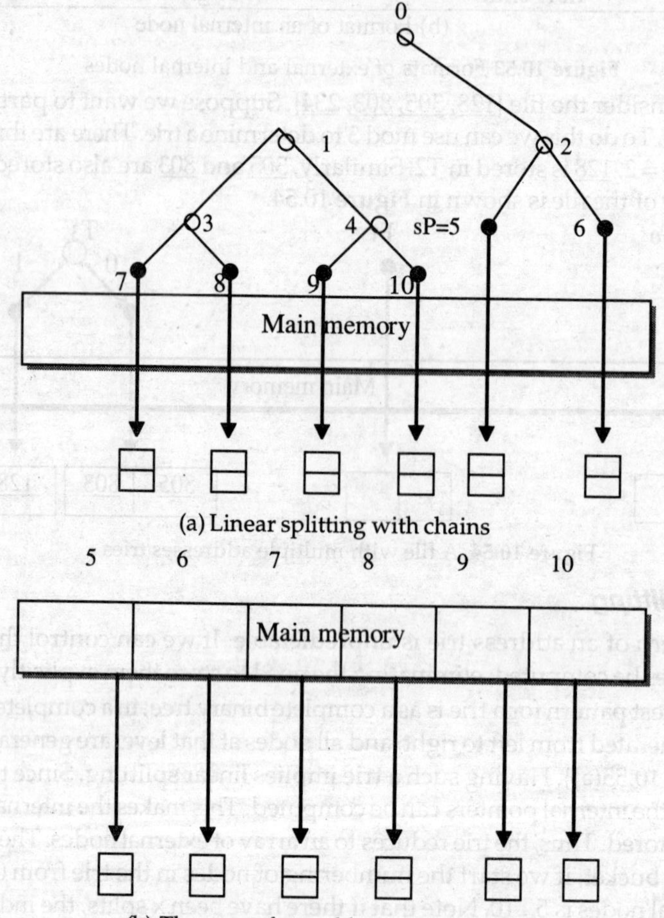

Figure 10.55 Linear splitting

Implementation of Hash Table creation module has been given in Chapter 9.

10.9 B-TREE (REVISITED)

In this section we will introduce B-trees in respect to file structures more details will be found in Chapter 11. B-trees are perhaps the most mysterious of all file structures. The origin of "B" in "B-tree" is not known. However, "B" does not stand for binary. In fact a B-tree is a search tree where the fanout is at least 3, precisely ruling out the case of a binary search tree. It is useful to put search trees in the context of our discussion. Most readers are probably familiar with binary search trees. A m+1-ary search tree, or a search tree with a fanout of m +1, where m+1 ≥ 2, is a generalization of a binary search tree. In the previous two sections we have seen splitting as a fundamental mechanism to expand a file gracefully. In this section we will introduce splitting in search trees. We will see that, the binary search trees (m+1=2) are the least interesting of all search trees. The reason for this is that they do not easily accommodate splitting. Therefore, binary search trees do not readily support graceful dynamic expansion of the address space.

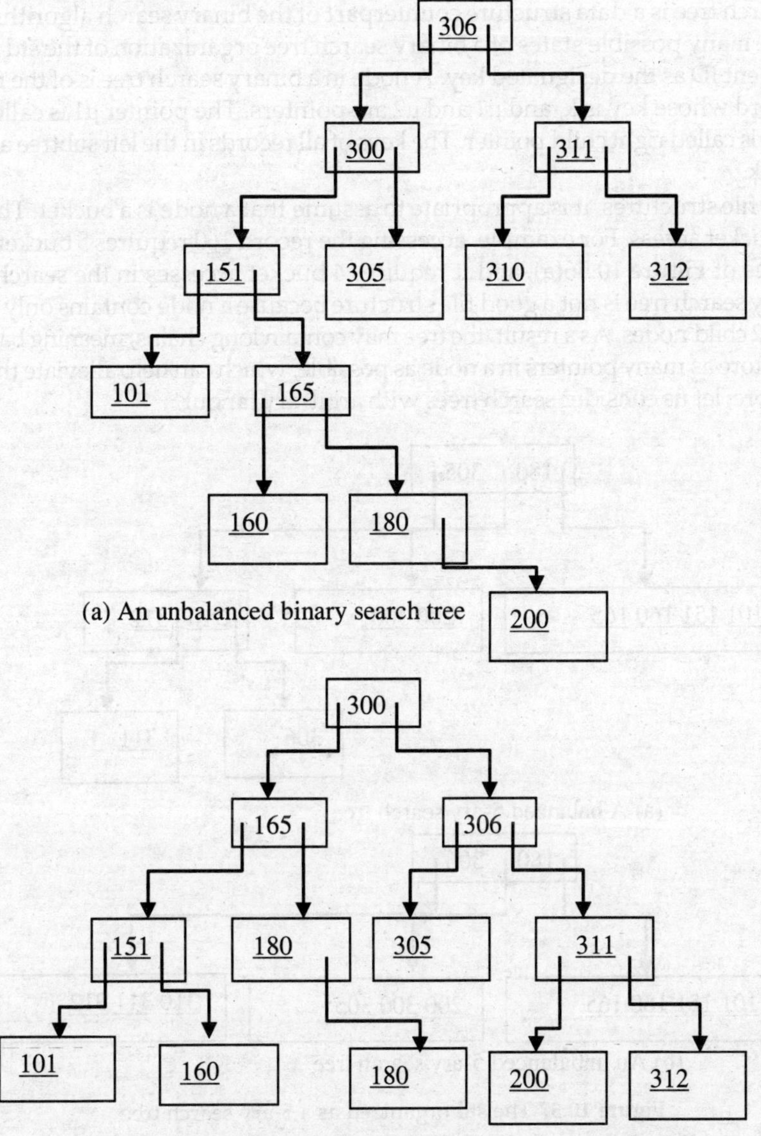

Figure 10.56 The std file organized as a binary search tree

The concept of splitting in a search tree directly gives rise to the definition of a B-tree. A B-tree by definition is a balanced search tree with at least 50% space utilization (except in small degenerate cases). This guarantees a reasonable fanout and a shallow tree, which is good for performance. We will observe that in a B-tree, records are stored in every node, even though the structure of the tree only depends upon the keys. This limits the fanout of a B-tree, making them less than optimal file structures. In the next section we will introduce variants of B-trees that are excellent file structures. B-trees are still important to us from a pedagogical point of view. Because of their simple uniform structure they are ideal for developing a good understanding of operations such as insertions, deletions and retrievals.

A binary search tree is a data structure counterpart of the binary search algorithm. **Figure** 10.56 shows two of the many possible states of a binary search tree organization of the std file of Example 4.1, treating student ID as the designated key. A node in a binary search tree is of the form (μ1, k, μ2); where k is a record whose key is k, and μ1 and μ2 are pointers. The pointer μ1 is called the left child pointer, while μ2 is called right child pointer. The keys of all records in the left subtree are ≤ k and those of the right are > k.

In context of file structures, it is appropriate to assume that a node is a bucket. Thus, following a pointer costs 1 bucket access. For example, accessing the record 160 requires 5 bucket accesses in the binary search tree of **Figure** 10.56(a), and it requires 4 bucket accesses in the search tree of **Figure** 10.56(b). A binary search tree is not a good file structure because a node contains only 1 record, and it can have at most 2 child nodes. As a result, the tree may contain long chains, meaning bad performance. It is desirable to store as many pointers in a node as possible, which can help alleviate this performance problem. Therefore, let us consider search trees with arbitrary fanout.

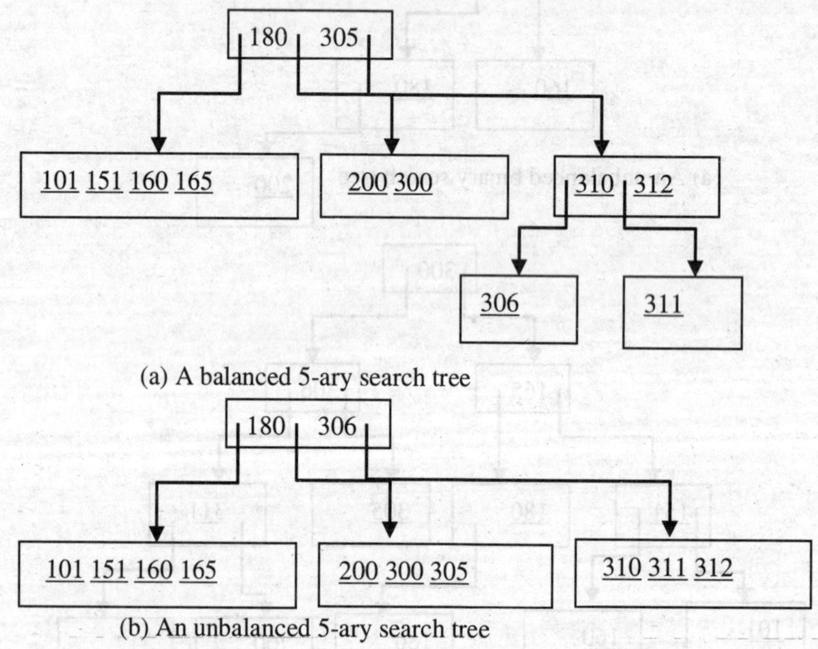

(a) A balanced 5-ary search tree

(b) An unbalanced 5-ary search tree

Figure 10.57 The std organized as a 5-ary search tree

A node in a search tree is termed a search node. The records and pointers alternate in a search node: pointer, record, pointer, ···, record, pointer. The number of pointers is always one more than number of records. For a given file we will only consider fixed size nodes (buckets) in which we can have up to a fixed number of records and pointers. The number of pointers in a node is called its fanout. Clearly, the fanout of a node in binary search tree is 0, 1, or 2. The maximum possible fanout of nodes in a search tree is called the fanout of the tree. Thus, the fanout of a binary search tree is 2.

A m+1-ary search tree is a search tree with a fanout of m+1. **Figure** 10.57 shows two of the many possible states of a 5-ary search tree for the same std file of Example 4.1. The tree in **Figure** 10.57(a) contains 6 nodes. Note that all the 6 nodes have the same physical size. Each is capable of holding up to 4 records and 5 pointers. Three nodes contain 2 records and 3 pointers each; not shown in these nodes is the unutilized space for 2 records and 2 pointers. Similarly, there are 2 nodes containing 1 record and 2 pointers each. Lastly, there is 1 node with 100% space utilization, containing 4 records and 5 pointers.

Example 9.1. Suppose buckets consisting of 1024 bytes each is to be used as nodes in a B-tree. Suppose the record size is 80 bytes, and a pointer requires 2 bytes. Then $80 \times m + 2 \times (m+1) \leq 1024$. Optimal value of m is 12. Note that 38 bytes are wasted in every bucket (wastage amounts to 3.7%).

It should be clear by now that a rule of thumb for a good performance for a m+1-ary search trees it to keep the tree balanced. Formally, a leaf is defined to be a node with at least one child pointer that is null. A tree is balanced if all its leaves are at the same level. **Figure** 10.57(b) shows a balanced 5-ary search tree. The binary search tree for the std file as shown in **Figure** 10.56(b) is not balanced according to our definition because all leaves of that tree are not at the same level.

In addition to having a larger fanout, a 5-ary tree has a critical advantage over the binary search tree. This advantage is the fact that a 5-ary search node is elastic. Although we have assumed that all nodes in the 5-ary tree have the same physical size, a node can contain anywhere from 1 to 4 records, and consequently 2 to 5 pointers. This choice is not available with a binary search tree. In fact, any m+1-ary tree for m+1 > 2 has elastic nodes.

Having defined a balanced tree, we now can focus on how to control the height of the tree. The problem is that even a 100-ary tree can degenerate into a binary search tree, and this is where the concept of splitting comes to the rescue. When a node (bucket) is splitted into two nodes, each node still contains about half as many records, thereby preventing a tree from getting degenerating.

Note that in data structures, a binary search tree is commonly defined to be balanced if all its leaves are at the last two levels. According to this definition, the binary search tree of **Figure** 10.56(b) would be balanced.

10.9.1 Splitting In A Search Tree

As in other file structures, we have some expectations of splitting in a search tree. In every search node, there is a tight relationship between the number of pointers and the number of records: the number of pointers is always one more than the number of records. A split has to break a search node into two search nodes. We have to be careful about the correspondence between numbers of records and pointers in each node. A split should disturb only a small portion of the tree, and the new node obtained after the split has to be integrated into the system at the same level of importance as the original node.

Figure 10.58 shows the split of a 9-ary node. One record is used as a pivot, around which the split is performed. In this case the pivot is X_3. Usually, the middle (or closest to middle) record may be used as a pivot, but this by itself is not a theoretical necessity to carry out a split. When a node is splitted, a new node μ' is created in addition to the existing node μ. The ⟨record, pointer⟩ pair $\langle X_3, \mu' \rangle$ is added to the parent. Note that in **Figure** 10.58, the node μ' has been added at the same level as μ. Therefore, if the original tree was balanced, after the split the tree would also be balanced.

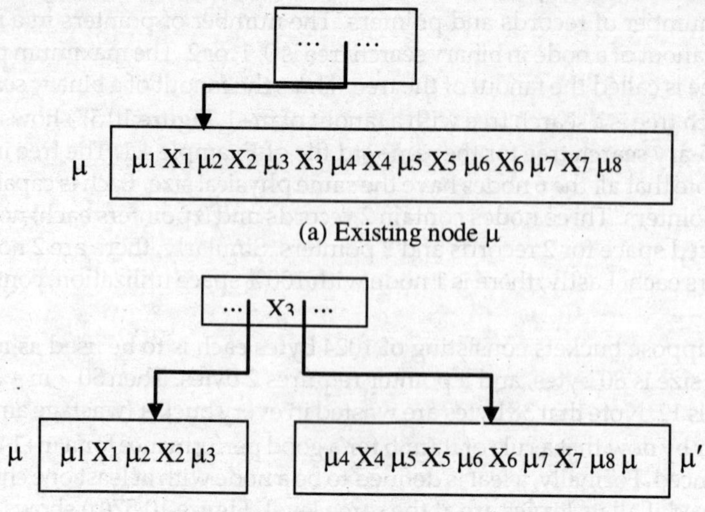

Figure 10.58 Splitting a search node

10.9.2 B-tree (Revisited)

Before formally defining a B-tree, it is important to state our intention is to split a node in a B-tree only when it overflows. The split is performed around a pivot, which is the middle, or closest to the middle, record. This controls the space utilization in the resulting nodes to a minimum around 50% and prevents the tree from degenerating into a binary search tree. We note that the splits do not destroy the balanced property of a search tree. The splits in a B-tree start at the leaf and migrate upward as needed. In the worst case, a new root is created. We have to allow root this to be an exception: it may contain as few as one record.

A B-tree with a fanout m+1 is a balanced m+1-ary search tree such that every node, except possibly the root, contains $\lfloor m/2 \rfloor$...m records.

Note that guaranteed space utilization and balanced properties are built into the definition of a B-tree. The feasibility of such a definition follows from the concept of a split introduced in section 10.9.1. Next we will consider the performance of retrievals in B-trees.

10.6.3 Retrieval Performance

In this section we estimate the performance of retrievals in a B-tree. The main consideration will be direct access; i.e., given a key, we want to retrieve the record that has that key. A search ends in a success if the record is in the tree, and in failure if the record is not in the tree. A node in a B-tree is stored as a bucket. Every time a child pointer is followed, it costs us an additional bucket access. Therefore, the performance of retrievals in a B-tree is directly dependent upon the height of the tree. We want to estimate the height h of the tree in terms of the number of records n and the fanout m of the tree. For brevity, we will denote $\lfloor m/2 \rfloor$ as d.

To facilitate counting, let us imagine that we have an extra level in the tree, which consists of the failure nodes {**Figure** 10.59}. Recall that N denotes the number of nodes (buckets) in the tree. The following are the auxiliary parameters:

- h = height of the tree, i.e., the number of levels, counting the root as level 1
- f = the number of (imaginary) failure nodes

The term failure arises from searches that fail because a record we are searching for is not in the file. The parameter f makes it easy for us to give a counting argument. We will calculate f in two different ways in terms of the other parameters and then eliminate f to obtain a relationship among the other parameters.

Let us imagine that the set of all possible keys forms the real line. The n keys (records) contained in the tree are points on that real line. If we remove these points, we are left with n+1 disjoint line segments on the line. These line segments have an interesting property. Suppose we fix one of the line segments. Then a search of every key in the line segment forces us to traverse a unique path in the search tree leading to the same failure node. Thus, there is a one-to-one correspondence between the line segments and the failure nodes. Therefore,

$$f = n + 1 \qquad ...(1)$$

Now we try estimating f in another way. At level 1, we have at least 1 node. At level 2, we have at least 2 nodes.

At level 3, we have at least 2(d+1) nodes. At level 4, we have at least $2(d+1)^2$ nodes, and so on. At level h+1, we have at least $2(d+1)^{h-1}$ nodes. Thus, we obtain

$$2(d+1)^{h-1} \le f \qquad ...(2)$$

From (1) and (2) we can eliminate f, giving us the following relationship between d, h, and n:

$2(d+1)^{h-1} \le n+1$

Hence $(d+1)^{h-1} \le ½(n+1)$

Thus $h - 1 \le \log_{d+1} ½(n+1)$

Finally we have the following estimation for the height of the B-tree in terms of m and n.

$h \le \log_{\lfloor p/2 \rfloor+1} ½(n+1)$

B-tree of height h

F F ... F

Imaginary level of failure nodes

Keys in B-tree

F F ... F

Imaginary level of failure nodes

Figure 10.59 Failure nodes

Example 9.2. Suppose a file has n = 1000000 records. We want to store this file as a B-tree with m = 200 and we want to estimate the height. Clearly,

$$= 1 + \log_{100+1} ½(1000000+1)$$

$= 1 + \log_{101} 500000.50$
$= 1 + \log 500000.50 / \log 101$
$= 3.85$

Since h is an integer, $h \leq 3$. Directly from the definition of a B-tree, it is easily proved that $h > 2$. Thus, $h = 3$.

The above example is significant because it tells us that if we can choose m to be 200, a file containing as many as 1000000 records can be stored as a 3-level B-tree. This means that a record with a given key can be accessed within 3 bucket accesses. In fact the above argument can be strengthened to prove that even 2000000 records with the given fanout will require only 3 levels.

It turns out that in a B-tree a node (bucket) contain records, and it may be difficult to pack 200 records in it. However, the next section will introduce a variant of the B-tree called a B^+-tree. In all but the last level of a B^+-tree we store keys instead of records, and m = 200 is not unrealistic for such a tree. For the above file, we will have a B-tree of height of 4. As the root can be replicated in the main memory requiring only 1 buffer, a performance of 3 bucket accesses can be achieved. This will be discussed in detail in Section {10.10}. In fact in that example we argue that if we can afford merely 20 buffers to replicate the first one or first two levels in the main memory, we can achieve a guaranteed performance of 2 bucket accesses.

Now let us switch the attention towards insertions and deletions in B-trees. These operations have to maintain all the properties of a B-tree.

10.9.4 Insertion

We will assume that a B-tree with a pointer, b, to its root is given. We are given a record, x, which is to be inserted in the tree.

The algorithm for insertion is directly inspired by the concept of split in a search tree introduced earlier. First we traverse down the tree and find a leaf node where x logically belongs {See path P in **Figure** 10.60(a)}. Next we would like to add the x to that leaf node. But we cannot add a record to a node in a search tree without also adding a pointer. Thus, addition to a node must consist of a ⟨record, pointer⟩ pair. Because all pointers in a leaf are null, the record pointer pair to be added to the leaf node in this case is ⟨x, null⟩. If the node has space in it to accommodate a pair, the insertion is completed. On the other hand, if the leaf overflows, it is splitted and a ⟨record, pointer⟩ pair is added to the parent node. The record in this case is the middle record of the overflowing node, and the pointer is the address of the newly created node by the split. If the parent node has space in it, the insertion is completed, or else the parent is splitted, and a ⟨record, pointer⟩ pair migrates to its parent. This continues until a node that can absorb a record is encountered {**Figure** 10.60(b)}. In the worst case, the root may have to be splitted, and a new root would be created {**Figure** 10.60(c)}. Note that while splitting we need to revisit the parent nodes backwards along the path P.

We assume that we have 1 buffer, α, which allows us to traverse the tree starting from the root to a leaf node. With 1 buffer we do not have the capability of memorizing a parent. Therefore, we maintain a stack, denoted as parent $h \leq 1 + \log_{\lfloor p/2 \rfloor + 1} \frac{1}{2}(n+1)$, to store the pointers of all the parent nodes. For example, in the 4-level tree of **Figure** 10.60(c), we would push 2 parent pointers on to the stack before the leaf node is reached. The leaf node is not pushed on to the stack. We also assume that there is an additional buffer, β, so that a split can be composed in the main memory in the 2 buffers, α and β. When a split is performed, 2 child nodes are written, and the parent node is read; the address of the parent is found on the top of the stack. Finally, the parent node has to be modified. The algorithm **BTreeInsert** is given in **Figure** 10.61. This algorithm uses the following procedures.

FindLeafAndStackParents (b, k, parentStack, μ, α) searches for the leaf node where the record k logically belongs, stores parent pointers in **parentStack**, sets μ to point to the leaf node, and reads the contents of μ into the buffer α.

α, **midKey**, β ← α ∪ ⟨k, ν⟩ facilitates a split. It identifies the middle record of α ∪ ⟨k, ν⟩ as the pivot, stores all the records and pointers in α ∪ ⟨k, ν⟩ on the left of the pivot in α, and those on the right of the pivot in β.

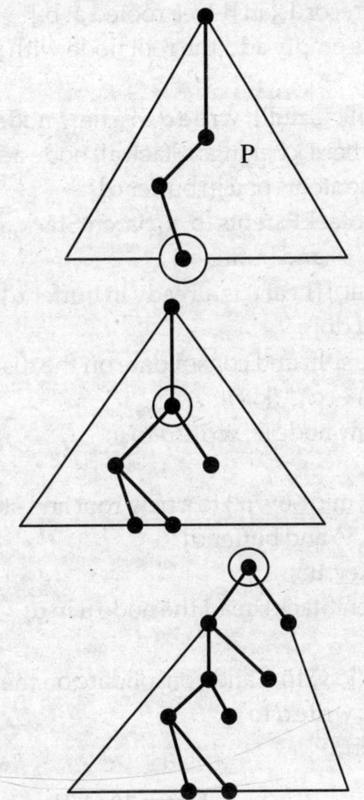

Figure 10.60 Insertion in a B-tree

Example 9.3. In this example we illustrate insertions in a 5-ary B-tree. For a 5-ary B-tree m = 4. Every node, except possibly the root, will have 2 to 4 records and 3 to 5 child pointers. The root is an exception: it can have 1 to 4 records and 2 to 5 child pointers. In a B-tree the child pointers in leaves are nulls. Every child pointer in every internal node is non-null.

We will start with an empty B-tree and insert a sequence of 20 records in the tree. The records to be inserted are 07, 15, 02, 05, 11, 03 10, 01, 04, 13, 06, 19, 12, 08, 14, 16, 20, 18, 17, 09. Note that we have chosen consecutive records from 01 to 20 for the ease of reading. We start with the empty B-tree b, which is simply a null pointer. A null B-tree is shown in **Figure** 10.62(a).

The first record to be inserted is 07. Since the tree is empty, the statement α ← (null, x, null) is executed. It composes a node in the buffer α with the record 07 and two pointers that are null. The buffer α is then written to a bucket μ on the disk. The pointer b representing the tree is set to μ. **Figure** 10.62(b) shows the B-tree at this point. The B-tree consists of a single node. This node is the root as well as a leaf. Since this node is the root, it is allowed to contain only 1 record and 2 pointers. The pointers are currently null. Although not shown in the figure, the node contains additional space for three records and three pointers.

Next we insert 15. On entering the algorithm, we form the record pointer pair ⟨15, null ⟩. This pair is added to the leaf node by collating it with existing record and pointers in the leaf. The records 02 and 05 are inserted in a similar manner. The state of the tree at this point is shown in **Figure** 10.62(c). The single node in the tree is full: it contains four records and five pointers. All pointers are null.

```
BTreeInsert (b, x)
[Insert a new record x in B-tree rooted at b.]
[If the B-tree is empty add the root node with x in it]
If b is null,
then {α ← (null, x, null); write α to a new node μ; b ← μ}
[Find leaf μ where x belongs. Stack all node addresses from root to just before μ on the parent
stack. Leave contents of μ in buffer α]
FindLeafAndStackParents (b, x, parentStack, μ, α);
[Setup pair ⟨k, v⟩ and buffer α:]
⟨k, v⟩ ← ⟨x, null⟩; [Leaf μ is already in buffer α]
While α is full do
[Compose the split and consolidate on the disk]
(α, midKey, β) ← α ∪ ⟨k, v⟩;
write β to a new node μ'; write α to μ;
If μ is the root,
then {write (μ, midKey, μ') to a new root and stop}
[Setup pair ⟨k, v⟩ and buffer α]
⟨k, v⟩ ← ⟨midKey, μ'⟩;
μ ← pop (parentStack); read the node μ in α;
endwhile
[Add the last ⟨k, v⟩ to α and consolidate on the disk]
α ← α ∪ ⟨k, v⟩; write α to μ;
end BTreeInsert;
```

Figure 10.61 The algorithm BTreeInsert

Now we need to insert 11. On entering the algorithm, we form the record pointer pair ⟨11, null⟩. This pair has to be added to the leaf node μ. We know that this is going to split the node μ. In the algorithm a split is expressed as the assignment statement. (α, midKey, β) ← α ∪ ⟨k, v⟩. Here α and β are buffers. The buffer α contains (null1 02 null2 05 null3 07 null4 15 null5), the contents of the node μ. The pair ⟨k, v⟩ is ⟨11, nullnew⟩. We have added subscripts only for the visual inspection. The environment for the split is now set.

Now we see how the split is carried out by the assignment statement (α, midKey, β) ← α ∪ ⟨k, v⟩. Computation of α ∪ ⟨k, v⟩, the right hand side, leads to a hypothetical node (null1 02 null2 05 null3 07 null4 11 nullnew 15 null5). This node does not have to be computed explicitly, but it is only for the ease of understanding a split. This hypothetical node has 5 keys and 6 pointers, and we refer to this as an overflow. Now let us consider the left hand side of the assignment statement (α, midKey, β) ← (null1 02 null2 05 null3 07 null4 11 nullnew 15 null5). This is three assignments rolled into one: α ← (null1 02 null2 05 null3), the first half of the overflow node; midKey ← 07; and β ← (null4 11 nullnew 15 null5), the second half of the overflow node. This completes the composition of the split.

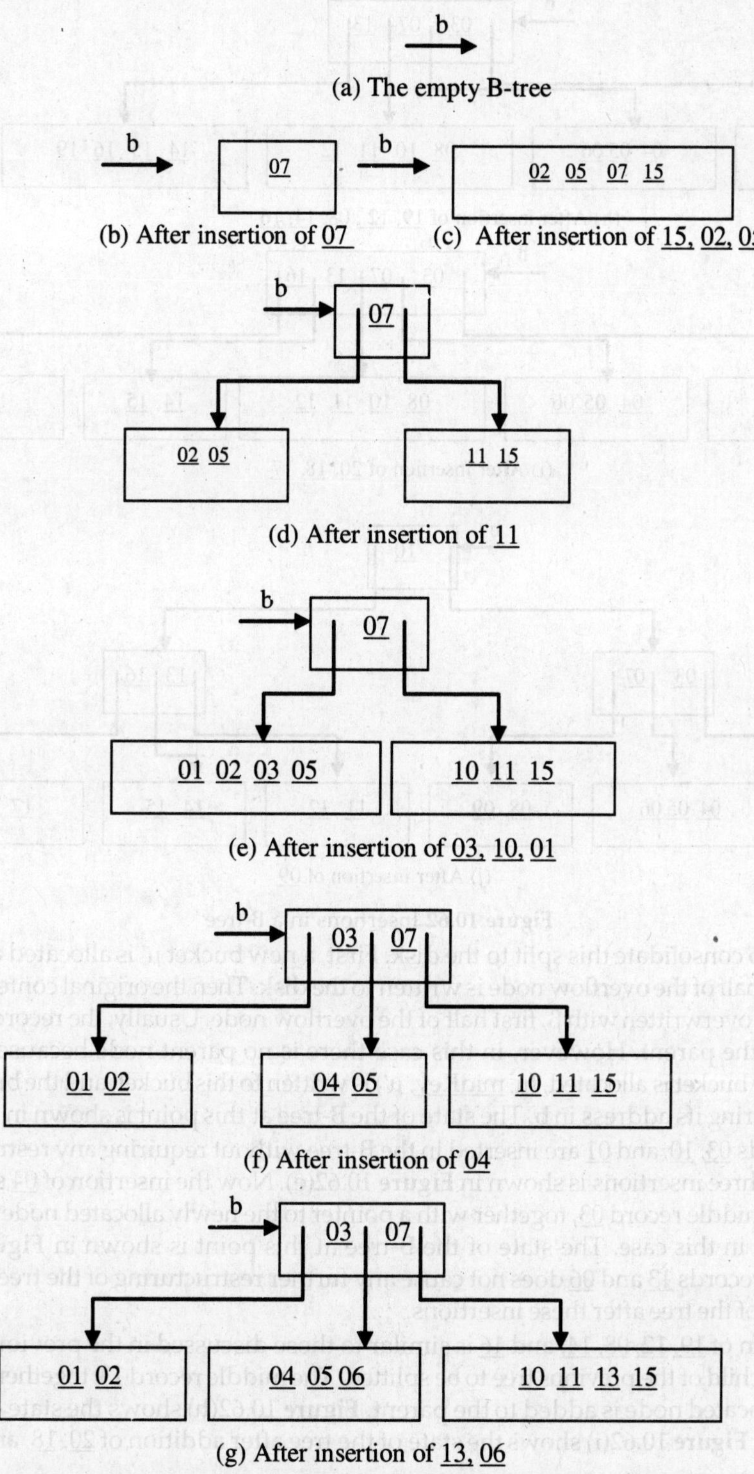

(a) The empty B-tree

(b) After insertion of 07

(c) After insertion of 15, 02, 05

(d) After insertion of 11

(e) After insertion of 03, 10, 01

(f) After insertion of 04

(g) After insertion of 13, 06

Figure 10.62 Insertions in a B-tree (Contd...)

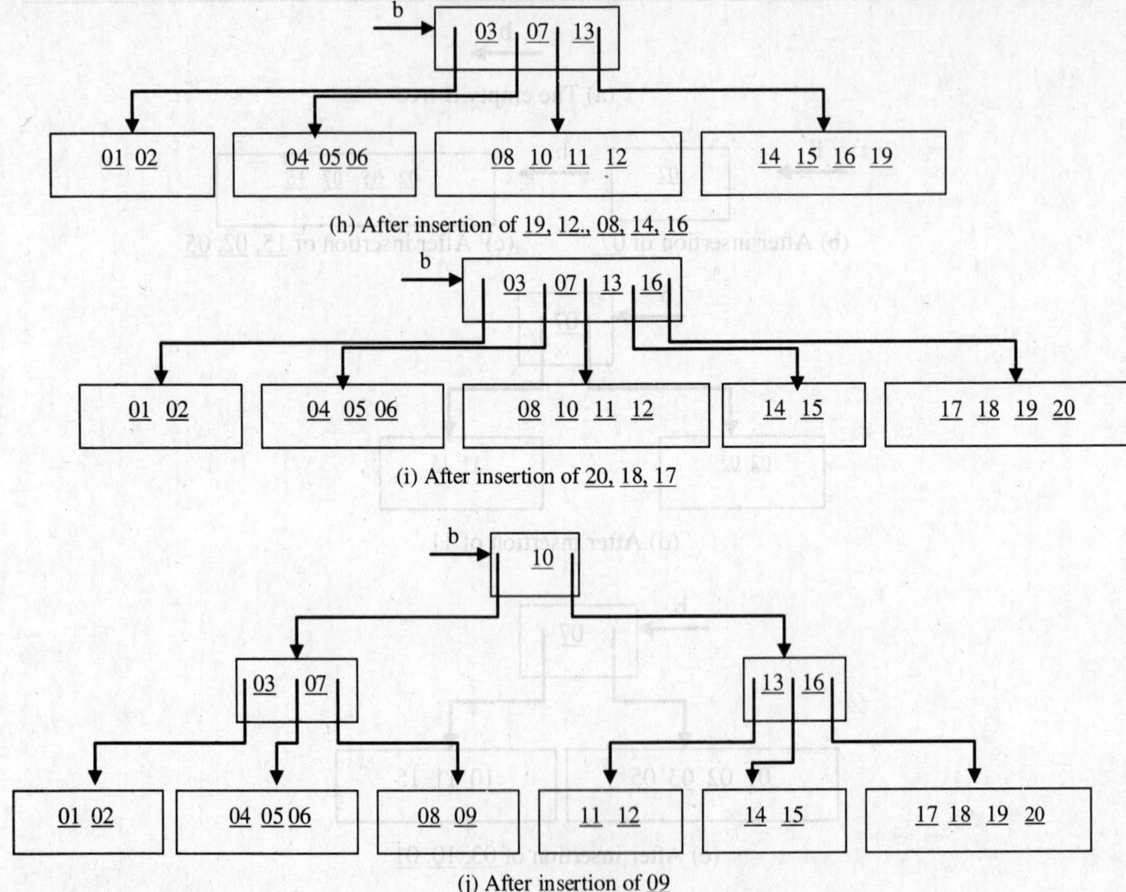

(h) After insertion of 19, 12., 08, 14, 16

(i) After insertion of 20, 18, 17

(j) After insertion of 09

Figure 10.62 Insertions in a B-tree

It remains to consolidate this split to the disk. First, a new bucket μ' is allocated and the contents of β, the second half of the overflow node is written to the disk. Then the original contents of the bucket μ on the disk are overwritten with β, first half of the overflow node. Usually, the record midKey would to be added to the parent. However, in this case there is no parent node because μ is the root b. Therefore, a new bucket is allocated, (μ, midKey, μ') is written to this bucket, and the bucket is made the root node by storing its address in b. The state of the B-tree at this point is shown in **Figure** 10.62(d).

Next, records 03, 10, and 01 are inserted in the B-tree without requiring any restructuring. The B-tree after these three insertions is shown in **Figure** 10.62(e). Now the insertion of 04 splits the left leaf in the tree. The middle record 03, together with a pointer to the newly allocated node are added to the parent, the root in this case. The state of the B-tree at this point is shown in **Figure** 10.62(f). The insertion of the records 13 and 06 does not cause any further restructuring of the tree. **Figure** 10.62(g) shows the state of the tree after these insertions.

The insertion of 19, 12, 08, 14, and 16 is similar to those discussed in the previous paragraph. 19 causes the right child of the previous tree to be splitted. The middle record 13, together with the pointer to the newly allocated node is added to the parent. **Figure** 10.62(h) shows the state of the tree at this point. Similarly, **Figure** 10.62(i) shows the state of the tree after addition of 20, 18, and 17.

Now we consider the insertion of 09. The addition of the record pointer pair ⟨09, null⟩ causes an overflow in the middle leaf of **Figure** 10.62(i). This node is splitted into two nodes, and the pair consisting of the middle record 10, together with the pointer to the node allocated by the split are added to the parent node, which is the current root. As the root is full, it is also split into two nodes, and the middle record 10 together with the pointers to the two split nodes are stored in the new root. **Figure** 10.62(j) shows the final state of the tree after all the twenty insertions.

10.9.5 Performance of Insertion

In this section we will give an informal and somewhat imprecise argument to estimate the cost of insertion. We will assume that we start with the empty tree, and insert one key at a time into it. Normally, in life of the B-tree some deletions would also occur, but we will ignore them here. Let us assume that the height of the B-tree is h. Disk accesses during execution of BTreeInsert can be logically divided into the following three phases:

The search phase: This consists of starting from the root, and following child pointers along a path, P, until a leaf is reached {**Figure** 10.60}. This phase requires h bucket accesses.

The splitting phase: If the leaf is not full, it can absorb the insertion and this phase terminates. Otherwise, the leaf is splitted and a ⟨record, pointer⟩ pair moves upwards along the path, P, possibly splitting some nodes. We denote the number of nodes being split by s. A split involves 2 bucket accesses to write the 2 nodes after a split has been composed in the buffers. If the node being split is a non-root node, an additional bucket access is required to read the parent node, whose pointer is found on a stack. On the other hand if the node being split is the root, there is no parent node to be read, but a new root is composed in a buffer and written to the disk. As will be clear shortly, the writing of a new root node is not counted toward the cost of the split. If all of the s splits are for the non-root nodes, the cost of splits is 3s, and if the root is involved then it is implied that all the h nodes in the path P have been splitted and the cost of splits is 3h – 1.

The final write phase: During this phase a single node is written back to the disk. If there are no splits, this node would be a leaf node. If a new root is created, it would be for writing the new root. Otherwise, it is the last parent that is updated. The cost of this phase is 1 bucket access.

Now we summarize the cost of an insertion. If there are s splits and the root is not splitted, the total cost of the insertion is h + 3s + 1. In the worst case the root is splitted, it is implied that all h nodes in the path P have been splitted and the cost is h + (3h – 1) + 1 = 4h. In the best case s = 0 and cost of insertion is h+1.

We observe that the variation in the cost of insertion in the best case (h+1) and the worst (4h) is rather large. Fortunately, the splits are rare if the fanout m+1 is fairly large, bringing the average cost of insertion much closer to the best case. We give a somewhat imprecise argument to estimate the average number of splits. We assume that we are starting with an empty tree, and keep on inserting records, and while doing this no deletions occur. Let us consider the following parameters:

- S = total number of splits
- S_{av} = average number of splits per insertion

It is easy to prove the equation S = N – h. Initially when N = 1 and h = 1, the number of splits S = 0. Therefore, S = N – h is satisfied. Subsequently, with every split both sides of the equation increase by 1. With every new split, the increase in S by 1 is obvious. The node being split is either a non-root node or a root node. In the former case N increases by 1, and h remains the same, and in the latter N increases by 2 and h increases by 1. In both cases N – h, the right hand side of the equation increases by 1. Therefore,

$$n \geq 1 + (N - 1)d$$

This is also easy to see: the root has at least 1 key, and each of the remaining N – 1 nodes has at least d keys. Now, for N > 1,

$$S_{av} = \frac{S}{n} = \frac{N-h}{n}$$

$$S_{av} \le \frac{N-h}{n} \le \frac{N-h}{1+(N-1)d} \le \frac{N-1}{1+(N-1)d} \le \frac{1}{\frac{1}{N-1}+d} \le \frac{1}{d} \le \frac{2}{m}$$

Thus, the average number of splits is bounded by 2/m, and the average cost of insertion is shown below. Assuming a reasonably large value of m, the performance is close to the best case. The average cost of insertion will be given by

$$= h + \frac{6}{m} + 1$$

10.9.6 DELETION

Deletion of a record from a B-tree is accomplished by removal of a record pointer pair from a node in the tree. Sometimes the removal of a record will cascade restructuring of the tree in the direction towards the root of the tree.

Recall that every node in a B-tee, except possibly the root, contains $\lfloor m/2 \rfloor$...p records. We say that a node can spare a record if it has at least $\lfloor m/2 \rfloor + 1$ records if it is a non-root node, and it has at least 2 records if it is the root node. Obviously, a node cannot spare a record if it is a non-root node and it contains exactly $\lfloor m/2 \rfloor$ records, or if it is the root node and it contains exactly 1 record. If a record pointer pair is removed from a node that cannot spare a record, a shortage of a record is said to be caused. A shortage leads to a temporary violation in the integrity of a B-tree that has to be fixed before deletion of a record can be considered as completed.

An understanding of deletion in a B-tree is reached by examining different scenarios surrounding a shortage. The shortage is fixed by restructuring of the tree. In order to save disk accesses, the scenarios for the shortage are classified with an emphasis to localize the restructuring as much as possible.

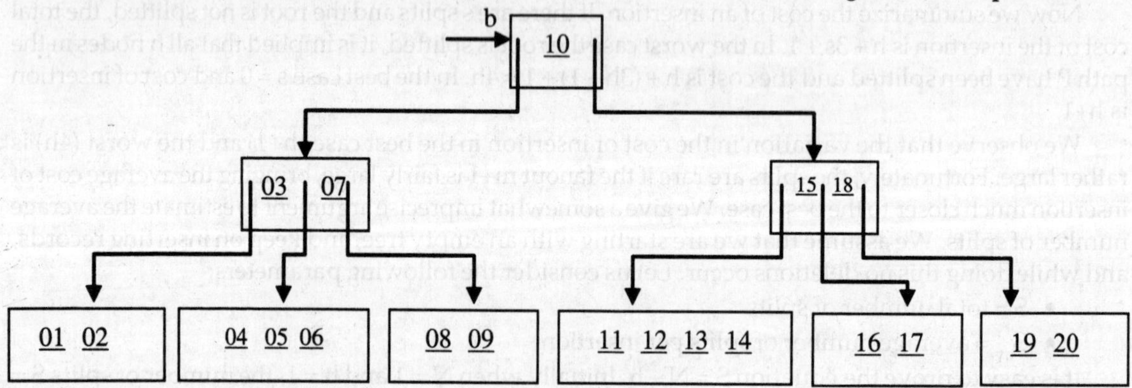

Figure 10.63 A B-tree

Suppose x is a record in a B-tree. Then a record y in the tree is called successor of x if the key value y is the smallest of all keys present in the tree that are larger than x. In the B-tree of **Figure** 10.63, the record 10 is in the root node, its successor, 11, is in the 4th leaf node. To reach the successor of a record, one starts with the child pointer to the right of the record, and then follows left most child pointers until a leaf is reached.

It is interesting to note that for every record x in a B-tree, either x or its successor is in a leaf node. This property allows us to pretend that a record to be deleted from the tree is always to be found in a leaf node. If the record to be deleted is not in a leaf node, it is swapped with its successor. After the swap, the record to be deleted is in a leaf node. This would violate the integrity of the B-tree in that the record x is not in correct place in the tree. This problem is fixed by removing the record x together with the pointer to its right from the leaf node. However, the leaf node may become short of a record. The scenarios surrounding this shortage and its remedy will be discussed later on.

We will use the B-tree of **Figure** 10.63 as a running example. It illustrates the concept of a successor and enumerates scenarios surrounding the potential shortage of record when removal of a record pointer pair from a node is to be attempted. Some of these scenarios require us to examine siblings of a node. Siblings of a node are the children of its parent. The immediate siblings are of particular interest to us. Immediate siblings are siblings to the left or right of a node. Note that the left most child of a parent has only right sibling and the right most child of a percent has only left sibling, and all other children have left and right siblings.

By inspecting Figure 10.63 we find: (a) The record 10 is not in a leaf but its successor, 11, is in a leaf. (b) The 2nd and 4th leaves have a record to spare. (c) The 1st, 3rd, and 5th leaves cannot spare a record, but have a sibling that can. (d) The 6th leaf and its sibling cannot spare a record. The same is true for each node at the first two levels.

The algorithm for deletion of a record x from a B-tree proceeds in two phases. The algorithm is illustrated in **Figure** 10.64. This figure illustrates a variety of scenarios for deletions. The reader is cautioned that every deletion is done starting from the original state of the B-tree in **Figure** 10.63 in isolation of other deletions. In the first phase we start from the root and search for x in the tree. If x is found in a leaf, the search is ended. On the other hand, if x is found in a non-leaf node, the search is continued for its successor reaching a leaf node. The record x is then swapped with its successor so that x is in a leaf {**Figure** 10.64(a)}.

In Phase 2 of deletion, the record x and the null pointer to its right are removed from the leaf. If this removal does not cause a shortage of a record in the leaf, the deletion is considered as completed. This scenario is illustrated in **Figure** 10.64(b). On the other hand, if the removal of a record pointer pair causes a shortage of a record in the node, the shortage is fixed by a local restructuring of the tree. Sometimes, this restructuring has to be cascaded all the way to the root.

The scenarios surrounding the removal of a record are listed below. In all these scenarios, we have a node L from which the record x and the pointer to its right have to be removed. The node L is not necessarily a leaf.

Case 1: The node L has a record to spare: This scenarios has been discussed before, but listed here for the sake of completeness, note that the record pointer pair to be removed from the node L that is not required to be a leaf. In this case the record x and the null pointer to its right are simply removed from the tree and the deletion is considered as completed. This scenario is illustrated in **Figure** 10.64(b).

Case 2: The node L cannot spare a record, but one of its siblings can: This scenario is illustrated in **Figure** 10.64(c). In this case the record x and the pointer to its right are removed from L. To fix the shortage of one record in L, a rotation is used. A rotation moves a record from the parent to node L, and a record from the sibling of L to the parent. A rotation preserves properties of a B-tree and it only involves movements of records. No pointers are moved. A rotation also completes the deletion in a B-tree without causing a structural restructuring of the tree.

Case 3: Neither node L nor any of its siblings can spare a record: This scenario is illustrated in **Figure** 10.64(d). In this case the record x and the pointer to its right are removed from L. In this case a sibling cannot fill the shortage of one record in L. In this case the node L and one of its siblings are collapsed to form a single node. But this necessitates the removal of one record pointer pair from their parent. So a record pointer pair is also pulled from the parent into the combined node. This fixes the problem at the level of the node L. If the parent becomes short of a record pointer pair, the parent node becomes the candidate for the scenario of Case 1 or Case 2 and the respective measures are taken. Clearly removal of a record pointer can cascade all the way up to the root node. If the root has at least two records, it will spare a record pointer pair. On the other hand, if the root has only one record the nodes being collapsed will absorb the root and will become the new root of the tree. In this case the height of the tree will reduce by 1.

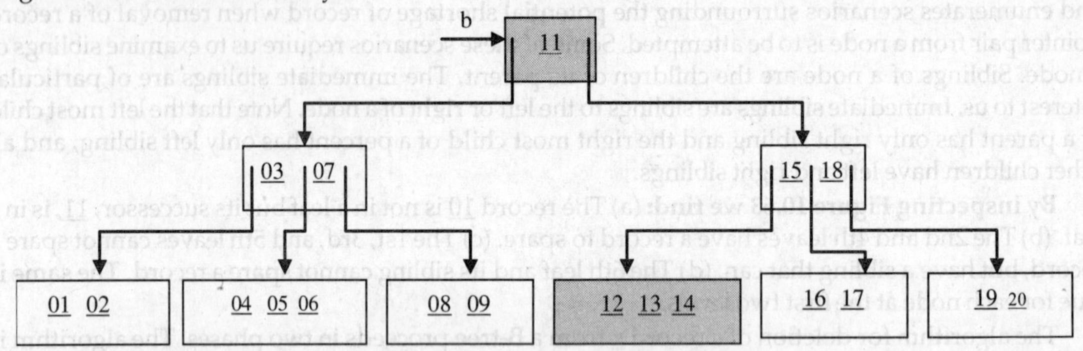

(a) Deletion of 10 that resides in B-tree of Figure 10.63 in a leaf node.

The record 10 is swapped with 11. Now 10 is in a leaf. In this case, the leaf has a record to spare; therefore, 10 and the pointer to its right are removed. In general the removal of a record and the pointer may be as in (b), (c), or (d) below.

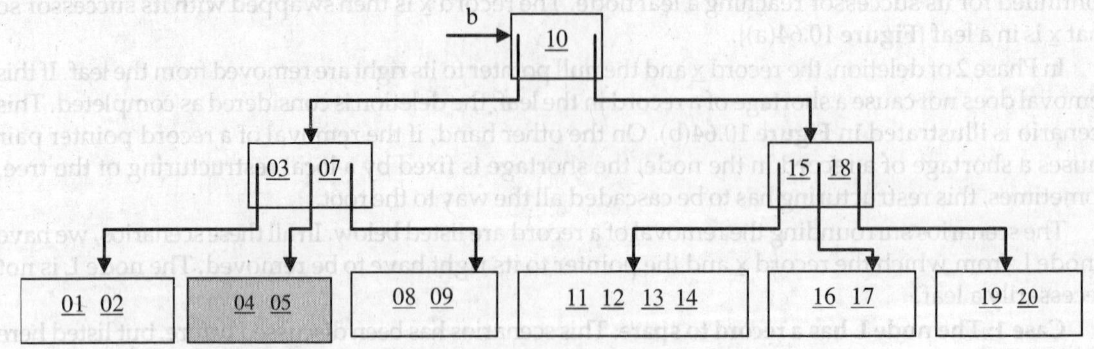

(b) Deletion of 06 that resides in B-tree of Figure 10.63 in a node that can spare a record. The record 06 and the pointer to its right are simply removed from the tree.

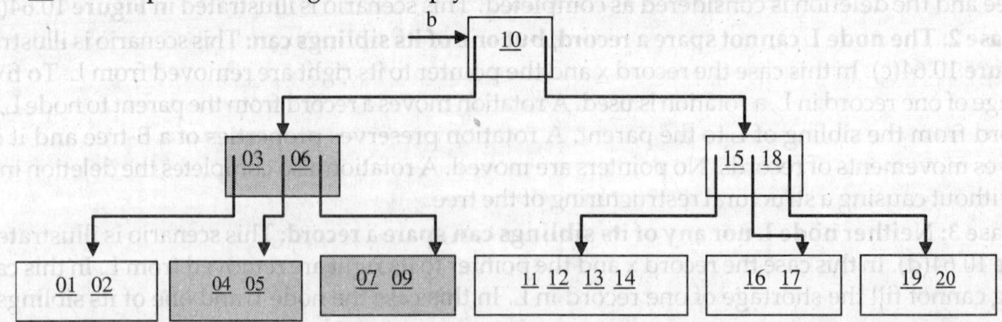

(c) Deletion of 08 that resides in B-tree of Figure 10.63 in a node whose sibling can spare a record. The record 08 and the pointer to its right are removed from the 3rd leaf, creating shortage of a record. The shortage is fixed by rotation of records: 07 is moved from the parent to the 3rd leaf, and the vacancy in the parent is filled by drawing 06 from the 2nd leaf. Rotation does not a movement of child pointers in the affected nodes.

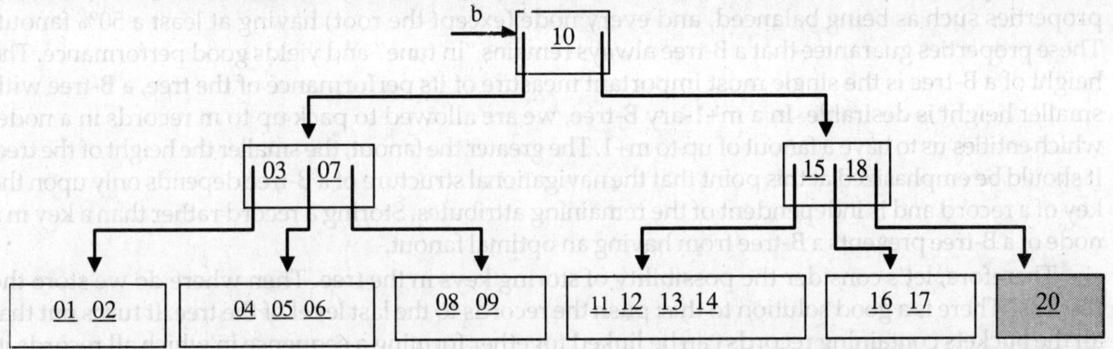

(d) Deletion of 19 that resides in B-tree of Figure 10.63 in a node that cannot spare a record and does not have a sibling that can spare a record. The record 19 and the pointer to its right are removed. This creates a shortage of a record in the leaf. The (only) sibling to its left cannot spare a record. Continued ...

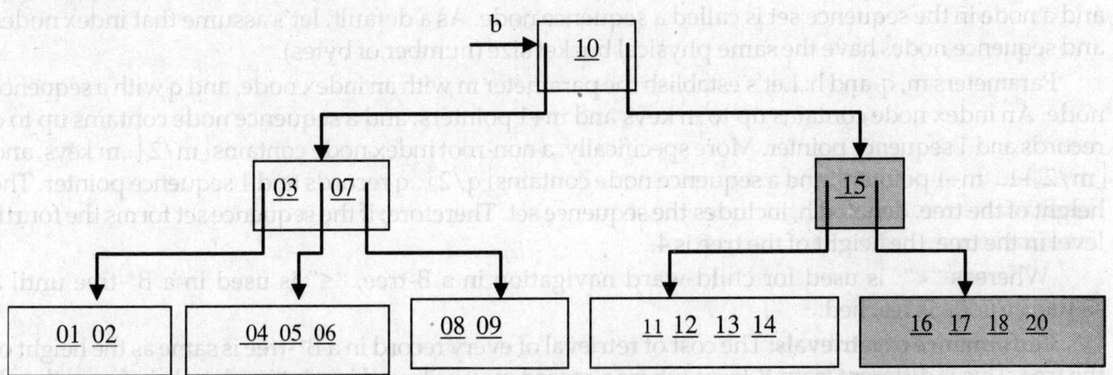

The two shaded leaves and the record 18 from the parent are collapsed to form one node. This creates a shortage of a record in the parent node. Continued ...

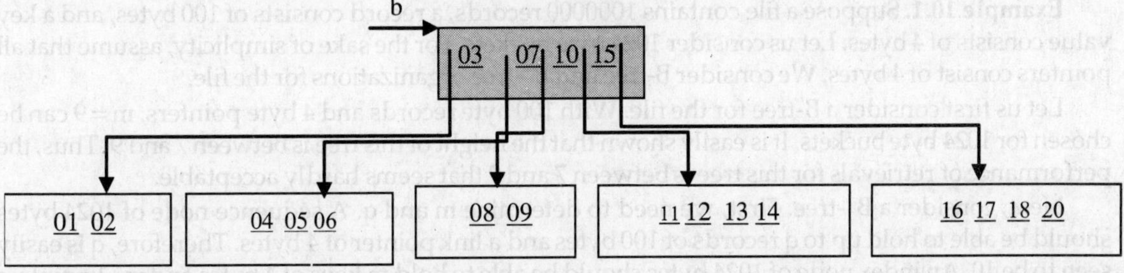

The contents of three nodes at the first two levels are collapsed to form a node that becomes the new root of the tree. This finishes the deletion of 19.

Figure 10.64 Various scenarios for deletion in a B-tree

Note: For each deletion- we start with the B-tree in **Figure** 10.63, here parts (a)-(d) corresponds to the scenarios (a) – (d) listed in **Figure** 10.63.

10.10 B⁺-TREE

In the previous section we have been introduced B-trees as m+1-ary search trees with some desirable properties such as being balanced, and every node (except the root) having at least a 50% fanout. These properties guarantee that a B-tree always remains "in tune" and yields good performance. The height of a B-tree is the single most important measure of its performance of the tree, a B-tree with smaller height is desirable. In a m+1-ary B-tree, we are allowed to pack up to m records in a node, which entitles us to have a fanout of up to m+1. The greater the fanout, the smaller the height of the tree. It should be emphasized at this point that the navigational structure of a B-tree depends only upon the key of a record and is independent of the remaining attributes. Storing a record rather than a key in a node of a B-tree prevents a B-tree from having an optimal fanout.

Therefore, let's consider the possibility of storing keys in the tree. Then where do we store the records? There is a good solution to this: push the records to the last level of the tree. It turns out that all the buckets containing records can be linked together forming a sequence in which all records in the file appear in the logical order of the key. The resulting tree will be termed a B^+-tree. A B^+-tree provides reasonable performance for direct access, and excellent performance for sequential and range accesses.

A B^+-tree consists of an index set and a sequence set. A node in an index set is called an index node and a node in the sequence set is called a sequence node. As a default, let's assume that index nodes and sequence nodes have the same physical bucket size (number of bytes).

Parameters m, q, and h: Let's establish the parameter m with an index node, and q with a sequence node. An index node contains up to m keys and m+1 pointers, and a sequence node contains up to q records and 1 sequence pointer. More specifically, a non-root index node contains $\lfloor m/2 \rfloor$...m keys, and $\lfloor m/2 \rfloor$+1... m+1 pointers, and a sequence node contains $\lfloor q/2 \rfloor$...q records and 1 sequence pointer. The height of the tree, denoted h, includes the sequence set. Therefore, if the sequence set forms the fourth level in the tree, the height of the tree is 4.

Whereas "<" is used for child-ward navigation in a B-tree, "≤" is used in a B^+-tree until a sequence node is reached.

Performance of retrievals: The cost of retrieval of every record in a B^+-tree is same as the height of the tree. This is different from B-trees where a record may be found in a internal node in fewer than h accesses. The height, h, of a B^+-tree is given as follows:

$h \le 2 + \log_{\lfloor p/2 \rfloor + 1} \frac{1}{2}(n / \lfloor q/2 \rfloor)$

Example 10.1. Suppose a file contains 1000000 records, a record consists of 100 bytes, and a key value consists of 4 bytes. Let us consider 1024 byte buckets. For the sake of simplicity, assume that all pointers consist of 4 bytes. We consider B-tree and B^+-tree organizations for the file.

Let us first consider a B-tree for the file. With 100 byte records and 4 byte pointers, m = 9 can be chosen for 1024 byte buckets. It is easily shown that the height of this tree is between 7 and 9. Thus, the performance of retrievals for this tree is between 7 and 9 that seems hardly acceptable.

Next, consider a B^+-tree. First, we need to determine m and q. A sequence node of 1024 bytes should be able to hold up to q records of 100 bytes and a link pointer of 4 bytes. Therefore, q is easily seen to be 10. An index node of 1024 bytes should be able to hold m keys of 4 bytes and m+1 pointers of 4 bytes. Therefore, q is set to 127. Hence, a non-root node of the tree has 63...127 keys and its fanout is 64...128. The height of a B^+-tree is easy to determine by estimating the number of nodes in the tree, bottom up, level by level. In order to determine the range for the height, we see thinnest and thickest trees. These calculations are shown in Table 10.7.

Table 10.7 Height of B + -tree of Example 10.1

Level L	Number of nodes at level L	
	The thinnest tree	The thickest tree
h	$\lfloor 1000000/5 \rfloor = 200000$	$\lceil 1000000/10 \rceil = 100000$
h-1	$\lfloor 200000/64 \rfloor = 3125$	$\lceil 100000/128 \rceil = 782$
h-2	$\lfloor 3125/64 \rfloor = 48$	$\lceil 782/128 \rceil = 7$
h-3	1	1
Conclusion	$h \le 4$	$h \ge 4$
	The height of the tree is 4	

It turns out that the height of this B$^+$-tree with 1000000 records is always 4. Therefore, the performance for retrievals is 4 disk accesses. If we are willing to replicate the root of the tree in a buffer, we can improve the performance by 1 disk access. An interesting observation is that the number of nodes in the first two levels of the tree ranges from 8 in the best case to 49 in the worst case. If we are willing to replicate these nodes in the main memory, a performance of 2 disk accesses can be guaranteed. Note that this requires 8 to 49 buffers. Clearly, the B$^+$-tree provides a much better performance than the B-tree. At some expense of main memory, a performance of 2 disk accesses could be guaranteed for retrievals.

10.10.1 Insertion Of A Record

A B$^+$-tree consists of a sequence set and an index set. The sequence set is a linked list of nodes (buckets), each containing $\lfloor q/2 \rfloor$...q records. The index set is just like a B-tree except that the index nodes contain keys and child pointers instead of records and child pointers. A non-root index node contains $\lfloor m/2 \rfloor$...m keys and $\lfloor (m+1)/2 \rfloor$...(m+1) pointers. The root node is an index node and it contains 1...m keys and 2...(m+1) pointers.

The insertion of a record $\underline{x}$ in a B$^+$-tree is accomplished in three phases. In Phase 1 one identifies the appropriate leaf node in the sequence set. In Phase 2 the record is added to the sequence set. If the leaf node has space for a record, the record is added to it and the insertion is completed, else, splitting is necessary. The record is collated with the leaf and the resulting sequence node is splitted into two nodes called the left node and the right node. In Phase 3, the pair consisting of the key of the highest record in the left node and the pointer to the right node is added to the parent of the original leaf in a way similar to that in B-trees. During this phase the splits can cascade upward and in the worst case a new root will be created. The three phases are described below in greater detail.

Phase 1. Identify a leaf node: In this phase one starts with the root of the B$^+$-tree and follows child pointers reaching a leaf node. This navigation is similar to that in B-tree. In the node being visited, the smallest key k satisfying $k \le x$ is identified, where x is the key of $\underline{x}$. If such a key exists, the child pointer to the left of the key is followed. Otherwise the last child pointer in the index node is followed. This will eventually lead to a leaf node in the sequence set. At the end of this phase, the contents of the leaf node are in a buffer.

Phase 2. Add record to the sequence set: If the buffer obtained from the previous phase has space in it; the record $\underline{x}$ is added to it. The buffer is then written to the disk in place of the original leaf, and insertion is completed.

On the other hand, if the buffer obtained at the end of Phase 1 is full (containing q records) a split will be composed using two buffers. For convenience, we refer two buffers as the left buffer and the right buffer. To compose the split, first buffer obtained from Phase 1 and the record x are collated. The result is an imaginary overflow buffer. Now a split is composed in the two buffers by splitting this node so that each buffer gets one half of the records. If q is odd, we let the left buffer have one record more than the right buffer.

We write the left buffer in the place of the original leaf node and link it to a new node containing the records from the right buffer. The new node should point to where the original leaf node was pointing. To accomplish this, a new node is allocated and the link pointer of the original leaf from Phase 1 is transferred to right buffer. The address of this newly allocated node becomes the link pointer in the left buffer. The composition of the split is now complete. The two buffers are then written to the disk.

Next the middle record of the overflowing node is designated. For this algorithm, the middle record is defined to be the highest record in the left buffer after the split.

Phase 3. Add key pointer pair to the index set: Now a key pointer pair is formed. The key is the copy of the key of the middle record identified at the end of Phase 2. The pointer is the address of the right node allocated in Phase 2.

Now this key pointer pair is added to the parent of the original leaf node from Phase 1. From here onward, the addition of key pointer pairs is identical to that in B-tree. The only difference is that in a B-tree one adds record pointer pairs, but here key pointer pairs are added.

Example 10.2. Now we give example of insertions in a B^+-tree with m = 4 and q = 3. The root is always an index node, and it can contain 1...4 keys and 2...5 pointers. Other index nodes can contain 2...4 keys and 3...5 pointers. A sequence node can hold 1…3 records. When we have a full sequence node with 3 records and add a new record to it, the sequence node splits into two nodes, each containing 2 records.

Starting with an empty B^+-tree, we insert the records 02, 17, 05, 09, 13, 03, 11, 01, 04, 15, 08, 19, 14, 16, 18, 12, 20, 07, 06, 10 in a sequence. The empty tree simply consists of a null pointer (to an index node). When 02 is inserted, one obtains a B^+-tree with one node in the sequence set and one node in the index set. The sequence node contains the record 02 and a null link pointer. The index node contains a pointer to the sequence node followed by the key value of 02. This is a small tree and it does not conform to definition of a search tree. For example, the index node contains 1 key and not 2, but 1 child pointer. Strictly speaking we should allow such exceptions to be built into the definition of B^+-tree. This is a bit tedious but simple. We ignore this detail for small states of the B^+-tree. **Figure** 10.65 shows the results at several stages in the sequence of insertions.

10.10.2 Performance Of Insertion

Analysis of performance of insertion in a B^+-tree is similar to that in a B-tree. If there are s splits and the root is not splitted, the total cost of the insertion is h + 3s + 1. In the best-case s = 0 and cost of insertion is h+1. In the worst case the h nodes are splitted, including the root, and the cost is 4h. On average, we can assume that s = 2/q. Therefore, the average cost of insertion is h + 6/q + 1, which is close to the best-case performance (and much better than the worst case).

10.10.3 B^+-tree As A Secondary Index

Every file structure can be used either as a primary structure or a secondary structure. This is also true for B^+-trees. When a B^+-tree is used as an indirect index, a sequence node contains up to q ⟨key, primary bucket pointer⟩ pairs, and 1 sequence pointer. The index nodes in a secondary B^+-tree are similar to the index nodes in a primary B⁺-tree. More specifically, a non-root index node contains $\lfloor m/2 \rfloor$...m keys and $\lfloor m/2 \rfloor$+1... m+1 pointers, and a sequence node contains q/2...q keys, the same number of primary bucket pointers, and 1 sequence pointer.

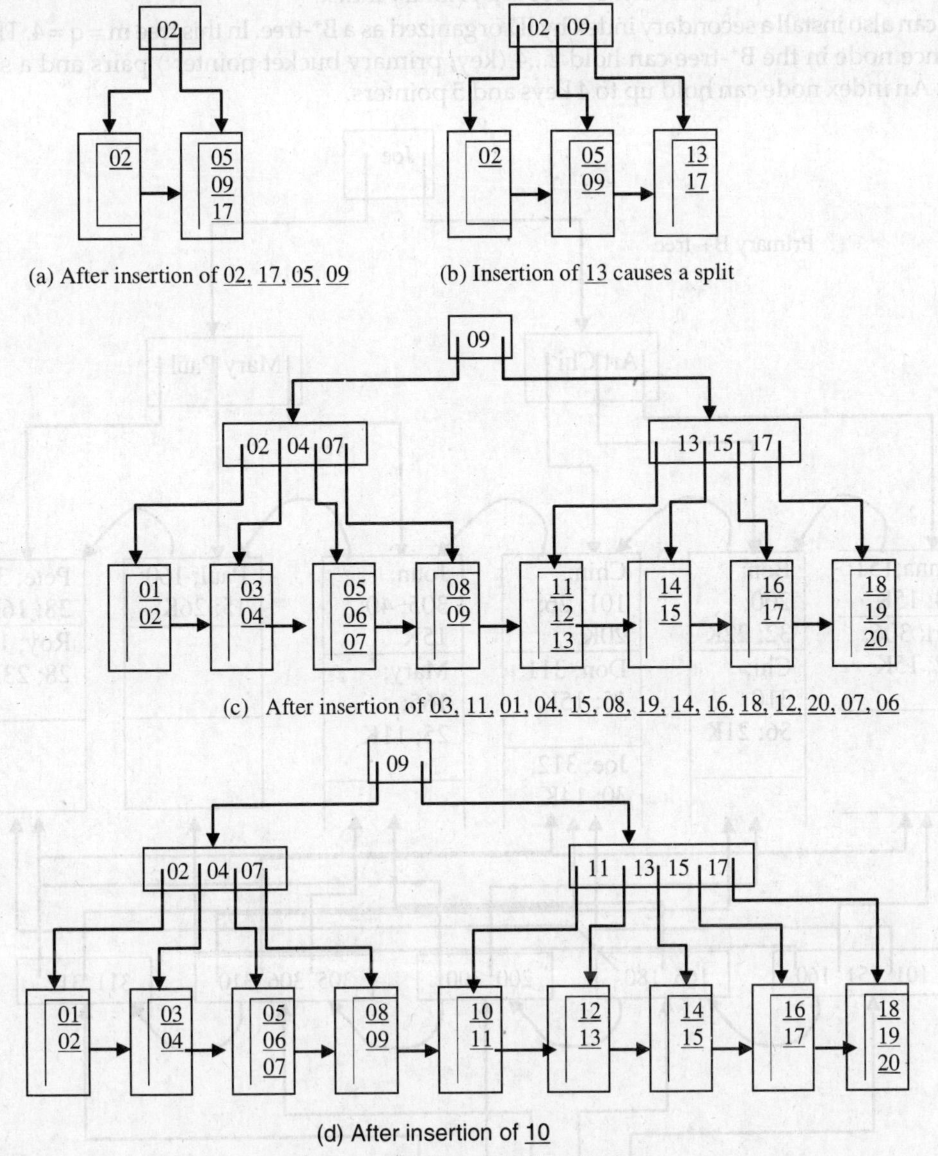

Figure 10.65 Insertions in a B+-tree

As in primary B^+-trees, we will assume that index and sequence nodes in a secondary B^+-tree use the same size buckets. Sometimes we can assume that a bucket pointer has the same physical size as an internal pointer. Under this assumption m = q. Otherwise m and q may be different. The height h of the secondary tree is same as the level of the sequence set. Therefore, if the sequence set is at the fourth level of the tree, the height of the tree is 4. This means that at the 4th level we only have pointers to the records; records themselves are elsewhere in a primary file that is separate from the secondary B^+-tree at hand. More details regarding B^+-tree and B^*-tree is given in Chapter 11.

Example 10.3. Figure 10.66 shows an example of a primary B⁺-tree and a secondary B⁺-tree. The std file of Table 10.5 forms the sequence set of the primary B⁺-tree. In this tree m = 4 and q = 3. Therefore, a sequence node can hold 1...3 records and 1 sequence pointer, and an index node (except the root) can hold 2...4 keys and 3...5 pointers. The B⁺-tree is a primary index.

We can also install a secondary index by ID organized as a B⁺-tree. In this tree m = q = 4. Therefore, a sequence node in the B⁺-tree can hold 2...4 ⟨key, primary bucket pointer ⟩ pairs and a sequence pointer. An index node can hold up to 4 keys and 5 pointers.

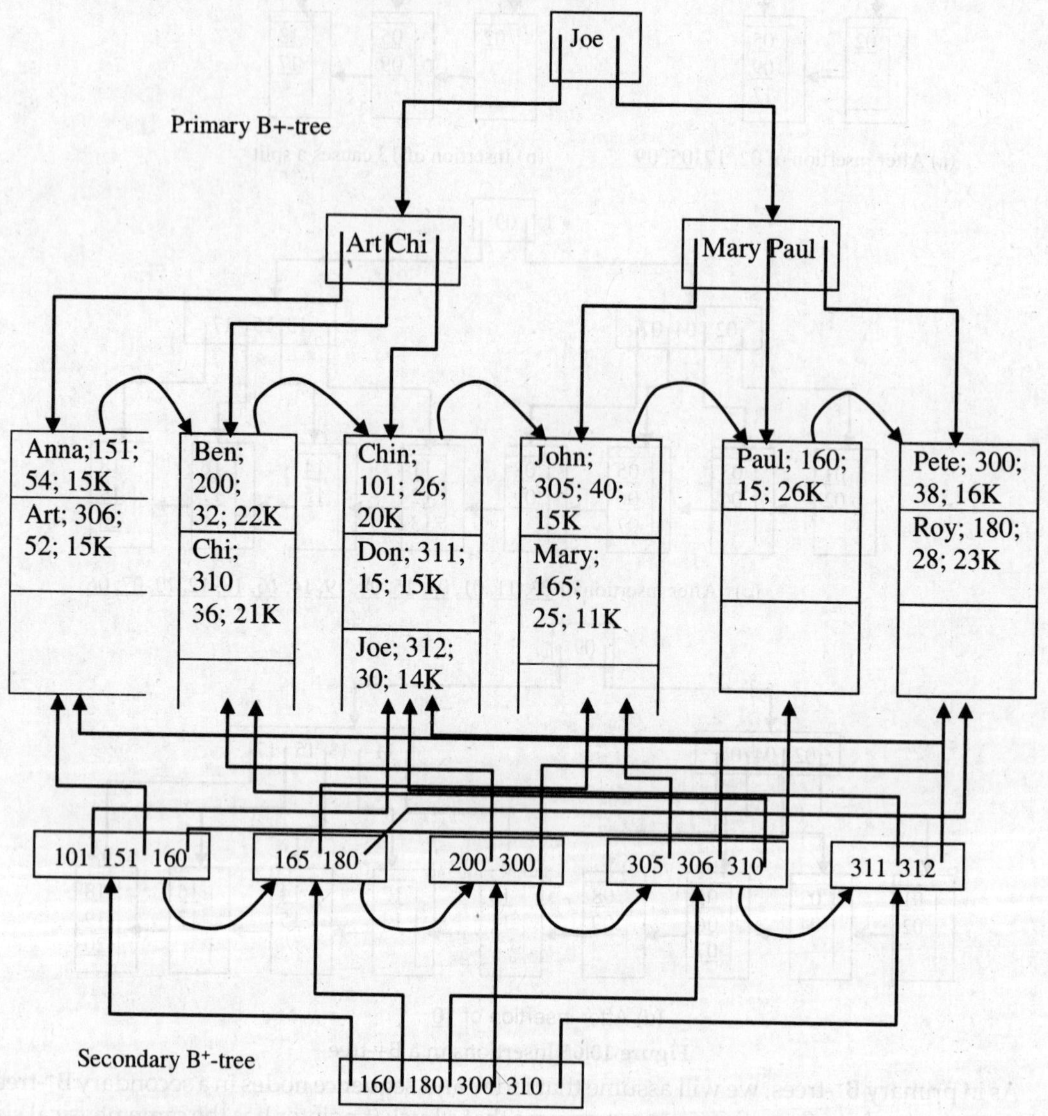

The std file of Table 10.5 is the sequence set of B⁺-tree with Names as the primary key (m = 4, q = 3). The B⁺-tree is a secondary index by ID (m = q = 4).

Figure 10.66 Primary and secondary B⁺-trees

FOR SUMMATIVE AND FORMATIVE ASSESSMENT

10.1 An old model of hard drives for IBM mainframe systems consisted of 9 disk platters, in which the bottom disk was not used to store actual file data, but as a mechanism to increase data reliability. What might be stored on the bottom disk?

10.2 To minimize head movement, hard disks often place related file data on tracks of the same cylinder rather than on adjacent tracks of the same surface. Why does this reduce head movement?

10.3 We have a disk drive with the following characteristics:
- seek time: 30 ms
- rotational delay (latency): 10 ms
- transfer rate: 5 Kbytes/ms

On average, how long would it take to read 500 bytes from this disk?

10.4 Why is it necessary, in general, for a checksum function to produce different values for different inputs?

10.5 Given 5 buckets, numbered 0, 1, 2, 3, 4, each with a capacity for two records, show the result of inserting the records with the keys: 16, 7, 15, 34, 24, 25, 75, 14, 39, into the appropriate buckets, using the linear probing hashing function
$h(K) = [K + (i-1)] \bmod 5$
(a) On average, how many buckets had to be read to insert each record?
(b) How would this number change (calculate it) if we used instead the non-linear probing hashing function $h(K) = [K + (i-1)^2] \bmod 5$ to insert the same records?

10.6 Double hashing overcomes secondary clustering by using two different hashing functions as in: $h(k) = (h1(k) + (i-1)h2(k)) \bmod N$. Is it possible to overcome secondary clustering with only a single hashing function? If so, describe the method, and if not, explain why?

10.7 In the virtual hashing method with a total of M initial buckets, and an initial hashing function of $h(K) = K \bmod M$ which of the following occurs when a bucket B overflows for the **second** time?
(a) Bucket 2B is allocated.
(b) Bucket B + 2M is allocated.
(c) Bucket B + 4M is allocated.
(d) Rehash some records using the hashing function $h(K) = K \bmod 2M$.
(e) Rehash some records using the hashing function $h(K) = K \bmod 4M$.
(f) Rehash some records using the hashing function $h(K) = K \bmod 8M$.

10.8 A certain file is stored in buckets using the simple table-assisted hashing method described in class. There are four buckets, each of which can hold up to 3 records. The initial contents of this file and of the maxKey table are shown in the figure below. The hash function is $h(K,i) = (K + i-1) \bmod 4$. Show the state of the file and of the maxKey table following the insertion of a record with key 28 into the file.

Bucket	maxKey	contents
0	16	4 16 8
1	43	9 43 25
2	26	18 26
3	19	7 3 19

(a) What is the maximum number of buckets that must be accessed during the search for a record?

(b) When a record to be inserted hashes to a full bucket, where is the record placed?

10.9 In the table assisted hashing method the attempted insertion of a record, R, into a full bucket may require that another record, R be removed from that bucket and re-inserted elsewhere. Is it possible that this re-insertion of record R would require record R to be re-inserted, and so on, thus resulting in an infinite loop? Explain.

10.10 Write a pseudo-code routine for the deletion of a record from a direct file, implemented using the table-assisted hashing method.

10.11 For the dynamic hashing method, a PseudoRandom function, B(K, i), is required to guide the traversal of a binary tree towards the bucket containing the record with key K. The function outputs either 0 or 1, based on the values of the key, K, and the tree level, i. What is wrong with using the following function for B(K, i)?

```
int B(int K, int i)
{
    int pos, bit;
    pos = 1 << i; /* calculates 2^i */
    bit = (K & pos) >> i; /* obtains the ith bit of K */
    return (bit);
}
Write a good function for B(K,i).
```

10.12 A certain file is stored in buckets as determined using the method of dynamic hashing. The hash function is h(K) = K mod 4 and the first few bits of the B string associated with each key in the file are given in the table below. Each bucket can hold up to 2 records. Show the state of the directory and the file after the records with keys 17, 13, 16, 5, and 25 are inserted.

Key	**B**
17	01101
13	00101
16	10110
5	11110
25	1(

10.13 What major issue can we ignore when deleting from a direct file using the dynamic hashing method instead of simple open addressing?

10.14 What is the major similarity between table assisted hashing and dynamic hashing? What is advantage there to using dynamic hashing?

10.15 In order to perform master file update with a single pass over the master file and a single pass over the transaction file, reading every record of each file at most once, which of the following conditions must hold?

(a) Transaction file must be sorted.

(b) Master file must be sorted by same key as transaction file.

(c) Software must provide direct access to an individual record.

(d) Hardware must provide direct access to an individual record.

(e) There can be at most one transaction per master file record.

10.16 (a) A sorted master file consisting of 1000 records and an unsorted transactions file, containing only change transactions (i.e., no insertions or deletions), are stored on disk. We are asked to use the on-line update method to apply the transactions file to the master file, ensuring that if a disk crash occurs, we can later recover the original master file contents. Assuming that only read operations count as record accesses, what is the maximum number of records in the transactions file one should accept before suggesting that the on-line file update method would be more efficient?

(b) How would answer to (a) change if a copy of the original master file were not required?

(c) How would answer to (a) change if the transactions file was initially sorted?

(d) Explain why answer to (a) would change if a large number of transactions were insertion operations. We do not need to provide any math for (d).

10.17 A sorted master file consisting of 1000 records and an unsorted differential file consisting of 128 records are stored on disk. We have just received a request to locate the record with key K. Assuming that the record is in the master file, but we first check the differential file, approximately how many disk accesses in total will it take before we find the desired record?

10.18 Is a B-tree of order m=4, containing all the letters of the alphabet unique? Explain.

10.19 For a B-tree of order 9, state the minimum and maximum number of records, which may be contained in (a) the root, (b) any internal node, (c) any leaf node.

10.20 A B-tree of order m=3 is given below. Insert a record with key N, making sure to show the evolution of the tree as the B-tree insertion algorithm proceeds.

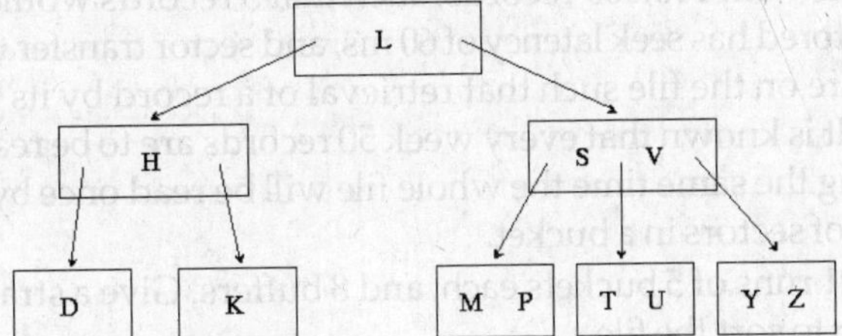

10.21 A B-tree of order m=3 allows nodes to have as many as three children. Why is a B-tree of order m=2 not necessarily a binary search tree?

10.22 If we have a B-tree of order 10, containing keys 10 bytes in length, calculate a lower bound on the block size. Assume that all pointers are 4 bytes in length.

10.23 (a) Construct a B-tree of order m=3 by inserting the following keys into an initially empty tree: A, B, C, D, E, F, G, H. Show the tree at each stage.

(b) Can a tree of lower height, also of m=3 and containing the same keys as in part (a) be constructed? If so, show such a tree, and if not, explain why not.

(c) If we now added a record with key I to the tree of part (a), would answer to part (b) change? Justify answer numerically.

(d) Delete the record with key B from the tree of part (a). Show the tree at each stage.

10.24 Consider a file consisting of chains. Suppose that the capacity of a bucket is 4 and the records within a chain appear in the increasing order of their key values. Further assume that a chain always remains compacted; meaning every bucket in the chain, except possibly the last bucket, is full, and that the last bucket contains at least one record. Write an algorithm to split a chain into two chains containing records with even and odd keys, respectively. The address of the home bucket of the chain containing records with even keys should be same as that of the old chain. De-allocate buckets to dismantle the old chain and allocate new buckets to assemble new chains.

10.25 A sorted file with 500,000 records occupies 50,000 buckets. We need to create a secondary index, also a sorted file, with respect to a unique key K. A K-value requires 8 bytes, and a secondary bucket consists of 1005 bytes. Assuming 80% space utilization for the secondary file, estimate the amount of disk space it requires.

10.26 We are given a chain containing records whose keys are divisible by a positive integer M. Give a criteria to attempt to split the chain into two chains, each containing about half of the records in the original chain.

10.27 On a given disk a cylinder contains 100 tracks, a track contains 12 sectors, and a sector contains 600 bytes. A file to be stored on the disk consists of 60 byte records, and it uses 2 block buckets. Disk architecture 25

(a) What is the bucket capacity?

(b) How many records would fit on one cylinder?

(c) How many records would a cylinder contain if the average space utilization in buckets is 40...80?

10.28 Suppose we make the assumption that a bucket is not allowed to be splitted across tracks. This is not a good assumption, as it will cause some space within tracks to be wasted. Suppose we are given a disk with 200 bytes per sector and 10 sectors per track. Consider a file contained 300 byte records. Calculate the minimum amount of space which will be wasted per track.

10.29 We are given a file with 100,000 records, such that 3 records would fit in a sector. The disk where the file is stored has seek latency of 60 ms, and sector transfer time of 2 ms. Assume that there is a structure on the file such that retrieval of a record by its key is accomplished in 2 bucket accesses. It is known that every week 50 records are to be read randomly by their key values and during the same time the whole file will be read once by buckets. Determine the optimal number of sectors in a bucket.

10.30 We are given 2401 runs of 5 buckets each, and 8 buffers. Give a strategy and calculate the I/O cost of merging to sort the file.

10.31 Suppose a file consists of 1024 runs of 10 bucket each. For merging we have 6 buffers. Suppose bucket access time is 50 ms. Consider the following three options for merging and give an appropriate answer.

(a) Estimate the cost of 5-way merging. To simplify the calculations pad the number of runs being merged so that it is divisible by 5. Do not pad the number of runs in the last pass. The number of runs will follow the following

(b) sequence: 1024 changed to 1025, 1025/5 = 205, 205/5 = 41 changed to 45, 45/5 = 9 changed to 10. Now do a 2-way merging.

(c) Estimate the cost of 2-way merging using 2-bucket cascades. Assume that the bucket transfer time is 10 ms.

10.32 Given a single disk with 15 ms of seek time, 10 ms of latency, and 2 ms of bucket transfer time. A file with 625 runs of 10 buckets each is stored on the disk. Assume that each run is stored as a cascade. We are given 20 buffers which are to be configured as follows: 5 cascades of 2 buckets each, for 5 input streams, and, 1 cascade of 10 buckets forming a single output stream. Calculate the cost of I/O in sorting the file using merging.

10.33 Suppose that for linear hashing, the starting value of the parameter M is 3. Enumerate the values of the variable sP just before each of first 20 splits.

10.34 Given current value of M = 48, sP = 20. How many chains does the file contain? Into what chain does 150 hash?

10.35 Suppose that the initial value of M = 3. A bucket can hold 10 records. Suppose that currently the file has 1,000 records, space utilization is exactly 40% and average chain length l_{av} is 1.25. Calculate the chain number where the record 300 is to be found.

10.36 Assume that we have a dynamically hashed file with linear splitting where average chain length of 1.5 is used to trigger splits. Suppose the file is expected to contain up to 150,000 records and the bucket capacity is 10.

(a) Calculate the main memory requirements for external nodes containing bucket pointers.

(b) Calculate the index of the external node where the chain address corresponding to the bit pattern consisting of all zeros is to be found.

10.37 We have a file for which we propose to use dynamic hashing with linear splitting with one address tree. Suppose 36,000 bits of main memory is available for the address tree. How many chains can be supported?

10.38 Assume a dynamically hashed file with linear splitting. At a given moment, suppose 25 is the index of an external node.

(a) What bit pattern would lead to this external node?

(b) Assuming no deletions have taken place, what is the minimum and maximum number of splittings that have occurred?

10.39 Given a B-tree with m = 200 and height 3, what is the range for n?

10.40 A certain file is stored in buckets as determined using the method of dynamic hashing. The hash function is h(K) = K mod 4 and the first few bits of the B string associated with each key in the file are given in the table below. Each bucket can hold up to 2 records. Show the state of the directory and the file after the records with keys 17, 13, 16, 5, and 25 are inserted.

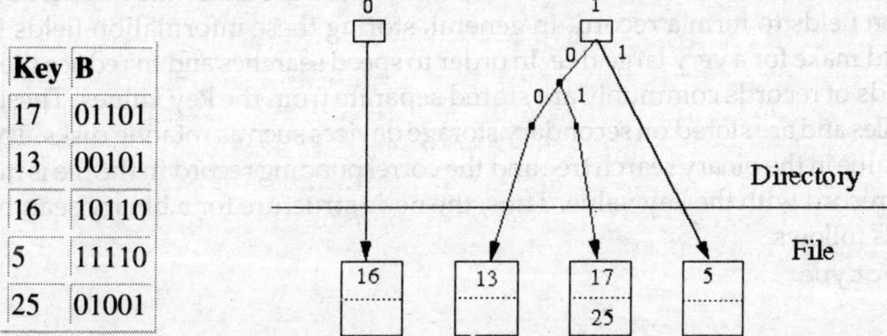

Key	B
17	01101
13	00101
16	10110
5	11110
25	01001

(a) Calculate the size of a B-tree node of order 10, containing keys 10 bytes in length. Assume that all pointers are 4 bytes in length.

(b) Assume a B-tree consists of three levels of completely full nodes. Locate a particular record, with key K, followed by the next record in the sequence, and report its key value. Illustrate the best case and the worst case in terms of numbers of file accesses for this task. How many file accesses would be required in each case?

❑

CHAPTER

11

Variants of B-Tree

Indexes support applications that selectively access individual records, rather than searching through the entire collection in sequence. One field (or a group of fields) is used as the index field. For example, in a banking application, there might be a file of records describing Branch Offices. It might be appropriate to index the file on Branch Name, providing access to Branch office information to support interactive inquiries. In this chapter, we introduce techniques for providing rapid access to particular records in a file. These techniques supplement the data collection using a tree that guides access to the desired records. We will start with a relatively simple tree-structured index and then progress to more complex structures

11.1 BINARY SEARCH TREES AS INDEXES

Let us first reconsider the binary search tree, which was discussed in Chapter 7, Recall that the nodes of a binary search tree are arranged in such a way that a search for a particular key value proceeds down one branch of the tree {Figure.11.1}. The sought key value is compared with the key value of the tree's root: if it is less than the root value, the search proceeds down the left subtree; if it is greater than the root value, the search proceeds down the right subtree. The same logic is applied at each node encountered until the search is satisfied or it is determined that the sought key is not included in the tree. Typically, a key value does not stand alone. Rather the key value is associated with information fields to form a record. In general, storing these information fields in the binary search tree would make for a very large tree. In order to speed searches and to reduce the tree size, the information fields of records commonly are stored separate from the key values. These records are organized into files and are stored on secondary storage devices such as rotating disks. The connection between a key value in the binary search tree and the corresponding record in the file is made to house a pointer to the record with the key value. Thus, the node structure for a binary search tree may be defined in C is as follows.

```
struct rectype
{
   int id;
   char name[100];
   int age;
};

typedef struct rectype recptr;
typedef struct nodetype nodeptr;

struct nodetype
{
```

```
    int key;
    recptr *infoptr;
    nodeptr *left;
    nodeptr *right;
};
```

where rectype is defined appropriately for the application. Key is defined here as integer data type; it could be of other types.

Figure 11.2 shows the binary search tree with pointers included to the data records. This augmentation of the binary search tree to include pointers (i.e., addresses) to data records outside the structure qualifies the tree to be an index. An index is a structured collection of key value and address pairs; the primary purpose of an index is to facilitate access to a collection of records. It is said to be a dense index if it contains a key value-address pair for each record in the collection. An index that is not dense is sometimes called a sparse index. There are many ways to organize an index; the augmented binary search tree is one approach.

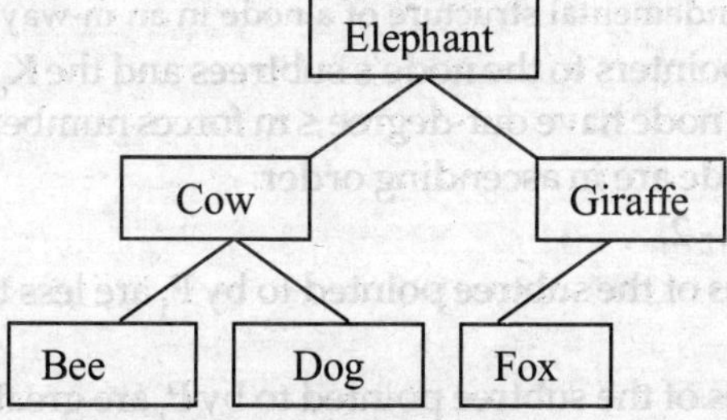

Figure 11.1 Binary Tree

We have not concern with the actual location of the records on primary or secondary storage. Suffice it to say that in contrast to relative files where the physical locations of records are determined by a hash algorithm applied to key values, there is significantly more freedom in the physical placement of records in an indexed file. Processing of this augmented binary search tree is the same as discussed earlier. When a search terminates successfully, the information pointer (infoptr) may be followed to find the data associated with the sought key. Just as a binary search tree can be used as an index, so can an AVL tree or a Balanced Binary tree. The maximum path length through an AVL tree is

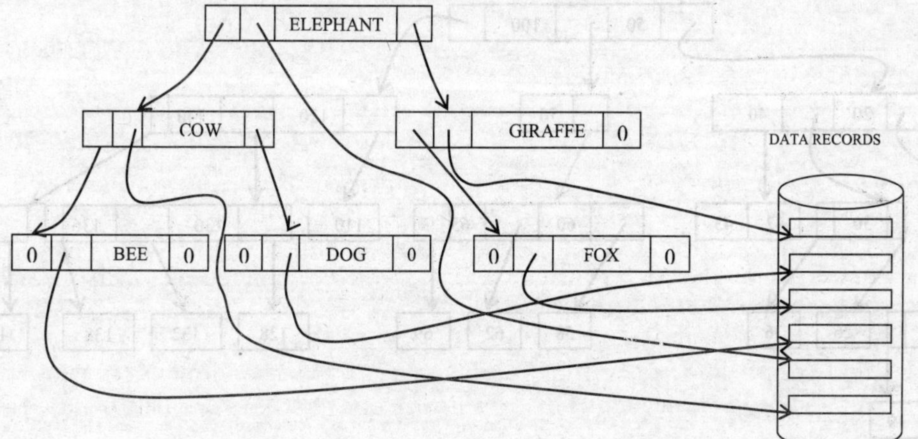

Figure 11.2 Binary search tree from Figure 11.1 used as an index

$O(\log_2 n)$. Thus, use of an AVL tree to house a flense index to n records would result in a maximum search path length of $O(\log_2 n)$ to locate the address of the sought record. Actually the maximum search length of an AVL tree is 1.40 $O(\log_2 n)$.

11.2 M-WAY SEARCH TREES (REVISITED)

The performance of an index can be enhanced significantly by increasing the branching factor of the tree. Rather than binary branching, m-way ($m > 2$) branching can be used. For expository purposes we ignore for the moment pointers out of the structure to data records and consider only the internal structure of the tree. An m-way search tree is a tree in which each node has out-degree $\leq m$. When an m-way search tree is not empty, it has the following properties.

1. Each node of the tree has the structure shown in **Figure 11.3**.

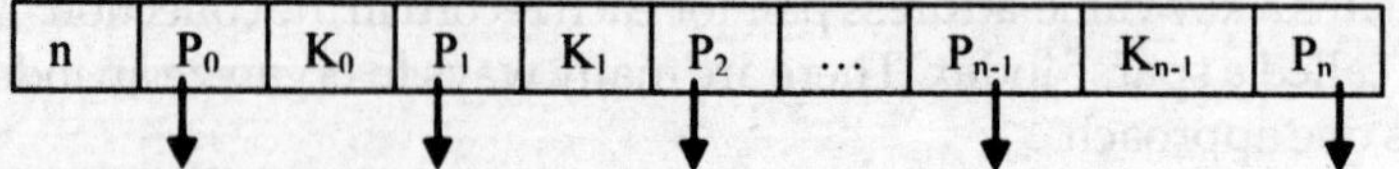

Figure 11.3 Fundamental structure of a node in an m-way search tree.

The $P_o, P_1, \ldots, P_n$ are pointers to the node's subtrees and the $K_o, \ldots, K_{n-1}$ are key values. The requirement that each node have out-degree $\leq m$ forces number of keys $n \leq m-1$.

2. The key values in a node are in ascending order:
$K_i < K_{i+1}$ for $i = 0, \ldots, n-2$.
3. All key values in nodes of the subtree pointed to by P_i are less than the key value K_i for $i = 0, \ldots, n-1$.
4. All key values in nodes of the subtree pointed to by P_i are greater than the key value K_{i-1}.
5. The subtrees pointed to by the P_i, where $i = 0, \ldots, n$ are also m-way search trees.

Note that the arrangement of key values in nodes is analogous to their arrangement in binary search trees. A five-way search tree has a maximum of five pointers out of each node, i.e., $n \leq 4$. Some nodes of the tree may contain fewer than five pointers.

For example, **Figure 11.4** illustrates a three-way search tree. Only the key values and the non-null subtree pointers are shown. In this figure, leaf nodes have been depicted as containing just key values. Each internal node of the search tree has the structure depicted in **Figure 11.3** with a maximum of three subtree pointers.

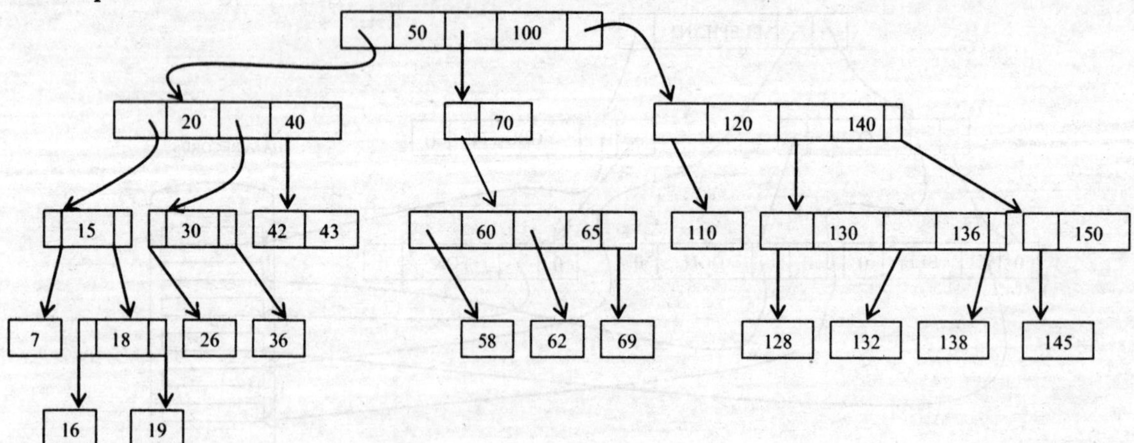

Figure 11.4 Three-way search tree

11.2.1 M-Way Search Trees as Indexes

When an m-way search tree is used as an index, each key-pointer pair (K_i, P_i) becomes a triplet P_i, K_i, A_i where A_i is the address of the data record associated with key value K_i. Thus, each tree node not only points to its child nodes in the tree, but also points into the collection of data records. If the index is dense, every record in the collection will be pointed to by some node in the index. In C we can define the nodetype for an m-way search tree index as follows.

```
struct rectype
{
    int id;
    char name[100];
    int age;
};

typedef struct rectype recptr;
typedef struct nodetype nodeptr;
typedef int keytype;

struct nodefield
{
    nodeptr *ptr;
    keytype key;
    recptr *addr;
};

struct nodetype
{
    int n;
    struct nodefield keyptrs[100];
    nodeptr *keyptrn;
};

nodeptr *root;

The key's type need not be integer; n ≤ m - 1.
```

11.2.2 Searching an M-Way Search Tree

The process of searching for a key value in an m-way search tree is a relatively straight-forward extension of the process of searching for a key value in a binary search tree. A recursive version of the search algorithm is as follows. The variable skey contains the sought key value; node initially points to the root of the tree. The search tree is assumed to be global, with variable root of nodeptr and local with node of nodeptr. Here node receives the root information.

```
recptr * search (keytype skey, nodeptr *node)
{
    int i =0;
```

```
    recptr *foundrec;
    if(node == NULL)
    {
        printf("Tree is empty");
        foundrec = NULL;
    }else
    {
        while((i<node->n)&&(skey > node->keyptrs[i].key))
            i++;
        if((i < node->n) && (skey == node->keyptrs[i].key))
            foundrec = node->keyptrs[i].addr;
        else if(i < node->n)
        {
            node = (node->keyptrs[i]).ptr;
            search(skey, node);
        }else
            search(skey, node->keyptrn);
    }
    return(foundrec);
}
```

The primary task is that the array of keys in each node of the m-way tree is to be scanned to find the appropriate pointer to follow either down to a child node or directly to the data record.

11.2.3 Analysis

The maximum search length is the height of the tree. No more than one node is ever visited on any given level of the tree. To minimize this height for a tree containing n keys, the tree should be as bushy as possible. A three-way tree can provide shorter path lengths than a two-way tree for the same set of keys. In general, the higher the order of branching of the tree, the shorter is the maximum search length. Each node visitation causes a selection from among a greater number of possible branches. Consider an m-way tree with height h. The maximum number of nodes in this tree is $\sum_{i=0}^{h-1} m^i = \frac{m^h - 1}{m-1}$. Each node carries a maximum of $(m - 1)$key values. Thus, $n = \left(\frac{m^h - 1}{m-1}\right)(m-1) \Rightarrow m^h - 1$ is the maximum number of keys in the tree of height h. $n = m^h - 1$ taking log of both sides we get minimum height $h = \log_m(n+1)$ of m-way search having n keys. The maximum search length of an optimal m-way tree of n keys is $O(\log_m n)$. Setting m = 2 gives the expected results for optimal binary search trees. In order to have an m-way search tree of n keys have a maximum height of h, m must be at least $(n+1)^{1/h}$.

For example, to ensure a maximum path length of 4 with 255 keys, the tree must have at least four-way branching; to ensure a maximum path length of 4 with 65,535 keys, the tree must have at least 16-way branching. The extent of branching is not the only factor that determines the performance of an m-way search tree. As it is mentioned for binary search trees, performance can be improved by keeping the tree balanced. Note that the definition of an m-way search tree does not ensure that each interior node of the tree will have m non-null pointers to subtrees. The tree of **Figure 11.4** could have improved search performance, if it is balanced. As discussed binary search tree, keeping an m-way search tree completely balanced may not be worth the effort. Rather, it may be sufficient to constrain the extent to which we allow the tree to deviate from complete balance. Just as AVL trees enjoy more widely spread use than do their completely balanced binary search tree counterparts, so are almost -balanced m-way search trees called B-trees more popular than completely balanced m-way search trees.

11.3 B- TREES (REVISITED)

In this section we review the basic structure of B-tree first and then introduce some of the variations of it, such as B*-tree and B+-tree.

1. Each node of the tree, except for the root and the leaves, has atleast $\left\lceil \frac{1}{2}m \right\rceil$ subtree and no more than m subtrees
2. The root of the tree has at least two subtrees, unless it is itself a leaf.
3. All leaves of the tree are on the same level

The first constraint ensures that each node of the tree is at least half full. The second constraint forces the tree to branch early. The third constraint keeps the tree nearly balanced.

The size of a B-tree of order m and its search path lengths may be larger than for the optimal m-way search tree for the same collection of keys. However, as we will see in the next section, maintaining a B-tree is significantly easier than maintaining an optimal m-way search tree. The reasons for using a B-tree of order m rather than an optimal m-way search tree are the same as the reasons for using an AVL (or Balanced binary) tree instead of a completely balanced binary search tree. Less overhead is required to maintain the B-tree structure when key values are inserted or deleted; yet maximum search lengths are nearly as good as those of an optimally structured, balanced m-way search tree of the same order.

For example, **Figure 11.5** illustrates a B-tree of order 3 that contains the keys of the three-way search tree of **Figure 11.4**. Each node has been marked with a letter to facilitate later references to this example tree. Not shown for each node is an indicator of the number of non-null subtree pointers that it contains. The leaves need not have space for those pointers. B-trees of higher order are certainly more interesting but become difficult to draw. Each node of a B-tree of order m has the same structure as a node of an m-way search tree. When a B-tree is used as an index, its nodes contain pointers to the records corresponding to each of the key values.

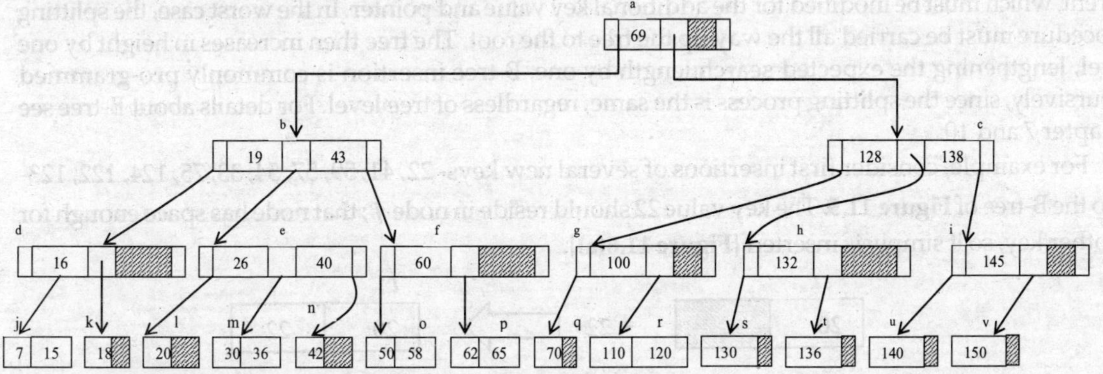

Figure 11.5 B-tree of order 3 containing keys of the three-way search tree of **Figure 11.4**.

11.3.1 Searching a B-tree

The search for a particular key value in a B-tree follows the same procedure as does the direct search of an m-way search tree. How well does a B-tree search perform? Consider first the question of the minimum number of keys in a B-tree of order m with height h. By definition, the root of a B-tree has at least two children. Each of these nodes has at least $\lceil \frac{1}{2}m \rceil$ children, and so forth down the tree to level h-2 (the leaves are on level h-l). Thus, the tree must contain at least $1+2+\sum_{i=3}^{h-2} 2*\lceil \frac{1}{2}m \rceil^{i-2}$ interior nodes and at least $2*\lceil \frac{1}{2}m \rceil^{h-2}$ leaves. Each interior node except the root must contain at least $\lceil \frac{1}{2}m \rceil - 1$ keys; the root and each leaf must contain at least 1 key. Thus, the minimum number of keys in the tree is

$$n \geq 1+\left(2+\sum_{i=3}^{h-2} 2*\lceil \tfrac{1}{2}m \rceil^{i-2}\right)\left(\lceil \tfrac{1}{2}m \rceil - 1\right)+2*\lceil \tfrac{1}{2}m \rceil^{h-2}$$ which reduces to

$n+1 \geq 2*\lceil \frac{1}{2}m \rceil^{h-2} \Rightarrow \frac{n+1}{2} \geq \lceil \frac{1}{2}m \rceil^{h-2}$ taking log of both sides we get the maximum height of the tree that is $h \leq 2+\log_{\lceil \frac{1}{2}m \rceil} \frac{n+1}{2}$ for m>2.

The leaves will all appear on a maximum level of h - 1. Since the tree's height determines the maximum search length, we now know that the B-tree performs very well for direct searches.

11.3.2 Inserting into a B-Tree

The insertion and deletion algorithms for B-trees are somewhat more interesting. Like operations on AVL and balanced binary trees, operations on B-trees must preserve the balanced character of the data structure. Insertion or deletion in an AVL or balanced binary tree may force rotation to keep the tree in balance. The algorithms for keeping a B-tree balanced are conceptually simpler than are those rather complex rotation algorithms.

First a B-tree search (which is the same as an m-way tree search) must be done to find the correct location for the key value in the tree. Then the key is inserted, especially with higher-order trees, the node has space available for another key value and pointer. Some-times, however, the node is already full and cannot accommodate another key value. The node must be split into two, with half the key values and pointers going into one node and half into the other. These "twin" nodes have the same parent, which must be modified for the additional key value and pointer. In the worst case, the splitting procedure must be carried all the way up the tree to the root. The tree then increases in height by one level, lengthening the expected search length by one. B-tree insertion is commonly pro-grammed recursively, since the splitting process is the same, regardless of tree level. For details about B-tree see Chapter 7 and 10.

For example, consider first insertions of several new keys- 22, 41, 59, 57, 54, 33, 75, 124, 122, 123- into the B-tree of **Figure 11.5**. The key value 22 should reside in node l; that node has space enough for another key, so it simply is inserted {**Figure 11.6(a)**}.

l			l	
20		+ 22 ⇨	20	22

Figure 11.6 (a)

Similarly, key value 41, which should reside in node n, may be inserted there because space is available {Figure 11.6(b)}.

Figure 11.6 (b)

Note that the proper sequence of key values must be maintained; key value 42 is shifted right to make room for key value 41.

Key value 59 should reside in node o. However, node o already contains the maximum allowable number of key values for a B-tree of order 3. Whenever a key needs to be inserted in a node that is already full, a split occurs. The one node becomes two nodes; half of its keys go in one of the two nodes and half in the other. The remaining value is moved up to the parent node. The parent node also be must adjusted to include a pointer to the spawned node. Here, nodes f and o both are modified {Figure 11.6(c)}.

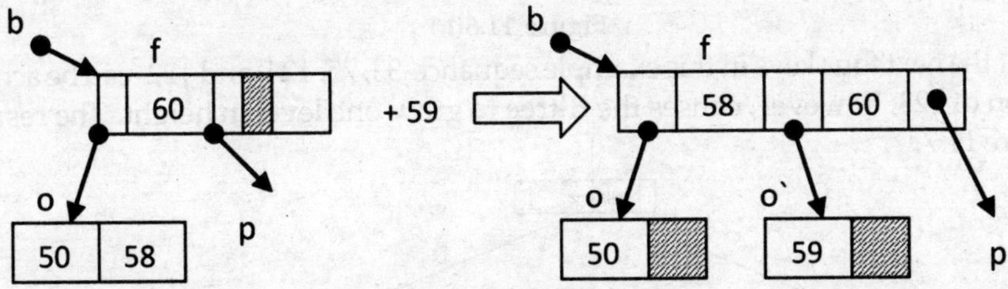

Figure 11.6 (c)

Now, insertion of 57, the next key value, proceeds by simply placing 57 in node o {Figure 11.6(d)}.

o
50
+ 57
o
50 57

Figure 11.6 (d)

Key value 54 also should be placed in node o, but node o is again full. The same splitting algorithm is applied (Figure 11.7(e)).

o
50 57
+ 54
o
50
o¨
57
+ 54 into the parent f

Figure 11.6 (e)

However, the parent node f is also full and cannot accommodate another key value and a pointer to node o". The splitting algorithm is again applied, this time to node f {Figure 11.6(f)}.

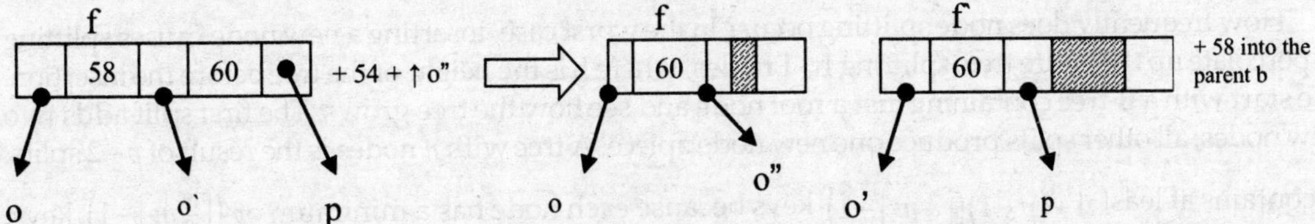

Figure 11.6 (f)

Again, the parent node b happens to be full and cannot accommodate another key value and a pointer to f'. The splitting procedure is now applied to node b {Figure 11.6(g)}.

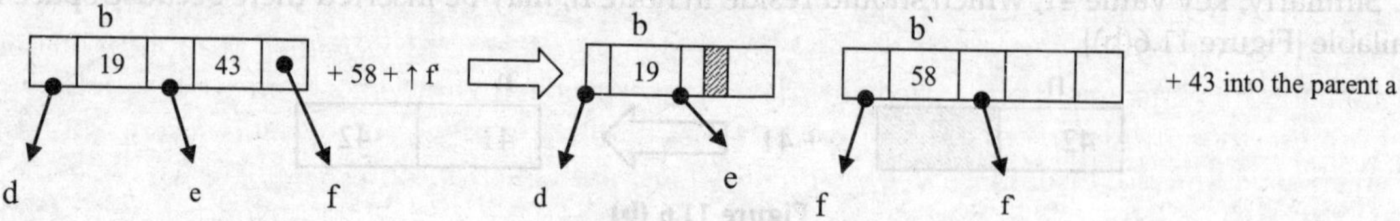

Figure 11.6 (g)

The parent node a does have space available for another key value and a pointer to b′ {Figure 11.6(h)}.

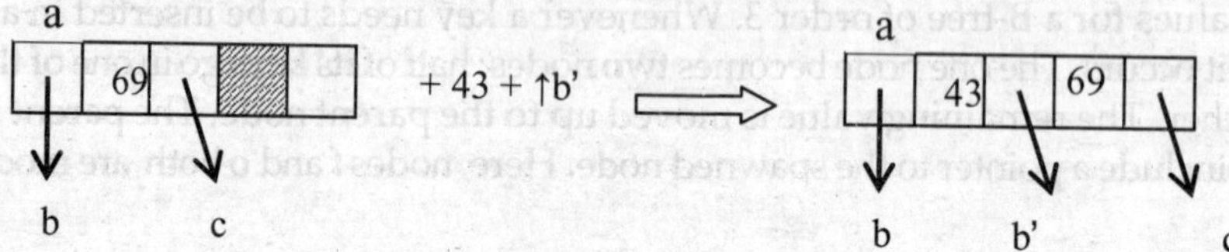

Figure 11.6(h)

Insertion of the next four keys in this example sequence-33, 75, 124, and 122 -can be accommodated easily. Insertion of 123, however, causes the B-tree to grow one level in height. The resultant tree is shown in Figure 11.7.

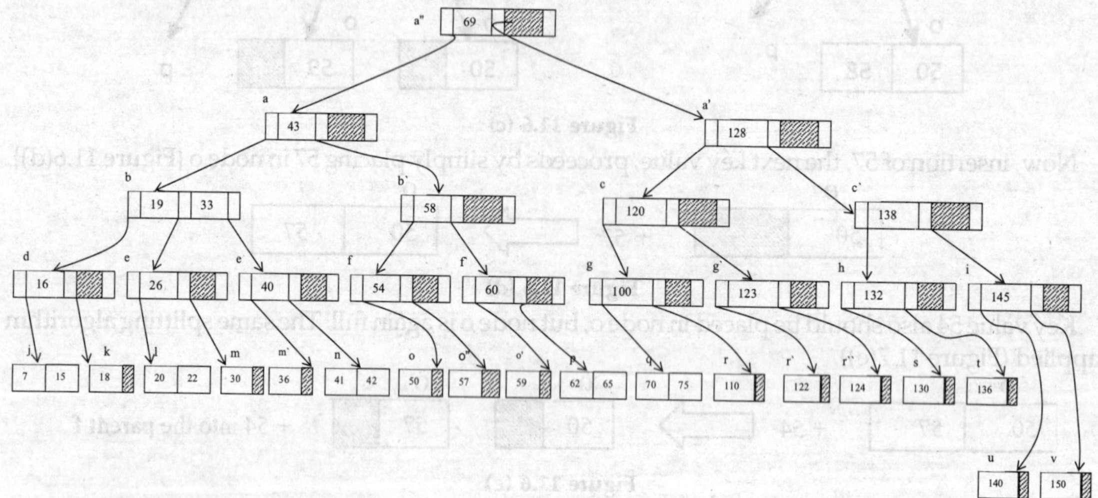

Figure 11.7 B-tree resulting from sequence of instance into the B-tree of **Figure 11.5.**

11.3.3 Analysis

How frequently does node splitting occur? In the worst case, inserting a new node causes splitting to percolate up the entire tree, splitting h - 1 nodes, where h is the height of the tree before the insertion. We start with a B-tree containing just a root node and see how the tree grows. The first split adds two new nodes; all other splits produce one new node apiece. A tree with n nodes is the result of $p-2$ splits. It contains at least $1+(p-1)\left(\left\lceil \frac{1}{2}m \right\rceil -1\right)$ keys because each node has a minimum of $\left(\left\lceil \frac{1}{2}m \right\rceil -1\right)$ keys, except the root, which must have at least one key. The probability that an additional split is required upon insertion of a key value is less than the ratio of splits to keys: $\frac{p-2}{1+(p-1)\left(\left\lceil \frac{1}{2}m \right\rceil -1\right)}$ which is less than 1 split per $\left(\left\lceil \frac{1}{2}m \right\rceil - 1\right)$ key insertions (since $\frac{1}{p-2}$ approaches to 0 for large p and $\frac{p-1}{p-2}$ is approximately 1). For m = 10, the split probability is 0.25; for m = 100, the split probability is 0.0204; for m = 200, the split probability is 0.0101. The higher the order of the B-tree, the lower the probability that key insertion will cause a node to split.

11.3.4 Deleting From a B-Tree

Deletion of a key from a B-tree is only slightly more complicated than insertion. In order to keep the B-tree, two nodes need to be merged when one node would have fewer than, the minimum required keys and pointer. For deleting a key value from a B-tree as with an insertion, a B-tree search must first be done to find the node containing the victim key. If the key to be deleted is in an interior node, the tree is transformed to move this key into a leaf because it is easier to delete a leaf. Once the deletion is made, other keys may need to be shifted or leaves be combined to meet the minimum key and minimum pointer requirements for a B-tree. These node combinations may be needed for several levels. If a merge percolates all the way to the highest level, a new root is formed and the height of the B-tree is decreased by 1. As with splitting, the probability of node merging decreases as the order of the B-tree increases.

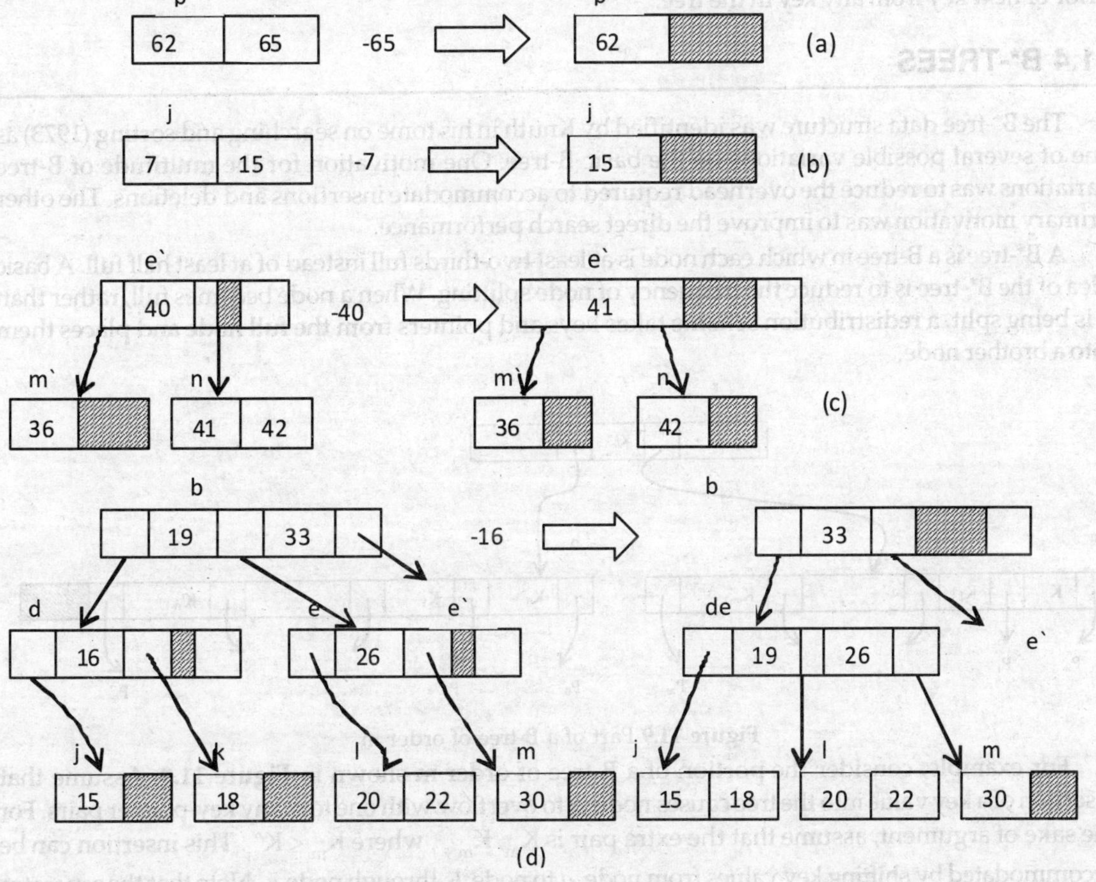

Figure 11.8 Deletion in B-tree

For example, consider deletion of the following sequence of keys from the B-tree of **Figure 11.7:** 65,

7, 40, 16. Removal of key value 65 from node p is easy {Figure 11.8(a)}. Removal of key value 7 from node j is also easy (Figure 11.8(b)). Note that 15 has been shifted left to maintain proper key sequencing.

Removal of key value 40 leaves node e′ with two pointers but no keys. Some key must be found to place in e′ so that the minimum key requirement is met. A proper key value is the leftmost key of the subtree pointed to by the pointer after the deleted key; here that key value is 41 in node n {Figure 11.8(c)}.

Sometimes keys are distributed in such a way that nodes must be merged to maintain compliance with B-tree constraints. Deletion of 16 from node d gives us such a case. Not only d and e are merged, but j and k are also merged and ancestor node b is also affected {Figure 11.8(d)}. More details about deletion can be found in Chapter 7.

Understanding the insertion and deletion operations on B-trees will increase readers' comprehension of why B-trees are defined as they are. Splitting of a full node is resulting in two nodes that both meet the requirement for a minimum number of keys and pointers. A sub-minimal and a minimally loaded node fit together nicely without violating the constraint on maximum number of keys and pointers when two nodes must be merged. The key arrangement makes it easy to find the prior or next key from any key in the tree.

11.4 B*-TREES

The B*-tree data structure was identified by Knuth in his tome on searching and sorting (1973) as one of several possible variations on the basic B-tree. One motivation for the multitude of B-tree variations was to reduce the overhead required to accommodate insertions and deletions. The other primary motivation was to improve the direct search performance.

A B*-tree is a B-tree in which each node is at least two-thirds full instead of at least half full. A basic idea of the B*-tree is to reduce the frequency of node splitting. When a node becomes full, rather than it is being split, a redistribution scheme takes keys and pointers from the full node and places them into a brother node.

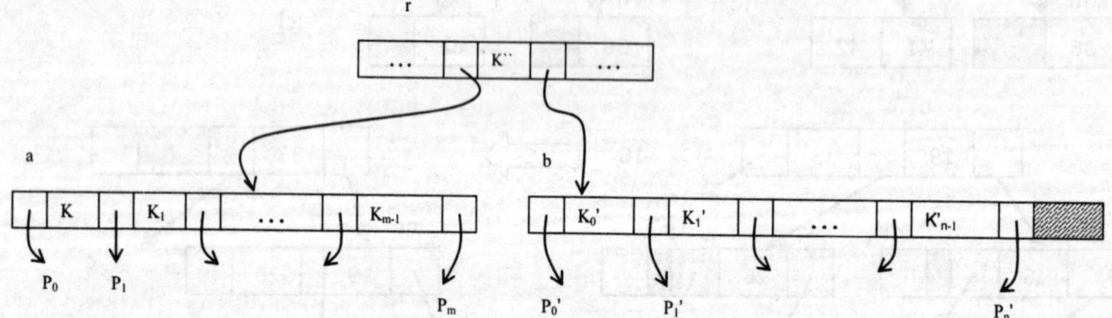

Figure 11.9 Part of a B-tree of order m

For example, consider the portion of a B-tree of order m shown in **Figure 11.9**. Assume that insertion of a key value into the tree causes node *a* to overflow with one to many key-pointer pairs. For the sake of argument, assume that the extra pair is K_m, K_{m+1} where $K_m < K''_j$. This insertion can be accommodated by shifting key values from node *a* to node *b* through node *r*. Note that the separator key value in node *r* must be changed to reflect the rotation.

The keys may be redistributed in several ways. One approach is to place half the total number of keys, here m + 1 + n, in each node a and b, as shown in **Figure 11.10**. Node a then contains c keys, where $c = \lceil (m+1+n)/2 \rceil$, Key K_{c+1} is the middle key of the collection $K_0, K_1, \ldots, K_{m-1}, K_m, K_j'', K_o''$, $K'_1, \ldots, K'_{n-1}$, from nodes a, r, and b. K_{c+1} is placed in the parent node r. The free space from brother node b has been used to accommodate the overflow from node . Moreover, that free space has been redistributed between nodes *a* and *b* such that each now has about half of it.

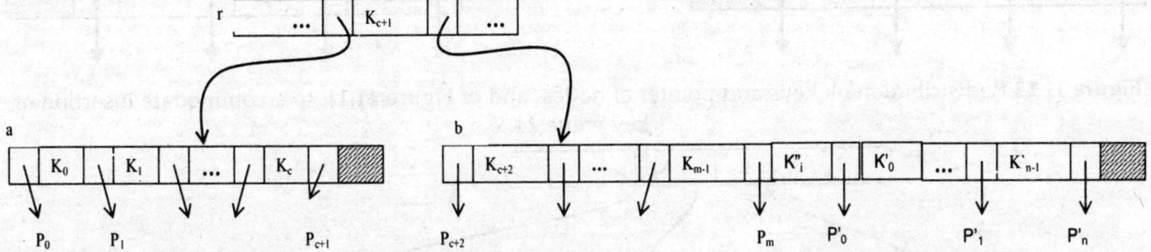

Figure 11.10 Redistribution of keys and pointers in nodes and from **Figure 11.9**

11.4.1 Insertion into a B*-tree

Consider the situation shown in **Figure 11.11**. Adding a key value 24 to node *a* will cause overflow because node *a* is already full. However, the insertion can be done by shifting key values from *a* node *b* to node through node *r*. The total number of keys involved is seven {18, 20, 22, 24, 26, 33, 35}. About half (i.e., of the keys {18, 20, 22} would be placed in node *a*; the middle key {24} would become the separator key in node *r*; the remaining keys {26, 33, 35} would be placed in node *b*, as shown in **Figure 11.12**. Free space from node has been used to accommodate the overflow from node . Moreover, the remaining free space has been redistributed between nodes *a* and *b* such that each now has half of it. What if node *b* was also full and did not have free space to accommodate node *a's* overflow? In a B*-tree, two nodes are split to form three nodes, each of which is about two-thirds full. The total number of keys involved is 2m + 2 (m from each *a* and *b*, 1 in *r*, 1 to be added). The resultant three nodes should contain each about 2m/3 keys; two keys are placed into the parent node to act as separators. A diagram illustrating the result of the split is shown in **Figure 11.13**.

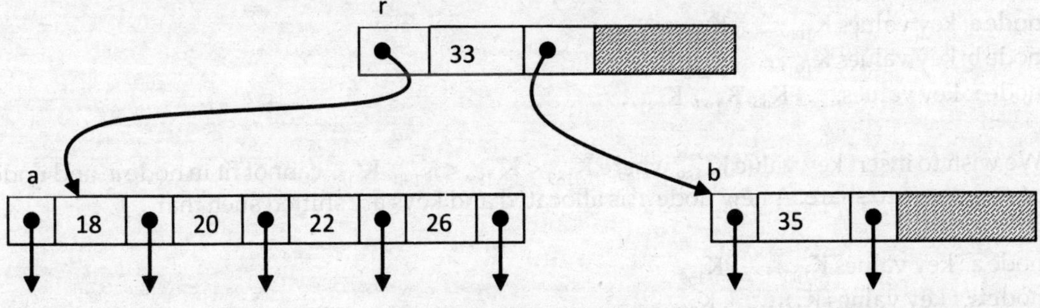

Figure 11.11 Part of B* -tree

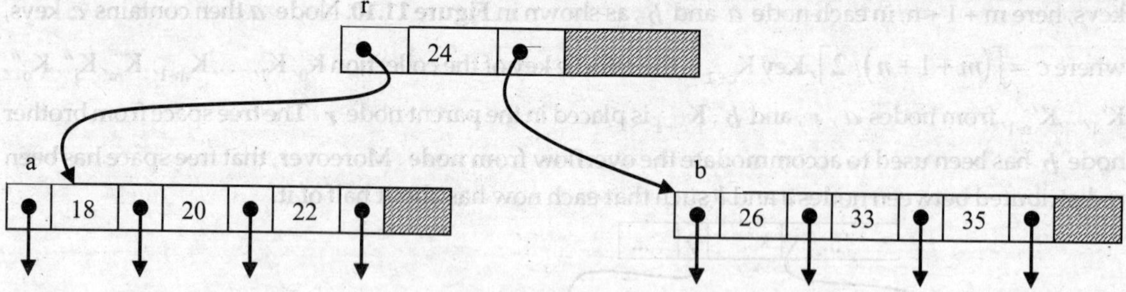

Figure 11.12 Redistribution ok keys and pointer of nodes and of Figure 11.11, to accommodate insertion of key value 24.

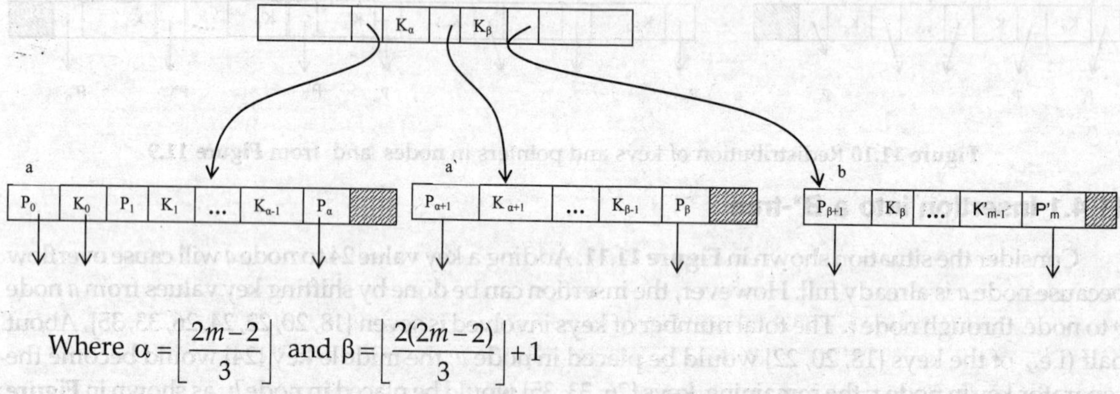

Where $\alpha = \left\lfloor \frac{2m-2}{3} \right\rfloor$ and $\beta = \left\lfloor \frac{2(2m-2)}{3} \right\rfloor + 1$

Figure 11.13 Result of splitting nodes *a* and *b* from B* -tree

Now consider the situation shown in **Figure 11.14**. The insertion of 24 cannot be accommodated by shifting key values from node *a* to node *b* , because node *b* is already full. Instead we split nodes *a* and *b* into three nodes, each of which is about two-thirds full. The total number of keys involved is 10. About one-third of the keys that are not separators are placed in each node *a*, *a′* and *b* as shown in **Figure 11.15**. Let us see another example, consider a B*-tree of order m = 90. Assume that nodes *a* and *b* are both full. Say

node a: key values $K_{100}, \ldots, K_{189}$
node b: key values $K_{191}, \ldots, K_{280}$
node r: key values, $\ldots, K_{99}, K_{190}, K_{281}, \ldots$

We wish to insert key value K'_{189} where $K_{189} < K'_{189} < K_{190}$, K'_{189} cannot fit in node *a*, and node *b* has no free space to share. A new node *a′* is allocated and keys are shifted such that

node a : key values $K_{100}, \ldots, K_{159}$
node a′ : key values $K_{161}, \ldots, K_{219}$
node b : key values $K_{221}, \ldots, K_{280}$
node r :key values, $\ldots, K_{99}, K_{160}, K_{220}, K_{281}, \ldots$

Nodes *a*, *a′* and *b* each has free space for 29 key values. The new key K'_{189} resides in node *a′*.

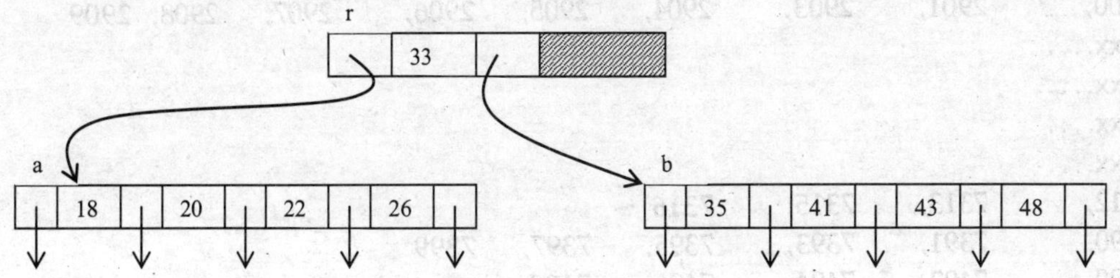

Figure 11.14 Example part of B* -tree

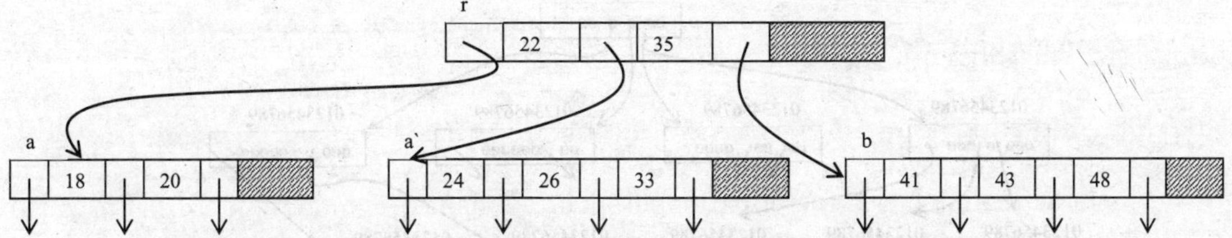

Figure 11.15 Result of splitting nodes *a* and *b* of B* -tree of Figure 11.14, to accommodate insertion of key value 24.

11.4.2 Tries (Revisited)

A trie is a data structure that uses instead the representations of key values as sequences of characters or digits to guide searches through the structure. The name trie was suggested by E. Fredkin (1960) because it is part of information retrieval.

A trie is an m-ary tree. It is not a search tree of order m, i.e., the ordering of key values in the nodes do not conform to the rules of an m-way search tree. The order of a trie is determined by the radix used to represent key values. The radix of key values represented by 10 digits; the radix of key values represented by alphabetic characters is 26 (or 27 if the space is included). Each node of a trie of order m is essentially a one- dimensional array of m pointers. Each element in the array corresponds to one of the elements of the radix set. A node in a 10-ary trie is shown in **Figure 11.16**.

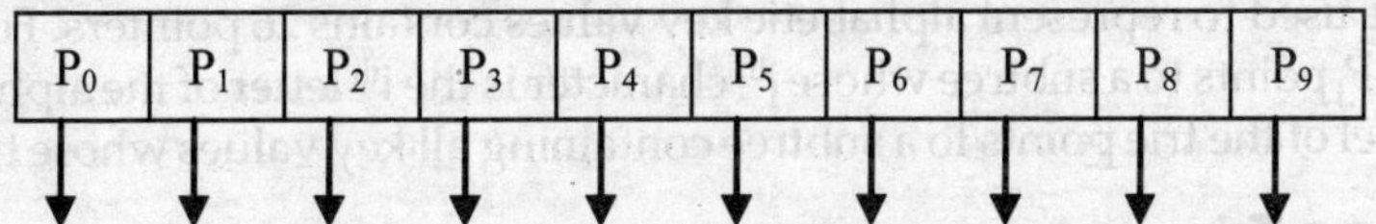

Figure 11.16 Node structure for 10-ary trie.

Note that the node is composed entirely of pointers. The position of a pointer in the node determines the value to which it corresponds.

The height of a trie is determined by the length of the key field. For a node on the jth level of a 10-ary trie, P_i points to a subtree representing all key values whose j^{th} digit is i. For example, P_4 on the sixth level of a 10-ary trie points to a subtree representing all key values whose sixth digit is 4.

For example, **Figure 11.17** illustrates part of a trie for structuring a collection of 4-digit key values. This example trie represents the following collection of key values:

2302, 2303, 2305, 2306, 2307, 2308
2350; 2352, 2353, 2355, 2356, 2358, 2359
2581, 2582, 2584, 2585, 2586, 2588, 2589
2590, 2591, 2593, 2594, 2596, 2597, 2599

2900, 2901, 2903, 2904, 2905, 2906, 2907, 2908, 2909
32xx....
35xx....
52xx....
59xx....
7312, 7313, 7315, 7316
7390, 7391, 7393, 7395, 7397, 7399
7490, 7492, 7494, 7496, 7498

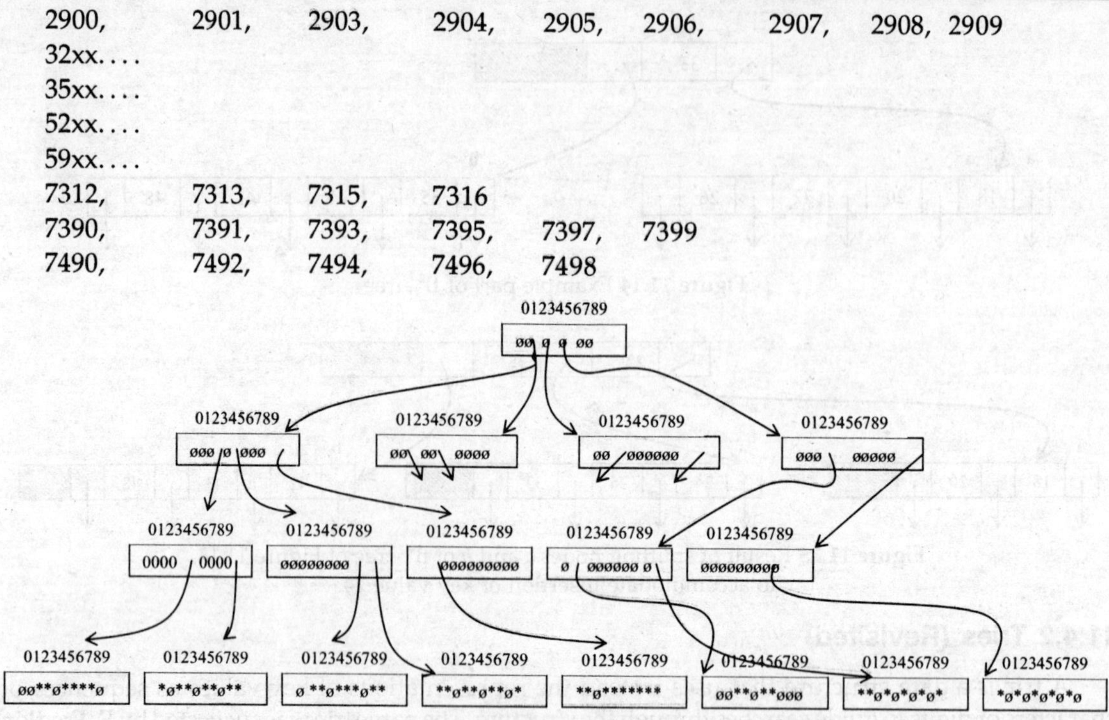

Figure 11.17 Trie for a collection of 4-digit key value

When a trie is used as an index, the leaf nodes contain addresses of data records with the corresponding key values. A trie can also be used to represent a collection of values, without a file of associated data. In that case, the leaf nodes would simply contain placeholders indicating the presence or absence of a corresponding value.

A node in a trie used to represent alphabetic key values contains 26 pointers. For a node on the jth level of such a trie, P_i points to a subtree whose j^{th} character is the ith letter of the alphabet. For example P_{10} on the third level of the trie points to a subtree containing all key values whose third character is j.

11.4.3 Searching a Trie

Successful direct searches in a basic trie must terminate at leaf nodes. To find the pointer to a particular record requires visiting all levels of the tree. At each level, the next branch to follow is determined by the pertinent digit of the key value. Thus, the length of a successful search is determined by the height of the trie which is determined by the length of the key field. The length of a search in an m-way search tree is determined by the number of key values represented. In the trie of Figure 11.17, a successful search requires visiting four nodes regardless of whether there are three key values represented or 10^4.

On the other hand, an unsuccessful search terminates when it is determined that a sought key value does not reside in the structure. In a trie, an unsuccessful search may terminate on any level of the structure. For example, visiting only the root node of the trie of Figure 11.17 is enough to determine that there are no key values in the trie with high-order digit from the set {0,1,4,6,8,9}. This good performance for unsuccessful searches is a major attractive feature for use of the trie in some applications.

11.4.4 Maintaining a Trie

Inserting a new key value in a trie is relatively easy. The correct leaf to represent the new value is located using a direct search. It may be that the correct leaf does not exist. In this case, nodes must be added properly to the index part of the structure to direct a search to the new leaf node. The correct element of that leaf is found and changed from non-null to a place-holder value or, if the trie is used as an index, to the address of the related data record.

Note that even though the maximum structure of the trie is fixed by the key set's radix and the key field's length, the basic trie shown in **Figure 11.17** does not include all possible nodes. With radix and key length, there may be *k* levels, with r^{i-1} nodes on each level *i*. The nodes that contain only null pointers are not shown. These empty nodes have the potential to exist and can be inserted into the tree when key value insertion makes them nonempty.

Not storing empty nodes makes better use of memory when the distribution of key values is such that there are many null nodes. This may be a case especially when the key range is sparsely used. For example, consider a company with 250 employees. Assume that the 9-digit social security number is used as the key field to identify employee payroll records. A basic trie built upon this key field would have nine levels and potentially space for 10^9 employee record pointers on the leaf level. Only 250 of these elements (0.000025%) would be occupied.

Deletion of a key value also requires locating and modifying the proper elements to have null values. Note that there is no node splitting or merging, although nodes may need to be added when a new value appears the first time in a particular position of the key.

11.4.5 Trie Variations

There are several variations possible on the basic trie. For example, a trie can be modified slightly to accommodate more efficiently a variable-length key field. Consider an alphabetic key field with values that are people's last names. Some of these names are very short. Others are quite long. Building a 26-way trie to structure names of up to 30 characters means that even searches for short names requires 30 node visitations. Assume that 80% of the names to be represented are no more than eight characters in length. The trie can be built with the following node structure. Each internal node can contain 27 elements; 26 are for the letters of the alphabet, and one (say) is to represent key values that terminate at the represented length. Each name is represented as if its low-order character were Θ. For example, IGOR is represented as IGOR Θ. A name that terminates with a Θ on level j would be a name with j characters. For example, the name IGOR would be represented with an I on level 0, pointing to a G on level 1, pointing to an O on level 2, pointing to an R on level 3, pointing to Θ on level 4.

The trie itself could be constructed with eight levels because 80% of the names have a maximum of eight characters. Each leaf node could contain the 27 usual elements, plus pointers to auxiliary indexes (for example binary search trees) containing the remaining parts of the names with more than eight characters. Thus, 80% of the searches would require a maximum of eight node visitations; 20% of the searches would travel completely through the trie and into another index.

Another alternative for improving the space requirements of a trie is to reduce node sizes by not making provision for all possible values of the radix in each node. Instead, only those values that are actually in use might be represented. Trie in **Figure 11.18** shows uses of this variation in storing a small set of three-letter girls' names. Each internal node of the trie contains both pointers and the radix value corresponding to each pointer; each leaf of the trie contains one or more radix values. Each leaf could contain pointers indexing into a file of data records about the girls.

Prior knowledge of distributions of key values can be used to further reduce memory needs. For example, if the trie of **Figure 14.18** is used only to store names (not an index to corresponding data records), we take advantage of the fact that N and M appear frequently in leaves. There could be a single N node shared as a leaf by multiple parents. Similarly, a single M node may be shared, as shown in **Figure 11.19**.

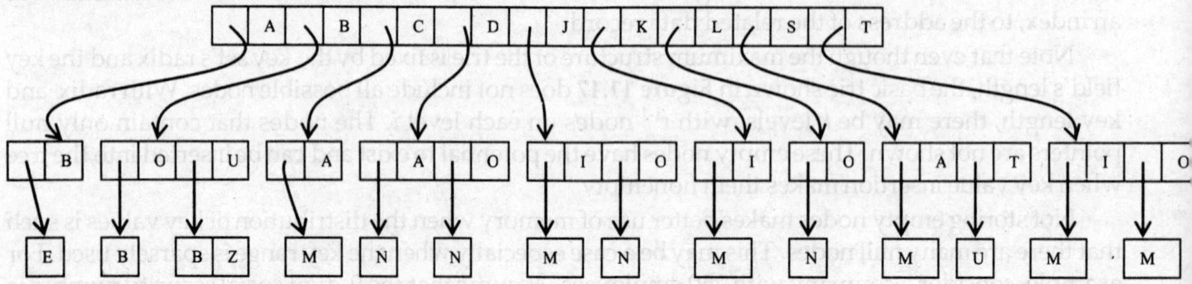

Figure 11.18 A trie for collection of three-letter girl's names

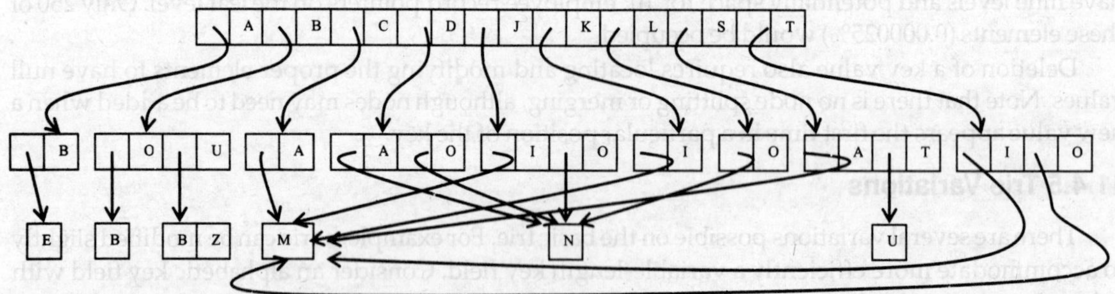

Figure 11.19 Variation on the trie of **Figure 11.18**, with sharing of some leaf nodes

11.5 INDEXED SEQUENTIAL FILE

An effective way to organize a collection of records when there is need both to access the records sequentially by some key value and also to access the records individually by same key is indexed sequential file organization. An indexed sequential file provides the combination of access types that are supported by a sequential file and a relative file. There are several approaches for structuring both the index and the sequential data portions of an index sequential file. The most common approach is to build the index as a tree of key values. The tree is typically a variation on the B-tree introduced earlier in this chapter and also in Chapter 10. The other common approach is to build the index based on the physical layout of the data in storage. This section will discuss both the approaches.

For example, one way to think of the structure of an indexed sequential file is as an index with pointers to a sequential data file as shown in **Figure 11.20**. In this example index is structured as a binary search tree. The index is used to service a request for accessing to a particular of a record. The sequential data file is used to support sequential access to the entire collection of records.

We are familiar with this approach for structuring a collection of information to facilitate both sequential and direct access. For example, consider a dictionary: the thumb tabs provide an index into the sequentially organized collection of words. In order to find a particular word, say "SYZYGY" we usually do not scan the dictionary sequentially. Rather, we select the appropriate thumb tab, S, the first letter of the word, and use that tab to direct the search into the approximate location of the word in the data collection.

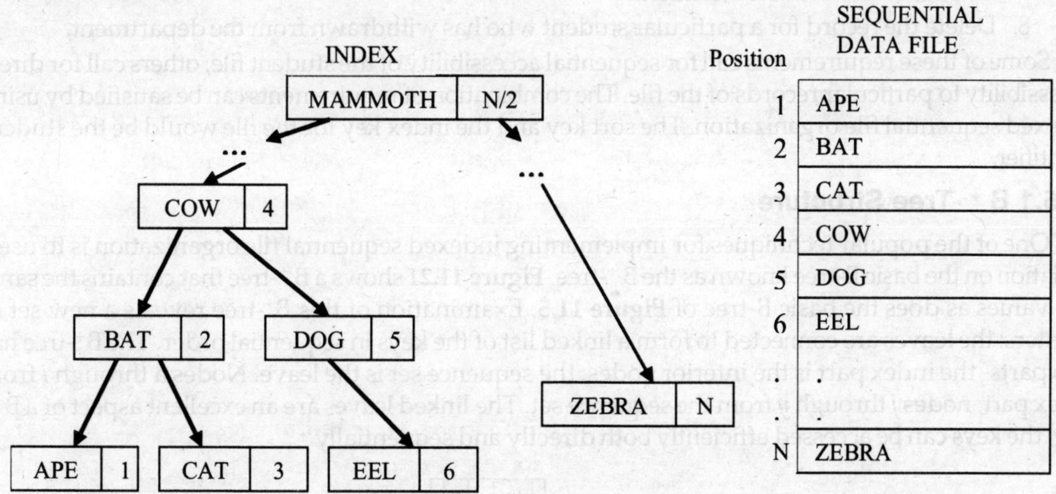

Figure 11.20 Use of a binary search tree and a sequential file to provide sequential access

Again we do not proceed with a sequential search from the beginning of the S's to find the target word, "SYZYGY." Instead we use the column headings on each page which indicates the first and last elements on that page. Once we have located the proper page, the search might proceed sequentially to find the sought word.

It is important to note from the dictionary example that the key that is used to sequentialize entries is the same as the key that is used to search directly for an individual entry. The thumb tab and column-heading index structure does not work unless this point is true.

Because of its capability to support both sequential and direct access, indexed sequential organization is used frequently to support files that are used for both batch and interactive processing. For example, consider a credit card billing system with an indexed sequential master file of customer account information. An appropriate key for the file will be the account number of each record. The file will be accessed in batch mode, monthly, to generate customer invoices and to prepare summary reports of account activity. Each account record will be accessed once in this processing. The bills and the detail lines on the summary report will appear in account number sequence.

The credit card management agency wants to use the master file of account information also to support interactive inquiry of the current credit status of any account. When a customer makes a purchase, the master file will be consulted to determine the credit limit and then to update the remaining credit amount. This kind of processing is not be supported well by sequential access to the customer account file. Rather, the need to access an individual account, given its account number, dictates use of the index of the indexed sequential file organization.

Another example of an application that calls for support by an indexed sequential file is a class records system. Processing requirements for this system include the following:

1. List the names and addresses of all students.
2. Compute the average age of the students.
3. Compute the mean and standard deviation for students' grade point averages.
4. Compute the total number of credit hours for classes in which the students are presently enrolled.

5. Change the classification of a particular student from probational to regular.
6. Display the grade record for a particular student.
7. Insert a record for a new student.
8. Delete the record for a particular student who has withdrawn from the department.

Some of these requirements call for sequential accessibility of the student file; others call for direct accessibility to particular records of the file. The combination of requirements can be satisfied by using indexed sequential file organization. The sort key and the index key for the file would be the student identifier.

11.5.1 B + -Tree Structure

One of the popular techniques for implementing indexed sequential file organization is to use a variation on the basic B-tree known as the B +-tree. **Figure 11.21** shows a B +-tree that contains the same key values as does the basic B-tree of **Figure 11.5**. Examination of this B+-tree reveals a new set of pointers: the leaves are connected to form a linked list of the keys in sequential order. The B+-tree has two parts- the index part is the interior nodes; the sequence set is the leave. Nodes a through *i* from index part; nodes *j* through *y* from the sequence set. The linked leaves are an excellent aspect of a B+ -tree; the keys can be accessed efficiently both directly and sequentially.

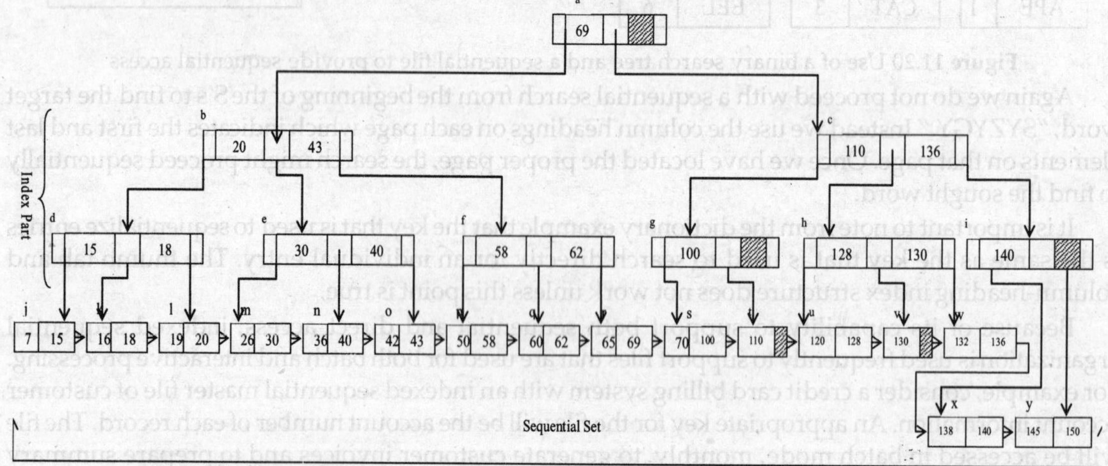

Figure 11.21 A B+-tree containing the same key values as the B-tree of **Figure 11.5**

A B-tree can also support sequential access to the key values it contains. The tree can be traversed sequentially by visiting the nodes in inorder. Each internal node will be visited more than once since it contains several keys. The subtree associated with each key must be visited before the next key of the node is accessed. In fact, sequential access to the keys of a B-tree does not exhibit very good performance, especially when requirements to trace the path through the tree are considered. The sequence set of a B+-tree remedies the problem. When a B+-tree is used to provide indexed sequential file organization, the key values in the sequence- set are the key values-in the record collections; the key-values in- the index part exist solely for internal purposes of directing access to the sequence set.

The B+-tree is discussed such that pointer P_i in the index points to the subtree containing key values greater than those in the subtree pointed to by P_{i-1} and less than or equal to key value K_i. Sometimes B+-trees are designed such that pointer P_i in the index points to the subtree containing key values greater than-those in the subtree pointed to by P_{i-1} and less than key value K_i. The leaf containing key value K_i then is in the subtree pointed to by P_{i+1}.

11.5.2 Manipulating a B⁺-tree

Inserting a new key value into a **B⁺**-tree is done in almost the same way as insertion of a new key value into a basic B-tree. When a leaf node is split into two nodes, a copy of a low-order key value from the rightmost node is promoted to be the separator key value in the parent node. The new node also must be inserted in the linked list of the sequence set. Deleting a key value from a **B⁺**-tree is somewhat easier than if the tree is a basic B-tree. When a key value is deleted from a leaf, there is no need to delete that key value from the index of the tree. This key value still can direct searches to the proper leaves.

11.5.3 Searching a B⁺-tree

A direct search in a B⁺- tree must terminate in a node of sequence set. If there is a key in the index that matches the sought key, the preceding pointer is followed until finally the correct leaf is reached. Not every key in the index part need to appear in the sequence set. A key may be deleted from the sequence set. When its corresponding records was deleted from the record collection, but the key may be retained in the index part of the B⁺- tree for the purpose of guiding access to the sequence set. A B⁺-tree provides as good performance for direct searching as does a basic B-tree of the same order. The maximum height of a B⁺- tree of order m with n key values is $\left(\log_{\lceil 1/2m \rceil} \frac{n+1}{2}\right)$. Sequential access to the data indexed by a **B⁺**-tree is provided by scanning the sequence set. Typically, as an indexed sequential file, the sequence set contains not only key values, but also the corresponding data records. If data records are variable length or relatively large, the file alternatively might be structured in a way that the sequence set nodes contain pairs of key value and address that point to the data records stored elsewhere.

For example, **Figure 11.22** shows an indexed sequential file of animal information, structured using the B⁺-tree approach. The nodes of the index file are labeled index block. The nodes of the sequence set are called data blocks and reside in the data file. This example contains *n* data blocks and three levels of index. Each entry in the index is a pair of lowest key value and pointer. The pointer is to another block in which the key value is the lowest key value that appears. Each level of index block points to all of the blocks that form the next lower level of the index, except for the lowest level index blocks, which point to the data blocks. This B⁺-tree is a 4-way search tree.

Direct Access: When a request for access to a particular record, say one with key value BAT, is received, first the highest level of index (here block 3.1) is searched. In this example, the pointer from AARDVARK is followed to index block 2.1. The appropriate pointer out of that box is one found with AARDVARK and leads to index block 1.1. The pointer followed out of that box is one found with BABOON and leads to data block 2. The data block is then searched for the record with the target key BAT and the record is made available.

Sequential Access: A request to access the data in sequential order is serviced by accessing the data blocks in sequential order. The data blocks are the sequence set; they are logically consecutive, but are not necessarily physically consecutive.

Inserting Records: Let us now consider a series of requests for inserting new animal records. Assume that each data block has space adequate to hold five records. The requests

INSERT APE

INSERT AIREDALE

are easy to do. Only data block 1 is affected, and it results in the contents shown in **Figure 11.23**. Note that the entries in the block must be kept in ascending sequential order.

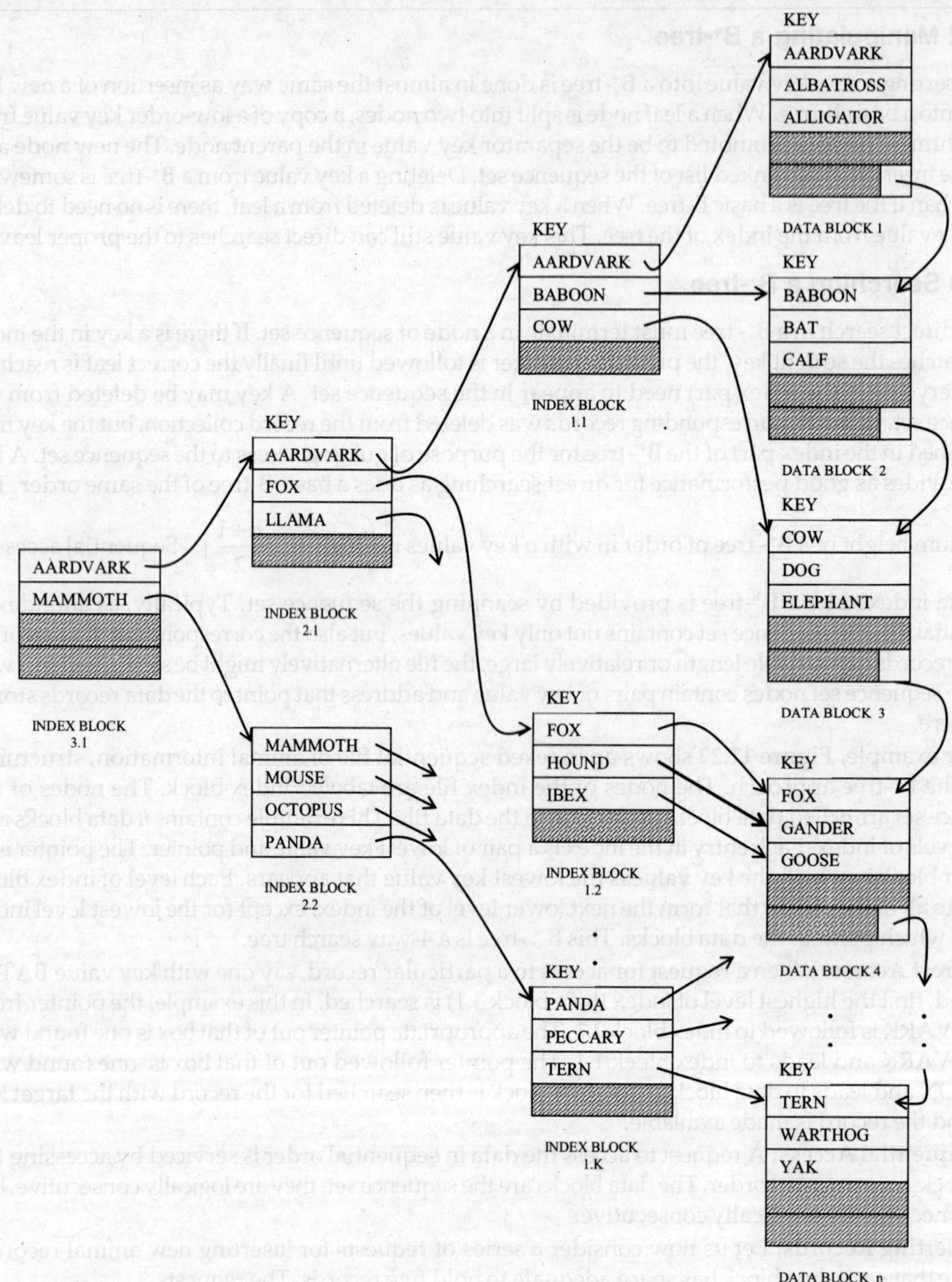

Figure 11.22 Indexed sequential file structured using a B$^+$-tree.

Key

AARDVARK
AIREDALE
ALBATROSS
ALLIGATOR
APE

DATA BLOCK 1

Figure 11.23 Data block 1 of **Figure 11.22** after inserting APE and AIREDALE.

The request INSERT ARMADILLO is a bit more difficult to handle. Search of the index structure reveals that ARMADILLO should reside in data block 1, but that block is already full. This condition necessitates a split of data block 1, with accompanying modification of index block 1.1, as shown in **Figure** 11.24 half of the contents of data block 1 remain there; the other half are moved to the newly created block: data block 1A. The requests

INSERT CAT
INSERT BEAR
INSERT BOBCAT

fill data block 2, then cause it to split, forming data blocks 2 and 2A **Figure 11.25**. Index block 1.1 is already full and cannot accommodate a pointer to block 2A, so it also must split, with the change percolating up to index level 2. When the index block at the highest level (here level 3) becomes full, then splits, a new level is added to the index tree. All direct searches would then requires four index block accesses and one data block access.

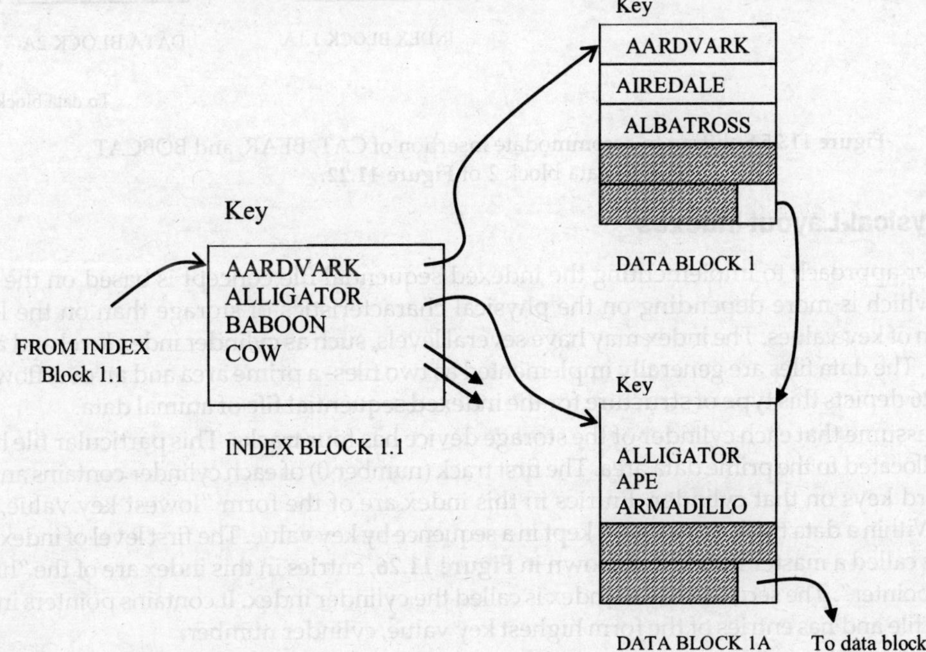

Figure 11.24 Splitting to accommodate insertion of ARMADILLO into data block 1 of **Figure** 11.23

Use of B+-tree to implement indexed sequential files is common. For example, it is used in International Business Machine's (IBM's) key-sequenced VSAM files. In VSAM terminology, a data block is referred to as a control interval. When the records in a control interval are stored in ascending order by a given key (as they are in index sequential file), the records are said to be in a key-sequenced data set.

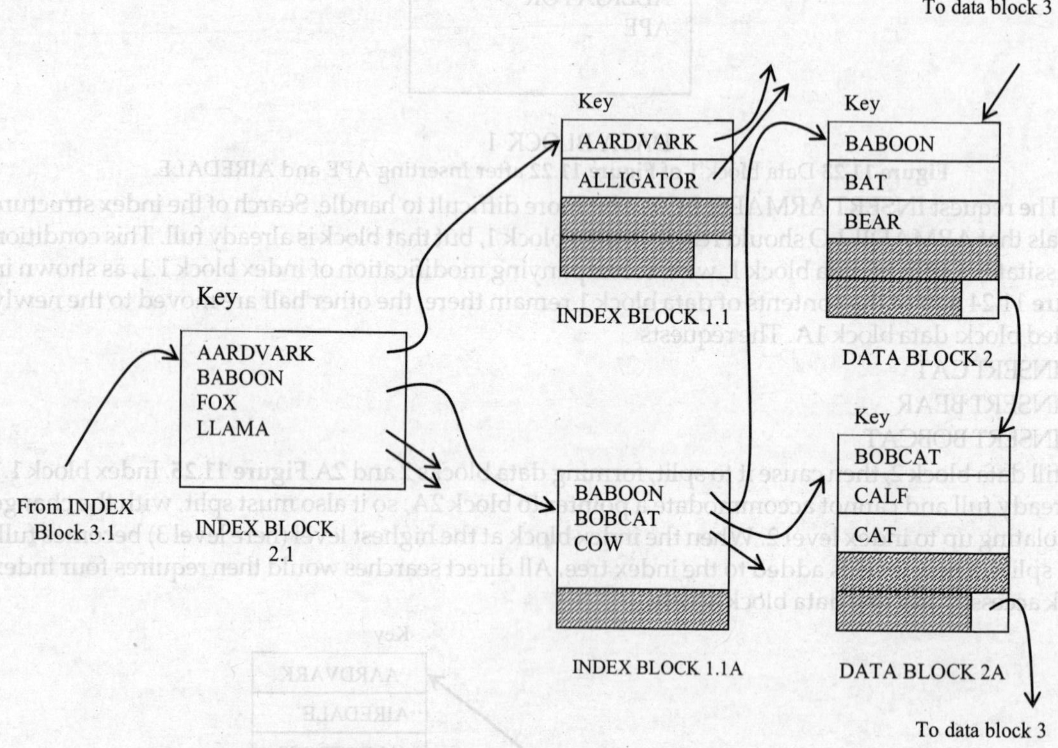

Figure 11.25 Splitting to accommodate insertion of CAT, BEAR, and BOBCAT into data block 2 of **Figure 11.22.**

11.5.4 Physical-Layout Indexes

Another approach to implementing the indexed sequential file concept is based on the index structure which is more depending on the physical characteristics of storage than on the logical distribution of key values. The index may have several levels, such as cylinder index level and a track index level. The data files are generally implemented as two files- a prime area and an overflow area. **Figure 11.26** depicts this type of structure for the indexed sequential file of animal data.

Let us assume that each cylinder of the storage device has four tracks. This particular file has six cylinders allocated to the prime data area. The first track (number 0) of each cylinder contains an index to the record keys on that cylinder. Entries in this index are of the form "lowest key value, track number". Within a data track, records are kept in a sequence by key value. The first level of index in the index file is called a master index. It is shown in **Figure 11.26**, entries in this index are of the "highest key value, pointer". The second level of index is called the cylinder index. It contains pointers into the prime data file and has entries of the form highest key value, cylinder number.

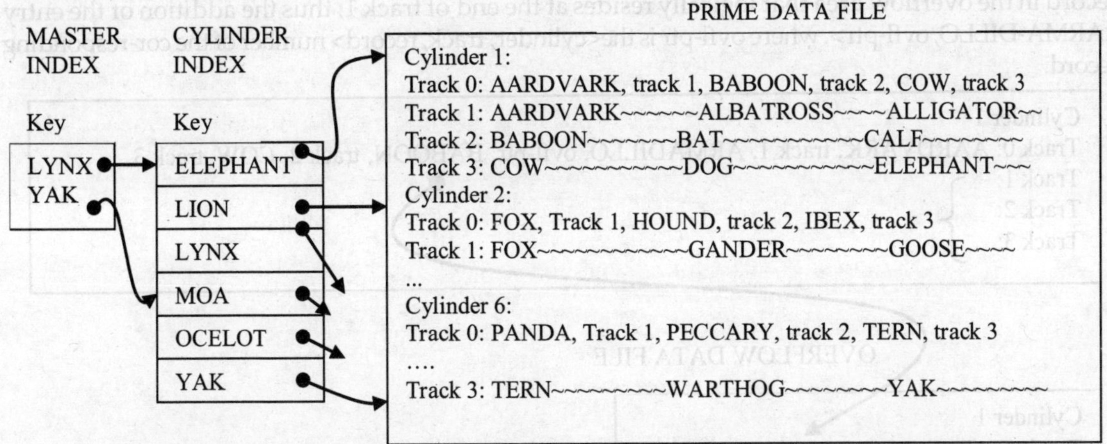

Figure 11.26 An animal file structured using physical-layout index approach.

Accessing Data Records: When a request to access a particular record, for example one with key value BAT is received, first the master index is searched. Because BAT precedes LYNX, the pointer from LYNX is followed into the cylinder index. Because BAT precedes ELEPHANT, the pointer from ELEPHANT is followed to track 0 of cylinder 1. Because BAT follows BABOON and precedes COW, the pointer from BABOON is followed to track 2, which is searched sequentially until BAT is found and made available or is determined not to exist. A request access the data in sequential order is serviced by accessing the cylinder and tracks of the prime data file in the physical sequence.

Inserting Records: Let us now examine the handling of updates to an indexed sequential file which is implemented based on this technique. Assume that each track of the prime data file has enough space for five records. If insertions and deletions to the file are expected, then it is created with empty spaces distributed through the data records. This space is called free space or padding. In example, we have considered the prime data area with 40% free space as it is similar to the case for the structure of **Figure 11.22**. The requests

```
INSERT APE
INSERT AIREDALE
```

are easy to do. Only data track 1 of cylinder 1 is affected and it results in the contents shown in **Figure 11.27**. Note that the entries in the track must be kept in ascending sequential order.

Cylinder 1
Track 0: no change
Track 1: AARDVARK~~AIREDALE~~ALBATROSS~~ALLIGATOR~~APE~~
Track 2: no change
Track 3: no change

Figure 11.27 Cylinder 1 of **Figure 11.26** after inserting APE and AIREDALE.

The request INSERT ARMADILLO is a bit more difficult to handle. Search of the index structure reveals that ARMADILLO resides in track 1 of cylinder 1, but that track is full. This condition necessitates use of the overflow data area. This overflow area is in a separate file from the prime data area but is pointed to by entries in the prime data area. **Figure 11.28** shows the result of adding ARMADILLO. Because ARMADILLO belongs after the five existing entries of track 1 of cylinder 1, it must be placed in the overflow data area. The track index for cylinder 1 must be modified to show that there is now a record in the overflow area that logically resides at the end of track 1; thus the addition of the entry <ARMA-DILLO, ovfl-ptr>, where ovfl-ptr is the<cylinder, track, record> number of the cor-responding record.

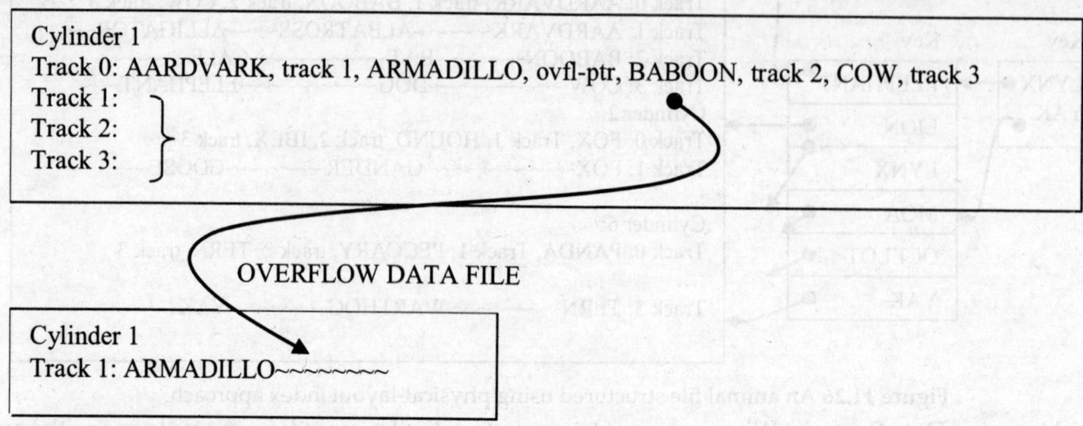

Figure 11.28 Cylinder 1 of **Figure 11.27** with overflow area to accommodate inserting ARMADILLO.

The requests

INSERT CAT

INSERT BEAR

INSERT BOBCAT

fill track 2 of cylinder 1 of the prime data area, then cause use of the overflow area {**Figure 11.29**}. Note that CAT is moved to the overflow area because not only must the entries in a prime track be in sequence, but also those entries must precede any overflow entries from that track. Now service the request

INSERT ANT.

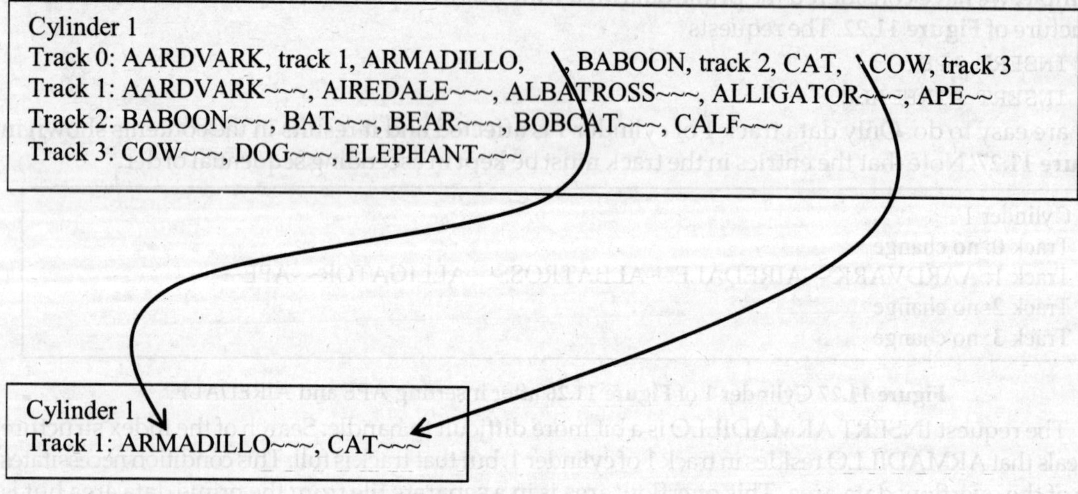

Figure 11.29 Cylinder 1 of **Figure 11.28** with overflow area after inserting CAT, BEAR, and BOBCAT.

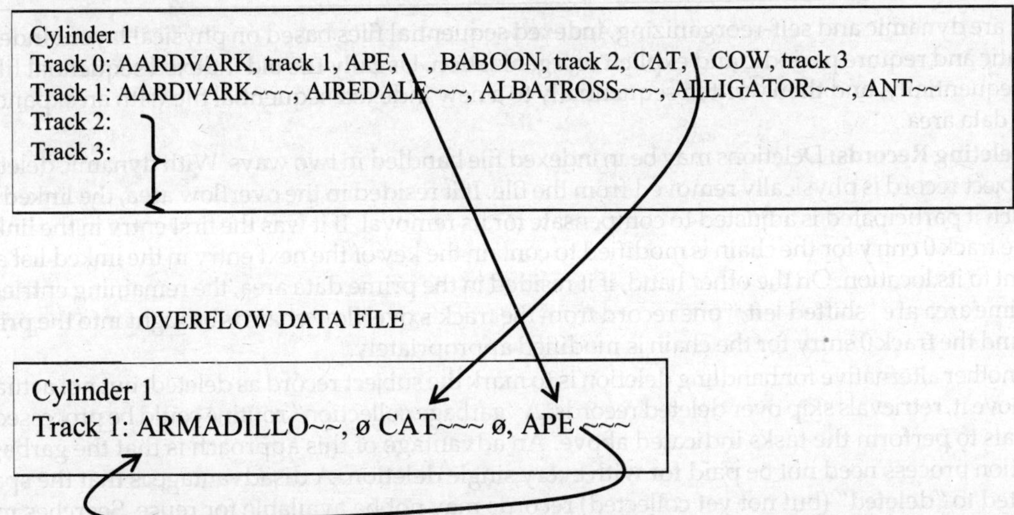

Figure 11.30 Cylinder 1 of **Figure 11.29** with overflow area after inserting ANT.

Search of the index structure reveals that ANT resides in track 1 of cylinder 1. Again, the proper ordering of keys in the prime area must be maintained, so ANT is placed in track 1 of cylinder 1 and APE is bumped to the overflow area {**Figure 11.30**}. Track 1 now has more than one entry in the overflow area. To be able to access the records sequentially and in fact, to be able to find a record with direct access, the overflow from a track must be chained together in proper sequence. Thus, the format of records in the overflow area is "key value, rest of record, pointer to next overflow record for this track". A given track of the overflow area may contain records that represent several prime tracks and that the overflow chain for a particular prime track may span multiple overflow tracks. The file can be defined with either one overflow area per cylinder or a combined overflow area containing records from all the prime cylinders. Entries are made in the overflow area in order by time of insertion. The linked lists in the overflow area show the key sequencing

Wrinkles: The processes of direct and sequential retrieval from the indexed sequential file actually are somewhat more complex than we have presented here. When a request for a particular record is received, the master and cylinder indexes are used to locate the correct cylinder in the prime data area for the target record. Then index in track 0 of that cylinder is searched. The pointer accompanying the key in the track index that is the largest key value not greater than the sought key value is followed. If the pointer is to a track in the prime area, the keys of records on that track are compared in a sequence with the target key value. On the other hand, if the pointer is to a record in the overflow area, the linked list of records pointed to, is searched. These records will be linked in ascending key value order but may be located physically anywhere in the overflow area. A request to access the data in sequential order is done by accessing the next prime track and then following its overflow chain, and so forth until the prime and overflow areas have been exhausted.

It is easy to see that with many records insertion, long overflow chains could result. Direct access to a record that resides in the prime area generally requires four I/O-devices accesses: two for the index file, one to the track-0 index, and one to the appropriate prime track. Direct access to a record that resides in the overflow area could require as many as 3+K I/O-device accesses: two for the index file, one to the track 0 index, and K to the overflow area, where the target record is K^{th} on the overflow chain. Access to each record on the overflow linked list could require a distinct I/O-device access.

Indexed sequential file that are implemented with prime and overflow data areas are susceptible to degradation of performance over a period of insertion activity. In contrast to B^+-tree-structures which are dynamic and self-reorganizing, indexed sequential files based on physical layout indexes are static and require periodic and explicit reorganization. Usually the old indexed sequential file is read sequentially, and then written sequentially to a new indexed sequential file with an expanded prime data area.

Deleting Records: Deletions may be in indexed file handled in two ways. With dynamic deletion the subject record is physically removed from the file. If it resided in the overflow area, the linked list in which it participated is adjusted to compensate for its removal. If it was the first entry in the linked list, the track 0 entry for the chain is modified to contain the key of the next entry in the linked list and to point to its location. On the other hand, if it resided in the prime data area, the remaining entries in the prime area are "shifted left," one record from the track's overflow chain is brought into the prime area, and the track 0 entry for the chain is modified appropriately.

Another alternative for handling deletion is to mark the subject record as deleted, but not actually to remove it, retrievals skip over deleted records. A "garbage collection" routine could be processed at intervals to perform the tasks indicated above. An advantage of this approach is that the garbage-collection process need not be paid for with every single deletion. A disadvantage is that the space allocated to "deleted" (but not yet collected) records may not be available for reuse. Searches may extend into the overflow area because of deleted records in the prime area, and chains in the overflow area may include deleted records. The physical layout index approach with prime and overflow areas for implementing indexed sequential files was developed before the B^+-tree approach.

FOR SUMMATIVE AND FORMATIVE ASSESSMENT

11.1 Given both a B-tree and a B^+-tree of order m=3, consisting of three levels of completely full index nodes, how many disk accesses would it take to perform the following tasks? Fill in the table and show your calculations, below.

task	B-tree		B+ tree	
	at most	at least	at most	at least
locate an arbitrary record				
locate sequentially next record				

11.2 We are given a file with 1,000,000 records, organized as a B^+-tree. The sequence set of the tree contains 100,000 nodes. We want to create a secondary index with respect to a secondary key. A secondary key value requires 63 bits. The secondary index is to be a dynamically hashed file consisting of 1,000 byte buckets. (Pure dynamic hashing, not the one with linear splitting.) We expect the hash file to achieve a space utilization of 80%. Estimate the disk space required by data buckets in the secondary index.

11.3 Under what conditions would we choose a B^+-tree over a B-tree?

11.4 A B-tree of order m=3 is given below. Delete the record with key N, making sure to show the evolution of the tree as the B-tree deletion algorithm proceeds.

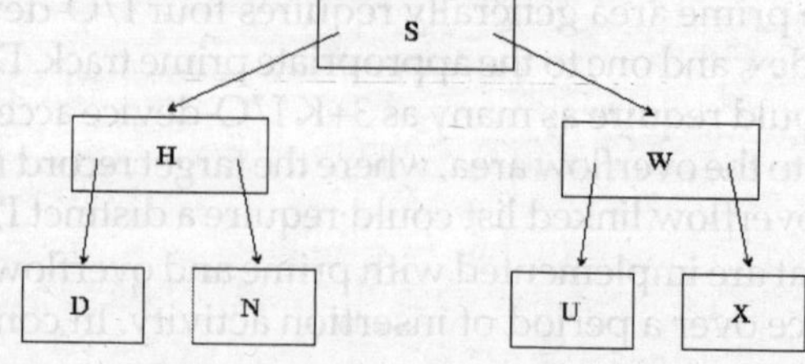

11.5 Why is it that the B-tree of the previous question cannot be considered a legal B^+-tree?

11.6 What are usages of B^+-tree discuss with the help of suitable of example.

11.7 What is B^+-tree? Discuss with the help of suitable examples.

11.8 What is B^*-tree? Discuss with the help of suitable examples.

11.9 What are usages of B^*-tree discuss with the help of suitable of example.

11.10 What is an index? Discuss.

11.11 What is index sequential file? Discuss with the help of suitable example.

11.12 Suppose a file with attributes A and B is given. The file is organized as a B^+-tree with A, a string of characters, as its unique key. The file contains 10,000 records, and on average a node in the sequence set holds 10 records. The sequence set is at the 4th level. Give a good strategy to execute the query "compute the count of records A, B such that rev(A), B is also a record in the file." Note that rev(A) is the reverse of the string A. Compute the cost of executing the query.

11.13 For a B^+-tree, residing on the disk, with m = 18, q = 4, and 16,000,000 records, what is the minimum and maximum possible cost of retrieval of a record by its key value?

11.14 A B^+-tree with m = 198 and q = 4 has 15,000 data nodes. What is the cost of insertion in the worst case?

11.15 We are given a primary file with 20,000 records. We want to build a secondary B^+-tree with at most 3 levels to index primary file. Assume m = q and estimate the node size for the tree if a key requires 6 bytes and every pointer requires 4 bytes. (Hint: Set up an inequality involving m. First compute a reasonable approximation for m, and then by trial and error, find the best solution for m.)

11.16 Suppose we want to index a file containing 500,000 records by a secondary index that is a B^+-tree. The height of the B^+-tree is required to be 3. A key value needs 6 bytes and all pointers need 4 bytes of storage.

(a) Estimate the node size for the B^+-tree. (Hint: Setup an inequality involving m, solve it for m approximately, and then determine exact value of m.)

(b) Assuming value of m from part (a), estimate the cost of accessing the file in the sequential order of the key in the B+-tree.

Quiz-9 (based on the complete data structures studies)

1. A priority queue is implemented as a Max-Heap. Initially, it has 5 elements. The level-order traversal of the heap is: 10, 8, 5, 3, 2. Two new elements 1 and 7 are inserted into the heap in that order. The level-order traversal of the heap after the insertion of the elements is:
   (a) 10, 8, 7, 3, 2, 1, 5
   (b) 10, 8, 7, 2, 3, 1, 5
   (c) 10, 8, 7, 1, 2, 3, 5
   (d) 10, 8, 7, 5, 3, 2, 1
2. Consider a hash table with 9 slots. The hash function is h(k) = k mod 9. The collisions are resolved by chaining. The following 9 keys are inserted in the order: 5, 28, 19, 15, 20, 33, 12, 17, 10. The maximum, minimum, and average chain lengths in the hash table, respectively, are
   (a) 3, 0, and 1
   (b) 3, 3, and 3
   (c) 4, 0, and 1
   (d) 3, 0, and 2
3. Special node in tree structure which has many child nodes and one parent node is called
   (a) descendant nodes
   (b) root node
   (c) leaf node
   (d) search node

4. Tree structure diagram in which pointers of data are stored at leaf nodes of diagram is classified as
   (a) b tree (b) B^+ tree
   (c) b^2 tree (d) B^* tree
5. In tree structure, node which is free of child nodes is called
   (a) descendant nodes (b) root node
   (c) leaf node (d) search node
6. Search value which is present on each node in search tree diagram of order 'p' is as
   (a) p - 1 (b) p - 2
   (c) p + 1 (d) p + 2
7. In tree structure diagrams, non leaf node is called
   (a) search node (b) descendant nodes
   (c) external node (d) internal node
8. Consider a B^+-tree in which the maximum number of keys in a node is 5. What is the minimum number of keys in any non-root node?

   Since the maximum number of keys is 5, maximum number of children a node can have is 6. By definition of B Tree, minimum children that a node can have would be 6/2 = 3. Therefore, minimum number of keys that a node can have becomes 2 (3-1).

   (a) 1 (b) 2
   (c) 3 (d) 4
9. Which of the following is FALSE about B/B^+ tree
   (a) B/B^+ trees grow upward while Binary Search Trees grow downward.
   (b) Time complexity of search operation in B/B^+ tree is better than Red–Black–Trees in general.
   (c) Number of child pointers in a B/B^+ tree node is always equals to number of keys in it plus one.
   (d) A B/B^+ tree is defined by a term minimum degree. And minimum degree depends on hard disk block size, key and addresses sizes.
10. The order of an internal node in a B^+ tree index is the maximum number of children it can have. Suppose that a child pointer takes 6 bytes, the search field value takes 14 bytes, and the block size is 512 bytes. What is the order of the internal node?

    Key size = 14 bytes (given) Child pointer = 6 bytes (given)
    We assume the order of B+ tree to be 'n'.
    *Block size = (n - 1) * key size + n * child pointer 512 >= (n - 1) * 14 + n * 6 512 >= 14 * n – 14 + 6 * n n = (512 + 14) / 20 n = 526 / 20 n = 26.3 n = 26*

    (a) 24 (b) 25
    (c) 26 (d) 27
11. With reference to the B^+ tree index of order 1 shown below, the minimum number of nodes

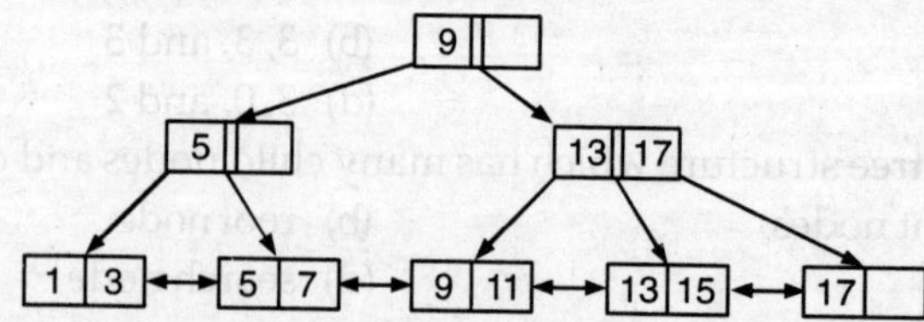

(including the root node) that must be fetched in order to satisfy the following query: "Get all records with a search key greater than or equal to 7 and less than 15" is ______.

(a) 4 (b) 5
(c) 6 (d) 7

12. Consider B^+ tree in which the search key is 12 bytes long, block size is 1024 bytes, record pointer is 10 bytes long and block pointer is 8 bytes long. The maximum number of keys that can be accommodated in each non-leaf node of the tree is

Let m be the order of B^+ tree
m(8)+(m-1)12 <= 1024
[Note that record pointer is not needed in non-leaf nodes]
m <= 51
Since maximum order is 51, maximum number of keys is 50.

(a) 49 (b) 50
(c) 51 (d) 52

13. B^+ Trees are considered balanced because
(a) the lengths of the paths from the root to all leaf nodes are all equal.
(b) the lengths of the paths from the root to all leaf nodes differ from each other by at most 1.
(c) the number of children of any two non-leaf sibling nodes differ by at most 1.
(d) the number of records in any two leaf nodes differ by at most 1.

14. A B^+ -tree index is to be built on the Name attribute of the relation student. Assume that all student names are of length 8 bytes, disk block are size 512 bytes, and index pointers are of size 4 bytes. Given this scenario, what would be the best choice of the degree (i.e., the number of pointers per node) of the B^+ -tree?

Size of 1 record = 8 + 4 = 12. Let the order be N.
No. of index values per block = N - 1
(N - 1) 12 + 4 = 512
12N - 12 + 4 = 512
16N = 1009, i.e., N = 43.3333

(a) 16 (b) 42
(c) 43 (d) 44

15. A B-tree of order 4 is built from scratch by 10 successive insertions. What is the maximum number of node splitting operations that may take place?

(a) 3 (b) 4
(c) 5 (d) 6

16. The order of a leaf node in a tree B^+ is the maximum number of (value, data record pointer) pairs it can hold. Given that the block size is 1K bytes, data record pointer is 7 bytes long, the value field is 9 bytes long and a block pointer is 6 bytes long, what is the order of the leaf node?

Disk Block size = 1024 bytes, Data Record Pointer size, r = 7 bytes
Value size, V = 9 bytes, Disk Block ptr, P = 6 bytes
*Let order of leaf be m. A leaf node in B+ tree contains at most m record pointers, at most m values, and one disk block pointer. r*m + V*m + p <= 1024 16m <= 1018 m =< 63*

(a) 63 (b) 64
(c) 67 (d) 68

17. A B-Tree used as an index for a large database table has four levels including the root node. If a new key is inserted in this index, then the maximum number of nodes that could be newly created in the process are
    (a) 5 (b) 4
    (c) 3 (d) 2
18. B Trees are generally
    (a) very deep and narrow (b) very wide and shallow
    (c) very deep and very wide (d) cannot say
19. A B-tree of minimum degree d can maximum .... pointers in a node.
    (a) d–1 (b) 2d–1
    (c) 2d (d) d

❑❑❑

INDEX

A

B

C

D

E

F

G

H

I

K

L

Q

R

S

T

U

V

W

□□□